International Banking

1870–1914

International Banking
1870–1914

EDITED BY

RONDO CAMERON
V. I. BOVYKIN

WITH THE ASSISTANCE OF

Boris Anan'ich, A. A. Fursenko,
Richard Sylla, and Mira Wilkins

New York Oxford
OXFORD UNIVERSITY PRESS
1991

Oxford University Press

Oxford   New York   Toronto
Delhi   Bombay   Calcutta   Madras   Karachi
Petaling Jaya   Singapore   Hong Kong   Tokyo
Nairobi   Dar es Salaam   Cape Town
Melbourne   Auckland

and associated companies in
Berlin   Ibadan

Copyright © 1991 by Oxford University Press, Inc.

Published by Oxford University Press, Inc.,
200 Madison Avenue, New York, New York 10016

Oxford is a registered trademark of Oxford University Press

Library of Congress Cataloging-in-Publication Data
International banking, 1870–1914 / edited by Rondo Cameron and
V. I. Bovykin with the assistance of Boris Anan'ich . . . [et al.].
p.   cm.
Includes bibliographical references.
ISBN 0-19-506271-X
1. Banks and banking, International—History.   I. Cameron, Rondo E.
II. Bovykin, Valerĭ Ivanovich.   III. Anan'ich, B. V.
HG3881.I575123   1991
332.1'5'09034—dc20   89-26656   CIP

2 4 6 8 9 7 5 3 1

Printed in the United States of America
on acid-free paper

Royalties from this book accrue to the
International Research and Exchanges Board,
an affiliate of the
American Council of Learned Societies.

Preface

The idea of carrying out a collaborative study, the results of which are submitted here, first arose at the Eighth International Economic History Congress in Budapest (1982), in the course of the work of Section B–10, "Transformation of Banking Structures in the Industrial Period."

The interaction of production and credit in the process of capitalist development, and the role of banks therein, has long been the subject of study by economists and historians. The problems involved have been discussed more than once at congresses of the International Economic History Association. The Second Congress (Aix-en-Provence, 1962) focused on the problem of capital formation in the early stages of industrialization. The Fifth Congress (Leningrad, 1970) examined the role of bank credit in economic development. While these studies were aimed at establishing the role of banks as factors in economic development and, in particular, pursued the task of defining their place in the course of industrialization of individual countries, the participants in Section B–10 at the Budapest Congress were concerned with elucidating the reciprocal effects of industrialization processes on the banks and the changes occurring in them as they adapted themselves to the requirements of industrial development. The papers presented there and the discussion of them showed that in order to understand the mechanism of transformation of bank structures in individual countries at the end of the nineteenth century and the beginning of the twentieth, when the integration and internationalization of capital markets intensified sharply, it is especially important to examine the international aspects of the development of banking.

Originally, we planned to examine two aspects: (1) the impact of international factors on the formation of financial systems in separate countries, and (2) the relationship between banks and multinational enterprises. But in the process of elaborating the structure of the project we decided to treat specially the activity of foreign banks as channels of foreign investments through case studies of several countries in the history of which foreign capital played a particularly conspicuous role. Because this role differed from country to country, countries were singled out as objects of study that differed in the character and level of economic development and also in their political status. It should be stressed that both Part I (International Factors in the Formation of Banking Systems) and Part II (Foreign Banks and Foreign Investment) examine the integral process of internationalization of bank structures. But in Part I the accent is on the development of domestic banks, whereas in Part II it is on the activity of foreign banks. This is why chapters devoted to the United States and Russia appear in both sections. Other countries are discussed either in Part I or in Part II depending on whether the accent is on elucidating the processes of formation of banking systems in these countries or defining the impact produced on them by foreign banks.

Although we have included many countries and regions in our study, and hope thereby to have a representative sample of both capital-exporting and capital-importing nations, it was obviously impossible within the limits of our finances to include all countries and regions of the world. It is a matter of regret, nevertheless, that we did not include chapters on two small but important capital exporters, Switzerland and the Netherlands. Initially the difficulty of identifying appropriate participants constrained us; and the quantitative dimensions of their capital exports did not seem to make their omission important. As our study developed, however, the strategic international importance of their banking systems, especially that of Switzerland, became clearer. We hope that other scholars will remedy this deficiency.

Professor A. A. Fursenko of the Institute of History of the USSR in Leningrad first suggested undertaking the project at the Budapest Congress. The preliminary plan of the study, which became an activity of the US–USSR Commission on the Humanities and the Social Sciences of the American Council of Learned Societies and the Academy of Sciences of the USSR, was drawn up in April 1983 at a meeting in Moscow of Professors Bovykin and Cameron, in which Professor Fursenko and Professor Boris Anan'ich, also of Leningrad, likewise participated. A further planning conference took place in Atlanta in September 1984, in which Professors Richard Sylla and Mira Wilkins participated, along with Anan'ich, Bovykin, and Cameron. Meanwhile, the other participants had been identified and contacted, and permission was received from the Rockefeller Foundation to hold a conference at the foundation's Study and Conference Center in Bellagio, Italy. At that meeting, August 19–23, 1985, preliminary drafts of all the chapters were discussed. Most of the participants presented brief résumés of their studies at the Ninth International Congress of Economic History in Berne, Switzerland, in August 1986. A final editorial meeting took place in San Francisco in September 1987, in connection with the annual meeting of the Economic History Association, with the participation of Anan'ich, Bovykin, Cameron, Sylla, and Wilkins. Dr. Ruth Roosa also participated in that meeting. The book was substantially complete by the summer of 1988, at which time Oxford University Press agreed to publish it. We had hoped to present it at the Tenth International Economic History Congress in Leuven, Belgium, in August 1990, but unforseen delays repeatedly postponed publication.

Because we believe this project to be unusual if not unique in the annals of collaborative international research in history and social science, a few words about the nature of our collaboration are in order. It should be obvious from our nationalities and institutional affiliations that the participants do not all belong to the same school of historical or social science research, yet we are all conscientious scholars seeking to discover the truth about the past. Although we sometimes differ in our interpretations of the significance of past events—that is the reason for two separate concluding sections in the final chapter—at no time in our collaboration have ideological differences prevented fruitful discussions of the facts or hindered full and frank consideration of the issues. We hope that our fortunate experience, along with parallel developments in the loftier spheres of international politics and statecraft, augurs well for the future of peaceful, productive international collaboration in all aspects of the human endeavor.

Administrative and financial support for the project has been provided by the International Research and Exchanges Board, an affiliate of the American Council of Learned Societies, and by the USSR Academy of Sciences under the agreement on scientific cooperation between the Soviet Academy and the American Council. The Rockefeller Foundation generously provided hospitality for the Bellagio meeting, and additional financial support for travel expenses for that meeting came from the Maison des Sciences de l'Homme (Paris) and the British Council. Individual participants received support from their institutions or governments.

In the course of our work on this book the several participants have accumulated obligations to many individuals too numerous to list here. Collectively, however, we wish to acknowledge the aid and assistance of three exceptional persons: Dr. Wesley A. Fisher, Secretary to the Commissions with the USSR of the American Council of Learned Societies; Ms. Susan E. Garfield, Coordinator of the Bellagio Study and Conference Center; and Ms. Arlene DeBevoise of Emory University, coordinator of the project, who also undertook the laborious task of processing and reprocessing the numerous drafts of the manuscript. Dr. Irina Diakanova, of the Institute of History of the USSR, served as coordinator of the project in Moscow.

V. B.
R. C.

Contents

Part II. Foreign Banks and Foreign Investment

Part III. International Banking and Multinational Enterprise

List of Contributors

B. V. Anan'ich, Professor in the Institute of History of the USSR, Leningrad.

Hubert Bonin, Professor of History in the University of Bordeaux III, Bordeaux, France.

V. I. Bovykin, Professor in the Institute of History of the USSR, Moscow.

Albert Broder, Professor of History in the University of Lille, France.

Rondo Cameron, William Rand Kenan University Professor, Emory University, Atlanta, GA; during academic year 1988/89, exchange professor, University of Augsburg, German Federal Republic.

Fred V. Carstensen, Professor of Economics, University of Connecticut, Storrs.

Vincent P. Carosso, Kenan Professor of History, New York University.

P. L. Cottrell, Department of Economic History, University of Leicester, England.

Ian M. Drummond, Professor of Economics, University of Toronto, Canada.

A. A. Fursenko, Vice Chairman, Presidium of the Leningrad Scientific Center, Academy of Sciences of the USSR.

Martine Goossens, Fellow of the National Fund for Scientific Research in Belgium, University of Leuven, Belgium.

Peter Hertner, Librarian, European University Institute, San Domenica di Fiesole (Florence), Italy.

Kanji Ishii, Professor of Economics, University of Tokyo, Japan.

Hans Christian Johansen, Professor of Economics, University of Odense, Denmark.

Frank H. H. King, Professor Emeritus, Center of Asian Studies, University of Hong Kong.

György Köver, Professor of Economics, Budapest University of Economics, Budapest, Hungary.

Maria Bárbara Levy, Professor of Economics, Federal University of Rio de Janeiro, Brazil.

Ragnhild Lundström, Department of Economic History, Uppsala University, Sweden.

Ruth AmEnde Roosa, Research Associate, Harriman Institute of Russian Studies, Columbia University, New York.

Richard Sylla, Henry Kaufman Professor, Stern School of Business, New York University.

Jacques Thobie, Professor of History in the University of Rennes, France.

Richard Tilly, Professor of Economic and Social History, University of Münster, German Federal Republic.

Herman Van der Wee, Professor of Economics, University of Leuven, Belgium.

Ulrich Wengenroth, Professor of History, Technical University, Munich, German Federal Republic.

Mira Wilkins, Professor of Economics, Florida International University, Miami, Florida.

International Banking
1870–1914

Introduction

Rondo Cameron

The papers collected in this volume deal with international banking and investment in an important historical era, the generation or so before World War I. In that period international investment reached dimensions previously unknown, and the banking systems of the world achieved a degree of internationalization also without precedent. It should not be thought, however, that either international banking or international investment were novelties. On the contrary, each had centuries-long histories. This brief introduction is intended to provide a context for appreciating the developments that occurred after 1870.

I

A strong argument can be made that banks constituted the first multinational business firms.[1] Although it can be argued in rebuttal that the Italian bankers who frequented the fairs of Champagne were only engaged in international trade, and thus were not true multinationals,[2] such was clearly not the case for the Italian bankers in England in the thirteenth and fourteenth centuries.[3] The Bardi and Peruzzi were the largest business enterprises in Europe before being forced into bankruptcy by the default of Edward III in the 1340s; nor were they the only Italian bankers in England. The Medici bank, although somewhat smaller than the Bardi and Peruzzi, was nevertheless the largest business enterprise in the fifteenth century. It pioneered the holding company form of organization in order to avoid the kind of catastrophe that had overtaken the Bardi and Peruzzi, and had branches in Rome, Venice, Naples, Pisa, Milan, Geneva, Lyons, Basel, Avignon, Bruges, and London in addition to its headquarters in Florence.[4]

As with international banking, with which it was closely connected, international investment can also be traced to the High Middle Ages. The Italians initially went to England to engage in the wool trade, but they soon became involved in lending to the sovereign, which ultimately proved to be their undoing. They could also be found in Bruges, Antwerp, and several other cities of northern Europe, as well as in the Levant. As in England, it was probably the opportunity for trade that first lured them to such locations, but in time they engaged in both public and private finance. In the fifteenth century a number of Tuscan merchant bankers financed the silver mining industry of the Balkans.[5]

Italian bankers clearly dominated the banking industry throughout the Middle Ages, with the Catalans, especially those from Barcelona, as runners-up; but at the end of the fifteenth century they began to encounter stiff competition from bankers in south Germany who, in the next century, emerged as leaders of the industry.[6] Of these the Fuggers and the Welsers were, of course, most prominent, but there were many others.[7]

The Fuggers owed their prominence in large part to their dealings with the House of Habsburg, in particular with the Emperor Charles V. In the end they suffered the fate of other financiers, such as the Bardi and Peruzzi, who loaned too liberally to sovereigns. In their heyday, however, from the end of the fifteenth century to the middle of the sixteenth century, the House of Fugger was preeminent in European finance. Under Jacob Fugger II (1459–1525) the family firm, with headquarters in Augsburg, operated branches in several German cities, in Hungary, Poland, Italy, Spain, Lisbon, London, and Antwerp. Through their relations with temporal rulers they obtained control of the silver and copper mines of the Tyrol and Hungary from which they supplied the monetary needs of Antwerp before the influx of Spanish silver from the New World.[8] From Lisbon and Antwerp they largely controlled the distribution of spices in Central Europe, for which they exchanged the silver and copper needed to purchase the spices in India. They also accepted deposits and dealt extensively in bills of exchange. The rise of the Fuggers more or less coincided with the rise of the Antwerp market, but the timing was less than coincidental.[9]

The decline of Antwerp, after the initial success of the Dutch revolt and the closure of the Scheldt, was even more rapid and dramatic than its rise, but it was paralleled by the equally rapid and spectacular rise of Amsterdam. The ease with which Amsterdam achieved its rank as the principal entrepôt of Europe was due in part to the influx of merchants and financiers from fallen Antwerp, who brought both their capitalist know-how and their liquid capital.

The seventeenth century appears to have witnessed a mild trough or slowdown in international investment, although the rise of the Dutch and English East India companies absorbed funds that might otherwise have been used for more conventional foreign investments. (The establishment of English and other colonies in North America may also be regarded as a form of foreign investment.) On the one hand the examples of the Spanish kings in repudiating their debts, followed to some extent by the French and other absolute monarchs, discouraged lenders from trusting their disposable funds with political sovereigns. On the other hand the financiers with the most liquid capital—that is, the Dutch—found ample opportunities for investment in shipping, trade, and the public securities of their own country. The Dutch did, nevertheless, initiate a pattern of lending to foreign governments that they expanded greatly in the following century.[10]

In the first half of the seventeenth century Louis de Geer, a Walloon from Liège who became a naturalized Dutchman and operated from Amsterdam, became the principal financier of Sweden's Gustavus Adolphus. De Geer, along with his in-laws of the Trip family, likewise from Amsterdam, also introduced modern technology into Sweden's iron and copper industry, in which he invested heavily.[11] Dutch investors also participated in financing the reclamation of the fenlands of eastern England, employing Dutch engineers and Dutch technology.

Genoa and Geneva continued to function in the seventeenth century on a small scale as markets where funds could be procured for international uses, but it is significant that neither produced great banking dynasties to be compared with those of earlier or later centuries.

The eighteenth century experienced a revival of both international banking and international lending. The Dutch were chiefly responsible for both. The relative decline of Dutch commercial superiority left them with ample reserves of liquid funds but comparatively few profitable outlets for investment. As a result the Amsterdam capital market attracted borrowers—for the most part, deficit-ridden governments—from all of Europe and even, from 1781, the fledgling United States.[12] The principal debtors included Great Britain, Austria, Denmark, Sweden, Russia, Poland, Spain, and France. The process of international lending also produced a new international banking dynasty, Hope & Company, whose founder claimed descent from Scottish nobility.[13] Geneva likewise took part in the eighteenth-century revival of international lending, largely as a result of the dispersal of French Huguenots after the Revocation of the Edict of Nantes in 1685.[14]

The wars of the French Revolution and the Napoleonic era wrought havoc with international financial relations, bringing with them repudiations, inflation, and the disruption of ordinary commercial and financial processes. Indirectly, however, they set the stage for the next episode in the drama of international finance by bringing into prominence those "five gentlemen of Frankfurt," the brothers Rothschild, and by creating the need for the first large international financial operation of the nineteenth century, the financing of the French indemnity. They also opened the way for the classic era of international merchant banking.

Virtually all of the bankers mentioned above were merchants as well as bankers; indeed, most of them became bankers by way of their mercantile activities. In the literature of banking history, however, the period from the end of the Napoleonic Wars to the rise of the great international joint stock banks in the latter half of the nineteenth century is generally regarded as the classic era of merchant banking.[15] In that period private bankers in international commerce and finance proliferated, and a few of them became so rich and powerful that they numbered among the movers and shakers of the nineteenth century.

What, exactly, were their functions, and what were their characteristics? Since they were, in the first place, merchants, the import and export of commodities were, in the beginning at least, of major concern; and some of them continued active in such business until the first half of the twentieth century. The international movement of commodities was financed in large part by bills of exchange and acceptances, thus requiring a familiarity with these instruments on the part of the merchants. Some of them, generally the more prominent ones, began to specialize in granting acceptance credits on bills of exchange for others, thereby making the transition from merchant to banker. According to Chapman, this transition was especially marked in Britain between the crises of 1825 and 1836.[16] In the frequently quoted words of Baron Schroeder, a prominent merchant banker of the late nineteenth century, acceptances were the "bread and butter" of merchant bankers, but some of them helped themselves to the "jam" of the issuance of public securities. With time a few—the London House of Rothschild, for example—specialized in the latter almost entirely.

Another common characteristic of the merchant bankers was their international orientation. Many (of the founders, at least) were natives of countries other than the ones in which they made their marks as bankers. A few of the merchant bankers of Paris could trace their origins to the Old Regime, but others were foreigners, mainly Protestants from Switzerland and Jews from the Rhineland who moved to Paris during the Empire or soon after. The foreign-born or foreign-descended also played prominent roles in the English, especially the London, banking community, which helps to account for its cosmopolitan outlook. The Barings, for example, came originally from Germany. Others were of Dutch and German origin, both Jewish and Gentile; French Huguenots; Greeks and others from the eastern Mediterranean; a goodly number of Americans; and of course the Scots from north of the border. Across the Atlantic in America all of the bankers were of course descended from European stock, but many had come directly and recently from England, Scotland, France, Germany, and elsewhere.

A brief listing of some of the leading figures and families of this international financial community will serve to highlight both the similarities and diversity. At the end of the Napoleonic Wars the Hopes of Amsterdam and the Barings of London were unquestionably the leading international bankers. They had financed a large part of the British war effort and assisted in financing Britain's allies. In 1803 and afterward they helped finance Jefferson's Louisiana Purchase from France. In 1817 they took the lead in organizing France's "liberation loans," the funds for which were raised mainly through the London market although French bankers and investors also participated.

The Rothschilds did not participate directly in the liberation loans, but they soon began to play a major role in virtually all international financial operations. The family bank originated during the Napoleonic Wars when the Elector of Hesse-Cassel, in flight from Napoleon, engaged Meyer Amschel Rothschild of Frankfurt, the founding father, to look after his fortune.[17] Meyer Amschel had five sons, one of whom, Nathan, had gone to England as early as 1798 and in 1804 established the firm of N. M. Rothschild & Co. in London. In 1810 Meyer Amschel took his sons into partnership in the Frankfurt firm as M. A. Rothschild & Söhne. Shortly afterward the youngest son, James, established a branch in Paris where, under the nose of Napoleon, he cooperated with the other branches in financing the allies. After Napoleon's defeat the firms reorganized. The eldest son, Amschel, had already taken over the management of the Frankfurt house after the death of their father in 1812. The Paris branch became an independent firm, and in 1816 Salomon set up a branch in Vienna to help restore the shattered finances of the Habsburg Monarchy. Karl did likewise in the Kingdom of Naples in 1820.

The principal business of the Rothschild banks, like that of all merchant banks of the period, consisted in the finance of international trade by means of bills of exchange drawn on one another and on other correspondents in the principal centers of commerce. Like the Barings and Hopes before them, however, the Rothschilds quickly began to specialize in government finance, underwriting the issues of government bonds that proliferated in the great restructuring of public finance that occurred after the Napoleonic Wars and in the wake of revolutionary upheavals in the 1820s and 1830s. Baron James soon acquired a virtual monopoly on the issue of French government *rentes* and the securities of other Latin governments.

In the mid-nineteenth century the third most important London merchant bank, after Rothschilds and Barings, was Brown, Shipley & Co., the London branch of the American firm of Brown Brothers, which had originated in Baltimore and had branches in New York, Boston, Philadelphia, and Liverpool as well as London.[18] In the 1860s and 1870s it was overtaken by another American firm, J. S. Morgan & Co., whose principal had begun as a partner of George Peabody, one of the pioneer American bankers in London, and whose son, Pierpont Morgan, Sr., was destined to become one of the most powerful private bankers of all time.[19] There were, in addition, numerous other Anglo-American firms based in London.

London also attracted many German-Jewish and other German bankers hoping to follow in the footsteps of the Rothschilds. These included the Stern brothers, R. Raphael & Sons, the Seligman brothers, the Speyer brothers (both also in New York), Alexander Kleinwort (founder of the forerunner of Kleinwort, Benson & Co., eventually the largest acceptance house in London), C. J. Hambro & Son (actually from Copenhagen), Frederick Huth & Co., Ludwig Knoop & Co., and William Brandt.[20] Most of these firms, which also maintained branches on the Continent—Hamburg, Frankfurt, St. Petersburg, and elsewhere—specialized in commercial and financial relations between continental Europe and the rest of the world through London.

Although James de Rothschild was undoubtedly the preeminent private banker in Paris during his lifetime (he died in 1868), he both competed and cooperated with numerous old established Catholic and Protestant firms as well as more recent Jewish arrivals from the Rhineland and Central Europe. Among the former were Jacques Laffitte, a governor of the Bank of France (1814–1819) and an important financial innovator before his death in 1844, and the Perier family, who produced several regents for the Bank of France as well as some prominent politicians. Notable Protestant banking dynasties included the Mallets, established as bankers in Paris from 1723, and the Delessert, Hottinguer, André, Odier, and Vernes families. Among the Jewish financiers the Foulds came to Paris from the Rhineland soon after James de Rothschild. Adolphe d'Eichthal was the first Jewish regent of the Bank of France (1839–1849).[21] Later Jewish arrivals included the Bischoffsheims, the Goldschmidts, and the Sterns, all of whom had relatives and correspondents in both London and Central Europe. All of the above banking families, along with others, were known collectively as *la haute banque parisienne*.

In the second half of the nineteenth century the private merchant bankers encountered the competition of large joint-stock banks. The transition from private to joint-stock banking in the international economy has been dubbed a "financial revolution," and its crucial years have been located in the 1850s and 1860s.[22] Such terminology may be overly dramatic, however, as there was no abrupt shift in either the methods or instruments of international finance. The private banks continued their traditional activities until World War I and even afterwards, and in many instances the joint-stock banks were merely the creations—and creatures—of the private bankers. The transition might more aptly be described as the natural evolution of financial institutions as they responded to changes in the technology of production and communications and to the increase in the capital requirments of both industry and government.

II

The concept of joint-stock investment banking may be traced to the ideas of the utopian theorist Count Henri de Saint-Simon. Saint-Simon argued that the true natural leaders of society were the great bankers and industrialists, and that the means for achieving the reconstruction of society were to be found in the role of credit and the "spirit of association." Among Saint-Simon's acquaintances was the banker Jacques Laffitte, who subsidized a number of the former's publications and who, less than a year after his summary dismissal as governor of the Bank of France, proposed the creation of a company with a capital of 240 million francs to construct all of the canals to be authorized by the French government. The reactionary government of the day, however, fearing the concentration of financial power in the hands of the liberal opposition, of which Laffitte was one of the leaders, rejected the proposal. Four years later Laffitte came up with a new proposal for a Société Commanditaire de l'Industrie to be capitalized at the slightly more modest figure of 100 million francs. The proposed company would function in part as an investment bank, in part as a gigantic holding company for industry. Laffitte enlisted the support of the leading financiers and industrialists, including Casimir Perier, Charles Mallet, and James de Rothschild, as potential investors and officers, but the government, relying in part on the advice of the Bank of France, again rejected the proposal in October 1825. The financial crisis of the following month temporarily dissipated enthusiasm for the project, and the stubborn attitudes of the government and the Bank of France successfully resisted all similar proposals for more than two decades.[23]

Meanwhile more practical steps toward the introduction of joint-stock investment banking occurred in the southern Netherlands, soon to become independent Belgium. There the foundation in 1822 of the Algemeene Nederlandsche Maatschappji ter Begunstiging van de Volksvlijt, known after 1830 as the Société Générale de Belgique, laid the foundations of modern investment banking. A somewhat more detailed account of the activities of the Société Générale and its companion and rival, the Banque de Belgique, in promoting the industrialization of Belgium will be found in Chapter 5. What merits emphasis here, in addition to noting the origin of practical joint-stock investment banking, is the international aspect: that is, the role of the French capital market and in particular the cooperation of the merchant bankers Rothschild and Hottinguer with the Société Générale and the Banque de Belgique, respectively.[24]

For the next act in the drama of international finance the scene switches back to Paris. (The British joint-stock banks, which developed apace from the 1830s, did not engage in international banking until the end of the century, leaving that function to London's merchant banks.) After the *coup d'état* of 1851 and the proclamation of the Second Empire the following year, Napoleon III sought to lessen the dependence of his government on Rothschild and other members of the *Haute banque* by creating new financial institutions. He found eager collaborators in the brothers Emile and Isaac Pereire, former employees of Rothschild who had struck out on their own. With the blessings of the Emperor they founded in 1852 both the Société Générale de Crédit Foncier, a mortgage bank, and the Société Générale de Crédit Mobilier, initially intended as a "railway bank."

The Crédit Foncier at first restricted its activities to France, especially in providing mortgage credit for the reconstruction of Paris undertaken by Napoleon's prefect of the Seine, Baron Haussmann; but in 1863 its directors participated in the establishment of the Allgemeine Oesterreichische Boden-Credit-Anstalt, popularly known in France as the Crédit Foncier Autrichien. In subsequent years it assisted in the formation of the Preussische Central Bodencredit A.G. (1870), the United States Mortgage Company (1871), the Banco Hipotecario de España (1873), and played a large role in Egyptian finances. It also served as the model for the state-owned Sveriges Allmänna Hypo-teksbank (Swedish General Mortgage Bank), founded in 1861, and for German mort-gage banks generally, which played an important role in financing late nineteenth-century urbanization.[25]

Unlike the Crédit Foncier, the Crédit Mobilier launched immediately into interna-tional finance. In the spring of 1853, only a few months after its own establishment, it participated in the syndicate promoting the Bank für Handel und Industrie in Darmstadt (Darmstädter), the first of the German "great banks."[26] From there it went on to promote banks, railways, and industrial enterprises in Switzerland, Austria, Russia, Spain, Italy, the Ottoman Empire, even London! In addition to its own activities, it inspired a host of imitations by both French and other promoters. Some, like the Stockholms Enskilda Bank, were soundly conceived and administered and contributed significantly to the economic development of their countries; others, like the Credit Mobilier of America, which had no connection with the original except the pirated name, were fraudulent from the beginning.

The *Economist* noted with amazement that

> the manner in which the French capitalists are extending their relations is most remarkable. At present they have under their control railways in Switzerland, in Austria, in Italy, in Spain, in Holland, and in Belgium; they have established Crédit Mobiliers in Madrid and Turin, are about to do the same in Lisbon, and are trying to do the same at St. Petersburg and Constantinople; they are endeavoring to obtain concessions of railways in Russia; they have established a large bank at Darmstadt, and will not rest until they get one at Constantinople; . . . they hold important con-cessions of mines and coal pits in Spain, in the Rhenish provinces, and in Silesia; they hold a large and in some cases a predominating interest in numerous railways, iron works, coal pits, and banks in Belgium; they are about to establish lines of gigantic steamers . . . ; they are taking the lead in the project for cutting through the Isthmus at Suez; and they have a pretty considerable interest in the omnibuses of Lon-don. . . .[27]

James de Rothschild observed the progress of his former employees with growing concern. Although he did not immediately sever relations with them—in April 1852 Emile Pereire presented the annual report for the directors of the French Northern Railway and was reelected as director for a term of four years—Rothschild withdrew his support from the Pereires' projected Midi Railway, and thus indirectly—and unintentionally—turned them to promote the Crédit Mobilier. When they offered him a token participation in the first block of shares he replied by drafting an indignant letter to none other than the Prince-President in which he charged them with speculation, monopoly, and irresponsibility![28] The following year, during the promotion of the Darmstädter Bank, Rothschild organized a countersyndicate to depress the price of the shares, thereby depriving the promoters of most of their expected profits.[29]

Of all the Pereires' successes, their purchase of the Austrian State Railway by the Crédit Mobilier in 1854 galled Rothschild the most. The public finances of the Habsburg Monarchy had been regarded by the Rothschilds as virtually an exclusive fief, and they resented any transgression on it. Even more ominous, rumors circulated in the spring of 1855 of the impending formation of a large joint-stock bank in Vienna by interests affiliated with the Crédit Mobilier. Isaac Pereire, in his annual report to

Crédit Mobilier stockholders in April 1855, outlined a program for the creation of affiliated banks in all countries of Europe:

> In creating these establishments it would be necessary, while assuring them of independence of action for the development of their own national industries, to avoid the dangers of isolation. It would be necessary, in fact, to attach them to one another in order to develop their powers of expansion and association. . . .[30]

Soon afterward Isaac himself was in Vienna with a number of proposals for the economic development of the monarchy, including plans for the bank.

The Rothschilds had been handicapped in opposing the purchase of the railway by the absence of any family members in the Austrian capital. Salomon, in charge since 1816, had fled the country with Metternich in 1848, leaving the bank in the care of employees; he died near Paris early in 1855. James, now stung into vigorous action, dispatched Salomon's son Anselm, whom he had trained personally in his Paris countinghouse, to prevent further encroachments on the family preserve in Austria. Anselm joined forces with a group of Viennese aristocrats and bankers of the second order who had already petitioned the government to charter a *mobilier*-type bank. Alexander Bach, the interior minister, and Baron von Bruck, the finance minister, at first favored the Pereires' proposal, but with the return of the Rothschilds they suggested an amalgamation of the two groups. The Pereires reluctantly agreed, but Baron James, hastily making amends with the imperial government in Paris, persuaded it to attach conditions that made it impossible for the Crédit Mobilier to participate. Thus on November 6, 1855, the Austrian government formally chartered the K. K. Privilegirten Oesterreichischen Creditanstalt für Handel und Gewerbe to a group dominated by the Rothschilds. Baron James, who along with other merchant bankers had frequently denounced the joint-stock form of organization as inconsistent with the banker's function, allowed himself to be persuaded of its utility.

With the Rothschilds' example before them, other merchant bankers flocked to create joint-stock banks. In 1856 the Rothschilds themselves, through their Berlin correspondent Gerson Bleichröder, took part in establishing the Berliner Handels-Gesellschaft, a creation of the principal merchant bankers of Berlin. Unable to secure a charter as an *anonym Gesellschaft* from the Prussian administration, the founders organized it as a *Kommanditgesellschaft*.[31] In the same year David Hansemann reorganized the Diskonto-Gesellschaft, also a *Kommanditgesellschaft* founded in 1851 as a simple discount bank on the model of the French Comptoir d'Escompte, as a *mobilier*-type operation.

Although the Prussian administration was adamant in refusing charters for true joint-stock banks, other German principalities were more liberal: In the single year 1856 no fewer than a dozen joint-stock banks, mostly modeled on the Crédit Mobilier, were established in such German cities as Breslau, Coburg, Dessau, Hamburg (two), Leipzig, and Oldenburg.[32] That same year, also saw the creation of banks in other countries, with three Switzerland, three in Spain (all with French capital, including affiliates of Rothschild and the Crédit Mobilier), and others in Sweden, the Kingdom of Sardinia (Piedmont), and Constantinople. Attempts to establish *mobilier*-type banks were also made in Belgium, the Netherlands, Rumania, and Serbia, but in all cases the proposals were refused by the respective governments.

Why were there no new banks in France in 1856? In fact, Rothschild and several other prominent merchant bankers, a group known informally as the *Syndicat des banquiers* and the *Réunion financière*, had planned to establish one, but the government, fearing a financial crisis (a year prematurely, as it turned out) announced on March 6 that it would approve no further *sociétés anonymes* for the remainder of the year. The next French joint-stock bank, the Crédit Industriel et Commercial, came in 1859. Its founders, who included David Hansemann and William Gladstone of London (*not* the politician) as well as several French bankers, announced that they intended to create a large deposit bank on the English model and "naturalize" in France the English practice of payment by check; in fact, its operations in its early years resembled those of the Crédit Mobilier. Meanwhile the Comptoir d'Escompte de Paris, created as a temporary emergency measure in 1848, received a new charter as an independent *société anonyme* in 1854, doubled its capital in 1856, and by 1870, with a capital of 100 million francs, had branches in London, Alexandria, Bombay, Calcutta, Hong Kong, Saigon, Shanghai, and Yokohama.

The next great wave of financial promotions reached a peak in 1863, with dozens of new banks and credit companies setting up throughout Europe: in France, Switzerland, Italy, Belgium, the Netherlands, Sweden, the Czech Crownlands and Hungary as well as Austria proper, Russia, and even in well-banked England. The names of two of these new institutions will appear frequently in this volume: the International Financial Society of London, the details of whose founding are sketched in Chapter 1; and the Banque de Paris et des Pays-Bas (Paribas).

The latter began as a nominally Dutch institution, the Nederlandsche Credit en Deposito-Bank of Amsterdam. Although it had a Dutch charter, the majority of shareholders owning more than three fourths of its shares resided in France, and it immediately opened a branch in Paris that quickly outran the main office in Amsterdam in its volume of business. Its energizing spirit was Louis Bischoffsheim, a Jewish financier who moved from Amsterdam to Paris in 1850 and set up a private bank, which he subsequently merged with the new institution. From the beginning it operated internationally; by 1870 it had branches in Geneva, Antwerp, and Brussels, and participated in banks and industrial enterprises in France, Belgium, and overseas. In 1872 it amalgamated with the recently established Banque de Paris, changed its name, and moved its headquarters to Paris.

In 1863 the Crédit Industriel established a filial, the Société de Dépôts et de Comptes Courants, also in Paris. More auspicious for the future, Henri Germain, using the new law permitting free incorporation with limited liability for companies capitalized at not more than 20 million francs, founded the Crédit Lyonnais with exactly 20 million francs as a purely local bank. It did not long remain such. In 1864 it established a branch in Paris, which became its head office in 1878.[33]

Rothschild and his friends in the *Réunion financière* had intended to launch their long-delayed rival of the Crédit Mobilier, the Société Générale pour favoriser le développement du Commerce et de l'Industrie en France ("Société Générale"), in 1863, but bureaucratic foot-dragging in the *Conseil d'Etat* held up approval of their request for a full year. Meanwhile the English friends of the *Réunion financière* had succeeded in bringing out the Société Générale's "twin," the General Credit and Finance Company.[34]

Germany did not participate significantly in the financial promotions of the 1860s.

In part, perhaps, the creations of the 1850s sufficed; but more important was Prussia's continued refusal to permit joint stock banks. When the law was modified in 1870 to permit free incorporation—together with the euphoria generated by the victory over France later the same year—the *Grunderjahren* of 1870–1872 made the experience of 1856 pale by comparison. In little more than three years more than a hundred new banks were founded in Germany alone. The crisis and depression of 1873 wiped out almost three fourths of those, but of the ones that survived the Deutsche Bank and the Dresdner Bank were destined to play a large role.[35] A new chapter in the history of international banking had begun.

III

The following decades, until the outbreak of World War I, witnessed the creation of a truly worldwide economy.[36] International commerce increased at unprecedented rates: more than 3 percent per annum for the world as a whole, and much higher than that for the leading commercial nations. As trade grew, the international division of labor became more pronounced, with the nations of Western Europe (and, increasingly, the United States) exchanging their manufactures for foodstuffs and raw materials from the rest of the world.

International investment likewise reached unprecedented heights and involved, as either creditors or debtors, virtually every inhabited region of the globe. Table 1 provides a quantitative basis for the analysis that follows.[37]

As is well known, a handful of West European nations provided the bulk of foreign investments. Great Britain alone was responsible for more than 40 percent of the total. (Actually, some of the investments made through London belonged to nationals of other countries.) The only major lender outside Europe was the United States, which was also, however, the largest gross debtor. Among the borrowing nations, other than the United States, the Russian Empire was the largest gross and net debtor, although on a per capita basis Canada, Australia, New Zealand, the Scandinavian countries, and perhaps a few Latin American nations exceeded it. The Austrian half of the Habsburg Monarchy was a creditor with respect to the Hungarian half, but the monarchy as a whole was a net debtor.

Among the creditor countries all except Great Britain and possibly the Netherlands had been debtors earlier in the nineteenth century (and Great Britain in the eighteenth, with the Netherlands its principal creditor). France became a net exporter of capital in the 1820s, and Belgium in the 1850s. The Netherlands, the world's leading capital exporter in the seventeenth and eighteenth centuries, may have become a net debtor in the first half of the nineteenth century; but if so it soon recovered its status as a capital exporter. The German states, especially Prussia, were significant net debtors before about 1870, but with the rapid growth of industry and trade after the formation of the new German empire in 1871 Germany quickly became one of the major capital exporters. Switzerland—more specifically, the city and canton of Geneva—had been historically an exporter of capital; but in the second half of the nineteenth century it became a net debtor, principally on account of railways. By the beginning of the twentieth century Switzerland had apparently recovered its position as a capital exporter, but that is by no means certain; because of its geographical and political position,

TABLE 1. Gross Foreign Investments as of 1914 (in billions of 1914 U.S. dollars)

By Lending Region and Country			By Borrowing Region and Country		
Europe		40.0	*Western Hemisphere*		19.6
United Kingdom	18–20.		United States	7.1	
France	9–10.		Canada	3.7	
Germany	6–7.0		Argentina	3.0	
Netherlands	2.0		Brazil	2.2	
Belgium	1.5		Mexico	2.0	
Switzerland	1.5		Other Latin America	1.6	
Rest of the world		5.0	*Europe*		11.0
United States	3.5		Russia	4–5.0	
Other[a]	1.5		Spain and Portugal	2.0	
			Austria-Hungary	1.5	
			Italy	1.0	
			Balkans	1.0	
			Scandinavia	1.0	
			Asia		8.0
			Near and Mideast[b]	3.0	
			India and Ceylon	2.0	
			China	1.5	
			Other	1.5	
			Africa		4.0
			South Africa	1.7	
			Other	2.3	
			Oceania		2.4
			Australia	1.7	
			Other	0.7	
TOTAL		45.	TOTAL		45.

Sources: Herbert Feis, *Europe, the World's Banker, 1870–1914* (New York, 1939); William Woodruff, *Impact of Western Man: A Study of Europe's Role in the World Economy, 1750–1960* (New York, 1967); W. Arthur Lewis, *Growth and Fluctuations, 1870–1913* (New York, 1978); Rondo Cameron, *France and the Economic Development of Europe, 1800–1914* (Princeton, 1961); Mira Wilkins, *The History of Foreign Investment in the United States to 1914* (Cambridge, MA, 1989), 145.

[a] e.g., Japan and Russia in China and Korea, Portugal in Brazil.

[b] Ottoman Empire, Egypt, and Persia.

Switzerland became a favorite site for the location of international holding companies, especially in the electrical industry, resulting in myriad inflows and outflows of capital.

The geographical distribution of foreign investments reveals interesting patterns. Table 1 shows the overwhelming predominance of the Western Hemisphere as a destination, with more than 40 percent of the invested funds. Of those, the United States and Canada took more than half, accounting together for almost as much as all of Europe, the second largest recipient. Great Britain, appropriately, furnished the lion's share, with German, French, and other European investments distinctly secondary. In Latin America, Great Britain was also the largest investor, with roughly 40 percent of the total; but Germany, France, other European countries, and the United States and Canada (from the 1890s) also contributed.

Europe, surprisingly perhaps, absorbed almost one quarter of the foreign investments in 1914; but the recipients belonged primarily to those countries on the periphery of Europe, geographically and economically. (In the mid-nineteenth century several countries in Western and Central Europe, which later became capital exporters themselves, figured prominently among the recipients of investment.) France was the major creditor, especially for Russia, the Iberian peninsula, and Scandinavia. Germany had larger investments in Austria-Hungary. The smaller European creditor countries also invested in Europe, as did Great Britain to a lesser extent, and even the United States (especially in the electro-technical industries of Western and Central Europe).

Investments in Asia (excluding Russian Siberia) were widely scattered. The Near and Middle East (Ottoman and Persian empires, Egypt) was most important quantitatively. The French had invested massively in the Suez Canal and Egypt, although by 1914 Great Britain was also a major creditor. All creditor nations vied for the opportunity to lend to the decrepit Ottoman Empire, with the French in the lead, followed by Germany and England. Persia's minimal demands were supplied almost exclusively by Britain, with a token participation by Russia under the aegis of the government. Britain, of course, was also the principal investor in India and Ceylon, and the Netherlands in Indonesia. In China, as Frank King vividly demonstrates in Chapter 17, all of the creditor nations, joined as well by Russia, Japan, and the United States, impelled by a mixture of pecuniary and political motives, participated in the scramble for the privilege of granting loans. The other Asian recipients included Japan, Thailand, and the various colonial dependencies.

Investments in Africa, other than Egypt, went primarily to the European colonies there, including South Africa, which obtained dominion status in 1910. Although France, Germany, Belgium, and even Spain and Portugal participated, British investment was paramount.

Britain, of course, also dominated investment in Oceania, primarily Australia and New Zealand. Although investments in that area were the smallest of the geographical regions considered, they were in terms of the size of the host population among the largest recorded anywhere.

IV

What was the role of banks in the investment process? Great Britain had both the largest foreign investments and the most highly developed banking system, but these two facts were not strictly related in a cause-and-effect nexus. As Cottrell shows in Chapter 1, the foreign investments were orchestrated in large part by London's private bankers, with their widespread international connections, operating through the London Stock Exchange. The domestic banks were scarcely involved before the 1890s, and even then their role was distinctly secondary to that of the private banks. Insofar as they participated in international finance they did so indirectly, by placing their deposits at the disposal of bill brokers and discount houses, and that for the purpose of financing trade on a short-term basis.

This state of affairs had its mirror reflection in the United States, the largest capital importer, where private bankers, mainly in New York, directed the inflow of foreign capital in cooperation with their counterparts in London. For a variety of reasons detailed by Carosso and Sylla and by Wilkins, domestic joint-stock banks did not participate significantly in international capital flows—not even in short-term trade finance. Subsequently, in the 1890s and afterward, when the United States began to export capital on a large scale, it was again the private rather than the joint-stock banks that played the leading role. (A major exception should be made for direct investments abroad by America-based multinationals, such as Standard Oil Company, the large electrical manufacturers, and International Harvester.)

In the countries of continental Europe, on the other hand, both those that exported and those that imported capital, the joint-stock banks played a much larger role in the mobilization and deployment of capital for foreign investment. This was due in part to the closer relations—one might almost say an identity of interests—of the private and joint stock bankers. Even so, significant national differences existed in the manner in which the banks played their roles.

French industry, with its tradition of self-finance, had few direct links with the banking system—or so it is alleged by some authorities. Whether or not this was so, and if so whether it reflected the strength or weakness of industrial enterprises, is still a subject for debate. It is also maintained by some that French banks had an aversion to industrial finance—the experience of the Crédit Lyonnais with the artificial dyestuffs industry in the late 1870s is frequently cited in this connection—which inverts the direction of the argument. In either case, according to the proponents of this line of argument, the absence of strong bank-industry relationships within France predisposed the banks to nonindustrial investments when they sought investment outlets abroad. They had invested—or guided the investments of their customers—in railroads and some other public works in France, and did so as well abroad. For the greater part, however, they tended toward the "safe" investments represented by government securities. Thus they neither supported French industry in its search for foreign markets, nor did they seek to build up complementary industrial aggregates abroad. (The strength of this argument is diluted somewhat by the evidence on security issues in France for the period 1892 to 1914, the only one for which comparable reliable figures exist. They show nongovernmental issues rising from 25 percent of total foreign issues in the 1890s to slightly more than one-half for the years 1910 to 1913.)[38]

Another argument sometimes advanced to account for the character of French foreign investments and the role of the banking system in promoting them invokes the low rate of interest in France (indicating a slack demand for capital, for whatever reason) and the situation of the French balance of payments. From about 1867 onward, except for the Franco-Prussian War and its immediate aftermath, the income from existing foreign investments generally equalled or exceeded the total of new foreign investments. Although there was no mechanism to guarantee the automatic reinvestment abroad of income received from abroad, the availability of such funds gave the bankers considerable leeway in advising their clients, and numerous studies have shown the greater profitability *to the banks* of foreign over domestic securities.

The situation with respect to Belgian foreign investments and the role of the banking system is far more straightforward than for France. Prior to about 1850 Belgium was a net importer of capital, mainly from France. As is well known, and as briefly recapitulated in Chapter 5 on Belgium, the Société Générale de Belgique and other Belgian banks played a major role in channeling that capital into Belgian heavy industry. After about 1850, when Belgium became a capital exporter, the Société Générale, again followed by the other banks, played a similar role in channeling Belgian capital abroad. It did so in the first instance by participating in the establishment of railways, tramways, and industrial enterprises that purchased equipment from Belgian firms patronized by the banks. At a later stage, in the 1890s, the Société Générale took the lead in creating holding companies and similar financial institutions abroad in which it maintained a controlling or at least a preponderant interest. These firms, in turn, catered to the needs of government and industries in the countries in which they were located. In this way the Société Générale, in particular, became the center of a vast worldwide network of financial and industrial interests.

Germany's position in the international financial network was again different, and more complex than that of Belgium, but perhaps less so than that of France. As Professor Tilly makes clear, Germany's rapidly growing industries required large domestic investments of capital. The banking system that developed from the 1850s, and especially from the 1870s, catered directly to the needs of German industry for capital, and also accompanied it abroad in the search for foreign markets. The booming export surplus of German industry generated the funds for foreign investment, and the banks saw to it that those funds were utilized in ways that contributed to further foreign demand for German industrial products. They did this in part like the Société Générale de Belgique, by patronizing foreign enterprises, especially railways, that placed orders for German industry. They also attempted to exert diplomatic pressure on needy foreign governments to the same end, occasionally with success. (In some instances the German government pressured the banks for primarily political reasons. The Deutsche Bank's involvement with the famous *Baghdadbahn*, for example, was undertaken at the urging of the German foreign office.) German banks also engaged in what can best be described as cooperative ventures, both with one another and with banks of other nationalities (including the French, in spite of diplomatic and political tensions). The complexity of these alliances defies simple summary, but some of the details will be found in the chapters that follow, not only in the chapter on Germany.

One of the most striking aspects of the Russian banking system is the extent to which the creation and growth of that system was an integral part of the process of foreign investment itself. The first major instance of foreign investment in Russia, apart from occasional borrowings of the tsarist government in Holland in the eighteenth and nineteenth centuries, was the Great Russian Railway Company of the late 1850s. It was financed by French, British, Dutch, and German bankers with token participation by a couple of private bankers in St. Petersburg and Warsaw.[39] The formation of the "modern" Russian banking system dates from the foundation of the State Bank in 1860, and more especially from the proliferation of joint-stock banks after 1868. Most of the joint stock banks not only employed Western capital (a majority in some, at least in the 1900s), but also obtained their executives and managers from banks in Western Europe. This did not mean that Russian banks were mere slavish imitations of Western banks, but, as Bovykin and Anan'ich point out, they "developed through a process of adapting borrowed experience to indigenous conditions."[40] Western banks invested in Russian banks not only as a profitable use of their funds but also, especially in the 1890s and afterwards, as a means for obtaining contracts for Russian government loans and for overseeing their numerous investments in Russian industry.

The banks of Denmark and Sweden also followed the models of their more advanced neighbors, especially France and Germany; but unlike the Russian banks they were financed and managed by indigenous entrepreneurs. For the most part they engaged in purely domestic activity, where they were heavily involved in the finance of domestic industry. To the extent that they participated in international affairs, apart from the short-term finance of international trade, they served as conduits for the introduction of foreign capital, much as the Société Générale de Belgique had done in Belgium before 1850.

The Austro-Hungarian banking system (the treatment of which might have been placed in Part I equally as well as in Part II) was likewise an integral part of the continental "model," with strong affinities to, as well as intimate relations with, the French and German—and even the British—systems. On the whole, however, insofar as joint operations were concerned, the Austro-Hungarian banks appeared most often as junior partners to other banks, at least with respect to foreign operations in southeastern Europe and elsewhere.

Professor Hertner's assignment, which he has acquitted extremely well, was expressly confined to delineating and analyzing the role of foreign capital in the Italian banking sector. Thus the reader should not expect to find a complete exposition and evaluation of the Italian banking system. Instead, readers will discover, first, the preponderant role of French capital and influence in the formation and development of Italian banking, and second, in the 1890s, the important stimulus of German capital and methods. By the early twentieth century, however, the Italian system had been assimilated into the larger Western European model.

Outside Europe and the United States, banking systems developed along lines already pioneered in those two entities, sometimes by explicit design, at other times in more random fashion. This did not result, however, in a uniform pattern—far from it. To an even greater extent than in Europe and the United States, local circumstances of geography, politics, and historical tradition shaped and modified the evolving financial structures. The final outcome was a bewildering mosaic of bits and pieces that requires a practiced and perceptive eye to detect the common elements.

Professor Drummond's chapter on Australia and Canada is especially successful because the author consciously adopted an international comparative perspective and explicitly compared the distinctive features as well as the common elements in his two cases. In both the banking systems resembled—as might be expected—the British and American patterns more than the continental European, without being merely derivative in either. With respect to their roles in the process of international investment, the latter was incidental rather than determining.

The Japanese case is also especially important and interesting for several reasons. In the first place, Japan was the only nation entirely outside the Western cultural tradition before 1914 successfully to adopt Western technology and institutions while preserving its own. In the more limited sphere of banking and finance, Japan consciously and explicitly adopted Western models—that of the United States in 1872, then those of Europe a decade later, after the first had proved unsatisfactory—yet the final, successful result was distinctly Japanese. With respect to the role of banks (and government) in the process of international investment, Professor Ishii shows how Japan was able to utilize foreign investors and their funds without allowing them to dominate the Japanese economy. His chapter (10), which relies almost entirely on Japanese-language sources, is certain to become the definitive English-language article on the subject.

It is a matter of regret that Latin America is distinctly underrepresented in our sample of banking systems. Brazil is scarcely typical of the region as a whole for a number of reasons, including its size and history. Its economy did, nevertheless, exhibit a number of characteristics in common with the remainder of Latin America. The most obvious of these, of course, was the dependence on foreign, mainly European, markets for the export of primary products. For the rest, the economies were mostly of the subsistence variety, with only limited market orientation. The correlative of the dependence on foreign markets was a similar dependence on foreign sources of capital. This was true of both long-term and short-term capital, the latter for financing the export of the primary products and the import of manufactures, capital as well as consumer goods. The intermediaries for the long-term investments were chiefly European private bankers, especially the Rothschilds for Brazil (the Barings played a similar role in Argentina until the crisis of 1890), although near the end of the nineteenth century some joint-stock banks, especially German, became active in this area. The need for short-term capital was ministered to by expatriate merchants and bankers, mainly British, although again near the end of the century German and other joint-stock banks participated. Domestic private and joint-stock banks also existed, but they were concerned mostly with domestic commerce, industry, and especially agriculture.

Frank King's fascinating account of European banks on the China coast reveals that almost all of them were originally established to finance international trade. Even the exceptions, such as the Russo-Chinese Bank and its successor, the Russo-Asiatic Bank, proclaimed the finance of trade as their ostensible purpose. (The Banque de l'Indo-Chine, on the other hand, which also established branches in China, began as an all-purpose bank, including the issue of banknotes, for France's Asian colonies.) The most successful of all, the Hongkong and Shanghai Banking Corporation, was even founded as a "local bank" to finance regional trade within China. Eventually, however, they were all drawn into the competition to secure concessions from the imperial government and to grant it loans to cover its ever-widening deficits. The chapter will be of interest to both political and economic and banking historians.

The same can be said with even greater emphasis with respect to the chapter on the Middle East. The banking systems there were to a large extent merely the overflow of systems already existing in Europe, but they encountered and became enmeshed in the tangle of great-power diplomacy and politics that already characterized the relations of the European powers with polities in the area. The first joint-stock bank in the area, the British Bank of Egypt, dated from 1855, but it encountered the economic competition and political opposition of numerous French private banks that already operated there. In time the French established their own joint-stock banks, and banks of other nationalities, both private and joint-stock, soon proliferated. The predominant financial institution in the whole of the Middle East, however, was the Banque Impériale Ottomane. Established as a British overseas bank in 1856, it received a large infusion of French capital and management in 1863, and by the end of the century it was regarded as an almost exclusively French institution. Even so, it was the only foreign bank to have direct discounting access to the Bank of England. In 1889 British interests established the Imperial Bank of Persia. All European banks in the Middle

East, including branches of European joint stock banks, such as the Crédit Lyonnais and the Deutsche Bank, engaged in ordinary commercial banking, especially the finance of international trade; and most of them also became involved in various developmental projects, especially railways and other forms of infrastructure investment. Their most characteristic activity, however, was government finance, with its inevitable political complications.

V

Readers may be curious about the relative brevity of Part III. As we explain further in our conclusion, the organizers of this project (Bovykin and Cameron) initially expected to discover that large banks with international interests played a major role in organizing and financing multinational industrial enterprises. We did not, and that is one of the major conclusions of our study. The reasons we did not—that is, the reasons the banks did not play the role we expected to find—may be deduced from the four case studies we do present, and are explicitly stated by Carosso and Sylla with respect to the House of Morgan, probably the largest and most influential private bank in operation at the end of the nineteenth century: International banking in both its private and joint stock forms was a highly specialized profession.[41] Its most successful practitioners recognized this and stuck to their lasts as assiduously as a skilled shoemaker to his. Banking involves risk-taking, to be sure, as does any market-oriented activity, but the risks bankers are exposed to—even investment bankers—differ in kind from those of industrial entrepreneurs. Only rarely did bankers succumb to the temptation to become industrial entrepreneurs, and they usually regretted it when they did. Evidence for this is found throughout the chapters that follow, and especially in the four case studies of Part III.

Fursenko clearly shows that in the oil industry large integrated multinational companies maintained their independence vis-à-vis the banks, regardless of the latter's wishes or intentions. This was notably the case with the Standard Oil Company, which served in effect as its own investment bank, but the larger European firms followed a similar pattern. Ludwig Nobel and his son and successor, Emmanuel, the most successful entrepreneurs in the Russian oil industry, made frequent use of banks, foreign as well as Russian; but at no time did the banks dictate company policy. The Paris Rothschilds had a major interest in the Russian oil industry, but as industrial entrepreneurs rather than as bankers. Their oil concerns were entirely separate from the family bank, and they eventually sold them to Royal Dutch-Shell. The German banks, in spite of repeated efforts both individual and collective, never succeeded in controlling even the German market. Finally, the Anglo-Persian Oil Company (later British Petroleum) owed its existence not to the banks but to that role model of laissez faire, the British government.

Wengenroth tells a similar story for the iron and steel industry. There, as he points out, "technological and organizational economies of size and scale acted as strong imperatives to concentrate operations as much as possible in one place,"[42] rather than duplicate facilities across political boundaries. Insofar as the enterprises did seek foreign properties it was in an effort to secure vertical integration by obtaining control of raw materials (iron ore and coal). Banks facilitated this process, especially by providing useful contacts and information, but they did not supply the initiative. They played a similar role when changes in Russian tariff policy and slack domestic demand suggested to Belgian, German, and French iron and steel makers the profitability of transferring their operations to the newly opened coal and iron resources of the southern Ukraine. The one instance in which a bank played a distinctly entrepreneurial role was the involvement of the Deutsche Bank with the Mannesman tube steel companies, but that came about when the traditional support of the bank for innovative entrepreneurs resulted in large and seemingly unending losses. The bank was obliged to take over the management of the enterprise in order to salvage its investment, but when the companies were finally viable the bank disposed of them on the market.[43]

Carstensen's account of McCormick/International Harvester, although dealing only with a single enterprise and thus not generalizable for an industry as a whole, nevertheless has the merit of subjecting that enterprise to a detailed, almost microscopic, treatment. He finds that the firm's "financial operations, though occasionally influenced by the internal struggle for corporate control, remained entirely separate from production and marketing strategies, domestic and foreign."[44] McCormick personally, and subsequently International Harvester, had financial dealings with many banks, but none was able to influence company policy significantly. In the one instance when a large bank might have been able to play a significant role, that role was in fact taken over by a single individual, John D. Rockefeller, who apparently acted from family motives as the father-in-law of Harold F. McCormick.

The electrical industry presented a different aspect from those previously considered. It was even newer than petroleum and agricultural machinery, technically more sophisticated, and subject to a high rate of technological obsolescence. It was also highly capital intensive and susceptible to economies of scale, like iron and steel. The remarkable success of the German industry in Europe, rivalled only by that of the United States overseas, undoubtedly has a very complex explanation, of which the role of banks and finance is only one element. It may well be true, as Broder asserts, that the German banks were both better equipped and more willing than those of other large nations to finance the expansion of the industry both domestically and abroad; but, on his own evidence, it was the electrical entrepreneurs rather than the banks who conceived the successful strategy, to which the banks had to conform.[45]

In addition to the few industries included in Part III, the organizers had initially intended to present a chapter on the chemical industry, but our consultant and potential author, Professor Paul Hohenberg, persuaded us that there was too little bank involvement to be of interest in this connection. Here human capital and technical knowledge, rather than physical or financial capital, were the relatively scarce factors. The textile industries, as is well known, made relatively little use of long-term bank finance. The fledgling automobile industry at the beginning of the twentieth century, like the oil industry, developed largely on the basis of reinvested profits with minimal participation by banks. At the Bellagio conference mentioned in the Preface, Dr. Ragnhild Lundström presented a brief paper on the finances of the Nobel dynamite "trust," which we intended to include in our collection; but again, the findings were largely negative— that is, they showed that the role of banks was incidental and of little consequence.

We return, therefore, to the original stimuli of our project: international factors in the formation of banking systems and the role of banks in foreign investment. International banking firms were the first multinational business enterprises. As such they influenced, in greater or lesser degree, the character of the various national and regional banking systems in which they were imbedded. Their role as conduits of foreign investment was particularly important to the rapid growth of the international economy from 1870 to 1914. But that role was relatively much greater in short-term trade finance and in foreign portfolio investment of a passive nature than in the active, entrepreneurial financing of industry across national borders. The essays that follow illuminate these and many other points.

I

INTERNATIONAL FACTORS
IN THE FORMATION
OF BANKING SYSTEMS

1

Great Britain

P. L. Cottrell

Although Great Britain's industrial leadership declined in relative terms during the half century before the World War I, its international financial power increased both absolutely and relatively.[2]

The distinguishing feature of the British economy from the mid-1850s was its high propensity to export capital, so much so that the ratio of net overseas assets to gross domestic product (GDP) increased from 0.8 in 1873 to 1.8 in 1913, with the income from net overseas assets being 8.5 percent of GDP in the latter year. Between the early 1870s and 1914 the proportion of British savings devoted to the export of capital was the highest of that in the history of any major country. Whereas from the early 1870s until 1914 Britain, Germany, and the United States had broadly similar rates of savings of the order of ll to 15 percent of gross national product (GNP), British domestic investment was only 7 percent of GNP as compared with 12 percent for its two growing industrial rivals. The balance of British savings was sent abroad.[3] In 1914 Britain's international investments were more than double those of France, more than three times those of Germany, and nearly six times those of the United States.

Between 1870 and 19l4 Britain was also the center of international trade. Its exports rose rapidly and its imports even more rapidly.[4] In 1870, based on the total value of imports and exports, Britain's four principal trading partners were the United States, France, British India, and Germany. In 1912 the top four were the same, but in a slightly different order. In the years between 1870 and 1914, however, the eastern coast of South America (Brazil, Uruguay, Argentina) had moved from tenth rank to fifth rank in the list of Britain's trading partners. In 1912 British trade with these three countries almost equaled that with France (£90 million versus £92 million).[5] These trade figures are highly relevant in discussions of British international banking.

For reasons of economy in exposition, historians often refer to the British capital market during the fifty years before 1914 as "London," thereby implying an almost unchanging monolithic institution. Such an approach, although understandable at high levels of generalization, ignores provincial and Scottish developments and may give the wrong impression to the reader in suggesting that there was no structural development after 1870. Actually the British financial sector did not achieve anything like its modern form until the beginning of the twentieth century, as major changes that began during the mid-century period were not fully worked out until the early 1900s. The liberalization of company law with respect to banking between 1857 and 1862, along with other factors, led to a major boom in joint stock bank formations, of which the most novel element was the establishment of corporate overseas banks. Expansion of the financial sector was tempered by crises in 1866 and 1878, which led the domestic commercial banks to a greater concern for liquidity and reserve requirements and may have brought about a sea change in lending behavior.

With regard to English domestic banking, the industry in 1870 still consisted largely of unit banks, both private and joint-stock, and a national banking system only developed from the 1890s as a result of amalgamation and branch expansion. Until the full emergence of "nationwide" banks with "balanced" branch networks in the early 1900s, the system of unit commercial banks was integrated merely through correspondent relationships with the metropolis, involving certain London banks either holding balances, or arranging the rediscount of bills, for country banks. "Surplus" funds were invested as deposits in the London money market—Lombard Street—in which the principals were the discount houses, which also took bills either directly or indirectly from the provincial commercial banks.

Not only was the structure of the commercial banking system transformed during the last quarter of the nineteenth century, but the London money market also underwent profound changes. These consisted of the development of corporate discount houses from the mid-1850s, their dominance after the 1866 crisis in which the major private house—Overend, Gurney, & Co.—had failed, and, owing to declining domestic inventories and the growing liquidity of domestic commercial banks, their main stock-in-trade from the 1880s became international bills rather than inland bills of exchange. Therefore, although the commercial banking system centered on the London money market from the 1830s, following the appearance of the discount houses in the City, the commercial banks themselves did not become London-centered until almost the Edwardian period, when they had grand City head offices that administered branch networks covering the whole of the English economy. Scottish banks, a product of a different development, had London offices from the 1870s, many years after the emergence of commercial joint banks with extensive branch networks centered either on Edinburgh or Glasgow.

Generally, until the 1880s, English joint-stock banks were concerned with the accumulation of deposits and their mobilization primarily but not entirely through the provision of short term credit facilities. Their customers, both depositors and borrowers, were usually members of the local economies that the banks had been established to serve, and were quite frequently shareholders in the banks. International dealings were largely the concern of London-based financial institutions, frequently of foreign origin, a development that had begun in the last quarter of the eighteenth century but which grew apace from the mid-1850s. The main principals were private merchant banks that provided international acceptance credits—the bill on London—and some of which undertook the flotation of foreign loans. Their numbers grew from the 1850s with the increase in international financial activity, and they were joined from the 1860s and 1870s by new corporate concerns—"Anglo-International" and "Anglo-Imperial" banks—through which they were linked by merchant bankers acting as their promoters and subsequently their directors. The community of overseas bankers within the City was augmented after the 1870s by the establishment of further merchant banks and the transformation of a number of local and "offshore" mercantile firms into investment groups, which undertook new issues activity. London's pivotal position in the world economy before 1914 was further underlined by the growing number of foreign banks that opened offices in the City from the 1870s.

The English financial sector in the 1870s was marked by a division of labor through specialization of function, but the parallel financial markets that this characteristic produced did, to some degree, coalesce from the 1880s. This came about not so much as a result of London's merchant banks taking an interest in the capital needs of provincial industry, but rather through a growing involvement on the part of the emerging nationwide joint-stock banks in overseas dealings. This took a variety of forms but was marked by the commercial banks entering the international acceptance market, becoming investors in certain classes of overseas securities, underwriting foreign issues, and, finally, acting as issuing houses for international flotations.

At the center of the system was the Bank of England, a very special commercial bank, with responsibilities in public finance and a lender of last resort. Its customers included the British government, the London clearing banks, the merchant banks, British overseas banks, some foreign banks, and the discount houses. It also dealt with the public, individuals, and business enterprises. The Governor of the Bank had a statutory duty to maintain the convertibility of the note into gold coin, that is, it was his task to maintain the gold standard. Nothing was more crucial to British financial superiority. The pound in these years was as good as gold. The gold standard contributed importantly in assisting the developing British institutions in providing for the world's financial needs.

All historians of international finance have acknowledged the remarkable role that London's institutions played in the development of the international economy during the nineteenth century. Nevertheless, doubts have arisen over the volume of finance that the London markets provided for global development, while, more recently, it has become clearer that Britain was not simply a "rentier" investor in foreign securities. Consequently, the first question that needs to be addressed is the quantity of finance that Britain exported, paying at the same time some attention to its character.

I

Adjusting a previous estimate made by Paish, Herbert Feis calculated that British overseas holdings, in terms of publicly issued securities on the eve of World War I, amounted to £3,763 million, to which he added £300 million for foreign direct investment.[6] Subsequent historical scholarship until the 1980s has only confirmed the Feis estimate made in the 1920s, often rounded for convenience to £4 billion.[7] Imlah, using the indirect method as given by his reconstruction of Britain's nineteenth century balance of payments, arrived at a total of £3,534.7 million for the stream of net overseas investment for the period 1865 to 1913.[8] Applying better estimates of bullion flows arrived at by Feinstein, Edelstein has modified the Imlah aggregate to £3,487 million.[9] This is in accordance with Simon's estimate of money subscribed to foreign issues between 1865 and 1913 of £3,879 million.[10] Recently the work of Simon has been extended by Davis and Huttenback who have examined in particular Britain's financial relations with its Empire.[11] They have arrived at a range of estimates of subscriptions to public issues between 1860–1861 and 1910–1911 that aggregate from a minimum of £3.1 billion to a maximum of £4.8 billion.

Comfort, if not confidence, has been taken because of the broad agreement of these various estimates arrived at in different ways, while at the same time it has been acknowledged that they should not agree too closely since they attempt to measure different things.[12] Platt, the chief critic of earlier estimates of British overseas investments, argued that these estimates are greatly overstated because they account inadequately for purchases of new securities by foreigners on the London market as well as for subsequent repatriation of foreign securities initially—but only temporarily—sold to British investors in London's markets. Platt also argued, however, that British direct investment overseas likely was underestimated by earlier analysts.[13] Platt's revaluation of the role of direct investment arises from the growing attention that has been recently given to this aspect of international finance. It needs to be understood that in nineteenth-century parlance "direct" investment was that which occurred without the intermediation of the public market, whereas "portfolio" investment was the acquisition of securities through the public new issue market. In the late twentieth century the term "direct" investment now carries with it concepts of control. Consequently, modern studies are often only concerned with the transnational development of companies through the establishment of overseas branches or subsidiaries, normally financed by internal, nonpublic, flows of funds.

If the twentieth-century concept of control is applied to overseas acquisition before 1914, then the pre-1914 notions of portfolio and direct investment become inapplicable. Rather, substantial proportions of what contemporaries classified as portfolio investment can now, in terms of assets controlled "effectively" by nonresident investors, be described or classified as direct investment. By applying modern usage Svedberg felt able to categorize 44 to 65 percent of foreign private investment in underdeveloped countries in 1913/14 as direct.[14] In the case of Latin America, Stone has estimated that 48 percent of British foreign private investment in 1913 was direct.[15] Using a classification based on ownership and management of a foreign operation, it now seems probable that two-fifths of British overseas investment before 1914 was direct.[16]

Recategorizing British pre-1914 investment is not to conjure up a Victorian world of international business in terms of the late twentieth century multinational corporation. Much nineteenth century British direct overseas investment consisted of what Mira Wilkins has termed "free-standing firms."[17] These were not proto-multinationals but rather largely seem to have been a type of business unique to the nineteenth century, with few surviving World War I for reasons still to be discerned. They were British companies, registered under British company laws, which in contrast to laws in America and continental Europe were highly permissive. Their British offices were largely administrative and perhaps no more than a brass plate on a door in the City, while they operated a railway, a mine, a plantation or an oil installation in but one overseas country. Although British-registered, these companies need not necessarily have been "British," as many were cosmopolitan in terms of ownership, combinations of French, German, and British capital and management, with the registered office in Britain because of the ease of company formation and access to the London market.

Stressing the importance of free-standing firms in British overseas direct investment is not to overlook the arrival of multinational corporations in the 1880s.[18] S. J. Nicholas, drawing on a variety of sources, has enumerated 119 British manufacturing firms that, between 1870 and 1939, undertook direct investment overseas, involving the ownership or control of either sales facilities or production plants in the United Kingdom and at least one foreign country.[19] The character of the investment that Nicholas has established from the activities of the firms in his sample is rather more aggressive in terms of an international strategy than the conclusions reached earlier by Stopford.[20] Indeed, it now seems that the British economy, rather than lagging behind the United States in terms of the number of multinationals that it generated, was the world's most prolific multinational investor before 1939.[21]

Tracing the roots of the modern British manufacturing multinational may be misleading, however, for an understanding of nineteenth-century British international business. Not only does it largely ignore the free-standing firm, the outstanding characteristic of British direct foreign investment before 1914, but it also omits consideration of commercial and financial multinational investment.[22] In practice, the multinational during the first half of the nineteenth century was frequently a mercantile firm, dealing in goods internationally, but increasingly providing short-term credit facilities to other shippers. Often this was undertaken through a correspondence network, but some firms used branch houses.[23] Whereas American and continental European mercantile firms established offices in London (hence the increasing cosmopolitan nature of the City over the course of the century), large numbers of British firms developed international networks of branches.[24] The global multibranch commercial house was a feature almost unique to British trading activity during the first three-quarters of the nineteenth century as continental mercantile firms tended to restrict such networks to Europe, while American mercantile enterprises relied generally on visiting agents, or in the Orient continued to use the supercargo.[25]

In the late 1840s there were about 1,500 British mercantile houses overseas, compared with 150 American and 500 French, with about half the latter located in the Mediterranean and the Levant.[26] It was from such commercial houses that many British merchant banks emerged during the middle decades of the nineteenth century. But the description "British" is a misnomer; although the head offices of these international houses were located in London, they were largely cosmopolitan in nature, a reflection of both their frequent emigré origin and the extrovert nature of the British economy. From mid-century they were joined by British corporate international banks, often founded by London merchant bankers, which were concerned with the finance of international trade and sometimes with the movement of long-term capital. These banks built up extensive international branch networks, although usually of a regional nature, under the control of a London head office, following the path blazed by British mercantile enterprise.[27]

Feis, when writing in the 1920s, was concerned with the connection between international finance and diplomacy and, while colonial historians have now given us a clearer picture of the "new" imperialism of the 1880s, little attention has so far been paid to the concurrent parallel spread of business imperialism.[28] The political "scramble for Africa" was relatively brief, but its economic and financial dimensions took longer to establish, not being clearly delineated until the 1930s. From the 1880s there was a moving frontier of business imperialism, the pace of advance being determined by political agreements, armed force, or the diplomacy of commerce. Much of the initial dynamism for this expansion of business imperialism came from chartered and concessionary companies. The British North Borneo Company of 1881 provided a model not only for subsequent British companies but also similar institutions of other nationalities, with Bismarck seeing the chartered companies as fit for emulation by his imperial Reich.

The chartered company was a particular form of direct overseas investment and the British companies had varying experiences. The North Borneo Company was not designed to be an operating company per se but instead was to gain its revenue from the sale of lands and concessions to others, particularly rubber and tobacco plantations. As a result of sustained local resistance, it failed to generate dividends for its shareholders. In contrast, the Royal Niger Company of 1886, modeled on the North Borneo Company, was extremely profitable, its gains coming from commercial activities that extended British trading influence in West Africa. The experience of that epitome of British business imperialism—the British South Africa Company of 1889—was more like the North Borneo Company. It was designed to sell concessions to others, but until 1922 it did not distribute a dividend, a result largely due to London Stock Exchange speculations undertaken by members of its board and other major "insider" shareholders. Chartered companies were established by the British, Germans, and the Portuguese because they offered a flexible form of business organization untrammeled by the petty restraints of bureaucracy and parliamentary control. They were tools of expansionist business policies unofficially sanctioned by government. In the British case they created the administrative, judicial, and infrastructural framework for the growth of private investment in particular areas and regions.

From the 1880s a significant proportion of British overseas direct investment was undertaken to obtain raw materials required by the growth of the industrial economies of Western Europe and the United States. Chartered companies provided the "shells" for such activity, much of which was unsavory, as were the parallel activities of concession hunters. They operated in economically and politically weak nations, such as the Latin American republics, China, Persia, and the Ottoman Empire. Often these carpetbagging activities were undertaken by individuals out to make a fortune, like those who had gone to India a century and a half before: "simply an Englishman of the old school who believed in taking anything that was worth taking, and troubled his head about it no further."[29] They preyed on financially embarrassed governments by advancing substantial sums of money, sometimes subsequently funded by publicly issued loans, to secure fiscal and other state monopoly rights ranging from petrol to matches. At the beginning of the twentieth century the proliferation of patented technology provided other opportunities, especially in the area of wireless, postal, and telegraphic enterprises. The resulting concessionary companies, which often arose out of deals struck by free-booting Western entrepreneurs with local rapacious and unstable power groups, in the cases of German and Portuguese as well as British based-enterprises, were often international in terms of ownership, control, and sphere of operations. Before 1914 political boundaries rarely constituted a constraint for either raising or investing capital.

In summary, recent research has altered to a considerable degree the interpretation of the estimates of British overseas investment in 1914 that Feis put forward almost sixty years ago. The overall global sum of £4 billion may be on the high side; certainly it was not solely British in origin. Rather, London was the major geographical center of an international capital market that drew on resources from the whole of Western capitalism, from the money markets of the United States on the western seaboard of the North Atlantic to Berlin in east-central Europe. A sizable proportion of those resources was invested in assets that were not only owned but also controlled by Western capitalists. It is this aspect of late nineteenth-century British overseas investment that has slowly come into focus in recent years. Much of this only recently recognized direct investment abroad consisted of free-standing firms, but they operated in a world already populated by multinational mercantile banks, both private and corporate, that had developed from the beginning of the century. These were joined from the 1880s by increasing numbers of British-based multinational manufacturing firms, which by the eve of World War I were beginning to produce abroad, following earlier overseas investments in selling branches. In the 1880s a railway company in a temperate region of recent white settlement may have been the most typical British overseas firm. But by the early 1900s the extraction of new products such as oil and rubber was becoming more important, and often such exploitation of natural resources was guided by the dynamic of business imperialism.

II

Until the 1880s foreign dealings were largely the province of a group of specialized private mercantile houses and corporate overseas banks in London, nearly all of which undertook acceptance credit business (i.e., short-term credit), while some made loan issues on behalf of foreign governments and railway companies. In sharp contrast, the domestic commercial banks were generally local, occasionally regional institutions, concerned with the financial servicing of the particular economies of which they were a product. The number of domestic commercial banks continued to mount until the late 1870s, but increasingly the industry consisted of joint-stock as opposed to private banks. Its unit structure began to fade with the rising tally of amalgamations in the 1860s and 1870s. These consisted primarily of the acquisition of private banks by joint-stock banks, but from the late 1880s the dominant pattern was the merger of the latter, which led to the appearance in the 1900s of twelve nationwide joint-stock commercial banks.

From 1870 to 1913 the number of English commercial banks, both private and joint-stock, fell from 365 to 70.[30] Although forces within the banking industry were responsible for the emergence of nationwide English joint-stock banks through the amalgamation movement, this change in the structure of the system was also a result of the impact of the Baring crisis of 1890, Chancellor Goschen's call for increased banking reserves, and the decline in the price of consols (government securities) after 1902. These various factors led to the typical Edwardian English commercial bank being a joint-stock limited company with a branch network covering London and the provinces. In 1904 there were a dozen such banks with a total of 2,721 branches. One important consequence of this development was that the major banks from 1900 had "balanced" branch networks, being able to offset regional surpluses and deficits of credit internally without recourse to rediscounting on the London money market.[31]

Scottish banking, a product of a different legal system and historical development, was badly affected by the 1857 crisis, which resulted in the closure of five banks, and again, and more seriously, by the crash of the City of Glasgow Bank in 1878. The City of Glasgow Bank's failure had repercussions north and south of Hadrian's Wall. Scottish bank liabilities reached a cyclical peak of £111.81 million in 1876, fell to £95.27 million in 1878, and in current prices did not regain the level of 1876 until 1888. In England joint stock banks established before 1857 rapidly reconstituted themselves as limited companies, usually on the basis of reserve liability following legislation of 1879, with twenty-seven doing so between 1879 and 1885. As a result, by the 1890s hardly any English joint-stock bank was organized as an unlimited company.

The post-1870 change in the nature of bank assets had become clearly apparent in Lombard Street by the mid-1880s. Inland bills were now scarce, a function not only of provincial banks retaining them until maturity but also of the decline in inventories due to transport improvements. The shortage of bills led to an appreciation of their price with the corollary of a decline in yields on them. It also brought about a gradual reappraisal of their attributes as assets by some London bankers in the 1890s. Their bill holdings now increasingly arose from purchases in the London money market and were the product of international transactions in which the banks' goodwill was not involved. Such bills could be considered as secondary reserve assets, the holdings of which could be varied with the requirements of the banks. With the fall in the price of consols from 1902, foreign trade and international finance bills came to be regarded as more liquid than bonds, since they were self-liquidating. Consequently, between 1891 and 1904 the London banks' holdings of inland bills as a proportion of total liabilities fell, while with the rapid growth in the number of international bills, the proportion of open market bills discounted by the banks increased sharply in relation to discounts of domestic bills for customers.[32]

Some London banks went further and became acceptors of international bills, a development largely initiated by Scottish banks when they opened London offices in the 1870s. The London, City and Midland, together with the Union Bank of London, figured among the fifteen largest acceptors of bills held by the discount house of Gilletts in 1903, along with long-established acceptance houses such as Schroeders, Kleinworts, Barings, and Frederick Huth.[33] From the 1870s the specialization of function in the English banking system began to diminish very gradually as the emerging nationwide joint-stock banks began to play roles not only in the acceptance market but also in the overseas new issues market.

Not only did the paper in which Lombard Street traded change in character during the last quarter of the century, becoming predominantly international with the decline in inland bills, but also the organizational structure of the discount market was altered. The fabric of the market had been rent by the failure of Overend, Gurney in the 1866 crisis. To fill the void that this created, during the late 1860s eleven new private discount houses were established, while one finance company, the General Credit, which had been formed during the 1860s boom, transformed itself into a discount house. These new entrants made some headway, but from 1866 until the mid-1880s the market was dominated by National Discount, the first joint-stock discount house to have been formed. Its position was challenged in 1885 by the formation of the Union Discount, however, the product of a merger of two other joint stock houses. By 1889 Union Discount had a greater turnover than did National Discount, and by 1894 held more deposits, so becoming the largest house in the market. The last step in this structural change was the incorporation of Alexanders, the biggest of the private houses, in 1891, although it did not become a public company until 1911. These three corporate houses, together with more than twenty private firms, constituted the fulcrum of Lombard Street in the early 1900s, which by then was "no longer a purely English or even a British institution; it belongs to all nations."[34]

III

An important development in British banking in the last half of the nineteenth century was the establishment of Anglo-International and Anglo-Imperial overseas banks. These institutions, with some exceptions, were run from London head offices and their senior executives were British. Often they have been described as exchange banks, but actually they undertook a very wide variety of activities, including acting as banker to local governments, issuing local currency, and performing the functions of a quasi-central bank. Their commercial business ranged from the issue of long-term loans at one end of the spectrum of financial activity to branch deposit banking at the other. By 1914 most of these British overseas banks attempted to finance their local business from local deposits, with overdrafts on the London head office being used only to cover sterling bills in transit. It was a method of business by which exchange risks could be minimized. Local deposits were mobilized in self-liquidating commercial transactions, either by bill discounting or credits. Long-term advances to local industry or agriculture were generally avoided, but in the Middle East, for instance, British banks were prepared to make unsecured loans, accommodating thereby British practice to local custom.

One of the main functions of these banks from their inception was the finance of trade, but in 1914 the leading group of London acceptors of international trade bills still consisted of seven merchant banks: Rothschild, Baring, Kleinwort, Schroeder, Hambro, Brandt, and Gibbs. It has been estimated that they were responsible for about 45 percent of foreign trade commercial credit granted by the London acceptance market on the eve of World War I.[35] In 1913 London prime acceptances, both home and foreign, totaled £350 million of which 60 percent, some £210 million, were finance bills arising from the working of the international gold standard. Finance bills were created to take advantage of arbitrage, their volume being related to the level of short-term interest rates prevalent on the London money market. The shift of British domestic commercial banks into the international acceptance business from the 1890s led to their group having a share of some 24 percent by 1913.

Although Oriental trade grew in importance in the creation of London acceptances, the United States was still the most important single recipient of London commercial credit on the eve of the Great War. The United States accounted for a third of London's international trade credit in 1913, followed by Germany with a quarter and Russia with a sixth. Sixty years earlier the United States had dominated London's international credit business, but with the American protectionist tariff of 1864 and the full integration of the world economy during the last quarter of the century, London's international acceptance business diversified. It was through the acceptance market that the British merchant banks gave domestic manufacturing firms their greatest assistance, by the provision of credits to finance imports of raw materials and exports of finished goods. Otherwise there was little contact, with domestic industrial firms looking generally to their local branch bank for other financial services. Only very rarely did some London merchant banks undertake the flotation of securities on behalf of domestic firms.

London's links with foreign trade centers were strengthened from the 1870s by the opening of offices of foreign banks in the City. German banks were in the vanguard, led by the International Bank of Hamburg in 1871; thereafter each upswing in world trade brought others, with a notable increase in the number of foreign banks opening offices in London during the late 1890s. Foreign banks could not themselves engage in London's first-class acceptance business, however, because their offices ranked as "agencies" on the money market, and therefore they were not eligible for prime rates.[36] Rather, the growing foreign presence in the City augmented London's connections with other developing centers of trade and finance, which in turn increased the business of London acceptance houses, both the old established merchant banks and the newer houses that grew in number after 1866. Nevertheless, the head offices of European commercial banks became strong competitors in the international acceptance business during the last quarter of the century with, for instance, the Dresdner in 1913 having a greater volume of acceptances than Kleinwort, probably the then London market leader. Similarly, the Crédit Lyonnais had a business equivalent to that of Barings, which admittedly had much diminished since 1890, while the acceptances of the Russian Bank for Foreign Trade exceeded those of Brandt.[37]

Care must be taken, however, when comparing the published volume of credits granted by continental banks with London acceptances, as it is evident, at least with German banks, that a large proportion of the credits in their balance sheets were not for the finance of the international movement of goods but rather provided clients with capital, often in terms of a revolving credit, or supported stock exchange speculation. In 1900 sterling was still the world's premier trading and financial currency, with nine bills being drawn on London by foreign countries for every one bill drawn in London on foreign countries; but other currencies, especially the mark and the franc, and to some extent the dollar, had gained key currency status.[38]

Baron Schroeder called the acceptance the "bread and butter" of a merchant bank, but the "jam" was security flotations, almost all overseas issues. Merchant banks collectively accounted for almost 40 pecent of overseas issues undertaken on the British capital market between 1870 and 1914.[39] The other major intermediaries in this business were overseas banks and agencies, mainly Anglo-International and Anglo-Imperial banks, with a share of about 15 percent, and the English commercial banks with a share of 10 percent, the latter being an increasing force in the flotation of overseas issues from the mid-1890s. The balance, some 35 percent of new overseas issues between 1870 and 1914, was undertaken by a variety of intermediaries, of which the most important were the companies themselves making their own issue through their bankers. This form of self-issue, albeit with some of the services provided by a London bank, accounted for just over 20 percent, while the Bank of England and the Crown Agents were responsible for nearly 10 percent.[40] Some £248 million, about 5 percent, was undertaken by special-purpose syndicates, members of the Stock Exchange who also undertook some new issues activity, and investment trusts.

The Anglo-International banks' place in the foreign new issues market was assisted by their strong personal connections with the merchant banks, partners of which sat on their boards of directors. In 1870 there were seventeen such British financial institutions with branches predominantly in the Far East, South America, and Europe. By 1910 this group had expanded to twenty-five, while its geographical sphere of interest had changed slightly with a retreat from Europe but an expansion in the Middle East.[41]

Other new entrants to the overseas capital market from the 1890s were London and "offshore" mercantile firms that became involved in such flotations as a result of the growing exploitation of new raw materials. Eastern agency houses established plantation companies and provided their proteges with local management and financial services. While agency houses acted solely for companies in which they had a significant financial interest, some of the new mercantile issuing houses had more diverse activities; Harrison Crossfield, for instance, raised capital for tea estates and tobacco firms in Java and India, Borneo timber companies, and Japanese silk undertakings, as well as rubber companies.[42] The issuing activities of these largely Eastern mercantile firms were a facet of the transformation in their underlying business, which began in the 1870s and resulted by 1914 in many of them calling themselves bankers, rather than merchants.

In many respects these houses were following the path already mapped out by the London *haute banque* of the Victorian period half a century or so before. During the mid-century period Eastern mercantile houses had made their profits chiefly from the consignment business; but the increased speed of world communications from the 1870s, due especially to the growth of a global telegraph network, contracted the chain of middlemen involved in international dealings in goods. As a result, some firms of general merchants disappeared after 1870, but many, along with other specialist suppliers of raw materials, turned themselves into investment groups. They used their well-established names in the City to float subsidiary overseas companies concerned with trading, manufacturing, mining, or finance. The parent mercantile banking houses usually remained organized as partnerships, or from the 1880s as private limited companies, but developed networks of foreign subsidiary companies, usually registered abroad under local commercial law, and overseen by junior partners or managers. This particular form of business structure allowed decision-making power to remain concentrated in the hands of the London partners or directors, but its very nature often completely cloaked the size and ramifications of the business. These activities largely filled the gap created by the wariness of the old merchant banks and other established London issuing houses toward the risks involved in mining and manufacturing overseas. For the mercantile houses these new investment banking activities allowed a redeployment of mercantile capital and diversification of their interests.

To Indian agency houses (Indian branches of British trading firms) this form of activity was hardly new, but from the 1870s involved different resources: partners' capital, retired partners' capital, and the funds of friends and well-established clients. Increasingly from the 1820s Indian houses had used local deposits to finance investments in indigo factories, sugar plantations, ships, docks, and loans to mercantile firms in the East Indies. During the last quarter of the century they invested in tea, jute, shipping, and cotton manufacturing, now using primarily London-centered funds. By the 1900s their geographical horizon had widened beyond the Indian subcontinent to embrace investments in Malaysia, the Dutch East Indies, and Russia. China houses followed the same path of diversification and redeployment, and from the 1880s some were investing in South African gold. This transformation of mercantile enterprises is at present best documented with regard to British/Oriental mercantile houses, but all British international houses found that mercantile profits thinned if not disappeared from the 1870s and so were forced for their own survival to undergo a metamorphosis, some becoming what Chapman has termed "British-based investment groups."[43]

The provision of international capital and credit was largely a metropolitan affair, but regional developments should not be overlooked. In the 1840s provincial markets, particularly Liverpool, had provided finance for foreign railways, and this Atlantic port, with branch houses of Anglo-American merchant banks, was the center of an important credit market for the shipment of cotton.[44] With the decline of the local tin mining industry from the 1850s, Cornish capital financed the expansion of the industry abroad: Mexico in the 1860s and Malaya from the 1890s.[45] Scottish capital from Edinburgh and Aberdeen had gone to Australia and the United States in the 1820s and 1830s[46] and this flow resumed from the 1870s in much greater volume.[47] It has been estimated that by the late 1880s Scottish solicitors were placing for clients between £2 million and £4 million of new funds annually in Australian bank deposits and debentures of specialized Anglo-Australian pastoral finance companies.[48] Similarly, Scottish investment trusts, established in Dundee, Edinburgh, Glasgow, and Aberdeen from the 1870s, invested heavily in the United States; in the next decade this Caledonian financial enterprise broadened out to include investment in free-standing overseas ranching, mining, and timber companies, a trend that reached its apogee after 1900. The magnitude of this activity can be gauged from Dundee alone having invested at least £5 million in the United States during the 1880s.[49]

The British financial sector matured during the last quarter of the century with some breaking down of the institutional divisions between its parallel markets. Specifically, the joint-stock domestic commercial banks entered both the acceptance business and the overseas new issues market. The function of undertaking security flotations is often used in British financial history to distinguish merchant from commercial deposit banking, universal banking not developing until the 1970s and 1980s. British corporate overseas banks undertook security flotations in some measure before 1914, however, while from the mid-1890s British domestic commercial banks played a not insignificant role in the overseas new issues market, building on long-established connections. These developments have often been overlooked by historians who have largely stressed the role of London's growing community of private merchant banks in the flotation of overseas issues.

Since at least the mid-1820s English domestic commercial banks had lent at short term to London stockbrokers and thereby became linked to the metropolitan capital market, albeit the secondary securities market.[50] It is likely that by 1914 half of the banks' reported volume of money at call and at short notice consisted of loans on stock exchange security.[51] This type of business grew apace from the 1870s and provided the banks with an alternative investment to the declining volume of bills available on Lombard Street. Loans for the stock exchange account offered a considerably higher yield than call money placed with the discount houses, but generally the English commercial banks were very particular about the nature of the securities against which they would lend, normally only officially quoted securities and therefore not paper in process of being issued.[52] The development of this business eventually gave the commercial banks well-established connections with brokers, jobbers, and dealers who made the secondary market.

The next stage in the domestic commercial banks' gradual involvement with overseas new issues was their acquisition of foreign securities for their own investment portfolios, initially government and municipal bonds, but after 1900 railway bonds as well. Accordingly, the banks' investments became more diversified from the 1880s, a result of the falling yields on consols following their conversion, and increasingly the English commercial banks obtained some of the foreign paper in their securities through underwriting new issues, a cheaper if not always certain method of acquisition. This latter activity, together with the banks coming to act as servicers of foreign debt, led to the final step being taken: undertaking new issues.

The movement in this direction was led by an early pioneer, the London and Westminster, which by most other criteria was a conservatively managed institution. As early as 1857 it issued, in conjunction with Barings, a loan for the Australian state of Victoria, and by the 1880s it was acting for other Australian states as well as South African colonies, becoming in the process almost a central bank for parts of the British Empire. The London and Westminster supported the secondary market in the securities of some of its imperial customers and acted as a jobber of last resort for members of the stock exchange for the bonds that it had issued.[53] By the 1880s such behavior was no longer exceptional, as Parrs performed similar functions for the governments of China and Japan, while the London Joint Stock Bank became associated with German issues.

Although new intermediaries entered the overseas capital market after 1870, the core of principals continued to be the merchant banks. Not all such houses became fully fledged issuing institutions, however. A considerable number of the most profitable houses retained their mercantile and acceptance business or at most retailed a tranche of an issue made by another house. Until the crisis of 1890 Barings and Rothschilds retained their early established lead in the business of foreign issues.

It has been argued that underwriting consortia become prevalent for overseas issues only from the 1900s, being adopted by Rothschilds in 1907 and Barings somewhat earlier. Certainly the "lead" houses may have been slow to change their practice in undertaking flotations; it was both an affront to their name and it reduced their gross profits, but it is evident that underwriting consortia, or at least the sharing of risks in a new issue, was prevalent by 1870, indicating that this business had developed even earlier. Syndicates were used in London for the Egyptian loan of 1868 and the Turkish loan of 1869 and thereafter became general during the foreign loan boom of the early 1870s. *The Bankers' Magazine* commented:

> It is not too much to say, that, by the means of these combinations of capitalists, not only were loans issued for larger amounts than could otherwise have been possible, but that a certain class of loans was introduced which otherwise could in all probability have never been adopted.[54]

Some overall view of the processes at work in the flotation of overseas issues is provided by the experience of the International Financial Society, which was well placed to obtain participations in foreign securities through the connections of its merchant bank directors and its links with the Imperial Ottoman Bank and the Anglo-

Austrian Bank. With J. S. Morgan as a director it is not surprising that the society received blocks of a number of loans made by J. S. Morgan and Co., including the £1 million nominal 5 percent loan for Chile of 1870, the St. Louis Bridge bond issue of the same year, as well as the 6 percent French loan. Similarly, through Morgans the International Financial Society was able to join the syndicate headed by the Oriental Bank for the £2.4 million nominal 7 percent Japanese loan of 1873. Invitations to join syndicates came not only from established connections of the society, but also from other houses and firms such as Morton, Rose and Co., an Anglo-American house established in London in the mid-1860s, and from stock exchange brokers, including Knowles and Forsters, and Walker and Lamsden.[55]

The way in which a syndicate operated is indicated by the International Financial Society's involvement in Peruvian loans. Two were issued in the early 1870s: the first for £11.9 million nominal at 6 percent by Schroeders in 1870, and the second in 1872 by Schroeders with Stern Brothers, consisting of £1.5 million nominal at 5 percent. Through Cazenove, London stock brokers, the society took "firm" £10,000 nominal of the 1870 loan together with an option on a further £14,000 of the £5 million nominal tranche to be issued in London. In addition, by way of F. Huth and Co., the society took another £14,000 "firm" and obtained an option on £22,000 out of the Paris tranche from Dreyfus. After the public flotation the International Financial Society was called upon to take up £20,000 of the £24,000 constituting its London "firm" commitment, but it was able to sell immediately £10,000 in London at a premium of 15 shillings. Actually, the 1870 public issue was a failure, as a considerable amount of stock was left in the hands of the principal loan contractors. In this situation brokers now bought the stock directly from the contractors with, in October 1871, the International Financial Society joining a syndicate headed by Walker & Lamsden, which initially took £200,000, once having secured the engagement from the contractors that there would be no public sales for a month. This syndicate successfully sold this parcel of stock together with another of £400,000 in November 1871, but at only a narrow turn, the thin profit margin being an indication of the unreceptiveness of the private investor. The market took nearly a year to digest the issue in two stages: first an underwritten public issue made in a number of European financial centers and, second, the remaining balance being retailed to the public through stock exchange syndicates. These processes eventually cleared the way for another public issue made in March 1872, of which the International Financial Society obtained a participation of £72,000 in a London syndicate that took £1.2 million nominal out of the £1.5 million being issued. This case study suggests that the overseas issues market in London by the end of the third quarter of the nineteenth century was already a complex mechanism involving various processes for the sale of securities, of which the public issue by prospectus was but one.

Public long-term loans were only one aspect of lending to foreign governments. The International Financial Society also participated in private advances made to foreign states by groups of bankers. It had been a member of such syndicates in 1869, and during the early 1870s it continued to operate in this private capital market, taking shares in loans to the governments of Egypt, Turkey, Portugal, Spain, and Argentina. All these countries were financially unstable during the early 1870s, and their governments raised a series of public loans on increasingly worsening terms to meet the servicing of previously issued external debt, to close budgetary gaps, and to fund maturing private short term advances.[56]

Between the 1870s and the early 1900s the share of government loans in British foreign lending declined from over 60 percent to under 40 percent. Railway finance became the increasingly dominant feature to the 1890s, mainly as a result of public issues, but also other arrangements involving private short- and medium-term loans and arbitrage between London and New York. This can again be illustrated from the activities of the International Financial Society, which became a participant in the American railway market in the late 1870s. With J. S. Morgan as a director, the society had the relevant expertise and connections at hand, which were of particular importance in the late 1870s when there was a sudden decline in the confidence of the private British investor in American railroad securities, triggered by the failure of the Philadelphia and Reading to declare a dividend in January 1876. Like other British and Anglo-American merchant banks, Morgan continued to have to meet the needs of his American railroad clients but now by raising funds privately. The first operation of this type was the joint purchase by the International Financial Society and Morgans of £1.6 million 5 percent first-mortgage bonds from the Baltimore and Ohio at 80. At the same time through J. P. Morgan in New York a two-year loan at 7 percent was made to the Delaware and Hudson Canal in which the lenders had the option of buying the collateral, 6 percent sterling bonds deposited at 90. A private sale of Pennsylvania Railway currency bonds was also undertaken by J. S. Morgan and Co. and the International Financial Society.

As well as providing medium-term loans, the Society bought both sterling and currency bonds of American railroads as prices tumbled down. Accordingly, it speculated in Lehigh Valley, Philadelphia and Reading, Central New Jersey, and Allegheny Valley securities, while J. S. Morgan bought on the Society's behalf shares of the Delaware and Hudson Canal and the Lackawanna and Western Railroad. The Society sold these various holdings of American transport securities, which it had accumulated from 1876, on the New York market during the autumn of 1877 and in 1878 as prices recovered, with a change in market sentiment following increased freight rates that heralded the resumption of dividend payments.[57]

These kinds of transactions continued on into the early 1880s. In 1879 the International Financial Society operated only in the securities of first-class lines as their prices appreciated on both the London and New York markets, but from the middle of 1880 it spread its interest, buying unlisted stocks through British brokers as well as Morgans. These operations came to an end in 1881: In March, Morgans correctly anticipated a price reversal on the New York market by a number of months, while the interest of the London market as a whole in American railroad securities waned at the close of the year. Generally, British investment in American railroad securities was not to revive again until the mid-1880s.[58]

From the mid-1870s until the early 1880s the International Financial Society, along with many others, had acted as an arbitrage dealer, buying and selling in both New York and London. It was well placed to do this as a result of its connection with J. S. Morgan and Co., which by the early 1880s was one of the premier Anglo-American merchant banks concerned with U.S. railroad securities. Although arbitrage is essentially concerned with short-term gains, these operations did lead to some permanent British investment in American railroad stocks, and the private nature of their transatlantic movement did cause some disquiet, especially on the part of the London Stock Exchange authorities.

It is clear from these case studies of the activities of a well-connected but relatively minor institution that British merchant banking in the 1870s and early 1880s with respect to foreign security issues took on a multitude of forms that went well beyond the publication of a prospectus and making an allotment. They often involved international groups and syndicates, some long established as the result of the finance of transatlantic economic intercourse.

Syndicating had been used in the flotation of loans ever since the finance of the Napoleonic Wars and had become a feature of the London market by the early 1870s, but Barings and Rothschilds disliked it. Chapman has claimed that such leading London issuing houses only resorted, with considerable reluctance, to syndication to meet the competition of the American houses that opened in the metropolis in the late 1860s.[59] Syndicates became even more general in the 1880s when they often had a continental bank at their head, while after the Baring crisis of 1890 pan-European syndicates were commonplace. These developments finally led to changes in the practice of even the "lead" houses. The Rothschild consortium consisted of the three family private banks, four German-Jewish private banks, three incorporated Austro-Hungarian banks in which there were Rothschild interests, together with the Disconto-Gesellschaft and the Darmstädter Bank. These syndicates, even when bound by family interest, religious ties, and interlocking share holdings, were not always stable and, in the case of the Rothschild consortium, the Hungarian General Credit Bank obtained increasingly better terms so that it had parity of membership by 1910.[60] Syndicates were established not only to spread the risks of issuing but came about also as a result of government pressure, with the British government from 1900 promoting such combinations to issue loans for areas where British politico-economic interests were threatened, as in Egypt, Turkey, Persia, and China.

IV

In this broad survey of the development of the British financial sector after the initial phase of industrialization, there remain at least two further questions to be considered: the relationship of banking and bankers to society, and the interconnection of finance and the state. In viewing such links—societal and politico-economic—one contextual point must be borne in mind, namely that Britain was the first nation to experience industrialization and that that industrialization involved largely the structural transformation of the textile and iron industries, along with the growth of a railway construction industry. These developments have probably led to a misdirection of the historian's effort, as its focus has been mainly upon changes in the growing industrial regions in the North and West Midlands, thus losing sight of the continuing and growing importance of the "service economy" of the Southeast centered upon London. From the beginnings of industrialization the export of manufactures was insufficient to pay for the import of raw materials, augmented by an increasing stream of foodstuffs from the 1830s. The balance of payments remained in surplus, a growing surplus from the mid-1850s, as a result of invisible exports, predominantly shipping until the 1870s, after which income from overseas assets became increasingly important. These earnings became particularly crucial with the very substantial growth of food imports over the last quarter of the nineteenth century, joined by a mounting tally of manufactures from the 1890s as new technologies were but partially incorported within the domestic manufacturing sector.

The incomplete transformation of the production of goods in Britain during the nineteenth century, with the continuance of small-scale workshop production involving skilled labor rather than machines, is possibly reflected in the generation of wealth in Victorian society. The typical nineteenth-century industrialist left an estate of about £100,000; few became millionaires. Rather, in 1914 as in 1815, it was commerce and finance that produced considerable fortunes, with Victorian millionaires coming predominantly from the ranks of merchants, bankers, shipowners, and stock and insurance brokers. The center of wealth in Victorian Britain was London, and in particular it was the City that produced plutocrats; not just those who have become household names such as the Rothschilds, Barings, Rallis, Sassoons, Gibbs, and Montefiores, but also generally totally unknown men like the Morrisons, merchant bankers and financiers, and Hugh McCalmont, stockbroker and foreign merchant. Only late in the century did some provincial fortunes begin to rival those made in London, and even then these provincial millionaires were predominantly involved with commerce and finance.

Not only were members of the London middle class richer than their provincial counterparts, having higher incomes per capita, but they were also socially differentiated. The greater wealth of the London middle classes, together with the extrovert character of the Southeast service economy, may explain differences in investment behavior as, when allowing for population distribution, Londoners were twelve times more likely to buy foreign company shares than were people from the provinces. Beyond London, only Lancashire stands out as a regional center of investment in publicly quoted foreign equity securities during the period before World War I. In marked contrast, the holding of domestic shares was spread across the country with no significant regional differences. In addition to geographical contrasts in investment patterns, there were also occupational differences, with manufacturers as a social group being the least interested in overseas shares, while merchants, together with financiers, had the strongest affinity for foreign equity.

In terms of investment in the formal Empire, the major group of shareholders consisted of peers, both metropolitan and provincial, along with gentlemen.[61] These divisions within the Victorian middle class and its elite groups also ran along lines of social and political behavior. Whereas the middle class in the midland and northern manufacturing towns and cities were typically nonconformist, participating in chapel-centered society, their London counterparts continued to adhere to the Established Church and accordingly sent their sons to the major public schools and then on to Oxford and Cambridge. Moreover, the London middle class supported the Unionist party following the Liberal/Unionist split. Therefore the middle class of the metropolis was closer in attitudes and social mores to the old preindustrial elite; indeed, the two came increasingly together from the 1880s with the growing participation of landed society in City business life. London bankers, particularly long-established merchant bankers, became ennobled landowners, while members of the peerage became company directors and their daughters married bankers' sons.[62]

Just as the merchant groups behind the chartered trading companies formed in the City at the end of the seventeenth century were absorbed into the leading elements of society over the course of the eighteenth century, so by the 1890s senior London bankers had become assimilated into the continuing aristocratic elite. Furthermore, by the end of the nineteenth century they had become largely a self-perpetuating caste. These processes had gone furthest with London private bankers, long-established merchant bankers, and directors of the Bank of England; by 1900, about 87 percent of this group were sons of bankers. The confluence with older, landed wealth had become marked by the 1850s when significant proportions of London bankers had been educated at the major public schools. Accordingly, during their school days they had rubbed shoulders with future cabinet ministers while increasingly their fathers-in-law were members of the House of Lords. By the 1890s two-thirds of senior London bankers—partners in private companies and directors of corporations—lived in the fashionable suburbs of the West End and nearly half had a country residence as well. Many joined the leading London clubs or gained membership of smaller, but select, social institutions such as the Royal Yacht Squadron, competing ill-fatedly with their American counterparts.

Not all bankers joined the aristocracy by way of marriage. Jewish merchant banking dynasties and Quaker private banking families were characterized by intermarriage, as was a group of old-established banking families. This latter set had at its core three of the most prestigious merchant bankers—Barings, Hambros, and Morgan, Grenfell—and three of the longest-surviving private banks: the Smith group, Glyns' bank, and Robarts, Lubbock. Although the families behind these institutions did intermarry both with other banking dynasties and the aristocracy, their outstanding characteristic was the high degree of interrelatedness among them brought about by marriage.

London banking families became landowners, ennobled and involved in politics, but over generations did not move away from the bank. For most of these families the bank—whether private, joint-stock, or merchant—remained the hub of the family's activities, and where younger sons could not be accommodated within it, they were often placed within the City, in a discount house, a stockbroking firm, or a legal practice. These filial strands were important in the fabric of the City, not only for reasons of social structure but also as an information network. At a senior level—a partner's desk or a seat on the board—banking accorded considerable free time, with most of the day-to-day routine being handled by clerks, whereas much of the administration could be handed over to managers. Accordingly, senior bankers had potentially ample leisure time, which many devoted to their estates, to parliamentary careers, and to the social life of the metropolis: the Season and country weekend house parties. Directors of the nationwide joint-stock banks, which emerged at the turn of the century, adopted a similar life-style, though having other City commitments through directorships of insurance companies and investment trusts.

These are broad generalizations, and their precise incidence varied from family to family, bank to bank, and apply least to the newest institutions—those that joined the City from the 1870s—whose senior staff were still developing a business and were not yet accepted by the older elite. Leisure too had its perils; the major reason for Barings' failure in 1890 was that at least one of its senior partners spent insufficient time in the City. It is clear that few senior London bankers had direct and formal contact with British manufacturing industry. Only 7 percent of London bankers between 1890 and 1914 were directors of domestic industrial companies, and they came mainly from recently established nationwide commercial banks and reflected these banks' recent regional and local origins.

Although forming an important segment of the membership of Parliament, bankers seldom made use of their presence in the House to forward their particular private interests; indeed, few intervened in debates in the House of Commons during the quarter of a century before World War I. Usually bankers sat for county constituencies, often representing localities in which their country residences were situated. Therefore they formed within the Commons a section of the "Knights of the Shire," with Parliament being for many banker members a part of their social activities.[63] This does, however, ignore the unquantifiable: the extent to which the lobby, the club smoking room, the country house party could be used to influence the formation of government policy; but that can only be a matter for conjecture or, at the most extreme, lurid conspiracy theory based upon circumstantial evidence.

This is not to put out of court the question of the exact relationship between the state and finance and especially the interplay in the formation of economic foreign policy. Some historians of imperial Britain have argued that the government throughout the nineteenth century tried to establish and maintain British paramountcy by whatever means. Indeed, Gallagher and Robinson, when putting forward what has come to be called the "Imperialism of Free Trade," went beyond the generally accepted view that the British government was concerned to establish security for trade and contended that policy consisted of "trade with informal control if possible; trade with rule when necessary."[64]

Drawing on examples in Africa, China, Latin America, and the Middle East, Gallagher and Robinson argued that throughout the nineteenth century the British government opened up interiors in other continents and assisted the expansion of British influence inland from ports in order to develop their hinterlands, thereby creating complementary satellite economies that would supply the metropolitan economy with food and raw materials, which would in turn take in British manufactures. Accordingly, they contend that the alleged inactivity of the British government, particularly during the mid-Victorian era, is an illusion, as it overlooks informal developments. Following Britain's forced entry into Latin America in the 1820s, China in the 1850s, and the Ottoman Empire in 1855, diplomacy, Gallagher and Robinson maintain, was employed to encourage stable governments in these countries so as to minimize risk for British overseas lending and, where this was not possible, coercion was employed against weaker and unsatisfactory states to induce more cooperative attitudes.

The "Imperialism of Free Trade" has come under increasing criticism, particularly by Platt, who maintains that Gallagher and Robinson have taken the occasional rhetorical flourish in speeches by Canning and Palmerston and translated them into a grand design of policy taken up by other foreign secretaries.[65] Although accepting that the British government was bound to open the world to trade, Platt argues that it is also equally clear that the range of policy options available to ministers was very limited, particularly before the 1880s. In trade negotiations the official stance was that of equal favor and open competition and, above all in international relations, nonintervention was one of the most respected principles of British diplomacy through the century. Even at the sacrifice of British trade and finance, the British government remained detached from political alignments. This was the case as late as the 1890s, when the international arena had changed completely; but even so the British government did not bow to City pressure either to intervene in the Chilean and Argentinian revolutions or to assist in the regeneration of Argentinian finance.

This continuity of policy can be followed from Canning in 1807 to Sir Edward Grey in 1911. Likewise, senior civil servants, the administrators of policy, took the same stance, as can be seen by looking at the comparability in the views of Bowring, at the Board of Trade in 1860, and his successor, Sir Courtenay Boye, in the 1890s. All in all, the government was reluctant to extend its responsibilities beyond the minimum required to guarantee free play for British merchants and financiers abroad. Ministers and their civil servants saw the state's main role as supplying and augmenting the flow of commercial intelligence available to the mercantile and financial community. Accordingly, the British government preferred "open-door" stipulations in commercial treaties in terms of a "fair field and no favor," and therefore would not promote individual private interest. Very rarely would it take any responsibility for the issue or expenditure of a foreign government loan; it would not back commercial or financial enterprises outside of the formal Empire, and saw no role to play in defaults and debt-collecting, providing British creditors were dealt with on the same terms as other external creditors. Consequently, the use of the gunboat by consuls or diplomatic representatives would only be sanctioned by Whitehall under the most stringent conditions.

This is not to deny that the British government undertook no annexations, but these usually were in order either to safeguard existing imperial frontiers or to exert discipline over existing British communities. British paramountcy before the 1880s was not the result of the British government following an expansionist economic policy designed to bring nominally sovereign nations under informal control so as to maximize the market for British goods and finance. Rather, the undeniable British paramountcy over the world economy was a result of Britain's earlier industrialization, which gave it a quasi-monopoly over the machine production of goods, and which private investors and traders utilized in pursuing their private pecuniary advantage.

Actually, British traders and financiers before the 1860s were largely indifferent to distant markets, such as Latin America, the Levant, and China. Trade to these areas before the 1860s mainly consisted of speculative flurries that did not lead to continuing and growing international economic intercourse. British exports before the 1860s went primarily to Europe, the United States, India, and the white colonies of the Empire. The countries of Gallagher and Robinson's "informal empire" were unattractive to most British mercantile houses because they offered little in the way of return cargoes by which to transfer remittances back to England, coupled with the time, up to eighteen months, that it took to make those settlements.

In Latin America, Brazil was an exception, but remittances from Brazil, because of the nature of Brazilian exports, particularly coffee, had to come back via either continental Europe or the United States, and over the mid-century period a direct trade developed, cutting out the entrepôts of London and Liverpool.

Until the 1850s the Levant could offer nothing in the way of return cargoes except some vegetable dyestuffs and specie, while with China the British market for its teas and silks, despite all the glamour of the clipper races, was limited. The main British export to these areas was manufactured cottons, and often before the 1860s they could not compete at the local subsistence level with either the rural cottage industry or the traditional urban mill and workshop. Further, these areas had the cost advantage of cheap labor and established tastes and habits, perhaps forsaken by the proto-middle class in the town but not by the rural peasantry that made up the mass of the population.[66] Change came only in mid-century, and in the case of China not until the 1890s, when capital goods came to characterize British trade with these areas, moving in parallel with British lending.

There was an informal empire in the mid-Victorian period but it had little to do with trade and finance. It consisted of a string of territories in the tropical world, where British consular officials and political residents influenced, guided, or controlled native regimes in order to maintain political stability along the frontiers of the formal Empire. Informal control in the Gallagher and Robinson sense grew only from the 1880s as a result of much greater international competition for markets, the rise of tariff barriers, greater jostling for concessions, and heightened rivalry for foreign loans. Formal empires, particularly in Africa, were rapidly delineated at the conference table if not on the ground, while there was greater and heightened recognition of the equation between economic and political power. If anything, contemporaries gave too much credence to economic influence leading to political control. The result was that often the gaining of a foreign loan by a particular banking house, group, or syndicate was regarded as the securing of politcal sway over the borrower, whereas the successful tender for a railway concession was equated with mapping out a sphere of political influence. The gradual division of Europe into two warring camps during the *belle époque* gave such contemporary calculuses of economic and political power added weight, certainly in terms of diplomatic anxiety.

As far as Britain was concerned these new pressures arising from the confluence of economics and politics were most acute in the Middle East and China. Here greatpower rivalry was too finely balanced to allow colonial division; indeed, even if it had been possible, none of the great powers wanted the formal responsibility that would have followed. Further, both areas were controlled by native regimes that had auras of faded grandeur. Nevertheless, the Ottoman Empire, Persia, and China were disintegrating as a result of both internal and external forces. Moreover, the penetration of Western capitalism, if not political systems, had forced the governments of these countries to allow in foreign capital, so much so that in the case of the Ottoman Empire the longevity of the sultanate came to depend on the willingness of Western markets to lend. By the 1890s the British government could no longer rely on supporting the native regimes to maintain the integrity of their sovereignty, while in each area the British government had political interests greater than the British commercial and financial stake. To support its political interests Whitehall now turned to financial power in order to augment the efficacy of traditional diplomacy.[67]

The British interest in the Ottoman Empire was a long established one of maintaining a barrier at the Bosphorus to Russian expansion into the Mediterranean and Asia Minor, which could threaten the imperial route to India, whether by sea or over land. Accordingly, British policy consisted of supporting the Sultan's regime to prevent the partition of the Empire. From the 1890s resident British influence given by the British financial adviser, the British customs controller and the British reorganization of the Ottoman navy was bolstered by diplomatic support to those seeking concessions.[68] The greatest concern, however, arose from the state of the Ottoman fiscal accounts and the Turkish ability to service externally held debt. The British Foreign Office had long recognized that the financing of the Sultan's regime did provide a means to encourage administrative and financial reforms, which in turn would stabilize the government economically. Pressure now came through the competition for Ottoman foreign loans, however, particularly as German tenderers did not seem to recognize publicly the anarchy that could result from Ottoman debt default or, perhaps in a more Machiavellian vein, were trying to produce that very end in order to prepare the way for German penetration.

In the 1900s the Foreign Office cast about for a strong group of British financiers who would act as a conduit for a flow of British funds into Turkey. Initially it had looked at the London committee of the Imperial Ottoman Bank, but that body did not represent the caliber of financial power that the diplomats were seeking. In seeking financial support to buttress diplomacy, the British Foreign Office remained conservative, only considering first-class names of the highest prestige. In 1908 the solution was found in Cassel's group behind the National Bank of Turkey, but even then the Foreign Office would make no definite commitment to it, relying on the financial group's own magnetism to draw further high-class support to it. Both Cassel and Sir Edward Grey, however, recognized the particular and largely exceptional relationship that the bank had with the British government. The Foreign Office, in its exclusive support, did help in finding senior management for the National Bank and fended off other London competitors, such as Morgans, for Turkish loans. Nevertheless, it proved to be an abortive experiment, with the bank failing in 1913 without fulfilling either its business or its political objectives. This forced the Foreign Office back to its earlier strategy of strengthing the London branch of the Imperial Ottoman Bank, recognizing at the same time that this would largely augment French economic and political power, now allied in the Entente, rather than British.

In Persia, which acted as another buffer state against southward Russian expansion, the Foreign Office during the 1900s supported the Imperial Bank of Persia, which had been founded in 1889. This state bank, which held the important lien on the customs revenues of the Persian Gulf ports as security for external borrowing for the Shah, was seen by Whitehall as the key to maintaining the British presence in southern Persia. Accordingly the Foreign Office in 1910 choked off the attempt of Seligman Brothers to obtain a loan contract, while in 1912 it ensured that the Imperial Bank obtained a share of the loan to be issued by Barings.

With China it was not the case of a stragegic political interest as in the Middle East, but the maintenance of British prestige and the protection of commerce in the Yangtsze River valley. The Foreign Office from the late 1880s began to support the Hongkong and Shanghai Banking Corporation, a local bank but with a London committee, particularly to secure the second and third indemnity loans for British finance.[69] This support gradually developed into preferential treatment for the Hongkong and Shanghai Bank, which was publicly evident by 1905. With the growing political divisions within Europe, the Foreign Office encouraged Anglo-French financial cooperation, as in the Ottoman Empire.[70] In China this applied to railway concessions, often regarded as establishing spheres of political influence, as well as foreign loans. The international loan consortium of 1909/10, controlled by the Hongkong and Shanghai Bank, met precisely the diplomatic aims of the Foreign Office, but after 1911 the preferential treatment by Whitehall of the Hongkong and Shanghai Bank was subject to increasing public criticism in London. This embarrassed the Foreign Secretary, especially as the bank was now turning the relationship about with its insistence on a monopoly of state support. The Foreign Office was successful in obtaining the admittance of four other City houses into the international consortium for the loan to the new Republic of China.[71] Yet at the same time the government still restricted its diplomatic support to only a few institutions, one result of which was the official but private dissuasion of Hambros to enter the new China loan group.

The coming together of finance and British diplomacy in a few areas during the decades before World War I was not the relationship that Gallagher and Robinson have attempted to establish for the whole of the nineteenth century. Instead of the government using state power to open up the world for British commerce and finance, diplomats attempted to use British financial organs in a limited number of cases to augment British presence and secure goals of foreign policy. Although Britain had the largest commercial stake of the European powers in the Middle East and China, in terms of the pattern of British overseas trade and investment these were areas of minor interest, with overseas dealing with Europe, North and South America, and the white southern dominions being far more important.[72]

2

U.S. Banks in International Finance

Vincent P. Carosso and Richard Sylla

In the United States of America banks and bankers were players in a drama of international finance before 1914, but their roles were small ones compared to those of British, French, and German bankers. Because the U.S. economy by 1914 was approximately as large as those of the other three nations combined, the bit parts allotted to U.S. bankers may seem surprising. Our investigation points to the regulatory environment in which U.S. banks operated as the primary factor that undermined a larger international role for American banks. The analysis also accounts for the fact that the most important U.S. bankers internationally were private, unincorporated bankers least subject to U.S. banking laws and regulations. At the end of the period, on the eve of World War I, the regulatory constraints were relaxed. That—and the results of the war—opened a new era in U.S. international banking.

The U.S. in the International Economy: Trade and Finance

Measured on the scale of nations, the economy of the United States moved from being merely very large in 1870 to becoming gigantic by 1914. In the former year, although known in the world economy mainly as a producer and exporter of primary products, the United States stood second only to the United Kingdom in manufacturing. The two English-speaking nations were far in front of other countries in manufacturing industry, accounting together for some 55 percent of the world's output of manufactured products. After 1870, the United States, with huge land areas coming under settlement, continued to be a large producer and exporter of primary products. But output of manufactured products grew even more rapidly, and in the decades preceding 1914 the United States became a major exporter of manufactures. By 1913, the United States produced some 36 percent of the world's manufactures, a share that roughly equaled the combined percentages of Germany, the United Kingdom, and France, the next three largest producers.[1]

The remarkable growth and development of the North American republic made it an increasingly important factor in world trade, but not as much as might have been expected on the basis of its high rate of economic growth in comparison with other leading national economies. The share of combined U.S. exports and imports in the world totals rose from roughly 6 percent in the late 1860s to 11 percent in 1913, but even the latter figure is small in relation to the U.S. share of world output. Moreover, the ratio of U.S. foreign trade (exports plus imports) to U.S. production declined in these years—from about 15 percent in the early 1870s to only 11 percent in 1913.[2] This U.S. trend of decreasing relative importance of international trade in relation to total production is in marked contrast to the trend in other leading national economies, where foreign trade/output ratios rose. Two factors probably account for the U.S. deviation.

First, the United States was a continental economy of great size and diversity, with distinctly greater opportunities for internal specialization and exchange than existed *within* other nations. Internally, the U.S. economy was a vast free trade area with falling transport costs resulting from massive railroad building. Second, the United States was a high-tariff nation throughout the period, and this external policy stance reduced the nation's relative role in the international trading economy from what it would have been with less protectionist policies. The policy of protection to manufactures promoted import substitution, and with considerable success: the share of finished manufactures in United States imports declined from 35 percent between the years 1869 and 1878 to 21 percent during the years 1904 to 1913.[3]

Trends in the U.S. balance of payments in these decades indicate a maturing industrial economy. The commodity trade balance (exports minus imports), almost invariably negative in earlier American history, turned positive in the 1870s, and—with a few annual exceptions—remained so until 1914 (and thereafter, until recent years). The more encompassing current account balance also turned positive (and capital was exported) in the late 1870s. But it returned to a negative position in most years until the mid-1890s as trade surpluses were more than offset by interest and dividend payments to foreigners, tourist expenditures, transportation charges, and immigrant remittances. Then the current account turned positive, and the United States began its long tenure (again, until recent years) as capital exporter to the rest of the world. The weight of earlier capital imports kept the United States a net debtor to the rest of the world until World War I, but the export of American capital had begun in earnest two decades earlier.

The gross *stock* of U.S. foreign investment around 1913 is estimated at some $3.5 billion. Comparable figures for other leading industrial nations are as follows: United Kingdom, about £4 billion or $19.5 billion; France, $9 billion to 10 billion, and Germany, $5.2 billion to $5.9 billion.[4] The European powers were thus well ahead of the United States in foreign lending and investment. This point is driven home even more emphatically when foreign investment is related to national wealth. The figure for Great Britain was about 25 percent of that nation's wealth, while the French and German figures were about 17 and 7 percent, respectively, of their national wealth. In the United States, by contrast, the stock of foreign investment was only 2 percent of the stock of wealth. If the United States had invested in absolute terms as much abroad as had the United Kingdom, the ratio to total wealth in 1913 would have been only 11 percent compared to the United Kingdom's 25 percent.

Why was the United States, one of the first countries to industrialize and, by 1913, the wealthiest of all the industrial nations by a good margin, relatively backward in terms of foreign investment? The standard answer is that, in the words of Jonathan Hughes, "Americans had found sufficient investment opportunities at home."[5] Because the United States not only absorbed most of its own funds available for investment but also continued to 1914 to act as a magnet for the funds of investors in other nations, there is a certain truth in Hughes's statement. Geography probably played a supporting role: How much easier it must have been for an English investor to invest in Germany or a French investor in Russia than for an American to invest in any of these countries. But what does that mean? From the vantage of this research, it is worth asking whether (and why) the mechanisms of foreign investment were less developed in the American case than in those of the United Kingdom, France, and Germany. In particular, were American bankers relatively backward in their foreign-investment capabilities compared to their European counterparts?

Evidence pointing toward an affirmative answer to this question is not difficult to find. Here the distinction between foreign direct and portfolio investment is relevant, for it may safely be assumed that bankers have more to do with the latter. Of the $6.75 billion of foreign long-term investment in the United States in 1914, according to the estimates of Cleona Lewis, 81 percent was portfolio and 19 percent direct investments.[6] But of America's foreign investments of $3.51 billion, only 25 percent was portfolio and 75 percent direct.[7] In other words, it appears that foreign financiers had a comparative advantage over nonfinancial enterprises when it came to investing in the U.S. economy, but that American nonfinancial enterprises—manufacturers and sellers of commodities, resource extracters, and the like—had a comparative advantage over American bankers when it came to investing American funds outside of the United States. This may come as no surprise to devotees of the Visible Hand, but on the whole the differences in the portfolio/direct proportions between investment flowing into the United States and that flowing out are striking if not surprising.[8] Alfred Chandler's American managers appear to have been relatively better than America's bankers at foreign investment, at least when the comparison is with the nonbanker business managers and bankers in other nations that engaged in foreign investment. But why were U.S. bankers relatively backward compared to U.S. nonbank business managers and to European bankers? The answers may be found in the peculiar development of the U.S. banking system before 1914.

The U.S. Banking System and International Finance

Recently the German economic historian Karl Erich Born has drawn attention to what, from a European's historical perspective, was a striking peculiarity of the development of banking in the United States:

It is a very astonishing phenomenon in the history of banking that in the United States a few big private bankers were able to uphold their position among the greatest financial powers in the country; what is more: well into our own century, the most influential money and credit institution in America was a private banker! This is remarkable because the large private banks in Europe were already financially powerful and influential undertakings with many international ties at the time when joint-stock banks were first promoted; and yet they were relatively quickly overtaken by the most successful joint-stock banks. In America, the private bankers who had played a significant role at the turn of the century had won their preeminence only in the last quarter of the 19th century while competing with big joint-stock banks. What probably explains their success is that they had collaborated in the formation of big trusts at the end of the 19th and the beginning of the 20th century, thereby not only gaining opportunities for control and influence in industry and transport, but also making considerable profits.[9]

Born is correct in his assessment, but his tentative explanation of the U.S. peculiarity leaves much unsaid.

The importance of the big American private bankers, especially in international finance, during the period between 1870 and 1914 resulted from the long and variegated history of U.S. joint-stock banking. This history had tended by the late nineteenth century to bind the joint-stock banks in a web of regulatory constraints that made it difficult, if not impossible, for them to take advantage of new opportunities arising in the international sphere. Because joint-stock banking, beginning in the 1780s when the new Republic was formed, had received one of its earliest and largest developments in the United States, this late–nineteenth-century result might well be considered one of the disadvantages of being a pioneer, which are sometimes contrasted by economic historians with the advantages of being a latecomer.

Between the 1780s and the 1860s each of the states of the Union developed its own joint-stock banking laws, albeit with some copying of one another. In this era of state-chartered banking the federal government promoted two early attempts at central banking with its First (1791–1811) and Second (1816–1836) Banks of the United States. But these were ultimately rejected on constitutional, states' rights, and local self-interest grounds. Some of the state banking laws were liberal and enlightened; others were strict to the point of prohibiting joint-stock banking altogether. By 1860, the resulting U.S. banking system was made up of some 1,600 individual, independent banks chartered under state laws, and about 1,100 private, uncharted bankers, whose very existence on such a scale is indicative of the restrictiveness of the state laws and regulations.[10] The private bankers, unlike the state banks, were generally forbidden by law from issuing circulating bank notes, but they could engage in all other banking operations, including some that the state banks legally could not.

During the American Civil War (1861–1865), when the influence of states' rights arguments was substantially lessened in Washington, D.C., the federal government enacted and put into operation the National Currency and National Banking Acts of 1863 and 1864. These laws and related legislation were designed to replace the state-chartered banks with federally chartered national banks and to give the nation a uniform bank note currency backed by U.S. government bonds. The latter goal was successfully achieved; the former was not. A prohibitive tax drove state bank note issues out of existence. But the federal legislation took over many of the regulatory restrictions of state laws and added to them. National banks were not allowed to have branches unless state laws allowed them, and most state laws did not. National banks had minimum capital requirements that were not overly restrictive in the developed Northeast but were too high to encourage bank formation in much of the developing southern and western regions of the country. National banks were restricted in the types of loans they could make and the types of collateral they could accept; in particular, they were restricted from accepting real estate as loan collateral, and this was the only type of collateral many Americans possessed.

These restrictive regulations had predictable effects. The prohibitive tax on state bank note issues drove most state-chartered banks into the National Banking System. In 1870 only 261 state banks remained in operation, whereas there were 1,612 national banks. But there were in 1870 some 1,903 private banks, or more than the combined total of state and national banks. The result of the federal government's attempt to unify American banking under one system of federally chartered banks thus turned out to be that a majority of American banks in 1870 operated under no charter at all (see Table 2–1). Thereafter, the states revamped their own banking laws, in part to overcome the inhibiting effects of national bank regulations. The state systems then began to gain on the national system in terms of bank numbers, capital, and deposits, creating in the process the so-called dual banking system that persists to this day. In 1890, however, private, unchartered banks were still more numerous than either national or state banks. By 1910, nonnational (state and private) banks together surpassed national banks in numbers, capital, and deposits (Table 2–1). The proliferation of independent unit banks—contrary to the contemporary trends of merger, amalgamation, and consolidation in other nations, and unique in the history of banking—emphasizes the great antipathy to branch banking that characterized the United States in this period. Old, established unit banks used the public's fear of monopoly to stifle the competition that branch banking threatened to provide for the unit banks.

There were three great drawbacks to international banking in the development of this peculiarly American banking system. First, the sentiment against branch banking embodied in federal and state banking laws prohibited most American joint-stock banks from establishing branches abroad as well as at home. National banks, which included the largest American banks and the logical candidates for foreign expansion,

TABLE 2–1. U.S. Commercial Banking Structure, 1870–1910

Year	Type of Bank	Number of Banks	Capital ($ million)	Deposits ($ million)
1870	National	1,612	427	542
	State	261	165	383
	Private	1,903	n.a.	n.a.
	TOTAL	3,776	592	925
1890	National	3,484	642	1,522
	State	2,830	439	1,095
	Private	4,365	n.a.	510
	TOTAL	10,679	1,081	3,127
1910	National	7,138	989	5,300
	Nonnational	17,376	1,000	6,985
	TOTAL	24,514	1,989	12,285

Souce: Richard Sylla, The American Capital Market, 1846–1914 (New York: Arno, 1975), 278.

were precluded from establishing overseas branches until the Federal Reserve Act made it possible to do so starting in 1914. Second, American joint-stock banks—national and state—were either legally forbidden or (what amounted to the same thing) lacked specific authorization to accept drafts or bills of exchange. Since acceptances were the main instrument by which banks participated in the finance of international trade, the inability to accept bills and drafts placed the American joint-stock banks at a competitive disadvantage relative to banks in other nations. Again, the Federal Reserve Act relaxed this restriction for national banks in 1914, as had a few state banking laws in the years immediately preceding. But it is substantially correct to say that American joint-stock banks did no accepting before 1914. Clyde William Phelps, the author of a fine study of the foreign expansion of American banks in the 1920s, argued that the inability to accept was not a binding constraint on American banks before 1914 because lower discount rates in centers such as London than in New York would have given those centers most of the international acceptance business in any case.[11] One may ask, however, why U.S. short-term interest rates were greater than those in foreign centers?

The answer, we think, lies in the third great drawback to U.S. international banking before 1914, namely the absence of a central bank and a discount market for acceptances and other short-term instruments such as was facilitated by the central banks of other leading nations. In a few years before the mid-1890s, and for about half the years from then until 1914, average rates on call loans (short-term loans backed by stock exchange collateral) in the New York money market were below the market rate of discount in London.[12] Call loans, to be sure, were not equivalent to 3-month bills, and it must also be recognized that U.S. commercial paper rates and rates for stock exchange term loans were usually above the London rate of discount before 1914. But that is the point. The U.S. financial market in those years could, and on occasion did, generate short-term interest rates as low as London's, but the lack of a central bank and a discount market for bankers' acceptances meant that the United States could not compete on the field where the contest of international short-term finance was played. The problem, it seems, was institutional rather than purely economic.

At the long end of the interest rate market the institutional barrier working against U.S. bankers was not a serious problem in the decades before 1914. Yields to maturity on U.S. government bonds fell below the yields on British government consols, a roughly equivalent security, as early as 1882, and the American rate remained below the British rate from then until 1914, with the exception of four years in the mid-1890s.[13] If long-term rates in New York, at least at times, were as low as, if not lower than, rates in other markets from 1880 on, one might expect to see that foreigners raised money there. This expectation was in fact realized. The Canadian province of Quebec borrowed $3 million in New York in 1879, and Cleona Lewis lists a number of foreign governmental and private loans in the 1880s and 1890s.[14] After the turn of the century, the flotation of foreign securities in New York became quite large, some $460 million between 1901 and 1905. The British and Japanese governments were the largest borrowers; others included the London Underground, Canadians, Germans, Filipinos, Mexicans, Cubans, Russians, Costa Ricans, Nicaraguans, and the European cities of Vienna and Copenhagen. Understandably, but somewhat prematurely, the American Secretary of State, John Hay, declared in 1902, "The 'debtor nation' has become the chief creditor nation. The financial center of the world, which required thousands of years to journey from the Euphrates to the Thames and Seine, seems passing to the Hudson between daybreak and dark."[15]

American long-term rates thus were as low as those elsewhere at times during the two to three decades before 1914, and American banks could on those occasions compete effectively in long-term loan markets against bankers in other financial centers. These points reinforce the argument that institutional factors rather than financial or economic immaturity were the barriers to greater U.S. joint-stock bank penetration of foreign markets. Moreover, American banks that did compete effectively in the international arena were not joint-stock banks but rather private bankers not subject to all the legal and regulatory barriers of U.S. banking laws. We are about to describe the work of these big private American bankers in some detail. But before we do that, there is one more feature of the U.S. joint-stock banking system that should be discussed because it aided rather than hindered the rise of the New York market to world prominence.

Besides creating regulatory barriers to the development of national and state banks, the national banking laws of 1863 and 1864 established a peculiar legal reserve system for national banks. These banks were divided into three classes: non-reserve-city (or "country") banks, reserve-city banks, and central-reserve-city banks. The minimum reserves that were required by law could be "pyramided" among the three classes. That is, the small country banks were required to hold a reserve of 15 percent against their deposit liabilities, but of this, three-fifths or 9 percent could be held as a deposit in a reserve-city bank. The reserve-city national banks were required to hold a 25 percent reserve against deposits, but half of this reserve or $12\frac{1}{2}$ percent could be held as a deposit in central-reserve-city banks, which essentially meant the national banks of New York City.

Because the reserve-city and central-reserve-city banks paid interest on reserve deposits or, more generally, any balances deposited with them by other banks, the myriad banks throughout the United States found it convenient and profitable to hold their legal reserves as well as their excess or secondary reserves in the larger city banks toward the top of the pyramid.

In fact, the American banking system, with its thousands and, eventually, tens of thousands of independent unit banks, came to be bound together in an elaborate system of correspondent banking relationships that to a great extent was the American substitute for the prohibited branch banking.[16] State banks, either by law or by choice, also kept required reserves and other balances in the national banks, as did the numerous private bankers who were unregulated. At the top of the pyramid were the large national banks of New York City, which essentially functioned as the nation's central banking group holding the nation's ultimate reserves and acting as lenders of last resort before 1914. The inflow of bankers' balances to the New York banks is estimated by John James to have averaged approximately $1 billion per year in the decade between 1900 and 1910, and one of us has calculated that net bankers' balances on deposit in New York City national banks amounted to 34 percent of the assets of these banks in 1900 and 31 percent of their assets in 1910.[17] One, the Chase National Bank, received 70 percent of its $45 million of deposits from other banks in 1900. The New York joint-stock banks, lacking a discount market such as existed in London, typically employed these resources on the stock exchange call loan market. They also placed considerable amounts of their resources at the disposal of the big private bankers who before 1914 were the leading American houses in the short-term finance of international trade and the long-term finance of domestic and foreign governments, transportation enterprises, public utilities and manufacturing corporations, including multinationals.

The Big Private Bankers

In the decades before 1914 private banks (unincorporated proprietorships and partnerships) occupied a strategic and powerful place in American finance. Though not much is known about these institutions because they did not have to make a public record of their affairs, the available evidence suggests they were more numerous, more widely located, and more significant than has been generally acknowledged.[18] Apart from their legal status and the fact that they were barred from issuing their own notes for circulation as money, private banks provided all the financial services offered by the state and federally chartered institutions but were far less regulated. The lack of regulation was among the greatest advantages of the private banks over their joint-stock counterparts.

Not all private banks were alike. The differences among them were as great as those that existed among incorporated banks. The oldest and most prestigious private banks were located in New England and the Middle Atlantic states, and nearly all of them were situated in three cities, New York, Boston, and Philadelphia, the country's principal financial centers. The leading private bankers in these cities, probably no more than a score altogether, conducted most of the nation's foreign banking and securities business. Between 1870 and 1914 they financed most of the country's foreign trade that was not foreign financed, and were involved in negotiating nearly all the international loans raised to refund the United States government's Civil War debt and to help pay for the expansion, consolidation, and reorganization of the nation's rail system. They also provided the funds to organize the industrial giants of the late nineteenth and early twentieth centuries.

That America's private banks should occupy so dominant a place in the country's international financial transactions is understandable. They were the firms with the longest tradition, most varied experience, and strongest connections in overseas business, and they were relatively unhampered by federal and state banking regulations. Most of the nation's top private banks, like many of Europe's leading merchant banks, had started as mercantile firms, commodity dealers, foreign exchange traders, or stock brokers. The transition from these occupations to banker was gradual, often imperceptible. The financial services these firms provided their clients, such as buying and selling bills of exchange, extending credit, holding deposits, and dealing in securities, were a natural extension of their original business. This was as true of the major pre–Civil War private banks, notably Baltimore's Alexander Brown & Sons, Boston's J. E. Thayer & Brother, Philadelphia's Drexel & Co., and New York's Winslow, Lanier & Co., Duncan, Sherman & Co., and August Belmont & Co., as it was of those founded in the 1860s, among them Jay Cooke & Co., J. & W. Seligman & Co., Kuhn, Loeb & Co., Dabney, Morgan & Co., and Morton, Bliss & Co.[19]

America's principal post–Civil War international banking connection, as it had been since the founding of the Republic, was with the City of London, then the world's premier financial center. The strongest link in this relationship was between the two countries' private bankers. The American banking presence in London generally took either of two forms: the organization of Anglo-American partnerships or the establishment of agency arrangements between British and American private banks. Baltimore's Alexander Brown & Sons, the leading nineteenth-century Anglo-American merchant bank, operated mostly through a system of branch offices. The American firms (Alexander Brown & Sons, and Brown Brothers & Co., Philadelphia, New York, and Boston) were represented in Britain by William and James Brown & Co., Liverpool, which became Brown, Shipley & Co. in June 1839. The latter name was used for the London branch, which opened in 1863.[20] By the beginning of the next decade upwards of a half-dozen American private banks had opened London offices, among them J. & W. Seligman & Co., Morton, Bliss & Co., and Jay Cooke & Co. A few of them, such as Drexel & Co. and Lazard Frères (the latter began as a New Orleans dry goods concern) established themselves at Paris before they opened in London. The notice announcing the opening of Drexel & Co.'s Paris house in May 1868 described the firm's business in these words: "We shall issue letters of credit, buy and sell bills on the United States and elsewhere, cash American coupons on presentation, make advances on American securities, and fill orders for transactions at the Paris Bourse or in America."[21]

Many of the same financial services also were provided by representatives of European merchant banks in the United States. New York's Speyer & Co., the American branch of the centuries-old and eminent Frankfurt international banking house, L. Speyer-Ellissen, helped place the Union government's Civil War bond issues with European investors and, after the war, concentrated on originating and underwriting railroad loans. James Speyer, the nephew of the founder of the New York house, told a Senate investing committee that in the last quarter of the nineteenth century his firm had "sold millions of dollars of American securities in Germany, Holland, Switzerland, and all over Europe, especially for railroads in California, such as the Southern Pacific and Central Pacific, which were built with European money secured by us acting as intermediaries . . . ."[22]

Importing European capital for and financing the overseas trade of American businesses were also the principal occupations of several other agents of European houses. August Belmont & Co., founded in 1837, at the time of the great panic, served as the Rothschilds' American agent from pre–Civil War times well into the twentieth century, and Boston's Kidder, Peabody & Co., the exclusive agent of London's Baring Brothers since January 1886, continued to occupy that position until the beginning of the 1930s. Throughout those years Kidder, Peabody's circular letters of credit were issued jointly with Barings, which was also a major participant in the Boston firm's underwriting groups, among them those set up to sell the debt offerings of the American Telephone & Telegraph Co.[23] Unlike the Belmont–Rothschild connection, which appears to have remained a purely agency relationship throughout its duration, the 1886 arrangements between Kidder, Peabody and Barings involved fundamental changes in the makeup of the Boston firm's partnership. Thomas Baring, a partner in the family's London house, was made a member of Kidder, Peabody, serving at the firm's New York branch, which was then headed by George C. Magoun, an expert in railroad finance. In April 1891, six months after the Baring crisis led to the London firm's reorganization, Kidder, Peabody's New York and Boston offices were made into separate partnerships. The Boston firm kept the Kidder, Peabody name; the one at New York, with Cecil Baring as a partner, was styled Baring, Magoun & Co. In March 1906, after the four original partners had retired, Hugo Baring organized Baring & Co., which continued in business for two years, when the firm was taken over by Kidder, Peabody and made a branch of the Boston partnership, as it had been before 1886.[24] Throughout these years Kidder, Peabody and Baring Brothers shared each other's commercial accounts and participated in each other's government and corporate loan accounts.

One of the most important transatlantic private banking connections of the late nineteenth and early twentieth centuries was the one that developed among the Morgan houses. The founder of the family banking business, Junius Spencer Morgan, was a Boston merchant who became a London merchant banker in October 1854. Morgan started his career in international finance as a junior partner in George Peabody & Co., an Anglo-American private banking house. Peabody, a former Baltimore dry goods merchant, had moved to London late in 1837; less than a year later he opened a small office in the City to serve the financial needs of American traders doing business in Britain and other countries, not only in Europe but also in South America and the Far East. To these operations, Peabody added others. He accepted deposits, made some loans, arranged credits for English bankers, and dealt in American state and corporate securities. The firm prospered, and by the time Junius Morgan joined the partnership, it was, along with the Brown and Baring houses, a leading English merchant bank specializing in American finance. As long as Peabody headed the business, the firm remained primarily an American house. On his retirement in October 1864, Morgan took over the firm, renamed it J. S. Morgan & Co., and, over the next quarter-century, turned it into a full-fledged international merchant bank.

Junius Morgan's rise to prominence as London merchant banker owed much to his American connection. Many of the Morgan firm's major commercial credit and loan accounts originated with its New York agent, first Duncan, Sherman & Co., then through his son's firm, J. Pierpont Morgan & Co., which opened for business in September 1861. From then until Junius Morgan's death in April 1890, the London house conducted most of its American business through Pierpont Morgan & Co., which became Dabney, Morgan & Co. in November 1864, Drexel, Morgan & Co. in July 1871, and J. P. Morgan & Co. January 1895.[25] The London and New York firms were totally separate partnerships; each served as the other's agent and attorney but did not share in each other's profits and losses. Junius Morgan never was a partner in the American houses, and Pierport Morgan did not become a partner in the London firm until he succeeded to his father's place. Pierpont Morgan remained the London firm's "senior" until December 1909, when the old partnership expired and Morgan, Grenfell & Co. was established to succeed to the business of J. S. Morgan & Co. The new firm, unlike its predecessor, was formally tied to the American houses through an interlocking partnership arrangement.[26]

None of the partnership changes altered the close relations between the London and New York houses. What changed was the locus of the Morgan banks' leadership. As long as Junius Morgan was alive, it rested in London; after his death final authority was centered at Pierpont Morgan's Wall Street office. Junius Morgan's place at London and the intimate ties with his son, a major financial power in his own right since the

1870s, made for a unique transatlantic relationship. No other Anglo-American banking connection was quite like it, either in the strength of the ties that bound the firms together or in the significance of the business they shared.[27]

What was the business that occupied the Morgan banks and other international banking partnerships like them? The heads of these firms considered themselves merchants engaged in providing a variety of financial services to a limited clientele. "We are a private firm of merchants . . . for a long time . . . merchants in securities as well as in money," said Thomas W. Lamont, a Morgan partner from December 1910 to April 1940, when the firm became a New York incorporated commercial bank and trust company.[28] The totality of private banking services included most of those generally associated with present-day commercial and investment banks. Not all private banks offered a full range of services. Some stressed one function over another. The Brown's post–Civil War business, for example, centered more heavily on financing trade and dealing in exchange than in selling government and corporate loans.[29] The Drexels, on the other hand, moved forcefully from money trading into the securities business, especially after they allied themselves with Pierpont Morgan. Whatever financial speciality they stressed, most of the leading houses provided a mix of international domestic and foreign banking services.

Between 1870 and 1914 the international operations of private banks encompassed two broad areas. They financed the movement of goods across the world, including the purchase and resale of a few commodities on their own account, and they dealt in government and corporate securities. For most of the period private banks dominated both the commercial credits and the long-term loan business. The Browns, as Edwin J. Perkins has shown, were "the single most important international banking house serving the trade sector of the American economy" for much of the last half of the nineteenth century.[30]

Financing international trade involved a variety of services. Private banks extended their clients short- and long-term credits, both covered and uncovered, provided them with foreign exchange, arranged payments, and often also held their deposits. The commissions and brokerage fees generated in satisfying the financial needs of importers and exporters provided private banks with a steady and substantial source of income. The business also enabled the partners in these banks to gain a close knowledge of commodity markets and prices, information they often used to buy and sell goods on their own or on joint-account with their agents and correspondents. Not all private banks dealt in merchandise; nor did all those engaged in the business pursue it to the same extent or continue in it permanently. There was great diversity among the different houses. During the late 1860s London's Morgan & Co., for example, gradually abandoned dealing in cotton, silk, and tea. By then the firm had limited its commodities business to buying and selling iron for America's railroads and, to a lesser extent, trading in gold.

None of the J. S. Morgan & Co. merchandise business yielded the firm larger profits than did the iron trade, most of which was conducted on joint-account with New York's Dabney, Morgan & Co., sometimes with a third party, usually another Wall Street banker or a London mercantile house. Exporting British rail iron remained an important aspect of the London and New York firms' business until the end of 1873, when the number of American steel mills producing the product increased and their output grew both in volume and quality. Technological and industrial advances in

America soon put an end to a once large and profitable trade.[31] The Morgan firms and a few other transatlantic partnerships, notably the Browns, continued to trade in iron and some other commodities until the early 1880s, but on a greatly diminished scale. By then most private bankers had quit dealing in commodities on their own account and confined themselves to financing trade and providing their mercantile clients with the other banking services they required.

Serving the financial needs of traders gave private banks detailed knowledge on businesses in many different countries, as well as much other useful information on general economic and political conditions that enabled them to serve their clients in a variety of capacities, including some nonbanking ones. Cyrus H. McCormick, the inventor of the reaper and a commercial-credit and deposit client of London's Morgan & Co., for example, relied on the firm to secure the English, Australian, New Zealand, and German patents for his harvesting machines.[32] The firm agreed to assume the responsibility, not only to satisfy a client, but because it promised additional business for McCormick and Morgan & Co. The fact that private banks stood ready to provide their clients with nonfinancial services brought them much business. None of it was more important than the opportunity to satisfy the client's long-term capital requirements. The private bankers' preeminence in managing the export and import of long-term capital grew out of the knowledge, experience, and connections accumulated in financing trade. Corporations turned to private banks for the funds they needed to expand and improve their enterprises, and governments looked to them to help finance the modernization of their economies, influence diplomatic policy, pay for wars, balance budgets, and meet interest payments on earlier loans.

Between 1870 and 1914 private banks satisfied the long-term capital needs of governments and corporations by issuing bonds, many of which they sold through international banking syndicates. Most of the same firms that managed government loans also headed corporate offerings. The techniques employed to place government issues also were used to sell the bonds of) transportation, industrial, and public service companies. During the 1870s the largest government loan accounts were for the U.S. Treasury, which issued almost $1.4 billion of bonds to refund the Union's long-term Civil War debt. The huge operation was conducted almost entirely through two transatlantic private banking groups, a London one co-headed by N. M. Rothschild & Sons and J. S. Morgan & Co. and, after the failure of Jay Cooke & Co. (September 1873), an American syndicate led by four Wall Street firms with strong British connections— August Belmont & Co., Drexel, Morgan & Co., J. & W. Seligman & Co., and Morton, Bliss & Co.[33] All these houses, and a few others of comparable stature, continued to compete and cooperate for the federal government's business. In February 1895 New York's J. P. Morgan & Co. and August Belmont & Co. co-headed the American issue of the Treasury's $62.3 million bond sale, with N. M. Rothschild & Sons and J. S. Morgan & Co. co-managing the London offering, each group taking one-half of the entire offering.[34] Similar transatlantic arrangements were made to sell American state and municipal government issues.

The same houses that facilitated the flow of European capital to the United States also directed the migration of American funds abroad. In the case of New York's J. P. Morgan & Co., for example, most of its international loan accounts originated with the London house, which usually offered the Wall Street firm an underwriting participation in its foreign government issues. The New York firm's sole function in these operations was to lighten the London partnership's risk. Not until the close of the 1890s, when American investors developed an interest in foreign securities, did the New York firm place any of the issues it underwrote in the United States. Lack of a strong American market for foreign securities also was largely responsible for Pierpont Morgan's repeated refusal to issue any of them at New York. The Wall Street firm's first co-management of a foreign government loan occurred in July 1899, when it headed the American sale of £47 million of Mexican bonds (£2.5 million of which represented the rising, joint-stock National City Bank's interest in the account). The balance of the issue (£18.0 million) was sold through an international banking group, with Morgan's London house heading the English offering, while S. Bleichröder, the Deutsche Bank, and the Dresdner Bank co-managed the Berlin and Amsterdam markets, and the National Bank of Mexico represented its country's financial interests.[35]

Publication of the Mexican loan prospectus elicited wide comment in the British press. Early in June 1899, when the London financial community first learned that J. P. Morgan & Co. was among the issuing houses, the City's press was quick to note the significance of the event. "The strangest fact of all," noted *The Daily Mail*, "is the appearance for the first time of an American banking house on a foreign loan prospectus. New York is flapping its wings over the new departure of Messrs. J. P. Morgan & Co., who well deserve to be congratulated on their courage and enterprise."[36] The successful placement of the issue, the paper suggested, would lead the firm to undertake other similar commitments.

So it did. During the first dozen years of the twentieth century New York's J. P. Morgan & Co. and a few other Wall Street firms moved aggressively into the foreign government loan business. Morgan, for example, served as the Bank of England's sole American agent for the sale of a part of the British National War Loan of 1900, and together with its Philadelphia partners (Drexel & Co.); Kidder, Peabody; and Baring, Magoun, the firm co-managed the U.S. sales of the British Exchequer's three subsequent war issues, the last of which was offered in April 1902. Kuhn, Loeb & Co. provided much the same services to Germany and Japan. In September 1900, the Morgan bank and New York's National City Bank co-managed the American offering of an 80 million mark issue of German imperial bonds, and in April 1905 the house headed the sale in the United States of $75 million of Japanese war bonds.[37] With the possible exception of Speyer & Co., no other pre–World War I American issuer of foreign securities matched Morgan & Co. and Kuhn, Loeb's records, either in the size or in the geographical spread of their offerings. They were the recognized leaders, the firms that sponsored, co-sponsored, or held syndicate participations in most of the foreign government and corporate loan groups. They were also the tutors of joint-stock banks, such as National City, that were becoming interested in investment banking (see discussion in this chapter).

Between 1900 and 1913 nearly 250 foreign issues with a total par value of some $1.14 billion were sold in the United States. Many of them, nearly one-third ($374 million), represented the obligations of Latin American governments and businesses. The Far East, principally Japan, accounted for the next largest sum ($310 million), followed by Europe ($278 million), and Canada ($175 million).[38] Except for Canada, which continued to issue its securities chiefly through English syndicates, most of the other large foreign loans were sold through international groups. (Very few Canadian issues originated at New York. A few firms, such as Boston's E. H. Gay & Co. and

New York's W. A. Read & Co., and Blair & Co., made a specialty of trading Canadian government and corporate bonds, but none of them was a major sponsor of these securities.)[39]

Financing new security issues through international banking groups was an old practice. All the leading European houses of issue usually included in their syndicates firms in other countries, either as underwriters, distributors, or both. Some of the earliest foreign issues that New York's Morgan & Co. participated in came to it through the London partnership and C. J. Hambro & Son. These two firms, together with several others, subsequently became regular participants in groups headed by Morgan's New York and Philadelphia houses.

Unlike most nineteenth-century international banking groups, which were generally informal combinations used to sponsor the issues of a single client, those established in the early years of the twentieth century were of a more formal and comprehensive nature and, not infrequently, were pushed or supported by governments intent upon using finance as an arm of diplomacy. The U.S. State Department, not the bankers involved, was chiefly responsible for American participation in China's pre–World War I external loan accounts. In 1909 Secretary of State Philander C. Knox, with the enthusiastic support of President William Howard Taft, moved to increase America's presence in China by urging four of the country's top banks to join together and, with the government's backing, seek admission to the recently organized British, French, and German international banking consortium, which was then engaged in negotiating a loan for the construction of the Hukuang Railway. The American Group, formed in June 1909 and composed of Kuhn, Loeb & Co., New York's First National and National City banks, with J. P. Morgan & Co. as its lead banker, struggled for almost a year to win admission into a four-power consortium. Neither the administration nor the American Group gained what it sought. Dollar diplomacy in China failed to advance either America's national or business interests and yielded no advantages at all to the bankers that Secretary Knox had recruited to implement the administration's policies.[40]

China was not the only borrowing country where different national banking groups joined together to issue government and corporate loans. The Mexican loan of July 1899, as noted, was managed by an international banking syndicate. In July 1910, when the issue was refunded, the managing group was expanded to include five French banks led by the Banque de Paris et des Pays-Bas.[41] Similar international banking groups existed to finance other countries. In July 1909, a month after the organization of the American Group for China, the same four New York City banks formed the North American Group for the purpose of expanding their Latin American business. The unstated reason for the group's organization appears to have been to strengthen the members' competitive posture against rival houses, most notably Speyer & Co., their most consistent and determined challenger for Latin American and other international accounts. Secretary Knox commended the North American Group's members for having joined together in so "laudable an enterprise," and he assured Morgan & Co., the group's leader, that the combination could count on the administration to assist it "in every proper way." [42]

Organization of the North American Group marked no radical departure from previous practice. The group's members continued to lead or participate in each other's old Latin American accounts much as they had done before. The 1909 agreement applied only to new business. It required the contracting banker to offer all the group's members an equal participation on original terms. No one need accept every invitation, and few did so. Kuhn, Loeb, for example, did not participate in the North American Group's 20 percent interest in the international syndicate that sponsored Argentina's £1.25 million internal gold loan of August 1910.[43]

The role of private banks in government finance was essentially that of an intermediary, employed to provide a specific service—arrange a short-term advance, sell a loan, or buy gold or exchange. The influence that bankers exercised in these operations was modest at best and generally did not extend beyond shaping the terms of the contract.

Such was not always the case with the bankers' role in the affairs of the businesses they served. The relationship between bankers and their business clients ranged far more widely than the ones that usually prevailed between bankers and governments. Besides extending businesses all the standard financial facilities that they provided governments, such as taking their deposits, arranging credit advances, negotiating security issues, and acting as fiscal and transfer agents, bankers also served the enterprises they financed in a variety of other entrepreneurial capacities when circumstances compelled them to do so. Generally they did not interfere with the business policies of capably managed companies with adequate credit and satisfactory earnings. The bankers' relationships with such clients was largely "passive," a term that business historians have applied to bankers who exercised no managerial or other entrepreneurial functions over the enterprises they financed.[44]

Active banker participation in the management of enterprises to which they extended credit occurred most frequently at times of uncertainty or when the business was in financial trouble. Bankers intervened as aggressively in the business of their mercantile clients as they did in the management of the railroad and industrial corporations they served. London's Morgan & Co., the firm with which the American and French houses conducted most of their commercial credit accounts, not only determined the standards upon which the business was to be done, but also decided when it was necessary for the firm that had originated the credit to supervise its disposition. "You are a conservative good man of business and will, I am sure, agree with me that the aggregate am't [of credits in force] is too large," wrote Junius Morgan in 1870 to Egisto P. Fabbri, then the head of his own New York City mercantile firm (Fabbri & Chauncey) and soon to become Pierpont Morgan's partner. "This being so," Junius Morgan added, "let us see how we can reduce it."[45] The two men spent several months deciding upon a mutually satisfactory plan to reduce the amount of Fabbri & Chauncey's outstanding credits, and, when the agreement finally was reached, Drexel, Morgan & Co. was appointed to supervise its enforcement. During the next three years, while the plan was being put into effect, Fabbri & Chauncey shared most major decisions on the conduct of its credit accounts with the Morgans' London and New York houses.

Bankers assumed many more entrepreneurial functions when ministering to financially ailing and bankrupt clients. The nonfinancial functions they performed in a railroad or industrial reorganization included all those commonly associated with the role of a business executive. Reorganization of the Cairo & Vincennes (C&V), a strategically located 157-mile railroad in Illinois, by the Morgans' London and New York firms illustrates the range of entrepreneurial functions that bankers assumed when called upon to save a financially troubled client. Rehabilitation of the property took eight years. It began in June 1873, some two months after the road had missed a scheduled interest payment on a £700,000 bond offering sponsored by London's Morgan & Co., and continued until July 1881, when the road was leased to the Wabash, St. Louis and Pacific Railway. During that period the London house was in total control of the property. With the help of the New York firm, the London partners arranged a £45,000 loan to cover the missed interest payment and keep the road in service; won the reluctant assent of the C&V's builders and suppliers not to demand immediate payment on their bills; and, as a majority stockholder, forced the resignation of the company's board and the election of another of its own choosing. Once in unquestioned control of the property, the bankers imposed tight financial controls, assigned a partner to monitor all receipts and expenditures, hired engineers to inspect the road, and advanced funds for necessary repairs, new equipment, and the purchase of connecting lines to make the C&V more attractive to potential lessees.

When these measures proved insufficient to assure the road's full recovery, Morgan & Co. sold the road under foreclosure for $2 million to the holders of its first mortgage. The sale and reorganization that followed were designed to accomplish two purposes: reduce the road's fixed charges and protect the interest of the first mortgage holders by exchanging their bonds for the new C&V's common shares. The road's former mortgagees were made its owners, sharing their equity in the property with the preferred shareholders, the investors who put up the $2 million purchase price. Pierpont Morgan, the C&V's real boss for a half-dozen years, was elected its president. The change in his status did not alter any of his duties. He continued to manage the property from New York, much as he had done before, and with the same repeated complaint: that it was "pretty hard to manage a railroad . . . and a business besides, particularly when those for whose interests you are striving are so far off."[46] Pierpont Morgan's association with the "miserable business" (his words) continued until 1881, when the property was leased to the Wabash and the London Morgan house's control of the C&V finally came to an end. Salvaging the C&V proved costly both in time and money. The London firm's losses on the business totaled a hefty £472,500.[47]

The Morgans' experience in managing the C&V was not unique. Other bankers occupied the same entrepreneurial role in the affairs of their troubled clients. Kidder, Peabody and Baring Brothers—the Atchison, Topeka & Santa Fe Railroad's longtime lead bankers—used their large holdings of the company's stock to rescue the financially pressed railway's faltering credit and guide it back to profitability. The bankers won the power necessary to achieve their objectives at the Santa Fe's May 1889 annual meeting. Thomas Baring, the American representative of the London house and a Kidder, Peabody partner, voted his huge block of stock (71 percent of the shares outstanding) to elect a new board, a majority of whose members (four out of six) were Kidder, Peabody partners. One of them, George C. Magoun, the firm's railroad expert, was made chairman and charged with supervising the company's finances. The bankers also assured themselves majorities on the executive and finance committees. Once these arrangements were in place, the bankers reorganized the Santa Fe's finances, simplified the company's administrative structure, and tightened accounting practices. The execution of the reorganization plan, widely hailed at the time as "a brilliant conception," was entrusted to a recently appointed Santa Fe executive, an expert in railroad operations and accounting.[48] The financial, administrative, and managerial changes that Kidder, Peabody imposed on the Santa Fe, like those the Morgans enforced on the Cairo & Vincennes, were subsequently employed to rehabilitate most of the railroads that went into bankruptcy during the depression of the 1890s.

Private banks played a similar entrepreneurial role for the industrial companies they financed. Drexel, Morgan & Co.'s organization of the General Electric Company grew out of more than a decade of business with Thomas A. Edison, not all of it financial. Pierpont Morgan's partner, Egisto Fabbri, was one of the Edison Electric Light Company's organizers, a subscriber to its stock, and he also served the new corporation, set up in October 1878, as a director and treasurer.

Drexel, Morgan was the company's banker. The assignment involved much more than holding the company's deposits and arranging its time loans. The banking firm was given "sole control" over Edison's electric light inventions in Portugal, New Zealand, and parts of Australia; it was authorized to arrange demonstrations, secure the necessary patents, and manage their disposition, all at the firm's expense, and it was to be given a percentage of the proceeds from these transactions. Morgan's London house negotiated the consolidation of Edison's English company with Swan Electric Light (October 1883), and Drexel, Morgan merged the inventor's five American properties into Edison General Electric (May 1889). Three years later (April 1892) Drexel, Morgan combined the latter company with Thomson-Houston Electric to form General Electric, a $50 million consolidation.[49]

The structure and management of the new corporate giant was largely determined by Drexel, Morgan & Co., not by the Edison Company, which had initiated the merger talks. The consolidation plan that finally was adopted was largely the work of Pierpont Morgan and his partner, Charles H. Coster, the firm's expert corporate reorganizer. They, more than anyone else, were responsible for the shape of the new company, which proved to be entirely different from the one originally proposed by the Edison Company's president, Henry Villard. He and Edison had planned to have their company, with its greater assets and output, take over Thomson-Houston. Morgan and Coster, acting more like industrial entrepreneurs than bankers, achieved the exact opposite, Thomson-Houston's absorption of the Edison Company. The bankers' decision to reverse the form of the consolidation rested primarily on business, not financial, considerations. Morgan and Coster considered Thomson-Houston the better-managed property. Its president, Charles A. Coffin, was an able administrator, the kind of leader the new company needed to organize its operations, push sales, and develop a strong maintenance service for the users of its heavy equipment. Morgan decided to make him president of General Electric, and he did so by getting Villard to resign as head of Edison General Electric and endorsing Coffin, who was promptly elected to head the consolidation.[50]

Industrial mergers, like railroad reorganizations, involved bankers in numerous entrepreneurial decisions of far-reaching importance; Morgan and Coster were entrepreneurs as well as bankers. It is probably no exaggeration to say that the Morgan partners, perhaps as many as half of them at any one time, were as heavily engaged in shaping some of their clients' business decisions as they were in satisfying their financial needs. The part that private bankers played in the great merger movement that swept the United States at the turn of the century, together with their presence on the boards of the corporations they financed, led to widespread charges that America's biggest businesses were the captives of their bankers. Though the charge never was proved, the evidence used to support it, imperfect as it was, underscored the central place that the private banker occupied in the American economy. "Without the aid of their invaluable enterprise and initiative and their credit and financial power," reported a special committee of the House of Representatives in February 1913, "the money requirements of our vast ventures could not have been financed in the past, much less so in the future."[51]

Nor could a number of the pre–World War I decade's foreign enterprises have been financed without the direct or indirect participation of the same private bankers who had helped organize America's giant corporations. Private bankers facilitated the course of late nineteenth- and early twentieth-century industrial development in a multiplicity of ways. Their chief contribution, which was also the ultimate basis of their strength and influence, was their access to the world's principal sources of capital. But they also assisted the enterprises they financed in other important ways. They helped introduce advanced technological equipment, scientific and engineering skills, and improved business and management practices.

The Morgan firms' long association with the Argentine Great Western Railway is a case in point. Besides managing the railroad's foreign bond offerings, arranging its short-term sterling advances, maintaining a market for its stock, and acting as its fiscal agent, London's Morgan & Co., which headed the account, also provided the company with many other nonfinancial services. It participated in—indeed, often guided—the company's legal negotiations with the government, which guaranteed the road's bonds. It helped to arrange (and reviewed) all equipment purchases, and it advised the road's officers on construction and maintenance contracts. When the Argentine boom of the early 1880s collapsed and was followed by a prolonged contraction, rampant inflation, and political instability, Morgan & Co.'s relations with the Great Western grew more involved. By April 1891 the firm's holdings of the company's preferred shares, then valued at well over £100,000, gave Morgan & Co. "practical control" of the property.[52] For the next eight years, Morgan & Co. held and exercised final authority over the company. The Morgan bank, aided by its own hired engineers, auditors, and its Buenos Aires agent, instituted a drastic retrenchment program, imposed strict accounting controls, and informed the road's president that it would not approve the general manager's reappointment. The firm had been "making inquiries in America" for a suitable replacement, and advised its Buenos Aires agent to get the company's officers to institute a search of their own, emphasizing that the new manager should be experienced, prudent, and willing to accept a modest salary until he had proved that he could restore and develop the property. Morgan & Co.'s supervision of the Great Western operations, aided by a reviving economy, restored the company to financial stability.

"Financially, the A.G.W. is now in an enviably strong position," the firm informed its Buenos Aires agent in May 1897. Assured that the rail company's officers intended to continue the conservative policies the firm expected of them, Morgan & Co. agreed to provide the company with £500,000 for needed improvements.[53]

The large entrepreneurial role of Morgan & Co. in the management of the Great Western Railway was no different from the commanding position the New York firm and other private banks occupied in the affairs of their troubled clients. Bankers generally undertook nonfinancial responsibilities out of necessity—to protect their own interests and those of the investors to whom they had sold the company's securities. These were the reasons that motivated the Morgan partnerships' interventions in the management of the companies to which they extended credit. Neither Junius Morgan, nor his son, nor any of their partners wanted to be railroad or industrial entrepreneurs. So opposed were they to assuming management responsibilities that they declined to finance many enterprises that might have required them to accept nonfinancial tasks. The Morgans preferred to serve the banking needs of well-established, prudently managed companies. That, more than anything else, accounted for the Morgans' reluctance to finance new industries and untested companies doing business in countries where the partners had few strong connections.

Not all the new promotions that came to the Morgan firms' attention were rejected. Those in which they did participate usually were undertaken as members of a small group, most often composed of a few partners acting on their own accounts, other bankers, and the promotion's sponsors. Arrangements of this type had several advantages. They limited the firms' exposure, while allowing them to earn interest, fees, and commissions on the banking services they extended the group, which generally also participated in selecting the venture's managers. London's Morgan & Co., for example, was both a promoter of and banker for the Caucasus Copper Co., Ltd., an English corporation set up to explore and develop mining properties. The firm's initial interest in the business occurred in August 1901 with a £50,000 loan at 7 percent, of which the house kept £12,500 and subdivided the balance.[54] Morgan & Co. continued to arrange the copper company's loans for another dozen years, but avoided assuming any direct business responsibilities, except to review the choice of managers.

Much the same relationship existed between Morgan's New York firm and the Alaska Syndicate, the well-publicized group set up in June 1906 to exploit the territory's copper, coal, and other resources. Organized for a period of ten years and originally capitalized at $10 million (subsequently increased to $15 million), the syndicate's shares were divided equally between M. Guggenheim & Sons and J. P. Morgan & Co. They, in turn, subdivided their interests among a small group of friends. Morgan & Co.'s role in the promotion was to serve as the syndicate's bankers. The firm took no part in planning its extensive Alaskan operations. These were conducted through the syndicate's newly organized and wholly owned Katalla Company.[55]

Promotions like the Morgans' participation in the Alaska Syndicate and Caucasus Copper Co. accounted for an insignificant share of the firms' total business. Nor does it appear that other leading U.S.-headquartered international private banks were any more involved in similar promotional ventures, though more research into the business of these houses is needed to assess the nature and extent of their contribution to the development of new, high-risk enterprises. But if the record of the Morgan houses is any indication, the private bankers' principal work in the years between 1870 and 1914 was financing trade, arranging government loans, and satisfying the capital needs of established corporations. Their role in the affairs of the corporations they sponsored sometimes required them to assume entrepreneurial responsibilies they generally would have preferred to avoid. The fact that they were capable and stood ready to assume these tasks when the occasion demanded it gave the private bankers immense influence, far beyond the amount of money they themselves commanded. It was their role as bankers and entrepreneurs that allowed the partners in the major firms to influence significantly the structure and operations of the pre-1914 era's largest transportation and industrial companies. More than any other group of financial intermediaries, the private bankers were largely responsible for facilitating the rise of giant enterprises, the consolidation of industries, and the organization of the earliest multinational companies. But around the turn of the century the private bankers were increasingly joined in these activities by aggressively expanding joint-stock banks.

The Joint Stock Banks

At the beginning of this century the big private bankers of New York City dominated America's international financial relationships because of their close connections and affiliations with foreign houses, and because they were relatively unhampered by a web of inhibiting laws and regulations in which the national and state joint-stock banks found themselves entangled. Nonetheless, some of the joint-stock banks began to play a larger role in the international financial arena. A few state-chartered institutions actually established branches abroad, which national banks were legally precluded from doing before 1914. Others were chartered by a few states specifically to engage solely in overseas banking.

The big national banks, chiefly those in New York City, moved into trade finance by developing correspondent relationships with foreign banks, relying on foreign discount markets—chiefly London's—because the United States did not have one of its own. The huge flow of bankers' balances from the thousands of banks in the U.S. domestic system into the large New York joint-stock banks also made these institutions the natural allies of the big private bankers in investment banking, both domestic and international. Banking groups made up of private and joint-stock banks were formed, but usually with the old and well-connected private bankers as leaders. By the time that the Federal Reserve Act paved the way—at the close of the period we are considering—for an American discount market and the establishment of branches of the U.S. joint-stock banks overseas, there were already signs that the big joint-stock bankers were ready to become co-equal competitors, rather than merely junior partners, of the big private bankers.

New York law, like federal law, did not allow banks to have foreign branches until 1914, but trust companies, which carried on a full line of banking business, were allowed to have such branches. Trust companies began in the United States as savings banks for the wealthy *rentier* class. They were given the legal power to receive deposits of money in trust and to invest in the securities of business firms. Between 1870 and 1914 the trust companies became important competitors of national and state-chartered banks, largely because the latter were subject to many regulations that trust companies were not. For all practical purposes trust companies became full-fledged banks. Because they were not organized as "banks" under banking laws, however, they grew rapidly by moving into areas of financial business that "banks" were forbidden from entering. Foreign branching was one such area.[56]

The first U.S. joint-stock company to branch abroad, according to Phelps, was the Jarvis-Conklin Mortgage Trust Company, which opened an office in London in 1887. After several parent company reorganizations and name changes, the branch became the property of New York's large Equitable Trust Company in 1912. The Equitable (which in 1930 was merged into Chase National Bank, later Chase Manhattan) had already opened a Paris branch in 1910.[57] Three additional New York trust companies also opened foreign branches before 1914: the Guaranty Trust Company (in London,

1897), the Farmers' Loan and Trust Company (in London and Paris, both in 1906), and the Empire Trust Company (in London, 1913).[58] These trust company branches were the only foreign branches of domestic U.S. banks before 1914.

Two American corporations were chartered under state laws before 1914 to engage solely in foreign banking. The International Banking Corporation (IBC) was chartered by Connecticut in 1901. Before 1914, the IBC had opened branches— sixteen in all—in China, England, India, Japan, the Philippines, Panama, Singapore, and Mexico. A similar but smaller enterprise, the Continental Banking and Trust Company of Panama, was incorporated under West Virginia law in 1913 and opened three branches in Panama and one in Colombia.[59]

These trust company and foreign banking company branches, numbering twenty-six in all, were the only foreign branches of American joint-stock banks established before 1914. At the time they were not of much importance in either U.S. or foreign financial markets. Their late arrival and meager numbers are significant mainly in illustrating the inhibiting effects of American law on joint-stock bank expansion abroad.

The more important international work of U.S. joint-stock banks before 1914 involved the large national banks of New York City. Here the leading institution—as the House of Morgan was the leading private bank—was the National City Bank (today's Citibank). Under the dynamic leadership of James Stillman (from 1891 to 1909), Frank Vanderlip (from 1909 to 1919), and Charles E. Mitchell (in the 1920s), the National City Bank was transformed from a minor New York commercial banking institution to "the greatest bank in the Western Hemisphere" and the first American bank to have a worldwide branch system.[60] Stillman brought National City Bank to prominence by building its ties to other banks as well as large corporations and their leaders, and by engaging it on a large scale in investment banking and foreign trade finance. During the 1890s Stillman formed alliances with the Rockefellers and Standard Oil, to the benefit of National City's commercial and investment banking business, and with the private investment bankers Kuhn, Loeb & Co. Kuhn, Loeb was a natural ally for National City because it had the ability to originate security issues as well as European investment connections, both of which National City at the time lacked, but it itself lacked the resources of a large commercial bank, which National City could provide.[61] From 1895 to 1898 Kuhn, Loeb and National City joined forces to reorganize the Union Pacific Railroad. By 1900 the two banks sold a $20 million issue of German government treasury notes, mostly to American investors, and National City alone sold a $10 million Swedish loan.[62]

National City's ties to large corporations were instrumental in building its deposit base and in generating both domestic and international loan business. By 1904 leaders of Standard Oil, Union Pacific, American Sugar Refining, International Harvester, National Sugar, and Armour & Co. were represented on the bank's board of directors. National City had established a foreign exchange department in 1897 to serve its large, multinational corporate clients. It was not the first U.S. joint-stock bank to do so; First National of Chicago had entered this field in 1873, as had The Bank of New York in 1893. But National City quickly became a leader in foreign exchange. In 1902 it was reportedly able to pay out any sum of money in any city in the world within 24 hours. Its ability to do so, in the absence of foreign branches, rested on a large international correspondent network. In 1912 there were 132 such correspondents, including the

London City and Midland, the Deutsche Bank, and the Hongkong and Shanghai Bank.[63] American imports and exports were financed by National City through drafts and acceptances handled by its London correspondent. Because the United States lacked a discount market for acceptances, the big American banks relied on those overseas. But the extra costs of relying on overseas markets—double commissions and the like—became one of the main arguments for establishing a U.S. discount market, soon to be made possible by passage of the Federal Reserve Act.

Until 1907 National City had been the junior partner of Kuhn, Loeb in their joint investment banking ventures. The bond market collapse in the panic of that year presented the opportunity for the big joint-stock bank to become an equal partner of the private banking house. National City, with its large deposit base, was able to make short-term loans to its and Kuhn, Loeb's mutual client firms until the latter could sell their own bonds on a reasonable basis. Kuhn, Loeb, as specialized investment bankers, did not have this short-term lending capability. When Armour & Co. asked National City in 1909 to underwrite a $50 million bond issue to expand its meat packing operations in Argentina, National City and Kuhn, Loeb handled the issue as joint bankers rather than with National City as junior partner. In these years National City also became an ally of the Morgans, the private bank that was the acknowledged leader in U.S. investment banking. Morgan partners were represented on the National City board of directors from 1896 on, and National City had participated in Morgan syndicates as early as the Mexican loan of 1899. With the Morgans as with Kuhn, Loeb, National City then became a member of the originating group of investment banking syndicates, an advantage over its former role as a member only of selling syndicates.[64]

By this time expansion-minded National City along with other large national banks began to realize the confining character of the legal and regulatory constraints imposed by the banking laws under which they operated. The big banks joined in the call for a true central bank that would free them, as holders of the nation's ultimate bank reserves, from responsibility for the stability of the U.S. banking system. Such freedom would allow the pursuit of new profit opportunities. At the same time, following the lead of New York's First National Bank, which had formed a state-chartered securities affiliate in 1908, National City in 1911 launched the National City Company, a similar affiliate that was owned and managed by National City Bank but free to enter lines of business not specifically authorized for national banks. The National City Company quickly became a nationwide bank holding company—holding shares in seven New York banks, eight non–New York banks, and also in the Cuban Banco de la Habana. This was National City's way around the national banking law's prohibition of branch banking. The holding company gave National City less influence with its affiliates than it would have had with branches, but much more influence than it had with the 1,889 out-of-town correspondent banks with which it dealt in 1912.

The passage of the Federal Reserve Act in effect ratified many of the goals and actual operations of big joint-stock banks such as National City. The new central bank assumed the reserve functions of these banks, freeing them to pursue more profitable opportunities in commercial and investment banking at home and abroad. The big national banks were allowed to open branches oveseas and, for the first time, to create trade acceptances, which could be discounted at the Federal Reserve banks rather than through an overseas correspondent. Moreover, the move of the big national banks into investment banking, although raising many suspicions, was implicitly endorsed by the new federal banking law.[65]

Under this law National City opened the first foreign branch of a U.S. national bank in Buenos Aires in November 1914. By 1920 it would have fifty-seven foreign branches, far and away the largest number of any American bank.[66] Much of the impetus for this expansion came from National City's large corporate clients, American firms that had extensive overseas operations, including U.S. Steel, DuPont, W. R. Grace, International Harvester, Armour, and Standard Oil of New York. These firms and their subsidiaries offered to furnish National City with branch deposits and exchange commercial information with it. In return, National City would finance their trade and investments abroad.[67] The U.S. banks—finally—were able to compete on equal terms with the great banks of other nations in international financial markets. The worldwide financial consequences of the Great War would speed up this American overseas expansion, but pre-1914 trends indicate that it was already well underway when the war began.

Conclusion

Two issues of political economy arise from our analysis of the international role of U.S. banks between the year 1870 and 1914. One has to do with the influence of bankers on public policy. Specifically, given that bankers are typically important and influential members of most business communities, why did it take so long for American bankers to achieve a relaxation of the legal and regulatory restraints on international banking? Why—uncharacteristically—didn't the bankers get the regulations they wanted? A second and related issue has to do with so-called finance capitalism and imperialism. Did U.S. bankers dominate the firms they financed at home and abroad, and did they—while seeking foreign outlets to invest the funds at their disposal for higher returns—push the federal government into greater foreign involvement?

The first issue is the easier to handle. The more numerous and influential U.S. bankers did tend to get the regulations they wanted. They were the thousands of unit (single-office) bankers scattered throughout America's cities and towns. These bankers were almost totally oriented to their local and regional economies. Conservative and self-interested, they had no use for branch banking at home or overseas. With a nativism bordering on isolationism, they shared with other Americans an antipathy to foreign financiers and the eastern U.S. money-center bankers who had foreign connections. These U.S. bankers got the regulations they wanted from state and national legislatures—regulations that promoted unit banking and local control over the interests favoring branch banking and the opening of financial markets to outsiders, including foreigners. The tiny minority of American bankers who had overseas interests and ties could not by itself overcome the great majority's antipathy or lack of interest in altering the bank regulatory climate in directions that would have facilitated a greater presence of U.S. bankers in international finance or of foreign bankers in U.S. domestic finance. But growing perceptions of defects in American banking arrangements—especially their periodic tendency to collapse in financial panics—created a movement for banking reform starting in the mid-1890s. During the subsequent two decades the internationalist minority used this movement to create openings for greater American involvement in international banking.

On the issue of finance capitalism and its relation to imperialism, the evidence does not lend itself to clear conclusions. It does appear that the big private and corporate bankers of New York and other eastern financial centers worked at home and abroad to open foreign markets to greater U.S. foreign lending during the two decades before 1914. But most examples of such lending seem to be better described as conservative rather than entrepreneurial. Moreover, in the clearest example of American bankers and government working in concert, namely the involvement with China, it was the government prodding the bankers rather than the other way around. More scholarly work is needed on these complex interactions and relationships. Our preliminary impression, however, is that "finance capital" influences and motives were not very strong in the U.S. case. The urge to invest abroad and to involve U.S. governmental policies in the process seems to have come more from nonfinancial corporations—manufacturers, trading companies, and the like—than from American bankers.[68]

3

The Case of the French Banks

Hubert Bonin

The present state of research does not yet permit a definitive synthesis of the history of the French banking system or of its internationalization for this period. Although historians have scrutinized the activities of French banks abroad, the archives have scarcely been consulted in order to reconstitute their operations in France at the turn of the century, except for the Crédit Lyonnais.[1] The field of investigation is virgin territory.[2] It is necessary to gauge the maturity of the French banking system at the turn of the century in order to isolate three major debates and to judge whether the banks were useful instruments of industrialization domestically or abroad. Did they contribute to the economic power of France?

The Maturity and the Mobility of the French Banking System

When the "second banking revolution" was completed at the beginning of the 1870s, the French banking system acquired a lasting configuration. The "first banking revolution," from around 1750 to 1840, saw the emergence of local banks and, above all, of the great private banks. The latter prospered through the financing of French state loans and those of Metternich's Europe, from operations on the Bourse, and from the management of great fortunes. Because of the vigor of industrial self-finance, French banks did not contribute greatly to industrialization in the first half of the nineteenth century, apart from providing commercial credit. Nevertheless, the *Haute banque* did support, by medium term-credits and participations *en commandite*, the iron industry and railways in particular.[3]

The pace of growth slackened at the end of the 1840s. The crises between 1845 and 1851 revealed the debility of the capital market, the lack of financial strength of enterprises and banks, and the necessity of enlarging the bases of industrial development.[4] That was the role of the "second banking revolution" between the years 1848 and 1875.[5] This brought forth banks with large capital bases, both their own funds obtained under the joint-stock form of organization, and deposits collected by a massive appeal to savings. The model of the Crédit Mobilier dominated, inspired by St. Simonian theories and by the Société Générale de Belgique.[6]

Private banking houses and associations of financiers and industrialists formed groups, which then transformed themselves into great banks. The group around the Crédit Industriel et Commercial (with the Société de Dépôts et de Comptes Courants, the Société Lyonnaise de Dépôts, the Société Marseillaise de Crédit, and the Société Nancéienne),[7] the Crédit Lyonnais, and the Société Générale,[8] promoted the idea of mixed banking more durably than the Crédit Mobilier, which failed in 1867.[9] The bank expansion of the 1850s and 1860s was completed at the beginning of the 1870s with the formation of the Banque de Paris et des Pays-Bas (Paribas) by merger. The *Haute banque* (Rothschild, Mallet, et al.) evolved, amplifying its financial means and enlarging its capital, in order to meet this competition.[10] Industrialization was sustained by the collection of savings by the bankers, and by their participation in investments in railways, public works, metallurgy, and chemistry. The "mixed bank" seemed to have rooted itself in France, as in Belgium and Germany.

The 1880s reversed that process. Financial weakness (the *grève du milliard*), reinforced by political, social, and military tensions, and the irregular path of economic growth, left the banks with a bitter taste.[11] Investments resulted in losses.[12] The depression of those years accentuated the recoil of the bankers from industrial finance. The majority of deposit banks adopted "liquidity" as their watchword, making them suspicious of industrial immobilizations. Only the Société Générale and the Société Marseillaise de Crédit maintained some aspects of mixed banking.[13] Paribas specialized as an investment bank (*banque d'affaires*), as did the Banque de l'Union Parisienne (B.U.P.), reorganized in 1904 by several members of the *Haute banque*. This "banking dualism" has been accused of contributing to the weakness of French economic growth during the last quarter of the nineteenth century. In this view, the banking system by its excessive prudence, often symbolized by the *doctrine Germain* (from the name of the president of the Crédit Lyonnais, Henri Germain), prevented the banks from stimulating sufficient domestic expansion and from contributing to the spread of French capitalism abroad.

Given that the enlargement of the development base proved necessary in order to conquer capital goods markets in new countries and to supply consumer goods to middle-class markets in old ones, it is legitimate to inquire into the capacity of the banks to amplify that tendency to internationalization as a stimulus to French growth. Three debates have emerged: Were the banks sufficiently aggressive? Did their foreign investments contribute to French industrialization? Did the internationalization of the banks create a new type of banking system?

The Debate on the Strength of the Internationalization of the French Banks

French Banks and International Financial Flows

French banks undertook intense relations abroad, a heritage of the precocious internationalization of the *Haute banque*, which, in the years 1780 to 1848, became involved in European networks. They depended on the solidarity among immigrants (German, Swiss, or Italian) from a particular city, on family and religious ties (Jewish, Protestant, etc.), then on the affinities among correspondents taken on afterwards. These relations were compromised after 1870 by the reorientation of European business. The Parisian market saw its function as a clearinghouse for foreign exchange between continental Europe and the anglophone world reduced. The surplus of the French trade balance with the United Kingdom diminished by half between 1897 and 1913, whereas the latter's surplus with the Mediterranean, Scandinavian, and German nations also narrowed. The role of the Paris banks in intra-European transfers was shaken. Other negative factors added their effects, such as the policy of the Bank of France in favor of a low interest rate after 1865, and the introduction of inconvertible paper money between 1870 and 1878. The amount of foreign exchange in the country was reduced by the decline of the transit and international intermediation function of the Rhône Valley due to the completion of Alpine tunnels, the spread of steam navigation, and the losses of the Lyons silk industry in the face of competition from Milan and the English. The *Haute banque* gradually lost its role as broker for the precious metals. The arbitrage that resulted from variations in prices from market to market in foreign exchange and private and public securities gradually became less profitable as a result of the circulation of paper money and the use of the telegraph.

The slender resources of the French banks became evident. They lacked deposits in comparison with their English competitors. The depression of the 1880s encouraged deposits in public savings banks or investments in *rentes* and other liquid placements, even if the agrarian crisis created flows toward the stock market. The great enterprises—by the criteria of French capitalism at the time—born in the years between 1850 and 1870 did not become "money trusts" between 1870 and 1914.

Nevertheless, the French banks maintained their European connections, their networks of correspondents, and their collection of information. They also maintained their place in short-term international financial flows, and the circulation from market to market of international liquidities. The Paris market regained its function as a clearinghouse, serving as an intermediary between Russia and its suppliers and customers, whether in Europe or overseas. It fed this traffic thanks to its financial surplus with Russia, as a result of annual interest payments on the Russian debt and deposits of the Russian State Bank in Paris. France obtained the foreign exchange of the south European and Mediterranean countries, in deficit to it, but in surplus with the American continent as a result of tourist revenues and emigrant remittances. The banks circulated commercial paper labeled in foreign currencies, accepted bills of exchange, and profited from short-term capital movements as a result of variations in the rate of interest and rate of exchange. They participated in the international trade in colonial products, precious metals, and raw materials. They provided a secondary market for state securities and facilitated, as brokers, the investment of savings and investors in foreign financial markets.

The Participation of French Banks in International Groups

The banks participated in international groups that brought together several French and foreign establishmemts. These consortia pooled the financial means of their members and divided the risks. They created "omnia," which undertook audacious operations, in progressive rupture with tradition, because they presupposed the engagement of large sums and even their immobilization. A notable example was the Banque Impériale

Ottomane (B.I.O.). English banks participated in a syndicate in 1863 with French banks under the aegis of the Pereires to launch that establishment specializing in advances to the Ottoman State, from which it obtained the privilege of issuing money and the direction of its Treasury in Constantinople.[14] Some banks were created in France with foreign participation. The Crédit Industriel et Commercial (C.I.C.) attracted English and German interests in 1859. The Société Générale in 1864 brought in English and Dutch interests, which permitted it to establish itself abroad from the beginning.

The Société Générale succeeded in enlarging its relations, in spite of its rupture with the English in 1868, then with its ally, the Comptoir d'Escompte de Paris (C.E.P.), and its Dutch and German partners. It rooted itself in Central and Eastern Europe, where it pushed business opportunities offered by the opening of the Danubian countries. In association with the Austrian Länderbank and the Anglo-Austrian Bank, it created a consortium with German banks interested in southeastern Europe and the Ottoman Empire. In 1909 it entered the Bank of Salonika, created in 1888 by the Länderbank. The general manager of the Société Générale directed these networks and was himself a director of two Hungarian banks: the Ungarische Hypotheken Bank in which were associated Paribas and the Société Général, which, in 1910, participated in the coalition with the Länderbank to purchase the Ungarische Escompte und Wechslerbank.

Paribas followed the same strategy. In Rumania it was associated in the years between 1887 and 1894 with the English banks Hambro and Baring, the Dutch Hope and Company, and the interests involved with the C.E.P. It added to that, in the 1890s, collaboration with the Diskonto-Gesellschaft and Bleichröder. It assisted the Deutsche Bank in 1903 in buying the petroleum firm Steaua Romana; in 1905 German and Hungarian banks made a place for it in the capital of the Marmorosch Blank bank. The actions of Paribas cannot be understood without taking into account its integration into European "pools," durable or temporary. In Central Europe it formed a trio with the Deutsche Bank and the Wiener Bankverein.

The B.U.P., a kind of alliance or "cooperative" of several Protestant members of the *Haute banque* (Mallet, Neuflize, Mirabaud, Vernes, Hottinguer), allied itself in the decade before 1914 with the Wiener Bankverein and the Banque de Crédit Foncier Hongrois (Ungarische Hypotheken Bank). In 1906 it created the Banque Commerciale Roumaine with the Anglo-Austrian Bank, the Wiener Bankverein, and the Greco-Rumanian house of Economos, of Trieste.

The French banks were not isolated on the international scene, but worked in concert with their counterparts, including German establishments, without regard to official political differences. In Russia, when the monopoly of the Rothschilds on state loans, effective from 1862 to 1875, came apart, the syndicates that succeeded them included French and German banks—for 65 percent and 15 percent, respectively, in 1888. The French government encouraged that cooperation at the beginning, in order to undermine English influence and to thwart the Anglo-German financial accords undertaken between 1896 and 1898. French banks worked in the Balkans with German partners; in Greece, the public loans were subscribed by an Anglo-Franco-German association. In Serbia the B.I.O. and the Berliner Handels-Gesellschaft shared business (such as public loans) in 1895. In Bulgaria an international group under the leadership of the Banque Internationale de Paris (B.I.P.) gave 28 percent of its business to Austro-

German elements. In 1894 an understanding between German and French banks divided the percentages of Turkish public loans without bidding. The Deutsche Bank and the B.I.O. agreed in 1905 that 25 percent of the contracts concluded by one would be offered to the other.

The French banks undertook an authentic cosmopolitanism. Some important managers were recruited abroad from a European pool of talent, which permitted them to overcome compartmentalization in the formation of management. For example, the C.E.P. was managed during the 1870s and 1880s by the Hungarian Ulmann.

> In the great international operations French bankers did not hesitate to practice a true financial collaboration. In many regions of the globe German and French bankers worked hand in hand, respecting scrupulously their zones of reciprocal interest. They took part together in Russian, Balkan, Turkish, Iberian, Scandinavian, and South American business. They grouped themselves in financial syndicates, under the leadership of a Frenchman or a German. The negotiation of large foreign loans provoked numerous contacts among French and German bankers . . . who ignored the frontiers. They gave a perfect image of financial cosmopolitanism which was unaffected by national antagonisms. By means of tacit accords or contracts, they assured one another reciprocally of participation in their business.[15]

The Networks of Agencies and Relations: Bastions and Breaches

The French joint-stock banks created foreign branches almost from the beginning. The Société Générale had a sister institution in London, the General Credit and Finance Company, even before its statutes were approved, and after 1871 it organized its branches in German Alsace-Lorraine as the Société générale alsacienne de banque (Sogenal); it also had affiliates in Brussels and Antwerp. Paribas had agencies in Amsterdam, Brussels, and Geneva. The C.E.P. was established in London, Liverpool, Manchester, and the Near East and Far East. The Crédit Lyonnais had fourteen foreign branches in 1913, 7 percent of its total.

The traditional bastions, 1870–1900. French banks took root in several bastions. The Rothschilds conducted multiple operations with the Italian government between 1861 and 1882, being especially important in the formative years 1861–1865. The Crédit Lyonnais undertook business with the silk district of northern Italy. Some French bankers specialized in Mediterranean business. The Crédit Lyonnais provided capital for the floating debts of the states all around the Mediterranean, including Turkey. The reestablishment of the Spanish monarchy in 1875 called forth a rush of bankers attracted by large profits. The Crédit Lyonnais set up in Egypt in 1875; it participated in loans to the khedive in 1875/76, then devoted itself to advances on cotton. In 1881 it was the most important French enterprise in Egypt, after the Suez Canal Company.

French banks were also active in Central Europe. The Crédit Lyonnais undertook intense relations with Switzerland, both for commerce and for employing short-term funds in Geneva. The crisis of 1873 and its sequels, and the vigor of Jewish and German banks, deterred it from a lasting implantation in Austria. But French bankers made numerous short-term investments in Vienna, taking advantage of the higher rate of interest. From 1901 the Crédit Lyonnais and the C.E.P. placed funds with Czech banks. The German market also attracted funds by its rates of interest; the banks granted acceptances, discounted commercial paper, and made advances. Sometimes they refinanced their German partners—as in 1898, for example. The Atlantic world was not neglected. The banks had correspondents in London where they maintained surplus funds. The Crédit Lyonnais looked after the finances of the silk industry and undertook a large volume of acceptances. Other banks dealt in commercial paper, exchange with Paris, and the German banks in South America.

The breaches. The French banks were not strong in the areas where the Germans controlled too much business for the establishment of direct agencies to be profitable, or even possible, because of nationalist political susceptibilities. Germany, Austria-Hungary, and Central Europe generally frequently repelled the Parisian bankers. In Austria, the French Rothschilds did not invest so as to avoid conflicts with their Viennese cousins, bankers of the Triple Alliance. The Crédit Lyonnais closed its Vienna agency in 1879. The French had some influence in Austrian banks: the role of Bontoux in the creation of the Länderbank assured them of a substantial part of the capital, even in 1914, but a weak role in the management of the bank. The Boden Creditanstalt had French interests from its foundation in 1863, with eight French directors on its board and a Committee of Paris; French influence gradually declined, but did not disappear. In 1878 Paribas replaced the Crédit Foncier as the principal French correspondant.[16] In Rumania the German banks predominated even if some French capital was associated with them, as the Paribas in Marmorosch Blank.

In the 1890s the Germans entered the Italian peninsula. The participation of Paribas in the equity capital and on the board of the Banca Commerciale and of the C.E.P. in that of the Credito Italiano did not change their pro-German nature.[17] No French bank was active in Greece, when the Germans created the Banque d'Orient there in 1905. The participation of the B.U.P. in 1904 in the Bank of Athens concerned, above all, business with Egypt.

The French market for acceptances was only one-eighth of the London market, which had become the center for international transactions in foreign exchange. The French bankers appeared timid compared with the specialized English bill brokers and discount houses. Although some French firms participated in trade, they were light-weight in comparison with their British counterparts. The French banks were able to capture only a very small part of the international business in London.

The French presence in new countries appeared weak. The large banks abstained. The Crédit Lyonnais remained in New York only from 1879 to 1882! The C.E.P. had an agency in Chicago only from 1893 to 1900, and in New Orleans from 1895 to 1903. The Lazard bank appeared, before 1914, more Anglo-American than French. In Latin America the French bankers were feeble compared to the solid German presence. The C.E.P. and the Société Générale organized in 1896 the Banque Française du Brésil, and Paribas created an agency in Chile in 1893. These efforts were timid, lacking all continuity and strategy. The initiative was abandoned to the English and the Germans in spite of protests by French diplomats. The merchants were isolated and obliged to depend upon banks that financed their European rivals. The bankruptcy of French firms in Rio de Janeiro was linked to the impossibility of getting support from banks of national origin. The French consul in Valparaiso reported in 1902, "Without French banks and French steamers we are isolated in Chile. We are dependent upon our rivals."[18]

Only the C.E.P. made a significiant effort in the Far East. But its failure and reorganization in 1889 weakened it, and its influence in China declined. The push of the Banque de l'Indochine, created in 1875, which established agencies in Hong Kong in 1895, Bangkok in 1897, Shanghai in 1899, and Singapore in 1905, was not followed up by the other banks, which abstained in the face of the German offensive and the English dominance. A French diplomat noted, "In order for this policy of railways and mines to succeed, we must have in China an independent financial institution. The establishment in Peking of a French bank has become the necessary complement of our political and diplomatic activity in China."[19]

The international location of French banks left large gaps: "With the exception of the eastern Mediterranean, where French banks established branches, the other regions of the globe lack filials capable of sustaining French commerce."[20] The large deposit and investment banks imposed geographical restrictions on themselves and required immediate profitability, perhaps to the detriment of a future return on nonmaterial investment, which constitutes an aspect of relations. The private banks appeared less internationalist and imaginative than comparable English houses, although their basic structure was very similar. They did not benefit from the close connections among American, English, and German banks made possible by emigration, marriages, and common interests.[21] Noetzlin, of Paribas, had contacts with Jacob Schiff of Kuhn, Loeb of New York, and the Paris Rothschilds profited from their relations with the London Rothschilds, but the French Jewish banking community did not appear as open to international influence as those in Germany and the United States.[22] The members of the *Haute banque* offered a very thin financial and relational "surface." The creation of the B.U.P. as almost a banking cooperative revealed the weakness. Did that reflect the narrow dimensions of the capital market, of French familial capitalism, or of the inventiveness of the participating firms? Were great bankers lacking?

The French banks thus lacked the information flows provided by international agencies. Lacking a solid basis, one observer noted:

> Quite often, French capital was placed in the hands of foreign banks and companies, which disposed of it freely, whereas the employment of German capital could be controlled by the network of officials of German banks installed throughout the world. In addition to the role of purveyors of German commerce, these banks assured a presence; they offered to German merchants and industrialists an information service, and, to the local clientele, credit conditions provided by German banks.[23]

French industry and commerce missed out on these business opportunities because the banks did not have sufficiently rich information to sell them.

The Debate on the Role of Banks in French Foreign Investments

The Conditions of Banking Activity in France and the Need for Internationalization

Near the end of the century French banks appeared to be "loaded with deposits," and they experienced difficulty in finding suitable employment for them. The growth of the great deposit banks since the Second Empire, their collection networks for savings, the liquid assets from firms placed in banking current accounts, large fortunes, the liquid savings of the bourgeoisie, all offered substantial reserves of money.

The depression of the 1880s reduced the possibilities of employment of funds by way of discount or industrial engagements. The banks sought to export capital as "a way of enlarging the limits of elasticity of the rate of profit."[24] Both to place their own surplus funds, and as intermediaries for the savings of their customers, they sought out foreign operations susceptible of profitable returns.

> Their principal objective remained that of finding a higher rate of return on capital, that is to say, the hope of finding abroad good business with high dividends. . . . France, like the other advanced capitalist countries, those who already had an important accumulation of capital, needed to find abroad profitable employment for its surplus capital.[25]

The "end of the crisis" around the years 1896–1899 scarcely modified the quantitative or intellectual conditions of banking decisions. Although the growth of "the second industrialization" was more capitalistic, self-finance, family structure, and entrepreneurial reticence to depend on banks seemed to conserve their essential place. The change in mentality was imperceptible and took place, partially, over more than ten years between 1895 and 1906. The behavior of the banks evolved little. To be sure, some of the larger regional banks granted unsecured loans for six months, renewable with regularity, in order to better participate in financing the working capital of companies. Even if the financial needs of enterprises grew, the economic recovery brought revenue and profits that could satisfy the needs. There remained a surplus of capital for export.

The Banks and the Supply of French Capital

The rhythm of the flows of French capital. According to Rondo Cameron's data, the connection between global prosperity and the amplitude of the exportation of capital is undeniable. After the 550 million franc annual average of the years 1852–1870, and the 700 million franc annual average of the years 1871–1881, followed the 500 millions of the years 1882–1897, then 1,350 million in the years 1898–1913.[26] Maurice Lévy-Leboyer notes the fall in exports of capital of which the quinquennial annual average slid from 1,241 millions in 1865–1874 to 377 millions in 1875–1879 and 80 millions in 1880–1884.[27] Such a fall is explained by the sale of foreign securities corresponding to the Liberation loans of 1873 to pay the war indemnity; by the appearance of a lasting deficit in the balance of trade; by the banking and monetary crises of London, Rome, and Madrid in the years between 1866 and 1869, and of New York and Vienna in 1873; by the repudiation of their debts by the countries of the Middle East and Latin America, as well as the consolidation of the Ottoman debt. Then the exports of capital rose again, from 195 million annually between 1880 and 1889 to 675 million between 1890 and 1899, 1,254 million between 1900 and 1909, and 1,142.5 million between 1910 and 1913.

To be sure, the penetration of Russia began in 1877/78, amplified in the 1880s, and reached very high figures between 1888 and 1896. The average real flows to Russia amounted to 496 million francs between 1888 and 1896; it fell to 166 million between 1897 and 1903 and only rebounded to 325 million between 1904 and 1913. (These figures refer only to state loans and state-guaranteed loans.)[28] Figures relating to the totality of Russian issues in France (both public and company securities) are convergent: 578 million between 1885 and 1894, 338 million between 1895 and 1904, 386 million between 1905 and 1913, as if the Russian placements were a derivative of the depression.[29] But the trough at the beginning of the century corresponded as well to the tensions both in the economy and in the sociopolitical system of Russia. The sums intended for the public coffers and those guaranteed by the state had to compete with flows through private financial circuits, which sustained direct investment.

René Girault notes that a third of all the French investments in Russia took place between 1906 and 1914—that is, 3.5 billion francs—of which a billion went in the single year 1906. The private investments earned 7.1 percent annually between 1907 and 1914, as against the 3.38 percent for the investments in public securities. The issues of company securities aggregated 26 million annually between 1888 and 1894, 83 million between 1895 and 1914, and 112 million between 1905 and 1913. The chronology established by Jacques Thobie of French investments in Turkey appears within the general evolution of the export of capital: 15 million between 1896 and 1903, 63 million between 1904 and 1909, and 130 million between 1910 and 1914.[30] The national economy and the export of capital languished or flourished simultaneously.

The role of the banks. On the international financial market the French deposit banks themselves organized the issues of public or private securities without resorting to specialized investment banks in the American style, so that this function did not become a monopoly of the *banques d'affaires.* They had at their disposal their branch networks to retail to the public the issued securities, and their liquid assets to sustain the syndicates that guaranteed the issues of shares and bonds. The *banques d'affaires* also set up underwriting syndicates in which they played the role of *chefs de file,* but they could not by themselves place all the securities. Their relations with large savers or investors, with their banking "friends," and with provincial banks did not suffice, as was proved by the growing difficulties of the Rothschilds to hold on to the Franco-Russian business. When they made the conversion of 1,243 million francs of the Russian debt in 1889, they had difficulty in placing the securities, which demonstrated the archaic quality of the triptych, Rothschild-*Haute banque*-provincial banks, in the placement of international loans. The B.U.P. was reorganized by the Protestant bankers in 1904 specifically to deal with this problem.

The investment banks allied themselves thereafter, until 1914, with the great deposit banks. An informal consortium was established by the Crédit Lyonnais, the Société Générale, the C.E.P., the C.I.C., and certain investment banks: Paribas, the Banque Française pour le Commerce et l'Industrie (B.F.C.I., created in 1901), the B.U.P., and the Crédit Mobilier Français. That was the permanent structure of successive underwriting syndicates. The financial establishments succeeded in tapping between a fifth and a fourth of disposable savings in France to feed the exports of capital. Between 1901 and 1913 the percentage of issues of foreign securities on the Bourse of Paris, in relation to the total issues there, oscillated between a minimum of 56 percent in 1913 and a maximum of 87 percent in 1904, with the average close to one-half. These securities accounted for 25 percent of the total portfolio of French securities between 1892 and 1893, and 33 percent between 1908 and 1914.

The Polemic Over the Connection between the Export of Capital and National Industrialization

The banks' responsibility? One can see an imbalance between the importance of the financial support to certain countries and the weakness of the commercial ties with them. The new loans and the conversions raised in France by the Turks went to purchase military materiel in Germany, in particular between 1881 and 1903. The Russian loans of 1901 and 1904 gave rise to scarcely any orders in France. What could have incited the banks to neglect French interests? The French banks paid little attention to national considerations of macroeconomics and limited themselves to the simple circulation of money, and to exchanges of working capital: "The principal, not to say the unique, aim of our Eastern agencies is to employ a part of our surplus funds," said the president of the Crédit Lyonnais in 1875. They looked for short-term profits to the detriment of the establishment of durable relations: "Sacrifice everything to our security and our liquidity. Do not lend more," telegraphed a director of the Crédit Lyonnais in 1904 to the agent in St. Petersburg, who then repatriated a maximum of funds.[31] To be sure, the Crédit Lyonnais was not typical of all French banks; and 1904 was a year of panic and depression in Russia.

The tendency to separate banking action from commercial penetration appears evident, however. "Not finding directly with the banks the means to finance its sales," the Schneider firm could only obtain a large Turkish order for warships in 1906 thanks to diplomatic pressure.[32] At the limit, a connection appeared between the negotiation or the issue of a loan on the French market and an order, but without financing appropriate to facilitate the presentation of the industrial offers, as Thobie showed for the project of Ottoman naval rearmament in 1910/11 and Poidevin showed for the construction of the Thessaly-Macedonia Railway in 1913. The Banque d'Orient remained pro-German in spite of participation of the C.E.P., and the Bank of Athens, friend of the B.U.P., "poorly defended French interests." Were not the French banks only "merchants of paper"? They hesitated to go beyond the role of intermediary for the placement of securities, to grant advances on current account, to make unsecured loans, or renewable credits at medium term. They did not provide the technical or intellectual assistance for the finance of exports, the submissions of offers of military or railway equipment, or direct industrial investments. The banks conducted their affairs without sufficient collaboration with French industrial capitalism. Because of the absence of a "franc diplomacy" in the Franco-Russian relations during the years between 1887 and 1893, "The bankers . . . were independent and consulted only their own interests and the sentiments of the public."[33]

The governmental geopolitical initiatives appeared, at the turn of the century, to take place without a parallel mobilization of the banks. The banks favored loans that later paid for German sales. They associated themselves with common undertakings with their German counterparts. They refused to tie orders to loans, or to create filials in Italy or in South America in spite of the pressing recommendations of the diplomats. Even when the government attempted between 1902 and 1905 to require the Rumanians to make purchases in France, the banks refused to extend the Franco-German syndicate: The loan in 1905 of 100 million francs resulted in 40 millions of orders to Krupp and almost nothing for the French. The French bankers were "little conscious of the general interest," or to "defend the interest of Creusot. They voluntarily undertook private agreements to assure themselves financial benefits, even if these agreements resulted in a reduction of orders to French industry."[34] Paribas protested against an "immixture in its affairs" in 1905 when the industrialists demanded some Brazilian orders. The banking strategy insisted on the necessity of a Franco-German financial understanding in Latin America, and Central and Eastern Europe, and in Turkey, with a division of the industrial orders, and rejected the urgency of a permanent connection between banks and industry, which risked putting an end to the balanced divison of loans and sometimes of orders. The B.I.O. was "essentially a financial group" that did not undertake "organic connections with industrial capital."

Two financial strategies confronted one another. As Thobie notes, there were

> two possible ways for the reinforcement of French interests in the Ottoman Empire. One led to the development of an international financial association, in view of the constitution of powerful consortia exercising their activity in the whole of the Ottoman Empire . . . representing a capitalism which did not fear to march step by step with its foreign counterparts. The other way was that which did not undertake any economic or financial action in the Empire except in a purely French framework in order that, given the danger represented by foreign capitalism, only French business would obtain the aid and protection of the government, enveloped in the protective folds of the tricolor."[35]

The absence of bank–industry ties. A poor articulation between banks and industry was one of the causes of the relative weakness of French firms in comparison with their German rivals. They acted without coordination, and their financial means were insufficient to extend credit to their customers, who were obliged to borrow in order to buy. Schneider wanted to penetrate the Turkish market but did not have the means to finance the sale itself, whereas the B.I.O., at least from 1901 to 1905, neglected the interests of French industry. Albert Broder notes the absence of a "real investment policy" of the French in Spain, unlike the Société Générale de Belgique and the English, who looked upon investments as instruments permitting them to obtain orders for equipment, with the former being liquidated as the latter were realized.

The French, on the other hand, looked for stable returns, without mobility or arbitrage. Spain purchased English mining equipment, Belgian railway equipment, and German locomotives and generators, thanks to French money, because the banks lacked a strategic plan for the development of the Iberian economy and its potential feedback to France.[36]

The French banks did not favor the creation of financial holding companies for industry, unlike the German, Belgian, or Swiss conglomerates, which served as spearheads for penetration of markets for capital goods in the new countries. From the close alliance between German bankers and industrialists a polyvalent capitalism emerged, apparently more efficacious for the "second industrialization."[37] What prevented the French banks from doing likewise? One must question their intellectual agility, "the degree of internal maturity of French capitalism, the degree of fusion of banking and industrial capital."[38]

Banking or industrial responsibilities? Could the banks alone have animated commercial expansion abroad? The internationalization of French banks in the 1960s accompanied the export strategies of the large enterprises in parallel development.[39]

The weakness of the instruments in the French commercial agencies abroad was often criticized. The industrialists hesitated to open offensives in markets under German commercial influence, where they begged for diplomatic, financial, and banking support, lacking the will to create by themselves the necessary structures for seeking new customers. The high cost of production posed an additional obstacle, as well as the lack of rigor in the treatment of orders. Purchasing power was sluggish during the depression of the 1880s and also at the beginning of the second industrialization; although exports per capita rose, and France remained the fourth commercial power from 1871 to 1914, the relative position of France in European and world commerce slipped between 1860 and 1913.[40] The rate of growth of French exports fell from 4.56 percent in the period 1815–1875 to 0.86 percent between 1875 and 1895, and rebounded to 2.75 percent in the years 1895–1915. "The national industry has begun to look out for itself," observed the minister Caillaux in 1908, but its efforts appeared too timid.[41]

The structure of French industry, and in particular its comparative advantage for exports, placed the French at a disadvantage in certain strategic industries such as iron and steel, mechanical and electric equipment, and so on. One can understand why French investments in Eastern Europe took place in what Maurice Lévy-Leboyer has called "sheltered sectors," such as banks, urban public services, mortgage credit, and real estate, and why French investments concentrated so much in Europe, neglecting equipment for the developing countries overseas. The bankers made their choice within the new international division of labor, which required industrial redeployment at the turn of the century. They could not alone counterbalance the tendencies of an industrialization in which France failed to participate in the emegence of several new branches. Thus, the Rothschilds gave up the direct exploitation of Russian petroleum and turned it over to the Royal Dutch-Shell group.[42] French bankers likewise participated in the financing of German-Belgian electro-technical industries.[43] The banks scented the opportunities of the market and accompanied the growth of the firms; but they could not substitute for the entrepreneurs in the long term. "Banking backwardness existed only as a function of another backwardness, that of the degree of economic development; indeed, it was not backwardness, but a reflection."[44]

The Debate on the Appearance of New Formulas of Banking Activity

Is it true that, after the buffeting of the 1880s, the French banking system revivified itself at the beginning of the twentieth century in the first step of a movement that lasted until the crisis of 1931–1934?

A New Type of Bank?

One senses a new attention of certain bankers to the birth of markets, whether for investing in them, accompanying industrial and commercial investors, taking advantage of their deposits and their needs for credit, or for collecting savings and making loans in imitation of the banking revolution that occurred in France itself in the 1850s and 1860s. French banks invested in Russian banks in accompaniment of direct industrial investment or in anticipation of the opening of mobile, liquid fortunes. The French were dominant in the Banque du Nord, created by the Société Générale in 1901, with a participation of the B.U.P. from 1906 to 1910, and later participated in the Azov-Don, two of the eight largest banks in Russia. In 1910 the fusion of the Banque du Nord with the Russo-Chinese Bank created the Russo-Asiatic Bank, the largest bank in Russia in 1914 in terms of assets. The French owned about two-thirds of the capital of the latter, in which Maurice Verstraete, the former French consul in St. Petersburg and former co-manager of the Banque du Nord, was one of the animators. The French also had minority holdings and influence in the Petersburg Private Commercial Bank, the Bank of Siberia, and the Union Bank. In the latter the B.U.P. was strongly represented from 1908 to 1913, having helped create it by merger of the Banque internationale du commerce de Moscow, the Banque de commerce d'Oural, and the Banque de commerce du Midi de la Russie. The amount of French capital invested in Russian banks increased tenfold from 1891 to 1914 (277.5 million francs); it doubled from 1902 to 1907, then again from 1907 to 1914.[45] Specialists such as Girault and Bovykin maintain that ownership did not necessarily imply control, and that the Russian banks frequently functioned autonomously; but the French banks were less interested in day-to-day operations than in opportunities for large operations. The bank investments became the lever of penetration.

In Turkey the French controlled 77 percent of direct foreign investments in banks. The French influence within the B.I.O. intensified with respect to the English. Paribas launched the Banque Générale de Bulgarie in 1906, whereas the B.U.P. and the Société Générale took over the Banque Balkanique between 1908 and 1910, which had been a filial of the Wiener Bankverein since 1905. The C.N.E.P. (Comptoir Nationale d'Escompte de Paris, as the C.E.P. was known after its reorganization in 1889) entered the Banque d'Orient in Greece and took away its pro-German orientation. Jacques Thobie has signaled the existence of a *trompe l'oeil*, such as "the Ottoman group," which participated in the launching of the Crédit Foncier Ottoman, which in turn issued from the Bank of Salonika controlled in fact by the Société Générale and Paribas. In 1909/1910 the Banque Française et Italienne pour l'Amérique du Sud, associating French and Italian capital, squeezed into Brazil. In 1911 French shareholders took control of the National Bank of Mexico.

A mutation occurred between 1902 and 1914. In place of "antenna" agencies or branches created solely to provide short-term government credit, a new strategy called for putting down local roots abroad, diffusing banking instruments developed in France, and infiltration of the local economy. The French were to short-circuit the whiffs of nationalism blowing up in Russia by means of a subtler form of international-ization: The relation between a "center" and its "periphery" would give way, at least temporarily, to a multipolar system. While a number of industrial branches appeared to be falling behind in the competition to escape the crisis, the banks hit upon a unique method for stretching the structural limits of the French market: They would open the international market, not only to invest French funds or manage government debts, but to exploit the layers of autochthonous savings.

Industrializing Banks

Cyclical and structural pressures. The chronological field of our study covers the completion of the first trend of banking investments when the banks supported the creation of European railway networks between 1855 and 1880, and when the French banking system adopted the Crédit Mobilier model. The Crédit Mobilier Espagnol of the Pereires, which controlled two railway firms, survived the fall of the original Crédit Mobilier in 1867 and lasted until 1903, when it merged with the Banco Español de Credito. But the railway networks in Italy were bought up little by little by the state. In Austria the lines begun by the Banque de l'Union Générale of Bontoux were taken over at its failure in 1882 by the C.E.P., which lost them in its fall in 1889. The Rothschilds were evicted from the *Südbahn* when the state purchased its lines in the years between 1906 and 1908. The entry of the C.E.P. in three Swiss networks around 1876 ran aground with the fall of that bank in 1889; they were repurchased by the Swiss government in 1897/98.[46] The years between 1870 and 1900 were no longer a period of railway initiatives by the banks, which either disengaged or contented themselves with managing what they had acquired.

The depression of the 1880s and its financial embarrassments seemed to dull the offensive capacity of the French banks. Thus the crisis of 1873 made the banks skittish of industry in Austria, which had seduced some French investors in the 1860s.

> In Europe, as in the rest of the world, the Parisian banks scarcely bothered with anything but loans and current account business, and consented only with a great deal of reticence to take part in French industrial business. They refused any operation that did not give rise to immediate profit and, unlike the German banks, they systematically rejected all long-term investments. Even the few so-called investment banks, like Paribas, preferred loans.[47]

Did the French banks at the turn of the century envisage a return to a strategy of international industrialization?

After 1895 a burst of creation of companies with French capital appeared in Turkey. French investments in Ottoman enterprises doubled between 1895 and 1914 (over 510 millions francs). In Russia private investments reached 181 million francs between 1888 and 1895, and 708 million between 1895 and 1902. But the business cycle remained uncertain. Tensions in Russia in 1899 and 1901 to 1903, and stagnation in Austria from 1900 to 1904, were signs of this uncertainty. The French thus hesitated to create companies in Russia from 1901 to 1904. Then the growth of Russian industrial production accelerated from 1907 to 1913. The European upswing and the burst of industrialization caused direct investments to swell.

The industrialists animated that push. But, in spite of the case of Huta Bankowa, which preserved its financial ease, many enterprises in Russia could scarcely assemble funds sufficient for growth, internal or external, and to maintain their working capitals. The opening of firms to outside capital—shareholders for new capital or bankers for current accounts—was in itself a blow to both mentality and management.[48] Putting at their disposal the ability to mobilize savings was a reorientation of the banks from public securities to private issues. A strategic alliance came into being for the development of Russia. "French heavy industry lacked the necessary resources for independent expansion abroad; it had to rely on French banks. . . . Schneider had to obtain the support of Paribas to establish Volga-Vichera (1896), Châtillon-Commentry did the same with the Banque Internationale de Paris for the Ural-Volga (1896–1900)."[49] Moreover, as Girault observes:

> Industrial companies and French investment banks tried to impose themselves in Russia without having solid bases on the scale of international competition; the direct

investments in Russia came from companies less powerful than their German competitors, less capable of successfully sustaining a strictly industrial struggle. Schneider or Châtillon-Commentry could not take on Krupp and Mannesmann, at least not without the support of the banks."[50]

The simultaneous reinforcement of the extroverted banking system and of the will to Europeanization of the industrialists permitted them to profit from the cyclical upswing. The strategic redeployment of the banks needed both the industrialists and the cycle to succeed, because they could not by themselves be the lever of international growth.

Audacious and pioneering banks? The banks more and more were confronted with the need to return to the forms of prudence adopted previously. Girault notes:

> French bank management had the duty to choose. It was no longer a question of considering the immediate profits to be drawn from a new issue of shares or bonds, but of judging beyond the immediate operation, the likely future profits and the risks. In effect, to launch a company or to take one over permitted the banks to assure themselves of the current accounts, the contracts, the cash advances, and the exchange transactions (without counting the dividends), which would give the banks appreciable profits.[51]

The difficulty lay with the selection of the business opportunities and the risks.

The majority of firms concluded understandings with banking partners in order to obtain credit, sell their shares to the public, gain the moral guarantee of having bankers on their boards of directors, and participate in the share capital. The diffusion of the latter among numerous stockholders conferred on the banks a strong influence in the Russian companies quoted in Paris because they controlled blocks of minority shares that gave them the right to vote. The banks regarded themselves as the lookouts of French capitalism, promoters of the intensification of European industrialization. Thobie described the B.I.O. of 1907 as a "mixed bank." Alongside its activities as a commercial bank it swelled its portfolio of securities (80 million francs), even though its holdings were modest and classic, as in railways, tramways, and gas.[52] According to a tendency already noticeable between 1890 and 1914 in the French provinces, where regional banks were guided by local capitalists, but perceptible at the national level above all in the 1920s, "mixed bank" behavior spread as though the banks were seeking to get around the principle of liquidity, by moving through the provinces or abroad. Internationalization played a role in promoting the "universal" or "mixed" bank in France, prior to acclimatizing it within the frontiers.[53]

Nevertheless, with the B.I.O. one discerns not a strategy of industrialization of Turkey, but the simple desire to construct minimal infrastructures.[54] The bank could not substitute for entrepreneurs, public or private, or for autochthonous savings in the Ottoman Empire. Austria-Hungary, with the Czech lands, which seemed able to undertake self-sustained growth, closed itself to French capitalism for political reasons. The states of its periphery offered only their agriculture, if one excludes the mining and petroleum deposits with which the French had little to do. Russia thus appeared as the prime field for French banking offensives, along with the Balkans and North Africa. Beginning in 1886, Rothschild pursued an obstinate strategy for the oil of the Caspian

Sea.[55] Girault has the impression that Paribas had a "coherent strategy." It played a major role in the negotiations and leadership of the underwriting syndicates for Russian loans, public and private. It invested in the metallurgical enterprises of the Urals from the later 1880s. In 1907 it attempted to put together a consortium uniting the *Haute banque*, the Société Générale, and stockbrokers, in order to mobilize their capital and lend to Russian firms whose orders for material would come to France.

The strategy of the Société Générale was not to disperse its business but to concentrate on a few key companies, stable and firmly controlled. It remained faithful to its initial behavior as a mixed bank, which flowered in Russia as a *politique à la Talabot*.[56] Although it held only 25 million francs in industrial participations in Russia in 1901, in coal mines and metallurgy, it saw its Russian filial, the Banque du Nord, as an instrument for freeing from the official accounts of the mother company its industrial engagements in order to avoid the suspicions of French savers. It took over the direction of the metallurgical company of Briansk in 1901, and attempted in the Omnium (Société Générale de l'Industrie Minière et Métallurgique en Russie) to create a conglomerate.[57]

"Financial nebulas" can be discerned where the banks assembled capital and undertook to find business where it would be profitable. The B.U.P. led a kind of syndicate for Russian business from 1908 until the war with the houses of the *Haute banque* that created it, along with Belgian and English banks. The Société Générale entered an informal agreement with Paribas in 1905 to unite their capacity to mobilize savings and their business networks. The banks offered to foster Russian capitalism.

> An international capitalism of audacious entrepreneurs, supported by several deposit banks, acted from afar with a concerted strategy and with continuity: the export of capital was not just an outlet for overabundant savings; it was a means of undertaking profitable business on an international scale.[58]

The banks at the heart of the diptychs? If, in furnishing railway material in Southern and Eastern Europe, German industry affirmed its power, the competition of French firms took place in part thanks to banking support. The Rothschilds insisted on participating in Russian loans in the 1880s for the purpose of obtaining orders for material for the Trans-Siberian Railway, but we don't know if their participation in the Baku petroleum industry resulted in purchases of materials in France. The steady participation of Paribas in the negotiation of loans, as in the Russian program for economic and strategic railways in 1913, is explained by the desire to further the interests of the French and Russian firms with which it was connected. The banks participated in the Smyrna-Cassaba Railway in 1894, and in the Syrian-Palestinian Railway during 1899–1901. The B.I.O. supported the specialized French group in railway management, the Régie Générale des Chemins de Fer. Coalitions occurred between public works firms and banks: The Omnium d'Entreprises united three banks and two entrepreneurs to obtain the Smyrna-Dardanelles Railway in 1914. That explains the penetration of French interest in the control of Ottoman railways, which balanced the German force in 1914, if one takes account of lines in operation and those for which the concession had been accorded. The banking dynamism was reinforced in that branch favorable to French talent.[59]

But was there creation of new markets for French enterprises? Although the Régie

Générale furnished management and thus obtained orders for "gray matter," we don't know the amount of the material delivered in Russia and Turkey or the place of French firms in construction. Some projects got started on the base of common interests. In 1913 the Banque Franco-Serbe and the B.I.O. agreed with the Société Franco-Serbe d'Entreprises Industrielles et de Travaux Publics, founded by the Banque Franco-Serbe in 1912, to obtain a large contract: The banks furnished the money that permitted French contractors to place their orders. Multiple examples are available: The B.I.O. patronized the association between Schneider, the industrialist, and Hersent, Batignolles, and Vitali, the contractors, who in the Consortium des Ports de l'Empire Ottoman negotiated the construction of ports and in 1913/14 carried away the contracts for five great ports. In 1910 the Banque Française pour le Commerce et l'Industrie brought together Fougerolle, Giros-Loucheur, and the Grands Travaux de Marseille in the Société Générale d'Entreprises dans l'Empire Ottoman; the bank provided finances and financial services to the company and participated in obtaining a large contract for road construction in 1910. Participations in share capital and loans permitted the banks to provide equipment for the Ottoman Empire. If diplomatic pressure and sometimes technical military collaboration facilitated obtaining orders for armaments or ships, the efficacy of the banks in these successes does not appear clearly. The coupling of an issue of a loan by the banks, the authorization for quotation on the Bourse, and the signing of orders grew. It is not easy to discern whether the industrialists finally learned the necessity of constant promotional campaigns and the delivery of technical services before or in association with the furnishing of materials, or if the establishment of the "triptych finance-industry-diplomacy" brought about a change in banking habits.

The essential acquisition seems to have been the web of regular relationships between bankers and industrialists who acquired the habit of working together. Informal or structured understandings among the furnishers of money and those of techniques or materials outlined, on a common front, the French interests who also associated with European business centers.

During establishment of the "diptych," who was most active, the industrialists or the bankers? During the campaign of the B.U.P. and Schneider for naval and other construction projects in the Baltic between 1910 and 1914, the bank became the financial axis of an integrated multinational ensemble led by France: Austria-Hungary (Skoda) and Russia (Poutiloff) participated in an interaction between the dynamism of the industrialists and the suppleness of the bankers: "Bank and industry shoulder to shoulder."[60] But the B.U.P. was reticent in the face of the initiatives of Schneider, which led to their rupture, and the creation in 1920 by Schneider of the Union Européenne Industrielle et Financière. The manager of the B.U.P. wrote in 1913, "Our friends march ahead, signing contracts without informing us, looking after their interests, but scarcely bothering about ours and demanding that we take all the risks. Besides, they use the name of the B.U.P. excessively."[61] The growth of firms involved in international business added to their autonomy in finance and decision making. So didn't the bank follow the entrepreneur? Did the banks request ties with the enterprises? Did they hope to create a "financial capitalism"? Did they have the means, not only monetary, but also intellectual, conceptual, and human (engineers, technicians, analysts, etc.) to develop the profession of "business banking"? The banks could not "dominate" capitalism unless they habitually took part in strategic decision making, and increased their "financial engineering," as in the United States and Germany.

Conclusion: A Multinational Capitalism?

A new model gradually took shape. Whereas the *mobilier*-type banks, dominated by the Parisian center, led industry in a type of development that seemed to run aground at the end of the 1870s, the new model saw banks and industry as equal partners, often in a double binary structure. This central Parisian "couple" corresponded, in fact, to a "peripheral couple," decentralized, rooted in the fertile soil of the growth of developing countries. It was a "multinational capitalism" as much as "financial capitalism" that arose.

In spite of their size in relation to the whole of the French economy, and in spite of the renewal of their flows of savings by the returns on foreign investments, the banks did not control an inexhaustible supply of resources. They could not substitute for the imagination of entrepreneurs in order to devise financial contracts attractive for their customers or offer capital goods at competitive prices. The bankers "maintained, within these limits, a certain amount of autonomy with respect to development; they had, one might say, a certain margin of freedom of action, which left them the possibility of playing the role of motor—or of brake—in economic development."[62] They could mobilize themselves for investments and credit in periods of lively growth despite their reputation for paralysis.

The initiatives of the banks on international capital markets and their participation in the industrialization of certain developing countries have contributed to defining the new banking behavior. From these practices and these men a new "tradition" had to appear. The difficulty is in understanding the integration of these changes in domestic banking behavior.[63]

Is it anachronistic to detect the formation of a French "financial capitalism" by means of French participation in international industrialization? Bouvier notes:

> Everything happened as if, in the case of France, the process of the "fusion," of "interpenetration" of banks and industry was less developed. The "financial capital" in France at the beginning of the twentieth century was only in process of slow formation. It was far from complete. The increasing concentration of banking capital and industrial capital had not yet created a single mechanism. . . . But it was in foreign operations, because of the necessity of the union of industrial and banking interests, that the "fusion" began to develop a few years before 1914.[64]

In the end, "the export of capital played a major role in the origin of 'financial capital,' although that development was not very far advanced in France on the eve of the first World War."[65]

Did the foreign operations of the banks, in association with industrial capital, sketch the outline of a pioneer economic system largely based on exports and credit, like that which flourished in France in the 1920s, and again after 1950? We must be prudent: Can we maintain that the companies included in the "diptych" were representatives of French capitalism? Is their preeminence due more to the sagacity of historians who have resurrected them from the archives, or to their place in the avant-garde of the second industrialization? Does our subject concern only that small group of exporting firms who tried to sniff the air of the whole?

4

International Aspects
of the Development
# of German Banking

Richard Tilly

The leading characteristic of the German banking system as it evolved in the second half of the nineteenth century was certainly not its international orientation. Like the German economy itself during this period, German banks were dominated by the financial opportunities created by domestic social overhead and industrial investment. Many ways exist for demonstrating the primacy of Germany's domestic financial needs, but the most convenient one for present purposes is to cite figures collected by Walther Hoffmann in his book on German economic growth and by Raymond Goldsmith in one of his earlier comparative studies (Table 4–1).

Note the increasing importance of residential construction on the investment side of Table 4–1. Its counterpart on the finance side in 1913, for example, consists of the assets of the mortgage banks plus some 20 billion marks in mortgage credit supplied by saving banks, insurance companies, and other miscellaneous institutions. This point is worth stressing here, for it bears on an important contemporary debate concerning Germany's capital market; in particular, it bears negatively on the thesis that Germany's foreign investments were excessive relative to the country's financial resources.[1]

Nevertheless, Germany's foreign investment and international financial ties had more than negligible importance in the period under investigation, especially when viewed from the international perspective. According to the sources cited by Hoffmann, the value of German foreign investment rose from roughly 7 billion marks in 1882, or nearly half the estimated national income, to around 20 billion, or 41 percent of the latter figure in 1913.[2] This made Germany third in the world ranking of nations exporting capital at that date. Moreover, over the same period, Germany's foreign trade expanded considerably—indeed, more rapidly than the country's rapidly rising income.[3] The growth of trade necessitated an expansion in the volume and complexity of Germany's foreign payments and led inevitably to the increasing involvement of German banks in the international payments and short-term lending business. By 1913 this business had reached a scale sufficiently large to make the

TABLE 4–1. Net Investment by Major Sector and Assets of
Financial Institutions in Germany, 1860–1913

	Investment/Assets[a] (millions of marks)		
	1860	*1880*	*1913*
Sector			
Agriculture	630	80	1,580
Industry and trade	160	450	3,200
Residential construction	150	340	1,750
Transport[b]	240	260	790
Construction[c]	80	200	850
TOTAL	1,260	1,330	8,170
Financial Institutions			
Credit banks	390	1,350	22,040
Private bankers	1,500	2,500	4,000
Savings banks	510	2,780	22,560
Mortgage banks	90	1,850	13,550
Land banks	680	1,760	7,200
Life insurance	70	440	5,640
Other	1,010	2,820	16,010
TOTAL	4,250	13,500	91,000

Sources: Walther Hoffmann *et al., Das Wachstum* (see note 2 below); Raymond Goldsmith, *Financial Structure and Development* (New Haven, 1969), Appendix D-13.

[a] Investments and assets are expressed in current prices.

[b] Railroads.

[c] Streets and canals, harbors, sewer and lighting systems and public buildings.

German mark one of the world's "key currencies" and also to have repercussions on the
domestic monetary system.[4] The subject of the following pages thus represents rather
more than an insignificant part of Germany's banking history.

The principal actors in the story of German international banking in the second half
of the nineteenth century are the private bankers, the joint-stock ("credit") banks, and
the central bank of issue—until 1875 the Prussian Bank and from 1875 to 1914 the
Reichsbank. Private bankers dominated the international banking business well into the
1870s; from that point on, at the very latest from the 1880s on, joint-stock banks stood
in the forefront. This development matched that in domestic banking. The reason is
that free incorporation laws in the 1870s made it easier for private bankers to found
joint stock bank enterprises with limited liability, while the pressures of day-to-day
business led to ever-greater autonomy of joint-stock banks from their original founders.
Owing to the greater ease with which they could attract equity capital, they soon
outstripped the private bankers in size and in volume of business—both domestic and
international.

The parallel between the domestic and international banking business extended to
the predominance of "mixed" or "universal" as opposed to specialized commercial or
investment banking. Like the private bankers who founded them, German joint-stock

banks came to engage equally in short-term lending and payments business on the one hand and in long-term investment, mainly in the form of the promotion and issue business, on the other. Explaining this institutional development, however, requires a look at the story's third principal character: the central bank of issue. By the 1870s a handful of banks closely controlled by the German governments all but completely monopolized German note circulation, with one of them, the Prussian Bank, alone accounting for close to 80 percent.[5] In 1875 this monopoly of issue was transferred to the imperial government's newly founded Reichsbank. This meant that joint-stock banks had to move into areas other than the liquid payments and very short-term credit business. Those other areas became the field of "mixed banking." At the same time, the joint-stock banks relied on the central bank of issue for refinancing and payments facilities; and the Reichsbank proved willing and able to accommodate their needs and thus fully justify their reliance. Knut Borchardt's remarks apply equally to domestic and foreign demands:[6]

> . . . the credit system rested on the assumed liquidity guarantee of the Reichsbank. More, this was the prerequisite for the heady expansion of the system of "universal banking" in the last decades before World War I. The mixed banks more and more forced the Reichsbank out of the business of lending directly to industry and trade, but at the same time they increasingly laid claim to a service which was not originally designed for them, namely the right to raise credit on good-quality bills in unlimited quantity. . . . This right contrasted ever more sharply with the Reichsbank's ability to accommodate it. For in the last analysis, even the bank of issue had to make payments in a means of exchange it could not itself create—in gold.[6]

The above quotation is an appropriate conclusion to this section, for it properly identifies a mixture of international and institutional constraints on the functioning of the German banking system that must be borne in mind in the discussion of institutions and behavior patterns that follows.

German Banks and the Foreign Investment Business

During the first half of the nineteenth century German private bankers participated actively in the field of international investment. They did so mainly by marketing the securities of foreign governments and principates in such nascent financial centers as Berlin and Frankfurt/Main. This was by no means a trivial business, and it has therefore puzzled historians, for a relatively backward economy such as that of the German states in the first half of the century might have been expected to *import*, rather than *export*, capital.[7]

With the advent of railways and correspondingly large financial demands in the 1830s, German private bankers *did* begin to organize that expected import of capital. But though some compelling examples of capital import can be cited—the role of Cologne bankers in the 1830s in fashioning a Belgian market for Rhenish Railway Company securities is one such case[8]—it is unlikely that a substantial net inflow of financial capital (corresponding to portfolio investment abroad) developed. One reason why such a flow is unlikely is that private bankers—especially in centers such as

Berlin or Frankfurt—were increasingly committing their resources to *foreign* railways at this time, not just to domestic ones.[9] That is, outflows may have just balanced inflows. Another reason is that most of the adequately documented examples of foreign investment in Germany during the early industrialization period (to 1870) were closely associated with foreign entrepreneurs and really amounted, in effect, to direct rather than portfolio investment.[10]

Perhaps the most significant form of capital import during this period derived from the use of short-term foreign commercial credits—significant in the sense that such credits demanded lower interest payments than did domestic credits and thus set resources free for other purposes.[11] Like long-term foreign investment, this short-term flow also passed largely through the private banking houses. The period of early industrialization thus anticipated the later period from 1870 to 1914 in two respects: (1) the predominance of German portfolio investment abroad over foreign portfolio investment in Germany, and (2) the net negative balance on short-term capital account.

The 1870s marked some very significant shifts in the German capital market with consequences for the international banking business. One such shift was the introduction of free incorporation, which contributed to the enormous increase in the numbers and size of German joint stock banks in the early 1870s. In the financial crash of 1873 and the long depression that followed it, many of these banks disappeared and others wrote down their capitals.[12] Nevertheless, the gains of the early 1870s were not erased. Many of the surviving banks held their ground and some even grew; thus, by the end of the 1870s, joint-stock institutions clearly occupied a place in German banking—both domestic and international—that rivaled that of the private bankers.[13]

From an international perspective, the most important of the new banks was the Deutsche Bank, organized by a group of private bankers in 1870 for the purpose of capturing a greater share of the foreign short-term credit and payments business that was "needlessly" flowing into British hands.[14] To this end the Deutsche Bank founded branches or new dependent banks abroad (e.g., in Asia in 1872, and London in 1871 and 1873) in addition to cooperating with other banks in the organization of new overseas banks such as the Argentinian creation, Deutsch-Belgische Laplata-Bank. This creation was relatively unsuccessful; indeed, the Deutsche Bank's foreign business in general proved disappointing over the first decade or so. In consequence, the Deutsche Bank revised its program and began to concentrate on domestic business, a change not welcomed by its founders (and principal shareholders)—who were themselves bankers largely engaged in domestic financing activities and who had seen the Deutsche Bank only as a complementary instrument for handling the business they did not want or could not easily handle.[15] Nevertheless, these initial creations proved important for the Deutsche Bank and for German banks in general, and for two reasons: (1) As the volume of German foreign trade expanded, so too did the foreign payments and short-term credit business that these banks carried out, i.e., their existence became justified; (2) these institutions, even if their local volume of business was small, served as valuable sources of information on foreign economies and as contact centers that could ease the development of the foreign investment business.

The financial crash of 1873 and ensuing depression, in and of themselves, enhanced the attractiveness of foreign investment to German bankers and capitalists by virtue of the destruction of domestic investment opportunities with which they were associated. In addition, the Prussian government's purchase of the extensive private railway network beginning in the late 1870s increased the domestic supply of funds in search of higher (if riskier) returns on portfolio investment than domestic, nonrailway securities offered.[16]

In the wake of these changes, German bankers and banks appear to have ridden a first and substantial wave of foreign investment running through the decade of the 1880s. It involved a wide range of government and railroad investments in Eastern Europe (above all, Imperial Russia) and South America. It also included some important banks in South America and China. This first wave received a setback in 1887 when Bismarck, on foreign policy grounds, banned Russian bonds from the list of securities eligible as collateral for Reichsbank credit.[17] It really broke in the early 1890s, however, when a number of foreign governments, above all Argentina (the Baring crisis), but also Portugal and Greece, temporarily ceased servicing their debts.[18] A smaller wave recurred in the mid–1890s (to 1898), once again including Eastern Europe and South America as recipients of new capital, but this time also marked by a penetration of Italian banking and industry. Thereafter, foreign investment played only a relatively minor role in German capital issues, rising to a substantial sum in but one year—1905—the result of an unusual coincidence of heavy foreign demands, including those of both participants in the Russo-Japanese War of 1904/05.

Taking new issues of securities on the Berlin Stock Exchange as an indicator, Table 4–2 attempts to sum up the chronological story.

Taken as a whole, the story is one in which certain phases of especially pronounced foreign engagements occur, as already mentioned, but in which the amount of foreign business in general tends to reflect the amount of *total* business—i.e, foreign issues depend to a significant extent on the buoyancy of the domestic capital market rather than on changes in opportunities abroad.[19] Of course, foreign portfolio investment differed from its domestic counterpart in that fixed-interest securities dominated the former; moreover, German banks also implemented projects involving large amounts of *direct* foreign investment and not necessarily having the same temporal pattern as portfolio investment.

No great claims of precision can be made for these foreign investment data, either as total figures or as estimates of the geographic distribution. Nevertheless, they are probably good enough to support statements about long-term trends and broad distributional tendencies. That, at least, appears to be the opinion of the historical literature on the matter.[20] Table 4–3 presents three different, though related, estimates of the geographical distribution of German foreign portfolio investment before World War I.

Note the rough equality of European and overseas investments as of 1914. The leading role of the United States as target of German capital exports is apparent here, but note also the "Europeanization" of foreign investment in the years immediately preceding World War I (Table 4–3, column 2) as North American portfolio investments declined.[21] It is interesting to observe, finally, that Latin America gained in relative importance in this latter period. In the following discussion of German banking practice in relation to foreign investment, therefore, these three geographical areas are singled out for special attention.

Before taking up that discussion of largely qualitative matters, however, I should like to comment briefly on one obvious but difficult quantitative aspect of Germany's foreign portfolio investments—their profitability. Unfortunately, for Germany there is no study comparable to Edelstein's important analysis of London Stock Exchange

TABLE 4–2. Foreign and Total New Issues in Germany's
Capital Market, 1883–1913 (in millions of marks)

Year	Foreign Issues (1)	Total Issuesª (2)	Total Issuesᵇ (3)	(1)/(2) %
1883	300	563	754	53
1884	530	717	905	74
1885	510	745	899	68
1886	485	763	1,015	64
1887	410	793	1,008	52
1888	667	1,160	1,985	58
1889	584	1,336	1,742	44
1890	386	1,229	1,521	31
1891	245	676	1,218	36
1892	172	511	949	34
1893	342	916	1,266	37
1894	384	860	1,420	45
1895	318	875	1,375	36
1896	568	1,408	1,896	40
1897	633	1,461	1,944	43
1898	710	2,042	2,407	35
1899	234	2,164	2,611	11
1900	275	1,651	1,777	17
1901	210	1,420	1,631	15
1902	454	1,700	2,111	27
1903	242	1,101	1,666	22
1904	232	1,489	1,995	16
1905	1,108	2,522	3,091	44
1906	221	2,336	2,741	9
1907	153	1,886	2,212	8
1908	228	2,780	3,416	8
1909	348	2,943	3,590	12
1910	546	2,342	3,022	23
1911	460	2,087	2,709	22
1912	270	2,730	2,934	10
1913	604	2,589	2,646	23

Source: Arthur Spiethoff, *Die Wirtschaftlichen Wechsellagen* (Tübingen, 1955), Vol.
2, Tafel 3.

ª Without mortgage bank debentures.

ᵇ Including mortgage bank debentures.

securities.[22] It is likely, however, that German foreign portfolio investment, like that of the United Kingdom investigated by Edelstein, paid relatively well. Knowledgeable contemporaries said it did; and for Germany's Russian investments in the period we have some quantitative evidence substantiating that claim.[23] For purposes of illustration, contemporary opinion can be utilized to assemble a "portfolio" of foreign securities traded on the Berlin Stock Exchange and to present a picture of that "portfolio's" average returns. Appendix A at the end of this chapter lists those securities and their returns. The average rate of return of 6.7 percent per annum (1870–1911) is 2.4 percentage points above that earned on Prussian consols, though more variable. On the other hand, it is at least as far from the returns earned on domestic industrial shares in

TABLE 4–3. Geographical Distribution of German Foreign
Portfolio Investment, 1897–1914 (in billions of marks)

Regions	New Issues 1897–1906 (1)	New Issues 1907–1914 (2)	Estimated Total Foreign Investment, 1914
Europe	7.1	5.5	12.5
Austria-Hungary			3.0
Russia			1.8
Turkey			1.8
Balkan states			1.7
North America	4.0	1.1	3.7
Central America (including Mexico)	0.7	0.6	
South America	0.2	0.8	
Latin America	0.9	1.3	3.8
Asia	1.7	0.9	1.0
Africa		0.2	2.0
TOTAL	13.7	9.0	23.5

Source: Herbert Feis, Europe, the World's Banker (note 16), and Paul Arndt, "Wesen und Zweck der Kapitalanlage im Ausland," Zeitschrift für die gesamte staatswissenschaft, N.F. 6 (Leipzig, 1915).

the period.[24] These results are worth pondering, though the data base is as yet too uncertain to justify more than highly speculative pondering.

If the data underlying Table 4–3 can be trusted, the United States was the largest single recipient of German foreign investment in the late nineteenth century. Apart from profitability, one possible explanation for this may lie in the closeness of personal ties between German and American bankers in the period. More than one historian has noted the importance of German-Jewish immigrants for the development of the New York banking community in the nineteenth century.[25] A well-known example is the connection between the Warburgs of Hamburg and Kuhn, Loeb & Co. of New York. In 1895 Felix Warburg, one of the principal's five sons, married Frieda Schiff, the only daughter of the New York firm's senior partner, Jacob Schiff; and in the same year Paul Warburg, another one of the five sons, married Nina Loeb, daughter of Solomon Loeb, a founding partner of the firm.[26]

Another example is Arthur Gwinner, an important director of the Deutsche Bank in the 1890s, who was related by marriage to owners of the New York banking house of Speyer & Co., which had additional family ties to a private banking firm in Germany.[27] Yet another case is the close relationship between the Berliner Handelsgesellschaft, a large bank controlled by Carl Fürstenberg, and the New York bankers W. G. Hallgarten & Co., in which Fürstenberg's stepson was partner.[28] It would be easy to extend the list of such connections.

Such ties had their reflection in many large international transactions involving some of the names just mentioned, and particularly because they were an internationally familiar asset, involving American railways securities. The story of the Northern Pacific Railroad and Henry Villard, an adventurous financier who had emigrated from Germany in the 1850s, is only one of the more notorious and negative cases of a series containing many positive ones.[29]

It was Villard's ability to persuade influential directors of the Deutsche Bank, such as Georg von Siemens, that American railways were a promising investment that gave him his strength and leverage within the field of American railroad finance in the 1870s and 1880s. He was, so to speak, an "information intermediary," playing in Germany his "American card"—information about American railroads and their economic and legal context—and in the United States his "German card"—which was access to a hitherto (as of 1870) only weakly exploited source of funds and a source that could only be tapped by someone who could speak the proper language—in both the figurative and literal sense of the word.

Villard's great chance to exploit his cross-cultural position came with the business crash of 1873 and the related collapse of Jay Cooke's financial empire—which included the Northern Pacific Railroad. In 1874 a committee of Frankfurt investors in American railway securities hurt by the crash and led by the private banking firm of Jacob S. H. Stern, hired Villard to represent their interests in the United States and especially with respect to the Northern Pacific. On the basis of this support, Villard soon built up a position of great strength in railroad affairs; by 1879 he was president of the Northern Pacific. In the 1880s the rail line again ran into difficulties and in 1883 went into receivership. Nevertheless, German banks, above all the Deutsche Bank, continued to support Villard and the Northern Pacific. First, second, and then third mortgage bonds were introduced by the Deutsche Bank onto the Berlin and Frankfurt markets in 1886, 1887, and 1888. By this time, it seems in retrospect, a point of no return had been reached, and the Deutsche Bank held firm, even when the railroad again went into receivership in 1893. By now, however, the Berlin bank had lost confidence in Villard; moreover, partly due to Villard-made difficulties, the bank's leadership had developed alternative sources of information on American railroads and no longer needed Villard. So out he went.

Without Villard and through close cooperation among the Deutsche Bank, J. P. Morgan & Co., and James J. Hill of the Great Northern Railway, which competed with the Northern Pacific, the troubled road was once more reorganized (1896).[30] In the subsequent "battle of the titans" (Morgan-Hill vs. Schiff-Harriman) for control of the road in 1901, the Deutsche Bank and its investors then sold out their holdings at a reportedly handsome profit. According to at least one banking historian, the happy end to this particular episode appears to have been an important factor keeping German investor interest in American railroad securities strong in subsequent years.[31] That happy end, however, resulted not simply from a lucky break, but from improved informational flows that eased international cooperation among bankers.

The historian of German investment in the United States, it appears, will have to take account of personal ties between bankers as a factor of considerable importance. There are two difficulties with an explanation that builds primarily on such ties, however. First, many cases can be cited in which close, personal ties evolved out of business connections.[32] Second, German bankers had close ties with banking houses in many of the other foreign centers in which they operated. The first difficulty, indeed, points to an alternative explanation: Owing to American banking regulations, German bankers could not establish branches in New York, America's principal banking center; they had to ally themselves with resident American firms, either by becoming partners in a private firm, by becoming major shareholders in a joint-stock bank, or by simply cultivating strong, though informal, links. Historically observed personal and family connections, that is, may well have *followed* from such circumstances. Nevertheless, the fact of close personal ties is indisputable and remains important as an element of international banking—not just for the American business.

Our story of international connections can fruitfully continue by moving southward to Latin America. German financial penetration of Latin American countries in the same period also involved the use of personal and family networks, but in a much less pervasive manner. For here the emigré financial community of German origins was much smaller, and the barriers to setting up dependent banks with branches much weaker. Partly as a means of offsetting the greater strength of British merchants and bankers there, the Cologne private bankers, Sal. Oppenheim Jr. & Co., the Berliner Diskonto-Gesellschaft, and the Austrian Creditanstalt, together with Belgian bankers, founded the Deutsch-Belgische Laplata-Bank in 1872. This was a bank with a nominal capital of 10 million thalers (roughly 30 million marks) and branches in Buenos Aires and Montevideo. The bank did poorly from the outset, for political reasons and also because of the depression of the 1870s. It has therefore remained somewhat puzzling that the Deutsche Bank of Berlin was so keen to buy into this enterprise—which it did in 1875, when it became principal owner.[33] After a decade of disappointments, marked, for example, by a change of regime in Uruguay and that country's cessation of debt servicing, the Deutsche Bank liquidated the bank in 1885.[34]

In 1886, however, the Deutsche Bank founded a new bank in the old one's place: the Deutsche Übersee-Bank (D.Ü.B.) This bank built on the preparatory work of the old, initially had a capital of 10 million marks and headquarters in Berlin and Buenos Aires, but soon set up branches elsewhere in Argentina, in Chile, Bolivia, and Uruguay.[35] Apparently impressed by this step, the Diskonto-Gesellschaft and the Norddeutsche Bank founded together in 1887 the Brasilianische Bank für Deutschland with headquarters in Hamburg and plans for branches (subsequently realized) in five Brazilian cities. In 1890 the same German pair added an independent branch in Buenos Aires and in 1895 a new bank, the Bank für Chile und Deutschland, to its Latin American operations.[36] Other institutions followed, but these three German banks were the most important. They did well and, but for the continued strong competition from British banks and growing competition from Americans, might have done still better. The striking weakness of German financial penetration of Mexico, for instance, probably reflects the relative strength of American competition there.[37]

As mentioned earlier, these banks owed their importance largely to their role in financing German trade with Latin American countries and to their significance for their German founders as sources of information on Latin American financial conditions and opportunities.[38] The first aspect receives some attention in a later discussion; the second is difficult to assess. It is difficult to assess because of a built-in source bias: The German banks remained formally and firmly in control of their overseas offshoots; if large business opportunities emerged, they tended to be perceived, negotiated, and decided very largely in the German headquarters.[39] The smaller day-to-day operations contributed to the success of these overseas banks, both directly and indirectly—as producers of information and contacts going into the large transactions. But the sources, and thus the histories of these banks, tend to be dominated by the large transactions.

By far the most significant set of such large transactions involved the founding and development of the Deutsch-Überseeische-Elektrizitäts-Gesellschaft (D.Ü.E.G.), a public utilities enterprise begun in Buenos Aires in 1898, which became by 1913 one of Germany's largest overseas enterprises.[40] Emil Rathenau and his Allgemeine Elektrizitäts-Gesellschaft (A.E.G.) initiated this project in 1895 in close association with a group of Berlin bankers led by the Deutsche Bank.[41] Negotiations between this group and the City of Buenos Aires, interestingly, were conducted by the local representative of the D.Ü.B., and once the D.Ü.E.G. was launched (with an initial capital of 20 million marks), that representative remained as permanent member of the local board of directors.[42] The D.Ü.E.G. was conceived to build, own, and operate power stations and urban transport and lighting facilities, at first in Buenos Aires, later in other parts of Argentina and other South American countries. This program called for the mobilization of large sums of money—its capital amounted in 1913 to over 200 million marks—most of which was raised in the German capital markets through a syndicate that included virtually all important Berlin banks.[43] The Deutsche Bank remained in charge of this syndicate, and as the bank's historian has observed (of the pre–1914 period):

> Stock exchange interest in D.Ü.E.G. shares never abated. The Deutsche Bank could at all times expect from its customers a readiness to take up the shares it offered them. Here we have Crédit Mobilier banking in its best possible form. In the case of the Mannesmann enterprise, the Deutsche Bank found itself in the position of having to finance a defective, unripe innovation for many years during which no recourse to the stock exchange and, hence, no substantial sales of the company's shares was thinkable. In the case of the D.Ü.E.G., in contrast, the enterprise's (and Emil Rathenau's) technical plans proved feasible from the outset, and the young power stations in Buenos Aires functioned without fault, serving as a magnet, so to speak, for investors. The capital which banks had advanced was thus never in jeopardy.[44]

The last sentence quoted above is an exaggeration, for the history of the D.Ü.E.G. ran a course characterized by much uncertainty—about the politics of the host country and about potential competition—which was reflected in shifting *ex ante* market judgments on the company's prospects.[45] Nevertheless, the point implied about a parallel between domestic and international banking procedures is well taken.

The case of the D.Ü.E.G., however, is doubtless unrepresentative of German banking experience in Latin America. Most financial projects were of smaller scale and involved more local initiative. We have an example that reflects this, though imperfectly. It involves successful negotiations between a local representative of the D.Ü.B. and Latin American officials, this time, of the central government of Chile. In connection with the negotiation of a 3.5-million mark loan on behalf of the Deutsche Bank and those internationally connected private bankers, Speyer & Co.—in the years between 1904 and 1906, the local D.Ü.B. representative—persuaded the Chilean government to hold a major share of the proceeds on deposit with the Deutsche Bank on terms reportedly favorable to the latter. In the words of an involved contemporary, Hermann Wallich: "The negotiations with the government proved the usefulness of having a permanent financial representative in the country's capital, Santiago."[46] The example is interesting, for it involves a flow of funds opposite to the normal one. It is imperfect, however, in the sense that here, too, the main impulses came from headquarters in Germany.

A better example of local initiative concerns the real estate development business.

In the period between 1900 and 1913, a substantial railroad building program in Argentina produced rising land values and great interest in real estate investment. This led to much D.Ü.B. activity as intermediary between European capitalists and local landowners, even, eventually, to the establishment of a local mortgage bank.[47] This was the kind of business for which local representatives were absolutely indispensable. As Hermann Wallich once pointed out, the local real estate business was one in which European banks in South America, for lack of other forms of acceptable collateral, were inevitably involved.[48]

Despite the considerable attractive force of the New World in the years 1870 to 1914, German bankers did most of their foreign investment business on the European continent. Given the variety and complexity of the European business, this brief chapter can make no attempt at a balanced account. Only a few general points can be made, supplemented by some relevant illustrative observations.

One such point concerns the continued importance for international banking of close personal and family ties, related to the continued importance of private bankers in this branch of activity. The Rothschilds are the classic multinational example, of course, though for German banking an example of diminishing significance in the sense that Berlin—increasingly since 1866 Germany's financial capital—had no Rothschild. To be sure the Rothschilds maintained close ties with the Bleichröder bank and regarded the latter as their Berlin representative.[49] Thus, most important instances of German foreign investment in Europe organized by the Rothschilds or the Bleichröders in the period included both houses. In fact, this "special relationship" between two leading Jewish banking firms was paradigmatic for German international banking, albeit on a less exalted scale. There was, for example, the relationship between the Rothschilds and the Hamburg bankers, Behrens & Sons[50;] and to take another example, one may cite the connection between the Hamburg bankers, the Warburgs, and the St. Petersburg bankers, the Günzburgs. This latter example is significant, for it includes initially distant family ties leading to closer business links and eventually through these to still closer family relations.[51] The story is a familiar one in German banking and thus requires no further discussion here.

With the growing importance of joint-stock banks, the organization of German foreign investment became increasingly formalized. The best-known example is undoubtedly the "Rothschild Consortium," a kind of cartel-like collection of roughly a dozen firms, five of them German, formed to handle all types of large-scale financing involving security issues by Austro-Hungarian government bodies or firms. It began in the 1860s as an ad hoc arrangement to limit competition among bankers for Austrian government loans and developed in subsequent years into a virtually permanent organization.[52] Its origin, one may add, lay in the challenge made to the Rothschild's previous monopoly of the Austrian business by a rival group led by the Diskonto-Gesellschaft.[53] Smaller and somewhat less formalized groups materialized in the same period in connection with Russian loans (for which a consortium led by the Berlin bankers Mendelssohn & Co. was generally formed), or with large industrial enterprises that operated on a large scale abroad such as the Siemens & Halske group (led by the Deutsche Bank) or the A.E.G. group (led from 1897 on by the Berlin Handelsgesellschaft).[54]

A third form of financial penetration related to foreign investment was the acquisition of an interest in foreign banks. This could take the form of a partnership (or *Kommanditär* stake) or a shareholding sufficient to ensure influence over the foreign bank. As early as the 1850s and 1860s some German banks and bankers such as the Darmstädter Bank or Sal. Oppenheim Jr. & Co. sought foreign influence as *Kommanditäre* or major shareowners, alone and in cooperation with other German banks.[55] In spite of disappointments and shutdowns, the practice spread in subsequent years.[56]

German foreign investment in Europe was much more closely linked with international politics than was its counterpart in the Americas. Historians have written at length and in depth on this subject,[57] and it thus requires no further documentation here. What merits reemphasis, however, is the frequently overlooked fact that bankers, principal vehicles of Germany's European foreign investment, acted primarily in response to purely financial stimuli. For reasons largely beyond their individual control, international political issues insinuated themselves into foreign investment questions and thus became part of the bankers' profit calculus.[58]

Indirectly, international political interests and controversies built upon the results and expected results of foreign investment; but the latter, in contrast to the large-scale intergovernmental transfers of our own times, were primarily profit oriented. The problem was that no mechanism existed that would ensure that the same strict profit and loss calculus governing private foreign investment decisions could be extended to decisions about political spheres of influence. And there remains the still unresolved question of whether there is something about foreign investment that dazzles or distorts the vision of political decision-makers concerning national interests. Although such issues go far beyond the aims of this discussion, it is well to raise them, for the fact remains that Germany's considerable European foreign investments had become, by 1914, an important part of any European political leader's assessment of Germany's claim to Great Power status. The question of their origins and the role of banking remains relevant. This section of the discussion concludes, therefore, with a very brief account of one of the most important chapters in the history of German banking activities abroad—namely, German operations in the Habsburg Empire and the Balkans, followed by a somewhat longer discussion of another aspect of the same theme, the case of German investment in Imperial Russia, 1870 to 1914.

The importance of the Austro-Hungarian investments lies in the sheer magnitude of the financial involvements, in their economic impact, and in their possible political ramifications. Note, however, the use of the word "possible" here, for the retrospective view of the Dual Alliance (between Austria-Hungary and the German Reich) may well suggest a closer and more direct connection between politics and finance than the pre–1914 facts can support.[59] Unfortunately, this contribution can do little more than call attention to the issue; lack of space, of time, and of competence forbid a proper treatment. Three brief points must suffice.

First, German bankers did a relatively large financial business in Austria-Hungary, mainly in government and railway securities. The "breakthrough" into the Austrian government loan business achieved by Hansemann and his Diskonto-Gesellschaft in the 1860s (leading to the formation of the so-called Rothschild Consortium) has already been mentioned. Subsequently, this business grew substantially, especially in the 1890s. By 1900, according to John Komlos, Germans held something like 3 billion crowns' worth of Austrian and Hungarian government securities (or approximately 2.5 billion marks).[60] In addition, bankers facilitated German investment, mainly direct, in private industrial enterprises (for example, in the manufacture of electrical equipment) in these years.[61]

Second, these foreign investments seem to have generated economically satisfactory returns, both for German capitalists and for the Austro-Hungarian economies. On the former point we have an estimate of the rate of return realized on a sample of eleven securities between the years 1870 and 1909: At 6.1 percent per annum it exceeded the rate estimated for the Russian foreign security portfolio (discussed later in this chapter) by a considerable margin. On the latter, we have the argument by Komlos on Hungarian economic development to the effect that government spending on the infrastructure helped, while the ability to finance such overhead investments by capital imports set domestic savings free for other modernizing investments. Austrian development in the period is rather less impressive, government spending for unproductive purposes perhaps more so. Nevertheless, the argument could hold for Austria as well, though with diminished force.[62]

Third, German banking operations did not lead to much penetration of the Balkan countries. Apart from a few bank enterprises in Bulgaria, the only involvements worth mentioning concern investments in Rumanian oil. As early as the 1860s German banks had played an active financial role in Rumania, mainly in connection with railroad and government finance.[63] By the 1890s oil had become an attractive prospect. In 1895 Bleichröder and the Diskonto-Gesellschaft founded a Rumanian bank, the Banque Générale Roumaine, to help finance oil exploitation. In 1902 the Deutsche Bank took over control of the large Rumanian oil company, the Steaua Romana, while in 1904 the Dresdner Bank and Schaaffhausen'sche Bankverein entered the same industry by forming yet another company. By 1906 close to half the capital of Rumania's oil industry lay in German hands.[64] This was an important achievement, both for the German banks and for Rumania, though by no means unambiguously positive for the latter. On the whole, however, this engagement was exceptional, and German banking activities in the Balkans lagged far behind those of the French.[65]

German foreign investment in Russia in this period flowed into four major areas: government finance, railroads, banking, and heavy industry.[66] The first two of these took the form of portfolio investment; the latter two represented mainly direct investment. German banks were major intermediaries in all four areas, however, although least important in heavy industry. The German investment was large, absolutely and relatively. Between 1870 and 1914 it amounted to over 3 billion marks, according to one estimate.[67] The cumulated total of around 3.8 billion marks as of 1913 could have represented something like one-seventh of Germany's total foreign investments at that date.

Germany's investment in Russia was subject to a number of significant shifts, political and economic in origin, that affected both its size and its composition. In the 1860s and 1870s substantial portfolio investment in government and railway securities occurred (see Table 4-4). At that time, also, the backwardness of Russian banking attracted German capital, leading, for example, to significant participation in the St. Petersburg Discount Bank by the Diskonto-Gesellschaft, S. Bleichröder & Co., and Mendelssohn & Co. (all of Berlin) and in the St. Petersburg International Trading Bank by the Hamburg bankers, Berenberg, Gossler and Co., and the two Frankfurt bankers, the Bethmanns and Erlanger & Sons.[68] This banking investment, to be sure, was *direct* investment, for such shares could not yet be marketed in Germany. Moreover, its importance was probably dwarfed by the movement of financial techniques and technicians from Germany to Russia.[69]

Be that as it may, the depression of the 1870s led to a virtual cessation of new

TABLE 4–4. Estimated German Portfolio Investments in Russian Government and Railway Securities, 1870–1913 (in millions of marks)

Year	(1) Government Securities	(2) Railway Securities	(3) Total (1) + (2)
1869	375.8	360.2	736.0
1870	448.3	360.2	808.2
1871	586.3	383.7	908.0
1872	628.7	486.9	1,115.6
1873	739.1	491.9	1,231.0
1874	739.1	512.7	1,251.8
1875	848.3	522.8	1,371.1
1876	848.3	522.8	1,371.1
1877	1,106.3	522.8	1,629.1
1878	1,293.8	522.8	1,816.6
1879	1,471.7	522.8	1,994.5
1880	1,832.8	546.1	2,378.9
1881	1,832.8	675.4	2,508.2
1882	1,832.8	675.4	2,508.2
1883	1,848.9	725.3	2,558.1
1884	2,115.9	725.3	2,841.2
1885	2,139.2	867.6	3,006.8
1886	2,148.8	900.8	3,049.6
1887	2,148.8	905.7	3,054.5
1888	2,148.8	909.3	3,058.1
1889	780.8	930.5	1,711.3
1890	390.8	904.7	1,295.5
1891	164.8	897.0	1,061.8
1892	164.8	897.0	1,061.8
1893	148.8	897.0	1,045.8
1894	243.8	869.5	1,113.3
1895	243.8	992.2	1,236.0
1896	280.7	1,048.7	1,329.4
1897	280.7	1,275.9	1,556.6
1898	280.7	1,511.5	1,792.2
1899	280.7	1,511.5	1,792.2
1900	280.7	1,511.5	1,792.2
1901	287.5	1,642.5	1,930.0
1902	549.4	1,642.5	2,191.9
1903	555.1	1,642.5	2,197.6
1904	555.1	1,642.5	2,197.6
1905	862.9	1,642.5	2,505.4
1906	862.9	1,642.5	2,505.4
1907	862.9	1,642.5	2,505.4
1908	862.9	1,642.5	2,505.4
1909	862.9	1,753.3	2,616.2
1910	862.9	1,823.3	2,686.2
1911	862.9	1,881.8	2,744.7
1912	862.9	1,943.8	2,816.7
1913	862.9	1,979.8	2,842.7

Source: See note 67.

portfolio investment for a time. In 1877, however, Russia's increased military expenditure (related to the Russo-Turkish War of 1877/78) necessitated a series of new loans, this time "gold loans" (the principal of which was payable in paper rubles, although interest was guaranteed in gold).[70] These were raised to a substantial extent in the German capital market, with the two Berlin bankers, Mendelssohn and Bleichröder, playing the leading role in placing the securities.[71] In the early 1880s there followed a number of further loans related to the Russian railroad-building program.[72]

In the second half of the 1880s there occurred a deterioration in the political relations between Russia and Germany. Although other factors were involved, the sign of this deterioration in the economic sphere was the beginning of a tariff war. Bismarck's special political "allies," the East Elbian landowners and the heavy industrialists, in addition to a widening circle of nationalist opinion-makers, demanded a political reaction, while Bismarck himself hoped to exploit Russian dependence on the German capital market as a means for influencing its foreign policy. His answer was the famous *Lombardverbot*, the ban on using Russian securities as collateral for loans from the Reichsbank.[73] This action, coming at a time of growing interest of French bankers in Russian loans, led to a wholesale movement from the German to the French capital market (see Table 4–4). This marked the beginning of an enormously significant shift in international capital flows, significant especially because of the political realignment it ushered in.

Needless to say, most German bankers opposed this measure, for the Russian business had not only been profitable as a transaction in its own right, but had also brought business to German industry—hence to German bankers—that would otherwise have gone elsewhere.[74] The Berlin banker Gerson Bleichröder, Bismarck's financial advisor, also opposed the measure, and Bismarck himself appears to have had misgivings.[75] Bleichröder attempted to repair the damage to the "Russian connection," and this attempt resulted in 1889 in a lucrative Russian loan conversion transaction for his bank and the Diskonto-Gesellschaft. Via a chain of relationships discussed elsewhere, however, this only further contributed to both Bismarck's and Bleichröder's political downfall.[76] And in any case, Russian government loans were all but totally lost to French banks, for the German capital market was structurally unable to compete with the low-interest French market, at least for this type of business.

In 1906, after the Russian government had renewed its use of the German capital market in 1905 (in consequence of the Russo-Japanese War of 1904/05) and wished to negotiate a further German loan, Germany's political leaders intervened and sought to make such a loan conditional upon a Russian vote against the French in the famous Morocco conference (in Algeciras) of that year.[77] This intervention failed, we know, for Russian dependence upon French capital was too great by this time. But the incident is instructive, nevertheless, for it suggests that German political leaders saw in foreign investment an important foreign policy instrument.

The cooling of political relations and the stagnation of the government loan business by no means put an end to German investment in Russia. From 1887 on, instead, this investment concentrated itself in Russian railroads, and then from the mid-1890s on, in heavy industry and in banking. The industrial investments tended to concentrate in areas of German comparative advantage: electrical engineering and heavy chemicals. But of particular interest is the fact, noted long ago by Olga Crisp, that foreign investment tended to concentrate increasingly in banking (rather than industry) from 1900 on, in large part because investors came to realize that banks were more likely to receive Russian government support than were industrial enterprises.[78] By 1914 German banks took second place behind the French in their penetration of the Russian banking system, but their hold—as exemplified by the influence exercised in three large St. Petersburg banks by the Diskonto-Gesellschaft and the Deutsche Bank—was also strong and not far behind; relatively speaking, it was even larger.[79]

German banks thus tended to direct investment in Russia into areas in which German relative superiority was strong and in which, therefore, relatively high profits could be expected. Banking itself represented, as already mentioned, a sector of extreme Russian backwardness, resulting in much German penetration. Railroads were another such sector. Capital scarcity in Russia was so general that Germany's bankers could appear, at least initially, as the financial answer to Russia's development problem. It would be most interesting to raise—and answer—the question of the profitability of such investment. Unfortunately, an answer is out of range at the moment. What can be given, instead, is a summary of the payments made by Russian governments and railroads to German security holders in the years between 1870 and 1913.[80] That summary, based on contemporary observations of the German capital market and on assumptions about holding periods for German investors—reflected in Table 4–4— is reproduced in Table 4–5.

If German ownership had been as implied by Table 4–4, the mean rate of return on these securities would have been approximately 5.4 percent annually. Given the comparable rate of return on German government bonds in this period of around 3.8 percent (Prussian consols around 4.3 percent), the return on Russian securities would explain their marketability in Germany. The return to German bankers, one may assume, was a good deal higher, although systematic evidence is lacking.[81] To this one may add the dividend returns on German-held Russian shares of joint-stock industrial companies (of roughly 534 million marks in the period),[82] in themselves a modest 5.2 percent annually (excluding capital gains). The sum total of over 4 billion marks in returns, interestingly, was larger than estimated German capital exports to Russia in the

TABLE 4–5. Estimated Balance of Payments Flows between Germany and Russia, 1870–1913 (in millions of marks)

Flows from Germany to Russia	
German portfolio investment	2,843
German direct investment	850
Balance of trade deficit	12,608
TOTAL	16,301
Flows from Russia to Germany	
Interest payments	
Government securities	1,797
Railway	1,975
Dividends on direct investment	534
TOTAL	4,306
Net balance in favor of Russia	11,995

Source: See note 80.

period. It was much less, however, than the estimated import surplus for these years, which had a cumulative total of nearly 12 billion marks, and which represented the country's aggregate real return on Russian use of German savings.[83] German foreign investment in this part of Europe, it seems, paid quite satisfactory returns, although not in political terms.

Banks, International Trade Finance, and Payments Problems

Many of the institutions and networks described in the previous section served—and were developed to serve—short-term trade finance and payments needs. In the 1860s and 1870s, German bankers, as well as business journalists and politicians, appeared to have believed that the dominance of the British pound sterling as international currency represented an unnecessary payments drain and foregone profits, in addition to being an affront to growing national pride. The problem was that overseas trading partners had a strong preference for taking and making payments in sterling bills on London. The alternative for German exporters and importers was bullion or German bills at a substantial discount relative to London bills or—if German bills were wholly unacceptable—no trade at all. According to one contemporary calculation, frequently cited, British bankers earned in the late–1880s about 500,000 marks per year in commission on bills used in Germany's trade with Chile alone (amounting to about 60 million marks per year).[84] Extrapolated to Germany's total South American trade, the former payments would have amounted to about 6 million marks per year; and a global extrapolation takes us to still higher figures.[85] Needless to say, German bankers could have been interested in this potential business, even if their services would have imposed higher costs on the German exporters and importers who might have utilized them.[86]

Much of the history of the development of international banking in Germany from 1870 to 1914 can be seen against the background of this Anglo-German difference. Contemporaries saw in two major developments steps to the "solution" of the problem: in the establishment of a unified German currency, the mark, on the basis of the gold standard; and in the establishment of a network of foreign and especially overseas banks. With historical hindsight, however, it becomes clear that the originally posited cost-benefit calculus of alternative systems of international payments was by no means certain or clear-cut. Understanding the development of international banking in Germany thus requires a look at one further aspect of our subject: the role of international links between national money markets.

Establishing the new gold standard currency called for the use of German bankers' foreign contacts for two purposes: (1) to obtain the desired amount of gold, and (2) to sell the redundant silver. The first of these tasks was associated with the war indemnity that Prussia imposed upon France in 1871: The famous 5 billion gold francs represented the foreign exchange fund from which the new Reich's increased gold supply derived. Some gold was transferred directly; the rest had to be purchased on the market. Virtually the entire transfer involved German bankers at one stage or another. At the very first stage, concerning decision making on the mechanism of transfer, Bleichröder reportedly advised Bismarck as to which French bankers could be called upon to guarantee the initial indemnity payment of 200 million francs.[87] German bankers such as Bleichröder and the Diskonto-Gesellschaft also participated in the syndicates formed to market part of the French government loan raised in 1871 to finance indemnity payments (since part of the loans were raised outside France).[88] And bankers, especially Hamburg bankers such as the Norddeutsche Bank, Behrens & Sons, or the Warburgs, served as collection points for foreign remittances (which they held while transferring the corresponding amount in cash or credit to the German government).[89] This whole set of transactions has been discussed elsewhere.[90] Suffice it to say that most of the necessary new gold was purchased by the Reich government through German banks working with their correspondents abroad, especially in London. Arbitrage held the movements in European money markets within relatively narrow limits, but there were occasional signs of strain, nevertheless.[91]

By 1871 sentiment among Germany's political leadership sufficiently favored adopting the gold standard to end the purchase and minting of silver. Since over 80 percent of the metallic circulation was silver and since, moreover, the French war indemnity itself added a substantial amount of silver (five franc) coins to the already-existing stock, measures for withdrawing and eventually disposing of this stock had to be contemplated. The problem was to execute these massive sales without depressing the market price of silver too rapidly. The government authorities entrusted this task to none other than Hermann Wallich, one of the directors of the newly founded Deutsche Bank, mainly because of his knowledge of the silver-based Chinese and Indian money markets (in which Wallich had successfully operated in the 1860s).[92] Wallich successfully unloaded the French coin in France itself, and the rest of the Deutsche Bank's consignment in other markets at such good prices that they reportedly compared favorably with the publicly quoted market prices of those years (1872–1876) and even more favorably with the losses subsequently taken by the government on the silver it sold via the Reichsbank.[93] By the end of the 1870s, at least in retrospect, the German mark had clearly become a gold-standard currency.

Expansion of Germany's foreign trade from the 1870s on eased, just as it spurred, the extension of German banks' international connections by means of overseas dependent banks or branches. More German exports stimulated the demand for means to pay for them, and institutions that could satisfy that demand could induce more exports. The role of the overseas banks was to provide credit and payment services to the local merchant communities. Their presence reduced the risks to home-country banks of the export credits they extended. Their presence also recruited both additional customers for German exports and additional suppliers of exports to Germany. As Hermann Wallich, one of the architects of the Deutsche Bank's D.Ü.B., put it, the business of an overseas bank was simple. It had two main parts based on two important principles: (1) credit on "long bills" to local merchants, a business that should be carried on with deposits mobilized locally, and (2) the finance of international trade, a business that should be carried on with the bank's capital but in such a manner that opportunities for all types of arbitrage were exploited and the capital at all times covered against possible exchange rate losses.[94] Such principles were naturally more easily articulated than practiced.

For example, in the early years of the D.Ü.B., local deposits were scarce so that the bank's own capital had to be invested locally, with the result that coverage against foreign exchange losses was far from complete, and—in a country like Argentina, whose currency's value fluctuated relative to gold over long stretches of our period—such losses were possible.[95] Moreover, given the absence of "thick" secondary financial markets for first-class securities or bills, credit was largely on a personal basis, and liquidating such collateral as was available could be a difficult and time-consuming process. This fact and the great distance from headquarters meant that the fortunes of an overseas bank depended significantly upon the good judgment and ability of its local management, at least in the medium run. According to observers such as the Wallichs (on the D.Ü.B.) or Franz Urbig (on the Deutsch-Asiatische Bank), good judgment and ability were often missing. And to these lacunae came the additional factors of physical climate and social environment, for the former could sap a local director's energy, the latter his loyalty to the bank.[96]

Despite such dangers, Germany's overseas banks did quite well in the years before 1914, quite apart from their role in furthering foreign portfolio investment. The D.Ü.B., for example, paid average dividends of close to 7 percent between the years 1886 and 1913, and the "realized rate of return" (dividends plus capital gains) for shareholders between 1896 and 1913 was about 10 percent. The Deutsch-Asiatische Bank paid average dividends of close to 9 percent between 1899 and 1910, slightly less than the average of 10 percent paid by the Brazilian Bank for Germany between 1890 and 1910, but rather more than the 6.1 pecent paid by the Bank for Chile and Germany in the years 1896 to 1909.[97] These returns were higher than German banks were earning at home in these years, and just about equivalent to what German industrial corporations were yielding their shareholders.[98]

In one respect, however, these banks did not fulfill the hopes that contemporaries had placed in them; and in that sense they failed: They did not free German foreign trade from its dependence upon sterling or London bills as key currency and means of cheap credit. Indeed, one of the most significant of post–1870 developments in German international banking was the strengthening of its London connection. The Deutsche Bank, characteristically, made the first move, founding together with two other German banks and two British firms a dependent bank, The German Bank of London, as early as 1870. This firm, in which the Deutsche Bank had a 25 percent share, did not yield the desired increase in business, so in 1873 the Deutsche Bank established its own London branch, the "London Agency." This move, dependent upon a reciprocity treaty between Great Britain and the German Reich concluded in 1872, paid off in a large increase in business. It was through this branch that the Deutsche Bank executed most of the bullion transactions on behalf of the German government in the 1870s. In the mid-1870s over half of the bank's foreign business was London business (representing about 10 percent of the bank's total volume). By the beginning of the twentieth century, the agency's share in the Deutsche Bank's total turnover was close to a quarter; and this was Germany's largest bank![99] Underlying this expansion was the desire to give German overseas merchants and banks a German address in London upon which they might draw sterling bills. In this way the Deutsche Bank, and its German overseas correspondents, could capture that part of the German business in which preferences for sterling dominated and which would have otherwise gone to British bankers. This program, it appears, was a success.

If the London business were so attractive, it is somewhat puzzling that the Deutsche Bank remained for so long (until 1895) the only important German bank to have a London branch. Perhaps one reason was that the margin of advantage (over working from Germany with a London correspondent) was small and the volume of German-intermediated business that the market could bear was limited. Foreign banks operating in London suffered a competitive disadvantage relative to British banks in that the Bank of England refused to grant foreign banks access to its rediscount facilities.[100] This fact, added perhaps to a certain amount of skepticism toward new, foreign banks, made their acceptances less attractive for money market investors than British ones— i.e., they represented a somewhat more expensive form of credit. If foreign banks pursued a cautious policy of "modest" expansion of their acceptances, however, they could still enjoy part of the discount and commission rate differential that tended to persist between London and most of the money markets (including expecially Berlin). In any case, when the other large Berlin banks followed the Deutsche Bank's example and opened London branches, (e.g., the Darmstädter in 1895, the Diskonto-Gesellschaft in 1899, and the Dresdner Bank in 1910), they also reportedly paid off in terms of a significant increase in business.[101]

By the eve of World War I the presence of German banks in most of the world's important commercial centers, in association with the rapid growth of German foreign trade, had made the mark an international currency. It had not become a challenge to the pound, but in certain areas it had become a "key currency"—for example, in trade with Sweden, Denmark, Rumania, Italy, Austria-Hungary, and even for part of the German-American business.[102] And in many other areas—in South America and Asia, for example—the mark bill had become a possible alternative, increasingly utilized.[103] If the international use of a currency is regarded as a measure of success, then the international expansion of the German banks in the late-nineteenth century was successful. By the same token, however, the German challenge to the British banks would have to be deemed a failure, for the pound had become, if anything, more important for Germany's economic well-being. Indeed, by establishing London houses based on sterling, the German banks had themselves, so to speak, "joined the enemy."

One may doubt whether this line of argument concerning Germany's failure has much validity. German banks made increasing use of British banking and money market facilities because they were generally more efficient or cheaper than any other. Franz Urbig, a German banker well versed in international affairs, observed that Germany's use of British credit facilities in the late nineteenth century far exceeded its "real" trading needs.[104] His explanation was that British short-term credit was cheaper than German and most other sources of short-term capital. He failed to add that the French money market was an additional, frequently still cheaper, source of short-term capital for German banks than the British. This is a feature of Germany's international situation noted by others (e.g., by Borchardt in his study of German currency and banking development, 1870–1914; and by Bloomfield in his study of short-term capital movements among gold-standard countries in the period).[105] Germany, indeed, had likely become by the beginning of the twentieth century the world's largest net debtor on short-term capital account.[106] This situation followed from the country's rapid economic expansion in the period with its resultant demands upon the financial system, for that combination produced high levels of debt and relatively high interest rates. It was not necessarily a dangerous situation, for Germany had some valuable and fairly liquid claims on the asset side of the ledger. Moreover, thanks to the country's international banking activities, its currency—or rather its short-term debt—had become an attractive and relatively secure form of investment for foreign banks (including some central banks).[107] In times of greater pressure, as Lindert has shown, holders of short-term claims against the mark did not, on balance, liquidate their holdings; or, to put it differently, relatively modest interest rate changes could suffice to induce such investors to hold on to their mark-denominated assets.[108]

It is nevertheless true that contemporaries saw danger in this situation. In such perceptions, indeed, lay the essence of pre–1914 central banking debates, both in Germany as elsewhere. That is worth stressing, for the essence of the debate did not consist in discussion of the magic or automatic properties of a gold standard, as is sometimes implied, but in the fear that the complex system of international payments and debt claims built up by the profit-seeking activities of banks and bankers contained weak elements (i.e., bad debts), which changing expectations could suddenly expose, leading to a quick rush for liquidity that no single bank or even a single central bank of issue could satisfy. On the belief in the time-honored adage that "an ounce of prevention is worth a pound of cure," experiments in the theory and practice of central banking were begun. In Germany, they found expression in official investigation of the banking system (with particular attention to its liquidity), in semiformal consultations between the big banks and the central bank, and in agreements among the banks themselves. [109] The story of these experiments is a fascinating one, but one into which this brief discussion cannot enter, for lack of time, space, and also for lack of good, easily mobilizable, data. Over twenty-five years ago one scholar wrote:

> Twenty-five years ago Viner wrote that "international short-term lending still awaits its historian."[110]

Unfortunately, fifty years later this gap is still largely unfilled. From what we know of German monetary and banking history, this gap has not remained unfilled because it has no bearing on that national history, but rather because filling it faces daunting barriers.

APPENDIX

Foreign Securities Traded on the Berlin Stock Exchange, 1870–1911

Security	Years Traded	Average Return[a]	Standard Deviation
Governments			
Argentinian			
5% bonds	1886 (1887–1911)	.085	.157
Argentinian			
4.5% gold bonds	1888 (1889–1911)	.088	.166
Austrian			
4% gold rente	1876 (1876–1911)	.062	.043
Austrian			
4% state rente	1892 (1901–1911)	.031	.008
Chilean			
4% state rente	1889 (1889–1911)	.046	.062

Security	Years Traded	Average Return[a]	Standard Deviation
Chinese 5% state rente	1896 (1896–1911)	.052	.023
Greek 4% state rente	1889 (1889–1911)	.040	.149
Hungarian 4% gold rente	1881 (1881–1911)	.053	.040
Hungarian 3% gold bonds	1895 (1895–1911)	.029	.036
Italian 5/4% gold rente	(1876–1911)	.056	.053
Japanese 4.5% bonds	1905 (1905–1911)	.049	.039
Rumanian 4% bonds	1890 (1890–1911)	.052	.047
Russian 5% premium bonds	1864 (1880–1911)	.085	.149
Russian 4% consol bonds	1880 (1881–1911)	.058	.059
Russian 4.5% bonds	1905 (1905–1911)	.053	.029
Turkish 4% consol bonds	1903 (1904–1911)	.068	.076
Russian 3.5% gold gonds	1894 (1894–1911)	.027	.058
Rumanian 4% bonds	1890 (1890–1911)	.052	.047
Egyptian 3.5% bonds	1890 (1890–1911)	.044	.022
Buenos Aires 4.5% gold bonds	1888 (1889–1911)	.102	.314
Norweigan 3% bonds	1888 (1888–1911)	.039	.046
Swedish 3.5% bonds	1880 (1895–1911)	.033	.014
Greek 5% railway bonds	1890 (1890–1911)	.082	.433
Italian 3% railway bonds	1860 (1878–1911)	.081	.046
Portuguese 4.5% tobacco bonds	1891 (1891–1911)	.074	.111
Serbian 4% bonds	1895 (1895–1911)	.080	.054
Railways			
Austrian Kaiser-Joseph 4% silver bonds	1884 (1884–1911)	.049	.032
Austrian Südbahn 5% bonds, Series B	1869 (1869–1911)	.065	.038
Austrian Südbahn 4% bonds, Series E	1885 (1885–1911)	.040	.039

(*continued*)

Foreign Securities Traded on the Berlin Stock Exchange, 1870–1911 (*continued*)

Security	Years Traded	Average Return[a]	Standard Deviation
Austria-Hungarian State Railway			
5% prior bonds	1873–74 (1890–1911)	.045	.021
Russian Trans-Causasian Railway			
3%	1889 (1889–1911)	.059	.072
Illinois Central			
4% gold bonds	1888 (1889–1911)	.043	.024
Northern Pacific			
3% gold bonds	(1896–1911)	.074	.078
Northern Pacific			
4% gold bonds	(1896–1911)	.054	.040
St. Louis & San Francisco			
6% general mortgage bonds	(1884–1911)	.084	.052
Bagdadbahn			
4%	1903 (1904–1911)	.040	.018
Gotthardbahn			
shares	(1872–1911)	.084	.165
Galizische Karl-Ludwig			
4% bonds	1890 (1890–1911)	.051	.039
Moscow-Kiev-Volronesch			
4% (tax-free)	1895 (1895–1911)	.029	.037
Anatolian			
5% gold bonds	1894 (1894–1911)	.060	.034
Italian Mediterranean			
shares	(1895–1911)	.037	.070
Chicago, Burlington, & Quincy			
4% bonds	1887 (1887–1911)	.048	.042
Central Pacific			
4% first refunding mortgage gold bonds	(1900–1911)	.038	.030
Banks (shares)			
Austrian Credit-Anstalt	(1870–1911)	.089	.187
Österreichische Länderbank	(1889–1911)	.085	.092
Bank für Elektrische Unternehmungen			
	(1896–1911)	.089	.106

[a] These rates of return implicitly assume successive holding periods of one year and equal weights for each year. Investors did not "learn from the past" in this sample.

5

Belgium

Herman Van der Wee and Martine Goossens

During the period between 1870 and 1914 Belgium played an active role in the internationalization of banking activities and industrial finance. In 1913 Belgium was one of the five major creditor nations of the world.[1] Its foreign interests at that time were estimated at 7.5 billion pre-1914 francs.[2]

In this chapter we will argue that the expansion of financial activities in Belgium took place within the framework of a specific financial system—that is, the "mixed banking" system. Originated in the early 1830s, the Belgian mixed banking system quickly developed into a remarkable and successful financial institution that became the main engine driving industrialization in Belgium. The Belgian mixed banks first focused their strategies on domestic activities. Gradually they widened their scope to form an appropriate basis for the internationalization of Belgian financial activities. Internationalization had reciprocal effects on Belgian banking: It led to the consolidation of the mixed banking structure and to the successful innovation of the modern holding company.

In the first part of the chapter we describe the emergence of the Belgian mixed banking system; in the second part we deal with the internationalization of the mixed banking activities and the effects it had on the Belgian banking system as a whole.

The Creation of a Specific Belgian Financial System: The "Mixed Bank"

The Société Générale and the Origin of Mixed Banking in Belgium, 1822–1850

The economic and financial situation in the Southern Netherlands before the creation of the Société Générale (1800–1822).[3] At the beginning of the nineteenth century the Southern Netherlands (later Belgium) entered its era of modern industrialization. The mechanized Walloon heavy industry was the driving force behind it. At least four historical and geological reasons may explain Belgium's early industrial transformation. First, decisive innovations in agriculture during the early modern period had led to an agricultural surplus that made possible the absorption of rapid demographic growth. Second, substantial improvements in the transport infrastucture had provided the country with a fairly good system of roads and canals. Third, the evolution of an important rural industry, based on the putting-out system, had given rise to a dynamic and wealthy class of merchant-entrepreneurs. Finally, the immediate availability of two crucial raw materials—coal and iron—formed the basis for a rapid industrialization of the Walloon heavy manufacturing industries.

Notwithstanding rapid mechanization, the textile industry, unlike that in Great Britain, failed to become a leading sector in Belgian industrialization. England's technological advance in textiles was a serious handicap for Belgium in foreign markets. Furthermore, the political tribulations of Belgium during the first half of the nineteenth century disrupted export-led growth of the textile sector. The production of food did not become a modern industrialized sector either; neither did production of consumer durables. The small scale of the internal market was one of the main causes of that double failure. The very low level of wages in Belgium was a second determining factor: The unequal distribution of income indeed inhibited the growth of the home market for consumer goods.

The financial structure of the Southern Netherlands at that time was still very primitive. No central institute of issue, such as the Bank of England, existed. A modest private banking system prevailed. Most private bankers in fact combined their financial activities with commercial transactions. This was especially the case in Antwerp, which along with Brussels was an important financial center in Belgium during the period. The private bankers mainly supplied short-term commercial credit; they worked mostly with their own means, deposits being not yet very important. During the second quarter of the nineteenth century, however, far-reaching changes occurred in the traditional banking system. The concentration of wealth, which was itself a consequence of the low level of wages and the unequal distribution of income, generated a new leading sector in Belgium, notably, banking. From the 1830s onward the rise of banking and, close in its tracks, of a modern financial system became a driving force of industrialization in Belgium.

The Société Générale and the origin of mixed banking in Belgium. In 1822 William I, king of the United Netherlands,[4] created the first corporate bank in Brussels, the so-called Algemeene Nederlandsche Maatschappij ter begunstiging van de Volksvlijt, later referred to as the Société Générale. Although from the very beginning intended to develop as an investment bank,[5] the Société Générale originally concentrated its activities mainly on traditional banking functions: Accepting deposits, extending short-term commercial loans, issuing bank notes,[6] and—in its function of cashier and banker of the state—managing the public debt.[7]

Before 1830 the Société Générale's role as industrial banker remained limited to the field of short-term commercial and industrial loans. Only in a few cases did it grant long-term industrial loans, *inter alia* to the Franco-Belgian canal undertakings in 1825 and to the modern metal and coal works of the big entrepreneur John Cockerill in 1829.[8] Short-term commercial and industrial loans were more welcome and much sought by the Société Générale. In fact, such loans laid the foundation for the mixed banking system in Belgium; during the sharp economic crisis brought about by the Belgian Revolution in 1830 and continuing throughout the following years, the Société Générale was forced to accept shares of companies in financial trouble in return for extinguishing the debts of those companies. Thus several companies of the Borinage coal mining and metal sectors came under the direct influence of the Société Générale. That was the real beginning of mixed banking in Belgium: As the board of directors of the Société Générale gradually saw investment banking's potential for growth and power and as they experienced the profitable character of "industrial banking," a specific long-term industrial strategy was worked out. It favored in particular the development of the coal mining and metal sectors in the Hainault region, and in a later stage favored the development of a national railway network.[9] The rise of the mixed banking system in Belgium in the second quarter of the nineteenth century is best illustrated by the evolution of the industrial portfolio of the Société Générale: It rose from 3.8 million francs in 1835 to 38.7 million in 1840 and to 54.8 million in 1850.[10]

The development of an industrial portfolio was accompanied by the sale of the Société Générale's most important asset—the royal domains that William I had donated to the company in exchange for shares.[11] Between 1830 and 1842, there were 28,108 hectares of forests auctioned off; the proceeds of those sales, as well as the deposits of the savings bank of the Société Générale created in 1832, were used to finance the long-term investment policy.[12] The sale of the domain land is illustrative of the changing mentality of the board of directors of the Société Générale: Throughout the 1830s the bank gradually put more faith in its industrial participations, to the extent that it was prepared to give up the security of investment in real estate.

The Société Générale was not the only bank to develop as a mixed bank. The Belgian liberals suspected that the sympathies of the Société Générale lay with the Dutch House of Orange. For that reason they founded the competitive Banque de Belgique in 1835.[13] The rivalry that inevitably emerged between the Société Générale and the Banque de Belgique in the following decades would cause more damage to the latter than to the former. Indeed, the investment policy of the Société Générale always remained cautious, whereas the Banque de Belgique sometimes threw itself into outright speculative undertakings.

In tandem the Société Générale and the Banque de Belgique formed a dynamic financial power and a motive force of Belgian industrial development. The total amount of money invested in the 150 newly created joint-stock companies between 1833 and 1838 reached about 288.5 million francs, of which the Société Générale accounted for 102 million, or 35 percent, and the Banque de Belgique 54 million, or 18 percent.[14] The banks' industrial participation went along two lines: directly by taking up shares and indirectly by granting long-term loans.[15]

Between 1835 and 1837 the Société Générale and the Banque de Belgique introduced an even more sophisticated form of industrial banking: Both banks founded subsidiary companies whose task it was to look after industrial investment, mainly in the coal mining and metal sectors. In addition to the management of their own portfolios, these subsidiary companies were also entrusted with the expansion of the parent company's participations in industry and transport. Moreover, they had to stimulate, coordinate, and control the modernization of the patronized companies and reduce the number of family businesses so as to integrate them into a few big joint-stock undertakings. In this way the portfolio administration contributed to the development of more centralized company techniques (horizontal and vertical integration). Above all, the subsidiary companies were already *holdings avant la lettre*. Indeed, they also took capital from outside the parent company.[16]

One can of course wonder why the system of mixed banking was so successful in the early stages of Belgian industrialization. We posit that the link of the mixed banks with the heavy industries fueled the Belgian industrialization process: The need for long-term fixed capital being very high in the industrial sectors, the mixed banks could supply the necessary capital where self-finance could not suffice.[17] It is indeed remarkable that both the Société Générale and the Banque de Belgique concentrated their activities on the expanding industries of Wallonia. One can find little sign of interest in the more slowly modernizing and less capital-intensive industries of Flanders (textiles, wood, and leather).

The rise of mixed banking in Belgium was thus indissolubly linked with the emergence of the heavy industries. The increasing collaboration between the Walloon heavy industries and the Brussels system of industrial banking, even the osmosis of both interests, or still better the absorption of the interests of industry by the banks— the so-called *Bruxellisation de la Wallonie*[18]—meant an organizational progress that, in setting the pace for growth, became the real core of the Belgian industrialization pattern. The organizational progress was especially important when it came to making decisions on long-term investments: Owing to the system of mixed banking, the decision-making process was transferred from a decentralized, segmented capital market to a strong center of power, a sort of mini-capital market, which clearly had better information and better instruments of coordination and control at its disposal.[19]

Closely linked with those main explanations for the successes of the mixed banks in Belgium from about 1835 onward was a juridical-institutional factor. The creation of new joint-stock companies was liberalized with Belgian independence. The Société Générale and the Banque de Belgique therefore could expand their supply of capital in a very efficient and flexible way.[20]

The inherent dangers of the mixed banking system. Notwithstanding the success of the mixed banks, the formula was not without danger. Because of the long-term immobilization of a large part of their assets, both the Société Générale and the Banque de Belgique worked with low liquidity ratios. Such ratios increasingly threatened the smooth functioning of deposit and, especially, issue banking. Indeed, the low liquidity ratio caused acute problems when the banks faced sudden panic withdrawals. The danger was enhanced by the nonexistence of a central bank that could act as a lender of last resort in cases of real emergency.

The Belgian financial crisis of 1838 underscored the shortcomings of the system. Both the Société Générale and the Banque de Belgique temporarily suspended payments. The situation of the Banque de Belgique was particularly strained; its bankruptcy was prevented only by governmental support.[21] The Société Générale resisted the crisis better because it was able to sell its French assets on the French capital market.[22] After the crisis the Banque de Belgique liquidated a part of its portfolio, and during the following decade it concentrated more on its commercial activities. On the other hand, the Société Générale remained strongly attached to the formula of mixed banking. In a reflex of precaution, however, it did not engage immediately in large new undertakings.[23] In 1848 international events badly affected the Société Générale. This time the formula of mixed banking was put in question for the Société Générale, too. It became clear that no mixed bank, not even the powerful Société Générale, would ever be able to combine the functions of bank of issue, deposit bank, and industrial bank in a satisfactory way, the constraints of liquidity in deposit and issue banking being fundamentally irreconcilable with the long-term requirement of investment and industrial banking. To perform satisfactorily their task as deposit banks in times of sudden panic withdrawal, the banks should be able to issue more bank notes, but at that very moment the public insisted on redeeming its bank notes for gold or silver![24] The situation seeming insoluble in the long run, the Belgian government in 1850 withdrew the right of issuing bank notes from the mixed banks and at the same time created the National Bank of Belgium, conferring upon it a legal monopoly of issue.[25]

The restructuring of the Belgian banking system after the crisis of 1848 did not weaken the position of the mixed banks. On the contrary, it became the starting point for consolidation and swift development of the system. By losing the right of issuing bank notes, the mixed banks at the same time lost a great deal of their liquidity problems. Moreover, if liquidity problems in the field of deposit banking eventually arose, they could now be solved by appealing to the central bank of issue through the technique of discounting and rediscounting. In that sense the creation of the National Bank of Belgium in 1850 can be considered an important variable in the swift development of the mixed banking system during the second half of the nineteenth century.

The smaller mixed banks. For the sake of completeness, we must comment on the development of other Belgian banks during the period under study. Notwithstanding their relative unimportance compared with the Société Générale and the Banque de Belgique, some provincial banks played an active role in the promotion of economic development of their respective regions. Such was the case for the Banque Liègeoise among others. Created in 1835, the Banque Liègeoise developed into a modest mixed bank. Later on it cooperated with the Banque de Belgique in financing the Liège heavy industries. In Flanders, the Banque de Flandres played an important role in industrial promotion, but it always confined itself to short-term transactions. The outstanding commercial city of Antwerp also accommodated many commercial banks. The most important independent ones were the Banque Commerciale d'Anvers and the Banque d'Industrie. Antwerp also possessed an important subsidiary of the Société Générale, the Banque d'Anvers. Created in 1827, the Banque d'Anvers developed into a vital commercial intermediary and soon became the most prosperous and the most autonomous subsidiary of the whole Société Générale group.[26]

International aspects. As already mentioned, Belgian bankers during the period between 1830 and 1850 showed little interest in foreign investment. Indeed, with few exceptions (for example, the Société Générale's participation in the French Sambre-canalization project), bank transactions on foreign capital markets were limited for the most part to buying bonds issued by foreign governments.[27]

On the other hand, foreign penetration into the Belgian capital market was of great importance during this period. The unsteady state of public finance during the first years of Belgian independence forced the Belgian government to borrow large amounts of money in foreign countries. As is well known, the House of Rothschild handled the launching of many of those long-term Belgian government loans on the markets of Paris and London.[28] From about 1840 onward, however, the interest of foreign lenders in investing in Belgium shifted more toward the industrial sector. French capitalists subscribed increasingly to the capital of newly created Belgian joint-stock companies, mainly in the coal mining and metal sectors. The English investors concentrated on railway construction but showed some interest in the financial sector, too. The Banque de Flandres, for example, was launched with considerable English support.[29]

The Belgian Mixed-Banking System, 1850–1870s

During the third quarter of the nineteenth century the Société Générale and the Banque de Belgique remained by far the most important mixed banks of Belgium. The investment strategy of both banks, however, showed important differences; while the Société Générale created the image of a "cautious" mixed bank, at the same time interested in promoting the national economy, the Banque de Belgique developed into a sometimes openly speculative industrial bank. To nobody's surprise the Banque de Belgique failed, first provisionally, then definitively in 1886. The Société Générale, on the contrary, remained faithful to the strict rules of orthodox mixed banking; only its capital and reserves were invested in shares and in long-term risk capital. The cautious policy of the Société Générale was rewarded by a very successful development of its industrial portfolio. Its investment strategy therefore proved to be the right one.

Many new banks arose during the same period. The favorable economic situation certainly furthered this development. A few of the newly created banks developed as mixed banks, too, but they never threatened the hegemony of the Société Générale or the Banque de Belgique. During the same period the first signs of internationalization of the Belgian banking activities took place. One can hardly make mention of a systematic foreign investment policy, however. In many cases speculation was the underlying motivation of the bankers. Once again, exception should be made for the Société Générale; during this period the Société Générale laid the foundation for a very successful foreign investment policy that would bear its fruit in the period between 1880 and 1914.

The Société Générale between 1850 and the 1870s: A success story. Between 1850 and the 1870s the Société Générale concentrated increasingly on its strategy of acquiring participations in Belgian heavy industry and related sectors. It lost to some extent its mixed banking character to become more or less a portfolio company.[30] The Société Générale took few if any risks in its long-term strategy. An extensive investigation always determined the credibility and profitability of the companies that were the objects of its investment policies. It also always kept a close eye on its own financial structure; the discount activity was kept high, and special efforts were always made to limit the payment of excessive dividends in order to increase the capital reserves and to prevent liquidity problems.[31]

As the figures presented in Table 5–1 show, the Société Générale focused its investment strategy during the third quarter of the nineteenth century on the heavy industries, railways and coal mines in particular. To do so meant an accentuation of the strategy developed during the former period. The involvement of the Société Générale in railway promotion is especially striking. Within one decade the share of participations in railway companies in the total portfolio rose from 4.2 percent to 25.9 percent. At least three reasons may explain that special interest. First, the need for fixed capital was very high in railways and it took some years before the investment yielded a significant return. From that point of view it is understandable why entrepreneurs

TABLE 5–1. Composition of the Industrial Portfolio of the Société Générale, 1851–1879

Sectors	1851		1860		1870		1879	
	Nominal Terms (francs)	Relative Terms (percent)	Nominal Terms (francs)	Relative Terms (percent)	Nominal Terms (francs)	Relative Terms (percent)	Nominal Terms (francs)	Relative Terms (percent)
Infrastructure								
Railways	2,318,400	4.2	13,633,925	25.9	15,779,250	22.0	11,809,000	15.1
Canals	6,376,700	11.4	6,115,600	11.6	7,335,500	10.2	4,673,000	6.0
Heavy Industries								
Coal mines	20,473,133	36.4	19,268,860	36.6	26,410,142	36.8	32,024,114	41.0
Metal industry	6,649,646	11.8	5,164,922	9.8	8,087,500	11.3	5,731,200	7.3
Financial Institutions	13,368,150	23.8	5,526,900	10.5	6,368,325	8.6	12,643,053	16.2
Real estate	—		—	—	6,126,912	8.5	8,554,510	11.0
Miscellaneous	7,006,200	12.5	2,865,335	5.4	1,701,959	2.4	1,627,752	2.1
TOTAL	56,192,229	100	52,575,542	100	71,809,588	100	78,062,629	100

Source: Marie-Anna Trooskens, De Société Générale als Promotor van de Belgische Industriële Ontwikkelung (Unpublished dissertation, K.U. Leuven, History Dept., 1974), p. 129.

turned to credit institutions, particularly mixed banks, when creating railway companies. Second, since railway construction induced an enormous demand for the products of the patronized iron and steel companies, the interest of the Société Générale for that modern transport sector is again obvious. Third, in 1865 the Société Générale even created a subsidiary company, the Société Belge des Chemins de Fer, that concentrated exclusively on the construction of railways.[32] In a later, international stage, the Société Belge des Chemins de Fer developed into one of the first specialized holding companies.

The declining share of the railroad participations after 1860 was mainly due to the increasing saturation of the domestic market. Another interesting aspect is the rising share of the financial sector after 1870 (Table 5–1).[33] It was the result of the Société Générale's strategy to create, in addition to agencies in Brussels, Antwerp, and the industrialized areas, a close financial network in the more remote provinces as well, in order to drain savings from the smaller towns in Belgium and to promote the development of medium- and small-sized enterprises outside the main industrial areas. With that aim in mind, the Société Générale bought, from about 1870 onward, many existing local or regional banks and transformed them into joint stock companies. New companies were also created.[34]

The Société Générale proclaimed explicitly that one of its main goals was the promotion of domestic industry: "We think that an establishment like ours should not merely seek bank commissions, but has an implicit moral responsibility to the community. Without pretending to do everything . . . we will always attempt to assist Belgian enterprises."[35] It is against this background that the first international transactions of the Société Générale must be interpreted. Because new railway companies induced a high demand for iron and steel, which favored the patronized heavy industries in Belgium, the Société Générale deliberately supported the creation of foreign railway companies. It usually acted as issuer of bonds or shares to the Belgian public. The proceeds of the issues were then used to pay the Belgian companies supplying the rails, the rolling stock, and any other equipment connected with railway transport. Sometimes the foreign companies paid the Belgian steel and metal companies directly with bonds or shares, which were then sold by the Société Générale to the public on behalf of the companies. In most cases, however, the Société Générale acted as issuer of the shares and bonds of the foreign companies.[36] One important exception must be mentioned. The Société Générale, together with the Banque de Belgique and the Crédit Mobilier, not only created the Société des Chemins de Fer du Nord d'Espagne but also remained great shareholders of that company.[37] This Spanish railway company was for more than six years an important market for the Belgian iron and metal industries.[38] The investment of the Société Générale in Spain can be considered a representative example of its foreign investment policy; as soon as the construction of the Spanish railroad was finished—that is, as soon as the demand for Belgian materials ceased— the Société Générale started to sell its shares on the Paris exchange.[39] Apparently, in the view of Société Générale, the development of a Spanish railway network was beneficial for Belgian industries.

The Banque de Belgique between 1850 and the 1870s: A reckless adventure.
Originally, the Banque de Belgique focused its attention on the railway sector. Like the Société Générale, it took care of issuing foreign railway securities, but, in contrast to

the Société Générale, it also got very much involved in speculative participations in those foreign companies.[40] That strategy led to serious difficulties in 1863/64; the value of the foreign assets being very much affected by the international financial crisis of those years, the Banque de Belgique's industrial portfolio underwent a serious depreciation. The bank was forced to liquidate many foreign assets and suffered great losses.[41]

The Banque de Belgique was hit once again by the industrial and financial crisis of 1873; the financial structure was not strong enough to support the speculative strategy the bank pursued. Still worse, the bank confronted a case of embezzlement that resulted in the loss of nearly half the company's capital. Bankruptcy could not be prevented, and in 1876 the bank collapsed. The bank was refounded, but that operation of *sauvetage in extremis* could not prevent the definitive disappearance of the Banque de Belgique in 1886. Moreover, during the last decade of its existence, the bank was no longer important.[42] The demise of the Banque de Belgique meant the end of the long-lasting rivalry between the two largest private financial institutions of Belgium.

The other mixed banks. Between 1850 and the 1870s many provincial banks emerged, and some of them also got involved in long-term industrial investment. Most of these provincial mixed banks concentrated on sectors that were neglected by the big Brussels banks: sugar, chemicals, fertilizers, glass works, and others. Like the Banque de Belgique, the provincial banks sometimes followed very speculative investment policies. The results were not at all surprising; some of the banks, unable to overcome the crises of 1857, 1866, and 1873, collapsed. On the whole, however, the mixed-banking activities of the provincial banks were rather limited.[43] In fact, in 1870 only four of them possessed an important portfolio and could thus be qualified as real mixed banks: The Banque Générale pour favoriser l'Agriculture et les Travaux Publics, the Banque de l'Union, the Crédit Général Liégeois, and the Banque Liégeoise.[44]

The period from 1850 to the 1870s also witnessed a revival of private banking, especially in Brussels. According to B. S. Chlepner, the names of Bischoffsheim, Oppenheim, Errera, Brugmann, Cassel, Frank, Model, and Philippson were the most important ones in that respect.[45] The names of Tiberghien, Allard, Nagelmackers, and Mathieu could be added to the list. It is noteworthy that many of those private bankers were Jewish, and, above all, many of them were immigrants. Just a few examples will illustrate this international character of Belgian private banking in the nineteenth century. J. R. Bischoffsheim descended from the famous international banking house of the same name with branches in Amsterdam, Paris, London, and elsewhere. Emigrating from Amsterdam, Bischoffsheim arrived in Antwerp in 1828 and created the Antwerp branch of the house. After 1830 he moved to Brussels and became one of the leading Belgian financiers of the nineteenth century.

J. Errera, born in Venice, arrived in Brussels in 1857 as a consul-general. His career as banker started in 1864 when, with his father-in-law, the Brussels banker J. Oppenheim, he created the bank Errera-Oppenheim. This new private bank soon became one of the leading Brussels houses. Errera was also the man behind the creation in 1871 of the Banque de Bruxelles. The capital of this new joint stock bank was subscribed partly by the bank Errera-Oppenheim and, because of Errera's contacts in the international financial world, partly by Jewish bankers in London, Amsterdam, Rotterdam, and Frankfurt. The Banque de Bruxelles experienced a spectacular rise during the following decades, soon becoming a new competitor of the Société Générale. Errera also introduced F. Philippson to the Belgian financial world. In 1865, at the age of sixteen, Philippson, having emigrated from Magdeburg, started his career as an apprentice in Errera's bank.[46] The favorable Belgian fiscal and institutional regime with respect to bank creation is undoubtedly one of the major reasons why foreigners created banks in Belgium.[47] And Belgian neutrality in the strained international situation on the eve of the Franco-Prussian War can only have strengthened the preference for founding banks in Belgium. Nevertheless, besides fiscal, institutional, and political factors, personal circumstances (for example, in the case of the Errera-Oppenheim bank) and even geographical factors played a significant role in the creation of Belgian banks by foreigners. More investigation on this topic is needed to confirm this hypothesis.

The private bankers invested in industry (for example, the private banker Nagelmackers in the Liège heavy industries)[48] and in finance (for example, the participation of Errera-Oppenheim in the Banque de Bruxelles). On the whole, however, during the third quarter of the nineteenth century the private bankers, and the Jewish bankers in particular, specialized, as in the case of the Banque de Belgique, in the introduction of foreign railway shares and bonds into the Belgian capital market.[49] As such, the private banking houses were an important link in the rise of an internationalized Belgian banking system. Again, personal factors—that is, the existence of an international network of Jewish bankers—may have furthered these international transactions.

The Internationalization of the Belgian Mixed Banking System

From the 1870s onward, especially after 1895, the foreign expansion of Belgian mixed banks was a general phenomenon. Once again, the Société Générale played a dominant role. And once again, its initiatives were soon successfully imitated by other banks.

The foreign expansion of the Belgian banks did not remain limited to Europe. Belgian bankers (and industrialists) also invested on a large scale in America, Africa, and Asia. They were active mainly in the transport sector (rail and tramways), but neglected neither heavy industry nor light manufacturing. At the end of the century the quickly developing electricity industry and the financial sector were also integrated into the foreign investment strategy of the mixed banks. The consequences for the development of the banking structure were far-reaching: The modern holding company came to maturity and a large and very active Belgian financial network abroad was created. Both factors consolidated more firmly the success and power of the Belgian banking system. During the same period a revival of foreign penetration into the Belgian capital market occurred. German bankers especially tried to infiltrate the Belgian domestic and foreign financial network.

The Société Générale as Promoter of Financial Expansion Abroad

The Société Générale was the first Belgian bank to extend its international activities in a systematic way. Foreign expansion could be reconciled perfectly with the traditional investment policy of the bank. The national railway market being nearly saturated from the 1870s onwards, and the national tramway market being not large enough to absorb the output of its patronized domestic iron and steel firms, the Société Générale had to widen the geographical range of its investment policy to guarantee sufficient outlets for the patronized firms. Whereas in the former period, the Société Générale acted only as issuer of shares and bonds on behalf of foreign railway companies, it now started, from about 1870 onward, to participate directly in the creation of new foreign companies. The active participation of the Société Générale in the Franco-Belgian Société d'Etude de Chemin de Fer en Chine, which had obtained the Pekin-Hankow concession, is illustrative in this respect. That important railway project (1,200 km) created for about ten years (1898–1908) an important demand for railway equipment produced in Belgium.[50]

The Société Générale did not follow a strict strategy of *direct* participation in foreign companies. It also began to act similarly via its subsidiary companies, such as the Société Belge des Chemins de Fer, created in 1865. Facing, like the mother company, a saturated domestic market, the Société Belge obtained, between 1877 and 1883, many concessions for the construction of railways in France, Germany, Austria, Italy, Spain, the Netherlands, Russia, China, and Central and South America. The exploitation of those lines was entrusted to branch and filial companies of the Société Belge, in which the latter kept a major share.[51] For this reason, the Société Belge des Chemins de Fer can be considered as a financial trust, a holding company in the modern sense of the word. As the internationalization of Belgian financial activities proceeded, that formula became very popular; it proved to be perfectly well adjusted to the requirements of international mixed banking. In this sense, the rise of the modern holding company is undeniably linked with the emergence of international mixed banking and should be considered as an important result of it.[52] Thus, between 1880 and 1913, the Société Générale, whether directly or via specialized holding companies, got actively involved in railway construction abroad.[53] The patronized domestic heavy industries all took advantage of those foreign investments.

The international railway market in turn becoming saturated from about the 1890s, the Société Générale once again changed its investment strategy. It did not shift, as many other mixed banks did, to participation in the tramways sector but instead focused its efforts on creating outside Belgium a powerful international financial network.[54] A first step was taken in 1891, when the Société Générale became an important shareholder of the Banque Parisienne. During the following years the Société Générale, among others, participated in the Banque Russo-Chinoise (1896), the Anglo-Argentine Bank (1897), and the Banque Française de Brésil (1899). The real starting point of the creation of an international banking system, however, is usually situated in 1902, when the Banque Sino-Belge was created under the control of the Société Générale. In 1913 this bank was transformed into the Banque Belge pour l'Etranger with a broader international outlook.

Meanwhile, in 1904, the Banque Parisienne had been restructured and transformed into an important French investment bank, the Banque de l'Union Parisienne.[55] In 1909 a branch of the Société Générale opened in London and in the same year the Société Générale participated in the creation of the Banque Italo-Belge, which specialized in financial activities in South America. The Société Générale also launched then the Banque du Congo Belge.[56] The few companies mentioned here are only the most outstanding examples of foreign financial investment by the Société Générale: Between 1891 and 1913 the Société Générale gained interests in at least nineteen foreign banks or financial institutions.[57] This quick development of the foreign financial portfolio of the Société Générale shows the dynamism and vigor of the Belgian mixed-banking system during the prewar period. Thanks to its financial participations, the Société Générale often acquired seats on the boards of directors of the patronized banks. Indirectly, this could benefit Belgian industrial interests in foreign countries—for instance, in the granting of concessions. That was, for example, the case in Morocco; thanks to the Société Générale's control (since 1907) of the Moroccan State Bank, Belgians could gain a place in the Moroccan urban tramways and tobacco industries.[58]

The Société Générale's rising interest in international banking was backed by a strategy of domestic financial expansion. In 1900 the Société Générale already controlled twelve regional and local banks with branch services in fifteen different places. In 1913 the number of regional and local banks patronized by the Société Générale had risen to eighteen; these banks now disposed of a network of sixty-one branches throughout Belgium.[59] The combined strategy of expanding the control over international and domestic banking resulted in an impressive increase of the share of financial participations in the total portfolio of the Société Générale; it rose from 16.42 percent in 1880 to 39.67 percent in 1913.[60]

The internationalization of the Société Générale's investment policy was not limited to the railway and finance sectors. Mining and heavy industries were also integrated into the international investment stragegy. A famous example is the Société Métallurgique Russo-Belge. Created in 1896 in St. Petersburg by the Société Générale and the Société des Aciéries d'Angleur, this joint-stock company created many metal companies in the mining region of North Donetz, and was considered one of the most important industrial growth centers of tsarist Russia.[61] The creation of the Société Métallurgique Russo-Belge fitted perfectly well in the general Belgian capital export movement toward Russia, and more specifically to southern Russia, between 1886 and 1899. After the French, the Belgians were the second most important creditor nation of Russia in 1913;[62] if we can believe the *Moniteur des intérêts matériels* of 1901, the Belgian interests even exceeded the French, at least in the industrial sector.[63] The total value of Russian securities circulating on the Paris and Brussels bourses was estimated at 1.3 billion francs. According to the *Moniteur*, "we don't believe ourselves mistaken in saying that 75 percent is Belgian and 25 percent French. If we add the numerous tramway companies created in Russia by Belgians, which are not included in the exchange estimates, we reach a much larger proportion in favor of the initiative of Belgian capital."[64] In 1899, ten of the twenty-nine joint stock companies in Odessa were of foreign origin, and of those ten, eight were Belgian.[65]

Belgians were active also in the Russian textile, glass, brick, and ceramic industries, and above all in the metals industry.[66] This activity was mainly due to the success of the Cockerill companies in Russia. In the 1830s contacts had been established between John Cockerill and the Russians. During the 1860s those contacts intensified and led to the creation in 1888 of an important Belgian steel company, the South Russian Dnieper Metallurgical Company. This Belgian firm was the most successful steel company in Russia during the late nineteenth and early twentieth centuries.[67] Another creation of Cockerill, the Almaznaia Coal Company (1894), on the other hand, was a failure. Created as a coal and coke producer in 1894, the company expanded into pig-iron production, but went bankrupt in 1904.[68]

The success of the Cockerill companies was carefully watched in the mother country and may explain the rapid growth of a Belgian capital export flow to Russian industry, especially to the Russian metals industry, during the last decade of the nineteenth century.[69] In that respect the Société Générale's Société Métallurgique Russo-Belge is a perfect illustration of the "Cockerill effect." The Société Générale also played an important role in the formation (1897) of the Société Générale de l'Industrie Minière et Métallurgique en Russie (the "Omnium") and in the creation (1908) of the Russian Metallurgical Trust.[70] In the latter, its famous, highly qualified engineer J. Jadot, who later became governor of the Société Générale, played a dominant role.[71]

The Société Générale's interest in heavy industries was not limited to Russia. From the 1870s onward the Société Générale and its subsidiaries acquired important participations in companies in Luxembourg, the Saarland, German and French Lorraine, China, Morocco, and Canada. Later, many colonial companies, such as the Union Minière du Haut Katanga and the Société International Forestière et Minière, were also integrated into the investment strategy.[72]

Finally, we must refer to the Société Générale's investments in other industries, such as chemicals in the United States, sugar in Italy, and tobacco in Portugal and Morocco.[73] To conclude: In 1870 the Société Générale was the most important Belgian mixed bank; in 1913 it was the center of an important financial and industrial network extending over the world.

The Other Belgian Mixed Banks Between 1870 and 1913: Following the Société Générale's Lead

Between 1870 and 1914, more specifically between 1895 and 1913, the total number of Belgian banks increased rapidly. In 1913 the total number of banks was estimated at between 250 and 300. Most of them were founded after 1895. Between 1895 and 1900 not less than fifty-eight new banks emerged in Belgium. Simultaneously, the number of mixed banks increased also. In 1870 only six banks had a mixed character; in 1913 at least thirty banks could be considered mixed banks.[74] The spectacular increase of the number of mixed banks was due largely to the favorable economic conditions after 1895. The movement was undoubtedly strengthened by institutional factors as well. In 1893 the Belgian Parliament completely lifted the legal restrictions on the founding of joint stock banks.[75]

The Crédit Général Liégeois, the Banque Générale Belge, the Banque de Bruxelles, and the Banque d'Outremer were, according to their total capital resources, the most important joint-stock banks next to the Société Générale. When their long-term industrial investment portfolios are compared with the similar portfolio of the Société Générale, however, the importance of these banks appears limited; even their combined portfolios were not as important as the single portfolio of the Société Générale.[76] Among the private banking groups, the group E. Empain was without doubt the most important one. Also prominent were Nagelmackers, Allard, Lambert, Philippson, Cassel, and Mayer.[77]

In the wake of the Société Générale, the other joint-stock banks as well as the private banks actively participated in international long-term investment. The Banque de Bruxelles, the Banque Internationale de Bruxelles, the Banque d'Outremer, and again, the Empain group, were the most important investors in this respect. Although successful from the very beginning in its Italian transport undertakings, the Banque de Bruxelles developed as a really important mixed bank only after World War I.[78]

The Banque Internationale de Bruxelles was founded in 1898. Its most important shareholders were the Banque Centrale Anversoise and a number of German banks. The Banque Internationale de Bruxelles participated in many undertakings abroad, mainly in Italy, Spain, and Russia. The bank was considered to be the representative of German interests in Belgium. In 1917 it was absorbed by the Banque de Bruxelles.[79]

The Banque d'Outremer (Compagnie Internationale pour le Commerce et l'Industrie) was created in 1899 by the Société Générale, three important French banks (among them the Banque de Paris et des Pays-Bas), and two German banks. From the very beginning this institution was meant to develop as a dynamic colonial bank. It undoubtedly fulfilled the high expectations placed on it. Together with its filial holding company, Compagnie International d'Orient, it actively furthered the industrial development of the Belgian Congo. The bank also participated in other foreign undertakings—for example, the Belgian Canadian Pulp and Paper Company, and mines in Kaiping (China).[80]

Whereas the Société Générale originally was interested mainly in railway construction, the other banks specialized more in the construction of urban and rural tramways.[81] The case of Italy is illustrative: Between 1874 and 1885 Belgian financial and industrial groups created thirty-two transport companies, which, taken together, constructed about 1,481 kilometers of tramways.[82]

Following the example of the Société Générale, the other banks usually participated directly in foreign industries. But they also acted through subsidiary companies, namely financial trusts, which usually took the form of holding companies. This last strategy resulted in a big increase in the number of holding companies between 1870 and 1913. On the eve of World War I, holdings were considered an integral part of the Belgian financial system.

One of the most important subsidiary companies was the Société Générale des Tramways, created by the Banque de Bruxelles and J. Errera in 1874 and concerned mainly with the development of the Italian tramway network.[83] In 1882 the company was absorbed by the Société Générale des Chemins de Fer Economiques, founded in 1880 by the Banque de Bruxelles, the Banque de Paris et des Pays-Bas, and a group of private bankers. By 1914 the Société Générale des Chemins de Fer Economiques had become one of the most powerful holding companies. It possessed tramway companies in many cities in Italy, Egypt, Spain, and in other countries of Europe and elsewhere. The Compagnie Générale des Chemins de Fer Secondaires, founded in 1880 by the Banque Centrale Anversoise, the Philippson-Horwitz bank, the Empain group, and a German group, also created many tramway companies, mainly in Italy, Germany, Austria, and Brazil.[84] The cities of Buenos Aires and Constantinople were supplied with urban transport, respectively, by the Compagnie Générale de Tramways de Buenos-Ayres (1907) and the Société des Tramways et Electricité de Constantinople (1914), both founded by Belgian, German, and French banks.[85]

The great Belgian industrialist E. L. Empain created many new holdings in the rail and tramway sectors, not only in Europe (e.g., Spain and Russia) but also in Egypt and China. In 1880 Empain had founded a bank in Brussels, the Banque E.L.J. Empain, for extending short-term loans and other financial services to his many industrial enterprises and transport companies in Belgium and abroad. In 1919 he merged it with his Banque Industrielle Belge, which developed as a very active and powerful financial institution.[86]

From the end of the nineteenth century onward Belgian foreign investment shifted from railways and tramways to the rising electrical industry. In 1895 the Banque de Bruxelles, the Banque de Paris et des Pays-Bas, and two holding companies—the Société Générale des Chemins de Fer Economiques and Compagnie Générale des Chemins de Fer Secondaires—together with a German group, created the Société Générale Belge d'Entreprises Electriques, which participated in many new undertakings in Belgium and abroad. It was a forerunner of the current holding company Electrobel.

In 1898 the Banque Liégeoise, a group of private bankers, and, again, a German group, created the Société Financière de Transport et d'Entreprises Industrielles (SOFINA), to become, after World War I, the most important electrical holding company in Belgium. On the eve of World War I the latter two holdings and the Société Générale des Chemins de Fer Economiques together represented a capital of more than 700 million francs in tramway and electricity companies.[87]

Not all holding companies were successful undertakings. Some of them ended in tragic failure, due mainly to speculative investments or involvement in too many sectors.[88] The mother companies, often mixed banks, carried a large responsibility in that respect.[89] From a general point of view there is a certain resemblance between the relation of the Société Générale and the Banque de Belgique with regard to the introduction of the mixed-banking system in the second-third of the nineteenth century and the relation of the Société Générale to the other mixed banks with regard to the introduction of holding companies at the end of the century. The Société Générale always opted for a cautious investment policy in solid sectors. The returns were never spectacular, but safe and satisfying at the same time. The other mixed banks or their subsidiary companies often undertook spectacular experiments, but by doing so frequently obtained disastrous results.

Of course, not all international investments passed through holding companies; direct investment occurred as well, as illustrated in the person of the Liège private banker Nagelmackers. Nagelmackers was the direct concessionaire of the Mandaria-Brasse railway (42 km) in the Ottoman Empire (1891), and in Russia he owned the Taganrog Steel Company. Above all, Nagelmackers was the creator-director of the international company Wagons-Lits. Wagon-Lits provided, among other things, a weekly sleeping car with restaurant between Moscow and Vladivostok.[90]

Foreign Interests in Belgium

Foreign interests in Belgian banks and holding companies increased as well during the last third of the nineteenth century and the beginning of the twentieth. French capital had always been very important for Belgium. As already mentioned, fiscal and institutional factors to a great extent explain the large French capital-export movement toward Belgium. The Franco-Prussian War of 1870 and the unification of the Belgian and French monetary systems in the Latin Monetary Union (1865) reinforced the trend. The Banque de Paris et des Pays-Bas, the Crédit Lyonnais, the Comptoir Nationale d'Escompte de Paris, and the Société Française de Banque et de Dèpôts (a branch of the

Société Générale Française) were the most important representatives of French interests in Belgium in 1913.[91]

The British penetration reached its culmination during the railway era. Afterwards, British capital export to Belgium decreased, but it did not stop, as the presence of the London and River Plate Bank in Antwerp in 1913 bears witness.[92]

From 1880 onwards German capital, which never before had been very important, came strongly to the fore. On the eve of World War I German capital had infiltrated deeply into the Belgian metallurgical, chemical, electrical, and colonial sectors.[93] In the financial sector the Banque Internationale de Bruxelles and the Banque Centrale Anversoise in particular were considered to represent German interests in Belgium. Finally, the Deutsche Bank and the Diskonto-Gesellschaft created subsidiaries in Brussels and Antwerp, respectively.[94] German participation in the Belgian electrical holding companies has to be mentioned also.

German penetration was not always appreciated. It was suggested that the Germans used Belgian firms as a cloak for their imperialistic motives.[95] Newspapers even used the term *vasselage industriel*.[96] The German penetration into Belgian colonial affairs in particular was considered a great danger—for instance, the important German interests in the Compagnie du Congo pour le Commerce et l'Industrie, the Compagnie Maritime du Congo-Belge, and the Banque d'Outremer.[97] In 1913 the French minister in Brussels, M. Klobukowski, wrote: "the German danger focused especially on the Belgian Congo, but the offer of German financial collaboration was obstinately refused by the Empain group."[98] The "active" German infiltration was, according to contemporaries, reflected also in the social status of the German directors in Belgium. Belonging to the high commercial and industrial bourgeoisie, they had close connections with the aristocracy in Germany. Such was not the case, again according to contemporaries, with the French; they generally belonged to the low commercial bourgeoisie and did not have explicit connections with the industrial world.[99]

Conclusion: The Internationalization of Long-Term Investment, A Decisive Stage in the Development of the Belgian Mixed Banking System

The internationalization of long-term investment by the Belgian banks and holding companies marks the third stage in the development of the Belgian mixed banking system. The first stage in the rise of the Belgian mixed banks took place between about 1835 and 1850 and consisted in the creation of the system. It was accompanied by a certain overestimation of the capacities of the system in a still primitive economic environment. The first financial trusts also were founded during that period, but they all failed.

The creation of the National Bank of Belgium in 1850 initiated a second stage, which lasted until the 1870s. It was the system's consolidation stage. The Société Générale and the Banque de Belgique increasingly directed their investment stragegy toward long-term industrial financing at the expense of their traditional banking activities. A few new mixed banks joined the two leaders. The Belgian railway revolution was, in fact, the driving force behind the consolidation stage of the mixed banking system. For that reason the saturation of the domestic railway market ended that stage.

Slowly a third stage emerged, characterized by an internationalization of the industrial investments of the Belgian mixed banks. The formula of holding companies was now successfully introduced, and an international network of banks was organized.

In this historical overview two constants can be found: first, the initiating role of the Société Générale and the imitation strategy of the other mixed banks; second, the cautious investment policy of the Société Générale and the more speculative policies of many of the imitators. The second constant might be explained by the attempts of some of the imitating banks to overtake the Société Générale. Some of those attempts ended in tragic failure; before World War I the bankruptcy of the Banque de Belgique was the most spectacular.

The cautious policy of the Société Générale and of other mixed banks had a negative aspect as well. It evolved in the course of the twentieth century into a rigid investment strategy, imprisoned in traditional sectors without economic future. Only after World War II did American and German multinational companies shift long-term industrial investment strategy in Belgium toward the modern growth sectors.

6

The Role of International Factors in the Formation of the Banking System in Russia

V. I. Bovykin and B. V. Anan'ich

Structure and Stages of the Formation and Development of the Commercial Credit System in Russia

The formative stage of the Russian banking system was the 1860s and 1870s, a period when capitalist relations were being significantly strengthened in the country. Previously, the country lived under serfdom (not abolished until 1861), which fettered and deformed the growth of production, commerce, and credit. Faced with the threat of a revolutionary overthrow of the outdated feudal regime, Russian landowners sacrificed serfdom and embarked upon a gradual bourgeois transformation of the agrarian system and adaptation of the landowner stage to burgeoning capitalism. As a result, capitalist relations in Russia arose under conditions where landowners retained political dominance in the state and a monopoly of a considerable (and the best) part of the country's land resources.

While the landowner state took the initiative in promoting a bourgeois reconstruction of the social order, it did all in its power to gear the course and rates of change to the requirements of a capitalist evolution in the former serf owners' latifundia (estates). In essence, that meant a tendency to restrain the spontaneous processes of capitalist growth in order to give the landowners greater opportunity for the least painful adaptation of their estates along capitalist lines. That policy, in turn, however, obliged the state to contribute to the development of certain branches of capitalist business that were of particular importance and interest to the ruling class.

One such branch was the railway, the construction of which would open markets for noble estates and enable them to become commercial operations. But the growth of the railways had broader ramifications, for it made the development of corollary branches—the production of rails, wagons, steam engines, and the like—a vital necessity. Put succinctly, railway development could not be achieved in a vacuum; growth in selected industrial branches could only be attained under conditions favorable to overall development. The result was a fundamental shift in state policy in the late 1880s and early 1890s, from encouragement of special, privileged sectors (with concomitant tariff protection) to promotion of broad-based industrial growth. The new policy found its clearest expression in a new system of inclusive protective tariffs and a gold standard designed to stimulate direct foreign investment.

Compared to these changes in the industrial and commercial sectors, the capitalist reorganization of landed estates proceeded extremely slowly. A key factor was the terms of the 1861 reform, which enabled the landowners to stretch out its implementation over a long period of time. By giving the manumitted serfs minimal land allotments (which, with the prevailing agricultural technology, virtually precluded extensive agriculture), by saddling them with onerous redemption payments and taxes, and by restricting free purchase and sale of allotments, the reform served at once to assure landowners of labor and shielded them from competition by peasants who had become capitalist farmers. As a result, the reform—in the interest of latifundia reorganization—had sacrificed peasant households and placed them in conditions that retarded their shift to capitalist commodity production. Despite the landowners' numerous privileges, for the most part they nevertheless proved incapable of making the requisite adjustment and reorganization. Only lavish credits by the state, which meant a diversion of internal savings from productive utilization, could sustain the continued existence of their estates.

Consequently, the main dynamic in the formation of a market for large-scale industry in Russia was the development of capitalism "in breadth"—i.e., along geographically extensive lines. Unable to overcome the resistance of estate owners who were concentrated in the agricultural center of the country, agrarian capitalism spread to outlying areas that were less inhibited by the relics of serfdom. The peasant colonization and economic development of the southern Ukraine, the foothills of the Caucasus, the trans-Volga country and Siberia turned these regions into areas of advanced capitalist agriculture. And these regions were not only the main suppliers of agricultural products; they were also a growing market for manufactured goods. It follows too that the development of capitalism "in breadth" and its extension to new territories necessitated the further expansion of the railway system. And that railway construction, in turn, provided additional impetus to industrial growth.

Because the regime diverted considerable resources to unproductive subsidy of gentry estates (to maintain the landowners' economic and political predominance), it was able to ensure railway construction and industrial development only by turning to foreign money markets and giving foreign capital ever broader access to Russia. All the circumstances noted here would have a major impact on the formation and development of the credit system in late Imperial Russia.

The available statistics do not suffice for a quantitative assessment of the structure and development of the Russian economy in the 1860s and 1870s. Apart from the want of suitable data, the analysis of Russian economic growth—and its comparison with that of other states—is made still more complex and difficult because of the uneven development of different sectors and geographical regions of the country.

Only a few credible estimates of Russia's national income are currently available. On the basis of these we calculated the relative share of agriculture, forestry, and fishing (group I) and industry, construction, transport, and communications (group II) in the total annual product of these branches (see Table 6–1). According to calculations

TABLE 6-1. Sectoral Shares of Total Material Product

Author, Time of Publication of the Estimate, Territory Covered	Period Covered by the Estimate	I Agriculture, Forestry, Fishing (percent)	II Industry, Construction, Communications, Transport (percent)
1. Prokopovich, 1918, 50 gubernias of European Russia	1900	60.0	40.0
	1913	58.8	41.2
2. Strumilin, 1927, Russian Empire (without Finland)	1913	60.4	39.6
3. Falkus, 1968, Russian Empire (without Finland)	1913	61.1	38.9
4. Gregory, 1982, Russian Empire (without Finland)	1883–1887	71.0	29.0
	1897–1901	62.7	37.3
	1909–1913	61.1	38.9

Sources: S. N. Prokopovich, *Opyt ischisleniia narodnogo dokhoda 50 gub. Evropeiskoi Rossii v 1900–1913 gg.* (Moscow, 1918); S. G. Strumilin, *Perspektivy razvertyvaniia narodnogo khozaistva SSSR na 1926/27–1930/31* (Moscow, 1927); M. E. Falkus, "Russia's National Income, 1913: A Revaluation," *Economica,* N.S. 35, No. 137 (February 1968); Paul R. Gregory, *Russian National Income, 1885–1913* (Cambridge, MA, 1982).

by S. N. Prokopovich in 1918 for the fifty provinces of European Russia (i.e., excluding the Kingdom of Poland), the relative shares of groups I and II were 60.0 and 40.0 percent, respectively, in 1900 and 58.8 percent and 41.2 percent in 1913.[1] Later studies by S. G. Strumilin,[2] M. E. Falkus,[3] and Paul R. Gregory[4] for the Russian Empire as a whole produced very close results for 1913; their figures show 60.4 percent to 61.1 percent for group I and 38.9 percent to 39.6 percent for group II. The higher figure that Prokopovich obtained for group II in 1913 can be easily explained by his smaller geographic focus: The territory covered in his estimate included the main industrial areas and a larger part of the railway network of the country. When allowance is made for this, Prokopovich's estimates for 1900 and Gregory's estimate for 1897–1901 are also fully compatible.

The comparison of the results obtained by Prokopovich for 1900–1913 and by Gregory for 1897–1901 and 1909–1913 shows that the share of group II increased at the expense of group I by 1.2 percent within the boundaries of the fifty gubernias (provinces) of European Russia and by 1.6 percent within the boundaries of the Russian Empire. As suggested by Gregory's estimates for 1883–1887 (71.0 percent for group I, and 29.0 percent for group II), the shift in the relative share of the economy in favor of group II occurred at a much faster rate in the last fifteen years of the nineteenth century than after the beginning of the twentieth century. That tendency was also apparent from the mid-1860s to the mid-1880s, when agricultural output grew at a rather sluggish pace but manufacturing production more than trebled and the length of railways increased nearly sevenfold. All this means that the share of group II output in the national economy was sharply lower in the mid-1860s than it was two decades later. In a word, at the onset of our period the Russian national economy stood under the overwhelming predominance of the agricultural sector.

The terms of serf emancipation in 1861 and specific features of the postreform agrarian order were the fundamental causes for the slow growth rates in agricultural production in the first two decades after the reform (see Table 6–2).[5] It was not until the early 1880s that the serf emancipation finally achieved full implementation, but once this was completed, it made continued operation of landed estates on traditional, feudal lines utterly impossible. Processes of change, indeed, were already at work: Compared to the stagnation in agriculture in the 1850s, the next two decades witnessed signs of increasing vitality as the 1861 reform gradually took effect. Still more striking evidence of the transformation of the agrarian system was apparent by the 1880s and 1890s—a steady growth of commercial grain production, a change in its geography (a sharp rise of grain production in the south, a parallel decline in the old farming center), development of commercial animal husbandry, expansion of industrial crops, and broader utilization of machines. Although remnants of serfdom still retarded the capitalist development of the village, even the slow pace of structural and social change was a spur to accelerated rates of industrial growth, considering the scale of the country.

Russian industry entered the postreform era bearing the marks of its prolonged operation under the conditions of serfdom. In essence, prior to 1861 Russian industrial development proceeded along two main courses. One was the adoption of Western organizational forms of large-scale manufacturing production, but based on the utilization of serf labor. This pattern prevailed in such sectors as the mining industry of the Urals, in coarse cloth and linen production, glassmaking, winemaking, and in part also in sugar refining, which formed the sphere of predominant activity of the landed gentry. The second course was the establishment of industrial enterprises that were based on hired labor. One important source of such labor was in fact the serfs, whom some landowners had transferred from dues in kind or labor to money payments. To pay this quitrent (*obrok*), such serfs either had to go to towns as hired labor or to engage in subsidiary handicrafts in their home village. The latter gave rise to the Russian cotton industry that later played a major role in the industrialization process and particularly in the formation of large, mechanized textile mills. Such mills, in fact, had even gained dominance in cotton spinning before the reform. At the same time, the growth of the cotton industry was further abetted by the incorporation of small-scale peasant (handicraft) production.

While the abolition of serfdom sounded the death knell for enterprises based on forced labor, the fact that implementation dragged on for more than twenty years enabled such enterprises to hang on for some time, and to seek to adapt (with scant success) to the new order. Hence, the development of Russian industrial organization after 1861 was integrally tied to the process of serf emancipation, with two major patterns prevailing: a decline of the landowners' manufacturing based on serf labor, and expansion of purely capitalist factories that relied upon hired labor and peasant handicrafts. Without question, application of the advanced technology and organizational techniques of Western countries helped to accelerate the development of large machine production in Russia.

Russian industrial growth after 1861 brought not only the recasting of old branches along new capitalist lines, but also the emergence of entirely new sectors. The latter included steam-engine and wagon manufacture, coal mining and coke production, oil extraction and refining, and the production of steel rails, copper rolled stock,

TABLE 6–2. Main Indicators of Russia's Social and Economic Development, 1861–1914

Year	Population (millions)	January 1		Grain Output (50 gubernias of European Russia) (millions of puds)[a]	Per Year			
		Length of Railways (1,000s of kilometers)	Liabilities of Joint-Stock Banks (millions of rubles)		Industrial Value of Output (millions of rubles)	Turnover of Commercial Establishments (millions of rubles)	Exports (millions of rubles)	Imports (millions of rubles)
1861	73.6	1.6	—	1,649	—	—	177.2	167.1
1875	90.2	18.2	595.3	1,847	—	—	381.9	531.1
1880	97.9	22.7	431.4	1,991	1,177.4	—	498.7	622.8
1887	113.1	27.3	568.5	2,395	1,400.9	4,111	617.3	399.6
1893	121.5	31.2	728.7	2,627	1,824.3	4,438	599.2	449.6
1900	132.9	49.8	1,380.2	2,842	3,086.0	6,995	716.2	626.4
1908	152.5	65.5	2,007.3	3,259	4,297.3	7,813	998.2	912.6
1913	—	—	—	4,240	6,521.7	10,855	1,520.1	1,374.0
1914	175.1	70.2	6,233.0	—	—	—	—	—

Sources: See note 5.

[a]Five-year average except for 1913. One pud equals 36.1 pounds avoirdupois.

and cement—all the result of the technological revolution then under way. Moreover, these branches arose chiefly because of an infusion of capital, and that in turn enabled large capitalist enterprises, many of which operated in the form of joint-stock companies, to establish a dominant position. Another group of young industries (for example, flour milling, oil, and timber production) invaded the processing of agricultural products. But, organizationally, these industries emerged gradually from the agricultural sector itself and, for the most part, were dominated by small family firms.

Table 6–3 delineates the general structure of industry in the fifty provinces of European Russia in the 1860s (excluded are those industries subject to internal taxation, such as sugar refining and distillation of spirits).[6] As Table 6–3 suggests, cotton manufacture occupied a special position, and textiles as a whole accounted for more than two-thirds of the total manufacturing output. Later, the expansion of other branches and emergence of some new sectors reduced cotton's predominance, yet the latter continued to hold a leading position.

Data for the 1880s, which embrace not only the fifty provinces of European Russia but also the entire Russian Empire (as well as the taxed industries and mining), demonstrate that Russian industry had largely taken its final shape. Its largest branches were textile and food industries, which had grown as a direct result of the capitalist development in agriculture. Together, they accounted for more than half the value of total industrial output. The food-processing industry, which had achieved a considerable output by the early twentieth century (for such products as flour, sugar refining, oil, alcohol, and tobacco), bore witness to the progress in commercial agriculture. At the same time, the high level of development in the textile industry, and especially cotton production—which relied chiefly upon imported raw materials and served primarily a domestic, rural market—reflected a division of labor that was well advanced. Next in importance was metallurgy and metalworking, which had developed initially to satisfy the demands of railway construction, but which by the end of the century had become increasingly oriented toward a broader producer and consumer market.

By the turn of the twentieth century, Russia was in the ranks of the five largest industrial powers in the absolute volume of industrial production, coming close to France in the total value of industrial output and surpassing that country in such important industrial indices as pig iron and steel, machine and toolmaking, and cotton consumption. But if measured in per capita terms, production in Russia still lagged far behind that of the advanced capitalist countries. Most notably, agriculture, which had undergone such a contradictory and uneven development, remained the dominant sector. Hence, even in the European part of the Russian Empire, giant industrial centers and pockets of advanced commercial agriculture existed alongside areas with backward agrarian relations that retarded economic development.

An important stimulus to economic growth was the creation of the railway network, which connected both the center with outlying provinces and agricultural regions with major cities and seaports. Virtually this entire network was constructed in the four decades following the reform of 1861.

The main features of Russian economic development also shaped the country's international commercial ties. These ties, which reflected the formation of an international system of the division of labor, played a major role in the evolution of capitalism in Russia. Thus, the growth of Russian grain exports contributed to the capitalistic restructuring of agriculture. Likewise, the transfer of modern industrial technology,

TABLE 6–3. Value of Output of Industrial Production in Russia, 1867–1913 (millions of rubles)

| | Food | | | | Manufacturing | | | | | | |
| | | | | | Textiles | | | | | Mixed Materials Processing | Animal Product Processing |
Year[a]	Flour mills	Taxed Branches[b]	Others	Total	Cotton	Wool	Silk	Flax and Hemp	Total		
1867 I	—	—	—	—	104.7	49.2	4.3	9.1	167.3	0.2	20.6
1874 I	21.3	—	5.3	26.6	140.9	58.1	7.6	25.8	232.4	2.3	33.6
1880 I	76.5	—	11.6	88.1	216.3	99.9	8.4	31.8	356.4	4.2	55.1
II	110.3	158.7	22.9	291.9	242.3	130.4	12.0	34.6	419.3	4.8	66.9
1887 I	131.9	—	9.3	141.2	251.8	71.1	10.8	30.4	364.1	6.1	41.6
II	155.1	265.1	30.8	451.0	288.9	113.7	15.2	36.0	453.8	10.2	53.8
1893 II	158.5	328.4	45.6	532.5	399.3	138.7	16.9	38.7	593.6	15.6	53.9
1900 II	234.9	429.7	102.8	767.4	526.0	180.3	31.0	67.9	805.2	33.5	85.3
1908 II	479.6	570.6	165.5	1215.7	886.2	241.8	37.5	94.3	1259.8	52.5	124.1
1913 II	464.2	681.4	298.1	1443.7	1277.7	368.2	53.8	155.2	1854.9	76.6	163.8

[a]I, within the boundaries of 50 gubernias of European Russia; II, within the boundaries of the Russian Empire.

[b]Sugar refining, alcohol, tobacco, etc.

(continued)

TABLE 6–3. Value of Output of Industrial Production in Russia, 1867–1913 (millions of rubles) (Continued)

| | Manufacturing | | | | | | | | | | | | | | |
| | Chemicals | | | | | | | Silicates | | | Metal-working | | | | Total Mfg. |
Year[a]	Basic Chemicals, Paints, Varnishes	Rubber	Match-making	Fats and Perfume	Total	Paper	Wood-working	Porcelain and Faience	Building Materials	Total	Engineering	Metal Products	Precious Metals	Total	
1867 I	5.8	0.7	0.5	13.1	20.1	5.3	—	4.7	—	4.7	14.0	3.7	—	17.7	235.9
1874 I	7.8	3.9	1.3	23.4	36.4	12.5	2.3	8.6	1.8	10.4	38.9	12.4	—	51.3	407.8
1880 I	9.9	5.9	2.0	35.8	53.6	14.1	17.5	10.3	11.7	22.0	50.8	33.0	—	83.8	694.8
II	11.3	5.9	2.1	40.4	59.7	16.1	23.4	12.1	16.1	28.2	59.1	38.6	23.0	120.7	1031.0
1887 I	14.4	7.1	2.3	22.4	46.2	19.1	20.3	11.8	11.4	23.2	41.8	30.2	—	72.0	733.8
II	18.7	7.2	2.6	26.3	54.8	21.7	26.4	14.0	15.0	29.0	51.7	37.0	25.7	114.4	1215.1
1893 II	32.8	17.1	5.6	28.7	84.2	28.8	39.7	16.1	18.6	34.7	—	—	—	173.4	1556.4
1900 II	61.1	28.7	8.5	32.9	131.2	55.4	97.9	34.0	46.7	80.7	—	—	—	357.8	2414.4
1908 II	93.3	64.8	11.2	47.8	217.1	90.3	123.5	45.9	51.9	97.8	—	—	—	407.2	3588.0
1913 II	214.6	169.3	11.8	82.9	478.6	94.4	221.0	70.3	117.4	187.7	—	—	—	769.0	5289.7

[a] I, within the boundaries of 50 gubernias of European Russia; II, within the boundaries of the Russian Empire.

(continued)

TABLE 6–3. Value of Output of Industrial Production in Russia, 1867–1913 (millions of rubles) (*Continued*)

Year[a]	Mining							Total Industrial Production
	Coal	Oil	Other Minerals	Non-Ferrous Metallurgy	Ferrous Metallurgy	Metal Articles[c]	Total Mining	
1867 I	—	—	—	—	—	—	—	—
1874 I	—	—	—	—	—	—	—	—
1880 I	—	—	—	—	—	—	—	—
II	—	—	—	—	—	—	148.5	1179.5
1887 I	—	—	—	—	—	—	—	—
II	14.7	11.3	46.8	5.7	69.9	37.4	185.8	1400.9
1893 II	26.0	18.8	68.2	5.7	117.8	27.2	263.7	1820.1
1900 II	84.8	197.0	66.8	8.7	269.4	44.9	671.6	3086.0
1908 II	145.7	224.0	84.8	17.2	205.8	31.8	709.3	4297.3
1913 II	187.3	429.3	108.6	31.8	365.3	60.1	1182.4	6472.1

Sources: 1867 I, 1874 I, 1887 I: *Svod dannykh o fabrichno-zavodskoi promyshelennosti v Rossii za 1867–1888 gg.* (St. Petersburg, 1890). 1880 II: *Obzor devatelnosti Ministersrva finansov v tsarstvovanie Imperatora Aleksandra III (1881–1894)* (St. Petersburg, 1902). 1887 II–1912 II: *Dinamika rossiiskoi i sovetskoi promyshlennosti v svlazi s razvitiem narodnogo khozaistva za sorok let (1887–1926)*, Vol. I, Parts 1–3 (Moscow–Leningrad, 1929–1930).

[a] I, within the boundaries of 50 gubernias of European Russia; II, within the boundaries of the Russian Empire.

[c] Produced at metallurgical plants.

machines, and capital from Western European countries helped to accelerate Russian industrial development. This was, however, a two-edged sword, for competition of more developed countries also posed a threat to domestic industry in Russia. As a result, a high protective tariff became a vital precondition for the survival and growth of Russian industry.

This tariff structure served to reinforce Russia's relatively autochthonous course of economic development, which was oriented primarily toward domestic rather than foreign trade. It bears noting that, in contrast to Western European states, which had overseas colonies, the Russian Empire was a single state–territorial complex that included both industrial and agrarian regions, each of which differed greatly in both natural and geographical conditions as well as general level of social and economic development. Commodity exchange between those sections, which could be viewed as the metropolis and the colonial regions, remained within the framework of the domestic market. And both industrial and agricultural production in Russia was aimed mostly toward this market, not export. Hence, the all-Russian market protected by a wall of protective tariffs constituted a relatively autonomous sector of the world economy, and commodity flows within this Russian sector were not registered by world trade statistics. But, most important, external trade played a relatively minor role in the division of labor that functioned within the framework of the Russian Empire.

Nonetheless, foreign trade was of considerable importance. Very detailed and reliable statistics are available for the entire postreform era and provide a clear picture of trade.[7] These data show that not only did Russia's foreign trade increase significantly (more than eightfold) but that it also underwent a basic structural change. Most noteworthy was the importance of grain in Russia's export trade: By the mid-1870s it constituted 50 percent of all exports and remained at this level (with some fluctuations) up to the 1900s, when it began to fall. By the end of the nineteenth century timber ranked second to grain; some traditional export items like flax remained important, but the export inventory also included some new industrial products, such as oil and sugar. Nevertheless, Russia failed to gain a foothold in the Western European industrial market, and the share of these goods in the Russian export trade declined at the beginning of the century. More significant was the export of timber and the output of intensive agriculture, such as eggs and dairy products. As a result, between 1909 and 1913, when the average annual export volume stood at 1,501.5 million rubles, the main export items were grain (676.1 million rubles a year, or 45.2 percent); timber (145.0 million rubles, or 9.7 percent); flax (77.3 million rubles, or 5.2 percent); eggs (76.4 million rubles, or 5.1 percent); and butter (62.2 million rubles, or 4.1 percent).

But in comparative terms, the absolute value of such trade was not very substantial. Thus, on the eve of World War I, Russia's share of the world market was only 4.2 percent and, according to available estimates, the country's exports constituted only some 6–8 percent of its total output. Among the major export items only flax and butter were produced mainly for export. In 1913 Russia exported 54 percent of its flax output and 76 percent of its butter. As for other prominent commodities, the amount exported constituted a much lower share of total production: 15 percent in the case of wheat, 3 percent for rye, 4 percent for oats, 34 percent for barley, 17 percent for eggs, 8 percent for sugar, and 12 percent for oil. In the five years preceding the Great War, when the production of these goods expanded considerably, the proportion exported exhibited unmistakable signs of decline.[8]

With respect to imports, the dominant items in 1861 were consumer goods: food products and textiles. But by the end of the nineteenth century about one-half of the value of Russian imports consisted of producer goods and raw materials—cotton, machines, metals, wool, dyestuffs and other chemicals, and coal. Nevertheless, the volume remained relatively low; by 1914 Russia's share of world imports was even smaller than its exports, about 3.5 percent. During 1909 to 1913 the total import trade amounted to approximately 1,140 million rubles annually, of which the main import items were machines (135.5 million rubles a year, or 11.8 percent); cotton (108.3 million rubles, or 9.6 percent); wool (62.0 million rubles, or 5.5 percent); tea (59.9 million rubles, or 5.3 percent); and coal (49.8 million rubles, or 4.2 percent). Machine-tool imports had increased sharply during industrial booms and at their peaks (1878–1880, 1898–1900, and 1911–1913) substantially surpassed the import of cotton. But in all other years cotton ranked at the top of the Russian import list. Its share was most significant during the second half of the 1880s and in the early 1890s (over one fifth of total imports). But thereafter it began to decline, for the brisk and growing demand could be increasingly satisfied by domestic cotton from Central Asia and Trans-caucasia, which provided over 50 percent in the prewar years.

On the eve of the war, when the import of machines reached its peak, the domestic suppliers produced about 44 percent of the machinery requirements. One half of imports consisted of production machines (chiefly machine tools), one quarter of agricultural machines and implements, and one-tenth of electrical machines and equipment. The rest was taken up chiefly by machine parts. The demand from Russian railways for locomotives and rolling stock was satisfied by domestic producers. In general, producer goods, intended chiefly for use in production (primarily in industrial manufacturing), prevailed over commodities needed to satisfy consumer demand.

This special line of economic development in Russia determined the extraordinary role that the state played in the formation of the capitalist credit system.[9] Characteristically, the system traces its origins back to the State Bank, which was established in 1860 to replace the Treasury banks that had operated to funnel savings into agriculture and thereby help to maintain serfdom. The State Bank, which arose on the ruins of the prereform credit system, and in some measure assumed its functions, was at the same time to contribute to the "revival of commercial exchange." It became the first commercial bank in Russia.

But once the government founded the State Bank, it at first responded rather cautiously to the rising demand that a joint-stock commercial bank be opened as well.[10] In the end, the need for a capitalist credit system was met through the formation of private banking houses and small credit institutions. In the late 1850s and early 1860s, the old banking firms of Stieglitz, Jacobi, and Jadimirovsky, symbols of an earlier age, went out of existence and surrendered their place to new banking firms—Meyer, Günzburg, Kaiger, and others. Moreover, municipal banks also took root in the early 1860s, the first of which was the St. Petersburg Mutual Credit Society, opened in 1863. It was followed the next year by the St. Petersburg Private Commercial Bank and, in 1865, by the Moscow Merchant Bank, the first joint-stock bank in Russia. Such joint-stock commercial banks were extensively promoted after 1868 and within six years thirty-seven more had opened their doors, not only in St. Petersburg and Moscow but also in twenty-seven provincial cities.[11] Over the same years branch banks likewise proliferated. But all these banks experienced acute difficulties during the crisis of

1873, which led not only to bankruptcy (the failure of the Moscow Commercial Loan Bank in 1875), but also marked the beginning of a long decline in the development of joint-stock commercial banks. Thus, over the next five years the number of banks and their branches shrank and the sum of deposits dwindled considerably (see Table 6–4); not until the mid-1880s did the picture improve. Thereafter the total number of banks remained highly stable (with little change over the next three decades), as these opened numerous branches, chiefly in the provinces.

By the early 1890s the total assets of joint-stock commercial banks surpassed those of the State Bank and also ranked above the mutual credit societies and municipal banks. Whereas the latter fell into decline in the 1880s (and thereafter ceased to play a substantial role), mutual credit societies fared better, continuing to grow at a rather slow pace and by the eve of World War I could claim to be of some importance.

Development of the State Bank, an exceptionally important component of the postreform credit system in Russia, was exceedingly complex. To begin with, its role was hardly uniform, but varied at different points in the development of the system. Then, too, the State Bank was principally an instrument to effect the government's economic policy, and its activity was as contradictory as the policy itself. According to the estimates offered by I. F. Gindin in a special study, the State Bank allocated just 28 percent of its assets in the years between 1866 and 1875 to commercial credit.[12] During the next five years it increased the proportion to 53 percent, and to 63 percent in the 1880s.

At first glance it would appear only natural that the State Bank increased its credit to the national economy at the time when joint-stock commercial banks were experiencing a sharp decline and had neither the resources nor the incentives to extend credit to industry and trade. But, in fact, the State Bank had become a new source of venture capital. As Gindin has observed:

> Credits to industrial enterprises by the State Bank were least of all a commercial operation aimed at higher profits, and its customers were not at all thriving and expanding enterprises. On the contrary, nearly all of them were enterprises in financial difficulties or even with their finances in disarray. Predominant among them were stagnating old metallurgical enterprises that resisted capitalist reorganization, transport engineering enterprises that had run into formidable difficulties, unsuccessful railway and other promoters and, lastly, landowners who tried to establish sugar refineries on their estates.[13]

The State Bank also extended its support and aid to joint-stock commercial banks. The salvaging of banks on the verge of bankruptcy, and support of specially favored industrial enterprises, seriously limited the capacity of the State Bank to be a major creditor for trade and industrial turnover. Its activities were further limited by investment in government loans (which essentially signified financing of the state), and also by diversion of resources to subsidize landowners (through mortgage credits). As a result, the numerous branches of the State Bank strewn throughout the country served less to promote trade and industrial activity than to siphon money from the provinces for purposes of furthering state economic policy.

In the 1890s this function passed in the main to Treasury savings banks. Amidst the extraordinary boom taking place at the time, the State Bank greatly expanded the

TABLE 6–4. Resources of State and Private Credit Institutions (millions of rubles)[a]

Jan. 1	State Bank					State Savings Banks		Joint-Stock Commercial Banks			Mutual Credit Societies			Urban Banks		
	1	2	3	4	5	6	7	8	9	10	11	12	13	14	15	16
1861	15.0	30.3	—	31.9	62.2	—	—	—	—	—	—	—	—	—	—	—
1875	23.0	30.3	0.7	224.7	255.7	72	5.0	39	108.4	299.7	—	—	—	—	—	—
1880	28.3	42.1	0.8	224.8	267.7	76	8.1	33	95.2	197.0	84	23.5	110.6	235	19.1	115.1
1887	28.2	117.9	1.4	288.0	407.3	439	41.8	34	122.7	255.1	102	17.9	84.5	281	27.6	171.7
1893	29.1	147.7	52.4	226.5	426.6	2439	239.4	34	148.4	285.4	101	26.7	115.1	242	33.7	89.9
1900	53.1	594.0	23.0	195.6	812.6	4781	608.3	39	275.2	547.9	117	37.7	168.1	241	38.9	97.0
1908	55.0	357.4	51.3	231.1	639.8	6710	1149.2	35	311.2	818.1	304	54.6	228.9	267	48.1	111.0
1912	55.0	951.2	13.9	263.1	1228.2	8553	1685.4	47	836.5	2539.0	1108	150.9	595.3	317	59.5	198.3

Sources: I. F. Gindin, *Russkie kommercheskie banki* (Moscow, 1948); *Russkie aktsionernye kommercheskie banki po otchotam za 1914 g.* (Petrograd, 1915).

[a] 1 = Own capital, State Bank; 2 = Treasury resouces, State Bank; 3 = Current accounts of savings banks, State Bank; 4 = Private accounts, State Bank; 5 = Total deposits and current accounts, State Bank; 6 = Number of state savings banks; 7 = Deposits, state savings banks; 8 = Number of joint-stock commercial banks; 9 = Own capital, joint-stock banks; 10 = Deposits and current accounts, joint-stock banks; 11 = Number of mutual credit societies; 12 = Own capital, mutual credit societies; 13 = Deposits and current accounts, mutual credit societies; 14 = Number of urban banks; 15 = Own capital, urban banks; 16 = Deposits and current accounts, urban banks.

availability of credit, especially for commodity circulation, and thereby directly promoted the nationwide development of Russian capitalism "in breadth."

When recession and crisis gripped the Russian economy after the turn of the century, the State Bank again sallied forth as the savior of tottering banks and industrial and commercial enterprises. It shouldered a considerable part of the crisis burden, and only its lavish support accounted for the survival of some leading St. Petersburg banks—the St. Petersburg International Bank, the Commercial and Industrial Bank, and the Private Bank.

During the prewar industrial boom (1909–1913) the State Bank concentrated its activities in two areas, already foreshadowed. As one of the largest commercial banks in the country, it again expanded credit to trade, especially on the periphery, in areas not yet served by joint-stock commercial banks. It also took a rather prominent role in financing the grain trade. At the same time, it continued to expand, on an ever-grander scale, credit to joint-stock commercial banks, and began to turn into a bankers' bank.

Despite all these changes in its activities, the State Bank—after 1894 directly under the control of the Finance Ministry—remained primarily an instrument of government economic policy. The concern for supporting state credit and monetary flows was always at the center of its attention.

In their initial stage of rapid development the joint-stock commercial banks concentrated their activities on discount operations, which showed a stupendous rate of growth (almost eightfold between 1870 and 1875), yielding more than two-fifths of gross profits.[14] The joint-stock commercial banks also had close ties to railway and industrial promoters and began to grant them ever-larger loans. This policy was in fact one major cause of the problems that beset the banks in the mid-1870s. To deal with the ensuing outflow of deposits, bank authorities had to make sharp cutbacks in their active operations and to be more discriminating in their credit decisions. As a result, in the years 1876 to 1880, bill discounting shrank by nearly one-half and remained at this level over the next decade, not rising again until the 1890s. Until then, joint-stock commercial banks had little connection to the growth of industrial production, preferring instead to invest a large part of their resources in state bonds and government-guaranteed railway loans—"solid" paper with a fixed rate.

The 1890s proved a major watershed in the development of the banking system in Russia, as the capital stock of commercial banks and their liabilities more than doubled over the decade. This time the Russian banks did not stand aside from the general economic boom or, in particular, from the vigorous industrial growth. The main thrust of their activity was the rapidly expanding trade turnover; bill discounting, credits against goods, and promissory notes increased nearly two and a half times. This growth constituted over half the increase in assets of joint-stock commercial banks. By 1900 about three-fifths of bill and commodity-secured operations were conducted in the provinces, an expansion of geographical framework largely attributable to the proliferation of branches of St. Petersburg banks (their number increased more than two and a half times). And if in the past St. Petersburg banks, engaged mostly in operations with state and guaranteed securities, were weakly connected with the provinces, they now began to establish their presence across the entire country.

Although by 1900 securities took second place to credits against bills and commodities, the operations of joint-stock commercial banks nevertheless remained of first-rate importance (see Table 6–5). But they had acquired a quite different form in

TABLE 6–5. Structure of Basic Assets of Joint-Stock Commercial Banks

	Bill and Commodity-Secured Operations[a]		Operations with Guaranteed Bonds		Operations with Non-Guaranteed Bonds[b]		All Basic Assets	
	(millions of rubles)	(%)	(millions of rubles)	(%)	(millions of rubles)	(%)	(millions of rubles)	(%)
January 1								
1900	602.3	49.4	169.9	13.9	345.1	28.3	1,218.9	100
1908	1,086.9	62.4	221.7	12.7	284.9	16.3	1,742.7	100
1914	2,584.2	52.6	381.2	7.8	1,619.8	33.0	4,913.8	100
Growth in								
1900–1908	484.6	80.5	51.8	30.5	−60.2	−17.4	523.8	43.0
1908–1914	1,497.3	137.8	159.5	71.9	1,334.9	468.5	3,171.1	182.0

Sources: I. F. Gindin, Russkie kommercheskie banki (Moscow, 1948).
[a] Bill discounting, on-call bills, credits on merchandise, etc.
[b] Own bonds, loans, on-call bills, etc.

the 1890s, for the main focus was nonguaranteed securities, primarily involving railways. Amid unprecedented industrial boom and the concomitant surge in joint-stock company promotion, these banks played a vital role not only in the formation of new companies and placement of their capital but also in the issue of additional shares and bonds for existing enterprises. According to I. F. Gindin's rough estimate, their participation in the growth of share capital and industrial enterprises between 1893 and 1900 amounted to about 150 million rubles.[15]

The economic crisis that erupted in Russia at the end of the 1890s took many joint-stock commercial banks by surprise. They were deeply involved in operations with industrial securities and had overloaded their portfolios with shares that could not be realized. The ensuing losses caused some of them to fail. But these were chiefly lesser banks, for larger ones obtained support from the State Bank and weathered the crisis. They scaled down their financing of industry, but continued to develop commercial credit, promoting its expansion to peripheral areas and the integration of sectors that were still weakly tied to the national economy. But, encouraged by the new industrial boom of 1909–1913, joint-stock commercial banks not only increased their commercial credit but also, with redoubled zeal, resumed their activities in industrial finance. It was in these final prewar years that they became undisputed leaders of the entire Russian banking system.

The formation of a banking system commenced in Russia at a time when it was nearing completion in Western Europe. It was only to be expected that the experience of Western European banks provided a model for the development of banking in Russia. The founders of joint-stock commercial banks in Russia significantly did not simply draw upon second-hand information and reports on European banks; erstwhile servants of foreign credit institutions even helped to form the backbone of the top executive personnel of the first Russian banks.[16]

Not that the Russian banking system replicated that of the West. On the contrary, the content and forms of activity of banks in different countries, though relatively uniform technically, could differ widely, depending on the local conditions—

economic, political, and legal. Hence, the banking system in Russia, just as in other countries, developed through a process of adapting borrowed experience to indigenous conditions. The assimilation of foreign personnel graphically illustrates the process: The chief officers of St. Petersburg banks, though foreign in origin, usually regarded themselves—and acted—as Russian businessmen.[17]

Foreign banks also influenced the development of the Russian credit system through direct participation in the establishment of joint-stock banks in Russia and the placement of shares. For the period before the beginning of the twentieth century we do not have proof that this participation led to the establishment of foreign control over Russian banks. Moreover, there are grounds to believe that foreign banks began to seek this control only when Russian banks sharply increased their role during the economic upsurge of the 1890s. Though due primarily to internal factors, the growth was also encouraged by the cooperation of Russian and foreign banks in two major areas: (1) the placement of government loans and state-guaranteed loans of railway companies, and (2) the financing of Russian industry.

Russian Banks in the International Financial Network

As is well known, the earliest Russian connections with international finance took the form of foreign state loans. The first such transaction dates back to a loan in 1769 from Holland. From that time onward the tsarist government resorted incessantly to foreign capital markets in search of funds to cover budget deficits. To make these loans, the Russian government usually enlisted the mediation of private banking houses. A striking example of this pattern is afforded by the court financier A. Stieglitz, who played a rather conspicuous role in securing loans in Britain and Holland in the 1850s. After his appointment as first director of the State Bank in 1860, Stieglitz—together with such bankers as Anton Fraenkel and Leo Rosenthal—continued for some time to play a prominent role in establishing companies or banks to attract foreign capital, either under the aegis of the Russian government, or jointly with representatives of European banks. The latter type of financial activity in the 1860s and 1870s gave rise to several key institutions: the Great Russian Railway Company, the Mutual Land Credit Company, and the Central Russian Land Credit Bank.

The Great Russian Railway Company

Founded in 1857, this company set for itself the goal of building and operating about 4,000 versts (verst = 0.6629 mile) of railways to link the main agricultural regions of the country with St. Petersburg, Moscow, Warsaw, and also with the Baltic and Black Sea coasts. Its founders included A. Stieglitz (St. Petersburg), S. A. Fraenkel (Warsaw), Francis Baring (London), Hope and Company (Amsterdam), Henri Hottinguer (Paris), Mendelssohn & Company (Berlin), and several directors of the French Crédit Mobilier, including Auguste Thurneyssen and Emile and Isaac Periere.[18] The capital stock of the company was fixed at 275 million rubles in silver, which was to be realized through a gradual issue of stock and bonds; the shares yielded 5 percent income, which was backed by a government guarantee, but the European and American financial crisis in the autumn of 1857, the Russian stock exchange crisis in 1859, and the company's speculative machinations and embezzlement had already plunged it into a deep crisis in early 1860. By 1868 the company, which was supposed to have promoted an influx of foreign capital for railway construction, had become deeply indebted to the tsarist government, its debts amounting to some 89 million rubles.

To support the company, the government sold to it the best state-owned railway line, which operated at a profit—the Nikolaevskaia Railway (Moscow–St. Petersburg). The sale, set at 144,437,500 rubles in specie, was arranged through two 4 percent loans, which were contracted on behalf of the board of the Nikolaevskaia Railway but with state guarantee through a foreign syndicate (the Baring Brothers in London; Hope and Company in Amsterdam; Hottinguer and Co., and the Comptoir d'Escompte de Paris). The first issue of the Nikolaevskaia Railway bonds in the amount of 75 million rubles in specie (300 million francs) appeared on the basis of the decree of July 18/30, 1867; a second issue in the amount of 69,437,500 rubles in specie (277.5 million francs) was authorized by a decree of March 25/April 6, 1869.[19] On September 1/13, 1868, the railway passed into the ownership of the Great Russian Railway Company.[20] In 1867 the Russian government used the capital obtained from the sale of the Nikolaevskaia and other government-controlled railways to establish a special fund for financing private railway construction. Further contributions to the fund were raised through the issue of consolidated railway bonds on foreign markets. These loans were contracted by the government after 1870, when it prohibited the issue of bond loans abroad by individual companies.[21]

By the early 1880s the government had reversed its policy of privatization of railways and had begun to consider the purchase of the Great Russian Railway Company, the largest private enterprise in the nation. The sale of the Nikolaevskaia Railway had consolidated the company's position, and by the early 1870s its securities enjoyed wide currency on foreign markets. That is evident, for example, from the total volume of shares represented at its general meeting on July 20, 1870 (Table 6–6).[22]

It is noteworthy that, despite the company's broad international connections, about 70 percent of its shareholders resided in Russia. The company's debt to the tsarist government continued to grow, and in order to repay it the company contracted new loans abroad guaranteed by the government. Thus, in 1883, to pay a part of the government debt (15 million paper rubles), the company issued a 4 percent loan through Hope and Company, Baring Brothers, and the Banque de Paris et des Pays-Bas for the nominal capital of 11,800,000 gold rubles (£ 1,880,000) at a rather low price— 71 percent. Real receipts from the loan amounted to 8.378 million gold rubles.[23] In

TABLE 6–6. Total Volume of Shares, Nikolaevskaia Railway, July 1870

Number of Persons	Location of Shares	Number of Shares	Number of Votes
470	St. Petersburg	79,149	1,765
34	London	13,401	335
28	Amsterdam	9,846	245
71	Paris	19,505	459
32	Berlin	12,000	300
TOTAL 635		133,901	3,104

1890, to settle accounts with the government but also to make improvements in the Nikolaevskaia Railway and to underwrite various other projects, the company concluded a new 4 percent loan for 15.625 million rubles in specie (£ 2.5 million) from a syndicate of banks (Hope and Company, Baring Brothers, and the St. Petersburg International).[24] Nevertheless, despite bond issues on the domestic and foreign markets and despite the company's control of such profitable railways as the Nikolaevskaia, St. Petersburg–Warsaw, and Moscow–Nizhnii Novgorod lines, by the 1890s it had become the biggest debtor of the Treasury for guaranteed capital; by 1894 its debt stood at 170.5 million rubles, which was 2.3 times higher than its share capital.[25] In November 1893 the government decided to have the Treasury take over the various railways belonging to the company.

In January 1894 an international syndicate of banks was formed to carry out the purchase of the company by the government. At the talks with the government the syndicate was represented by Baron Rosenthal (from the Dutch banking house of Lippmann, Rosenthal and Co.) and A. Rothstein (director of the St. Petersburg International). Participants in the syndicate included Lippmann, Rosenthal and Co., and a number of French, German, and Russian banks. The French controlled the single largest bloc in the syndicate, which immediately authorized, to meet current expenditures, the 50,000 francs that had been contributed by the bankers.[26]

By a decree of February 9/21, 1894, a large foreign loan was issued for exchanging the shares and bonds of the company. The loan was quoted at Amsterdam, Berlin, and Paris, and in St. Petersburg, Moscow, and Riga in Russia. The nominal loan capital equalled 113.6 million gold rubles (or 170.5 million paper rubles).[27] Thus, in 1894 the Great Russian Railway Company ceased to exist, all bond issues being converted into 4 percent government bonds.

In the 1860s and 1870s the Mutual Land Credit Company and the Central Russian Land Credit Bank, following the example of the Great Russian Railway Company, made attempts to attract foreign capital by means of mortgage credit.

Mutual Land Credit Company

Formed in St. Petersburg in 1866, this company held the right to issue 5 percent mortgage bonds denominated in metallic currency. This enabled it to place its securities abroad, and the company became very active in seeking foreign capital. Thus, the company issued thirteen series of 5 percent mortgage bonds amounting to 10 million rubles in specie each, and it placed a considerable part of them on European exchanges. The company signed four contracts with foreign bankers to handle these transactions for distributing 5 percent mortgage bonds. On December 15/27, 1867, the company signed a contract with the banking houses of M. A. Rothschild and Sons in Frankfurt and Rothschild Brothers in Paris for the issue of the first five series totalling 50 million rubles in specie. Though the company signed the contract with the Rothschilds, it was able to carry out the transaction only through the assistance of Berlin bankers Gerson Bleichröder and Friedrich Leman, who had close ties with the Rothschilds.[28] The banking house of Bleichröder and Co. took 6.2 million of the 10 million rubles issued in the first series.[29] The contract for the issue of the next five series (i.e., from the sixth to the tenth), signed on February 8/20, 1872, involved the same foreign banks as before, but this time included as well the Bleichröder banking house. This contract was later supplemented with a special treaty (signed on January 20/February 1, 1874, in Berlin), which bore witness to the growth of ties between the company and foreign bankers.[30]

On December 6/18, 1874, it signed a further contract with Rothschild and Sons in Frankfurt and Bleichröder in Berlin for the remaining series of mortgage bonds (the eleventh to the fifteenth). In July 1877 the company issued its thirteenth series and this, in fact, proved to be its last: By the late 1870s the company experienced a period of crisis and ceased all its foreign operations. In 1890 the Mutual Land Credit Company was transferred to the jurisdiction of the State Land Bank for the Nobility and its mortgage bonds remaining in circulation were then recognized as state bonds.[31]

The Central Russian Land Credit Bank

When the Khar'kov Bank appeared in May 1871 it was the first joint-stock mortgage bank in Russia, but within roughly a year nine more had appeared—the Poltava, Tula, Kiev, Moscow, Nizhnii Novgorod-Samara, Vil'na, Yaroslavl'-Kostroma, Bessarabian-Tauridian, and Don banks. In the autumn of 1872 the bankers Anton Fraenkel and Leo Rosenthal proposed to establish a joint-stock company called the Central Russian Land Credit Bank, for the specific purpose of placing mortgage bonds on European markets. In April 1873 the tsar approved the statutes of the bank. Apart from Fraenkel and Rosenthal, its founders included a group of commercial houses of St. Petersburg and Odessa as well as the Diskonto-Gesellschaft in Berlin, the Austrian Creditanstalt in Vienna, and the banking houses of Baring Brothers in London and Hope and Company in Amsterdam.[32]

The main function of the Central Land Bank was to purchase mortgage bonds of Russian mortgage banks and the bonds of urban credit societies and then, on their security, issue its own mortgage bonds at a lower interest but in metallic currency and dispose of them on foreign stock exchanges. The activity of the new bank was strictly controlled by the government. From 1873 to 1875 the bank issued five series of mortgage bonds. The first, fourth, and fifth series of 5 percent mortgage bonds totaling 35 million metallic rubles were issued in France through the Comptoir d'Escompte de Paris and with the assistance of the Paris banker Dutefois.[33] But in 1877, as a result of the fall of the exchange rate, the bank began to incur losses. Its revenues shrank even more after 1891/92, with the conversion of 6 percent mortgage bonds of Russian mortgage banks into 5 percent bonds.

In 1894 the government was forced to liquidate the bank and announced the exchange of its 5 percent mortgage bonds for state bonds of the 3 percent gold loan. The Russian 3 percent gold loan of 1894 (second issue), launched for this purpose and set at 41,625,000 metallic rubles of nominal capital, was placed mostly on the Paris Bourse. Organizers of the loan were the banking house of Hottinguer and Co. and Adolf Rothstein from the St. Petersburg International Bank. Apart from Hottinguer and Co., the participants included the Comptoir d'Escompte de Paris, the Banque de Paris et des Pays-Bas, the Crédit Lyonnais, and several private banks as well as the Société Générale de Belgique, and Lippmann, Rosenthal and Co. in Amsterdam. About 40 percent of the total was assumed by Russian banks: St. Petersburg International, the Russian Bank for Foreign Trade, the Volga-Kama Bank, the St. Petersburg Discount and Loan Bank, the Moscow Discount Bank, and others.[34]

Hence, all three companies examined here—the Great Russian Railway Company, the Mutual Land Credit Company, and the Central Russian Land Credit Bank—had the same fate: By the 1890s all had ceased to exist, having been liquidated or redeemed by the state with the active participation of the State Bank and through the issue of foreign loans. Nor was the record of these Russian credit institutions very impressive. Thus, the Great Russian Railway Company, in P. P. Migulin's view, caused an export of capital from Russia, for foreign bankers bought shares and bonds of the company at a nominal price, resold them to Russian investors at a higher price, and transferred the difference abroad.[35] Nevertheless, the joint participation of Russian and foreign banking houses in establishing these companies did contribute to stronger ties and further expansion of loan operations, especially for the purpose of financing Russian railway construction. Railway loans became a major dynamic in the formation and evolution of the Russian banking system.

Prior to the 1850s railway construction in Russia drew primarily upon internal resources and turned to foreign countries chiefly for the purchase of equipment and materials.[36] But in the 1860s Russian railway construction began to draw heavily on foreign capital to finance further expansion. To attract it, railway companies either applied directly to foreign banks or enlisted the mediation of Russian banking houses.[37] Thus the Odessa banking houses of Ephrussi and Co. and Raffalovich Brothers that took part in founding the Central Land Bank signed an agreement in October 1868 with the founders of the Kharkov-Kremenchug Railway Company for the issue of a bond loan for 10,725,000 metallic rubles (£ 1,716,000) and agreed to place it in London through Henry Schröder and Co. and in Berlin through the Diskonto-Gesellschaft. The main part of the loan was placed in London with the participation of Baring Brothers.[38]

These operations were supervised by the Ministry of Finance and the State Bank. The role of the State Bank as a major instrument of tsarist financial policy and its relations with European banking circles constitute a separate, complex problem; it should be noted here, however, that the State Bank helped to attract foreign capital to Russia (operating indirectly through other Russian banks by serving as guarantor or providing support), but also directly participated in some loan operations abroad. Thus, in the 1870s the third, fourth, fifth, and sixth issues of the consolidated bonds of Russian railways, carried out through the Rothschilds in London and Paris, proceeded with its participation.

As far as the participation of Russian commercial banks in railway construction in the 1860s and 1870s is concerned, very little information is available. All that is known is that the St. Petersburg Private Commercial Bank placed the bonds of the Riga-Morshansk Railway Company in 1866 and later supported the construction of the Orel-Witebsk, Brest-Graevsk, and other railways.[39]

Large Russian commercial banks began to participate on a regular basis in consortia formed in the early 1880s to float bond loans for Russian railway companies on foreign markets. In 1881 the St. Petersburg International Bank and the Russian Bank for Foreign Trade, which had strong ties with various German banks, concluded a syndicate agreement on joint operations of this type and, as members of a German consortium (Mendelssohn & Co., Deutsche Bank, and Diskonto-Gesellschaft), assumed responsibility for placing nearly half the loan for the Ivangorod-Dombrowsk Railway.[40] That same year the Deutsche Bank, jointly with the Wiener Bankverein, underwrote a new issue of the shares of the Russian Bank for Foreign Trade.[41] By the mid-1880s the Russian group of the German banks' consortium had been joined by the St. Petersburg Discount and Loan Bank. When 4 percent bonds of the Kursk-Kiev Railway were issued on the Berlin market in 1887, this St. Petersburg bank undertook to place 20 percent of the total loan, while the St. Petersburg International and the Russian Bank for Foreign Trade acted as subparticipants with the leading banks, the Diskonto-Gesellschaft and Mendelssohn & Co. In 1888 these three Russian banks took part (each bearing 25 percent of the total) in placing 4 percent bonds of the Nikolaevskaia Railway; the balance was taken over by English and Dutch banks. At the close of the 1880s the St. Petersburg International and St. Petersburg Discount and Loan Bank acted as intermediaries in arranging large conversion loans for the Russian Finance Minister, I. A. Vyshnegradskii, with French banks playing the leading role. Thus the share of Russian banks was 50 percent in the first conversion loan of 1889 (for 125 million metallic rubles) and 33 percent in the second loan (for 175 million metallic rubles).[42]

By the outset of the 1890s a syndicate of four Russian banks was active in financing railway construction: the St. Petersburg International, the Russian Bank for Foreign Trade, St. Petersburg Discount and Loan Bank, and the Volga-Kama Bank. Throughout the 1890s these four institutions placed both internal and external railway loans through a consortium of foreign banks, sometimes with the participation of the Moscow Merchant Bank, the Russian Bank for Industry and Trade, Russo-Chinese Bank, the Warsaw Commercial, and other banks. Relations in the syndicate of the four Russian banks were far from idyllic. The role of the leader was played by the St. Petersburg International Bank, which usually took a larger share of a loan than did the other Russian participants and, at the invitation of the German banks, participated in operations outside Russia.[43] But the St. Petersburg Discount and Loan Bank and also the Volga-Kama Bank tried to challenge the position of St. Petersburg International as the leader.[44]

By the terms of contracts the share of Russian banks in foreign consortia for the issue of Russian loans varied considerably (from 6 percent to 60 percent), but on the whole remained rather high. But this formal share did not always correspond to reality and could be revised by a special syndicate agreement of the participating banks. Russian banks, just as foreign banks, often ceded a part of their share to subparticipants (either Russian or foreign banks and banking houses) that, ordinarily, had belonged originally to the consortium.

The role of Russian banks in financing Russian railway construction increased sharply during the prewar industrial boom. From 1908 to 1914 nine Russian banks—the Russo-Asiatic, St. Petersburg International, Russian Bank for Industry and Trade, St. Petersburg Discount and Loan Bank, Russian Bank for Foreign Trade, the Siberian Trade Bank, St. Petersburg Private, Volga-Kama, and Azov-Don banks—controlled most operations for the promotion of railway companies, their reorganization, financing, and the purchase and sale of railway bonds and shares.[45] These same banks were active participants in the multilateral foreign (mostly French) consortia that issued the bonds of Russian railways. For example, these banks participated in issuing the bonds of the West Ural Railway in 1912 and Semirechensk Railway in 1913; although the original contract in both cases set the Russian banks' share at 64 percent, additional syndicate agreements limited the participation of Russian banks in profits to 30 percent.[46]

The same group of Russian banks also played a conspicuous role in placing the loans of Russian cities abroad. Thus, when the sixth and seventh St. Petersburg loans were issued in France for 29 million rubles (104 million francs), the Crédit Lyonnais assumed 20 percent of the total loan sum, while Russian banks had 80 percent. The Russian Bank for Foreign Trade, the Volga-Kama, Azov-Don, St. Petersburg Discount and Loan, and St. Petersburg International banks took 13 percent each, the Northern Bank 9 percent, the Russian Bank for Industry and Trade 4.5 percent, and the Siberian Trade Bank 1.5 percent.[47]

The factors that determined the share of participation of Russian banks in consortia for the issue of Russian loans abroad could differ and did not necessarily correspond to the interests of the banks themselves. For example, when a Russian 4.5 percent loan for 231.5 million rubles was issued in Germany and Holland in 1905, the Russian banks underwrote 24 percent. Finance Minister V. N. Kokovtsev himself insisted that the Russian group assume so large a share, hoping thereby both to satisfy the domestic demand for bonds of Russian foreign loans (which arose after the outbreak of the Russo–Japanese War) and to reduce the drain of Russian gold caused by purchases abroad.[48]

Beginning in 1899, Russian banks, under the aegis of the State Bank, took part in syndicates formed to counter fluctuations of exchange rates on the St. Petersburg exchange. On the eve of World War I a qualitatively new phenomenon appeared in this sphere of activity of Russian banks. In June 1911 a syndicate of five Russian banks (St. Petersburg International, Volga-Kama, St. Petersburg Discount and Loan, Russo-Asiatic, and Russian Bank for Industry and Trade) was formed for the purpose of buying and selling Russian securities on foreign exchanges. The syndicate was headed by the St. Petersburg International Bank. The share of each member bank of the syndicate was 20 percent. The syndicate agreement was originally concluded for one year, but was later prolonged and became permanent. The State Bank opened credit for the syndicate in the amount of 100 million to 200 million francs against securities.[49]

This attempt to regulate the purchase and sale of Russian securities on foreign exchanges reflected the growing influence of Russian banks in the system of international financial ties.

Russian Banks and Industrial Finance: International Aspects

Participation in the placement of state and government-guaranteed railway loans in the 1880s and the first half of the 1890s gave the Russian banks a kind of schooling in issue operations. They established contacts with banks and banking houses that acted as co-participants and subparticipants in issue consortia, and acquired a rather wide clientele for placing bonds. They developed such forms of bond placement as the granting of on-call loans on this security, which was then widely practiced by Russian joint-stock banks to perform operations with shares and bonds of industrial companies. All this provided Russian joint-stock banks with preparation for financing industry.

From the mid-1890s operations for placing industrial shares and bonds, both from existing and newly created companies, occupied a central place in the activity of Russian joint-stock commercial banks. To perform such operations and also to handle the issue of state or railway bonds, they formed bank consortia. These consortia usually included several "friendly" banks that attracted as subparticipants bankers and industrialists closely affiliated with them. Such operations gradually generated a complex network that facilitated the mutual participation of banks in industrial and various other joint-stock enterprises.

A study of the extant archival materials of the St. Petersburg International, St. Petersburg Private, and St. Petersburg Discount and Loan banks shows that by the end of the 1890s these banks had come to participate in industrial enterprises of broad scope.[50] Unfortunately, the bank archives are too incomplete to provide a full documentary picture of participation by Russian banks. But the main contours are evident from their connections with other joint-stock enterprises. The simultaneous presence of the same people in the governing bodies of two or more companies was an important tell-tale sign of "participation," for as a rule, such participation was a matter of direct personal control.

To be sure, overlapping leadership merely indicates such relationships and does not disclose the specific terms of content. But taken together, they provide an important index to the increase in such "participations" as a whole. Thus, by the early 1890s, the largest Russian bank, the St. Petersburg International, had ties with forty-eight joint-stock enterprises. These included two commercial mortgage banks, two insurance companies, three railway companies, three shipping companies, and over thirty industrial enterprises in such varied sectors as metallurgy and engineering, ore mining and coal, oil, chemical, glassmaking, sugar refineries, and flour mills. Similarly, another leading St. Petersburg bank, the Russian Bank for Foreign Trade, had connections with thirty-six enterprises. Such overlap in leading personnel also emerges from a study of the St. Petersburg Discount and Loan Bank, the St. Petersburg Private Bank, the Russian Bank for Industry and Trade, the St. Petersburg-Azov, the Kiev Discount Bank, and the Warsaw Commercial Bank.[51]

Thus, the banks gradually developed definite spheres of interest from what, at first, was a rather motley conglomeration of diverse enterprises. When banks acted jointly to place the shares of a particular enterprise, they divided up their participation in it and, consequently, mixed together the participation and placement of shares in the most bizarre fashion possible. Joint financing of industry, furthermore, directly abetted the process of grouping and aggregation of Russian commercial banks. The result was clusters of specific banks, intimately linked through their participation in various industrial enterprises. One group formed by the end of the 1890s included the St. Petersburg International, St. Petersburg Discount and Loan Bank, and Russian Bank for Industry and Trade. But despite this cooperation they were locked in fierce rivalry for leadership. The Russian Bank for Foreign Trade occasionally joined this group, but it generally strove to pursue its own independent policy. A special position was occupied by the St. Petersburg Private Bank, which cooperated in issue operations mostly with secondary banks and banking houses.

The rise of banking groups in Russia was closely connected with the incipient interlocking of finance capital. In founding industrial enterprises, Russian banks in the 1890s often acted jointly with foreign banks. As the Russian banks moved into industrial finance, they initially sought at least the symbolic support of the more experienced foreign credit institutions with which they had cooperated in handling state and guaranteed bonds.

At the same time foreign banks were founding industrial enterprises in Russia in the late 1890s, and they relied increasingly upon cooperation with Russian banks. Although the archival materials provide only an incomplete picture of such joint promotion operations, somewhat richer data exist for one role of the St. Petersburg International in such operations. Between 1895 and 1900 this bank collaborated with foreign banks and banking houses to found more than ten joint-stock industrial companies in Russia and abroad. Its partners included the Banque de Paris et des Pays-Bas (for establishment of the Russian Gold Mining Company, the Tula Copper Rolling and Munition Plants, and Bibi-Eybat Petroleum Co.), the Banque Internationale de Paris (for the Société Metallurgique de l'Oural-Volga), the Rothschild banking house of Paris (for fuel oil and electricity companies), the Dresdner Bank (in the Russian company for Hartman's engineering plants and the Russian Union Company), and the Deutsche Bank (Russian works of Siemens-Halske).[52] The fragmentary information available for other Russian banks suggests that they engaged in similar operations as well.

When French banks and affiliated stockbrokers began setting up special companies in Paris and Brussels between 1896 and 1898 to handle Russian industrial securities or gain control over them (Société de l'industrie houillère et metallurgique en Russie—Omnium), they found it necessary to solicit the participation of Russian banks.[53] Russian banks entered into the Great Russian Syndicate, a multinational association of banks and electrical engineering firms formed in 1899.[54]

To judge from archival materials on the St. Petersburg International and St. Petersburg Private banks, in their contacts with Western European partners in financing industrial enterprises in Russia they energetically stood up for their own interests and at times even tried to impose their will on them. Such ambitions are evident, most notably in the active role the St. Petersburg International Bank played in setting up the Société Générale pour l'industrie en Russie (SGIR) and the Great Russian Syndicate. A further instance was the attempt by the St. Petersburg Private Bank to infiltrate an electric lighting company that was founded in 1886 as a filial of the German Siemens and Halske Company.[55]

It is no simple matter to disentangle the relations between Russian and foreign banks in the late 1890s, all the more since they were partners in some matters, rivals in others. Yet there were certain tendencies toward aggregation and association here too. Thus, as the St. Petersburg International Bank developed ties with different French credit institutions (Banque de Paris et des Pays-Bas and Banque Internationale de Paris, the Rothschilds, and other *haute banque* firms), it eschewed cooperation with the Société Générale. By contrast, the St. Petersburg Discount and Loan Bank, the Russian Bank for Industry and Trade, and the St. Petersburg Private Bank gave preference to the Société Générale.[56] Among German banks, partners of the St. Petersburg International were chiefly the Dresdner Bank, Diskonto-Gesellschaft, and the banking houses of Mendelssohn & Co. and Warburg & Co. In rare instances it also cooperated with the Deutsche Bank, which ordinarily inclined toward ties with the Russian Bank for Foreign Trade.[57]

The crisis of 1899 to 1903 and ensuing period of flux and change temporarily disrupted the investment and placement activities of Russian banks. Then, too, the inflow of direct foreign investments also fell off sharply. It was not until the new economic upsurge that occurred between 1909 and 1913 that Russian–European bank ties reemerged, and this new era of collusion and cooperation has become the source of considerable controversy. Paradoxically, by 1914, amid a rapid growth of the internal money market and consequent reduction in the share of foreign capital in total direct investments, European banks actually increased their involvement—and influence—in a number of major Russian banks.

As previously noted, prior to 1900 European credit institutions participated in the capital stock of Russian banks, but rarely laid claim to co-management. Instances where the foreign banks appointed representatives to the boards of Russian banks were both rare and short-lived; the only significant exceptions here were the Russo-Chinese and Northern banks. The former, founded in 1895 at the initiative of the tsarist government but with the participation of both French banks (headed by the Banque de Paris et des Pays-Bas) and Russian banks (under the aegis of the St. Petersburg International), was a credit institution specifically designed for conducting operations abroad. The Russian government allotted foreign banks representation on the board but reserved for itself control over its activity.[58] The Northern Bank, created in 1901, was virtually a branch of the Société Générale and fully subject to its control. It was only in 1906, when the Société Générale decided to increase the bank's capital, that management came to be shared with another French credit institution, the Banque de l'Union Parisienne.[59]

But the prewar industrial boom brought a substantial new presence of foreign banks on the boards of Russian banks. Thus, in early 1910 the Russo-Chinese and the Northern banks (the former eking out a miserable existence, the latter on the verge of bankruptcy) merged to form the Russo-Asiatic Bank, soon the largest credit institution in Russia. A large block of its shares belonged to the Banque de Paris et des Pays-Bas and the Société Générale. The French and Russian participants had equal board representation; a Paris Committee—formed solely from representatives of the Banque de Paris et des Pays-Bas and the Société Générale—actually controlled the board's activity.[60] Similar changes were apparent in the St. Petersburg Private Bank and the Moscow United Bank: As a result of reorganization and increase in the participating capital stock, two French banking groups (Crédit Mobilier Français and Crédit Français in the Petersburg case; Banque de l'Union Parisienne in the Moscow case) obtained representation on the boards of the reorganized banks.[61] At the same time, board chairman A. A. Davidov was elected to the board of the Crédit Français.[62]

Further instances of foreign intrusion were apparent in ensuing years. Thus in 1911 a large packet of shares of the Russian Bank for Industry and Trade passed to the well-known London dealer Birch Crisp, who organized a special financial company in London called the Anglo-Russian Bank. As its representative, Crisp was elected to the board of the Russian Bank for Industry and Trade.[63] In 1912, when the Siberian Trade Bank prepared a new issue of shares to increase its capital stock, it admitted to its board two representatives of the Banque Française pour le Commerce et l'Industrie. Simultaneously, a board member of the Siberian Trade Bank was elected to the council of the French bank.[64]

In most cases, however, these incursions were short-lived. Thus the attempts of the Banque de l'Union Parisienne to dominate the Moscow United Bank came to naught; by 1912 the French bank lost its control and shortly afterwards its representation on the board of the United Bank.[65] Another example is provided by the experience of the Banque Française pour le Commerce et l'Industrie: In 1913 its representatives on the council of the Siberian Trade Bank were not reelected.[66] Although Birch Crisp retained his seat on the board of the Russian Bank for Industry and Trade, he failed to exert any practical influence on its activity.

But the question of French influence in the Russo-Asiatic and St. Petersburg Private banks is much more complex. It is also more important, considering the paramount role that the Russo-Asiatic Bank played in the economic life of the country on the eve of World War I. Although the matter requires further study, some preliminary observations can be made on the basis of correspondence between the head of the Russo-Asiatic Bank, A. I. Putilov, and the head of the Société Générale, Louis Dorizon.

From the outset of their collaboration, Putilov and his Paris partners were at odds over various matters. Part of the problem was the system of the bank management—"Board-Paris Committee," which proved to be very unwieldy. Moreover, Putilov and the heads of the Société Générale and the Banque de Paris et des Pays-Bas—Dorizon and Edouard Noetzlin, respectively—held different views on the proper direction of the Russo-Asiatic Bank's activities. The setbacks that the bank experienced in its first year—a result of the French side's refusal to support Putilov's proposals—precipitated the conflict. By mid-1911 Putilov had sent a number of letters to Dorizon, alternately threatening resignation and demanding greater freedom of action.[67] The outcome is evident from Putilov's letter of February 12, 1912 to Dorizon: "Since autumn, when more intimate and, I dare say, more cordial relations were established between us, I have regarded the Société Générale and the Banque de Paris et des Pays-Bas more as friends than as masters of the Russo-Asiatic Bank."[68] Judged by the materials of the Russo-Asiatic Bank and the documents of the Société Générale in the years 1912 to 1914, the Société Générale and the Banque de Paris et des Pays-Bas continued to exercise control over the Russo-Asiatic Bank's shares, but in its practical activity the Russo-Asiatic Bank was guided by its own program. In its realization the Russo-Asiatic Bank collaborated not with the Société Générale and the Banque de Paris et des Pays-Bas but with other foreign banks, in particular with the Banque de l'Union Parisienne. This was the basis of the subsequent activity of the Russo-Asiatic Bank, which, however, has so far received only fragmentary study.[69]

The history of Russian banks provides numerous instances where credit institutions were formed specifically for operations abroad. Two of these—the Persian Discount and Loan Bank and the Russo-Chinese Bank—have been the subject of substantial research and provide valuable insight into Russian foreign policy, since both banks were established in response to government interests.[70]

Prior to the early 1890s Russian banks had a mere three branches abroad. Between 1893 and 1900 they increased this number to twenty-four, but that was chiefly the result of activities by the Russo-Chinese Bank. By 1914 the total number of foreign branches amounted to thirty-four; half of these belonged to the Russo-Asiatic Bank in the Far East and had been acquired at the time of the Russo-Chinese Bank's liquidation in 1910. Its name notwithstanding, the Russo-Asiatic Bank turned its attention elsewhere and had little need for these branches; the only reason it did not liquidate them, apparently, was to maintain good relations with the Finance Ministry. The other seventeen branches were in Europe, including five in Paris and three each in London and Berlin. Although historians have advanced different views on the mission of these bank branches, it is difficult to offer any definitive answer: The branch archives have not been preserved, and the archives of Russian bank boards contain little correspondence with branches.[71] To judge from annual bank reports, the main task of branches was to conduct operations with Russian securities and payments on them.[72]

Sporadic references in the press, memoirs, and literature also touch upon the establishment of filial banks by Russian banks abroad, chiefly in France. Some of these pieces of information can be confirmed by the materials of the archives. In 1912 the Azov-Don Bank took part in the augmentation of the capital of the Banque des Pays du Nord, and as a result the president of the Azov-Don Bank, Boris A. Kamenka, was elected to the French bank's board.[73] According to the archives of the Banque de Paris et des Pays-Bas, the Azov-Don Bank possessed the majority of the shares of the Banque des Pays du Nord.[74] In 1913 the Siberian Trading Bank founded in Paris a filial, the Société Française de Banque et de Crédit.[75]

While this fragmentary evidence on Russian bank filials in France requires further verification and elaboration, their participation in financial or holding companies abroad is much better known. While the first activities date back to the 1890s, in the immediate prewar years the Russian banks no longer confined themselves to a partnership role in foreign financial groups, but took the initiative in founding a number of companies, especially in Britain, to acquire the shares of Russian enterprises and establish control over them. The most conspicuous of these was the Russian General Oil Corporation (RGOC), registered in London in 1912. It was a joint enterprise of a large group of Russian banks headed by the Russo-Asiatic and St. Petersburg International banks, and their partner for contact with the Western capital markets was the Paris banking house of A. O. Rosenberg et Cie. The participation of a British MP (Lord Carrick) in this undertaking, as a member of the board, was purely symbolic. The RGOC enabled the Russo-Asiatic and St. Petersburg International banks in 1914 to form a gigantic, if loose, association of no fewer than twenty oil-producing, processing, drilling, mechanical, transport, and commercial enterprises holding an aggregate share capital of more than 120 million rubles.[76] A similar case is offered by the Russian Tobacco Company, which served to establish an association of Russian tobacco enterprises. Founded in London in 1913, its main impetus came from the Russo-Asiatic Bank, which collaborated with a number of Russian banks and the English banking firms of M. M. Haes and Co., Higgins and Co., and Gers.[77]

Conclusion

It is clear that the formation of the banking system in Russia proceeded under conditions of close interaction with West European credit institutions. The primary determinant in this interaction was the fact that Russia embarked on capitalist development later than the countries of Western Europe. In the early stages this interaction consisted chiefly in the transfer and assimilation of commercial credit know-how from the West to Russian banks. The growth and maturation of the latter, however, altered the terms of this mutual interaction and gradually led to various forms of cooperation between Russian and foreign banks.

While the influence of Western banking capital on the development of Russian banks is indisputable, the primary dynamics and patterns of development derived from internal, not exogenous, factors. Foreign investment and banks, in fact, catered to the demands of the existing social system in Russia. They met the demand for railway loans, and supplied funds for the maintenance of landed estates, the conduct of wars, and the struggle against revolution.

While Russia's industrial growth and the capitalist evolution of its national economy dictated this high reliance upon foreign investment, cooperation between Russian and Western banks gradually became the central characteristic of the credit system in prerevolutionary Russia. As the role of Russian banks expanded, so too did the scale of cooperation, from the mere placement of state and guaranteed railway loans in the 1870s to joint ventures of industrial finance in the 1890s. As Russian banks branched out into trade at the turn of the century, they began to cooperate with foreign banks in financing foreign trade. All this left its mark not only on the structure of bank operations but also on the very organization of banking activity. Thus, joint operations to place state and guaranteed railway loans led to the formation of issue consortia, the primordial stage in the development of international banking groups. Joint financing of industry stimulated the growth of international and even multinational financial societies and holding companies. With respect to Russian foreign trade, cooperation of Russian and Western banks led to mutual participation in commercial and shipping companies.

Despite the lacunae in the data and literature, the development of Russian and foreign banking relationships passed through several distinct stages. The first was the decades of the 1860s and 1870s, when the Western banking model impressed itself upon a new, still emerging system of commercial credit in Russia. Although foreign credit institutions did help to found the first Russian joint-stock commercial banks and promoted the subsequent expansion of their capital, the available evidence does not suggest active business cooperation between Russian and foreign banks before the mid-1880s. From the late 1850s to the mid-1870s, some banking houses exhibited initiative, together with foreign credit institutions, in organizing enterprises to place Russian railway and mortgage securities abroad. But such efforts were unsuccessful and bore no broader, long-term significance.

In the 1880s Russian commercial banks became deeply involved in operations with state and guaranteed securities and, as a consequence, gradually developed business contacts with foreign banks. From the mid-1880s, Russian banks became more and more regular participants in consortia that had been formed by foreign banks to place state and guaranteed loans.

A further stage of development was the second half of the 1890s, when Russian–foreign bank relations focused increasingly on Russian industrial growth. But that came to a grinding halt in the next decade. The crisis and depression between 1899 and 1903, the Russo-Japanese war 1904/05, and the revolution between 1905 and 1907 triggered a serious overhaul in the relationship between Russian and foreign banks. Particularly conspicuous was the role of loans, which bore a clear political overtone, as intended for waging war and suppressing revolution.

These long years of crisis and depression left many Russian banks, even the largest, on the verge of collapse. To help save them the Russian government chose to tap foreign capital to finance their reorganization. As a result, the prewar economic upsurge in Russia was characterized by a greater participation of foreign capital in Russian banks coupled with the attempts of foreign banking groups to establish control over the premier Russian banks. But under the conditions of rapid economic growth and a substantial increase in the role of national capital in the industrial development of the country, these attempts led chiefly to closer cooperation between Russian and foreign banks. Relying on their connections with foreign credit institutions, Russian banks stepped up their foreign operations and even created a number of large financial companies abroad. The result was still closer connections and collaboration of national and foreign capital.

7

Banking and Finance
in the Danish Economy

Hans Christian Johansen

Industrialization came late to Denmark. In 1870 the economy was still dominated by agriculture, and about three-fourths of the population lived in rural areas.

In the previous years Danish agriculture had specialized in grain production, a large part of which was exported to England. The expansion of grain production had needed some investment in better tools, which, however, mainly was paid for from current earnings. Investment in new farm buildings had been less heavy and mortgaging on farms was therefore most likely to take place in connection with changes of owners. Loans would then often be provided by the seller or through special credit associations (see below).

The export revenue was mainly used to pay for the import of manufactured products and colonial goods, such as coffee, sugar, and tobacco. Most of the imports came from, or by way of, England and Germany[1].

Danish manufacturing used mainly handicraft methods and worked for a limited market. At the industrial census of 1871/72 only about 400 undertakings used steam power and most of the engines were small, less than 20 horsepower. The only exceptions were a few textile mills, some iron foundries, and a shipyard. The tobacco industry occupied many workers, but only three factories used steam power. Nearly all the industrial firms were owned by one or two entrepreneurs, and the requisite capital was provided by the owners themselves or by family members or friends.

Economic Development, 1870–1914

Between 1870 and 1914 great changes occurred in this structure. Agriculture's share of national production declined and the shares of manufacturing, construction, and services increased (Table 7–1). The period was also characterized by a high growth rate of total output, on average 2.8 percent per year with the best years after the mid-1890s, but with economic crises in 1877, 1885/86, 1901, and 1907/08.

The government adhered throughout the period to a liberal policy. There was little protection in the tariff act of 1863 and the rates were lowered still more in 1908.

TABLE 7-1. Changes in Danish Gross National Product, 1870–1914

Years	Annual Real Growth Rate (%)	Share of GNP in		
		Primary (%)	Secondary (%)	Tertiary (%)
1870–74	2.4	48	20	32
1875–79	1.6	44	20	36
1880–84	2.2	42	20	38
1885–89	2.1	37	22	41
1890–94	2.8	37	23	40
1895–99	3.5	31	25	44
1900–04	3.6	31	26	43
1905–09	3.0	30	25	45
1910–14	3.7	30	24	46

Source: Sv. Aa. Hansen, Okonomisk vaekst i Danmark, Vol. II, pp. 209ff.

Discussions in Parliament focused on other types of public intervention in economic affairs, but these did not materialize in actual legislation. The only types of economic activity administered by the state were the main railway lines and the postal and telegraph services.

Development within agriculture was influenced by the gradual changes in the relative prices of vegetable and animal products, which had started in the 1860s when increasing quantities of overseas grain arrived in Europe. Danish farmers reacted to this by a transition to greater animal production, especially between 1875 and 1900. At the same time an increasing proportion of the vegetable production was used as fodder, and new crops with higher nutritional values, such as turnips, were introduced. From the 1880s Denmark became a net importer of grain, and the grain export of previous years was replaced by an export of live animals, beef, pork, and butter. The largest customer for the new products was Britain, with small quantities exported to Germany. The new products emphasized high quality because of the rationalization obtained by centralizing part of the processing in newly established cooperative dairies and slaughterhouses.[2]

During this period agricultural production doubled. Early in the period new land was reclaimed, especially in moor areas in Jutland and through the use of dikes. Investment in new stables and other farm buildings and in livestock was also intensive, whereas there was only an insignificant increase in the demand for labor, in spite of the fact that animal production is regarded as more labor-intensive than is vegetable production. The surplus population in rural areas migrated to the cities or to overseas destinations.

Because the transition was accomplished in a period with declining prices and low incomes for the farmers, part of the investment costs had to be financed from outside agriculture, and capital import was one of the ways used to secure the necessary funds.

In manufacturing, the first wave of industrialization reached Denmark in the period between 1870 and 1914, and the highest rates of growth occurred between 1895 and 1906. Value added in constant prices quadrupled, and among the larger firms the growth of the production was even greater. The labor force, on the other hand, only doubled, which means that worker productivity increased significantly. This was due, among other factors, to mechanization. In 1914 about 16,000 enterprises used a total of 229,000 horsepower. The new industrial firms that were established or that expanded during the 1870s were beetsugar works, breweries, paper mills, and shipyards. Along about 1900, mechanization reached margarine, cement, and sulfuric acid production, among other industries. In several industries the mechanized firms captured market shares from old artisan workshops; in others they ousted foreign suppliers.

In contrast to agriculture, manufacturing in 1914 was still oriented to the home market. Only a few branches had exports of importance. Among them were the sugar works, the cement industry, the shipyards (which in 1912 had launched the world's first diesel-powered ocean-going ship, the *Selandia*), and part of the machine industry, which supplied a worldwide market with rotary kilns for cement production, cold storage plants for dairies, and lifts and other electrical transport equipment.

The industrial expansion before 1914 called for investment in buildings and machines to an extent that could not be financed from the traditional circles of owners and relatives. Most of the larger firms were incorporated, and a stock market developed in Copenhagen. Long-term funds were also raised by issues of debentures, whereas most of the short-term capital came from commercial banks.

Foreign capital played only a modest role. Among the few examples of foreign shareholdings were Hamburg merchants who subscribed for one third of the shares in the largest cement works in 1889, and British interests that tried to start another cement works, but failed, in 1891. British capital also participated in the largest railway coach factory, the "Scandia," in the city of Randers. The only example of loans raised directly abroad by Danish industrial firms was the borrowing undertaken by the sugar refineries in 1875 through the Merchant Banking Company in London.

Neither did subsidiary companies of foreign corporations play a role in Danish industrialization in the period under discussion. Among the few examples are a cigarette factory in Copenhagen established in 1913 by the American Tobacco Company, and Siemens and Schuckert, which set up a small factory for electrical products in 1904. It produced part of the larger installations undertaken by the German parent company.

A few Danish companies had foreign branch factories located in other Nordic countries and in Russia, Germany, and England. Among them were the margarine enterprise Otto Monsted and the engineering firm F. L. Smidth.

Much of the Danish infrastructure was modernized in the period between 1870 and 1914. The first railway line had been opened in 1847, but it was not until about 1870 that the trunk lines were built, and most of the branch lines were constructed even later in the century. To these lines ferries and railway bridges were added to connect the systems.

The first lines were built by private companies that were granted concessions from the state, each for an individual line. Several of the early concessionaires were British, and they also contributed part of the capital. Later Danish banks acted as middlemen, and also sold some shares abroad. Between 1866 and 1880 the state gradually took over the most important trunk lines and set up the Danish State Railway Lines as a special board under the Ministry of the Interior. Private interests continued in the branch lines.

The banks were also active in establishing new shipping companies in these years and in supplying them with sufficient capital to finance the transition from sailing ships to steamships. Danish and foreign capital was united from 1869 in Det Store Nordiske Telegrafselskab (The Great Northern Telegraph Co.), which laid cables in many places in Europe and the Far East.

The Capital Market

In 1870 the stock of negotiable bonds was still rather limited. Most long-term loans were, as mentioned earlier, obtained on an individual basis, and the state had not floated new domestic loans for half a century except for some small amounts during the two Schleswig-Holstein wars. The circulating stock of old state bonds had a value of 160 million krone.

In 1851 an act made it possible to establish so-called *Kreditforeninger* (credit associations or building societies). They offered loans against first mortgages on real property up to 60 percent of the value of the property. The money was raised by issuing negotiable bonds for which all debtors were guarantees. The half-yearly installments were used to redeem the bonds, which were issued in small denominations, and the joint liability made them a safe investment. In the first years the activities of the new associations were relatively modest. In 1870 there were seven associations in operation and they had issued bonds for 86 million krone, which was about the same amount as that of foreign securities owned by Danish citizens.

Between 1870 and 1914 few changes took place in the institutional structure, but the activities of the credit associations increased greatly to meet the growing demands from residential building and the trades.

A rough approximation of the capital market around 1914 is shown in Table 7–2.

Foreign Trade and International Capital Movements

The rich grain sale years had secured Denmark an international creditor position by 1870. In 1872 a bill introducing a new stamp duty on foreign securities was passed. Those securities that were registered added up to a value of 81 million krone (state-owned securities included). The most usual types were Swedish, Russian, and Nor-

TABLE 7-2. Estimates of Bonds and Shares in Circulation, 1914 (in millions of krone)

Debtor		*Creditor*	
Government bonds	350	Public authorities	60
Municipal bonds	250	The Nationalbank	30
Credit associations	1,900	Commercial banks	250
Shares	900	Savings banks	210
Debentures	110	Public trustees	50
		Life insurance companies	170
		Other Danish creditors	1,740
		Foreign creditors	1,000
TOTAL	3,510	TOTAL	3,510

Source: Balance sheets of the various debtors and creditors.

wegian state and railway bonds, but securities from several other European countries and the United States were also included. At the same time it was estimated that Danish securities of a value of 25 million krone were owned by foreigners.

From the mid-1870s the trade situation changed. Imports grew rapidly owing to increased demand for raw materials used by agriculture and the new industrial enterprises, whereas exports rose more slowly. The result was a deficit in the trade balance, which was only partly compensated by higher earnings of foreign exchange obtained by the Danish shipping companies (Table 7–3).

The resulting capital import was in the first years mostly undertaken by private persons. Foreign securities were sold off, and Danish securities were sold to foreigners. From the late 1880s the capital import was to a large extent institutionalized. Commercial banks participated during years of low interest in an effort to refund much of the internal debt, and they tried to sell many of the new securities abroad. From the mid-1890s both the state and private credit associations sold many of their newly issued bonds abroad, later in the period partly through a new public institution, Kongeriget Danmarks Hypotekbank (The Royal Danish Mortgage Bank), established

TABLE 7–3. Balance of Payments and Changes on Capital Account
(in millions of krone)

Years	Current Account		
	Merchandise (net)	Invisibles (net)	Current Account
1870–74	−88	101	13
1875–79	−258	235	−23
1880–84	−361	281	−80
1885–89	−411	321	−90
1890–94	−403	317	−86
1895–99	−572	395	−177
1900–04	−554	371	−183
1905–09	−675	327	−348
1910–13	−455	210	−245

Years	Changes on Capital Account				
	The Exchequer	The Central Bank	Commercial Banks	Other	Total
1870–74	47	14	7	−55	13
1875–79	13	25	−1	−60	−23
1880–84	6	6	3	−95	−80
1885–89	−1	12	10	−111	−90
1890–94	−51	6	13	−54	−86
1895–99	−91	−5	−11	−70	−177
1900–04	−44	15	24	−178	−183
1905–09	−45	−9	−12	−282	−348
1910–13	−52	18	8	−219	−245

Sources: Dansk Pengehistorie, Vol. I, 1968; Kj. Bjerke and N. Ussing, *Studier over Danmarks Nationalprodukt, Statistiske Undersogelser*, No. 24, 1958; yearly balances of the Nationalbank; public accounts.

TABLE 7-4. Geographical Distribution of Danish Foreign Trade, 1875-1914

Years	Britain (%)	Germany (%)	Norway–Sweden (%)	United States (%)	Other Countries (%)	Total (%)
Exports						
1875-79	41	31	22	—	6	100
1880-89	44	29	19	1	7	100
1890-99	58	22	12	1	7	100
1900-09	56	20	11	4	9	100
1910-14	60	28	4	1	7	100
Imports						
1875-79	25	36	15	2	22	100
1880-89	23	36	16	5	20	100
1890-99	20	32	15	8	25	100
1900-09	16	32	10	15	27	100
1910-14	17	37	11	9	26	100

Source: O. B. Henriksen and A. Olgaard, *Danmarks udenrigshandel, 1874–1958*, 1960.

in 1906. The Hypotekbank bought domestic bonds and issued new state-guaranteed securities, payable in French francs.

By 1914 Denmark had thus become a debtor nation. It has been estimated that the foreign debt in 1912 was about 1,012 million krone, i.e., about half a year's GNP, whereas Danish citizens only owned foreign securities valued at about 134 million krone. Table 7–3 shows part of this process. Among the changes on capital account listed under "Other," which totals 1,124 million krone for the entire period, there is probably included an export of about 300 million krone in state bonds, about 300 million krone of credit association bonds, and about 200 million krone of bonds issued by Danish municipalities. The remainder consists of shares, foreign credits given to Danish companies, and so on.

The Danish bonds were sold on a wide European market and were quoted on the exchanges in Hamburg, Berlin, Amsterdam, London, Brussels, Antwerp, Paris, and Zurich. The geographical distribution of foreign trade, on the other hand, was not influenced very much by the structural changes in the period. Britain and Germany remained the main partners (Table 7–4).

The Monetary System and Central Banking

In 1873 an act, which was effective January 1, 1875, replaced the Danish silver standard with a gold standard and introduced a new money of account, the kroner (DKr), in place of the rix dollar. (Two krone had the value of one rix dollar, and one kroner had the value of 0.403225 grams of fine gold. The par values to the most important international currencies were 88.89 DKr to 100 Reichmarks, 18.76 DKr to £ 1, and 3.73 DKr to 1 $ U.S.) Denmark retained the gold standard until 1914, but the rules were changed several times. For example, the Nationalbank (the central bank), which held the international reserves, was also permitted a fiduciary issue of notes in addition to those that had to be backed with metallic reserves; the fiduciary issue was adjusted from time to time to satisfy the increasing transactions demand for money.

In the first half of the nineteenth century the Nationalbank, which was owned by private shareholders, also functioned as a commercial bank, accepting deposits and lending to individuals. After the middle of the century, with the establishment of commercial banks, the Nationalbank gradually withdrew from that type of business and adjusted itself to the role of a bankers' bank. In 1907/08, when several commercial banks were in difficulties, it combatted the crisis by acting as a lender of last resort.

Between 1870 and 1914, therefore, the most important international aspects of the operations of the Nationalbank were to see that the reserves were large enough to back the note issue. As the commercial banks only kept small amounts of foreign assets, most of the changes in the stocks of gold and foreign exchange in the central bank were caused by foreign trade and international capital movements. To counteract unwanted effects from these transactions the central bank borrowed occasionally from foreign correspondents, mainly in Hamburg, Berlin, and London, and had a close cooperation—nearly a monetary union—with the Norwegian and Swedish central banks.

Foreign borrowing took place in 1874/75, but during the succeeding period with declining prices and an unchanged fiduciary issue there were normally ample reserves. After the mid-1890s the fiduciary issue was again increased, but even so the metal backing rules were not fulfilled around the half-yearly interest settlement dates in June and December. It was not until 1908, when a proportional reserve system was re-introduced, that sufficient reserves once again were secured (Figure 7–1).

FIGURE 7–1. Note issues of the Nationalbank, 1870–1914.
Source: Annual accounts of the Nationalbank.

TABLE 7–5. Currencies Used in the Bill-of-Exchange Transactions of the Danish Nationalbank, 1869/70 to 1913/14

	Currency (in millions of DKr)					
Years	German	British	Norwegian-Swedish	French	Dutch	Austrian
1869/70–1873/74	91	128	15	9	3	—
1874/75–1878/79	81	91	45	5	1	—
1879/80–1883/84	119	57	34	4	1	—
1884/85–1888/89	135	60	17	7	2	—
1889/90–1893/94	156	128	41	8	2	—
1894/95–1898/99	199	136	19	18	7	5
1899/1900–1903/04	132	107	21	28	1	—
1904/05–1908/09	185	125	12	8	1	1
1909/10–1913/14	372	359	192	67	3	15

Source: Annual reports of the Nationalbank.

Another international aspect of the Nationalbank's transactions was the trade in bills of exchange. Bills were rediscounted for the commercial banks and sent to foreign correspondents or used to meet the demand from commercial banks, which needed money for foreign payments undertaken by Danish importers. It is not known to what extent commercial banks had their own direct links abroad, but at least the big banks undertook important international transfers.

The volume of the transactions of the Nationalbank can be seen in Table 7–5. Most important, naturally, were the currencies of the great trading partners, but when the capital import started, the role of the French franc increased, as that currency was used both on several of the state bonds and on the mortgage bank bonds. The transfers to and from the Norwegian and Swedish central banks are not included in the amounts in Table 7–5.

The Danish Banking System, 1870–1914

In the early nineteenth century several savings banks began operating in Denmark. Their main business was to care for small depositors' savings, and right up to 1914 these banks had larger deposits than the commercial banks, although the difference was very small from about 1912. Because the savings banks had no international contacts at all, no further analysis of their development will be undertaken.[3]

By 1870 eighteen commercial banks were in existence, but about half of their total balances belonged to Copenhagen's largest bank, the Privatbank, established in 1857, and many of the smaller provincial banks were dependent on the Privatbank.

This bank's main transactions consisted of discounting foreign and domestic bills and lending on various forms of security. In some periods, such as the early 1870s, the bank also had a substantial holding of bonds and shares, and it is normally assumed that most were shares, since the bank played a decisive role in incorporating many firms in that period, acting as a *Grunderbank*. This became a very risky business when the boom ended, and in 1875 and 1876 all the bank's reserves were used to cover losses mainly from speculations in the shares of the Great Northern Telegraph Company.

Being that type of bank, it had to have a large share capital, and deposits played a more modest role in the balances.

There was in several influential circles in the capital a distaste for the *Grunderbank* idea, and shortly after 1870 that resulted in the foundation of two new large banks, the Landmansbank and the Handelsbank, each with its own specific profile. These banks are still today "the big three" in the Danish banking world.

The basic concept behind the Landmansbank came from Scotland. The idea was that the bank should open branch offices all over the country and especially in rural districts, where its concern should be to supply agriculture with operating capital financed by interest-bearing securities of low denominations. The financing scheme was, however, abandoned when it was realized that it would be considered a violation of the note-issuing monopoly of the Nationalbank. Instead, the Landmansbank, when it opened its doors in 1872, was divided into two sections, a "normal" commercial bank and a bond-issuing mortgage bank. The commercial section introduced cash credit loans in the Danish banking system, but its holdings of bonds and shares was very small until the 1890s, in contrast to the policy of the Privatbank. It was expected that Danish estate owners would subscribe for a large part of the shares in the Landmansbank, but they turned out to be very reserved in their attitude. The founders then raised about half of the share capital in Hamburg and Berlin, and in spite of several extensions of the share capital about half of the shares were still owned by Germans in 1914. The German influence on the daily transactions of the bank was, however, slight.

The prime mover behind the Handelsbank was the Copenhagen merchant banker D. B. Adler. He had close relations with England and was well acquainted with English banking practice. His aim was therefore to establish a commercial bank, the main business of which should be discounting of bills and other short-term lending to commerce, manufacturing, and agriculture. It was also in this case necessary to raise a considerable part of the capital in Germany (Hamburg) and smaller amounts in Sweden. The business started in April 1873 and a branch system was built up outside Copenhagen in competition with the provincial savings banks.

Between 1870 and 1914 many new independent commercial banks were also established in the provinces. The total number of Danish banks in 1914 was 140, but most of them were fairly small and the three big banks held more than half of the balances.

The structure of commercial banking changed also during this period. In the industrial expansion of the 1890s the Privatbank, now accompanied by the Landmansbank, was still actively engaged in company formation and in share-issuing operations, and shares most likely constituted a large part of the stock of bonds and shares in these two banks' balances. Several banks were also represented in the boards of many of the larger industrial and commercial enterprises.

In the following years up to 1914 the importance of this part of the banks' activities declined. The companies were now more likely to raise their long-term loans as debentures sold in an anonymous market and even abroad, so that the influence of the banks was exerted through short-term loans, where cash credits gradually took over the leading position, while discounting of bills lost ground (Table 7–6).

Coming thus closer to the English banking system, Danish banks had less need for large share capitals and large reserves; an increasing part of the available funds resulted

TABLE 7–6. Balances of Danish Commercial Banks, 1870–1914

	Assets						
Year	Domestic Bills (%)	Foreign Assets (%)	Other Loans (%)	Bonds and Shares (%)	Cash in Hand (%)	Other Assets (%)	Total (%)
1870	49	6	30	9	4	2	100
1880	28	7	29	15	6	15	100
1890	19	9	33	18	5	16	100
1900	22	6	41	13	3	15	100
1910	17	4	44	18	2	15	100
1914	16	3	46	19	2	14	100

	Liabilities			
Year	Share Capital and Reserves (%)	Deposits (%)	Other Liabilities (%)	Total (%)
1870	36	58	6	100
1880	38	54	8	100
1890	27	68	5	100
1900	23	69	8	100
1910	23	67	10	100
1914	19	71	10	100

Source: *Statistiske Undersogelser,* No. 24, *Kreditmarkedsstatistik,* 1969.

from deposits. By 1914 the deposits in the commercial banks had nearly the same size as those in the savings banks. In 1870 they had only amounted to one-quarter.

The growing importance of the commercial banking system can also be seen from a comparison with the size of the gross national product. In 1870 the total assets of the banks had a value of 7 percent of GNP. In 1913 it had increased to 59 percent. Similar comparisons with national wealth are not possible, as no reliable figures exist.

International Transactions of the Commercial Banks

The small banks had few, if any, direct contacts abroad. When they had to undertake international payments for their customers, they normally used one of the three big banks as a middleman. This division of labor also turns out in the distribution of the foreign assets of the commercial banks, where the three big banks after the late 1870s held more than 90 percent (Table 7–7).

The printed yearly accounts of the three big banks in their annual reports are very summary in their information about the nature of their international transactions. The Privatbank and the Handelsbank give the yearly turnover in foreign bills of exchange according to currency used, but not by types of transactions these capital movements cover. The distribution makes it probable, however, that the great majority were payments connected with foreign trade (Table 7–8).

Most of the business in bills of exchange took place with a limited number of foreign correspondents—banks and merchant bankers—in the large European cities. There were almost daily notifications of the transactions in letters or telegrams between the two banking partners in the payments. The content of the correspondence follows simple and formal rules. Two typical examples of letters received from British correspondents will illustrate the technique used.

London, 11 October 1879

Dear Sirs,
We confirm our respect of yesterday and received your favor of 8. inst. enclosing

	£ 2000.0.0 of 11. Jan.
%92 days 1%	£ 5.0.10
% stamp	£ 1.0.0

£ 1993.19.2

to your credit, val. 11. Oct. and advising your draft on us for £ 14.2.10 v. 20. Oct. Mess. Jacobsen and Steenberg drew on us £ 200.0.0 12. January for which we debit you.

We remain Dear Sirs
Yours truly

Manchester, Oct. 7th 1879

Gentm.,
We refer to our letter of 1st inst. and have today received your favour of 3d which brought us
£ 37.12.6 London and Westminster Bank
which is placed to your credit together with Kr. 6.62.
Enclosed we beg to hand you
£ 23.0.0 3/m from 3d inst., Th. Wessel and Vett with which please credit us in the usual way.

We remain Gentm.
Yours truly

An important international transaction undertaken by the Danish commercial banks in the period under discussion was issuing of Danish and other loans on the European capital markets. The normal procedure was that the Danish bank entered a consortium with participants from several other countries. The consortium took over the bonds from the issuing public authority and guaranteed the sale and the proceeds of the bonds on payment of a commission. Besides the Danish loans the most frequent types were Norwegian, Swedish, and Russian. The foreign banks that most often entered consortia, where one of the three big Danish banks were members, were the Stockholms Enskilda Bank, the Stockholms Handelsbank, the Centralbanken for Nor-

TABLE 7–7. Foreign Assets of Danish Commercial Banks (year end in millions of DKr)

Year	Privatbank	Landmansbank	Handelsbank	Other Copenhagen Banks	Provincial Banks	Total
1870	3.3	—	—	0.6	0.9	4.8
1880	9.0	5.7	3.9	0.1	0.5	19.2
1890	7.8	5.7	2.7	—	0.6	16.8
1900	8.5	6.3	7.2	0.2	0.9	23.1
1910	9.1	20.2	16.3	0.8	1.3	47.7
1913	7.8	17.4	17.7	1.1	0.8	44.8

Source: *Statistiske Undersogelser*, No. 24, *Kreditmarkedsstatistik*, 1969.

TABLE 7–8. Currencies Used in the Bill-of-Exchange Transactions of the Handelsbank, 1875–1913 (in millions of DKr)

Years	German	British	Swedish-Norwegian	French	Dutch	U.S.
1875–79	3	8	2	—	—	—
1880–84	2	9	2	—	—	—
1885–89	3	10	1	—	—	—
1890–94	5	21	5	1	—	—
1895–99	10	35	10	2	1	1
1900–04	26	50	16	2	1	1
1905–09	39	72	14	7	1	—
1910–13	48	98	11	12	2	—

Souce: Annual reports of the Handelsbank.

ge (Norway), Crédit Lyonnais, Banque de Paris et des Pays-Bas, Norddeutsche Bank (Hamburg), L. Behrens und Söhne (Hamburg), and C. J. Hambro & Son (London).

Conclusion

The Danish banking system that developed in the period between 1870 and 1914 played an important role in financing Danish industrialization. Only a few Danish industrial firms established branch factories outside the country, and the number of foreign-owned industrial undertakings in Denmark was rather limited, so that there was little international business for the Danish banks connected with multinational enterprises.

The two most important types of international financial relations were therefore import/export payments and participation in placement of state and municipal loans abroad. This business reached a stage late in the period where it was felt that a closer connection to the large Western European capital markets was desirable for the big banks. In 1911 a group of Scandinavian banks founded the Banque des Pays du Nord in Paris with a capital of 25 million francs, and in 1912 the same banks established the British Bank of Northern Commerce in London having a capital of £ 2 million.[4]

Appendix

Geographical Extension of
the Danish Banking System in 1914

The 140 Danish commercial banks that existed in 1914 had their domiciles spread all over the country. Only twelve were situated in the capital but had 68 percent of the assets; eighty-seven operated in seventy-three provincial towns with 28 percent of the assets, and forty-one small banks were situated in smaller market centers or other rural surroundings with only 4 percent of the balances.

The normal thing for a bank was to have all its business in one place. Only the Handelsbank and the Landmansbank were exceptions. The Handelsbank had a few branch offices in the capital and in seven of the larger provincial towns, and the Landmansbank had three offices in the capital and eleven more in provincial towns. The yearly balance sheets do not state the business of each of these branch offices. They have only figures for the headquarters and for the total business. During 1913/14 the branch offices had 27 percent of those of the Landmansbank. When working with geographical regions it is consequently impossible to distribute the transactions of these offices to the regions.

Nevertheless, some quantitative evidence of the penetration of the banking business into the various parts of Denmark has been reproduced in Table A7–1.

If bank resources per capita (column 5 in Table 7A–1) are used as a measure, the capital of Copenhagen comes out with a much higher ratio than the provinces, and

TABLE 7A–1. Commercial Banking Balance Sheets, 1913/14

Region[a]	Number of Banks	Balances (in millions of krone)	Population	Urban population	Balances per capita (in thousands of DKr) Total	Balances per capita (in thousands of DKr) Urban areas
Copenhagen	12	920.0	559	559	1,646	1,646
Copenhagen without branch offices	12	741.4	559	559	1,326	1,326
Provinces without branch offices	128	426.8	2,198	551	194	775
Provinces with branch offices	146	605.4	2,198	551	275	1,099
Sealand	38	83.6	537	96	156	871
Bornholm	5	7.0	43	19	163	368
Lolland-Falster	5	13.4	116	32	116	419
Funen	15	76.2	303	91	251	837
East Jutland	26	119.6	482	176	248	680
North Jutland	19	61.5	352	79	175	778
West Jutland	20	65.5	365	58	179	1,129

Source: Statistiske undersogelser, No. 24, *Kreditmarkedsstatistik*, 1969.

[a]For the regions, figures are without branch offices. They were distributed with 4 in Sealand, 1 in Bornholm, 2 in Lolland-Falster, 1 in Funen, 6 in East Jutland, 1 in North Jutland, and 3 in West Jutland.

TABLE 7A-2. Deposits of Danish Commercial and Savings Banks, 1913/14

	Deposits per capita (DKr)			Commercial Banks' Share of Deposits (%)
Region	Commercial Banks	Savings Banks	Total	
Copenhagen	1,109	343	1,452	76
Copenhagen without branch offices	736	343	1,079	68
Provinces without branch offices	153	311	464	33
Provinces with branch offices	248	311	559	44
Sealand	131	340	471	28
Bornholm	140	402	542	26
Lolland-Falster	75	321	396	19
Funen	186	561	747	25
East Jutland	190	270	460	41
North Jutland	141	252	393	36
West Justland	148	173	321	46
Denmark	347	318	665	52

Souce: Statistiske Undersogelser, No. 24, Kreditmarkedsstatistik, 1969.

TABLE 7A-3. Provincial Danish Banks Distributed According to Size of Cities, 1913/14

Size of City (population)	Number of Banks	Assets (millions of DKr)	Average (millions of DKr)	Number of Cities	Population (1,000s)	Assets per Capita (DKr)	Number of Branch Offices
Above 20,000	9	99.7	11.1	5	184	542	5
10,000-20,000	11	65.6	6.0	9	123	533	8
7,000-10,000	13	52.1	4.0	9	80	651	2
4,000-7,000	22	95.7	4.3	16	83	1153	2
Under 4,000	32	63.3	2.0	34	81	781	1

Source: Statistiske Undersogelser, No. 24, Kreditmarkedsstatistik, 1969.

outside Copenhagen the highest ratios are found in Funen and East Jutland. Since the two latter regions were the most urbanized, and it is well known that farmers joined the banking system as customers relatively late, it may be thought more appropriate to use column 6 as a measure, but the variations are now more difficult to explain, especially that the least urbanized region, West Jutland, has so high a ratio. There must have been many farmers in that part of the country, which have used the local banks, and especially the Varde Bank, the fourth largest outside Copenhagen, although Varde was a small town with only 4,816 inhabitants.

One reason for the local variations could possibly be the density of the savings bank system, since for small business this could be an equally well-suited monetary institution as the commercial bank. For the average savings banks the best available measure of their penetration of society is their deposits, and in Table 7A-2 these deposits are compared to those of the commercial banks. Total deposits per capita seem to reflect what is known about the relative income position of the regions—Copenhagen being the richest part of the country, and Funen, Sealand and East Jutland the richest parts of the provinces, whereas West Jutland was the poorest. The relative positions of the commercial and the savings banks, on the other hand, seem to have no connection to how rich the region was—with West and East Jutland as those with the highest commercial banking share—and that even though the branch offices of the Handelsbank and the Landmansbank, which were especially strong in these regions, are excluded from the calculations.

A different geographical division is made in Table 7A–3, where cities are grouped according to size. Most of the larger provincial banks are, as expected, found in the larger cities, but the bank resources per capita are, surprisingly, to some extent rising when smaller cities are considered. One explanation could be that the banks in the small cities had a larger proportion of rural customers; another was that the branch offices played a larger role in the big cities than in the small ones. If it is assumed that these branch offices on average had the same size as the banks in the same cities, the difference would disappear except for the group of cities that had from 4,000 to 7,000 inhabitants.

The main conclusion to be drawn from this modest investigation is that the Danish banking system had its greatest strength in the capital, which is natural as large-scale commerce and manufacturing was gathered there more than in the provinces. By 1914 the Danish banking system had, however, also penetrated into all urban areas in the country, whereas the savings banks still dominated in rural districts.

8

Sweden

Ragnhild Lundström

The Swedish Economy, 1870–1914

By 1870 most of the privileges and regulations of the "old society" had been done away with in Sweden. In some cases this had only implied a codification of what was already practiced. In many instances, however, it had been the result of a liberal policy embraced by a great number of the more influential Swedes, including the late king. The bank reform of 1864 contained both these elements. The ban on bank interest rates above 6 percent was abolished, but it had earlier been circumvented by banks charging commissions of various kinds and dealing in bills of exchange as sales and purchases instead of lending. The other part of this reform, which greatly facilitated the founding of note-issuing banks with unlimited liability, was the final result of a long political struggle concerning banks that dated from the early 1820s.

The parliamentary reform of 1865/66 replaced the Diet of the Four Estates by a two-chamber parliament, and also officially did away with the classification of the Swedish population into farmers, burghers, clergymen, and nobility, which for more than four centuries had formed the basis of representation but which in the middle of the nineteenth century was clearly obsolete. It came as no surprise that in this new parliament, when it first met, the landowners/farmers formed the largest interest group, soon to develop into the agriculturists' party.

The Swedish economy was still predominantly agrarian. Only one-eighth of the population lived in cities or towns, compared with one-fourth of the population of Denmark and two-thirds of that in England. This does not imply that the rest of the population was solely engaged in agriculture, however. In those days Swedish industry was to a considerable degree located in the countryside. This was true for both the old iron industry and for the sawmill industry that had started slowly at the end of the eighteenth century and by the middle of the nineteenth had developed fast enough to make Sweden the world's largest exporter of timber and lumber products. These industries were part of agricultural life, and vice versa. The fact—much lamented by economic historians and national income statisticians—that sawmill production was not included in official industrial production statistics until 1896 (exports were of course recorded) depicts the actual situation rather well. A great number of sawmill workers, and for that matter iron workers, did not work a full year in the industry until around the turn of the century. Most of the many seasonal workers also had their small

174

farms, and one can say that agriculture subsidized industry for quite some time. Cutting, transporting, and floating timber were classified as agricultural endeavors until well after World War II.

This was the period of Sweden's industrialization. It had all started before 1870, but the pace quickened notably, particularly during the 1870s, and even more so from the second half of the 1890s. Although recent estimates—by raising the initial relative level—indicate a somewhat less dramatic rise in GNP per capita from 1870 to 1914 than has hitherto been assigned to Sweden, the increase was substantial, approximately 2 percent per annum at constant prices.[1] It was among the highest in Europe and comparable to that in the United States.

The contribution (value added) to GDP of the industrial sector surpassed that of the commercial sector around 1901, that of agriculture about 1905 (see Table 8–1).

Sweden had a well-balanced, if still small, industrial sector before the big spurt. In the early 1870s capital goods accounted for 46 percent of total manufacturing output, almost totally made up by the iron and timber industries. Both capital and consumer goods industries developed at about the same pace except at the end, when the capital goods industries grew faster. In 1912 capital goods accounted for 52 percent of total manufacturing output.[2]

The consumer goods industries employed fewer workers in 1870. Also at the end of the period these industries had a considerably higher output per worker than did the capital goods industries. The malt beverage industry alone, with its 6,000 workers, had an output almost exactly the size of the iron ore mines with their 10,000 workers.[3]

This fact is very seldom stressed, if even mentioned, in Swedish textbooks on the period. The capital goods industries somehow seem more intriguing, and there were perhaps more dramatic changes within that sector. Manufacture of wood pulp increased while that of lumber products stagnated. Iron ore began to be exported. The engineering industry became more specialized, and the so-called genius industries were started: the cream separator, the telephone, ball bearings. The capital goods sector became more diversified.

When focusing on banks, however, one ought to consider these differences in output per worker between the capital goods industries and the consumer goods industries. More research on this matter is of course needed—there is also the question of the costs of raw materials—but profits and savings were most likely larger in the consumer goods sector, sheltered as that sector was behind tariff barriers from the early

TABLE 8–1. Contribution of Various Sectors to Swedish GDP, 1871–1915 (in millions of Swedish kronor)

	Agriculture	Manufacturing and Mining	Commerce	Total GDP
Average				
1871–75	460	158	246	1,295
1901–05	599	570	523	2,395
1906–10	770	838	679	3,130
1911–15	935	1,128	898	4,039

Source: Östen Johansson, *The Gross Domestic Product of Sweden and Its Composition, 1861–1955* (Stockholm, 1967), p. 150.

1890s. On the other hand, capital was much needed in the capital-intensive capital goods sector during this period.

Exports accounted for almost 20 percent of GDP in the early 1870s as well as in the early 1910s. This ratio rose to somewhat above 22 percent in the early 1890s, whereafter it declined. If exports are related only to production within the sectors that exported, this quotient was about twice as large in the end of the 1880s as it has been around 1850. From the end of the 1880s until around 1905 it declined, however. Both these ratios indicate that the home market became more important during the very period that showed the greatest increase in GDP per capita.[4]

Swedish exports became more diversified during this period. In the beginning forest products dominated, and there was also a sizable amount of agricultural goods, mainly oats, exported. The share of more highly processed commodities (pulp and paper, food, and engineering products) increased.

From the banks' point of view, the development of imports was probably more important. They surpassed exports in most of the years during the period we are examining. They had to be financed short term, but once sold to customers in Sweden they usually meant large profits to importers and a good source for the banks' deposit and other business.

Already by 1870 Sweden was well integrated in the international economy. Even though exports declined in importance at the end of the period they still represented a large share of industrial output—as in most countries with a small population—and Sweden was influenced by the fluctuations in the international economy. A boom in the 1870s ended with a crisis in 1878; another low point toward 1885 was followed by rising figures from the middle of the 1890s, then another slump in 1901 and somewhat of a crisis again in 1907.

Investment rose as a proportion of GNP; that was, of course, the vital element in the entire process. The ratio went from 7.7 percent in the early 1870s to 9.5 percent in the late 1880s, to 13.6 percent in the late 1890s, and above 15 percent after 1900. During the first five years of the 1870s, agriculture, transport, and building and construction each accounted for 25 percent, manufacturing for 18 percent. Investments in manufacturing did not surpass those in agriculture until toward the end of the 1880s. All through the 1880s they amounted to about one-quarter each. Only after 1905 did industrial investments surpass those in the transport sector.[5]

Investments in transport varied a great deal from one year to another, reflecting the pattern of Swedish railway construction, which was at its height in the period under study. In 1854 the Swedish Diet adopted a railway program according to which the trunk lines were to be built by the state, and bonds issued by private railways were to be guaranteed by the state. Loans were to be issued abroad for the actual construction, which was to be carried out gradually so that traffic on the lines already built could pay for the interest on the loans. Thus the Swedish rail network was complete by World War I. One-third had been built by the state and two-thirds by private companies, in which some foreign capital, mainly British, was involved.

The building of the railways was probably the single most important factor influencing the Swedish economy during this period. Although a study shows that most of the material, except rolling stock, was imported, the impact of the railways was still great in many other respects.[6] Railways brought market integration for large parts of the country, provided access to new natural resources, and meant decreasing costs of inventories, to mention only a few benefits. For the Swedish banks railways were of great importance. Railway bonds created a Swedish bond market. The foreign loans increased contacts with foreign capital markets and supplied welcome short-term deposits.

The Banking System

In view of its stage of development in 1870, Sweden already had at that time an exceptionally advanced and diversified banking system. The banking system had developed along two different lines because of differences of opinion between the government—the king in council—and the parliament, or Diet. Ever since 1668 the parliament had controlled the national bank, the Riksbanken, which originally had a monopoly on the issuing of notes. The government, to counterbalance this power, advocated imitating the Scottish banking system and gave charters to *enskilda* banks, banks with unlimited liability that were allowed to issue their own notes. The Riksbanken responded by giving subsidized loans to so-called filial banks, affiliates of the Riksbanken, although founded by influential inhabitants in several provincial towns and nominally independent enterprises.

This rivalry was partly solved in the early 1860s. The Diet of 1862/63 decided that subsidies were no longer to be given to the affiliates. A royal—i.e., government— decree in 1864 facilitated the founding of note-issuing joint-stock banks with unlimited liability. Obtaining a charter for such banks was now made a mere formality. In 1864 and 1865 twelve new unlimited banks were founded, thus doubling their number.[7]

The more liberal attitude of the Diet, which was clearly manifested in several new acts easing old regulations on trade and industry, also opened up possibilities of yet another type of bank, the joint-stock bank with limited liability but without the note-issuing right. Three such banks were opened in 1864. They were chartered under the Company Act of 1848 for ordinary joint-stock companies, and until 1886 there were no other laws regulating the business of limited banks.[8] Unlike the banks with unlimited liability, these joint-stock banks could therefore own shares. In fact, that was one of the purposes of these banks, or credit companies as some of them were named. They were modeled on the Crédit Mobilier.

The largest of these limited banks, the English and Swedish Bank Ltd., went into liquidation as early as 1870. It was an English firm with offices in both Gothenburg and Stockholm. During the few years of its existence it was by far the largest bank in Sweden with a share capital, both nominal and paid up, far exceeding the equity of any of the existing Swedish banks. Banks of the Crédit Mobilier type were premature, however, considering the stage of development of the Swedish economy. The English and Swedish Bank Ltd. had invested sizable amounts of money in Swedish ironworks and railroads, which did not yield immediate profits.[9]

The mistake of the English and Swedish Bank became obvious after only a year or so and thus provided a lesson for the other limited joint-stock banks. Skandinaviska Kredit, which opened its office in Gothenburg in 1864 and a branch office in Stockholm in 1865, rather soon concentrated on more regular bank business, although it had at times a larger portion of long-term lending than did other banks. Stockholms Handelsbank, founded in 1871 by dissenters from Stockholms Enskilda, upheld a very cautious policy from the start. These two banks were later—toward 1920—to develop into the two largest banks in Sweden, after having merged with several other banks. It is rather difficult to get at the exact number of Swedish banks in 1870. In 1864 there were twenty-four *enskilda* or unlimited joint-stock banks with the right to issue their own notes. The number of filial banks was twenty-two. As their charters lapsed they either discontinued their business or turned into or were merged with *enskilda* banks. There were also four limited joint-stock banks. When the regular bank statistics start in 1874 they record thirty-five banks, twenty-seven unlimited and eight limited joint-stock banks. These were and are here called *commercial banks*.[10]

In the early 1870s there were also over 300 savings banks and over forty mortgage institutes. Many mortgage associations were founded early but their number increased in the 1840s. At that particular time the need for mortgage credit was pressing, for the law giving equal rights of inheritance for both daughters and sons was extended to embrace also the estates of the nobility and the farmers. In the 1870s several new mortgage associations were founded, especially in the towns and municipalities.

As shown in Table 8–2, the mortgage institutions held the lead in lending until the beginning of the 1880s.

The period from 1860 to 1875 is considered one of the most expansive and crucial in Swedish banking. In addition to the introduction of joint-stock banking, the innovative role of A. O. Wallenberg and Stockholms Enskilda Bank, founded in 1856, merits attention. Stockholms Enskilda Bank assumed the role of a quasi-central bank that the Swedish national bank, Riksbanken, until 1897 refused to play. The note-issuing *enskilda* banks with unlimited liability—there were more than forty such banks, all in the provincial towns around Sweden—had to keep a reserve of legal tender, the Riksbank notes, for exchange on demand. As Stockholm was the center of commerce, all banks had to have representatives there, usually merchants for this exchange business. Wallenberg offered to assume this role for the provincial banks and to pay interest on the funds deposited. He also introduced bank money orders, which became a great success in Sweden, where they were not subject to a stamp tax as in Britain and Denmark. This naturally resulted in Stockholms Enskilda Bank receiving sizable amounts of short-term deposits for the beginning.[11]

Undoubtedly this had a credit multiplying effect, especially since the transport system of Sweden was still so slow. G. B. Nilsson, who has analyzed bank policy in general and the role of A. O. Wallenberg in particular, has pointed to other fundamental changes in banking that were attributable to Wallenberg. Stressing the role of bank

TABLE 8–2. Lending by Swedish Credit Institutions, 1870–1910 (in millions of kronor)

	Riksbanken (National Bank)	Commercial Banks	Savings Banks	Mortgage Institutions	Other Institutions	Total
1870	43	121	57	156	38	415
1880	66	287	121	289	64	827
1890	89	457	241	361	107	1,255
1899	130	1,046	382	353	192	2,104
1910	191	2,093	728	507	319	3,808

Source: I. Nygren, *Från Stockholms Banco till Citibank,* (Stockholm, 1985), p. 140.

money orders in making money more efficient, he also shows the devastating effect of the great reliance on note-issuing that the unlimited banks hitherto had had. They had been founded on the Scottish model but had become complacent with regard to deposits. The large proportion of notes outstanding on the banks' debit side made them keep large, unused reserves. Wallenberg considered it important to fulfill the idea of the Scottish/English commercial bank by increasing deposits; he introduced deposits on somewhat longer terms with higher interest rates. Wallenberg also introduced a completely different outlook on banking. Banking was business, and turnover should be fast. High liquidity was essential. His dream was that people would eventually regard banks as bakeries, to which they came daily. His banking policy also stressed short-term lending; he catered in the beginning particularly to the business in drafts and bills of exchange.

Wallenberg's policy was on the whole adopted by other commercial banks. The profits recorded by Stockholms Enskilda served as an extra impetus. Undoubtedly the Swedish banking system benefited from this change in attitude and performance. Circulation of the comparatively little money that there was became faster; velocity increased. Cooperation between the banks also gave a greater elasticity to the banking system.[12]

For a rather long time the structure of the Swedish commercial banking system remained as it had been formed during this transitional period of the 1860s and 1870s. No great changes occurred until the middle of the 1890s, and the number of banks remained virtually constant. In the 1890s the *enskilda* banks expanded by opening a great number of branch offices, mostly in the surrounding provinces and regions, and several of them also in Stockholm.

There was hardly any competition between the commercial banks themselves except as regards the three largest commercial banks in Stockholm. Nor was there any competition between the commercial banks and other credit institutions. In contrast, several regional networks were formed consisting of various credit institutions, insurance companies, and local authorities. One example of such a regional network is from the province of Skane, at this time one of the richest and best-developed parts of Sweden both with regard to agriculture and manufacturing. Skanes Enskilda Bank, founded in 1830, was the largest note-issuing bank, and during most of this period was also the largest commercial bank in Sweden. In 1885 it had a dozen members on its board. Five of these were at the same time directors, some even chairmen, of savings banks in the area; five were on the board of mortgage institutions, five served on the board of local railroad companies, one was on the board of two insurance companies, five were members of parliament, five were members of local or county representation, one was a mayor, etc. These were not the same people; there were only two of the board members who did not hold any such position, and one of them was the bank's vice president. The bank had fifteen branch offices, each with its own small board of directors consisting of a similar group of people. This example can be multiplied by practically all other banks.[13]

This picture of calm—and stagnation—started to change during the second half of the 1890s. In 1895 there began a new, much more rapid expansion of banking. The number of banks increased to forty-five in 1895, to sixty-four in 1900, and to eighty-three in 1908. All new banks were joint-stock banks with limited liability. From 1900 the number of *enskilda* (unlimited) banks started to decline. The issuing of notes was made a monopoly of the Riksbanken again by an act passed in 1897. All private issues had to be discontinued after 1903. It was also enacted that the Riksbanken would serve as a national bank and as lender of last resort. In 1900 the total assets of *enskilda* banks were still 50 percent larger than those of limited banks. In 1908 the figures were reversed.

The largest number of banks is recorded for 1909. Several new banks were founded after 1909, but this was counterbalanced by a large number of mergers. The merger movement had started earlier but its pace was much faster now and it embraced also the largest banks. The mergers resulted in banks with a countrywide net of branches. Seasonal and regional differences in demand for, and supply of, credit were now leveled out within the banks.

Commercial Banks and Swedish Industry

It is difficult to estimate to what degree the expansion of the commercial banks in the period 1860 to 1875 meant to new deposits and an extension of the bills of exchange business. There did exist a well-functioning private credit market at least in the larger cities. It consisted of merchants, merchant bankers, private bankers, bill brokers, and credit societies, most of whom accepted deposits and arranged for credit.

With better communications between themselves to even out regional and seasonal differences, and with different ideas about banking, the commercial banks offered a strong competition to the existing credit market. The banks took over and were eventually to dominate the credit market. The Swedish credit system became more standardized with commercial banks handling all kinds of business of their customers. The more specialized system that had existed gradually disappeared. But exactly when is difficult to say. Unfortunately, very little is known about this private credit market.[14]

It is very likely that a great part of the increase in bank deposits was due to the fact that several large bankruptcies had occurred in merchant circles during the 1860s and that banks were now considered safer. Greater safety also from the lenders' point of view played a role for the breakthrough of commercial banks. Joining together in a bank, even in one with unlimited liability, meant a spreading of the risks. Merchant houses, merchants, and private lenders were among the largest shareholders in the banks in the 1860s and 1870s; sometimes they were the initiators of new banks.[15] Banks became a new form for organizing their lending, as joint-stock companies became the new form for organizing other business.

From the borrowers' point of view, banks began to appear to be more efficient— lowering transaction costs—than the old "arms-length" system. Before, most large firms had had a special "loan manager" of their own to scout around for credits and to arrange for sales and purchases of bills of exchange.[16] From now on, they only had to turn to a bank, and the banks even offered their services.

Merchants served several functions. They were in charge of the sales of Swedish export products, they arranged credit until deliveries could be made, and they supplied long-term credit as well. The last part, though, was not included in the new program of the commercial banks. Several of the large merchants and merchant bankers were born abroad and had good connections on the Continent and in Britain. When the commercial banks began to trade in export and import bills of exchange they had to open accounts with banks abroad. Stockholms Enskilda Bank was the first Swedish bank to trade in foreign bills, and Skandinaviska Kredit followed. Both these institutions also started doing arbitrage business, apparently taught so by the Danish Privatbanken and its director Tietgen, who was said to be a master in such business.[17]

During this period when the banks gradually took over the bill-of-exchange business, Swedish export firms began to get their agents abroad. Even the banks took over some of the functions of the merchants and began to be market makers for their customers. The whole export structure of Sweden also changed. The importance of the old iron industry declined, which even stagnated in absolute terms. Later exports of lumber products stagnated. These were the two fields where the merchants had been experts and where contacts especially with the British market had been established. With the new markets of more processed products the old merchant houses were less familiar. Thus, the importance of the banks as intermediaries between producer and market grew in several ways. If the commercial banks wanted to keep their new customers they had to acquire better knowledge of both product and credit markets.

After the big increase in both manufacturing and banking in the first quinquennium of the 1870s, the period from 1875 to 1895 was surprisingly dull (Table 8–3). Many banks had invested rather heavily in railroad bonds that were offered in the railroad boom of the 1870s. Railroad bonds could be used as security for the reserves necessary for deposits. As deposits increased or when share capital was raised, the amount of bonds had to be increased. At times deposits increased so quickly that it was impossible to find safe lending to counterbalance them. Several banks, especially Stockholms Enskilda, were stuck with a large amount of railroad bonds, which they had acquired with the intention of selling, when they were hit by the crisis of 1878. Some banks were in great difficulties, and the Swedish Parliament decided to help Swedish banking by granting loans from the railroad fund.

Thanks to such a loan and to another loan from its correspondent bank in Britain, namely the Union Bank, Stockholms Enskilda Bank barely escaped bankruptcy. This

TABLE 8–3. Gross Swedish Investments, Bank Lending, and Capital Imports, 1871–1910 (in millions of kronor)

		Increase in Lending			
	Gross Domestic Investments during Period	All Credit Institutions	Commercial Banks		Capital Imports during Period
			Total	Loans	
1871–75	588	284	143	—	120
1876–80	741	128	23	15	184
1881–85	644	279	130	54	305
1886–90	667	149	40	40	304
1891–95	666	142	103	64	92[a]
1896–1900	1,242	707	486	195	246[b]
1901–05	1,496	680	411	268	437
1906–10	1,844	1,024	606	299	386

Sources: Ö. Johansson, *The Gross Domestic Product of Sweden and Its Composition 1861–1930*, pp. 130ff; I. Nygren, *Från Stockholms Banco till Citibank* pp. 140ff; E. Lindahl, K. Kock, *National Income of Sweden 1861–1930*, II, pp. 573ff.

[a]Capital exports, 8 million kronor.
[b]Capital exports, 23 million kronor.

situation was not to be forgotten for many years. In Stockholms Enskilda Bank it was spoken about as late as the 1920s. This traumatic experience forced the bank to maintain a high liquidity and large reserves thereafter.

Most banks now concentrated on consolidating. All the banks built up their reserves. Investments in manufacturing were also at a standstill during this period, until the middle of the 1890s. Investments in building and construction were substantial, however. Urbanization had begun, and investments by both central and local authorities were kept at a high level. A considerable number of bonds were issued during this period, both in Sweden and abroad (cf. Table 8–3).

Toward the end of the 1890s there began a new and much more rapid expansion of both industry and banking. Deposits, lending, and total assets of the commercial banks increased sharply (see Fig. 8–1 and Table 8–4). Commercial banks' assets followed manufacturing output (or vice versa) more closely than they did national income.[18]

An attempt has been made (Table 8–5) to find possible causal relationships. The factors involved are so many and so intricate that it is very difficult to do so. It appears that in the beginning of the 1890s bank lending—in connection with capital imports—led, and deposits followed. This may indicate (1) that capital imports were of immediate importance for the banks by supplying the negotiating and participating banks with temporary and short-term deposits; or (2) that it was important for the individual banks to keep their lending within their sphere of permanent customers and/or sphere of influence to avoid a leakage out to the rest of the system. In this last respect the networks of associates formed by the banks—as described in the case of Skanes Enskilda Bank earlier—would fit in well. When relating lending to domestic investments, though, it seems as though investments were leading. In 1893, for example,

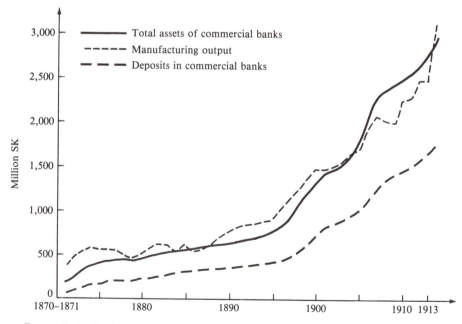

FIGURE 8–1. Total assets of, and deposits in, Swedish commercial banks, 1870–1913.

TABLE 8–4. Commercial Bank Deposits and Lending, Yearly Average, 1871–1913
(in millions of kronor)

			Lending		
		Bills of		*Current*	*Total*
Deposits	*Equity*	*Exchange*	*Loans*	*Accounts*	*Lending*
1871	90	55	48	42	29	119
1875	192	91	94	95	74	264
1880	243	100	94	109	65	266
1885	323	109	159	164	81	404
1890	346	106	165	203	69	437
1895	417	130	186	262	89	537
1900	738	250	321	454	215	990
1905	1,016	360	428	710	274	1,413
1910	1,457	562	579	993	470	2,044
1913	1,671	638	558	1,186	508	2,252

Sources: Sveriges Riksbank 1668–1924, Statistiska tabeller. For 1871, *Svenska Handelsbanken, 1871–1921.*

investments fell by 10 percent and capital was exported instead. The banks' receivables on their foreign accounts increased.[19]

In both boom periods, the early 1870s and the latter part of the 1890s and onwards, the amount of share loans increased more than other types of loans (Table 8–6). In the 1870s there were only a few banks that gave such loans, one of them Stockholms Enskilda Bank, which accounted for around 25 percent of share loans given at that time. Still in the early 1900s the percentage of share loans varied from one bank to another, but such loans were now much more common. It was not only the

TABLE 8–5. Increase in Deposits, Lending, and Capital Imports, 1890–1900
(in millions of kronor during year)

					Capital Account	
	Commercial Banks				*Capital Issues*	*Capital*
	Equity	*Notes*	*Deposits*	*Lending*	*Abroad*	*Imports[a]*
1890	1	—	5	30	42	69
1891	3	—	24	21	6	42
1892	18	—	3	36	—	35
1893	3	—	21	5	—	+7[b]
1894	7	2	9	14	27	15
1895	3	—	14	24	—	+1[b]
1896	2	4	21	32	—	+23[b]
1897	20	7	36	97	2	4
1898	31	7	71	112	16	62
1899	63	1	105	121	43	95
1900	4	2	88	91	61	85

Sources: Sveriges Riksbank 1668–1924, Statistiska Tabeller. E. Lindahl, E. Dahlgren, K. Kock, *National Income of Sweden 1861–1930,* Part I, pp. 268ff.

[a]As from balance of payments estimates.

[b]+ = capital exports.

TABLE 8–6. Types of Collateral for Commercial Bank Loans,
1875–1910 (percentage of all loans)

	Mortgages (%)	Bonds (%)	Shares (%)	Personal Guarantee (%)	Total Loans (in millions of kronor)
1875	30	7	24	39	95
1880	42	11	14	33	109
1885	54	7	13	26	164
1890	58	10	15	17	203
1895	53	12	19	16	262
1900	50	8	28	13	454
1905	52	8	27	13	710
1910	54	6	29	11	993

Source: Sveriges Riksbank 1668–1924, Statistika Tabeller.

large Stockholm, Gothenburg, or Malmö banks that lent against shares. Many provincial and very small banks had a large percentage of their outstanding loans through shares. Some of the new banks even seem to have been founded for the main purpose of giving share loans to their founders.[20]

There was now much more of a share market. Stockholm had a regular stock exchange and the banks were accepted as brokers. A somewhat wider circle of people began to be interested in shares with the introduction of the Grängesberg shares on the stock exchange.

As regards the banks' lending against shares, there are two factors that led to the increase. One was that a great number of mergers took place from the end of the nineteenth century onward. There was a sizable amount of both vertical and horizontal integration. Therefore, it rather often happened that firms borrowed with shares of acquired companies as collateral. The second factor was that several banks (or directors of banks) now took a more active part in the issuing of shares. Usually a consortium was formed and its members were promised loans against the shares issued. Banks themselves were not allowed to own shares until 1909 and even thereafter the amount allowed was still very small.

Although loans increased as a percentage of total bank lending after 1900 and although share loans as a percentage of all loans also increased, this fact must not be over-emphasized. In 1908, when such a comparison is possible, share loans given by banks only accounted for 15 percent of the total share capital of all Swedish limited joint-stock companies (exclusive of banks). In that same year, when share loans amounted to 272 million Swedish kronor, bonds issued by the joint-stock companies and placed in Sweden amounted to 432 million kronor and bonds placed abroad to 63 million kronor.[21] All the bonds had been placed by the banks.

Commercial Banks and International Relations

After several decades without a state debt, which was unusual for a former warrior country like Sweden, the parliament decided on the state railroad program, which implied large foreign debts. From 1856 until 1910 Sweden was in general a net importer of capital. Only around 1870 and in a couple of years in the early 1890s was

Sweden a net exporter of capital. Then rather dramatically Sweden became a net exporter of capital from 1911 onwards for more than fifty years. It has been estimated that Sweden in 1908 had a foreign debt of 1,200 million kronor, which is said to have equalled half of Sweden's national wealth. Of those 1,200 million, 250 million kronor were short-term debts of industry and banks. The state debt amounted to 460 million, and the General Mortgage Bank owed 135 million, almost exactly the same amount as did the city of Stockholm.

The debts of the cities and municipalities had increased with urbanization. The geography and demography of Sweden implied expensive urbanization. Water, electrical, and sewage services had to be duplicated many times over, and there was little to be gained from scale economies. Even before the welfare state Sweden had a larger public sector than did several other countries.

During and immediately after the World War I, Sweden purchased most of its foreign debt under very favorable conditions, when the Swedish currency was very strong as compared with those of other nations. Swedish bonds for 360 million kronor had been purchased before the truce at the end of 1918, around half of that from Germany. In the succeeding years another 300 million worth of bonds was purchased, of which two-thirds was from France.[22]

The first institutions to enter the foreign capital market were the mortgage associations. Sweden had a number of small local mortgage associations, but these found it difficult to raise funds on reasonable terms. In 1861 Sveriges Allmänna Hypoteksbank (Swedish General Mortgage Bank), modeled after the French Crédit Foncier, was founded. Its bonds, guaranteed by the state, were to a large degree issued abroad. At first the German market was most important, but later the French took over: In 1914 the French owned 99.5 percent of all Sveriges Hypoteksbank's bonds issued abroad.[23] The loans were negotiated either directly or by private bankers, of whom Stockholm had several. Private bankers continued to negotiate loans for both mortgage banks and cities during all this period; they did not quite disappear, although their number decreased, and very often they later cooperated with the banks.

The Danes were well ahead of the Swedes, more advanced and closer to the Continent as they were. They had rather early formed consortia with private bankers in both Germany and England. The Skandinaviska Kredit was admitted to the Privatbanken's consortium and Stockholms Enskilda Bank into the Landmansbanken's consortium, where the bank's director Glückstadt had good connections both with Hamburg bankers and with C. J. Hambro & Son in London. Stockholms Handelsbank engaged as its manager one of the most successful negotiators in the German market, Louis Fraenckel, who had extremely close cooperation with Warburg and Co. in Hamburg.[24] Stockholms Handelsbank headed the first Swedish consortium for issuing loans for Sweden. These produced good profits for the banks, and competition between the various consortia was keen.

Until the early 1890s the German and British capital markets were approached alternatively. K. A. Wallenberg, son of the founder of Stockholms Enskilda, who served an apprenticeship in the Crédit Lyonnais, managed to get into the French consortium. The Crédit Lyonnais cooperated with Wallenberg and did not act without his approval when approached by other banks. This was fortunate for Sweden because both the German and British capital markets had other interests. When large loans were issued in the 1890s and the first decade of the 1900s, practically all were first placed on the French capital market. Stockholms Enskilda Bank of course benefited from this; it received commissions and also short-term deposits. It returned the courtesy of Landsmansbanken and let Glückstadt have parts of "their" loans. K. A. Wallenberg, married to a Norwegian, also came to dominate the Norwegian loan market, mainly perhaps because the Crédit Lyonnais was the best contact to have on international capital markets in those days.

Competition increased, however, especially from Stockholms Handelsbank. In 1907 an agreement was signed by Stockholms Enskilda, Stockholms Handelsbank, and the Warburgs stipulating the terms of future cooperation. K. A. Wallenberg continued to act as the sole negotiator for Nordic loans on the French market. He had an agreement to the same effect also with the Crédit Lyonnais, which in its turn had agreements with the other large French banks that it would lead the French consortium. Warburg and Co. was to approach all other markets including the British. Side agreements were signed with the largest Danish and Norwegian banks as to their share.

There were great difficulties, not least for the foreign parties, to stick to the old consortia agreements when Norway, which had denounced its union with Sweden, wanted to negotiate its own loans (or rather its bankers did). New agreements were signed in 1910 and 1912. Stockholms Enskilda Bank still negotiated in France, but negotiations in Norway and Denmark were carried out by Norwegian and Danish bankers. Warburg and Co. lost its "right" to negotiate in Britain for the consortium. This was now left open to the Danish Landsmansbanken and to Stockholms Enskilda as well. Hambro & Son was approached first regardless of the negotiator. Warburg and Co. still had the monopoly to negotiate for the Scandinavian consortium in Germany, Switzerland, the Netherlands, and the United States.[25]

This does not imply that the Scandinavian foreign bond market was completely monopolized. Skandinaviska Kredit did not belong to the consortium. This bank, however, which earlier had been very active on the foreign bond market, had become quite complacent in this respect. New banks were founded, though, and some of them were very active in this field, especially the Sveriges Privatbank, founded in 1912.

The connections that the largest Swedish banks made by negotiating state and city loans were valuable also for Swedish industry, and this in many ways, both direct and indirect. Between the banks in the various consortia there was a rather genuine cooperation. Although Sweden was a net importer of capital during most of this period, it did not mean that foreign bonds and shares were not sold on the Swedish market. As for Stockholms Enskilda Bank and its connections, the Crédit Mobilier business of Paribas came to be of importance. The Wallenbergs and others around Stockholms Enskilda Bank were often offered shares in French consortia. In this field reciprocity was of course important. Neither Norsk Hydro nor the Swedish-Danish Telephone Co. would have been founded had it not been for the cooperation of the Crédit Lyonnais and, through it, Paribas. It was important for Swedish firms that wanted to go abroad that Swedish banks belonged to a brotherhood of bankers.

Conclusions

The Swedish economy developed in two steps during this period, one in the early 1870s, and the second from the middle of the 1890s onwards. The parallelism with the economic situation in Europe and Great Britain is striking. How much of the Swedish development was actually Swedish? Swedish capital imports were naturally of tremendous importance and must have raised the line above which the Swedish economy oscillated. From the middle of the 1870s until 1890 these capital imports were larger than internal savings.

It seems as though the Swedish banks in the 1860s took over at least the bill brokerage business from merchants and merchant bankers but that they did not to any considerable degree add to the proportion of industry's external financing. In the 1860s there might have been a credit multiplier effect from the decrease in reserves necessary and from the greater velocity of bank credit.

By 1870 Sweden had already a well-developed banking system. In fact, it was more developed and more diversified than even that of several economically more advanced countries. It did not stand back for the banking system of France, for instance. This indicates that the *idea* of deposit and commercial banking was the prime mover. The concept and system was first adopted. The development of the economy and of industry followed, although rather independent of the existing banking system.

Deposit and commercial banking was an innovation that had spread to Sweden from Scotland. These new types of banks were to the credit market what joint-stock companies were to production. It was a new way of organizing credit, which implied spreading of the risks involved as compared to the old type of merchant-house or private lending. The volume of credit need not necessarily have increased by the new banking system. The velocity did, though, and to a considerable extent. Lending on shorter terms and cooperation both between the commercial banks themselves and between the commercial banks and other credit institutions—savings banks, mortgage and insurance associations—meant a faster turnover of money. The institutionalization of credit contributed to the monetarization of the Swedish economy. It also implied lower transaction costs for borrowers of money.

Investment banking was premature in the 1870s, considering the stage of development of the Swedish economy. Those that tried, either as banks of the Crédit Mobilier type or as mixed banks investing in bonds or granting large proportions of share loans, got burned. Such experience usually discouraged other banks from trying for quite some time.

An internal market had first to be developed. Capital imports contributed to such development. They helped in building the Swedish infrastructure. Railroads, telegraph and telephone lines, harbors, schools, gas works, water powerplants—all implied not only more workers in construction but also more workers in transport, service, and maintenance—viz., more people in nonagricultural pursuits who needed to purchase their food and clothing in markets.

Sweden began to urbanize. The close cooperation between local authorities and credit institutions helped to finance this urbanization. The banks functioned as intermediaries between the Swedish and foreign capital markets.

Around the turn of the century Swedish banks took a more active part in the financing of industry. The banks' equity also rose considerably, both because new banks were founded and because the existing banks raised their share capital. The relation of bank equity to deposits increased to a level that was higher than even in the German banks.

Yet it must be said that investments in industry led and that banks followed.

Despite the difference in stage of development and pace of industrialization between Sweden and the rest of Europe, the trend of bank lending in Sweden looks almost exactly the same as in other countries. This does not mean that banks were of little importance for industry. On the contrary, banks were to industry what railroads were to transport and market integration.

9

Banks and Banking in Canada and Australia

Ian M. Drummond

In many respects Canada and Australia possessed similar financial systems. But in many ways the systems were very different. Our survey treats not only the commercial banks but also the "near-banks" and "semi-banks" that shared the field with the more conventional banking institutions; we also discuss the financial context, both domestic and international, in which these institutions worked. Summary financial data appear in Table 9–1.

By 1870 the financial systems of the two countries had taken the fundamental forms that they would maintain for the next forty years or more. Both lands possessed complicated and reasonably sophisticated systems of bank and banklike institutions, together with life insurance and other insurance companies, both domestically and externally headquartered. The period between 1870 and 1914 saw very considerable financial development, and considerable additional sophistication, especially in Canada. It also saw a perceptible displacement of externally headquartered financial institutions by domestic ones, even though there was no formal legal discrimination in favor of the domestic firms. Furthermore, one detects a noticeable extension of the spheres of action of the domestic firms, as they added branches and business activities outside their national boundaries. These new developments were important, but they should not be seen as a transformation. Nor did the domestic financial institutions become subordinate to external ones; although with the development of their own external businesses they certainly formed new links with British and American financial firms, these links involved no more than cooperation; they certainly did not involve subordination.

Before discussing financial history we must treat the constitutional framework. With the emergence of "dependency theory," both in its Marxist and its non-Marxist variants, there has come a renewed tendency to write of "dependent economies" only in their relation to the "metropolitan" power or powers. Where the dependencies are actually components of a formal empire, as with Canada and Australia before 1914, the temptation is even harder to resist. When writing about trading economies, which are capital-importers and are also on the gold standard, it is naturally not possible to ignore the capitalist world-system. Trade and payments do matter, especially for the financial

189

TABLE 9–1. National Outputs and Financial Statistics, Canada and Australia, 1870–1914

| | Canada (millions of dollars) | | | | | | | | Australia (millions of pounds) | | | | | |
| | Chartered Banks | | | | | | | | | Trading Banks | | | | |
	GNP	Total Assets	Total Canadian Deposits	Total Notes in Circ.	Total Assets P.Q.[a] Svgs. Banks	Total Assets Dom. & P.O. Svgs.	Total Assets Mtge. Cos.	Total Assets Trust Cos.	GNP	Total Assets	Total Aust. Deposits	Total Notes in Circ.	Net Liabil- ities[b]	Total Assets Svgs. Banks
1914	na	1,556.0	1,044.0	106.0	42.0	54.0	255.0	62.0	419.6[c]	175.1	155.5	0.3	−15.0[d]	87.8
1910	2,235	1,229.8	855.8	87.7	37.1	58.0	193.4	34.4	310.1[c]	138.8	126.5	3.7	−13.8	57.7
1905	na	815.5	523.7	70.0	29.1	61.9	149.4	20.4	221.0[c]	114.0	94.9	3.0	−7.3	38.3
1900	1,057	501.5	305.4	50.8	20.8	56.1	134.7	9.6	187.7	116.7	87.4	3.3	−0.3	30.3
1895	na	322.2	194.4	32.6	16.4	46.8	137.3	na	138.1	129.5	84.9	3.0	11.7	21.6
1890	803	260.1	139.6	35.0	12.8	39.4	122.0	na	203.2	151.3	98.6	4.5	20.2	14.6
1880	581	192.5	89.2	27.3	8.9	15.8	71.4	0	134.0	60.2	46.0	3.5	−6.0	6.2
1870	459	111.0	52.1	18.5	3.9	4.6	13.7	0	82.8	33.0	19.9	2.4	−0.7	3.1

Sources: M. C. Urquhart and K. Buckley, eds., *Historical Statistics of Canada* (Toronto: Macmillan, 1965), Series E 224, H 151 through H 234; E. P. Neufeld, *The Financial System of Canada* (Toronto: Macmillan, 1972), Appendix Table B; N. G. Butlin, *Australian Domestic Product, Investment, and Foreign Borrowing* (Cambridge: at the University Press, 1962), Table 1; Reserve Bank of Australia, *Australian Banking and Monetary Statistics 1817–1945* (Occasional Paper No. 4A) (Sydney: Reserve Bank, 1971), pp. 112–15, 125–6, 502–3. Australian trading-bank data are averages of weekly returns; Australian savings-bank data are totals of balance sheets ending in each year—predominantly on 30 June. Canadian chartered-bank data are year-end figures; data for other Canadian financial institutions are totals of annual balance sheets, and thus apply to no particular date within the year. Except for Canadian GNP, full annual runs of data are available in the sources cited here. Gross national product data are reported in current market prices.

[a]Quebec Province.

[b]Trading bank liabilities in Britain.

[c]Year ending.

[d]1913.

na, not available.

systems of small economies where prosperity depends in large part on exportation and investment. But local circumstances, aspirations, and policies matter also, and it would be the crudest sort of reductionism to see Canadian or Australian banking merely as the reflection of circumstances, pressures, and desires in the United Kingdom.

In 1914, as in 1900 or 1867, Canada and Australia were "self-governing colonies." The imperial Parliament in Westminster created them by linking colonies that had already enjoyed both internal self-government and "responsible government," whereby local cabinets were responsible to elected local legislatures on the Westminster model. The federating Acts transferred some powers from these old colonial legislatures to the new ones, but they did not add or delegate powers. In particular, they did not create something called "dominion status." In 1914 the governors-general could "reserve" local laws for consideration in Whitehall, which in turn could "disallow" such local enactments. Earlier in the nineteenth century such powers had been used with vigor, and financial measures, in particular, had frequently been "reserved" and sometimes "disallowed."

By 1867, however, that practice had fallen into desuetude; although the Colonial Stock Acts prescribed some of the terms on which colonial government securities could qualify for trustee status, Westminster neither regulated the financial affairs of the self-governing colonies nor legislated with respect to these affairs. Local autonomy was effectively complete, even in matters such as the currency, where colonial governors were supposed to refer all local enactments to Whitehall.

Thus in the Australian financial crisis of 1893 both Victoria and New South Wales enacted measures that affected the financial system. But in neither colony did the acting governor think of consulting London by cable. Both men assented, justifying their actions in seaborne dispatches. Six weeks later, meditating on these dispatches and on supporting documentation from the Agent-General of New South Wales, the Colonial Office routinely endorsed the colonies' actions.[1] In fact, except for routine statistical materials there is remarkably little in the Colonial Office records that in any way reflects financial developments in the self-governing colonies. Westminster could incorporate companies, especially banks, insurance companies, and various sorts of land and loan companies, which would do business wholly or largely in the self-governing colonies. But the colonial legislatures could regulate such firms, and could incorporate their own. Local law might sometimes prescribe special rules for externally headquartered businesses—as in Canada, for American and United Kingdom insurance companies. Imperially chartered firms, such as the Hongkong and Shanghai Bank or the Royal Exchange Insurance Company, had no automatic right to do business in Canada or in Australia. But United Kingdom firms were not thought to be "foreign," nor would it have been sensible to see them in that way, given the facts of common citizenship and common allegiance. Nor were there measures that discriminated against externally headquartered firms, or denied them access to local opportunities, although such firms were naturally required to submit themselves to local law and regulations. Discriminatory measures would not come until much later.

Canada's Banks and Near-Banks

The British North America Act of 1867 explicitly gave the new Dominion of Canada the power to incorporate banks and to regulate "the business of banking"; furthermore, the Dominion's own note issue, which co-existed with the Canadian banks' issues, superseded the preexisting note issues of the federating colonies. These colonies, however, now called "provinces," were given power over property, civil rights, and all matters of a purely regional or local nature. Their enactments, therefore, could indirectly affect the ways in which financial business would be done. Until 1891 the imperially chartered "Anglo-imperial" Bank of British North America enjoyed some minor special powers on account of its charter, but these were then legislated away.

Not only the Dominion but also the provinces could charter most types of companies, whether by letters patent under general legislation or by special acts that could and often did confer special powers. The so-called near-banks—building societies, mortgage loan companies, trust companies, and, after 1900, cooperative credit unions—thus enjoyed two routes to incorporation, with which went a choice between regulatory regimes. While the Dominion could "reserve" or "disallow" any provincial statute, these powers were not employed to bring about uniformity in financial matters.

By 1870 the framework of Canadian commercial banking had long been established, the pioneering days having occurred in the second decade of the century. There had always been unincorporated "private banks," operating essentially on English models, sometimes issuing currency in their earlier days. Even though in most regions they had lost the power of note-issue in 1838, their numbers would expand greatly in the last decades of the nineteenth century.[2] Yet although there is almost no statistical information about the operations of the private banks, it is agreed that if we could compare assets and liabilities of private and incorporated banks we would find that the private banks were of slight importance compared with the incorporated commercial banks, which were called "chartered banks," a term that by 1870 meant simply that a bank was a limited liability company. A few were Anglo-imperial banks, incorporated in the United Kingdom: In 1867 these included the small Bank of British Columbia, which had branches in that colony and along the American Pacific Coast, and the much larger Bank of British North America, which had branches in all the central and eastern British colonies of the North American continent. Much more numerous and important were the locally incorporated banks, each of which at first largely operated in its own locality. Branching, however, was in no way proscribed, although by 1870 branch networks were anything but extensive. Indeed, there were then several incorporated branchless banks. Among the chartered banks there was also one oddity: a limited-partnership note-issuing bank where the sleeping partners' liability was limited.

Locally incorporated banks did the larger share of the banking business, and that share tended to increase from 1870 to 1913. By 1913 the Anglo-imperial Bank of British Columbia had been bought by the Toronto-based Canadian Bank of Commerce, so that the only surviving imperial bank was the Bank of British North America, which had only 3.9 percent of the assets of the commercial banking system.[3] Furthermore, locally incorporated banks were as active in the larger world as were the Anglo-imperial banks. The Canadian banks had extensive dealings in New York, London, Chicago, Minneapolis, California, and the West Indies; in some of these places, especially in London and in New York, they held liquidity balances and operated an exchange business, while in other places, such as Chicago, they made extensive commercial loans, and in still others, as in the West Indies and to some extent even in London, they functioned as ordinary "retail bankers," operating branches and, in the West Indies as in Canada, circulating their own notes.[4] There was no systematic or important difference, in these respects, between the domestically incorporated banks and the imperial ones. They all did much the same things, in much the same way. It follows that if we were to concentrate our attention on "foreign banks" in Canada we would have remarkably little to say, and almost everything with respect to Canadian banks and foreign investment would be left out of account. Of course, if we redefine our topic so as to include Canadian borrowings through American-based or British-based banks, such as Glyn Mills, our story would become rather different. But our task is to describe local banking, not metropolitan arrangements. If we widen our focus so as to include the near-banks the story becomes a little richer, in that British and French firms were somewhat more significant in this sector of the financial system. Nevertheless, only two important mortgage companies—the Trust and Loan Company of Canada and the Crédit Foncier Franco-Canadien—were owned abroad, and, although these firms were large, they did not dominate the industry, nor did their practices differ in any important respect from the much more numerous locally owned near-banks.

Again, it is better to discuss the near-banks as a whole, not to make an artificial differentiation between domestic and foreign-based institutions. Admittedly the two big externally owned firms were unusual in depending wholly on external finance, neither attracting nor seeking to attract any funds within Canada. But this was, from the point of view of international capital movements, merely a difference of degree.

Savings banks were of some importance, although in Canada savings banks were, proportionately, far less important than they were in Australia, as Table 9–1 reveals. There were incorporated savings banks in Montreal and Quebec; these concentrated on lending to government, and after 1900, on such liquid assets as they could find. As for government savings banks, in 1867 the several provinces transferred their banks to the Dominion, which thereafter operated branch savings offices in some places, and a postal system everywhere; net receipts were treated as ordinary Dominion revenues. The chartered banks themselves, which offered interest-bearing deposit accounts of various sorts, did most of the savings business, leaving little role for the specialized savings banks.

On 31 May 1870, twenty-seven chartered banks were listed on the Canadian Government bank return. One had been erased through merger thirteen days earlier; one had already failed. Of the remainder, one was an Anglo-imperial bank, three had their head offices in New Brunswick, five in Nova Scotia, and eleven in the Province of Quebec. Although this last group included the very large Bank of Montreal, the banks of the three eastern provinces were, on the whole, small institutions, most of which as yet operated no branches, and some of which could not manage even to file the required financial return. Six head offices were in Montreal, and of these six banks, three small institutions were largely run and owned by French-speaking businessfolk.[5] In the Province of Ontario there were five banks, two of which were based in Toronto. But branch banking was far better established in Ontario than elsewhere in the Dominion; of the 123 branches existing in 1868, 100 were in that province.[6] Thereafter branch banking would develop rapidly and extensively. In 1902 the enlarged Dominion contained 747 branches; in 1905, 1,145, and in 1920, 4,676. The uniform Dominion Bank Act of 1870 explicitly provided that banks could establish branches when and where they liked. It also placed few barriers, beyond a minimum figure for paid-in capital, to hinder the creation of new banks. The result, thanks to new creations, mergers, failures, and the physical expansion of the Dominion, was as follows. In 1881 and 1891 there were thirty-six chartered banks; in 1901, there were thirty-four, and in 1913, twenty-five.

The geographical growth of the Dominion did not add many head offices: In 1873 the new Province of Prince Edward Island contained only two small banks, of which one failed in 1881 and the other was bought out two years later, while in 1871 the colony of British Columbia contained only the somewhat larger Bank of British Columbia, an Anglo-imperial bank, which had only two British North American offices in 1868 and which was bought out by a Toronto bank in 1900. In addition, there had certainly been some unincorporated private banks in western British North America when these territories became part of the Dominion, but most of them quickly passed from the scene.

Some interest attaches to the necrology of Canadian banks during our period. Mergers were comparatively few: only nineteen banks were erased through absorption from the beginning of 1870 to the end of 1913. Failures were rather more common—in all, twenty-three over the same period. These failures were quite evenly distributed through time, a fact suggesting that the usual explanation was individual incompetence, dishonesty, or bad luck, rather than any general panic or similar trouble. For instance, neither 1873 nor 1907 leave any particular mark on the Canadian bank-failure series. The failures, furthermore, were mostly of "small" banks—generally, indeed, of branchless "unit" banks. Only three of the twenty-three failures might be said to have involved "large" banks, and seven of the twenty-three were in the small towns of the Maritime Provinces, while another nine were in Quebec, of which four were francophone banks and two were in small towns.

Similarly, of the nineteen banks that vanished through merger, nine were in the comparatively small centers of the Maritime Provinces, and all but two or three were certainly small, even when based in Toronto or Montreal. Thus it would seem that a small bank, or a bank in a small town, had little long-run chance of survival. Furthermore, it is quite certain that in spite of considerable entrepreneurial activity in the smaller centers, head-office banking activity became strongly concentrated in Toronto and in Montreal, especially after 1900. Indeed, that date has some symbolic value, for in that year one Halifax bank moved its executive offices to Toronto; soon afterward, another Halifax bank moved its head office to Montreal, at the same time abandoning its locally oriented title in favor of a markedly nationwide one. Anglo-imperial banks, meanwhile, became comparatively unimportant, as the Bank of British Columbia was bought out and the Bank of British North America was outgrown and outmerged by the domestically headquartered banks.

Summary data on bank assets appear in Table 9–1. In Canada these assets grew almost continuously. In real terms, also, bank assets were rising. Intermediation was increasingly important, as bank assets outgrew national income.

Regrettably we can provide no summary data on Canada's unincorporated private banks, because they neither filed official returns nor, in general, published their financial statements. Even their numbers are only roughly known, in that counts of private banks have to be made from the commercial directories of the period. Although there were private banks everywhere in the Dominion at one time or another, these institutions were always concentrated in Ontario, which had at least thirty soon after Confederation and at least 137 in 1895, at which time there were at least 180 in the entire

Dominion.[7] Many private banks were in very small localities where there was insufficient business to support a chartered-bank branch, but where a private banker could
survive by combining his banking with other activities. Even in larger centers such
combinations were not unknown, although the city private banker was likely to specialize in exchange transactions. Such bankers often evolved into full-time brokers, while
in rural areas the private bankers were generally displaced sooner or later by chartered
banks as branch networks were extended, especially after 1900.[8] By the 1920s few
private bankers remained.

It is not generally thought that the displacement of the private banks, all of which
were domestically owned, caused any particular disruption of the financial fabric.
Some private banks, of course, went messily bankrupt. But these tended to be in out-
of-the-way places. Many private bankers became the branch managers of the chartered
banks that bought them out; some, presumably, continued to cultivate the other lines of
business in which most of them possessed footholds. Meanwhile, the contraction of
private banking was paralleled by development in other parts of the financial system—
in particular, the development of the mortgage companies and the growth of a much
more active new-issue market—so that by 1910 the financial help of the private
banker, who could lend as and how he liked with no regulation at all, was presumably
less necessary than it had been in earlier decades. Furthermore, the new industrial
development of the period was concentrated in cities and in larger towns, places where
chartered banks were well established and where the private bankers had no obvious
role to play.

As far as we know, after Confederation no private bank ever converted itself into a
chartered bank. One important chartered bank, however, was founded by interests that
had once been active in private banking. Additionally, it is possible that some mortgage
and trust companies were founded by private bankers, or by persons who would have
become private bankers if the profit potential for the near-banks had not become so
attractive.

Canada's chartered banks worked within a fully developed and elaborate code of
nationwide banking law—one that was refined and altered, largely on the basis of the
bankers' own representations, every ten years. Furthermore, the Canadian Bankers'
Association, after its formation in 1892, possessed powers of persuasion and regulation. The regulatory system could not and did not prevent all speculative excess, bad
lending, or the occasional bank failures; indeed, given the prominent role of the banks
themselves in the drafting and revising of the Dominion Bank Acts, it is reasonably
clear that if the bankers had wanted somewhat laxer legislation they would have gotten
it. Bankers' own caution, therefore, was at least as important as regulation, and the
failures among Canada's smaller banks suggest that Canadian bankers were not nearly
as cautious as they wanted the public to think. There was no domestic lender of last
resort, and none of the banks were bankers of international groupings that could be
counted on for automatic support in case of need, although some had friendly relations
with particular banks in London or New York.

Today we know little about such arrangements, and in any event it should be
remembered that relative to the New York banks of the time the large Canadian branch
banks were very considerable businesses. Hence, the importance of maintaining large
external reserves rather than relying on the circulation of one's own paper in London or
New York.

Among Canada's failed banks, the general pattern was obvious enough. Small chartered banks, or small private banks, would become unduly committed to a narrow range of local activities, commonly commercial but very often industrial. Bad trade superimposed on this sort of bad judgment would bring them down. For the sake of the note holders and depositors, and to protect the reputation of the banking system as a whole, the larger banks often absorbed the failing ones before actual suspension was necessary.

Another pattern appeared in the Great Canadian Boom of 1900–1913, when several new banks were formed. It later became apparent that the standard of banking practice among these new banks was not as high as one might have desired—perhaps, in part, because rapid expansion was putting great strain on the banks' ability to generate competent management through their traditional systems of in-house training and on-the-job experience. The Farmers Bank, the Sovereign Bank, and the Home Bank, all based in Toronto and all new, rapidly growing, rapidly branching firms, had short and unpleasant lives. The first two were messily insolvent by the end of 1910, and the third survived, with some difficulty, until 1923. Here there are obvious parallels with the Australian experience of 1889–1893, even though in Canada it remained the exception, not the rule, to find a bank in trouble.

Canada contained nothing closely resembling the puissant private banker of New York, London, or Amsterdam. It will be noticed that Canada's private banks were small affairs, and that most of them operated in rural areas. Nevertheless, among the brokers and the bond houses were to be found by 1914 certain specialized businesses that performed some of the same functions with respect to the issue of securities, not only at home but abroad. In this work they relied not only on financial assistance from the incorporated banks but, now and then, on deposits from the public. Furthermore, for all such businesses a network of personal contacts and "friendly relationships," not only at home but also in New York, Paris, Brussels, and especially London, was of crucial importance.

Besides the commercial banks, both incorporated and unincorporated, and the savings banks, Canada possessed numerous financial institutions that it is convenient to call, following present-day Canadian usage, "near-banks." The term may conveniently be used of financial institutions that were neither called banks nor regulated as such, but that received deposits, made loans, and sometimes, or generally, allowed some or all of their depositors to write checks. Such institutions, in Canada, were the mortgage loan companies, the building societies, some of the trust companies, and, after 1900, the Quebec-based credit unions known as *caisses populaires*. The *caisses* were of little importance until well after 1914, so we can ignore them here.

Because Canada's chartered banks could not lend on mortgage in the ordinary course of business, other financial institutions found a wide field in which to work. The first domestic building societies had appeared in the 1850s, although an imperial mortgage firm, the Trust and Loan Company of Canada, had been at work before that time. In the 1870s the domestic firms increased greatly in size and in number, partly by the issuance of capital stock within Canada, partly by receiving domestic funds on deposit, and partly by the issue of debentures, both in Canada and in Britain. In due course they were joined by a Paris-controlled enterprise, the Crédit Foncier Franco-Canadien, and, especially after 1900, by a variety of United Kingdom-based land companies that raised their funds in Britain, and in Canada held agricultural land and lent upon it.[9] The parallels with the Australian developments of the 1800s, which we shall later survey, are reasonably close. In 1913 only three non-Canadian mortgage companies were licensed to do business in Ontario, although some firms did business only in western Canada. The Trust and Loan Company, which had 4.9 percent of the industry's assets in 1899, had withdrawn from the province, and the total assets of the three remaining non-Canadian companies were 35 percent of industry assets; almost all of these assets, furthermore, belonged to the Crédit Foncier Franco-Canadien.

As for Canada's trust companies, the first was founded in 1882, and, like such firms in Australia, it was genuinely anxious to concentrate on trust and agency business; for forty years it refused to take deposits or to borrow in any way. Other trust companies, of which the number increased rapidly from the mid-1890s, proved less pleasant. Indeed, the later years of the Great Canadian Boom saw an efflorescence of dubious near-banks, almost all called trust companies, along lines that were broadly similar to those of Australia during the late 1880s. By 1913 the western provinces, in particular, were full of such firms, which financed much of the land and building speculation that was characteristic of these provinces between 1909 and 1913. The western cities were thickly spread with headquarters buildings and boosterish enthusiasm. By the end of 1913 the weaker of such firms, in a fashion that Melbournians would have found familiar, were already going to the wall, creating rage and dismay among their creditors in the United Kingdom.

All the Canadian near-banks faced some limitations on their powers of borrowing and of placement, but these statutory controls became less stringent with the passage of time, so that it is doubtful if any firms were ever really prevented from doing what their owners wanted, either in borrowing funds or in placing them: Legislators seem generally to have been willing to change laws in accordance with companies' requests. In the 1870s and 1880s, for instance, the mortgage companies' powers of placement were rather narrowly restricted to mortgage paper and some sorts of government security. But during the 1890s, when neither kind of placement was plentiful or remunerative, the companies pressed for relaxation, and legislatures obliged. Thus by 1900 many mortgage companies enjoyed almost unlimited investment powers, and some firms employed these powers to make loans on bonds and stocks, and to develop new business as bond houses.

Canada's near-banks became adept at tapping the flow of savings in France and Britain as well as in Canada. France was relevant because the Crédit Foncier Franco-Canadien, with one-third of industry assets in 1913, borrowed exclusively in Paris. As for Britain, Canadian and Australian overseas arrangements were much the same: United Kingdom agents would be appointed, especially in such cities as Edinburgh, where nonnegotiable debentures for terms of up to five years would be available on tap. In some periods, such as the later 1890s, the Canadian mortgage companies were able to reduce their dependence on overseas funds; in other periods, as in the later years of the Great Boom, they drew ever-larger amounts from the United Kingdom. All the near-banks made some effort to match the terms of assets and liabilities, although insofar as they relied on domestic deposits this was obviously not possible. Furthermore, in choosing between domestic and overseas sources of funds, they were responsive to the comparative interest costs of borrowing in the two markets. Thus the balance between domestic and external finance changed from time to time. In 1913, 37.5 percent of loan company liabilities were owned in the United Kingdom and in

France; in 1900 the figures had been only 20.5 percent for the United Kingdom and only 4.5 percent for France.[10]

There were friendly links between certain near-banks and certain chartered banks, although it does not seem that joint ownership was at all common. The National Trust of Toronto had close fraternal connections with the Canadian Bank of Commerce; the Bank of Montreal was linked with the Royal Trust Company; presumably to cause confusion, the Montreal Trust Company established some community of interest with the Royal Bank. These connections underline the fact that a Canadian trust company was not a bank. Its placement policies were subject to regulation on a different set of principles; it could not issue its own paper currency under any circumstances whatever; it could make mortgage loans, and usually did so on a very large scale, while many of its other assets would consist of long-term government securities—paper that the chartered banks would hold only in small quantities, or not at all. Yet a trust company would be a near-bank insofar as it took deposits and allowed depositors to draw checks; conversely, in that chartered banks operated very large savings departments, the Canadian banks themselves had certain resemblances to the near-banks of some other countries.

A rapid development of Canadian insurance firms, especially in life insurance, occurred during our period. As with banking, a large proportion of the new business was written by domestically headquartered companies, even though British and American firms were also present and active. The domestic firms extended their businesses beyond Canada's borders. Their accumulating funds provided important local markets for mortgage paper, government securities, and, especially after 1900, the bonds and stocks of utilities and industrial firms.[11] But by no stretch of the terminology can an insurance company be called a bank. Hence we shall give no space here to these large and thriving businesses.

In most respects the needs that Canada's banking system had to fill were not unusual. There was, first of all, the need for a circulating paper medium that could be converted into gold at a fixed price, and which the public would be willing to hold and use. In earlier days there was often a physical shortage of "hard money," combined with a general messiness arising from almost medieval perplexities about monies of account and the valuations of various circulating coins, both imperial and foreign. Economists would assert that there can never really be a "shortage of money," but we should not ignore the utility of circulating convertible paper.[12] Hence the central role of the incorporated commercial banks in the maintenance of external reserves and in the operation of the gold standard. It is true that the gold standard was "supported" throughout our period by government gold reserves, which ensured the gold-convertibility of the Dominion's own note issue. In that the role of such reserves appears to have been entirely legalistic and unmanaged, it was really the chartered banks that "operated" the gold standard. Any of the larger banks, regardless of ownership, might sometimes find itself supporting the external reserve position by borrowing in London, and Canadian banks might also borrow in New York, although it appears that they rarely did so. The overseas borrowings of the near-banks could also be important, from time to time, in supplying foreign exchange.

In the British North American colonies there was generally a lively demand for commercial credit and for funds with which production could be financed—important matters for economies where so much production was on an annual cycle and where markets and sources of supply were so far away. The chain of trade credit could meet many of these needs, but banks of discount and advance could find plenty of colonial business at remunerative rates. Because external trade and payments bulked large in these colonial economies, there was plenty of exchange business for colonial banks to do. Furthermore, there was a strong local demand for mortgage credit. Canadian chartered banks were not allowed to lend on mortgage, but the efflorescence of mortgage loan companies, the large flow of mortgage funds through the life insurance companies, and the rather later development of the trust companies, all helped to fill the institutional gap that might otherwise have emerged. And because interest rates were often higher in the colonies than in Britain and Europe, it was natural that banks and near-banks often borrowed overseas—partly by circulating their own paper, partly by taking deposits, and partly by issuing longer-term obligations on their own accounts.

With the development of locally owned manufacturing came demands for bank advances to manufacturers, not just to trade or primary production; the elaboration of local wholesale and retail trade would also create new demands, as would the commercialization and intensification of agriculture. The mining industry itself, as it adopted more capital-intensive methods and as new ore bodies were opened up, especially after the mid-1890s, became an eager absorber of capital. Canada's banks were often accused of shunning such very risky enterprises. But equity capital, whether domestic or external, generally proved easy to raise. Finally, insofar as Canada produced gold and silver in considerable quantity, from time to time the banks performed useful service with respect to the monetization, storage, and transfer of these precious metals.

The banking system, in turn, could grow insofar as it could convince the public to hold its liabilities. The rapid economic development of the period naturally created a growing demand for transactions and precautionary balances. And as far as the near-banks were concerned, overseas holders could be brought into the picture by the offer of attractive interest rates.

Because Canada was generally a capital importer it is natural to ask if the banks assisted in the process of capital importation and, if so, to what extent. It is now known that in London both the chartered banks and the trust companies became involved in floating the long-term obligations of others, especially of governments but also of Canadian-owned public utilities and industrial corporations. Furthermore, at least some large Canadian banks, in an effort to increase their turnovers, made serious efforts to attract American direct investment: These efforts, which seem to be concentrated in the years after 1900, would in due course involve credits from the domestic banks to the foreign-owned firms in trade, manufacturing, and perhaps mining.[13] Regrettably, the nature of the data, and the character of the international investment processes, make it hard to state what proportion of international capital flows were mediated, in one way or another, by the banking systems. Therefore, it seems better to describe the problems and procedures that can yield an impressionistic answer, rather than to present estimates in tabular form. We will begin with the years of the Great Boom.

From 1895 through 1914 Canada and its provinces raised some $187 million in London, almost all with the assistance of the Canadian banks. In addition, from 1897 through 1914 the overseas obligations of the Ontario-registered mortgage companies increased by $32.9 million. From 1900 through 1914, external capital invested in Canada rose by $2.6 billion.[14] Comparing these numbers, it appears that less than 10 percent of Canada's capital imports were actually mediated through the banking system. This percentage, however, ignores the raising of railway and municipal capital. During the years for which data are available the municipalities raised $216.4 million abroad. Most of these issues were purchased and then resold by the Canadian bond houses, but Canadian banks handled some directly, and in the background they were providing the finance on which the bond houses worked.[15]

As for the railways, although the Bank of Montreal provided interim finance to the Canadian Pacific, the Grand Trunk and Canadian Pacific made their own arrangements for London issues, while the newly fledged and high flying Canadian Northern (CN) relied on Canadian financial interests to manage its overseas borrowings, with the assistance of associated financial houses in London. By 1916 the CN owed $327.3 million, of which only $26 million of the general funded debt, $25 million in income-dependent convertible debenture stock, and $16.9 million in equipment bonds, had been denominated in dollars.[16] Thus at least $259 million of the railway's debt was owed in Britain, and sizable proportions of the dollar-denominated obligations were also owed there. The Canadian banking system, therefore, should be credited with mediating somewhere between $259 million and $327 million of capital import on railway account between the mid-1890s and the outbreak of the Great War. Adding our figures for provincial and national governments, the municipalities, the mortgage companies, and the railways, we get two totals: One is 27 percent of the capital inflow, and one is 29 percent. It will be noticed that the dates and coverages do not match precisely. But the comparison is sufficiently robust for our purposes. It appears that Canada's banking system managed somewhat more than 25 percent of the Dominion's capital importation between the mid-1890s and 1914.

Between 1870 and 1895, because the Canadian banks did not manage either provincial or Dominion borrowing and because there was no bank-managed railway borrowing to match the Canadian Northern's, the proportion would have been a great deal smaller than in later years. Matthew Simon's series on money raised through new issues, which covers 57 percent of the total capital imports between 1865 and 1893 as estimated by Hartland,[17] casts some light on the matter. It seems that in these years substantially all of the bank-related new issues must be included with "Finance, Land, and Real Estate," a category that accounts for only 6.1 percent of the total new Canadian issues. To this must be added the external obligations of the mortgage companies, which increased by $32.3 million between 1875 and 1895.[18] Adding this figure to the Simon data, we obtain a total of $38.8 million, which is 4.4 percent of the Hartland total for capital imports in the years between 1868 and 1895.

The above calculations, crude though they are, emphasize that Canadian banks were of importance for the importation of capital chiefly with respect to government, infrastructure, and the agricultural economy; they had little relation to the inflow of external direct investment, thus functioning very differently from the banks in Imperial Russia. We should remember that capital flowed both into and out of Canada's economy, and that not all long-term investment consisted of portfolio investment. Canadian businesses invested abroad, especially in the United States. Canadian banks had substantial businesses abroad, not only as lenders in the United States but as deposit-takers in the West Indies.

Banks experienced considerable swings in their external positions, so that from time to time they appeared directly as net lenders to the rest of the world, or net borrowers therein. There were substantial external, direct investments, and these give rise to great perplexity. No one can hope to disentangle the financing of the initial acquisitions, although it does not appear that local banks, whether or not they were headquartered abroad, ever played any significant role. Later growth and expansion of an externally owned business, however, could be and no doubt often was financed at least in part by advances from local banks. On the other hand, the ploughing-back of locally earned profits could finance expansion.

The accumulation of such profits could be considerable. In 1926 Canada's gross external liabilities were $6.4 billion, of which direct investments were $1.8 billion; in 1914, when the total of external capital invested in Canada was $3.8 billion, direct investments were certainly proportionately much less important than they later became, but we do not know precisely how large they were, and even if a figure were available, it would be surrounded with valuation problems.

From 1900 through 1913 American investment in Canada is said to have risen from $200 million to $800 million; much of this was direct investment, and none or almost none of the direct investment would appear to have been mediated through the Canadian banking system. On the other hand, some unknown proportion of the comparatively small flow of American portfolio investment certainly came through the banks. United Kingdom investments are said to have risen from $1 billion to $2.8 billion, an increase of $1.8 billion, of which, according to Paterson, only $139 million represented additional equities.[19] Thus there was, proportionately, more room for the banks to be important in transatlantic capital movements than in transborder ones. Finally, there was an inflow of capital from other countries, whose claims on the Dominion rose from $14 million in 1900 to $173 million in 1913.[20] Apart from the external borrowings of the Crédit Foncier Franco-Canadien, the Canadian banking system is thought to have played little role in these capital inflows from continental Europe.

One would like to parallel this discussion of international capital flows with a statistical account of the banks' domestic placement policies. Regrettably, there are no useful summary statistics. Banks were not required to report their advances or their investments by industry, location, or term, and the information as to purpose is not revealing. Banking histories are numerous, but they cast little light on this topic, partly, it appears, because the banks themselves did not organize their internal records in the ways that we would find appropriate or helpful. Discussion of the connections between banks and the financial system, whether at home or abroad, must therefore be constructed from many sorts of evidence, and there are some distressing gaps. Nevertheless, a reasonably intelligible picture can be constructed, even though some parts of that picture remain topics for controversy.

In 1870 Canada's chartered banks were quite definitely "commercial," concentrating on short-term lending whose purpose was to facilitate the production cycle and the movement of commodities in trade, both external and internal. By 1914 their involvement in the producing economy had become much more complicated. They were helping Canadian entities to borrow abroad, involving themselves de facto not only in long-term lending but in railway promotion, and, in general, operating in much more adventurous ways than they had done in 1870. There were, naturally, differences among the banks. Some institutions were far more "entrepreneurial" and far less risk-averse than others.

Domestic financial markets had begun to develop by 1914, although few present-day observers would find them impressive in terms of sophistication or levels of activity. Certainly there was nothing resembling a short-term money market, so that New York was necessary for the placement and management of the banks' short-term funds. Local advances and overdrafts were often a great deal less liquid than they appeared. Furthermore, from the banks' point of view local long-term obligations, whether governmental or private, were very illiquid indeed, because bond markets were thin, transactions few, and secondary markets often completely absent. Bonds, therefore, were normally bought to hold, and precisely for this reason the banks fought shy of them. As new issue markets and stock markets became somewhat more active, the banks became somewhat more willing to support these markets. These trends were especially noticeable after 1895: Chartered banks appeared as underwriters and distributors of securities, and they supplied increasing amounts of "call money" in Toronto and Montreal, along the same lines that they had long employed in New York, where such loans, of course, were far more genuinely liquid than in the cities of the Dominion. Banks also came to provide bridge finance when mergers were envisaged, and they financed the inventories of the bond houses, some of which, in turn, had developed from private banks. Also, by 1900 the private bankers in the larger Canadian cities were using the deposits of the public to support promotional activities of various sorts, and some may have borrowed from chartered banks for the same purpose. One private bank and bond dealer, having failed in the crisis of 1903, reappeared as an incorporated securities dealer, and shortly acted as "midwife" at the birth of a moderately successful chartered bank, the Metropolitan of Toronto. Another chartered bank was erected at the same time on the basis of a near-bank that had specialized in call loans and securities transactions.

Canada contained no "universal banks" on the German model, or overtly promotional banks of the Crédit Mobilier type. The banks, whether incorporated or not, had generally been founded by persons who came from the worlds of commerce and finance, not from industry or transportation. In Canadian historiography this fact has combined with the conservative safety-first propaganda of the leading Canadian bankers to produce what Inwood has called the Structural Immobility Hypothesis, or SIH.[21] According to SIH, capital funds and entrepreneurial talent did not flow readily from commerce and finance to industry, and they flowed to transportation only insofar as transport improvements could be seen to serve the interests of commerce, especially in the import-export trades. To SIH-theorists, therefore, indigenous industrial capitalism appears to be stunted, and the way is cleared for externally based industrial capitalism, especially American, to establish factories and mines in the Dominion.[22]

The SIH was first proposed at a time when little was known either of bank activity or of industrial development. As such knowledge has accumulated, it has become clear that the Canadian economy was not segmented as the SIH would suggest. We now know that Canadian industrial development was respectably rapid between 1870 and 1914, that Canadian entrepreneurs were active not only in older branches of industry but also in newer branches, not only in finance but also in manufacturing and mining, and that Canadian banks played an important role in the financing of these developments, even though they rarely functioned as industrial promoters. Some banks bought industrial bonds; some financed individual entrepreneurs; some private banks provided mortgage finance; some incorporated banks and some private banks provided capital to the emerging domestic securities industry, which generated and distributed corporate bonds and common stocks to a wide public not only within Canada but also abroad. Furthermore, banks provided short-term credit to manufacturing industry, and such credit continued to be of much greater proportionate importance than SIH-theorists realize. Naturally no one can prove that there was no segmentation at all, or that every worthwhile project was considered seriously by the Canadian banking industry. But the SIH does not appear to be consistent with the evidence that is now at hand.

Indeed, when we consult the available data on the accumulation of capital in manufacturing, and on apparent surplus value, along Marxian lines, it becomes clear that Canadian manufacturing industry did not need much external finance, whether from within the Dominion or from outside it. Manufacturing was sufficiently profitable to finance the recorded additions to its land, buildings, machinery, and work in progress.

Thanks to Canada's decennial censuses, we have information on the reported values of capital in manufacturing.[23] The census records an increase in manufacturing capital from $78 million in 1870 to $1,247,600,000 in 1910, of which 52.5 percent was land, buildings, and plants, and the rest was working capital. In 1890 the composition of capital was much the same as in 1910, although working capital was proportionately somewhat more important in 1890; data for 1870 and 1880 are available only as totals. Applying the 1890 composition-of-capital figures to the capital accumulation of the whole period, we might suppose that Canadian manufacturers had to accumulate $570.7 million of additional land, buildings, and plants; the 1910 figures imply an accumulation of $614 million under those headings. These are the figures that interest us, because few historians doubt that the banks were perfectly happy to supply the working capital needs insofar as trade credit did not do so.

For land and buildings there was plentiful mortgage finance, not from the chartered banks but from the near-banks, from private lenders, and, in Ontario's smaller towns and rural areas, from private banks. Nonmortgage finance, therefore, was needed for a considerably smaller sum than $614 million. But Canada's manufacturing firms were quite profitable, and aggregate profits clearly increased with the passage of time. Decennial censuses reported the receipts and payments of industrial firms in a form that generates a figure we can call "surplus." It was not pure profit, for from it had to come interest, taxation, the cost of electricity and gas, as well as depreciation allowances, insofar as these were then calculated at all. But since few firms practiced depreciation accounting and since our capital figures are almost certainly gross of depreciation, we can ignore the last item; as for the other costs, they cannot have been very large. Interpolating in a linear fashion between census years, and summing the results for the entire period between 1870 and 1910, we can construct a very rough estimate of "total surplus." The figure is surprisingly large—$4,997,800,000.

However rough the calculations, and whatever adjustments we might want to make in the basic data, it is obvious that genuine profit must have been several times larger than new spending on buildings, land, and plants. Furthermore, the great bulk of that profit came into the hands of Canadian residents: External direct investment, though long established in some lines of business and rapidly advancing in some others, was not sufficiently prominent by 1914 to capture any large share of it.

New firms, of course, might or might not be able to tap the flow of profit from older, established businesses. That is to say, capital and entrepreneurial talent might in principle have been immobile within the manufacturing sector. Again, there may have been some tendency of this sort, but it does not seem to have been particularly important. New Canadian-owned firms appeared, not only in such old industries as textiles and papermaking but in such new ones as iron and steelmaking, automobiles, rubber goods, and the electrical trades; in manufacturing, American and United Kingdom ownership was a complement to Canadian ownership, not a substitute for it.

The mining industries might constitute a separate case in that beyond the eastern seaboard there was little mining activity anywhere in British North America in 1870, whereas by 1914 there was a great deal of mining in central and western Canada, and a considerable amount of British and American capital was active in these new mining areas. Funds, therefore, might be imagined to be immobile either intersectorally or interregionally, thus accounting for the prominence of American and British firms. However, as Peter George has recently reminded us,[24] the externally owned firms did not dominate the mining industry, where plenty of very large Canadian-owned firms were active, and where great Canadian fortunes were made.

In petroleum the story is more complicated but the conclusion may very well be the same. Oil production and refining were begun before Confederation by a myriad of small Canadian-based firms, which for at least thirty-five years had no apparent trouble in raising capital. Several merged into a Canadian-owned company, Imperial Oil, which was, in turn, bought by Standard Oil in the mid-1890s, and then was used as a means for establishing Standard's monopoly of Canadian refining. By 1914, however, Canadian interests had set up other oil-refining companies, and most of these firms continued to thrive, generally under Canadian ownership, for many years. It has been suggested that the Canadian owners of Imperial Oil sold out to Standard because they could not raise capital for a western distribution network. But this is an ex post facto justification, not encountered at the time, and there are good reasons for refusing to believe it. For one thing, the banks were perfectly happy to provide working capital; for another, by 1895 there was still not much of a western market for Imperial to supply with kerosene.[25] If tank cars had been needed, it would have been easy to organize a separate rolling-stock company, as several Canadian entrepreneurs would shortly do.

Although from our perspective the financing of industrialization is especially interesting, to contemporaries the most obvious and pressing financial problems related to government, transport, and mortgage lending. With respect to mortgage finance, we have already noted the several ways in which the financial system mobilized and channeled funds, both domestic and external, toward mortgages. As for railways and governments, the precise pattern of financial demand was much affected by two circumstances: the distribution of functions between public and private sectors, and the allocation of activities among levels of government. In Canada the railways were largely private, while the municipal and federal governments were far more significant than the provinces; in Australia the state governments were much the most important borrowers even in 1914, while railways and most public utilities were government enterprises. The flows of securities, and the arrangements for financial intermediation and marketing, evolved in different ways, in part as reflections of these structural and constitutional differences.

From governments' financial needs came problems of intermediation, both at home and abroad—especially in London. Each level of government could and did sell securities either in Britain or at home; some Canadian provincial and municipal bonds, furthermore, were sold in the United States, especially during the Great Boom. Few Canadian municipalities were large enough to make public issues, especially in London; indeed, they were generally eager to sell their bond issues en bloc, by private negotiation or by tender to single buyers, who might, in turn, hold the bonds or resell them, either in Canada or abroad. The private bankers of Toronto and Montreal were doing some such business in 1870, and so was the Bank of Montreal. As the specialized bond houses developed, they worked largely on the basis of dealings in municipal bonds, later adding industrial securities, especially after 1900. The commercial banks, as we noted earlier, assisted chiefly by financing inventories for the bond houses.

The incorporated commercial banks were not anxious to hold government bonds. Even in 1914 Canadian chartered banks held only 0.7 percent of their assets in the form of Dominion and provincial securities, and these holdings were only 3.7 percent of the Dominion funded debt.[26] However, with respect to the attracting of external funds the commercial banks came to play an important role. As for railway finance, Canadian banks were not much interested in holding railway securities for any length of time. Even in 1913 their holdings of all railway, corporation, municipal, and foreign securities amounted to only 12 percent of railway funded debt, and constituted only 10 percent of their own assets.[27] Yet bank involvement might take any or all of the following alternative forms. A bank might provide personal advances to railway promoters, or working capital advances to railway constructors. It might buy and hold railway bonds and stocks, preferably for short periods. It might arrange for the issue or underwriting of railway securities in London. This last sort of involvement could and often did spring naturally from the first and second forms.[28]

The private placement of Canadian municipal securities in Britain, in a volume that compares favorably with the amount the Dominion itself was raising, was effected almost entirely by the Canadian bond houses and chartered banks, which also made public issues from time to time. The Bank of Montreal was especially active in this line of business. Thus, for instance, in 1908 that bank agreed to handle a single Winnipeg bond issue of $7.5 million—about half as large as the entire funded debt of the province wherein Winnipeg lies.[29] Thirty-two London merchant banks also handled Canadian municipals between 1900 and 1914, but their public flotations were less than half as large as those that the Canadian banks and bond houses put on the open market. Furthermore, to a large extent the London merchant bankers were acting on behalf of Canadian institutions that had bought the securities from the municipalities but which lacked the will or the apparatus to handle a London flotation themselves.[30] The role of the Canadian financial institutions, therefore, was even larger than our statistics suggest.

It is worth emphasizing that substantially all of this new issue work was handled by Canadian-headquartered banks and bond houses, at least after 1891. The Anglo-imperial Bank of British Columbia had handled the London business of "its" province, but with absorption into the Canadian Bank of Commerce that business went to the absorber, which later developed the London offices it had acquired through the merger as the base for a considerable new issue business. The Bank of British North America was not active in such transactions. As far as the mortgage markets were concerned the picture is a more mixed one, in that not all the active firms were based in Canada, so that some mortgage funds certainly flowed from Britain through other channels. But the Canadian firms appear to have provided the more important route through which Scottish solicitors could place their clients' funds in prairie mortgages.

Banks and Semi-Banks in Australia

By 1870 Australian banking, like Canadian banking, had taken on the form that would characterize it for many decades to come. The Australia Act of 1900 seemed at first to make little difference: Although the new federal government acquired all relevant powers with respect to currency and banking, the preexisting regulatory arrangements continued in force for the time being.[31] In the 1890s there had been a great deal of interest, both inside the banks and outside them, in a common legal code for Australian banking; this, however, did not come about until 1945. Although the powers of the various banks might differ according to the precise way in which each had been established, there was no systematic nationwide regulation, and no differentiation among "domestic," "external," and "foreign" banks. Only in 1910/11 did the new Commonwealth Government proceed to change the inherited arrangements through new legislation that provided for a Commonwealth note issue and for a government-owned Commonwealth Bank. The other banks had foreseen as early as the mid-1890s that they might lose the note-issue power, and some, at least, were not reluctant to do so.[32] By the outbreak of war in 1914, nevertheless, the federal authorities had not tried to regulate the banking system, although they had taxed the commercial banknote issues almost out of existence, as Table 9–1 reveals. In other respects the system remained much as it had been before federation.

Locally incorporated trading banks did the larger share of the banking business, and that share tended to increase from 1870 to 1913. In 1878 those Australian banks with head offices in New Zealand and London held 38.8 percent of bank assets in Australia; by 1913 they held 26.4 percent, while the Comptoir National d'Escompte, the only non-British bank, had only 0.06 percent of banking assets.[33] The Australian incorporated banks, whether locally owned or not, held liquidity balances in London, and from time to time they took very large sums on deposit there. Their external positions, therefore, were subject to very large swings, as Table 9–1 reveals. There was no systematic or important difference, in these respects, between the domestically incorporated banks and the Anglo-imperial ones. They all did much the same things, in much the same way, although in London it was believed that some of the locally headquartered banks were likely to be more reckless than the larger London-headquartered ones. The summary data on bank assets, which appear in Table 9–1, reveal that after rapid growth in the 1870s and 1880s, the system suffered a severe crisis and contraction, which lasted until 1905. Nonetheless, as in Canada, intermediation was increasingly important. By 1870 the Australian "private banks" were utterly insignificant, and they would not increase in number or importance. The brokers were beginning to evolve into securities dealers, but there were still no merchant banks, nor would any appear until many years had passed.

Savings banks were of large and growing importance in Australia, where their proportionate significance, both in the asset and liability structure of the financial system and in the financing of government, was very much greater than in Canada. All the savings banks were locally owned and controlled—largely though not entirely by governments. In some Australian states it seems that small amounts of savings bank finance may have flowed into industrial uses, and that in earlier decades small sums were placed in commercial bills. But in the period we are examining, funds were provided to governments and for the finance of building.

In 1870 Australia contained twenty-one note-issuing, check-paying banks, and one bank that paid checks but did not issue notes. Of these twenty-two incorporated banks, six were headquartered in London. Included in this group were two of the largest banks, the Bank of Australasia and the Union Bank of Australia. In 1914 there were again twenty-one banks that had once issued notes, and there were six banks that paid checks without issuing notes; in addition, there was the government-owned Commonwealth Bank, which began its trading-bank operations in 1912. Four of the surviving banks were still based in London, and one new entrant, the Comptoir National d'Escompte, was based in Paris. Among the note-issuing trading banks there had been twelve new foundations, seven failures (four during the extended crisis of 1889 to 1893), and five mergers or absorptions. Furthermore, the "great banks" of 1870 had all survived and had been responsible for all but one of the mergers, each of which had involved only comparatively small and short-lived banks.[34] Bank branches, also, increased in number, from 380 in 1870 to 2,061 in 1914.[35] Even so, in 1914 as in 1870, the world of Australian banking contained both whales and minnows. Also, it was perceptibly less geographically centralized than was the Canadian system: In spite of failures, mergers, and the spread of branch systems from one state to another, each Australian state capital was home to at least one domestic bank.

The Australian banking system did not grow or develop in a smooth or untroubled way. Special difficulties always plagued it because of its commitment to agricultural and pastoral lending, and to mortgage lending, both rural and urban, on a continent where markets, prices, and rainfall were all uncertain. Furthermore, its entire fabric was disrupted by a major financial crisis, beginning in 1889 and coming to a peak in 1893. This crisis, the origins of which were almost entirely local, has no parallel in Canadian experience. Besides the asset-decline, which is recorded in Table 9–1, the number of branches fell by 21 percent from the peak in 1891 to the trough in 1896. Although there were no further failures or mergers from 1893 to the end of our period, Australia's financial fabric recovered only slowly from the crisis. Frozen assets had to be nursed, and frozen deposit liabilities gradually liquefied. Nor was the drought of the later 1890s conducive to the comfort of bankers. Deposit liabilities and assets, therefore, declined for more than a decade, and thereafter grew more slowly than in Canada, apparently because Australia did not experience anything like Canada's Great Boom.

The Australian troubles of 1889–1893 had occurred in a banking environment that was, in accordance with United Kingdom practice, but not with Canadian, essentially unregulated. Although some banks were restrained by the specific terms of their charters and by local banking codes, regulation was much less systematic and serious than in Canada. Most of the banks had no legal trouble lending on mortgage, and where prohibitions existed they were commonly evaded or ignored,[36] so that the urban building boom of the late 1880s readily could and certainly did give rise to overlending and illiquidity. As in Canada, there was no domestic lender of last resort, nor were the banks members of international groupings. But the Australian "big nine" were by no means small in relation to London, where they held large external reserves and where they also sought deposits, sometimes, as in the 1880s, on a very large scale. One element in the Australian crisis of 1889–1893 was certainly a lack of domestic liquidity, of the sort that central banks exist to provide.

In Australia a few building societies, apparently only three in number, became near-banks in the Canadian sense during the period between 1874 and 1890. Most Australian building societies, however, did not evolve in this way, nor did Australia's trust companies.[37] Nevertheless, there were many Australian financial institutions that had some resemblance to banks, either in their reliance on deposited and other borrowed funds or in the character of their lending. For such firms it is convenient to use the label "semi-banks."

Among Australia's most important semi-banks were the pastoral finance companies, most of which originated as proprietorships and partnerships.[38] These firms would advance funds to graziers and market the growers' wool crops. In the early 1870s these older firms were joined by several Anglo-Australian mortgage and finance companies, which shared with the established trading banks and private firms the financing of pastoral activities and the marketing of the wool crop. Among these firms were the Australian Mortgage Land and Finance Company (AML&F), the Land Mortgage Bank of Victoria, and the Trust and Agency Company of Australasia, all of which existed by 1872. By 1882 there were at least nine more, including R. Goldsbrough and Company, Ltd., The Mortgage Company of South Australia Ltd., and the Queensland Investment and Land Mortgage Company Ltd., which worked in close association with the Queensland National Bank, an incorporated trading bank headquartered in Brisbane. In 1882 it was estimated[39] that all the Australasian companies could dispose of some £ 20 million. In addition there were still many unincorporated firms that did the same sort of business, advancing to graziers on long term and on short, and marketing the wool that had been pledged. Among such firms were Dalgety, Du Croz and Company, Sanderson, Murry and Company, L. A. Elder, and Young, Ehlers and Company. These firms were not unimportant. For instance, in 1882 Dalgety alone received and marketed more wool than all the banks, while the largest four unincorporated firms handled more wool than the largest six mortgage and finance companies.[40] In due course such firms would incorporate, largely so as to borrow on debentures in Britain, and would themselves shower medium-term debentures on the United Kingdom market, where such imperial firms as the AML&F had always raised the bulk of their finance.[41] The step was not always taken willingly: Dalgety, for instance, resisted for years, eventually issuing a London prospectus only in 1883.[42] Goldsbrough Mort also incorporated in the early 1880s, and by March 1891 the firm had raised over £ 2 million on debentures, over £ 500,000 in fixed deposits, and over £ 400,000 in call and current accounts; in addition, it regularly ran a large bank overdraft.[43]

The pastoral finance companies were of immense importance during the sheep boom of the 1870s and 1880s, when the pastoral economy was expanding and when many squatters were obliged to raise mortgage money so as to buy land from the colonial governments. They, like the building societies and mortgage companies, also provided competition for the commercial banks.[44]

Also to be included in the ranks of the semi-banks were most of Australia's building societies. As in Britain and Canada, these began as "terminating" societies, which usually operated under the general regulations governing friendly societies. They then evolved into "permanent" societies that came to resemble ordinary financial corporations.

In the boom conditions of the 1880s, the building societies became a great deal more numerous, and to all appearances far more financially important. Within the colony of Victoria there were forty-seven building societies in 1880, and in 1889/90, seventy-two; over the same period the deposit and current-account liabilities of Victoria's building societies rose from £ 830,000 to £ 5,062,000—some 13 percent of the deposit liabilities of the colony's trading banks.[45] In the other Australian colonies, building societies developed in a comparably dramatic way. Furthermore, they were joined, especially in Melbourne, by various sorts of "mortgage company," "mortgage bank," and "land bank," all much concerned with property speculation.

To the financial historian this development can cause perplexity because so many of these institutions took to themselves the name "bank," without exercising many banking functions. Their funds came partly from the receipt of deposits, and partly from the sale of medium-term debentures both in Australia and in Britain, where an extensive network of agencies gathered funds for them; it is also possible that some were financed, at least in part, by the trading banks. Butlin has found that in 1891 there were at least sixty-four such institutions that solicited deposits and that called themselves "banks" but that were not included in the official banking data.[46]

Early in this century the Victorian banker-historian H. G. Turner reported that in 1885 there were sixty-two building societies in the colony of Victoria alone, almost all in Melbourne. Because of mergers and liquidations there were only fifty survivors by October 1891, and by 1893 all but two or three were in liquidation. Also, Turner found that by 1888 Melbourne contained twenty-eight listed financial institutions that called themselves banks but that were not "genuine banks" at all.[47] In the crisis of the early 1890s only two of these twenty-eight Melbourne semi-banks managed to avoid suspension, while six made terms for reconstruction; the rest had to be liquidated. Moreover, in 1888 there were also twenty-two "land and investment companies," some of which were certainly known as "land banks," and all of which went out of business. In addition, there were fifty newly created and registered financial companies that were not listed on the stock exchange, and almost all of these Melbourne semi-banks collapsed in the early 1890s.

Developments in Sydney and Brisbane during the late 1880s, though perhaps less frenetic than those in Melbourne, were broadly parallel. Coghlan reports that besides the Anglo-Australian land and mortgage companies mentioned earlier, there were twenty small and dubious Sydney land companies that suspended in 1891/92; in addition, three Sydney building societies "of excellent repute" had to suspend.[48] In Brisbane, during 1890, more than a hundred firms called themselves "banks." But, Coghlan tells us, apart from the banks of issue, not more than two or three did any banking business "or even attempted to do so."[49] Many of these firms were building societies that were converting themselves into public companies so as to speculate in land. Few survived the crisis of the early 1890s.

The banking system had to fill much the same needs in Australia as in Canada. Two differences should be noted: In Australia the pastoral economy was of immensely greater importance than in Canada; Australian industrial development was comparatively slower, and certainly later, than was Canadian development. As we shall see, these structural differences were reflected in the asset structure of the Australian banks; furthermore, they were responsible for the specialized semi-banks that were so prominent on the Australasian scene, and which had no parallel in Canada.

Because the Australian near-banks and semi-banks were so heavily dependent on their overseas borrowings during the 1800s, the withdrawal of such deposits would at once create severe balance-of-payments pressure. It was widely feared that such liquidations would be a problem during the Australian financial crisis of 1893, although Coghlan has argued authoritatively that this was not the case.[50] More recently, Butlin[51] has argued explicitly that the problem was an *internal, domestic* drain—the result of a collapse of confidence that followed upon a collapse first in building activity and then in land prices. By May 1893, Butlin explains, at least half of all Australian bank deposits had been frozen, "and at least half the note issue had ceased to be freely negotiable." To this should be added the impact of prior collapses among banks and semi-banks. Of the nine banks that survived intact, 88 percent of deposit liabilities and 84 percent of the note liabilities appertained to only three banks—The Bank of New South Wales, headquartered in Sydney, and the Bank of Australasia and the Union Bank of Australia, both headquartered in London.[51]

Australian financial institutions were much more inclined than Canadian institutions to obtain overseas funds by issuing their own shares and by seeking deposits and debenture finance; before 1890 they were also much more active as channels for the public issue of others' securities. Butlin[53] has calculated by the "direct method" that from 1871 through 1900 total overseas borrowing amounted to £ 280 million, of which £ 17 million came through the banks, £ 15.5 million through the pastoral finance companies, and another £ 7 million through other finance companies, so that the banks, near-banks, and semi-banks provided 13.9 percent of Australia's capital inflow. During the financial boom of the 1880s, however, they provided 30 percent. Since Australia was a consistent capital exporter from 1901 through 1911, while even in 1912/13 capital imports were not large enough to swamp the contrary movements of 1901 to 1911, there is little point in pursuing the question in Butlin's terms after 1900.

So much for the equity capital and the direct obligations of the Australian banks, near-banks, and semi-banks. As for the flotation of government stock in the London market, Hall tells us that, with the exception of Western Australia, which before it obtained responsible government in 1890 had to borrow through the Crown Agents, in the 1870s and early 1880s the Australian states borrowed overseas with the aid of Australian banks, some locally headquartered and some imperial. But, he writes, "in the mid-eighties the major borrowers transferred their issuing business to leading London banks," and when Western Australia left the care of the Crown Agents it did the same.[54] Only South Australia continued to borrow in London through an Australian bank. Hall explains the shift as a "desire of the Australian governments to make use of the prestige surrounding such names as the Bank of England, and the London and Westminster."[55]

Municipalities, however, continued to issue through the banks. Hall finds little evidence that other Australian entities did so, although he notes that the banks and semi-banks themselves generally managed their own new issues. Totaling Hall's figures for total new issues and his data on colonial and municipal new issues up to the dates at which London banks took over the issue function,[56] we find that, from 1870 through 1914, 26 percent of the nominal value of Australian new issues were floated through Australian banks. In that government and municipal issues were fully "paid up" while corporation issues generally were not, the percentage of cash actually raised on the new-issue market through the intermediation of the Australian banks was some-what higher than this figure.

Because the Butlin and Hall figures are constructed on different conceptual bases, and relate to different periods, it would not be correct to add the two percentages and conclude that 40 percent of Australia's capital importation came through the banking system. Nevertheless, this appears to be the right order of magnitude, although it would certainly be far too high for the years after 1890, and is probably somewhat too high for the period as a whole.

In Australia the trading banks were at first heavily committed to commerce, but because of their involvement in mortgage and pastoral finance they were never as obviously "commercial" as Canada's chartered banks. Australian productive functions were so distributed that Australian banks could never become entrepreneurial on Canadian lines, because such things as railways and public utilities were securely in the public sector. Nevertheless, there is some hint of widening interests during the first decade of the twentieth century and even before. The National Bank of Australasia was lending on mining shares well before the turn of the century—apparently in the 1880s, or even earlier.[57] The Bank of New South Wales was banker to the Colonial Sugar Refining Company, which operated plantations and refineries not only in Queensland but in Fiji. Writing of this bank, the largest Sydney bank and one of the largest in the country, Holder explains that "Board minutes in the first year or so record decisions to grant new or extended [credit] limits for coal mining, gold mining, hat manufacture, flour milling, sugar mill machinery, and provision of meat cold storage facilities."[58] Nevertheless, Holder has to admit that "many of the records that would allow a detailed study and assessment of lending policy have not survived,"[59] so that the first comprehensive asset distribution for this bank is for 1912. Pastoral advances were then 36 percent of the value of all productive loans, and 25 percent were agricultural; 23 percent consisted of advances to merchants, storekeepers, stock and station agents, sawmillers, and manufacturers. These three categories consist wholly of simple advances—overdrafts or cash credits. The fourth category, "bills discounted for collection" (6 percent), could not be broken down as to industry of origin.[60]

We have to wait until 1927 before we find any comprehensive Australian data on the industrial structure of bank assets. The figures cover the "big nine" trading banks, both domestic and imperial. It is reasonable to suppose that in 1914 things would not have been very different.[61] In all, 41.5 percent of all outstanding advances had been made to agricultural and pastoral industries, 22.6 percent to commerce, transport, and distribution, 11.9 percent to manufacturing and mining, 10.1 percent to finance, insurance, the professions, and the entertainment and personal service industries, and 13.9 percent to "other pursuits, including advances for building and to public bodies." Australian banking obviously had not ignored manufacturing or mining, but its chief commitments were still to commerce, the other service trades, and the land; as in Canada, there were no "universal banks" and no overtly promotional ones.

If the SIH applied in Canada it ought to apply in Australia, since the economic structures and financial systems were so similar. We cannot prove conclusively that it did not. But Australian industrialization, though laggard in comparison with Canadian, did get well under way before 1914. And Australian mining developed most impressively. External direct investment in either sector was not of great importance until well after the Great War. We cannot duplicate our "surplus" calculations for Australia, but it is certainly reasonable to suppose that, because Canadian industrial development was essentially self-financing before 1914, Australian development may well have been equally autonomous.

As we noted in the last section, the requirements for financial intermediation followed to a considerable extent from the political structure. In Australia, state governments built the railways and operated a wide range of infrastructural services that in Canada were handled by municipalities or private firms. Thus the financing of the states was of special developmental importance. Political predilections and economic accidents, furthermore, may have played some special part. Hence, it is noticeable that Australian governments were at least twenty years ahead of those in Canada in the development of savings banks as protected channels through which governments and mortgage lending could be financed. The attractiveness of the government savings banks, in turn, may well reflect the difficulties in which Australian banks and semi-banks were mired after the financial crisis between 1889 and 1893. With respect to mortgage finance, Australian trading banks were certainly helpful. But with respect to government they certainly were not: In 1914, they held less than 6 percent of their assets in such forms, and their holdings were less than 4 percent of the Commonwealth and state funded debt.[62]

After the early 1890s the Australian financial firms were much less active in Britain, chiefly because of the crisis of those years, and also thanks to the droughts and the general Australian slump, which lasted until after 1900.[63] When the Australian economy again began to grow, the domestic financial system had changed. The state savings banks had become much larger in relation to the commercial banks. Since the savings banks lent almost entirely to the state governments, and on mortgage, the domestic flows of funds had been decisively altered: Government debt and mortgage debt had, in effect, acquired prior claims on the domestic flow of savings. For these two sectors, therefore, overseas intermediation probably mattered less than before 1893.

Conclusion

In many respects both of our banking systems might be called successful. Overexpansion and overoptimism certainly occurred, nor was bad judgment unknown, but financial institutions showed considerable skill in adapting to changing demands and in surviving under circumstances that were often difficult. They also became adept at drawing overseas funds and in managing their external assets so as to maintain gold convertibility and exchange-rate stability. Depositors and note holders experienced a good deal of disappointment, especially in Australia, and borrowers, of course, were not always satisfied. Indeed, it might be said that borrowers are seldom completely satisfied, and that if they are, the financial system is working very badly. Nor would one want to suggest that every worthwhile project was financed, or every potential borrower treated with objectivity and fairness. At least on the Canadian scene, and especially in connection with industrial development finance, railways, and the stock market, there are plentiful examples of an "old boy network" at work. Such things are inevitable in small and rapidly growing economies.

A different sort of banking structure—something along German lines—might have accelerated industrial development. But manufacturing and mining certainly grew quickly, especially in Canada, and with respect to industrial finance the Canadian banks were much more forthcoming than had once been thought, while the Australian banks and semi-banks labored mightily, especially in the 1880s, to finance not only the pastoral economy but also the urban one. If there was some sort of gap, why did no one come forward to fill it? In both countries there was certainly plentiful evidence of financial adaptability, entrepreneurial energy, and innovativeness. Nor would the law have proved a barrier: Legal codes and incorporating charters were, if anything, rather too open to change along the lines that the financiers desired. Furthermore, the financial systems did not depend on externally headquartered firms; financial talent and innovativeness were very largely local. Of course, the banks did staff themselves to some extent with expatriates from Britain.

Finally, both Canada and Australia were "lands of opportunity" for the adventurous Briton. But it would not be sensible to say that if the Englishman or the Scot or the Irishman comes to a colony and begins a financial business there, his business is "really foreign." As far as Britain, Australia, and Canada were concerned, common citizenship was a reality, and the intra-imperial movement of persons was not a cause for surprise; indeed, nothing could have seemed more natural.

10

Japan

Kanji Ishii

Development of the Japanese Banking System

Economic development of modern Japan. The growth rate of real GNP of Japan from 1887 to 1913 was once estimated at 3.6 percent per annum, one of the highest rates in the world at that time,[1] but a new estimate by Kazushi Ohkawa in 1974 reduced it to 2.4 percent,[2] which led to a hot controversy about the correct rate. For lack of reliable data, we can only say that the rate was around 3 percent, which was not the highest rate but a fairly high one at that time.[3]

Concerning the impetus to sustained growth, there are two prevailing views. The first may be called "growth-from-above," which stresses the role of the government and large-scale enterprises, and the other "growth-from-below," which argues the importance of small-scale enterprises. Hugh T. Patrick regards the first view as applicable to the earlier period and the other to the later period.[4] I do not agree with this view because these two kinds of growth-courses coexisted from the earlier period to the later and are closely related to each other. I will explain the point later in this chapter.

Development of the credit system before 1870. Patrick has already offered a clear account of the history of the banking system in modern Japan, to which I have little to add.[5] Here I discuss only the importance of the development of the credit system before 1870. It is commonly agreed among historians that the credit system in the Tokugawa period (1603–1867) developed to a very high level, particularly in Osaka, the largest center of commerce. But it is also agreed that this highly developed system was destroyed during the Meiji Restoration (1859–1877), so that a modern banking system had to be imported from Western countries.

Many of the Osaka merchant banking houses did not survive the Meiji Restoration, but some famous ones such as Sumitomo, Konoike, Kajimaya (Hirooka), Chigusaya (Hirase) established modern banks later in Osaka.[6] After the opening of Yokohama port in 1859 Edo (Tokyo), near Yokohama, became a major center of commerce equal to Osaka, and Edo merchant banking houses began to finance Yokohama merchants.

For example, the merchant banking house Chogin (Choji-ya Kobayashi Ginemon), which had offices in Edo and Kyoto, sold remittance bills to Yokohama tea merchants who wanted to send money to the tea-producing area near Kyoto, and bought exchange bills from importers in Yokohama who wanted to collect the proceeds of imported goods from merchants in Kyoto or Osaka. The sum of the money provided by Chogin to Yokohama merchants amounted to 1,093,000 yen in 1875, which is comparable to the sum provided by the larger urban banks later.[7] Without such financial support, Yokohama merchants could not have transacted with foreign merchants on equal terms and could not have prevented them from invading interior markets. The Kyoto office of Chogin had a current account with Banjin (Yorozu-ya Jinbei), a larger merchant bank in Kyoto, and paid merchants in or near Kyoto with bills drawn on Banjin.[8] This is very similar to the check system of modern banks. The national banks and private banks, most of which were founded after 1876, superseded the activities of merchant banking houses. We should recognize the continuity between the traditional credit system in the Tokugawa period and the modern banking system in the Meiji period (1868–1912). Such a highly developed credit system before 1870 was one of the reasons why Japan could imitate the modern banking system of advanced foreign countries.

Banks and the Import of Capital

With respect to the import of capital, the role of banks in Japan changed drastically again and again, so that we must divide the entire period of 1870 to 1914 into at least three subperiods. From 1870 to 1881 a considerable amount of foreign capital was imported even though the new Japanese government, established in 1868, struggled to exclude it. The second period (1882–1903) began with the establishment of the Bank of Japan in 1882. In this period Japanese industrialization went on rapidly without any support from foreign capital. The third period began with the outbreak of the Russo-Japanese War in 1904 and continued to 1914. In these years Japan was compelled to import a large amount of foreign capital.

The First Period (1870–1881)

The role of the national banking system. During the first period Japan did not have a central bank. Instead, many national banks issued their own bank notes. Why had these national banks been established before the Bank of Japan?

In 1871 the Japanese government attempted to adopt a gold standard system, minting new gold coins containing 1.5 grams of gold per yen. But Japan also minted new silver coins equivalent to the Mexican dollars that dominated East Asian trade. As the exchange rate between the new gold coins and the new silver coins was legally fixed, the Japanese monetary standard at this time was actually bimetallic. In addition to these coins, a large amount of inconvertible government paper money circulated.

In order to eliminate the paper money, the government promulgated in 1872 the National Bank Act, mainly on the American model. National banks were to buy government bonds with paper money and issue an equivalent amount of bank notes convertible into gold coins, with the intent that convertible bank notes would replace the inconvertible government paper money. But only four national banks were founded between 1872 and 1875, and the bank notes issued by them could not circulate in the market because the government continued to issue paper money. Simultaneously, the decline of the silver price in the world market caused a sudden export of gold coins from Japan.

In 1876 the government provided the samurai class and feudal lords (daimyo) with pension bonds instead of paying them feudal dues every year. At the same time it amended the National Bank Act to allow national banks to issue inconvertible bank notes using the pension bonds as security. As a result, 153 national banks were soon founded by samurais, merchants, and landowners. The newly issued national bank notes circulated smoothly, and national banks supplied various developing industries with funds. In 1877, however, when a large issue of government paper money (to finance military expenditure to suppress the Satsuma Rebellion in southwestern Japan) was added to this issue of national bank notes, the result was severe inflation. Replacement of inconvertible paper money and bank notes with convertible bank notes of a central bank became the most urgent task for the government.

For this purpose a leading official, Shigenobu Okuma, proposed to issue £ 10 million in foreign bonds, but his colleagues in the government rejected the proposal.[9] Then in 1881 Masayoshi Matsukata became the Minister of Finance and initiated the famous deflation that bears his name by increasing taxes and reducing expenditures. By 1886 the difference between the paper yen and the silver yen disappeared. In 1885 the Bank of Japan began to issue bank notes convertible into silver coins, and in the next year the government also began to convert its paper money into silver coins. Eventually the silver standard system was established in Japan.

Japan failed to establish a gold standard in the 1870s because the government continued to issue inconvertible paper money and to mint silver coins that were considered indispensable for East Asian trade. Far from supporting the gold standard, the national banks supplied another kind of inconvertible money. But the history of the national banks should not be treated as an unnecessary mistake. To eliminate the government paper money, the public finances had to be improved by cutting the expenditure on the samurai class and the nobility. To accomplish this peacefully, the amendment of the Bank Act in 1876 was indispensable. It is true that the adoption of the national bank system was a roundabout way to establish the Bank of Japan and a standard currency system, but it was an effective strategy for the government officers who had to take feudal privileges away from their colleagues as peacefully as possible. Establishing a standard currency system is not only an economic issue but also a highly political one.

Foreign trade and foreign banks. Most of Japan's foreign trade during the 1870s was in the hands of foreign merchants such as Jardine, Matheson and Co. (hereafter Jardines), Siber and Brenwald, and others. Japanese merchants dealt with them in the foreign settlements of the treaty ports. Foreign banks in the settlements supported the activities of foreign merchants. The first foreign bank operating in Japan was the Central Bank of Western India, which opened its Yokohama branch in 1863. The Oriental Bank Corporation, the biggest exchange bank in Asia, also opened a Yokohama branch in 1864.[10] The Hongkong and Shanghai Banking Corporation, founded in China in 1865, established its agency in Yokohama by the end of the year.[11]

The amount of bills of exchange sold and bought between Jardines, a leading

TABLE 10-1. Bills of Exchange Bought and Sold Between Jardines and Foreign Banks, 1863-1873 (in Mexican dollars)

Year	Central Bank of Western India	Mercantile Bank	Oriental Bank Corp.	Comptoir d'Escompte	Hongkong Bank	Deutsche Bank	Total
1863	222,051	138,500					360,551
1864	170,000	50,000					220,000
1869			487,713		700,138		1,187,851
1870		90,188	193,969		297,998		582,155
1872			106,645	24,946	231,153		362,744
1873		22,642		6,400	39,102	22,326	90,470

Souce: Kanji Ishii, "Reorganization of British Colonial Banks in Japan and China from the 1870s to the 1880s," *The Journal of Economics,* Vol. 45, No. 1, No. 3, 1979.

foreign company in Yokohama, and foreign banks in the same city is shown in Table 10-1.

Jardines in Yokohama had a current account with the Central Bank of Western India from 1863. But two years later, when Jardines foresaw the coming economic crisis in Bombay, it closed the account at once and opened a new account with the Oriental Bank Corporation. As expected, the Central Bank went bankrupt in the crisis of 1866. Jardines's transactions with the Oriental Bank, however, did not continue long. In 1872 Jardines in Yokohama transferred its current account to the Hongkong Bank, as did Jardines in Shanghai. Jardines in Hong Kong also closed its current account with the Oriental Bank in Hong Kong. The Hongkong Bank's progress gradually weakened the dominant position of the Oriental Bank in East Asia. Confronted with these powerful foreign banks, Japanese merchants had difficulty in establishing their own exchange banks. The Yokohama Specie Bank, which was founded in 1880 as the first exchange bank in Japan, was supported and controlled by the Japanese government in order to provide Japan with an entry into the exchange market.

Capital imports and banks. The new Japanese government decided on a policy to prevent the inflow of foreign capital. The commercial treaties concluded by the Tokugawa government with foreign countries in 1858 prohibited foreign merchants from traveling for business beyond the border of their settlements at treaty ports. But foreign merchants tried repeatedly to expand their activities beyond the border of the settlements and advanced much money to Japanese merchants, the Tokugawa government, and local governments (Han). The new Japanese government, which was more cautious about the invasion of foreign powers into the domestic economy than was the Tokugawa government, feared such advances might nullify the prohibition clause in the treaties.[12] The government repaid all the debts (amounting to 5.77 million yen) that the Tokugawa government and the local governments owed to foreigners.[13] They also recovered the right of an American legation attaché to construct the railway between Edo and Yokohama, which had been granted by an official of the former Tokugawa government, and bought back the Takashima coal mine, which had been developed by a British merchant, T. B. Glover.[14]

The Japanese government, however, had to ask the Oriental Bank to issue public bonds for £ 1 million in London in 1870 to construct the national railway,[15] and to issue £ 2.4 million of public bonds there again in 1873 for buying out the feudal rights of the samurai class. After that, until 1896, the government did not depend on foreign capital at all, for fear that it would lose its sovereignty (as Egypt did) if it could not repay the debts regularly.

Despite the effort of the government to prevent the inflow of foreign capital, many Japanese entrepreneurs who intended to enlarge their businesses tried to borrow abroad. For example, former high official Shojiro Goto, who owned the Takashima coal mine disposed of by the government in 1874, borrowed 1.3 million Mexican dollars from Jardines secretly. Because investment by foreigners in the mining industry had been forbidden, Yataro Iwasaki, a near relative of Goto who succeeded him in the management of the mine in 1881, repaid the debt to Jardines and developed it into one of the most profitable firms of the Mitsubishi zaibatsu.[16] The largest financial house, Mitsui, overcame the economic crisis of 1874 by borrowing a million yen from the Oriental Bank, while two other famous financial houses, Ono and Shimada, went bankrupt.[17] No matter how loudly the Japanese government appealed to native entrepreneurs not to import foreign capital, those entrepreneurs who intended to enlarge their businesses tended to rely on foreign merchants or bankers. What the government should have done was to provide funds to them. In this regard, the foundation of the Bank of Japan in 1882 was significant because it had the effect of stopping the inflow of foreign capital to the private sector.

The Second Period (1882–1903)

Foundation of special banks. The convertible bank notes issued by the newly born Bank of Japan increased rapidly from 1885, while the circulation of government paper money and the national bank notes disappeared by 1899. In 1897 the Japanese government promulgated a law to mint gold coins containing 0.75 grams of gold per yen. Thereafter, the bank notes of the Bank of Japan became convertible into gold instead of silver. Compared with the old gold coins minted in 1871, the value of the yen in terms of the new gold coins had decreased by half, which corresponded to the depreciation of silver in the world market from 1871 to 1897. The adoption of the gold standard in 1897 therefore had no influence on prices in Japan.

Matsukata, the Minister of Finance, intended at first to develop the Bank of Japan, which was founded on the Belgian model, as a center of commercial finance. As for long-term finances, other special banks were to be founded. But because of political circumstances before the Sino-Japanese War (1894–95), the plan was delayed, and only after the war were such special banks as the Hypothec Bank of Japan, the Industrial Bank of Japan, and others established. The delay in establishing the special banks was one of the reasons why the Bank of Japan and the ordinary banks had to provide not only short-term finance but also long-term finance.

Activities of the Yokohama Specie Bank. The proportion of total Japanese foreign trade handled by Japanese merchants increased from 9 percent in 1882 to 35 percent in 1900. The share of total foreign exchange bills accounted for by the Yokohama Specie Bank reached 39 percent in 1900.[18] The Specie Bank opened branches abroad in

London, Lyons, San Francisco, Hawaii, Bombay, Hong Kong, Shanghai, Tientsin, Niu-Chuang and Peking by 1903, and established an agency in New York in 1883.[19] From 1889 the Bank of Japan supplied the Specie Bank with up to 10 million yen at 2 percent interest, which was far lower than the common level of the interest rate in Japan.

The Specie Bank provided foreign as well as Japanese merchants with foreign-exchange services. For example, Jardines in Yokohama sold a franc bill to the Specie Bank at 4.77 francs per Mexican dollar on November 2, 1883, while having sold one to the Hongkong Bank at 4.80 francs on the same day. In 1884 Jardines sold bills for $1.19 million to the Specie Bank and only $520,000 to the Hongkong Bank.[20]

Furthermore, the crisis of other exchange banks in Asia aided the development of the Specie Bank. The foreign banks in Japan suffered seriously from the depreciation of silver after 1873, and the Oriental Bank went bankrupt in 1884. The Japanese government, which had close connections with it, let the Specie Bank promote its London agency to branch status in order to take over the government business of the Oriental Bank.

It is often said that the Hongkong Bank was the model for the Specie Bank.[21] Perhaps it is true that the foreign-exchange policy of the Specie Bank during this period was similar to that of the Hongkong Bank. But the organization of the Specie Bank was quite different from that of the Hongkong Bank. For example, only Japanese could be stockholders of the Specie Bank, while those of the Hongkong Bank were composed of British, American, German, French, and other nationals. The liability of the stock-holders of the former was limited to the face value of the stock, while that of the latter was double the face value. The former was supported and controlled by the Japanese government, while the latter was comparatively free of regulation by the Hong Kong government.[22]

Capital imports and banks. The period under study overlaps the period of the beginning of Japanese industrialization (in my view, from 1886 to 1907).[23] Many cotton-spinning factories were established during the 1880s, and the export of cotton yarn exceeded its import by 1897. Increased exports of raw silk brought money needed for the import of raw cotton and machinery. The national and private railways extended from 174 miles in 1882 to 4,495 miles in 1903, and the Nihon Yusen Co., the largest steamship line, started regular service to the United States, Europe, and Australia in 1896.

The capital for industrialization in this period came mainly from internal sources in Japan. It is true that Japan received an indemnity for the Sino-Japanese War amounting to £ 38.08 million (equivalent to 364 million yen), but at least £ 17.53 million of that money was spent to import warships and new weapons. Industrialists and merchants united in the Chamber of Commerce criticized the expansion of armaments and requested the government to repay the war loan, but in vain.[24]

In 1897 the government sold 43 million yen of the war loan held by the Yokin-bu (a section in the Ministry of Finance that utilized post office savings) in the London financial market through Samuel and Co. in Yokohama. This was the first import of foreign capital since 1873. In 1899 the government contracted for a £ 10 million foreign loan with the syndicate of Parr's Bank Ltd., the Hongkong and Shanghai Banking Corporation, the Chartered Bank of India, Australia and China, and the

Yokohama Specie Bank. Parr's Bank had been closely connected with the Yokohama Specie Bank for many years, as Alan Shand, the assistant manager of the London branch of Parr's Bank, had been employed by the Japanese government from 1872 to 1877 to teach bankers how to manage banks. A part of this loan was invested by the government in the national railway, the national telephone service, and the Yawata ironworks, but the greater part of it was used for the expansion of armaments.[25]

During this period no debentures were issued abroad. Some officials planned to establish a special bank that would issue bonds in the United States guaranteed by the Japanese government, but J. P. Morgan rejected their proposal, and it was also opposed by the Bank of Japan and the large ordinary banks, which feared their business might be taken away by the new special bank.[26]

The adoption of the gold standard in 1897 and the revision of treaties in 1899, which permitted foreigners to do business anywhere in Japan, seemed to open chances for them to make direct investments in Japan. But few direct investments took place because foreigners thought Japan, which was preparing for the war with Russia, was a very risky place for investment.

The Third Period (1904–1914)

Capital imports and maintenance of the gold standard. In this period the amount of imported capital showed a rapid increase (Table 10–2). Most of it resulted from public bonds issued abroad, and the Japanese government held a considerable part of the funds in the United Kingdom and elsewhere for foreign payments. When it wished to use them in Japan, the government sold these foreign funds to the Bank of Japan in exchange for bank notes, and the bank in turn held the funds abroad. On January 11, 1908, the Japanese government had on deposit with banks or merchant bankers in London, Berlin, and Paris, foreign funds equivalent to 235 million yen, and the Bank of Japan had foreign funds equivalent to 162 million yen with banks and merchant bankers in London.[27] The Bank of Japan issued some of its bank notes based on specie held abroad, and it prevented the outflow of gold from Japan by selling bills of exchange on London to the exchange banks, which otherwise would have demanded gold, at a price that overvalued the yen.[28] In this respect, the Japanese gold coin standard resembled a gold exchange standard. Artificially maintaining the value of the

TABLE 10–2. Balance of Payments, 1870–1914 (millions of yen)[a]

| | | Increase of Long-Term Capital | | |
| | Merchandise | (1) Import of Foreign Capital | (2) Export of Japanese Capital | |
Total	Export-Import			(1) − (2)
1870–1881	−162.5	5.1	—	5.1
1882–1893	−23.0	−9.1	—	−9.1
1894–1903	−399.1	184.6	28.4	156.2
1904–1914	−522.9	1,453.6	212.9	1,240.7

Source: Ippei Yamasawa, Yuzo Yamamoto, *Foreign Trade and Balance of Payments*, 1979.
[a] Japan proper (excluding colonies).

TABLE 10-3. Bills of Foreign Exchange in 1911
(in millions of yen)

Bank	Export Bills	Import Bills	Total	(%)
Yokohama Specie Bank	202.3	230.3	432.6	(45.4)
Hongkong Bank	137.1	146.1	283.2	(29.7)
Chartered Bank	49.9	68.5	118.5	(12.4)
International Bank	24.0	41.8	65.8	(6.9)
Russo-Asiatic Bank	12.0	14.8	26.8	(2.8)
Deutsche-Asiatische Bank	11.0	14.4	25.4	(2.7)
TOTAL	436.3	515.8	952.1	(100.0)

Source: Japanese Ministry of Finance, *The History of the Public Finance in Meiji and Taisho Periods,* Vol. 17, p. 480.

yen higher than its real value, however, stimulated the import of goods. The capital imports, which brought about an increase in the money supply having no connection with the balance of trade, also inhibited automatic control by the gold standard. Thus, just before the outbreak of World War I, the Japanese government was anxious about the maintenance of the gold standard itself.

Development of the Yokohama Specie Bank. The financial activities of the Japanese government and the Bank of Japan in London were mainly performed by the London branch of the Yokohama Specie Bank. In the field of foreign exchange in Japan the Specie Bank ranked first among the banks (Table 10–3). Supported by the low interest funds of the Bank of Japan as before, the Specie Bank also began to depend on increasing deposits in the United States, China, and India.[29] The big Japanese merchants such as Mitsui Bussan and Co. depended both on the Specie Bank and foreign banks. In 1911, when Japan recovered the autonomy of its customs duties, about half of the foreign trade was handled by Japanese merchants.

Capital imports and banks. The sudden increase of capital imports was occasioned by the war loans for the Russo-Japanese War (1904–05). Of the war expenses of 2 billion yen, Japan raised 686 million yen abroad. Korekiyo Takahashi, vice president of the Bank of Japan, went to London and succeeded in raising four loans amounting to £ 82 million, having Parr's Bank, the Hongkong Bank, and the Specie Bank underwrite them. Kuhn, Loeb & Co., an American financial house, underwrote these four loans in the amount of £ 36 million, and German bankers also underwrote the last loan in the amount of £ 10 million. The proposal of Jacob Schiff, president of Kuhn, Loeb, surprised and overjoyed Takahashi. After the war De Rothschild frères also underwrote the public loans raised for converting or redeeming the former bonds.[30]

While the balance of the central government loans raised abroad was 1,606 million yen at the end of 1914, municipal government loans and debentures raised or sold abroad were only 177 million yen and 167 million yen, respectively.[31] Over four-fifths of these loans and debentures were underwritten by the Industrial Bank, which had been ordered by the government to control these loans and debentures. The nationalization of the railways in 1906 also decreased the volume of the debentures.

After the Russo-Japanese War the Japanese government was eager to decrease the balance of the imported capital and to protect domestic industries from an invasion of foreign capital.

On the other hand, direct investment from abroad increased considerably during this period. There were two famous cases, one by the General Electric Co. in the Tokyo Denki Co. and the Shibaura Seisakusho (in 1939 they united as Toshiba), and the other by Armstrong and Co. and Vickers and Co. in Nihon Seikosho, which produced weapons for the Japanese army and navy. But the total direct investment at the end of 1911, estimated as 44 million yen, was only 2 percent of the total amount of the capitals of the companies at that time.[32]

It is not easy to decide how much the capital imports in this period contributed to industrialization. Considering the fact that the war expenses paid to foreign countries were only 234 million yen, the greater part of the four war loans raised abroad (net receipts amounted to 686 million yen) must have served to promote the expansion of the domestic economy. Public loans raised abroad after the war also developed the domestic economy. But the direct investments were limited and most of the debentures were used for the development of Manchuria and Korea. What is important is that the deficit in foreign trade increased year by year and threatened the gold standard of Japan. It is true that a considerable part of the imported capital contributed to the expansion of Japanese economy, but owing to the weakness of heavy industry the import of machines, iron, and steel contributed to the growing deficit in foreign trade.

Banks and Industrial Finance

Earlier views. It thus appears that the role of imported capital in promoting Japanese industrialization was comparatively limited. Our examination turns now to how the banks promoted industrialization without importing foreign capital. Concerning this point we already have the two opinions of Hugh Patrick and Kozo Yamamura.[33] Patrick asserted in accordance with common opinion in Japan that the ordinary banks before World War I provided funds for fixed investment as well as for working capital. On the other hand, Yamamura, criticizing this opinion, insisted that the nature of Japanese ordinary banks changed during World War I from commercial banks on the British model to investment banks like the German.

It seems to me that Yamamura made a serious mistake in analyzing the accounts of the banks. Until the change of the accounting method in 1916, *waribiki tegata* (bills discounted) usually contained *tegata kashitsuke* (loans against accommodation bills), which should be classified as long-term loans. From Table 10–4 we should not conclude that the nature of banks changed suddenly in 1916 from commercial banks to investment banks.

When Yamamura examined the financial records of industrial firms he omitted the analysis of industries such as silk reeling, coal mining, and railways that borrowed much money from banks, and neglected the analysis of the cotton-spinning industry before 1905.

On the other hand, Patrick insisted that the larger urban banks gradually shifted their lending emphasis from agricultural and small-scale industrial units to large-scale

TABLE 10–4. Ratio of (1) *waribiki tegata* (bills discounted) and (2) *kashitsukekin* (loaned-out money) in Total Loans[a]

At the End of Year	1899 (%)		1910 (%)		1915 (%)		1916 (%)	
	(1)	(2)	(1)	(2)	(1)	(2)	(1)	(2)
Mitsui Bank[b]	74.8	5.8	46.3	45.0	55.4	36.5	49.3	41.7
Daiichi Bank	61.5	26.3	82.8	7.3	79.2	13.1	31.0	62.0
Mitsubishi Bank	52.7	42.7	81.3	11.5	70.2	22.7	10.8	81.8
Yasuda Bank	30.0	29.3	48.1	37.2	48.6	24.7	14.2	66.3
Sumitomo Bank	82.6	10.4	95.8	0.4	94.9	0.2	32.0	63.3
TOTAL	63.5	20.5	67.2	24.0	70.9	19.9	30.4	61.4
All ordinary banks	45.7	34.9	55.1	29.3	62.1	24.1	22.2	66.5

Source: Histories of the banks.
[a] Total loans = (1) + (2) + overdrafts.
[b] The Mitsui Bank changed its accounting method in 1910 rather than in 1916.

industrial enterprises. But this opinion was mistaken insofar as it overlooked the continuity of indirect finance to the raw-silk manufacturers by the larger urban banks.

Our focus next turns to the industrial finance provided by the banks, first to the cotton-spinning industry as the leading sector of Japanese industry, second to the silk-reeling industry as the most important export industry, and third to the railway industry, which required the largest amount of funds.

The cotton-spinning industry. The total paid-up capital of the cotton-spinning industry amounted to 30,313,000 yen at the end of 1899, which ranked first among manufacturing industries.[34] Table 10–5 shows the financial data of the five firms that would form the Big Three after 1918.[35] In 1890 most of the equipment fund was raised by paid-up capital. But we must remember that banks sometimes financed stockholders in order to encourage the payment of this capital. For example, the Yokkaichi branch of the Daiichi Bank financed the stockholders of the Mie Spinning Co., taking the shares of the company as security to the amount of 6,000 shares in 1897, which was about one-fifth of the total shares issued by the company or about one-third of the shares owned by stockholders in Mie prefecture.

During the 1890s the funds needed for expansion exceeded the accumulation of internal reserves and paid-up capital, so that the insufficiency of equipment capital had to be covered with debentures and bank loans, including short-term loans. The Osaka Spinning Co. drew accommodation bills on the Naigai Men Co., a trading company in raw cotton and cotton goods, and had the Daiichi Bank discount these bills. The Kanegafuchi Spinning Co. depended on a loan of a million yen from the Mitsui Bank when the company purchased three bankrupt firms in 1899 and 1900. By 1910, however, the insufficiency of equipment capital tended to diminish.[36]

The cotton-spinning firms used to draw bills on the trading companies, such as Mitsui Bussan, Nihon Menka, and Naigai Men, from which they bought raw cotton. During the 1890s these bills were soon discounted by the ordinary banks in Osaka or

TABLE 10–5. Financial Data of the Five Leading
Cotton-Spinning Firms, 1890–1910

	End of Year		
	1890	1899	1910
Item	(in thousands of yen)		
Fixed assets (1)	3,267	10,410	39,261
Paid-up capital (2)	3,154	7,600	22,530
Internal reserve (3)	518	1,532	16,576
(2) + (3) − (1)	405	−1,278	−155
Liabilities—long (4)	214	832	5,885
Liabilities—short (5)	932	2,163	7,336
Firm	Fixed-Asset Ratio (%)		
Osaka	92.1	119.6	105.7
Mie	87.9	90.1	94.3
Kanegafuchi	81.2	134.5	109.1
Amagasaki	—	113.4	66.0
Settsu	97.0	86.5	97.5
TOTAL	89.0	114.0	100.4

Source: Kazuo Yamaguchi, ed., History of the Industrial Finance in Japan (cotton spinning industry), Tokyo, 1970.
Notes: Fixed-asset ratio = (1)/[(2) + (3)]. (3) = reserves and balances carried forward. (4) = debentures and loans. (5) = overdrafts and promissory notes.

Tokyo, and re-discounted by the Bank of Japan. For example, all of the bills drawn by the Osaka agency of the Kurashiki Spinning Co. from 1895 to 1897 (amounting to 1,214,000 yen) were soon discounted by the ordinary banks in Osaka, and three-fourths of these bills (920,000 yen) were re-discounted by the Osaka branch of the Bank of Japan. Considering the fact that the discount fee was paid, not by the trading companies on which bills were drawn, but by the cotton-spinning firms themselves, these bills should be looked on as instruments by which the cotton-spinning firms asked banks for loans secured by the credit of the trading companies.[37]

Until they accumulated enough internal reserves after the turn of the century, the cotton-spinning firms and their stockholders had to depend on bank loans that were used not only for working capital but also for fixed capital, directly or indirectly.

The silk-reeling industry. According to company statistics, the status of the silk-reeling industry was very low, for most of the filatures (silk-reeling factories) were not incorporated at this time. During the 1870s many small filatures with ten to thirty reeling basins were constructed on the model of the Tomioka filature with 300 basins of French style, completed in 1872 by the Japanese government. Soon, however, the reeling equipment in these small filatures was transformed into much simpler and cheaper ones than those in the Tomioka filature. At Suwa in Nagano prefecture, the cost of construction of these small filatures was only 10 to 20 yen per basin, while that the Tomioka filature was about 660 yen.[38] (The basin is an apparatus with hot water from which a female laborer reels raw silk off cocoons.) It has been said that Japanese raw-silk manufacturers, starting their business on a small scale, expanded the filatures usually by investing most of their profit in reeling equipment because they could borrow working capital.

They borrowed the working capital to buy raw cocoons from silk merchants of Yokohama, an export port for raw silk, and from local banks of silk-producing areas. For example, the S. Hayashi family in Suwa, which had 300 basins and bought about 100,000 yen of cocoons from June to July in 1895, borrowed a like sum from Ono and Co. in Yokohama and the Nineteenth National Bank in Nagano prefecture.[39]

Such Yokohama silk merchants and local banks in turn borrowed money from the larger urban banks in Yokohama and Tokyo (Table 10–6). The Second Bank and the Seventy-fourth Bank in Yokohama depended almost entirely on funds from the Bank of Japan. Although the Bank of Japan and the larger urban banks tended to avoid direct transactions with small silk manufacturers, the funds of these banks were provided abundantly to them by way of Yokohama silk merchants and local banks. Consequently, the raw-silk manufacturers had to pay the greater part of their gains to the merchants and banks as commissions (1.0–1.5 percent) or interest (10–15 percent per annum), so that they could hardly provide their own working capital.[40]

In Suwa there were many manufacturers who were expanding their filatures so fast that they borrowed money from the Nineteenth Bank even though they had not repaid their old debts. Few manufacturers had sizable deposits in the bank (Table 10–7). Katakura was an exceptional case, and such manufacturers as Yamaju, Oguchi, and Ozawa expanded their filatures by means of virtual long-term loans of the Nineteenth Bank. The loans from Yokohama silk merchants also often became virtual long-term loans.[41]

The development of the silk-reeling industry, which has usually been regarded as the typical case of "growth-from-below," was in fact supported by the indirect finance

TABLE 10–6. Financing from the Larger Urban Banks (thousands of yen)

	To Yokohama Silk Merchants 9 July 1907	To the Nineteenth Bank 25 July 1907
Bank of Japan	—	1,187
Yokohama Specie Bank	5,000	354
The Second Bank	1,600	—
The Seventy-fourth Bank	900	—
Mitsui Bank	3,200	260
Daiichi Bank	1,500	250
The Third Bank	800	—
Mitsubishi Bank	—	640
Sumitomo Bank	—	200
Others	—	1,335
TOTAL	13,000	4,226

Source: Historical Materials of the Mitsui Bank, Tokyo, 1978, p. 94; Kazuo Yamaguchi, ed., *The History of Industrial Finance in Japan (silk-reeling industry),* Tokyo, 1966, pp. 146–147.

TABLE 10–7. Debit Balances of Silk Manufacturers of the Nineteenth Bank, 1908–1914 (thousands of yen)

	Katakura	Yamaju	Oguchi	Hayashi	Okaya	Ozawa
End of May						
1908	−269	19	48	23	—	81
1909	−177	42	—	46	−5	77
1910	−363	93	—	11	−1	73
1911	−575	88	2	−1	−8	−36
1912	−364	180	37	8	−2	225
1913	−425	189	54	30	5	159
1914	−658	146	11	−3	−10	115
Basins						
1908	3,536	1,445	1,606	1,729	2,131	1,621
1914	6,195	6,061	3,674	2,920	2,570	2,083

Souce: The History of the City of Yokohama, Vol. 4–1, Yokohama, 1965, pp. 68–69.

Note: Minus means a credit balance.

of the larger urban banks, the central figures of "growth-from-above." Such a close connection was one of the reasons for the extraordinary development of the Japanese silk-reeling industry.

The railway industry. From Table 10–8 we see that most of the construction expenses were met from paid-up capital, particularly in the cases of the six largest companies. Although the government granted permission for foreigners to invest in Japanese railway companies in June 1900,[42] their investments were negligible until the nationalization of railway companies in 1906, when such opportunities ended. One of the reasons why the large volume of shares of the railway companies could be sold internally in Japan was the development of stock-secured finance by the ordinary banks, supported by the Bank of Japan. In order to help the banks, which fell into difficulties by the sudden depreciation of the shares taken as security in 1890, the Bank of Japan discounted bills secured by the shares of main railway companies. In spite of

TABLE 10–8. Financial Data of the Railway Companies (thousands of yen)

1900 (year-end)	Paid-up Capital over 5 Million Yen (6 companies)	Paid-up Capital under 5 Million Yen (35 companies)	Total (41 companies)
Construction expenses (1)	134,326	63,188	197,514
Paid-up capital (2)	130,283	50,984	181,267
Internal reserve (3)	3,092	544	3,636
(2) + (3) − (1)	−951	−11,660	−12,611
Debentures	4,759	6,259	11,018
Liabilities—long	338	2,160	2,498
Liabilities—short	1,365	6,068	7,433

Source: Department of Railways, *The Annual Report for the Year 1900.*

Note: The six companies with paid capital of over 5 million yen were the Nihon, the Kyushu, the Sanyo, the Kansai, the Hokkaido Tanko, and the Hoshu Railway Companies.

this violation of its own regulation, the Bank of Japan continued to discount such bills until 1906.[43]

In the case of the smaller companies, debentures and bank loans were indispensable for the construction of railways. There were some cases in which the railway companies borrowed virtual long-term funds by discounting bills at banks. For example, the Ohmi Railway Co., which had 901,000 yen of paid-up capital and no internal reserve at the end of the year 1900, had to draw 832,000 yen in bills to pay construction expenses amounting to 1,614,000 yen. These bills, drawn by the president of the company and endorsed by all of the directors, were discounted by banks in Shiga (Ohmi) prefecture, Osaka, Kyoto, Tokyo, and elsewhere. The first bill discounted by the Kitahama Bank in Osaka on August 20, 1900, was renewed twenty times until October 30, 1904. Between 1900 and 1904 the Ohmi Railway Co. drew 426 bills amounting to 9,734,000 yen.[44] Among the bills for unsecured debt discounted by banks in Osaka and Kyoto at the end of January 1901, amounting to 24,001,000 yen, those drawn by the railway companies for 3,328,000 yen occupied the second rank, following those drawn by cotton-spinning companies totaling 4,838,000 yen.[45] Most of the bills drawn by the railway companies were accommodation bills like those drawn by the Ohmi Railway Co.

From this it is clear that finance by banks played a crucial role in the capital accumulation of the railway companies.

Having examined the finances of the three main industries, we can now conclude that the role of banks was decisive for the development of these industries. The banks provided them with funds for both fixed capital and working capital. Of course, we should admit that the situation changed through the 1900s because the leading cotton-spinning companies accumulated enough internal reserves and the main railway companies were nationalized. From the early 1900s on, however, heavy industry began to develop in Japan and demanded a large amount of funds. In this chapter we concentrated our analysis on the three most important industries of the 1890s. At that time the larger urban banks headed by the Bank of Japan financed small-scale industrial units as well as large-scale ones, directly or indirectly via local banks, merchants, or stockholders.[46] This highly organized financial system permitted rapid development of Japanese industries without importing foreign capital.

Banks and the Export of Capital

As we have seen, there was no surplus capital in Japan to export at that time, but Japan actually did export some capital to Korea, Formosa, and China. Why and how was such export of capital possible?

The First National Bank in Korea. In 1876 the Japanese government forced Korea to open the country in much the same way that Commodore Perry opened Japan in the 1850s. In 1878 the Daiichi Kokuritsu Bank (the First National Bank) set up a branch at Pusan, a treaty port in Korea, another at Wonsan in 1880, and a third at Inchon in 1882. The Daiichi Bank, established in 1872, was one of the biggest banks in Japan, and its president, Eiichi Shibusawa, was also the president of the Tokyo Chamber of Commerce. Kohachiro Okura, who later became vice president of the Tokyo Chamber of Commerce, had previously been asked by a leading official, Toshimichi Okubo, to begin transactions with Korean merchants; he requested Shibusawa to set up branches of the Daiichi Bank in Korea.[47]

In addition to the Daiichi Bank, the Eighteenth National Bank of Nagasaki opened an Inchon branch in 1890, as did the Fifty-eighth National Bank of Osaka in 1892.[48] These banks provided Japanese merchants in Korea with funds. In 1884 the Daiichi Bank succeeded in getting the deposit of customs duty revenue of the Korean government. Gradually it became a kind of central bank of Korea.[49]

After the conclusion of the Sino-Japanese War, Shibusawa set about establishing the Keijin Railway Co. Ltd., and the Keifu Railway Co. Ltd. The latter was to construct a long railway between Seoul and Pusan. Shibusawa and his supporters traveled to various places in Japan to persuade local landowners and merchants to buy shares of the company.[50] He also attempted to gain foreign capital from the United States, Belgium, and the United Kingdom, but his efforts failed for several reasons, including opposition by the Japanese army, which was planning to rule Korea itself.[51] At last the 4 million yen debenture of the company was underwritten by a syndicate of big Japanese banks including Mitsui, Mitsubishi, and Daiichi.[52]

Following the protocol between Korea and Japan concluded at the outbreak of the Russo-Japanese War, Korea gradually became a kind of protectorate of Japan, and finally lost its independence in 1910. The branches of the Daiichi Bank accounted for two-thirds of the total deposits, loans, and profits of all banks in Korea in 1908, and the profit of its Korean branches was about one-third of the total profit of the Daiichi Bank.[53] As the amount of bank notes issued by Korean branches increased, Korea became a part of the gold realm of Japan, for their bank notes could be converted into those of the Bank of Japan.

In 1909 the Japanese government ordered the Daiichi Bank to transfer the main business of its branches in Korea to the newly established Bank of Korea, the central bank. The Keifu Railway Co., was absorbed by the Japan National Railways in 1906. The energetic activities of Shibusawa in Korea were from beginning to end closely connected with the Japanese government, which endeavored to rule Korea politically.

The Bank of Taiwan in Formosa. In 1895 Taiwan (Formosa) became a colony of Japan as a result of the Sino-Japanese War, and the Bank of Taiwan was established as the central bank in 1899. Of the bank's entire capital of 5 million yen, the Japanese government held one fifth and most of the remainder was collected from Japanese landowners and merchants.

As Formosa had been in the silver realm of China, the Bank of Taiwan at first issued bank notes convertible into silver coins. But when the Bank of Taiwan began to issue new bank notes convertible into gold coins in 1904, Formosa became a part of the gold realm of Japan. On such a common currency basis the direct investments in Formosa by Japanese sugar companies increased.[54]

Capital exports to China. The balance of Japanese capital exports to China in 1914 was $219.6 million, which is far less than that from the United Kingdom ($607.5 million), but comparable to those from Russia ($269.3 million), Germany ($263.6

million), and France ($171.4 million). Approximately 88 percent of the Japanese total was direct investments, which were represented by that in the South Manchurian Railway Co., and about half of the remaining 12 percent represented loans from the Industrial Bank of Japan and the Yokohama Specie Bank to the Hanyang Ironworks located in central China.[55]

In 1899 the Japanese government contracted with the Hanyang Ironworks to import iron ore for the government-controlled Yawata Ironworks. From 1904 the Japanese government advanced funds repeatedly to the Hanyang Ironworks through the above-mentioned special banks. By a loan of 15 million yen in 1913 the Japanese government obtained the total assets of the Hanyang Ironworks as security for loans, and sent engineers and an account advisor to the ironworks. Thus the Hanyang Ironworks, which had been sending iron ore and pig iron to the Yawata Ironworks, became actually a mere branch factory of the Yawata facility.[56] The funds advanced were mainly provided by the Ministry of Finance of Japan, which gathered them through the post offices in the entire country. The post office saving system in Japan was characterized by extremely small deposits. It was estimated in 1908 that the size of deposit per depositor in Japan was about one-tenth of those in Britain, France, Belgium, or Russia. Another characteristic of the system was that the Minister of Finance had the right to use the funds without consulting any authorities. As a result, the Japanese government was able to export capital to Asian countries whenever it thought necessary.[57]

When South Manchuria, located in the northeastern part of China, became a sphere of influence of Japan by the Treaty of Portsmouth in 1905, the main concern of the Japanese government was how to get funds to manage the South Manchurian Railway. Although a memorandum of agreement to form a syndicate to provide the capital for the railway had been exchanged between E. H. Harriman, president of the Union Pacific Railroad Co., and Taro Katsura, the Prime Minister of Japan, it was cancelled by the strong opposition of Jyutaro Komura, the Foreign Minister, who had just returned from the Portsmouth peace conference. The proposal of P. C. Knox, the U.S. Secretary of State, to put the railway under joint control of the Powers was also rejected by the governments of Japan and Russia.[58] Having rejected the attempts of American capitalists to participate in the railway, the Japanese government had to let the South Manchurian Railway Co. issue debentures amounting to £ 14 million in London from 1907 to 1911, mainly through the Industrial Bank of Japan.

The Yokohama Specie Bank, which had opened many agencies in Manchuria during the war, tried to unify the currencies after the war by issuing its bank notes convertible into silver coins. Although its bank notes were fitted to the silver realm of China, the attempt ended in failure, partly because the South Manchurian Railway Co. and Japanese merchants in Manchuria insisted on using the notes of the Bank of Japan, convertible into gold coins, and partly because financial institutions of the Chinese local government began to issue their own paper money. The lack of enough funds of the Specie Bank to control the Chinese local government prevented it from unifying the currencies of Manchuria, as had been done in Formosa and Korea.[59]

Concerning capital exports to China from Japan, the direct investment by the cotton-spinning industry was important, too, but mainly after World War I. Prior to that time capital export to China from Japan was mainly promoted by the Japanese government. The funds were provided by issuing debentures in London and by gathering small savings through post offices. These are the reasons why Japan could export considerable capital to China before the onset of the Great War.

Conclusion

International factors played a decisive role in the formation of the modern Japanese banking system. The Japanese government investigated assiduously the modern banking systems of the advanced foreign countries and tried to emulate the most developed systems. We should admit, however, that a highly developed credit system before 1870 in Japan had enabled the Japanese government to imitate such banking systems.

Although the Japanese government expected to have the ordinary banks develop as commercial banks on the British model, such banks had to provide major industries from the beginning with funds for both fixed capital and working capital, as the German banks did. The larger urban banks headed by the Bank of Japan financed not only large-scale industrial units but also the small-scale ones, directly or indirectly via local banks, merchants, or stockholders. Such a highly organized financial system in Japan promoted industrialization without depending upon foreign capital.

Finally, Japan exported some capital to other Asian countries despite a shortage of capital of its own. The funds for capital export were provided by issuing debentures in London and by gathering small savings through post offices located all across Japan. Thus it was that Japan became the sole imperialistic power in East Asia.

II

FOREIGN BANKS AND FOREIGN INVESTMENT

11

Foreign Banks and Foreign Investment in the United States

Mira Wilkins

America in 1914 was a debtor nation in international accounts, owing more money abroad than was owed to it.[1] Long-term foreign investment in the United States on the eve of World War I totaled in excess of $7 billion.[2] The United States had the largest foreign obligations of any country in the world.[3] The foreign investment in the United States, which had mounted from 1870 to 1914, contributed to making the American economy the wealthiest in the world.

Foreign investment came from European countries, from Canada, and to a far lesser extent from elsewhere. Throughout these years, Britain was by far America's greatest source of foreign capital, followed by Germany, Holland, and then France, Canada, Switzerland, Belgium, Sweden, and so forth.[4] Part of this foreign investment was by multinational enterprises and, in many such cases, no financial intermediaries aided the entries. Some of the "foreign direct investments"[5] were, however, assisted by foreign banks. As for the substantial portfolio interests, banks—foreign and domestic—played a major role in expediting the transfer of capital. The use of the word "banks" here includes merchant banks as well as banks of deposit. This chapter deals with such banks. Foreign-headquartered investment trust companies, mortgage companies, mortgage banks, and insurance offices were other channels through which Old World savings were transferred into American investment. These are excluded here from the definition of banks and, accordingly, from this chapter, basically because of space limitations.

This chapter deals exclusively with long-term nonresident foreign investment.[6] Excluded are short-term trade-related credits or other short-term obligations; only when a bank's international behavior was altered by foreign trade financing in a manner that affected long-term foreign investments in the United States or affected the extension of the bank itself internationally will data on foreign trade financing be included.

In 1870 long-term foreign investment in the United States—as estimated by the U.S. Commissioner of Revenue for year-end 1869—came to about $1,390.5 million, of which $1 billion was in U.S. federal government securities, $107.5 million in state government and municipal bonds, $243 million in railroad bonds and shares, and $40 million in other securities, real estate mortgages, "and so forth." For 1914, economist

Cleona Lewis divided the long-term foreign investment in the United States, which she put at $7,090 million, in the following manner: $4,170 million in U.S. railroads, $1,710 million in other securities, and $1,210 million in foreign-controlled enterprises.[7] While I have some reservations about the accuracy of these estimates, a total of $1.4 billion for January 1870 and $7.1 billion for July 1, 1914 seems legitimate.[8] As these figures suggest, over the years from 1870 to 1914 not only did the totals increase but the sectors attracting investment changed. The most conspicuous difference between the 1870 and 1914 allocations lies in the relative position of government versus railroad securities. Likewise, Ms. Lewis included what we now define as "foreign direct investment," while the Commissioner of Revenue did not put "foreign-controlled" enterprises in a separate category. In 1870 government securities attracted the most foreign investment. From the 1880s onward foreign investment in America went overwhelmingly into productive private-sector activities.[9]

The Nature of the Foreign Investment and the Banker's Role

In the 1870s there were important foreign investments in American federal government securities, but by 1914 such stakes were minimal. Financing the American Civil War (which ended in 1865) had required formidable public expenditures. Most of the winning side's financing had been done at home. Yet, when the victory of the North seemed assured, speculators on the European continent bought existing American government securities at well below par, gambling on appreciation. Thus, U.S. federal government securities, initially taken up at home, had drifted abroad.[10] In the early 1870s two large U.S. dollar-denominated refunding loans were in the main placed abroad—although with difficulty;[11] and in the years between 1874 and 1879, the country sought to resume a specie-backed currency (the nation used "greenbacks"— fiat paper currency—during and after the Civil War). Foreign investments assisted the process of specie resumption. N. M. Rothschild & Sons, London, played a significant role.[12] In 1879 America went—on a *de facto* basis—onto the gold standard. In early 1895, when the U.S. Treasury worried about the outflow of gold, N. M. Rothschild & Sons helped stem the tide (foreign investment serving that function). The Rothschilds were not, however, prepared to pursue a similar course in late 1895.[13]

Aside from the foreign investments of the 1870s and 1895, for the years 1870 to 1914 foreign holdings of U.S. federal government securities—which in 1870 (as noted) had represented the largest single sector in the foreign indebtedness statistics— had no significance. In 1914 the *Stock Exchange Official Intelligence,* London, listed only three U.S. government bonds: the 4 percent U.S. loan issued in February 1895 (and selling at between $111\frac{1}{2}$ and $118\frac{1}{2}$—i.e., well above par); a 3 percent loan that had been offered at par in 1898 (that had virtually no buyers in Britain); and a 2 percent issue of March 1900 that was exchanged for certain U.S. bonds bearing a higher rate. The manual also noted other outstanding U.S. federal government loans (at 2 or 3 percent).[14] The interest rate was too low to be attractive to foreign investors. In 1914 foreign investments in U.S. federal government securities—aside from the holdings of foreign-based insurance companies that were in business in the United States—were negligible. The American market absorbed these securities.

As for bonds of American state governments, the post–Civil War years saw substantial foreign interest in these issues—and then in the early 1870s many southern state governments defaulted.[15] For the last two decades of the nineteenth century and in the early twentieth century, state government securities (which at one period in pre–Civil War American history had been the most important sector for foreign investment)[16] virtually disappeared from foreign portfolios. Here again, American domestic money markets proved adequate for state government needs. Some American cities had in times past sold, and continued from 1870 to 1914 to sell, securities abroad. By the early twentieth century, however, only New York City went on a regular basis to foreign markets for financial assistance.[17]

Far more important in the period between 1870 and 1914 were the formidable foreign private sector investments. American railroads were the magnet for the most foreign capital from 1880 to 1914. It is not clear precisely when the level of foreign investment in U.S. railroads surpassed that in American government securities—probably during the mid-1870s, but certainly by 1880. From the 1880s to 1914 foreign stakes in railroads took first place.[18]

Foreign investments in American railroads were awesome. The geographical size of the United States created a demand for transportation that could only be met by giant expenditures. Americans wanted a railroad network connecting the east and west coasts and the intervening areas. The country in 1870 had 53,000 miles of railroad track in operation; the comparable figure at year-end 1913 was 380,000.[19] To build such a vast railroad system required far more capital than the nation could provide. To mobilize foreign as well as domestic investment called for a new sophistication—for "professional" finance. Railroads depended on bankers and money markets. Foreign savings flowed into U.S. railroad bonds and shares, more to the former than to the latter. Banks facilitated the process.[20]

Sometimes a bank (foreign or domestic) acted as a loan contractor. More often in these years, the bank served as an underwriter, or more often still, part of an underwriting syndicate. Often there were participations, involving American and foreign banks. The leader(s) in managing an issue would assemble a group. Frequently the initiative was taken by an American bank or banks that either had houses abroad or had close associations with foreign banks (Morgan; Morton, Bliss; Kuhn, Loeb; Speyer; Seligman, for example); sometimes the initiative was taken by a foreign bank—Baring, for instance.

Stanley Chapman has written that "the main period of issue of American railway securities in London (1865–1880) saw numerous [merchant banking] firms involved—with the Barings, Bischoffsheim & Goldschmidt, J. S. Morgan, and Morton, Rose the key ones."[21] J. S. Morgan & Co., London, was headed by J. P. Morgan's father; Morton, Rose was an American house in London. Chapman's emphasis on the years 1865 to 1880 neglects the many subsequent issues, both in London and on the Continent.[22] The later issues—especially those in the early twentieth century—were huge. In 1906, for example, the Pennsylvania Railroad marketed a $50 million loan in Paris.[23]

In the case of a new issue of a security, banks helped the railroads to decide in what currency it should be denominated (dollars, pounds, or francs). If denominated in dollars, bonds could have a fixed exchange rate specified for interest and principal, or just for the interest payments. Some bonds were specified as gold-backed. There were first and second mortgage bonds and general mortgage bonds. Some were convertible. Bonds were issued on divisions of particular railroads, or subsidiaries of railroads. There were "serial debentures," "first collateral trust mortgage gold bonds," "refunding and extension mortgage gold bonds," "first consolidated mortgage gold bonds," and numerous other types of securities. A single railroad might have a whole battery of differently backed bonds.[24]

After a banker or bankers were chosen, the American railroad and its bankers would determine not only the currency in which the issue would be denominated but also the type of issue (what the backing would be). In addition, the banker would, in collaboration with the railroad, establish the appropriate interest rate, the duration of the bond, the price at which it would be offered, and the timing of the issue.[25] For example, among the numerous bonds of the Atchison, Topeka, and Santa Fe Railway "known in London" in 1913 were "General Mortgage Four Per Cent, 100 Year Gold Bonds," "Four Per Cent, 100 Year Adjustment Bonds" (secured by a mortgage), "Ten Year Five Per Cent Convertible Gold Bonds," and "Four Per Cent 50-year Convertible Gold Bonds." All of these were denominated in dollars, with maturities in 1995, 1995, 1917, and 1955, respectively.[26] The banker was essential in helping the railroad's management decide what the market would absorb and in working out the logistics of the issue. This required a professional with knowledge of foreign investors' preferences. That professional could be an American or a foreign banker, but often was the latter.

It was, however, not only in the origination and marketing of new issues that bankers participated; in the years between 1870 and 1914 existing American railroad securities were increasingly introduced into foreign markets and traded. The level of foreign investment is *not* reflected in the total of "new issues." Foreign investors bought and sold existing American "rails" on a regular basis. Merchant bankers expedited these trades. Foreign bankers often served a brokerage function, buying and selling American railroad securities on behalf of clients in London, New York, or elsewhere.[27]

Bankers arranged for listings on foreign stock exchanges for both new *and* existing securities. That a security was listed on a foreign stock exchange did not necessarily mean that there had been an "issue" in that country. In January 1873, the nominal value of American railway securities quoted on the London Stock Exchange was £ 82.7 million; on December 31, 1913, the same figure was £ 1.7 billion.[28] These numbers do *not* indicate foreign investment in American railroads, or British investment; what they reveal is the growing availability on the London market of American railroad securities. Such accessibility made transactions easier. In Amsterdam, American railroads figured prominently among the foreign ones.[29] Likewise, American railroads were traded on the Frankfurt, Berlin, Paris, and other European exchanges.[30]

Bankers arranged for dividends, interest, and principal (when appropriate) to be paid to the investor in a familiar currency. Investors did not want to worry about foreign exchange. Bankers aided in the routine of security transfers. The foreign investor in American securities wanted liquidity. By 1914 the *Stock Exchange Official Intelligence*, London, contained detailed information on how American railroad securities could be transferred. Typically the signature of the transferor had to be guaranteed. A bank or banking house often performed that function. In some cases the name of the banking house was specified—for example, Baring Brothers for the Atchison,

Topeka, and Santa Fe Railway.[31] American railroads had London banks that acted as their "agents"; thus, in 1914, Speyer Brothers, London, served the Baltimore & Ohio Railroad Co., and the London Joint Stock Bank, Ltd. acted for the Pennsylvania Railroad Co.[32] In addition, bankers in London and on the Continent offered financial advisory services and were well versed on American railroads' prospects. It was aptly said that investors trusted the banker, not the borrower.[33]

If an American railroad had problems meeting its obligations, which was frequently the case, foreign bankers joined American ones in participating in financial reorganizations, attempting to restructure the railroad's debt, and sometimes in selling certain assets so as to assure the railroad's financial performance.[34] Dutch bankers were particularly active in this regard. A. A. H. Boissevain of Amsterdam was, for example, on the reorganization committee of the Union Pacific in 1893.[35] European bankers—cooperating with American ones—were catalysts in the American railroad mergers at the turn of the century. The Deutsche Bank, for instance, was involved in discussions leading to the entry of Northern Pacific into Northern Securities.[36]

By 1914 American railroads had become a typical part of the investment portfolios of British businesses as well as those of individual investors.[37] A number of British, continental European, and Canadian banks held American railroad securities as part of their assets—as purely portfolio investments, having nothing whatever to do with the day-by-day operations of either the banks or the railroads.[38] By contrast, Dutch bankers frequently held shares of American railroads for individual investors, providing the latter with certificates that paid dividends in florins; the Dutch bankers in these cases voted the shares on behalf of the individual investors and did have influence.[39]

When in 1905 a private donor made a large contribution of American railroad securities to King Edward's Hospital Fund, those selected as administrators (as a "finance" committee) were leaders in the London financial world and all were highly knowledgeable on American railroad matters: Hugh Colin Smith, former Governor of the Bank of England (1897–1899) and in 1905 a director; Lord Rothschild, head of N. M. Rothschild & Sons; Lord Revelstoke, head of Baring Brothers; Sir Ernest Cassel, a private banker, long active in American railroad finance; and the Scot, Robert Fleming, the pioneer in British investment trusts and in 1905 a merchant banker in London.[40]

Sometimes foreign bankers made loans directly to American railroads and then were repaid through the issues. In an earlier era securities of American railroads had moved overseas in payment for iron rails. This was *not* common after 1870. By 1914, for an investor in Britain or on the Continent or in Canada for that matter, American railroad stocks and bonds were readily available through securities markets. Financial markets were well integrated. A London–New York message by cable could be sent *and* a reply received in two and a half minutes.[41] Transactions could take place on any exchange on behalf of foreign investors.

While railroads were without question the largest single sector attracting foreign capital to America in the late nineteenth and the early twentieth centuries, foreign investments also went into numerous other endeavors. Although railroad finance is now relatively easy to document,[42] international "industrial investments"—those in American mining and manufacturing—were more complex because of the various methods by which long-term foreign capital was introduced. Whereas the greatest part of the foreign monies that went into American railroads (1870–1914) passed through money markets, it is less clear that this was the case with industrial investments. Some foreign investments, to be sure, did mirror the financing of U.S. railroads and were strictly portfolio ones. In 1871 Bischoffsheim & Goldschmidt, which, as noted, participated in American railroad financing, issued in London shares of United States Rolling Stock Company, a firm formed to provide equipment for the Atlantic and Great Western Railroad. The very next year Bischoffsheim & Goldschmidt offered securities of the Atlantic and Great Western Railroad in London.[43] In 1874 the Joliet Iron & Steel Company raised money in Britain; a promoter, David Chadwick, made the arrangements. Chadwick had earlier handled similar transactions for American railroads.[44] When at the turn of the century the giant Amalgamated Copper Company required capital, its securities were offered in London;[45] so, too, when American Smelting and Refining Company sought financial resources it arranged through banking intermediaries to have its securities sold in London and Paris;[46] in 1911 Studebaker Corporation raised money in Europe.[47] In each of these last three cases an issue of an American company was floated and listed on a foreign stock exchange, or exchanges.

Just as with railroads, so with industrial enterprises a company might be listed on a foreign stock exchange with no securities floated abroad. If a new issue were floated, normally a banking house, or several, would participate. Likewise, if the security were listed on a foreign stock exchange, a banker typically arranged the listing. In the *Stock Exchange Official Intelligence,* for example, such industrial companies would usually have a foreign "banker" named.[48] Especially after 1900, the largest American industrials were traded on foreign exchanges. In these instances, the American industrial corporations used basically the same financial infrastructure set up in Europe many years earlier that had served to move European monies into U.S. city, state, and federal government bonds, and then into railroad securities.[49]

It should be noted that, just as in the case of railroads, foreign investors—through banking houses or brokers—could and did buy American industrial securities on Wall Street as well as abroad; the absence of a listing on a foreign exchange did not make the stocks and bonds inaccessible. Canadian and European bankers and brokers had contacts in New York to handle such transactions.

In mining and oil, in London, Paris, Frankfurt, and Berlin, a group of bankers specialized in handling these particular securities. Many of the bankers took part directly in the metals trade, and their banking and trading were associated. Because mining, smelting, and refining enterprises often required substantial capital, this encouraged the integration of the trader-banker with the actual mining and mineral processing. The Metallgesellschaft group, for example, had a banking house; the group's American operations were represented by American Metal Company.[50] The London and Paris Rothschilds were active in the metals trades and in related American industrial investments.[51] While one large British trader (Balfour, Williamson) had interests in American flour mills, it is not possible to establish in agricultural commodities the banker-cum-trader investment relationship in U.S. industrial finance that seems so evident in the mineral industries.[52]

A significant subset in the pattern of banker-trader relationships in "mineral industries" is identified with gold, a monetary metal. Merchant bankers traded in gold. They also had interests in American gold mining. Likewise, there was a silver connection. These investments in monetary metals offer special cases of "industrial finance."[53]

Another important type of U.S. industrial finance from overseas took a different path, with its genesis in an American and/or foreign promoter. A corporation would be set up abroad, typically (but not necessarily) in London, to buy an existing American enterprise or to develop an American mine. If established in the United Kingdom, the company would have a British board of directors, a secretary in Britain, and would be designed to control the American operations. I have labeled such enterprises "free-standing" firms.[54] What characterized a free-standing company was that it had no operations in the place of incorporation, but was formed there principally to facilitate the mobilization of capital. Established merchant bankers were often wary of these ventures.[55] British free-standing companies channeled foreign capital into U.S. mining, steel, breweries, flour milling, and meat packing, as well as in numerous other sectors. The infamous Emma Silver Mining Company, Ltd., was a typical free-standing venture. It was promoted in London; its board of directors was decorated with celebrities; it raised substantial money. It turned out to be a scam.[56]

Take another case—that of Pillsbury-Washburn, America's leading flour maker: A British parent was formed to acquire it; the parent was floated in London.[57] Likewise, a British "syndicate" took over Hammond, one of the four principal U.S. meat packers.[58] Numerous American brewery combinations were floated in London.[59] British bankers' roles in this type of activity ranged from carrying on banking functions for the headquarters company in Britain, to arranging the transfers of securities, to giving advice and assistance when something went wrong.[60]

The key rationale behind the establishment of a British-headquartered company was financial; it was important that the securities be denominated in pounds and be liquid.[61] That they were easily traded was a crucial part of both speculation and industrial finance. The free-standing company was a form that was used for business not only in America but also in other host countries. Its principal advantage was that the investors, who were being courted, had no need to worry about foreign exchange (the investor bought securities denominated in a home currency); the headquarters was at home. The investor made a "foreign investment" by investing in a domestic corporation, which in turn did business abroad. Often, however, at least in the American context, these free-standing enterprises were notoriously unsuccessful—that is, they were not satisfactory sources of profit to the investors. They were often over-capitalized. In the main, their boards of directors (intentions notwithstanding) failed to control, much less monitor, the business. Under American law incorporation frequently had to be in the United States, so these free-standing units became holding companies. They had costs, but no effective continuing function once the initial capital had been raised. Overseeing operations by directors (who had other directorships plus additional full-time commitments) from a British headquarters with at most one full-time person (the secretary), proved virtually impossible. Nonetheless, monies were moved into American industry through such arrangements. There were literally thousands of such free-standing companies.

Most of the free-standing companies in America were set up for the promoters' gain.[62] They can be differentiated from other free-standing companies formed in England by British businessmen in the same industry with an eye to undertaking business in the United States. Thus, British iron masters established iron mining and manufacturing companies in the American South. These were *not* extensions of their existing firms, but were directly related to the business know-how of the British-headquartered founders. For example, the Southern States Coal, Iron, and Land Co., Ltd., incorporated in 1875, would fit into this category; it was organized by English iron masters. Such ventures were for the British-founder-owner's gain. These too had difficulties in continuity. When the original entrepreneur died, the American venture had no parent enterprise to rely on for managerial guidance.

In yet another type of industrial finance, some foreign bankers financed individuals in America. A member of the Swedish Wallenberg family started a cream separator company in New York State. The family firm, Stockholms Enskilda Bank, financed the new manufacturing enterprise.[63] Sometimes a foreign banker took the initiative in U.S. industrial finance: The Deutsche Bank involved Siemens & Halske and Allgemeine Elektricitäts-Gesellschaft (AEG) in the Edison General Electric Co., the predecessor of General Electric.[64] At other times, banks followed industrial companies: Clive Trebilcock reports that Vickers attracted to Electric Boat Company (an American manufacturer of submarines) the investments of the Rothschilds; the Speyers; Ladenburg, Thalmann; and Chaplin, Milne, Grenfell.[65]

Still another prevalent form of foreign investment in U.S. industry was that of the modern multinational enterprise variety: in the factories of Nestlé, Lever, Lipton, J. & P. Coats, Bayer, and the refineries of Royal Dutch-Shell, for example. Sometimes foreign banks played no role whatsoever in these ventures; on occasion they facilitated such investments. When, for instance, Lever invested in the United States, there is no evidence of any bankers having been involved. The Deutsche Bank representative in the United States served Siemens & Halske *after* the latter retreated from its second foreign direct investment in this country—providing a conduit for information and helping the German electrical company solve specific problems that had stemmed from its earlier stakes.[66] The more capital required for the U.S. activities, the more prominent the bankers' role. Thus, when l'Aluminium Français, which comprised the principal French aluminum producers, decided to build an aluminum plant in the United States (1911/12), its initial financing came from Banque Franco-Américaine and then from Crédit Lyonnais and Banque Louis Dreyfus.[67]

These many diverse sorts of foreign participation in U.S. industry were not entirely separate from one another. The purely portfolio foreign investments in U.S. Steel in 1914 (according to corporate records, as of June 1, 1914, $150 million of the common and preferred shares were held outside the United States)[68] in part (probably small part) had their origins in earlier foreign *direct* investments in America by British iron masters. In liquidating their unsuccessful interests, the direct investors had sold out to U.S. Steel (or to its predecessors) and received in exchange—in the typical pattern of mergers—securities in (portfolio investments in) the acquiring company.[69] When Royal Dutch-Shell made a direct investment in oil production in Oklahoma in 1912, the French Rothschilds (who had participated in the oil industry elsewhere) joined with Royal Dutch-Shell; the Rothschilds were in a minority position but did make a contribution to equity.[70]

In the period between 1870 and 1914 other foreign investments in the United States existed, aside from those in federal, state, and municipal government securities, railroads, mines, and manufacturing. These, too, were numerous—from investments in agriculture (including sizable ones in cattle ranches) to those in the telephone system (American Telephone & Telegraph), to those in insurance companies; indeed, very few aspects of the American economy failed to be touched by foreign investment.[71] In these many ("nonindustrial") sectors, the roles of foreign banks as intermediaries covered the spectrum.

Foreign investments in American agricultural land, for example, ranged from backward integration by multinational enterprises (with no banking involvement)—for instance, the Fine Cotton Spinners' and Doublers' Association in cotton plantations— to free-standing companies (with a minimal banking role)—cattle ranches are the leading example. Sometimes foreign investments in agricultural land occurred through mortgage defaults; foreign-owned "investment trust companies" and mortgage companies had large stakes in granting U.S. farm mortgages. British merchant bankers— Benjamin Newgass and Robert Benson & Co.—had investments in American land and farm mortgages.[72]

Foreign interests in American Telephone & Telegraph Co. were strictly portfolio ones. A.T.&T. raised substantial monies abroad in the early twentieth century, and both U.S. and foreign bankers took part in underwriting the new issues.[73] By contrast, the business of the British Marconi company in radio communications was in the form of modern multinational enterprise. In 1912 when Godfrey Isaacs, managing director of the Marconi Wireless Telegraph Co., Ltd., wanted to raise the capital of its American affiliate, he traveled to the United States accompanied by Percy Heybourn, a member of the Stock Exchange firm of Heybourn & Croft, who were the largest jobbers in the Marconi market. Isaacs and Heybourn worked out the financial reorganization of the American Marconi Company. Heybourn was present, for he would introduce some of the new shares of the enlarged capital on both the London and New York markets.[74]

Foreign insurance companies made major investments in the United States. To sell insurance in America they needed a presence there and, accordingly, made the sizable investments, especially in American railroads. These were "foreign investments" (even though the transactions took place in the United States) because they represented, ultimately, a claim on U.S. assets by a foreign beneficial owner. No banks seem to have been involved; the insurance companies were themselves financial intermediaries. While British firms ranked first among foreign insurance companies in America, would anyone have expected that the fourth largest foreign insurer in the United States as measured by net premium income was the Rossia (sic) Insurance Co. of St. Petersburg?[75]

In sum, this brief overview, covering the period between 1870 and 1914, reveals the wide variety of long-term foreign investments in the United States and the involvement of the various foreign banks.[76] To repeat, from the 1880s to the end of the period under discussion, 1914, foreign investments in the United States were principally in private, not public sector, activities.

Bankers' Transatlantic Associations

Foreign banks, as indicated, expedited the transfer of capital to America. Their close associations with American banking institutions assisted the process. J. S. Morgan & Co., the successor to George Peabody and the predecessor of Morgan, Grenfell & Co., headquartered in London, worked with Drexel, Morgan & Co. and its successor, J. P. Morgan & Co., New York. Brown, Shipley & Co., London, was the British house of Brown Brothers. Morton, Rose in London had Levi Morton, an American, as the principal partner; but Chaplin, Milne, Grenfell (the successor to Morton, Rose)—which continued to have a large U.S. business—does not seem to have had an American partner. The Seligmans migrated to the United States from Germany, and then set up (from a U.S. base) branch houses in foreign cities. The Seligmans were an American-based bank; the direction was from the United States. The Lazard brothers migrated to America, opened houses in the United States, and then, in turn, ones in Paris and London. The latter appear to have been more independent than the Seligmans' foreign banks, yet I think it is legitimate to call the Lazard firm American; there are Frenchmen who call it "French"; and Lazard Brothers is often included in lists of London banks. Blake, Boissevain & Co., London, had American and Dutch partners; when it went into liquidation, January 1, 1901, the Swiss Bankverein, which already had sizable U.S. business, took over many of that firm's customers. The Swiss Bank Corporation's historian writes that the firm of Ad. Boissevain in Amsterdam and its "branch" in New York were retained as "connections."[77] The Speyer firm began in Frankfurt, and then established New York and London houses. In 1870, it was probably a "German" firm, since the Frankfurt bank was still the center of its activities. By 1914 the New York house was of key importance. Yet, Sir Edgar Speyer in London was a leader in his own right. I include the Speyer firm below under co-partnership relations.

The difficulty in defining a "foreign" (as distinct from American) headquarters is not the only problem facing the student of foreign banks in America.[78] For example, the evidence indicates that in the late nineteenth and early twentieth centuries, the British and the French Rothschild houses made decisions independently. The cousins corresponded, kept each other informed, yet neither London nor Paris was the Rothschild "headquarters."

Such problems in pinpointing foreign headquarters notwithstanding, this chapter deals solely with the banks that had their key decision making abroad (defining foreign headquarters as the location of such decision making). Examples are provided of the various forms of operations in the United States of foreign-headquartered banks. (I leave the American-headquartered ones to Professors Carosso and Sylla; see Chapter 2.)

In order to intermediate monies into the United States, a foreign bank did not require a physical presence, that is, "operations" in the United States. Typically, however, if a foreign bank handled substantial American business it would normally have some sort of regular "connections" in the United States. Such "connections" were diverse, changed over time, and comprised a complicated (and still not very well documented) web of interrelationships. Sometimes a foreign bank's American "presence" had nothing (or little) to do with the influx of capital into the country. Many relationships appear to have been informal. The Barings and the Rothschilds had long been involved in intermediating capital to America. Because of their special importance vis-à-vis foreign investment in the United States, we shall examine their American connections in some detail, and then give a sampling of the various forms of "operations" of other foreign banks.

The Barings had developed their American business from the end of the eighteenth century.[79] In 1870 Thomas Baring (1799–1873) was close to retirement; after him, Russell Sturgis (1805–1887) became the senior partner. Sturgis was an American, but more interested in East Asian than in U.S. business (he retired in 1882). In the

1880s the key partner in Barings was Edward Charles Baring, as of 1885 the first Lord Revelstoke (1828–1897). E. C. Baring had become a partner in 1856; he was concerned with American finance, and under his direction in the 1880s Baring Brothers enlarged its American investments. After the 1890 Baring crisis, Lord Revelstoke yielded the leadership of the house to his eldest son, John Baring (1863–1929), who became, in 1897, the second Lord Revelstoke. John Baring, with the aid of his cousin Francis Henry Baring (1850–1915), son of Baron Northbrook, headed the firm. When Francis Baring retired in 1902, Gaspard Farrer became a partner in the House of Baring. While the second Lord Revelstoke had interests in American finance, this was even more the case with Gaspard Farrer. Before joining Barings, Gaspard Farrer had been a partner in H. S. Lefevre, London, and through his clusters of friends had many American involvements.[80]

Meanwhile, across the Atlantic, until 1885, the Barings were represented in New York by the firm S. G. & G. C. Ward. Samuel Grey Ward and George Cabot Ward were sons of the Bostonian Thomas Wren Ward (1786–1858), who in 1829 had become Baring's U.S. representative.[81] While the Wards still acted for the Barings in New York, in 1878 Kidder, Peabody & Co., Boston, became the Barings' "correspondents" in both New York and Boston.[82] When in January 1886 Baring Brothers, London, appointed Kidder, Peabody its exclusive U.S. agent, this substituted for its now terminated relationship with the Ward family. That year, 1886, Thomas Baring (1839–1923), brother of the first Lord Revelstoke, became a partner in Kidder, Peabody, joining another Kidder, Peabody partner, George C. Magoun, in the New York office of the Boston house.[83] This arrangement persisted until after the Baring crisis; then, in 1891, for the first time in their entire history, the Barings set up a house in New York that carried the family name, Baring, Magoun & Co. They contributed $2 million to the capital of the new New York house, while Kidder, Peabody matched that sum. Cecil Baring (1864–1934), son of E. C. Baring and brother of John Baring, joined his uncle as a partner in Baring, Magoun & Co., New York. Thomas Baring withdrew as a partner in Kidder, Peabody at this time. Magoun died in 1893, but the New York firm kept his name until 1906, when it was restyled Baring & Co.; the Baring then in America was Cecil's youngest brother, Hugo. Hugo Baring (1876–1949) returned to England in 1908, and Baring's New York business had a new title, becoming as it had been from 1886 to 1890, a branch office of Kidder, Peabody, Boston.[84] The fundamental difference was that there was now no Baring partner involved. Kidder, Peabody was the exclusive agent for Baring Brothers, but with no interlocking partnership relations.

At the same time, Baring Brothers had many associations with other American banks. In the important American Telephone & Telegraph issue of 1906, for example, J. P. Morgan, Kuhn, Loeb & Co., Kidder, Peabody & Co., and Baring Bros. & Co., Ltd. served as managers of the underwriting syndicate.[85] Gaspard Farrer was a long-time friend of the New York lawyer John W. Sterling, who in turn was intimate with James Stillman, president of National City Bank.[86] Farrer was also very close to Lord Mount Stephen—an important foreign investor in James Hill's railroads.[87] In international banking such personal relations were of the greatest importance. In short, the Barings continued to be active in American finance, especially but not exclusively in American railroad finance in the late nineteenth and early twentieth centuries. The 1890 Baring crisis shocked the firm, but it survived and in the years between 1891 and 1914 retained its prominent role in American investment.[88]

Likewise, the Rothschilds in Paris and London during the years from 1870 to 1914 participated in an information network that encompassed the United States. These two Rothschild houses were the main participants in American business, with the role of the other Rothschild houses subordinate. In 1870 the "Rothschild world" was about to change. Baron James de Rothschild (1792–1868), who for decades had been *the* Paris Rothschild—the head of finances in Europe, as he once called himself[89]—was now succeeded by his eldest son, Baron Alphonse de Rothschild (1827–1905), who was the principal French Rothschild of this new generation. On Alphonse's death, his son Edouard (born in 1868), assisted by Alphonse's two brothers, Gustave and Edmond, led the Paris house.[90] In London a generational change also occurred; on the death of Baron Lionel N. Rothschild (1808–1879) the new head of the London house was his eldest son, Nathaniel M. Rothschild (1840–1915), who in 1885 became the first Lord Rothschild. Between the cousins in Paris and London a constant stream of mail kept each house well informed; a sampling of this correspondence reveals that events in America were important to both houses.[91]

In the United States, in 1870, August Belmont & Co. represented the Rothschilds in New York. August Belmont (1816–1890) had arrived in that city in 1837, traveling on behalf of the Rothschilds. His visit was to be short, but by chance it came at the very time that the existing New York agent of the Rothschilds went bankrupt; young Belmont then settled in the United States. He set up his own banking house, which acted for the Rothschilds. In addition to August Belmont in New York, in 1849 Davidson & Co., whose head was a member of the Rothschild family (by marriage), had become the firm's "agent" in California.[92] In the 1880s, as the new generation of Rothschilds assumed leadership in London and Paris, so, too, August Belmont's son, also August, increasingly took charge in New York.[93] In 1880 the London Rothschilds appointed the Bank of California as a correspondent, replacing its own California agency.[94]

The relationship between August Belmont & Co. and the Rothschilds was not always cool, calm, cordial, or even close. The London and Paris Rothschilds depended heavily on their American representative; the new generations in both houses, however, had a difficult time adapting to one another. A clear loyalty persisted, but because a recommendation came from New York did not mean that it would be adopted; the Belmonts, father and son, did not hesitate to express themselves freely with the Rothschilds. There was a regular flow of correspondence between New York and both London and Paris.[95] When August Belmont, Sr., died in 1890, his son at once dropped the "Junior." Accordingly, all references to August Belmont after 1890 are to the son. The long associations notwithstanding, in the early twentieth century August Belmont was addressing Nathaniel Rothschild as "Lord Rothschild." (His father had been more familiar, calling the latter Nathaniel.) In 1907, when Belmont was in financial difficulty, having borrowed excessively against Interborough Rapid Transit bonds, the Rothschilds feared that Belmont's failure might extend the American panic of 1907 and have serious consequences in the United States. They had no doubt that they should rescue him, which they did.[96]

In 1901 the London Rothschilds inaugurated a formal association with Lee, Higginson & Co., Boston. This was in addition to the house's continuing relationships with August Belmont & Co. The London Rothschilds' American account books show a "general account," "our account," and a "securities account" with Lee, Higginson in 1913.[97] In addition, the Rothschilds had informal friendships with numerous other

American bankers. Thus, Edward Adams, long with Winslow, Lanier & Co., and then the Deutsche Bank representative in the United States, always visited with Lord Rothschild on his London trips.[98] In 1895, when the U.S. Treasury wanted to stop the outflow of American gold, J. P. Morgan and N. M. Rothschild & Sons cooperated in the process. Lord Rothschild knew Jacob Schiff of Kuhn, Loeb & Co. well.[99] In short, while the Rothschilds did not have their own bank in New York, they had many contacts with the principal private investment bankers in America and enjoyed excellent access to information about business in the United States.

There was an added way that the Barings and the Rothschilds were *au courant* on American money markets, and which involved them in indirect, informal relations with American banks. The London banking world was small. The Barings and the Rothschilds knew personally the heads of the American houses in London. While there was secrecy and competition, there was also cooperation on many levels.[100] And there was in particular the extraordinary interchange of information that ranged from the sharing of credit ratings, to general economic insights, to psychological profiles on the motivations of American business leaders.

Other European and Canadian banks also had formal associations with American banking institutions that sometimes did, and sometimes did not, relate to the inflow of foreign investment to the United States. These arrangements ranged from American correspondent banks, representatives, agencies, branches, and affiliates, including co-partnerships. An individual foreign bank would often have different relationships over time. Likewise, a single foreign bank might coincidentally use more than one of these forms of doing business in America.

London City and Midland Bank, one of the world's largest deposit banks, had by 1914 forty-five correspondent banks in the United States. These included thirteen in New York City; five in Philadelphia; three each in New Orleans, Boston, and San Francisco; two each in Chicago, St. Louis, and Minneapolis; and one each in Milwaukee, Indianapolis, Hutchinson (Kansas), Pittsburgh, Seattle, Oakland and Santa Barbara (California), Dallas, Manchester (New Hampshire), Kalamazoo and Detroit (Michigan), and Cincinnati. Lloyds Bank had twenty-one correspondent banks in the United States.[101] The correspondent banks do not appear, however, to have been of major importance in the intermediation of foreign *investment* into the United States.

The route of having an American representative was followed by the Deutsche Bank, which did make large American investments. Its first U.S. representative was Henry Villard, an extraordinary German immigrant who was at one time president of the Northern Pacific Railroad, and at a later point president of Edison General Electric Co., the predecessor to General Electric. Edward D. Adams, from an important American family, followed Villard as the Deutsche Bank's next representative in America. Adams had been a partner in the private American bank, Winslow, Lanier & Co., before becoming the representative of the Deutsche Bank in America. He was the principal developer of power facilities at Niagara Falls.[102]

Some foreign banks had "independent" banks as American agents. R. Raphael & Sons, London, had Louis von Hoffman, New York.[103] Gaspard Farrer of H. S. Lefevre referred (in 1901) to the Bank of British North America as "Our New York Agents."[104] The Diskonto Gesellschaft seems to have had a regular business connection with Kuhn, Loeb & Co.[105] Paul Emden writes that "in order to enlarge the German market for American securities, the Dresdner Bank . . . in 1905, entered into a working arrangement with J. P. Morgan & Co., of New York."[106] Sometimes in banking terminology the words "correspondent," "representative," and "agent" were used interchangeably, indicating a certain American bank was authorized to act on behalf of a foreign one in specified roles. Such alliances were typically nonexclusive, that is, the American bank acted for others as well as the particular foreign bank.

Often, however, the word "agency" in banking terminology meant an extension of the foreign bank—i.e., salaried employees. By 1914, twenty banks from abroad had "licensed agencies" in New York, licensed under New York State law. While the purposes of their licensed agencies varied, none of the banks that chose this route was a large expediter of monies to the United States.[107] The banks with licensed agencies in New York City included the major British "foreign and colonial banks" that did business in Africa (the African Banking Corporation; the Bank of British West Africa); Canada (the Bank of British North America); the Caribbean (the Colonial Bank); South America (the Anglo South American Bank; the Commercial Bank of Spanish America; the London & Brazilian Bank; and the London & River Plate Bank); South Africa (Standard Bank of South Africa); and Asia and Australia (Chartered Bank of India, Australia, and China, and the Hongkong and Shanghai Banking Corp.).[108]

The principal Canadian banks—Bank of Montreal, Bank of Nova Scotia, Canadian Bank of Commerce, Merchants' Bank of Canada, and Royal Bank of Canada—also had licensed agencies in New York. Likewise, a handful of other foreign banks had such agencies, namely the Banco di Napoli, Naples; the Bohemia Joint Stock Bank, Prague; the Yokohama Specie Bank, Yokohama; and the National Bank of Cuba, in Havana.[109] (Perhaps the Cuban bank should not be classified as a "foreign" bank, since in 1914 it seems to have been owned primarily by American capital.)[110]

In earlier years (before the licensing provisions came into effect in 1911), other foreign banks had had their own agencies in New York City, for example, Crédit Lyonnais (1879–1882)[111] and Nederlandsche Handel-Maatschappij (known to have had the agency from 1879 to 1881, not clear when closed).[112] The Comptoir National d'Escompte had an agency in New Orleans from the mid-1890s to 1903.[113] Other foreign banks had their own agencies in American cities, often short-lived ventures.

In contrast to an agency that was an extension of the bank (as distinct from an "independent agent") but had limited functions, a *branch bank* could take deposits. Canadian banks that branched in Canada set up "branches" in certain American states, where state law permitted. Likewise, both the Hongkong and Shanghai Banking Corporation and Yokohama Specie Bank had "branches" in California, which with changes in state law were later transformed into separately organized "banks."[114] In Chicago for many years a "branch" of the Bank of Montreal did regular commercial banking, taking deposits and making loans.[115] Sometimes it was not clear whether a foreign bank's presence was as an agency or branch; thus, the Comptoir National d'Escompte, Paris, had a "branch" (or agency) in Chicago between 1893 and 1900.[116]

Another form of entry was that of co-partnerships (or partnerships in existing American banks). Baring's 1886 relationship with Kidder, Peabody fits into this category. Earlier, J. K. Gilliat & Co., London, had a partner in Maitland & Phelps, New York.[117] This approach was a particularly prominent mode of doing business for German banks. The Darmstadter Bank had in 1854 acquired an interest in G. Vom Baur & Co., New York, while the Deutsche Bank in October 1872 obtained a "silent partnership" in Knoblauch & Lichtenstein, New York.[118] Neither venture survived the

1880s. The Darmstadter Bank sold out in 1885, while the Deutsche Bank terminated its association in 1882. Both American banks were then closed down.[119] When this occurred, the large German banks continued to do business in the United States; they just employed other channels.

In 1904, the Berliner Handels-Gesellschaft, which was very much involved in selling American securities in Germany, had two partners in Hallgarten & Co., New York.[120] One of the two, Hans Winterfeldt, before he left for New York, had been on the board of the Schweizerischer Bankverein; he retained that board membership.[121] Private German banks, likewise, had partners in American firms. Lazard Speyer–Ellissen & Co., Frankfurt, and Speyer & Co., New York, had interlocking partnerships.[122] S. Bleichröder, Berlin, was said "for a time" to control Ladenburg, Thalmann & Co., New York.[123]

Hope and Co., Amsterdam, had invested in at least one existing bank in New Orleans in the 1830s. Fifty years later it still held an interest in the Citizens' Bank, New Orleans. But by 1902 this stake no longer existed.[124]

Yet another method of entry seems the equivalent of the "free-standing" company described earlier. Such foreign banks had no single foreign parent, but were controlled from abroad. In this category were The London and San Francisco Bank, Ltd., San Francisco (1864–1905),[125] the Swiss-American Bank, San Francisco (1873–1877),[126] and the Banque Franco-Américaine de Paris, New York (ca. 1906–1914).[127]

In sum, before 1914 a number of foreign banks participated in U.S. business through correspondents, representatives, agencies, branches, and interlocking partnership arrangements. Some foreign banks had investments in individual banks. How, or whether, a foreign bank actually extended itself into the United States was a function of (1) the constraints established by American law and (2) the bank's particular strategies.

The Legal Environment

The legal environment influenced the form and functions of foreign banks engaged in business in America. Banking institutions in the United States were regulated by both federal and state law. A foreign bank operating in the United States had to conform to American rules. Neither the National Bank Act of 1864 nor the Federal Reserve Act of 1913 prohibited foreign ownership of "national" banks, but under both laws directors of national banks had to be U.S. citizens. This meant that a foreign owner could not have a representative on the bank board of his own nationality. Likewise, under the National Bank Act, national banks were not permitted to branch out of state (or in state, for the most part). Thus, there were statutory limitations on the growth in their size. Both the inability to exercise direct control and the size restrictions seem to have made national banks unattractive to foreign investors—and more particularly foreign banks. The Federal Reserve Act for the first time allowed national banks to branch abroad.

Prior to 1914 American federal law, as interpreted by the courts, denied national banks the privilege of accepting drafts or bills of exchange in international transactions.[128] Clyde Phelps has called the "acceptance privilege" "one of the most important powers possessed by banks doing foreign business."[129] In July 1915, W. P. G. Harding, of the Federal Reserve Board, Washington, wrote

> We hear a good deal nowadays about dollar exchange as applied to the financing of transactions arising from our trade with foreign countries. A year ago this was almost an unknown expression, and generally speaking, long bills drawn against international transactions were in sterling, in reichsmarks or in francs. Our great incorporated chartered banking institutions were not permitted to engage in the acceptance business, and when a cargo of grain or cotton left an American port for Liverpool, drafts against the shipment were drawn in sterling, or when a vessel laden with dyestuffs or jute bagging cleared from Bremen or Hamburg for Boston or for Savannah, credits covering the invoices were expressed in reichsmarks, so the foreign banker exacted his toll in both directions.[130]

This changed when the Federal Reserve Act of December 1913 specifically allowed national banks, in transactions involving the import and export of goods, to accept for amounts not exceeding 50 percent of their capital and surplus (not long thereafter, the law was amended to extend to the full amount of capital and surplus).[131] These rules were important in molding the activities of foreign banks doing American business, for the inability of major American banks to accept left a gap that American private banks and, more important, foreign banks filled.[132]

It was not only federal legislation that affected foreign banks; each state passed its own body of laws regulating the entry and the behavior of banks within its boundaries. New York City (America's financial capital) was where foreign banks would wish to be, yet under New York State law, no out-of-country institution could take part in a "banking business" any place within the state. As explained by the British Consul General (October 1886), foreign banks in New York City could not "receive deposits, discount notes or bills, or issue any evidence of debt to be loaned or put in circulation as money." This applied to "foreign corporations"; private individuals could as "private banks" "receive deposits and discount notes or bills."[133] In 1911, an amendment to the New York State banking law provided for the licensing of agencies of foreign banks:

> a license shall be issued by the Superintendent of Banks to such companies only after a careful investigation of the nature of the business conducted by such foreign bank and its financial standing, with a view of being satisfied that the company may be safely permitted to conduct business of a foreign bank within this state or through an agent.[134]

"Foreign" under state law always meant out-of-state (which included out-of-country).[135] In April 1914 a new New York State banking law restated the prohibition on foreign bank *branches* and reconfirmed the licensing of foreign bank *agencies*. An agency under New York law could not take deposits.[136]

New York State law also restricted the activities of state chartered banks. Not until the April 1914 legislation did the New York legislature, by statute, permit banks incorporated in that state to accept drafts and bills of exchange drawn against not only shipments of goods to and from foreign countries, but also against domestic transactions.[137]

Each state had different laws.[138] In Illinois, banks from other states and countries were allowed to enter.[139] In Louisiana, in 1902 a new law provided that the banking business in that state could be carried on only by such incorporated institutions as shall have been organized under the laws of this state and the United States, by individual citizens of the state and by firms domiciled in the state, whose active members shall be citizens of this state.[140]

Texas in 1905 prohibited "foreign" corporations, except national banks of the United States, from engaging in banking in that state.[141]

In California, for years out-of-country banks had been able to do business without special restrictions. Then, the 1909 California Banking Act forbade foreign banks from having "branches" in the state.[142] One with a "branch" already there could, however, under this statute, "incorporate" its branch, that is, set it up as a distinct entity. In 1913 California law on foreign banking became more restrictive. A "branch" of a foreign incorporated bank that had operated in California prior to that year could stay, but it had to comply with the new law. Its capital and all the funds and deposits received by it had to be kept separate from that of the parent corporation. This appears to have been a reiteration of the 1909 rules. After 1913, however, no *new* foreign banking arrivals could take deposits in California, although such banking corporations could be allowed by the Superintendent of Banks to issue letters of credit, to pay or to collect bills of exchange, or to have an office, which did not entail doing a banking business.[143]

The state of Washington in a 1905 law let foreign banks do business under rules that barred them from taking deposits; existing foreign bank branches were unaffected.[144] Oregon remained open to foreign banks, permitting them to do a general banking business in the state.

This brief summary of some state laws relating to foreign banks indicates the variety and the changes. Both federal and, more important, state legislation provided the legal environment for foreign banks. The rules, especially those in New York State, influenced the outsiders' entries and their operations in America.

Functions of the Foreign Bank

The functions of a foreign bank in the economy of a particular host country can be twofold: (1) the bank can play a role in that nation's external economic relations, coping with international needs, such as foreign trade finance, foreign exchange, and capital intermediation (inflows and outflows), and (2) the bank can serve the internal domestic economy, operating within that economy in exactly the same manner as a domestic bank. It is possible to distinguish a foreign bank's activities into these two spheres, recognizing that a single bank could undertake both functions. While foreign banks did engage in both activities in the United States in this period, the former was of far greater importance because within America domestic banking institutions were well equipped to provide domestic credit, whereas they were less well equipped to handle international transactions.

Before 1914 foreign banks were important because expanding U.S. international commerce meant that trade had to be financed, because of their role in relation to newly arrived immigrants, and because of America's formidable capital requirements.[145] They were not alone in serving in any of these capacities; rather they supplemented the activities of American banking institutions. In part owing to the legal restrictions on national and some state-chartered banks, America remained very dependent on foreign banks for foreign trade financing.[146] British banks, in particular, had long experience in such activities and real advantage in carrying out such functions. America's international trade volume was sizable. The United States ranked in first or second place in the world in its exports in the early twentieth century.[147] To perform this foreign trade financing, correspondent banks or agencies were adequate for the foreign banking house.

Foreign banks had expertise in dealing with foreign exchange. Thus it was natural that they undertook a role related to immigrant remittances. On the West Coast, the Hongkong and Shanghai Bank and the Yokohama Specie Bank served the Chinese and Japanese communities, remitting monies to the families back home. The New York agencies of the Italian bank (Banco di Napoli, Naples) and the Czech bank (Bohemia Joint Stock Bank, Prague) seem to have served a similar function in that city.

Most important, for purposes of this chapter, because large American corporate banks were restricted in international trade transactions, they developed little expertise with foreign-exchange dealings and with the intermediation of capital to the United States. Foreign banks joined with American private banks, playing a major role in this sphere. Investment banking in America had developed in a healthy manner. Private American bankers had experience in mobilizing both U.S. and foreign monies. They did the latter, however, either through their own houses abroad or in concert with "friends" in Europe. The "friends" were foreign bankers.[148] The principal British merchant banks took part in expediting the flow of British capital to America, especially into railroad investments, and then from 1889 to 1914 into industrials as well. Stanley Chapman divided the London merchant banks in the mid-1870s into the "Jewish," the "Anglo-American," and the "Anglo-German" groups.[149] All three participated in American business.

Other British banks—deposit banks—also played a role, but a far smaller one. Some of the merchant banks had close connections in Amsterdam and Paris, and the Dutch and French banks, through their London associations, directly handled American securities. In American business, the Deutsche Bank often cooperated with Speyer, in New York, London, and Frankfurt, and with Stern Bros., London, and more important, Jacob S. H. Stern, Frankfurt.[150] All of the large German banks were involved in American finance, as well as the private banks. Edouard Noetzlin of the Banque de Paris et des Pays-Bas was a longtime friend of Jacob Schiff of Kuhn, Loeb.[151] By the 1880s the Banque de Paris et des Pays-Bas appears to have introduced in Paris many of the same U.S. securities that Baring Brothers and Morton, Rose were introducing in London.[152] There was throughout an international network of contacts and information. In the late nineteenth and early twentieth centuries, as the volume of international transactions rose, banking relationships seem to have become more rather than less personal. Having information was fundamental and knowing what others were doing the *sine qua non* of success. Capital flowed easily into American securities assisted by such contacts.

In many ways the personal, informal channels were more important in the intermediation of long-term foreign monies into America than a bank's "presence" per se in the United States. The long-existing Anglo-American cultural and social ties, as well as faster transportation and communication (as noted earlier, by 1913 cable messages took minutes across the Atlantic), contributed to low-cost international transactions.

Even before airplanes, travel had become simple, and travelers shared information. Robert Fleming, whose investment trusts and then his merchant bank were heavily involved in American securities, had no "American house." Yet, in the year after the panic of 1893, when all American stocks and bonds seemed in peril, he made seven trips across the Atlantic. He often dealt with fellow Scots in the New York banking community, and was also close to Jacob Schiff. German immigrants to America cemented the financial links between Germany and the United States. "Family" associations persisted. German bankers could conduct business in the United States in the German language. Dutch monies since the eighteenth century had gone to America, and between 1870 and 1914 the Anglo-Dutch banking connections bridged the Atlantic with no difficulty. Dutch banks handled American securities based on long experience. The Société Générale, Paris, did not need a large New York presence to become involved in financing Westinghouse.[153] The same was true of Swiss bankers, who often moved French monies into American investments.

The existence of the gold standard made payments easy. Foreign exchange values after 1879 were quite stable. European bankers saw opportunities for profit in American finance and found they could, in the main, participate in the intermediation of capital from Europe to the United States without extending the banks themselves in an important manner into the country.

By contrast, to undertake domestic banking a bank must be on the spot, dealing on a daily basis with customers. Between 1870 and 1914 there was no need for foreign banks to provide domestic banking in America. Within the nation, American banks proliferated.[154] Banking developed in the United States to meet everyday requirements. Here there was no vacuum and little reason for foreign bank participation. The one possible exception was in mortgage banking, where foreign financial intermediaries did play a role (as noted at the start of this chapter, space precludes a discussion of such institutions). Domestic banks, federal, state, and private, handled the taking of American deposits and the making of most American loans. Now and then a foreign bank took part in domestic banking. In California, foreign banks or foreign-owned banks had been important in the immediate post–Civil War period,[155] but they came to be replaced by fully adequate and more efficient domestic ones.[156] Foreign banks had no advantage in purely domestic activities. Interestingly, when the latter did participate in domestic banking they were, more often than not, Canadian banks simply extending their branching over the border. The Bank of Montreal in Chicago, which financed foreign trade, and also took part in domestic banking, was unique in its size and importance.[157] Some American banks had foreign portfolio owners, but the amount of shares held abroad was negligible.[158] By 1914 American domestic banking was undertaken by domestically owned and controlled banks.

Conclusions

Substantial long-term foreign investment entered America between 1870 and 1914. Some of it bypassed financial intermediaries and money markets. Because this chapter has been concerned with foreign banks and foreign investment, little attention has been paid to long-term investments that did not involve foreign banks.[159] When investments went through money markets, British, German, Dutch, French, and Swiss banks often played a role in the intermediation process. Sometimes foreign banks became involved directly in long-term loans, or even equity participations. Most of the time the foreign banks were intermediaries, moving American securities—bonds, but also some shares—to other owners abroad.[160] Foreign banks had correspondents, representatives, agencies, branches, and co-partnerships in America. Such outlets were numerous, but scattered. Most frequently the crucial banking relationships identified with international finance were informal ones, syndicates that temporarily joined individual American and foreign bankers who trusted one another, information networks rather than structured bureaucratic organizations.

British, continental European, and Canadian banks were significant in American international finance—short-term trade financing as well as long-term capital transfers—since there was a need that they could fill with advantage. Foreign banks engaged in information gathering and dissemination, foreign trade financing, handling foreign exchange, and shipping specie. In Britain and on the European continent, bankers helped to make American securities attractive to their countrymen.

By contrast, while some foreign banks did regular banking business in America, these were insignificant in U.S. *domestic* banking, in part because of American legislative restraints, but more importantly because they had no advantage in that sphere and domestic institutions sufficed. While foreign investment in the United States was sizable in this period, foreign investment in American *banking* as such represented a very small part of that foreign stake. Finally, foreign banks played a major role in the flow of British and continental European savings into American investments; they were key participants in the intermediation process. Such functions could be carried out, in the main, through collaborative relations with American investment bankers rather than a massive entry onto American soil.

12

Foreign Banks and Foreign Investment in Russia

B. V. Anan'ich and V. I. Bovykin

Types and Volume of Foreign Investment in Russia

A key dynamic in the industrial development of capitalist countries was the diffusion of advanced technology. The process of technological modernization, synchronous with the construction of railway networks, generated an exceptionally high demand for capital, which in most cases was supplied largely by foreign investments. Russia was no exception. Calculation of just how important a role foreign capital played has been an object of continuing controversy; the problem is complex in the extreme and requires further study and analysis, but two aspects seem clear.

First, estimates of Russia's balance of payments—made at different times, based on different data, calculated on different methodological principles—testify to one thing: As early as the beginning of the 1880s, payments on foreign investments in Russia exceeded their inflow. This excess was not covered by Russia's surplus foreign-trade balance. The balance of payments equilibrium was maintained only by new loans and the inflow of foreign capital into Russia's national economy.[1]

Second, it has been long noted that the demand for foreign capital in Russia resulted not so much from inadequate internal accumulations as from its diversion from productive investment because of the state credit system. Further evidence for this conclusion is provided in a recent study by Paul Gregory demonstrating the high level of internal accumulation in Russia.[2]

Because of ample opportunities abroad to obtain resources to develop a railway network and industrial sectors of direct state interest, the government was able to divert internal accumulations for nonproductive expenditures that served to maintain the economic and political power of the dominant landowner class. Thus, foreign capital contributed to the growth of some branches of Russia's national economy while the main obstacle to Russia's capitalist development—the political power of the landowners and landed estates—remained intact. This "aid" from foreign capital resulted in the pumping out of a steadily rising share of the national income abroad (in the form of interest and dividend payments). At the beginning of the twentieth century such indirect support given by foreign capital to the landowner state proved insufficient, and between 1905 and 1907 the government was obliged to borrow abroad for the suppression of the revolution.[3]

When statistical data are used in the study of foreign investment, it is particularly important to know their origin. During the period under consideration, the registration of international capital movements was just beginning. For this reason we can account for the fact that the estimates of foreign investments in the Russian economy, in particular the data on the investments of various national origin adduced by different authors in this book, are not in full concord. Table 12–1 shows the structure of foreign investments, their dynamics, and place in the main branches of the national economy. The data on state loans, on government-guaranteed loans of railway companies placed abroad, and also on the liabilities of state mortgage banks (columns 1–4) for 1908 and 1913 were taken from official publications of the Finance Ministry. These data are reliable, for the Ministry annually collected information about foreign payments on state and guaranteed securities. Analogous data for 1893 and 1900 were calculated from official data indirectly characterizing the distribution of these securities. This gives some certainty that they approximate the actual figures. Finally, the data for 1861 and 1881 are the result of rough estimates; it is to be hoped that they are a reasonable approximation of reality. Data on foreign investment in Russian urban loans (column 5) have been derived from information about their issue; the volume was relatively small and potential errors or omissions will not distort the overall picture. For columns 6 and 7, showing foreign investment in joint-stock enterprises, the well-known figures of P. V. Ol' were used. Figures on the shares placed abroad by enterprises in Russia (column 9) were obtained by subtracting L. E. Shepelev's sums of share capital of foreign companies operating in Russia (column 8) from the data given in column 7. To determine the foreign investment shares of total investments in separate categories of securities the following information was used: official data on the sums of state and guaranteed bonds in circulation at that time, data on the loans to Russian cities published in statistical reference books, and Shepelev's data on the capital of joint-stock societies operating in Russia.[4]

As for the figures (from Ol') used in Table 12–1, many researchers considered them to be exaggerated. After comparing those figures with the data on the increase of all joint-stock capital, I. F. Gindin concluded that the figures in Ol' are consistent with these other data up to 1909, that is, the prewar industrial boom. But for the boom period itself, Gindin argued that they "absolutely cannot be reconciled with the figures for joint-stock statistics," and the correct figures for January 1, 1915, are "at least 250 million or 15 percent lower." The exaggeration by Ol' of foreign investments in Russian banks was, in Gindin's view, even greater.[5]

That Ol' overestimated the scale of foreign investment in joint-stock companies in Russia is also evident when one compares the Ol' figures on French investments with a French registration of shares and bonds of Russian joint-stock enterprises in 1919. Those latter data, supplemented with data from other sources, yield a sum (650.1 million rubles) for 1919 that is nearly 10 percent smaller than what Ol' calculated for 1915 (715.8 million rubles).[6] Table 12–2 gives the Ol' data and those from the above-mentioned registration of French investments in Russian joint-stock commercial banks. It is highly unlikely, to say the least, that amidst revolution and civil war Russian bank shares placed in France were transferred to Russia. Indeed, as some documentary and memoir evidence suggests, precisely the reverse movement occurred. In addition, the

TABLE 12–1. Structure of Foreign Investments in Russia, 1861–1913[a]

Years (as of Jan. 1)	State and Government-Guaranteed Securities					Shares and Bonds of Joint-Stock Enterprises Operating in Russia				
	1	2	3	4	5	6	7	8	9	10
1861	[400] (25)	[350] (?)	[50] (?)	—	—	8 (?)	8 (?)	?	? (?)	[408] (?)
1881	[2,345] (48)	[1,615] (?)	[730] (?)	—	—	115 (?)	110 (?)	?	? (?)	[2,460] (?)
1893	2,713 (46)	2,090 (43)	623 (59)	—	—	238 (23)	203 (21)	89	114 (13)	2,951 (35)
1900	3,995 (51)	3,325 (53)	568 (53)	102 (18)	4 (19)	911 (35)	762 (32)	365	397 (19)	4,910 (40)
1908	5,266 (47)	4,642 (53)	528 (42)	96 (8)	26 (24)	1,187 (40)	989 (38)	399	590 (26)	6,479 (39)
1913	5,461 (43)	4,410 (50)	865 (52)	186 (9)	164 (39)	1,960 (35)	1,701 (33)	553	1,148 (25)	7,585 (35)
1913[b] with 15% amendment	5,461 43	4,410 50	865 52	186 9	164 39	1,666 31	1,446 30	551	895 21	7,291 34

Sources: V. I. Bovykin, Formirovaniye finansovogo kapitala v Rossii (Formation of Finance Capital in Russia) (Moscow, 1984), pp. 157–68.

[a] 1 = Total; 2 = Bonds of state loans; 3 = Bonds of guaranteed railway loans; 4 = Bonds of Nobility and Peasants' Bank; 5 = Bonds of loans by Russian cities; 6 = Total; 7 = Shares of joint-stock enterprises operating in Russia; 8 = Shares of foreign enterprises; 9 = Shares of enterprises founded in Russia; 10 = Total foreign investments. Totals are expressed in millions of rubles and as percentage of total domestic and foreign investments (in parentheses). Numbers in square brackets are estimates.

[b] The amendment is introduced into columns 6, 7, 9, and 10.

TABLE 12–2. French Investments in Russian Joint-Stock Commercial Banks (according to P. V. Ol's estimates and the results of 1919 French registration of the shares and bonds of Russian joint-stock enterprises placed in France)

Banks	Joint-Stock Capital on Jan. 1, 1914	P. V. Ol's Data for 1915	Results of the Registration on Jan. 1, 1920
	(in millions of rubles)		
St. Petersburg International Bank	48.0	1.0	ND
Azov-Don Bank	50.0	10.0	19.5
Russo-Asiatic Bank	45.0	36.0	19.2
Siberian Bank	20.0	4.0	ND
St. Petersburg Private Bank	40.0	22.8	7.3
Commercial and Industrial Bank	35.0	4.0	0.3
Russo-French Bank	18.0	4.0	6.3
United Bank	30.0	18.0	8.0
Moscow Private Bank	12.5	7.5	6.4
Rostov-on-Don Merchant Bank	5.0	2.3	ND
Russian Bank for Foreign Trade	50.0	ND	1.9
TOTAL	—	109.6	68.9

Sources: P. V. Ol', Inostranniye Kapitaly v Rossii (Foreign Capital in Russia) (Petrograd, 1922); France, Archives Nationales, F30.1091.

ND, No data.

registration revealed far fewer Russian commercial bank shares in France than Ol' presumed.

Since the evidence seems to suggest that the Ol' figures are inflated, two variants of data for 1913 are given in Table 12–1: (1) one set consistent with the Ol' estimates; and (2) another based on the 15 percent adjustment proposed by Gindin.

Data given in Table 12–1 show that, among Russian securities placed abroad, the predominant type was state and government-guaranteed securities—state loan bonds, government-guaranteed bonds of railway companies, and liabilities of the State Mortgage Banks for the Nobility and Peasantry. But their share, which in the early 1890s exceeded 90 percent, gradually declined to about 80 percent between 1900 and 1908, then to about 75 percent by 1913. Concurrently, the proportion of shares and bonds of joint-stock enterprises operating in Russia increased, amounting to one-quarter of all foreign investments in 1913.

The share of foreign investments in the total sum invested in Russian securities rose before 1908 and then began to decline. After 1900 the share of foreign investments in state and guaranteed securities began to decrease. After 1908 new domestic investments in joint-stock enterprises surpassed foreign ones.

The rise of domestic vis-à-vis foreign investment is supported by the Russian Finance Ministry's information on the placing of new issues of Russian bonds in the years 1903 to 1912: Whereas 37 percent was placed outside Russia between 1904 and 1907, the corresponding figure for 1908 to 1912 had declined to 30 percent. Only the bonds of railway companies and the bonds of city loans continued to be placed primarily abroad.[7] Although it may be assumed that some portion of the securities placed in Russia was subsequently shifted to the West, the Russian capital market on the eve of World War I was obviously gaining in significance. Nevertheless, the share of Russian securities held abroad, despite its decrease by 1913, was still substantial, mainly because of state and railway funds, more than half of which were owned by foreigners. As for foreign investment in the shares and bonds of joint-stock companies, its proportion of the total was one-fourth—or one-fifth, if the securities of foreign enterprises operating in Russia are excluded from the sum of foreign investments.

These are some quantitative indicators giving a general picture of foreign investments in Russia at the end of the nineteenth century and beginning of the twentieth.

Participation of the Foreign Banks in the Placement of Russian State, Railway, and Municipal Loans

The extent of participation by Dutch, English, German, French, or Belgian banks in the placement of Russian state, railway, and municipal bonds and the mortgage bonds of Treasury mortgage banks depended primarily on the general political relations between Russia and the nations that these banks represented. The impact of overall political relations was particularly evident in the case of state loans.

Ever since Russia had concluded its first foreign loan in Holland in 1769, the banking houses of Amsterdam, especially Hope and Company, were regular creditors of the tsarist government. Later, from the mid-nineteenth century, the banking house of Lippmann, Rosenthal and Co. also played a major role in Russian finance. Although the Russian government also sought loans from Italian and English bankers in this period, Holland remained Russia's main capital market until the 1840s.[8]

After the Napoleonic Wars English banking houses (especially Baring Brothers and N. M. Rothschild & Sons), in cooperation with the Dutch banks, became more frequent creditors of the Russian government. After the Crimean War of 1853 to 1856, Russian securities were mostly placed on the English market. Many operations were conducted jointly by Baring Brothers and Hope and Company, and in 1857 these two houses helped to establish the Great Russian Railway Company. In 1864 and 1866 they issued two major Anglo-Dutch loans that enabled the Russian State Treasury to meet its international payments. Together with the Barings, the English banking house of J. Henry Schröder and Co. also participated in the placement of the Russian railway companies' bonds. In 1862 the London banking house Frühling and Göschen established the Dünaburg and Witebsk Railway Co. with a share capital of £ 2 million.[9]

From 1870 to 1884 the tsarist government offered seven issues of consolidated Russian railway bonds. The bonds of the first four issues and the seventh issue yielded 5 percent, the fifth issue 4.5 percent, and the sixth 4 percent; all were for a special state railway fund to provide government subsidies to railway companies. Of the first five issues, two for £ 12 million (nominal) and the rest for £ 15 million were underwritten by the banking houses of N. M. Rothschild & Sons in London and de Rothschild frères in Paris, with no participation of the Dutch market.[10] The total sum of £ 15 million of the fourth issue, however, was divided into three parts: The Rothschilds took £ 8 million, the State Bank handled another £ 4 million and £ 3 million was left in the hands of the government. A portion of the bonds of this sum (£ 175,000) was realized through Hope and Company in Amsterdam and £ 1,730,000 through Verne and Co. in

Paris.[11] When the fifth issue in the amount of £ 15 million was placed in 1875, £ 8.5 million was realized through the Rothschilds and £ 6.5 million through the State Bank.

After 1875 the London Rothschilds withdrew from the syndicate for Russian consolidated railway bonds, and the last two issues were carried out with the active participation of German banks.[12]

The sixth issue of consolidated bonds (May 1880) was issued at 4 percent for 150 million metallic rubles. Although the government intended to carry out the operation without resorting to foreign bankers,[13] the bonds were in fact issued with a guaranteed exchange rate by Lippmann, Rosenthal and Co. in Amsterdam; the Diskonto-Gesellschaft, Bleichröder, Mendelssohn, and Warschauer in Berlin; A. Behrens and Sons in Hamburg, M. A. Rothschild and Sulzbach Brothers in Frankfurt, and the Comptoir d'Escompte in Paris.[14] The bonds were admitted to quotation in Amsterdam, Brussels, Berlin, and Paris.

The seventh and the last issue of 5 percent consolidated bonds of Russian railways was made in April 1884 for £ 15 million. The main organizers of the loan were Bleichröder in Berlin and the St. Petersburg Discount and Loan Bank. About a third of the total loan sum was raised in Russia.[15]

Rothschilds' refusal to participate in the two final issues of consolidated Russian railway bonds and the active participation of German banks in these operations were, to a considerable extent, the result of changes in the political situation. In the second half of the 1870s Anglo-Russian political relations were exacerbated by events in the Middle East, and the role of Russia's main creditor passed from Britain to Germany.

Even before the Russo-Turkish war of 1877/78 the tsarist government had already exhausted its foreign currency reserves to meet the payments on outstanding loans. In July 1876 the government shipped abroad some 22 million rubles in gold from its exchange fund to replenish the foreign reserves. But this sum lasted only until April 1877. It was then that the director of the St. Petersburg Discount and Loan Bank, A. I. Sack, and the head of the Mendelssohn banking house in Berlin, Franz Mendelssohn, came forward in the role of saviors of the government. Acting on instructions from the Finance Ministry, Sack bought a large package of bills of exchange and gold totalling 98 million metallic rubles on the St. Petersburg Stock Exchange, which accrued abroad to the account of the Finance Ministry. The operation was carried out secretly so as not to cause a rise in the exchange rate.[16] Simultaneously, the Russian government entered into talks for an external loan through Mendelssohn & Co. Tense political relations with Britain led not only to the closing of the English market for Russian securities but also the reselling of Russian securities already in quotation to other markets at reduced prices.[17] Under the circumstances the Russian government resorted to an extraordinary operation—an advance against the future loan.

Mendelssohn & Co., who organized the operation, invited Dutch banks to participate. Although Hope and Company flatly refused, Lippmann, Rosenthal and Co., who cooperated with German banks, accepted the invitation.[18] In early May 1877 Mendelssohn & Co., Lippmann, Rosenthal and Co., and also the Comptoir d'Escompte agreed to grant a 90-million mark advance to the Russian government. This advance was to be covered by bonds of a 5 percent loan in the amount of 307.5 million marks that the tsar authorized for issue on May 26/June 7, 1877. The consortium held the price of the new bonds at 94 percent of par, and only at the end of 1877, when the financial situation for Russian securities improved somewhat, did they begin their gradual sale, completing it in early 1878.[19]

Since the 1860s, with some interruptions, the German market actively participated in the placement of Russian railway securities. In 1859 the 5 percent bonds of the Moscow-Riazan railway were accepted for quotation on the Berlin Stock Exchange. The loan was carried out through the Darmstädter Bank für Handel und Industrie and the Cologne banking house Oppenheim and Co., with the Diskonto-Gesellschaft participating.[20]

In the second half of the 1860s the German banks F. W. Krause and Co., A. Siebert (later Mitteldeutsche Creditbank), Gebrüder Sulzbach, and the Berliner Handelsgesellschaft in cooperation with the Dutch banking houses of Lippmann, Rosenthal and Wertheim and Gompertz placed a large group of loans of Russian railway companies, including those belonging to the Russian dealer S. S. Poliakov.[21] By 1879 the German banks had participated in seventeen such loans and had acquired Russian railway securities worth 300 million marks (100 million rubles).[22] Another dimension of these activities was the German-Russian railway union, formed in 1875. It enabled members to pay for the transportation of goods between Russia and Germany through Mendelssohn and the Great Russian Railway Company.[23]

By the beginning of the 1880s a group of major German banks—the Diskonto-Gesellschaft, Bleichröder, M. A. Rothschild, Mendelssohn, Warschauer, and the Berliner Handelsgesellschaft—comprised the so-called Russian syndicate, which carried out the placement of Russian loans.[24] The syndicate was often joined by Lippmann, Rosenthal.[25] The German banks acquired not only bonds but also shares of the Russian railway companies, chiefly for the lines close to the Prussian and Austro-Hungarian borders, as well as of the Kiev and Vladikavkaz railways, which played a major role in transporting oil exports.[26] These Russian railway securities were often distributed in Germany among minor holders. That practice gave rise to a joke among contemporaries that Russian railways were built with the money of Berlin cooks.[27]

But the development of Russo-German financial relations was interrupted in November 1887, when Bismarck imposed a ban on loans on the security of Russian bonds. This break lasted until the end of 1894 when a Russo-German trade agreement was signed and the ban was lifted. French banks exploited the opportunity and with their active participation a considerable portion of Russian securities was transferred from the German to the French capital market in the late 1880s. This was the financial foundation upon which the edifice of the Franco-Russian political and military alliance was later built. Indeed, from the late nineteenth century to World War I France was to remain Russia's main creditor.

A syndicate headed by the Crédit Foncier with the participation of Hottinguer, Verne, Mallet, and other banks was formed in Paris to buy Russian securities on the German market. De Rothschild frères also began to purchase Russian securities.[28] The transfer of Russian securities from Germany to France was accomplished through a series of conversion loans, placed mostly in France at the initiative of Finance Minister I. A. Vyshnegradskii at the very end of 1888. The exchange of Russian 5 and 6 percent bonds for loans with lower interest and a longer repayment period was designed to reschedule Russia's state debts.[29]

In October 1888 E. Hoskier, a Paris banker acting as representative of a syndicate consisting of Paris credit institutions (Banque de Paris et de Pays-Bas, Crédit Lyonnais, Comptoir d'Escompte, the Société Générale, the Crédit Industriel et Commercial), approached Vyshnegradskii with a proposal to convert 5 percent bonds of the Russian external loan of 1877.[30] To carry out this operation, a Russian 5 percent loan for 125 million gold rubles was floated in 1889. In addition to the French banks mentioned above, Barings, Hambro, Mendelssohn, Warschauer, the Berliner Handelsgesellschaft, and Hope and Company also participated.[31]

In January 1889 representatives of the St. Petersburg International and St. Petersburg Discount and Loan banks handed over to Vyshnegradskii a proposal from de Rothschild frères, M. A. von Rothschild, Bleichröder, and the Diskonto-Gesellschaft to convert the 5 percent consolidated bonds of Russian railways. For this purpose, by a decree of February 20/March 4, 1889, a loan with the title "Consolidated Russian 5 percent Railway Bonds, First Series" was issued. The first series for 175 million gold rubles was taken by the consortium participants at the firm price of 86.875 percent of par in the following proportions:[32]

de Rothschild frères and M. A. von Rothschild	$33\frac{1}{3}\%$
Bleichröder	$16\frac{2}{3}\%$
Diskonto-Gesellschaft	$16\frac{2}{3}\%$
St. Petersburg International Commercial Bank	$16\frac{2}{3}\%$
St. Petersburg Discount and Loan Bank	$16\frac{2}{3}\%$

The loan was designed to carry out the conversion of the first through fourth and seventh issues of the 5 percent consolidated bonds of Russian railways. Under the decree of April 16/May 7 the same syndicate issued the second series for 310,498,000 gold rubles. This sum was taken by the syndicate participants at the rate of 88.875 percent. The bonds of the 4 percent loans of the first and second series were to replace all the 5 percent consolidated bonds of Russian railways. The same syndicate, under the decree of December 30, 1890/January 11, 1891, undertook to place the third series for the nominal capital of 80 million gold rubles, which was to convert the 4.5 percent consolidated bonds.[33]

In 1892 Sergei Witte replaced Vyshnegradskii as Finance Minister. Under Witte the last conversion, the "Russian 3.5 percent Gold Loan of 1894" in the amount of 100 million rubles, was concluded with the assistance of the Rothschilds. From the end of 1888 to 1894 the price of one basic type of Russian security (the 4 percent) rose on the Paris exchange from 83 to 100 percent. In Russia itself the years 1893/94 marked the beginning of a period of rapid industrial growth and rising quotations on Russian stock exchanges. The government succeeded in stabilizing the ruble and carrying out a monetary reform. To guarantee the introduction of the gold standard, Witte floated one more loan in 1896, this time at 3 percent for 100 million gold rubles, with a consortium headed by the Paris Rothschilds.[34] But at about this time the Russian government's idyllic relations with the Paris stock exchange came to an end. In 1895/96 the French press mounted a campaign against Russian loans. The French Finance Ministry was worried by the large amount of the Russian securities in France and by the preference given to them by the holders.

During 1898/99 Witte attempted to open the American market for Russian loans and restore relations with the English market. But these efforts came to naught. All that the Finance Ministry managed to accomplish was to place in London, in June 1899, through Schröder and Co., government-guaranteed bonds of the Moscow-Vindava-Rybinsk Railway Company for £ 2,975,000, and this only with the assistance of banking houses in Berlin (Mendelssohn in the first place) and Amsterdam. Most of the bonds were purchased in Germany and Holland.[35] In October 1899 a $10 million railway loan, likewise guaranteed by the tsarist government, was concluded in the United States. Eighty percent of the sum was advanced by the New York Life Insurance Company, which had a branch in St. Petersburg, and 20 percent by the St. Petersburg International Commercial Bank. Of the total, $3.2 million was intended for the Southeastern Railway Company, and $6.8 million for the Vladikavkaz Railway.[36] The Finance Ministry conducted negotiations through the St. Petersburg International Commercial Bank with J. P. Morgan and also with National City Bank chairman James Stillman about possible cooperation and conclusion of a large loan in America, but these ended without any results.[37] By the end of 1900 it was clear that the tsarist government could not count on large financial operations in New York and London, mainly for political reasons.

After 1894 financial relations with the German money market resumed. The Berlin exchange, however, did not have the same surplus of free capital as the Paris Bourse, due to the constant demand for capital by Germany's growing industry. The Finance Ministry held the view that Germany successfully performed the role of banker in relation to Russia, enjoying credit in France and Britain, and that such firms as Bleichröder, Mendelssohn, and Warschauer made fortunes by operating as middlemen between Russia and French and British capitalists.[38] Thus, the French Bourse remained the main creditor for the tsarist government.

At the end of the 1890s the Finance Ministry considered it unprofitable to place railway bonds in France because of high taxes. The Ministry preferred state loans, and also attempted to sell the securities of Treasury mortgage banks, in particular the mortgage bonds of the Land Bank for the Nobility.

Mortgage bonds of the Bank for the Nobility were placed by the State Bank and Finance Ministry. Usually the Bank for the Nobility transferred its bonds at a definite price to the State Bank, which, with the consent of the Finance Ministry, chose the most convenient way of realizing them. It could deposit them in the portfolios of savings banks, announce the underwriting of the total sum of mortgage bonds transferred to it, or sell them gradually on the stock exchange. Thus, with the help of State Bank and on the basis of the imperial decrees of April 4/16, June 20 and 27/July 2 and 9, 1897, the first issue of 3.5 percent bonds of the Bank for the Nobility was floated for the nominal capital of 100 million rubles, this time on the London and Paris markets. The operation was carried out with the participation of C. J. Hambro & Son and also Seligman Brothers in London, the Crédit Lyonnais, and Hoskier and Co. in Paris.

The second issue of 3.5 percent bonds (authorized by a decree of January 16/28, 1898) was floated in Paris for the nominal capital of 172,785,200 rubles, and the third issue (through a decree of June 17/29, 1898) for 100 million rubles, was likewise transacted in Paris.

In 1899 the Finance Ministry attempted to place a further 50 million rubles worth of 3.5 percent mortgage bonds of the Land Bank for the Nobility held in savings banks, in the hope this would release a part of the resources of the savings banks for railway construction. Talks were conducted with the Crédit Lyonnais. Despite the very low price the bank proposed, a mere 91.45 after commission and taxes, or nearly 4.7 percent below the price of the bonds of 1897 and 1898, the Finance Ministry agreed. For political reasons, however, the French government refused to allow the bonds to be quoted. In October 1899, during the visit of the Russian Foreign Minister, M. N. Murav'ev, to Paris, the French government proposed issuing in France, instead of the mortgage bonds, a railway loan of 400 million francs on the condition that it be used for building a strategic railway line from Orenburg to Tashkent or from Uralsk to Chardzhou in the eventuality of war with Britain. The idea for this railway reflected France's concern with the recent Fashoda conflict. Witte, however, declined the proposal, noting that securities by railway companies were more heavily taxed in France. He sought to persuade the French government to place mortgage bonds for 200 million rubles on the French market in 1900 and 1901. In the event that the French agreed, Witte expressed readiness to undertake construction of the Orenburg–Tashkent rail line with domestic funds. In the end, the bonds were sold at the beginning of 1900, but for only 50 million rubles, a quarter of the original sum.[39]

The crisis that began after 1898 on European exchanges affected the prices of Russian securities, including one of the main types, the 4 percent rente. In 1894 a 4 percent rente had been issued in Russia to replace a number of 5 percent internal loans subject to conversion. Over time the 4 percent rente replaced the majority of internal Russian loans and also a number of shares and bonds that passed into the treasuries of the railways.[40] The Finance Ministry considered the rente form of loan to be most beneficial for Russia because of the absence of reissues, and it granted a number of advantages to these bonds over other securities. In March 1898 the Finance Committee decided to permit the sale of the rentes on foreign markets. By the end of 1900 more than 2 billion rubles had been issued, but foreign markets took only 300 million. With the onset of the crisis one-third of the rentes were sold by the foreign holders and returned to Russia. In order to stem this influx, in late 1900 the Finance Committee decided to exempt the 4 percent rentes held by nonresident foreign nationals from the 5 percent income tax (which had been deducted from interest payments). As a result, at the beginning of 1901 the government was able to place 159 million rubles (424 million francs) of the 4 percent consolidated rente in France through the Paris Rothschilds.[41]

Meanwhile, not only in the late 1890s but also after the turn of the century, Russian railway bonds continued to be placed in the German and Dutch markets. By 1902, however, the total sum of these bonds amounted to more than 500 million rubles, and the demand for them fell off. Nonetheless, a Russian state loan of 181,959,000 rubles of nominal capital, proposed by Mendelssohn, was issued in Germany in the spring of 1902. Foreign banks participating in the syndicate (Mendelssohn, Bleichröder, Warschauer, Diskonto-Gesellschaft in Berlin; Lippmann, Rosenthal and Co. in Amsterdam) underwrote 80 percent of the total, while Russian banks (St. Petersburg International, St. Petersburg Discount and Loan Bank, the Russo-Chinese Bank, Russian Bank for Foreign Trade, and the Volga-Kama Bank) took the remaining 20 percent. The syndicate took 139 million rubles at a firm price of 94.875 percent; the balance (approximately 43 million rubles) was placed in the portfolio of Russian savings banks for a minimum term of seven months, to be realized later by a special arrangement with Mendelssohn.[42]

For the rest of 1902 and 1903 Russia raised no further state loans abroad. But in 1904, 1905, 1906, and 1909 the state did have to float new loans to support the gold standard, to finance the Russo-Japanese War, and to cover expenditures incurred in suppressing the revolutionary movement.

During the Russo-Japanese War, in particular, French banks played a decisive role in financing Russia's military spending. On April 29/May 12, 1904, the tsarist government signed a contract with a syndicate consisting of Hottinguer and Co., the Banque de Paris et des Pays-Bas, and the Crédit Lyonnais to issue on the Paris market 5 percent State Treasury bonds for 300 million rubles (800 million francs), at a price of 94 percent, with provision for a public subscription at a price of 99 percent. The bonds, issued for a term of five years, were exempt from all Russian taxes.[43] Six months later the Russian government applied to German banks, and on December 15/28, 1904, an imperial decree authorized a 4.5 percent state loan in 1905 for a nominal capital of 231.5 million rubles (500 million marks). The loan was underwritten by German and Dutch banking houses in the following proportions: Mendelssohn, $31\frac{1}{8}$ percent; Diskonto-Gesellschaft, $16\frac{5}{8}$ percent; Lippmann, Rosenthal and Co., $3\frac{1}{12}$ percent; S. Bleichröder, $12\frac{3}{8}$ percent; Berliner Handelsgesellschasft, $12\frac{3}{8}$ percent. The balance (a hefty 24 percent) was assumed by Russian banks.[44]

The 5 percent state loan of 1906 was concluded for 2.25 billion francs, of which 1.2 billion was taken by France, 830 million by England, 165 million by Austria, 55 million by Holland, and 500 million by Russian banks. Although the tsarist government intended that the loan bear an international character, the French government imposed a political condition: Russia's unreserved support in the French conflict with Germany over Morocco. As a result, German banks withdrew altogether. Witte was unsuccessful in his attempts to win Morgan's participation, and America remained aloof from Russia's credit operations abroad. The English market opened for Russia in connection with the Anglo-Russian rapprochement that began in late 1905 and culminated in a political agreement in August 1907. Still, participation by English banks in the Russian 5 percent loan of 1906 and 4.5 percent loan of 1909 was essentially symbolic, and the lion's share in each case was taken by French banks—Banque de Paris et des Pays-Bas, Crédit Lyonnais, Hottinguer and Co., Comptoir d'Escompte, and the Société Générale. Other participants in the operation were Baring Brothers, Hope and Company, and Lippmann, Rosenthal. The loan of 1906 was issued by public subscription in Russia, France, and Austria at 88 percent, in Britain at 89 percent, and in Holland at 88.8 percent. After the bankers' commissions the government realized 83.5 percent of the face value.[45]

All syndicate members involved in the 5 percent loan in 1906 also participated in the last Russian external loan before World War I, namely the 4.5 percent loan of 1909, for a nominal capital of 525 million rubles (1.4 billion francs). The French group took most (1.2 billion francs), with insignificant participation by English and Dutch banks (150 million and 30 million francs, respectively).

After 1909 the government abandoned the policy of placing state loans abroad, preferring government-guaranteed railway loans, which was a more convenient form of credit that did not require special approval by the Duma and was less vulnerable to external political conditions.

By this time the role of French banks in the placement of Russian railway loans and in various forms of cooperation with Russian banks had grown immensely. As early as the end of 1906 Maurice de Verneuil, chairman (*Syndic*) of the Paris Bourse, proposed to the Russian Finance Minister the formation of a powerful group of Russian and French banks that would use French capital to promote the development of Russian commercial and industrial enterprises. In Verneuil's view, the biggest Russian commercial banks (such as the St. Petersburg International Bank, the St. Petersburg Discount and Loan Bank, the Russian Bank for Foreign Trade, the Volga-Kama Bank, and the Azov-Don Bank) would share responsibility for the new undertaking with French banks.[46]

Although Verneuil's proposal received an enthusiastic welcome in St. Petersburg, its realization was hampered by political events connected with revolution in Russia. But the cooperation proposed by Verneuil commenced in 1908 and reached its apogee on the eve of World War I. During the revolution of 1905 to 1907 the government made no attempt to place railway loans abroad, but after their resumption in 1908, such loans soon became the main type of external loans.

In 1908, after a long break, three government-guaranteed railway loans were placed on the French market for a total of 120 million rubles (nominal): for the Volga-Bugulma, North Donets, and Southeastern railways. Together with other French banks, the Banque de Lyon et Marseille took an active role in these transactions, assuming almost all responsibility itself for placing the bonds of the Volga-Bugulma Railway. In 1910 the Banque de Lyon et Marseille reissued the bonds of the Volga-Bugulma Railway in the amount of 37,950,000 rubles (nominal).[47]

On the eve of World War I Franco-Russian financial relations were characterized by joint operations by Russian and French banks. French provincial banks began to participate actively in Russian affairs along with major credit institutions. The character of syndicate contracts changed: They became long-term contracts including agreements on issuing bonds and shares not of single railways but several railways at once. For example, in June 1911 a meeting of Russian and French bankers ended with an agreement between nine Russian banks and the Banque de Paris et des Pays Bas, the Société Générale, and the Crédit Mobilier Français to finance construction of several railways in Siberia and the Urals.[48]

In January 1914 the Finance Ministry signed an agreement with a group of French banks to issue a joint railway loan for 665 million francs (249,375,000 rubles nominal). The bulk of the loan was undertaken by banks already active in Russian loans: the Banque de Paris et des Pays-Bas, the Comptoir d'Escompte, the Crédit Lyonnais, the Société Générale, and Hottinguer and Co. Provincial banks of a minor syndicate were also permitted to participate for a sum of 70 million francs; the group included the Crédit Mobilier Français, the Société Générale des Banques de Province, the Société Marseillaise, the Crédit du Nord, the Crédit Foncier d'Algérie et de Tunisie, the Société Nancienne, the Banque de Pays du Nord, the Compagnie Algérienne, the Banque de Bordeaux, Renauld et Cie, Thalmann et Cie, and Günzburg et Cie. The loan yielded 603.5 million francs (226.3 million rubles) net. The proceeds went to the Bukhara, the Achinsk-Minusinsk, the Fergana, the Moscow-Kazan, the Moscow-Kiev-Voronezh, the North Donets, the Olonets, the Podolsk, and the Ryazan-Ural railways.[49]

Although German banks for political reasons did not participate in the last two Russian external loans of 1906 and 1909, Russian banks and the Finance Ministry maintained active relations with the German market almost until the beginning of World War I. Between 1908 and 1913 German banks placed loans for the Moscow-

Kazan, Moscow-Kiev-Voronezh, and Vladikavkaz railways. The last loan (for the Vladikavkaz Railway) was issued in 1913.[50] At a meeting in April 1912 the Azov-Don Bank council announced that it had joined a group of German banks (Mendelssohn & Co., Bleichröder, Berliner Handelsgesellschaft, and Bank für Handel und Industrie) to place Russian railway loans.[51] The Russian government maintained special relations with Mendelssohn, who, over many years, regularly informed the Finance Ministry of the situation on the international money market.[52]

After 1909 the London market again showed interest in Russian railway bonds, in particular the bonds of the Armavir-Tuapse, Kokand-Namangan, Troitsk, and Black Sea-Cuban' railways.[53] The Russo-Chinese Bank (subsequently reorganized as the Russo-Asiatic Bank) and the Russian Commercial and Industrial Bank cooperated with British banks engaged in issuing Russian railway loans. For example, in 1910 bonds of the Kokand-Namangan and the Troitsk railways were both placed by the same syndicate of banks: Lloyds Bank Limited, the Anglo-Russian Trust in London, Birch Crisp and Co., and the Russo-Chinese Bank. In 1912 bonds of the Kakhetiia Railway amounting to 13,230,000 rubles (£ 1.4 million) were placed through Crisp and Co. and the Anglo-Russian Trust. Fifteen days after the Finance Minister's approval of the contract the amount of the loan was credited to the Kakhetiia Railway Company through special accounts opened in five London banks: Lloyds Banks Limited, the London Southwestern Bank, the Anglo-Russian Bank Limited, the Russo-Asiatic Bank, and the Russian Commercial and Industrial Bank.[54]

In addition to the ties with French and British banks, the Finance Ministry showed interest in the markets of Belgium and Switzerland. This was demonstrated in the 1912 loan for the North Donets Railway Co., which was raised in Antwerp, Basel, Brussels, Geneva, and Zürich.[55]

Between 1908 and 1914, along with railway bonds, the Russian government attempted to sell municipal bonds and mortgage bonds of land banks on foreign markets. As before, the mortgage bonds were mainly placed on the domestic market, whereas the municipal bonds were distributed primarily abroad. London's role in municipal bonds grew markedly. In the 1890s Germany had been the main market for these, and Moscow loans in particular were raised in Berlin and Hamburg. But after 1900 St. Petersburg and other Russian cities were granted credits in Paris, and beginning in 1908 British banks showed an interest in Russian municipal loans. In 1912 Moscow loans amounting to 36 million rubles, loans of Nikolaev amounting to 6.5 million rubles, and loans of Vilna amounting to 42 million rubles were raised in London, as was a major St. Petersburg loan in 1913.[56] Belgian banks also participated in placing Russian municipal bonds. The Moscow loan of 1910, for example, was placed in Brussels through the Caisse Générale de Reports et de Dépôts and in Antwerp through the Banque Centrale Anveroise and Crédit Anverois.[57]

Before 1912 only the mortgage bonds of the Land Bank for the Nobility were accepted for quotation on foreign stock markets—in Paris, London, and Amsterdam.[58] At the beginning of 1912 Finance Minister V. N. Kokovtsev decided to place the 4.5 percent state certificates of the Peasants' Land Bank in Paris. In February 1912 the second series of these certificates for a sum of 100 million rubles (nominal) was issued. The French members of the consortium were headed by the Banque de Paris et des Pays-Bas and the Crédit Lyonnais. The group also included the Société Générale and Hottinguer and Co. Russian participants in the consortium were represented by the

Russo-Asiatic Bank and the St. Petersburg International Commercial Bank. The Volga-Kama and the Azov-Don Commercial banks also took part in the operation, which redeemed the 6 percent bonds of the Peasants' Bank issued on the domestic market.[59]

The cooperation of French and Russian banks in exporting capital to those regions of the world where Russia and France had common interests, or where France was ready to support Russian interests, has not yet been studied adequately. The Russo-Chinese Bank was established in 1895, on the initiative of the Russian Finance Ministry. Its founders were the St. Petersburg International Commercial Bank and a group of French banks: Hottinguer and Co., the Banque de Paris et de Pays-Bas, the Crédit Lyonnais, and Comptoir d'Escompte. The initial capital of the bank amounted to 6 million rubles, of which three-eighths were placed in Russia and five-eighths in France. Three members of the bank's board represented French shareholders and five members, including the chairman, represented Russian shareholders.[60] In 1910 the Russo-Chinese Bank was liquidated and replaced by the Russo-Asiatic Bank, marking yet another stage in the development of Franco-Russian cooperation.

In January 1912, at the initiative of the Crédit Français, talks were begun on establishing the Balkan Commercial and Land Bank in cooperation with Russian banks. The Russian ambassador in Sofia told the head of the Crédit Français, that he would like to see the Russian group include not the Russo-Asiatic Bank or the Private Commercial Bank, which operated with foreign capital, but the Volga-Kama and St. Petersburg Discount and Loan banks, which represented "pure Russian capital."[61] In April a Russo-Bulgaro-French bank named the Commercial and Mortgage Bank of the Balkans opened. It had a capital of 10 million francs: 5 million from the Crédit Français, 2.5 million from the Bulgarian People's Bank, and 2.5 million from four Russian banks (the St. Petersburg International, the Volga-Kama, the St. Petersburg Discount and Loan, and the Russian Bank for Foreign Trade). In May, however, the Russian group conceded 1 million francs to the Crédit Français.[62] Prior to the outbreak of World War I the activities of the Commercial and Mortgage Bank of the Balkans remained on a small scale, partly because of the complicated political situation in the Balkans.

Russian banks acted as subparticipants or French banks' partners in loan operations that were carried out by various countries after the 1890s. At the beginning of the 1890s the International Bank, in particular, acted as a subparticipant in Serbian and Bulgarian loans from the Paris International Bank.[63] In 1899 the St. Petersburg International Bank conducted negotiations with the Banque de Paris et des Pays-Bas on their joint participation in an Iranian loan, which, for political reasons, was not floated.[64] In March 1898 the Russian, British, and French governments signed a convention for a joint guarantee of a Greek loan amounting to 170 million francs. The following month bankers of the three countries realized the first portion of the loan, amounting to 124.5 million francs. A group of Russian banks took one third of the total sum, dividing it among the State Bank (two-sevenths), the Volga-Kama, the Russo-Chinese, the Russian Bank for Foreign Trade, the St. Petersburg International Bank, and the St. Petersburg Discount and Loan Bank (one-seventh each). A subsequent separate agreement between the State Bank and the St. Petersburg Private Commercial Bank allowed the latter to acquire the State Bank's share.[65]

In 1902 the Banque de Paris et des Pays-Bas in cooperation with the State Bank floated a Bulgarian loan amounting to 106 million francs. The State Bank's share was only 14 million. Since the State Bank's participation in the operation was not for commercial purposes, the Russian government passed the bank's profit gained from realization of the loan to the Bulgarian government.[66]

Foreign Banks and Direct Foreign Investments

The only foreign bank to maintain branches in Russia before World War I was the Crédit Lyonnais. It opened an agency in St. Petersburg in 1879 and twelve years later added offices in Moscow and Odessa.[67] Studies by Bouvier and Girault, however, have demonstrated that its operations in Russia actually had little to do with direct foreign investment.[68] In fact, the bank's management categorically forbade its Russian branches to participate in industrial undertakings, to grant long-term credits, to purchase local securities, or to engage in commercial operations. The management's aim was to make "major deals with the tsarist government," which was then placing its loans in France.[69] When the Crédit Lyonnais helped to place the 4 percent Russian external loan of 1889, it was the first step toward this objective. This same bank was subsequently to play a prominent role in placing not only Russian state and municipal loans but also mortgage bonds of the Noble Land Bank.

Russian agencies of the Crédit Lyonnais ordinarily did not take part in these operations. Their primary task was to carry out remittance and exchange operations for clients requiring international payments.[70] They were also to supply information on economic conditions in Russia. As early as 1868 the head of the Crédit Lyonnais (Henri Germain) wrote: "It is important for us to have people in Russia in a good position to inform us of all major financial, trading, and industrial affairs so that at appropriate times we might involve ourselves in them and if need be take the initiative."[71] And it was the Russian branches of the Crédit Lyonnais that gathered such information for the bank's "financial studies" service.

To judge from the records of its St. Petersburg branch, the service took a keen interest in virtually every aspect of economic life. For example, it painstakingly collected thousands of Russian press clippings on such subjects as state finance, industry, credit, trade, and transport. Analyses of these data (as well as information obtained from other sources) are preserved in the archives of the Crédit Lyonnais in Paris. Apart from translations of the Russian newspaper articles, the files include letters written by branch heads as well as reports and summaries by the experts of the bank's industrial studies service in St. Petersburg. All these documents contained detailed analyses of the economic condition and technical operation of many industrial enterprises.[72] Though the Crédit Lyonnais had no "industrial business" in Russia, it displayed an interest in Russian industrial development that was anything but abstract. In addition to regular reports on major industrial enterprises (which most likely were under regular observation), the Paris office sent numerous instructions to St. Petersburg to obtain information on specific firms and businessmen.[73] This information-gathering effort doubtless reflected a vigorous economic interest in Russia, and the Crédit Lyonnais in satisfying this demand indirectly influenced the development of foreign enterprise in Russia.

By the late 1870s, as the Crédit Lyonnais opened its branch in St. Petersburg, foreign entrepreneurship in Russia had acquired some distinct new features. Previously, foreign investments had been closely tied to the immigration of businessmen, and it had concentrated mainly on cotton production, the fastest growing sector of Russian industry.[74] In the 1860s interest spread to sugar refining, which was just then entering a period of rapid growth. Foreign businessmen contributed to the formation of some new industries, such as electrical equipment, rubber, perfume, and confectionary production. They also took a rather prominent place in trade.

Already by mid-century, the Russian Empire had a fairly numerous set of joint-stock companies, including some industrial firms.[75] Enterprises established by foreigners usually had an individual or narrow family character; only the successful minority subsequently turned into joint-stock companies, a process often abetted by indigenous investors and businessmen. At the same time most of the original foreign owners became naturalized citizens and gradually assimilated into the local population.

On the other hand, from the first, some foreign-owned enterprises in Russia continued to operate abroad. Normally in such cases an industrial or commercial affiliate was established first; at some later point a Russian joint-stock company was founded to manage and operate the affiliated enterprise. One of the earliest such cases was a cotton mill in St. Petersburg, established in 1844 by the British firm E. Hubbard and Co.; only in 1851 did the firm establish a Russian joint-stock company to operate the mill. In 1852 and 1865 two more such companies were founded.[76] It bears noting that, in some instances, there was a protracted hiatus between the time that a foreign firm established an affiliate in Russia and reorganized it as a Russian joint-stock company. For example, the branch of Siemens & Halske (Germany), which had been active since the 1850s, did not become a joint-stock company until 1898.

By contrast, in the 1870s and 1880s foreign entrepreneurs were increasingly drawn toward sectors of heavy industry (such as mining, metallurgy, metalworking, and chemicals) as well as public works and utilities. Although foreign entrepreneurs continued to immigrate, it was not individuals but foreign companies that assumed the principal role in founding industrial and other capitalist enterprises.

The first foreign company specifically constituted to operate as an industrial enterprise in Russia was the New Russian Company, Ltd., registered in London in 1869. It was soon followed by the Lodz-Gas-Gesellschaft (Berlin, 1870), Azoff Colliery Company (London, 1872), and Odessa Waterworks Co., Ltd. (London, 1873). Of particular import were the French companies, of which there were eleven in operation by the early 1880s.[77] Although two represented simply an extension of their operations elsewhere, nine had been formed specifically to operate as Russian enterprises. The Société Minière et Industrielle, which owned coal mines in the Donbas, also had lead and zinc mines in northern Spain and manganese deposits in the Upper Pyrenees.[78] But more numerous was the other, newer pattern, whereby foreign companies added Russian divisions to their complex of industrial enterprises either by forming affiliates or by receiving permission to start operations in Russia. The latter path appealed particularly to German firms. In the 1880s they formed a number of affiliates in the Russian Empire, mainly in Poland and the Baltic provinces.[79] As a result of such processes, the number of foreign companies operating in Russia had increased substantially by the mid-1880s. It was to continue over the ensuing fifteen years, accounting for a sixth of all new joint-stock companies in Russia and more than a fifth of the increment in joint-stock capital.[80]

It should be noted that, with rare exceptions, the foreign companies organized their Russian operations with the participation of local investors and businessmen. In part, such collaboration was due to the fact that, especially in the 1880s, foreign entrepreneurs sought not only to establish enterprises in Russia but also to reorganize the financial and plant operation of indigenous firms.[81] The first influx of foreign capital into Russian joint-stock companies also occurred at this time.

Amid the rapid economic growth of the 1890s and proliferation of enterprises, foreign entrepreneurs and local capital combined to form an intricate system of interrelations in which banks assumed an increasingly pronounced role. The enormous growth of capitalist production in the last third of the nineteenth century, the replacement of family firms by joint-stock companies, the interest in the potential profits of industrial finance—all underlay the banks' growing involvement in capitalist entrepreneurship. Not surprisingly, this process developed differently from one country to the next, depending on the peculiarities of capitalist development in both the investing and host country. As will be seen, these factors shaped the behavior of Western banks that provided direct foreign investments in Russia, leading to significant differences in scale and organizational form of their entrepreneurial activities.

The first known participation, dating back to the early 1870s, was that of the Société Générale. As Bertrand Gille has shown, its interest was first sparked by an "incidental" loan in 1865 to three British entrepreneurs using Dünaburg-Witebsk Railway bonds as collateral. That impelled the bank in 1870 to send an engineer to study Russian railways and, in the spring of the same year, to make an advance to the Kremenchug-Kharkov Railway and to participate in the Smolensk-Brest Railway.[82] Although the Franco-Prussian War temporarily interrupted activities, it immediately resumed these after the war.

In 1872 it obtained concessions for steamship service for St. Petersburg-Kronstadt and the Moscow River. It transferred these operations to the Société Industrielle Franco-Russe, an affiliate that the bank established with a capital of 20 million francs. The latter also became interested in mineral deposits and, most notably, took a lease on a rich coalfield in the Donets Basin. Inasmuch as the interests of the Société Industrielle Franco-Russe were not limited to Russia, in 1873 it was reorganized as the Société Minière et Industrielle.[83] Although this undertaking suffered from the deteriorating economic situation and had to give up its steamship companies,[84] the bank retained control of its claims to the rich coalfields in the Donbas. Until 1897 it exploited these through the Société Minière et Industrielle de Rutchenko, which the bank had founded earlier in Belgium.[85]

In the 1870s and 1880s the initiative in foreign entrepreneurship in Russia was taken by major Western firms or groups, chiefly French and German and to a lesser extent Belgian.[86] Although bank involvement is known in a few cases, it was exceedingly rare for banks to provide direct support to these foreign enterprises in Russia. Even when Siemens & Halske established its electric lighting company in Russia in 1886, the role of the Deutsche Bank was not apparent, notwithstanding Siemens' close ties to the bank.[87] Nor was there evidence of direct bank participation in the enterprises of Lyons industrialists Jean Bonnardel, Eugene Verdié, Gabriel Chanove, and Eugene Pasteur, who established the Société des Forges et Aciéries de Huta-Bankova in 1877 and the Kama Steel Company in 1883.[88] The same can be said of numerous other companies founded in Russia in the 1880s by French, German, and Belgian entrepreneurs. Nevertheless, the decade of the 1880s also marked the first cases where foreign banks, particularly French, began to invest directly in Russian industrial business.

The pathbreaker was a newly founded Paris bank, Union Générale. Already in the summer of 1879, its Lyons branch undertook to place 4,000 shares (nominally worth 2 million francs) of the Société Franco-Russe de l'Oural, established in Paris.[89] This was followed by establishment of a number of other French companies intending to operate in Russia.

In 1880 the Société Générale participated, along with Union Générale and two metallurgical firms from the Loire valley, in founding the Société des Usines Franco-Russes in Paris. They purchased the shipyards of George Baird, a Scottish-born St. Petersburg factory owner, and proceeded to modernize and enlarge them. Two members of the bank's board of directors joined the company board. The following year the Société Générale participated in the formation of the Société de Minerai de Fer de Krivoy-Rog.[90]

The same year another new bank, the Banque de Lyon et de la Loire, of Lyons, created two more companies: the Société Foncière et Forestière (for the exploitation of large tracts of forest near Mozyr) and the Société des Naphtes et Petroles du Caucase.[91] Although the bankruptcy of the Union Générale and the Banque de Lyon et de la Loire in 1882 put an end to their initiatives,[92] the Société Générale survived and its two companies, the Société des Usines Franco-Russes and the Société de Minerai de Fer de Krivoy-Rog, turned out to be viable. To judge from the records of the Société Générale, the bank continued to support these companies by directing the placement of additional issues of share and bonds.[93] As the industrial interests of the Société Générale in Russia took shape, its involvement was facilitated by its ties with French industrial groups. Thus, the bank was induced to participate in the Société des Usines Franco-Russes by the Marine-Marrel group. The Société de Minerai de Fer de Krivoy-Rog was founded at the initiative of the Talabot group; it was headed by Paulin Talabot, a director of the Société Générale.[94]

A similar role at the Comptoir d'Escompte was played by one of the bank's directors, Louis Saint-Paul de Sinçay, a well-known businessman on whose proposal in 1883 the Société des sels gemmes de la Russie méridionale was founded in Paris.[95] Sinçay managed to attract the private banking firm of Demachy et Seillière, in addition to the Comptoir d'Escompte, to join the venture.[96]

The Laveissière group, which joined with the Belgian firm Chaudoir to open the Copper-rolling and Tube Works Co. (formerly Rosenkranz) in 1881, was also connected with the Comptoir d'Escompte. In 1888 it placed the bonds of the Briansk Steel Works, which planned a metallurgical plant near Ekaterinoslav. In addition to the Comptoir d'Escompte, this operation included the participation of the Banque de Paris et des Pays-Bas, the Crédit Mobilier Français, and the Banque de Brabant.[97]

By the early 1890s, as Girault has noted, it was clear that French industrial groups could keep pace with the rapid economic growth in Russia only with bank assistance.[98] For their part, French banks displayed a far more lively interest in such operations. As early as 1886 the Rothschilds had acquired a controlling interest in the Caspian-Black Sea Company, a penetration of the Russian petroleum industry with long-term objectives.[99] This set an example for the Comptoir d'Escompte and the Banque Internationale de Paris, which, in 1891, bought a controlling interest in the Société des sels gemmes de la Russie méridionale.[100] By the mid-1890s banks replaced industrial groups as the driving force of direct French investment in Russia.

The most important of these were the Société Générale, the Banque de Paris et de Pays-Bas, and the Rothschilds. At first their spheres of interest did not intersect. The Rothschilds operated in the petroleum industry of Baku and Grozny, the Société Générale concentrated on coal mining and metallurgical industries in southern Russia, and the Banque de Paris et des Pays-Bas really had no specialized interests. The bulk of the latter's diverse enterprises (mining, metallurgical, metalworking, and machine-building) were in central Russia and the Volga River Basin. But as the Société Générale and the Banque de Paris et des Pays-Bas expanded their operations they soon found themselves in the same areas, with conflicting interests.

Together with the French banking giants, credit institutions of lesser rank also became active in Russia in the second half of the 1890s. One of the more important was the Banque Internationale de Paris, which functioned as a sort of vanguard for larger forces. A similar role was played by professional promoters (H. Legru, F. Maes, E. Gauthey, M. Gorgeu, Th. Motet, L. de Chatelier, A. Josse, L. Laport, F. Schmatzer, and others), who acted as initiators of many enterprises in Russia. The Banque de Paris et des Pays-Bas generally tended to follow the Banque Internationale de Paris, whereas the Société Générale skillfully used promoters to meet its needs.[101]

As the French banks expanded their spheres of interest in Russia, they had to design suitable organizational forms for their participation in Russian industry. Thus, in October 1896 and February 1897, French banks established two new companies to serve as intermediaries between themselves and the Russian enterprises they financed.

The first company was the Société Générale pour l'industrie en Russie (SGIR); founded by the Banque Internationale de Paris, it represented a financial group that included the Banque de Paris et des Pays-Bas, banking houses from the Haute Banque, the Société des Forges de Châtillon et Commentry, and the St. Petersburg International Bank.[102]

The second company was the Sociéte Générale de l'industrie minière et metallurgique en Russie (also known as l'Omnium russe), which the Société Générale established in Brussels with the participation of three Russian banks (the Commercial and Industrial Bank, the Discount and Loan Bank, and the St. Petersburg-Azov Bank) and a great number of French and Belgian financiers and industrialists.[103]

Amid this vigorous activity in enterprise formation, another intermediate layer had also emerged—the *sociétés financières* registered in Belgium. Sponsored by promoters, these companies were highly speculative, undertaking operations that the major banks deemed too risky or inappropriate. In McKay's words, the Sociéte Générale used the Société Financière Internationale, of Brussels, "as screen and agent for Russian activities of doubtful morality."[104] But Belgian industrial firms and banks operated in Russia not only in alliance with the French, but also independently. In the second half of the 1890s there occurred a sharp increase in Belgian investments in Russian industry. The main trends of Belgian investments in Russia are well elucidated by Van der Wee and Goossens in this book (Chapter 5). Chapter 21 by Wengenroth also contains interesting material.

German firms, similarly, made considerable direct investments in the 1880s and 1890s. They established subsidiaries as well as affiliates closely connected with them in terms of production. In the case of affiliates it is often well-nigh impossible to assess the role of the banks, for the German firms did not organize affiliates as separate companies, but simply obtained permission to conduct their operations in Russia. But when affiliates were reorganized as formally independent companies under the Russian code, in the second half of the 1890s, it was clear that German banks had participated in virtually all of them. Particularly notable for their Russian operations were the Deutsche Bank (the Siemens & Halske Company of Russian electrotechnical plants, the Kramatorskaya Metallurgical Company, the Sosnowice Tube-rolling and Iron Works, etc.) and the Dresdner Bank (the Union Company, the Hartman Machine Company, etc.).[105]

Very little is known about British investment, unfortunately. The main involvement did not come until 1897, when two competing groups in London almost simultaneously purchased the Baku enterprises of the oilmen G. Z. A. Tagiev and S. M. Shibaev.[106] After the turn of the century this investment spread from petroleum to copper mines and gold fields in the Caucasus and in Siberia. Whether acquiring old enterprises or founding new ones, the British normally employed a system of multitier financial and holding companies, making it easier to explore the lower layers of this financial pyramid than to discern its apex.

Foreign banks at first tended to finance Russian industry independently of Russian banks, but from the mid-1890s began to cooperate with the major St. Petersburg banks (International; Discount and Loan; Private; Commercial and Industrial). The St. Petersburg banks at first acted as junior partners, but as time passed they began to claim a greater role. This is particularly evident in the case of the St. Petersburg International Bank, which often aspired to have a leading role, especially in the organization of SGIR. By working with a variety of banking groups, it occupied an independent position in its relations with foreign partners, sometimes resulting in rather interesting situations.

By the end of the 1890s the Société métallurgique d'Oural-Volga, founded on the initiative of the Banque Internationale de Paris with some participation of the St. Petersburg International Bank, found itself on the verge of bankruptcy. New investments were urgently needed. The director of the Banque International de Paris, T. Lombardo, asked the director of the St. Petersburg International, A. Rothstein, to involve the Rothschilds in the affair.[107]

As early as the 1890s some banking groups active in Russian industrial finance were multinational. It was particularly characteristic in the electrotechnical industry, which became the area of competition among several international financial corporations. Along with Russian banks, German, French, Belgian, Swiss, Austrian, and Dutch banks and banking houses participated in the great Russian syndicate formed in 1899 to finance the electrification of urban transport.[108]

The crisis of the early 1900s was a severe test for the Russian enterprises financed by foreign banks. As is clear from the minutes of the boards of the Banque de Paris et des Pays-Bas and the Société Générale for the 1900s, the banks regarded these enterprises as an enormous burden and had to make major efforts to save them or to terminate them with minimal losses.[109] This analysis confirms the observation by McKay and Girault that the character of French banks' involvement in the Russian economy changed in the immediate prewar years. McKay describes the changes as a switchover to "passive investments,"[110] and Girault discerns a "new strategy" and "new forms" of investment.[111]

As the minutes of the two leading French banks demonstrate, they renounced their leadership as entrepreneurs in Russian industrial development and elected to confine themselves to undertakings proposed by Russian banks, with the French role reduced to assistance in placing the shares on the Paris stock exchange. These two banks began to attach more importance to operations concerned with the reorganization of the Russian banks and to the establishment of railway companies. To be sure, exceptions can be found; it should be pointed out that the Banque de l'Union Parisienne tried to play a more active role in Russian industry before the war.[112] But, as McKay has convincingly shown, this bank did not fare well even in relations with a relatively weak enterprise like the Bogatyr Company, and was finally forced to liquidate its participation.[113] It is a fact of some import that precisely at this time the Rothschilds ceded their oil enterprises in Russia to Royal Dutch-Shell (in exchange for 20 percent of its shares).[114]

The prewar relations between German banks and Russian industry have received less attention, have been less studied, but appear to have undergone no major changes. As Diakin's study of German capital in the electrotechnical industry shows, however, under conditions of the prewar industrial upsurge German banks managed to maintain their positions in this industry only by establishing closer relations with Russian banks and industrial groups.[115]

The sphere of British investments, by contrast, widened noticeably in the prewar years. The influx of British capital moved in the same directions as before: oil extraction in the Caucasus and the mining industry of Siberia and the Urals (chiefly gold and copper). The threads of control over British enterprises in Baku and the North Caucasus led to oil concerns competing in the world market. And British companies founded to exploit Russian gold and copper mines were the offshoots of financial groups dominating the world gold and copper industries. They were all interconnected. It is indicative that the founders of one of the first British companies for financing mining enterprises in Russia, the Russian Industrial and Mining Co., Ltd., were the prominent oilmen Frederick Lane and Calouste Gulbenkian.[116] This company, connected with the Union Bank of London and Smiths Bank,[117] founded the Jenisei Copper Co. in 1902.[118]

At first such companies did not include Russian businessmen. This is true not only of the Industrial and Mining Co., but also for the Siberian Syndicate established in 1902,[119] which joined with the Union Bank of Scotland to found the Spassky Mine Society.[120] Nor did the Anglo-Siberian Co.[121] (registered in 1906) incorporate indigenous elements as it (together with the banking firm of Brown, Shipley & Co.) founded the Perm Corporation in 1907 or (with the London and Country Banking Co.) the Kyshtym Corporation in 1908.[122] To cite one exception, Russian businessmen did participate in 1906 in establishing the Russian Mining Corporation that (with the London Joint Stock Bank) founded the Lena Goldfields Company in 1908.[123]

Later, however, businessmen did join the boards of such companies.[124] For example, when the disbanded Anglo-Siberian Co. was replaced in 1912 by the Russian-Asiatic Corporation, the new company included representatives of St. Petersburg banks A. Putilov, A. Davidov, and F. Kon on its board.[125]

The prewar period was also marked by an increase in the proportion and significance of foreign investments in Russian banks. This tendency was particularly evident in the activity of French banks and embodied the substance of their "new strategy." To a certain extent, this pattern was also apparent in the case of German and British financial groups.

Foreign banks, particularly German, participated in the formation of several Russian banks. For this reason some Russian banks, the St. Petersburg International and the Russian Bank for Foreign Trade in particular, are often described in the literature as the German banks' affiliates. But the extensive documents of the St. Petersburg International Bank do not sustain that view; nor does the scholarship on German banks demonstrate any influence upon the activity of the St. Petersburg International Bank.[126] Moreover, the proceedings of shareholders' meetings (including those of the St. Petersburg International) indicate that foreign banks did not even make an attempt to exert such influence, an observation that holds true as well for the stockholders' meetings of some other major Russian banks.[127] It is significant too that, before the mid-1890s, foreign banks were even without formal representation on the boards of Russian banks. Not until 1895 did a Russian bank—the Russo-Chinese Bank—include the heads of foreign credit institutions as permanent members of its board, but this was a rather special case, since its creation was linked chiefly to government foreign policy.

When the Northern Bank opened its operations in St. Petersburg in 1901, the first authentic affiliate of a foreign bank in the history of Russian credit institutions made its appearance. At first the bank had one patron, the Société Générale, but in 1906 it added the Banque de l'Union Parisienne. But, as Girault demonstrated, the Northern Bank's position as the Société Générale's affiliate soon clashed with its functions as a Russian bank, particularly the need to occupy a place in the Russian banking system, without which it had no chance for success.[128] Several years after its creation, the director of the Northern Bank, T. Lombardo, wrote in a melancholy mood: "We have to do what is convenient for the Société Générale. But these are affairs which exceed the bounds of our operations."[129]

The crisis of the early 1900s entailed bankruptcies, subsequent economic stagnation, and a slump in the rate of exchange. All this put Russian banks under considerable pressure. Some were on the verge of collapse and could be rescued only through the intervention of the State Bank. Under the circumstances, foreign credit institutions played an important role in the financial reorganization of many Russian banks and in the increase of their capitals.

When the Russo-Asiatic Bank was erected in 1910 on the ruins of the Russo-Chinese and Northern Banks, the reorganization had required a considerable participation by the Banque de Paris et des Pays-Bas and the Société Générale. As a result, representatives of French credit institutions were on its board. At about the same time, a consortium of banks (including the Crédit Mobilier Français, two Paris banking houses, J. Loste and Co. and Thalmann and Co., and also the London firm Hirsch and Co.) revitalized the St. Petersburg Private Bank, which had virtually become bankrupt. Foreign banks also helped increase the capital of the United Bank, the Siberian Trade Bank, the Azov-Don Bank, the Russian Bank for Foreign Trade, and the International Commercial Bank. As a result, representatives of foreign credit institutions joined the boards of several Russian banks.[130]

The consequences of this are not entirely clear. Both McKay and Girault addressed the question of the foreign banks' influence upon Russian banks and came to different conclusions. But the study of the Russo-Asiatic Bank based on the archive's materials demonstrates that this bank was by no means a blind tool of the Banque de Paris et des Pays-Bas and the Société Générale.[131] The problem is admittedly a complex one and requires considerably more research and analysis before any broad conclusions can be drawn.

Conclusions

The interest of foreign banks in Russian securities during the prewar period was due to Russia's demand for capital, the profitable terms of investment, and government guarantees. The influx of foreign capital was promoted by the government's adoption of the gold standard in 1897, the ensuing stabilization of the ruble, and the government measures to attract capital for industrial development and railway construction.

Before the beginning of railway construction in Russia, foreign banks invested mainly in Russian state loans. These transactions were carried out with the assistance of court bankers. Before the Crimean war of 1853–1856 Dutch bankers played a special part in placing Russian state loans. With the onset of railway construction, government-guaranteed loans of railway societies became an increasingly popular form of foreign capital investment. In the 1870s the government itself concluded a number of loans for railway construction purposes.

From the mid-1850s the main role in placing Russian securities passed from Dutch to British banks. In the 1860s and 1870s foreign banks conducted their operations in Russia through the State Bank and also through a group of influential private banks that, together with foreign banks, actively participated in the formation of the Great Russian Railway Co., the Central Land Bank, and also in the foundation of the larger Russian commercial banks.

In the second half of the 1870s Germany assumed the role of Russia's main creditor. By the beginning of the 1880s a group of major German banks formed a consortium especially for placing Russian railway loans. By this time Russian commercial banks began acting as foreign banks' partners in placing Russian loans. Russian banks' participation in German and later in French consortia became an important stage in the formation and development of the Russian banking system.

At the end of the 1880s a considerable portion of Russian securities was transferred from the German to the French market. This occurred with the active participation of French banks, which played a decisive part in the conversion loans of the tsarist government. France became Russia's main creditor and retained this position up to World War I.

The predominance of state and government-guaranteed paper among Russian securities placed abroad by the end of the nineteenth century determined, firstly, the important role of these transactions in relations between foreign and Russian banks and, secondly, the great influence political interests had upon the development of these relations.

On the one hand, this influence manifested itself in the attempts of creditor countries to use the tsarist government's need for foreign loans to exert political pressure. Such attempts were made by the German government at the end of the 1880s when Bismarck imposed the infamous Lombard *Verbot*. Similar attempts were later made by the French government. The dominant role of French capital in Russian loans after the 1890s formed a basis for diplomatic and military relations between France and Russia. The French government tried to exploit the Russian Finance Ministry's interest in credit and its right to admit Russian securities to quotation on the Paris Bourse. It demanded that the Russian State Bank support French entrepreneurs who experienced difficulties during the crisis years and insisted that Russian contracts be granted to French industrialists on profitable terms.

On the other hand, the Russian Finance Ministry was constantly searching for alternate markets for Russian securities. The attempts by Witte simultaneously to use the services of various European and even American money markets and to impart an international character to Russian state loans reflected this policy.

The participation of Russian banks in consortia for the issue of railway securities between 1870 and 1914 bears eloquent witness to the accelerating evolution of the Russian banking system. Two stages in this development merit particular attention: the second half of the 1890s and the period immediately preceding the outbreak of the Great War in 1914 (see Appendix Table 12A–1).

As components of consortia for the issue of bonds, the Russian and foreign banks acted as two separate, independent groups. Each side had its own leaders (one or two banks), which bore comparatively greater responsibility for the operation and received a correspondingly greater return for its efforts. It was, further, these leading banks that determined the composition of the subparticipants and their share of participation. Within the Russian group, until 1904 it was ordinarily the St. Petersburg International Bank exercising this leadership role. Thereafter other banks—the Russo-Asiatic, Azov-Don, St. Petersburg Discount and Loan Banks—also assumed a leadership role. Among German banks, in the 1880s it was the Diskonto-Gesellschaft that dominated as leader; in the next decade that role shifted to the banking house of Mendelssohn & Co.. Among French banks, the leadership function was held at various times by a wide variety of banks—the Banque de Paris et des Pays-Bas, the Société Générale, Crédit Lyonnais, Hottinguer and Co., and Crédit Mobilier Français.

Relationships between the Russian and foreign components in such consortia were exceedingly complex and variable, depending upon specific circumstances. The relative status of the Russian and foreign banks in the consortia organized by Mendelssohn and the St. Petersburg International Bank in the 1890s and after the turn of the century was ordinarily one of virtual equality. But that relative equality was not invariably the case. Thus the lines of Franco-Russian consortia for the issue of Russian railway bonds in 1912/13 plainly show the predominance of the French banks. In this case the Russian banks had no role in determining either the price or the conditions for the issue of the loans; they took 25 to 30 percent of the bonds (their quota) into their portfolio without a French stamp and deposited them in their own holdings.

Between 1908 and 1914 Russian banks participated in the realization of the bond capital of new railway companies simultaneously appearing as their co-founders and largest stockholders. In these cases, as co-founders of the companies they received from the French group part of the profit from the nominal capital of the loan (0.38 to 0.05 percent). This practice was quite typical for consortia headed by the Banque de Paris et des Pays-Bas and the Crédit Mobilier Français.

Some instances are known where the St. Petersburg Private Commercial Bank entered the French rather than Russian side in a consortium (for the bond issue of the Northeastern Urals Railway in 1912 and of the Akkerman Railway in 1913). But these were rather exceptional cases due to the very intimate ties between the Private Bank and Crédit Mobilier Français after 1910, when the Private Bank teetered on the verge of liquidation and was saved through the infusion of French capital.

As a rule, however, Russian banks acted independently when they cooperated with the banks of various countries, depending upon the market where the railway securities were to be placed. The St. Petersburg International Bank, which had solid ties with Mendelssohn & Co., the Diskonto-Gesellschaft, and other German banks, nevertheless collaborated simultaneously with the leaders of the French group—the Banque de Paris et des Pays-Bas and Hottinguer and Co.

The joint participation of Russian and foreign banks in issuing loans contributed to their readiness to cooperate in financing Russian industry. Although direct foreign investments began before the reform, foreign banks began to participate only from the 1880s. By the 1890s they cooperated with Russian banks and this contributed to the growing significance of Russian banks in the national economy.

The losses suffered by foreign entrepreneurs and banks in Russia during the crisis of 1900–1903 led to changes in the strategy of direct foreign investments in Russia. This was manifested in the attempts by French and some German banks to establish control over Russian banks and by British capitalists to develop various holding companies; the available data, however, do not indicate how successful such attempts in fact were. At the same time, by World War I the growth of the domestic credit market became an important factor in Russian economic life.

Appendix

Table 12A–1 contains data only on those bonds issued at parity with foreign currency. Although the table makes no claim to exhaustiveness, it embraces the overwhelming majority of bond operations of this type.

In assessing the nominal value for the issue of one or another bond issue, it is necessary to take into account the fact that, prior to the introduction of the gold standard, the ruble represented $\frac{1}{10}$ of the imperial, reduced to $\frac{1}{15}$ after the reform.

In most cases, the information included in Table 12A–1 is taken from contracts concluded between banks and railway companies, a kind of document bearing the greatest amount of detail. In those instances where contracts were unavailable, it was necessary to rely upon other sources (the correspondence between the representatives of banks and railway companies, or to various reference works, or the secondary literature), or to be satisfied with incomplete information.

Sometimes, in the course of the operation, the acquisition or issue price of a bond would change. If information of such changes was available (through marginalia, contracts, supplementary codicils to consortia, or references in later documentation), the table has included the data in the chronological sequence (the final information appears in the bottom row).

If the veracity of the data is in doubt, these are given in brackets. The table was compiled with the participation of S. K. Lebedev.

Abbreviations

Currency

F	franc (France)
Fl	P-B florin (Dutch)
£	pound sterling (U.K.)
M	reichsmark (Germany)
R	ruble (Russia)
T	thaler (Prussia)

Russian Banks

A-D	Azov-Don Commercial Bank (Azovsko-Donskoi kommercheskii bank)
B	Russian Bank for Foreign Trade (Russkii dlia vnerschnei torgovli bank)
DL	Discount and Loan Bank of Persia (Uchetno-Ssudnyi bank Persii)
LP	L. S. Poliakov (Bankirskii dom Poliakova)
MD	Moscow Discount Bank (Moskovskii Uchetnyi bank)
MM	Moscow Merchant Bank (Moskovskii Kupecheskii bank)
MT	Moscow Trade Bank (Moskovskii Torgovyi bank)
PI	St. Petersburg International Commercial Bank (Petersburgskii Mezhdunarodnyi kommercheskii bank)
PL	St. Petersburg Discount and Loan Bank (Petersburgskii Uchetnyi i Ssudnyi bank)
P-M	St. Petersburg-Moscow Commercial Bank (Petersburgsko-Moskovskii kommercheskii bank)
PP	St. Petersburg Private Commercial Bank (Petersburgskii Chastnyi kommercheskii bank)
R-A	Russo-Asiatic Bank (Russko-Aziatiskii bank)
R-C	Russo-Chinese Bank (Russko-Kitaiskii bank)
R-F	Russo-French Commercial Bank (Russko-Frantsuzskii kommercheskii bank)
RI	Russian Bank for Industry and Trade (Russkii Torgovo-Promyschlennyi bank)
SB	Siberian Trade Bank (Sibirskii torgovyi bank)
UB	United Bank (Soedinennyi bank)
V-K	Volga-Kama Commercial Bank (Volzhsko-Kamskii kommercheskii bank)
WB	Warsaw Commercial Bank (Kommercheskii bank v Varschave)

German Banks

B	S. Bleichröder and Co.
BHG	Berliner Handels-Gesellschaft
BHI	Bank für Handel und Industrie (Darmstadt)
DB	Deutsche Bank
DG	Direktion der Diskonto-Gesellschaft
DrB	Dresdner Bank
Krause	F. W. Krause Co. Bankgeschäft (Berlin)
M	Mendelssohn & Co.

MCB   Mitteldeutsche Creditbank (Berlin)
NBD   National Bank für Deutschland (Berlin)
R   M. A. von Rothschild and Co. (Frankfurt am Main)
RW   Robert Warschauer and Co.
SBV   Schlesische Bankverein (Breslau)
Siebert   August Siebert (Frankfurt am Main)
Sulzbach   Gebrüder Sulzbach (Frankfurt am Main)

French Banks
BEP   Banque d'Escompte de Paris
BPL   Banque Privée à Lyon
BUP   Banque de l'Union Parisienne
CEP   Comptoir National d'Escompte de Paris
CF   Crédit Mobilier Français
CL   Crédit Lyonnais
EH   E. Hoskier
H   Hottinguer and Co.
L-M   Banque Privée Industrielle, Commerciale, Coloniale—Lyon, Marseille
Pbs   Banque de Paris et des Pays-Bas (Paribas)
Rf   Rothschild Frères
SFR   Société Franco-Russe des Entreprises Industrielles et Travaux Publics
RG   Régie Générale de Chemins de fer et Travaux Publics
SG   Société Générale pour favoriser le développement du Commerce et de l'Industrie en France

English Banks
ARB   Anglo-Russian Bank, Ltd.
A-R   Anglo-Russian Trust, Ltd.
BB   Baring Brothers and Co., Ltd.
BC   Birch Crisp and Co.
C&M   London City and Midland Bank, Limited
FT   British Bank for Foreign Trade, Limited
H&S   Hambro and Sons
S-W   London South-Western Bank

Dutch Banks
Ho   Hope and Company
LP   Lippmann, Rosenthal and Co.
W&G   Wertheim and Gompertz

Belgian Banks
BA   Banque d'Anvers
Bal   Balser and Co. (Bruxelles)
CA   Crédit Anversois, Anvers
SB   Société Belge de Banque à Bruxelles
SGB   Société Générale de Belgique

TABLE 12A–1. Participation of Banks in the Placement of Russian Railway Company Bonds (1870–1914)

1	2	3	4	5	Course		Banks and Relative Share of Bank Participation	
	Name of Loan	Year of Issue	Nominal Value	Term	Bank Purchase Price	Bank Resale Price	Russian (%)	Foreign (%)
1	1. 5% Bonds: Warsaw–Vienna RR. Ser. 3	1870	R. 3,255,000 = T. 3,500,000	—	—	93	—	Müller & Co. (Berlin)
2	2. 5% Bonds: Rybinsk-Bologoe RR	1871	R. 3,000,000 = T. 3,264,000	81	—	71.375	Meyer & Co. 16.3	Sulzbach; Siebert; Müller & Co. (Berlin); Richter & Co. (Berlin)
3	3. 5% Bonds: Rybinsk-Bologoe RR	1872	R. 7,500,000 = T. 8,160,000 = £. 1,203,600	81	78.25	81.75	St. Petersbourg Mutual Credit Company 90.5	Sulzbach; Siebert; Müller & Co. (Berlin); Richter & Co. (Berlin)
4	4. 5% Bonds: Baltic RR	1872	R. 4,500,000 = T. 4,896,000	—	—	84.75	Meyer & Co. 39	Sulzbach; Siebert; Müller & Co. (Berlin); Richter & Co. (Berlin)
5	5. 5% Bonds: Warsaw–Vienna RR Ser. 4	1872	R. 4,999,959 = T. 5,376,300	50	86.6	—	—	Müller & Co. (Berlin); MCB 71.4 28.6
6	6. 5% Bonds: Riga-Dünaburg RR	1872	R. 1,500,000	—	88.44	—	—	—
7	7. 5% Bonds: Kursk-Khar'kov-Azov RR	1872	$. 11,000,000 = T. 11,968,000 = £. 1,760,000	83	—	—	—	BHG; Krause; H&S; LR; W&G
8	8. 5% Bonds: Warsaw–Vienna RR Ser. 5	1875–1879	R. 3,249,978 M. 10,574,400	50	82.8	—	—	Bonds distributed partly in Germany
9	9. 5% Bonds: Warsaw–Vienna RR Ser. 6	1880	R. 7,588,800 = M. 24,480,000	50	85.7	—	—	Bonds distributed mainly in Germany

Bond	Year	Amount		Price		Syndicate			Banks
10. 3% Bonds: The Great Russian Railway Company, 3 Issue	1880	R. 13,147,000 = / F. 52,588,000 = / M. 42,280,752	70	66.4	—	—		—	M: Banque Russe et Française[LR] / 50 50
11. 4½% Bonds: Ivangorod-Dombrova RR, 1 Issue	1882	R. 16,566,000 = / M. 54,071,424	50	83	87.5	PI; BF / 24.1 24.1			DB; DG; M / 20.6 10.1 12.1
12. 3% Bonds: Transcaucasian RR	1882	R. 55,651,250 = / M. 181,645,680	70	51 1/9	—	PL			M: RW; CEP; H; BB; Ho
13. 4% Bonds: Vladikavkas RR	1885	R. 20,531,500 = / M. 67,014,816	68	74.57 / 76.13	76.221 / 79.6	PI; BF; V. Tenishev / 17 12 10			DG; R; DB / 56 5
14. 4% Bonds: Southwestern RR	1885	R. 29,535,750 = / M. 96,404,688	68	74.57 / 76.13	76.221 / 79.6	PI; BF; ? / 17 17 5			DG; R / 61
15. 4% Bonds: Moscow-Riazan RR	1885	R. 9,895,833 = / M. 32,300,000	60	82.5	88	PI; BF / 2.58 2.42 } as subparticipants DG			DG; R
16. 4% Bonds: Riazan-Kozlov RR	1886	R. 15,014,000 = / M. 48,645,000	62	86.25	—	PI; BF / 1 1 } as subparticipants DG	20	PL / 20	DG; BHG; RW; M; [R] / 20 30 15 15
17. 4% bonds: Moscow-Kursk RR	1886	R. 6,480,000 = / M. 21,000,000	66	87.61 / 87.85	—	V - K	20	PL / 20	NBD: Jacob Landau (Berlin); L. Behrens & Söhne (Hamburg)
18. 4% Bonds: Kursk-Kiev RR	1887	R. 20,500,000 = / M. 67,286,500	68	87.25	92.25	PI; BF / 1.5 2 } as sub-participants M: DG	20	PL / 20	DG; DHG; RW; M; [R] / 20 30 15 15
19. 4% Bonds: Koslov-Voronezh-Rostov RR, Ser. A	1887	R. 6,108,058 = / M. 19,792,800	65	87.25	—	PI:		PL	B: [DG]; [R]; E. Heimann (Breslau); Breslauer Diskonto-Bank; L. Behrens & Söhne (Hamburg); W. Blumenthal's Nachfolger (Hannover); Ephraim Meyer & Sohn (Hannover)

(continued)

TABLE 12A–1. Participation of Banks in the Placement of Russian Railway Company Bonds (1870–1914) (*Continued*)

					Course		Banks and Relative Share of Bank Participation	
	Name of Loan	Year of Issue	Nominal Value	Term	Bank Purchase Price	Bank Resale Price	Russian (%)	Foreign (%)
1	*2*	*3*	*4*	*5*	*6*	*7*	*8*	*9*
20.	4.5% Bonds: Ivangorod-Dombrova RR, 2 Issue	1887	P. 1,518,125 = F. 6,072,500 = M. 4,955,160	47	84	—	—	M: Bonds distributed in 1888
21.	4% Bonds: Orel-Griazi RR, Ser. A	1887	R. 2,819,000 = M. 9,133,200	63	87.25	—	[P-M]	B: [DG]; [R]: E. Heimann (Breslau); Breslauer Diskonto-Bank; L. Behrens & Söhne (Hamburg); W. Blumenthal's Nachfolger (Hannover); Ephraim Meyer & Sohn (Hannover)
22.	4% Bonds: Nikolaevskaia RR (The Great Russian Railway Company RR)	1888	R. 11,800,000 = £. 1,888,000	64	71	—	PI; 25 BF; 25 PL 25	Rf as subparticipant PL BB: HO } 25
23.	4% Bonds: Kursk-Khar'kov-Asov RR, Ser. A	1888	R. 12,184,838 = M. 12,732,600 = £. 1,287,200	67	87.25	—	[P-M]	BHG; Krause; H & S; LR; W & G; Danske Landsman Bank in Copenhagen; B
24.	5% Bonds: Transcaucasian RR	1890	R. 6,861,500 = F. 27,446,000	63	—	97.25	PI; 25 20 BF; 25 20 PL; 25 20	DB; 25 20 LR — 20
25.	4% Kursk-Khar'kov-Azov RR, Ser. B	1889	R. 43,873,000 = M. 142,157,000 = F. 175,563,895	65.5	87.25	90 1/8	P-M — — 2.5 LP; 21.375 22.5 15	Bonds distributed in 1893 B: 21.375 22.5 15; DG: 21.375 22.5 15; R: 9.5 10 9; LR: 5 — 5; Rf: — 5 21

No.	Bond	Year	Amounts													
26.	4% Bonds: Kozlov-Voronezh-Rostov RR, Ser. B	1889	R. 4,669,136 = M. 15,128,000	63	87.25	90 1/8	PI; 21.375 22.5 15	PL; 21.375 22.5 15	LP; — — 2.5	P-M — — 2.5	B; 21.375 22.5 15	DG; 21.375 22.5 15	R; 9.5 10 9	LR; 5 — 5	Rf — — 21
27.	4% Bonds: Orel-Griazi RR Ser. B	1889	R. 15,446,106 = M. 50,177,000	61	87.25	90 1/8	PI; 21.375 22.5 15	PL; 21.375 22.5 15	LP; — — 2.5	P-M — — 2.5	B; 21.375 22.5 15	DG; 21.375 22.5 15	R; 9.5 10 9	LR; 5 — 5	Rf — — 21
28.	4% Bonds: Warsaw-Vienna RR	1890	R. 21,535,000 = F. 86,140,000 = M. 69,601,120 = FL.P-B. 41,174,920	41.5	91.5	— (91.125)	PI; 10.5	BF; 10.5	PL; 10.5	BW 12	B; DG; M; MCB; SBV; R; BA; LR; Bal — 8.25 16.5 8.25 3 3 3.5 10 2 2 / 9 18 9 3 3 3.5 7 2 2				
29.	4% Bonds: The Great Russian Railway Company, 4 Issue	1890	R. 15,625,000 = £. 2,500,000 = FL.P-B. 30,000,000	61	87	90	PI; 10	BF; 10	PL; 10	V. Polovtsov 3 1/3	[Pbs] [EH]; DB; Ho 66.67				
30.	4% Bonds: Warsaw-Vienna RR, 9 Ser.	1894	R. 8,031,250 = M. 25,957,000	37	96	—	PI; 9 10 (H. Wavelberg 4)	BF; 9 9	PL; 9 9	V-K; 9 8	WB; 10	B; DG; M; MCB; SBV; R; Bal; LR 8.5 17 8.5 2.75 2.75 3.5 2 5			
31.	4% Bonds: Riazan-Ural'sk RR	1894	R. 18,750,000 = M. 60,600,000 = FL.P-B. 35,850,000	52.5	95.75	98	PI; 9 10	BF; 9 9	PL; 9 9	V-K; 9 8	RI; 4 4	B; DG; BHG; RW; M; R; LR 10.2 10.2 10.2 10.2 10.2 4 5			
32.	4% Bonds: Vladikavkas RR	1894	R. 12,500,000 = M. 40,400,000 = FL.P-B. 23,900,000	62	95.25	97.25	PI; 23.75 18	BF; 23.75 14	PL; 18.75 10	V-K; 18.75 10	B; DG; BHG; RW; M; DB; DrB; Les fils Dreyfus & Cie successeurs Les Fils d'Isaac Dreyfus (Bâle) 3 3 3 3 3 3 2 } 3			

V. Tenishev, H. Schlesinger 12 0.5

F. Birkenfeld 0.5

as subparticipants PI

LR 15 15

as sub-participants PI

of quota PI

(continued)

Table 12A–1. Participation of Banks in the Placement of Russian Railway Company Bonds (1870–1914) (Continued)

Name of Loan	Year of Issue	Nominal Value	Term	Bank Pur-chase Price	Bank Resale Price	Russian (%)	Foreign (%)
				Course	*Course*	*Banks and Relative Share of Bank Participation*	
33. 4% Bonds: Rybinsk RR	1895	R. 21,121,510 = M. 68,443,000	59	97	99	PI; BF; PL; V-K 12.5 12.5 12.5 12.5	B; DG; BHG; RW; M; R; LR 8.5 8.5 8.5 8.5 8.5 3¹/₃ 4¹/₆
34. 4% Bonds: Vladikavkaz RR	1895	R. 17,508,730 = M. 56,736,000 = Fl.P.-B. 33,616,080	60	97	99.5	PI; BF; PL; V-K; MM 9 9 9 9 4 17.5 7 7 7 4 2.5 for PI	B; DG; BHG; RW; M; R; LR 10.2 10.2 10.2 10.2 10.2 4 5
35. 4% Bonds: Moscow-Kiev-Voronezh RR	1895	R. 27,704,874 = M. 89,776,000	59	97	99	PI; BF; PL; V-K 10 10 10 10	B; DG; BHC; RW; M; R; LR 10.2 10.2 10.2 10.2 10.2 4 5
36. 4% Bonds: Vladikavkas RR	1897	R. 19,750,400 = M. 64,000,000 = Fl.P.-B. 37,920,000	58	98.375	100.5	PI; BF; PL; V-K; MM 10: 7.5 7.5 7.5 7.5 16.75 6.25 6.25 6.25 6.25 15 6.25 6.25 6.25 6.25	B; DG; BHG; RW; M; R; LR 10.2 10.2 10.2 10.2 10.2 4 5 3 for PI
37. 4% Bonds: Moscow-Iaroslavl-Archangel RR, 3 Issue	1897	R. 10,183,800 = M. 33,000,000	46	98.375	100.5	PI; BF; PL; V-K; MM 10 7.5 7.5 7.5 7.5 15 6.25 6.25 6.25 6.25	B; DG; BHG; RW; M; R; LR 10.2 10.2 10.2 10.2 10.2 4 5
38. 4% Bonds: Moscow-Vindova-Rybinsk RR	1897	R. 6,820,060 = M. 22,100,000	57.5	98.375	100.5	PI; BF; PL; V-K 12.5 12.5 12.5 27.5 7.5 7.5 7.5	B; DG; BHG; RW; M; R; LR 8.5 8.5 8.5 8.5 8.5 3¹/₃ 4¹/₆
39. 4% Bonds: Riazan-Ural'sk RR	1897	R. 23,762,200 = M. 77,000,000	49.5	98.375	100.5	PI; BF; PL; V-K; MM; RI 10 6.5 6.5 6.5 4 13 5.5 5.5 5.5 4	B; DG; BHG; RW; M; R; LR 10.2 10.2 10.2 10.2 10.2 4 5
40. 4% Bonds: Southeastern RR	1897	R. 14,538,146 = M. 47,110,000	55	98 ³/₈	100.5	PI; BF; PL; V-K; R-C; MM 10 6 6 6 6 6 11.6 5.8 5.8 5.8 5.8 5.2	B; DG; BHG; M; R; LR 11.75 11.75 11.75 11.75 4 5

1 2 3 4 5 6 7 8 9

41. 4% Bonds: Moscow-Vindava-Rybinsk RR	1898	R. 32,683,054 = M. 70,605,000	56.5	98 5/8	100.75 99.25	PI; BF; PL; V-K; R-C 13 1/3 6 2/3 6 2/3 6 2/3 6 2/3 20 6 6 6 6	B; DG; BHG; RW; M; R; LR 10.2 10.2 10.2 6.2 14.2 4 5 65
42. 4% Bonds: Vladikavkas RR	1898	R. 15,321,990 = M. 33,100,000 = Fl.P-B. 19,529,000	57	98.375	100.75	PI; BF; PL; V-K; R-C; MM 11.6 5.8 5.8 5.8 5.8 5.2 16.75 6.25 6.25 7 5/16 — 6.25	B; DG; BHG; RW; M; R; LR 10.2 10.2 10.2 6.2 14.2 4 5 3 for PI
43. 4% Bonds: Riazan-Ural'sk RR	1898	R. 39,832,545 = M. 86,050,000	48.5	98 5/8	100.75	PI; BF; PL; V-K; R-C; MM; RI 11 5.5 5.5 5.5 5.5 4 3 11.25 5.5 5.5 5.5 5.5 4 3	B; DG; BHG; RW; M; R; LR 10.2 10.2 10.2 6.2 14.2 4 5 59.75
44. 4% Bonds: Southeastern RR	1898	R. 20,632,453 = M. 44,570,000	54	98.375	100.75	PI; BF; PL; V-K; R-C; MM 11.6 5.8 5.8 5.8 5.8 5.2	B; DG; BHG; RW; M; R; LR 10.2 10.2 10.2 6.2 14.2 4 5
45. 4% Bonds: Moscow-Smolensk RR (Conversion of 5% Bonds 1869)	1898	R. 16,511,781 = M. 35,670,300 = Fl.P-B. 5,827,000	52	—	—	—	[DG; BHG; M; Sulzbach]
46. 4% Bonds: Moscow-Vindava-Rybinsk RR	1899	R. 28,113,750 = £. 2,975,000 = Fl.P-B. 35,700,000	55	96.75	99	PI; BF; PL; V-K; R-C 11 5.5 5.5 5.5 5.5	B; DG; BHG; RW; M; LR; 8 5/6 8 5/6 8 5/6 5 2/6 12 1/6 6 Henry Schröder & Co. (London) 17
47. 4% Bonds: Vladikavkas RR	1900	R. 13,212,400 = $. 6,800,000	56	—	—	PI 20	New York Life Insurance Company 80
48. 4% Bonds: Southeastern RR	1900	R. 6,217,600 = $. 3,200,000	56	—	—	PI 20	New York Life Insurance Company 80
49. 4% Bonds: Lodz Factory RR	1901	R. 5,397,414 = M. 11,660,000	38.5	93.6	96	PI; BF; PL; V-K; R-C 8 8 8 8 8 10 for M	B; DG; BHG; RW; M; LR 11 11 11 6.5 15.5 5
50. 4% Bonds: Warsaw-Vienna RR, Ser. 10	1901	R. 15,864,045 = M. 34,271,000	31	95.5	—	—	B; DG; MCB; SBV; M; LR; Bal 17.5 35.1 4 4 23.4 10 6
51. 4% Bonds: Moscow-Kazan RR	1901	R. 16,608,852 = M. 35,880,000	43.5	93.6	96	PI; BF; PL; V-K; R-C; MM 6 2/3 6 2/3 6 2/3 6 2/3 6 2/3 6 2/3 10 for M	B; DG; BHG; RW; M; LR 11 11 11 6.5 15.5 5

(continued)

TABLE 12A–1. Participation of Banks in the Placement of Russian Railway Company Bonds (1870–1914) (Continued)

Name of Loan	Year of Issue	Nominal Value	Term	Course Bank Purchase Price	Course Bank Resale Price	Banks and Relative Share of Bank Participation Russian (%)	Banks and Relative Share of Bank Participation Foreign (%)
1	3	4	5	6	7	8	9
2							
52. 4% Bonds: Warsaw-Vienna RR, Ser. 11	1901	R. 9,591,750 = M. 20,721,000	60	95.5	—	—	B; 17.5 DG; 35.1 MCB; 4 SBV; 4 M; 23.4 LR; 10 Bal 6
53. 4% Bonds: Southeastern RR	1901	R. 15,025,734 = M. 32,460,000 = Fl.P-B. 19,151,400	51	93.6	96	PI; 6⅔ BF; 6⅔ PL; 6⅔ V-K; 6⅔ R-C; 6⅔ MM 6⅔ {10 for M}	B; 11 DG; 11 BHG; 11 RW; 6.5 M; 15.5 LR 5
54. 4% Bonds: Moscow-Vindava-Rybinsk RR	1903	R. 11,625,000 = F. 31,000,000	51	—	—	PI	The consortium headed by Pbs
55. 4% Bonds: Moscow-Kiev-Voronezh RR	1903	R. 17,625,000 = F. 47,000,000	51	95	—	PI	The consortium headed by Pbs
56. 4% Bonds: Riazan-Ural'sk RR	1903	R. 35,625,000 = F. 95,000,000	60	—	—	PI	The consortium headed by Pbs
57. 4.5% Bonds: Volga-Bugulma RR	1908	R. 13,095,000 = F. 34,920,000	77	80	—	PP; [A-D]	L-M
58. 4% bonds: Moscow-Kazan RR	1908	R. 2,226,549 = M. 4,810,000	37	—	—	—	Bonds distributed mainly in Germany
59. 4.5% Bonds: North-Donez RR	1908	R. 87,859,875 = F. 234,293,000	81	81.5	88.25	PI; 9 Northern Bank 9	Pbs; 9 BUP; 9 CEP; 9 SG; 18 SFR; 13.5 A. Spitzer & Cie; 4.5 SGB: 9 CL 10
60. 4.5% Bonds: Southeastern RR	1908	R. 19,531,937 = F. 51,818,500	44	84.25	90.5	PI; 7.5 BF; 7.5 PL; 7.5 V-K 7.5	Bonds distributed mainly in Germany

No.	Year	Amount					Notes
61. 4.5% Bonds: Armavir-Tuapse RR	1909	R. 33,499,872 = £. 3,544,960	81	85.5	90	PL; R-C; A-D	BC; C&M
62. 4.5% Bonds: Vladikavkaz RR	1909	R. 6,786,191 = M. 14,657,000	46	—	—	PL; BF; PL; V-K; [MM] 5.6 5.6 5.6 5.6 5.6	—
63. 4.5% Bonds: Moscow-Kiev-Voronezh RR, 1 Issue	1909	R. 12,038,000 = M. 26,000,000	46	—	—	—	Bonds distributed mainly in Germany
64. 4.5% Bonds: Moscow-Kiev-Voronezh RR, 2 Issue	1909	R. 27,780,000 = M. 60,000,000	46	-	—	—	Bonds distributed mainly in Germany
65. 4% Bonds: Moscow-Kazan RR	1909	R. 9,610,491 = M. 20,757,000	60	—	6	PL: PL: R-C	Bonds distributed mainly in Germany
66. 4% Bonds: Volga-Bugulma RR	1910	R. 37,950,000 = F. 101,200,000	76	86.75	90.5	—	L-M
67. 4.5% Bonds: Kokand-Namangan RR	1910	R. 3,799,845 = £. 402,100	81	97.5 94.25	—	R-C	BC: Lloyd Bank. Ltd: A-R
68. 4.5% Bonds: Moscow-Kiev-Voronezh RR	1910	R. 33,683,713 = M. 72,751,000	45	—	—	—	Bonds distributed mainly in Germany
69. 4.5% Bonds: Troitsk RR	1910	R. 5,631,822 = £. 595,960	81	97.5 94.25	—	R-C	BC: Lloyd Bank. Ltd: A-R
70. 4.5% Bonds: Podol'sk RR	1911	R. 19,758,062 = M. 42,674,000	81	$94^5/8$	—	PL; PL; R-A; BF $\{\frac{4.2}{28}\}$	M: Bonds distributed mainly in Germany and Holland
71. 4.5% Bonds: Chernomorsk-Kubansk RR	1911	R. 18,085,032 = £. 1,913,760	81	—	—	—	BC: Bonds distributed mainly in England
72. 4.5% Bonds: Moscow-Kazan RR	1911	R. 25,224,703 = M. 54,481,000	60	94.75	—	PL; $\{R\text{-}A \ 4^2/3\}$	M: Bonds distributed mainly in Germany
73. 4.5% Bonds: Vladikavkaz RR	1912	R. 37,000,000 = M. 80,000,000	60	—	—	PL; $\{R\text{-}A \ 4\}$	M: Bonds distributed mainly in Germany

(continued)

TABLE 12A–1. Participation of Banks in the Placement of Russian Railway Company Bonds (1870–1914) (*Continued*)

					Course		Banks and Relative Share of Bank Participation	
Name of Loan		Year of Issue	Nominal Value	Term	Bank Purchase Price	Bank Resale Price	Russian (%)	Foreign (%)
1	*2*	*3*	*4*	*5*	*6*	*7*	*8*	*9*
74. 4.5% Bonds: Altai RR		1912	R. 57,000,000 = F. 152,000,000	81	93.8 94	—	PI; BF; PL; V-K; R-A; RI; PP; SB; A-D {30}	CEP; CL; SG {7}
75. 4.5% Bonds: Northeastern-Ural'sk RR		1912	R. 22,875,000 = F. 61,000,000	81	94	—	PI; BF; PL; V-K; R-A; RI; SB; A-D {25}	CF; PP {75}
76. 4.5% Bonds: Western-Ural'sk RR		1912	R. 33,490,875 = F. 89,309,000	81	94	—	PI; BF; PL; V-K; R-A; RI; SB; A-D; PP {30}	Pbs; CEP; CL; SG 19.25 13.3 19.25 18.2 {70}
77. 4.5% Bonds: Kahetia RR		1912	R. 13,230,000 = £. 1,400,000	81	93.75	96.5	R-A; RI 20 20	S-W; ARB; Lloyd Bank, Ltd. 20 20
78. 4.5% Bonds: North-Donez RR		1912	R. 10,584,200 = F. 28,300,000	79	93.75	—	R-A;	BPL; SB CA
79. 4.5% Bonds: Armavir-Tuapse RR		1913	R. 20,999,979 = £. 2,222,220	—	—	—	[A-D; RI; PL]; UB	Bonds distributed mainly in England
80. 4.5% Bonds: Troitsk RR		1913	R. 29,295,000 = £. 3,100,000	—	91.75	96	PI; BF; PL; R-A; RI as sub-participants {33.3}	BC; FT; A-R {66.7}
81. 4.5% Bonds: Akkerman RR		1913	R. 5,625,000 = F. 15,000,000	81	—	96.65	R-A; SB; R-F	PP; CF; Bonds distributed mainly in France
82. 4.5% Bonds: Vladikavkaz RR		1913	R. 3,750,000 M. 8,099,351	—	—	—	—	Bonds distributed mainly in Germany

							L-M
84. 5% Bonds: Tavris RR	1913	R. 14,440,500 = F. 38,508,000	75	—	96	DL; PP 10	
85. 4.5% Bonds: RR Branch lines	1913	R. 27,434,813 = F. 73,159,500	60	91.125	—	BF; PL; R-A; RI; A-D; PP; UB 64	BUP; SGB; Thalman & Co.; L. Hirsch & Co., 36
86. 4.5% Bonds: Chernomorskaia RR, 1 Issue	1913	R. 38,408,625 = F. 102,423,000	81	91.125 91.17	94	PI; BF; PL; V-K; R-A; RI; SB; A-D; PP 24	Pbs; CEP; CL; SG 9.9 6.84 9.9 9.36 19.25 19.30 19.25 18.20
87. 4.5% Bonds: Chernomorskaia RR, 2 Issue	1913	R. 24,591,375 = F. 65,577,000	81	90.625 91.17	94	PI; BF; PL; V-K; R-A; RI; SD; A-D; PP 24	Pbs; CEP; CL; SG 9.9 6.84 9.9 9.36 19.25 19.30 19.25 18.20
88. 4.5% Bonds: Kol'chugin RR	1913	R. 12,528,000 = F. 33,408,000	81	—	—	PI; R-A; ? . . 8.75 33	RG; SG; N.J. & S. Bardac 67
89. 4.5% Bonds: Semirech'e RR	1913	R. 45,648,000 = F. 121,728,000	—	91⅛ 91.125	94.5	PI; BF; PL; V-K; R-A; RI; SB; A-D; PP 30	Pbs; CEP; CL; 19.25 19.30 19.25
90. 4.5% Bonds: The First Company for RR spur tracks in Russia	1913	R. 8,499,750 = F. 22,666,000	—	—	—	—	Bonds distributed mainly in Belgium
91. 5% Bonds: Oranienbaum RR	1913	R. 5,259,750 = FB. 14,026,000	—	—	—	PP	The consortium headed by Banque de Reports (Anvers)
92. 4.5% Bonds: Kulunda RR	1914	R. 3,297,000 = F. 8,792,000 = £. 347,000	81	91	—	Fund of savings banks	—
93. 4.5% Bonds: Achinsk-Minusinsk RR		R. 22,725,000 = F. 60,600,000				PI; BF; PL; V-K; R-A 6.4 6.4 6.4 6.4	Pbs; CEP; CL; SG; H 9.1575 6.3270 9.1575 8.6580 2.7000 36
94. 4.5% Bonds: Bukhara RR		R. 16,875,000 = F. 245,000,000				MW; RI; SB; A-D; PP 6.4 6.4 6.4 6.4 6.4 64	Provincial banks of a minor syndicate were also permitted to participate in the loan for a sum of 70 million francs. The group included:

(continued)

TABLE 12A–1. Participation of Banks in the Placement of Russian Railway Company Bonds (1870–1914) (*Continued*)

| | | | | | Course | | Banks and Relative Share of Bank Participation | |
					Bank Pur-chase Price	Bank Resale Price	Russian (%)	Foreign (%)
1	*2*	*3*	*4*	*5*	*6*	*7*	*8*	*9*
	Name of Loan	*Year of Issue*	*Nominal Value*	*Term*				
95.	4.5% Bonds: Moscow-Kazan RR		R. 56,250,000 = F. 150,000,000					Banque National de Crédit; Crédit Mobilier Français; Société Marseillaise; Crédit du Nord; Crédit Foncier d'Algérie et de Tunisie;
96.	4.5% Bonds: Moscow-Kiev-Voronezh RR		R. 62,400,000 = F. 166,400,000					
97.	4.5% Bonds: Olonets RR		R. 10,125,000 F. 27,000,000					
98.	4.5% Bonds: Podol'sk RR		R. 22,500,000 = F. 60,000,000					Société Nanceïenne: Banque des Pays du Nord; Compagnie Algérienne; Banque de Bordeaux; Banque Renauld et C-ie;
99.	4.5% Bonds: Riazan-Ural'sk RR		R. 22,500,000 = F. 60,000,000					Thalmann et C-ie; Günzburg et C-ie.
100.	4.5% Bonds: North-Donetsk RR		R. 25,875,000 = F. 69,000,000					
101.	4.5% Bonds: Fergana RR		R. 10,125,000 = F. 27,000,000					
	Sum Total		R. 249,275,000 = F. 665,000,000					
102.	4.5% Bonds: North-Donetsk RR	1914	R. 11,594,000 = FB. 31,000,000	78.5	92 1/8	93.5	R-A; 25 BI 25	SGB 50
103.	4.5% Bonds: Moscow-Kiev-Voronezh RR	1914	R. 5,812,500	—	91	—	—	New York Life Insurance Company

Joint railway loan 1914

13

Banking and Financial Relations between Russia and the United States

Ruth AmEnde Roosa

I

The crucial role of capital in the industrial development of Russia before 1914 is recognized by scholars both in the Soviet Union and in the Western world. Indeed, its critical importance was emphasized by Russia's most advanced economic leaders long before 1914, albeit not without opposition from agrarian interests. Although the state had generally sought to play a positive role in initiating industrial development, its economic policies had been subject to alternating change through both the eighteenth and nineteenth centuries. Even by the early 1890s, when Sergei Witte, the initiator of Russia's modern age of industrial development, became Minister of Finance, and in fact throughout the prewar years, there were still many influential voices, not limited to aristocratic agrarians but encompassing important sectors of the intelligentsia as well, that expressed opposition to industrialization and proclaimed the need for Russia to remain an agricultural country. Closely interconnected with this issue was that of the desirability of foreign capital imports, on which industrial development largely depended. While opponents of industrialization argued that capital imports represented a potentially dangerous infringement on national independence, supporters contended that the attainment of true national independence was impossible without financial help.

The attempt to draw a meaningful picture of the Russian-American financial relationship during the period under discussion is fraught with extraordinary difficulty and complexity. Indeed, one may well question whether a satisfactory description of that relationship will ever be possible, owing to the inadequacy, with a few notable exceptions, of the materials available. Scholarly progress in this field is hampered not only by the secretiveness that normally attends most financial relationships but also by the fragmentary, and sometimes contradictory, nature of the archival records. The records of some American financial institutions are in fact almost nonexistent.

The Russian situation is comparable. Until the early years of the twentieth century Russian banks were under a substantial degree of state influence, especially in the allocation of railroad credits. Official statistics were, until the later years, incomplete, if not lost altogether, although this deficiency is compensated in part by the publications of the Association of Joint Stock Commercial Banks (Komitet S'ezda predstavitelei aktsionernykh kommercheskikh bankov). These difficulties have been well demonstrated in a recent work by V. I. Bovykin.[1] Manifestly, more research is needed in the records of private companies and banking institutions before a truly reliable picture can begin to emerge. Professor Bovykin's forthcoming book will undoubtedly shed much light on the subject. Meanwhile, the present chapter must be viewed only as an attempt to summarize what is already known, supplemented by information that has been made available to the author, in both American and Soviet archives, regarding certain aspects of the Russian-American financial relationship.

The United States was still a debtor country, in overall terms, throughout the period under consideration. Nevertheless, despite the fact that on the eve of World War I its aggregate foreign indebtedness amounted to more than $7 billion, it had also begun to export capital. As of 1914 its total exports of capital amounted to about $3.5 billion, roughly half its total balance of imported capital.[2] Russia was a net importer of capital throughout the entire period, although it did serve as an exporter of capital to China at various times.[3]

The amount of American capital that found its way to Russia is impossible to estimate with any assurance of accuracy. As Arcadius Kahan has said with respect to Russia, "the distribution between foreign-owned and domestically owned industrial assets is difficult to establish"—indeed, impossible on the basis of secondary sources alone.[4] This judgment echoes the prior conclusion of two early American authorities on the Russian debt structure, Pasvolsky and Moulton, that "the exact figures of Russia's foreign indebtedness and its precise distribution among various countries may never be known. . . ."[5]

Much of the American capital that went to Russia undoubtedly represented anonymous investments in joint-stock enterprises or in state or railroad bonds, some of them purchased on European exchanges. American participation in European-controlled investments—a process greatly assisted by close ties between American and London banking houses—adds to the general obscurity that surrounds the subject. The establishment of marketing agencies in Russia by American commercial and industrial firms that were often under the effective control of foreign concessionaires, the establishment of branch enterprises by large American enterprises (frequently with the help of a well-established branch in another country), and the occasional establishment of smaller productive enterprises by venturesome individuals also contribute to the difficulty of a broad assessment. Nevertheless, it is generally agreed that the total amount of American capital in Russia on the eve of World War I was small, especially in comparison with European investments. The principal countries investing in Russia were France, Britain, Germany, and Belgium, in that order, with the United States trailing far behind in fifth place.[6] Yet the Russian-American involvement in successive financial negotiations, and the significance of such contacts for the broader pattern of economic and political issues, throws substantial light on the developing relationship between the two countries.

Perhaps the most detailed report of American industrial investment in Russia was submitted to William Howard Taft (U.S. President, 1909–1913) before World War I by the legal counsel for the large and respected German commercial and financial firm, the Hanseatic Company. "It is probably a conservative estimate," it observed, "to say that American investments in Russia at the present time amount to $125,000,000."[7] The brief report asserted that "the best information we have been able to obtain indicates the following investments of American capital in plants and business in Russia":

New York Life Insurance Co.	
(capital and reserve)	$ 22,500,000
Singer Sewing Machine Co.	12,000,000
Standard Oil Co. (in control of Russian	
Oil Co. "Nobel") capital	7,500,000
Equitable Life Assurance Society	
(capital and reserve)	5,000,000
Westinghouse Elec. & Mfg. Co.	5,000,000
Westinghouse Air Brake Co.	2,500,000
International Harvester Co. in Russia	3,500,000
International Harvester Co. of America	20,000,000
Vacuum Oil Co.	500,000
Worthington Pump Co.	500,000
International Taxicab Co.	100,000
J.C. Lenske	100,000
	$ 79,200,000

In addition to the foregoing, the report continues, "there are American investments in mining, street railroads and other enterprises in different parts of the Russian Empire, as to which, thus far, it has been impossible to obtain any data."[8] After the war, however, the U.S. Department of Commerce—using "Soviet official sources"—assessed the situation in somewhat different terms:

American investments in Russia presented a strong contrast with those of European nations. Investments by American nationals in industrial securities, railroad stocks, or those of small enterprises, especially on a partial scale, are practically absent; small individual holdings of Russian industrial securities are likewise negligible. Half a dozen large American concerns hold practically all of American claims against Russia. All of American capital was, with but two exceptions, invested in enterprises of trade, finance or insurance.[9]

These contrasting judgments, admittedly made a decade apart, serve as an example of the disparity of views that has prevailed with regard to total American investments in Russia on the eve of World War I.

II

A brief survey of economic conditions in both countries may serve as a useful background for our examination of the more detailed financial aspect of the Russian-American relationship. Unquestionably, the decade extending roughly from 1896 to 1906 represented the high point of this relationship. Although the overall flow of capital continued throughout the prewar period, those were the years when the thought of financial cooperation aroused the most excitement on both sides of the Atlantic. The period was marked, it is interesting to note, by an apparently deep-seated political interest on both sides in improving and developing Russian-American relations. But at the same time political forces in opposition emerged on both sides and contributed, along with purely economic considerations, to the final failure of the effort to establish a closer financial relationship. Although less came of this decade than many of the persons most involved would have wished, it is nevertheless revealing of many of the problems confronted by both sides. Russia and the United States learned much about each other's growing levels of sophistication in the financial and banking world at this time, as well as about each other's ambitions and internal problems. Above all, they learned much about the forces that favored cooperation and those that represented rivalry or even potential hostility, both within each country and between them. These conditions are relevant to an understanding of why Russia and the United States were drawn toward each other at the end of the nineteenth century and why they tended to be pulled apart during the immediate prewar years.

The United States and Russia had much in common during the last years of the nineteenth century. Both were developing countries with enormous potential and ambition for further economic growth. Both had internal frontiers (although Siberia was far more "open" than was the American West), which competed with foreign markets for the industrial and commercial initiative of their own more developed sectors. Both were richly endowed with natural resources, limiting their interest in the exploitation of external supplies. Yet both were keenly interested in promoting their own exports, particularly oil and agricultural commodities. In both countries, also, railroad construction had been and remained a major influence in advancing general economic development.

But here the resemblance stops. The industrial development of the United States far exceeded that of Russia, and its industrial interests already had turned, in some measure, toward the export of finished manufactures. As early as the 1850s, in fact, American technology had already so developed certain specialized metal products, such as machine tools, guns, reapers, and sewing machines, that the country enjoyed world leadership in these products. Indeed, by 1857 several American firms were selling locomotives, cannon castings, and a variety of machinery to the Russian government.[10] During the 1870s and 1880s many American firms were seeking markets abroad for their products, and toward the end of the century the combination of an economic depression and the rapid growth of mergers gave rise to a substantial number of large corporations that were eager for new markets.[11] One result was a steady rise in industrial exports during the 1890s. By the end of the century some of these enterprises were well established in European markets, and a few, most notably the Singer Sewing Machine Company, had operating sales agencies in Russia.[12]

Closely associated with the rise of the large corporation was the growth of large-scale investment banking in the United States. As early as the 1870s and 1880s American financial enterprises were growing at a rate comparable with the country's developing industrial interests. New York City became firmly established as the financial center of the country, followed by Boston, Philadelphia, and Chicago. By the end of the century the financial influence of the major life insurance companies—the New York Life Insurance Company, the Equitable Life Assurance Society, and the Mutual

Life Insurance Company—which were allied with the principal banks and investment houses, was also growing rapidly.[13] Moreover, these companies were interested in investment abroad, and, in the case of the first two, in investment in Russia.

American investment was still, during the last decade of the nineteenth century, largely deflected by the developmental needs of the United States, and such investments as were made abroad tended to be concentrated in Canada and Latin America. Commercial, industrial, and financial interests appeared, however, to be poised for a major advance into European and Far Eastern markets. During the early twentieth century the American economy continued to prosper, and President Theodore Roosevelt announced that "as a nation we stand in the very forefront in the giant international competition of the day."[14] Government support of business enterprise abroad was stronger during those years than it had ever been before. In 1909 President Taft declared that his administration was "lending all proper support to legitimate and beneficial American enterprises in foreign countries" and that the State Department was being reorganized to "make it a thoroughly efficient instrument in the furtherance of foreign trade and of American interests abroad."[15] Foreign countries were showing an increasing interest in borrowing from the United States, and between 1900 and 1913 some 250 foreign loans with a par value of nearly $1.1 billion were placed on its markets.[16]

Russia's pattern of development during these years was very different from that of the United States. In America, government stood largely apart from the free-wheeling growth of private enterprise. In contrast, industry and finance in Russia had to contend with the predominant role of the state in the national economy. Although the question of whether this official role was helpful or harmful has long been the subject of scholarly debate, it is usually agreed that it tended to stifle the spirit of enterprise and to cause business interests to look first of all to the state for guidance and assistance. Nevertheless, both the great expansion of railroad construction that occurred during the 1870s, which was largely dependent on state-guaranteed foreign investment, and the industrial demand that it generated were largely responsible for the beginning of the growth in the 1880s of the coal and metallurgical industries of southern Russia and the extraction and refining of Russia's vast oil resources in Baku. These industries, too, with the partial exception of the oil industry, were largely dependent on foreign financial investment. By contrast, the textile industry, which was already well established in the Moscow area, was far more financially independent.

It was not until the 1890s, however, that European capital began to flow into Russia on a large scale. Prior to that time the unstable and deficit-ridden condition of state finances had proven a serious deterrent to foreign investment. As late as 1892, Witte, the new Minister of Finance, had declared the Russian state to be on the verge of bankruptcy.[17] It was only with the introduction of monetary reforms in 1894, culminating in the adoption of the gold ruble in 1897 and the resulting stabilization of the currency, that the risk factor was significantly reduced and Russia became an attractive field for foreign investment.[18] The high profits earned by Russian enterprise at this time, when Russia experienced its first great burst of industrial expansion,[19] further enhanced the attraction. As the Soviet historian L. Ia. Eventov has observed, with the second half of the 1890s, "there begins the active history of foreign capital."[20]

The Russian government remained, at the end of the century, heavily in debt and desperately seeking new sources of foreign capital. At the same time its ally and greatest source of financial support, France, was showing a reluctance to make further loans to Russia on acceptable terms. England was also disinterested, for both economic and political reasons. Thus, Russia's interest in foreign loans, both for industrial and for state needs, coincided with the burgeoning American interest in financial investment and in commercial and industrial expansion.

The early years of the twentieth century were very difficult for Russia. The period of great economic expansion that it had recently enjoyed came to an end, abruptly halted by a severe depression that began in 1900. Then, when the economy began to show signs of recovery, came the disastrous war with Japan, beginning in 1904 and quickly followed by the revolution of 1905/1906. It was not until 1908/1909 that the economy began to show definite signs of recovery. The last years before the war were once again years of rapid economic growth.

During the final prewar years Russian-American financial relations never regained the promise that they had held during the years between 1896 and 1906. The Russian Ministry of Finance, under V. N. Kokovtsov, was primarily concerned with keeping foreign borrowing to a minimum in order to reduce the vast national debt that Russia had contracted as a result of the preceding years of war and revolution. In the United States political antagonism, founded on dislike for the tsarist system as a whole and for its anti-Semitic policies in particular, became increasingly a source of all-pervading influence. In 1911 the commercial agreement that had been in force since 1832, with its most-favored nation clause, was allowed to lapse. The Russians responded with bitterness, but half-hearted efforts to negotiate a new treaty were unavailing. Nevertheless, Russian commercial and industrial circles frequently expressed admiration for American economic achievements, and 1913 was marked by the establishment of the first Russo-American "Chamber of Commerce," which was designed to promote economic contacts between the two countries.

III

A complete survey of American financial and banking interests in Russia during the period under consideration will not be attempted here. Instead, the focus will be on two institutions that, while dissimilar in many respects, were also in all probability most intensely involved in Russian affairs: the New York Life Insurance Company and J. P. Morgan & Co. Mention will also be made of the National City Bank, which was the largest bank in the United States and very much interested in Russia.

Created in 1845, the New York Life Insurance Company began its activity in Russia in 1877, only seven years after beginning its first operations abroad.[21] Although little is known about its early activities in Russia, which probably were limited to the purchase of railroad securities, the company played a pioneering role in the introduction of American financial interests to the Russian financial market. On October 10, 1885, it was officially authorized to sell life insurance throughout the Russian Empire, although not without qualifications that proved to be a source of permanent antagonism between the company and the Russian government. During the same year the Russian government also established the rule that foreign-owned enterprises must be subject to state regulation. It was provided in the 1885 decision that the company's operations be conducted "as a self-contained Russian insurance business," with its headquarters in St. Petersburg.[22] New York Life thereupon opened an office in St. Petersburg, prestigiously located in the heart of the financial district at the lower end of the Nevskii Prospect, and offered its entire portfolio of life insurance policies for public sale. But a lengthy and detailed set of rules, known as the *Pravila*, which was to govern the company's operations, was not approved by the government until two years later, on October 21, 1887.

During the intervening period the first of many altercations between the company and the Russian government arose. In this dispute the government itself was not united. In fact, a triangular struggle emerged among the Ministry of Finance, which at that time wished to restrict foreign investments, the Ministry of Internal Affairs, which favored expanding such interests, and New York Life over the contents of the proposed *Pravila* and the requirements to be imposed on the company's operations.[23] In the judgment of New York Life, the Finance Ministry was "entirely in the hands of our enemies" and the only hope lay with the Minister of Internal Affairs.[24] The battle centered mainly on the Ministry of Finance's insistence that all profits should be invested in some way in Russia and deposited in the State Bank. New York Life did not object to investing its profits in Russia, but preferred to invest them in private banks. It also objected to the amount of the guarantees required. It did not succeed in winning any concessions, however.

As finally approved, the *Pravila* required the company to maintain three types of reserve funds: a Deposit Guarantee of 500,000 rubles; a Reserve Fund, consisting of ruble deposits maintained in the State Bank in the form of government bonds or securities guaranteed by the Russian government amounting to the "total outstanding reserve liability of all of its life insurance contracts" in force in Russia; and a Reserve Capital, consisting of 10 percent of the net annual profits of its operations in Russia, designed to meet a possible national disaster caused by famine, epidemic or such.[25]

Throughout these difficult times the company, in the words of its chairman, faced "a great danger of being not only stopped in our business but fined a heavy amount" for doing business without legal authorization.[26] New York Life concluded that its only recourse was to continue its business operations while trying to obtain a revision of the *Pravila*. Probably it was with this in mind that the company granted the Russian government a loan of 600,000 rubles, at 4 percent interest, early in September 1887.[27] This action was no doubt also motivated, in part at least, by competition from another American insurance company, the Equitable Life Assurance Society. The two comprised the only American insurance companies ever to operate in Russia. As early as December 1886, New York Life observed that the Equitable was "picking up quite a business." When the company's position has been legalized, its Paris office declared, the manager of the St. Petersburg office of New York Life, P. P. Moeller, "will do all he can to prevent them [the Equitable] from operating there."[28] Early in 1887 it was further noted that Equitable was "pushing on and they may get their concession before we do."[29] Thus the policy differences within the Russian government were in a sense matched by entrepreneurial rivalries on the American side.

The difficulties were overcome, and New York Life prospered, leaving Equitable far behind. Before the war, New York Life had major offices not only in St. Petersburg but also in Moscow, Kiev, Kharkov, Odessa, Rostov-on-the-Don, Riga, Lodz, and Warsaw. The banks in which these offices kept their funds were quite diverse, ranging from the Petersburg-centered Volga-Kama Bank in Kiev and Rostov to the French Crédit Lyonnais in Moscow and Odessa, and such local banks as the Riga Exchange

Bank in Riga, the Commercial Bank in Lodz, and, in Warsaw, both the German-based Warsaw Discount Bank and the Warsaw Bank of Commerce. The company had about 600 employees in its offices in St. Petersburg, Moscow, Odessa and Warsaw alone. In addition, in 1899 it opened negotiations with the St. Petersburg-based International Commercial Bank for the right to draw checks on its deposits in a very large number of towns throughout the Russian Empire. But as of 1900 it had only $2,796 on deposit with the bank, and had to transfer $5,094 from the Volga-Kama Bank.[30]

By the end of 1888 the company had more than $3 million in life insurance policies in force, against which it held over $350,000 in deposited securities.[31] A decade later, at the end of 1898, there were 9,233 policies outstanding, valued at $28,337,673, and the deposited securities amounted to over $4 million.[32] According to the figures presented by the St. Petersburg office, at the end of 1913 the company had 37,746 policies outstanding, with a total value of $90,064,769. Its required reserves in the State Bank amounted to $20,506,670, among its total Russian assets of $24,840,389.[33]

The proceeds from its expanding sales of insurance enabled the Russian branch of New York Life to become an active investor in the Russian market. By far the greater part of its investments was in railroad bonds, guaranteed by the state. As of 1894 (the first year for which such records are apparently available), when it had issued 5,733 policies valued at $21,280,859, it had on deposit in the State Bank, as required by law, the state-guaranteed bonds of four railroads, totaling $591,100 in par value, plus the "internal loan" granted in 1887 of $1,686,900. Thus the investments on deposit in the State Bank came to a total of $2,278,000.[34] A decade later the company had 25,405 policies in force, valued at $60,041,162, and had investments in twelve railroads, in addition to state bonds and bonds of the Nobles' Land Bank, the latter totaling $390,500 and $2,263,700, respectively.[35]

By the end of 1913 its holdings in railroad bonds totaled $20,379,275. In addition, it had on deposit in the State Bank $1,926,950 in shares of the Nobles' Land Bank, $390,500 in government bonds (Rentes), and $4,074,823 classified as policy loans. Thus, its total deposits, according to these figures, amounted to $26,771,648. Of the railroads included, the largest investment by far was in the Consolidated Railway, totaling $11,867,062, followed by the Vladikavkaz Railway with $3,279,732, the Southeastern Railway with $2,129,651, and the Moscow-Kazan with $1,069,096. Shares in the Chinese Eastern Railway, incidentally, were valued at $43,250.[36]

There is no reliable way of assessing whether any substantial sums of money were also held in other banks and therefore represented additional investments of New York Life in Russia. According to one statement of the New York office, however, the company in 1905 had about $411,629 on deposit in the International Commercial Bank.[37] Fairly substantial sums must have been deposited in the Volga-Kama Bank, since New York Life relied primarily on it for its payments on life insurance policies. Moreover, on various occasions the Paris office of New York Life asked the Volga-Kama to remit to it fairly substantial sums, such as 30,000 francs in 1908, and a total of 90,000 francs in 1909. The complexity of its banking relations is exemplified by the fact that with respect to the 1908 request the Volga-Kama reported to the Paris office of New York Life that the St. Petersburg International Commercial Bank had "turned over to us, for your account," the 30,000 rubles. A large amount of these dealings apparently represented small sums held in life insurance policies in the United States, the proceeds of which were being transmitted to their Russian heirs.[38]

It is also apparent that New York Life pursued an active role in trading and diversifying its holdings in the State Bank as opportunities arose. Such procedures required the assistance of a private bank, usually the International Commercial Bank, which had very close connections with the State Bank. Thus on February 7, 1897, an agreement was reached between the director of the International Commercial Bank and the manager of the State Bank authorizing the State Bank to accept some $792,550 in state bonds and $1,827,450 in internal loans for deposit in the State Bank.[39] Shortly afterward the Ministry of Internal Affairs contacted the International Commercial Bank to serve as the agent in arranging an exchange desired by New York Life of securities that it currently held for a large issue, amounting to $2,482,661, of the Nobles' Land Bank.[40] This transaction was initiated by a letter from George W. Perkins, vice president of New York Life to Alexander Koch, of the St. Petersburg International Bank, explaining that such a transfer of holdings would be profitable for New York Life.[41]

The most notable financial negotiation ever concluded between New York Life and the St. Petersburg International Commercial Bank took place during the month of October 1899. Perkins was then in Russia where he was setting up branch offices for the firm outside St. Petersburg. But one of his principal objectives was to prevent the Mutual Life Insurance Company from obtaining authorization to establish offices in Russia.[42] Apparently with this in mind, Perkins began negotiations with A. Iu. Rothstein, chairman of the International Commercial Bank, who was acting on behalf of Witte, the Finance Minister. Perkins' letter to Rothstein proposed the formation of a syndicate with the International Commercial Bank for the sale of a $10 million railroad loan, 80 percent of which was to be the responsibility of New York Life. The terms were favorable: a guaranteed interest of 4 percent at a price of $96\frac{3}{4}$. New York Life also wished to reserve for itself the option of taking an additional $23,149,119 (30 million rubles) at a later date. New York Life's only real concern, Rothstein reported in his letters to Witte (who was vacationing in Yalta), was "that after the [American] market has been prepared for the receipt of Russian railroad bonds and after it has gone to great expense for publicity, other groups of banks will profit from it." Therefore New York Life had made it a condition for granting the loan that the Russian government should not engage in talks with any other American insurance company. Rothstein concluded by saying that "Personally, I believe that this engagement cannot but serve you at the time of future negotiations and that it will actually facilitate business."[43]

Witte telegraphed his agreement to Rothstein. Although noting that he would prefer a loan of $25 million, he assured New York Life that he would "be against granting permission to install in Russia any new American insurance companies."[44] The contract was signed on October 27 by Perkins and Rothstein. The $10 million was to be divided into $6.8 million for the completion of the Vladikavkaz Railway, a line that was important to Standard Oil (and hence to both New York Life and the National City Bank, which was heavily involved with Standard Oil) in its struggle to gain additional means of exporting oil from Baku, and $3.2 million for the Southeastern Railway.[45]

The Soviet scholar B. V. Anan'ich contends that these negotiations were viewed by the Americans as an experimental operation, to accustom American investors to purchase Russian securities.[46] His point seems to be supported by Perkins' statement that the aim of New York Life was "to lay a firm foundation" for future large-scale Russian financial activities in the United States. But the aim was certainly also to assure New York Life against additional American competition. Indeed, when, some time later, rumors circulated that the Russian government was in fact talking with an American insurance company, New York Life protested and received a flat denial from the government.[47] In any event, Perkins' rejoicing at the terms of the agreement was manifest. On the train to Berlin he wrote to John A. McCall, president of New York Life:

> We are now on the same pleasant and friendly relations with the Russian [Insurance] Department that we heretofore established with Austria, Switzerland, and Prussia, and I wouldn't give a man five kopecs [sic] to guarantee us against trouble in any one of these four Governments. . . . They are our friends—they believe in us and even want to help us. The entire complexion of things, as existing four or five years ago, is changed and our future could not be brighter.[48]

Unfortunately, despite New York Life's continued progress, the spirit of these words would have to be retracted before many years had passed.

The years from 1885 to 1914 were for the Russian branch of New York Life a period of steady growth. It had overshadowed not only the Equitable but also major native Russian insurance companies such as the Rossiia and the Salamander. Moreover, the value of its policies compared favorably with branches of the company in other countries. In 1894 Russia occupied second place among the nations (outside of the United States) supplied with insurance by New York Life—first place being held by Brazil.[49] By the end of 1913, France had taken first place and Brazil had fallen to near the bottom of the list. Russia, however, was still in second place.[50]

What, one may ask, can account for the remarkable success of this American company in Russia? Its success was in part the result of its advertising campaign, which, throughout the years between 1885 and 1914 (and later), stressed the unique benefits to be derived from "a system of insurance with the accumulation of profits," or, in other words, a mutual company the aim of which was to share profits with its policyholders.

"In earlier times," according to a typical flier published in March 1887, "life insurance constituted for the insured only a sacrifice for the benefit of his family," but now, "the policy is a source of profits for the insured himself. It is possible to say without exaggeration that now life insurance is the most suitable method for the investment of savings."[51]

As late as 1911, New York Life was still emphasizing that it was a mutual company, all of the profits of which belonged to the policyholders. During the year 1911 alone, the company reported, it had paid them more than $698,775 (1,358,000 rubles) in dividends derived from profits, "more than the sum paid by all other Russian insurance societies together." Payments at time of death totaled an additional $1,079,530 (2,098,000 rubles). Moreover, in addition to sharing in profits, as well as death benefits, policyholders were said to benefit from the right to receive loans on their policies, the right to repurchase a policy at cost, and the right to obtain a payment-free prolongation of the full amount of the policy.[52]

Nevertheless, the emphasis on the benevolent "accumulation of profits" did not assure it of freedom from trouble with the Russian government. Indeed, throughout the period its relationship with the official world suffered a variety of difficulties. During 1893/94 the question came up in government circles of prohibiting New York Life from conducting its insurance business on the basis of "accumulation of profits." Officials were clearly concerned about protecting the interests of native Russian insurance companies.

In a pamphlet issued at that time, New York Life expressed its conviction that "the task of the administration of the life insurance society amounts to introducing into the policies an element of personal advantage for the insured *without raising the size of the premium.*"[53] The law introduced on March 25 (Russian style) of 1894 forbade the offering of such insurance and introduced a new schedule of rates. The company's grievance was clear—its rates had been raised in order to make its insurance more costly to the policyholder than that of certain Russian companies, and also the Equitable. Clearly the government's hope was to cause the Russian policyholder to drop his New York Life policies in favor of others that charged lower prices, although they did not pay the annual dividends that New York Life paid. The pamphlet concluded on a note of sarcasm and undisguised bitterness:

> How else to explain the fact that a rate without the inclusion of profits is cheaper, in the N.Y. Society, than in Russian Societies, and participation [in it] much more expensive than the others? This is clear to everyone, and we recommend that persons who have a feeling of sympathy for the American N.Y. company take insurance with it *only* at a rate *without the participation of capital.* We think that in this it will succeed with difficulty, if in fact it succeeds at all.

Thus for the first time the problem of competition with native Russian companies had made its appearance (in print, at least); but the issue must have been gathering strength for some time as a direct consequence of the extraordinary success of New York Life, and the government had clearly taken the side of the Russian companies. There is nothing in the records that would show how the issue was resolved, if, in fact, it was resolved at all.[54]

Another recurring issue was that of American competition. During the negotiations for the railroad loan at the end of the century, Witte was persuaded, as we have seen, to issue a guarantee against allowing any additional American insurance companies into the Russian market. In May 1914, however, when New York Life evidently still considered Russia a desirable market, the general director of New York Life for all of Russia, F.M. Kors, dispatched, without comment, to the board of directors of the Volga-Kama Bank a letter he had just received from L. Matveev, the head of his Kharkov branch. The problem had first been broached at the end of 1912, when Matveev had informed the Board that the manager of the Voronezh branch of the bank, named Koriagin, had been an "agent" for "Life" (presumably the Equitable Company), and had used his position to shift clients out of New York Life and into the other company.

In October 1913 the board of directors of the Volga-Kama Bank told Matveev that Koriagin was no longer an agent of "Life" and, moreover, that employees of the bank were not permitted to serve as agents for companies competing with New York Life.

But in fact, Koriagin had continued his activities in an unofficial capacity with one of his colleagues serving as his agent. This activity had recently become more open, and increasingly directed against New York Life, even to the point of making slanderous remarks against the latter for the edification of prospective clients. Apparently at this point a real trade war between the two companies developed. Hence, Matveev asked Kors to bring the case once more before the board of the Volga-Kama Bank.[55] Once again, we have not seen any record indicating what action, if any, was taken to resolve this issue. Probably, in view of past history, none at all.

But the principal source of irritation for New York Life lay in the financial restrictions imposed on it by the Russian government. Of these, taxation was the most serious problem, although the agreement of 1887 also continued to be a source of resentment.[56] In addition to the restrictions on profits introduced in 1887, additional taxes had been levied in the form of the stamp tax and a "supervisory" tax, to both of which nearly all businesses were subject. Against these taxes petitions were frequently, and unsuccessfully, filed by New York Life with the Governing Senate, Russia's highest court, beginning in 1900. Basically, it was the company's contention that it should be subject to special treatment because of its status as a mutual company. It was this that lay at the heart of the continuing dispute.

In 1907, when a "trade tax" on net profits was introduced, the problem escalated still further. The tax for that year was calculated at a rate of 23.7 percent of the company's profits. The fact that two Russian mutual insurance companies were not subject to the tax because they were mutual made it even harder to accept. It was quite clear, as the general counsel of the company in St. Petersburg wrote in November 1910, that the Russian government intended to continue to take one-quarter of the company's annual profits, while also compelling it to pay to its Russian clients the same dividends based on profits as it paid to its American clients.[57]

In the autumn of 1910 the company's anger peaked. In November the Russian branch of the company addressed a petition to the Grand Duke Nikolai Nikolaevich, asking to be received by the Emperor to discuss the Governing Senate's recent affirmation of the tax, "a question [which] actually involves the continuance of the operations of the Company in Russia. . . ."[58] This initiative apparently met with no success. In October the general counsel of the New York headquarters addressed a detailed memorandum on the subject to Baron Rosen, the Russian ambassador in Washington, protesting the tax as a matter of principle but in effect declaring the company's willingness to accept it provided profits were calculated differently, thereby arriving at a total of 1,241,962 rather than 2,140,683 rubles of net profit for 1907, and if the rate were reduced from 23.7 to 4 percent by applying its estimated net profits against the whole of its deposits in the State Bank rather than against only the smallest of the three, the Guarantee Deposit, amounting only to 500,000 rubles. By diminishing both estimated net profits and the rate of interest, the general counsel concluded that the tax for 1907 would be a tolerable 49,678 rubles.[59] Nothing came of these efforts either, and in May 1914 the Governing Senate again upheld its decision of November 1910.[60]

Despite its diversified holdings, New York Life was never a major force in the Russian bond market. It did make a significant contribution, however, to Russia's supply of financial capital through the channeling of indigenous Russian savings from the purchase of life insurance policies into Russia's banks, government bonds, and railroads.

IV

As the nineteenth century drew to a close both Russia and the United States were being increasingly drawn into the complex world of international finance; and during the years immediately preceding World War I the growing commercial and industrial development of Russia, in particular, led to an increasingly active role for banking institutions, especially those in St. Petersburg with their already close international connections. In 1910, the possibility of the establishment of an American bank in Moscow was discussed, although unsuccessfully, by an unidentified group of American financiers.[61]

On the Russian side, the main banking agent in international affairs was the St. Petersburg International Commercial Bank. The Volga-Kama Bank, among others, also served as the agent of the State Bank in the latter's dealings with New York Life.[62] In the American banking world, Kidder, Peabody & Co. had the most consistent record of involvement in loans to Russia, having participated in the sales of government bonds since 1889.[63] J. P. Morgan & Co. was notably less enthusiastic about investment in Russia, regarding it as unduly risky. Nevertheless, Morgan did take some initiative in establishing relations with the St. Petersburg Commercial International Bank; and in the Russian sale of 4 percent bonds in March 1898, which was widely supported throughout Europe, J. P. Morgan, August Belmont & Co., Kidder, Peabody, and the National City Bank constituted the American subscribers.[64] Morgan's ambivalence, however, was shown in a letter dated March 24, 1898 to Alexander Koch of the St. Petersburg International Commercial Bank in which Morgan indicated that he was not in a position to conduct additional business at the moment because of a variety of unfavorable circumstances, ranging from the death of his brother-in-law to "the complicated condition of politics in the United States, as well as in Europe." He did add, however, that "it is not unlikely that something can be done later, but at the moment I must ask you to let the whole matter remain in abeyance until political matters [settle] down somewhat, and this question between Spain and the United States has been definitely disposed of."[65]

Interestingly enough, the flow of funds occasionally went not from west to east but in the opposite direction. Thus, in the late 1890s the shares of a syndicate organized by Kuhn, Loeb & Co. on behalf of the Illinois Central Railroad were actively promoted in Russia by M. M. Warburg and Co. in Hamburg, with a resultant sale of $35,000 worth to the International Commercial Bank.[66] The Vereinsbank in Frankfurt am Main also represented the Illinois Steel Company of Chicago in St. Petersburg,[67] although the specific purpose of this representation is unknown. On one occasion the National City Bank wrote to the Volga-Kama Bank, offering the services of its bond department in the purchase, sale, and investigation of securities. On December 29, 1910, John E. Gardner, vice president of National City Bank, wrote to the Volga-Kama and thanked the bank for its decision both to open a checking account with National City and to close its account with the Deutsche Bank, London, which had been the agent for transmitting funds to Russia. "We trust," Gardner concluded, "that the business relations which have thus been established will prove mutually profitable. . . ."[68]

National City, the largest bank in the United States early in the new century,[69] was active in the transmittal of accounts between the two countries. For the most part these represented small sums, probably immigrants' gifts to relatives and friends in the old country, but small business interests were also included.[70] There are few indications of greater involvement, although National City was engaged at the turn of the century in negotiations with the International Commercial Bank with regard to the Far East. In August 1904 Frank A. Vanderlip, then vice president of National City, wrote to James Stillman, its president, who was in Paris at the time, that "we sold the last of the Russian bonds some days ago. . . ."[71] Yet by 1914, when Vanderlip was president of the bank, it had a total of thirty-eight correspondent banks serving its interests throughout the Russian Empire. Of these, the designated bank in St. Petersburg, Moscow, and Odessa was the Crédit Lyonnais. Elsewhere, the National City Bank's needs were met only by Russian banks. Among the many that carried out this role were the Volga-Kama, which was listed for Kazan, Perm and Saratov; the Azov-Don for Yalta, Kerch, Novorossisk, Samara, and Tiflis; the St. Petersburg International Commercial Bank for Ekaterinoslav and Kharkov; and the Discount Bank of St. Petersburg for Kiev and Rostov-on-Don.

The other banks listed included the Russian Bank for Foreign Trade and the Russian Bank for Industry and Trade, both also centered in St. Petersburg, as well as a wide variety of local banks. At the same time the Ministry of Finances maintained a balance of $892,000 with the National City Bank in New York—a very respectable sum, comparatively speaking.[72] Two years earlier Vanderlip, who had become president of the bank in 1909, wrote to Stillman, then its chairman, asserting the need for public "recognition of the supremacy of the City Bank now and always in the banking field."[73]

As of 1909 National City did the largest bond trading business of any banking institution in New York.[74] However, despite Vanderlip's long interest in Russia and his desire to promote the bank's interests in Europe, its bond investments in January 1914 included virtually none in Russia. Yet its funds in the State Bank were listed as of June 1, 1912, as amounting to $24,799.38 (or, more correctly, perhaps, $25,099.38), which did not compare unfavorably with $24,797.69 for Kidder, Peabody & Co., $27,721.01 for August Belmont & Co., and $27,543.69 for J. P. Morgan & Co.[75] These small sums seem to reflect only the needs of these banks for the fulfillment of the general financial requirement of American firms in Russia.

These were also years of growing commercial and industrial interest in Russia on the part of Americans, which brought financial interests in their wake. One of the earliest efforts to establish a firm financial relationship between the two countries was not a success. This was an attempt by one of the largest Philadelphia banks, the Fourth Street National Bank, to obtain an agreement with the International Commercial Bank for the establishment of mutual banking operations, including the conducting of affairs by the latter in the United States. Two overtures were made to A. Iu. Rothstein in 1896.[76] Rothstein responded favorably, hoping to obtain American credits for Russian industrial orders, which in turn led the Fourth Street National Bank, headed by F. G. Rogers, to seek a Russian contribution to the capital of the recently established Russian-American Manufacturing Company. The latter had been founded and was controlled by a group of Philadelphia bankers, the president of which was a Mr. Hollister. It was energetically represented by Edmund D. Smith, who headed an independent concern in his own name in New York. Smith corresponded actively with Rothstein beginning in August 1896, at first about such matters as Russian purchases of railroad equipment and the possibility of Russian investment in a French syndicate that was proposing to sell American pipe. In December Smith cabled Rothstein that he was engaged in forming a syndicate that would include Morgan and possibly Standard Oil for the purpose of purchasing American interests in the Russian-American Manufacturing Company, the holdings of which included the Russian Nikopol-Mariupol Mining and Metallurgical Co. in St. Petersburg, a large enterprise controlled by the International Bank. He asked Rothstein's assistance in holding the stocks in the latter enterprise on a temporary basis until he could gather together sufficient shareholders.[77] At his meeting with Morgan and Standard Oil, Smith also discussed the question of "the creation of conditions for the expansion of future enterprises in Russia and China."[78]

These ambitious plans rapidly came to a bad end. By the end of January 1897, Hollister and his colleagues had disavowed Smith's efforts and forced his resignation. Early in February, the latter received a telegram from Rothstein asserting that "After experience proved E. D. Smith the single respectable man among thieves, must give up all hope of finding credulous people [who] will probably do business with Americans," a message to which Smith carefully responded: "One setback need not condemn a whole nation! Americans have known very little of Russia in the past, but are now being educated in the belief that there is a great opening for business in your Country."[79]

J. P. Morgan & Co. in these years emerged as the leader of all private banking and brokerage houses in the United States. Morgan also began to show signs of a growing interest in Russian affairs. This, as it developed, was primarily an interest in Russian government bonds, in contrast with the emphasis of New York Life on railroad bonds. Morgan's relations with the Russians were also, one must hasten to add, largely unproductive. It is his negotiations, which lasted in fits and starts until the spring of 1906, that are of interest. The record shows J.P. Morgan, Sr. to have been extremely diffident about any investment in Russia. He was intensely fearful about the risks of placing his money in that relatively unknown part of the world and hesitant about coming to any firm agreement with the Russians.

On the Russian side, early attempts "to penetrate the American money market and even to broadly 'open' it for Russian government loans" were primarily associated with Witte. In fact, Witte was thinking about this possibility even before he became Minister of Finance in 1892, while he was still Minister of Communications. But his first move, sparked by a severe shortage of funds to support his currency reforms and unfavorable conditions on European money markets, did not come until 1898. The background for the steps he was taking at that time was contained in a note to the Tsar in November 1898 in which Witte described his fears of an approaching economic crisis, which would threaten his entire economic program, and stressed the need for foreign loans that could provide Russia with "resources against poverty."[80] This coincided with a similar proposal on the part of an American consul stationed in Germany, who was aware both of Russian needs and also of the growing interest of the American business and financial worlds in expanding their activity in Russia.[81]

The Russian-American talks began almost at once in New York, where A. I. Vyshnegradskii and M. V. Rutkovskii, representatives of the Ministry of Finances, arrived in early December.[82] It was most apparent that Witte was extremely anxious to keep the talks secret, and they were conducted under cover of negotiations for equipping Russia with grain elevators.[83] His object in pursuing this secrecy, it soon became clear, was to conceal the magnitude of Russia's need from European financiers. The talks came to nothing, but not before Morgan had taken rather half-hearted steps to form a syndicate with the British firm of Baring, Magoun and Co., the New York house of Baring Brothers, which proposed to offer an $80 million loan at $3\frac{1}{2}$ percent, at a cost of 92 to the dollar—terms that proved unacceptable to the Russians.

The failure of the Russian mission was explained in a lengthy letter, dated December 30, 1898, from William M. Ivens of the New York firm of Ivens, Kidder and Melcher. It was written from a sickbed in great perturbation to E. A. Hitchcock, the American ambassador in St. Petersburg. "Their presence [i.e., the two Russian representatives], under the circumstances," he observed, "did not help matters, inasmuch as it evidenced considerable anxiety on the part of Russia. It was quite natural what these gentlemen might say—to the effect 'that Russia did not need a loan, etc., etc.' Their presence was quite a sufficient contradiction of their statement."[84] Rutkovskii in particular made the rounds of American bankers in an effort to determine whether there were sufficient funds to be had in America to make the effort practical. The efforts of the Russians, according to Ivens, soon received widespread publicity, emanating first from Chicago. This became a source of great irritation to both sides, but particularly to Vyshnegradskii and Rutkovskii. Soon it "also became apparent that the strong Jewish and German influences were at work here for the purpose of injuring Russian credit in our market," Ivens wrote. Obviously these ethnic influences were not helpful. "To my intense annoyance and my sincere regret this all naturally had a very bad influence upon our Russian friends here. They immediately insisted on either closing with M. Morgan or retiring altogether." "Of course," Ivens noted, "our bankers are not to be driven under such circumstances."[85]

Morgan was unwilling to make additional concessions, although, as has been noted, he did offer the Russians 92. "They said that to accept that offer or anything near it would be ruinous to Russian credit."[86] The Russians left in some haste, alleging not only that the American terms were unacceptable but that the amount of free capital seeking investment "was hardly great."[87] Ivens explained the fiasco to Hitchcock mainly in terms of Russian failures. Essentially they did not understand how long a time would be needed to put together a loan of $80 million on this side of the Atlantic. But "this whole business has been rendered difficult by jealousies among the Russians themselves", according to Ivens:

> Mr. Routkowsky [sic] made it pretty plain to me that he did not care to further the business, and I am satisfied it was because he thought that the Consul General, rather than he, would have the credit for doing it, if anything were done. I learn from Washington that Count Cassini [the Russian ambassador] was not inclined to further it because the negociations [sic] had been taken up through your embassy instead of his. Mr. Wishnegradsky [sic] came before he was wanted, and when he got here, showed himself to be the embodiment of Timidity, and as a special envoy, interfering with the regular work of the Agent, Mr. Routkowsky, the latter was not particularly active in his desire to assist.[88]

Ivens concluded his account on a note that was both regretful and ambivalent. "The time was quite ripe, and I cannot help thinking that the negotiations could have been successfully carried through if it were not for some conditions peculiar to Mr. Witte's situation, which led to the adoption of the policy which was pursued by his representatives at this end."[89] Ivens' letter is revealing not only of the course of the negotiations but also of the extent of official involvement on both the American and the Russian sides. Yet Count A. P. Cassini wrote to the Russian Vice Minister of Foreign Affairs, saying that in his view political circumstances had not affected the outcome of the talks and expressing confidence that they would be resumed at a more favorable time.[90]

The extent of governmental involvement was made still more apparent when Morgan, who was then in London, received a letter dated April 27, 1899, presumably from Herbert H. D. Peirce, Chargé d'Affaires at the St. Petersburg embassy, and written at the suggestion of Ivens and with the advice of Hitchcock.[91] The purpose of the letter, clearly, was to reopen negotiations between the Russians and Morgan. According to Peirce, Rothstein had told him that "he [Rothstein] felt entirely confident that could he come into personal communication with you [Morgan], the question of taking up a loan of the Russian Government could be arranged between you and him upon terms entirely satisfactory to both parties and that he would for his part take one quarter part of the loan to be placed among his clients." Peirce strongly seconded these sentiments, pointing out Rothstein's closeness to Witte and the fact that Rothstein was also "a controlling factor in his own country." Peirce concluded by noting that his own sole interest lay "in the advancement of the diplomatic and commercial interests of the two countries, which during my residence in Russia in an official capacity for five years I have become convinced would be greatly enhanced by the placing of a Russian loan in America."[92]

According to this letter, Rothstein offered to meet with Morgan at any place in Europe which the latter might choose. He suggested Dover, England, as a place unlikely to attract attention. A scribbled reply by Morgan suggested Brussels. The hectic correspondence between Morgan and Peirce that followed during the next month showed Morgan, however, to be unenthusiastic about the proposed meeting. He postponed its date, and on May 19, 1899 declared it to be his considered conclusion that "a conference at Brussels [would be] quite useless," and suggested further delay.[93] These circumstances probably accounted in part at least for Rothstein's extraordinary letter of May 2/14 to the French banker, Rothschild, in which Rothstein not only made it clear that he had kept the latter informed about the results of his earlier talks with Morgan but also apprised him, along with warnings of the need for secrecy, both of the possibility of his meeting with Morgan and of a possible meeting also with Rothschild to discuss the floating of a loan on the English market, presumably if nothing came of the Morgan meeting.[94]

The meeting between Morgan and Rothstein took place on May 24, but the discussions were essentially only procedural, although they did contain a Russian agreement that the St. Petersburg International Commercial Bank would assume 25 percent of any future loan. Rothstein, in a subsequent letter to Morgan, informed him that he had told Witte that "I had convinced myself of your friendly disposition toward the Russian finances and of your wish of making eventually a Russian business . . . and that I had assured you that undoubtedly he would be very pleased to enter in direct intercourse with you and that your high standing, authority and position would be taken into consideration." Witte had replied that he agreed with what Rothstein had said and asked him to tell Morgan so, adding "that if there had been certain misunderstandings in the former negociations [sic], they would have been set aside by our conversation."[95]

Within a few days Rothstein also wrote to Peirce, informing him that rumors about a projected loan from Baring, Magoun and Co. in London were not true. The following day a letter from Peirce to Rothstein expressed "la satisfaction la plus vive que j'ai lu ce témoinage a l'entente et au bon rapport qui existent dans vos relations avec Mr. Morgan et que je suis convaincu ne peut que résultez [sic] heureusement pour les relations êntre les États Unis et Russie."[96]

The Soviet historian A. A. Fursenko (like Anan'ich on another occasion) makes the point that American financial circles, and Morgan in particular, favored a loan to Russia not so much for the profits to be derived therefrom but for the possibilities that were to be found in it for the further development of commercial relationships with Russia.[97] Certainly that was also the view of Peirce and Hitchcock, except that more friendly political relationships between the two countries were also envisaged. But whether Morgan himself was enthusiastic about undertaking a Russian loan is questionable. His clear reluctance to enter the Russian market despite repeated urgings by Grenfell in London to enter into active participation in Russian banking affairs and trading in Russian securities was based on his assessment of that market as relatively unattractive, both because it allegedly paid less in interest and because the outlook was more risky. Moreover, the American money market was too constricted, in his view, to risk involvement in Russian operations. This judgment may have been further supported by concern over both the current situation in China and the American war with Spain. In any event, the Russians had their railroad loan, which they had negotiated with New York Life, as a kind of consolation prize. Morgan, incidentally, was a member of the American syndicate, and probably the largest member, sponsoring the loan. This was to be the only loan to Russia in which the House of Morgan participated.

In the spring of 1900 Russian-American talks entered a new phase with the arrival of Rothstein himself in New York. Witte, it appeared, influenced by the unfavorable turn of events in China for Russia, was now ready to accept an American loan on terms that he had rejected during the previous negotiations. Rothstein, who was in constant communication with Witte, resumed negotiations with Morgan in June 1900. Morgan immediately offered to establish a syndicate with the International Commercial Bank, in which he would take $50 million, again at $3\frac{1}{2}$ percent interest and a price of 92. He also insisted on a commission for the house of Morgan of 1 percent. The amortization period would be 81 years, beginning in 1901, and he demanded an agreement by the end of February 1901. At the same time, Rothstein, in a telegram to Witte, noted that because of the approaching presidential election in the United States and also because of the bad news from China, Morgan would prefer to postpone the talks.[98]

Perhaps because of this, Witte at once declared these overall terms to be acceptable, although he declared his failure to understand either the commission to Morgan, thereby reducing the price to 91, or the latter's concern over the China question. But he apparently would have liked to change the terms of the syndicate in order to reduce the share of the International Bank from 50 to 10 percent. The remaining 90 percent would consist entirely of American financial enterprises, excluding completely European banks. This led to urgent pleas from Rothstein to Witte to permit the ratio between them to remain at 50–50 or, at the very least, to allow a 15 percent share for the International Commercial Bank and an additional 5 to 10 percent share for the Russo-Chinese Bank, a subsidiary of the International Bank. As he bluntly stated, he was in the difficult position of serving as the representative both of the Ministry of Finance and of his own bank. Witte's response at first was adamant,[99] but he later yielded and reverted to granting the International Bank a 50 percent share in the investment.

In the continuing negotiations, New York Life, National City Bank, and August Belmont & Co. were also participants. But Morgan knew, Rothstein reported to Witte, that with the exclusion of all European banks, on which Witte continued to insist, Morgan would bear a heavy responsibility in case the issue failed. Nevertheless, Morgan and Witte succeeded in reaching an agreement, and a contract was duly drawn up well before the end of June. Witte cabled Morgan on June 20 that he was "très content" with the terms of the agreement, and on the next day, apparently on the very eve of Rothstein's departure from New York, he sent Morgan a telegram declaring that "Your last despatches have dispelled my doubts of borrowing in dollars and pounds sterling in America."[100]

Despite various conditions that Morgan appended to the agreement on the following day, including one giving to the Morgan Company the sole right to determine the amount and timing of the issue, Witte apparently found the agreement satisfactory. On July 10 Rothstein wrote to J. P. Morgan, declaring that Witte had emphasized repeatedly

> that it was very important and gratifying to him to be assured of your cooperation in this, his first great American operation, and that he altogether defers to you the determination of the amount of the issue and the selection of the suitable time therefor, because, above all, the moral effect of the matter is of the greatest moment to him.[101]

This was even followed by an exuberant invitation from Witte to Morgan to visit him if he should ever be in St. Petersburg. At about the same time the Russian ambassador in Washington once again optimistically wrote to the foreign ministry, saying that the proposed agreement showed "the inclination of big American financial figures to promote in every way a financial and commercial rapprochement between the two countries, and in this, in my opinion, lies the basis for the development of friendly relations between the two young peoples."[102]

From then on, however, conditions deteriorated rapidly. Morgan telegraphed Rothstein the very next day, July 11, saying that he was "very sorry to report present indications less favorable than before your departure." Shortly afterward a letter arrived from Rothstein declaring Russia's intention of undertaking the "pacification of Manchuria" and declaring the Russians' "general distrust of the Chinese."

"It is unfortunate," Rothstein continued, "that through these occurrences our project has to be postponed." Witte, Rothstein intimated, did not want to appear to be concluding a war loan.[103] Morgan replied promptly:

> We regret very much that you found upon your arrival home the situation in China to have been much more serious than you had expected. . . . We appreciate that Mr. de Witte would not be willing to ever seem to be making anything in the nature of a War

Loan at the present time at least in this country, and perhaps it is just as well, as you can readily understand that in the present uncertain state of the markets of the world it would be impossible to carry out the proposed negotiations.[104]

The following letters and telegrams from Rothstein were devoted to two subjects: (1) an attempt to salvage something of the relationship that had been built up with so much effort by proposing a direct purchase of Treasury bonds, which Morgan rejected out of hand, and (2) informing Morgan of the receipt of a French offer of a large loan, which had the support of the French government. Apparently Witte had not yet agreed to the latter and was trying to use it to extract more favorable terms from the Americans.[105] These efforts were without success, however, and in November 1900 Morgan telegraphed his final refusal to conduct Russian operations of any type on the American market.[106]

It would seem that both Witte and Morgan shared the responsibility for the failure of the loan to materialize. The Chinese affair, while playing a part in it, cannot be regarded as the principal cause of the failure. Despite their expressions of happiness at the initial outcome of the negotiations, the terms of the agreement were in fact below the hopes and expectations of the Russians. Morgan no doubt still retained his fears of any dealing with the Russians, and especially so when the Russians were at war with China, where American financial circles were hoping for an improvement in conditions. Witte resorted once more to the French money market, from which he had sought to free himself, concluding in 1901 a loan of 159 million francs. During the course of these proceedings, he asked Rothstein to refrain from undertaking negotiations with foreign bankers on financial questions that were of concern to the Russian government, since that might lead "to the conclusion that the government needs money, seeks loans,—substantially damaging state credit. . . ."[107]

V

This was not the end of the story, however. Both Russian and American financial circles had been playing with the thought of instituting some kind of cooperative effort in the Far East. The American initially most closely associated with this endeavor was one Robert Porter, who was close to Morgan and had some slight semiofficial aura, having served as President McKinley's "Special Commissar" to Cuba and Puerto Rico in the wake of the Spanish-American War. Now he was clearly looking for new worlds to conquer. In May 1899 Porter visited St. Petersburg, where he had various talks concerning the establishment of closer Russo-American ties. In August of that year J. P. Morgan sent a letter to Rothstein, introducing Porter as "a quasi-official of the United States Government" who could possibly play a "helpful" role in matters of mutual interest. In a follow-up letter to Rothstein in the same month, Porter declared his mission to be that of "increasing the financial and commercial relations of the two great countries."[108]

Nothing came of the visit Porter had intended to pay to St. Petersburg in the fall, but in November he wrote to Rothstein, with whom he evidently had been in correspondence, telling him that in a recent visit with Morgan Porter had told Morgan of Rothstein's idea of "establishing a branch of your [Rothstein's] bank in connection with his [Morgan's] financial institution in this city."[109] Porter had stressed to Morgan the value of such a connection for American interests in the Far East (presumably because of the existence of the Russo-Chinese Bank, of which Rothstein was chairman). Morgan, however, had been characteristically noncommittal, merely requesting a more detailed statement in writing from Rothstein.

In the spring of 1900 the Russians again raised the question, which had been under discussion earlier, of a cooperative effort with the Americans in the Far East. These proposals were raised in early April by a member of the International Commercial Bank in correspondence not with Morgan but with National City Bank and its president, James Stillman. Adolf Werth, manager of the Russo-Chinese Bank in Shanghai, also participated in the triangular correspondence. The proposal was for the establishment of "a Russian-American banking association," composed of National City Bank and the Russo-Chinese Bank. It was to have a capital of 4 million rubles, not a great sum, which should be shared equally between them, as should all expenses and profits. Its headquarters would be located in St. Petersburg, while in New York its function would be the issuance and circulation of Russian securities on the market. Rothstein made it clear that the Russian government would be favorably disposed and would probably deposit funds with the new banking institution. Werth, he declared, was "of the opinion that a very lucrative business may be arrived at."[110]

Rothstein also observed that American commercial success in the Far East was more likely through cooperation with Russia, which already had entrenched interests in the area. Cooperation between the two countries would enable them to thwart more successfully competing British interests in China. In addition, Russia had not only further plans for the construction of the Trans-Siberian Railroad but also concessions for the construction of railroads in Manchuria and was ready to accept the aid of American capital in this.[111]

Stillman replied to these overtures with enthusiasm at the end of April 1900. "I trust," he wrote, "the result will lead to an immediate beginning in business between our two institutions, especially as relating to exchange transactions between this country and Asia."[112] In June, when Rothstein was in New York, Stillman sent him a letter, also addressed to Werth, stating his understanding of the terms of the agreement, which differed little from those originally proposed by the International Commercial Bank. "The financing of exports from America to China and East Asia in general is our aim," he declared, but it also included the diversion of exports from London.[113] Stillman and Rothstein also discussed various firms they regarded as prospective business clients, as well as all the more minute operating details. Included among the possible clients was the Standard Oil Company, with which National City Bank had had previous contacts.

In July, however, after Rothstein's return to St. Petersburg, the new relationship began to show signs of suffering from the Morgan shadow. Rothstein wrote to Stillman:

> I have in so far encountered a difficulty, that the Minister [Witte] at the moment does not like to make any special concessions in order to attract foreign money. He has with great interest taken cognizance of our arrangements, and held out to me prospects of approving of every desired facilitation. But at present he does not like to do anything that could give the appearance as though he were particularly endeavoring to attract to himself money from America. . . .[114]

Witte, however, stipulated only that bank notes to be delivered should be deposited with the State Bank rather than in New York, to which Stillman readily agreed. The relationship between Stillman and Rothstein continued to be most friendly, both with respect to the "joint account" and in personal terms. In November Stillman received a telegram from Rothstein, congratulating him on the reelection of President McKinley as "most welcome news," indicating "that the honesty and intelligence of the bulk of the people of the United States have again proved themselves enduring factors."[115] During the following months the two cooperated in their financial dealings with China, especially with regard to the payment for a Chinese war indemnity to the United States on which the Russo-Chinese Bank represented American interests, and also with respect to the shipment of silver directly to India rather than by way of London.

In the spring of 1901 Stillman sent Rothstein warm letters of introduction both for the Honorable Frank A. Vanderlip, who was leaving his post as Assistant Secretary of the Treasury to join the National City Bank, and for United States Senator Albert J. Beveridge, "one of our most esteemed friends."[116] As of the end of October 1901, the last date for which material is available, the relationship among the three (the St. Petersburg International Commercial Bank, National City Bank, and Russo-Chinese Bank) appeared to be a model of friendly cooperation.[117]

With this exception, Russian-American financial relations at the turn of the century seemed to enter a period of at least partial withdrawal. Even New York Life, at a special meeting of its finance committee with Perkins in the chair, decided in April 1900 not to avail itself of the 30 million-ruble option it had insisted on as part of its railroad loan of 1899, although the finance committee did vote to extend it until July 15, 1901.[118]

The troubles that beset the relationship during the early years of the new century have already been noted. Even the cooperation in the Far East could not long endure in view of the increasing problems between Japan and Russia, which the United States preferred to avoid. And a Russian agreement with National City Bank providing for the sale of American railroad equipment was not received at all favorably in some circles in Russia. Deploring what they saw as state support for the continuing dependence of Russia on foreign countries, the industrialists and their supporters firmly believed that such orders should be placed with domestic industry, especially in a time of economic depression.

In April 1901 Frank A. Vanderlip made an extended trip to Russia, as well as to other countries in Europe. In the course of a lengthy talk with Witte, Vanderlip "suggested instituting an American bank in St. Petersburg with branch houses in the interior whose duty it would be to pay the Americans cash for their goods and grant sound Russian firms the credit they would require." Such a bank would have another advantage: "Most of the drafts which now pass through London could go directly to New York." Witte was reportedly "greatly pleased with the idea" and suggested that such an agency would also be desirable in Siberia. The American ambassador, Mr. Hitchcock, and his chargé, Mr. Peirce, also supported the proposal, although the former also expressed his "doubt if there is a field for American investment in Russia."[119]

Especially interesting are Vanderlip's more general observations. Witte emphasized that he needed foreign capital, and especially American capital, primarily for railroad construction and industrial development.[120] Yet, according to a British consular agent in St. Petersburg at the time, "Witte feels that he will be ruined as Finance Minister if he borrows at any rate he is now able to command."[121] Referring obliquely to the recent failure of Russian efforts to obtain American financial assistance, Witte complained that "Our great misfortune is that you [i.e., the United States] do not understand us." To this he added with respect to that failure: "I think it is more due to political influence. Russia is misrepresented to the Americans." [122] Expressing his opinion on how commercial relations between Russia and the United States could be improved, Witte declared: "We could do it, but you, with your government, which must always listen to the people and shape its course for political reasons, could not." Witte also stressed Russia's need for peace, declaring that "Militarism is the nightmare and the ruin of every European finance minister."[123]

The subject of a major loan by American financial interests was not resumed until 1905, when Russia's unsuccessful war with Japan, combined with the outbreak of revolution, caused that country again to look to the United States. Even as early as March 1904, when the Japanese attack on Port Arthur had only recently occurred, Vanderlip wrote to James Stillman that McCall, the head of the New York Life Insurance Company, "Agreed perfectly with you that it would be inadvisable either to bring out or underwrite such a [Japanese] loan here. He thought it would have a bad effect in Russian [sic] upon the national attitude toward this country, and, specifically, would have a bad effect upon their business if the New York Life were in any way connected with bringing out such a loan."[124]

At the same time Morgan evinced a positive interest in taking advantage of the situation to establish better financial relations with Russia.[125] A year later, in March 1905, Morgan sent a representative to Russia to try to arrange for the construction of battleships, to be paid for by bonds floated by an American syndicate. The opportunity to begin talks with American banking circles concerning the possibility of large loan came in the summer of 1905, however, with Witte's journey to the peace talks with Japan at Portsmouth, New Hampshire, and his subsequent visit to New York. Russia's financial situation was now very critical, and talks early in the year concerning the possibility of a second French loan had broken down.[126] At the same time, the ongoing course of Russia's first revolution encouraged Morgan to consider such a loan in order to support the Russian government.

Immediately after the Portsmouth talks, Vanderlip had discussions with Witte in which Vanderlip responded favorably to Witte's suggestions.[127] During July, Witte, on instructions from V.N. Kokovtsov, the Minister of Finance (Witte had left the ministry in 1903), also conducted talks with Morgan and with George Perkins (whose connections lay not only with New York Life and the National City Bank but also with J. P. Morgan & Co., of which he was now an influential partner and on close terms with J. P. Morgan personally). Throughout the succeeding negotiations, Morgan insisted that his must be the only American bank to be involved, and he showed special concern that National City Bank not learn of the developing situation. Meanwhile, Witte, on his way to Portsmouth, had reopened talks with French bankers with the idea of forming an international consortium.

In August Witte proposed in his talks with Morgan that the Americans make a loan of $400 million to Russia as their share of an international effort on behalf of that country. Morgan immediately rejected the thought of a loan of such magnitude, but he agreed in principle to participate in an international syndicate, while limiting the American share to between $50 million and $100 million. Morgan also made this offer contingent on the granting of special privileges for the American market. Finally, he insisted that other American banks not be permitted to participate in any loan.[128] To these conditions Kokovtsov, the Minister of Finance, responded favorably in September and urgently pressed for a quick beginning of negotiations. Kokovtsov insisted that a Morgan representative be sent to St. Petersburg at once, and told Morgan that he was dealing "directly with you [Morgan]."[129] The continuing ambivalance of the senior Morgan was fully revealed, however, in a cable to his son, J. P. Morgan, Jr., who was in London:

> Think the whole matter very important but may decide to do nothing, but hope not. Witte and the Minister of Finance virtually agreed nothing will be done in U.S.A. except with J.P.M. and Co.[130]

On October 10, 1905, J. P. Morgan, Jr., met in Paris with a group of international financiers—French, English, and Dutch (Germany was not present but was expected to participate)—to discuss the terms of an international loan to Russia. J. P. Morgan, Jr., met there with George Perkins, who had just arrived from the United States bearing instructions from J. P. Morgan, Sr. The others had already been meeting for several days and planned to leave for St. Petersburg shortly. J. P. Morgan, Jr., soon returned to London, however, because he had been told nothing about the terms his company might grant and found his whole situation an embarrassment.[131]

Perkins and J. P. Morgan, Jr., arrived in St. Petersburg only when the talks had already been under way for several days. They were authorized by J. P. Morgan, Sr., to contribute $50 million to the syndicate, with the understanding that most of the bonds should be sold in the United States. The elder Morgan had also stipulated as a further condition for a grant that orders must be awarded to American industry.[132] The latter condition was rejected by Kokovtsov, who noted in his reply that he could not accept the slogan: "America for the Americans."[133] On October 17, J. P. Morgan, Sr., cabled both his son and Perkins to say that he had been

> examining the whole question and have reluctantly come to the conclusion that in the present conditions of our money market it would be absolutely impossible to make a successful issue here for some time. On this point all Financial Houses and banks coincide. . . . Another difficulty we should encounter in case of an issue just now is the public anxiety caused by the Insurance embroglio which is increasing. [We] also hear that the Jews are combining in opposition.[134]

In fact, the Jewish investment house of Kuhn, Loeb & Co. had organized a syndicate that was distributing $75 million in Japanese war bonds in the United States—a loan that was greatly oversubscribed. Its success "was especially gratifying to Jacob H. Schiff, under whose leadership the offering was made, because, in his opinion, it would help defeat the anti-Semitic and tyrannical Russian government, which he labeled the 'enemy of mankind.'"[135]

Perkins and J. P. Morgan, Jr., told Witte and Kokovtsov about the new attitude on the part of the senior Morgan and were assured in a spirit of great friendliness that the sum could be negotiable if only the United States would continue to participate in the group. J. P. Morgan, Sr., reiterated his decision, however, which impelled Perkins and J. P. Morgan, Jr., to mount a vigorous campaign to reverse his stand. The British and the Germans, they noted, as well as the Russians were most eager for the United States to continue to participate. Perkins and the younger Morgan also propounded the value to J. P. Morgan & Co. of an established position with this international group of leading banking houses in the first completely international transaction in history:

> "We believe this connection [to be] of utmost value, . . . for future Russian business and for possible affairs in other countries, and American affairs on the continent."[136]

They also reported that Witte, in a "long, confidential talk," had also asserted that "the entrance of America into this group would have the greatest possible political value." Finally, they reiterated their position, opposing the withdrawal of Morgan from the group not only because it would adversely impact on the credit of the firm as well as on the United States as a whole, but also because "we are most unwilling to drop the business and thereby show ourselves so weak that we disappoint the Russian Government and the strongest financial group ever formed in Europe."[137]

On October 24, 1905, J. P. Morgan, Sr., yielded. The following day, however, Perkins and J. P. Morgan, Jr., reported, for the first time apparently, on the railway strike that was currently underway in Russia, and on the two following days they reported further regarding the prospects for political reforms and the elevation of Witte to a high position. With the granting of the October Manifesto, which held out the possible prospect of the transformation of the Russian government into a limited monarchy, the international group disbanded and, leaving behind an unsigned contract for possible later use, quickly left the country on the advice of Witte. Before leaving, Perkins and J. P. Morgan, Jr., cabled the senior Morgan: "We have seen the death of the old and the birth of the new Russia."[138] Thus they left Russia in a spirit of optimism for the future.

The explanation for Witte's action, however, has baffled historians to this day, especially in view of Russia's ever desperate financial needs. Some Soviet historians contend that Witte must have assumed that with the granting of the October Manifesto and his own rise to head of the government, matters would soon quiet down and a loan would not be needed. But, as these historians also observe, these assumptions were quite mistaken, as Witte and Kokovtsov soon had to turn once more to the French.[139]

Succeeding months saw a dramatic reversal of roles both on the part of Witte and of the Morgans, father and son. On April 2, 1906 J. P. Morgan, Sr., who was then in Paris, cabled his son in New York:

> [We] have received the following cable from Witte.—We are renewing business commenced [in] St. Petersburg and suspended by us. We hope you will take part with same good will you showed then.[140]

J. P. Morgan, Jr., replied on April 7. "Hope very much Russian business will be turned down again for present, as under present circumstances here it would be most impolitic and very injurious to us to offer any foreign bonds. . . ." Presumably he was speaking about both economic and political conditions in the United States.

Three days later came his father's reply, favoring the offering of a loan to the Russian government of £111 million by a consortium composed of France, England, Holland, Austria, Italy, and, they all hoped, the United States. Only Germany remained outside the new effort. J. P. Morgan, Sr., proposed that the American share should be a small one, but he felt it desirable that the United States take part, "in view of what has already transpired, as well as our future relations with Russia and with the financiers we have been in association with. . . ."[141] The reply of J. P. Morgan, Jr., and Perkins came back the next day, April 11: "Greatly regret. Feel compelled to take position that business proposed would be absolutely unwise at present." The cable stressed the poor condition of the money market and the fact that any unsuccessful attempt to sell Russian bonds "would endanger the success of any future Russian business here." The financial world, they emphasized, was virtually unanimous in its opposition to the proposal. But in conclusion they declared:

> We are greatly distressed at the declining business, especially after your consideration last October, but we know we do not exaggerate difficulties, dangers. It is not a question of money but of public hostility which we ought not provoke.[142]

The following day Morgan Sr. regretfully followed his son's lead.

Thus ended the most active period of J. P. Morgan's financial involvement with Russia. The company's interest in later years shifted toward more entrepreneurial pursuits, although not with any very productive results. It thought of financing the construction of grain elevators and the irrigation of the cotton-growing lands of Turkestan. It also had some active industrial interests, but in January 1910, J. P. Morgan, Jr., proposed to Grenfell that its principal enterprise, the "Caucasus" (a copper-smelting firm in which the J. P. Morgan & Co. reportedly had some $10 million invested), despite "its great promise of success," be sold[143] along with the petroleum refining and electrical enterprises. Morgan's interests, it would seem, shifted away from Russia during these final prewar years and toward greater emphasis on Canada, Latin America, and, in a limited way, China. European peace seemed more and more endangered, while the United States was becoming increasingly conscious of its own latent economic power. The words of Vanderlip, in a letter to Stillman on the occasion of the death in 1913 of J.P. Morgan, Sr., were significant:

> The king is dead. All New York is at half-mast. There are no cries of "Long life the king" [sic], for the general verdict seems to be that there will be no other king, that Mr. Morgan, typical of the time in which he lived, can have no successor, for we are facing other days.[144]

VI

In the last prewar years J. P. Morgan & Co., Kidder, Peabody & Co., August Belmont & Co., and National City Bank were all listed by official Russian sources as having active accounts with the Russian State Bank.[145] The New York Life Insurance Company, however, stands out as by far the most successful American financial institution to engage in business in Imperial Russia. The relationship was not always a happy one, but the enterprise continued to thrive throughout the period. In its ownership of railroad securities especially, it made a modest contribution to the growth of the Russian economy. Much less can be said of J. P. Morgan & Co. in terms of practical achievements, despite its international renown. But its participation at the highest official levels on issues of finance and diplomacy is certainly of historical interest, revealing alternating propensities on both sides toward rivalry and friendly cooperation. As for National City Bank, if U.S. law had not prohibited national banks from having foreign branches (a ban that was removed in December 1913), it would in all likelihood have established a branch bank in Russia long before it finally did so in 1916.

What went wrong with a relationship that once, during the closing years of the nineteenth century and the early years of the twentieth, had seemed so promising? The answer is complex—a complexity not diminished by inclinations toward secrecy on both sides (for example, Witte's apparent reluctance to permit his European allies to know of his negotiations with American bankers, and Morgan's insistence in 1905 that National City Bank not know of his dealings with the Russians).

In Russia, during Witte's tenure at the Ministry of Finance and for several years thereafter, until 1906, there was an acute need for funds, first to promote economic growth and later in 1904 to 1906 to cope with the expenses of war with Japan and the 1905 revolution. During this period Witte, especially, looked toward the United States in the dual hope that it might be a new source of funds and a means of freeing Russia from its ever-growing dependence, political as well as economic, on the European powers. But these hopes were dashed. The American financial market proved to be smaller than anticipated, and the terms that were offered were not acceptable. After this, and with the clear establishment of V. N. Kokovtsov's position as Minister of Finance in 1904,[146] a new prudence governed official financial policy with the emphasis not so much on borrowing from abroad as on reducing Russia's foreign debt.

In the United States, despite the early interest of such persons as Vanderlip in creating the basis for a friendlier relationship with Russia, there never was anything approaching an equivalent interest in advancing loans to that country. In part this reflected the relative newness of international finance (apart from old, established ties with London) in American financial circles, and their fears of risking money in a largely unknown Russian market. The United States still had more opportunities that it could utilize for secure investments in Latin America, Canada, and the Far East. During the decade before the outbreak of World War I it was branching out, with governmental support, into all these areas.

But an assumption that these policies were pursued with unanimity by either Russia or the United States would be a mistake. In Russia, divisions within the government over the proper policy with respect to foreign investment were always present, going back in the case of American interests as far as the dispute between the Ministries of Finance and Internal Affairs in the years 1885 to 1887. Even more serious were class differences, especially after 1907, when the landowners were firmly entrenched in power and, aided by some members of the intelligentsia, were strongly opposed (for both political and economic reasons) to the intrusion of foreign capital in their homeland. The industrialists, on the other hand, with their own supporters both inside and outside the government, believed that increased foreign investment was essential not only in their own self-interest but also for the achievement of national economic development, prosperity, and power.[147] In the United States, especially during the final prewar decade, interest in financial investment in Russia was inhibited by a growing antipathy toward any action that could be viewed as promoting the interests of what was increasingly seen as a tyrannical and anti-Semitic tsarist government. Thus, financial interests tended to yield to political influences and the power of American public opinion.[148]

Finally, in both countries, despite the complexity of the issues involved, one overriding consideration stands out—the mutual interdependence of economic and political factors in determining the financial relations between the two nations. It is impossible, in the final analysis, to treat one without also giving due consideration to the other.

14

The Austro-Hungarian Banking System

György Kövér

In the eighteenth century the Habsburg Monarchy lost its international character and the Danubian monarchy became a multinational conglomeration. The dynasty did its best to make a genuine union of the empire. With this aim in view in 1754 a protectionist tariff system was adopted to establish close links on the basis of the differences of regional potentialities and a large-scale regional division of labor. In 1850 the last internal customs frontier, separating Hungary from the hereditary provinces, was abolished and the customs union created. The autonomist and separationist national struggles having been defeated in 1848/49, an unrestricted absolutism dominated the 1850s. This was implemented by a supranational bureaucracy and army. The empire of the young Francis Joseph seemed to be more stable and uniform than ever. The emancipation of serfs, the unified customs system, the introduction of industrial freedom, and the abandonment of railway construction to private enterprise all promoted the commercialization of both the economy and the society. The hopes of the dynasty were destroyed at Solferino and Königrätz, however. In 1867 a compromise, the *Ausgleich*, provided for a limited decentralization of the empire. In this way the Austro-Hungarian Monarchy came into being, and this constitutional form coordinated the centrifugal forces derived from its multinational character.

The per capita GNP of the Austro-Hungarian Monarchy was below the average of the European states. Thus it was considered to be a great power of secondary importance only (Table 14–1).

Even though growth was general in the period between 1870 and 1910, the distance between the great powers did not diminish but increased. At least this was true with respect to the Habsburg and Romanov empires. Prior to World War I, Germany overtook France, both of them got closer to Great Britain, and even the Monarchy advanced as compared to the European average, while the position of Russia worsened. No doubt these data are the result of guesstimation, and therefore cannot be exact. The conclusion they suggest, however, coincides with impressions based on historical records. Table 14–1 reminds us of a race where the runner starting with a handicap on the outer track may run even faster than the more fortunate rivals on the inner tracks, but cannot reduce the distance between them. With reference to Paul Bairoch's figures

TABLE 14–1. Per Capita GNP of the European Great Powers (in 1960 U.S. dollars and prices)

	1870		1890		1910	
	Per capita GNP	Index	Per capita GNP	Index	Per capita GNP	Index
Austria-Hungary	305	85	361	93	469	94
France	437	121	515	133	680	136
Germany	426	119	537	138	705	141
Russia	250	70	182	47	287	58
Great Britain	628	175	785	202	904	181
European average	359	100	388	100	499	100

Source: Paul Bairoch: "Europe's Gross National Product: 1800–1975," Journal of European Economic History, 5 (Fall 1976), p. 286.

contained in Table 14–1, the growth rate of the per capita GNP of the Austro-Hungarian Monarchy kept pace only with that of France from 1870 to 1890, while from 1890 to 1910, in spite of an undeniable increase, the Monarchy reduced its lag only with respect to Great Britain.

We have a number of calculations made with different methods concerning the economic growth of post–1867 Austria-Hungary. The specialists examining both countries agree that Hungary produced a higher growth rate. According to the calculations of László Katus, between the Compromise of 1867 and the start of World War I the gross domestic material product (GDMP) increased at an annual rate of 2.3 percent in Austria and 2.4 percent in Hungary.[1] The annual growth rate of agriculture was 1.3 and 1.7 percent, respectively, while that of industry was 3.9 and 4.2 percent, respectively. The dynamic growth of agriculture was especially important: In 1910, 57 percent of the working population in the hereditary provinces and 64 percent in Hungary were employed in that sector.[2]

With time series of industrial growth rates in the two halves of the Monarchy at our disposal the business cycles can be traced.[3] (See Table 14–2.) The data reflect not

TABLE 14–2. Industrial Growth Rate in Austria and Hungary (in manufacturing, mining, construction)

Austria (annual %)		Hungary (annual %)	
1861–1871	4.7	1861–1871	3.9
1871–1884	1.9	1871–1883	3.1
1884–1895	2.4	1883–1896	3.8
1895–1909	2.8	1896–1906	1.5
1909–1912	2.4	1906–1913	3.9
1867–1913	2.97	1867–1913	3.33

Source: John Komlos, The Habsburg Monarchy as a Customs Union (Princeton University Press, 1983), pp. 281–321.

only the fluctuations of economic activity throughout the entire period but also the asynchronism in timing and duration of the cyclical fluctuations in the two halves of the empire.

In domestic trade the two equal partners of the Monarchy were not equally interested. Austria had traditionally close links with Germany, the most significant foreign trade partner of the Monarchy. At the turn of the century the value of the goods delivered from the Austro-Bohemian provinces into Germany was only a little lower than that of the "exports" going to Hungary. In the three decades preceding the Great War the share of Austria in Hungarian "imports" fell from 83 percent to 74 percent while the share of goods exported to Austria remained about 71 to 74 percent of the total Hungarian exports throughout the period.[4] In the customs union, reaffirmed by contracts every ten years, the partners proved to be in need of each other in spite of their debates. Their dependence was not of equal intensity, however.

As for the actual foreign trade of the entire Monarchy, at the beginning of the twentieth century exports represented some 15 percent of national income and couldn't have been higher before. Between 1883 and 1913 the annual average rate of growth of exports of the Monarchy was 2.4 percent. Compared to Western Europe and Russia this was a low rate.[5] In Europe's total exports the Monarchy provided 7.4 percent in 1880 but only 5.6 percent in 1910.[6] Except for some short periods—e.g., 1870 to 1874 and 1907 to 1913—the Monarchy had a positive trade balance between the Compromise of 1867 and the start of World War I.[7]

At the same time the Monarchy was among the indebted states on European capital markets. One-third of the state debt accumulated by the time of the Compromise was owed to foreign creditors.[8] After the Compromise the national debt was divided between the two halves, leading to the exclusion of Austro-Hungarian securities from the London Stock Exchange in May 1870. In the meantime the Hungarian government ran up more debts, and by the summer of 1873 it became almost insolvent. In the late 1870s both governments raised more loans, this process goingon continuously until the war. In 1912, 24.7 percent of the debt of the hereditary provinces and 39 percent of that of Hungary were in foreign hands.[9] Throughout the era 30 to 40 percent of the budgets of both governments went to debt service.[10]

After 1855 the Monarchy tried to induce private enterprise to undertake investments in railway construction, guaranteeing the interest on the invested capital. When in the 1870s and 1880s the railways were nationalized on a large scale, the state-owned railway system went on serving the growth of transportation by subsidized fares and by orders for equipment. The Hungarian government went as far as the direct promotion of industry: Besides exemption from taxes given for industrial investments in the 1880s, in the 1890s credit and in the early years of the twentieth century even subventions were granted to promote manufacturing industry. These sums were very small as compared to the total industrial capital, however. The significance of these measures was, therefore, rather to recruit investors and create taxpaying consumers.

In the discussion thus far, the Dual Monarchy was considered as a state both in its outer and inner relations. In the following discussion we are going to focus on the banking system—on its inner structure and its international financial relations. Finally, the multinational and international banking system will be shown in relation to its industrial environment.

Development of the Banking Structure
in Austria-Hungary

When the first *Gründerzeit* took place following the Compromise of 1867, the components of the banking system of the Monarchy had already been established. The different components were formed in different periods, as if deposited one upon the other like geological strata, while their importance might change more than once with the system. Of course, some new institutions, even new types of institutions, were created after 1873, because the system itself was dynamic.

The oldest element of the banking structure was the *bank of issue* in Vienna, established in 1816. The Austrian National Bank opened its first branch in Prague in 1847, and the second one in Pest in 1851; by 1875 it had twenty-four branches in addition to the headquarters in Vienna. On local markets these branch offices played a decisive role in the distribution of Treasury notes (government paper money that had been issued again since 1866) as well as in the supply of its own bank notes. Even in the years of monetary ease (1867–1873), the Austrian National Bank could create money shortages by refusing to grant additional credit facilities to a local branch or by refusing an application for the establishment of an additional branch. For example, in November 1872 the Commodity Exchange of Kassa complained of "not being able to tolerate the money regulator that could put the reserves of the regional money market under critical financial conditions."[11] After the bank had been reorganized on a dualist basis in 1878 (the Austro-Hungarian Bank) it formed a widespread system. Before the Great War 55 branches and 83 *Zweiganstalten* (offices) belonged to it in the hereditary provinces and 43 branches and 107 *Zweiganstalten* in Hungary. When the Treasury notes had been retired from circulation at the beginning of the century the major components of the money supply were those created by the issuing bank (47.4 percent in 1912) and by the Austrian and Hungarian joint-stock banks in the form of liabilities on current account (32.2 percent and 15.9 percent, respectively).[12]

Savings banks were established as early as the beginning of the nineteenth century. The Erste Österreichische Sparcasse, established in 1819, had philanthropic aims, and it served as an example in other regions of the empire.[13] The first savings bank of Prague, established in 1825, as well as the Kronstädter Algemeine Sparcasse, operating from 1836, served the same aims.[14] The Pesti Hazai Elsö Takarékpénztár (First Domestic Savings Bank of Pest), which opened in January 1840, broke away from the philanthropic ideas and was organized as a corporation because of the peculiarities of Hungarian legislation.

The *Regulativum* (Regulations), issued in the hereditary provinces in 1844 and prescribing the humanitarian aims in the first place, was accepted in Hungary only in the time of neoabsolutism, in 1853, and it had little practical success. After the Compromise these bureaucratic limitations were eliminated (in Austria the articles of 1872 stressed the banking function), and by the turn of the century the savings banks didn't differ much from the joint-stock banks.

Owing to the crises of 1857 and 1873 a great number of the *private bankers*, who were considered to be the dominant financiers of the Vormärz era, disappeared from the scene and the function of those left was essentially transformed: They specialized in certain branches demanding great flexibility or joined larger banks established at that time. Perhaps the Rothschild house in Vienna was the only one to keep its former position.[15]

The first real banks to grant short-term commercial credit were established in the 1840s and 1850s in the most important trade centers—Pesti Magyar Kereskedelmi Bank (The Hungarian Commercial Bank of Pest), 1841; Niederösterreichische Escompte-Gesellschaft, Vienna, 1853; Banca Commerciale Triestina, 1859. They were *commercial banks* in the narrow sense, considering the discounting of bills as their main function. At first they had no part in promotions. By the turn of the century, however, they too became universal banks.

The first *mortgage banks* granting long-term agricultural credit opened in 1841. The Galizische Landstandische Credit-Anstalt followed the pattern of the Prussian *Landschaften*. From 1856 the Austrian National Bank also granted mortgage loans—an unprecedented practice in Europe. The Magyar Földhitelintézet (Hungarian Landcredit Bank), founded in 1863, also followed the model of the *Landschaften* to meet the needs of the big Hungarian landowners. Mortgage loans were of special importance also at the savings banks. The novelty of the 1860s, however, was the corporate "immobile" bank following the French example. The first and most powerful was the Allgemeine Österreichische Boden-Credit-Anstalt, authorized in 1863, followed by Magyar Jelzáloghitelbank (Hungarian Mortgage Credit Bank) in 1869. The Boden Credit-Anstalt was interested not only in mortgage transactions but dealt also in the issue of securities and after the turn of the century also took part in current business transactions.[16]

The really original mortgage banks of the Dual Monarchy were the provincial banks (*Landesbanken*). The first one was established in Prague in 1865 (Hypotheken-bank des Königreiches Böhmen), and fourteen additional ones were founded before the Great War. They were peculiar in having no proper capital and in having the government of the Land (province) guarantee their loans.[17]

The true carriers of the revolution of the banking system in the nineteenth century were the *mobilier banks*, which followed the pattern of the French Crédit Mobilier of the Pereire brothers. Their main business was issuing securities, and for this purpose they absorbed both short- and long-term financial credits from very different resources. The first *mobilier* bank of the Monarchy, the K.K. priv. Österreichische Credit-Anstalt für Handel und Gewerbe, was founded in 1855. Its business practice showed clearly that the old *haute finance* had abandoned the orthodox methods of private bankers.[18] Before the Compromise it had five branches, in Pest, Prague, Lemberg, Brünn, and Trieste,[19] but these were only involved in supplying short-term loans. In 1867 the Credit-Anstalt founded the Magyar Általános Hitelbank (General Hungarian Credit Bank) in Pest, which in 1871 incorporated the Pest branch of the parent company in Vienna. More exactly, they were jointly operated; that is, the Credit Bank got the $3 million forint capital of the former branch and in turn had to return 40 percent of the profit. This unilateral dependence did not cease until the turn of the century. The relation between them continued to be "cordial and friendly" even thereafter.[20]

A number of banks were established subsequently: The Anglo-Austrian Bank in 1863, which founded its first branch in Lemberg; the Anglo-Hungarian Bank, established in 1868 with its help, didn't survive the crisis of 1873 and had to be liquidated.[21] The parent company then opened a branch in Budapest and one in Prague in 1880.

The Živnostenská Banka pro Čechy a Moravu v Praze, established in 1868, had a dual function. On the one hand, it acted as a middleman channeling central bank discount credit toward the Bohemian savings banks. On the other hand, it issued securities like a *mobilier* bank. With a more effective realization of the latter objective in view, an independent institution, the Všeobecná Česká Banka, was founded in 1869.[22]

In 1869 the Boden-Credit-Anstalt created the Wiener Bankverein as a *mobilier* bank, and in 1870 the Unionbank came into being through the union of four minor banks in Vienna. The great banks of Vienna—to which the Österreichische Länderbank was added in 1880—had been founded as universal banks, and their efforts to extend their influence to the whole of the Monarchy through the establishment of branches and contractual obligations soon became obvious. The Bohemian and Hungarian banks followed the same path, trying to integrate their hinterlands as independent units into the multinational capital market of the empire. The difference still existed before the war, however: the starting capital of 80 million crowns of the Hitelbank or of the Živnobanká was far less than the 130 million of the Wiener Bankverein or of the Länderbank—not to mention the 150 million share capital of the Credit-Anstalt.

Finally, we should mention the *credit cooperatives*. Two types became significant in the second half of the nineteenth century. Both originated in Germany. The Schultz-Delitsche type cooperative served the needs of urban craftsmen, received deposits, engaged mainly in discount business, and promised high dividends to the members. The Raiffeisen cooperatives turned toward the rural communities. They didn't pay dividends but created social and cultural funds and supplied longer-term loans against bonds. The first cooperative of the urban type came into being in Klagenfurt, while in the same year the Saxons founded the Beszterczei takarek-és kisegitö egylet (Savings and Loan Association of Besztercze) in Transylvania. Owing to the depression in agriculture the Raiffeisen cooperatives sprang up like mushrooms from the middle of the 1880s onwards.

The assets grouped by the types of banking institutions show that after the crisis in 1873 the growth of joint stock banks was broken and the climax of the *Gründerzeit* would be reached again only in the early 1890s (Table 14–3). The savings banks were less retarded by the crisis and so they could play a leading role in lending, which they lost only in the first years of the twentieth century (1904–1912), in the second *Gründerzeit*.[23]

Beginning with the 1880s the importance of the mortgage banks and credit cooperatives also increased. The "second credit sector"—as März and Socher call these institutions—can't be considered as secondary, since they played a decisive role in financing agriculture, home building, and the local infrastructure.[24] After 1873 the general public and the banks were reluctant to take the risk of industrial investment, so the credit sectors organized mostly on a local basis could get ahead, which usually brought about the allocation of funds within a given region. As a matter of fact, the institutions themselves were arranged in a national framework within the multinational monarchy. Here we can mention the repeated but unsuccessful efforts to establish an independent Hungarian issuing bank. But only the "central" bank-creating activity of the savings banks brought results. In July 1901 the joint foundation of the German savings banks of Bohemia and their Austrian partners came into being: the Centralbank

TABLE 14–3. Total Assets of Financial Institutions (in millions of crowns)

	1873	1883	1893	1903	1913
Austro-Hungarian Bank	1,111.26[a]	1,186.26	1,531.04	2,523.04	3,344.59
Joint-stock banks					
Cisleithania	2,233.96	1,712.43	2,323.30	3,794.90	9,766.30
Transleithania	263.42	184.41	886.26	1,929.20	12,112.02[b]
Savings banks					
Cisleithania	1,030.000	1,894.90	3,242.40	4,813.30	7,092.90
Transleithania	375.26	401.92	1,499.80	2,643.90	— [b]
Postal savings banks					
Cisleithania	—	8.20	166.20	450.60	590.40
Transleithania	—	—	33.16	118.70	270.30
Mortgage companies					
Cisleithania	170.47	390.37	798.01	2,020.20	3,592.70
Transleithania	125.68	138.18	651.36	1,299.80	937.60[b]
Credit cooperatives					
Cisleithania	29.74[c]	452.05	839.06	1,822.26	3,880.24
Transleithania	39.74	39.43	168.54	443.67	816.53

Sources: For Cisleithania: D. F. Good, "Stagnation and Take-off in Austria, 1873–1913," *Economic History Review,* 27 (February 1974), Appendix 1. For Transleithania: Hungarian Statistical Yearbook.

[a]Osterreichische Nationalbank.

[b]After 1910 the Hungarian statistical sources published jointly the joint-stock banks (including joint-stock mortgage companies) and savings banks.

[c]This estimate is "clearly wrong," according to Komlos (1983, p. 247).

der deutschen Sparcasse, which was followed by a parallel Bohemian institution, the Ustredny Banka Ceskych Sporitelen (the so-called Sporobanca) in May 1903.[25] By that time the banks themselves had tried to get closer to the depositors; the concentration of banking capital went along with the decentralization of the institution. Whereas in 1896 the ten large banks of Vienna had thirty-four domestic branches, by 1905 they had ninety-two. In consequence the competition sharpened not only between the banks of the nationalities but also between the commercial banks and the savings banks. In 1913 the Sporobanka had branches in Vienna, Lvov, Krakow, Czernovitz, and Budapest, in addition to that in Brünn.[26]

Within the banking system of Austria-Hungary, international influence can be found not only in the case of the joint-stock banks but also the mortgage banks and the private banking houses, which, unfortunately, are not represented in Table 14–3. The latter made Vienna emerge as one of the international financial centers in the Vormärz era. The Austrian state debt made the stock exchange in Vienna, established in 1771, a site for the lending activities of the cosmopolitan dynasties of bankers.[27] The hierarchic dependence between the cosmopolitan and domestic influence can be best shown by David Landes' pattern:

"such a team might consist of a nucleus of two or three correspondents in different major markets . . . to all of which, either singly or collectively, were attached outside houses in other commercial centers. These outside firms would in turn work with their own regional networks of foreign and domestic bankers, who generally dealt with the great cosmopolitan houses only at second hand. . . . The solidity of the units in such a multiple network usually varied inversely with their distance from the center."[28]

So it is not by chance that—according to a survey of financial assets made in the 1870s—the most eastern of the Rothschild houses had the least capital and that Sina and Wodiáner of Vienna, who were in close business relations with the Rothschilds, were interested especially in the domestic accumulation of capital.[29] That's why Vienna was considered to be an international center of the money market—though only a secondary one. That was what Budapest and Prague would have liked to become.

Such aspirations manifested themselves at the first general meeting of the Anglo-Hungarian Bank in 1869:

> our main objective is to gain full independence and self-reliance as soon as possible so that we shall not always be the free ball of the money world of Vienna, and by spreading our attention to the best known money markets of our globe and with the help of our relations to be able to carry out not only in name but also in practice the role of an international bank.

The Anglo-Hungarian Bank failed to realize its ambitions, and in spite of the growing importance of the stock exchange of Budapest, at the turn of the century the general director of the Hungarian Commerce Bank of Pest—who himself greatly contributed to the internationalization of the Budapest bourse—could still declare his banker's *ars poetica* only in the conditional:

> emancipating the significant interests of the money market of the country from one-sided support and looking to international relations instead, our capital as the center of the Hungarian money market should participate in the organic systems of the universal European money centers."[30]

The Bohemian banks had even greater ambitions and they could have been more successful than the banks in Pest. Still, the director of the Živnobanka had to confess in 1919:

> Until this time all of our banks—including the Živnostekska banka—have been banks of local significance. Direct relations abroad were and still are relatively small and the road to the rest of the world lies through Vienna and primarily through Berlin."[31]

Austro-Hungarian Banks in the System of International Financial Relations

As we have seen, the credit institutions of the Monarchy were established along French and German patterns. In the case of the Prussian *Landschaften* and credit cooperatives there was a direct imitation, while the savings banks—at least in Austria—combined

German and English or French patterns. In the case of joint-stock banks the mechanism of imitation was far more complicated and indirect. At the same time the existence of such original institutional types as the *Landesbanken* beyond the River Leitha or the Austro-Hungarian Bank reorganized on a dualistic basis, as a binational bank, show that the Danubian Habsburg Monarchy had a peculiar financial climate. The adjustment to this climate is shown through institutional types (the *crédit mobilier*, the *crédit foncier*, and the foreign banks), while paying special attention to the foreign participation in the ownership and management of the banks.

Even the French archetype of the Crédit Mobilier and the Pereire brothers' plan of building a European system of banks tempted the Monarchy to follow them. Isaac Pereire openly declared the basic principles:

The gathering in great centers of the available capital now dispersed and possibly buried throughout the various countries of Europe; the direct application of this capital to the most useful, consequently the most profitable, employments; . . . the union which will exist among the principal European centers of credit will necessarily result in an augmentation of the amount and above all in the useful efforts of the available capital."[32]

This declaration meant an open challenge to the hegemony of the Rothschilds, which had already been shaken by the purchase of the Austrian State Railway Company by the Crédit Mobilier. The Credit-Anstalt, established in the end of 1855, brought about the Rothschilds' victory over the Pereires in Austria. In their application to the Ministry of Finance the founders guaranteed the subscription of the capital of 60 million florins, 40 percent of which was taken by the Rothschild houses in Vienna, Frankfurt, and Paris; 50 percent went to Austrian and Bohemian aristocrats (but including Louis von Haber from Baden); and 10 percent to Leopold Lämel, a private banker of Prague.[33] The occurrence of Haber's name is reminiscent of the joint foundation of the Pereires and Haber, the Bank für Handel und Industrie in Darmstadt (1853), as one of the prototypes of the Credit-Anstalt.[34] As for the statutes, those of the Crédit Mobilier and the Darmstädter served as examples. The differences can be seen at once, however.

The French ambassador in Vienna correctly noticed the differences as between the institution of Vienna and that of Paris, namely, that the Credit-Anstalt according to the founders' statement of intention could only undertake Austrian transactions, and that a representative of the state had a seat in the governing body.[35] Representatives of the Hungarian aristocracy also had seats in the first committee of the management. In this way the Credit-Anstalt wished to be an institution representing the Monarchy. As Anselm Rothschild wrote to his uncle James in Paris: "The institution must have as much national character as the national debt."[36] The final distribution of shares is not known exactly. One-quarter of the shares (15 million florins) was put up for public subscription, but the amount subscribed came to 644.5 million florins, so the subscribed sums had to be reduced.[37] After the reduction the subscribers of Paris got 3 million florins.[38] Thus 20 percent of the shares available for public subscription went into French hands, 5 percent of the total capital. In this way the Credit-Anstalt revealed its "national" character—of course, in the state-patriotic sense of the word, so that neither the dynasty (which also obtained shares), nor the aristocracy, nor the Jews of Vienna were excluded. The fact that the Pereire brothers' plan of international filials could not be realized was not by chance. From time to time the "national" interpretation in Vienna was a burden even for the Rothschilds of Paris: ". . . the Viennese House is in such close relationship with the Credit-Anstalt that they always proceed jointly."[39] On the eve of World War I not more than 3.9 percent of the capital of 150 million crowns of the Credit-Anstalt was in foreign hands,[40] so the clue to the international relations of the bank can be found not in the direct foreign share but in the close links with the Rothschilds of Vienna and the partnership with the large German banks.

The Crédit Foncier became part of the Monarchy's financial structure in a radically different way. Among the founders we can find big Austrian landowners and bankers as well as financiers from Paris. At the foundation of the Boden-Credit-Anstalt a number of familiar names appear: besides Louis von Haber, Samuel Haber, who was living in Paris at that time, and the Bohemian aristocrat Count Chotek, who had assisted also in the foundation of the Credit-Anstalt. A banker named Sina of Greek origin, who was known to have good French contacts, also appears. On the French side Isaac Pereire represented the Crédit Mobilier, while Louis Frémy and Baron de Soubeyran came from the Crédit Foncier de France, where they were governor and deputy governor, respectively.[41]

A truer imitation of the French prototype was due not only to the more liberal atmosphere of the 1860s but also to the fact that the prototype itself bore strong marks of state intervention.[42] As the French journal *L'Industrie* observed, the initial success of the Boden–Credit-Anstalt was due to the fact that "it has profited from all the experiences of its model; but it is proper to add that it has borrowed along with its traditions its most eminent directors."[43] As compared to the Credit-Anstalt, there was a significant difference in that the capital was stated in silver gulden (or in francs), and, according to the Austrian custom, 30 percent had to be paid upon the start. The entries of bookkeeping profits and losses were given in gold gulden in consideration of the significant proportion of the capital owned in France, however.[44] The proportion of shares held abroad was still about 45 percent at the beginning of the twentieth century, but by the outbreak of World War I it had fallen to 17.8 percent.[45] The close French links of the institution also changed, but this meant no more than selling its mortgage bonds in Western Europe through the Banque de Paris et des Pays-Bas instead of the Crédit Foncier in the late 1870s.[46] Within the Monarchy it was involved in state loan transactions as a member of the Rothschild consortium from 1886 on. We must say that this double dependence was characteristic in itself.

"The English foreign banks followed the pattern of English deposit banks in having only little share capital paid at the foundation; consequently they differed significantly from the institutions founded after the French pattern, which had a high capital of their own already at the beginning," wrote Carl Morawitz, president of the Anglo-Austrian Bank, retrospectively.[47] The first steps of the Anglo-Austrian Bank were directed toward current business, but from the beginning the bank had to adopt itself to its environment in the empire, and the typical continental *mobilier* bank strategy seemed to be the solution.[48] One of the founders, the head of Glyn, Mills and Co. in London, claimed that "the Government would so far encourage the creation of the Bank by giving it business and position, . . . " and that "satisfactory arrangement can be made for the local management of the Bank by means of existing banking interests [such as Sina's] being merged in the new Institution."[49] They didn't succeed in winning Sina: Instead of him another private banker of Vienna was incorporated into the international institution. The directorate was divided into two halves—one committee in Vienna and one in London. From the beginning, there was a separate office in London, whose appointed manager had "special experience of German financial and commercial business."[50] It should be mentioned that the bank wasn't chartered in England until 1921.

To meet international demands the capital was stated in both pounds sterling and silver gulden. At the start, however, there was no crowd of would-be shareholders as at the foundation of the Credit-Anstalt. George Glyn cooperated with other continental banking houses: In Berlin Mendelssohn received 1,500 shares; in Paris, Mallet frères received 1,000. But the majority of subscribers came from London and Vienna.[51] Up to 1872 the bank used the silver standard in its transactions but later on, owing to the falling price of silver, the share capital had to be converted into gulden of Austrian value. The same procedure was followed by the Anglo-Hungarian Bank in the same year. Revealing the motives, the president of the bank stated: "Up to now the conversion didn't seem timely and was hindered by the circumstance that as many shares were owned in England we had to pay attention to the interests of the shareholders there as well as to the international character of the bank in general."[52]

After 1873, however, the Anglo-Austrian Bank was transformed more and more into an Austrian institution. The first sign of it was that in the *Compasses* (official publication) the order of publication of the committees in London and Vienna changed, and the Austrian directors had more and more influence in management. In any case, it is a fact that on the eve of the Great War only three percent of the shares were in foreign hands.[53]

The above patterns of acclimatization had a decisive effect upon the international financial relations of the Austro-Hungarian banking system. Upon establishment all the *mobilier* banks of the Monarchy followed the statues of the Credit-Anstalt and those of the Hungarian General Credit Bank (established by the Credit-Anstalt), which the Ministry of Finance considered to be the standard. In order to enlarge its sphere of influence the Boden-Credit-Anstalt founded the Wiener Bankverein in 1869 and placed three of its directors on the board of the latter. Besides establishing the Anglo-Hungarian Bank, the Anglo-Austrian—in cooperation with the Credit-Anstalt—founded the Austro-Ägyptische Bank in 1869. This is an example of the occasional cooperation between former rivals beyond the frontiers.

In the years of the *Gründerzeit* a great number of quasi-international banks were also established—obviously with a purely speculative objective in view. For some of the establishments the Erlanger house was responsible. This private bank had headquarters in Frankfurt and agencies in Vienna and Paris at the time.[54] In 1869 it founded two institutions simultaneously: the Franco-Österreichische Bank in Vienna and the Franco-Hungarian Bank in Pest. These banks had practically nothing to do with France. (Fréderic-Emile, the second son of the Erlanger family, moved from Paris to London in 1870). An example of the expansion of the "Franco" banks in the Balkans was the Prva Srpska Banka (First Serbian Bank) in Belgrade, created in 1869 by the Franco-Hungarian Bank in collaboration with Belgrade merchants. A common feature of these institutions was that they issued bonds of railway and industrial companies; all of them were forced into liquidation during the crash of 1873.[55]

After the depression of the 1870s a new boom came in the 1880s, but without the radical change of the paradigms created in the 1860s. We have already mentioned the change of the Boden-Credit-Anstalt in connection with the Paribas. In the early 1880s the Wiener Bankverein raised its capital from 8 million to 25 million gulden with the help of the Deutsche Bank and the Crédit Lyonnais.[56] At the beginning of the century 30 percent, but on the eve of the war only 18 percent, of the shares of the bank were in foreign (mainly German) hands.[57] In spite of the obvious fall in the participation of foreign shareholders, the Bankverein still was one of the institutions—like the Boden-Credit-Anstalt—of more pronounced international character.

The most significant novelty, however, was the establishment of the Union Générale of the Frenchman Eugène Bontoux in Austria-Hungary. As we have seen when analyzing the 1860s, the power relations in the Monarchy could not be substantially changed without the approval or against the will of the state. The Minister of Finance, Dunajewski, enclosed a favorable opinion on Bontoux's proposal before delivering it to the Emperor. The concessionaires of the Länderbank wanted "the bank to carry the outer signs of the patronage of the imperial government" and the Minister of Finance didn't object. "In its own best interest the Austrian fiscal administration was firmly resolved to let the new bank take care of several state financial transactions in order to prevent the newly gained capital from flowing abroad again, on the one hand, and to keep the new institution on the path of sound development on the other."[58] With the help of the Austrian Länderbank (whose directorate was hallmarked with decorative names of French aristocrats) the Magyar Országos Bank (Hungarian Länderbank) was established in Budapest; it was even advertised as the Banque Nationale Hongroise until the Hungarian government protested.[59] The capital of the Pesti Magyar Kereskedelmi Bank (Hungarian Commercial Bank of Pest) was also increased and the "new" banking style was introduced.

The bankruptcy of the Union Générale in 1882 brought about a severe crisis in the financial markets of the Monarchy. The Hungarian Länderbank went bankrupt, too, but the Austrian Länderbank survived and even emerged as an international institution. It was obviously due to the fact that up to 1889 its capital had had to be paid in gold (or in francs). The conversion into Austrian value was performed only later. The Länderbank founded a branch in Paris in 1890 and another in London in 1903; it also obtained a majority of shares in a Frankfurt bank in 1911. It was one of the institutions pursuing effective policies in the Balkans. In 1881 it opened the Banque de Crédit Serbe (Srpska Kreditna Banka) in cooperation with the Comptoir d'Escompte de Paris,[60] and later, in 1911, the Živnostekska of Prague also got involved. The Länderbank, however, preserved a majority interest.

In 1888—together with French and local interests—the Länderbank founded the Banque de Salonique. During the Balkan wars, however, it gradually withdrew its capital.[61] In 1904 it transformed its *commandite* in Bucharest into a corporation named Banque Roumaine de Crédit.[62] The internationality of the Länderbank was due to the above but also to the fact that 31.4 percent of its capital was still in foreign hands on the eve of the Great War.[63]

After the transition to the "new" banking style the Hungarian Commercial Bank of Pest also turned its attention toward the Balkans. As early as 1883 it sent representatives to Belgrade and Bucharest to collect information. Closer business connections were established in the late 1880s. At the end of 1888 it took a portion of the Banque Andrejević et Cie in Belgrade; then on 1 January 1890 it participated in Marmorosch,

Blank et Cie in Bucharest. The Bank of Darmstadt was also interested in this fast-developing banking house. At the beginning of 1905 it was transformed into a joint-stock company in which the Paribas also joined in 1906. In 1906 the Banque de Commerce et de Depots in Salonika was founded with the assistance of the Bucharest bank but later, after the Balkan wars, when Salonika came under Greek protection, the Commercial Bank withdrew.[64] The Andrejević Bank, which was much smaller, followed a different path. At the time of the Serbian tariff war and the annexation of Bosnia it suspended its business activity, calling forth countermoves by the Serbian bank of issue, the Narodna Banka. When in 1909 the Commercial Bank—with the assistance of the Berliner Handels-gesellschaft—transfornmed the Andrejević Bank into a joint-stock company it could hardly increase its significance.[65] In Bulgaria the Commercial Bank founded the first corporation in 1898, and later, in 1906, collaborating with the Paribas, it transformed this corporation into another bank named Banque Générale de Bulgarie. Together with the Berliner Handelsgesellschaft and the Banque Internationale de Bruxelles, the above mentioned institutions were also involved in the foundation of the Banque Générale Hypothécaire du Royaume de Bulgarie in 1911.[66]

We can see that in the influx of capital to the Balkans, French and German banks cooperated with the Commercial Bank. In the case of Marmorosch, Blank et Cie of Bucharest we can follow the trend of participation through a longer period of time (Table 14–4).

The percentage distribution of the capital shows that in the time of the *commandite* (1890–1904), when the international security market did not yet play a role in providing the bank with capital, the number-one foreign creditor of Marmorosch, Blank et Cie was the Commercial Bank. The share of German and French banks grew when the bank was transformed into a joint-stock company and, subsequently, when the capital was increased. By 1912 German capital had gained a dominant participation

TABLE 14–4. Changes in the Distribution of Capital: Bank Marmorosch, Blank et Cie

	1848	1874	1890	1898	1905	1906[a]	1912[a]
Capital (1,000 lei)	30	172	2,500	5,000	8,000	10,000	15,000
			(percent of total capital)				
J. Marmorosch	100 }			19 }		—	—
	} 100	40		} 45			
M. Blank	}			19 }		10.5	10.5
Hungarian Commercial Bank of Pest			40	38	25	35	28
Darmstädter Bank			20	24	15	20	35
Berliner Handelsgesellschaft					15	11.5	11.5
Paribas						23	15
Form of the enterprise	Private		*commandite*		Joint-stock company		

Source: For 1848 and 1874, *Bank Marmorosch, Blank und Co. AG., 1848–1923*, p. 60; for 1890–1912, HNA Z34.
[a]Participation in syndicate for issuing new shares.

TABLE 14–5. Branches and Affiliated Banks in the Balkan States

	Branches	Affiliated Banks
Constantinople	2	—
Smyrna	2	—
Bucharest	—	4
Salonika	1	2
Belgrade	1	3
Sofia	—	2

Source: Nagy Magyar Compass, 1915/16, Budapest, 1916.

(46.5 percent). The Commercial Bank continued to have a decisive influence in management, however, in spite of the increase of the participation in the capital of other foreign interests. In addition to possessing two seats in the directorate it had also a letter from director-general M. Blank "promising to discuss all transactions of major importance with director Weiss in advance."

Branches of Austrian or Hungarian banks predominanted on the territory of the former Turkish empire (the branch of the Prazska Uverni Banka in Belgrade must be considered as an exception), but the Balkan states, as they gained independence, preferred to have separate banks founded with foreign participation. This was also preferred by the banks, whose primary functions were financing state loans and foreign trade. (See Table 14–5.)

Banks and International Investment

With the exception of the period between 1903 and 1908, the Dual Monarchy generally had an export surplus of securities—i.e., it was a net importer of long-term capital. We have no comprehensive data representing the trend of the circulation of securities for the whole era, but from 1892 on we can form a more exact notion.[67] Judging by the state loans floated between 1867 and 1914, the sources of capital imports into the Monarchy shifted, too. While in 1868 the majority of loans was taken by Amsterdam, Brussels, Frankfurt, and Paris, Berlin seemed to be the number-one foreign creditor on the eve of the Great War. The transfer of the most important foreign capital resources into Central Europe corresponded to the normal course of events and the expectations of the international money market. In 1869 the Economist, commenting on British investment in Austria, observed that "when a country was prosperous and when domestic confidence was established, the securities of that country would find their way home, or to be held in the neighbourhood."[68]

Government securities and railway priority bonds constituted the largest categories. Table 14–6 shows the distribution of government securities for various years. Table 14–6 is only a rough estimate, as our data don't come from homogeneous sources. The list prepared for the Compromise settlement in 1867 may have indicated a smaller volume of foreign holdings than was actually the case before 1868—i.e., before the panic following the announcement of conversion.[69] The parallel Hungarian data, however, represent the distribution of the subscribed part of an unsuccessful

TABLE 14–6. Austro-Hungarian State Securities Held
Outside the Customs Union (in millions of crowns)

	1868ᵃ	1890	1903	1913
	(percentage share in parentheses)			
Austrian total	6,959	4,404ᵇ	9,095	11,252
Abroad	2,016	2,368	2,423	2,778
	(33.3)	(53.8)	(26.6)	(24.7)
Hungarian total	62	3,244	5,029	5,817
Abroad	40	1,364	2,069	2,273
	(64.5)	(42.1)	(41.4)	(39)

Source: For 1903 and 1913, Bartsch, *Statistische Daten,* p. 22.
ᵃAustria: joint state debt only [Mulinen]. Hungary: February 1868. Results
of subscription to the first state loan [HNA].
ᵇ4 percent gold rente (1889/90) (*A valutaugyre vonatkozo statisztikai
adatok.* Budapest, 1891, 84–88).
4.2 percent paper rente (1879–1889).
4.2 percent silver rente (1879–1889).

issue. At the same time they reflect the idea of the Minister of Finance, who thought it possible to go directly to the Paris market, avoiding Vienna. (Perhaps Vienna could have been avoided, but it would have been hardly possible to elude the Rothschilds, as our story also says.) As for 1890, only the distribution of some Austrian state bonds was available. We think, however, that it may reflect the distribution of state debts between domestic and foreign creditors, and the trends of the 1880s can be summarized too.

Our data show that in the second half of the 1870s the fast-growing debt of the hereditary provinces was placed mainly abroad, and the proportion of it was much higher than that of the Hungarian state debt issued at the same time.[70] Partly owing to the nationalization of the railways, more than half of the Hungarian bonds were possessed by the Cisleithanian parts of the empire.[71] Since after 1873 the Viennese banks were especially interested in fixed interest-bearing government securities we can say that these banks could use their capital—preserved through the foreign placement of Austrian bonds—to finance to a greater degree the deficit of the Hungarian Treasury. After the stabilization of currency and the conversion of debts the importance of native capital was growing as domestic accumulation increased. The role of domestic resources in the Monarchy's finances was more or less constant after the turn of the century. This meant that about three-fourths of the total debt in the case of the joint state debts and those of the hereditary provinces, and about three-fifths in the case of the "customs inland" shares of Hungary. Within the latter more and more Hungarian government securities remained actually in Hungary or were repatriated (36 percent in 1912).[72] As we have already mentioned, Germany became the number-one foreign creditor for both halves of the empire.

In terms of state debts the Monarchy seems to have been a debtor toward Western and Central Europe, while at the same time it acted as a creditor—in most cases joining German capital—toward the Balkans (Table 14–7).

The combined German and Austro-Hungarian figures conceal the fact that in Serbia and Rumania the banks of the Monarchy were insignificant as compared to

TABLE 14–7. Sources of Long-Term Loans to
Three Balkan States, 1867–1912

	Serbia (%)	Rumania (%)	Bulgaria (%)
France	79	32	45
Germany			
Austria-Hungary	} 21	} 52	} 39
Domestic		11	—
Other	—	5	16

Source: J. R. Lampe and M. R. Jackson, *Balkan Economic History, 1550–1950* (Indiana University Press, 1982), p. 231.

French and German banks, and only in the case of Bulgarian state loans were they of some importance. Before World War I more than one-fourth of the Bulgarian bonds were possessed by Austro-Hungarian rentiers.[73] After 1878 most of the debts of the Balkan states financed railway construction. As Lampe and Jackson note: "The loans served not so much to introduce direct European influence as to push Balkan state budgets into permanent reliance on further loans in order to continue the rapid growth in state expenses."[74]

While lending for the infrastructural development of backward countries, the Monarchy built its own railways system with the help of foreign capital. After 1855, when the Austrian railways were sold to private enterprise and the system of guaranteed interest was introduced, foreign capital enjoyed many opportunities to penetrate the economy of the empire. Behind the railways there stood the financing *mobilier* banks that supplied the needed capital. The ambitious railway construction plan of the Hungarian government fit into this climate. As the Minister of Transport stated, the Hungarian railway system "would connect Pontus with the Adriatic on the one hand, and with the Northern and Eastern seas bordering the North-German fatherland on the other, and would fix the center of these major lines of transportation in our native land."[75] One of those "major lines," however, the Hungarian Eastern Railway, caused an international scandal and at the same time it placed Hungary's public finances (and state credit) in an awkward situation.

In the summer of 1873 the state-guaranteed coupons of this still unfinished railway, due in July, couldn't be cashed either by the company or by the state. The majority of the shares were subscribed in France, in the German states, and in Vienna in 1869.[76] In the summer of 1873 rumors spread among the excited shareholders from Prague (through Vienna, Lemberg, Munich, and Frankfurt) to Amsterdam, and nearly the whole of Europe became suspicious of Hungarian railway construction and even of the Hungarian state, which didn't keep its word.[77] The Hungarian Eastern Railway, finished by the autumn of 1873 but operated at a deficit, found the solution (as Hungarian railways in general) in nationalization. In Hungary 85 percent of the railway system was owned and run by the state as early as 1891, while in Austria only 55 percent was run by the state, which owned only 43 percent in 1897.[78] In spite of this, more than 70 percent of the railway priority bonds of the hereditary provinces were still in the possession of foreign investors at the beginning of the twentieth century, and this proportion was still more than two thirds by the time of the Great War.[79]

The actual "foreign investment directly in industry" was small, only 12 percent of all industrial shares and only 0.5 percent of all Austrian securities at the beginning of the century.[80] Taking into consideration that, in Austro-Bohemian industry, family enterprises were still very important at the turn of the century, this proportion must have been even smaller with regard to the whole of industry. Austrian capital investments, which had contributed directly to the establishment of certain industrial branches in Hungary in the time of neo-absolutism, were gradually withdrawn from the beginning of the twentieth century. They had a decisive role solely in some modern branches of industry with a high demand for capital (machinery and chemicals). The capital exports of the Monarchy to the Balkans are not inaptly called "reluctant imperialism" in modern literature.[81] There may be two exceptions: The Bohemian banks, which began a strong industrial expansion after 1908, could hardly be called either imperialist or reluctant, and the Rumanian banks controlled by foreign interests (first of all Marmorosch, Blank et Cie).[82]

The cooperation of the banks promoting the international movement of capital brought about the establishment of international banking groups. Legally, these groups were built as consortia of independent banks, where the holding of one bank in the stock of the others was of minor importance.[83] One time cooperating banks might become rivals on another occasion, or former rivals might be forced to participate in the same consortium. Business coalitions did change, but the groups showed a surprising stability.

This was especially true for the Austro-Hungarian Monarchy where the struggle between international banking groups meant, in the field of government loans, nothing else than repeated attempts to break the monopoly of the Rothschild-Credit-Anstalt consortium. The birth of the Austrian Rothschild group was linked with the silver loan of 70 million gulden in 1864, in which the Diskonto-Gesellschaft of Berlin, the head of the participating German banks, took a one-third quota. The close cooperation between the Credit-Anstalt and the Diskonto-Gesellschaft in the field of Austrian state finances goes back to this date.[84] From 1873 on the same group monopolized Hungarian state credit, and it preserved its key position until the outbreak of war. Owing to this very continuity, the Hungarian loan business can serve as an example through which the changing composition of the Rothschild banking group can be shown (Table 14–8).

The gold rente contract concluded in December 1875 clearly shows the dominance of the Rothschild houses of Vienna, Paris, and Frankfurt. The share of private bankers (Wodianer and Bleichröder included) in the total sum was not more than 50 percent. By 1908 the nearly one-third participation by the Hungarian General Credit Bank brought about the main change.

In the consortium the proportion of private bankers fell back to 29 percent in spite of the fact that in 1900 Mendelssohn also entered. When Wodianer died in 1885, his business discontinued, and after Gerson von Bleichröder's death in February 1893 the participation of the private bankers of Berlin was also coming to its end.[85] The shares of the Rothschilds fell also, and their house in Frankfurt closed. Among the new members of the consortium there was the former rival, the Boden-Credit-Anstalt (since 1886), while the Diskonto-Gesellschaft was losing importance within the Hungarian consortium. We should add, however, that the actual share of the Hungarian Credit-bank was not more than 20 percent. The rest was given to subparticipating Hungarian banks.

TABLE 14–8. Participation in the Rothschild-Credit-Anstalt Consortium for
Hungarian State Loans

	1875	1908
	6 percent gold rente (%)	4 percent crown rente (%)
Credit-Anstalt	18	17.7
M. Wodianer	5	—
Vienna Rothschild		21.7
Paris Rothschild	40	
Frankfurt Rothschild		
Boden-Credit-Anstalt	—	12.073
Hungarian General Credit Bank	9	32.663
Disonto-Gesellschaft	19.5	7.123
S. Bleichröder	5	3.373
Darmstädter Bank	3.5	1.5
Mendelssohn & Co.	—	4.498

Source: R. A. L. XI/111/10; HNA.K51 MAH. 16. cs. 226.t.

The first attack against the Rothschild consortium began in the period between its gaining the 1864 Austrian and the 1873 Hungarian loans. The Hungarian government obtained a railway loan in 1868 from the Société Générale, and the silver loans in 1871 and 1872 from the consortium of the Erlanger houses. When granting the 54 million gulden loan in 1872 the Erlangers in Frankfurt, London, and Paris as well as the Franco-Österreichische and the Franco-Magyar banks took 19 percent each. The Austro-German Bank (Frankfurt) and the Franco-Austro-Hungarian Bank (Paris) were also their creations. The Anglo-Hungarian Bank and its group joined in with 30 percent.[86] The issue was carried out through R. Raphael and Sons in London in January 1873, but had a poor result.[87] Although the Erlanger group made another offer to the Hungarian government after 1873, the Hungarian Minister of Finance reported in confidence, "In no case would I contact the Erlangers again."[88]

A totally different challenge toward the Austrian hegemony of the Rothschilds emerged in 1877 when the group of the Wiener Bankverein gained the right to the second issue of bonds of 70 million gulden (the first one was handled by the Rothschild consortium). This group was known by that name only in Austria; two other Vienna banks belonged to the group, the Boden-Credit-Anstalt and the Anglobank. Of the foreign partners of the three Austrian banks the Deutsche Bank and the Banque de Paris et des Pays-Bas were the most important. [89] The association was thus based upon the cooperation of modern joint-stock banks, but their contacts were strengthened by "personal interpenetration." Between 1874 and 1901 Georg Siemens of the Deutsche Bank was also a director of the Wiener Bankverein.[90] The success in 1877 was only a temporary victory for this really modern international group in Austria, however. They may have had a fine future in the international arena, but the Rothschilds regained their hegemony in Austrian state loans; moreover, they were so powerful as to have been able to integrate the Boden-Credit-Anstalt in their own group in 1886.

The monopolistic position of the Rothschild group in the Monarchy could no longer be broken by just depriving them of privileges. From 1897 on, the Postsparcassa also participated in state loan transactions without joining the consortium. In the conversion of 1903 five Vienna banks participated under the leadership of the Wiener Bankverein (and of course its French and German partners), and they joined the consortium of the Rothschild group.[91] These steps can be considered as the outer signs of the rearrangement of the principles of the formation of banking groups in the Austro-Hungarian Monarchy. This was due not only to the fact that the banks of Prague, Budapest, and Vienna established independent, native banking groups by means of the branch system and contractual relationships, but also to the increase of capital.[92] The increased capital and possession of securities of domestic banking institutions made it possible to place the bulk of the state loans within the Monarchy. The Rothschild group, which showed adaptability when cosmopolitan dynasties of bankers were transformed into international banking groups, couldn't react effectively with the speed demanded in the new phases of development, not even through the Credit-Anstalt.

The "court revolution"—that is how Bernard Michel describes it—took place in 1910, when the Austrian Minister of Finance concluded a contract for the issue of certain bonds only with the Postsparcassa. The established group was joined by regional German, Bohemian, and Slovenian banks and the issue proved successful.[93] In 1911, after Albert von Rothschild's death, his son reorganized the group by uniting the former rivals: the Credit-Anstalt, the Wiener Bankverein, and the Länderbank. The new group—together with other banks in Pest and Vienna—continued issuing Hungarian state loans, but in the hereditary provinces its activities were confined to the control of industrial transactions.

We must mention that not only the role of the Rothschild-Credit-Anstalt consortium had changed in the state loan transactions of the Monarchy, but also the importance of state loans shifted among the branches of business in the banks of the Monarchy. The banks left out of the loans of the dual governments after 1873, when the trends of the market were favorable, turned toward the Balkan states. For example, the Länderbank was involved in the issue of a Serbian state loan of 40 million francs as early as 1884, as a member of a consortium headed by the Comptoir d'Escompte de Paris on the French side and by the Berliner Handelsgesellschaft, the Mendelssohn, Warschauer (Berlin), Bethmann, Erlanger (Frankfurt) and the Norddeutsche Bank (Hamburg) on the German side.[94] In 1889, however, it cooperated with the Dresdner Bank and Wiener Bankverein to issue a Bulgarian state loan of 30 million francs. In 1892 it joined a wider international group including the Paribas and the Deutsche Bank for a Bulgarian loan of 143 million francs.

After the turn of the century the Balkans became increasingly a battlefield for the foreign policy of the great powers. In these political rivalries the international banking groups could hardly remain outsiders.[95] Into the German-French rivalry the Austrian banks could only occasionally intervene (and only with English assistance, as in the case of the Bulgarian loan of December 1909). They had to be satisfied with being occasional subcontractors for smaller shares. They may have been somewhat compensated with the incomes from their industrial investments, increasing from the turn of the century on. The banking groups of the Monarchy not only founded industrial concerns of their own; they also established the Osterreichische Kontrolbank für Industrie und Handel as a joint undertaking of ten Cisleithanian banks (the Anglobank, the Boden-Credit-Anstalt, the Credit-Anstalt, the Depositenbank, the Länderbank, the Mercur, the Unionbank, the Verkehrsbank, the Wiener Bankverein, and the Živnostenska) in 1914. We are right in saying that the Kontrolbank meant the beginning of a new era, since its declared objectives were the management of syndicates as well as the control of cartels and trusts.[96]

Patterns of Short-Term and Long-Term Credit in International Industrial Finance

Certainly it is due to the institutionalist view of Central European banking history that the industrial financing practice of banks in the Austro-Hungarian Monarchy cannot be analyzed in its full range. It is especially valid for international relations, which cannot be illustrated but by some patterns. The discussion in the the following pages attempts to prove that the connection between the foreign capital stock and international borrowings of the banks was not linear.

The differences of the credit system within the Austro-Hungarian state emerge immediately if the composition of *short-term bank credit* is studied in the economically dominant regions of the Monarchy (Table 14–9). It is all the more worth considering since the equalization tendency of regional interest rates seems to have improved from the 1880s on.[97] At the beginning of the 1880s the dominant form of short-term credit was the bill of exchange even in Austria proper (43.4 percent), although its priority was quite minimal compared to other forms. The dominance is far stronger in the case of Bohemian-Moravian banks, whereas in Hungary the bill of exchange was of overwhelming importance (79.7 percent). The volume of bills of exchange at the end of the year may comprise differing turnovers during the year because of different dates of expiration, but that can only slightly modify the picture. That current accounts took the lead over bills of exchange in Austria in the 1880s and Bohemia in the 1890s, whereas in Hungary it did not take place until World War I, is closely related to the progress of industrialization. Due to the dynamism of Bohemian industrialization the short-term assets of Bohemian banks contained 63.2 percent current account credit in 1912, even greater than the Austrian banks.

In international payments the bill of exchange kept its priority even in the Austro-Hungarian Monarchy. Disregarding the active foreign-exchange policy dominated by certain monetary considerations of the Austro-Hungarian Bank after the introduction of the gold crown (1892),[98] it is obvious that international bill transactions depended primarily on foreign trade (flows of goods and securities).[99] The unfavorable foreign trade balance of the Monarchy mentioned above accompanied its role as a net capital importer. But the deficit arising from time to time caused tension in the turnover of foreign bills. For example, it was in vain that the Anglo-Hungarian Bank opened its London branch in 1871, since its turnover of foreign bills began to decrease in the very year because of the deficit in the Monarchy's foreign trade.[100] It was symptomatic that the deficit of the two Vienna banks operating branches in London (Anglo-Austrian Bank and Länderbank) reached £3.5 million before the outbreak of World War I. At the same time the Deutsche Bank London agency could report an active balance.[101] In the pre-war decade the Vienna banks operating branches in London could not match their German rivals in the acceptance business either, although London acceptance bills passed through Berlin to Vienna, Prague, and Budapest.[102] Before the Moroccan crisis

TABLE 14–9. Short-Term Bank Credits (in millions of Austrian crowns)

		Austria (%)		Bohemian Provinces (%)		Hungary (%)	
1880	a	569.4	(42.2)	36.7	(31.1)	46.0	(11.9)
	b	586.1	(43.2)	68.9	(58.3)	307.9	(79.7)
	c	195.3		12.5		32.4	
a + b + c		1,350.8		118.1		386.3	
1890	a	955.5	(51.3)	64.2	(47.2)	167.5	(20.2)
	b	632.9	(34.0)	64.8	(47.7)	609.6	(73.4)
	c	273.5		6.9		53.9	
a + b + c		1,861.9		135.9		831.0	
1900	a	1,608.0	(53.5)	230.7	(50.2)	620.7	(31.2)
	b	1,109.6	(36.8)	194.7	(42.4)	1,242.4	(62.4)
	c	300.6		33.8		128.3	
a + b + c		3,016.2		459.2		1,991.4	
1910	a	3,812.3	(55.3)	ND		1,648.9	(35.3)
	b	2,466.9	(35.8)	ND		2,748.7	(58.5)
	c	613.0		ND		273.0	
a + b + c		6,892.2		ND		4,670.6	
1912	a	5,065.0	(56.)	1,046.8	(63.2)	2,052.8	(36.7)
	b	3,089.1	(34.2)	476.7	(28.8)	3,229.0	(57.7)
	c	884.2		132.2		310.5	
a + b + c		9,038.3		1,655.7		5,592.3	

Source: Richard Rudolph, *Banking and Industrialization in Austria-Hungary* (Cambridge, Eng., 1976), pp. 81–82; for Hungary: Hungarian Statistical Yearbook.

a = current account debtors.

b = bills of exchange.

c = advances on goods and securities.

ND = No data.

in 1911, however, Belgian and especially French short- term credits played main roles in the Vienna and Budapest money market.[103]

As far as foreign current account credits are concerned, the development cannot be considered linear. To illustrate that let us examine the accounting of Marmorosch, Blank et Cie.[104] Referring back to Table 14–4, note that in 1890 the *commandite* stock of the Hungarian Commercial Bank and Darmstädter Bank represented 60 percent of the total capital, but their current account deposits decreased from 75 percent to 15 percent over the next thirteen years (Table 14–10). The crisis afflicting all of Central Europe played a part, but the dominant factor of this process was the dynamic accumulation of Rumanian home deposits. That is why it was necessary to involve other German and French banks in forming the joint-stock company in 1905, since among the debtors of the Bucharest Bank several industrial (sugar, timber, petroleum) firms represented increasing items, and the debits of domestic customers grew from 7 million to 12 million lei in the period.

In the immediate prewar years Bohemian banks got involved more intensively in financing the Balkan area. The Prazska Uverni Banka, for example, used its Belgrade

TABLE 14–10. Current Account Creditors of Marmorosch,
Blank et Cie (end of year, in 1,000s of leis)

	1890	1895	1900	1903
Current accounts of domestic creditors and depositors	1,669	4,249	5,064	7,995
Foreign creditors	5,140	5,871	2,250	1,395
TOTAL	6,809	10,120	7,314	9,390

Source: HNA Z 34 48-108-1266.

affiliate and its Sofia agency to establish Serbo-Bohemian and Bulgarian-Bohemian sugar refineries in 1911 and 1912, and also organized commercial offices for them.[105] In these countries the same bank also played an active part in importing agricultural machines and exporting plums.

By prolonging short-term credits the business became a long-term one. When Marmorosch Blank et Cie became a share company the Hungarian Commercial Bank loaned 3 million francs for ten years "under the old conditions," and beyond that a 1 million franc "temporary seasonal credit for the July–November period."[106] Obviously, the seasonal credit had to be renewed annually because of the peculiar credit demand of the agrarian countries in the late summer–early autumn period.

The extended borrowings of Balkan countries should not be considered as an isolated phenomenon. In the summer of 1873, when the Hungarian state was virtually insolvent, the Hungarian Finance Minister obtained a 5 million gulden credit for three months from the Credit-Anstalt (50 percent), S. M. Rothschild & Co. (20 percent), Sina, and Wodianer (15 percent each). But at its expiration the cooperation of Berlin was also needed. At this time a 4 million thaler advance was given to the Hungarian state by the Diskonto-Gesellschaft (50 percent), S. Bleichröder, and the Rothschild house of Frankfurt (25 percent each) for Treasury bonds to be issued subsequently. Finally, in December 1873, when the bonds were issued for £7.5 million, the cooperation of the London Rothschilds became necessary too.[107]

One can often distinguish short-term credits from the long-term international transactions only because statistical information is available for the latter. This statistical information, however, must be scrutinized carefully. The data on international capital flows do not give information on direct placement of securities. Take the example of the Hungarian 4 percent crown *rente* issued in 1893 for 1,062 million crowns of nominal value: The contractual part of the German banks in the Rothschild consortium amounted to 15.625 percent, but according to the first report of interest payments in 1895 only 8.71 percent of coupons were paid in Germany. By 1900, however, payments of coupons increased to 13.5 percent in Germany (approximating the contractual part) while in Austria the proportion of payments diminished. The sales of the Austrian banks between 1895 and 1900 were already represented in statistics of security flow. But the fact that the Austrian banks eventually "exported" the share originally contracted in Germany is hidden.[108]

The above-mentioned characteristics of international transactions emphasize the importance of the banks in contrast to the registrations of the stock exchange in the Austro-Hungarian Monarchy. In 1912 the share of foreign bonds in total registered securities was 48 percent on the London Stock Exchange, 55 percent in Paris, 5.6 percent in Berlin, and in Vienna it was 0.7 percent.[109] The registration of foreign bonds undoubtedly measures the international importance of different stock markets, but it was also determined by the rules and regulations of the stock exchanges in each country. In Vienna the share of foreign bonds had not altered much since the 1890s. At the beginning of the century, however, an important change took place in the actual international turnover. While in 1903 domestic securities dominated in the foreign commerce of bonds of the ten largest banks showing a significant import surplus, the flow of foreign bonds surpassed the international trade of domestic ones and itself contributed to the export surplus.[110] In the years before World War I (mainly after 1909) the Austro-Hungarian Monarchy was not merely a capital importer, but owing to the leading banking groups it could also cover the deficit partly by reexporting foreign bonds.

In the case of a country of such agricultural importance as the Austro-Hungarian Monarchy it is important to analyze the turnover of mortgage bonds. Studies of this, however, are almost completely lacking. One cannot detect agriculture through the prism of industrialization. The turn of the century, however, brought essential changes in this field too. Whereas, for example, at the beginning of the 1890s Holland owned the largest proportion of Hungarian bonds, at the turn of the century Germany became the leading creditor. By this time 90 percent of total mortgage bonds held abroad were in Germany, Holland, and Switzerland.[111] The importance of this fact from the point of view of Hungarian agriculture is a question that can be evaluated subject to two restrictions. On the one hand, the mortgage bonds held outside the Monarchy hardly reached one-third of the total turnover; on the other, credit on mortgages issued by credit institutes in Hungary amounted to only 38 percent of the total encumbered mortgages. Thus neither bank loans nor the foreign placement of mortgage bonds took a dominant role in providing Hungarian agriculture with credit.

While at the turn of the century the supply of agriculture with long-term credits seemed to have been settled, in the fields of transportation and industrial finance new forms could be observed. This was especially conspicuous in such international branches as railways and modern energy producers (petroleum and electricity). The emergence of international holding companies occurred all over Central Europe. One of the first companies of this type was called into being in 1890 when the Deutsche Bank and the Wiener Bankverein obtained the majority of bonds from Baron Hirsch in the Betriebsgesellschaft für Orientalische Eisenbahnen, which operated railways in the European part of Turkey. In the same year those banks together with the Schweizerische Kreditanstalt founded in Zurich the Bank für Orientalische Eisenbahnen especially for the purpose of owning and controlling bonds of Balkan and Anatolian railways. Albeit a bank in name, the company did not actually operate as a bank, since it did not have any creditors and debtors and even in 1910 it held 45,000 of the 88,000 bonds bought from Hirsch twenty years before.[112]

The Wiener Bankverein was one of the pioneers in bringing Rumanian petroleum production to the international market, partly by establishing a finance company in Budapest with the name of Magyar Ipar es Kereskedelmi Bank Rt. in 1890, partly by taking an interest in a Rumanian petroleum company in 1892. The Magyar Ipar es Kereskedelmi Bank Rt. established the Internationale Petroleumindustrie A.G. in 1895, which took over the Rumanian interest of Wiener Bankverein and organized a

Rumanian company to exploit the oil fields. The producing company Steaua Romana was founded in 1897 with the participation of the above-mentioned companies. Yet the bonds of the new enterprise were transferred to the Rumanian Oil Trust Ltd., a newly established finance company in London. So the financing of Steaua worked through multiple transfers.

The Magyar Ipar es Kereskedelmi Bank overreached itself, however. In 1901 the Internationale Petroleumindustrie A.G. and in 1903 the Magyar Ipar es Kereskedelmi Bank Rt. itself were forced into liquidation.[113] After 1903 the Deutsche Bank took the Steaua in hand and secured its finances. At the same time it concluded an alliance with Shell in Europe and unleashed a price war against Standard Oil.[114] In spite of this, the Wiener Bankverein retained an interest both in the Deutsche Petroleum-Aktien Gesellschaft, established to buy bonds, and in Petroleum Producte A.G., the petroleum sales agency of the banking group.[115]

Banking groups joined to finance the electrical industry from the beginning. The penetration of German capital has been widely discussed in the international literature since the turn of the century.[116] Thus, I only mention that 70 percent of the bonds of the Austrian Siemens-Schuckert Werke were in foreign hands, but significant Swedish and Swiss interests are also well known (Ericksson, Brown-Boveri). As an illustration, consider the financial practices of Ganz and Co.

Ganz together with the Wiener Bankverein brought about the Internationale Elektrizitats-Gesellschaft in Vienna in 1889, which can be considered a fairly early established financing company on the Continent, although its "internationalism" was limited to the Austro-Hungarian Monarchy only. To finance the Ganz enterprise the A.G. für Elektrische und Verkehrsunternehmungen was established in 1895 in Budapest. It was, according to the contemporary view, "the only considerable financing company in Austria-Hungary."[117] In its foundation the main role was taken by Gesellschaft für Elektrische Unternehmungen, established in 1894 by the Berlin Union group and the Magyar Altalános Hitelbank. Germany took 25 percent of the nominal value of its bonds while the Hitelbank kept one third of the bonds in its portfolio during World War I.[118] The company—which was referred to shortly as a trust—financed first of all the building and maintenance of Hungarian electric works through share companies established for that purpose in several towns.

But to contribute to building electric works beyond the border of the Austro-Hungarian Monarchy it was necessary to found new financing companies. The Hitelbank and Ganz together had a 45 percent share of the Societá per lo Sviluppo delle Imprese Elettriche in Italia, a financing company established in 1898 in Milan; the rest of the bonds were taken by the Berlin and Vienna UEG, the Wiener Bankverein, and the Banca Commerciale.[119]

Similar measures were taken by the Ganz Villamossági Rt., a joint stock company formed in 1906 from the electric department of the Ganz factory when gaining the concession to build the electric works of Constantinople in 1910. In 1911 the foundation of the Société Anonyme Ottomane d'Electricité was made in the frame of a syndicate organized by the Belgians, led by the Banque de Bruxelles and the Hitelbank. The construction of electric works was part of the undertaking to build up the modern public utility network of Constantinople managed by the "Constantinople Consortium" uniting German, French, Belgian, Hungarian, and Swiss banks and financing companies.[120] In 1913 in Bucharest Ganz also participated in the Société Anonyme Roumaine d'Electricité Ganz.

I mention only one characteristic example of the connection between international business and foreign policy before the war. When the Skoda Works, with the cooperation of Niederösterreichische Escompte-Gesellschaft and the Credit-Anstalt, intended to enlarge its share of Russian heavy industrial investment by raising the capital of the Nevsky Works and by credits given to the Putilov Works, the director of the Credit-Anstalt asked the advice of the Foreign Minister and the Minister of Defense. In the summer of 1913 the ministers stated that "there are no obstacles to the business on the part of the state administration."[121] I consider the behavior of both parties characteristic: that the director of the bank should ask the responsible ministers for advice before undertaking the business, and also that the latter would not wish to hinder the operation of the banks even on the territory of the *entente cordiale*. This mutual tolerance reflected the altered relationship of the bank and the state, which was expressed in the most authentic way by Eugen Lopuszanski, an official of the Austrian Finance Ministry before World War I: "The great mobilier banks nowadays represent a significant power factor in the state in every respect."[122]

Concluding Remarks

What roles did international factors play in the Austro-Hugnarian banking system?

First of all, it should be stressed that the banking system, like the Monarchy itself, was *multinational*. Owing to the dualistic state system the central bank became *binational* in 1878, and for similar reasons binational companies came about too. The international practices of banks must be viewed through these multinational and binational lenses. In close connection with that, foreign banks were founded as either quasi-international banks or they soon had to adapt to the conditions of the empire hosting them. The Austro-German coalitions that proved to be effectively lasting (Credit-Anstalt and Diskonto-Gesellschaft, Wiener Bankverein, and Deutsche Bank) were not so much international in the ethnic sense of the word: In this set-up, Vienna, we may say, had the role of the "little brother."

A similar Central European division of labor can be observed in the lending and loan mediating activity of the banks. When the Austrian state debts were unified and the common state debts were repatriated in the Monarchy, the Hungarian government bonds were repaid on the international money market. From the second half of the 1870s on, when Austrian government credit regained its respect abroad, the Vienna banks placed the Hungarian government loans increasingly in Cisleithania. In the 1890s, however, after stabilizing the proportion of government debts being placed abroad and at home, the Vienna banks began transactions on their own, with German and French background or through the mediation of Budapest to finance international industrial and traffic business in the Balkans. Hungarian banks tried to introduce a similar practice (with the involvement of German capital), and before World War I the Bohemian banks also founded some international Slavic enterprises of considerable means. In these transactions the *international mediator* role of the Monarchy's banks can be considered as characteristic. For all that, before World War I they lost their ability to finance the Balkans government loans.

Finally, I wish to reemphasize that throughout the dualistic era the share of international finance of the banks was relatively low when compared with the business affairs inside the customs border. The latter became effectively international, however, only after the Monarchy had fallen apart.

15

Foreign Capital in
the Italian Banking Sector

Peter Hertner

The development of the Italian banking sector in the years between the unification of Italy and the outbreak of World War I has been described by Jon Cohen in *Banking and Economic Development*,[1] by Antonio Confalonieri in his monumental contribution, *Banca e industria in Italia* (beginning in the 1880s),[2] and by the present author in a few essays published since 1978.[3] The following notes concentrate on the specific role of foreign investment in Italian banking between 1860 and 1914 and on the way these foreign investments may have contributed to Italian economic development.

The First Wave of International Investments in the Italian Banking Sector during the 1850s and 1860s

It was especially with the help of foreign capital that Piedmont tried to establish not only political but also economic leadership among the Italian states during the 1850s.[4] Of the state loans raised first by Piedmont and then by the newly unified Italian nation between 1849 and 1863, 47 percent were placed abroad, and of these not less than 89 percent had been underwritten by the House of Rothschild.[5] Part of this foreign capital went into the gradual buildup of infrastructure; as a result, 46 percent of Italian railways in 1859 (1,829 km altogether) had been constructed in the comparatively small and peripheral Kingdom of Piedmont-Sardinia.

Considering this massive inflow of capital from abroad, one should not be surprised to find a considerable degree of foreign direct investment in the banking sector, which slowly moved from traditional private banking houses to joint-stock companies precisely during the 1850s and 1860s. The first two attempts, undertaken in Piedmont before Italian unification, did not, however, prove to be successful. The Cassa del Commercio e dell'Industria, established at Turin in 1853, was transformed in 1856 into a Crédit Mobilier type of bank by the House of Rothschild, but some years later, at the beginning of the 1860s, the Rothschilds withdrew and the future of the bank was in doubt.[6] The same holds for the Credito Mobiliare Sardo, founded in 1856 and backed by a second-rate Parisian bank that did not even succeed in introducing its shares on the Paris Bourse. The Credito Mobiliare Sardo had to be liquidated in 1861.[7]

For the 1860s and 1870s one can agree in part with Bertrand Gille who concluded that "banking development was . . . very slow and due mainly to foreigners."[8] It certainly holds true for the Societá Generale di Credito Mobiliare Italiano, which originated in 1863 from the ruins of the Cassa del Commercio e dell'Industria, which had been taken over by the French Crédit Mobilier. By its statutes and its operational strategies the Credito Mobiliare Italiano followed closely the Paris Crédit Mobilier even when the French founders abandoned their Italian offspring at the end of the 1860s.[9] Also in 1863 the Banca di Credito Italiano was created by French and British investors guided by the Paris Crédit Industriel et Commercial, but the Banca di Credito Italiano never played an important role in Italian banking and was finally taken over by the Credito Mobiliare in 1892.[10]

At first sight things seemed to be quite different in the case of the Anglo-Italian Bank, established in 1864 in London with a nominal capital of no less than £1 million. As one of the "Anglo-Continental Banks" and backed by the International Financial Society, "one of the then best known Crédit Mobiliers in London,"[11] the Anglo-Italian Bank clearly profited from the liberalization of English commercial legislation begun in 1855, which "moved to being the most permissive code from one of the most stringent in Western Europe."[12] Unlike the Anglo-Austrian Bank, created shortly before by the same London group, the Anglo-Italian Bank never became active in the field of state or railway loans, not to speak of direct investment in industry, but concentrated its efforts in real estate speculation where it lost the major part of its capital within a few years.[13]

The same speculative activity was true of the Banca Italo-Germanica, founded in Florence in 1871 by two distinguished private banking firms of Frankfurt who shortly after were joined by some major German joint-stock banks, such as the Berliner Handelsgesellschaft, the Deutsche Bank, and the Mitteldeutsche Kreditbank. The Italo-Germanica was a typical fruit of the so-called *Gründerjahre*; it engaged heavily in real estate business, especially in the new capital of Rome, lost its entire capital in that sector, and had to be liquidated three years after its establishment. It had already been abandoned by its German founders within the first year of its existence.[14]

Another child of this hectic atmosphere was the Banca Generale, also created in 1871. The Wiener Bankverein subscribed one-quarter of its nominal capital of 30 million lire, but one decade afterwards it no longer figured among its shareholders. Officially the Banca Generale declared itself to be interested above all in short-term operations, but it nevertheless engaged an important part of its assets in 1871–72 in long-term investments that could be liquidated only with painful slowness during the following two decades. The same holds true for the Credito Mobiliare; in both cases the turnover of assets, so essential for a successful investment bank, was extremely slow.[15]

Summing up, one might say that during this first period, comprising the first two decades of Italian unification, the role of foreign investment in Italian banking was rather limited. At best it provided the initial impulse, abandoning the field shortly afterwards. The reasons might be found in the particular state of Italian economic development: Foreign investment in state and railway loans, particularly between the early 1850s and 1865, did not necessarily require the establishment of intermediaries in the country itself—and this quite apart from the absolutely dominant position of the Rothschilds. In general, direct investment in the industrial and commercial sectors did not promise interesting returns given the backward state of the Italian economy; it became still less attractive when the convertibility of the lira was suspended in 1866 (to be resumed only in 1881 to 1883) and profit transfer became a risky operation given the fluctuations of the Italian paper currency. There remained the speculative engagement in real estate operations: there the establishment of financial intermediaries could be a rational undertaking provided it remained a short-term business. In any case, the contribution to Italian economic development was rather modest.[16]

The Introduction and Life of the German Model

Alexander Gerschenkron's views on the decisive role of the German banks, "which may be taken as a paragon of the type of the universal bank" and which "successfully combined the basic idea of the Crédit Mobilier with the short-term activities of commercial banks," are now well known.[17] We also know that he considered the German type of mixed banking a "strategic factor" not only in the German but also in the Italian case of industrialization, where he observed "a deliberate application of techniques of investment banking as evolved in Germany in the course of attempts to overcome its own economic backwardness."[18] As in the cases of French and British investment in the Italian banking sector, the establishment of banks that followed the German model and that owed their foundation to German direct investment was preceded by a decade of intense economic and financial relations between Germany and Italy. From 1884 it was German capital that financed new railway investment and the growing deficits in the Italian state budget.[19] The 1880s also saw the first German direct investments in Italian industry and infrastructure.[20] These new German interests certainly did not at once replace the much older positions of French and British capital, and even at the beginning of the 1890s the German share in the Italian state debt placed abroad just reached the French quota but never surpassed it. Nevertheless, for a country like Italy, which had depended for decades on the capacity and the goodwill of the Paris capital market, these changes were quite fundamental.

Of course, when the German banks decided in 1894 to found a new Italian bank that could replace the Credito Mobiliare and the Banca Generale, both of which had failed shortly before, they clearly profited from exceptional circumstances.[21] Among others, these consisted of a favorable political climate, due to the Triple Alliance, which had been renewed in 1887; thus the Italian government clearly encouraged a German initiative to found "a German bank in Italy."[22] Until 1893 the two Italian investment banks, especially the Credito Mobiliare, together with the largest bank of issue, the Banca Nazionale, had functioned as intermediaries between the Italian state and the Berlin banks as far as public credit was concerned. Now the Credito Mobiliare was eliminated and the Banca d'Italia replaced the Banca Nazionale and, under the new banking law, had to observe much more severe rules. By founding a new large institution in Italy the German banks hoped to re-create the now "missing link." Thus in October 1894 the Banca Commerciale Italiana was established at Milan. Its capital of 20 million lire was mainly subscribed by the big Berlin joint-stock banks and the House of Bleichröder, traditionally strong in the Italian business. Their share amounted altogether to 78.9 percent; 13.4 percent was taken by the Österreichische Credit-Anstalt; 7.5 percent went to three Swiss banks.

A few months later Warschauer & Co., a traditional family firm of Berlin, the Nationalbank für Deutschland of Berlin, and the Basler Handelsbank—none of them first-rate—participated in the refounding of the Banca di Genova, which had been first established in 1870. By the early 1890s it was, however, in bad shape and in urgent need of fresh liquidity. At the beginning of 1895 the Genoese bank changed its name to Credito Italiano and gradually shifted its main activities to Milan. The German and Swiss share of its capital always remained below 50 percent (in 1914 it amounted probably to less than 1 percent!).

Even in the case of the Banca Commerciale, the German and Austrian shareholders sold out their shares relatively fast. In 1895 these amounted to 74 percent; six years later their participation was reduced to about l0 percent, and it was only 2.4 percent in 1914, while at the same time Swiss shareholders owned 20.5 percent and the French 14 percent of the Banca Commerciale capital. From 1899 the Banque de Paris et des Pays-Bas became a stable partner of the Banca Commerciale. The Credito Italiano also began close collaboration with several French, Belgian, and Swiss banks who regularly took part in its increases of capital.[23]

There were essentially two reasons for the retreat of German shareholders and for the decreasing interest the German founding banks, particularly those of the Banca Commerciale, showed as far as their Italian offspring were concerned. On the one hand the rapid growth of German industry after 1896 required a maximum of funds at home, and the entire German capital export suffered from this fact. On the other hand, against all expectations the Italian state after 1894 gradually reduced its foreign debt instead of expanding it further. Thus the Banca Commerciale could no longer play the role originally assigned to it by its founders.[24] In 1914 the *Consiglio di Amministrazione* of the Banca Commerciale consisted of thirty-three members: fifteen Italians, eight Germans, four French, three Austrians, and three Swiss. In this respect, therefore, the changes were less drastic. It was, however, this distribution of seats on the board as well as the fact that until 1915 the two leading managers of the Banca Commerciale were of German origin, which induced public opinion and foreign diplomats to consider the Banca Commerciale a "German bank."[25] The Credito Italiano had a much lower percentage of foreigners on its board, but a considerable part of its upper management also consisted of Germans, Austrians, and Swiss.

It was certainly this personal element that guaranteed that the two banks behaved according to the German model of "mixed banking," and it was no accident that Otto Joel, the German-born managing director of the Banca Commerciale, in his correspondence with Noetzlin of Paribas, called the Deutsche Bank the model (*Vorbild*) that the Banca Commerciale should follow.[26] In a contribution published some years ago I tried to demonstrate that the two Italian banks came quite close to the behavior of the big German banks as far as their territorial expansion domestically and abroad was concerned.[27] This was equally true of their "industrial policy," i.e., the permanent contact between bank and industrial enterprise "from the cradle to the grave," the importance of current account credit, and the will of the bank to carry an enterprise through the difficulties of its infancy or through later periods of crisis. A look at the balance sheets (which, of course, has to be made with skepticism) reveals ratios (such as capital/assets or different types of liquidity) that were quite similar between Italian and German banks, both of them differing markedly from the English commercial banks and the French deposit banks. There can be no doubt that there existed a high degree of structural relationship between the two Italian banks and their German founders.

It is, of course, not easy to assess the concrete importance of these two banks for the process of Italian industrialization, which really set in about 1897–98, i.e., only a short period after their establishment. In 1897 the assets of the Banca Commerciale and the Credito Italiano taken together amounted to 20.7 percent of the total assets of all Italian "ordinary credit banks" (i.e., joint-stock banks); in 1913 their share had risen to 48.7 percent.[28] This higher degree of concentration could, of course, be taken as an indicator of success; it does not, however, tell us anything about their role in the process of allocation of capital. We know about their really important role in financing new industrial sectors, including iron and steel, engineering, electricity production and distribution, and, as a typical consumer goods branch, sugar production. Besides, we observe an increasing engagement in such a traditional sector as textiles where, at least in part, the family enterprise ceded to joint-stock firms after 1900.[29]

Curiously, there is not much of a link between these new banks and foreign, particularly German, direct investment.[30] Normally the foreign subsidiary—for instance, in the engineering sector—depended very closely on technical and financial support from the parent firm. At least during the first stage of the new subsidiary abroad finance was provided indirectly via the parent firm by its banks in the home country. In the electricity sector, where capital requirements were particularly high, foreign capital was invested through financial holdings. (For fiscal and juridical reasons these were very often situated in Switzerland or Belgium; see, for instance, the Banque pour Enterprises Electriques at Zürich or the Brussels-based SOFINA).[31] Only after the "maturing" of these investments in electricity production or electrified transport some of the shares were sold to Italian private investors, and only at that stage did the two banks effectively enter and offer their services.

Interestingly enough, the example of the two banks was soon followed by "national" competitors, the Società Bancaria Italiana of Milan, established in 1898, and the Banco di Roma, originally a Roman local bank founded in 1880. Both of them almost failed, the Società Bancaria during the crisis of 1907, the Banco di Roma in 1912–13, and they barely survived. In the case of the Società Bancaria the rescue operation was certainly facilitated by the participation of French capital in 1911. In the same year French capital participated also in the foundation of the Società Italiana di Credito Provinciale, which itself was the result of the transformation of the local Banca di Busto Arsizio, situated in the textile belt of northern Lombardy. At the end of 1914 the Società Bancaria Italiana and the Società Italiana di Credito Provinciale merged and formed the new Banca Italiana di Sconto, which was to become a formidable competitor of the German-founded banks during the years of World War I.[32]

A final question should be raised: How can one explain the relative success of Banca Commerciale and Credito Italiano, keeping in mind the failures of their two predecessors and of their two "imitators," all of which at least pretended to follow more or less the same model of the investment bank?

The answer could be twofold:

1. The timing of the foundation of Banca Commerciale and Credito Italiano was

particularly favorable since it came just before the beginning of the definitive break-through of Italian industrialization. According to Jon Cohen, "the two large banks picked their clients first and other banks chose from what remained."[33]

2. The participation of the international *haute banque* and its continuing interest in the Banca Commerciale and in the Credito Italiano through its representatives on the respective boards gave these two banks a solid reputation right from the start, and a sort of international control that prevented them from undertaking unjustifiable risks. Both their predecessors and their followers lacked these advantages.

Was Alexander Gerschenkron right? He certainly presented many of the necessary conditions. In order to be sufficient, his fruitful hypothesis needs our ongoing research.

16

The Banking System and Foreign Capital in Brazil

Maria Bárbara Levy

In Brazil the year 1870 saw the beginning of a substantial transformation of productive infrastructure with the progressive extinction of slavery and the spread of free labor. We aim in this chapter to show the various ways in which the Brazilian economy related to the world economy, the British in particular, through international finance.

Development of the Credit System before 1870

The first Banco do Brasil was founded in 1808; its objectives were to advance royal and public revenues to cover state expenses and, only secondarily, to impact on commercial discount operations.[1] The notes it issued soon became inconvertible, but this situation did not worry the bank's shareholders, who received generous dividends for their loans to the government. It did not take long for monetary circulation to degenerate, with all gold coins disappearing to be hoarded for foreign trade, especially for purchase of slaves and British manufactures. The recent opening of Brazilian ports and the free trade treaty with Great Britain (1810) stimulated the import of industrial products, creating a severely unfavorable balance of trade.

With a deficit that absorbed its capital, the Banco do Brasil supported financially the war of independence against Portugal (1822/23) and opposed the secessionist movements that erupted in many regions of the newly founded empire under Dom Pedro I, the crown prince. Very soon the Empire of Brazil had recourse to British loans. The first one, in 1824—ironically called the Independence loan—mortgaged the revenues of the main customs houses and established the Rothschilds as Brazil's principal agents in London.

From then on the policy of entering into new loans to cover interest and amortization of previous loans was adopted; pay old debts with new and larger ones. As balance of trade deficits also became usual, loans were regularly negotiated to finance imports. In 1826 political dissatisfaction increased, brought about by the fall in prices of export products, and when parliament reopened, the Banco do Brasil was used by the opposition to discredit the Emperor. The decree extinguishing the Banco do Brasil (1829) and Dom Pedro's abdication were both manifestations of the same political instability.

With the closure of the Banco do Brasil the country remained without any financial institutions until the creation of the Banco Commercial do Rio de Janeiro in 1838. Alongside the notes of the National Treasury, commercial houses offered their products to retailers for later payment against the issue of bills of exchange. Discount houses negotiated these bills with endorsement, thus permitting the original creditor to recover his capital before the maturity of the bill. Private monies circulated under different denominations: vouchers, receipts, notes, and bills. Merchants entered into financial relations freely organized outside the control of the state, based exclusively on mutual confidence, as not even a commercial code existed.

To establish some control over the government's expenses the Legislative Assembly institutionalized the public debt, subjecting new debts to its approval. Rio de Janeiro absorbed most of the new securities because these were assets that corresponded very much to the requirements of terms, guarantees, and liquidity of the large agricultural producers who resided there.

In the province of Rio de Janeiro coffee plantations became dominant by 1830. They took up large extensions of land, making much use of slave labor. Credit demand became extremely great and a group of merchants detected the opportunity of incorporating banks, which offered an alternative to the primitive relations of direct debt then available. The first commercial bank, the Banco Commercial do Rio de Janeiro, began its activities as a bank of issue.[2] It issued vouchers that paid annual interest, but the amounts were so small that they were rarely collected. The vouchers circulated freely, independently of maturities and amounts, and almost never returned to be cashed for Treasury bills at the bank's counters. The only limit to their circulation was the geographical radius of their acceptance and their uselessness for paying taxes. The practice spread to other regions as new commercial banks were created.

The emergence of commercial banks did not alter substantially the financing of agricultural activities, which remained similar to what it had been since colonial times. Farmers obtained from intermediaries advances guaranteed by the estimated value of their harvest, which would be mortgaged to the creditor. In critical situations slaves would also be mortgaged. This maintained the dominance of mercantile capital over production.

During the 1850s a number of new banks were founded in consequence of the coffee boom and the capital made available after the abolition of the slave trade. Within this same sequence of events, we find first a manufacturing boom in Rio de Janeiro, resulting from the greater diversification of investments permitted by the organization of Rio's Stock Exchange (1848) and by the institutionalization of the Commercial Code (1850). In 1852 a second semiofficial Banco do Brasil was created with a monopoly of issue.

In 1857 a new Finance Minister, Souza Franco, of liberal views, carried out a reform that authorized five regional banks to issue, terminating the Banco do Brasil's monopoly of issue. Reactions against Souza Franco's "paper" policy gained a greater number of supporters in the Legislative Assembly. In 1860 a new law was passed requiring the reimbursement of bank notes in gold. Together with monetary and credit restrictions, all stock companies were more tightly regulated. Numerous bankruptcies occurred, business enterprises were greatly diminished, and public revenues fell 10 percent in relation to the previous year. Conservatives, defenders of the agricultural vocation of the country, objected to the urban policy of business corporations. Lack of capital, scarcity of specialized labor, prospects of greater profits in commerce, and inadequate protection led to the slackening of industry.

From the 1820s there had been great interest on the London stock market in underwriting Latin American government and railroad bonds. Although investments in Latin America never exceeded one-fifth of total British foreign investments, Brazil held an important place among the countries of the South American continent. (See Table 16–1.)

It is true that a substantial part of these investments were loans to the government, and the Brazilian foreign debt increased considerably. Valentin Bouças, the first author to study the subject, presented the following information on Brazilian loans raised in London during the 1860s.

	Nominal	Net
1860	£ 1,373,000	£ 1,210,000
1863	£ 3,855,000	£ 3,300,000
1865	£ 6,936,000	£ 5,000,000

The conservative legislation of 1860 coincided with British interest in operating in a safer environment for its investments. The first British banks, which came to Brazil before any other Latin American country, were established in this context.[3] The London & Brazilian Bank began operations in 1862, with Edward Johnston, head of the trading company E. Johnston and Co., and president of the Royal Mail Steampacket Co., as bank president. The Brazilian and Portuguese Bank, founded in 1863 and which two years later became the English Bank of Rio de Janeiro, had as its directors John Knowles, of the import-export house Knowles and Foster, and James McGrouther of Janurin and McGrouther, both of London; later, Mathew Megaw of Megaw and Norton also became a director of this bank.[4]

These banks were not branches of the main English commercial banks, but associations of businessmen who traded with Brazil and saw in banking activities prospects for expanding their businesses. The coming of these foreign banks brought a level of competence previously unknown in the country. "Before long the private bankers were feeling the weight of the competition from the new British banks which attracted deposits away from them to an embarrassing extent."[5] They were quick to dominate the market, by specializing in foreign exchange opeations and by tending to the necessities

TABLE 16–1. Geographical Distribution of British Investments in Latin America, 1825–1865 (£ millions)

	Brazil	Total
1825	4.0	24.6
1840	6.9	30.8
1865	20.3	80.9

Source: Irving Stone, "British Direct and Portfolio Investment in Latin America before 1914," *Journal of Economic History,* 37 (September 1977), p. 695.

of the export trade. On the other hand, they were indifferent to the requirements of the domestic economy and to the aims of the central government in bringing equilibrium to the balance of trade. They did not care for agricultural credit operations, and dealt almost exclusively with export-import houses.[6]

The aims of the British banks were not limited to mere competition with Brazilian banks. By means of their deposits and drawing rights on their home offices' reserves, they obtained excellent positions for exchange rate speculation. But their most important role was to facilitate the entrance of British capital. These investments were made possible through the formation of stock companies, with the help of the banks, which remained responsible for the placement of shares and bonds in London, destined usually for the construction of railways, ports, and gas plants. This process was enlarged by the fact that the Brazilian government also obtained loans for the purchase of British machinery and equipment.

British investments assisted Brazilian exports inasmuch as they were mainly directed to transport, through direct investments or loans placed in London. The expansion of railways favored the extension of coffee cultivation into previously inaccessible regions of the Paulista western hinterland, and greatly reduced production costs of the commodity. At the same time, the radius of penetration of British manufactures was increased. The increase of exports led to the growth of cities, which required water supply, sewer systems, and illumination networks. These were brought to the main cities of the country by British investments.[7]

The introduction of modern technology promoted the expansion of the internal market and contributed to the dissolution of slavery. Railways and steamships reduced commodities' time of circulation, releasing floating capital and helping reduce domestic interest rates. The export base of the economy was solid. Coffee, in the southeast, presented larger harvests, and tobacco and cotton, in the northeast, benefitted from these products' scarcity in world markets due to the American Civil War. Textile and hat manufacturers adapted improved production processes.

The outbreak of the war with Paraguay (1866–1870) caused the stricter monetary policy to be abandoned. Importation of armaments increased substantially. As these expenses had to be paid in gold, the government reserved the metal for international trade. Internally the government issued paper money to finance its purchases in building the army. Textile and shoe factories received large orders. While in Rio de Janeiro the market for government bills was very active, São Paulo became the distribution center for the goods consumed in the war being waged in the South.[8] The boom in manufacturing activities during the war occurred not only because of the increased demand, but also because of the elevation of import duties to generate more revenue for war expenses, which also served to protect Brazilian production. This stimulus was not limited to the textile industry, but also affected other sectors such as chemicals, optical instruments, nautical materials, leather, glass, hats, cigarettes, and paper.

Foreign Banks and the Import of Capital

In the financial history of Brazil the period from 1870 to 1914 holds a marked subdivision in 1889. In that year important changes occurred in society—the first year after the abolition of slavery—in politics—the proclamation of the republic—and in economics—a year of active incorporation of companies. (See Appendix.)

The First Period (1870–1889)

The first period is specially characterized by the decline of slavery. The aging of slave laborers (resulting from the earlier halt of the slave trade and the decline of the existing slave population) and the exhaustion of land by traditional methods of cultivation brought the gradual loss of political power for coffee planters in the region of Rio de Janeiro. A new economic area appeared in the country, São Paulo, then known as the "new west," where production of coffee was based on free labor, mainly immigrants. The country was still largely rural, with only 8 percent in towns of over 20,000 inhabitants in 1872 (3.6 percent in Rio de Janeiro).[9] Foreign capital was invested mostly in public utilities and in the exploitation of natural resources, with only a secondary presence in industrial activities.

Quantitative data on the development of the economy are scarce. Goldsmith studied available aggregate financial data, criticizing them and proposing new estimates.[10] His new estimate, carried out by dividing a synthetic estimate of national product in current prices, shows the following annual rates for the period as a whole and for subperiods. (See Table 16–2.)

From these it can be concluded that real national product per capita followed a modest upward trend from 1850 to 1889, but that the growth rate was much higher during the first half of the period than during the second, when in fact it was negative.

There are no estimates for sectorial shares in the product. Census data show about two thirds of the active population dedicated to agriculture in 1872, 1900, and still in 1920.

There are no statistics covering this period that would permit an estimate of the volume of capital formation. Using Harrod's formula, Goldsmith suggests a range between 6 percent (corresponding to an average capital-output ratio of 3) and 12 percent (corresponding to one of 4) of national income. This would be compatible with the situation found by that author in other countries during the same period. The saving ratio would be well below this number, as an important part of investment was regularly financed by capital imports (about 1.5 percent of national product according to Goldsmith's estimate for Brazil).[11]

Four financial assets (paper currency, commercial and savings bank deposits, and government securities) together amounted to 478 million milreis in 1870, increasing to 840 million by 1889. In this last year these financial assets represented almost 50 percent of national product. For Goldsmith, this significant growth is an indication of the initial development of a modern financial superstructure.

In 1870 the Banco do Brasil was the country's most important financial institution, and accompanied the economy's growth. During the 1860s and 1870s the ratio of

TABLE 16–2. Real Domestic Product, 1851–1889 (annual growth rate)

	Aggregate	Per Capita
1851–1889	2.04	0.34
1870–1879	1.29	−0.52
1880–1889	0.74	−1.14

Source: Raymond Goldsmith, "The Financial Development of Brazil" (mimeo, 1981), p. 20.

its total assets to national product remained under 10 percent, falling to less than 7 percent in 1889. After the creation of a mortgage department in 1866, long-term loans to agriculture absorbed a considerable proportion of assets, between one-sixth and one-third.

Banco do Brasil's share in the whole of the banking system gradually fell from the mid–70s, in part because a few foreign banks became the most important commercial banks, particularly in the financing of foreign trade and in foreign exchange. Cash reserves and deposits doubled during these years in the London and Brazilian Bank and the English Bank. Another foreign bank, the Brazilianische Bank für Deutschland, was founded in 1887 by the German Diskonto-Gesellschaft.[12]

Domestic nonofficial banks increased their loan activities between 1870 and 1889, based on current accounts with guarantees. Cash reserves doubled during the period, but deposits grew only 50 percent for most Brazilian banks. In 1889 there were thirty-five banks in Brazil, mostly without branches.

The most important financial event of these years was the bankruptcy of the Empire's most important entrepreneur, Irineu Evangelista de Souza, Baron de Mauá, during the crisis of 1875. In that year the government had contracted a loan in London on which it intended to draw a balance. Local banks had to come up with the necessary funds in local currency to buy the drafts on London. The banks then tried to force their debtors to obtain more liquidity. Unable to provide such an immediate return, many companies declared bankruptcy, their number growing in waves. After the debtors' bankruptcies came that of their creditors, among them Mauá's banking house. Mauá's distress was compounded by the impossibility of liquidating quickly his assets in Uruguay. As he himself stated, at the end of the war with Paraguay his bank in Montevideo was overly engaged with the Uruguayan government, and the Uruguayan economy was too weak.[13]

Brazil had always been an important market for Portuguese maritime insurers. In 1862 the first branch of a foreign insurance company appeared, the Compania Garantia do Porto. It was followed by Royal Insurance in 1864; Liverpool, London & Globe in 1866; and others. As these were not regulated in any way they did not publish balance sheets in Brazil, and invested their reserves abroad.[14]

After 1848 the Rio de Janeiro Stock Exchange was the most important market for domestic securities. In 1870 the shares of only eighteen companies were traded. Between 1870 and 1880 trade in the exchange increased by 25 percent in relation to the previous decade. The increase was concentrated in railway shares, reflecting the building boom begun in this decade through British investment. The growth in importance of transactions on the exchange occurred in 1877 with the creation of the trading floor, when debentures and mortgage bills also began to be negotiated.[15]

The relative importance of foreign trade in the national product showed a downward trend during these two decades: from 30 percent in the late 1860s to 25 percent from the late 1870s on. A regular surplus, however, appeared in the balance of commodity trade after 1872, except for one year. (See Table 16–3.)

Export prices, where coffee and sugar dominated the few products traded, fluctuated much more than did those of imports. The share of coffee in total exports maintained itself at around three-fifths during the 1870s and 1880s, occasionally reaching two-thirds of the total near the end of the period. Sugar's participation fell sharply, from about 25 to 10 percent.[16]

TABLE 16–3. Export Surplus

	As Percentage of Imports	As Percentage of National Product
1860s	14	2.1
1870s	21	2.6
1880s	15	1.8

Source: Goldsmith, "Financial Development of Brazil," pp. 54–55.

Changes in the structure of imports were fairly small. Foodstuffs constituted about 20 percent of the total, while the share of textiles remained at 50 percent throughout the 1870s. The share of equipment showed a slow increase, but in the early 1870s it was still only one-eighth of the total.

Existing data on the federal government's foreign debt are much more trustworthy than the information available on direct private investment. A study of foreign investments from 1860 to 1875 found, for a total of £26,539,706 invested, 33.9 percent in railways, 21.3 percent in banks, and 11.8 percent in insurance companies.[17] This information must be considered with care as it refers only to the declared capital of the companies, and did not usually include reinvestments of profits, operational or other. It can offer, however, an indication of size and point to certain tendencies through time.

As to the countries of origin of these investments, the same source shows 93.6 percent from Great Britain, 4.7 percent from Germany, and 1.5 percent from France.

For the following period, from 1878 to 1885, Ana Celia Castro found a total of £20,132,900 in new foreign investment, with the following sectorial distribution: 58.8 percent in railways, 10.5 percent in public works, and 4.4 percent in light, telegraph, and telephone companies. The banking sector amounted to only 1.8 percent, as only one bank was incorporated. During this period 87.5 percent of the investments had a British origin and 10 percent French, this last with two railroads and a public works company.

Irving Stone separates foreign investment into direct and portfolio.[18] In direct investment, the foreign investors were able to exercise control over management through ownership of an effective share of stock with voting rights. Portfolio investments consisted of securities of overseas companies held primarily for income purposes, rather than for managerial control. Government bonds are also properly included as portfolio investment. This form was that mainly found in Brazil (see Table 16–4). Stone's information is especially valuable for the period studied, in which British capital predominated.

Direct foreign investment grew at annual rates of between 4 and 16 percent from 1840 onward. Growth was especially marked during the years 1865 to 1875 and immediately before World War I. Until the turn of the century it is supposed that almost the totality of these belonged to British investors.

Until the mid-1890s, non-British participation in the federal government debt was almost nil. The growth showed a cyclical pattern, increasing regularly at annual rates between 3.2 and 4.6 percent until the mid-1870s, decreasing then until the mid-1880s, and again growing. Until the 1880s foreign public debt was contracted exclusively by the central government without participation by provinces or municipalities.

TABLE 16-4. British Direct and Portfolio Investment in Brazil, 1865–1913 (millions of pounds)

	1865	1875	1885	1895	1905	1913
Total investment	20.3	30.9	47.6	93.0	124.4	254.8
Direct investment	7.2	10.6	22.4	24.0	29.6	56.7
Portfolio investment	13.0	20.4	25.3	69.0	94.8	198.1
Government loans	13.0	20.4	23.2	52.4	83.3	119.6
Corporate securities	—	—	2.1	16.6	11.5	78.1

Source: Irving Stone, "British Direct and Portfolio Investment in Latin America before 1914," *Journal of Economic History,* 37 (September 1977), p. 706.

The classic books on the Brazilian foreign debt omit information as to the various related financial flows, mentioning only incoming money. Systematic data on interest payments and amortizations are practically nonexistent. For lack of other sources, Paiva Abreu accepted the data published in the late 1950s by IBGE, the Braziian statistical agency. His conclusions are consistent with those of Irving Stone (see Tables 16–5 and 16–6).[19]

The "old" Brazilian public debt (before 1931) generated the issue of bonds through merchant bankers in the main international financial centers. These paid fixed nominal interest rates and were held by individuals or trust funds. International market variations in interest rates had no affect; thus, the amount of interest to be paid by debtors. The nominal interest rates moved within a small interval; between 1824 and 1914, the yield on British consols varied from 2.5 to 3.8 percent a year. Other governments, of course, had to pay more depending on the perceived risk. Though in some cases the discount on Brazilian issues reached 50 percent, they usually were limited to about 20 percent of the face value of the loans.

The Second Period, 1889–1914

The second period, from 1889 to 1914, witnessed an important transformation in the structure of the Brazilian economy. For an economic historian it is relevant to return to this period to reconstruct the first steps in industrialization. The great financial boom at the beginning of the Republic, which came to be known as the *Encilhamento* (horseracing slang for the moment before the start, when the horses cannot be held back anymore), and the austere monetary policy that came after it, in different ways contributed to the feasibility of the industrial process.

Between 1889 and 1913 Brazil's population increased at an average annual rate of almost 2.5 percent, or from 14 million to 25 million people. Immigration accounted for much of this substantial increment. The state of São Paulo, having adopted a policy of immigration subsidy, received the majority of immigrants. It was hoped that foreign labor would substitute for slave labor on the coffee plantations, but it was the main urban centers that benefitted most from the arrival of qualified labor. The increase of the industrial labor force was particularly felt in São Paulo, where from 1890 to 1900 the share of foreigners in the urban population rose from 10 to 14 percent. In the total population, foreign-born residents jumped from 2.5 percent in 1890 to over 6 percent in 1913. Southern Europeans continued to be the majority of these immigrants, with over 85 percent of the total.[20]

TABLE 16–5. Brazil: Nominal Stock of Foreign Capital, 1875–1914 (£ millions)

	Private Portfolio				Public Portfolio				Total			
	British	American	Others	Total	British	American	Others	Total	British	American	Others	Total
1875	10.6	—	—	10.6	20.4	—	—	20.4	30.9	—	—	31.0
1885	24.4	—	—	24.6	23.2	—	—	23.2	47.6	—	—	47.6
1895	40.6	—	—	40.6	37.5	—	1.5	39.2	78.1	—	1.5	79.6
1905	41.1	4.0	30.0	75.1	83.3	—	5.0	88.3	124.4	4.0	35.0	163.4
1913	135.4	10.3	110.4	255.9	129.1	—	22.6	151.7	264.3	10.3	133.0	407.6

Source: Marcelo Paiva Abreu, A Divida Publica Externa do Brasil, 1824–1931.

TABLE 16–6. Brazil: Public Foreign Debt, Balances on December 31 (1865–1914) (in millions of pounds)

	Federal			States and Municipalities			Total		
	British	Others	Total	British	Others	Total	British	Others	Total
1865	13.0	—	13.0	—	—	—	13.0	—	13.0
1875	20.4	—	20.4	—	—	—	20.4	—	20.4
1885	23.2	—	23.2	—	—	—	23.2	—	23.2
1895	35.7	—	35.7	1.8	1.5	3.3	37.5	1.5	39.0
1905	70.0	—	70.0	13.3	5.0	18.3	83.3	5.0	88.3
1914	90.6	12.9	103.5	38.5	9.7	48.2	129.1	22.6	151.7

Source: Marcelo Paiva Abreu, A Divida Publica Externa do Brasil, 1824–1931.

The evolution of Brazil's foreign trade before World War I was largely determined by the movements of coffee prices. The necessity of keeping a high surplus in the balance of trade, in view of the weight of the foreign debt, constrained imports in relation to export revenue. Imports were held back by tariffs and by devaluation between 1889 and 1898. After 1898 the restrictive economic policy affected foreign trade inasmuch as, to obtain exchange revaluation, it sought larger surpluses in the balance of trade. The collection in gold of customs duties was also established to restrain imports.

From 1903 to 1913 foreign trade enjoyed a long phase of expansion. Until 1908 this was due to foreign credits for public investments in equipping ports and railways. From 1909 the increase in coffee prices permitted an increase in import capacity, and foreign loans and direct investments also occurred. Importation of capital goods for the transport industry and construction had thus a substantial increment.

Exports continued to be mainly coffee, around which other products appeared, e.g., rubber, for a total share of 80 percent for primary products. The list of imports underwent many changes. Consumption goods, which had composed up to one-third of the total, decreased relatively, while a dependence on raw materials, fuel, and lubricants became more apparent. Within raw materials, chemicals and other more elaborate materials increased their share. But the most important change was the growth in capital goods imports. We can follow the evolution of capital formation in the economy by comparing the share of this item in 1901–1907 (7.1 percent) with that of 1908–1913, when capital goods made up 13.9 percent of imports.

All national product estimates reflect the abrupt price rises of the early 1890s and their sharp decline a decade later due to changes in financial policy. According to Goldsmith's estimate, which is the only annual index in existence, based on four current price indicators (money stock, exports plus imports, government expenditures, and the wage bill), gross domestic product increased from less than 1,800 million milreis in 1889 to over 6,600 million milreis in 1913, an annual average rate increase of 5.5 percent.[21]

All indicators point to a substantial decline in real per capita product during the 1890s, though they differ considerably as to its size. Contador and Haddad estimated 35 percent,[22] whereas Goldsmith arrived at 11 percent. Between 1900 and 1913, when for the first time an index is available that is based for a large part of the economy on quantitative series, both aggregate and per capita real product increased substantially, 77 and 34 percent, respectively, for annual rates of 4.5 and 2.3 percent.

In spite of all uncertainties, there can be little doubt that the Brazilian economy grew very slowly during the first years of the Republic. We can also be certain that per capita product declined during the 1890s, but increased substantially during the period from 1900 to 1913.[23]

Marked changes in the sectorial distribution of national product occurred between 1900 and 1913, with agriculture's share falling from about 45 percent to around 38 percent. While industry rose from 12 to 14 percent, both commerce and government showed small increases, the former remaining at a low 8.5 percent in 1913.[24]

The only information on important components of capital formation refer to railway construction and to the capital expenditure of the central government. The railway network increased at a rate of 625 kilometers per year from 1890 to 1913, for a total of 15,000 kilometers. Spending at least two fifths of the total on railways, the central government increased its spending from 0.5 percent of national product in the 1890s to 1 percent in the first decade of the century and to 2.4 percent from 1910 to 1913.

Paper currency, savings, bank deposits, and government securities increased during this period by at least 1.2 percent of the national product. Between 1889 and 1913 the increase by almost 180 percent in the four main financial assets gave rise to a new distribution, as follows: 30 percent in paper currency, 30 percent in demand deposits with commercial banks, 31 percent in domestic government securities, part of which was certainly absorbed outside the household sector, and around 9 percent in time deposits with savings banks.

Present historiography has accepted and contributed to Fishlow's revisionist appraisal, in which he shows the *Encilhamento's* importance in the initial industrialization of Brazil.[25] The origin of *Encilhamento* can be found in the final legislation of the Empire. Once the abolition of slavery had been consummated, and the impossibility of Congress approving any indemnification for former slaveowners was verified, Minister of Finance Ouro Preto raised a loan in London for agricultural credit, to be distributed through the banking system. In practice, this permitted the banks to clear their portfolios of previous debts from coffee traders, who paid old debts with new money, thus tranferring all debts to the government. Farmers themselves did not benefit from the scheme.

Besides this loan, Ouro Preto signed the Monetary Law of 1888, which authorized a few new banks to issue notes proportionate to their metallic reserves. This return to bank issue was justified by the greater necessities of credit to cover the costs of labor, now "free." New issuing banks and the agricultural credit created a climate prone to speculation. The shares of these banks were issued at a 45 percent premium, and the expectation of profits, assured by government policy, gave rise to gambling with stocks.

Rui Barbosa, the first republican Minister of Finance, after consulting the bankers of the capital, agreed to maintain the Empire's monetary policy as a condition for receiving support from the financial bourgeoisie. The class composition in power, however, had changed somewhat and turned to the interests of the small urban bourgeoisie, close to commerce, the liberal professions, manufacturing, and the bureaucracy. Financial policy directed funds for investments in urban production.

Rui Barbosa's legislation (decree 164 of 1890) set very liberal controls over the incorporation of companies, among other things requiring deposit of only 10 percent of the capital for incorporation and trade of stock on the exchange. The decree also created regional issuing banks, which policy was in line with the federalist aspiration then dominant. Operations expected of these banks were so varied that they seemed more like present-day investment banks. To his critics Rui Barbosa answered that banking credit should not be limited by the availability of gold. He deemed the velocity of monetary circulation too low because of economic dispersion, hoarding by the public, and the seasonality of agricultural production.

The policy of bank note issues considerably increased the volume of money, with an immediate effect on the cost of credit, making it more accessible and stimulating applications for real assets, especially productive assets. This can be verified through the change in electric energy installed to supply recently established industry. This industrial movement, in its turn, directed toward the market various financial assets, such as stocks, debentures, bills of exchange, and mortgage bills. As government debt securities had been absorbed by the issuing banks, the market became more receptive to stocks and debentures.[26]

All revisionist theses as to the *Encilhamento*'s role in industrialization are based on the performance of cotton textile manufacturers. Credit expansion favored their growth. It must be made clear, however, that most of these companies existed previous to the stock exchange boom. They were available to profit from current conditions to become publicly held share companies. Many of these "new" companies had been operating for some time as family concerns.

In 1898 the government's monetary policy turned to a rigid metallist perspective. Joaquim Murtinho was the Finance Minister to mold this policy. He began by negotiating with foreign creditors a moratorium on gold payments. This funding loan permitted Brazil to suspend the service of its foreign debt for 13 years, with, among other guarantees, the mortgage of the main custom revenues of the country. The changes in government policy were radical. Industry was considered "artificial" for depending on the import of some raw materials. For the new minister, Brazil was essentially an agricultural country, an activity in which it held important comparative advantages. There was no reason for producing expensive and badly manufactured goods that could be imported in better quality and at a lower price. Later, new measures were introduced to complement this policy. In 1900 the gold tariff was increased, and in 1901 a loan was contracted to substitute for previous contracts with railways, for which the government guaranteed interest payments on their bonds.

The immediate consequence of Murtinho's reform was the bank panic of 1900 that almost destroyed the financial system. Seventeen banks went bankrupt and Banco da Republica do Brasil itself almost went under, having to suspend specie payments. Congress granted it a £1 million loan to help out other financial companies. Banks operated at times with a 100 percent cash reserve, unemployment increased, and coffee export income in milreis fell by 20 percent annually from 1901 to 1904.[27]

Because of the major role the Banco da Republica played in the financial system and because of its semiofficial status as the government's banker, the Treasury intervened in 1905, reorganizing the bank under government control, originating today's Banco do Brasil. The Treasury bought one-third of the new bank's stock, the greatest single block of shares. By its new regulation, the President of the Republic had powers to appoint not only the bank's president but also one of its four directors. The federal government held great influence in this bank, both as its main client and for having the power to grant special privileges. The Treasury deposited its funds with Banco do

Brasil, and to stabilize foreign exchange made it the sole agent in foreign currency transactions. It thus was able to break the domination of the foreign banks in exchange operations.[28] But the Banco do Brasil was not a central bank, as it did not operate as lender of last resort nor did it have any rediscount function.

Murtinho's policy succeeded in its aim of foreign exchange revaluation. The entrance of new foreign investment and the suspension of external debt payments forced the exchange rate upward, by 25 percent from 1905 to 1906. This reduced coffee's profitability in Brazil. The expectation of a large crop for the next year strengthened the opinion that there should be government intervention in the coffee market.

The government of the state of São Paulo was forced to reduce taxes on coffee as well as to take other measures for financing it. Farmers and politicians from São Paulo, Minas Gerais, and Rio de Janeiro signed an agreement that established the first governmental intervention to maintain the price of a product for the benefit of producers. The main aim of the agreement was to guarantee a minimum price in milreis for coffee through the retention of excess stocks, purchased with funds from a large foreign loan.

Rothschilds, traditional bankers for Brazil, refused to participate in the financing scheme, thus losing its almost exclusive hold on Brazilian official foreign business. The loan was underwritten by the Brasilianische Bank für Deutschland (£1 million), National City Bank of New York (£1 million), and J. Henry Schröder of London (£2 million).

One of the results of the Taubaté Agreement was the creation of a foreign exchange stabilization fund, the *Caixa de Conversão*. Coffee farmers feared that revaluation of coffee would provoke an influx of foreign currency, which would depreciate the exchange rate. The *Caixa de Conversão* was to purchase gold coins at the rate of 15 pence to the milreis, a bit lower than that of the market (16 pence), through notes of its own issue. Farmers had guaranteed favorable rates for the foreign currency they were to receive and thus socialized their losses.[29]

Intense foreign-exchange speculations began soon after the stock market's retraction during 1892/93. The amounts involved were much greater than those of the *Encilhamento*. During normal harvest periods, the total amount of drafts in foreign currency reached £1.5 million. When foreign exchange speculation was running loose, £250,00 a day were traded (around £5.5 million monthly).

The origin of this process must have been due to the sale of drafts for future coverage, when exports were realized. As the advances were made in foreign currency, this demand helped depreciate the milreis, increasing gradually the amounts involved. Speculative foreign-exchange operations did not result from actual foreign trade, but from the expectation that future exchange prices would become profitable, and the operation could be liquidated at a profit. Foreign banks received almost all drafts for collection on imports by local traders. It was alleged that the banks would force an increase in the exchange rate during harvest time, when farmers and traders needed the money. Once this was over, the foreign banks would play with their home office's gold reserves, forcing on importers lower exchange rates. (Until the advent of the cruzeiro, exchange rates were quoted in pence per milreis. Thus lower rates meant more milreis per pound.)

The banks speculated not only with trade. It was alleged that, informed by their home offices as to the dates of interest and amortization payments on the foreign debt, they would reduce the flow of foreign currency drafts, forcing a decrease of the rate. When the inverse occurred, with the release of money, they would offer drafts in excess, forcing an increase in the exchange rate. Only foreign banks were able to carry out these operations, because only they were able to draw against their home offices in London the drafts called "pig on pork," uncovered advances that could be liquidated at a substantial profit.[30]

While these banks made enormous profits, the local banks, according to Goldsmith, suffered. The cash-to-deposits ratio fell sharply in 1890/91, remained low until 1896, and increased enormously during the deflation of 1900 to 1903. The absence of quantitative data is particularly serious in the case of foreign banks, which then constituted an important part of the banking system, concentrating in foreign-currency transactions and thus avoiding the difficulties domestic banks faced in the crisis of 1900.

The sources for this period contain the harshest criticisms of foreign banks. An editorial of the *Gazeta de Commercio e Finanças* stated: "Foreign banks do not serve the purposes of Brazilian development, as they are not credit institutions, but mere agencies set up among us with the sole aim of obtaining profit without risking capital."[31] Speakers for the coffee interest in Congress lamented that the capital so necessary to agriculture "remained inactive in the safes of foreign banks."[32] Another Paulista politician claimed that "the banking capital that comes here is a sort of suction pump, which drains out profits."[33] It was also said that foreign banks did not employ Brazilians in management positions so as not to spread knowledge of banking matters.[34]

In addition to the three foreign banks operating in Brazil at the time of the proclamation of the Republic—the London and Brazilian Bank,[35] the British Bank of South America,[36] and the Brasilianische Bank für Deutschland[37]—three new foreign banks initiated activities before 1903: the London and River Plate Bank,[38] the Banque Française du Brésil,[39] and the Banque Belge de Prêts Fonciers.[40]

Between 1903 and 1913 the number of foreign banks increased considerably. The Banco Alliança (1906) was the filial of a bank in Oporto, Portugal. The Banco Español del Rio de la Plata (1907) was the branch of a bank in Buenos Aires. The Banque du Crédit Foncier du Brésil (1907) had as directors Parisian bankers and proprietors. The Banque Française et Italienne pour l'Amérique du Sud, a joint operation of the Banque de Paris et des Pays-Bas, the Banca Commerciale Italiana, and the Société Générale, with its main office in Paris, entered Brazil in 1910. Besides having offices in Rio de Janeiro and São Paulo, it established branches in Ribeirão Preto, São Carlos do Pinhal, Botucatu, Espírito Santo do Pinhal, Jaú, Mococa, and Sáo José do Rio Pardo, all in São Paulo's hinterland coffee plantations. In 1911 it went farther south, opening agencies in Porto Alegre and Rio Grande do Sul.

The Banque Brésilienne Italo-Belge, with its main office in Antwerp, opened in São Paulo in 1911. Among the participants were the Société Générale de Belgique, the Banque de l'Union Anversoise, the Anglo-South American Bank, the Banque Centrale Anversoise, Banque Générale Belge, Banque d'Outre-mer, and the Crédito Italiano. It also had branches in Santos and other cities in the hinterland of São Paulo. The Deutsche-Südamerikanische Bank (1911), with headquarters in Berlin and an agency in Rio de Janeiro, was owned by the Dresdner Bank, A. Schaffhausenscher Bankverein, and the National Bank für Deutschland; it also had a branch in Buenos Aires.

The Banco Allemão Transatlântico, headquartered in Berlin, installed itself in 1912 in Rio de Janeiro. It had agencies in São Paulo, Niterói, and Petrópolis. The Banco Nacional Ultramarino of Lisbon started operating in Rio de Janeiro in 1912. Finally, in that same year the Banque Française pour le Brésil et l'Amerique du Sud installed itself in Rio de Janeiro. Its most important shareholders were French bankers and two Brazilians (Affonso Arinos de Mello Franco and Monteiro de Barros) living in Paris.[41] These new banks and others that already operated in the country enlarged their activity in the hinterlands.[42] In this way the foreign banks followed the changes in the economy, especially the movement of agricultural expansion. (See Table 16–7.)

The banks' performance as a whole can only be followed after 1912.[43] Rio de Janeiro, the federal capital, which concentrated most of the banking transactions, suffered immediately from the crisis that announced World War I. In the rest of the country, the banking system behaved differently from that in Rio de Janeiro. Taking as reference the year 1912, we find that the crisis promoted some dispersion among the banks. While the six largest ones held 56 percent of deposits in 1913, in 1915 their share had fallen to 35 percent. The Banco do Brasil alone held almost 31 percent at first, but only 15 percent afterwards. In times of crisis foreign banks still attracted deposits from domestic ones. Considering the six largest foreign banks, their share amounted to 33 percent in 1913, increasing to 41 percent in 1914 and 46 percent in 1915.

There were no substantial changes in regional concentration of banking activities, with Rio de Janeiro keeping its position of financial center, though losing a small percentage of deposits to São Paulo. Rio Grande do Sul appears in third place, followed by Bahia, Pernambuco, and Pará. Minas Gerais placed only seventh. Foreign banks had an important share in Bahia, Pará, Pernambuco, and in the Amazon region, while domestic banks concentrated in Rio de Janeiro and São Paulo.

Though rubber exports fell both in quantity and in price, the share of banks from the north did not fall. In the Amazon all was foreign, and in Pará 69 percent. The share of sight deposits in São Paulo in the total of the country shows that the crisis of 1913 was felt sharply, but that during the next years it regained its position. This was not the case of Rio de Janeiro. Rio Grande do Sul was not much affected by the crisis, increasing its share of deposits to 19 percent by 1913.

Together with the nationalist ebullience of the beginning of the Republic came a campaign in favor of the nationalization of insurance companies, a movement that sought to stop the outflow of currency. The first insurance regulation dates from 1895. It referred only to foreign life insurance companies. (There were no domestic ones in this area.) This law required that insurance companies publish all operational details and required that all reserves be invested in domestic currency, real estate, mortgages, stocks, or time deposits. The companies were authorized to transfer dividends and profits to their home offices. Finance Minister Joaquim Murtinho established a General Superintendency of Insurance to control the activities of life, maritime, and land insurance companies. Previous requirements of publication of details of each operation were reaffirmed, with a new one that no company should commit more than 20 percent of its paid-in capital to any single risk. This limitation mainly affected foreign companies, as they usually transferred funds abroad as risk premiums for any amount whatever. This system was responsible for a permanent outflow of funds, affecting the

TABLE 16–7. Share in Total Sight Deposits of Foreign Banks by State with Largest Deposits (1912–1915)

Place	State 1912	(%)	State 1913	(%)	State 1914	(%)	State 1915	(%)
1st	Sao Paulo	20.1	Rio Grande do Sul	18.9	Sao Paulo	21.7	Sao Paulo	25.7
2nd	Federal Capital	13.6	Sao Paulo	16.7	Federal Capital	15.2	Federal Capital	21.0
3rd	Bahia	2.1	Federal Capital	11.5	Bahia	2.9	Bahia	4.5
4th	Para	1.5	Pernambuco	2.1	Para	1.7	Para	1.9
5th	Pernambuco	1.5	Bahia	1.9	Pernambuco	1.6	Pernambuco	1.9
6th	Rio Grande do Sul	0.6	Para	1.2	Amazonas	0.4	Amazonas	0.4
7th	Amazonas	0.5	Amazonas	0.4	Rio Grande do Sul	0.3	Rio Grande do Sul	0.3

Source: Brasil. Ministerio da Fazenda. Comercio Exterior do Brasil. In: Movimento Bancario, Rio de Janeiro, 1910–1914, V.3, pp. 220–223. Brasil. Ministerio da Fazenda. Comercio Exterior do Brasil. In: Movimento Bancario, Rio de Janeiro, 1920, pp. 164–195, 1922, pp. 22–145.

balance of payments. The foreign companies, beginning a campaign to maintain their previous rights, ceased operations and, after a remonstrance sent to the President claiming a new decree unconstitutional for having legislated on established rights, Congress in 1902 invalidated the Regulamento Murtinho. The new decree (5072/03) maintained the general characteristics of the previous one, but required only a 20 percent reserve from net profits to be invested in domestic currency. Foreign companies were left free to transfer whatever premiums they wished, and allowed to transfer their excess reserves as reinsurance.[44]

Trade on the Stock Exchange, after the last traces of the *Encilhamento*, turned toward fixed-income securities. Preference for public debt bonds became even greater after the crisis of 1900; they represented an average of 65 percent of volume on the exchange. The companies listed on the exchange underwent a clear change. The most marked movement occurred in the textile industry, which from twenty-four companies listed in 1903 grew to fifty-two by 1913. Transport companies, despite government support, did not follow the trend. Companies dedicated to new commercial and industrial activities came to the board, corresponding to a gradual diversification of the economy.[45]

Until the turn of the century almost all direct foreign investment was of British origin. According to Paiva Abreu, by 1905 non-British European and North American capital represented around 40 percent and 5 percent, respectively, proportions that maintained themselves until 1913.[46] For the period from 1886 to 1896, A.C. Castro found that the most significant foreign investments were in insurance companies, of which 90 percent were British.[47] British capital held 62.3 percent of the new investments, but German capital already amounted to 8.6 percent, followed by France, the United States, Austria, and Italy. These numbers must be analyzed bearing in mind that these only deal with a total of £3,359,328 in new investments during the period.

Between 1897 and 1902, according to the same author, British insurance companies continued entering in great majority. New investments during the period came to £25,014,444, of which Britain was responsible for 73 percent. Canadian investments began to grow (9.9 percent of total) with the creation of light and urban transport companies. (On this, more is said below.) Next came Belgium with 6.8 percent and France with 6.1 percent of the total.[48]

Still considering only new investments, the period from 1903 to 1913 shows a marked difference: In a total of £189,522,477, the relative share of British investments decreased, while North American capital accounted for 19.9 percent of the total, at £32.6 million. If Canadian investments were added to this total, the share would pass 30 percent.[49]

It is important to repeat that these shares represent what was declared at the moment of requesting authorization to operate from the government, with no assurance that the capital was paid in, which would lead to an excessive estimate of the capital stock. It must also be remembered that Canadian and North American companies raised capital in Europe.

Foreign investment in manufacturing increased significantly, attracting 7.2 percent of the total, with machinery and equipment accounting for 5.7 percent. Of this, North American capital accounted for 89.8 percent and German capital for 10.2 percent.[50] French capital never held the position of British capital or even North American. According to the research of Saes and Szmreczanyi, however, between 1900 and

1914 "the financial market in Paris held the stage for the repeated underwritings of Brazilian bonds."[51]

The foreign banks in Brazil continued to finance trade and to support the activities of other foreign companies, especially those in the service sector. The urban economy began to have a relatively autonomous role, and foreign investment had an important part in this transformation. One cannot find an association between banking and industrial capital from the examination of foreign banks. Recent studies on the textile industry of Rio de Janeiro, however, have shown that domestic banks took an active part in the incorporation of companies, either as shareholders or through their directors. Recent studies on textile enterprises show that the foreign banks also had a much greater connection with industrial activity than was previously supposed. The food and beverage industries should also be studied in similar fashion with the aim of making it possible to affirm or deny that the main industrial sectors of this period were associated with foreign banks or their directors for the purpose of obtaining credit facilities.

From the mid-1890s the non-British European share of foreign government debt grew, although in 1913 it was still 16 percent of the total. This total increased between 1895 and 1913 by around 5 or 6 percent annually. Until the 1880s all foreign debt was contracted through the central government. From the end of the Empire on, state and municipalities' debts increased, reaching 8 percent in 1895, 21 percent in 1895, 21 percent in 1905, and 12 percent in 1913.

The inflow of funds in Brazil roughly corresponds to the cycles of capital export from Britain. The share of British capital exports directed to Brazil, though, varied considerably. The participation of Brazil is especially relevant from 1886 to 1913, initially due to the boom of the second half of the 1880s and to the conversion of the central governmental debt, then due to the refinancing of the foreign debt between 1898 and 1901 and to the redemption of railway guarantees, and finally due to the expansion of economic activity, especially after 1908.

British investments in Brazil should receive a more detailed treatment, based on Irving Stone's findings. Brazil's share in total British investments in Latin America remained roughly steady at about 20 percent. (See Table 16–8.)

Between 1905 and 1913 the portfolio component of railways in Latin America nearly doubled, to reach £65 million, of which the Brazilian Railway Co. accounted for more than £22 million. During the same period British investment in canals and docks in Latin America had grown from £1.8 million to more than £15 million, of which more than £10 million was invested in Brazil. American interests controlled the main part of this portfolio investment. Portfolio investment always predominated in Brazil. As for investment in private industry, Brazil was one of the few South American nations in 1913 in which British portfolio holdings were greater than direct investment.[52]

TABLE 16–8. Geographical Distribution of British Investment in Latin America (1875–1913) (£ millions)

	1875	1885	1895	1905	1913
Brazil	30.9	47.6	93.0	124.4	254.8
TOTAL	174.6	250.5	552.5	688.5	1,179.9

Source: Irving Stone, "British Direct and Portfolio Investment in Latin America before 1914," *Journal of Economic History*, 37 (September 1977), p. 695.

Conclusions

The establishment of British banks in the 1860s facilitated the entry of British investment in Brazil, but the banks specialized in foreign-exchange and foreign-trade operations, and did not lend much to domestic industry. Toward the end of the century banks from other European countries joined the British, and between 1903 and 1913 there was a veritable boom of foreign bank promotions. These benefitted by the recuperation of the export economy and by the progressive diversification of Brazilian production. The most important operations in this period took place in the export-import trade. Secondly came credit for the foreign enterprises in the service sectors, mainly ports, railroads, urban transportation, light and telephone, which contributed to the urban development of the country. In third place, far behind, came credit for the textile industries and probably beverages.

In view of the evidence presented here, it is clear that "finance capital" in Hilferding's sense was not present in Brazil. The foreign banks had no interest whatever in dominating the Brazilian infant industries. They were, above all, tuned to international trade. Investments in the service sector for urban development also attracted them, however. Furthermore, since financial activity remained concentrated in the city of Rio de Janeiro, whose export sector had for a long time been in a decline, the conclusion that the foreign banks furnished credits for enterprises of urban infrastructure, which were also foreign, becomes even stronger. These investments facilitated the expansion of Rio de Janeiro's industry, which was already quite apart from the agrarian export economy.

Although Brazil was not a capital exporter, the dividends and interest paid by foreign banks and enterprises to their American and European shareholders constituted a significant outflow of funds.

Finally, it should be noted that the Brazilian government did not try to influence the actions of the foreign banks, but offered them great liberty in their business. The banks' direction and administration was concentrated in the hands of expatriate Europeans with little participation by Brazilians.

Appendix

TABLE A-1. Foreign Banks by Incorporation Date and Capital

Date	Name	Nationality	Capital
1862	London and Brazilian Bank*a*	British	1901: 13.333 contos 1921: £ 1.25 million 1926: 26.667 contos
1863	British Bank of South America*b*	British	1901: 8.888 contos 1921: £ 1.0 million 1926: 17.777 contos
1888	Brasilianische Bank für Deutschland	German	1901: 10,000 contos 1920: 15,000 contos 1926: 20,000 contos
1891	London and River Plate Bank	British	1901: 3.500 contos 1920: 3.500 contos

(continued)

Table A-1. Foreign Banks by Incorporation Date and Capital (*Continued*)

Date	Name	Nationality	Capital
1897	Banque Française du Brésil	French	1901: 10.000 contos 1910: Ceased operation
1900	Banque Belge de Prêts Fonciers	Belgian	1909: Ceased operation
1906	Banco Alliança	Portuguese	1908: Ceased operation
1907	Banque du Crédit Foncier du Brésil	French	1909: 100,000 francs
1907	Banco Español del Rio de la Plata	Argentina	1918: 800 contos
1910	Banque Francaise et Italienne pour l'Amerique du Sud*c*	French	1913: 25 million francs 1926: 15,000 contos
1911	Banque Brésilienne Italo-Belge	Belgian	1913: 20 million francs
1911	Deutsche-Südamerikanische Bank	German	1920: 2,205 contos 1926: 7,500 contos
1912	Banco Allemão Transatlântico	German	1913: 3,000 contos 1920: 3,675 contos 1926: 7,350 contos
1912	Banque Française pour le Brésil et l'Amerique du Sud	French	1913: 15 million francs
1912	Banco Nacional Ultramarino	Portuguese	1920: 3,000 contos
1913	Crédit Foncier du Brésil et de l'Amérique du Sud	French	

Source: Steven Topik, *Capital Estrangeiro e o Estado no Sistema Bancario Brasileiro, 1889–1931* (Rio de Janeiro, 1979).

a The London and Brazilian Bank joined the London and River Plate in 1923 to form the British Bank of South America.

b The British Bank of South America was at first called the Brazilian and Portuguese Bank. In 1886 it became the English Bank of Rio de Janeiro and in 1891 the British Bank of South America. In 1920, the Anglo-South American Bank bought it.

c The Banque Française et Italienne absorbed the Banco Comercial Italo-Brazileiro and the Banco Suizo Americano in 1910.

17

Extra-Regional Banks and Investment in China

Frank H. H. King

with the research assistance of David J. S. King

Historical Survey

The opening of the Yangtze River to foreign trade and the extension of the Treaty Port*
system of open ports consequent to provisions of the 1858 Treaty of Tientsin created a
network of foreign-initiated intraregional trade at a time when refugees from the
Taiping rebels inflated the demand for real estate protected by the provisions for
"foreign settlements" in the larger ports, especially Shanghai. The consequent boom
was fueled in part by India-based banks with branches in Shanghai and the British
Crown Colony of Hong Kong.

By 1870, there had been two significant developments. The first was a shake-out
of the early foreign banking presence as a result of the collapse of real estate speculation in Shanghai and the mid–1860s financial crises in Bombay and London. The
second was the opening in 1865 of a "local bank," the Hongkong and Shanghai
Banking Corporation, by a committee of British, German, American, and Parsee
merchants with the task, *inter alia*, of developing through a locally elected directorate
the finance of regional trade.

Foreign banking on the China coast was dominated by British-chartered "exchange banks"—the Oriental Bank Corporation, the Chartered Bank of India, Australia and China, and the Chartered Mercantile Bank of India, London and China—by
the Hongkong Bank, and by the Comptoir d'Escompte de Paris. Of the Indian banks
none survived, and only the reconstituted Agra returned. The French bank, managed
by what its Shanghai manager, Hermann Wallich, described as either "Swiss Calvinists
or German Jews," lost its Calvinist—presumably Victor Kresser—to be the Hongkong
Bank's first chief manager; and it lost its Germans, in part as a consequence of the
Franco-Prussian War, to the Deutsche Bank, which, for a brief period in the early
1870s, maintained branches in the East.

*See Appendix A for definition of this and other specialized and unfamiliar terms used throughout this
discussion.

Exchange operations had been considered mercantile rather than banking business; at the least, exchange dealings and currency issue should not be combined in a single institution—hence in India the "Presidency Banks" on which the Hongkong Bank as "local" bank was ostensibly patterned, and the exchange banks. By the 1860s this distinction, when not embodied in legislation, had lost its relevance. Similarly the claims of the Hongkong Bank's founder that he was working on Scottish principles— that is, dependence on branch banking and note-issuing—have to be understood as a statement of his initial inspiration. The British banking traditions in the East come clearly from the colonial banking regulations and Royal Charters as developed from the early 1830s. Foreign banking on the China coast then developed pragmatically.

By the end of the century, although the banks had established additional offices in Treaty Ports formerly serviced by the banks' merchant agents, the foreign "exchange banking" scene was little changed. The doyen of the British exchange banks, the Oriental, failed in 1884 and its successor (the New Oriental) in 1892; the Chartered Mercantile had reorganized as the Mercantile Bank of India, Ltd., but had in the process been forced to abandon its charter; in 1900 the Agra Bank was in liquidation— all banks had been affected by the drop in the price of silver. Nevertheless, British exchange banking (a term including the Hongkong Bank) continued its dominance.

Despite the presence of three German directors (of twelve) on the Hongkong Bank's board, German industrial interests, as opposed to Hanseatic merchants, pressed for a German bank responsive to their investment banking priority; this resulted in 1889 in the founding of the Deutsch-Asiatische Bank (DAB), with head office in Shanghai but direction in Berlin.

The Comptoir d'Escompte, reorganized in 1889 as the Comptoir National d'Escompte, never recovered its Eastern role, and French representation in the East became the responsibility of the Banque de l'Indo-Chine, a consortium bank in which the Comptoir National d'Escompte participated. In anticipation of this competition the Hongkong Bank established its own offices in Lyon (1881) and Hamburg (1889).

In this same period, Japan's Yokohama Specie Bank (founded 1880), self-proclaimed as modeled after the Hongkong Bank, made a significant entrance into the field of Eastern exchange banking. China's own first attempt, the Imperial Bank of China (in Chinese known literally as "Chinese Foreign Trade Bank"), founded in 1897 and managed by the retired Tientsin manager of the Hongkong Bank, survived but was less successful.

The last twenty years of the century were characterized by unfulfilled expectations relative to the "opening of China," and China became the goal of concession-seekers, legitimate industrial missions, especially from Germany, and merchant banking schemes. These developments reached one climax in 1889-90 but collapsed; further interest in "opening" China was delayed by the Sino-Japanese War of 1894-95.

Political developments, including China's defeat by the Japanese, revealed China's weakness. The terms of the Treaty of Shimonoseki (1895) clarified the right of foreigners to undertake fixed investment in China; reformers seemed for a time in control, and China professed interest in railway development. Although once again encouraged, financiers had now to take into account the political pressures to which the Imperial Chinese government was subjected. If China were to be preserved as a sovereign entity, the Western Powers had to ration their demands—there was a limit to which each of the Powers could safely go, given the state of international competition and suspicion, with respect to concessions involving some surrender of sovereignty and/or grant of exclusive privilege. This in turn encouraged the development of national and international consortia—for example, the German Konsortium für Asiatische Geschäfte (KfAG), the British and Chinese Corporation (B&CC), and the various Belgian groups, including the Compagnie Internationale d'Orient and the Banque Sino-Belge.

The imbalance of political power and financial capabilities resulted in the establishment of financial institutions with multinational sources of funds; of these banks the Russo-Asiatic Bank, as a successor to the Russo-Chinese Bank, was a prime example—French, Belgian, even German financing using a Russian political front. The earlier Russian bank, moreover, was seen by Count Witte as a means of strengthening Russian economic influence in China, thus counterbalancing the British influence, which he ascribed to its administration of the Chinese Maritime Customs—a view, incidentally, wholly erroneous as to fact and consequence. Another solution was the development of interbank agreements—for example, the 1895 agreement between the Hongkong Bank and the Deutsch-Asiatische Bank, which, much modified, would lead through a complex of negotiations to the climax in June 1913—the formation of the Six-Power Groups involving thirty-eight financial institutions from six nations, whose immediate aim was the financing of the new republican government of China through a £60 million series of "Reorganization Loans."[1]

The leadership of Britain, France, and Germany in the formation of "groups" reflects the ability of their capital markets to handle the consequent business. The granting of concessions by China, however, reflected political pressures rather than economic reality. The consequent mismatching of potential with capability was at first adjusted, by the formation of, for example, a Russian bank with multinational investment of funds. By 1910, however, pressures had mounted for full-scale Russian and Japanese "groups"; hence the composition of the Russian Group in Table 17–1 appears almost entirely Belgian but also includes British financial houses excluded from their own national group.

The success of the group system would in turn foster the development of opposition groups, including the Anglo-Belgian and Crisp syndicates, each of which sought to exploit the weakened financial position of China and the political embarrassment created in European governments by their need to endorse, for however brief a period, one group or another as the legitimate negotiator under the terms of the concession.

Foreign Banks: Geographical Penetration and Distribution in China

By 1914 geographical penetration of foreign banks in Asia was still limited to the major ports and to Peking. Hong Kong was a base for international banking and important for penetration of the South China market, but the main financial focus of China was Shanghai.

Foreign relations in China were restricted by the various treaties and trade consequently based on "treaty ports," that is, ports that were open consequent to provisions of those treaties. Foreign banks were at first further restricted by lack of trained officers, and bank-staffed branches or agencies were established conservatively, other

TABLE 17–1. Sextuple Agreement of June 1912: Members of the Six Groups

A. BRITISH GROUP
The Hongkong and Shanghai Banking Corporation
[From December 14, 1912:
The Hongkong and Shanghai Banking Corporation (33%)
Baring Bros. and Co. (25%)
London, County and Westminster Bank (14%)
Parr's Bank (14%)
J. Henry Schröder and Co. (14%)[a]]

B. GERMAN GROUP

Direction der Diskonto-Gesellschaft	Nationalbank für Deutschland
S. Bleichröder	Deutsch-Asiatische Bank
Deutsche Bank	Jacob S. H. Stern
Berliner Handelsgesellschaft	Sal. Oppenheim Jr. & Cie.
Bank für Handel & Industrie	Norddeutsche Bank in Hamburg
Mendelssohn & Co.	L. Behrens & Söhne
Dresdner Bank	Bayerische Hypotheken und Wechselbank
A. Schaaffhausen'scher Bankverein	

C. FRENCH GROUP

Banque de l'Indo-Chine	Société Générale de Crédit Industriel
Banque de Paris et des Pays-Bas	& Commerciel
Comptoir National d'Escompte de Paris	Banque de l'Union Parisienne
Crédit Lyonnais	Banque Française pour le Commerce
Société Générale pour favoriser	et l'Industrie
le developpement du Commerce	Crédit Mobilier Français
et de l'Industrie en France	

D. RUSSIAN GROUP

Banque Russo-Asiatique	Société Belge d'Étude de Chemins de Fer
A. Spitzer & Co.	en Chine
J. Henry Schröder & Co.[a]	Société Générale de Belgique
Eastern Bank Ltd.[b]	Banque d'Outremer[c]
Banque Sino-Belge	

E. AMERICAN GROUP (all of New York City)[d]

Messrs. J. P. Morgan & Co.	The First National Bank
Messrs. Kuhn, Loeb & Co.	National City Bank

F. JAPANESE GROUP
The Yokohama Specie Bank

[a]British—from December 1912 a member of the British Group.
[b]British—Sassoon interests.
[c]This bank is also Belgian.
[d]Represented in the United Kingdom by Messrs Morgan, Grenfell and Co., in France by Messrs Morgan, Harjes and Co., and in France and Germany by Messrs M. M. Warburg and Co. of Hamburg.

open ports being covered by merchant-agents and through these outposts to the local banking system.

The Hongkong Bank, which considered itself a "China bank," unlike government-sponsored or controlled banks (for example, the Banque de l'Indo-Chine or the Russo-Asiatic), would open new offices only on commercial grounds, for this reason specifically rejecting the suggestion of Chungking, Changsha, and (until the very eve of the Great War) Tsingtau. By 1914 it had offices in seven Chinese cities and a second office in Shanghai. The payout of loan funds and the servicing of railway debts had encouraged some expansion of foreign bank networks; the viceroy of the Liang-Kwang provinces with his offices in Canton practically forced the Hongkong Bank to open there in 1909; the Deutsch-Asiatische Bank opened in Peking rather than forgo a share in the servicing of a debt domiciled, exceptionally, in the capital.[2]

The Russians made tentative banking moves in the Kingdom of Korea, but the Hongkong Bank considered a commercial agent sufficient, virtually conceding the Japanese early economic domination there. Similarly in Taiwan, by the time the province had become sufficiently developed to warrant a bank-staffed office of a foreign-exchange bank, the economy was subject to Japan and the restrictions that country imposed on foreign banking in its colonial territories; the Hongkong Bank's agent worked with the Yokohama branch, while the colonial Bank of Taiwan developed and eventually expanded into an international operation.

The development of "spheres of interest" led governments to encourage their national banks to offer a financial presence. Thus the Deutsch-Asiatische Bank was in Tsingtau and the Banque de l'Indo-Chine in Yunnan-fu (Kunming), while the northeast provinces, that is, Manchuria, were dominated by Russian and later by Japanese banks, with the Hongkong Bank, for example, establishing no office north of the Great Wall until 1915 (Harbin).

Foreign Banks: Elsewhere in the Far East

The pattern of foreign bank penetration was the same elsewhere in Asia. Until the great 1923 earthquake Yokohama remained the chief foreign-exchange bank center in Japan, with branch offices in Hiogo/Kobe (1869) and Nagasaki (1891). In 1872 the Hongkong Bank had opened in Osaka to assist with the movement of bullion relative to the new mint. There was no purpose in a foreign bank in Tokyo.

Singapore was early seen as a banking center; for example, the Bank of Rotterdam, with a focus on Netherlands East India trade, was there by 1870, together with the British exchange banks. The King of Siam and the heads of smaller states in the region kept accounts in Singapore banks before their own countries had facilities. The Hongkong Bank established its own branch in 1877. As for the other Straits Settlements, the Chartered Mercantile Bank was in Penang as early as 1860 and the Hongkong Bank moved up after the banking crisis in 1884, but quieter Malacca was reached only in 1909.

Banking penetration of the Malay States came with the positive encouragement of British administrators, and the Chartered Bank of India, Australia and China moved into the Federated States of Perak and Selangor—Taiping and Kuala Lumpur—in 1888; Klang followed in 1909, by which time the tin-mining center of Ipoh had become the capital of Perak. The Hongkong Bank established there in 1910, the Chartered Bank in 1912. The early offices were not at first profitable; some were subsidized by government and seen as an essential first step to modern administration and investment. Similarly it was a friendly sultan of the unfederated state of Johore who encouraged the Hongkong Bank to set up there in 1910. The Mercantile Bank of India established the only pre–1914 East Coast branch at Kota Bharu, Kelantan, in 1912.

In Siam the major port was the capital, Bangkok, although the Chartered Bank was also established in the tin-producing area of Phuket. The Hongkong Bank and the Mercantile Bank of India covered southern Siam from Penang. Both the Hongkong Bank and the Chartered Bank were well-represented in Manila, and then, in 1883, rushed to be first in Iloilo, close to the sugar-producing area in the western Visayas. The Chartered Bank also opened an office in the port of Cebu. In the Netherlands East Indies the British banks were established in Batavia (1884), but the Hongkong Bank also found it useful, as in the Philippines, to have an office in a subsidiary port, namely Sourabaya (1896).

Most foreign bank networks were based on needs as perceived from the metropolitan base, whether London, Berlin, Paris, or Amsterdam. These might be fulfilled for a time by merchant agents, but when these failed or the banking business grew, the bank would establish an office (agency or branch) staffed by its own officers.

Colonial networks were influenced by pressures in Singapore, Saigon, and Batavia on the British, French, and Dutch banks/trading firms, respectively.

The Hongkong Bank, exceptionally, radiated out from Hong Kong as the colony's trade development and the requirements of its Hong Kong-based constituents dictated. Thus the bank's early move to Saigon (1870) was influenced by its first chief manager's involvement in the sugar estates at Bien Hoa and by the rice trade, vital to Hong Kong's interests. Similarly, it was Hong Kong's sugar trade—and the failure of its merchant-agent—which took the bank to the Dutch East Indies where Chinese remittances offset Hong Kong sugar refinery purchases.

The pattern of expansion was affected by the location of decision-makers among the bank's constituents, the need to service their accounts up-country, and the location of exceptional sources of funds.

Singapore was the center of banking partly because it was there that the heads of the major trading agency houses and the managing agents of rubber estates could be found. Bank offices in Singapore were usually "branch offices" as opposed to "agencies." This meant not only that they could issue bank notes—subject to charter provisions and local legislation—but that the manager controlled his own exchange operations and administered his business with considerable independence consistent with the basic regulations of his bank and subject to his having (1) been assigned capital and/or (2) access to a source of funds. With these funds he could respond to the requirements of major constituents, participate, for example, in the development of the tin industry and, unfortunately, facilitate speculation in rubber shares.

In contrast, Malacca's Hongkong Bank agent rarely needed to make a banking decision. He fulfilled at the local level decisions made in Singapore, keeping the accounts of the branch offices of agency houses and handling the current account business of their employees—the estate managers and their subordinates. The compradore might be more ambitious, but the old city had its limitations.

On the other hand, a ruler who wished to keep his private and government funds closer to home might convince the Singapore manager that the bank would be wise to set up an agency in his capital—if the bank wished to retain the business. The Johore office pre-1914 was a "subagency" as compared to Malacca, which was an agency. Both reported to Singapore.

The foreign banks continued to use merchants as agents where setting up even a small office was ruled impractical; they also had a fully developed correspondent system both within the region and worldwide. In China the foreign banks could remit funds through the native banking system, and as modern-style banking developed usual relationships were established. The networks were all-inclusive.

The "Eastern" Banks in Europe and North America

Typically the foreign banks operating in the Far East had but a single base point in their country of national origin. This was in part from the logic of their operational requirements and in part due to their origins. The Deutsch-Asiatische Bank, for example, as the creature of the domestic banks which founded it, was at first forbidden to have an operating office in Germany; its Berlin office opened in 1896 for limited purposes and its Hamburg branch not until 1906; consequently, it was the Hongkong Bank that flourished in Hamburg and kept the account of the Ost-Asiatischer Verein—of which the British bank's manager was for several years the treasurer.

British chartered banks maintained a London head office, which undertook general commercial banking business and operated current accounts for its constituents, who were all oriented to the area in which the bank operated. There is record of deposit-soliciting offices in Edinburgh from time to time, but the Hongkong Bank certainly found it could obtain sterling deposits from any region of Britain through appropriate advertising and correspondence. These banks were not the creation of British domestic banks although their directors often sat on the boards of British overseas banks (or the London Committee of the Hongkong Bank), providing relationships between the several regionally oriented chartered banks and with the major London clearing banks.

Unique among the British exchange banks, the Hongkong Bank retained its head office in Hong Kong. Its London office was, however—like the London office of other British chartered banks—managed by returned senior executives. The London manager thus carried the prestige necessary to be effective in the City. In this task he was advised by a local committee, mistaken by some as the actual board of directors, the members of which provided a link with the Hongkong Bank's clearing bank, the London and County (and its successors to the National Westminster), and with China merchants like E. and A. Deacon and Company, T. A. Gibb and Company, or Matheson and Company. There were also financiers on the committee, men who, in addition to their general role in the City, had a particular Eastern interest, as, for example, [Sir] Carl Meyer of the Pekin Syndicate.[3]

The Hongkong Bank had its own agencies in Lyon and Hamburg and in New York and San Francisco, the last mentioned for purposes of bullion purchases. The geographical spread placed the bank in a unique position among exchange banks.

French and German exchange banks obtained their capital from their founding domestic banks. The London-based Eastern exchange banks' capital came in part from their Indian foundation (if any) and in part from the equity investment through the Stock Exchange. The Hongkong Bank's initial capital was found primarily in Hong Kong, the China coast, the Philippines, and India; expansion was financed by rights issues. The bank maintained three share registers, in Hong Kong, Shanghai, and London; transfer of shares from the Eastern to the London register was strictly limited in an effort to prevent the predominance of a London shareholding and pressure to remove the domicile of the directorate and/or the site of the head office to London.

The Legal Environment

Extraterritoriality

Foreign banks in the East operated under privileged conditions. In China there was extraterritoriality (extrality). This was particularly important in providing the banks a safe operating location, subject to the jurisdiction of consular courts, supported by a British supreme court for China located in the Shanghai International Settlement. As foreign/Chinese business contacts became more frequent, the Shanghai Mixed Courts provided the basis for cooperative justice that, supplemented by recognition of merchant practice, provided the mechanism for meeting the increasingly complex legal requirements of the foreign communities in China.

British Colonial Banking Charters and Their Provisions

The British exchange banks operated under the provisions (and restrictions) of their own charter or ordinance of incorporation in the specified region applied for. The most important of these provisions were (1) double (or reserve) liability for shareholders; (2) the right to issue bank notes limited to the value of paid-up capital; (3) the need to publish annual accounts and to provide to the chartering authority—in the case of the Hongkong Bank, the Governor of Hong Kong—any information required; (4) control relative to the opening and closing of branches and agencies; (5) limiting of business to "banking" defined broadly to permit virtually any financial operation; (6) an ineffective prohibition on lending against the security of its own shares; and (7) a specifically limited period of operation and reservation of rights to the Crown.

The benefits derived from the charters were the right to operate in different territories as specified in the charter without further formality, to issue notes, and to receive funds from British colonial government entities without further security. These rights were in fact qualified, and since the charters were hedged by provisions that enabled government to remove or qualify the rights as stated—for example, the note-issuing right in territories issuing their own notes—or by making government business subject to competitive tender, the privileges dwindled to "prestige."

The provisions calling for publication of balance sheets on a specified form and the ability of government to call for further information suggested a control that the government in fact did not have; the provisions might consequently give the public the false impression that the balance sheet had been in some real sense verified by government, or even that government stood behind the bank. Not surprisingly the implication of this provision was one of the key reasons for the abandonment of the chartered banking system in the years after 1870. Other provisions—for example, the opening of branches or the renewal of the charter—provided the authorities with the opportunity to act as "gatekeepers," perhaps to induce the bank to accept changes in its privileges, which, despite Crown-reserved rights, the government was reluctant to impose without a *quid pro quo*.

The Bank Note Issue

Colonial banks were seen as note-issuing banks, but the collapse of the Oriental Bank in 1884 with a large Ceylon issue outstanding, an issue which for political reasons had to be guaranteed by the government, was an important factor in the trend to colonial government issues. In fact, the note issue, however attractive it appeared to bank promoters in the period between 1840 and 1865, was becoming more a sign of prestige than a source of profit.

The value of foreign bank notes issued in China outside Shanghai was minimal. Hongkong Bank statistics indicate that in April 1889 of a total issue of 5.8 million Hong Kong dollars (HK$), there was HK$678,000 issued in China of which HK$500,000 was issued in Shanghai. The Hongkong Bank's note issue in Japan totaled HK$86,000, restricted to the foreign community; and its note issue in the Straits Settlements was HK$1.4 million in 1889. The balance, HK$3.0 million, was issued by the head office in the Colony. The Straits Settlements government took over the note issue in the early 1900s; the foreign banks' issue in Siam was small, temporary, and experimental.

As paper money became increasingly accepted in ordinary business the British banks in any case came against the limits of their authorized issue. Consequently, the limits imposed by replacement of bank notes by a government issue, as in the Straits Settlements, merely permitted the banks to go further in meeting the requirements in Hong Kong, where between 60 and 70 percent of the Hong Kong issue was probably circulating in South China.

By 1898 both the Hongkong and Chartered banks were in danger of exceeding their authorized issues. They were subsequently permitted to issue additional notes under provisions of special legislation that required the deposit of a 100 percent reserve in silver against the "excess" issue. As there was a 1 percent tax on bank notes, it did not always suit the banks to issue on demand; consequently, the exchange could and did vary from the theoretical limits set by the relation of the prices of silver and gold— Hong Kong ceased to be on a silver standard narrowly defined, and this could cause an impediment to the smooth transfer of funds.

Other Legal Considerations

The British colonial banking system was designed primarily to control those banks aspiring to issue bank notes and receive government funds on deposit. Non-British foreign banks were permitted after registration to engage in general banking business, including the acceptance of local deposits. The situation was similar in French and Dutch territories. Under Spanish rule in the Philippine Islands, the British banks operated under a commercial treaty subject to their own charters, but with American rule all banks were subject to such regulations as required by the U.S. Comptroller of the Currency, who was responsible for administration of the national banking system. Foreign banks were eligible, subject to the deposit of security, to become depositors for federal and insular government funds.

As for Siam, the Hongkong Bank was established in Bangkok in 1888; it was followed by the Chartered Bank of India, Australia and China, the Banque de l'Indo-Chine, and the Deutsch-Asiatische Bank. The first Siamese modern bank, the Siam Commercial Bank (founded 1906), became a scene of international intrigue involving German and Danish interests and British concern for its own role in the kingdom. In Bangkok the banks operated under conditions of extrality, subject to their own charters, but the right to issue bank notes was subject to the laws of Siam. The Siamese authorization for a note issue by the Hongkong and Chartered banks proved temporary, a testing period to see how the notes would be received; in 1903 the Siamese began their own exclusive issue.

The Impact of the British Precedents

The British chartered banking system comprised a series of private-sector corporations in a combination of activities including the finance of private trade on the one hand and the issue of bank notes and the handling of public funds on the other. This combination of profit motive and public service, of trade finance and note issue, was unique; it was not accepted as legitimate even in Britain's Indian Empire until the 1850s. Nevertheless, British traditions, adjusted to particular national banking proclivities, were to influence such institutions as the Banque de l'Indo-Chine and the Yokohama Specie Bank.

The former was established on the basis of memoranda submitted to the French colonial authorities by a Saigon entrepreneur and banker, Victor Kresser, who had been the Hongkong Bank's first chief manager. The bank's development, however, was affected by the tradition of continental *banques d'affaires*, just as the Yokohama Specie Bank's role, whatever the initial inspiration, was determined by Japan's changing overseas banking needs.

The Role of Foreign Banks in the East

Exchange and the Finance of Trade

In the 1830s and 1840s many informed commentators considered exchange operations as more suitable to a mercantile than a banking establishment; certainly exchange and note-issue rights, when combined in one institution, were dangerous. But trade had to be financed and the right to issue notes was often considered by bank promoters as a source of profit essential for commercial success; hence, the regulations under which the new "exchange banks" operated.

By 1870 these banks had set up a network of exchange and bullion operations based on London, Calcutta, Hong Kong/Shanghai, San Francisco, and New York. Additionally, the Eastern exchange banks facilitated such triangular trade finance as Hong Kong/Calcutta/London; Bombay or Madras/Colombo/Rangoon. By cooperating with banks specializing in the Atlantic trade finance, Eastern exchange banks were able to offer facilities for the sugar trade with North America as well as Europe. With the fall in the gold price of silver most of these transactions involved an increasingly serious exchange risk, and the ability of the banks to cover their operations by developing sources of funds in each area was the measure of their success or survival (See Table 17–2). In all this the London office, even of banks headquartered overseas, became crucial; with the growth of foreign investment, it could take on investment banking functions.

To be safely involved in medium- or long-term finance the foreign banks had to depend on sources of funds in silver-using territories. Here their connection with merchant houses, their provision of facilities to foreigners, and their contacts with the

TABLE 17–2. Exchange Rates: Hong Kong on London

	(i)	(ii)		(iii)
1872 (June)	4/6	100	(June)	100
1876 (December)	4/2	115	(December)	109
1880	3/8	122		116
1885	3/4	135		128
1890	3/5	132		121
1895	2/1⁵/₈	211		195
1900	2/1	215		201
1901	1/10¹/₄	242		233
1903 (June)	1/8	269	(February)	269
1914	1/10⁵/₈	237	(June)	228

(i) Rate per $, Hong Kong on London.

(ii) Index based on (i) but indicating number of dollars per pound, with 100 = 4/6; i.e., £1 = $4.44; at 269, £1 = $11.96.

(iii) Index of ounces of silver purchasable with £1; 100 = 60d/oz, 269 = 22⁵/₁₆ d/oz.

local money markets were determining factors in overall success, giving the advantage to those foreign banks whose origin or base was actually in the East and whose primary affiliations were with those merchant houses having themselves a significant presence in the East rather than with the domestic banking system. The founders of the Deutsch-Asiatische Bank understood this and set their head office in Shanghai, but the directors remained in Berlin, negating the advantage.

With the closing of the Indian mints to the free coinage of silver and the elimination or modification of the silver standard in Southeast Asia and Japan, these territories were able to retain a safer exchange relationship with Europe, and funds could move more freely through the exchange banks for investment in mining and plantation economies. Nevertheless, the remittance business between Southeast Asia and China continued with the exchange banks rationalizing this flow and facilitating the China trade.

The role of foreign banks as investment channels for China was therefore hampered not only by the political developments in China but also by China's adherence to a silver standard. Those banks with significant sources of silver funds were able to finance small-scale investment, despite the theory of banking operations, by "advances" secured against real estate and shares; they could also assist the various governments by issuing silver-denominated bonds on local markets. Their most spectacular contribution was, however, the raising of funds denominated in gold units of account (usually sterling) in European capital markets and handling of the consequent exchange operations.

The foreign banks acted as ordinary commercial and even savings banks for the foreign communities, but in the larger communities they also offered facilities for local people wishing the protection or security afforded by a foreign-owned bank. One or more foreign banks would be designated, be founded, or be successful in tendering for local government and/or imperial government business. Official funds, loan-servicing funds, or indemnity and related payments, and, after the 1911 Revolution, Chinese customs revenues were an important source of silver funds at a time when local investment and local government loans in growing foreign settlements had become important.

New Banks and Investment after 1895

After 1895 a new generation of foreign banks arrived in the East. These were seen as primarily supportive of national investment aspirations and were often without a local banking base. Unable to offer the facilities that the older established banks provided, they nevertheless were able to participate in the growing "modern-sector" economies. Often, however, they found their operations dependent on the cooperation of the older banks, especially the Hongkong Bank with its superior network and access to silver funds.

Whatever the underlying priorities at the time of their formation, many of the new banks also financed trade. Thus the Russo-Asiatic Bank competed for finance of the brick-tea trade from Hankow; "national" banks catered to the needs of their country's sphere of influence. American financial interests, absent since the 1891 fall of the great agency house, Russell and Company, and the consequent hesitant start of the compradore-sponsored National Bank of China, which Russells had hoped to manage, returned to the East, the most prominent of the new institutions being the International Banking Corporation (now part of Citibank).

The expectation of bankers post–1895 was, however, that they would be involved in the long-term financial requirements of their country's newly won concessions. But China, when appearing most subject, retained under the Empire the capability of directing her own external financial affairs; hard bargaining and long negotiations lay between the political concession and any financial agreement.

China Loans and the Fall of Silver

A high proportion of the funds raised for China by the foreign banks went for defense and indemnity payments. This was especially true from 1874 through 1896, but the Boxer indemnity was financed by the Western Powers; they took back the sum agreed by the Boxer Protocol of 1901 in the form of government-held gold loans at 4 percent to be amortized over a period of forty years. In 1888/89 and between 1903 and 1911, however, the focus was for a time on funds for mining and railways and, in foreign-controlled municipalities, for utilities and streetcar concessions. Once again, with the worsening financial situation after the 1910 rubber boom and sharemarket collapse in Shanghai, the 1911 Revolution, and the north/south political split, funds were required at all levels for "administrative" and military purposes. Consideration of new railway loans, against which advances were being made by, *inter alia*, the British and Chinese Corporation, was again in process at the time of the outbreak of the Great War in August 1914.

Financial relations between Europe and the East were endangered by the dramatic fall in the gold price of silver, especially after 1876. The position of the London-based exchange banks was insecure despite the reasonably rapid turnover of funds that characterized their operations. Even then a bank could be caught, as was the Hongkong Bank in 1886, by laying down uncovered silver funds to finance tea exports from Hankow, for example, and to face a fall of 8.8 percent in the Hong Kong/London exchange within a period of three months. This also accounts for the lack of interest shown by the oldest and, at the time, largest of the exchange banks, the Oriental Bank Corporation, in lending to the Chinese government.

TABLE 17–3. German Interests in the East

I. German banks involved in the founding of the Deutsch-Asiatische Bank (DAB)

	(in taels)
Diskonto-Gesellschaft	805,000
Deutsche Bank	175,000
Königliche Seehandlung	555,000
S. Bleichröder & Co.	555,000
Berliner Handelsgesellschaft	470,000
Jacob S. H. Stern	470,000
Bank für Handel und Industrie	310,000
Robert Warschauer & Co.	310,000
Mendelssohn & Co.	310,000
A. M. Rothschild & Söhne (Frankfurt)	310,000
Norddeutsche Bank (Hamburg)	380,000
Sal. Oppenheim jr. & Cie.	175,000
Bayerische Hypotheken & Wechselbank	175,000

Dresdner Bank, Schaaffhausen'scher Bankverein, Nationalbank für Deutschland, and Born & Busse joined the consortia later.

II. German Banks in the Konsortium für Asiatische Geschäfte (KfAG)

Deutsch-Asiatische Bank	Bayerische Hypotheken und
Diskonto-Gesellschaft	Wechselbank
Deutsche Bank	Königliche Seehandlung
S. Bleichröder & Co.	Dresdner Bank
Darmstädter Bank	L. Behrens & Söhne
Berliner Handelsgesellschaft	National Bank für Deutschland
Jacob S. H. Stern	A. Schaafhausen'scher Bankverein
Norddeutsche Bank	Born & Busse
Sal. Oppenheim jr. & Cie.	Bank für Handel and Industrie

Source: D. J. S. King's research report, "On the relations of the Hongkong Bank with Germany, 1864–1948," p. 16, in Hongkong Bank Group Archives, Hong Kong.

German interest in China investment (see Table 17–3) was in part a consequence of the German silver position following the Franco-Prussian War, but it was the Hongkong Bank that, by its role as a "local bank," a virtually cooperative venture of Hong Kong merchant houses, found itself able to keep what the bank's famous chief manager, Sir Thomas Jackson, referred to as an "even keel." That is, the bank obtained deposits in London to cover its gold liabilities; these funds never came East. Similarly, the bank's Eastern financial operations were covered by local funds. The accounts of the bank were denominated in a silver unit of account; even though its performance was judged on the London market and in terms of sterling, in which dividend payments were denominated, the solvency of the bank had been effectively isolated from the decline in silver.*

The importance of this exchange factor is shown by the speculative boom in Eastern "trust and loan" companies that were fostered by the sudden but, as it turned

Note: Exchange was quoted as so many shillings and pence per Hong Kong dollar. A rise in the exchange means a greater number of shillings and pence is required to purchase one Hong Kong dollar, as there are fewer dollars per unit of sterling.

out, temporary rise in the price of silver. Between June 1889 and September 1890, exchange—that is, the sterling value of the Hong Kong dollar—rose by 28 percent; by June 1892 it had fallen back 27 percent. The initial rise coincided with ambiguous statements from Chinese officials relative to China's willingness to consider railway construction and with confirmation by banking experts familiar with the East that silver had at last been stabilized. China investment companies, associated with Eastern banking and merchant interests, were formed in 1889, but within three years had disappeared.

The exchange risk could be shifted to China by denominating credits in sterling, but there were two limits to this device. First, the Chinese preferred denomination in silver and, secondly, to the extent the Chinese actually required funds for local expenditure, the proceeds of the gold loan had to be remitted to China. The Hongkong Bank, with its silver funds, was in the best position to accommodate China.

The Predominance of The Hongkong and Shanghai Banking Corporation

The predominance of the Hongkong Bank was virtually unchallenged by the mid-1890s, but the political pressures surrounding China's borrowing to meet the Japanese indemnity of 1895 taught the Hongkong Bank it could no longer operate alone. That it had been able to develop its position from a base in Hong Kong was due to a combination of factors illustrative of the problem of financing foreign investment in late nineteenth-century China.

First, the growth of trade made it impossible for the great merchant houses, which earlier had been self-financed, to stand uninfluenced by the growth of the Hongkong Bank. In the early 1870s Jardine Matheson and Company, the leading British merchant house in the East, recognized this fact, and in 1876 the company's Hong Kong *taipan* joined the Hongkong Bank's board of directors. The new relationship did not end the scope for financial competition, however, as Jardines remained interested in merchant banking operations and their London friends, Matheson and Company, were City merchant bankers. In the end, however, their rivalry was rationalized by the formation in 1898, on the eve of what was seen as a breakthrough in Chinese railway development, of the British and Chinese Corporation (B&CC) Ltd., for which both were joint agents, the Hongkong Bank handling the finance and acting as the corporation's bankers.

Second, when Russell and Company virtually turned on the Hongkong Bank in 1891 and attempted to establish a rival institution with the cooperation of "compradoric capital" in China, the company was caught in silver speculations and was destroyed a few months later.

Third, China's unwillingness to commit itself to development and its dislike of foreign borrowing in principle placed it in a surprisingly strong position. Preferring to operate in traditional terms, the Chinese authorities refused grandiose schemes proposed by European financiers unfamiliar with the East and turned to the Hongkong Bank, which accepted their requirements in terms wholly unfamiliar to the London market; for example, loans denominated in obscure *tael* units of account, interest expressed in *li* per lunar month, and payments at inconvenient intervals. The bank acted as an intermediary between East and West and, for a fee, translated the terms required by the Chinese into those acceptable in London.

Finally, neither the amounts involved nor the purposes were particularly exciting, and City houses were having their own problems, often at times when the Hongkong Bank might otherwise have faced competition from Rothschilds or Barings. Having learned its London end of the business in a time of relatively small loans, the Hongkong Bank had established itself as Britain's China bank and was able to maintain this position against increasing protest until 1912, when the bank in response to Foreign Office and City pressures enlarged the British Group. Meanwhile, the Hongkong Bank had long been associated with German and French banks.

Exchange Banks and Local Financial Markets

The City of London

The exchange banks required finance to cover maturing bills; typically, the Hongkong Bank negotiated the level of acceptance credit with the London and County Bank and adjusted its interest rates to attract sufficient additional deposits to cover its sterling requirements (Table 17–4).

Eastern branches of exchange banks channeled their operations through their London office, providing a degree of internalization that could isolate them from the market. This permitted the bank to pursue an overall policy designed to optimize the use of funds throughout the system.

The fall of silver and the policy of an "even keel" required Eastern banks to hold reserves, to the extent their performance permitted the luxury, both in the East and in London. London investment of reserves included Indian and colonial securities as well as holdings of sterling-denominated Chinese Imperial Government bonds. The Eastern exchange banks were one source of funds for worldwide developments financed through London.

The Hongkong Bank as investment bank worked in conjunction with Panmure Gordon, whose early experience had been in Shanghai and whose firm was to be important in the China and Japan loan markets through the period. The London managers in the 1890s developed close relations—and at times rivalries—with Baring Brothers (the British Eastern exchange banks subscribed to the Bank of England guarantee funds for Barings in 1890), and with the Rothschilds, the latter being instrumental in the cooperation that developed between the Hongkong Bank and the Deutsch-Asiatische Bank.

In the East: The Compradore and His Role

In the East the relationship between the exchange banks and the local money markets was complex and important. Basic to the relationship was the role of a local "native manager" who guaranteed transactions with local constituents and who might himself be the proprietor of a local bank. In China this manager was referred to as the "compradore"; in Ceylon he would be the "guarantee shroff."[4] In Japan there would be a Japanese manager, *banto*, as well as a Chinese compradore. In Southeast Asia, where the Chinese community predominated in the commercial sector, the compradore was also likely to be a member of the dominant Chinese communal group—usually Cantonese, but Hokkien in Singapore and Chiuchow in Bangkok. Through his contacts

TABLE 17–4. Foreign Exchange Banks in China Selected Years, 1870–1914 (£ millions, or sterling equivalent unless stated otherwise)

	1870	1880	1890	1900	1910
Hongkong and Shanghai Banking Corporation					
Capital (HK$)	4.0	5.0	9.3	10.0	15.0
Shareholders' Funds (HK$)	4.8	7.0	16.5	24.7	48.5
Capital (£)	0.9	1.1	1.6	1.6	1.4
Shareholders' funds (£)	1.1	1.3	2.8	2.6	4.4
Agra Bank					
Capital	1.0	1.0	1.0	—	—
Capital + reserves	1.0	1.2	1.2	—	—
Chartered Bank of India, Australia and China					
Capital	0.8	0.8	0.8	0.8	1.2
Capital + reserves	0.8	1.0	1.0	1.3	2.8
Chartered Mercantile Bank of India, London and China then *Mercantile Bank*					
Capital	0.75	0.75	0.75	0.56	0.56
Capital + reserves	0.79	0.81	1.00	0.60	0.84
Comptoir d'Escompte de Paris					
Capital		3.2	—		
Capital + reserves		4.0	—		
Oriental Bank Corporation then *New Oriental Bank Corporation, Ltd.*					
Capital	1.5	1.5	0.6	—	—
Capital + reserves	1.9	1.5	0.6	—	—
National Bank of China, Ltd.					
Capital				0.3	—
Capital + reserves				?	—
Yokohama Specie Bank					
Capital				Yen 12.0	£2.5
Capital + reserves				Yen 19.5	£4.2
Deutsch-Asiatische Bank					
Capital				0.68	0.88
Russo-Chinese Bank					
Capital				1.2	
International Banking Corporation					
Capital					0.7
Banque de l'Indo-Chine					
Capital (French francs)					1.4

with the local business community, especially with the local money market, he became vital to the success of the foreign bank.

The Hongkong Bank's first Shanghai compradore may have been the first to make "chop loans" to native banks—that is, overnight "clean loans" usually intended to be rolled over for long periods of time. The foreign banks acted in the role of clearing bank and as such had an intimate knowledge of the local market; the advancement of funds to small banks and to the *chettiars* or their equivalent made the exchange banks sensitive to the retail market.

Finance of Export Crops

The compradore also channeled funds to merchants dealing in export commodities; the tea trade from Amoy and silk in the Canton delta region were financed by exchange banks through their compradores to native banks, who in turn advanced to the merchants who were in contact with producers up-country, the ultimate recipient of the funds. Sugar in the Philippines and rice in Siam were similarly financed, right to the point of production. The exchange banks did not themselves penetrate the interior nor did they finance agricultural production directly, but through the compradore and "native" channels funds did reach the producer. One method by which export production was financed was the granting of "packing credits," clean advances to merchants obtaining products up-country, the export finance for which was covered by bills of exchange. The risks involved, especially since the banks did not have their own godowns for storage, were considerable.

Dependence on the compradore was a fact of business life in the East; schemes to bypass him failed. Fluency in Chinese would enable the foreign banker to read the Chinese *chops*; it would not enable him to evaluate creditworthiness or sense the state of the local markets.

Although (or possibly because) the compradore was usually either himself a wealthy merchant or member of a well-connected family, in times of general speculation he could be overextended and illiquid. Too late the bank would discover that he had, in the then current phrase, "gone Canton more far," that is, absconded. This would happen when the bank's own operations were in difficulty, possibly coinciding with a sharp fall in the exchanges, a combination of events threatening the bank with insolvency.

Finance of Fixed Investment

The opening of the Hongkong Bank in 1865 occurred, not by chance, the same year as the passage of the first Hong Kong Companies Ordinance granting general incorporation with limited liability. Companies incorporated locally in Hong Kong could operate in the Treaty Ports. The Hongkong Bank financed, directly through overdrafts granted the company or indirectly through loans to constituents against shares, the embryonic industry of Hong Kong: a sugar refinery, distillery, and docks. The bank was the "local" bank and its deposits came from a wide range of residents, including wealthy Portuguese in neighboring Macau; the chief manager had calculated the percentage of "permanent deposits" and thus the margin of liquidity he considered necessary. The failure of the companies and general depression of trade combined with unprofitable exchange operations forced the bank to suspend dividends for three successive half-yearly periods in 1874/75; the "permanent" deposits were in danger of being withdrawn, but the bank pulled through.

This example is illustrative of the actual practice of exchange banks, which, although based on the principle of profit through turnover of funds, could and did finance local industry in ways both direct and indirect.

The Hongkong Bank and, to a lesser extent, other exchange banks gave a general liquidity to the community and permitted savings to be mobilized for those who wished to invest in the stock market. Unfortunately, such development-oriented activity also fueled speculation, drove up the price of shares, and led to a series of crises that characterized the Treaty Port economy in the period through 1914. The charter provision that prohibited lending against the bank's own shares could be, and was, circumvented.

Despite the fact that the board of directors imposed special controls, it proved difficult to restrain local managers from granting an overdraft to a small-scale entrepreneur, such as the Port pharmacist who argued for the viability of a brick-making enterprise; the funds became, in effect, permanent capital. Not all such advances were unauthorized, however. In 1911 the Hongkong Bank's head office advances to local public companies exceeded HK\$5.5 million, to Shanghai HK\$3.1 million (of total loans of HK\$122 million, that is, 7 percent), and the list, which had to be submitted to the board of directors, included textile factories, tug boat companies, docks, steamships (the Philippines), hotels, and sugar refineries.

The prominence of the Hongkong Bank in such operations suggests conclusively that the funds originated in the East. The bank was mobilizing local savings for investment but did not itself make equity investments, although from time to time it would become responsible for the management of a debtor firm until a crisis was weathered.

A case study is provided by the Tientsin Gas and Electric Company, then capitalized at Ts (taels) 250,000 and operating under a fifteen-year contract with the British Municipal Council. In 1904 the Hongkong Bank's Tientsin manager obtained board sanction for the underwriting of the company's 7 percent debentures totaling Ts80,000 for a $2\frac{1}{2}$ percent commission. On such a transaction the bank had to be prepared to hold a high percentage of the issue for a period of time.

Before 1895 industrial investment had been limited by the unwillingness of the Chinese to permit modern enterprise under foreign control and by the reluctance the Chinese themselves showed to fixed investment unless sanctioned by officials in the *kuan-tu shang-pan* (official supervision, merchant management) system. In 1884 the Hongkong Bank issued on the Shanghai market the 7 percent China Merchants' Steam Navigation Company Loan of £300,000 (= Shanghai taels [ShTs] 1.2 million and issued at 105) and in 1899 China's first major railway loan for the Peking-Mukden rail line, the Chinese Imperial Railways 5 percent gold loan for £2.3 million (issued at 97 to the public by the Hongkong Bank for the British and Chinese Corporation).

This introduces the problem of foreign bank relations with both the Imperial and provincial Chinese governments.

International Finance and the Chinese Authorities

Early Loans and the Role of the Imperial Maritime Customs

Ch'ing finances had long been in disarray and foreign merchants and agency houses had been making local advances for short periods at least from the 1840s. Despite proposals for major public loan schemes by China merchants linked with European financial houses, the Chinese authorities did not in fact approve a public loan until

1874, when the Hongkong Bank was authorized to issue as agent for the Imperial government an 8 percent sterling loan for £628,000 (at 95), denominated as HK$2.4 million to meet a Chinese requirement for 2 million Yang-p'ing taels. This was followed by three loans to finance the Northwest Campaigns, and, in 1884/85, during the Sino-French War, six further nonproductive loans were issued. The pattern was varied only in 1888 when the authorities required a million taels for Yellow River conservancy.

Little was known in Europe of China's financial position; little needed to be known. China had a ready source of security that gave her a dangerously attractive creditworthiness. Her "maritime customs" administration, although responsible to and taking direction from the appropriate office of the Imperial Chinese government, was headed by an Irishman, Sir Robert Hart, and staffed by Europeans and Americans—and later Japanese—in the service of Imperial China. The Imperial Maritime Customs (IMC) only assessed the duties, but no foreign ship could leave port without the *chop* of the IMC given after evidence that the duties had been paid to the local Chinese "customs bank."[5] Loans were issued on the security of the customs revenues, the statistics for which were collected and published by the IMC. Foreign borrowing, at least public or significant borrowing, was permitted only with Imperial authority; Sir Robert Hart would agree to the customs revenue being designated as security only on instructions from the Tsungli Yamen (the rough equivalent of a Chinese Foreign Ministry). All this was, for a time, reassuring to European investors.

Relations to 1894: Waiting for the "Big" Loan

These early loans were not, by international standards, "big" loans. What interest there was in China, as displayed from time to time by European financial houses, was based on the hope that China would soon "open up" and that the government would seek a large loan for railway and other development. Those on the scene moved closer to the seat of power in the north—to be ready; the Hongkong Bank opened its Tientsin agency in 1881 and moved an officer, the Chinese-speaking E. Guy Hillier, quietly into Peking in 1885, where traders were not authorized by treaty, to open an agency that the bank did not publicly list until 1891. Jardines also moved north, operating from Tientsin, and making petty loans to minor officials, loans at least partially financed by funds provided at 7 percent by the Hongkong Bank. Both were ultimately rewarded but not without rivalry in Peking and London, despite an agreement reached between the two companies' managers in Shanghai.

Furthermore, the Hongkong Bank developed a special relationship with the Chihli Viceroy, Li Hung-chang. In 1894 the bank's Tientsin manager was specifically instructed not to join in "any movement that would give the Viceroy the slightest offense." Since the late-1880s the bank had granted the Viceroy an overdraft of Ts300,000, which was used, together with other bank-granted funds, in the finance of what would become the Peking-Mukden Railway. In 1886 the bank advanced up to Ts180,000 for exploitation of the Pingtu mines; the loan was repaid. In 1891 the bank's manager, acting against board instructions, advanced Ts1 million for Viceroy Li's new cotton factory, and additional funds were certainly channeled directly and through the bank's compradore, Wu Mao-ting, for various industrial and mining enterprises, some of which were owned by Wu, in the Tientsin area.

The movement of funds, once in the Chinese system, is difficult to determine, and the foreign banks had little or no end-user contact or control. Funds for the China Merchants' SN Co., for example, might be used for other ventures, including real estate speculation of the directors. For a brief time the Chinese put the American IMC official, H. B. Morse—famous for his later writings on the East India Company and on nineteenth-century China—in a control position over the steamship company, but despite the bank's intervention, this development proved short term.

Ch'ing government documents reveal other foreign banking involvement—for example, the Hupei government knitting "bureau" in 1890. Foreign banks were, by their restricted presence, passive participants in the first tentative steps to modernization, but progress was subject to successive political and speculative financial setbacks.

Throughout the 1880s, while the Hongkong Bank was financing the Chinese government and Jardines was playing with minor officials, other European interests, often represented by frustrated agents without full authority, tried unsuccessfully to land the big loan. At best they shared in the minor lending. The Warschauer Group, of which Jacob S. H. Stern and the Berliner Handelsgesellschaft were members, had a mission in China. In 1887 they concluded the first public China loan to be offered in Europe outside London; it was negotiated through Carlowitz and Co. and the Viceroy Li Hung-chang for 5 million marks (£250,000 or ShTsl million) at $5\frac{1}{2}$ percent and issued in Berlin, Frankfurt, and Hamburg at $106\frac{1}{4}$. Meanwhile, the Deutsche Bank, encouraged by the overly optimistic German minister, Maximilian von Brandt, formed a consortium, which in 1885 sent the Exner Commission to China. The Rothschilds were urged through Adolph von Hansemann to enlist the cooperation of the Hongkong Bank, but the time was not ripe and the latter's terms proved too onerous.

With the Sino-French War over, a French syndicate, representing the most important companies in France interested in the China trade, obtained a contract allegedly for harbor works at Port Arthur worth Ts1.15 million guaranteed by the Comptoir d'Escompte, but they were unsuccessful, as were all others, in obtaining any monopoly financial privileges.

In 1889 there was a break in the pattern. China appeared ready to admit railway construction; as noted above, silver—which had reached 42.2d/ounce in June 1888—was once again rising; it reached a peak of 54.6d in September 1890—the Hong Kong exchanges also rose from 3s/0d to 3s/10 $\frac{7}{8}$d per dollar. But two years later the exchange had fallen to 2s/8 $\frac{3}{4}$d; the Sherman Act was repealed and the Indian mints closed to the free coinage of silver; at the end of 1902 the exchanges were at 1s/7d.

In the heady year of 1889 senior officers of the Hongkong Bank in conjunction with major Eastern financial interests promoted the Trust and Loan Company of China, Japan and the Straits. This was also the year of the founding of the Imperial Bank of Persia (now the British Bank of the Middle East). William Keswick of Matheson and Company, formerly chairman of the Hongkong Bank, was then on the bank's London committee; he was instrumental in the promotion of both the Trust and Loan Company and the Imperial Bank, becoming chairman of both.

Capital raised for the Trust and Loan Company was transmitted to China; China was not prepared for major industrial investment, but there was a real estate and share boom in Shanghai, and the Trust Company invested its funds accordingly. By 1893 the

Trust's directors were watching helplessly as the China-coast boom collapsed and the fall in the exchange wiped out the company's reserves. Honest men with years of experience had miscalculated on the two basic issues—the price of silver and the attitude of the Chinese authorities.

Finance in the First Sino-Japanese War, 1894/95

By the time the foreign community had begun to recover from this and related financial problems, the first Sino-Japanese War had commenced, and China, unable to secure sufficient funds by a domestic loan, sought foreign loans—which might nevertheless be subscribed for by Chinese, who would thus be protected by the shield of extrality behind which the issuing banks operated. Once again development was postponed. The Hongkong Bank raised the equivalent of £1.6 million through a 7 percent silver loan, exhausting for a time the supply of loanable funds on the China coast. The remaining loans by the Hongkong Bank, the Nationalbank für Deutschland, and the Chartered Bank totaled £5 million—in sterling. They were not well received in the London market, and the Hongkong Bank and its underwriters together had to take up some £2 million of a £3 million loan.

The Hongkong Bank's directors had long been concerned with the need to underwrite their own loan issues; the potential "tie-up" of funds was contrary to all rules of exchange banking. The bank did have to set aside approved securities as security for the authorized note issue, and the board attempted to regain liquidity by substituting such China issues for more marketable securities. The British Crown Agents, however, severely limited and on occasion prevented this solution. The Hongkong Bank was learning that, as China's demand for funds grew, it would be unable to manage on its own.

This was confirmed by events relative to financing the Japanese indemnity. In the twenty-one years between 1874 and 1895 the Hongkong Bank had been responsible for the public issue of China loans with a nominal value of £12 million, of which the largest was the £3 million 6 percent gold loan of 1895. The Japanese set the indemnity at £20 million and China needed additional funds for rehabilitation. There were political advantages to China and economic benefits to Japan if the indemnity were paid without delay. The Hongkong Bank took up the challenge but authorized its Hamburg manager, Julius Brüssel, to negotiate with Adolph von Hansemann, who was the effective spokesman for the Deutsch-Asiatische Bank (DAB) and the Konsortium für Asiatische Geschäfte (KfAG); the bank proposed inviting the cooperation of the Crédit Lyonnais and the Banque de Paris et des Pays-Bas.

But the initiative was no longer with the Hongkong Bank. The China scene had changed. China was no longer able to offer sufficient purely financial security and the Hongkong Bank could not operate without international cooperation. By a series of maneuvers the Germans were induced to withdraw from their association with the Hongkong Bank in favor of cooperation with the French; when this fell through the Russians, with French financial support, moved to close the First Indemnity Loan, a 4 percent gold loan for 400 million francs (= £15.8 million) despite last minute efforts from the Hongkong Bank and the DAB, brought together once again by the Rothschilds, to make a counteroffer.

This failure of purely financial initiative resulted in an agreement between the DAB and the Hongkong Bank in July 1895 stipulating that all government loans and advances would be split equally between the two and that railway projects and non-guaranteed loans would be dealt with on a case-by-case basis. Through all the pre–1914 years of increasing anti-German "scaremongering" this agreement, although amended and marred almost from the first by the Hongkong Bank's lone position in the British capital market, by Germany's 1898 Shantung adventure, and by various national and personal differences over the years, nevertheless formed a theme in the history of China's international finance.

The first fruits of the agreement were the successful negotiation of the next (and last) two indemnity loans—the £16 million 5 percent sterling loan of 1896 and the £16 million 4½ percent sterling loan of 1898, issued to the public at 98¾ and 90, respectively, the latter figure reflecting the impact of a further fall in silver and the general state of concern for China's financial position. With only £1,460,000 of the £8 million British tranche taken by the public, the underwriters took up 75 percent of the loan, the Japanese themselves "took back" £1,760,000 to clear the market.

Postwar Euphoria: Concessions and Finance to 1900

This interruption ended, investors turned once again to the vision of a China "criss-crossed" by railways. By 1894 only 312 km of track had been constructed in China; by 1914 the total was only 9,680 km, and the great trunk Peking-Canton line had yet to be completed. Purely financial considerations were subordinated to the political impact of "spheres of interest," the consequent railway concessions, and the frequent irrelevance of this to the logical developmnent of railways and their finance. On the one hand this led to virtually exclusive areas—for example, the Northeast, where the Russo-Asiatic Bank and the Japanese Bank of Chosen predominated; on the other, especially where railways traversed several "spheres," it led to international consortia sharing the overall finance while various national contractors were allocated the responsibility of constructing designated sections of the track.

In preparation for railway development and mining concessions, various consortia developed. The British response to the German KfAG was the British and Chinese Corporation (B&CC), intended originally to represent a wide range of interests. Initial shareholders included the contractors Pauling and Co. and financial representatives such as Lord Rothschild, Barings, Ernest Cassel, Gibbs, Hambro, Henry Oppenheim, Sir Marcus Samuel, and the several Sassoon interests. By 1905 the list of subscribers included the great entrepreneur and railway official Sheng Hsuan-huai himself (under his literary name of "Tsu-yi") and Calouste S. Gulbenkian. Despite this apparently wide range of interests, the main subscribers were, however, Jardines and the Hongkong Bank, and the corporation never succeeded in becoming truly representative of British interests in the East. It remained associated with the two main shareholders and permanent agents and chairmen; firms based in China were unwilling, in view of their historical efforts and superior contacts, to share on a basis of equality with domestic latecomers showing only a "fair-weather" interest in China investment.

Chinese policy showed consistent opposition to confrontation by a monopoly, especially by international combinations, which they saw as lessening their range of maneuverability. In consequence, China continued to grant minor concessions to miscellaneous promoters, and the B&CC, if it hoped to maintain its pretensions, was faced with the necessity of coming to an arrangement first with the Pekin Syndicate (conceived originally as representing both Italian and British interests), which had obtained mining-cum-railway concessions north of the Yangtze, and then with the smaller Yangtze Valley Company, which included Belgian interests. The result of the former was the successful negotiation in 1903 for the incorporation of a joint B&CC/Pekin Syndicate company, the Chinese Central Railways (CCR) Ltd.; this was enlarged in 1905 to take in French interests to form a French Group, Belgian interests for a Belgian Group while the Belgian-influenced but British Yangtze Valley Company joined the British Group, placing their voting rights in trust with the B&CC and the Pekin Syndicate; British control of the CCR was to be maintained through the casting vote of the British chairman. With the sellout of British interests in the Pekin Syndicate and its domination by continental groups by 1910, the entire delicate compromise was threatened and the Chinese took advantage of the situation to renegotiate concessions.

Although in the last three years of the century the Chinese granted concessions for railway and mining development—most notably the Tientsin-Pukow, Peking-Hankow, and Hankow-Canton, Nanking-Shanghai, the Shanghai-Hangchow and Ningpo, and Kowloon (Hong Kong)–Canton lines—only one public loan resulted: the Chinese Imperial Railway's 5 percent gold loan of 1899 for £2.3 million issued by the B&CC—that is, by the Hongkong Bank as the corporation's banker, at 97 for the financing of the Tientsin-Mukden Railway.

The Impact of the Boxer Uprising, 1900

At this point the Boxer Uprising, the Siege of the Legations, and the emotional aftermath intervened.

During the uprising certain of the provincial authorities refused to follow Imperial direction, keeping their regions "neutral." After first refusing on purely banking grounds, the Hongkong Bank, at the instigation of the British government, which guaranteed the advance, made available £75,000 to the Hukuang Viceroy Chang Chih-tung for ten years at 4 1/2 percent. This time the British Treasury permitted the bank to restore its liquidity by substituting the government-guaranteed loan for gilt-edged securities as security for its note issue.

The Boxer indemnity was assessed at HkTs (Haikwan [Customs] taels) 450 million, which the Boxer Protocol stated as a gold debt of £67 million equivalent to be paid over a period at 4 percent. The Chinese at first insisted on treating the obligation as a silver debt, but eventually agreed to pay on a gold basis, the arrears being financed by a loan of £1.2 million from the Hongkong Bank and DAB in 1905.

International Finance to the 1911 Revolution

The Boxer crisis coincided with the impact of the Boer War on the London markets, and the flow of capital to China did not resume immediately. The first post-Boxer public railway loan was not issued until mid-1904 (the 5 percent Shanghai-Nanking Railway loan, first tranche of £2.25 million, issued for the B&CC loan at 97½). This was followed in 1907 by a £1.5 million B&CC loan for the Canton-Kowloon Railway (Chinese section), and only in 1908 by the 5 percent Tientsin-Pukow Railway loan of £5 million shared between the Chinese Central Railways (Hongkong Bank) and the DAB.

In the disturbed years from the Boxer Protocol of 1901 to the Revolution of 1911, foreign banks lost their independence of maneuver as they tried to form alliances consistent with political concessions and Chinese aspirations. The rise of Western-style nationalism and the consequent "Rights-recovery movement" led the Chinese to seek purely financial support—that is, support devoid of supervision as to use of funds or construction of the project, for modernization at a time when acceptable security was inadequate except in terms of the expected revenue from the investment. This in turn strengthened foreign resolve to control project expenditure and management to protect the interests of bondholders and thereby to justify including control information in the loan prospectus whereby the favorable terms demanded by the Chinese could be justified.

This dichotomy of approach could be resolved only after lengthy negotiations fraught with mutual misunderstanding.

The conflict of approach affected the development of such firms as the B&CC, which combined contracting and financial functions. The banks' basic interest was in supplying credit on acceptable security; if the Chinese were unwilling publicly to designate the purpose of a loan or agree to deal through the designated agency house, the combination represented in the B&CC or the CCR could become a disadvantage to the associated banks. Chinese "gentry," whose origins were now to be found as often in trading as in classical scholarship, declared themselves interested in railway construction. Suppliers' credits offered by banks in Europe to agency houses dealing in China became a relatively uncontrolled financial alternative.

The £5 million 5-4½ percent gold loan of 1908 issued at 98 by the Hongkong Bank and the Banque de l'Indo-Chine is an example of a loan, originally negotiated in the name of the CCR on a concession basis, which developed into a purely financial loan in which the actual purpose—namely the recovery of rights from Belgian interests in the Luhan Line (Peking-Hankow)—was not specified in the final agreement.

Despite the loss of operational freedom that the foreign banks suffered in China, their European negotiations appeared to be based on the assumption that they lived in an era of financial internationalization. Thus the Hongkong Bank/DAB association—to which the Banque de l'Indo-Chine was joined—continued despite the increasing popular political concern in Britain and Hong Kong and of many in the British community in China over German intentions. The single-minded apolitical approach of the Hongkong Bank's chief negotiator, Sir Charles Addis, was maintained until after the 1914 declaration of war. Nevertheless, the impact of British concern in any matter coming close to Hong Kong or affecting its "sphere of interest" in the Yangtze Valley was political. The financing of the British sector of the Canton-Kowloon Railway and the provision of £400,000 to permit the Hukuang Viceroy Chang Chih-tung to buy out the American China Development Company's interests in the Hankow-Canton line concession was undertaken with funds borrowed by the Hong Kong government not from the Hongkong Bank in Hong Kong but from the Crown Agents in London, thus avoiding the need to see the loan shared on a fifty-fifty basis between British and German (DAB) interests. Ironically, as the authorities could not at the last moment lay down the funds in New York on schedule, the Hongkong Bank became involved, purely as an exchange bank, to save the deal.

In consequence of this timely British intervention, Viceroy Chang (the "Fraser–Chang understanding") granted designated British interests, that is, the B&CC, priority relative to any concession for the construction of the Hankow-Canton line, providing the terms were competitive.

The subsequent events provide an illustration of the "control" issue; B&CC terms (with which French interests were associated) were relatively comprehensive; as the Chinese hesitated, the DAB, denied participation in this British sphere, offered easier control terms, which the Chinese accepted. There then occurred prolonged negotiations in which the Chinese won easier terms as the Hongkong Bank brought in the DAB to form the Three-Power Groups' "consortium" and prepared to sign a loan agreement with the Chinese authorities.

At this point President Taft intervened, successfully convinced J. P. Morgan & Co. that an American group ought to be involved, and secured the company's inclusion, with the International Banking Corporation acting for them in China, in a Four-Power Group "consortium" agreement that eventually concluded the 1911 £6 million 5 percent Hukuang Railways Sinking Fund gold loan, issued at $100\frac{1}{2}$; the Chinese signatory was the veteran "modernizer" and entrepreneur Sheng Hsuan-huai, acting on behalf of the Ministry of Posts and Communications.

Throughout the period China was arguing for more control over the exchange rate used in effecting repayments, for shorter periods for the deposit of funds in the contracting foreign banks, and for the use, where possible, of Chinese depositories. The representations, although often misconceived, had some impact on the fringe benefits to foreign banks.

The Chinese were not, however, able to prevent the development of foreign banking groups nor their international combination. The concessions were originally obtained by foreign political intervention; therefore the "gift" of such concessions was in political hands. The British took the position that if rival British groups developed, the Chinese must make the initial choice; the chosen group would then be supported exclusively by the Foreign Office. The role of the groups was seen as one of rationalizing China's overseas borrowing, maintaining China's credit standing, and depoliticizing lending by agreement among banking groups recognized by the Powers. To this "paternal" approach China remained opposed, at first for reasons of principle, later also for reasons of financial urgency.

Nor were the groups able to maintain an exclusive position relative to China loans. First, rival syndicates, especially combinations of British, Belgian, French, and Russian interests excluded from the "groups," solicited public support in opposition to what they incorrectly labeled as government monopoly-support. Second, as the groups were unable to control suppliers' credits, the British government was forced to persuade them to exclude industrial loans from the scope of government "exclusive support" in connection with the reorganization loans, the first and only one of which was issued by the groups in 1913. Third, following the conclusion of Hukuang loan negotiations in 1911, Japan and Russia exerted pressure for admission of their "groups" despite the inability of their own capital markets to provide investment capital for China. Their intervention was politically motivated, providing further justification for China's suspicion.

Although minor railway advances (unrepaid) would be made in 1913–14 against future loans (never made), the Hukuang Railways loan was the last public loan for productive purposes issued in the period before the Great War. But before this European debacle, there was to be another interruption to China's modernization, the signs of which were visible in the increasing number of hitherto forbidden "provincial loans," mainly for administrative purposes. These were issued in silver by all or selected members of the Four-Power Groups—usually with funds originating in China—with the purpose of meeting emergency fiscal problems.

The Origins of the Reorganization Loan

Under the terms of the Boxer Protocol the Chinese were obligated, *inter alia*, to attempt currency reform. In this the foreign banks were involved as advisors. Schemes to place China on a gold standard, while totally impractical, appeared less urgent as silver rose, fluctuated, but showed no signs of a renewed downward plunge. The focus was on efforts to control the plethora of virtually fiat bank notes and the erratic character of the coinage. In 1910 the Chinese approached the American banks for a currency loan, but the Americans, now members of the Four-Power Groups, brought it to their associates and a £10 million loan was planned for currency reform and various miscellaneous purposes. The matter was pending when the first incident of the Chinese Revolution, the Wuchang Uprising of October 10, 1911, occurred.

Banking Crises in Hankow and Shanghai, 1909/10

On at least two occasions foreign banks were involved in major rescue operations in the local money markets. In 1909 the Hongkong Bank made Ts1 million available in Hankow to the Viceroy and the Chamber of Commerce when local banks were unable to repay *chop* loans.

A more serious crisis developed in Shanghai in 1910 when it appears that speculation in rubber company shares, fueled by the deposit of funds from many parts of China—possibly funds collected in relation to provincial "gentry" railways—caused a virtual collapse of the local banking system. With the Hongkong Bank acting as lead negotiator, eight other foreign banks operating in Shanghai combined to lend Ts3.5 million at the nominal rate of 4 percent to the Shanghai *tao-t'ai* (or administrator); when this proved insufficient a further 7 percent loan by the Hongkong Bank, the DAB, and the Banque de l'Indo-Chine for Ts3 million was made to the Nanking Viceroy.

The 1910 crisis marked possibly the first time that a foreign bank reached over its compradore (who was in any case dangerously extended and whose guarantee could not be taken for further lending) to deal directly with Chinese borrowers. To accomplish this the Hongkong Bank declared its intention of extending Ts2 million to Chinese businesses against the security of real property; borrowers were to be introduced through the Chinese Chamber of Commerce, which, for a commission of Ts2.5 per mille, would assign an interpreter, provide a letter of introduction, and compile the necessary information to permit the Chinese firm to deal directly with the European manager.

The major foreign banks had become an integral part of China's banking system and money markets. The crisis also confirmed that, although in an emergency the banks could deal directly with their Chinese customers, the services of the compradore, except in emergencies, were still required.

The Financing of Republican China

In November 1911 Sun Yat-sen met the Hongkong Bank's London manager, Charles Addis, at night and in secret in the latter's Primrose Hill home. The bank refused to consider financing the revolutionaries until a stable and recognized government had been formed. In the meantime China defaulted on an international obligation; the Hongkong Bank itself advanced £25,000 to pay the interest coupon without recourse and the public accepted this as an indication of the bank's faith in the credit of China. The bond market reacted only slightly.

The debt-servicing foreign banks, which also held Boxer indemnity funds prior to their transfer to Europe, had now to be more closely involved in the internal affairs of China. At the suggestion of the Chinese Foreign Ministry customs revenues were to be collected and transmitted directly, in the first instance, to the Hongkong Bank in Shanghai. As customs banks failed or officials absconded, the actual collection of dues became a foreign responsibility. From this to wielding a political influence was but a short step.

With this problem temporarily solved the enlarged groups—the Six-Power Groups—began consideration of financing Republican China's administrative requirements. As matters were urgent and the revolutionaries in Nanking and the Peking forces of Yuan Shih-k'ai appeared united under the presidency of Sun Yat-sen and then of Yuan himself, the groups made advances of Ts12.1 million (= £1.8 million), covered by the issue of Treasury bills, against the promise of a series of larger loans expected to total £60 million—the first loan was planned at £25 million. In view of the size of the commitment, governments reluctantly gave their exclusive support to the groups, certainly for the first loan and, less certainly, for the series.

The problem was security. Thinking in terms of the £60 million series the groups sought for new revenues to be pledged and chose China's traditional salt gabelle (tax) as suitable, provided it were reformed and under some degree of foreign administration. The parallel was the Imperial Maritime Customs, but that had come about with China's agreement in a prenationalistic Imperial polity and was under China's control. A similar foreign role in the salt administration was not easily accepted, especially as the issue was raised at a time when the more nationalistic Nanking Parliament was already in political opposition to President Yuan Shih-k'ai, who had remained in Peking.

This impasse provided an opportunity for other financial groups, interested only in smaller loans where the existing security might appear satisfactory and concerned only with their "up-front" profits, to attempt to destroy the Six-Power Groups' exclusive position.

In March 1912 an Anglo-Belgian syndicate under the Banque Sino-Belge signed a £1 million loan agreement, but only £250,000 was paid.

In August 1912 a full-scale attack on the Hongkong Bank's role was launched by anti-German scaremongers, and popular support was urged for an international syndicate under Birch Crisp, a British financier closely involved in Russian finance, involving the Chartered Bank, Lloyds Bank, and the London, City and Midland Bank in association with Belgian and Russian interests. Noting the advances already made to China by the Six-Power Groups, including the British Group (then consisting solely of the Hongkong Bank), the British government withheld its support from Crisp and his associates, but it pressured the Hongkong Bank to broaden the base of the British Group. The Germans, holding the Hongkong Bank responsible by its exclusive policy, were critical of Addis's handling of the situation. In December 1912 the Hongkong Bank brought Baring Brothers, the London County and Westminster, and Parr's Bank into the "British Group" and also detached J. Henry Schröder's from the Russian Group.

Meanwhile, Crisp was in difficulties. The syndicate had signed an agreement for £10 million and had successfully issued £5 million of bonds. He now faced the opposition of the Hongkong Bank in transferring the funds at a reasonable price to China. The bank had established a position in local funds; others could compete in smaller amounts, but newcomers could not intrude except at considerable cost. Were they to allow for this in setting terms for their loans, they would be unsuccessful in obtaining the business.

China too realized that, although a rival group might be able to raise funds in Europe, without the cooperation of the banks in the Six-Power Groups these funds could not be laid down in China at reasonable rates. Facing the open hostility of the British Foreign Office, in December 1912 Crisp withdrew plans for a second tranche, and the initiative returned to the groups. In March 1913 President Woodrow Wilson withdrew support from the American Group's role in the Six-Power Groups' negotiations, pretending that the terms of the proposed Reorganization Loan violated Chinese sovereignty; the American Group, never particularly enthusiastic, left the groups, and the loan was signed by the Five-Power Groups under dramatic circumstances.

By May 1913 the political relations between Nanking and Peking had deteriorated; the Nanking Parliament insisted that it approve the loan first; Dr. Sun summoned the Hongkong Bank's Shanghai manager and through him informed the groups that the loan would provoke civil war; President Yuan used the situation to obtain better financial terms, the several foreign ministries ruled Yuan was acting within his authority, and, with the Hongkong Bank's Peking office virtually under siege, the loan was signed.

Although some £2 million of the loan was set aside for "reorganization," the balance and possibly the entire amount of the funds raised went for nonproductive purposes, including payment of troops and repayment of principal and interest on previous borrowings. But this loan was intended to be, after all, only the first of a series. It proved to be the last. China was not to be reformed under the tutelege of foreigners or with the funds provided through foreign banks, however motivated.

This main-theme survey should be understood in a context of growing diversity of foreign banks established primarily to foster bilateral trade between China and, for example, Italy and the Netherlands and its colonies. The activities of such institutions did not affect the role of the major banks nor the effectiveness of the consortium.

Nevertheless, despite the apparent success of the international groups that formed the pre-war consortium, it was in fact being undermined by a dual French policy. The alleged "inaction" of the Banque de l'Indo-Chine had long been responsible for vague plans for a wholly-French investment bank, free of the allegedly conservative restraints of exchange banking. The opportunity to realize these plans came when French interests gained control of the then highly liquid Pekin Syndicate and used its funds, with French ministry encouragement, both to finance a Sino-French Banque Industrielle de Chine and to lend funds, never repaid, to the Chinese government to enable it to obtain a substantial equity involvement. Despite its pretentions, the new bank began its operations by undertaking a major financial loan, the end-uses of which were uncontrolled, under the guise of financing the port works at Pukow on the route from Tientsin to Shanghai. Thus the worst fears of the consortium were being realized, and, on the eve of the Great War, the disarray of China's external finances, fully realized in the 1920s, had begun in the context of the Banque Industrielle's dramatic path to scandal and ruin.

International Finance Elsewhere in the Region: A Postscript

This story may be contrasted with the record of foreign banks elsewhere in the Far East.

As Kanji Ishii has pointed out in his chapter, Japan did not enter the foreign capital market between 1873, the year of its last major loan from the Oriental Bank Corporation, and 1897, when it sold part of a war loan on the London market through Samuel and Co. In the immediate pre–1914 decade the Anglo-Japanese Bank and the Banque Franco-Japonaise were established; the former had difficulty paying a dividend and withdrew from the East; the latter came into conflict with the Banque de l'Indo-Chine and similarly withdrew, leaving the field to the Yokohama Specie Bank, the Hongkong Bank, and major financial houses in London. Japanese financial operations within the region—as, for example, the role of the Bank of Taiwan—are outside the scope of this chapter.

Between 1897 and 1912 the Hongkong Bank participated in the London issue of twenty-one Japanese loans, but always in association with a Japanese house, usually the Yokohama Specie Bank, and other British houses including the Chartered Bank, Barings, and Rothschilds, under the lead of Parr's Bank. German participation was spasmodic; attempts to deal directly in Tokyo failed. At one time Germany's concern for its Russian investments lessened its interest, at another the German minister in Tokyo, being concerned with the actual purpose of the loan, gave negative advice. In fact, the loans were for both project and general purposes, the former covering construction requirements of the South Manchurian Railways, Yokohama waterworks, Osaka harbor construction, and including refinancing.

The peaking of Japanese lean demands in 1905 may provide an explanation for the formation of two financial companies, both of which had links with established China syndicates. The Anglo-Japanese Bank, Ltd., which was established in May 1905 with an initial paid-up capital of £1 million, had Japanese promoters, particularly Kihachiro Okura, senior partner of Okura & Co. The firm's London manager was a member of the board. Baron George de Reuter, a director of the Imperial Bank of Persia, was also involved. The British and Japanese Finance Corporation, Ltd., registered in September 1905 with a subscribed capital of £601,000, had connections with the Yangtze Valley Company and with the Chinese Central Railways. Rempei Kondo, the president of Mitsubishi's NYK Line (Nippon Yusen Kaisha), was a director, suggesting that the finance corporation's formation may have been in part a response to the initiative of Okura. The directors included Edmund Davis, Emile Francqui of the Compagne Internationale d'Orient, and Albert Thys of the Banque d'Outremer, names familiar in China finance. The decline in post-1905 Japanese requirements, the attitude of the Japanese government to "old friends," and the subsequent role of the Yokohama Specie Bank in the Sextuple Groups from 1912 explain why these companies did not become real competitors of Parr's Bank, the Hongkong Bank, and the others associated in their syndicates. It is also significant that experience in Eastern finance was not the key to success in Japan.

In the Philippine Islands the Hongkong Bank was involved in the finance of the Manila Railway. In 1888 the bank issued a £1 million loan unsuccessfully on the London market; 80 percent was taken up by the underwriters: the German underwriter, former Hongkong Bank Chairman Adolph von André, holding £300,000 of the unsubscribed German portion. The railway was refinanced in 1906 by a loan of £5.3 million issued by Speyer Brothers in New York, with Hongkong Bank participation, and a further £1.25 million was raised in 1908.

In Siam official funds were deposited in the foreign banks and one Hongkong Bank inspector considered the branch "awash with funds," a dangerous situation since it tempted the manager to make local and illiquid advances. The kingdom's first public loan was the $4\frac{1}{2}$ percent £1 million sterling loan of 1905 to cover railway expenditure; it was floated in London and Paris on an internationalized basis at $95\frac{1}{2}$ by the Hongkong Bank (with a subparticipation by the Chartered Bank) and the Banque de l'Indo-Chine. The terms were particularly favorable to Siam, leading observers to compare the credit of the kingdom to that of Imperial China and to note the reasons. With the financial position of Siam under the care of a foreign advisor and with its accounts fully published, Siam had established a sound credit position, while China, whose customs revenues were by now over-committed, remained "unknown."

In 1907 the Hongkong Bank was the lead bank in the issue of Siam's $4\frac{1}{2}$ percent £3 million sterling loan of 1907, specifically for railway development. The loan was ill-timed, owing to the impact on the market of the recent sale of American railway bonds in London, and was fully sold only in 1911. This time the Germans obtained a participation of £750,000 through the DAB. Siamese policy had always been directed at the retention of independence of action, and by 1907 the government had turned to Britain's National Provincial Bank to balance the business being given the exchange banks.

Conclusions

The major *hongs* in the East were anxious to promote China's modernization. They attempted to illustrate the advantages by small-scale operations that were commercially viable in themselves and could be financed by foreign banks already in the region. Despite the dictates of exchange banking theory, foreign banks also financed the early efforts of compradores and their associates in manufacturing enterprise and made funds available to the several *kuan-tu shang-pan* enterprises.

In the absence of an accessible local commercial banking system, the Eastern exchange banks provided all the usual banking facilities to the foreign communities, and to those local citizens wishing to use them and willing to follow Western business practices or deal through the local "manager," for example, the compradore.

Foreign banks remained for the most part in the port settlements, protected by extrality or colonial rule, working through intermediaries to gain access to the local money markets and to the producers of export products. Lack of quality control suggested the development of the plantation system where political control of the interior was possible; estate companies were financed both in Imperial capitals and in the East, with banks supporting the liquidity of the community and the flow of trade.

For major projects China possessed a ready security in the form of customs revenues, but the advantage was exhausted in necessary but nonproductive loans raised in Europe and in the East. The fall of silver impeded the transfer of capital from Europe, but the problem was partially met by the intermediation of, particularly, the Hongkong Bank, using silver funds garnered in "domestic-type" banking in the East and by currency reform between 1890 and 1910 during which all territories except China and Indo-China went off silver.

Discussion of China finance requires full consideration of the political situation. For a complex of reasons little could be done by the banks alone, despite efforts by the Hongkong Bank, acting as coordinator of the groups, to deal on a commercial basis. Syndicates representing manufacturing interests found it increasingly difficult to combine with financial houses because of Chinese preference for purely financial loans by which they intended to retain control of construction and operation.

The actual terms under which any particular project was financed were the subject of complex negotiations at both the political and commercial level. Banks and firms with a China background, while able to demonstrate their considerable expertise and to negotiate on the basis of long-standing contacts and "presence," had to beat back charges of unfair official support and requirements that they "share" with newcomers for political reasons. The established groups, planning long-term programs, geared their financial terms accordingly and had to seek support against syndicates interested only in a one-time operation. Foreign investment, therefore, took on peculiar characteristics, inseparable from political involvement.

Japan in contrast moved onto a gold standard, developed its own exchange bank, and participated as an equal with London merchant banks in the raising of capital funds. Siam retained freedom of maneuver by dealing always with international combinations, but its own banking system would develop later.

Movement of funds to British colonial territories (and Siam) was facilitated by the development of the currency board system, minimizing the exchange risk for areas on a sterling exchange standard. Similar monetary relationships existed between the American Philippines and the United States; French and Dutch agency houses and banks cooperated in their respective territories. Investment was encouraged, but in primary production rather than in industry.

Appendix A: Glossary

banto	office manager [Japan]
chettiar	"chetty," a South Indian caste of "native" banker found also in Ceylon and the Straits Settlements.
chop	a mark or brand name
godown	warehouse
hong	company
kuan-tu shang-pan	"official supervision, merchant management," referring to government-sponsored enterprises, usually financed, at least in part, and managed by the private sector
lac	one hundred thousand, usually written: 1,00,000
li	Ts0.001, i.e. a one-thousandth part of a tael
Haikwan tael	an imaginary unit of account in which foreign customs revenues were denominated (HkTs100 = ShTs111.4).
Shanghai tael	an imaginary unit of account in which Shanghai-based commercial transactions were denominated; the tael is qualified as is the pound in "pound sterling" (ShTs72 = HK$100).
tael	a silver unit of account, a weight, cf. pound.
taipan	chief executive
tao-t'ai	district officer/magistrate, intendant of a circuit
Treaty Ports	Before the first Sino-British War, China had successfully limited Western seaborne trade to the port of Canton; under the terms of subsequent treaties the Chinese agreed to open further ports—and in some cases opened them without foreign inducement (the so-called self-opened ports). Until 1895 foreigners were free to settle only in designated areas of the open ports, in some cases under a local foreign administration, the foreign concessions. For the purposes of this chapter, we are interested in the "principal" treaty ports as designated in the IMC statistics on a trade basis: Shanghai, Tientsin, the Yangtze Ports, especially Hankow, Canton, and also Amoy, Foochow, and Tsingtau. By 1914 all these ports had foreign bank agencies or merchant-agent representatives, as did several of the minor ports—for example, Chefoo.

Appendix B: Chinese Glossary

As in text	Pinyin	Characters
Chang Chih-tung	Zhang Zhidong	張之洞
chops		
hao	hao	號
tzu hao	zi hao	字號

As in text	Pinyin	Characters
hong	hang	行
kuan-tu shang-pan	guandu shangban	官督商辦
li	li	厘
Li Hung-chang	Li Hongzhang	李鴻章
Sheng Hsuan-huai	Sheng Xuanhuai	盛宣懷
[literary] Tzu-yi	Ciyi	次沂
Sun Yat-sen	Sun Yixian	孫逸仙
taipan	daban	大班
tao-t'ai	dao-tai	道臺
Tsungli Yamen	Zongli Yamen	總理衙門
Wu Mao-ting	Wu Maoding	吳楙鼎
yang-p'ing taels	yang-ping liang	洋平兩
Yuan Shih-k'ai	Yuan Shikai	袁世凱

Bibliographical Notes

This essay has been prepared from material collected in connection with a commissioned history of the Hongkong and Shanghai Banking Corporation. Material dealing with that bank comes from its archives and from the Public Record Office, the archives of the Auswärtiges Amt in Bonn, the National Archives of the United States, and the Hoover Institution. Reference has also been made to essays in Frank H.H. King, ed. *Eastern Banking: Essays in the History of The Hongkong and Shanghai Banking Corporation* (London, 1983); see especially Carl T. Smith on the compradores, David McLean on "International Banking and its Political Implications," David J.S. King, "China's First Public Loan"; reference is also made to research reports on "China's Early Loans" and "The Hongkong Bank and China" by David J.S. King, graduate student, The Johns Hopkins University; German sources are listed in these reports.

The loan agreements referred to in the text are found in John V.A. MacMurray, *Treaties and Agreements with and Concerning China, 1894–1919* (New York, 1921), 2 vols.; earlier agreements are in various sources, including the Foreign Office FO 371 series in the Public Record Office and the Hongkong Bank Group Archives; see also Chen Chung-sieu, "British Loans to China from 1860 to 1913 . . . " (PhD Thesis, University of London, 1940).

Primary sources of greatest use have been: Charles S. Addis papers and David McLean (Hongkong Bank London Manager) papers in the Library, School of Oriental and African Studies, London; CO 129 and FO 17 and 371 files in the Public Record Office; and, as cited in David King's studies, various China files in Bonn. Parallel material is to be found in the Foreign Ministry archives in Brussels, Paris, and Rome, references to which are cited in Kurgan-Van Hentenryk and Mancini (see below) respectively. J.O.P. Bland's correspondence with Addis, describing the developing rift between the Bank and the Corporation as represented by Bland, is in the Toronto University Library. Reference was also made to the papers of Hermann Wallich made available by Dr. Henry Wallich, Federal Reserve Board of Governors; the letter books of Carl Meyer by Sir Anthony Meyer, M.P., Bart; the journals of F.T. Koelle, Hongkong Bank Hamburg Manager to 1919, by Dr. W. Koelle; for the role of H.B. Morse, see his letters in the Houghton Library, Harvard University.

Neither reliable balance of payments nor national income statistics exist for the countries of the region (Japan excluded). Detailed trade statistics were compiled by the IMC, although they require interpretation; see Liang-lin Hsiao, *China's Trade Statistics, 1864–1949* (Cambridge, MA., 1974).

Statistics dealing with foreign banks in the East on a country-by-country basis, except for references to note-issue, are rare; published bank accounts are not separated by territory. See Table 4.

Research associates have searched collections of Ch'ing documents including the collected memorials of key officials. A clear picture has failed to emerge.

Studies which were particularly relevant to this chapter other than those referred to above, are:

Born, Karl Erich. *International Banking in the 19th and 20th Centuries.* Leamington Spa, England, 1983. German ed., *Geld Banken . . . .* Stuttgart, 1977.

Couling, Samuel. *The Encyclopaedia Sinica.* Shanghai, 1917.

Feuerwerker, Albert. *China's Early Industrialization. Sheng Hsuan-huai (1844–1916) and Mandarin Enterprise.* Cambridge, Mass., 1958.

Gonjo, Yasuo. *Hurans teikokushugi to ajia—Indoshina ginko shi kenkyu* (French imperialism and Asia—a history of the Banque de l'Indo-Chine). Tokyo, 1985.

Hart, Sir Robert. *The I.G. in Peking, Letters of Robert Hart, Chinese Maritime Customs, 1868–1907.* John King Fairbank et al., eds., 2 vols., Cambridge, Mass., 1975.

Huenemann, Ralph W. *The Dragon and the Iron Horse: the Economics of Railroads in China, 1876–1937.* Cambridge, Mass., 1984.

King, Frank H.H. *Money in British East Asia.* London, 1957.

————. *Money and Monetary Policy in China, 1845–1895.* Cambridge, Mass., 1965.

————. *The History of The Hongkong and Shanghai Banking Corporation.* Vols. I-III. Cambridge, 1987–89.

————."Chinese Money and Banking: an historical survey, 1840-1960," in King, ed. *Asian Policy, History and Development.* Hong Kong, 1979, pp. 69–82. Originally published (in German) in Brunhild Staiger, ed. *China-Handbuch.* Dusseldorf, 1974.

Kurgan-Van Hentenryk, G. *Léopold II et les groupes financiers belges en Chine: la politique royale et ses prolongements (1895–1914).* Bruxelles, 1971.

Lee, En-han. *China's Quest for Railway Autonomy, 1904–1911.* Singapore, 1977., cols. 91–7, 391–8, 1537–40.

McElderry, Andrea Lee. *Shanghai Old-Style Banks (Ch'ien-chang), 1800–1935: a Traditional Institution in a Changing Society.* Ann Arbor, Michigan, 1976.

Mancini, Claudio M. "Appunti per una storia delle relazioni commerciali e finanziarie fra Italia e China, dal 1819 al 1900." *Revista de diritto valutario e de economia internazionale* 31–33: 401–33, 659–05, 931–63 (1987).

Morrison, G.E. *The Correspondence of G.E. Morrison, 1895–1920.* Ed. Lo Hui-min. 2 vols. Cambridge, 1976.

Müller-Jabusch, Maximilian. *Fünzig Jahre Deutsch-Asiatische Bank, 1890–1939.* Berlin, 1940.

Romanov, B.A. *Russia and Manchuria*. Trans. Susan Wilbur Jones. Ann Arbor, Michigan, 1952.

Shinonaga, Nobutaka. "La Formation de la Banque Industrielle de Chine et son ecroulement— un defi des fréres Berthelot." Ph.D. thesis. University of Paris VIII. 1988.

Spalding, W.F. *Dictionary of the World's Currencies and Foreign Exchanges*. London, 1928. See also his other works on exchange and Eastern banking.

Sun, E-tu Zen. *Chinese Railways and British Interests, 1898–1911*. New York, 1954.

Young, Ernest P. *The Presidency of Yuan Shih-k'ai, Liberalism and Dictatorship in Early Republican China*. Ann Arbor, 1977.

18

European Banks
in the Middle East

Jacques Thobie

The basic approach of this chapter rests on an ascertainable fact: The intervention of European banks in the Ottoman Empire, Egypt, and Persia involved necessarily and intimately two processes, one of financial and economic technique, the other of politics. The emergence and development of the purely financial activity of British, French, Belgian, Swiss, Dutch, then Austrian, German, Italian and Russian banks, occurred at a time when banking institutions in Europe strove to adapt themselves to the changing requirements of the development of industrial capitalism. Their activity in the eastern Mediterranean took different forms, such as intervention by the banks short of permanent presence in the area, the opening of branches, and the formation of banks bearing local titles but controlled by European capital.

Based on the search for profit and for its security, the types of transactions differed, including the achievement and control of the stability of currencies, exchange, commercial credit, varied loans, management, and membership in syndicates to underwrite state loans and industrial investment. At the same time, however, the economic and financial difficulties of these scarcely developed countries and the advantages of their strategic position were such that these banking transactions came to subtend more or less worked-out political and economic strategies. They reinforced national groups despite some attempts at international economic and financial cooperation. They involved the history of international relations by way of the accords and conflicts among imperialist powers. Finally, they drew partition of the region into zones of influence or straightforward occupation.

Having functioned efficiently during the settlement of the Ottoman and Egyptian debts at the end of the 1870s, this complex process reached, despite formidable contradictions, a high degree of sophistication on the eve of the Great War.

European Banks and the Ottoman and Egyptian Bankruptcies (1875–76)

The Ottoman and Egyptian bankruptcies, respectively of 1875–76 and 1875, constitute an excellent laboratory to understand the activities of old and new European bankers in the Middle East. The organized meeting between capital accumulation, within north-western Europe, first in Britain, then in France, and the chronic needs of hard-pressed rulers led borrowers to default, a situation that allowed lenders to tighten their control on local finances while restoring them, and the British and French governments to deepen Ottoman and Egyptian dependence. With some differences, a similar process occurred in Persia.

Bankers in London and Paris were very largely responsible for the infatuation of British and French investors for "securities with a turban." As regards the Ottoman Empire, seventeen state or related loans were floated between 1854 and 1877 (twenty-three years) and produced a real sum of 3.21 billion francs (5.3 billion at face value). They were negotiated mainly on the markets of London (30 percent) and Paris (40 percent).[1] In order to respond to this continuous stream of loans, to guarantee them minimal security and the highest profit, it was necessary to set up an infrastructure for banking.

Thus in 1863 the Banque Impériale Ottomane (B.I.O.) was created by the association of the English group of the Ottoman Bank founded in 1856 (T. Bruce, Pascal du Pré Grenfell, L.M. Rate, W.R. Drake, John Stewart) with a French group bringing 50 percent of the capital of the new bank. The latter included eminent members of the *haute banque* (Hottinguer, Fould, Pillet-Will, Mallet, Seillère) and representatives of the Comptoir d'Escompte de Paris (Hippolyte Biesta) and the Crédit Mobilier (Isaac and Emile Péreire). Duality was a feature both in the capital and the functioning of the bank. It was managed by the committees of London and Paris, from which was constituted the day-to-day administration in Constantinople.

An essential characteristic of the B.I.O. was its double nature, making it at once a private Franco-British bank and a state bank in Constantinople.[2] Ottoman authorities relied on this solid banking group to provide for the momentary needs of the Treasury, and to act as a link between them and foreign capital. The B.I.O. was granted the privilege of issuing bank notes and entrusted with all the transactions of the State Treasury in Constantinople in return for the obligation of making certain short-term loans to the state. Although it did not obtain a monopoly, the B.I.O. had a privileged position for servicing the foreign debt. The bank arrived at the right moment. It reassured future lenders by guaranteeing the security of their investments and was in good position to draw maximum profits from the situation. As Bruce, its chairman, was to declare, the condition of the bank "was unexampled in the history of independent companies or financial institutions in the world."[3]

It did not remain alone for long. To benefit from the manna, several banks emerged from the association of European capital and that of local origin, in the hands of the so-called Galata bankers. Among these were the following Franco-British firms: the Société Générale de l'Empire Ottoman (1864), the Crédit Général Ottoman (1869, a creation of the Société Générale de France), the Banque de Constaninople, the Société Ottomane de Change et de Valeurs (1872). In 1875 the Crédit Lyonnais opened in the Ottoman capital a branch for which a bright future lay ahead. The withdrawal of the Paris market after the war of 1870–71 made Vienna for a short while a center of speculation on Ottoman securities and led to the establishment of the Banque Austro-Ottomane and the short-lived Banque Austro-Turque (1871).

By means of underwriting syndicates for the purchase and negotiation of loans, the banks were satisfied most often with the role of intermediaries between investors and borrowers. Their aim was mainly to make money with money, and earn commission and interest from each transaction. Conditions were particularly favorable, and commissions amounted to between 10 and 12 percent of the sums actually gathered.[4] The 2.64 billion francs that the Ottoman government in fact received were sunk in basically unproductive activities, such as restoring its military affairs after the Crimean War, recall of paper money, conversion of the external debt, partial reduction of the floating debt, and payment of the expenses related to the insurrection in Crete. The last loans only served to plug holes in the budget and to service the debt.[5] Financial management of this kind could only lead to bankruptcy.

Even if it was of the same basic nature, the Egyptian scenario presented some characteristics of its own. The "Oriental mirage" worked well for Egypt, both in Paris, where the tradition was already established, and in London. A new era opened in the 1860s with the loans of the khedive and the cutting of the Suez Canal. One loan followed another and fed the debts. Between 1862 and 1873 (twelve years), eight state loans tapped, in conditions similar to those in the Ottoman Empire, 1.3 billion francs (1.71 billion at face value), to which must be added 500 million to 600 million for the floating debt. The *haute banque* was first to arrive on the scene. Edouard Dervieu, a trader who became an intimate friend of the khedive, was French; Frühling and Goschen English (of German-Jewish extraction), and Oppenheim of Cologne, Paris, and Alexandria cosmopolitan.[6] Investment banks and commercial (deposit) banks came soon after. The B.I.O. set up its first branch in Alexandria in 1867, and by its side could be found the Société Générale, the Comptoir d'Escompte de Paris,[7] the Banque de Paris et des Pays-Bas (Paribas), the Crédit Lyonnais—which opened a branch in Alexandria in 1875 (see Table 18–1)—and the Crédit Foncier.[8] Other banks were also set up in Egypt, such as the Bank of Egypt (1856), which was owned by British capital; the Anglo-Egyptian Bank (1864); the Banque Austro-Egyptienne (1869); and the Banque Franco-Egyptienne (1870). Despite its name, the Anglo-Egyptian Bank was under direction of a French group led by J.R. Pastré, an important merchant from Marseille and founder of the Société Marseillaise de Crédit. From 1873 the khedive lived solely on advances, eagerly made by the Anglo-Egyptian Bank to be sold through the Crédit Agricole and the Crédit Foncier. By depriving the khedive of any possibility of floating a consolidation loan, the Ottoman bankruptcy rendered inevitable its Egyptian counterpart.

The search for a negotiated solution to the Ottoman and Egyptian bankruptcies implied an international settlement to be worked out on two closely related levels. At first, the banks played an essential role in safeguarding the immediate interests of

TABLE 18–1. Estimate of Capital Invested in the Middle East by the Crédit Lyonnais (1866–1881)

	1866–1870	1871–1874	1875–1881	Total
		(millions of francs)		
Egypt	18.5	24.5	20.0	63.0
Turkey	6.26	4.7	15.833	26.793
TOTAL	24.76	29.2	35.833	89.793

Source: J. Bouvier, *Le Crédit Lyonnais de 1863 à 1882* (Paris, 1961), vol. II, p. 731.

threatened creditors. The great battle was launched, for the Ottoman as well as the Egyptian debts, between partisans of the "floating" and those of the "consolidated" portions. French establishments were more deeply involved in the advances, the floating debts, than in the "consolidated," which was of greater interest to British bondholders if not bankers. Thus can be explained the appearance of very different projects that, after active diplomatic intervention, tended toward an indispensable compromise. The other level showed even greater collusion between governments and financiers. The aim was to prevent debtor states from shirking their obligations by intervening directly in those countries to take hold of the product of their collateral security by means of more or less sophisticated control of their fiscal system and their budget. It was a necessary condition permitting new loans and the aggravation of a process that dealt a great blow to the sovereignty of these countries.

Whereas the purchase by Disraeli—thanks to the good offices of Lionel de Rothschild—of the 170,602 Suez shares belonging to khedive Ismail I did not provoke tangible reactions in Paris, important differences appeared in the French and British projects for settling the debt.[9] The solution advocated by the Comptoir d'Escompte, urged on by the Duc Decazes and the Crédit Foncier, provoked such British protests that talks were undertaken and concluded with the compromise of November 18, 1876.[10] It put into place a Franco-British condominium, divided and reduced the debt, confirmed the Caisse de la Dette Publique controlled by four commissioners (British, French, Italian, and Austrian), created a Commission de la Dette Publique (two British, two French, and two Egyptian representatives),[11] and called for the nomination of two "Controllers General," one French, one British, empowered with extensive rights in the financial administration. Finally, the British and French governments and banking groups reached an essential agreement for the dismissal of Ismail, who was replaced by his son Tewfik in 1879, and for the promulgation of the Law of Liquidation of December 31, 1880, which was intended to guarantee a lasting solution to the Egyptian debt by alleviating the burden of the Treasury.

Overwhelmed by financial and military disasters, Abdul Hamid made a commitment in the Treaty of Berlin, which took concrete form in the Decree of Muharrem of December 20, 1881. The B.I.O. played a leading role in setting up the Administration de la Dette Publique Ottomane, which was henceforth to manage the old Turkish debt, reduced for all practical purposes to the amount really handed over to the Ottoman Treasury. The government had to yield certain revenues for the service of the debt, particularly those of the monopolies of tobacco, salt, stamps, and silk. The Conseil de la Dette was made up of seven delegates (one British, one French, one German, one Italian, one Austro-Hungarian, one Ottoman, and one representative of the B.I.O.) and the annual chairmanship was reserved by turns to the French and the British.

Cosmopolitan organisms endowed with extensive powers were thus put into place in Cairo and Constantinople, as they previously had been in Tunis. The credit of Turkey and Egypt was reinforced in the long run by these transactions, which should have facilitated the granting of new loans at more reasonable conditions than in the past. This reinforcement, however, went hand in hand with the takeover by foreigners of the management of these countries' revenues. The Administration de la Dette, backed by the B.I.O., directly controlled 25 to 30 percent of the wealth of the Empire. From then on Egyptian and Ottoman finances were to be under surveillance. Moreover, the new institutions played a political role deriving, not from any written text, but from their very existence. In that respect, the British and French banking groups and governments were the real decision-makers in Constantinople and Cairo. The Administration and Caisse were typical of the way in which the export of capital gave rise to institutions representing new instruments for intensifying foreign intervention.

The destinies of the Ottoman Empire and of Egypt were, nevertheless, somewhat different. Whereas, for reasons which cannot be discussed here, rival imperialist ambitions neutralized each other in Constantinople, allowing the Empire to survive, in Egypt the result was the occupation of the country by British troops and the crushing of the national movement. One question remains to be dealt with: Why did not France intervene in 1882 alongside Britain? Here again, financial interests and political authorities worked hand in hand. Involved in Tunisia and worried about reactions from Berlin, the French government had only interests in Egypt, but no imperialist project. As early as April 1877, the Consul des Michels had written to Decazes: "I tell those who question me: our sole interest in Egypt is to be duly paid." Concurrently, in the period between 1877 and 1882, the Crédit Foncier was able to liquidate on favorable terms a large part of its Egyptian loans, and place on firmer ground the debt still owed to it. When the Bourse crisis broke out in Paris in January 1882, "the various French groups were completely paralyzed."[12] In any case, Parisian business interests considered the advent of the British as a positive factor of order, an opinion confirmed by the rise on the Bourse of Egyptian securities, particularly those of Suez.

European Banks and Monetary Stability in the Middle East

Two examples will show the course adopted by banks founded by European capital and acting as state banks to create some coherence in the circulation of money and order in the exchange rate, thus guaranteeing greater security to the activities of foreign banks.

In the *Ottoman Empire* difficulties resulted from a fairly complicated system of monetary circulation, from the decline of silver, from counterfeit, and from the abandonment of the silver standard abroad resulting in a premium of about 8 percent on gold in 1879. At the instigation of the B.I.O., a decree promulgated in 1880 specified that the basic unit of currency was the gold Turkish pound, and created in fact three different rates for the silver *medjidie*.[13] And so was put into place a bivalent system, a twofold circulation, both gold and silver being accepted. Its basis was the gold standard (for the capitalist network opened toward the outside world), while silver fluctuated like a commodity (for traditional internal commerce) according to supply and demand.

Despite the minting of new gold coins, the money supply remained stagnant (due to hoarding), while the B.I.O. showed caution in exercising its privilege of issuing bank notes. This Malthusian policy—reinforced even more by the stinging effects of the crisis induced by speculation in 1895—can be explained by the fact that the bank had no need for an increase in the circulation of gold coins, or money backed by gold, insofar as it also controlled the market for silver currencies and determined their rate of exchange. This two-tier system lasted thirty years for two reasons. On the one hand, the system was profitable to all those who, within the Empire, were participants in capitalist monetary movements based on the gold standard, at the expense of those who engaged in local or regional trade on the basis of silver currency. On the other hand, this system favored, both at home and abroad, the interests of importers and exporters, insofar as it guaranteed a premium to the pound sterling over the Turkish pound.[14] After 1880 the B.I.O. established and maintained a fixed parity between the pound sterling and the Turkish pound, thus providing commerce and capital movements with stability and security. The bank avoided "sudden variations in the rate of exchange between the Turkish pound and the pound sterling by manipulating the internal rate of exchange between the gold Turkish pound and the silver *medjidie.*"[15] By means of this dual system, half-fixed, half-mobile, the B.I.O. avoided external devaluations by relying on internal devaluations. In the final analysis, this strategy avoided the major disadvantages inherent in the adoption of a completely fixed or floating system[16]; it also provided the opportunity to make substantial profits. (See Fig. 18–1.)

The system put into place in *Egypt*, under the aegis of Great Britain, was at once more simple and more radical. The commission of 1884 chose the Egyptian pound as the unit of currency on the basis of the gold standard. Pending the minting of Egyptian pounds, it was decided to keep three foreign currencies, the pound sterling, the Napoleon, and the Turkish pound in circulation, and to maintain among them the rate established under Muhammad Ali,[17] which put a premium first on the Egyptian pound, then on sterling. With the minting of Egyptian pounds practically at a standstill, the pound sterling continued, in fact, to hold a predominant position in the monetary circulation of Egypt, and an additional profit was made on all transactions in sterling.

When the London-based group of Sir Ernest Cassel, with the participation of local financiers, decided to create a National Bank of Egypt, it intended to repeat in Egypt what the B.I.O. was so successfully doing in Constantinople. The hostility of the B.I.O., which considered its notes to be legal tender throughout the Empire, the opposition of the Crédit Lyonnais, acting as banker of the Caisse, which viewed the matter as an indirect way of borrowing for the government; and the uneasiness of rival British banks paralyzed Sir Ernest's initiative.[18] The Egyptian bank note was eventually accepted by the Treasury but did not become legal tender. Until the Great War

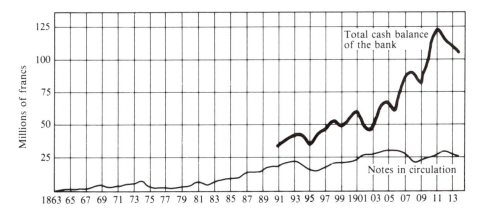

FIGURE 18–1. Paper money in the Ottoman Empire and the cash balance of the Banque Impériale Ottomane. *Source: J.* Thobie, *Intérêts et impérialisme français dans l'Empire ottoman,* p. 756.

the issue of notes was scant,[19] leaving the way clear for the pound sterling. In fact, this state bank accepted a system that actually deprived Egypt of any national currency, except a currency of account, or the potential for a monetary system. An economist correctly concluded about this institution, "a state bank so-called seemed much more to be an English colonial bank than a real Egyptian national bank."[20]

In *Persia*, the modernization of currency was led by the Imperial Bank of Persia (I.B.P.) As Geoffrey Jones humorously recounts, this bank was founded somewhat by accident.[21] Baron Julius de Reuter, whose surname is still a household word thanks to the news agency he founded, could not realize, as a result of Russian pressures on the shah, the concession for railways that he was granted in 1872. Article 20 of the concession gave de Reuter the first option should "the Persian government in the future . . . decide upon granting permission to start a bank." This article was the origin of the I.B.P. The new concession gave the right to establish a bank with unique privileges, notably the exclusive right of note issue in Persia; the royal charter of 1889 made this state bank of Persia a total banking institution. Its capital, amounting to £1 million, was not spectacular, but was entirely British; moreover, it had to be written down, in 1894, to £650,000. Considerable executive power was retained in London by a board of nine directors (George de Reuter Jr., Edward Sassoon, S. Ezekiel, David MacLean, Geoffrey Glyn, H. D. Stewart, A. Ph. Hotz, Sir Lepel Griffin, and finally, Chairman William Keswick, a former chairman of the Hongkong Bank). The post of chief manager in Tehran was offered to Joseph Rabino, the manager of the Cairo branch of the Crédit Lyonnais; he was the man without whom the I.B.P. might never have survived for two difficult decades.

Bank notes essentially represent for a bank an interest-free loan and also give it considerable prestige. The note issue grew slowly until 1899, then more rapidly until 1913 (53 million krans or £962,4l9), with a momentary decline between 1906 and 1908. Tehran's note issue was the largest. There were a number of obstacles to the rapid spread of the bank's notes: the activities of opponents and enemies of the bank, the obligation of maintaining a big cash reserve against the notes, the necessity for the

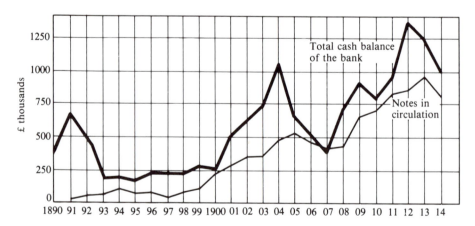

FIGURE 18–2. Bank notes in Persia and the cash balance of the Imperial Bank of Persia.
Source: Geoffrey Jones, *Banking and Empire in Iran,* p. 354.

notes to be payable only at the branch of issue. It can even be disputed whether they were really money.[22] In other respects, slowly but surely, in the disastrous situation of Persia, the bank became the Persian government's sole agent for importing silver. The bank received commissions and interest for advancing necessary sums for the purchase of silver. The fall of the exchange value of the kran (from 35 krans per pound in 1890 to 55.5 krans in 1913) resulted in a depreciation of the sterling value of the bank assets in Persia. Lastly, the bank gradually succeeded in withdrawing excess copper coinage from circulation, and in introducing a new nickel coinage. (See Fig. 18–2.)

European Banks and State Loans, 1880–1914

In a less "savage" context than in the preceding period, state and related loans were still the foremost business sought by European banks, of whose profits they formed an appreciable proportion. While the club of the chief underwriters of these major floatations was closed and carefully watched, the system of second- and third-line participation in syndicates widened the circle of banking establishments interested in these loans.

Thus, in the Ottoman Empire, thirty-four important operations were spread out from 1881 to 1914 (thirty-four years), represented by nineteen state and related (railway and municipal loans guaranteed by the state) loans, seven conversions, and eight issues of Treasury bonds. Of these thirty-four operations, twenty-four were carried out by French or near-French banks; the lion's share belonged to the B.I.O. with nineteen operations (respectively nine, six, and four). Three other French groups, the Count de Zogheb, the Banque Française pour le Commerce et l'Industrie (B.F.C.I.), and the Périer bank, split among themselves the five remaining operations. German banks became managers for seven operations (respectively five, one, and one). Lastly, three operations interested only British banks by way of the ambitions of the National Bank of Turkey.

Although British bondholders, hence British banks, shied away somewhat from Turkish state loans after 1881, they took a more active part in the Egyptian loans, without, for all that, surpassing the dynamism of French banks. Thus, of the seven operations (four loans, three conversions) launched in Cairo between 1880 and 1914, four were led by British groups dominated by high finance as personified by the Rothschilds of London and Sir Ernest Cassel, and three by the Rothschilds of Paris and by Paribas.

A Franco-British bank at first, the B.I.O. became more than 80 percent French in the 1880s. The Paris Committee was the only real decision-making body for all matters concerning Ottoman affairs, the London Committee concentrating especially—albeit without vigor—on investments in Egyptian affairs.[23] It is therefore easy to understand that the B.I.O. brought together the pick of banks in the underwriting syndicates it directed. In the first place, the faithful were always present, namely, the Société Générale, whose occasional fractiousness amounted to little; the Comptoir National d'Escompte; the Crédit Industriel et Commercial; and Paribas; the Banque de l'Union Parisienne (after 1905) and the Banque de Salonique (after 1909) were also included. Sporadically, the Crédit Lyonnais, the B.F.C.I. (Banque Rouvier), the Société Marseillaise de Crédit, as well as foreign banks, particularly German and Belgian, also took part in operations managed by the B.I.O. Through allies, friends, and third-line participants, cosmopolitan finance itself was involved. Figure 18–3 provides a simplified sketch of the process of subdivision. For the first syndicate of the 4 percent Ottoman loan of 1909 (500 million francs), the number of participants in the Paribas and Parunion groups alone reached a total of at least 152, including 45 French banks, 8 German, 7 Belgian, 5 Swiss, 3 Spanish, 3 Balkan, 2 Italian, 1 British, 1 Dutch, 1 American, and the Banque Centrale d'Haiti.[24] (See Fig. 18–3; Table 18–2.)

The B.I.O. thwarted two attempts by the Crédit Mobilier Français (in 1908 and 1910) to act independently in Ottoman affairs. It had to yield the management of operations, however, to the Count de Zogheb in 1893, then to the Banque Rouvier in 1911 and to Ferdinand Périer in 1909 and 1913.[25] At once minister and banker, Rouvier played a leading role in the consolidation of the Ottoman debt in 1903, and was rewarded with the management, jointly with the Syndicat des Banques de Province, of the Hodeida-Sanaa railway loan; he also enticed the Société Générale and the Comptoir away from the B.I.O. for a while. Périer et Cie., a well known bank in Paris, elbowed its way into the Orient, after some skirmishing with the B.I.O., with the municipal loan of Constantinople and the enormous issue of the "Périer bonds" (100 million francs), which saved the Young Turks from bankruptcy in December 1913.

Apart from the 5 percent bonds of 1914, all Ottoman securities issued on the Paris market were well received, so much so that it was sometimes necessary to reduce drastically initial applications. Although always higher than in Europe, profits were more moderate than in the preceding period. On the basis of the issue price, actual interest on Ottoman loans oscillated between 4.18 and 5.36 percent; on the basis of Bourse quotations, it ranged between 4.12 and 6.06 percent. Bank commissions tended to decline, the diminution for the period going from 5.8 to 2.37 percent of the amount collected. Table 18–3 furnishes an example, in summary form, of bookkeeping by a bank concerning the conversion of the 4 percent *Priorités* loan of 1906.

The Deutsche Bank initiated major and direct involvement in Ottoman affairs by taking responsibility for the so-called Fisheries 5 percent loan of 1888. By 1914 it had managed four other loans, including the first two series of the Baghdad railway. The entry of this new competitor could not but create difficulties for the established banks, first and foremost for the B.I.O. On the one hand, however, the Deutsche Bank could not fight on equal terms against the B.I.O. on account of the narrowness of the German financial market. On the other, it feared that unrestrained competition might cause an unfortunate fall in the value of Ottoman securities. The upshot was the agreements of Stuttgart and Paris (1894) by which each group undertook to reserve to its partner a certain interest (around 20 percent) in any future Ottoman loan it obtained. These accords did not mean the advent of an era of active collaboration between French and

TABLE 18–2. Breakdown of the Ottoman Public Debt in 1914

Thousands of francs	France		England		Germany		Others		Total	
	value	(%)	value	(%)	value	(%)	value	(%)	value	(%)
Face value	2,196	59.5	489.7	13	658.9	17.9	355.2	9.6	3,698.8	100
Real amount	2,002.6	59.8	458.3	13.7	542.3	16.2	343.8	10.3	3,347	100

Source: J. Thobie, *Interets et imperialisme francais, p. 521.*

TABLE 18–3. Net Profits of the B.I.O. in the Conversion of the 4 Percent *Priorités* Loan of 1906[a]

Summary of the accounts of the underwriting syndicate	Total amounts of the loan in francs	Amounts retained by the bank for	
		Expenses	Profits
1. Face value of 100% for 433,500 bonds of 500 francs	216,750,000		
2. Firm purchase by the B.I.O. at a net price of 85.5% (427.5 francs per pound)	185,321,250		
3. Firm purchase by the B.I.O. at a gross price of 87% (435 francs per bond)	188,572,000		
3 − 2 = 1.5% or 7.5 francs per bond			
breakdown: 1 × 216,750,000: 100 =		2,167,500	
0.5 × 216,750,000: 100 =			1,083,750
4. Firm purchase by the underwriting syndicate at a price of 88.75% (443.75 francs per bond)	192,365,625		
4 − 3 = 1.75% or 8.75 francs per bond			
breakdown: 1 × 216,750,000: 100 =		2,167,500	
amount retained by B.I.O.			
0.75 × 216,750,000 =			1,625,625
5. Average price of exchange and issue, 94.6% (473.03 francs per bond)	205,058,497		
5 − 4 = 5.85% or 29.28 francs per bond			
breakdown of the share of the B.I.O.			
Commission for the firm purchase, 19 francs per bond or 74,471 × 19 =			1,414,949
Commission for negotiation and exchange, 5 francs per bond, or 87,268 × 5 =			436,340
Commission for management of the syndicate, 1/8% of the face value of the loan, or 0.125 × 216,750,000 =			270,937
Total profits			4,831,601
2.2% of the face value or 2.6% of the net price of the firm purchase by the B.I.O.			

Source: Archives of the Société Générale and the Banque de Paris et des Pays-Bas.
[a] Issued July 5–12, 1906. First distribution to the underwriters (15 francs per share): August 6, 1906. Last distribution to the underwriters (4 francs per share): October 2, 1906.

German capital, but only the willingness to avoid irreparable harm and to set up a *modus vivendi*. It was a safety clause established to avoid overbidding, which would have a negative effect on profits, and to close the door to any possible intruder. All the same, each group kept its freedom of action to seek profitable business above all.

The Deutsche Bank was worried by the emergence in 1906 of the Deutsche Orient Bank (D.O.B.), formed by a rival group comprising the Dresdner Bank, the Schaffhausenscher, and the Nationalbank. Directed by Gutmann and supported by Krupp, this new bank proclaimed itself the defender of purely German interests, in contrast to the

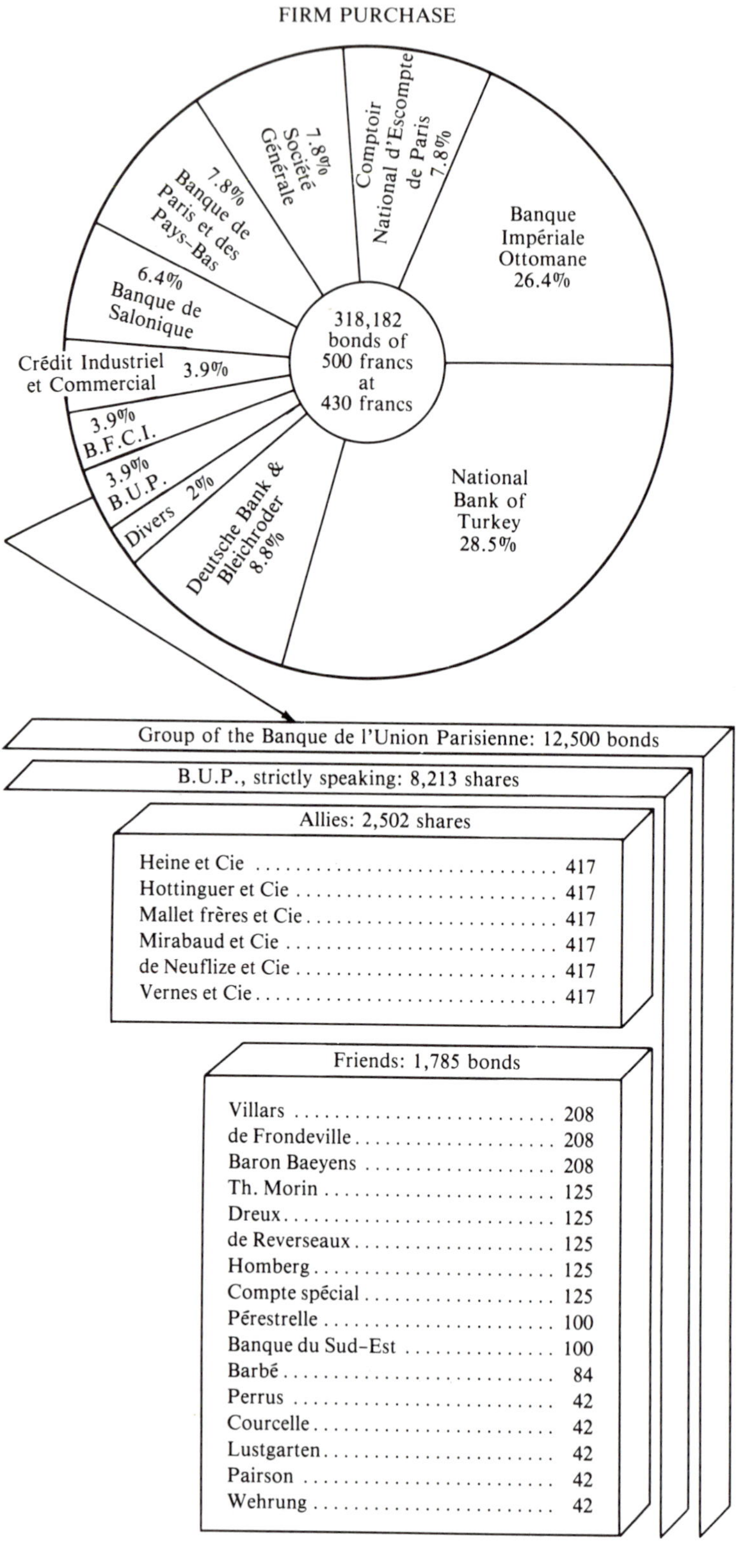

FIRM PURCHASE
318,182 bonds of 500 francs at 430 francs
Banque Impériale Ottomane 26.4%
National Bank of Turkey 28.5%
Deutsche Bank & Bleichroder 8.8%
Divers 2%
3.9% B.U.P.
3.9% B.F.C.I.
Crédit Industriel et Commercial 3.9%
6.4% Banque de Salonique
7.8% Banque de Paris et des Pays-Bas
7.8% Société Générale
Comptoir National d'Escompte de Paris 7.8%
Group of the Banque de l'Union Parisienne: 12,500 bonds
B.U.P., strictly speaking: 8,213 shares
Allies: 2,502 shares
Heine et Cie . . . 417
Hottinguer et Cie . . . 417
Mallet frères et Cie . . . 417
Mirabaud et Cie . . . 417
de Neuflize et Cie . . . 417
Vernes et Cie . . . 417
Friends: 1,785 bonds
Villars . . . 208
de Frondeville . . . 208
Baron Baeyens . . . 208
Th. Morin . . . 125
Dreux . . . 125
de Reverseaux . . . 125
Homberg . . . 125
Compte spécial . . . 125
Pérestrelle . . . 100
Banque du Sud-Est . . . 100
Barbé . . . 84
Perrus . . . 42
Courcelle . . . 42
Lustgarten . . . 42
Pairson . . . 42
Wehrung . . . 42

FIGURE 18–3. French and English syndicates of the 4 percent 1909 Ottoman loan.

EXPECTED SUBSCRIPTIONS

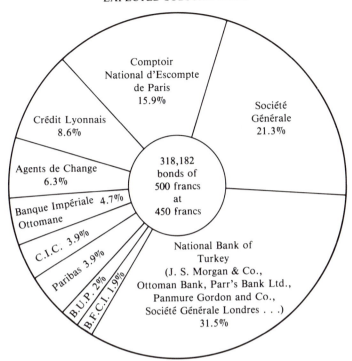

Comptoir National d'Escompte de Paris 15.9%

Société Générale 21.3%

Crédit Lyonnais 8.6%

Agents de Change 6.3%

Banque Impériale 4.7% Ottomane

C.I.C. 3.9%

Paribas 3.9%

B.U.P. 2%

B.F.C.I. 1.9%

318,182 bonds of 500 francs at 450 francs

National Bank of Turkey (J. S. Morgan & Co., Ottoman Bank, Parr's Bank Ltd., Panmure Gordon and Co., Société Générale Londres . . .) 31.5%

REAL SUBSCRIPTIONS

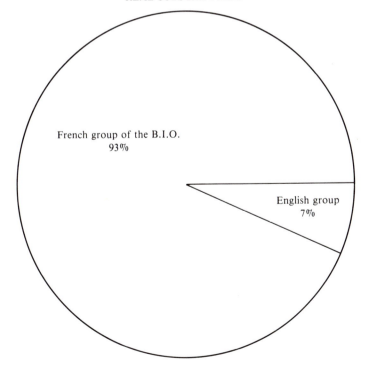

French group of the B.I.O. 93%

English group 7%

cosmopolitan compromises entered into by the Deutsche Bank. Despite certain limited successes, the D.O.B. did not succeed in wresting the management of German affairs in the Ottoman Empire from the Deutsche Bank.

The Deutsche Bank worked with a loyal associate, Bleichröder. Underwriting syndicates, of course, brought together many German and foreign banks. Tapping capital on a large scale was all the more necessary because the amount available from savings was limited. The fact was confirmed following the failure in France of the loan intended for 1910. With German capital only, the Deutsche Bank had to manage the subscription to the 4 percent loan of 1911. (See Table 18–4.) The operation necessitated the collaboration of thirty-one banks, twenty German, ten Austro-Hungarian and one Swiss. It was undeniable that in 1911, as in the case of other loans managed by the Deutsche Bank, agreements among banks, particularly through their branches or subsidiaries in Belgium and Switzerland, worked in such a way that many bonds actually entered French portfolios.

After 1881 the London financial market proved to be a poor subscriber to Ottoman securities. Such was the lack of interest that the London branch of the B.I.O. sufficed. In 1909, however, a British group led by Sir Ernest Cassel created the National Bank of

TABLE 18–4. Banks Underwriting the 4 Percent Ottoman Loan of 1911

Deutsche Bank	Berlin
S. Bleichröder	Berlin
Bank fur Handel & Industrie	Berlin
S. Behrens & Söhne	Hamburg
Berliner Handelsgesellschaft	Berlin
Gebrüder Bethmann	Frankfurt a/M.
Commerz & Diskonto Bank	Hamburg
Deutsche Orientbank	Berlin
Deutsche Vereinsbank	Frankfurt a/M.
Direktion der Diskonto-Gesellschaft	Berlin
Dresdner Bank	Berlin
Mendelssohn & Co.	Berlin
Mittledeutsche Creditbank	Berlin
Nationalbank für Deutschland	Berlin
Norddeutsche Bank	Berlin
A. Schaffhausenscher B.V.	Berlin
Lazard Speyer-Elissen	Frankfurt a/M.
Jacob S. H. Stern	Frankfurt a/M.
M.M. Warburg & Co.	Frankfurt a/M.
Württembergische Vereinsbank	Stuttgart
Boden-Credit-Anstalt	Vienna
Anglo-Osterreichische Bank	Vienna
Bömische Union Bank	Prague
Credit-Anstalt	Vienna
Ostereichische Länderbank	Vienna
Niederösterreichische Escompte-G.	Vienna
S.M. von Rothschild	Vienna
Ungarische Allgemeine Creditbank	Budapest
Union-Bank	Vienna
Wiener Bankverein	Vienna
Schweizerische Kreditanstalt	Zurich

TABLE 18–5. Distribution of the Egyptian Public Debt in 1914

	France		Great Britain & Others		Egypt		Total	
	Amount	*(%)*	*Amount*	*(%)*	*Amount*	*(%)*	*Amount*	*(%)*
Guaranteed debt	0.8	11.4	5.5	76.8	0.7	10	7	100
Unified debt	36.8	65.7	13.6	24.3	5.6	10	56	100
Privileged debt	19.7	63.3	8.3	26.7	3.1	10	31.1	100
Total billion £	57.3	60.8	27.4	29.2	9.4	10	94.1	100
Total billion F	1,400		685		235		2,320	

Source: J. Ducruet, *Les capitaux européens au Proche-Orient,* p. 64.

Turkey. Set up with the assistance of the Barings and of Sir Adrian Block, chairman of the Administration de la Dette, the new bank was intended, according to its founder "to compete with the B.I.O.," which had become "a purely French institution."[26] Sir Ernest, nevertheless, found it difficult to put together a million pounds. In spite of many international sympathetic reactions, Sir Ernest did not succeed in attracting the Société Générale or Paribas, and the "bluff" during the negotiations of the 4 percent loan of 1909 was called, as demonstrated by Figure 18–3. The National Bank of Turkey did, however, obtain the 5 percent municipal loan of Constantinople in 1909 and, along with the Banque de Salonique, led the issue of Treasury bonds in 1912.

Thus the B.I.O. maintained its primacy in Constantinople for state loans and its position was even reinforced with the 1914 loan. The Deutsche Bank was second, but far behind. Some Belgian, Swiss, Austrian, Dutch, and Italian banks were involved, but only as second-line participants.[27]

Information is much more sparse at the moment on the role of banks in the Egyptian loans.[28] The de facto dismantling of the Franco-British condominium and French attempts to internationalize the Egyptian question led the French party to adopt a policy of pinpricks, which hindered the British but left the way open for negotiated agreements aimed at safeguarding French interests. Such was the nature of the London accord of March 18, 1885, which sanctionned a new liquidation loan of over £9 million, guaranteed by six powers, underwritten by a British-managed cosmopolitan syndicate at a price of 95.5 percent and bearing interest at 5 percent.[29] The 1888 loan of £2.3 million was managed by the Rothschilds of London, along with those of Paris and Bleichröder of Berlin, one of the rare times German finance intervened in Egypt. Agreement was easily reached for the flotation of three conversion loans: for the Privileged Debt (1890), under the management of the Rothschilds of Paris, for the Daria (1890); and the Domains (1893), the latter two being managed by Paribas. British groups took in hand the irrigation works and railway loans (1902).[30]

That was the last prewar loan. The Franco-British accord of 1904 in effect changed nothing in that matter, for, with the achievement of budget surpluses, the time for paying off the public debt arrived. Financial rivalries and banking strategies were henceforth to be transferred to the fields of commercial credit and industrial investments.

In Persia a severe competition took place, concerning state loans, between the Imperial Bank of Persia and the Russian-owned Persian Loan Bank, founded in Tehran

TABLE 18–6. Distribution of the Persian Public Debt in 1914 (£ nominal)

RUSSIA	Russian government	Loan Bank of Persia	Total	Percent
	4,325,000	60,000	4,385,000	66.6
GREAT BRITAIN	British (and Indian) governments	London money market	Total	Percent
	954,300	1,250,000	2,204,300	33.4
TOTAL			6,589,300	100

Source: Geoffrey Jones, Banking and Empire in Iran.

in 1890. They led an endless policy of conflicting coexistence under the watchful control of their respective diplomacies. The signing of the 1907 Anglo-Russian Convention that divided Persia into spheres of influence, Russian in the north, British in the southeast, made clashes less hard, but did not change their attitudes toward the Persian government. Under the terms of its convention, I.B.P. had to make advances to the Persian government that could not exceed the sum of £216,666. If more were needed, a foreign loan would be necessary. The cancellation of the Tobacco Concession in 1892 forced Persia to join the ranks of Middle East borrowers to pay compensation to the Tobacco Corporation. Badly prepared by the I.B.P., the 1892 Persian loan was bound to fail: Only 164 out of the 5,000 bonds issued were allotted to the public. The Stock Exchange consistently refused to quote the bonds. No doubt the British bank had outwitted the Russian government, but its wish was to be repaid as soon as possible.[31] On the other hand, the only Persian loan floated on the London money market, in July 1911, was successful; for a nominal value of £1,250,000, the Persian government received 87.5 percent, and the issue was made at 96.5. Nine well-known houses of the City participated in the syndicate led by the I.B.P. The loan bred big commissions to the bank.[32] Following the initiative of the Russians the British government made several loans to Persia for specified purposes, amounting to more than £1 million between 1903 and 1914.

The Russians also took the field. Two entrepreneurial brothers, Lazare and Yakov Poliakov, obtained, in 1890, a concession for seventy-five years to set up a bank in Persia. The Loan Company of Persia (Sudnoe Obshchestov Persii, or the Société des Prêts de Perse) had a capital of only 5 million francs; the Poliakovs also opened a branch of the International Commercial Bank of Moscow in Tehran. In 1894, on the verge of liquidation, the Loan Company of Persia was taken over by Witte and became the Loan Bank of Persia (Susdnyi Bank Persii, or Banque des Prêts de Perse).

The bank led two big Russian government loans: in January 1900, a loan of 22.5 million rubles (£2.4 million), at 5 percent, repayable over seventy-five years, and a second Russian government loan of £1.1 million, issued in March 1902, whose exact conditions are not known. The I.B.P. reacted with anger: "The joint inaction of the money market and the Foreign Office has done England and the Bank great and lasting injury," Chairman Lepel Griffin wrote to the local director in February 1900.[33] Nevertheless, the repayment of the failed 1892 loan at par was a good thing for the I.B.P. The Loan Bank became more determined, opened new branches, and in 1902 was renamed the Discount and Loan Bank of Persia. Yet, by the spring of 1906, the Russian bank's incautious lending policies had brought it to insolvency. It continued, however, the service of three other Russian government loans for a total of £1,425,000.

A glance at the distribution of the Persian debt on the eve of the Great War suggests two remarks. (See Table 18–6.) First, the capital coming from Russia (and to a large extent, the Russian policy in Persia) was possible thanks to Russian loans raised on the Paris money market over three decades. Second, the small absolute figures, compared to those of the Ottoman and Egyptian debts, should be noticed.

European Banks and Banking Activity

It was only natural that, as European banks expanded in the world, they would seek to establish themselves in a market such as the Middle East, but the form differed according to the banking strategies adopted in their activities and, consequently, in the search for profits. The opening of branches in important cities (particularly ports) showed a desire to concentrate on commercial credit. The creation of more or less specialized banks corresponded to a more elaborate project of economic involvement in the various countries.

Competition among Branches

Except for the B.I.O., the only European bank to open a branch in the Middle East from 1875, the year the Crédit Lyonnais set foot there, to 1898 was the Banque d'Athénes (Alexandria, 1895).[34] Thereafter the economic recovery and the increase in trade from 1899 led to often intense competition, especially from 1904 to 1913.

The B.I.O. did not stand apart from this movement. The opening of branches was written into its contract, but it retained some room for maneuver. From 1863 to 1898 (thirty-five years) the B.I.O. opened thirty-one branches (agencies, sub-agencies, offices) in the Middle East—that is, a little less than one a year; from 1899 to 1914 (fifteen years), fifty-two branches were created, nearly four a year.[35] By 1914, even with the closure in 1913 of the branch in Tripoli on the Barbary Coast, the B.I.O. could claim 82 branches throughout the Middle East, apart from the head office in Constantinople. For all that, it had to confront bold competition in several cities. (See Fig. 18–4.)

At the turn of the century only the Crédit Lyonnais, established in Constantinople and Smyrna, competed with the B.I.O., which, in other respects, enjoyed a near-monopoly for the business of the government departments and large-scale trade.[36] The situation began to be change in 1899 with the arrival in Palestine of the Deutsche Bank, which opened branches in Jerusalem, Jaffa, and Haifa, in the hope of benefitting from pilgrimages and the settlement of German colonists in the area.[37] In 1902 the Crédit Lyonnais opened an office in Jaffa. The same year the Banco di Roma opened a branch in Alexandria "to engage in commercial transactions more than banking proper."[38]

From 1905 to 1907 a genuine rush was on. In 1905 the Banque de Salonique, the Bank of Athens, and the Banque d'Orient opened branches in Constantinople and Smyrna.[39] The latter installed itself in Alexandria and Cairo, while the Comptoir d'Escompte opened a branch in the great Egyptian port of Alexandria. In 1906 two

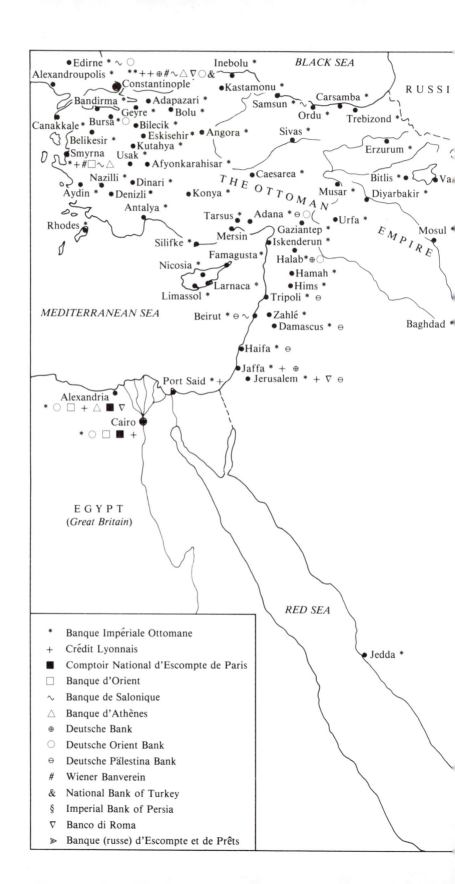

Banque Impériale Ottomane *
Crédit Lyonnais +
Comptoir National d'Escompte de Paris ■
Banque d'Orient □
Banque de Salonique ∿
Banque d'Athènes △
Deutsche Bank ⊕
Deutsche Orient Bank ○
Deutsche Pälestina Bank ⊖
Wiener Banverein #
National Bank of Turkey &
Imperial Bank of Persia §
Banco di Roma ∇
Banque (russe) d'Escompte et de Prêts ≽

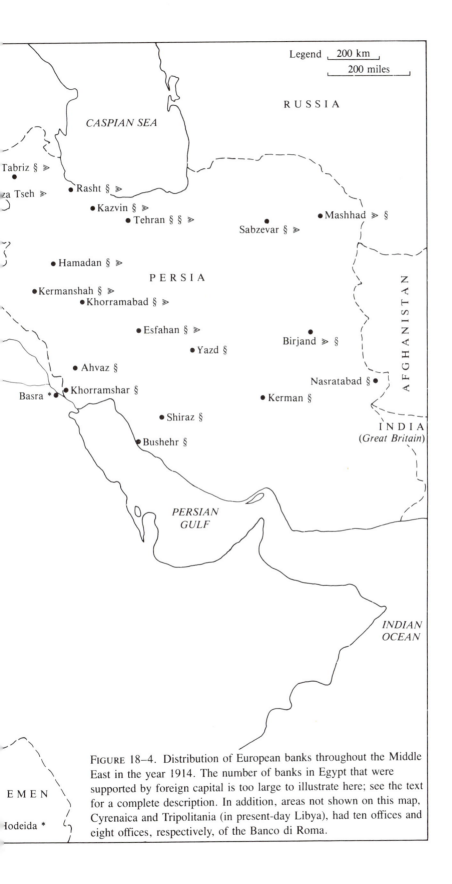

Legend

200 km

200 miles

RUSSIA

CASPIAN SEA

Tabriz § ≫
•

za Tseh ≫

• Rasht § ≫

• Kazvin § ≫

• Tehran § § ≫

Sabzevar § ≫
•

• Mashhad ≫ §

• Hamadan § ≫

PERSIA

• Kermanshah § ≫
• Khorramabad § ≫

AFGHANISTAN

• Esfahan § ≫

• Yazd §

Birjand ≫ §
•

• Ahvaz §

Nasratabad § •
•

Basra * • Khorramshar §

• Kerman §

• Shiraz §

INDIA
(Great Britain)

• Bushehr §

PERSIAN
GULF

INDIAN
OCEAN

FIGURE 18–4. Distribution of European banks throughout the Middle East in the year 1914. The number of banks in Egypt that were supported by foreign capital is too large to illustrate here; see the text for a complete description. In addition, areas not shown on this map, Cyrenaica and Tripolitania (in present-day Libya), had ten offices and eight offices, respectively, of the Banco di Roma.

EMEN

Hodeida *

offensives were mounted with consummate ability. Interested in deposits and business connected with the eastern railways, the Wiener Bankverein opened a branch in Constantinople, while the Deutsche Orient Bank did likewise in Constantinople, Alexandria, and Cairo. In 1907 the Deutsche Palästina Bank and the Banco di Roma did the same in Beirut and Tripoli, respectively.[40]

The economic and financial crisis of 1907/08 hit hard in the Orient and imposed a certain slowdown. The counterattack by the Deutsche Bank against the ambitions of the D.O.B. was launched in 1909–10; the Deutsche Bank itself got footholds in Constantinople and Aleppo, an important junction of the *Bagdadbahn*, while the Deutsche Palästina Bank opened branches in Adana and Tripoli on the Syrian coast. Pursuing its own offensive, the Banco di Roma opened agencies in 1911 in Constantinople and (perhaps) in Jerusalem.[41] In 1912 it had eight branches in Tripolitania and ten in Cyrenaica.

In Persia, the only modern banking services were provided by the branches of the Imperial Bank of Persia and the Loan Bank of Persia. In 1914 the I.B.P. had, besides the chief office in Tehran, eighteen branches: seven were opened between 1890 and 1895, four between 1896 and 1907, seven between 1908 and 1914—i.e., about one branch every sixteen months. The chief manager in Tehran was more enthusiastic than was the board in London over expanding the branch network. In fact, nearly all the branches were opened because of good commercial business, especially in foreign exchange. For instance, the branch at Mohammarah was designed to serve the new oil business of the Anglo-Persian Oil Company, and Sultanabad was a center of the growing carpet industry. Only the branch of Nasratabad, in spite of its poor results, was maintained for strategic reasons (see Fig. 18–4). All the branches played a prominent part in the expanding role of the bank as revenue collector for the Persian government, which was obliged to concede this function as a *quid pro quo* for advances.

After the opening of agencies in Baghdad (May 1890) and in Basra (June 1891), whose performances were very unsatisfactory, there was a growing fear that the B.I.O. would establish branches in Persia. In September 1893, therefore, the I.B.P. signed an agreement with the B.I.O. designed to defuse the danger of competition to its Persian business and to extricate itself from the Ottoman Empire. It closed the agencies in Mesopotamia in February 1894, and the B.I.O. agreed not to open any branches in Persia.[42] The chief manager believed firmly that his main task was to build a bank in Persia and not to try peripheral ventures. In this respect, it is interesting to observe that four of the seven branches opened in the last period were in the Russian-dominated north. St. Petersburg objected to the Sabzevar branch.

The Loan Bank of Persia had opened twelve branches by 1914, and eleven had to compete directly with branches of the I.B.P. This is doubtless, to a large extent, the reason why the performance of the branches of the Russian bank was so poor. In addition to the Loan Bank, the International Commercial Bank of Moscow maintained a branch in Tehran.

Thus, in the great centers of the Middle East, a hunt for customers was in progress. Attractive terms were proposed for hoarded money. The most favorable conditions were offered to those possessing savings, to merchants, traders, and notables as much to allow interest on their deposits as to respond to their need for credit. The gap between attractive conditions and the indispensable margin of security tended to diminish. Undoubtedly in a period of growth possibilities increased, but transactions both for silk, in Anatolia and Syria, and for cotton, in Egypt, were not without limits. Doubtless, the B.I.O. was in a better position than any of its competitors, from 1905 onwards, to reduce the gap between interest owed and interest due, and between the purchase and sale prices of foreign exchange. The new banks discounted commercial paper and, particularly on bills of exchange, offered terms of payment and rates that the older banks had to follow. The collateral (securities or commodities) they requested for advances made the very strict management of the Crédit Lyonnais shiver. In any case, it was to this competition and to downright "dumping" by the B.I.O. that the Crédit Lyonnais attributed the considerable counter-cyclical fall in the profits of the Constantinople and Smyrna branches between 1904 and 1911. While most banks retrieved their positions, some were not able to overcome the crisis of 1907 and disappeared, such as the Bank of Egypt and the Banque de Métélin in 1911.[43] On the whole, despite modest results, the aim was to maintain a presence that could permit later development.

European Bank Capital and On-the-Spot Constitution of New Credit Institutions

The major issue of investment in business in the region by European banks evolved first with the investment of bank capital, which could set the stage for industrial investment. Only the main stages of the process can be broached.

In the Ottoman Empire, the chief operation was the constitution of the Crédit Foncier Ottoman (C.F.O.). In fact, the industrial activities of the B.I.O., and the existence of a Crédit Agricole based on Ottoman capital, which had been lending to farmers on mortgage since 1887, left little room for other lending on real estate.[44] The constitutional government initiated important legislation designed precisely to make possible this type of loan.

Two French groups entered the lists. The first was led by the B.F.C.I., along with the Comptoir and the Banque de l'Union Parisienne (B.U.P.). It was not appreciated by the Ottoman government owing to its too exclusive French character. The second was led by Paribas, along with the B.I.O., the Société Générale, and the Banque de Salonique. With the utmost cleverness, the promoters put forward the Banque de Salonique (controlled by the Société Générale) as a member of the "Ottoman group," which made possible the inclusion of Ottoman personalities (see Fig. 18–5). With the active support of French diplomacy, these four banks in 1909 formed the Société Nationale pour le Commerce, l'Industrie et l'Agriculture dans l'Empire Ottoman. After agreement with the rival group and the granting of a traditional share to the Deutsche Bank, the Société Nationale created the Crédit Foncier Ottomane on May 4, 1914, with the considerable capital of 2 million Turkish pounds, of which one-quarter was paid-up (amounting to 11.5 million francs). One should not be misled by the official organization flowchart; the French were in complete control. Two vice presidents were French, as well as the governor, Leon Pisard, who left the general management of the Administration de la Dette to assume his new post on June 15, 1914.

Alongside this institution, the formation of the Banque du Liban (4 million francs) in 1913–14, by an exclusively French group, had a greater political than economic significance.[45] The aim was to set up an establishment destined in the long run to play vis-à-vis Mount Lebanon the role held by the B.I.O. in case Lebanon were to be completely detached from the Ottoman Empire. Such was, in any case, the wish of

SOCIÉTÉ NATIONALE POUR LE COMMERCE L'INDUSTRIE ET L'AGRICULTURE DANS L'EMPIRE OTTOMAN

Founding: October 6, 1909
Capital: 200,000 Ltq. (4.6 million F) into
20,000 shares of 10 Ltq., of which 65%
(2,990,000 F) was paid by 1913.

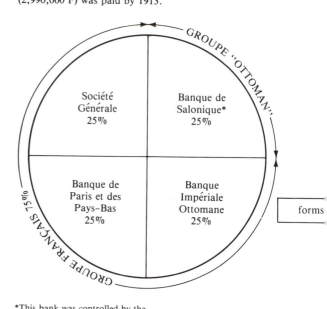

GROUPE "OTTOMAN"

| Société Générale 25% | Banque de Salonique* 25% |
| Banque de Paris et des Pays-Bas 25% | Banque Impériale Ottomane 25% |

GROUPE FRANÇAIS 75%

forms

*This bank was controlled by the Société Générale.

THE BOARD OF DIRECTORS (1909)
15 members: 9 French; 6 Ottoman

Isaac de Camondo (Paribas), *President*

Administrators (Paribas)
J.E. Moret
J.H. Thors
A. Turrettini

Administrators (Société Générale)
A. Bénac
G. de Frédaigues

Administrators (B.I.O.)
Albert Mirabaud
J. de Neuflize

Administrators
Léon Pissard (Director General,
   Dette Publique Ottomane)
Périd pacha (Ancient Grand Vizier)
Hamid bey (high official)
Is. Djénani bey
Azérian effendi
A. Salem (Banque de Salonique)
Sabbag bey (banker)

Sabbag bey, *Director of the Paris Committee*
Lanes (brother of Fallières' son-in-law),
   Secretary General in Constantinople

Correspondents in Constantinople
I. Fernandez, banker
J. Menasche, banker

FIGURE 18–5. The make-up of the Crédit Foncier Ottoman in the year 1914.

CRÉDIT FONCIER OTTOMAN

med: May 1914, to begin operations in June.
ital: 46 million F, of which 25% was paid in 1914.

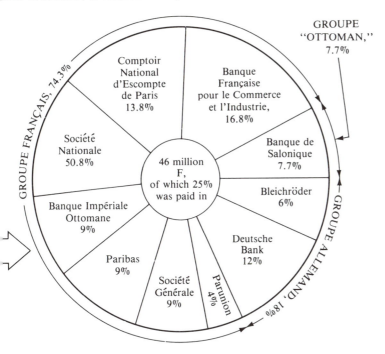

GROUPE
"OTTOMAN,"
7.7%

Comptoir National d'Escompte de Paris 13.8%

Banque Française pour le Commerce et l'Industrie, 16.8%

Société Nationale 50.8%

Banque de Salonique 7.7%

46 million F, of which 25% was paid in

Bleichröder 6%

Banque Impériale Ottomane 9%

Deutsche Bank 12%

Paribas 9%

Société Générale 9%

Parunion 4%

GROUPE FRANÇAIS, 74.3%

GROUPE ALLEMAND, 18%

THE BOARD OF DIRECTORS (June 1914)
24 members: 12 French, 9 Ottoman, 3 German

Marshal Ghazi Ahmed Mouktar pasha, *President*
(former Grand Vizier)

Férid pasha (former Grand Vizier, Senator)
Noury bey (Official of the Tobacco Monopoly)
Sabbag bey (Manager, Société Nationale)
Hamid bey (Director of Public Debt, Ministry of Finance)
Ismaël Djénani bey (Director, Société Nationale)
J. Ménasché (Director, Société des Routes)
A. Salem, (Attorney Director, Banque de Salonique)
Mahmoud Hamid bey (Proprietor)

. H. Thors (Paribas),
Vice President

Boudon (President, B.F.C.I.),
Vice President

A. Turrettini (Managing Director, Paribas)
Ch. de Gheest (Vice President, B.F.C.I.)
Georges Granjean (Manager, B.F.C.I.)
A. Bénac (Société Generale)
G. de Frédaigues (Société Generale)
J. de Neuflize (Banque Ottomane)
Ch. Chambefort (Comptoir)
E. Ullman (Vice President and Director, Comptoir)
Léon Pissard (Managing Director, Dette Ottomane)
X . . .
Karl Helfferich (Manager, Deutsche Bank)
Ed. Huguenin (Managing Director, Société d'Anatolie)
P. von Schwabach (Associate, Bleichroder)

Léon Pissard   appointed Governor of the Crédit Foncier Ottoman some Lebanese who supported this project, and of the French government, which adopted a benevolent attitude.

The situation was more troubled in Egypt.[46] As early as 1880, mortgage lending attracted French and British competitors. First, the Crédit Foncier Egyptien (share capital plus bonds in the year after its founding, 83 million francs) was established with the participation of most of the great Parisian credit institutions. More modest (15 million francs) was the Land and Mortgage Company of Egypt, constituted by British capital. The 1880s, however, did not represent a favorable period and the activity of the newcomers tended to stagnate. The Crédit Foncier Egyptien succeeded in stabilizing its position until 1898, and, only then, started borrowing on the bond market.

In the field of all-purpose banks, the Banque Générale d'Egypte, established in 1881 by the large Parisian banks and local financiers, went into liquidation as early as 1888. The old Banque Franco-Egyptienne (1870) ceased to exist in 1889.[47] Foreign capital established only one bank during this period, the Cassa di Sconto e di Risparmio. Its share capital was modest (200,000 francs), but it marked the arrival, in 1887, of Italian capital in Egypt.

The tangible revival of business in Egypt during 1897–98, and the Franco-British entente of 1904, stimulated the influx of foreign capital and the creation of new banks. In the field of mortgage lending the major fact was the constitution by Sir Ernest Cassel of the Agricultural Bank of Egypt (£3.5 million) in 1902. Did Sir Ernest have designs on the Crédit Foncier Egyptien, hard-pressed after the crisis of 1907? French diplomacy was preoccupied, but the loan granted the Crédit Foncier by a consortium of French banks in 1908 put it beyond the reach of English designs.[48] Sir Ernest "had to be content with the creation of the Mortgage Company of Egypt which, with one million pounds of equity, was not a serious competitor to the French company."[49]

As for French capital, it created in 1905 the Land Bank of Egypt (£2 million) and the Union Fonciére d'Egypt, through the initiative of the Société Marseillaise de Crédit and banks from Alexandria, Marseille, and London. When the full force of the crisis of 1907 passed, three banks were established in succession by French capital: the Crédit Foncier d'Orient (27.5 million francs), the Banque Hypothécaire Franco-Egyptienne (3.7 million francs), and the Banque Française Commerciale et Agricole d'Egypt. This multiplication of institutions drove into bankruptcy some competitors who were too accommodating, and the most recently established French banks went into liquidation in 1913.[50] Finally, French capital was invested in Belgian companies. Belgian capital controlled the Caisse Hypothécaire d'Egypte, founded in 1903, (16.8 million francs), as well as the Crédit Hypothécaire Agricole et Urbain d'Egypte, founded in 1908 with a share-capital of £500,000 (13 million francs in 1914). (See Table 18–7.)

Arriving late and at an unfavorable time, the Deutsche Orient Bank established the Egyptische Hypotheken Bank in 1911 with the modest capital of £130,000 to engage in mortgage lending.

In the nonmortgage sector, the vitality of French capital can be judged by the creation in 1905 of the Crédit Franco-Egyptien (13 million francs) and in 1907 of the Banque Française d'Egypte (5 million francs). On the English side, the originality of the Bank of Abyssinia should be mentioned. It was created in 1905 in Cairo, where its head office was located, by Sir Ernest Cassel's National Bank of Egypt. Its main branch was in Addis Abbaba and it had three other branches in Ethiopia. Its capital, amounting to £125,000, was British and it obtained the right to issue notes covered by

TABLE 18–7. French Capital in Egypt in 1911

| | In Millions of Nominal Francs | | Percent |
| | Total Foreign Capital | French Capital | French |
Type of Investment			
Egyptian foreign debt	2,352	1,250	53.1
Various joint-stock companies (shares and debentures)	2,384	1,200	50.3
Suez Canal Company (shares and debentures)	550	390	70.9
TOTAL	5,286	2,840	53.6

Source: F. Charles-Roux, "Le capital français en Egypte," in *L'Egypte Contemporaine*, 1911, pp. 465–582.

Maria Theresa thalers.[51] The bank was testimony to British penetration in Ethiopia at a time when the partition of the country into three zones of influence—French (with the Djibouti-Addis Abbaba rail line), British, and Italian—had been decided by the Tripartite Convention of 1906. The head office was in Cairo because Addis Abbaba was in the French zone.

European Banks, Economic Involvement, and Imperialism

It remains to examine the extent to which these banking interests included direct investment in industrial firms of the Middle East, and whether these interests served as the basis of imperialist projects on the part of the European governments. A distinction should be made, in that respect, among the Ottoman Empire, Egypt, and Persia.

Starting from different positions in the Ottoman Empire, European banks early in the twentieth century tended, whenever they opted for industrial investment, to follow comparable and most often competitive strategies.

As regards French banks, until the mid–1890s there were few connections between bank capital and industrial capital, despite the total amount exported. On one side the B.I.O. and other banks managed state loans; on the other, independent and often modest capitalists set up some businesses on their own, particularly in the field of communications (railroads and ports). Most of the time promoters even felt genuinely suspicious of banks, especially the B.I.O. Their fears were quite unjustified because the latter did not wish to make direct investments. No other attitude could be expected from the Crédit Lyonnais, staunchly opposed as it henceforth was to industrial investment.[52] Such a situation was on the whole harmful to French interests.

A change of outlook occurred in response to three factors. German successes were the first of these. French observers in Constantinople were impressed by the importance of military and railway orders won by German firms in the wake of the Fisheries loan and the concession of the Anatolian railway to the Deutsche Bank. Ambassador Paul Cambon believed that "the cause of their success must be sought in the unity of German industrialists and capitalists."[53] Moreover, nearly all banks opened in the 1870s in Constantinople disappeared, having been shaken by the bankruptcy and swept by the grave financial crisis of 1895. The B.I.O., whose French character became more marked, was consequently put in very advantageous position for carrying out French business. Finally, as will be seen, the hazards of the financial evolution of some firms drew banks in the industrial field. The B.I.O. tended then to adopt a strategy similar to that already tested by the Deutsche Bank, subsequently to be attempted by the National Bank of Turkey. The forms, however, were naturally linked to the level of capitalist development and the generally troubled context of international relations. Three stages may be distinguished, characterized by recourse to the state, the formation of mixed syndicates of banks and industries that sought out business opportunities, and the establishment of financial groups.

In the case of France, state intervention was particularly necessary for the effectiveness of the "tied loan," a device by which the borrower was obliged to devote a part of the loan to orders placed with the industrial firms of the lender country. The French government was able to play the role of an intermediary on account of the great liking French investors took to Oriental securities, and the system of authorization required for the quotation of foreign securities on the official list of the Paris Bourse. Indeed, from the beginning of the twentieth century manufacturers searching for markets laid siege to the Quai d'Orsay to achieve their end. For example, it was in the framework of the negotiations concerning the 4 percent loan of the 1904–05 firm that Schneider-Creusot picked up an order for warships from the Ottoman state. Worried by the success of Krupp, both ministers, Delcassé and Rouvier, wanted to give satisfaction to the Creusot company. Rouvier provided the link with the B.I.O., which in turn agreed to urge the Turkish government to accede to the request. Thus, by pressing on banks the grievances of often uncompetitive industries, the state created a link between them and industry, and mitigated to a certain extent the shortcomings in the integration of the economic-financial system in the center. Gaining in solidity until 1914, the finance-industry-diplomacy triptych represented one of the surest assets of French imperialism in the region.[54]

In that respect, the German way was operational earlier, and gave a somewhat different role to the state. The interpenetration of banks and industries being much more advanced in Germany, military and railway orders were linked with loans from the very first one floated on the German market (1888). The agonizing question remained that of the narrowness of the German financial market and the fear of the Deutsche Bank to commit itself beyond its financial capacity. The role of the German government was much less pronounced after the departure of Bismarck.

The British situation resembled the French, with particularly insistent lobbying by the shipyards. The absence of a system of authorization for the quotation of securities on the official list changed little, since a bank or an industrial firm was not likely to disregard advice from the Foreign Office. What set the British apart from the French and the Germans was that they did not have available for the Ottoman Empire and Egypt a financial institution comparable in size and dynamism to the B.I.O. and the Deutsch Bank. The Imperial Bank of Persia played a somewhat comparable role, but only in Persia.

Beginning in the years 1905–06, French banks and industrial firms set up joint companies for the purpose of research and study. If preliminary studies proved favorable, a permanent company consisting of the original partners would be established to channel orders to the manufacturers. Of the five syndicates actually operating in the Ottoman Empire, three were initiated by banks. The Participation d'Etudes Industrielles dans l'Empire Ottoman, enlarged in 1908 under the name of Société Franco-Ottomane d'Etudes Industrielles et Commerciales, brought together under the leadership of the B.I.O. six important Parisian banks, the Régie Générale des Chemins de Fer et Travaux Publics, and the Société des Batignolles. It played a great role in the search for railway concessions. The Association en Participation pour l'Etude d'Affaires Financiéres, Industrielles et Commerciales en Turquie united the Société Générale, the B.I.O., Paribas, and the Spitzer and Thalmann banks in 1909. In 1911 it added two electrical firms, the Société Centrale pour l'Industrie Electrique and the Société Thomson-Houston-France. Constantinople was its field of action. The Omnium d'Entreprises was set up in 1912 by the Périer bank with the Société Nancéenne de Crédit and the Banque Renauld (Nancy). The board of directors included four bankers, four banker-manufacturers, and two contractors. Its quest for concessions proved rather successful.

In 1910 Schneider and the contractor Hersent, with the assistance of the B.I.O. and the Regie Générale des Chemins de Fer, created the Consortium des Ports de l'Empire Ottoman. The Société Générale d'Entreprises, which undertook road construction and repairs, united the contractors Fougerolles fréres and the Grand Travaux de Marseille under the patronage of the B.F.C.I.

The establishment of this type of association was easier in the German context. It could be seen at work from the time of the creation of the group in charge of founding the Anatolian Railway Company, under the direction of the Deutsche Bank and with the participation of the Württembergische Vereinsbank. The same was true for the Société d'Etude du Chemin de Fer de Bagdad in which, under the leadership of the Deutsche Bank, several banks and the Holzmann company were assembled for the purpose of building the first sections; it placed most of its orders with German industry.[55] In 1908, with the Deutsche Bank in the lead, a consortium was constituted by fourteen banks (among them the D.O.B. and the Dresdner Bank) and two important electrical companies. The syndicate, headed by the Deutsche Bank, suffered from lack of capital in the quest for an oil concession in the Mosul region.

The British displayed much less vigor in that direction. Despite its ambitious aims, the syndicate formed by the Armstrong Shipyards and the London Committee of the B.I.O. marked time, evidence that the City would not bet on the Ottoman horse. The association made up of Royal Dutch-Shell and the National Bank of Turkey was in better position for oil exploration in Mesopotamia.[56]

These simple examples raise the issue of determining whether these syndicates united to create, according to need, powerful multinational companies, or whether, on the contrary, they sought consolidation on basically national lines. The answer is clear-cut, although not simple; international financial association failed and national groups were reinforced.

It could rightly be pointed out, however, that there were some examples of the establishment of multinationals. Indeed, the syndicate that best fitted this description was the Constantinople Consortium formed in Brussels in December 1911 to seek business in the field of energy and transport in the capital. It brought together a German group (seven representatives on the committee), a French (seven), a Belgian-Hungarian (six), a Belgian (six) and a Swiss group (one). Its first achievement was the founding in June 1914 of the (Belgian) Société des Tramways et de l'Electricité de Constantinople, the exact composition of which is given in Figure 18–6.[57] The company was con-

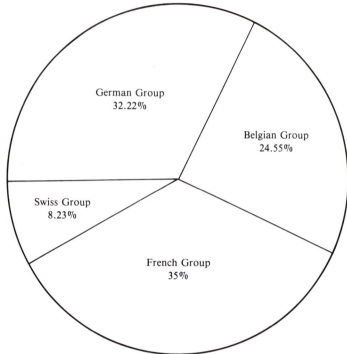

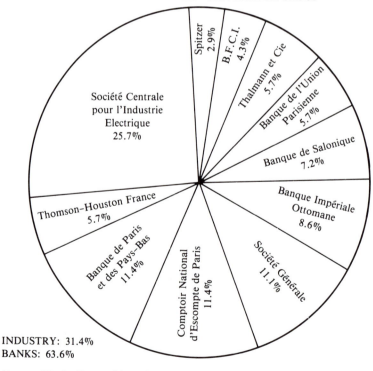

FIGURE 18–6. Composition of the Société des Tramways et de l'Electricité de Constantinople in the year 1914. The four graphs show the distribution of investments by the Constantinople Consortium members, by national groups.

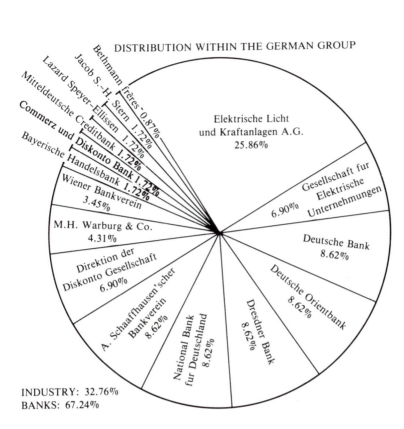

DISTRIBUTION WITHIN THE GERMAN GROUP

Elektrische Licht
und Kraftanlagen A.G.
25.86%

Bethmann frères 0.87%
Jacob S.-H. Stern 1.72%
Lazard Speyer-Ellissen 1.72%
Mitteldeutsche Creditbank 1.72%
Commerz und Diskonto Bank 1.72%
Bayerische Handelsbank 1.72%
Wiener Bankverein 3.45%
M.H. Warburg & Co. 4.31%
Direktion der Diskonto Gesellschaft 6.90%
A. Schaafhausen'scher Bankverein 8.62%
National Bank fur Deutschland 8.62%
Dresdner Bank 8.62%
Deutsche Orientbank 8.62%
Deutsche Bank 8.62%
Gesellschaft fur Elektrische Unternehmungen 6.90%

INDUSTRY: 32.76%
BANKS: 67.24%

DISTRIBUTION WITHIN THE BELGIAN GROUP

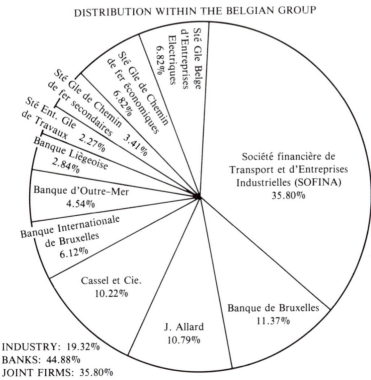

Sté Gle Belge d'Entreprises Electriques 6.82%
Sté Gle de Chemin de fer économiques 6.82%
Sté Gle de Chemin de fer secondaires 3.41%
Sté Ent. Gle de Travaux 2.27%
Banque Liègeoise 2.84%
Banque d'Outre-Mer 4.54%
Banque Internationale de Bruxelles 6.12%
Cassel et Cie. 10.22%
J. Allard 10.79%
Banque de Bruxelles 11.37%
Société financière de Transport et d'Entreprises Industrielles (SOFINA) 35.80%

INDUSTRY: 19.32%
BANKS: 44.88%
JOINT FIRMS: 35.80%

stituted in Belgium because this small country, a champion of neutrality, rendered acceptable to touchy public opinion the association of French and German capital.[58] The formal structure masked the reality of German domination, based on the weight of German capital in SOFINA, a legally Belgian company whose chairman presided in the Consortium. The other important example was the Anglo-German association in the Turkish Petroleum Co.; but a great disproportion existed in 1914 between the British group (70 percent of the equity) and the German group (25 percent). If one adds the Société du Téléphone de Constantinople (Anglo-Franco-American), the Port de Constantinople (Franco-British capital under the leadership of the B.I.O.), and the Franco-German syndicate of the company being formed to mine copper in Arghana, the list of multinational companies in the Ottoman Empire is complete.

The trend toward internationalization did in fact exist, but all large-scale projects for an international financial association failed. Explanations cannot be given here, but the great banks were not primarily responsible. The greatest failure was, of course, the unattainable internationalization of the Baghdad Railway. In December 1899 the (German) Anatolian Railway Company had obtained a right of priority for building and managing the Baghdad Railway. Between this date and the signing of the definitive convention of March 5, 1903, the main question for the group led by the Deutsche Bank was then to find international financial partners in order to carry out so big a business. Immediately the Russian government issued a flat refusal, considering that the projected line would make easier the concentration of Turkish troops at the Caucasian frontier, the management of the oil in Mesopotamia in competition with the Russian oil of the Caucasus and, above all, would deeply interfere with Russian influence in Persia. After a period of hesitation, the British government declined in April 1902; it was not possible to trust the German partner and the Baghdad line would affect economic and strategic British interests in the Tigris Valley and on the Persian Gulf. The Baring group then resigned. The problem was reduced to a Franco-German tête-á-tête.

From the beginning the condition put by the French Foreign Minister, Delcassé, was the following: a strict equality, both in the financial and construction companies, of rights and responsibilities. After a great number of propositions by the Deutsche Bank to the French group led by the B.I.O., the most sophisticated was the so-called Memorandum of Brussels of October 1, 1903: 40 percent for the German group, 40 percent for the French group, 20 percent for the others; the board of directors would include eleven Germans, eleven French, and seven others; the president would be German and the vice president French. Two ministers were mainly concerned, Delcassé and the Minister of Finance, Rouvier. They were divided: Rouvier wanted a Franco-German financial association, which might encourage better relations between the two countries. Delcassé distrusted all operations where the capital would not be entirely French; he wanted the German proposition to be refused. The government followed Delcassé and there was no authorization for the quotation of the Baghdad securities on the official list of the Paris Bourse. The financial participation of the B.I.O. in the Baghdad Railway, contracted long before this decision, became a simple private one. Several attempts were then opened, in 1911, 1912, and 1913, to find a means of reinternationalizing the question, but in vain. Finally, in 1914, a Franco-German agreement confirmed the disengagemnent of the French group. The Baghdad Railway was, indeed, a purely German business.[59]

Franco-British projects also fell through. The projected union of all French and British interests in the Ottoman Empire, led by Armstrong and the Société Française d'Entreprises, was rendered impossible by the creation of the National Bank of Turkey. Projects for the fusion of the latter with the B.I.O. came to naught (1911–12). The same was true of the mythical Homs-Baghdad rail line (1911). A gradual reinforcement of rival national groups ensued, and became especially pronounced from 1909 to 1911, as it rested on the partition of the Empire into spheres of influence. In that competition French groups carved the lion's share for themselves, thanks to the readily available resources of the Paris financial market for the great consolidation loan of 1914.

Only some French, British and German financial groups will be discussed here. I will first deal in detail with the B.I.O. group (see Fig. 18–7).

From the mid-1880s to the early years of the twentieth century the B.I.O. participated in various enterprises, not with systematic overall vision, but in a haphazard fashion, taking advantage of events that tended to favor the transport sectors. On the other hand, in the decade preceding World War I the bank, in keeping with the attitude of the French government, adopted a more dynamic policy of industrial investment, and made more systematic choices, testifying in that way to the ambitions of French imperialism in the region.[60]

Projects for municipal services were familiar to the founders of the bank and presented no real risk. The B.I.O., therefore, did not hesitate to take an interest in tramways and water distribution companies of Constantinople, as well as the gas company of Beirut. The authorities of the B.I.O. obeyed a more conscious purpose as they sought to take advantage of the two main sources of wealth in the country, tobacco and coal. In 1893, with the prior agreement of the Conseil de la Dette, the Régie Cointéressée des Tabacs de l'Empire Ottoman was created, the B.I.O. and its allies contributing 50 percent of the total capital.

It was through an important long-term loan that the B.I.O. consolidated its position in the Société des Mines d'Heraclée, which it founded in 1896. Along with its allies, it accounted for 80 percent of the share capital. Very modern equipment and excellent financial results in 1913 finally ushered in the take-off of profits.

In the transport sector the B.I.O. first took an interest in ports. A participant in the founding of the Compagnie du Port de Beyrouth in 1888, it took control in 1894 by dislodging the aging Count de Perthuis. It was feared that with the death of the initial promoter of the Société des Quais de Constantinople, the majority would pass to German capital; but, in cooperation with the Rothschilds of London, the B.I.O. managed to secure 52 percent of the capital. The B.I.O. did not play a pioneering role in the Asiatic railways of the Empire. It took a real interest in them only at the start of discussions about the Baghdad line in 1891. The B.I.O. could not but be favorable to the project, but could not arrive empty-handed at the discussions that were to ensue with the Deutsche Bank. Thus can be explained the takeover in 1894 of the Smyrna-Cassaba et Prolongements through the Franco-Belgian businessman Nagelmackers. In Syria, following the collapse of the Beyrouth-Damas-Hauran et Prolongements, the B.I.O. agreed to save the company with the more modest title of Damas-Hama et Prolongements.

The refusal by the French government of authorization for the quotation of Baghdad stock made the B.I.O. reexamine the situation and conclude that, in the hunt for concessions about to open, it could not prevail over its rivals (the Deutsche Bank

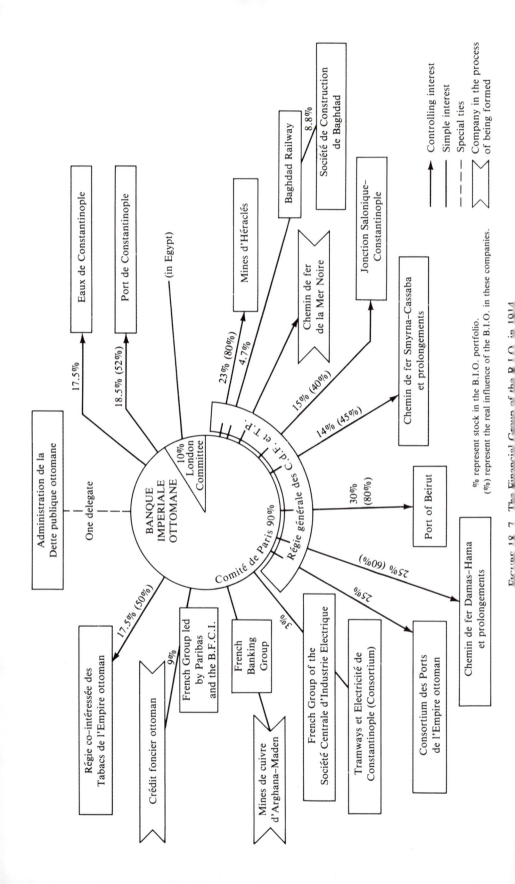

FIGURE 18.7. The Financial Group of the B.I.O. in 1914

and the National Bank of Turkey especially) without the support of French diplomacy. For its part, the French government could not effectively exercise its influence without relying on powerful French interests in the coordination of which the B.I.O. henceforth played a primary role. No doubt the B.I.O. would have preferred vast international associations on the scale of the Ottoman Empire. It seems to have adopted, however, without major difficulties, the process leading to partition into zones of influence, providing that the expected economic activities held out the prospect of being really profitable.

Apart from all the large research syndicates during 1905–06, it won the concession of the "Black Sea network" (2,344 km of track) and those of several ports on the Black Sea and the Syrian coast. It also obtained some minority interests.[61]

Roughly speaking, as is shown in Table 18–8, profits from industrial investment by the B.I.O. on the eve of the Great War represented 10 to 15 percent of its total profits. But its real authority in the Ottoman Empire went well beyond, thanks to its triple function as deposit bank, investment bank, and state bank. The analysis of the operational structures of the B.I.O. confirms the dynamic development of a potential financial group, with an entire sector evolving toward a bank holding.

In comparison, the achievements of rival groups were still embryonic. One must, nevertheless, note the successes and hopes of the Périer group between 1912 and 1914. In control of the Société du Gaz de Constantinople, the bank obtained firm concessions for the lighting, heating, and motor transportation of the Pera and Yaniköy districts of the capital, for the Tramways de Kadoköy, for the Smyrna-Dardanelles rail line (500 km), for the Société des Tramways, de l'Eclairage et des Eaux de Jérusalem-Bethlehem, and the Abattoirs de Constantinople. All this remained to be given concrete shape. The B.F.C.I. saw matters differently and the results were slim. The Hodeida-Sanaa rail project fell apart in the sand, and road construction remained a basically financial operation for the bank.

On the German side the Deutsche Bank flanked by many banks and industrial firms formed a practically unified whole around the Baghdad Railway. The shares and debentures of the Baghdad Company and its (Swiss) construction company amounted to 284 million francs. The Anatolian Company, the Port of Haidar-Pacha and that of Alexandretta, and the copper mines of Arghana (Metallgesellschaft), at the juncture of the zone of influence of the Baghdad line and the future Black Sea network, must also be taken into account. Finally, the bank held one quarter of the Turkish Petroleum Company (T.P.C.) and had a big influence in the Constantinople Consortium. It is, however, impossible to judge the weight of Ottoman business in the overall activities of the Deutsche Bank group.

The aims of Sir Ernest Cassel in Turkey did not materialize. Of small size, the National Bank of Turkey suffered in the final analysis from the allergic reaction of the London market to Ottoman securities. If our limited documentation provides any indication, the National Bank of Turkey registered two successes, its 20 percent interest as founder of the T.P.C. in 1911, and its winning of the concessions of the ports of Samsun and Trebizond in the same year. The massive entry of the Anglo-Persian in the T.P.C., however, led to the elimination in 1914 of Sir Ernest's bank; as for the ports, nothing had been done when the war broke out.[62]

The relationship between banks and industrial investment in Egypt seems considerably looser than in the Ottoman Empire. In any case, it is not possible to pinpoint

TABLE 18–8. The Financial Groups of the B.I.O. in 1913

Company	Number of shares	Share Price (francs)	Total Investment (Thousand francs)	% of the Total Capital	Dividend 1913 (%)	Profits 1913 (in franc
Eaux de Constantinople	7,000	500	3,500	17.5	3.68	128,8(
Régie des Tabacs	36,000	200	7,000	17.5	10	700,0(
Mines d'Héraclée	17,000	200	3,400	23	—	—
Port de Beyrouth	3,660	500	1,830	30	3.5	64,0!
Port de Constantinople	8,750	500	4,375	18.5	3.5	153,1:
Jonction Salonique-Constantinople	4,500	500	2,250	15	3	67,5(
Smyrne-Cassaba et prolongts	4,500	500	2,250	14	5	112,5(
Damas-Hama et prolongements	8,000	500	4,000	25	1.2	48,0(
Chemin de fer de Baghdad	1,400	500	700	4.7	6	42,0(
Sté de construction du Baghdad	1,758	500	879	8.8	6	53,7
Sté Fr.-Ott. d'ét.ind.et comm.	118	2,500	295	23		
Sté nat.p. Comm., ind., agric.	5,150	149.5	770	25.5		
Crédit Foncier Ottoman			1,035	9		
Consortium des Ports			50	25		
Constantinople Consortium	2,160	250	540	3		
Syndicat d'Arghana-Maden			20	4		
TOTAL			32,894			1,368,7

a bank that played a role equivalent to that of the B.I.O. or the Deutsche Bank in Constantinople. Land and real estate speculation absorbed more than half the capital invested in companies. To be sure, banks established firms, but some were ephemeral; for example, on the French side the Société Générale des Travaux founded in 1880 by the Anglo-Egyptian Bank and the Banque Franco-Egyptienne, or the Société Egyptienne d'Entreprises et de Travaux Publics founded the same year by large Parisian banks and local financiers. On the whole, business—municipal services, transportation, and food processing being the main sectors—appeared to evolve outside the control of banks. Such was the case of the Sucréries et Raffineries d'Egypte (of the Horace Say group), which achieved monopoly position in 1902 but found itself in a deep crisis in 1905 because of the difficulties it encountered in insuring its supply of sugar cane, and speculation by its chairman. The Suez Canal Company, controlled by French capital, represented a peculiar case. The largely steady growth of its profits gave it wide financial autonomy; it handled its own bond issues without having recourse to banks; it performed, as it were, its own banking functions. In effect, French capital was structured around two poles, Suez and the Crédit Foncier Egyptien, but the latter were not related. Thus, French companies developed each by itself "without the emergence of a leader seeking to constitute a group. They did not merge with British interests, but were not, as a result, engaged in a struggle against them."[63]

British companies did not behave differently. Like certain of their French counterparts, a number of them left their boards of directors in the hands of local financiers. Not surprisingly, the only exception was Sir Ernest Cassel. He alone had a somewhat coherent project for the Egyptian economy as a whole. He possessed, as was seen, interests in banks and mortgage institutions; he won the Aswan dam concession; he negotiated an agreement between the Sucréries and his own company of the Wadi Kom

Ombo, meeting no opposition from French diplomacy. There existed a willingness on his part to establish control of manifold interests through the constitution of a financial group. The concrete reality of the structures and operation of Sir Ernest's group in Egypt has yet to be brought to light.

A similar ambition seems to have manifested itself on the Belgian side in the group of Baron Empain in the fields of energy and electrical transportation. The subject remains open for research.

In the Ottoman Empire industrial activity by the banks was carried out in terms of partition of the country into zones of influence, and France held the upper hand. Such was not the case in Egypt. French diplomacy watched over the integrity of French interests, even if it was to use them as a means of exchange. French business and political circles agreed, as a compensation for the expansion of French imperialism in the western Mediterranean, that French financial and industrial interests were to be assured the profitable exploitation of Egypt in the shadow of British imperialsim, the guarantor of order and security.

The industrial involvement of the Imperial Bank of Persia was a long succession of failures. To be sure, domestic (endemic institutional and social disorders) and international events (the division of the country into spheres of influence) played a prominent role in these repeated disappointments. It is more difficult to appreciate the resonance of the intimate relationship between the bank and the British government in the industrial destiny of the I.B.P. The close relations between the board and the Foreign Office "would appear to confirm the Bank's role as an imperialistic tool" of the British government in Persia.[64] On the other hand, Geoffrey Jones notes that "Persia's situation would have been worse without the Bank."[65] As it is quite impossible to prove this remark, we will notice that, just as for the relationships between the B.I.O. and the French government, there was a convergence of common interests, not without possibly subordinate contractions. Thus, the bank was not ready to sacrifice profits on the nebulous altar of "national interest," but the directors knew also that the bank had little chance of surviving without the support of the British government.[66]

Actually, many factors converged to make the industrial plans of the I.B.P. a train of fiascos. Besides the Tobacco Monopoly, the I.B.P. took an interest in three sectors: mines, roads, and railways. Early in 1890 the bank formed a separate company to develop its mining rights, the Persian Bank Mining Rights Corporation, designed for a broad search for copper, cobalt, mercury, nickel, coal, and petroleum in all parts of Persia. The complete absence of results stopped the most optimistic engineers, and in November 1894 it was decided to put the Mining Rights Corporation into voluntary liquidation. This liquidation did not cause a financial loss, but the real damage was to the Imperial Bank's prestige.[67]

The Russian government pressured the Shah into a moratorium on the construction of all railways until 1910. This prohibition increased the financial value of the road concession. In January 1890 the I.B.P. acquired the Ahwaz-Tehran road concession. Only the Tehran-Qum section was completed. A foreign loan being obviously impossible, the bank decided in 1904 to sell the road concession to a new company, the Persian Transport Company.[68]

As in the Ottoman Empire, the decade preceding the Great War was rich in "development" projects for elementary infrastructure. Concerning mining, Jones notes the existence of personal relations. For instance, A. O. Wood represented the Anglo-

Persian Oil Company and the Persian Railway Syndicate; his deputy, D. Brown, looked after the interests of the Kerman Mining Syndicate and of F. Strick and Co. (ochre deposits in the Persian Gulf). "There was considerable intelocking at director level between the Bank and the British companies in southern Persia."[69]

Unfortunately, the author does not say if these personal links represented real financial structural associations of interests between the bank and the firms in question. The situation is clearer concerning railway projects that revived when the sterilizing agreement between Russia and Persia came to an end. The British government encouraged the I.B.P. to enter the formation, in 1911, of an Anglo-French-Russian syndicate, the Société Internationale du Chemin de Fer Transpersian. Alas! The Persian government decided that railway concessions were only to be given to Persians. The I.B.P. was qualified, as a Persian institution, to hold a railway concession. In August 1911 the bank sponsored the formation of the Persian Railways Syndicate Ltd., including the bank and seven partners.[70] The I.B.P. took 17 percent of the capital. On March 3, 1913, the Persian government granted the syndicate a two-year option for the construction of a 300-kilometer railway from Mohammarah to Khorramabad. Such a British railway would be tactically of great benefit as it would undercut a "German" Baghdad-Tehran route. More happily, the Russian government secured a concession for a Tabriz-Julfa rail line in February 1913. Two Franco-Russian groups were particularly interested in a line to Tabriz—the Syndicate des Affaires Russes (Banque de l'Union Parisienne) and the Banque Russo-Asiatique (Société Générale).[71] None of these plans materialized. Decidedly, the I.B.P. did not become an industrial holding company, as the B.I.O. was, but remained a regional institution, confined to its banking role.[72]

The diversity of forms and structures adopted by European banks in the Middle East from 1870 to 1914 is emphasized in this chapter. Both the complexity and the flexibility of the activities and strategies of these banks are confirmed. The gaps in the study indicate the additional research needed to complete our understanding and to clarify further the role of finance capital in the great and still controversial question of imperialism.

III

INTERNATIONAL BANKING AND MULTINATIONAL ENTERPRISE

19

The Oil Industry

A. A. Fursenko

The oil concerns that emerged in the late nineteenth century were the products of a profitable and rapidly growing business. The development of the petroleum industry constantly required new capital investments, and for the most part that took the form of reinvested profits, i.e., self-financing. Most of the large oil corporations, even if not averse to accepting credit from banks, nevertheless operated primarily with their own money. At the same time growth in the oil industry changed the companies' scale of operation: The expansion of foreign operations and rapid internationalization of the oil business turned national companies into transnational ones. Although such developments occurred in many branches of industry and trade, this process proceeded with particular intensity in the oil industry.

Banks played different roles in different countries. They were least important in the United States. For this reason this chapter will present only such information on the U.S. industry as is necessary to understand its multinational expansion. In Russia, where strict government control extended over a broad variety of matters such as the formation of new enterprises, the expansion of old firms, the establishment of foreign firms, and arrangements for oil exports, domestic and foreign banks were deeply involved. They made equity investments in the oil industry and mobilized capital to finance development. Since banks were important participants, a disproportionate amount of space is devoted to the Russian industry and its multinational behavior. In Germany the leading banks, encouraged by the government, took a direct role in efforts to secure oil supplies for the German Empire. In Britain a trading company turned merchant banker became allied with a Dutch oil company to become a principal participant in the international arena. French financiers were drawn into the Russian oil business and international oil marketing in Europe and in the East, sometimes in competition with and at other times in cooperation with British interests.

In pursuit of profits the oil corporations constantly sought expanded markets. The armaments race preceding World War I, including the conversion of navies to oil fuel, imparted a distinctly political hue to the problem of oil production—for which the histories of the Anglo-Persian Oil Company and the Turkish Petroleum Company offer cogent illustrations. The purpose of this chapter is to underscore the different roles of banks in the process of the rise of multinational enterprise in oil. To do this, it is important to provide some background on this international industry.

Standard Oil

The predecessors of the first Standard Oil Company emerged in the 1860s after the discovery of oil in Pennsylvania and Ohio. Many petroleum companies were formed to engage in oil exploration and extraction, and some of these also refined the crude oil into kerosene for illumination. In 1865 John D. Rockefeller invested $4,000 in a company that owned a single refinery, but within two years, after a company reorganization had consolidated Rockefeller's position, it already had five refineries. By 1870 the capital of Rockefeller's new Standard Oil Company of Ohio was $1 million.[1]

Capable management and economic efficiency enabled Rockefeller to cut prices, drive competitors out of business, and buy up their properties. The price war, indeed, was Rockefeller's primary tool for both eliminating competitors and expanding his own firm's productive capacity. By January 1872, when Standard Oil Company of Ohio's capital had reached $2.5 million, it continued to reinvest its profits, and to purchase other firms, paying with its own shares. As for the major entrepreneurs who survived the competition, Rockefeller signed agreements that gave them seats on the board of directors at Standard Oil. Some of them cooperated with Rockefeller by buying refineries under their own names, but it was Standard Oil that actually financed these transactions.[2] By 1875 the company's assets amounted to $3.5 million.

Initially Rockefeller and his associates concentrated on refining and transport. By 1880 Standard Oil controlled about 90 percent of U.S. refining capacity.[3] Rockefeller also made covert deals with railway companies for preferential rates. Transportation costs were an issue of paramount importance, for success or failure in competition depended heavily upon the railway tariff a company had to bear.[4] Standard Oil soon began to build and buy up oil pipelines, by far the most economical means of transportation. In the transition years from railway to pipelines, the company paid the railways a bounty for deliveries on its own pipelines as long as high freight rates were set for its competitors. But eventually the railways abandoned oil transportation altogether to the new system of pipelines. Here, too, Standard predominated: By the beginning of the 1880s it owned 35,000 of the 40,000 miles of all U.S. pipelines.

Standard also engaged in production of crude oil, but this was always a minor part of the enterprise. Between 1891 and 1911 Standard's net profits amounted to $1,280 million; of that, $532 million came from transportation, $307 million from marketing, $259 million from refining, and only $170 million from extraction.[5] Even though Standard owned the great majority of the nation's pipelines and refining capacity, its share of crude production was relatively modest: From less than 16 percent in 1889 it rose to 33.5 percent in 1898, then declined to less than 14 percent in 1911.[6]

By this time Standard Oil had grown into a gigantic integrated national and multinational enterprise. In 1882, to ensure its administrative integrity and to centralize the finances of the forty companies under his control, Rockefeller and his associates had reorganized Standard Oil as a trust. That meant that shareholders of the companies controlled by them (in extraction, refining, transporting, and marketing) surrendered their shares to nine trustees and, in return, received trust certificates. That assured their economic interests while denying them any voice in management. The trust's capital then totaled $70 million, an enormous sum for the time, and four-sevenths of this ($40 million) was in the hands of Rockefeller and his associates.[7]

The trust represented a new type of business organization, with much larger financial resources than usual. In the popular mind, in fact, the term "trust" was applied to any giant firm. The phenomenon was of course widespread in American industry during the Gilded Age, when a number of major trusts and large corporations were created under the aegis of leading banks, especially that of J. P. Morgan. Morgan had been involved in the formation of the General Electric Company (not a trust) in 1892. At the turn of the century he participated actively in some major railway mergers, the creation of the U.S. Steel Corporation, and other important enterprises. The Standard Oil trust, which had been formed several years earlier, was in fact the prototype of the trust, although it voluntarily gave up the trust form of organization in 1892. Unlike later amalgamations, where banks played key roles as catalysts and organizers, in the case of Standard Oil it was Rockefeller and his associates who took the initiative. To be sure, Rockefeller's companies had banking connections; most notably, at the turn of the century, they used the National City Bank of New York (whose president, James Stillman, had family ties with Rockefeller) for ordinary banking operations. But Standard Oil continued to serve as its own financier and regarded all financial operations, domestic and foreign, as an "internal affair." More creditor than debtor, Standard Oil was the most independent of all American oil companies.[8]

Standard Oil was a large-scale exporter; indeed, for a long time it was the only international trading company in the oil industry. By the mid-1870s kerosene exports constituted one-third of all Standard Oil trading operations and at times reached three-fourths of total production. Because of its near monopoly on foreign markets it could practice high price marketing and gain still another edge in the struggle for domestic markets; this was a key factor in the temporary consolidation of its monopoly. Standard Oil's international business expanded and the firm became a multinational enterprise.

In 1911 the U.S. Supreme Court decreed the breakup of Standard Oil. Out of this dissolution came thirty-four companies, including Standard Oil of New Jersey (now Exxon), Standard Oil of New York (now Mobil), and Standard Oil of California. Of the thirty-four companies, nine retained foreign facilities.[9]

Meanwhile, at home, even before the breakup of Standard Oil, the monopoly position of the company was being challenged. New, strong, independent firms were emerging: the Texas Company and Gulf Oil. Both had embarked on business abroad before 1914—albeit on a far more modest scale than the leading Standard Oil companies.

Russian Oil Corporations

In the early 1880s the American predominance in world markets was challenged by strong new rivals—Russian oil companies. The latter, whose operations were concentrated in a small area around Baku, had only made their appearance in the late 1870s. In 1879 the Nobels created the first big Russian oil company. Ludwig and Robert Nobel (brothers of Alfred Nobel, inventor of dynamite and creator of the Dynamite Trust) came from Sweden and settled in Russia. During the 1877/78 Russo-Turkish War they made a fortune from munitions sales to the Russian army and invested their profits in oil. Of the company's total capital of 3 million rubles in 1879, the two Nobels held 1,710,000; retired tsarist General Petz (Peter) Bilderling and his brother, Alexander, owned 980,000; a St. Petersburg merchant, I. J. Zabelskii, had invested

135,000; company managers owned 60,000, and Alfred Nobel held the remaining 115,000 rubles. By 1882 the company's capital had risen to 10 million rubles and two years later to 15 million.[10]

Alfred Nobel encouraged his brothers to solicit the support of the leading banks in Europe and thereby to augment operating capital. "As far as I understand," he wrote in 1880, "we shall need about 200 million rubles."[11] In those days that kind of sum was almost unimaginable; even Standard Oil's capital in 1882 amounted to only 140 million in rubles. But Alfred Nobel thought the Russian company could attract money from the Swedish, German, and French banks and various industrial enterprises that had supported the formation of his Dynamite Trust. When the company's capital stood at 10 million rubles in 1882, the two brothers in Russia held shares worth 4,575,000 rubles and Alfred had increased his holding to 1,375,000 rubles. After Ludwig Nobel died in 1888 and his son Emmanuel became head of the company, Alfred continued to solicit the participation of West European banks, suggesting that 60 percent of the stock go to shareholders living in Russia and the balance be held by himself and foreign financiers. But in 1896 the dynamite king died and took this project to the grave. Concurrently, his investments in Russia were recalled and ended this outside involvement, to the evident relief of the Russian company.[12]

Meanwhile, the Nobel Company did pursue Alfred Nobel's strategy of seeking bank support. It obtained loans from the Rothschilds of Paris and the Crédit Lyonnais, but its closest ties were with two Berlin banks, the Diskonto-Gesellschaft and the Berliner Handelsgesellschaft. For three decades these banks placed Nobel's shares and bonds on the German, Dutch, and Belgian stock markets.[13] The first major loan came in May 1884, in anticipation of a stock issue, and amounted to nearly 3 million rubles. The banks also established a successful syndicate for placing Nobel's shares and bonds and by June could remit 2 million from Berlin to the company's account in St. Petersburg.[14] The entire operation proved profitable, and in 1889 the banks loaned the Nobel company another 2 million rubles.[15] The company repaid the debt by 1894. For ten years (1884–1894) the German banks held 9 percent of Nobel's shares (amounting to 1,350,000 rubles) and continued the profitable business of selling Nobel's securities. In addition, they received big brokerage fees for such transactions. Finally, the value of the shares held by the banks rose steadily.

The Nobel Company maintained these ties to the German banks with the assistance of the St. Petersburg International Commercial Bank, which, from the beginning, had actively participated in placing Nobel's shares.[16] As a member of the German syndicate, it also held shares worth 30,000 rubles. Though the International Bank itself depended on credits from the Diskonto-Gesellschaft, it mediated Nobel's relations with European banks. In May 1899 the Diskonto-Gesellschaft asked the St. Petersburg International Bank whether the Germans could negotiate directly with Nobel on placing its shares.[17] As the ensuing correspondence demonstrates, the Petersburg bank preserved its role as a mediator and thereby helped Nobel remain independent.[18]

Like Rockefeller in the United States, Emmanuel Nobel first concentrated on refining and transport in order to establish control over oil marketing in Russia.[19] In 1879 the Nobel brothers' profits amounted to 128,000 rubles, but by 1889 these had increased to 2,499,000—a twenty fold increase.[20]

Because waterways remained the chief means of communication in Russia, Nobel relied primarily upon water as the most efficient method of oil transportation. But Nobel also made use of the expanding railway system; kerosene delivered to various points on the Volga was then shipped by rail to interior regions. That in turn led Nobel to develop its own transport infrastructure, from the construction of Volga wharfs to the purchase of American-style tank cars. It was no small venture. In the mid-1880s the company owned sixty trains (with twenty-five tank cars each), had storage tanks at forty junctions, and by the end of the nineteenth century the company owned thousands of tank cars, and had storage facilities at 129 ports. At the final stage of delivery kerosene was shipped in barrels by carts to remote points in Russia beyond the railway network.[21]

In the early 1880s the Nobel Company began large-scale sales of *mazut*, the residual oil left from the refinement of kerosene. *Mazut* was used as a combustible fuel for steamships, locomotives, and plant installations. Nobel had its own machine plant, which, from the early 1880s, organized the mass production of sprayers needed for the more efficient burning of *mazut* in steam boilers. *Mazut* profits rose steadily, increasing ten times between 1883 and the end of the century.[22] In sheer volume the *mazut* business exceeded that in kerosene and after 1893 was even twice as large; still, kerosene remained the more profitable because of large-scale exports. As company records clearly show, profits for kerosene were much higher than for *mazut*.[23]

As in the case of Standard Oil, Nobel initially had relatively small investments in crude oil production. In 1881 its drilling equipment represented only 5 percent of capital expenditures, rising to 8 percent in 1885. In the latter year most of the company's expanding investments were in refining (30 percent) and transportation (62 percent). Of the latter, 34 percent was for ships and barges, 20 percent for storage tanks, and 8 percent for pipelines.[24]

While Nobel achieved supremacy in the Russian oil business, the company did not achieve anything like Standard Oil's near monopoly. In 1883 Nobel controlled nearly a quarter of total oil production, and about one-half of the kerosene market. Significantly, the company was unable to conserve even this level of dominance. The emergence of strong local and foreign competitors in the 1890s and 1900s reduced Nobel's relative share of oil output to 10 to 12 percent and held its portion of the domestic market to 40 to 50 percent. Like Standard Oil (but on a more modest scale), Nobel assumed quasi-banking functions vis-à-vis its commercial suppliers and customers, extending various kinds of short-term credit. Unlike Standard Oil, however, that credit did not become a device whereby Nobel could eventually absorb smaller firms for purposes of vertical integration and monopoly.

It also bears noting that though the company founders were Swedes by origin, their firm could hardly be called foreign.[25] Apart from its strictly juridical status as a Russian firm, the Nobel Company also had close connections in high government circles, and frequently tapped these for various kinds of support, including financial aid. In the nationalist Russian environment, no "foreign" firm could or did receive such advantages. In 1883 the State Bank opened for the Nobel Company a special 2 million ruble current account at 7.5 percent annual interest, while private banks demanded 17 to 18 percent.[26] Although Nobel scarcely needed to make use of this credit (the State Bank reported in 1905 that Nobel had reduced its debts "to zero several times a year" and "had hardly used" an additional commercial credit of 2 million rubles), the preferential treatment shows clearly the firm's close ties to the tsarist regime.[27]

The state rendered the firm assistance, but at the price of control and oversight. The assistance took such important forms as preferential railway shipping rates, which were especially important for oil exports. Many exported oil products were delivered by the state-owned railways. The government reduced rail tariffs in order to encourage the export trade, and thereby to increase the inflow of specie, but the policy also meant larger profits, which were further augmented by the state's decision to exempt kerosene exports from excise duties. At the same time, the government subjected the petroleum industry to permanent surveillance. Thus the appropriate ministry had first to give its consent before an oil company could make decisions on such matters as the formation of new companies, determination of their spheres of activity, and increases of capital. Nobel, well aware of the importance of good state relations, made his headquarters not in Baku but in St. Petersburg—unlike most other oil firms. His decision paid off, for by the mid-1880s Nobel himself (or his representatives) regularly participated in various government meetings.

Nobel also had strong links with joint-stock commercial banks in Russia. It used them to issue shares and bonds and took short-term, low-interest loans in different securities, which were deposited in the State Bank as a guarantee for payment of the kerosene excise duty amounting to several million rubles annually. At the end of the 1890s and into the early 1900s the annual payment of excise duty by the company amounted to more than 10 million rubles. That was why in 1899 Nobel twice borrowed from the St. Petersburg International Commercial Bank for one-half and one million rubles each (at 1.195 and 2.5 percent annual interest).[28] Later documents of the Volga-Kama Bank likewise show that Nobel received short-term loans amounting to 10 million rubles at 2 percent annual interest.[29]

At the same time, Nobel developed relations with foreign banks. As noted above, the Paris Rothschilds loaned money to Nobel in the early 1880s and in 1884 negotiated to purchase 25 percent of the company's stock, which would have thereby increased its capital to 20 million rubles.[30] But precisely at that point Nobel entered into negotiations with the Diskonto-Gesellschaft. The Paris bankers took exception to these negotiations, and the whole Rothschild–Nobel agreement fell through. Frustrated in its negotiations with Nobel, the Paris bank then decided to acquire its own Russian oil enterprise, and in 1886 purchased the Baku Oil and Trading Company, which it renamed the Caspian-Black Sea Trade and Industrial Company, with a capital of 1.5 million rubles.[31] In 1898 two Petersburg banks, the Russian Bank for Foreign Trade and the International Commercial, participated in issuing company shares with a value of 900,000 rubles.[32]

Trying to avoid open confrontation with Nobel, the Rothschilds at first decided not to operate actively on the Russian domestic market where Nobel's position was particularly strong. Rather, they concentrated their efforts on the export business, and by the end of the 1880s had become the largest exporter of Russian kerosene. Like Nobel, the French financiers contracted with several dozen small and middle-sized firms for kerosene purchases in exchange for credits. Thus, the Rothschilds also formed a kind of bloc with its stronghold in Baku.[33]

While America followed a pure capitalist way of development, Russian capitalism developed under a semifeudal tsarist regime with multiform economic structure. Therefore, along with large-scale capitalist enterprises like Nobel and Rothschild, the Russian oil industry in Baku continued to include a number of smaller entrepreneurs with considerable total capital and investments. Interestingly, several of these tried to unite against Nobel. The leader was the firm of A. I. Mantashoff, who was originally involved in trade, local industry, and credit operations, but who later switched completely to the oil business and amassed considerable wealth.

Despite the growing power of Nobel and later the Rothschilds, Mantashoff and his allies still controlled a considerable part of Baku crude oil production as well as some domestic and foreign trade. The dearth of reliable statistics at the turn of the century admits no exact figures on production and trade, but the general picture is clear: Nobel and the Rothschilds together controlled nearly half the production in crude, two-thirds of the oil refineries, over half of domestic oil marketing, and three-quarters of the kerosene exports. A smaller but not inconsiderable share fell to Mantashoff's group, which held about one-third of the domestic refinery production and trade and about one-quarter of kerosene exports.[34]

In 1899 the Mantashoff firm was reorganized as a joint-stock company with a capital of 22 million rubles. The former owners received 13.3 million rubles in shares of the new company and 6.7 million rubles in cash.[35] The joint-stock company was formed with the active participation of Russian banks, which subsequently supported Mantashoff. On June 29, 1899, at the constituent meeting, more than half of the shares represented belonged to several Petersburg banks (International Commercial; Russian Foreign Trade; Russian Trade and Industry; Private Commercial; Volga-Kama; Discount and Loan); the Moscow bank of I. V. Junker and Co. also participated. It should be noted that immediately after this meeting the company's founders, A. I. Mantashoff and M. A. Aramiants (who held more than 10 million rubles in shares), borrowed 9 million rubles from the Russian Foreign Trade Bank, using their shares as security.[36] In short, Mantashoff, with the backing of many smaller, local firms and the credit of large banks, succeeded in maintaining independence. He successfully competed with even such giants as Nobel and the Rothschilds.

Multinationalization of the Oil Busines

The emergence of Russian oil companies represented a serious challenge to Standard Oil's position on the world market. Russian kerosene exports rose from just 2,000 tons in 1881 to 24,000 tons in 1882, and 117,000 tons in 1885; the Russian kerosene export of 556,000 tons in 1887 already comprised 22 percent of world exports. The remaining 78 percent was retained by the American company, but by 1891 the American share had fallen to 71 percent.[37]

The board of Standard Oil discussed the "Russian question" and decided to take urgent measures. At the end of 1883 Rockefeller's agents considered buying a large amount of Nobel stock but came to the conclusion that it would be "impracticable." They had nevertheless established contact with the Nobel people, and the American representatives hoped that in the future they could obtain information on the "financial standing and ability of the Russian company."[38]

The Rothschilds' activities in Baku likewise aroused interest at Standard Oil. In 1886, immediately after the Caspian-Black Sea Company had been formed, the board of Standard Oil discussed the possibility of an agreement with the Rothschilds' bank. In the following years Rockefeller representatives came regularly to Paris for negotiations and eventually obtained a draft agreement dividing the world market into spheres of influence. "I think you are following a right policy in the Russian affair," noted Rockefeller when informed of the agreement.[39] The arrangement would take effect, however, only if other Russian firms (most notably Nobel) agreed to join and if the tsarist government gave its consent. But neither condition could be met. Relations among Russian oil industrialists worsened as the Rothschilds' challenge to Nobel grew more formidable, and conflicts with the Mantashoff group increased. For its part, the tsarist government was not averse to a reasonable agreement with Standard Oil, but American proposals—which provided for a status quo on the European market—were manifestly contrary to the interests of a rapidly growing Russian export.

Although a U.S. industrial commission (1898–1902), which studied the international market for American products, recommended involvement of American banks "in the leading centers of world trade," and especially where credit institutions were poorly developed, that kind of recommendation had no practical significance for Standard Oil.[40] Rather this oil giant relied upon its earlier strategy and by the early 1890s Standard Oil had established a network of European affiliates in Great Britain, Denmark, Italy, Belgium, and Holland. Although nominally independent, these local firms were in fact controlled by Standard Oil. Thus, Rockefeller owned the entire stock of the English affiliate ($2.5 million), 51 percent of Belgian and Dutch stock ($2 million), and 60 percent of the Italian firm ($500,000). Like Standard Oil itself, these European enterprises had a full complement of transportation means, storage tanks, and other facilities to market the American kerosene. All this was but the starting point of a multinational business that would ultimately grow into modern transnational corporations. By the end of 1907 Standard Oil controlled fifty-five foreign enterprises with a capitalization of approximately $37 million.[41]

Almost simultaneously the Nobel and Rothschild companies established their own affiliates in Europe. Whereas the Rothschilds created affiliates in England, Belgium, and Holland, Nobel—who penetrated those countries, too—chose to base his chief affiliate in Germany. As in the Standard Oil case, the Russian companies owned the majority of their affiliate's shares, but their total investments were much smaller than those of the Americans, not exceeding $4 million to $5 million in comparable figures.

American and Russian affiliates concentrated on the European market where the largest sales were made but they also operated in the Far East. Prior to 1880 the Chinese kerosene market had been dominated ("virtually monopolized") by Standard Oil. Russian oil did not come into the picture until 1889. Imports from the Dutch East Indies and Borneo began in 1894 and 1901, respectively. Standard Oil of New York became the principal Standard Oil company in Far Eastern markets.[42] In 1891 Rothschild's contractor (Lane, MacAndrew and Co.) signed an agreement with the powerful British trading firm of Marcus Samuel and Company (later reorganized as The "Shell" Transport and Trading Co.) to make the latter its exclusive agent. But Samuel lost this privilege in 1895 when the newly formed Russo-Chinese Bank took over the sale of Russian kerosene in the Far East. The bank's capital came from several French banks, with the participation of the Russian Treasury acting under the supervision of the Ministry of Finance.

Meanwhile, in October 1893 the Russian government was instrumental in the formation of the Baku Union of kerosene producers, an export syndicate. After studying the organization of American corporations and the experience of Standard Oil, the Ministry of Finance summoned a group of local kerosene producers for a meeting in Petersburg, where they approved a draft agreement prepared by Nobel and the Rothschilds. Later, Mantashoff also joined the agreement. Under its terms the Mantashoff group was to control two-thirds of the kerosene trade in the Middle East and one-fourth in the Far East, but had to concede the entire West European market to Nobel and the Rothschilds. The government granted the Baku Union a six-month tariff reduction on the Trans-Caucasian Railroad and promised to prolong the privilege if negotiations with Standard Oil were successful. These negotiations, however, failed; Rockefeller demanded low export quotas and refused to take into account either the world market situation or the rise in Russian exports.

For its part, the Baku Union collapsed in 1897 because of growing internal differences. The Rothschilds increased sales in the British market; Nobel made separate deals with Standard Oil's European affiliates; and Mantashoff was constantly at odds with both Nobel and the Rothschilds. Several abortive attempts were made to resurrect the agreement, but the scheme for a unified Russian oil corporation was never realized.[43] Subsequent development of the oil business followed along the lines of gradual multinationalization, either through a strengthening of the established ties with foreign market partners and expansion of the affiliate network, or as a result of foreign capital flow into Russia.

Foreign Capital in Russia

Development of the Russian oil industry at the turn of the century was closely connected with foreign investments. Banks played an active role in this process: foreign banks as investors, Russian banks as intermediaries. During the industrial boom of the 1890s foreign banks showed great interest in the highly profitable Russian oil business.

This intense flow of foreign capital into Russia coincided with the tenure of Minister of Finance Sergei Witte, who wielded great authority. One essential component in Witte's economic program was the use of foreign investments for industrialization. As his chief agent in foreign financial operations, Witte relied upon the St. Petersburg International Commercial Bank, which actively participated in the creation of oil enterprises in Russia, and which also functioned as the government's liaison to the European capital market. The International Bank had some foreign shareholders, most notably the German Diskonto-Gesellschaft and (in the 1890s) some French institutions. On the whole, however, the Petersburg bank was quite independent because of large domestic investments as well as regular support from the Russian government. The bank was headed at this time by Adolf Rothstein, a shrewd businessman who had close connections to European financial circles and was considered Witte's "alter ego."[44]

Witte, at the same time that he encouraged foreign investment, also used government controls to block penetration by Standard Oil. Despite opposition by the nobility and agrarian interests (who feared that foreign capital and industrial development would undermine their position), Witte encouraged the French and British to invest in Russian oil. The effect of his policy was most evident in the case of the Rothschilds.

Prior to his advent, only a year after establishing their operation in Baku, they applied to the government for permission to increase the capital of the Caspian-Black Sea Company. But Witte's predecessor refused, and in 1887 the Rothschild bank had to lend the company 3 million rubles—twice the initial capital of 1.5 million rubles.[45]

But later developments, especially the Franco-Russian alliance of 1893, enabled the Rothschild bank to consolidate its position in Russian oil. It finally obtained the long-awaited permission to increase the company's capital at the end of 1895. The next year Jules Aron, the chief engineer of the Rothschild bank and its oil expert, visited Russia. "Since my last visit to Russia three years ago," he wrote to Rothstein, "the Russian oil industry has developed enormously, and I believe that, owing to the growing demand for liquid fuel in the regions which have transport communication with the Volga, we shall witness still more considerable progress in [the] future."[46] It was not exports, where the Rothschilds were already firmly established, but the domestic market that now attracted their attention.

Apprised of financial difficulties experienced by the Tagiev petroleum company of Baku, the Rothschilds tried to buy it by making use of Rothstein's "good offices." Their plan—to create a Baku merchant bank on the basis of Tagiev's enterprise—fell through, however. The next object of the Rothschilds' aspirations was Pollack and Sons Company, whose tankers provided oil transportation on the Volga. With Rothstein's assistance they elaborated a new plan to create a mazut (residual oil) firm. In March 1897, the International Bank finally persuaded the tsarist government to approve the Mazut charter for a company with an initial capital of 6 million rubles. This event was accompanied by the announcement of the Rothschilds' decision to participate in the subscription of yet another Russian government loan on the Paris Bourse.[47]

Although the new company was formed as a Russian enterprise, it was not such either by share distribution or by board composition. Of the 16,000 shares the Rothschilds kept 9,600, leaving 4,000 for the Pollacks and 2,400 for the International Bank (which distributed them among its traditional partners: the Russian Foreign Trade Bank; the St. Petersburg Discount and Loan Bank; and the Hamburg banking house of Max Warburg).[48] As provided in the agreement with Rothstein, his bank's partners pledged "to keep the shares in syndicate during five years at the disposal of the Rothschilds" and promised to act "in accord with all the actions that might be attempted by the Paris house." Of five seats on the board, Rothschild representatives occupied three and the Pollacks one, with Adolf Rothstein taking the other. At the Rothschilds' initiative, the board elected Rothstein as company chairman. In return, German Spitzer, a Rothschild associate who owned International Bank shares, was named to the bank's board of directors.

After the Mazut reorganization the International Bank rendered the company various services, opening a special credit account and receiving in deposit rather large amounts of company securities in exchange for short-term loans.[49] Like the Nobel Company, the Mazut Company granted short-term credit to some enterprises, including railroads, which bought fuel from the new company.[50]

At about this same time British investors invaded Baku and succeeded where even the Rothschilds had failed. At the end of 1897 they bought Tagiev's firm and formed the Oleum, with a capital of 12 million rubles, the largest British oil company in Russia. To ensure its success, Evelyn Hubbard, a director of the Bank of England, was appointed its chairman. Almost simultaneously a British financial group representing the interest of Marcus Samuel's steamship company acquired another local enterprise and formed the Shibaev Petroleum Company with a capital of 6.5 million rubles. Both firms proved to be highly profitable. By the end of the first year Oleum's profits returned the entire purchase price; the Shibaev accomplished the same feat in five years.

At a reception in the British Embassy in St. Petersburg in January 1898, Hubbard had a conversation with Witte and the latter promised the British favorable treatment. Witte later gave assurance in writing, and indeed, did all within his power to win approval for the charters of the newly formed British oil companies.[51] In return, the London Stock Exchange admitted Russian bonds for quotation in June 1898.[52]

At the beginning of 1899 the International Bank advanced a plan to create an Anglo-Russian Bank. When English promoters next requested new oil areas at Bibi-Eibat (near Baku), Rothstein proposed to reconstitute the Russian Bibi-Eibat Petroleum Co., something akin to an industrial credit bank with a branch in London, to distribute Russian shares and bonds in England. The International Bank was to exercise control over the new company. Although British financiers were ready to participate in the Anglo-Russian Bank, they worked out their own project and sent it to Witte. Ernest Cassel, an influential British banker who had just finished creating the National Bank of Egypt, took part in the negotiations. He accepted the main idea, which was to collaborate with the Banque de Paris et des Pays-Bas, but demanded "appreciable advantages" and "some temptations."[53] The differences between the British and Russians proved irreconcilable, however.

When Rothstein learned that negotiations were deadlocked, he dropped his initial plan and offered to sell the Bibi-Eibat Petroleum Company's shares to the British. As provided by an agreement with the International Bank, a British company was formed in London under the same name and purchased all 10,000 shares of the Russian company (with a nominal value of 2.5 million rubles) at a price of £455,000. The British paid £329,000 in cash and £126,000 in their company's shares.[54] The International Bank took half these shares and placed the balance among some of its traditional partners including the Azov-Don Bank; the Petersburg firms of Vavelberg and Hinzburg; the Banque de Paris et des Pays-Bas; the Société Générale pour l'Industrie en Russie; Lippmann, Rosenthal and Co.; and the German banks of Max Warburg and Robert Warschauer.[55] The Russian company continued to exist alongside the British as a subsidiary of the new British company. The British purchased the Bibi-Eibat sites after these had been examined by Boverton Redwood, a well-known British oil geologist, who compiled a special report.[56] Later, when the Anglo-Persian Oil Company was formed, he became its leading advisor.

In 1904 the International Bank participated in the Berekey Association. In this association the Bibi-Eibat Petroleum Company, together with the Shibaev Company, acquired new government-owned oil sites and undertook their exploitation. The total cost of 220,000 rubles was shared equally by the bank and the two oil companies, with proportional distribution of seats on the board of the association.[57]

Overall, the British acquired twenty-four oil companies in Russia. Apart from the Baku region, where British investors owned eleven firms with a combined capital of 40 million rubles, they also established a presence in the oil region around Grozny, where seven British firms had a combined capital of 11 million rubles. The first British companies were also being formed in the Maikop region, where, several years later, a major oil boom would occur. Altogether, by the early twentieth century British investments amounted to 65 million rubles and caused many to believe that the British position was close to that of the Nobel and Rothschild firms.[58]

At the end of the 1890s German capital also showed interest in Russian oil. A group of German bankers announced their intention to buy oil properties in Baku, construct a refinery on the Volga, erect warehouses and other installations, and acquire railway tank cars and oil tankers. The company planned to market part of its production in Russia. The German project not only resembled that of the Rothschilds' Mazut (which, with the assistance of the International Bank, had already been realized) but also solicited that bank's previously invited support and participation. Max Warburg, whom Rothstein had previously invited as subparticipant in the syndicate to distribute Mazut shares, was now counted among initiators of the German project and emphasized that German banks regarded the project "with great interest."[59]

The German bankers tried to entice the Russians with the advantages of the German market, and planned to establish the new firm's Central Kerosene Trading Agency in Hamburg, with branches throughout Germany. The Germans also approached the Rothschilds. Felix Wachenheim, a Frankfurt-am-Main banker, acting on behalf of a consortium that included the Warburgs of Hamburg and Bleichröder of Berlin, tried to interest the Paris bank in this project. Wachenheim emphasized that the German consortium planned to organize its own enterprise "apart from Nobel," the Rothschilds' chief rival in the Russian oil business.[60]

In May 1899, through the "good offices" of the International Bank, Wachenheim put forward a project to form "a kind of cartel" to counterbalance Standard Oil. The aim was to control the oil market not only in Germany but also in other countries by using "the bases which the Rothschilds have in England, Belgium, and Holland for selling their products."[61] But Nobel shrewdly countered by inviting the Rothschilds to join the board of directors of his German affiliate and to help raise its capital from 1.5 million to 2 million marks.[62] His offer was immediately accepted because of continuing friction and animus between French and German banks, and because Nobel's proposal promised to lead to broader collaboration between the two firms not only in the foreign but also in the domestic market. After the turn of the century, Nobel's proposal, in fact, became the subject of negotiations that ended in the cartel agreement, Nobmazut (1903). Under the terms of this agreement both firms were to coordinate trade practices in the Russian market.[63] As a government excise tax commission noted, the Nobel brothers and Mazut had acquired a dominant position.[64] Indeed, by 1901 their share of kerosene shipped to various home markets via the Caspian Sea amounted to 57 percent, with corresponding figures of 43.5 percent for mazut and 67.5 percent for lubricants.[65]

When Nobel applied to the International Bank for assistance in approaching the Rothschilds, Rothstein wrote that "if this combination is realized, Mr. Wachenheim will be of no interest to us."[66] The assistance of the International Bank was also instrumental in increasing the capital of Nobel's affiliate in Germany. Although the German banks of Warburg and Bleichröder acquired a modest number of shares from the International Bank subscription, they failed in their ambitious designs for a cartel— a striking contrast to the marked successes of the British and the French. All these activities led to major changes in the Russian oil business and at the same time facilitated a multinationalization of the entire oil industry.

Royal Dutch-Shell

In 1890 a group of wealthy Dutch businessmen in The Hague established the Royal Dutch Company (RDC) to extract oil in the Dutch East Indies. It opened a major producing, refining, and marketing enterprise in Sumatra and later developed business on other islands. Both at the initial stages and later, RDC, in the words of Frederick Gerretson, was "purely commercial in character"; it "financed industry" and operated as "an investment trust" to supply money to enterprises within its sphere of influence. As such RDC "exported capital to its foreign affiliates, which were to promote its interest as an international trade firm."[67]

In a short time RDC made considerable progress, profiting especially from the kerosene sales in China that started in 1894. In 1896 the RDC exported 5 million gallons, increased this to 15 million in 1897, and in 1898 it caught up with the Russian and ranked second only to the American firms. The richness of oil fields in the Dutch Indies, the proximity to the large kerosene market in China, and the availability of cheap labor enabled Dutch companies to reap high profits and constantly to expand production.[68] The Royal Dutch Company's dividends rose from 8 percent in 1894 to 52 percent in 1897 and, not surprisingly, its stock price soared. When the company's nominal capital was increased in 1897 from 1.7 million to 5 million florins, the sale of shares yielded 13 million florins.[69] After the emergence of Russian oil in the 1880s, the appearance of the Dutch oil company created a second challenge to Standard Oil's predominance in the international petroleum market.

In 1895 Rockefeller's representative, William H. Libby, proposed to August Kessler, the head of RDC, to form an alliance. "In this case," he explained, "RDC would enjoy the support of this powerful oil concern whose financial and technical resources are enormous."[70] Proposing a fourfold increase of RDC capital, Standard Oil wanted to purchase all newly issued shares, but RDC turned down the proposal.

Standard Oil then turned to another Dutch company, Moera Enim, second only to RDC. The two parties signed an agreement in February 1898. Under its terms Standard Oil was to pay 6 million florins and in return to acquire 60 percent of Moera Enim stock and two-thirds of the votes on its board. When the Dutch government refused to authorize the agreement, Standard Oil launched a price war that caused a catastrophic fall in RDC dividends, from 52 percent in 1897 to 6 percent in 1898/99. The Dutch government then authorized the issue of privileged shares, but forbade sales to foreigners—that is, to Standard Oil. Such measures, a common practice for financing oil corporations, enabled RDC to raise needed funds; the sum of the subscription considerably exceeded the nominal value.[71] The Paris Rothschilds also came to the aid of the Dutch businessmen with a loan that opened access to venture capital in France. The situation changed again when British interests gave financial aid to Moera Enim. In January 1899 the British Shell company (formerly Marcus Samuel and Company) signed an agreement with Moera Enim to increase the latter's capital from 1.2 million to 4 million florins. Although this agreement was made for only seven years, for all practical purposes Moera Enim had merged permanently with Shell.

Although the Shell company had little in the way of oil fields, it and its predecessor had a keen interest in the oil business. It had substantial capital, owned thirty ocean-going steam tankers and scores of storage tanks in various ports, and developed a network of agencies to sell kerosene throughout the East (by 1900 these numbered 320).[72]

The idea of a merger with the British company was first advanced by Henri Deterding, August Kessler's right-hand man and later his successor as chairman at RDC. It was during an inspection tour of Far East ports in 1896 that he realized the strength of Marcus Samuel's influence. Marcus Samuel and Company had begun as a general trading firm; it had served a merchant banker set of functions; and as we have seen had been involved in shipping Russian oil to Eastern markets. In 1897 Marcus Samuel formed The "Shell" Transport and Trading Co., which handled his oil business. In the early 1900s negotiations began between Deterding and Marcus Samuel that culminated in several agreements, the first of which joined Royal Dutch and Shell interests in Eastern markets and then, in 1907, resulted in the formation of Royal Dutch-Shell (RDS).

Frederick Lane, the head of Lane, MacAndrew and Co., played an important role as an intermediary and put his "good offices" at the disposal of Deterding. He represented the interests of both the British Shell and the Paris Rothschilds. In autumn 1901 Lane worked out details of a project to unite all the parties—save Standard Oil—that were interested in kerosene marketing in the East.

Despite the many obstacles to the Anglo-Dutch alliance, on May 17, 1903, Deterding and Samuel signed an agreement for creation of a trading enterprise uniting the "Shell" Transport and Trading Company with the Royal Dutch Company. It was more difficult to persuade Russian firms to sign on; although the Rothschilds were ready to join, Nobel and Mantashoff flatly refused. But in Deterding's view the Rothschilds' consent was sufficient. "If we unite with the Rothschilds," he wrote to Samuel, "everyone will realize the future is in our hands. Without their name we can do nothing."[73]

In June 1903 the Asiatic Petroleum Company came into being with a capital of £2 million; the stock was divided into three equal parts among Deterding, Samuel, and the Rothschilds. The new corporation, which unified the marketing interests of all these groups in the East, represented an important step in efforts to undermine the predominance of Standard Oil. In sheer geographic terms the agreement embraced literally half the world—not only Asia, but also Australia and Africa.

The alliance between Shell and Royal Dutch became worldwide with the merger of the two ventures in 1907—60 percent to Royal Dutch and 40 percent to Shell. Deterding became head of the new Royal Dutch-Shell group, establishing his main office in London. That city was the world's commercial and financial center and offered the ideal point for Deterding to fight Standard Oil.

Soon after Royal Dutch-Shell had been formed Deterding went to New York in an attempt to reach an agreement with Standard Oil, but he came away empty-handed. Rockefeller had quite other plans in mind: an alliance with Nobel against the Rothschilds that he hoped would give him over 50 percent control of the Russian export "through Nobel."[74] That was the main thrust of this strategy and it was incompatible with Deterding's intentions.

International oil rivalry had become even more complicated after 1900 with the efforts by German banks to establish footholds in the oil business, and with the entry of new American companies, which sprang up in Texas, Indiana, Oklahoma, and later in California, and operated beyond the reach of Standard Oil's influence. Whereas Standard Oil was said to control 95 percent of U.S. oil refinery output and 90 percent of exports in 1900, by 1910 it had lost about a third in each category to independent American companies.

At the same time the total volume of petroleum production steadily increased—from 24.3 million tons in 1902 to 35.1 million tons in 1907. Most of the increase was accounted for by a doubling of oil output in North America and by the rapid development of the oil business in such countries as Rumania. By contrast, production in the Dutch Indies leveled off, and it actually experienced a sharp decline in Russia after 1905. That shift posed a serious problem for Asiatic Petroleum, since it now had to buy large quantities of kerosene on the international market.[75]

To alleviate the situation, Deterding decided to expand Royal Dutch-Shell's activities and, as his first step, acquired oil fields in Rumania, where in 1908 he established the Astra-Romana Society. Royal Dutch-Shell almost simultaneously turned to Russia. The discovery of oil in the Maikop region in 1906 and the subsequent formation of several oil companies there signaled a new wave of British investments. But these activities were extended to Baku and Grozny as well as the promising Ural-Caspian region. As a result, the British doubled the total investments of the 1890s and by 1914 had about 180 million rubles tied up in the Russian oil business.[76]

According to Gerretson, an agreement between Deterding and the Rothschilds had been "in the offing since amalgamation"—that is, ever since 1907.[77] Royal Dutch-Shell acquired the Rothschild enterprises in the Grozny and Emba regions and the major Baku firms, the Caspian-Black Sea Company and Mazut, which along with Nobel's firm were the foremost concerns for the extraction and sale of oil in Russia. The Rothschilds sold these properties for more than 30 million rubles, and in exchange received 20 percent of Royal Dutch-Shell stock (which they pledged not to place on the market until January 1914). The Rothschilds remained stockholders of Russian enterprises, particularly of Mazut, until 1916.[78]

Royal Dutch-Shell's enterprises were among the most powerful oil-producing groups in Russia, their share capital amounting to more than 60 million rubles in 1914. These holdings included the Caspian-Black Sea Company (10 million rubles), Mazut (12 million rubles), three firms in Grozny (19 million rubles), the Ural-Caspian Company (7 million rubles), the Shibaev Company, and some lesser firms.[79]

Royal Dutch-Shell's success in Russia was complemented by Deterding's almost simultaneous success in acquiring oil enterprises in America. At the end of 1910 he approached Rockefeller's competitors with a proposal to create an American coalition against Standard Oil. The negotiations lasted for two years but came to nothing, and Deterding turned instead to Kuhn, Loeb & Co., a banking firm. With its assistance he tried to acquire large pieces of property, but here too he met with failure. In 1914 he founded the Shell Company of California, which would develop into one of the giants of American oil and absorb companies in Oklahoma and other states. With the help of Kuhn, Loeb & Co., Royal Dutch-Shell arranged to sell its securities on the American market in order to provide its U.S. enterprises with dollars.[80]

British Oil Corporations

Great Britain for a long time did not have its own oil fields. To be sure, the British formed some small companies to explore for oil in Burma and Borneo, but the results were of little consequence. By the beginning of the twentieth century the Burmah Oil Company produced only 1.5 percent of the world output, although this very company would later emerge as a key bastion of British influence in the East.[81] At the turn of the century British companies increased their oil investments as a result of successful undertakings in Russia. Still, the main thrust of British activity was oil transportation and marketing in the East. The Samuel Company, reorganized as the Shell Company and merged with Royal Dutch, was the leading "British" company.

A new era of British involvement began in 1909 with the organization of the Anglo-Persian Oil Company (APOC). In 1901 William Knox D'Arcy, a wealthy British financier, acquired an oil concession in Persia; he enjoyed the vigorous support of the Foreign Office and the Admiralty (which was planning to convert the Navy from coal to liquid fuel).[82] By the end of 1903 D'Arcy had spent £160,000 on oil exploration, but without evident success. When the British government refused to grant a subsidy of £120,000 he applied to private banks, including Joseph Lyons and Co. (London) and later the Rothschilds in Paris. D'Arcy also approached Sir Ernest Cassel, a friend of King Edward VII, but here, too, met rebuff. He even sought a loan from the Americans, who, however, made it clear that nothing could be done before oil was discovered.

Under the circumstances, a special commission of the Admiralty (headed by Ernest Pretyman, who had studied the issue of expanding British oil property) recommended that the Burmah Oil Company—a British government contractor—extend financial support to D'Arcy. Founded in 1886 by a group of Scottish financiers, and reorganized in 1902, this company with share capital of £2 million was a prosperous enterprise. Accordingly, Burmah Oil and D'Arcy signed an agreement on May 5, 1905 to create Concessions Syndicate, Ltd., which was to finance the work in Persia.[83] Three years later oil was discovered.[84]

Talks then began to reorganize the company and its finances. The result was an agreement on April 14, 1909, which established the Anglo-Persian Oil Company with an initial capital of £2 million: A million ordinary shares with a nominal value of £1 each were allotted as fully paid (570,000 to Burmah Oil, 400,000 to Concessions Syndicate, and 30,000 to Lord Strathcona, the company chairman), and £1 million in preference shares. As compensation for his expenses D'Arcy received 170,000 Burmah Oil shares worth £900,000 and an honorary post as APOC director, but he lost virtually any voice in company affairs.[85]

Leading British banks began selling APOC securities. Although the Bank of England refused to participate, pleading that industry was not its business, the company approached a variety of other leading banks—the National Provincial Bank, the Bank of Scotland (the Scottish origin of Burmah Oil was taken into account), and the Imperial Bank of Persia (an important instrument for British penetration into Persia).

When the securities were first issued (£600,000 in preference shares and a further £600,000 in 5 percent bonds), both issues were a great success. The company elected to direct most of the money to expand oil fields in Persia, and APOC announced plans to build a major pipeline (from the fields to the Persian Gulf) and a big refinery on Abadan island. The third subscription in October 1911 included a further £300,000 in preference shares and another £300,000 in bonds. Again, success: The preference shares were oversubscribed some fifteen times.[86]

On February 18, 1914, the British Cabinet decided to buy into APOC, and three months later, on May 20, the Admiralty came to terms with the company. The Exchequer, according to the agreement, was to increase the company's capital from

£2 million to £4 million, and in exchange was to receive a thirty-year contract for regular oil deliveries to the British Navy at reasonable prices. Two government representatives with veto rights were also appointed to the board of directors. At the same time the Admiralty confirmed all standing contracts with Royal Dutch-Shell and ordered that contractual relations with Deterding be on a long-term basis.[87]

The agreement with APOC paved the way for the future creation of the British Petroleum Company Ltd., one of today's major multinational oil corporations. In the early twentieth century direct state intervention in a major commercial enterprise was exceedingly rare. But the British decision on oil derived from a variety of concerns, only one of which was the Navy's need for oil. Rather, the arms race and the mounting tensions between the Entente and Central Powers encouraged the development of new forms of business organization, most clearly in the case of oil corporations. By 1914 Britain lagged behind the United States and Germany in large-scale industrial enterprise. While colonial possessions had long compensated for the retarded level of company organization in Britain, multinationalization of the world economy finally impelled the British government to reinforce the underpinnings of the weaker British corporations.

The political dimension of the British oil venture in Persia was obvious from the moment D'Arcy acquired the concession and obtained formal acknowledgment of the 1914 agreement. The British government used the company as a means to promote its policy throughout the Middle East, not just in Persia. Indicative, too, were the negotiations to form the Turkish Petroleum Company (TPC), which were concluded at the very time that the government decided to finance APOC. Acting on the advice of the Foreign Office, APOC acquired 50 percent of TPC stocks.[88]

Parliament formally ratified the agreement with APOC on June 17, 1914 and appropriated the requisite funds on August 5, 1914, shortly after the outbreak of World War I. This was highly symbolic, for preparation for war had been a prime motive for purchasing APOC.

German Banks

After the abortive cartel project in Russia at the end of the 1890s German banks redirected their energies to Rumania. In 1903 the Deutsche Bank gained control of the Steaua-Romana Company and increased its capital from 10 million to 17 million lei (and, three years later, to 30 million lei). The Diskonto-Gesellschaft and Bleichröder bank next bought up a number of minor Rumanian companies. As a result, by 1905 total assets of Rumanian firms controlled by German banks amounted to 97 million lei, or 64.3 percent of all investments in Rumanian oil. By contrast, Standard Oil's affiliate (Romana-Americana) had a capital of only 2.5 million lei in 1904; although that was later increased to 5 million lei ($100,000), it still represented just 3.3 percent of capital assets in Rumanian oil.[89]

In 1904 the Deutsche Bank, together with its allies, founded the Deutsche Petroleum Aktiengesellschaft with a share capital of 20 million marks. This holding company managed all the Deutsche Bank oil enterprises in Germany, Rumania, and Austria-Hungary; majority control of the company lay with the Deutsche Bank. Then in 1905 the Diskonto-Gesellschaft with Bleichröder and their allies formed a similar combination, the Algemeine Petroleum Industrie Aktiengesellschaft, with share capital of 17 million marks; it was charged with managing the German and Rumanian enterprises of the latter banks (whose oil interests were transferred to the holding company). Both companies were independent but worked in close cooperation.[90]

To counter Standard Oil the Deutsche Bank in 1906 founded a marketing company called the Europäische Petroleum Union (EPU), in which the Russian firms of Nobel and the Rothschilds participated. This time they accepted the German proposal to collaborate mainly because the Russian petroleum industry and kerosene exports had suffered great reverses during the Russo-Japanese War and the revolutionary upheavals in 1905/06. The EPU was capitalized in 1906 at 20 million marks, but in 1907 increased to 37 million marks (of which 20 million was contributed by the Deutsche Bank and its partners).[91] Apart from kerosene marketing, the EPU founders intended to supply Germany with fuel oil. According to American intelligence reports, Berlin demonstrated a "growing interest" in the naval oil fuel conversion.[92] When the Deutsche Bank analyzed industrial and technical developments at the beginning of the 1900s it stressed oil's potential significance as a fuel for diesel and internal combustion engines. It also stressed Germany's need for secure oil supplies. While kerosene imports retained high, stable levels (approximately a million tons annually from 1901 to 1911), other liquid fuel imports grew at a rapid pace—from 6,000 tons in 1901 to over 250,000 tons in 1911.[93]

Despite its original intentions, in mid–1907 the EPU ended up signing an agreement on market division and kerosene trade quotas with Standard Oil of New Jersey representatives. The agreement granted 75 percent of German kerosene imports to Standard Oil, allotted only 20 percent to the Deutsche Bank and its companions, and left just 5 percent for outsiders. This agreement aroused much bitterness in Germany and inflamed anti-American sentiments. In the end, the EPU also failed to satisfy the hopes of the Russian participants. By 1910 Nobel, for example, had increased its kerosene exports to Europe nearly threefold, but the price of kerosene delivered to EPU was only 40 percent of that on the Russian market. In 1910 the Nobel Company's profits fell to an unprecedented low level—352,000 rubles; even in the worst previous years they had never dipped below 2 million to 3 million rubles. As a result, Nobel came to the conclusion that EPU "fails to serve our interests" and that it must above all consider "the way to expand our market in Russia."[94]

Hoping to improve the situation, the Deutsche Bank's manager, Arthur von Gwinner, turned to Henri Deterding. In July 1910 Gwinner attempted to reach a large-scale agreement and in exchange for wider compensations even offered to relinquish the bank's stock in EPU. The Deutsche Bank also participated in construction of the Baghdad Railroad and sought oil concessions in a region of the Ottoman Empire adjacent to Persia. In the Gwinner-Deterding talks this question was closely linked with the future of EPU. When the Rothschilds learned of the talks, they offered Deterding 6 million to 7 million francs so that Royal Dutch-Shell could buy shares in EPU.[95] Although Deterding almost reached agreement with the Deutsche Bank, he in fact failed to do so and thereafter avoided any participation in German undertakings.

In March 1911 the Reichstag adopted a resolution calling for a government-controlled Kerosene Trading Organization, i.e., a state monopoly. The plan was to form a joint-stock company with capital of 40 million marks, to be furnished by the major banks. To this end the Treasury began negotiations with the Deutsche Bank and Diskonto-Gesellschaft.[96]

The latter, meanwhile, established a new holding company, the Deutsche Erdöl Aktiengesellschaft, to unite their oil interests in Germany, Rumania, and Austria-Hungary, and as an affiliate included the Austro-Hungarian marketing firm, the Oesterreichische-Ungarische Petroleum Produkte. Of the fifteen members on the Deutsche Erdöl Aktiengesellschaft board, ten were bank representatives. This alliance did not last for long, however. Whereas the Diskonto-Gesellschaft accepted the 1907 quota agreement with Standard Oil, the Deutsche Bank was determined to disrupt it, and in early 1912 the EPU cancelled the agreement. When Deutsche Erdöl indicated an inclination to resume negotiations with Standard Oil of New Jersey, the Deutsche Bank representative resigned from the board. The Deutsche Bank vigorously campaigned for a German state oil monopoly, but the Diskonto-Gesellschaft took a more cautious wait-and-see attitude. Gwinner persistently negotiated with different competitors of Standard Oil of New Jersey (Pure Oil, Gulf Oil, and Texaco) and sought to persuade them to make an agreement on oil supplies for Germany. But Standard Oil of New Jersey negotiated with the same companies and offered them a higher bid, depriving Gwinner of any hope.[97]

Heinrich Riedemann, the head of the Deutsche-Amerikanische Petroleum Gesellschaft—the main and most successful Standard Oil of New Jersey European marketing subsidary—reported to the company's board in New York that the German government, in event of war, wanted to be independent of outside oil supplies for at least a year. Riedemann explained to the Germans that Standard Oil was simply unable to deliver such a stock because of a tanker shortage, and the Germans seemed to be at a dead end. The closest oil fields, in Rumania and Austria-Hungary, annually produced about 3 million tons between 1911 and 1913, less than half of which was exported. Deliveries to Germany hardly amounted to 20,000 tons, less than 20 percent of German annual consumption.

In the early 1900s German banks had dominated the Rumanian and Austro-Hungarian oil business, but they subsequently lost their positions. For example, their relative share of Rumanian oil investments declined from 64.3 percent in 1905 to just 27.4 percent in 1914, notwithstanding the fact that their absolute investment increased from 97 million to 110.2 million lei in the same period. British and Dutch company investments, by contrast, had swollen from 13.2 to 47.9 percent of the total. Deterding's affiliate, the Astra-Romana, which was founded in 1910, was particularly successful, controlling 25 percent of Rumanian oil extraction and 40 percent of the country's refinery capacity. On a more modest scale, a Franco-Belgian group increased its share from 4.3 to 8.6 percent, and Standard Oil of New Jersey from 3.3 to 6.2 percent. Under the circumstances it was highly doubtful that Rumania could be relied upon as a source of German oil, still more after an open break between Gwinner and Deterding over the marketing of Royal Dutch–Shell Rumanian gasoline in Germany.[98]

Like the Deutsche Bank, the Diskonto-Gesellschaft was concerned over Germany's oil supplies. It adddressed the problem with the help of its long-time Russian connection, the Nobel Company. When the latter announced an increase of its share capital from 15 million to 20 million rubles in late 1911, the Berlin banks that had previously helped to distribute Nobel's securities were quick to offer their services.

Ultimately, the Diskonto-Gesellschaft and Berliner Handelsgesellschaft signed the agreement with Nobel and organized a banking syndicate of German (75 percent) and Russian (25 percent) groups.[99] The Germans were joined by Swedish and Dutch financiers, and the Russian group was represented by a long-term Diskonto-Gesellschaft partner, the St. Petersburg International Bank. The agreement designated the Diskonto-Gesellschaft as head of the syndicate. The new issue of Nobel shares appeared extremely profitable. Issued at 180 percent of the nominal value, they were quoted at 350 percent at the beginning of 1912, and in September 1913 hit a "sensational" peak of 455 percent.[100] The Diskonto-Gesellschaft acquired 6 million rubles in stock.

After the shares had been admitted to quotation, the Diskonto-Gesellschaft recalled that the Nobel representatives had spoken earlier of the possibility "to undertake a long-term delivery commitment." By this time, however, Nobel was on its feet and in good financial condition; its net profits for 1911 amounted to 3.5 million rubles—ten times that of the previous year. Nobel had, however, achieved this recovery mainly by domestic operations and had no desire to negotiate with the Germans.[101]

Still hopeful of changing Russian policy, the German government placed the oil question on the agenda of the meeting between Kaiser Wilhelm II and Tsar Nicolas II in the summer of 1912. The Kaiser had already met with Emmanuel Nobel six months earlier and wished to discuss a "joint effort" to supply their countries with liquid fuel and other petroleum products, "without the aid of the oversea markets." The Kaiser maintained that both Russia and Germany would profit.[102] But the effort foundered on opposition in the Russian government. The thinking in the Russian Navy General Staff is plainly evident from a memo of early 1912: ". . . of two of our main enemies [England and Germany] Germany is presently the most dangerous."[103] The German policy only redoubled suspicion, and it was evidently naive on the Germans' part to expect Russia to supply Germany with oil.

In late 1912 the German government nonetheless submitted a kerosene monopoly project to the Reichstag. In his opening speech, Minister of Finance Kühn, who had earlier denounced the aggressive actions of Standard Oil, appealed to the Americans to help assure future oil supplies for Germany.[104] But Standard Oil of New Jersey flatly refused to hold any talks with Gwinner, and the oil question became increasingly acute. In 1913 total oil imports in Germany amounted to 282,184 tons, while Germany's own crude oil production was only 121,000 tons. According to U.S. Navy Intelligence estimates, the German navy needed 60,000 to 70,000 tons of fuel oil annually.[105] Nevertheless, Germany failed to secure regular oil supplies not only because of international economic and political rivalries, but also (as the kerosene monopoly project showed) because of internal differences between the Deutsche Bank and Diskonto-Gesellschaft.

In 1913 and early 1914 international tensions became so inflamed that the Diskonto-Gesellschaft disposed of its Nobel stock; by May 1914 it had only 696 rubles in its possession.[106] During the same period it also disposed of 1.5 million rubles in shares of another Russian oil company, Neft', which it had bought earlier through St. Petersburg banks.[107] In a conference of July 1914 in Berlin, Gwinner, the manager of the Deutsche Bank, took aside Karl V. Hagelin, a director of the Nobel Company, and told him that "a war will break out soon," putting the blame on Russia's refusal to sign a trade treaty with Germany.[108] The conversation was a fitting epilogue to the history of relations between a major German bank and a leading Russian oil corporation, testifying to their involvement in international politics.

Banks and Oil Concerns on the Eve of World War I

By the outbreak of World War I the oil business had changed greatly since its early days. New production areas had emerged. The system of trade and financial relations had become more complicated. And substantial changes occurred in the structure of the oil industry in those countries where it originated, namely America and Russia, which remained the two largest producers.

In 1911 Standard Oil was the world's largest transnational corporation, with net assets of $660 million.[109] When the U.S. Supreme Court found it in violation of antitrust legislation and ordered the company's dissolution, it had sixty-seven foreign affiliates.[110] By that time John D. Rockefeller had retired and relinquished the administration to experienced managers. After the dissolution many foreign affiliates of Standard Oil continued their operations. Standard Oil of New Jersey was particularly active in international business. For this reason the historians of Standard Oil of New Jersey named the new period of the company's activity after 1911 "the resurgent years."[111] As in times past, the role of banks in the company's international expansion was not significant.

By 1914 the Russian oil companies had consolidated their positions. Having bought the Rothschilds' enterprises, Royal Dutch-Shell financed them and reorganized the management. Royal Dutch-Shell persuaded two Nobel directors, E. K. Groube and G. P. Eklund, to join them on the Russian board. Attempts were made at agreement between Deterding and Nobel, but they failed. The Nobel Company retained its leading position, at once keeping close relations with the government and expanding its ties with banks, both domestic and foreign, but principally the former. Although Russian crude oil production declined in absolute terms and its share in world production decreased even more sharply (from 53 percent in 1901 to 16 percent in 1914), the Nobel Company remained an important and profitable enterprise. While its share in Russian crude oil production fell from 11.9 to 10.9 percent between 1901 and 1910, it nearly doubled its kerosene production; it also expanded its share of kerosene and mazut deliveries inside Russia and in kerosene exports. Profits of the company from 1879 to 1914 are shown in Table 19–1. Company dividends went up from 12 percent in 1910 to 26 percent in 1914.[112]

Although a 1911 report on American investments in Russia listed Nobel as an American company, the assertion was clearly false.[113] Nobel did adhere to his agreement with Standard Oil for marketing allocations, but neither Rockefeller nor his partners owned Nobel stock: The latter remained a fully independent, self-financing enterprise. As chairman of the Volga-Kama Bank and making use of his influence in the Azov-Don Bank, Emmanuel Nobel also controlled the stock of other oil enterprises. His close personal ties with leaders of Stockholm's Enskilda Bank assured further credit, as in 1910, when that bank helped him to repay an earlier debt of 4 million marks owed the Diskonto-Gesellschaft.[114]

Taking advantage of the waxing interest of Russian commercial banks in oil during the prewar industrial boom (1909–1913), Nobel placed large portions of his

TABLE 19–1. Nobel Company Net Profits,
1879–1914 (thousands of rubles)

Year	Profits	Year	Profits
1879	128	1897	1,432
1880	1,005	1898	2,020
1881	1,443	1899	4,482
1882	1,770	1900	6,911
1883	2,072	1901	3,833
1884	1,793	1902	2,159
1885	859	1903	2,730
1886	1,755	1904	2,232
1887	1,755	1905	2,971
1888	1,658	1906	5,480
1889	2,499	1907	5,653
1890	2,337	1908	4,151
1891	1,451	1909	2,978
1892	1,484	1910	352
1893	612	1911	3,499
1894	1,795	1912	11,238
1895	2,171	1913	14,695
1896	2,032	1914	13,142

Source: MKNPR, p. 750.

company's shares among leading Petersburg and Moscow banks. Shortly after the 1912 increase of company capital, he sold 1,250,000 rubles in shares to a syndicate of St. Petersburg banks headed by the Russo-Asiatic, by that time one of the largest. Soon afterwards the Azov-Don Bank formed another syndicate to place 3,750 million in shares.[115] Likewise, the agreement with German banks for the 1912 issue included a cluster of Russian banks—the St. Petersburg International Bank, the Volga-Kama, Azov-Don, Russo-Asiatic, Russian Foreign Trade, St. Petersburg Discount and Loan banks, and several other banking institutions acting as subparticipants.[116]

After successfully increasing his company's capital by more than 25 million rubles, Nobel put 15 million into joint-stock capital and the rest into the reserve fund. In 1913 Nobel's nominal capital stood at more than 78 million rubles (30 million rubles in shares, 16.3 million rubles in bonds, and 32 million rubles in a reserve fund).[117] The price of Nobel's shares kept rising and it was no surprise that banks readily purchased them. A meeting of Nobel Company shareholders in May 1914 showed that of 30 million in shares, 18 million rubles were held by Russian banks.[118] As indicated above, by that time most German banks had sold Nobel securities.

A new stage in the development of a major Russian oil concern was marked by stronger ties with Russian banks. But even then the Nobel Company continued to operate as a trust, financing both its own organization and other companies under its control. In 1914 the firms within Nobel's sphere of influence had a capital exceeding 10 million rubles.[119] From the turn of the century the Nobel family operated a machine-building plant in St. Petersburg (which produced steam boilers, diesel engines, mazut sprayers, and other equipment), and in 1913 it invested 4 million rubles in the shipbuilding company Noblessner, which monopolized submarine construction in Russia.[120]

The Nobel Company encountered serious opposition with the formation in 1912 of the Russian General Oil Corporation (RGO), a powerful amalgamation of the holding company type that combined numerous producing, refining, and trading companies and whose capital amounted to 120 million rubles. Although it was registered in London as a British corporation, RGO was founded by St. Petersburg banks. Major Russian banks participating in RGO included the Russo-Asiatic Bank, the International Commercial Bank, the Discount and Loan, the Trade and Industrial, the Siberian, and the Russian Foreign Trade banks. Only the Volga-Kama and Azov-Don banks, the closest to Nobel, declined to join the operation since RGO obviously was contrary to Nobel's interest. The firms that formed RGO left no doubt of the corporation's anti-Nobel orientation. The idea of creating an independent "third force," first suggested in the 1890s, was realized with the formation of the RGO. The well-known Baku firms of Mantashoff, Lianozov, Goukasov, and Neft' formed the nucleus of RGO, but they also gathered a host of smaller oil firms.[121]

The RGO itself did not engage directly in oil production and marketing, but acted as a holding company. In accordance with the initial idea, its function was to help Russian banks carry out large-scale operations in placing Russian oil shares abroad. One such RGO member, the banking house of O.A. Rosenberg and Co. (together with its London and Paris branches as well as the French bank of Louis Dreyfus and the Belgian bank of Baron Margulis), conducted transactions for the corporate participants and arranged the issue of shares on the London, Paris, Brussels, and Amsterdam markets. In its first year and a half the bank syndicates raised RGO's initial capital of £2.5 million (about 23.7 million rubles). Simultaneously these same syndicates arranged new issues of shares of oil companies within RGO's sphere of influence. In 1912/13 these efforts succeeded in increasing the capital of the three main firms— Lianozov, Mantashoff, and Neft'—from 24.5 million rubles to 76.8 million rubles. Particularly impressive was the growth of the Lianozov Company (from 8 million to 30 million rubles) and the Neft' (from 5.5 million to 27.5 million rubles).[122] Together with the Russian banks, the underwriters earned about 3.6 million rubles on the RGO issues.[123]

The issue of new shares brought the oil companies enormous sums, which were further augmented by millions in loans. These funds, however, were used not so much to expand oil production as to acquire new companies and transport facilities. Having added a considerable number of firms, RGO far outstripped the other leading Russian oil groups, the Nobel brothers and Royal Dutch-Shell. (Table 19–2.)

TABLE 19–2. Crude Oil Production in Russia (1913–1914) (millions of tons)

Enterprise	1913	1914
RGO	2.1	1.9
Nobel Brothers	1.3	1.2
Royal Dutch-Shell Group	1.3	1.5
Other enterprises	4.4	4.3
TOTAL	9.1	8.9

Source: MKNPR, pp. 656–657.

In 1914 the three largest Russian groups accounted for 52 percent of total crude oil production and 75 percent of the marketing. Small and medium, more or less independent, enterprises operating alongside the trust-type organizations accounted for the rest. Credit from Russian and foreign banks was the most important source of their independence.

In the race for profits, RGO cast down a challenge even to Nobel itself, forming a syndicate to buy up its shares. From April to December 1913 the syndicate, headed by the Russo-Asiatic Bank, cornered a large bloc of Nobel shares on the Berlin and St. Petersburg stock markets. Similar attempts were made again later by another syndicate under Russo-Asiatic, but were no more successful than before.[124]

The RGO may have started with a bang, but it soon fizzled out. The St. Petersburg banks that participated in RGO's foundation provided powerful financial backing, but found it difficult to attract foreign capital. The French financial press sounded the alarm that the banks demanded unjustifiably high commissions.[125] In the autumn of 1913 contractors of Russian banks in Paris had reported "great difficulties" and "strong resistance" offered by French investors to the introduction of new Russian securities.[126] Despite the RGO board's reassurance in early 1914 that, because of the "excellent state of affairs," shareholders "may be sure that their shares are solid and highly profitable," the RGO had suffered a devastating blow to its reputation.[127] The price of RGO shares began to fall, and in February 1914 the management of the Russo-Asiatic Bank learned that "even the directors of Crédit Lyonnais" (which traditionally supported Russian enterprises) "advise their clients to get rid of RGO shares."[128] The month of May brought reports of serious difficulties in selling shares on the Paris Bourse; there were also reports that the financier Noel Bardac, who had earlier participated in issuing shares, refused to join the new syndicate.[129] Alarming news also came from London. As a result, the St. Petersburg International Bank requested the London Midland Bank not to sell the next issue of RGO shares on the market, but to distribute them equally among Russian and British banks. "The Russian banks, without hesitation, at their own expense, without applying to London, relieved the subscribers," stated the International Bank. "We hope that the Midland Bank, the representative of the British group, will follow suit not to discredit the enterprise."[130] Though Midland agreed, the speculative character of RGO became increasingly obvious, particularly when it was learned that its profits for 1913 were far less than Nobel's. Whereas the latter paid a handsome 26 percent dividend, RGO paid an average of only 6 percent, with some RGO members (including Lianozov and Mantashoff) failing to pay any dividends at all. Thus, the comparatively ephemeral success of RGO was followed by a steady decline, which ended in late 1916 and early 1917 with the exchange of stocks between Nobel and RGO and the settling of common interests to Nobel's advantage. With that the whole RGO challenge to Nobel came to an end.[131]

Conclusions

The role of banks in the oil business was that of catalysts, facilitating the growth of corporations and strengthening their multinational character. At the same time many oil corporations grew by way of self-financing, acting not only as trade, industrial, and transport enterprises, but also as financial enterprises. In this way they retained their financial independence from the banks while employing their services.

Alfred D. Chandler noted that Rockefeller's oil trust was an integrated amalgamation that controlled a complex set of operations. It must be kept in mind that the key element was its financial independence. Chandler finds it surprising that few American corporations imitated the Standard Oil structure, and names only two major oil firms, Sinclair Oil and Pan American Oil. At the same time, as Chandler notes, many European corporations followed the example of the American Oil Trust.[132] It also bears stressing that it was in the operation of highly profitable oil corporations that principles of a self-financing organization, acting as its own bank, were most fully realized. In many respects, Royal Dutch-Shell conducted its business in the same manner as did Standard Oil. A more complicated system was used by the Russian Nobel Corporation, although the same features could be observed in its activity. The company's accounts show that it fulfilled banking functions, namely lending, borrowing, and investing money.

The banks contributed to the transformation of the oil industry into a modern capitalist business, as is particularly obvious in the Russian case. Most important, however, banks did not maintain control over major firms. Thus, the Rothschild enterprises in Russia were sold to Royal Dutch-Shell (an integrated international oil enterprise); German banks' endeavors in oil all proved to be abortive; no British bank was willing to take the risks required to finance the Anglo-Persian Oil Company. The Russian General Oil Corporation, which had been founded on the eve of World War I by leading banks in Russia, failed to overcome the entrenched power of the Nobel Company.

Before World War I the oil business was the most "advanced" form of enterprise in terms of production, capital concentration, and financial and industrial development. Oil became the largest multinational business, with a major role not only in the world economy but also in international relations.

20

Banking and the Electrotechnical Industry in Western Europe

Albert Broder

Banks rarely appear as structural elements in studies of industrial history. If they do it is as suppliers of short-term working capital or seekers after the profits of capital export (for example, in France and Great Britain), or as the creators of cartels or trusts to reduce competition (Germany, perhaps the United States). This situation results from the difficulty of finding precise documentation. Unlike most economic properties, bank assets are volatile and variable. The "bottom line" is often deceptive as a measure of what banks actually do. The economic historian may look at the banks' activities and follow their policies, but measuring their role is far more complex.[1]

The "national" character of banks until the last third of the twentieth century is another source of difficulty. More than any other economic activity, banking is subject to national pressures. Even in the most capitalistic countries public opinion is suspicious, all the more so in countries like France, Austria, or Spain. At a given time technology, industrial production, and public utilities (water, gas, electricity, transport, etc.) and their means of finance do not differ from country to country, or at least are not contradictory; but not so with banking systems. Strictly conditioned by national legislation, which often reflects public opinion; by traditions, which even if recent are nevertheless respected; and the object of continual debates and contradictory requirements, the behavior and policies of banking were more closely tied to national traditions than any other economic activity of the nineteenth century.[2] The age of the gold standard and the free movement of capital was not that of free international banking.

Until the last third of the century that peculiarity of the banking system did not pose a problem, since the modes of international finance were relatively simple and did not necessarily imply actual flows of capital.[3] The finances of the electrical industry (central power stations, networks of lines, and electrotechnology), from the 1880s onward, required something quite different, all the more so in that the new form of energy required the simultaneous installation of the means of production, distribution, and utilization: public lighting, urban transport, electrometallurgy. Moreover, to permit the expansion made indispensable by the enormous investments required by electricity and electrotechnics, the latter industry developed new devices to replace other forms of power, such as the steam engine, by the continual improvement and enlargement of electric motors. There followed an intensity of research, innovation, and accelerated obsolescence of material unprecedented in any other industry. All this required an accelerated turnover of capital. Except for the United States, the national space was not suited to the economies of scale involved in this new industrial model. A new geography of national and international finance was created to which national banking systems had to adapt themselves.

Banking Factors

The technical complexity of electrotechnology (like that of organic chemistry) posed problems of evaluation for banking personnel accustomed to the relative simplicity of the industries of the middle third of the century. The engagement of financial establishments thus depended in part on their ability to obtain technicians capable of furnishing the necessary information. That, in turn, depended on the existence of qualified scientists and engineers able and willing to engage not only in industry but also in banking. The success of the electrotechnical complex depended as much on the combination of these factors as on the existence of abundant savings and of banks organized to tap them.

It would thus be useful to know the connections between the world of electrical technology and that of the financial decision-makers. The ideal would be to have dossiers of investment decisions or detailed reports of the discussions of the boards of directors. Unfortunately, banking history is very deficient in that respect; hence the relative fragility of the data on which to base an analysis.[4]

Few published works deal with the technical competence of bankers other than on financial questions. With respect to the situation in Europe, several cases can be examined:

1. An engineer sitting on the board of a bank linked to an industrial enterprise or, more often, representing one or more banks on the board of an enterprise. That was typical of railways, public works, mining, and metallurgy. Often "elected" at the end of a long career within the enterprise, these individuals brought competence and solid managerial qualities, but their experience and their age did not predispose them to innovation. But in the electrical industry that was necessary from the beginning.

2. The connections between scientists or technicians and financiers were close from the beginning in the electrical industry. The classic examples are German: those established in 1883 between Emil Rathenau and Carl Furstenberg,[5] and also those of Siemens with the Deutsche Bank.[6] Jeidels notes, "as in metallurgy, the banks wanted from the beginning to participate in the electrotechnical industry and to tie themselves as closely as possible to an enterprise in order to be its only bank, and to take care of all its business."[7] Thus the banker appeared in the electrical industry but, even more important, technicians joined the boards of banks, as in the relations between the Loewe firm and the bankers Bamberger and Born.[8] Also significant is the Swiss case of Walter Boveri, who married the daughter of a Basel banker.

On the other hand, neither in France nor the United Kingdom does one find similar examples. Before 1895 no representative of an important bank appeared on the board of an electrical company. Occasionally a third-rate bank might participate in a promising but risky enterprise requiring a very modest investment. These banks were never connected with the big ones, however. It was in no way a question of screening. The rare cases in which a polytechnician, for example, directed the distribution of electricity in a Paris company are not really exceptions, since such companies were not industrial in the strict sense.[9]

That situation changed slightly near the end of the century, after the international success of the industry was assured. Then the banks ventured out, but only in the limiting case of the French filial of General Electric, the French Thomson-Houston Company, or in 1898 the Compagnie Générale d'Electricité.

In England as well, the banks remained true to their traditions of prudence and caution. As in France, the awakening was tardy in comparison with Germany and America. The only study analyzing the participation of bankers in industry, that of Cassis, shows the very weak representation of industrialists on the boards of banks—7 percent at the end of the century—and the very small number of university graduates among the directors of banks.[10] The only exceptions are for the important bank shares in telegraph and cable companies, in which the British had a virtual monopoly.

It thus appears possible to affirm that the intervention of banks in the European electrotechnical industry depended in large part on the links between the former and the universities and the technical schools. Where those links were strong—Germany, Switzerland, even Italy—the active participation of the banks was notable from the first years of the industry. On the other hand, where tradition separated the two worlds an historic lag appeared in the financial and organizational roles of the banks.

3. Then there is the question of financial capacity. One of the classic methods of considering it is to measure investment in the electrical industry in relation to the capacity of the national financial market and the competition of other large national investment projects. Maurice Lévy-Leboyer used this method for the French case, but with so many assumptions that the results are difficult to utilize. Without going into hypothetical and imprecise calculations, it appears that the problem in France boils down essentially to a phenomenon of economic climate. The crisis of 1882 and the deep depression that France endured for almost fifteen years was certainly a factor. But the early years, those that saw the birth in the United States and Germany of the future great companies of the industry, corresponded in France to the rapid payment of the German indemnity and the great expense of the Freycinet plan for a "second" railway network, as catastrophic economically as it was politically useful. Together, the two projects absorbed 10 billion francs. In addition, if we consider the financial speculation that occurred and its effect on the steel industry, the amount of capital squandered was out of all proportion to the requirements of the electrical industry. On the other hand the guaranteed interest on the railway securities, the low risk of the state loans, the old connections of the banks with the steel industry, and above all the recollection of the remarkable synergy between the steel industry and the railways of previous decades reassured financial circles but made them reticent about the unknown electrical industry, especially after the unhappy experience of the Crédit Lyonnais with organic chemicals.[11]

In Germany the situation was quite different. If the France of 1871 felt the necessity to make up for the deficiencies that brought defeat, the same event confirmed for the audacious industrialists of the young empire their successes since the 1850s.

Victory brought about a feeling of optimism not without an effect on confidence in economic growth. The climate was thus favorable to innovation: renovation of the educational system and the introduction of new technologies. Add to this easily quantifiable financial factors: the French indemnity and the anticipated repayment of the Prussian war loans, some of which turned out to be unnecessary. The result was a great increase in bank resources. The five great banks of 1856, with a combined capital of 91 million marks, had become eight in 1872, with 160 million marks; in 1899 the Berlin banks alone were capitalized at more than a billion marks with 225 million in reserves, that is, more than six times the capital of all German banks a quarter century before.

A third major protagonist, the United Kingdom, did not lack capital, even if the actual amount is not known. Should we accept Cottrell's assertions on the atomization of the British banking system, its external orientation, and its refusal to take risks like the German banks?[12] But one should also consider the poor financial results of the first electric companies, the competition of the entrenched gaslight industry, and the legal consequences of "municipal socialism," which hindered large networks with their economies of scale.

Although this comparison of the financial strength of the three countries is not conclusive, the facts are significant. To the extent that share capital (including reserves) is the ultimate guarantee of banking risk, its evolution measures the capacity of financial institutions, at least over the medium term. Between 1870 and 1890 the German banks doubled or trebled their capital. The same did not occur in France, and apparently not in Great Britain. One should not neglect that fact.

Faced with the appearance of a new technology whose industrial consequences were uncertain, complex, and costly, the responses of the banks differed greatly. Only the German banks—and later the Swiss—reacted positively. The British and French were more cautious, hesitant, and reticent.

Banks and the Electrotechnical Industry, 1880–1898

France

It is useful to recall the unfavorable context: the war indemnity, possibly paid too rapidly; the Freycinet plan for railways, which flooded the market with unprofitable securities; speculation and the crisis of 1882; the unhappy experience of the Crédit Lyonnais with synthetic dyes; and the long, dramatic crisis of agriculture, which affected all sectors of the economy. The bankers who twenty years earlier had taken fright at the creative imagination of the Pereire brothers set out again on the route—or rut—of French and foreign state loans, the creation of mortgage banks, and the sale of railway bonds. As a result, savers were not only ill-prepared but kept in ignorance of the opportunities of the new industry. The financial press, including the market bulletins subsidized by the banks to tout their offerings, remained silent on electricity. Not even the international expositions modified the content of these publications, an obvious sign of the lack of interest of their banker-sponsors. In fact, the entire industry was the object of discredit. What dominated their pages were public issues, railway securities, gasworks, and mines, including those in the most distant regions unknown to investors, which allowed fantastic promises on doubtful conditions. Neither the business cycle nor the climate favored new domestic industries whose progress could be observed. Moreover, in this first period the level of investment did not recover that of the best years of the Second Empire.

The exposition of 1881 is a good indicator of the situation. The inventors mentioned in the press were almost all foreigners: Brush, Edison, Siemens, Swan. The French—Breguet and Gramme—occupied a modest place. The inventions that were the object of the most elegaic articles were not French: the electric tramway (Siemens) and the incandescent lamp (Edison and Swan). From that moment the banking background was important: Edison's invasion of Europe was supported by Morgan, whereas Siemens had bank connections (including the recently founded Deutsche Bank), which were consolidated in the wake of the international success of his telegraphic branch.

What little we know of the portfolios of the large French banks shows a total absence of any connection with electricity. Neither the Crédit Lyonnais, nor the Société Générale, Paribas, nor Rothschild owned any electric shares. The few companies producing and distributing electrical current were also poorly appreciated. Only the Cristofle firm, engaged in electrometallurgy, had a personal connection with the Comptoir d'Escompte through Olivier Christofle, a director of both. But that was a coincidence; none of the sixty-two other professional members of the bank's discount committee had either a close or a distant connection with electricity except Rostand, a shareholder of two stillborn companies. The large number of French exhibitors at the 1881 exposition were all small enterprises, some ephemeral, none with substantial bank support.

Systematic study of the minutes of the general assemblies of the large French banks for 1881 and 1882 does not reveal any interest in the new technology. At most they regarded it as a scientific novelty without an industrial future. And that at a time when American industrialists expected a great deal from the French market.

To be sure, the abstention was not total. In 1880 the Compagnie Générale pour l'Eclairage Electrique appeared, patronized by the Crédit Industriel et Commercial, the Comptoir d'Escompte, and some of their directors (Durrieu, Rostand, and De la Bouillerie), and even by a member of the *haute banque*, Lehideux. But in spite of the quality of its patents (Gramme and Zypernowski) and projects involving public lighting and industrial applications, the company never got off the ground. Although the intended capital was 8 million francs, the shares were never issued, and it isn't possible to determine why.[13]

It was the same with the Compagnie Générale d'Electricité, where one finds the same Durrieu of the Crédit Industriel et Commercial.[14] It was liquidated before issue of its shares, intended to raise 10 million francs. And the same was true with the Compagnie Lyonnaise de Constructions Electriques, which, in spite of owning the French rights to the Brush patents, was unable to obtain any bank support either locally or nationally.

The three cases cited here cannot be explained by the crisis of 1882. The enterprises appeared at a time when the Bourse was euphoric. Between 1878 and 1882 the combined capital of the twenty-five largest commercial banks in France increased by 53 percent (365 million francs), and during those same three years twenty-five new banks appeared with an effective capital of 364 million francs (1,075 million nominal).

Thus these fifty banks raised an effective capital of 729 million francs. The crisis itself was at first looked upon by qualified observers as having a positive effect, by curbing speculation and liquidating doubtful undertakings; credit would thus be abundant and cheaper for healthy firms. In a word, the crisis should have favored the spirit of enterprise.[15] Such was not the case. The abstention of banks in the first years of the electrical industry cannot be imputed to the market, to a lack of savings, or to the business cycle. In addition to the factors already mentioned plus France's weak urban dynamism and the inadequacy of its machine tool industry (especially after the loss of Mulhouse), the credibility of a national electrical industry was in question. On one hand the obstacles to public electric lighting in the large cities, including Paris, resembled the British case; on the other the industrialists of the capital goods industry— Schneider, Fives–Lille, and Cail—showed no interest in electrical technology. It is true that Schneider participated in a small electricity distributing company on the Left Bank in Paris, but without thought for a long time of developing a real industry. The situation is all the more surprising in view of Schneider's strong connections with the powerful Société Générale.

There remained a few modest enterprises, such as Sautter-Lemoine and Bréguet. The latter is symbolic of the comparative evolution of the French and German industry. Heir of a brilliant tradition of marine chronometry, Bréguet entered the telegraph industry concurrently with Siemens in Germany, but for internal reasons had only modest growth in France and none at all abroad. In 1883, confident of its technology, the company began simultaneously the construction of a central power station in Paris at the Palais Royal and a factory in Douai. The blindness of the Paris city government and the absence of any bank support led it to abandon the Paris works in 1885, and it converted the Douai factory to the production of naval armaments (as did Sautter-Lemoine).

The field was thus open to more dynamic and financially better supported foreign firms, but the results did not live up to the hopes. Bolstered by the brilliant success of his tramway at the 1881 exposition, Siemens in 1882 built a central power station in Passy, west of Paris, but abandoned it in 1886 in view of the attitude of the municipal authorities. Also in 1881 the International Thomson-Houston Company sought to build a tramway in Paris but could not find financial support either abroad or in France. Moreover, the hostility of the Compagnie des Omnibus de Paris, which had a legal monopoly of municipal transport, left little immediate hope for the tramway. Thomson-Houston therefore contented itself with protecting its patent rights by sharing them internationally, and built nothing in France.

Edison, also flushed with his success at the 1881 exposition, and supported by several American and French banks (Seligman; Speyer; and Drexel, Harjes from the United States), created three companies: Continental Edison (1 million francs), holding his European patents; the Société Industrielle et Manufacturière Edison (1.5 million francs), intended for the production of material under license; and the Société Electrique Edison (1 million francs), intended for the production of isolated small-scale systems. It is obvious that the initial capital, 3.5 million francs, was ridiculously inadequate. The future could be realized only with access to the French financial market, and thus with the support of French banks. Only three of them participated in the Edison enterprises, two of them quite modest. The most important, the Banque d'Escompte de Paris, was a relatively new one (1878) in search of promising business, but it was not well established. It was obliged to reduce its capital in 1891 and it disappeared in 1895 leaving a large debt.

One needn't suppose that Edison's French partners were trying to cheat him in order to understand their failure.[16] The hostility of the Paris gas and omnibus companies was certainly a factor. The tergiversations of the municipal authorities, which in 1888 divided the city into six small sectors for the distribution of electricity and authorized concessions for only twelve years, banished any prospect of long-term profits. The French bankers were not mistaken; from 1880 to 1895 only 96.5 million francs were invested in electric lighting and not one tramway was electrified.[17]

Studies of the market would not persuade the bankers to take a major risk, especially after the depression got underway. Alfred Neymarck, one of the most respected financial experts, advised his readers against risk:

> For purchases of shares one must choose companies with a *long history*, having produced beneficial results and about which regular information is available. . . . In no case should industrial shares constitute more than 5 percent [of one's portfolio].[18]

The rebuff of the electrical industry before 1895, and the abstention of the banks, cannot be explained by the crisis or the lack of financial means. Poorly prepared, poorly informed, little disposed to wait for profits over the medium term, the banks did not interest themselves in the new industry as long as other, more profitable and less risky alternatives existed. Once the depression set in, the fifteen-year absence of any industrial or urban dynamism only served to reinforce their attitude.

Germany

It isn't necessary to recall the financial situation of Germany. Certainly it had experienced a severe economic crisis in 1873/74, and the industrial difficulties didn't disappear entirely until the end of the decade; but the economic dynamism of the country was in no way stifled. What Leroy-Beaulieu had hoped for from the French crisis of 1882 actually took place in Germany after 1873/74. In 1881, at the time of the Paris exposition, Germany stood on the threshhold of a powerful and durable economic expansion: industrial mutation (mechanics, chemicals, electricity), reinforcement of traditional industries (coal and steel), demographic and urban expansion, rapid growth of foreign commerce, and, after the tariff of 1879, growth and modernization of agriculture. So many contrasts with the situation in France and the United Kingdom, and also Austria and Italy!

One result was a great expansion of banking capacity. Moreover, contrary to the French case, the German banks took little interest in foreign investment except in Russia and Austria-Hungary. When they did invest abroad, however, a part of it went into filials of German industries or to finance the export of capital goods, which almost never happened with French investments.

The banking expansion corresponds to the demand for capital by German industry, which the banks largely satisfied. According to Hoffmann fixed capital in German industry doubled in twenty-two years, from 75 billion marks in 1873/74 to 152 in 1895/96.[19] In this favorable context the bankers were disposed to participate in new industries inasmuch as their ties with the mechanical industries—Thyssen, Krupp, Börsig, as well as Loewe and Siemens—had produced such favorable results for a generation. It is thus not surprising that Carl Fürstenberg of the Berliner Handelsgesellschaft easily saw the logic and the future of the projects that Emil Rathenau proposed to him for his first enterprise, the Edison Gesellschaft für angewandte Electrizitäts, and gave him the financial support required by the American firm before turning over the patent rights. The bank continued to support Rathenau, in particular during the transformation of his firm into the Algemeine Elektrizitäts Gesellschaft (A.E.G.) in 1887 and his collaboration with other electrical manufacturers.

The ties between the Siemens family and the Deutsche Bank were even closer. Georg Siemens, along with Delbruck and Bamberger, was one of the founders of the bank and sat on its board for thirty years.[20] The absence of recent work on German banking (in terms of relations with industry) does not allow us to measure the extent of the financial engagement in electricity at its beginnings. Several questions need to be answered. What was the banks' effective participation in industrial capital? Under what conditions, to what extent, and at what price did the banks lend their support? One fact is certain, however: Given the secondary role of securities markets in the Germany of that time, it was interbank exchanges of securities that determined their prices, and consequently their placement with investors. Whatever the importance of the value of shares they finally held, their early engagement required the banks to hold stocks and bonds in their portfolios in order to support the price for their customers.

An example is provided by the intervention of the banks in the rationalization following the crisis of 1901. Such precocious and important engagements cannot be established solely on confidence. Another fundamental aspect resides in the technical collaboration between banks and industry and the creation of complex structures. The close personal relations between Rathenau and Siemens can be explained in part by the role of bank personnel. When the Deutsche Union Bank merged with the Deutsche Bank in 1876, Wilhelm Kopetzky, a manager of the Union Bank, assumed the same function in the Deutsche Bank. Kopetsky had collaborated with Rathenau even before the latter became interested in electricity. In similar fashion two other of Rathenau's collaborators, Felix Deutsch and Paul Mamroth, were financiers with long banking experience, in particular in the Jewish banking circles of Berlin to which Bamberger and Fürstenberg also belonged. Without pushing speculation too far, one can see an element of the rapprochement of Siemens with the Deutsche Edison Gesellschaft. By the same token, one can see the role of the Berlin bankers in the formation of Rathenau's group, which led to the Berliner Elektrizitäts Werke, thereby giving the young German industry a unique position in Europe.

The originality of the German case resides in the fact that the two groups mentioned, in spite of their early importance, were in no sense isolated. When the American Thomson-Houston firm implanted itself in Europe, it established its international base in France but created in Berlin an industrial ensemble in association with Ludwig Loewe, the great specialist in armaments and machine tools who had old ties with American industry. Thus was born the Union Elektrizitäts Gesellschaft (U.E.G.) in which the Berlin industrialist's two banks, the Darmstädter and the Dresdner, participated from the beginning (for unknown amounts). In the same way the conversion of the venerable cable factory of Felten et Guilleaume to electrotechnics was supported from the beginning not only by its regional banker, Salomon Oppenheim (Cologne), but also by the Berliner Handelsgesellschaft in the person of Carl Fürstenberg. Thus connections among electrical manufacturers were created through the intermediation of the banks. Those connections became important during the crisis at the beginning of the twentieth century, and they played a large role in the cartellization of the industry so remarked upon in the years preceding the Great War.[21]

To that list one can add the case of the engineer Schuckert who, after working for Edison in America, returned to Nuremberg to create his factory for dynamos with the support of the Schaafhausen'schen Bankverein. He also obtained support from the Bayerische Vereinbank through the intermediation of his industrial associates, Mann and Maffei, both of whom sat on the bank's board. In the same way enterprises such as Hélios, Lahmeyer, and Kummer obtained support from regional banks from the beginning. No doubt the political autonomy of the German states and the economic competition among them that ensued played an important role not found in overcentralized France or Great Britain. (But one should note the support of the Hungarian banks for the Ganz firm.)

Germany's tardy urbanization, in comparison with Great Britain and even in some respects with France, coupled with the rapid growth of the cities late in the century created favorable conditions. The gas and omnibus companies did not have such strong monopolistic positions as in the other countries. The urban expansion created a new, virgin field of action. Free to install lighting and transport facilities, the means were available.

It is also evident that the interpenetration of technical and banking groups; the success of the machine industry (in addition to that of Siemens with the telegraph); and the original contacts with the American industry, which permitted a better knowledge of the advance of the new technology across the Atlantic—all favored the banking support, which, in any case, the growth of the economy made easier than elsewhere in Europe.

The brilliant and precocious success of Rathenau was due only in part to the acquisition of the Edison patents for 350,000 marks. It is interesting only because there existed an industrial and public utility sector capable of absorbing a large production. The entry of Siemens in the capital of the Deutsche Edison Gesellschaft (D.E.G.) brought with it the support of the Deutsche Bank after that of the Berliner Handelsgesellschaft had permitted the easy placement of a first issue of 5 million marks and the simultaneous creation of the Grosse Berliner Strassenbahn (G.B.S.) and the Berliner Elektrizitäts Werke (B.E.W.). From the beginning the necessary (but not sufficient) conditions for economic success were present: D.E.G. and Siemens (electrotechnology); B.E.W. (production of current and lighting); G.B.S. (consumption of traction current). The last two were also obvious consumers of machinery and material.

Very soon, with the rupture between Rathenau and Siemens and the transformation of the D.E.G. into the A.E.G., the means of finance were seen to be inadequate. The success of the German industry rested on the concomitant development of electric manufacturers and their customers, on the one hand, and the control of the latter by the former, on the other. There was a double logic, industrial and financial, with the control of the markets guaranteeing the profitability of the industrial investments. Another essential element of that logic, previously absent from historical analysis, concerns the technical advantage flowing from control of the customers, the producing companies. The knowledge of the technical problems of production, maintenance, and expansion of networks of electricity, tramways, and electro-industry rebounded without delay, permitting the parent firm to resolve well in advance of the independents the inevitable problems, to have efficient maintenance, and to foresee future demands for material. That was the secret of success of General Electric in the United States and of the German groups. But the demand in capital and finance became such that even the associated banks could not supply them. On the other hand the placement of securities with the public was not satisfactory. The ups and downs of the business cycle could upset the process, as in the crises of 1890 and 1901 in Germany.

It was the crisis of 1890 that revealed the need after a decade of rapid growth. With the Allgemeine Lokal und Strassen-bahn A. G., the A.E.G., the Berliner Handelsgesellschaft, and the Deutsche Bank created the first "trust" or holding company, for electric tramways. In the decade that followed nine other "trusts" were created by the electrotechical companies and their associated banks. Thus control was assured at a minimal cost. Once established, the holding company issued securities that the banks sold, with the proceeds used to acquire control of existing enterprises and to provide working capital. The system was advantageous for the banks in several ways: It limited their financial engagement and protected their portfolios against the hazards of the business cycle, since the securities of the holding companies were less subject to price fluctuations than were those of industrial companies. Finally, the banks obtained firmer control over the latter to the extent that they issued fewer securities directly in the market.

Such a structure reduced risks but did not eliminate them altogether. It will not do for historians to extrapolate the profits of the successful enterprises only, for there were many failures and fusions. On occasion the failure of an industrial enterprise brought about the failure of the bank as well. For example, the bankruptcy of the Kummer group (A. G. für Elektrische Anlagen) in the crisis of 1901 resulted in the fall of the Kreditanstalt für Handel und Industrie of Dresden.

It is not easy to measure the importance of bank investments in the industry. Tables have been compiled to show, for example, the number of securities issues in which banks participated and the amount of capital raised, but these can be deceiving. For one reason, several banks usually participated in a given issue, and it cannot be determined in what proportions. Moreover, although the banks frequently had to hold some of the securities until they could be sold to the public, that was their ultimate goal, and without detailed balance sheet data it is impossible to say what proportion of the capital the banks actually owned.

Another way to seek to determine the role of banks in the industry is to look at their participation in the supervisory boards (*Aufsichtsräte*) of the companies. At the beginning of the century the Deutsche Bank had fourteen members of its board on the boards of electrical companies; the Berliner Handelsgesellschaft had ten, the Darmstädter eight, the Diskonto-Gesellschaft and the Dresdner six each, and the Schaafhausen'scher two.[22] (The Schaafhausen'scher had had more, but in 1898, after the failure of its attempt to merge the Schuckert group with the Loewe group, it seceded from the former.) A more detailed analysis for the period 1897–1902 shows an even greater penetration of the electrical industry by the banks. Without prolonging the analysis, it is clear that that engagement was not only important but that it represented the major sector of the banks' intervention. This finding modifies somewhat the traditional view of the banks' role in the metallurgical industries. For the six banks mentioned above, for the period between 1897 and 1902, we find 105 participations in the electrical industry and 164 in the field of transport (which included many tramway companies) as against 88 in machinery and shipbuilding and 74 in metallurgy and railway equipment.

This banking intervention poses the question of the role of financial power in the policies of the electrotechnical groups. It is not possible to resolve it within the limits of this discussion. The problem is certainly complex, and in the absence of internal analyses of the banks it can scarcely be broached. The known facts are contradictory. Thus in spite of the direct intervention of the Deutsche Bank the rapprochement of A.E.G. and Schuckert could not be realized. As mentioned, the Schaafhausen'scher in 1898 was unable to merge Schuckert with the Loewe group. Finally, after Schuckert was severely damaged by the crisis of 1901, the Deutsche Bank brought about its merger with Siemens in 1903. But in spite of all his efforts, and of other powerful financial interests in the two firms, Georg Siemens of the Deutsche Bank was unable to bring about his dream of merging the A.E.G. and Siemens. The operation with Schuckert was only a "second best."

More characteristic still was the fusion in 1904 of the A.E.G. and the U.E.G. (Union Elektrizitäts Gesellschaft—the Loewe group). Industrially it resembled the fusion of a dozen years earlier of Thomson-Houston and Edison in the United States. The consequences for the "cartelization" of the industry in Europe and Latin America were enormous.[23] Financially, it appears that the operation was brought about by Emil Rathenau. According to Felix Pinner, "Rathenau was not only independent of the great financial institutions, but he had created a situation in which they had to regroup around him and hasten to participate in his affairs."[24] Jeidels goes even further and asserts that the fusion between A.E.G. and U.E.G. that Rathenau brought about forced the bankers of the two groups to work together, rather than the reverse.[25]

Whatever the dominant sector, either banks or industry (but at that level it may be a false analysis of the historians), the cooperation of the two had remarkable positive effects. In spite of the crisis of 1901, the German electrotechnical industry was the equal of the American and the only one in Europe truly independent of it, financially and technically—apart from the small but interesting cases of Switzerland and Sweden, which are discussed later in the chapter.

German Banks and Industry: International Expansion

The growing requirements of investment, the necessity to amortize in a reasonable period equipment rendered obsolete by innovation, the search for the lowest cost of production by means of mass production, and the growing costs of research—all required control and domination of markets. The companies thus tried to duplicate abroad the combinations that had been successful within Germany: acquisition of concessions for public lighting, tramways, and eventually, when conditions required, the installation of production units.

The capacity of the national financial market, although in full expansion, was insufficient; moreover, the fragile balance of payments caused interest rates to rise. The partial failure of the financing of Rheinfelden and the recourse to Swiss and French banks demonstrated the necessity of an international structure for the accumulation of capital. The decision to apply the technique of holding companies was in the logic of the system; the choice of Brussels and Switzerland (Zurich and Basel) depended on political and legal considerations.

The first holding company, the Bank für Elektrische Unternehmungen (Elektrobank), was established in Zurich on July 25, 1895, by the A.E.G. and the Deutsche Bank in cooperation with the Crédit Suisse, and with the participation of other German, Swiss, and Italian banks.[26] (The Banca Commerciale Italiana and the Credito Italiano had recently been created by the same German interests in the Elektrobank, and were largely owned by them.)[27] Capitalized at 300 million francs (one half paid in), it was strictly controlled by the German interests (71 percent), which included the Berliner Handelsgesellschaft and several lesser banks. For obvious reasons the Crédit Suisse furnished the president—it was desirable on the French and even the English market that the bank appear Swiss—but the Germans had a majority of three-fifths on the board of directors.

In principle the function of the holding companies located abroad was identical to those in Germany. In practice the range of their operations was broader. The share capital of the Swiss (or Belgian) companies was not large, so as to minimize the investment of the industrial enterprise and its associated banks; the trust then issued bonds on the markets of Switzerland, France, Belgium, the United Kingdom, Italy—never in Germany. With the proceeds it acquired the securities of the subsidiaries created abroad by the principal firm (A.E.G. in the case above). In this way A.E.G. established filials in Italy,[28] Spain,[29] Austria-Hungary, Russia, and Latin America, which then ordered their capital equipment and material from it.

Financially, two mechanisms were in play:

1. The Electrobank, which held the securities of the filials in its portfolio, received interest and dividends from them. After paying the interest on its own bonds, the balance of its income was distributed as dividends to the owners of the "Swiss" holding company.

2. It sometimes happened (especially in Italy) that for reasons of local politics the A.E.G. sold material at prices below cost (i.e., dumping). In this case the German firm did not profit directly, but the correlative reduction in amortization charges in Italy increased the flow of funds to Switzerland. The Elektrobank could thus participate in increases in the capital of the A.E.G., thereby realizing a transfer of profits not subject to taxation and facilitating the control of its filials by the A.E.G.—a strategy that some financiers of the late twentieth century believe they invented.

Finally, the system permitted German intervention in politically sensitive regions, such as France and Latin America. It was in this connection that Brussels, an important international financial market (a position that Zurich had not yet obtained) with close ties to Paris, entered the picture. Important operating trusts were established there: IMATRA and especially SOFINA, inherited from the Loewe group.[30] By means of the latter, German firms participated in French industrial enterprises (Thomson-Houston) and in electricity and tramway networks: the Société Centrale pour l'Industrie Electrique and the Hydroelectrique de la Truyère, and also in Spain and Latin America. In these Belgian holdings the A.E.G. and the German banks were rarely represented directly, but indirectly through the Belgian banks they controlled—Banque de Bruxelles, Banque Internationale de Bruxelles, and the Banque Allard—and by SOFINA. Here again the Germans practiced market control, with A.E.G. obtaining a statutory part of all installations in France by the French Thomson-Houston Company, which had 60 percent of the French market.

Siemens, more directly engaged in filials in its own name in Austria-Hungary and Russia, did not develop a comparable international strategy. Nevertheless, in 1896 it created is own Swiss holding in Basel, the Société Suisse pour l'Industrie Electrique (S.S.I.E.), with a capital of 10 million francs (only 20 percent—i.e., 2 million francs—paid in). The banks associated with it were, apparently at least, less important: in Germany, Warschauer (a filial of the Darmstädter from 1904) and the Rheinische Kreditbank (connected with the Deutsche Bank from 1904); in Switzerland, the Basler Handelsbank, Dreyfus & Sohn, and Riggenbach (both Basel private banks), and D'Epine Fatio of Geneva, connected with the Union Financière of Geneva. An Austrian private bank, Rosenthal of Vienna, was also a partner in the S.S.I.E.

Great Britain, France, Switzerland, and Sweden

The German case has been presented in some detail, not because it was a model for others, but because it was unique in Europe.

The British electrotechnical industry on the eve of the Great War ranked third in the world, with 16 percent of the market. Although the price of gas, municipal socialism, and the archaic practice of hiring consulting engineers braked the growth of the industry domestically, why didn't the possibilities of the imperial market stimulate the initiative of the banks? To date no study of the British banking system has satisfactorily explained their absence.

Foreigners were the main beneficiaries of that unexplained absence. The British did not lack for patents in the beginning—for example, Swan, Parsons, Ferranti—but it was characteristic that the first large-scale Parsons turbine to be installed in a central generating station took place in Elberfeld, Germany, in 1900. In 1907 three of the four largest British manufacturers were foreign—Westinghouse, Thomson-Houston, and Siemens—and they also accounted for most of the exports. Imports also rose. Around 1900 about one-fourth of the generators and virtually all of the tramway and underground motors were imported. Also about 1900 the construction of large central stations got underway with imported material, especially from Germany (A.E.G.). The largest factories in the industry were those of Westinghouse (which acquired the Parsons patent in 1896) at Manchester and General Electric (British Thomson-Houston) at Rugby.

After 1900 the weight of the foreign companies was such as to limit the chances of growth of the local firms, and thus the engagement of the banks. In 1904 the British industry joined in the German-American cartels, such as that for incandescent bulbs. The only real industrial client other than the British Empire itself was France, and that was due to the presence of American and German filials within the country. Even that was for products of small added value, which was characteristic of British production in the industry.[31]

Thus the reserve of the bankers is clarified if not justified. It was only with the war, the difficulties of Westinghouse, and the dynamism of the Vickers group that a powerful national industry developed in Britain, and the banks had nothing to do with it. One might conclude, as did two British scholars, that "no amount of special pleading 'could acquit British manufacturers of electrical equipment of the charge of ineptitude and indifference and . . . organizational chaos'. . . ."[32]

The French situation scarcely differed and the bankers seem to have arrived like the carabineers in a comic opera. The firms that survived the crisis of 1882 were modestly capitalized and did not require bank assistance. Bréguet, with 3 million francs in 1882 and 4.35 million in 1914, and Gramme, whose assets never reached 2 million francs, did not have room for a financial partner. If they had, it would have been at the decision-making level of a third-rate bank or the regional director of a large one.

We reach the same conclusion for firms that apparently were more important. Lombard et Gérin owned the Ganz patent rights for France, had a capital of a million francs, and its major stockholder was Schneider-Creusot. The latter entered the electrotechnical industry at the beginning of the 1890s, as did Fives–Lille, but it would be erroneous to view that as an evolution of the type of U.E.G. of the Loewe group, even though they were leaders of the French mechanical industry. Electrical products never amounted to as much as 20 percent of their turnover, remaining a secondary activity not requiring modification of the financial relations of either firm. The Schneider case is slightly ambiguous, with a timid opening abroad; but also when the project for the electrification of the railways in association with Siemens was discussed, the latter was to be responsible for all of the electrical infrastructure, with the contracts going to its French filial, the Compagnie Générale d'Electricité de Creil.

The question of bank intervention arose in new terms during the upswing of the French economy in the 1890s when two more ambitious firms appeared: the Compagnie Française Thomson-Houston (CFTH, 1892) and the Compagnie Générale d'Electricité. The first, descended from filials of Edison and Thomson-Houston, quickly became the largest producer of electrical equipment in France, with 60 percent of the market. It established a structure of control over its customers quite different from the American and German models. In effect, it created or purchased electrical and transport companies without using a holding company; it simply kept in its portfolio enough shares (generally less than 20 percent) to guarantee orders for material. It was able to do that for lack of a real competitor in the domestic market and international agreements that controlled the French business of Westinghouse and A.E.G. In these conditions the great French banks were not asked for assistance. A few eminent bankers appeared on the board of the CFTH, but without an integration of interests. The American parentage sufficed to obtain financial support for Bourse operations; collaboration and a community of interests was neither necessary nor desired. Anyway, faithful to their tradition, the French banks preferred to participate in public utilities such as the distribution of electrical current and tramways. The true association was there, between the CFTH and the Marseillaise de Crédit in the Energie Electrique du Littoral Méditerranéen, or with Benard and Jarislowski in the Paris Metro.

The special case of the CFTH resulted from its hegemony of the French market and its international contacts. In the majority of cases the German example was at the origin of a banking movement. But whether from ignorance of the industry, excessive prudence, or more profitable opportunities abroad, as for Paribas and the Union Parisienne, the great French banks were not really interested in electrotechnics. The terrain was open for second-rate banks looking for dynamic business, but whose resources did not allow them to wait for long-term results and who could not afford large losses.

After 1901 the majority of Paris tram companies accumulated large deficits that resulted in the bankruptcies of their bankers, such as Genty, Henrotte et Muller, the Banque Française pour l'Afrique du Sud (tied to the former in the Compagnie Générale de Traction), and the Banque Internationale de Paris.[33] The attitude of the large banks with respect to three attempts at the beginning of the century was quite typical. The Banque Française pour le Commerce et l'Industrie, the Banque Mallet, and above all the Société Générale took part in the Société Westinghouse Française in 1901. It was less a question of supporting a French enterprise than of assisting the efforts of an American company in Europe. When the American firm suspended payments and went into receivership in October 1907 the issue of shares of the French filial (for 20 million francs) was dropped and the French bankers disappeared from the board. The bankers no doubt hoped to penetrate with Westinghouse, and without risk, a market that the success of the CFTH had shown to be quite profitable, but once again Offenbach's carabineers arrived too late. Contrary to expectations, the agreements of Westinghouse USA with General Electric and with A.E.G. and Siemens not only prohibited the filial from competing abroad, but also required it to face the competition of Westinghouse (Great Britain) in France without the reverse being possible. Arriving too late, not having a choice of partners, and unwilling to take long-term risks, the French banks could only retire from the fray.

The Banque Française pour l'Afrique du Sud took part in the origin of the Compagnie Générale d'Electricité (CGE), created in 1898 by Paul Azaria. The purpose of the CGE, which united a generating company, the Société Normande d'Electricité (Rouen), with several small manufacturing companies, was to create an ensemble along the lines of the CFTH. The beginnings were difficult, and before 1914 the CGE remained a medium-sized enterprise on the international scale. Nevertheless, thanks to bank support it managed to attract close to 60 million francs in various forms.[34] The support was complex. In the beginning the Swiss firm of Brown-Boveri supported Azaria. Although that didn't last, the CGE obtained the support of a provincial holding company with Swiss participation, the Omnium Lyonnais, and the Parisian antenna of Zurich finance, the Banque Suisse et Française (the future Crédit Commercial de France). The Société Générale joined the board as early as 1899, but for both it and the Banque Suisse et Française it was not a question of direct engagement. In any case, the capital grew little, from 15 million francs in 1898 to 25 million in 1913. Meanwhile the long-term debt rose from 10 million to 25 million nominal.

It is unnecessary to recite other more modest cases. They would only confirm the attitude of French banks with respect to industrial risks. The analysis defended by some historians with respect to the equilibrium of the French market or explaining the attitude of the banks and the industrialists by the limited scope of the domestic market doesn't wash.[35] It neglects (or ignores) the essential variables of a strategy including foreign markets from the beginning, the cohabitation of financiers, technicians, and merchants in the management of both banks and industry, and collaboration among otherwise competing banks. It was the combination of these factors that explains the German success and the British and French failures.

If confirmation of this is necessary it will be found in the brilliant case of the Swiss chemical industry, but also in the electrotechnical industry. In spite of limited capital and a minute market, Brown-Boveri had striking success. With the English engineer Charles Brown, inventor of the tri-phase motor, Walter Boveri obtained (in part by his marriage) support from banks in Basle and Zurich. The oldest member of the group, however, was the Alioth firm, which developed around two production units in Muenchestein (Basel) and Lyons (France) with the support of the Basler Handelsbank. Brown-Boveri, in Oerlikon, was supported from the beginning by the banks of German Switzerland: the Basler Handelsbank, Swiss Union Bank, Swiss Bank Corporation, and A. G. Leu. It was this support (the exact amount of which is unknown) that appeared as in Germany in the double liaison at the directors' level in both bank and industry, and in collaboration among the banks. The strategy resembled that of the northern neighbor, with industrial filials abroad: in Germany (Deutsche Brown-Boveri), Norway (A. K. Norsk BBC), France (Compagnie Electro-mecanique, which absorbed the French Westinghouse in 1917), Italy (Tecnomasio and Dinamo holding company). In Switzerland itself the group created with its bankers the Motor holding company, which in the 1930s brought together the great hydroelectric combines Aare-Tessin and Hinterrhein Kraftwerke.

As with all Swiss business, the financial details are not well known. Nevertheless, that structure permitted the BBC group to create a market on a European scale and to open, via its Milan holding company Dinamo, the South American market.[36] It was also the Swiss banks that defeated the attempt of A.E.G. to take over BBC by putting the future of Elektrobank in doubt. During the slowdown in hydroelectric investment around 1908 the Basler Handelsbank organized the fusion of Alioth and Brown-Boveri, reenforcing at the same time the position of the industrial group in France and that of the banks in the industry.

Apart from Brown-Boveri, the most remarkable case of an industry developing an independent technology in a country with such a small market is the Swedish firm Allmänna Svenska Elektriska AB (ASEA). ASEA's success in the beginning was due in large part to its patronage by Stockholms Enskilda Bank (SEB), which not only provided capital—at one point the bank owned a majority of the company's shares—but also sought out and even created markets for it. It accomplished the latter by founding new firms that ordered equipment from it. This was notably the case with the Norwegian as well as the Swedish hydroelectric industry, and also with the electrochemical and electrometallurgical industries. It is not without interest that the SEB frequently obtained funds for these operations from French banks, especially the Crédit Lyonnais and Paribas.[37] A final point of interest is that in 1987 ASEA and Brown-Boveri came together in a fifty-fifty merger.

Conclusions

The analysis of the relations between banks and the electrotechnical industry can only be provisional given the present state of research. Further advance will require the cooperation of bankers and industrialists in making available documents other than those that the law makes public. Progress made in this respect in the United States, Great Britain, and Germany has not been matched—far from it—in France and Switzerland. The shortage of researchers and their narrow, national horizons, frequently reenforced by the absence of a comparative spirit, are also major handicaps.

In spite of its lacunae, the present study does highlight certain features. The perceived disequilibrium, at first in favor of Germany and later Switzerland, is faithful to the reality. The German electrotechnical industry alone furnished more than half of European production. The Germans, Swiss, and their filials in Europe really had no competition except from the filials of the American General Electric Company, with whom the German groups were allied by means of financial participations, sharing of patents, preferred markets, and even, in Latin America, common operations. The explanations of such a disequilibrium, which no one at the beginning of the 1880s could have foreseen, are complex. The dynamism of the German and American growth played a definite role; we have mentioned the role of scientific education and the scales of social values. The existence of a modern capital goods industry also played a role, as did the ability to envisage the internationalization of markets. These two factors clearly favored Germany and Switzerland against France, but do not help explain the British case.

There remains the spirit of enterprise, both of the industrialists and the bankers, a taste for well-calculated risks and the capacity to adapt structures to the needs of finance, and for the bankers to work, not merely in relation to the industrialists, but to participate in common enterprises. The German and Swiss banks did this; not so the British and French, so cautious and secret. It must be emphasized that the syndicates so favored by French banks for certain operations were in no way comparable to industrial collaboration.

The fact that a similar structure appeared in both the German and Swiss chemical industries can only reenforce our hypothesis.

Finally, it remains that our analysis is above all a presentation of facts. The explanation may not satisfy other recent, more or less quantitative presentations. The contemporaries who were acquainted with the problem were not content with mere figures. Their analysis was often polemical, short, and simple; but it cannot be rejected out of hand, and the completion of the work remains to be done.

21

Iron and Steel

Ulrich Wengenroth

There were not so many true multinational iron and steel companies with plants and operations in more than one country before World War I, at least not if one has in view the manufacture of iron and steel proper. Production was still heavily centralized, and foreign subsidiaries of steel companies were mostly engaged in the acquisition of raw materials and kept under tight control by their headquarters. On the other side, quite a few steel companies, especially in Eastern Europe, were promoted by or with the help of foreign capital, including major European steel makers. It is difficult, however, to regard all these new companies as subsidiaries, since the Western parents did not seem to have had much influence on their policy—at least not in the long run. The clearest case of a multinational iron and steel company—manufacture of marketable products in several countries—was the rarest, and closely connected to superior know-how or patent rights. But since steel making was essentially a simple process, this kind of advanced technology usually took the company more into the field of engineering and armaments production, which is beyond the scope of the steel industry proper.[1]

The role of banks in these various cases was very important, but also very different. In a first approach one could say that banks exhibited most initiative when it came to erecting completely new steel plants in distant countries, not just across the border. In these cases we sometimes even find banks pushing firms to go abroad to run or help an enterprise in which the bank had an interest. While managers in iron and steel companies always had shown a keen interest to secure ample supplies of raw materials and were readily prepared to extend their operations across frontiers and "use" banks for this purpose, they were less enthusiastic about smelting, refining, and rolling units abroad.

To a certain extent this unwillingness to transfer the key processes of steel making to foreign countries can be explained by the development of the industry's economies of size and scale through the years prior to World War I. The growth of steel production in that period was remarkable, but so was the growth of the size of units of production. The size of a viable modern steel plant, benefitting from most known economies of scale, rose from between 30,000–50,000 tons output per annum in the 1870s to ten times as much in 1914, i.e., on average about 6 percent per year. Consequently, the *internal* growth of an individual steel plant had to be considerable to keep it abreast of technological and organizational progress.[2]

In the perspective of the industry's managers, to meet the growing demand for steel products did not necessarily require more units of production. Technological and organizational economies of size and scale acted as strong imperatives to concentrate operations as much as possible in one place. The most common investment behavior therefore was adding to existing equipment and resources to overcome or prevent bottlenecks in the flow of production, rather than duplicating plant, whether at home or abroad.

While new equipment and additional work force could usually be added to the existing works, this was not always true with resources of raw materials. The geological limitation to further expansion on the site was the most important incentive for steel companies' management to invest in distant regions and eventually to go abroad.[3]

Foreign Direct Investment in Raw Materials

The new steel processes that had been behind the enormous growth of production and rising economies of scale required iron ores different from those used until mid-nineteenth century and found in the vicinity of the works. Depending on the process employed, these new ores had either to be completely free from phosphorus or particularly rich in this mineral.[4] Both kinds were more abundant in the European periphery than in the old iron districts and therefore created a widespread effort among steel companies during the half century before World War I to get foreign ore fields under their control. Over this period, however, foreign direct investment (FDI) in raw materials became more and more difficult since it not only had to overcome financial and technological problems but also national jealousies and rising protectionism. This created very different conditions for the early wave of FDI in phosphorus-free ores in Spain and the later attempts to acquire the Swedish deposits of highly phosphorus ores.

A great number of the British steel companies together with a few continental makers had been lucky enough to secure ample supplies of suitable iron ores in the 1870s in Spain, before the protectionist tide set in. Never again was the acquisition of foreign raw materials made so easy by local and national authorities; and probably never again was it so cheap. Most of the ore was situated close to the northern coast of Spain and could be quarried and shipped with little expense. According to the historians of foreign investment in Spanish iron ore, capital expenditure in these undertakings was usually low and did not require much assistance by banks.[5] Even in the greatest investment scheme, the Orconera Iron Ore Company, with a capital stock of £600,000, most of which was used to build a railway, we could not find a single sentence on banks' assistance in the archival documentation of the three steel companies of the partnership consisting of Consett and Dowlais of Great Britain and Krupp of Germany. The Orconera, like most other Spanish mining companies, was floated and registered in London, and whatever banking services were involved in these operations remained in the obscurity of the City.[6]

Very different was the situation at the turn of the century, when the Swedish ores for basic steel making came in demand. It was mainly the German steel companies of the Ruhr district, closely affiliated to the great Berlin banks, that tried to get hold of concessions for iron ore in Sweden to guarantee the further supply for their expanding Thomas steel production. Although the joint efforts of German banks and steel companies in Sweden eventually ran aground, they are very instructive in showing the role and operations of German banks in the pursuit of the steel companies' foreign investment policies.

Swedish iron ore deposits were concentrated in two regions. In central Sweden the old mining district around Grängesberg had been developed by British capital in cooperation with local ironmasters.[7] During the 1870s the London bank of Bischoffsheim & Goldschmidt had brought together three railway companies and several small ironworks under the name of the Swedish Association. It was run by Swedish management and obviously unconnected to any steel producer. Like its predecessors, the association failed to thrive, and when its director, C. Weguelin, died, Ernest Cassel, who had come from Cologne to join Bischoffsheim & Goldschmidt, was left with the control over what seemed to be a very unattractive foreign investment. Since the iron ore could not be profitably processed in Sweden, an export company, the Grängesberg Grufveaktiebolag, was promoted in 1883 and merged with the Swedish Association in 1896 to form the Trafikaktiebolaget Grängesberg-Oxelösund (TGO). This was again under Swedish management with Cassel holding the majority of shares. Unlike its predecessors, TGO was profitable and had a bright outlook for the future in the advent of strong German demand for Swedish iron ore. As soon as the new company had established its reputation and quotations were rising, Cassel started to sell out his share in equity to the Swedish public—but not without striking the most spectacular deal in Swedish mining.

Development of the northern Swedish ore field was begun in a similar way by British capital unrelated to iron and steel producers. The mining proper was undertaken by the New Gellivara Company, which was transformed into a Swedish company, the Gellivara Aktiebolag, in 1882. All its capital was held by Sir Giles Loder, of London, who had made a fortune in Russian railways.[8] When Loder died in 1889 his heirs were almost immediately deprived of their mining concessions in a very debatable trial and the ore fields fell into the hands of the Swedish financier Gustav Emil Broms.

The shipping of the ore was to be undertaken by the Swedish and Norwegian Railway Company. But under pressure from central Swedish ironmasters, who were connected to the TGO, the Swedish government, in the same year 1889, closed the railway, drove the company into bankruptcy, and took the line and rolling stock over for little more than a quarter of the sum invested. The major damage in the event was suffered by the Amsterdamsche Bank and its partners. After the Swedish banks had refused to cooperate with the British company, the Dutch had issued and subscribed bonds for the railway with a nominal value of £1.5 million and a rate of 34 percent under par. However, the risk was obviously higher than the margin.[9]

The striking difference between Cassel's successful TGO and the unlucky British in northern Sweden was that Cassel cooperated closely with Swedish banks and ironmasters and thus managed to win acceptance for his company as a Swedish enterprise, while the British investors in the North were always seen as intruders who had come to strip the country of its mineral wealth.

This lesson was not lost on the German steel companies and their banks. When August Thyssen in 1902 went to Stockholm and the northern provinces to investigate the possibilities of acquiring Swedish mines for his steel works, his banker in the Deutsche Bank immediately started a major intelligence operation on the financial and institutional situation of Swedish mining. At no stage in the following negotiations did the Deutsche Bank pursue its own policy different from or parallel to that of Thyssen. It saw its own interest, not in some attractive loans on the way, but only in what was considered to be a healthy expansion and strengthening of one of its major clients. Thyssen was advised to get into contact with Wallenberg of the Stockholms Enskilda Bank, with whom the Berlin headquarters of the Deutsche Bank said they had "very good" relations.[10] The bank's director in Paris had to keep an eye on the French capital market and investigate the nature of the relationship between Broms and the Banque de Paris et des Pays-Bas, which had negotiated a bond-loan of several million crowns for the northern mines.[11] The Hamburg branch of the Deutsche Bank was set on Possehl, the merchant who had obtained the exclusive rights for Broms' export trade in exchange for extensive loans.[12] These loans, the so-called winter advance, were in fact the working capital for the mines, which could ship their ores only during a few months in summer. A similar bargain had been struck by the Norddeutsche Bank of Hamburg, a subsidiary of the Berlin-based Diskonto-Gesellschaft, on behalf of a group of German steel companies that were closely tied to this bank.[13]

The Hamburg branch of the Deutsche Bank was particularly lucky since Possehl soon turned up and asked for assistance in negotiating a 20 million to 25 million mark loan for Broms' two companies, the AB Gellivare Malmfält (AGM) and the Luossavaara-Kiirunavaara AB (LKAB). This, however, made him vulnerable to the Deutsche Bank's intelligence operation, and every bit of information was squeezed out of him as long as he could be kept in the air.[14] On the basis of Possehl's valuable information on the accumulated debts of Broms and the policy of the Swedish banks and government, Thyssen could develop his own strategy.[15] Since only a Swedish company would be tolerated, Swedish partners were essential. Thyssen, as suggested earlier by the Deutsche Bank, now got in contact with Wallenberg of Stockholms Enskilda Bank, who was the greatest creditor of Broms and had both a great interest in the reorganization of AGM and LKAB and intimate knowledge of the Swedish government's position vis-à-vis the northern mines.

This plan to strike the deal alone with Wallenberg soon ran aground, however, when Broms, in an effort to circumvent his Swedish creditors, offered his shares via the Berlin merchant bank of Aron Hirsch to the Diskonto-Gesellschaft.[16] Until then the policy of the Diskonto-Gesellschaft had not been to strive for ownership but rather to pool the demand of its clients and guarantee the sale of the ore at fixed prices over a long period of time. The Deutsche Bank now was in an awkward situation. Although it was still convinced that the information on the Swedish banks and the policy of the Diskonto-Gesellschaft was poorer than its own, it could not be ruled out that the Diskonto-Gesellschaft would manage to float a Swedish holding for the shares. In this case Thyssen could no longer afford to rely on the Deutsche Bank and had to change sides to guarantee the further supply of his works.[17]

The Diskonto group on the other side did not feel too confident that the proposed deal was a bona fide transaction and could eventually withstand a Swedish claim in court. Earlier, in 1902, Wallenberg had already wrecked the sale of the majority of AGM shares to the United States Steel Corporation via their agent S. W. Clark-Harrison, since most of these shares were kept by the Swedish banks, among them Wallenberg's Stockholms Enskilda Bank, as securities against direct loans.[18] Therefore, on the initiative of Thyssen, the two rival German groups joined forces. In a contract they agreed to sidestep Hirsch and instead cooperate with Wallenberg to work

out a scheme for a form of German governance over the mines that would be accepted
by the Swedish authorities.[19]

In the end the great scheme to bring the richest European iron ore resources under
German control failed. It was not the allied Stockholms Enskilda Bank, Deutsche
Bank, and Diskonto-Gesellschaft with their steel companies, but Cassel and Fraenckel
of the Stockholms Handelsbank who managed to acquire Broms' shares for the TGO,
thus achieving what had been Thyssen's first plan, the amalgamation of the two
greatest ore producers in Sweden.

Less ambitious projects were more successful. In 1897 the Viennese Rothschild
bought the Koskullskulle mines in the vicinity of AGM and for their Witkowitz steel
works in Bohemia. A Swedish company, the Bergverks AB Freja, was floated in
Malmö and was officially run by Franz Kockum, of the Malmö firm of Kockums
Mekaniska Verkstädter, who was a personal friend of Emil Holz, then director of the
Witkowitz works.[20] Since Freja, like the other northern mines, had a very short
shipping season it had to rely heavily on annual direct loans for working capital, the
"winter advance" Possehl had granted to Broms. These loans invariably and regularly
came from Rothschild via Witkowitz.

After their failure in Sweden the German steel companies turned to France;
although less documentation on the role of banks in these more successful ventures
survived, we can find similar patterns in the little we have.[21] In the case of Thyssen and
the Deutsche Bank it was again information and introduction to influential persons of
the host country's financial and political network. These services were not limited to
joint operations. When Thyssen met great difficulties over the acquisition of Lorraine
ore fields in 1903 the Deutsche Bank, although it obviously had nothing to do with the
financing of his newly floated French enterprise, introduced him to Rouvier, French
Minister of Finance and founder of the Banque Française pour le Commerce et l'Industrie (Banque Rouvier).[22] The Banque Rouvier was from the beginning designed to be a
kind of tacit intermediary for German capital in France, and Rouvier himself was
always amenable to support Franco-German industrial and financial cooperation
against a hostile and suspicious environment.[23]

This vital exchange of information and introductions naturally went both ways.
Thyssen always kept the bank well informed about his observations in France and
Sweden and sent very frank characterizations of bankers and industrialists he met.
Apart from this the only return the Deutsche Bank consistently and firmly asked for its
immaterial services was to be made bank of payment (*Zahlstelle*) for each of Thyssen's
foreign undertakings.

Foreign Direct Investment in Russian Steel Making

Foreign direct investment in Russian steel making took place in a political and economic environment very different from that of Sweden or France in the case of iron ore. In
1877 the Russian government had embarked on a new policy to support the erection of
a modern domestic steel industry that would be able to meet the nation's demand.
Protection was granted both through high tariffs and premiums on domestic products.
For steel rails, which were soon to become the most important product of this new
industry, they together amounted to the equivalent of 80 percent of production costs in

the leading West European works. To further minimize risks for potential investors the Russian government offered extensive orders for the first years of production at very generous prices.[24] Parallel to this protective legislation the state sold its possessions in mining and iron smelting in the western provinces to private entrepreneurs.[25]

All this encouragement to invest in Russian steel making came in the middle of the deepest recession the European iron and steel industry had to suffer prior to 1914. A number of plants, especially of the most recent Bessemer steel works, had been made redundant, not because of declining demand but rather as a result of newly won "economies of speed" that had multiplied the capacity of a given plant with only little capital expenditure.[26] Since there were few chances for continental steel makers that additional markets could be opened in the near future—the Russian tariff was only one of several discouraging events—they had to find new employment for their excess plants. One possibility was to dismantle a plant and ship it to a new place where its output would find a guaranteed market. Some German, Belgian, and French steel companies, which had been supplying the Russian market with rails and beams in the past, followed this policy and went to Russia to substitute direct investment for trade.

While there is no doubt about the motives of the eastern German steelmasters in Upper Silesia, who shifted the finishing stages of production a few miles across the border to overcome the new tariff with as few changes in the fabric of their enterprise as possible, the situation with French and Belgian investment is less clear.[27]

The first ones to be successful in setting up a complete Bessemer steel works in Russia after the 1877 tariff were the Belgian bankers Ernest Nagelmackers and Barthold Suermondt, both closely associated with the Belgian steel companies Angleur and Cockerill respectively.[28] For this purpose, however, they "used" neither of these two but rather the Rheinische Stahlwerke of Duisburg in western Germany, in which they held the majority of share capital. Whether they were joined by the Russian prince Galitzin, who was also on the board of the Rheinische Stahlwerke and had large possessions in Russian iron making, cannot be established.

The Rheinische Stahlwerke had been floated as a French company in Paris in 1870 and was managed by Georges Pastor, a Belgian financier and steel master, son of the director general of the Cockerill steel works.[29] Only after the Franco-Prussian War of 1870/71 was the company registered under Prussian law. The steel works were run like a foreign subsidiary of the two Belgian companies, especially of Angleur, in the first years, although they had no formal ownership.[30]

Successful application of the new "economies of speed" in the early 1870s increased the productive capacity of each of the company's two Bessemer plants from 20,000 tons to 50,000 tons.[31] Because demand did not keep pace with this rationalization, one of the two plants was shut down. At the same time the company suffered heavily from large long-term pig iron contracts at boom prices and had to rely increasingly on securities given by its Belgian owners to keep the credit lines with the German banks.[32]

In this situation French and Belgian bankers, among them the owners of the Rheinische Stahlwerke, were approached by Russian landlords and industrialists for capital to float new steel companies in Russia in view of the imminent protectionist legislation. Suermondt brought the two most promising schemes, a plant in the Dombrova and the projected Praga steel works of the already successful Lilpop, Rau, and Löwenstein group in Warsaw, before the management of the Rheinische Stahlwerke for evaluation.[33] A detailed cost calculation on the basis of the company's own practice for both locations came out in favor of the location near Warsaw.[34] Suermondt and Nagelmackers now opted for Praga and joined Lilpop, Rau, and Löwenstein in floating the Towarzystwo Warszawskiej Fabryki Stali.

Whether this decision was based purely on an impartial cost assessment remains doubtful since Wilhelm Rau of the Polish company, himself of German origin and a former assistant to John Cockerill, had married his daughter to Barthold Suermondt's son Robert, who held 4.5 percent of Lilpop, Rau and Löwenstein shares.[35] Wilhelm Rau was made president of the new steel company with Barthold Suermondt as a member of the board and their sons Mikolaj and Robert as substitutes.[36] Director-general was Georg Pastor, who had come from Angleur via the Rheinische Stahlwerke.[37] The staff of the Rheinische Stahlwerke had to dismantle the idle plant, reconstruct it in Warsaw, and put it back to work according to Duisburg standards.[38]

For their redundant plant the Rheinische Stahlwerke received shares of the Russian company at 120,000 rubles nominal value (total capital 1.5 million rubles), which eventually paid an average dividend of 18.9 percent.[39] Pastor held privately another 3.3 percent, the Rau family 11.7 percent, and the Suermondts 2 percent, while the Lilpop, Rau and Löwenstein Company and its subsidiary the Towarzystwo Starachowickich Zakladów Górniczych had more than 50 percent.[40]

The Praga steel works were started like a foreign subsidiary of the Rheinische Stahlwerke, a meticulous copy of which they were.[41] The Belgian financiers had effectively created a chain in multinationalizing the companies under their influence for a limited period of time to start a new enterprise in another country, which then gave better prospects for investment in iron and steel: from Angleur and Cockerill to the Rheinische Stahlwerke, and from there to Praga. The third step in this direction brought the two ends of the chain together. Against the vote of the German directors of the Rheinische Stahlwerke, who rather wanted to invest in the extension of the Duisburg works, the predominantly Belgian board in 1886 decided to join Cockerill and float the Société Métallurgique du Midi de la Russie, the so-called Dniépro-vienne.[42]

Cockerill's management had become interested in Russia when looking for new sources of iron ore.[43] At Krivoi Rog, in southern Russia, they found excellent high-grade ore the concession for which they secured in 1885. Their plans to erect a huge steel works on the spot and a shipyard on the Black Sea, however, met strong resistance from Russian ironmasters, who were still suffering from the depression of the early 1880s and had started a campaign against this "invasion by foreign industry."[44] The new company at Krivoi Rog had to be or at least to look like a Russian enterprise to neutralize opposition. On the other side the Praga steel works were about to lose a major part of its market because of a new inner Russian regional protectionism.[45]

The Belgian group now could kill two birds with one stone. In moving the old but by no means outdated German plant a second time over a new tariff barrier, they could float the Dniéprovienne as a Russian company in which at first sight Praga held 50 percent and Cockerill only 16 percent. The remaining 34 percent of Cockerill's half had been distributed among friends and directors.[46] On the other side the Rheinische Stahlwerke alone had another 8 percent via Praga, not including the direct participation of its Belgian directors.[47] In the document on the foundation of the new company we find the two members of the Rheinische Stahlwerke board, Georg Pastor and Robert

Suermondt, the latter representing the Warsaw steel company and the first acting on behalf of the Belgian group.[48] But in spite of the German management's hostility to this new Russian investment, once again it is difficult to maintain that the Rheinische Stahlwerke was "used" to its disadvantage. The Dniéprovienne was at least as profitable as its predecessor in Warsaw and frequently paid dividends as high as 40 percent of par value.[49]

The key to the successful operations of the Dniéprovienne was seen in its excellent technical management and well-conceived plant. The steel and rail production had come together with the foremen from Praga and was an offspring of Rheinische Stahlwerke experience. Blast furnaces and equipment for special products were installed and set in operation by Cockerill's engineers, most of whom left Russia as soon as the plant functioned smoothly.[50]

So successful was the direct investment of the Cockerill group in Russia that soon it was emulated by other Belgian groups. One of the best disciples was the Société Générale de Belgique. Following the well-tested pattern the bank took "its" steel company, Angleur, which had collaborated with Cockerill in getting the Rheinische Stahlwerke going, to promote the Société Métallurgique Russo-Belge in 1896—allegedly the only company to undercut the Dniéprovienne's production costs in one year.[51]

While the Belgian investors, advised by the management of their German steel works, had gone to Warsaw in 1877, the French at the same time opted for the other alternative, the Dombrova, where they started their business in a similar way.[52] Huta-Bankova had been an ironworks and mining complex of the tsarist government. It was sold to the large landed proprietors Riesenkampf and Plemiannikov, vice-director of the Russian Land Bank, who paid 25 percent of the purchase price. The rest was guaranteed by the French Banque Franco-Italienne through its director, E. Pasteur.[53] To exploit the coal mines the bank floated the Société Anonyme Française et Italienne des Houillères de Dombrova, of which it kept 75 percent of equity. Of the remaining 25 percent an unspecified share fell to Eugène Verdié and Gabriel Chanove, while Riesenkampf and Plemiannikov held the iron ore mines and the ironworks.[54]

Since the plant of the old Huta-Bankova ironworks was hopelessly outdated a new iron and steel works had to be built to make use of the Dombrova's coal and benefit from the government's premiums and long-term contracts for domestically produced rails. For this purpose Plemiannikov and Verdié undertook to float a second company with the assistance of a well-established French steel producer. This was the Société Anonyme des Forges et des Aciéries de Firminy, run by Eugène's father, François Felix Verdié.[55]

Firminy had difficulties similar to those of the Rheinische Stahlwerke. The domestic demand for rails had been declining since 1875 and with its location in central France Firminy was in a very unfavorable position for both imports of raw materials and exports of finished goods.[56] It was no sacrifice then to offer part of the company's redundant equipment for the production of rails to the Huta-Bankova.[57]

In the summer of 1877 the Crédit Lyonnais floated the Société Anonyme des Forges et Aciéries de Huta-Bankova (Etablissement Plemiannikov et Verdié) through its branches in Paris, Lyons, St. Etienne, and St. Petersburg with a capital stock of 6.3 million francs in 12,600 shares of 500 francs each. As proprietors of the premises of the Huta-Bankova, Riesenkampf and Plemiannikov received jointly 12,000 registered vendor shares for ceding the works and the iron ore mines for thirty-six years, and of the remaining 600—these were bearer shares paid in cash—35 percent went to representatives of Firminy. Only the paid-in shares were to be amortized and then replaced by rights to second dividends.[58]

Control, too, was firmly with the French group and Firminy. The articles of association, worked out by F. F. Verdié, stipulated that ten shares carried one vote and fifty votes was the maximum for a single shareholder. Since Riesenkampf and Plemiannikov owned their registered shares jointly they had fifty votes as opposed to sixty votes of the French group.[59] On the first board of directors the French had six out of nine members, among them Gabriel Chanove, Emile Crozet, and Eugène Verdié of the Banque Franco-Italienne's Dombrova coal company, and F. F. Verdié of Firminy as president.[60] Investment and working capital for the Huta-Bankova steel works was raised in 1880 through bond issues in Lyons with a nominal value of 4 million francs issued 20 percent and 30 percent under par.[61]

In 1877 it still looked as if Huta-Bankova was a fully controlled subsidiary of Firminy, with F. F. Verdié president of both companies' boards. Three years later it had become evident that Firminy's multinationalization had little to do with the firm and its further growth. In the meantime Jean Bonnardel had become president of the Huta-Bankova after Verdié's death. His only contact with Firminy apart from the Russian enterprise had been an abortive attempt to amalgamate his own company, the Société de l'Horme, with Firminy, with the support of the Crédit Lyonnais.[62]

Bonnardel, whose empire rested on river navigation in France, had been investing in Russia since 1871, and now made the Huta-Bankova the starting point of a whole group of Russian metallurgical enterprises in whose greatest company, the Forges et Aciéries du Donetz, we find again Eugène Verdié, Gabriel Chanove, and Edouard Pasteur of the Franco-Italienne on the board. The third major steel company of the Bonnardel group, the Société des Forges et Aciéries de la Kama, was directed by the president of the Forges de l'Horme.[63] This was French direct investment in the Russian steel industry but certainly not subsidiaries of de l'Horme or Firminy, the latter of which in 1880 had already started to sell its Russian shares.[64]

In these joint ventures of steel companies and banks, as in those of the Société Générale and the Aciéries de la Marine, or the Banque Internationale de Paris and Chatillon-Commentry, or Paribas and Schneider,[65] the bank was always the dominating partner—unlike the direct investment in raw materials and the undertakings of the Upper Silesian companies across the border in Polish Russia.[66]

Foreign direct investment in Russian steel making by French and Belgian capital was largely an example of how steel companies could be "used" by banks and financial groups. The transitory multinationalization of a well-established steel company was probably the safest way to start an industrial investment abroad and at the same time win the confidence of the future bondholders at home who had to supply capital. French authors like Girault, Griault, and Silly argue that the French steel industry, when it had exhausted the potential of the home market, transferred capital and technological and organizational know-how to Russia where it could find a field large enough to allow for further growth.[67] They cannot, however, show permanent organizational structures embracing both the French and Russian steel works of one group other than those via the banks. There was no multinational steel company visible that could be defined in administrative terms, and the only particular interest the Western parent company had in the new Russian undertakings was to get rid of its redundant machinery on favorable terms.

At the turn of the century, finally, when French banking syndicates and Belgian omniums had been formed to extend and coordinate the Russian possessions, there is no more direct influence of any West European steel producer discernible.[68] West European banks and capital, however, played a decisive role in the organization and domination of the Russian steel industry. The Russian steel cartel (Prodameta) was initiated by the Société Générale and largely run from Paris, but it was exclusively a cartel for the Russian market and had no links to any international agreements. In fact, the French- and Belgian-dominated steel companies did behave like national Russian companies although they were financed internationally. With their monopolistic policies the Western banks were defending their foreign direct investment on a single national market and not a multinational network of companies. Their eastern and western belongings and interests in steel were treated quite independently. While the banks had clearly become multinational in the process of their Russian operations, the steel companies among their clientele did so for a very limited time only and without the intention to stay abroad. The international dimension of Russian steel making was one of finance, not of industrial enterprise.

Multinational Manufacturing

Probably the least disputed example of a multinational iron and steel producer before World War I was the Mannesmann concern with tube works in Germany, Austria-Hungary, Great Britain, and Italy. The company was exploiting the patent rights of the brothers Mannesmann for the manufacture of weldless tubes, and instead of selling licenses had created subsidiaries in the major European markets. The Mannesmann brothers were supported by the Cologne manufacturer Eugen Langen and Werner and Friedrich von Siemens, who provided most of the funds for floating the Mannesmann tube companies in Komotau (Bohemia) in 1889, and Landore (South Wales) in 1888, where the Siemens steel works of Sir William Siemens had just been wound up. The Mannesmann brothers in each case received 50 percent of share capital for their patent rights and the technological expertise to get the plants working properly.[69] This, however, they failed to do. It took them much more time and money than expected to transform their experimental apparatus into a sturdy rolling mill. Capital requirements grew constantly with only great heaps of scrap being turned out.

In 1890, eventually, the Siemens brothers felt unable to guarantee personally more loans and approached their cousin Georg, director of the Deutsche Bank, to help them with the reorganization of the German and Austrian Mannesmann companies: They wanted to concentrate on Landore, which at that time seemed to be closest to profitable operations.[70] Eugen Langen, on the other side, was negotiating with the Schaafhausen'scher Bankverein of Cologne and the Diskonto-Gesellschaft, both of which had a large clientele among the Ruhr steel companies and much more experience than did the Deutsche Bank in financing and organizing metallurgical enterprise. The Deutsche Bank, however, which had granted most of the loans before and tried to win more influence among West German steel producers, refused to cooperate with its main competitors.[71]

In its decision to participate in the new tube company, the management of the Deutsche Bank relied on the favorable account Werner von Siemens had given on the technological and commercial potential of the Mannesmann inventions. Werner von Siemens was certainly one of the best authorities on production technology in the 1890s but he was not an ironmaster. His cousin Georg had to subscribe privately and, in proportion to his means, extensively to the new shares to win the confidence of his board.[72]

In June 1890 the Deutsch-Österreichische Mannesmannöhren-Werke, Berlin, was launched by the Deutsche Bank with a capital stock of 35 million marks. Of these, 17.5 million marks were vendor shares given to the Mannesmann family for patent rights, licenses, and equipment; 5.5 million was given to the owners of the Austrian and the German works; 12 million was paid in at 120 percent by a syndicate under the leadership of the Deutsche Bank.[73]

Despite this fresh capital and Werner von Siemens' optimism, the manifold technological problems could still not be overcome. In 1892 both the bank's board and Werner von Siemens at the board of Mannesmann had lost their patience with the expensive but fruitless test runs. The company's deficit was at 1.65 millions and 5.17 millions had been additionally written off (*Sonderabschreibungen*).[74] The brothers Mannesmann were pushed out of the company in the following year and, after having been taken to court, had to return 10 millions in vendor shares for which they received 2 million marks in bonds.[75] The Deutsche Bank, having granted loans in 1888/89 and supplied fresh capital in 1890, in 1893 found itself with a multinational tube manufacturer on its hands; and it was resolved to run it on its own as an industrial enterprise. Looking back to these years Max Steinthal, one of the bank's managers and director of Mannesmann, said in 1898: "Hitherto we bank directors had kept to those kinds of business we knew all about; now we take up things we still have to familiarize ourselves with."[76]

Tellingly, the first step in the "bank-only" era was to move the company's headquarters from Berlin to Düsseldorf, closer to the works. Two well-proven rolling mill experts were hired, a lot of staff discharged, and a new organizational structure created for the German and Austrian works. When in 1899 the Landore company, which had been kept separate from the Deutsch-Österreichische, went into liquidation, the Düsseldorf firm felt already confident enough to purchase the plant and reorganize it as the British Mannesmann Tube Company Ltd. Like the Bohemian Komotau works, it was now a full subsidiary of the Deutsch-Österreichische.[77] In the same year the first German subsidary, the Deutsche Röhrenwerke AG in Dusseldorf, started production of welded tubes to cover the whole range of steel tubes and counter other tube manufacturers' discriminatory sales policies.[78]

So convinced was the bank of the future commercial success of its involuntary acquisition that in 1903 it even refused to sell the company to Thyssen, its major client in the steel industry.[79] After compensating for previous losses of 12.9 million marks out of undivided profits, the first dividend of 5 percent could be paid in 1906. At the end of that year the Deutsche Bank had little difficulty in selling Mannesmann shares at 175 percent and issuing bonds for over 3.2 million marks at 4.5 percent interest.[80] With dividends rising to 12 percent in 1907 the lean years were well behind. In 1910, eventually, the long-standing credit with the Deutsche Bank and the Berliner Handelsgesellschaft was relieved by the issue of new shares.[81]

External consolidation followed internal. In 1905 the company purchased the majority of shares of the Röhrenwerke AG Schönbrunn in Austrian Silesia and made it a 100 percent subsidary within three years.[82] Like the Deutsche Röhrenwerke in Germany, Schönbrunn complemented the range of products of the Komotau works with conventional tubes and gave Mannesmann a commanding position in the whole southeastern European tube market. On the eve of the Great War the Austrian works alone accounted for about a third of the Mannesmann turnover. In 1908 the German and Austrian groups were formally separated and reconstituted as Mannesmannröhrenwerke AG, Dusseldorf and Österreichische Mannesmannröhrenwerke m.b.H., Vienna. To all appearances the Wiener Bankverein, in which the Deutsche Bank had an interest since 1874, played a vital role in this reorganization.

Only one year after the acquisition of the Schönbrunn works Mannesmann went to Italy and there promoted, together with the Societá Metallurgica Italiana of Livorno, the Societá Tubi Mannesmann in Dalmine.[83] The Metallurgica Italiana was clearly the junior partner, with only 24 percent of the 5 million lire capital stock. One percent was held by the Mannesmann representative of Genoa, and the remainder by the Deutsch-Österreichische Mannesmannröhren-Werke. Steinthal of the Deutsche Bank was again president of the board, and with him were Alessandro Centurini of the Italian partner, Hugo Markus of the Wiener Bankverein, and Giuseppe Toeplitz of the Banca Commerciale Italiana. The Banca Commerciale had been floated in 1894 with the help of the Deutsche Bank, and was taken on the board with a view to future credits once the new branch had been established on the Italian market.

Operations in Dalmine began in 1909 and caused heavy losses in the first years, when only sales of German and Austrian manufactured tubes was profitable. The Metallurgica Italiana soon lost confidence in the joint enterprise and did not participate in the same year's increase of capital to 7.5 million lire, which was then wholly subscribed by the Deutsch-Österreichische. In 1911 the representative of the Metallurgica Italiana finally left the board of the Societá Tubi and most likely returned the Italian partner's shares. Despite the liabilities of the Societá Tubi against the parent company, these had further increased to 3.5 millions by 1911 before a 4 percent dividend could be paid.[84]

In 1913, as in 1909 before, the parent company's claims were converted into share capital. For this purpose the capital stock of the Societá Tubi was first reduced from 7.5 million to 6 million lire and then increased to 10 million lire with all new shares being taken by the Mannesmannröhren-Werke. Only now, as a profit making company on a sound footing, did the Societá Tubi negotiate a credit of up to 2 million lire with the Banca Commerciale.[85]

If Mannesmann was a typical multinational enterprise almost from its beginnings, it was a very untypical steel company since it did not produce steel. The Mannesmann works were rolling mills for the manufacture of tubes and bought their steel on the market. The main assets of the company were the Mannesmann patents, and they were exploited first through horizontal expansion across borders. As long as Mannesmann did not produce its own steel it did not have to take into account the economies of size and scale in steel making, and the least common multiple for its plant was identical with a single patented rolling mill. Among locational factors markets were paramount, while accessibility of raw materials was less important.

This situation changed as output and competition grew in the early 1900s, and after 1906 the growth of Mannesmann more and more followed the standard path in steel making: vertical integration and concentration of plant. The necessity for integrating backwards into steel making and eventually also iron smelting and coal and ore mining arose from two sides. For welded tubes production costs had to be lowered to withstand competition; for seamless tubes very high quality standards had to be guaranteed to justify their higher prices.

In Italy, with its specific disadvantages for the production of pig iron, a steel works based on scrap consumption was added to the Dalmine rolling mills, while in Germany vertical integration had to go the whole way backwards to coal to achieve the lowest possible prime costs. Hence, investment after 1910 was heavily focused on the completion of a fully integrated steel concern in Germany that would also deliver steel to the subsidiaries abroad.[86]

Conclusions

From this short overview a few common points emerge. In the bank-enterprise relationship the part played by the bank seems to have been more innovative when expansion abroad went horizontally.[87] Banks were bolder in taking the entire industry to new markets while steel managers would only go abroad to strengthen their home base. When plants were duplicated abroad the technological and managerial ties between the parent and the subsidiary company usually did not survive for long, unless the two branches were only a short distance from each other on the two sides of a border cutting through what might be called a major enterprise. This was the case with most investment of the German companies of Upper Silesia, right across the border in the neighboring Polish provinces.

Over greater distances what had begun as a direct investment of a steel company usually turned into a portfolio investment. For a simple and uniform product like steel, there was little the parent company could offer over a long period of time. After a few years of practice, external control had no more technological or organizational rationale. The links became purely financial and unless the parent company did develop specific management resources for financing, like the Cockerill group, for instance, it was only natural that the bank would assume the dominating role in this relationship.

Foreign direct investment in raw material, on the other hand, was largely governed by steelmasters. Because they produced rather homogeneous goods they were a very cost-conscious race of managers; and highest on their cost sheets ranked iron ore and coal. As long as the parent company had good prospects for profitable growth there was little the bank could do to improve the yield of their joint investment. Interrupting the vertical integration established by foreign direct investment in raw materials was certainly a temporary solution only. Complementarity of processes and a continuous flow of goods from foreign subsidary to parent was obviously a stronger bond of cohesion than was the transfer of know-how that was not exclusive. No indications existed before World War I that a steel company lost control over foreign raw materials sources once it had managed to get hold of them, nor did a bank show an interest in running mines on its own account.

The situation was quite different but had a similar outcome when the production technology was not easily transferable because of patent rights or the inherent complexity of processes. This created another kind of dependency between the parent and the subsidary that guaranteed the cohesion of the multinational company. In this respect it was the patent for rolling seamless tubes that stood behind the multinationalization of Mannesmann and not the bank-specific advantages of its owner. Elaborate financing and access to credit beyond all customary lines was decisive for the successful development of the Mannesmann concern, to be sure. It seems very likely, however, that making seamless tubes a commercial success would have cost less money and anxiety had this been undertaken by a well-established steel manufacturer and not by amateurs like the rifle makers Mannesmann and the bankers of the Deutsche Bank. Success, after all, came only when experienced steel managers entered the company and reorganized production according to best business practice.

The painful early history of Mannesmann stressed the great importance of technical assistance in the initial phase of direct investment by banks—or any other outsider for that matter. In securing this assistance from their domestic clients the French and Belgian bankers were certainly well advised in their foreign undertakings. But unlike Mannesmann, these new companies had no particular advantage over their competitors and did not interfere with the parent's interest in its traditional markets. On the other hand, the Deutsche Bank could not ask for this kind of assistance as long as it wished to defend its profit-promising innovation against the major potential competitors. To achieve this as a newcomer in the trade it took the financial resources of a great bank, as the failure of the Mannesmann and Siemens families had shown. For the multinational expansion of Mannesmann, however, control and ownership by the bank was not essential. Had Thyssen been successful in his attempt to take over the company in 1903, the international operations would in all probability not have been very different, with the Deutsche Bank helping him as it had done before in Sweden.

Finally, even if there were not many true multinational iron and steel companies for reasons that are largely attributable to the nature of the product, this industry did generate quite extensive and sophisticated international banking activities with small private banks and personal, often kinsmanlike relationships still playing a vital role.

22

International Harvester and Its Competitors

Fred V. Carstensen

On May 1, 1851, the Great Exhibition of the Works of Industry of All Nations opened in London's Crystal Palace. In the midst of the thinly populated American exhibition sat Cyrus McCormick's "huge, unwieldy, unsightly and incomprehensible" mechanical grain harvester.[1] But in two demanding field trials McCormick's machine demonstrated its virtue—it offered farmers the first effective mechanical means for harvesting wheat, oats, and other grains, a machine that both reduced the labor requirement by four-fifths and cut the loss of grain from handling; the exhibition jury awarded McCormick its highest award, the prestigious Council Medal. McCormick used this signal victory as a cornerstone for American advertising for years afterwards and established a pattern of using victories in such European field trials to enhance the McCormick reputation. But these visible successes led to no significant European sales before 1880. And only in 1886 did the McCormick company begin to seek foreign markets seriously, building marketing organizations first in the United Kingdom, then in France and Germany, and finally, after 1895, in Russia, Mexico, Australia, and New Zealand. Even so, the company refused to use the full array of marketing tools common to the trade in the United States, and thus invested comparatively little in foreign markets. But the internal logic of marketing and the external pressure of competition ultimately forced International Harvester (successor firm to McCormick) to increase its effort, and thus its marketing investment, to sell machines.

Finally, in 1909, International Harvester took the final step—accepting itself farmers' notes—which brought marketing in Europe, Australia, and New Zealand in line with North American practice. This development, together with high dividend payments and poor management of factory inventories, forced International Harvester to seek increasingly large loans in American and British money markets. Even so, policies governing production and distribution of its machines remained independent of the sources of its capital.

McCormick (and Others) in Europe: 1850–1886

Cyrus McCormick had a special understanding of the publicity value of victories in competitive field trials and of the praise of leading agricultural societies. He had used

499

both effectively to establish his first markets in Virginia and to expand them in the upper Midwest. By the summer of 1849 he had struck on the idea of presenting a special display model of his harvester—made of highly varnished Michigan ash and bronzed metalwork—to the Royal Agricultural Society of England. He expected that the society's attention would translate into a national reputation for himself, his machine, and his company. But before the display model was finished Prince Albert announced plans for the first great world exposition, to be held in London in 1851.[2] McCormick's most serious competitor, Obed Hussey, left the fate of his machine in the hands of an English representative who had never seen it operate. In two field trials— one on a "sour, dark drenching day," when the McCormick machine was the only reaper that worked, a second in ripe wheat—Hussey's machine failed miserably.[3]

The McCormick reaper won additional competitive victories in Britain in 1852 and at the great French exposition of 1855. But Cyrus had no serious interest in developing direct sales; the competitions were for the benefit of his ego and of American marketing. He did sell a number of licenses to make his reaper to British firms and to two French firms. All but one of the licensees found they could sell almost no machines and quit; one licensee, Burgess & Key, did produce McCormick reapers for a few years with some success. The market was limited: McCormick insisted on a hefty license fee, which kept the price of his machine high; the McCormick machine was heavy and difficult to maneuver in small British fields; British farmers wanted the cut wheat delivered in swath rather than in gavels.[4] Other makes did respond to these imperatives. By 1860 the machines of Obed Hussey, Walter Wood, and others enjoyed significantly larger sales than did those of McCormick.[5]

During the early 1850s McCormick had little incentive to look for wider markets. The company had some difficulty expanding production before 1854. When, in 1855, production reached 2,500 machines, demand from farmers, eager to exploit the dramatic productivity of the reaper, was so strong that virtually all were sold in the upper Midwest, close to the company's Chicago home. The McCormick reaper established its reputation as simple, durable, reliable; with attractive installment credit and excellent support from the company's agents, it was the reaper of choice among American grain farmers. Moreover, its Chicago location, though advantageous for the American market, put it at a significant disadvantage when dealing with European markets. Competing manufacturers, such as Wood and Hussey, located in the eastern United States, had good access to only a limited domestic market, but they faced much lower shipping costs to Britain; they also built smaller, lighter machines, which were more popular in Britain and continental Europe than in America. Thus it was these smaller American companies that took the lead in developing foreign sales.[6]

By 1860 McCormick's production of more than 5,000 machines was outrunning demand in its midwestern markets, and the company looked further afield—to Texas, California, Oregon, to eastern states and some foreign markets. But the company enjoyed no enduring success in any of these areas. As a result, it treated these areas as dumping grounds for excess and outmoded machines, a practice that undermined goodwill and prevented development of a solid sales organization. Thus by 1860 McCormick, though perhaps the largest manufacturer of grain harvesters, was primarily a regional firm with few sales and little network outside of its established midwestern markets.[7]

McCormick's machine was also essentially unchanged from ten years earlier when it won awards at the Crystal Palace. But the industry had largely shifted to self-rake reapers, on which a set of arms periodically swept the cut grain from the platform and left it in gavels to be bound into sheaves. This both cut the labor needed to complete a harvest and improved the productivity of the machine itself. Cyrus McCormick clearly enjoyed his reputation as inventor of the mechanical grain harvester and refused to concede the field to competitors. He finally resolved to build his own self-raker and to introduce it to the market through the International Exposition in London in 1862. Again Cyrus ordered the factory to build a special show machine of "beautifully grained" ash, with "planished copper" on the platform, highly polished iron parts, and fine gold striping, and twelve machines for field trials. He sent a cadre of assistants to London to assure the machine's proper handling. And he also dispatched James T. Griffin, who had been superintendent of sales since 1858; Cyrus hoped that Griffin would turn the anticipated victories at the International Exposition into a significant volume of sales in Europe.[8]

McCormick won. In two trials—the first in "badly tangled and flattened" wheat, the second in rain—the new self-rake performed admirably.[9] *Bell's Weekly Messenger* declared it "beyond all doubt, a triumph of mechanical genius" that would become "the reaper of *the* day."[10] After taking the highest award bestowed at the exposition, the McCormick machine defeated all comers in a series of contests in Britain and on the Continent. Orders flowed in from the nobility of Europe—the Duke of Atholl, a Russian prince, the Marquis de Sambuy—promising a new market for McCormick machines. Griffin set eagerly to work, signing up agents from Madrid to Moscow.

If Cyrus McCormick had followed up this beginning with serious attention to marketing, his machine might have replaced Walter Wood's as the leader in European markets. But he neither gave the business his best attention, nor permitted his brothers William and Leander, who were actually managing the company while Cyrus enjoyed life in London, to use their own judgment to develop sales strategies and complementary products. As a result, foreign sales were few. More importantly, the company lost ground in America: In 1861 McCormick accounted for nearly 20 percent of harvester production in the United States; in 1866 the company produced less than 5 percent.[11]

In 1867 Cyrus McCormick again went to Europe for a competition, this time in France. Emperor Napoleon III, hoping to outshine the London Exposition of 1862 and shore up his sagging popularity at home, staged a magnificent, even extravagant international exposition. Though McCormick's self-raker was virtually unchanged and his newly developed mower an indifferent machine, he insisted on competing. Griffin, still trying to find a market for McCormick machines in Europe, worked diligently to bring his employer victory. In the mower competition, the Wood machine took first, McCormick third. But the McCormick self-rake performed beautifully. The Emperor invited McCormick to his estate at Chalons, and there ordered three McCormick self-rakers for use in his own fields. A triumph. The Associated Press cabled a long story. McCormick's Chicago office reported that it was "published in every newspaper in the U.S. Half a million will not give the advertising that you are getting gratis." But before Cyrus sailed for America he broke with Griffin and found it impossible to reach an agreement with Burgess & Key. Within a year Griffin began working for Wood, soon pushing sales over 2,000 machines a year.[12] And other American competitors—

Adriance-Platt, Johnston and Osborne—developed significant, profitable European sales. McCormick, first in victories but last in sales, virtually disappeared from the European market for ten years.

The victory in France in 1867 was a brief aberration from a long-term pattern of general decline for McCormick. By 1871 the company had slipped to at best fifth among American harvester manufacturers. It had significant sales in only four upper Midwest states and had no marketing hierarchy; everything was handled out of the factory offices in Chicago. In contrast, Wood was selling two-and-a-half times as many machines, including thousands in Europe, making special models for a new market opening in South America, and had established formal branch offices to supervise a growing trade in the American Midwest and in Europe. At least three other American competitors had also established branch sales offices in Chicago to push their trade.[13]

The great Chicago fire destroyed the McCormick factory on October 9, 1871. Cyrus had not lived in Chicago for nine years, and had given his business only occasional attention. For several years he had had a running feud with his brother Leander, who managed the factory. The sales organization was clearly in disarray and living on borrowed time; the old factory site, on the north bank of the Chicago River near Lake Michigan, could not accommodate a factory large enough to expand output. The company's general manager had already told Cyrus that he should either "quit" the business or "build a *No. 1* factory."[14] Aged sixty-two, wealthy without his Chicago real estate or company, McCormick probably would have abandoned the business if the choice had been his alone. But his wife, Nettie Fowler, with a clear eye on the future careers of her three sons, insisted on rebuilding. She then took a prominent role in directing the reemergence of the McCormick company as the industry leader and, in 1902, in the creation of International Harvester.[15]

In January 1873 the McCormick company began manufacturing in its new, spacious factory, located on 130 acres of prairie southwest of Chicago. Rebuilding cost about $619,000, a relatively modest sum given McCormick's wealth of $5 million to $7 million.[16] Of course, by itself rebuilding the factory would not restore the business. Neither the products nor the sales organization had been changed: In 1873 it sold only three-quarters of the 11,000 harvesters and mowers the factory turned out; agents deluged management with complaints that they were losing traditional customers to the new Marsh harvesters (on which two workers rode, hand-binding the sheaves) and wire-binders (which automatically tied the gavels of cut grain into sheaves with a twist of wire). A redesigned McCormick self-raker was of such poor quality that the company simply dropped it after one season. A small combined machine (one that could be used for both harvesting grains and mowing hay by changing a few parts) found few sales because McCormick had virtually no marketing organization in the regions where such machines were popular. The net result was that the McCormick company, which had once sold every machine it made, was carrying huge inventories of unsold machines.[17] Management finally responded, appointing an experienced, tough salesman, E. K. Butler, to rebuild the marketing organization, and committing the company to designing a competitive machine for the 1875 harvest.[18]

Butler, the new general manager, took decisive steps to restore the company. In his first two years he cut the number of McCormick agents by three quarters, making it clear that the company would no longer indulge failure to make sales. Each of the remaining thirty-seven agents became a full-time, salaried employee of the company with authority over a territory large enough to command his undivided attention. Butler also began developing standardized reporting and accounting procedures with which to assess the performance of each general agent. He pushed the company into new markets. Using special agents to audit marketing efforts, he drove the entire organization with an intensity it had not seen in at least twenty years. His efforts paid off: The company was soon setting sales records. In 1877 it had a positive cash flow, probably for the first time in four years, and was rapidly regaining its position. In 1878, for the first time since the early 1860s, it had the best designed grain harvester on the market; sales reached 18,500 machines. Moreover, the company had so much cash it borrowed nothing from banks or outsiders; it had regained its position among the industry leaders.[19]

Butler gave no attention to foreign sales because Cyrus McCormick handled those as his personal business, not company business, buying the machines at cost on his own account, and keeping whatever income their sales generated. In 1875 Cyrus had sent Abel Westengaard to Copenhagen to try to sell McCormick harvesters, but despite years of effort, appointment of over seventy agents, and extensive advertising, Westengaard failed completely. In 1876 Cyrus persuaded Rush Mason, a Chicagoan then residing in London, to show his new wire-binder at the important Smithfield Cattle Show. It drew very favorable attention; eighteen-year-old Cyrus McCormick, Jr. followed up with a series of field trials. In part because of this experience, he joined his mother in persuading Cyrus McCormick, Sr. to turn the potentially important foreign activities over to the company.[20]

The Paris Universal Exposition of 1878 offered yet another opportunity to earn valuable prestige and publicity. But others had already developed markets for mowers and simple reapers, capturing virtually all established implement dealers. If the McCormick operation wanted to build a good foreign marketing organization, it had to do so around a new product. It had that in its wire-binder. If leading retailers agreed to sell it, then, in time, the company could expect them to take on the McCormick reaper and mower, dropping the lines they were already handling. Management decided to run only the wire-binder in the obligatory field trials, passing up mower and reaper competitions. The exposition jury gave McCormick the top award, a decision confirmed in nearly a dozen subsequent trials in France, England, and Scotland.[21]

While still in Europe, Cyrus McCormick contracted with Waite, Burnell, Huggins & Co. of London to serve as the company's agent for the United Kingdom and the Continent for two years. Waite promised to buy a minimum of 200 harvesters for the 1879 season, with immediate payment in full. It would then either sell the machines directly to farmers or distribute them to smaller retail implement dealers. Such conditions meant that McCormick was making no significant investment (and taking no risks) and Waite would buy no more machines than it believed it could sell for cash or on very short time; it was unlikely that it would commit any of its own financial resources to provide credit, either to the retail dealers or to the farmers, limiting demand to what a cash trade could generate. This was in striking contrast to the techniques used in the American trade. McCormick had offered installment payments in the 1840s because farmers rarely had sufficient cash to buy a machine outright and available distribution institutions would not themselves provide the necessary credit. Moreover, acquiring a reaper meant a farmer could harvest more acreage, so he planted more acreage in grains—and the larger crop produced the income needed to pay for the new machine. The company relied on its salaried general agents and canvassers to do much of the actual selling; the local retail dealers all worked on straight commission contracts, simply providing a base of operations for selling. McCormick thus did not rely on the financial strength of these dealers, but itself assumed all the costs and risks of marketing, an approach that assured as wide sales as possible.

Moreover, local retailers only had annual contracts and were quickly and easily replaced when they failed to fulfill their role in marketing. But in the foreign markets (besides Waite, McCormick had contracts with firms to cover sales in New Zealand and Australia)[22] McCormick was insisting that the agent assume all the costs and risks of marketing. Such an approach minimized McCormick's investment in overseas sales and gave firms representing McCormick in those markets virtually no incentive to develop significant sales. This policy left McCormick behind Wood, Osborne, and other firms that had salaried agents in Europe, Mexico, and South America, and which placed machines with retail dealers on a commission basis.[23] But McCormick was well ahead of these competitors in the American market, and it made little sense to devote resources to developing foreign markets until the company had made the most of the large and still rapidly expanding American market.[24]

For the next several years the McCormick management virtually ignored foreign sales.[25] It focused entirely on developing an excellent twine-binder and improved mowers and self-rake reapers, on expanding the Chicago factory, and on building a first-class national marketing organization. By 1882 it was probably the largest harvester manufacturer in the world, with a new company, Deering Harvester, in second place. Walter A. Wood had lost a significant share of its domestic American market, though it remained the leader in foreign markets. Other firms important in foreign markets—Osborne, Johnston, Adriance-Platt—also lost ground domestically. Increasingly they were selling products that were marginally competitive in America; when the leading American firms turned their attention to foreign markets, these smaller firms would not be able to hold their position there either.

Though McCormick management took no active interest in foreign sales during these years, the company had, fortuitously, found itself with a strong European representative. When Waite, Burnell & Co. (Huggins had left) failed in 1880, Percy Lankester, a former employee, took over the business. He was an energetic, effective salesman for the McCormick binder, and in 1883 the company gave him authority over all European sales outside of Russia and Rumania. He traveled the Continent, signing up firms to sell binders in France, Spain, Portugal, Italy, and Greece. Butler praised his "interest and perseverance," which was finally building a market for McCormick machines. In July 1886 Butler decided to focus on Lankester's work, traveling to Europe to learn the market and to meet potential agents. This initiated a series of twelve annual summer trips for Butler as he, with Lankester, slowly built a European marketing organization that put McCormick into first place.[26]

Building the Foreign Marketing Organization: 1886–1902

In the summer of 1887 the French Agricultural Society conducted an important field trial of harvesters. Cyrus McCormick, Jr., who had succeeded his father on the latter's death in 1884, brought to the competition both the company's new steel-frame twine binder, which boasted a much simplified knotter, and an older wood-frame machine. But Walter Wood's French agent, "a man of grey hairs, wide reputation and high standing," had matters firmly in hand. The jury hardly looked at the machines, and awarded the gold to Wood; the silver went, absurdly, to the McCormick wood-frame binder. Cyrus Jr. judged the awards "humbug," but learned the hard lesson that Wood had cultivated the French market diligently for two decades, and had as its agent the dominant farm implement firm in France, with its headquarters in Paris. McCormick's agent, in contrast, was a competent but small firm located in Tonnerre, half-way between Orleans and Dijon in central France.[27] The problem in France was repeated in almost every major market; McCormick did not have leading houses to represent it. In Russia a couple of strong firms had taken the McCormick line, but sold it along with other machines, which often got most of the attention.

If Cyrus Jr. had not learned the lessons first-hand, the *Farm Implement News* declared the same point in a long article about Wood. That firm had had continuous foreign representation ever since 1858, and full-time salaried agents since 1868. It had given consistent, careful attention to foreign sales. The *News* justly claimed that "no American manufacturer of harvesting machines has done so much to establish a *foreign market* for machines *made at home*" in America. Wood had the best network of agencies in Europe, had developed a similar network in South America, and had agencies in Constantinople, Smyrna, North Africa, and in Zululand in southern Africa. Wood even had agencies in British India. Other firms, American and British, had also established networks for their harvesters and mowers. Cyrus realized that being the leader in America did not immediately or easily translate into leadership in other markets.[28]

Though Butler and the McCormick management were not yet prepared to make major changes in the European organization, they did make one critical change to strengthen foreign marketing. In a new contract with J. Mohr Bell & Co., covering Argentina, McCormick provided two years' credit on the machines purchased and, for the first time, assumed much of the cost for three factory experts to go to Argentina to assure machines were properly assembled and serviced. This was the first time that the company dropped a long-standing, consistent requirement that the agent firm pay the full cost of experts. The company made similar arrangements elsewhere in South America, including one unprecedented four-year contract, to secure good distributors to handle its machines. By providing more generous credit, longer-term contracts, and paying for experts, management believed these outside firms would take more machines and invest more of their own resources in marketing efforts.[29]

In 1888 luck gave McCormick's European sales effort a big boost. H. J. Mot & Co., which stood second only to Wood's agent in France and which controlled a network of more than 800 local retail implement dealers, wanted a new line of American harvesters. It had handled Johnston machines, but that firm had gone into receivership and was considering abandoning its European trade. Mot quickly settled for a three-year contract, which included provisions for McCormick to send self-rakers and mowers on consignment. At the same time, Percy Lankester became McCormick's salaried European manager, responsible for supervising business in France, Austria, Hungary, and Germany. His former employer retained the agency for Great Britain, Italy, Spain, Portugal, and Cyprus.[30] (Russia, which generated few sales, still had its own salaried agent, George Freudenreich, but it received little attention or resources.)

In making Lankester European manager the McCormick organization was beginning to impose the same type of structure on foreign sales that Butler had brought to domestic sales after 1875, and this reflected the serious attention that management was giving to foreign markets.

In 1889 Paris hosted yet another international exposition. For this one the Eiffel Tower, a statement of French status, was the centerpiece. Cyrus McCormick, Jr., Butler, and Lankester all attended. The company made a reasonable effort to win in the field trials, but did not view these contests as being as important as they once had been. Now what counted was the quality of the sales organization. The three McCormick officials focused on improving the network of agents in Germany. Cyrus reported that "Lankester has appointed some capital agents" and concluded that the company could expect a "neat trade in Germany" hereafter. Indeed, the trade there grew so rapidly that in 1890 Lankester appointed a full-time salaried assistant to supervise it.[31]

After the dramatic improvements in the European organization in 1888 and 1889 Cyrus McCormick, Jr. did not go to Europe again for nearly a decade, but Butler went every summer. He concentrated on those areas that he and Lankester thought offered the most promising market. In 1891, for example, Butler spent most of his time on the developing German organization, visiting Cologne, Berlin, Dresden, Leipzig, Frankfurt, Strasburg, and Hildesheim to meet new agents and impress upon them the company's commitment to pushing the German trade. He also drew up a new contract with Mot, who finally abandoned all other harvester lines.[32]

McCormick's exclusive contract with Mot reflected the shifting conditions of the American market and the wisdom of Cyrus McCormick, Sr. in locating in Chicago. Eastern manufacturers like Osborne and Johnston, facing higher overland freight rates than transatlantic ones, from the 1860s gave increasing attention to developing a European trade while McCormick, Buckeye, Champion, and, after 1880, Deering took the trade in America's great agricultural heartland. But as all transportation costs fell and, with the shift to steel machines after 1885, economies of scale grew, the leading American manufacturers located in that heartland were increasingly able to compete in those European markets that the eastern companies first developed. McCormick, building on its leadership in binders, was now securing that European market, taking agencies away from those eastern firms. This was to be McCormick's decade in foreign markets.

By 1894 McCormick, Butler, and Lankester had built solid organizations in Britain, France, and Germany. (European markets looked so promising that management seriously considered beginning some manufacturing in Great Britain in 1893, but the panic that erupted in April of that year soon ended such talk.) The only major European grain-producing region that Butler had not visited was Russia. It now made sense to turn his attention there. He spent three weeks traveling the territory. George Freudenreich had been working the country for thirteen years, sending constant criticisms to Butler about the lack of resources and the company's inattention to the potential of the Russian market. But Freudenreich had done a poor job of developing and managing his marketing organization. Few of his retail agencies showed much life.[33] After surveying the situation Butler decided that Russia did have potential, but that Freudenreich would have to be replaced by a new man, George Tracy. At the same time Butler took the unprecedented step of permitting Freudenreich to open a retail implement store in Odessa, where Freudenreich's largest and most strategically placed agent had dropped McCormick in favor of Deering. There was such a paucity of reliable merchants that Butler believed that was the only way in which McCormick could maintain its presence in the important Odessa market.[34]

When Tracy took charge in Russia he quickly began using a new approach; he appointed as agents numerous smaller firms located in towns around major centers such as Odessa, giving them credit for up to one year on machines they purchased. He also let them carry an inventory of repair parts on commission, assuring better support for machines already sold. This began to move the company away from a reliance on large, established trading houses. Such firms, with a diverse line of goods, had little incentive to advertise McCormick machines, educate customers in the care and operation of machines, or train a staff of experts necessary to service a large trade. Nor were they willing to risk their own resources to provide credit to farmers. The loss of its Odessa representative thus forced the McCormick management to begin to rethink the problem inherent in relying on such large mercantile houses and how better to generate foreign sales.[35]

The McCormick organization's record for 1895 revealed its growing strength. Foreign sales were up by two-thirds from 1894 levels; domestic sales were up nearly 35 percent; sales of binders alone had risen 43 percent. Profits were so plentiful—$2.62 million—that the company borrowed only $150,000 from its Chicago banks to help cover operating costs. The U.S./Canadian sales organization had grown to 48 salaried general agents supervising 5,698 retail agents. Two salaried agents—Lankester and Tracy—and 21 wholesalers handled distribution to foreign markets. McCormick had clearly moved well ahead of Deering, its nearest competitor.[36]

By 1898 McCormick's foreign sales exceeded 23,000 machines, worth nearly $2 million, and represented a seventh of total sales. With such a volume of sales Butler's continued direct supervision of all sales, domestic and foreign, was clearly unwieldy. Fortunately, Butler wanted to retire, opening an opportunity to reorganize the management structure of the company, including responsibility for foreign sales. Cyrus McCormick, Jr. divided Butler's old duties among a group of old and new departments and officials. He replaced Lankester with one of the strongest American general agents, William Couchman, and simultaneously raised the position of European manager to departmental status, making it equal to the officers in the Chicago home office.[37]

Couchman viewed the European market as "practically virgin soil" because no company had yet applied the marketing strategies standard in the American trade. He immediately improved support for the European organization by carrying a large inventory of parts in Hamburg free port, ready for shipment wherever they were needed. He also brought experts from the factory to study local conditions and to make adjustments to machine designs that responded to these conditions. Finally, he argued successfully for the right to create American-style branch houses under salaried general agents. To hasten this transition McCormick simply bought out its German jobber and Lankester's old firm, which still handled sales in England. By 1902 McCormick had seven European branch houses responsible for business in England, Germany, Switzerland, Russia, and Austria-Hungary; twenty-one independent jobbers handled the rest of Europe. A salaried employee—the general agent—managed each of the branch houses, which carried its own inventory of machines and parts, had its own staff of travelers and mechanics to contact, support, and control the firms that sold retail implements for the McCormick machines.[38]

McCormick's approach was quite successful. Between 1898 and 1902 foreign sales more than doubled, to $4.3 million, and represented one-fifth of company sales. They were also extraordinarily profitable. Between 1898 and 1900 profits in Russia, Germany, France, and Australia sometimes exceeded 50 percent; sales in Great Britain in 1900 returned a meager 27.74 percent. That very success encouraged competitors— Milwaukee, Deering, Plano, Massey-Harris—to begin building similar organizations under salaried, resident foreign agents. But these marketing strategies required little investment, and, as McCormick's profits showed, returns initially could be very, very good, as companies picked up easy sales. Moreover, none of the companies offered credit directly to the final user, the farmer. Thus, the primary financial pressure came from efforts to compete in the American market; for that, retained earnings, owner loans, and short-term financing from local banks typically provided the necessary funds. McCormick, for instance, earned nearly $35 million in profits between 1884 and 1899, but paid out less than half in dividends.[39] Loans from the McCormick family members provided a regular, major source of operating capital, and during most of the 1890s they were larger than the aggregate of bank loans (see Table 22–1). When the company undertook major expansion after 1898, it broadened the base of bank borrow-

TABLE 22–1. Family and Bank Loans of the McCormick Company: 1885–1902

Year	Family Loans	Bank Loans	Total Liabilities as Percent of Assets[a]
1885	$ 310,000	1,000,000	10.9
1886	161,194	480,000	6.8
1887	292,329	1,910,000	12.3
1888	842,000	780,000	15.5
1889	879,586	660,000	13.6
1890	266,467	520,000	6.7
1891	1,578,513	1,210,000	9.4
1892	930,481	1,520,000	9.3
1893	1,042,163	900,000	9.2
1894	1,554,074	300,000	6.9
1895	2,890,499	150,000	9.4
1896	2,985,976	1,746,150	13.0
1897	2,327,768	900,000	14.1
1898	269,161	1,150,000	4.7
1899	493,148	4,300,000	12.8[b]
1900	1,304,534	11,402,705	19.9
1901	494,115	3,300,000	18.7
1902	n.a.	11,100,000	22.2

Sources: Analysis of Family Loans at September 30, 1880 and 1881 to 1902 inclusive. Analysis of Bills Payable Account at September 30 (1880 and 1881 to 1902 inclusive). Statement Showing Gross Assets, . . . [Compiled 12/29/1895?] IH 202.

[a]Calculated at the end of each accounting year when family and bank loans had often been repaid out of current collections.

[b]The company made major investments in its own factory, added a twine mill, and acquired or built a number of distribution warehouses, activities that help account for the heavy borrowing in 1899 to 1902.

TABLE 22–2. Sources of McCormick Company Loans, 1900–1902[a]

Bank Name	1900	1901	1902
Chicago			
Merchants' Loan & Trust	$800,000	600,000	1,000,000
Northern Trust	500,000	—	—
Corn Exchange National	400,00	—	—
Illinois Trust & Savings	1,000,000	500,000	1,000,000
Commercial Bank	250,000	500,000	500,000
Crerar Library	400,000	—	—
American Trust	—	550,000	—
Merchants National	—	400,000	—
New York			
National City	800,000	400,000	1,000,000
U.S. Trust	400,000	—	—
J. D. Rockefeller	—	2,500,000	2,500,000
Boston			
Atlas National	200,000	—	
Third National	200,000	—	[$1,000,000]
National Shawmut	300,000	—	No distribution
Second National	150,000	—	available.
State National	250,000	—	
Massachusetts Hospital Life Ins. Co.	200,000	—	
Others			
Scottish Provident Inst.	1,002,705	—	—
National Bank of Commerce–K.C.	100,000	—	—
Iowa National	—	150,000	—

Sources: Comparative Statement of Money Borrowed and Sources, MC:2CBx 30:F: Consolidation: McCormick Harv. Mach. Co., Financial Statements: 1879–1902.
[a]The table does not include family loans (See Table 22–1). Most loans were for less than one year. For instance, in 1900, $5,050,000 was repaid during the year; $2,690,000 was borrowed for periods of fifteen months to four years; President's Annual Report [for year ending August 31, 1900], June 1901, MC:M/I: Bx 18:F:5.

ing from the Chicago, New York, and Boston banks shown in Table 22–2 for additional operating capital. But even this wider network did not create a basis on which to establish a special relationship with large, internationally active New York banks.

The Final Steps: International Harvester in Foreign Markets, 1902–1914

The creation of International Harvester in August 1902 brought together the five leading American harvester manufacturers—McCormick, Deering, Champion, Plano, and Milwaukee—in a single company that controlled more than three-quarters of the world market. In its first ten years growth came largely from foreign sales—they grew from less than 18 percent to more than 44 percent of total sales between 1902 and 1912, more than a fourfold expansion in dollar terms. But making such foreign sales was costly, especially after 1909 when management decided to use American credit policies in most foreign markets. In 1912 the ratio of investment to foreign sales was 2:1; for American sales only 1.3:1. At the same time, pressure, principally from

George W. Perkins and the Deerings, to pay a regular, hefty dividend on common stock meant the company retained only a quarter of its net earnings, and uneven management often left the company carrying huge inventories of raw materials and finished products. These three factors combined to increase company borrowing dramatically compared to the pattern of McCormick and other predecessor companies, reaching 44 percent of net investment in 1913 (see Table 22–3). Even so, International Harvester continued to rely largely on short-term loans and found no difficulty in raising whatever monies it needed in New York and London. Moreover, financing operations was a routine activity that had no significant influence on manufacturing or marketing developments during these years.

At its first meeting the board of directors decided to maintain the old companies intact as separate divisions. There was surely no other choice. Each company had had different internal procedures and geographic divisions; the harvesters, reapers, mowers, and hay rakes that each company manufactured varied slightly. There was no easy way in which to blend these variations in policies, structures, or product designs. The board did establish a special committee to evaluate marketing in both America and abroad. The committee recommended renaming the Milwaukee company the International Harvester Company of America and using it as a wholly owned marketing subsidiary for North America. For foreign markets, the committee tentatively recommended creating a series of sales subsidiaries for France, Germany, Great Britain, and Russia. But before implementing that plan it asked the company's New York law firm

TABLE 22–3. International Harvester: Statement of Maximum Annual Borrowings, 1903–1912

Year	Short-Term[a]	Total	As Percent of Invested Capital	Borrowed in Europe[a]	As Percent of Total
1903	$9,000,000	$14,974,000	12.48	—	—
1904	10,000,000	15,630,000	12.81	—	—
1905	15,800,000	21,470,000	17.47	$3,772,000	17.6
1906[b]	11,500,000	23,774,000	18.93	5,740,000	24.1
1907	22,800,000	34,915,000	27.25	7,558,000	21.6
1908	18,500,000	25,988,000	19.69	9,237,000	35.5
1909	22,200,000	29,922,000	21.89	10,252,000	34.3
1910	29,400,000	37,048,000	25.14	12,279,000	33.1
1911	n.a.	54,930,000	35.20	17,950,000	32.7
1912	n.a.	65,920,000	40.34	19,264,000	29.2
1913[c]	40,200,000	75,530,000	44.02	19,608,500	26.0

Sources: Defendants' Exhibit 210, U.S. *vs.* International Harvester. (Volume 13 of the printed transcript, p. 120.) Statement Showing Maximum Liability on Loans and Bills Payable, 1903–1910, MC:2C:Bx 33:F: IHC:Consolidation:Liability, Profits, Dividends. Miscellaneous Financial Statistics:1902–1929 Inclusive, MC:17:Bx 2: F:IHC:earnings. Agreement between John D. Rockefeller and International Harvester Company, February 16, 1911. National Archives: International Harvester Investigation, 4921/25.

[a]All of the European loans were short-term (less than one year); thus, that money market provided about half of the short-term loans from 1908.

[b]In January 1906 International Harvester borrowed $7 million from John D. Rockefeller, repayable between 1910 and 1913. This loan was replaced in 1911 with a ten-year, $20 million loan. Rockefeller also bought $5 million of the 1912 issue of three-year gold bonds.

[c]Based on Table 22–4 figures. Total borrowing may have been slightly higher in August, which typically showed the highest monthly indebtedness. Thereafter collections began to come in quickly and all short-term debt was retired.

to conduct an investigation of possible legal problems that might arise from the creation of locally incorporated companies. Roberts Walker conducted that survey.[40]

Walker spent nearly four months touring the European offices of the five divisions. He reported that legal questions were "less complicated than expected," and immediately turned his attention to business issues. The real problem, he argued, was choosing a marketing strategy. The old companies had used two different approaches— one "price," the other "exploitation." When entering a new market, just cutting prices produced good sales. The second approach required a slower start, higher prices, "vigorous canvassing," and a supporting service organization (i.e., both more time and much more investment). This was, in the long run, "vastly more effective," as the experiences of McCormick and Deering demonstrated. Walker specifically recommended that International Harvester develop standard policies on terms of sale, shipment, and settlement; that the company establish clear lines of communication among European managers; that it create a uniform system of experts, organize joint warehouses in at least five primary locations (London, Hamburg, Odessa, Rostov, Riga), and consider establishing several European twine mills. Walker gave the most detailed attention to the issues in the large Russian trade, and he invesigated the feasibility of both a twine mill and a fully operational factory for Russia.[41]

Walker's detailed and thoughtful analysis got virtually no attention among company managers. Bitter rivalries between the McCormicks and the Deerings split top management and paralyzed corporate decision making. International Harvester could not take advantage of the presumed efficiencies in production, distribution, and marketing that the merger was supposed to provide. In fact, it barely made money; in the first fifteen months, net earnings on assets were less than 1 percent. The foreign organizations (a sixth was added when International Harvester acquired Osborne in 1903) continued on their separate courses, even organizing three separate sales subsidiaries in Great Britain.[42]

Before 1906 the board of directors agreed on only two relatively small steps to change foreign operations. In 1904 it restructured supervision of foreign sales, giving Charles Haney direct authority over all foreign sales, and dividing supervision over the European divisions between Deering's Paris office and McCormick's Hamburg office. And in 1905 the board responded to a dramatic loss of market share in Scandinavia by buying a small factory in Sweden; this permitted the company to compete effectively against the burgeoning competition in that territory. But both decisions were defensive reactions to self-evident shortcomings in the organizational structure and to the rapidly increasing competition in European markets; they were not creative responses to the enormous potential of foreign markets. Management could not respond; it was wallowing in internecine warfare. The Deerings and McCormicks disagreed over virtually every policy; the Deerings essentially withdrew from active management during 1905 and threatened to pull the assets of their old company out of International Harvester; in the lower echelons, rivalry between former employees of each predecessor company was rife. Management had been reduced to the worst variety of constituency politics, unable to act decisively on any front, and earning poor profits.[43]

In late 1906 the leadership issue was settled. The board restructured management, giving Cyrus McCormick, Jr. much strengthened authority as company president; adding a new position of general manager, which it filled with Clarence S. Funk, a man unconnected to either the McCormicks or the Deerings; and the board eliminated the

Deerings from active management. Over the next five years International Harvester moved quickly to make up lost ground in foreign markets.

Until 1907 foreign sales continued on a conservative basis. Dealers worked on straight sales contracts—not commission contracts—and had to pay for all machines, typically within one year. The credit-worthiness of each dealer, not the size and quality of the market among farmers, limited the size of orders. International Harvester had established inventories of repair parts and used commission contracts to encourage dealers to maintain an adequate supply during the critical harvest season, and it had made available increasing numbers of mechanics to assure that machines were properly assembled and adjusted. But nowhere had the company used the one device that had been central to full development of the American trade; that device was providing credit directly to farmers. To do that necessarily meant relying on commission contracts with dealers and building an organization to supervise and assist those dealers and to make the necessary collections from individual farmers. But such a policy also permitted using small merchants who, with limited resources, could not buy machines on their own account for resale, and thus assured much easier access by farmers to the machines. It would also be expensive, requiring a vastly increased investment. Strengthening competition from European manufacturers and the absence of marketing intermediaries in Siberia finally forced International Harvester to apply its full marketing strategy in foreign markets.[44]

Marketing in Siberia had raised unique problems. Originally the Russian organization followed regular policy, looking only for "responsible firms," specifically those with "sufficient financial responsibility" to buy machines "for their own account." But Siberia had "no material from which to create regular agencies," and the company had had to rely on the few large mercantile houses that controlled much of the general trade in Siberia. Each of these firms maintained a string of "small houses located at the principal trading points." They sold farm implements "as they would market any merchandise, hardware or flour," and were utterly unwilling to develop demand with canvassing, service, credit, or stores in new markets. But without alternative marketing intermediaries (i.e., small merchants), International Harvester could bring little pressure to bear on these representatives. Charles Haney realized that if the company lost one of the big jobbers who handled the Deering and McCormick brands, its own organization was "not in position to take up the work and continue to hold the trade." The only solution was for International Harvester to take the extreme step of opening its own retail stores, a step that meant that it would not only have to carry implements manufactured by other firms—it had to offer a full set of complementary products to attract the trade—but also to give customers—the farmers—credit. Such a strategy was, Haney acknowledged, "not pleasant to contemplate," but it was the only way both to protect the company against the large jobbers and to assure development of the increasingly important Russian market.[45] Once the company was prepared to accept farmers' notes in Russia, commission contracts necessarily followed, thus bringing small, financially weak merchants into the retailing system. So the decision to begin retailing in Siberia led unavoidably to a new credit policy, and that policy inherently opened up marketing to a whole new category of retail agents.[46]

In 1907 International Harvester's branch house at Omsk opened five retail stores; by 1912 the Omsk and Vladivostok offices operated ninety-one Siberian stores. They were to be used only to "develop an organization." The stores would open the trade in

International Harvester products, thereby demonstrating that such a trade was profitable, and attracting independent agents who could then take over. Thus the company consciously appointed agents in villages surrounding its retail stores, ultimately eliminating its own retail trade, and converting the store to a wholesale distribution center. The experience gained in Siberia soon led management to the decision to use the policy as widely as feasible, working "where possible, to obtain more collateral paper," i.e., farmers' notes.[47] Thus, from 1909, International Harvester finally used the same strategies and marketing structures standard in the American market wherever it could follow that approach.

The intensifying effort to increase foreign sales was expensive. Developing an organization, building inventories, developing factories, and finally taking farmers' notes drove the investment required to make sales higher than it had been in America. Poorer transportation required larger inventories; rougher conditions required extra spare parts; operating factories required large investments in capital equipment and buildings; buying raw materials and paying a work force demanded significant working capital. Finally, these farmers did not pay off their notes as rapidly as did American farmers, so the company had to carry its receivables for a longer time. But International Harvester had been learning how to borrow more money at minimum cost virtually from its inception; the demands created by foreign marketing were simply subsumed within the aggregate needs of the company, needs met through borrowing in the U.S. and the London money market.

International Harvester's London Connection

At its May 2, 1904 meeting the board of directors resolved to appoint Wentworth P. Johnson "Assistant Treasurer of the Company for Great Britain and Europe." Johnson had served as controller for the McCormick organization but had been passed over for any significant position in the new organization. The McCormicks had pushed him forward for at least the position of controller and were undoubtedly looking for a way to keep him in the company. Moreover, the company was borrowing increasingly large amounts of money; given its excellent financial standing, some members of management—possibly Morgan partner George Perkins—knew the company could borrow cheaply in the London market. Whatever the reason, Johnson immediately resettled in London and began securing loans for International Harvester.[48]

Johnson's London operation was soon an important source for operating capital, as Table 22–4 reveals. The London loans were almost always for nine months or less. This policy of "clearing up annually" was the preferred practice in London financial circles; using it meant that International Harvester got the lowest rates in the market. In 1909 and 1911 the management, at the suggestion of some of the banks, considered going over to a revolving plan. In a 1911 meeting with one of the bankers, Cunliffe sternly warned Cyrus McCormick, Jr. against changing the established practice. Cunliffe declared, "You have reached a position by which you secure the cheapest money anyone can get in London, and now you proceed to alter the basis on which this credit has been given, just because you feel that you can do it—in other words you are *working* us a little."[49] Further interviews confirmed Cunliffe's "preference" for the annual cleanup of loans. The company continued to rely heavily on the London market

TABLE 22–4. Outstanding Term Notes and Current Borrowings, 1913

Term notes		
Issue of February 16,1911		10,000,000
Gold notes of February 15, 1912		20,000,000
Notes for steamship *Harvester*		275,000
John D. Rockefeller note due in 1913		5,000,000
Current borrowings due in 1913		
Chicago banks		
First National Bank	3,570,000	
Merchants' Loan & Trust Co.	1,250,000	
Corn Exchange National Bank	1,250,000	
Illinois Trust & Savings Bank	2,500,000	
State Bank of Chicago	200,000	
Country banks	1,946,000	
Miscellaneous	1,545,000	
Total		12,261,000
New York banks		
National City Bank	3,000,000	
First National Bank	2,000,000	
Bankers Trust Company	2,000,000	
Guaranty Trust Company	500,000	
Liberty National Bank	250,000	
Total		7,750,000
Foreign banks		
London City & Midland Bank, Ltd.	3,853,000	
Morgan, Grenfell & Co.	2,880,000	
Kleinwort Sons & Co.	720,000	
Samuel Montagu & Co.	960,000	
C. J. Hambro & Sons	480,000	
Fredrick Huth & Co.	480,000	
Koenig Brothers	960,000	
Cunliffe Brothers	360,000	
Seligman Brothers	480,000	
British Bank of South America Ltd.	480,000	
Frueling & Goschen	240,000	
Lazard Bros. & Co.	480,000	
Brown, Shipley & Co.	192,000	
Morgan, Harjes & Co.	961,538	
Comptoir National d'Escompte	192,307	
Commerz und Diskonto Bank	476,190	
Hope & Co.	200,000	
Nederlandsche Handel-Maatschappij	200,000	
Rotterdamsche Bankvereeniging	200,000	
I. H. Co. of Gt. Britain, Ltd.	600,000	
Compagnie Internationale des Machines Agricoles-Paris	2,884,615	
German houses	1,328,571	
Total		19,608,423

(*continued*)

TABLE 22–4. Outstanding Term Notes and Current Borrowings, 1913 (*Continued*)

Drafts Macleod & Co. (fiber purchases)	437,940
Cable remittances (no details)	200,000
Total bills payable, June 30, 1913	75,532,363

Sources: Statement of Bills Payable, July 31, 1913. W:MC:2C:Bx 37:F: IHC:R. Rockefeller asked for such monthly reports of loans and bills payable. Under the loan agreement of 1911 the company could "not borrow more than $65,000,000 during any one year without advising" Rockefeller in advance. J. D. Rockefeller to C. H. McCormick, 4–25–13. W:MC:2C:Bx 37:F: IHC:R The General Ledgers for 1911 through 1914 (earlier years were not available) confirm that these banks were the regular lenders to International Harvester. Ledgers in IH Archives.

(see Table 22–4), but made no further effort to move its London financings away from the short-term loans.

But with the rising use of loans, there was increasing concern about the potential dangers of using only short-term loans. If for any reason the company was slow in making collections on its notes, it would not have the cash to pay off the loans on time and might face severe penalties when it tried to refinance them. The first significant long-term loan was taken in January 1906, when John D. Rockefeller lent International Harvester $7 million, repayable in installments between 1910 and 1913. Rockefeller, father-in-law of Harold F. McCormick, Cyrus, Jr.'s brother, had become increasingly interested in the harvester business after Cyrus Jr. and Harold consulted him about a possible merger in 1899. In 1901 and 1902 Rockefeller had made large loans to the McCormick organization, and he had played an important role in the successful merger talks of 1902. He then contracted to lend the McCormicks up to $14 million to finance their required contribution to International Harvester's initial operating capital. He also was a close ally of the McCormicks in their ongoing struggle with the Deerings, George Perkins, and Judge Elbert Gary, including his stock holdings with theirs in calculations of which faction controlled a majority. While Rockefeller insisted that the loans to the company were strictly business, he clearly wanted the McCormicks to control the company; moreover, he constantly supported long-term strategies to strengthen the company.

In October 1910 another management crisis was building at International Harvester. The company had been controlled through a voting trust created in 1902 as a means of preventing an immediate fight for control between the principal stockholding factions, namely the McCormicks and the Deerings. Though the McCormicks had been firmly in control since 1906, the Deerings still hoped to climb back into management. Part of the strategy was to force the McCormicks to agree to an additional stock issue of $20 million in new stock and simultaneously to raise the common stock dividend from 4 percent to 6 percent. If carried through, this would have reduced McCormick holdings to a plurality of outstanding shares, reduced the ability of the company to finance its ongoing activities and growth out of current income—thus forcing it to borrow more from the financial community, and produced a rise in the market price of shares.

Frederick Gates, Rockefeller's business manager, suggested that George Perkins' insistence on raising the dividend was both to force placement of the new shares (which the Morgan house would handle for a commission) and the opportunity it would give Morgan to sell its own shares at a handsome premium. Indeed, Gates accused Perkins of running the stock up in a thin market as a way of pressuring the McCormicks to increase the dividend and issue the new shares; Gates rejected the whole idea as harmful to the company as well as to the McCormick/Rockefeller financial interests. After a strategy meeting between the McCormick brothers Cyrus and Harold and a principal advisor, John Wilson, Cyrus approached Rockefeller about another major loan to the company. Negotiations quickly led to a Rockefeller loan of $10 million in early 1911 and the defeat of the Perkins-Deering plan. Interestingly, the loan contract required that International Harvester limit its other borrowings to $50 million a year unless it had Rockefeller's permission; this provision reflected Rockefeller's long-standing concern over the company's tendency not to manage its business as tightly as he thought proper.[50]

By June 1911 it was evident the company had to develop a clear policy to handle its growing financial needs. Borrowings in 1911 were 40 percent above those of 1910, and represented an unprecedented 35 percent of invested capital (see Table 22–3). A financial expert, J. E. Blunt, was asked to evaluate the company's accounts and suggest "some method of furnishing. . . additional cash to offset the constantly increasing volume of bills receivable, consisting of agents' and farmers' notes."[51] Blunt recommended going over to a policy of placing serial debentures with maturities of one to three or five years; these debentures plus other long-term obligations would be kept below 80 percent of outstanding receivables; any additional financing would be handled with short-term loans. Blunt also suggested an alternative plan: authorizing an issue of $50 million in twenty-year sinking fund debentures. This would give the company needed flexibility in financing its continued expansion.[52]

Blunt's suggestions apparently produced no new policy, because management was forced to focus on an impending antitrust suit by the U.S. Justice Department. The only step taken to put financing on a sounder basis was to place a three-year, $20 million loan (with a large part taken by Rockefeller) through the Morgan organization in early 1912. Cyrus McCormick, Jr. simply deferred "the general question of broader financing" for a later date.[53]

International Harvester's financial operations, though occasionally influenced by the internal struggle for corporate control, remained entirely separate from production and marketing strategies, both domestic and foreign. Because all of the principal countries in which International Harvester operated were on the gold standard with fixed exchange rates, little reason existed to link specific investments in factories or markets with local credit availability. The company borrowed most of the money it needed in the primary money markets of New York and London because those were the cheapest places in which to raise funds.

Finally, beginning in late 1910 it began to sell longer-term notes, but management in fact gave little thought to more complex financial strategies, and the individual strength of Cyrus McCormick, Jr. as company president, backed by John D. Rockefeller's advice and wealth, kept the company from the influence of financiers who might have pushed different policies. Here at least the pace and pattern of transnational development of an important industrial enterprise provide virtually no hint of influence from the international financial community.

Conclusions

As noted in the Preface, we present two separate conclusions. They were drafted independently of one another and only lightly edited thereafter in the interest of stylistic consistency.

V.I. Bovykin

I

At first glance the reader may well be overwhelmed by the diversity of the material presented in this team project. Despite the contributors' obvious desire to do as they were advised—that is, to present a unified analysis of general processes—their respective chapters proved to be quite divergent. They differ in the range of questions under review, the nature of their analysis, and, last but not least, specific historical content. This was only to be expected; after all, the authors represent different national historiographic traditions and theoretical schools, which influenced their perception of the problems at hand and their selection and interpretation of facts. Moreover, they faced unequal conditions: Some were able to use extensive literature, others had to draw mainly from their own works, and still others, those who dealt with the least-studied subjects, had to begin almost from scratch.

But the root cause of the divergence among individual chapters lies undoubtedly in the diversity of the historical reality examined in them. And the fact that, for the sake of reflecting that diversity, the authors departed from the proposed scheme is not reproachable but commendable. This helped to bring out the complex and contradictory nature of the processes under review.

Despite their diversity, the chapters of this team project link up with each other surprisingly well to form a fairly integral historical picture. Naturally, many of its details still have to be filled in; some of the others, drawn from different angles and on different scales, are blurred as it were, and there are also some blank spots. And yet we do have at least an outline of the formation of national banking systems in their interaction, that is, the evolution of international banking in the latter part of the nineteenth and early part of the twentieth centuries. Further research will certainly make the picture more detailed and precise, but the key development trends are clearly seen from the outline: the internationalization of banking and the emergence of specific features intrinsic to national banking systems; the increasing uniformity of the development of banking and the growing diversity of its concrete manifestations in individual countries. While discharging essentially identical functions everywhere, banking proved to be remarkably adaptable to the economic, social, legal, and political specifics of individual countries with due regard for their position in the world at large. This is why a unique banking system took shape in each country under the impact of internal and external factors. At the same time every such system, connected with other national systems, was an integral component of international banking.

The two major factors influencing the internationalization of banking were the growth of world trade and the activation of the international movement of capital, as can be seen from, among other things, the materials of this study. Moreover, the international movement of capital, closely associated in its early stages with the movement of commodities, acquired independent status during the period under review and came to play a crucial role in the integration and internationalization of the world economy as it brought the expanding trade contacts and increasing international division of labor under its control.

Significantly, the uneven economic and social development and differing positions of countries in the world economy predetermined some major differences in the evolution of their national banking systems and accounted for the dissimilar impact of external factors upon them.

In the case of countries that were the first to embark on the road of capitalist evolution and industrialization the significance of external factors was determined by the existence of a less developed environment that could serve as an object of colonization, commercial and industrial expansion, and export of capital. Naturally, competition among them also played an important role.

In forming their environment, the advanced industrial states oriented their development on it increasingly using it as a market for manufactured goods, a source of raw materials and food, and a sphere of investment.

This tendency, most vividly expressed in Britain's economic development, was also manifested in the formation of its banking system. As demonstrated by Cottrell, it was largely shaped by the requirements of British foreign trade and export of capital. Moreover, when London became a world commercial center, its banks began to service the trade and cargo shipping needs of not only Britain but also other countries. This is why the British banking system was characterized by the development of special banking institutions engaged in crediting international trade, notably in bill acceptance, and operations with foreign securities and investments abroad. Overseas banks also associated themselves with this system.

As other countries developed along capitalist lines Britain and its banking system began to feel the reciprocal influence of the surrounding world. This influence, as evidenced by the penetration of continental banking experience into the British Isles, including the establishment of branch offices of continental banks in London, and, of course, the tougher competition with foreign banks on the world monetary market, became especially conspicuous in the late nineteenth and early twentieth centuries, as the British banking system underwent a profound change in line with the imperatives of the day.

The banking system that took shape in France was quite different in regard to its institutional forms, but its evolution was also largely influenced by the interests of foreign capitalist expansion, primarily the objectives of export of capital. Admittedly, the French way had its special features. Thus, British capital was mainly exported to other parts of the world: the British colonies (Canada, Australia, India, South Africa, etc.), the United States, and various countries in Latin America, the Middle East, and the Far East. Only a small portion of that capital was placed on the European Continent, whereas the bulk of French capital was exported to countries in Europe, though some of its also found its way to America, the Middle East, and the Far East, French colonies included. Hence the differing geographic distribution of the foreign ties of British and French banks and the dissimilar structures and organization of the international financial institutions and bank groups established by them. As can be seen in the chapters by Cottrell, Bonin, and other authors, however, these distinctions were made less conspicuous by the intertwining interests of the British and French banks. As a result, their relations in Europe and beyond, particularly in the Middle East and Far East, were marked by an increasingly more complex combination of competition and partnership.

While the evolution of banking in Britain and France witnessed an early orientation on serving foreign trade and the export of capital, the corresponding process in other countries, which pioneered capitalist modernization (Belgium, Germany, the United States), was much more geared to the objectives of their industrial development. Characteristically, it was in Belgium that a "mixed banking system" first emerged as the most efficient tool in the industrial strategy of banks. As Van der Wee and Goossens show in their chapter, that system served as a major vehicle of industrialization and ensured a fast growth of large-scale heavy industry in Belgium. Initially focused on domestic problems, the Belgian mixed banking system gained in strength and enlarged its sphere of operations by the late nineteenth century to become "mature enough" for expansion abroad—an especially vigorous process from the 1890s.

In Germany, too, according to Tilly, internal rather than international factors were instrumental in the formation of a banking system in the latter half of the nineteenth century. As can be seen from the figures he cites in this book, industrial growth was the main factor behind it. It is indicative, therefore, that German banks largely emulated the Belgian example in their drive to help their country's industrialization. In the 1870s, just like their Belgian counterparts, German banks began to show interest in international business and got actively involved in it within a decade. Yet it was only for a brief period in the 1880s that Germany's investments abroad exceeded its domestic investments. According to Tilly, the external activity of German banks in the late nineteenth and early twentieth centuries was more dependent on the market situation in Germany than on the foreign stock market situation. Nevertheless, his chapter offers convincing testimony that even the German banks played an important role in international economics, placing foreign loans in Germany, providing for German investments abroad, and financing foreign trade.

The formation of the U.S. banking system was also primarily shaped by internal factors, as can be seen from the chapter by Carosso and Sylla. Of special importance here were the unique legal conditions in which the U.S. banks had to operate. The U.S. example is highly interesting in this respect as it shows how the requirements of international business superseded the fettering legal norms and encouraged the development of those institutional forms of banking not covered by those norms. Its unique and autonomous nature notwithstanding, the U.S. economy was bound with the world economy by numerous ties. Its rapid growth resulted not only in the expansion of these ties but also in their changed character, which can be seen from, among other things, the fact that in the late nineteenth and early twentieth centuries the United States, previously a major importer of goods and capital, began to export more than it imported. And since the U.S. joint-stock banks had a limited overseas operational capability, private banks took it upon themselves to promote American economic expansion in the world. That, according to Carosso and Sylla, explains the secret behind the unusual flourishing of private banks in the United States.

The above-mentioned five countries, which had made the biggest headway in capitalist modernization by the end of the nineteenth century, determined the external conditions for the development of other national economies in the period under review. Their example and direct impact on the surrounding world in the course of their growing external expansion, and their fierce competition for markets, sources of raw materials, and investment spheres were among the more general international factors behind the formation of banking systems in other countries.

As demonstrated by the materials presented in this survey, the effect of these international factors varied from country to country, depending on the level of economic development, the character of social organization, and the degree of political independence there. The better ground was prepared in such countries for the development of capitalist credit, the more intrinsic was the relationship between external factors and domestic conditions. This provided the basis for the emergence of fairly independent national banking systems arising from the fusion of domestic needs and outside influences.

As regards the countries studied in this survey, this was the case in Russia, Austria-Hungary, Sweden, Denmark, Italy and Japan. They were very different countries and yet all of them embarked on industrialization at the close of the nineteenth century and made use of the experience of more advanced nations and the opportunities involved in trading with them and importing their capital, even if with varying success. Naturally, the specifics of each country could not but affect the emerging national banking systems, lending them some distinctive features.

In Canada and Australia, for example, given their status as self-governing dominions of the British Empire, autonomous banking systems grew up in the late nineteenth and early twentieth centuries in conformity with the economic structures prevailing there. Characteristically, banking in these two countries, which had taken shape under various kinds of foreign influence, eventually developed an interest in doing independent business abroad.

In countries where the domestic requirements for the development of banking were either insufficient or lacking altogether, foreign banks played a more active and independent role, resulting in the transplantation of institutional forms of banking devised in advanced capitalist states. Various options of such development are analyzed in the examples of Brazil, China, and countries in the Middle East. In Brazil the intrusion of foreign, mostly British, banks overshadowed the weak sprouts of local banking, leaving that country with a network of affiliates of the banking systems of more advanced states. That was also the case in China and the Middle East though, owing to the dominance of traditional economies, the ground was less prepared there for accepting the capitalist banking brought in from without. Hence the important role of intermediary (compradore) links, the emergence of foreign sectors and so on. As banks of various foreign origin operated in all those countries, very complex multinational structures emerged within their banking systems involving some local elements as well.

The present study of the role of international factors in the formation of banking systems in various countries highlights aspects of the relationship between banks and industry that were not quite clear heretofore.

Various views have been expressed in the literature on the subject concerning the mechanism of interrelationship between banks and industry in the process of industrialization of different countries. None of the scholars, however, disputed the fact that the role of banks was an important factor of industrial growth, though the operation of this factor varied from country to country depending on concrete historical conditions. At the same time, we hardly need to prove that, in a setting where the capitalist development of the national economy focuses on industrialization the needs of industrial growth acquire special importance in shaping the tasks and ways of development of capitalist credit. The various works on the history of the relationship between banks and industry in the early stages of industrialization have shown that everywhere—in Britain, the European Continent, the United States, and also in Japan—the banks contributed to the growth of industry, providing it with circulating capital through short-term credits. And there were many cases of short-term credits developing into long-term credits. The long-term investment needs of the developing industry arose everywhere in the early stages of industrialization. But, on the one hand, these needs were relatively unimportant and could largely be met through the reinvestment of profits, family savings, and transfer of capital from the outside (from old to new branches, from more developed to less developed countries) in the framework of credit relations between industrialists, without referring to banks. On the other hand, in view of their inadequate development and legal restrictions, the banks were not prepared for long-term investment in industry.

For nearly a century, through trials and mistakes, at the cost of much sacrifice, banks evolved their industrial finance techniques. Though they embarked on this road in different periods, the banks of different countries operating in the differing social, economic, and legal conditions of the time faced similar tasks—viz., ensuring liquidity, sharing responsibility, and exercising control. A contribution to the accomplishment of this task was made by Scottish joint-stock banks; by British "country," "commercial," and "merchant" banks; by the Belgian Société Générale and Banque de Belgique; by banking houses in France, Germany, and the United States; by banks of the *crédit mobilier* type and their offshoots in the shape of business banks in France; universal banks in Germany; the "investment trust" in Britain, and national banks and "trust companies" in the United States.

Large-scale industrial finance and the establishment of permanent and stable ties between banks and industry through "participation" and "personal union" systems expressive of the interlocking of productive and loan capital became possible and necessary only on the basis of a very high concentration of production and capital as exemplified by the rapid expansion of joint-stock companies. Before turning to operations with the shares of industrial enterprises, the banks had passed, as the present study shows, through long apprenticeship in the placement of government bonds and the securities of railway companies. Consequently, it was only in the last third of the nineteenth century that the interlocking of banks and industry (in the process of which banks began to establish industrial enterprises, supervise their operation, and even interfere in the settlement of production questions while the growing industrial enterprises began to carry out not only production but also commercial, credit, and financial operations) first emerged as a clear-cut capitalist development trend and not a transient, isolated phenomenon.

The process differed from country to country in its starting point, rates, and forms. Banks in Belgium and Germany, where the exceptionally high pace of industrial growth could not be secured by profit reinvestment, were the first to provide funds for industrial development. The coalescence of German banks with industry imparted a new dimension to their foreign expansion: They began to act jointly with the industrial corporations under their control. This cooperation was also characteristic of Belgian banks, which went over to foreign investment only after a period during which they had gained some experience in financing domestic industry.

In Britain and France, where the rates of industrial growth declined in the last third of the nineteenth century, industry's demand for long-term investment was not so high. As the findings of our study indicate, however, the interlocking of British and French banks with industry proceeded largely via the establishment and financing of industrial enterprises abroad. In other words, the interlocking of banks and industry tended to become an international process.

Perhaps the most impressive result of the study is the picture of the evolving relationship between the banking systems of different countries drawn by the joint efforts of its participants.

The starting premise for this evolution was the cosmopolitan nature of many private banks operating in European countries and the United States in the early half of the nineteenth century and that served as an important element in the formation of banking systems. These banks were frequently linked not only by traditional business cooperation but also by ties of kinship. But, as the materials of the study amply illustrate, the basis for cooperation between national banking systems was the emergence of the international division of social labor, which gathered momentum as a result of industrialization and grew in scope as this process spread to ever-new countries, enlarging the scope of their national economies. It was this process that gave rise to international cooperation between banks.

Banking's main functions were the crediting of world trade, making loans to states and cities, financing railway construction and industrial growth, floating securities, holding working balances, and collecting deposits in major financial centers. Its main forms were the formation of branches and affiliates abroad, participation in foreign banks, joint participation of banks of different countries in industrial and other companies, and the formation of international banks and bank groups.

The result was a kind of international interlocking of national banking systems, which represented nothing less than socialization of capital on a world scale. It is easy to see that this interlocking had a distinctly hierarchic structure. The main centers of financial ties that enmeshed the whole world were Britain, France, and Germany. The division into creditors and debtors, as indicated by data on international migration of capital, was also evidenced by the international bank ties elucidated by the participants in the present study.

II

The question of the role of foreign investment in the economic and social development of nations importing capital has been studied for some time. In the present survey, in conformity with its general idea, this question was examined in terms of the activity of banks as agents of such investment. For the sake of comparison we chose as objects of study several countries that were big importers of capital but differed in the level and character of their development, geographic position, and the place they occupied in the world capitalist system. Despite these differences their import of capital had some obvious common features. Everywhere the basic forms of foreign investment were bond loans to government authorities and railway companies. Participation in joint-stock companies, including industrial ones, played a considerably smaller role. But the relationship of different forms of foreign investment and the conditions and mechanisms of its placement by banks differed substantially from country to country. And, of course, foreign investment could also be made without the banks' assistance.

A special place among the importing countries was held by the United States—the biggest international debtor that from the late nineteenth century began to act simultaneously as creditor in relation to some countries. As distinct from most other countries, in the United States total external government loans declined steadily from the late 1870s to constitute only a small fraction of the country's foreign debts in 1914. Another important feature characteristic of foreign investments in the United States was the partnership established between American and foreign banks by the turn of the century on the basis of division of labor among them.

Considering the scope of the U.S. national economy, foreign investments, notwithstanding their stupendous size, played an important though auxiliary role. They dissolved, as it were, in the rapidly growing economic organism of the country. While facilitating international cooperation involving American banks, they did not pose any threat to their independence.

Russia lagged far behind the United States in economic and social development. But by its vast resources, high rates of industrial growth at the end of the nineteenth century, and its resultant ability to assimilate foreign investments in the national economy, it was very much like the United States. But Russia's semifeudal political regime, which absorbed an inordinately large share of internal accumulation, held back the country's capitalist evolution and fettered the potentialities of its economic growth. This accounts for the significant role played by foreign capital, primarily as a factor ensuring Russia's capitalist evolution and perpetuating its reactionary political regime and also as a means of direct financial support for the regime. By 1914 the share of foreign government loans to Russia constituted over three-fifths of its foreign debt; moreover, the proportion of nonproductive government loans had increased considerably at the beginning of the twentieth century. All this explains the close contacts between those foreign banks that placed Russian government securities abroad and their respective governments and the political strings attached to the settlement of issues related to this placement.

Political considerations did not play any notable role in foreign bank investments in Russia's industry, however. Being unable to open branches in the country on account of legislative restrictions, foreign banks participated extensively in Russian banks and strove to use them as intermediaries in industrial finance. Apparently, however, they did not succeed in establishing control over the Russian banks.

Roosa's analysis of financial and banking relations between the United States and Russia is of definite interest in the context of the present comparative study. Noteworthy is her mention of the failure of the attempts made by the tsarist government in the 1890s and early 1900s to place a Russian government loan in the United States. This failure can hardly be explained by subjective causes alone. According to Carosso and Sylla, in the late 1890s the United States did not yet have a fully developed security market. American banks were just beginning to place government loans abroad. At the same time the Russian experience of companies like Singer and International Harvester indicated that the U.S.-born pattern of a large corporation integrating both production and marketing functions was quite applicable and efficient in Russian conditions.

The Italian example analyzed by Hertner highlights some of the common features related to the impact of foreign capital on the development of banking in a number of European countries following the road of advanced capitalist nations. As a rule, foreign banks operated in those countries via local credit institutions that had already existed there for some time or that they had helped establish locally themselves. Their involvement in such institutions was phased out, however.

According to Levy, foreign banks with a negligible involvement of local capitalists gained a foothold in Brazil. Although these banks focused primarily on granting loans to the government and promoting foreign trade transactions, they could not avoid participating in the provision of the country's domestic economic needs by financing the establishment of an infrastructure, the development of the services sector, and, even though on a minor scale, the boosting of industrial production.

China and the Middle East countries dealt with in the chapters by King and Thobie were the key fields of activity of the "colonial" banks representing the interests of the bank groups of advanced capitalist countries. Irrespective of whether they operated as foreign or quasi-national institutions, these banks generally enjoyed a privileged (and often even extraterritorial) status and acted in exceedingly close conjunction with the colonial policies of the great powers. Therefore, one cannot interpret the activity of "colonial" banks in an adequate and comprehensive manner in isolation from the political context. The highly contradictory nature of that activity makes unequivocal evaluation impossible.

King showed in his chapter that, given the economic philosophy prevailing particularly in Britain and France at the time, the colonial bankers considered they were making positive contributions not only to trade finance but also to the local economies in which they operated and that by providing access to Europe's capital markets they were furthering the region's development and modernization. At the same time we have good grounds for making a critical assessment of the activity of the "colonial" banks both in China and the Middle East. Loans offered by those banks were instrumental in propping up reactionary political regimes and, thereby, in preserving backward social structures in the Middle East and Far East.

The dialectics of the development of colonial banks, which profited from these backward structures, however, actually led to the latter's gradual disintegration. This is evidenced by, among other things, the effect of their financing of railway construction in countries of the Middle and Far East. But it was limited in scope. Foreign investments had generally a superficial effect on the local economies.

While the previous section of the text focused on issues related to cooperation between banks of different countries and their intertwining interests, the materials of this section demonstrate abundantly that this interlocking not only did not remove the competition and contradictions between banks and their groups but, on the contrary, complicated them. These contradictions were extended to the level of international economic relations, with competition involving not only banks of different countries but also multinational bank groups. Moreover, the cosmopolitan interests of these multinational groups often clashed with the state interests of the countries of origin of member banks of such groups. The processes involved in the internationalization of capital and economic partition of the world served to aggravate the already acute imperialist contradictions.

III

Banks were, in fact, the first multinational enterprises. Considering the tendency toward the interlocking of banking and industrial capital that took shape in the late nineteenth and early twentieth centuries, it would be pertinent to discuss the role of banks in the formation of multinational industrial enterprises. Strange as it may seem, this aspect of their evolution has attracted less attention from researchers than its other aspects. That is probably why the interesting materials in the third section of our study raise more questions than they give answers.

The chapters of this section discuss different variants of relationship between banks and multinational corporations in the process of the latter's rise and growth. Wengenroth examined cases in which banks played an active role in establishing such corporations. He showed that banks financing the establishment of affiliate enterprises by firms controlled by them in other countries created the prerequisites for the rise of multinational enterprises. As he notes quite rightly, however, this did not always lead to the formation of really integrated enterprises with their departments in different countries linked to each other not only by financial but also production and commercial ties. Nonetheless, such cases did occur and the examination of one of them—the Mannesmann concern—enabled Wengenroth to form an opinion of the factors that played the key role in the formation of multinational corporations. Among these factors he lists the narrow specialization of production and the monopoly possession of technology. A bank's assistance, he believes, was important but not decisive. The record of International Harvester and the Nobel Dynamite Trust testifies that highly specialized multinational corporations could also emerge without any visible aid from the banks. According to Carstensen, however, at the development stage where their expansion assumed global proportions, aid from a bank became essential.

Of special interest is the comparative history of multinational corporations in the electrical engineering and oil industries. The banks' leading role in the former case is indisputable. Banks also showed an obvious interest in the oil industry. But here they were pushed into the background by three multinational monopoly corporations— Standard Oil, Royal Dutch-Shell, and Nobel—which, as studies have shown, successfully evaded the establishment of banks' control. What is the reason for the differ-

ing relationship between banks and industry in the formation of multinational corporations in electrical engineering and the oil industry?

It should be pointed out that the fact of self-financing identified here as the main
source of growth of the three oil corporations, important as it is, does not remove the
problem of their relationship with banks. Having enterprises in different countries and
carrying out large-scale operations in oil drilling and refining and the transportation,
storage, and sale of oil products, the companies needed not only large credits but an
apparatus for settlements and accounts. Judging by the Nobel Company balance sheets
in the early 1900s, the credits it received were considerably larger than its joint-stock,
bond, and reserve capital stocks. The value of its property constituted less than 15
percent of its assets. A large stock (over 5 percent of the assets) of shares of affiliate
enterprises instituted by the Nobel Company abroad for the sale of oil products and its
vast working capital showed, first, that this company had assumed the functions of a
holding company and, second, that it could not operate without close and lasting
cooperation with the banks. I think that the relations of Standard Oil, Royal Dutch-
Shell, and Nobel with the banks call for further elucidation.

And the problem as a whole obviously merits further study.

As early as the turn of the century economists and sociologists noted some newly
emergent trends in the economics of capitalist countries and international affairs generally. Some of the scholars interpreted them as signs of capitalism's entry into a new
development phase. They gave it different names to suit their own interpretations of
contemporary economic changes and their possible social repercussions, viz., imperialism, the era of finance capital, monopoly capitalism, organized capitalism, joint-
stock capitalism, etc. Irrespective of their differences, however, all of them attached
prime importance to the contemporary processes involved in the internationalization of
capital and production. Subsequent developments have borne out the fact that these are
long-term processes leading to irreversible change.

This study, analyzing the place and role of banks in the processes of internationalization of capital and production at the turn of the century, provides a deeper insight
into the driving forces, intrinsic nature, forms, and directions of these processes and
contributes to a better understanding of the profound qualitative changes that have
shaped the image of the modern world.

Rondo Cameron

At the outset of this project the organizers titled it "International Banking and Industrial
Finance, 1870–1914." We stated that "The purpose of this project is to study the
relationship of international banking to the development of banking structures (including the bank as a multinational firm), to international movements of capital, and to the
formation and operations of multinational industrial enterprises, 1870–1914." It was our
expectation that we would discover that banks, especially those with an international
orientation, played an important role in the creation and finance of the multinational
corporations that came into existence and prominence in that period.[1]

The clearest conclusion to emerge from this study is that banks were *not*, with few and minor exceptions, responsible for the emergence of multinational industrial enterprises. In that respect the expectations of the organizers were unfulfilled; but that in itself is a significant positive, not merely negative, conclusion.

Banks did play a significant role in mobilizing and channeling the unprecedented international investments of the period. But for the most part—the exceptions will be noted subsequently—the banks provided funds directly or indirectly for the needs of governments and for social overhead capital, especially railways. They also, in many instances, facilitated or assisted the expansion of multinational enterprises by means of short-term advances of working capital and especially by financing the international movement of commodities; but they did not, with few exceptions, take the initiative in organizing multinational industrial concerns, nor did they as a rule control large volumes of equity capital.

Apart from this major conclusion, our studies provide many findings and insights of interest to students of banking, international finance, international relations more generally, and to all who are cognizant of the significance for the contemporary world of the period 1870–1914. It is the purpose of this concluding chapter to point out the more significant of those findings and insights, not by recapitulating the earlier chapters, but by highlighting the comparative aspects. The entire project was originally conceived as a study in comparative economic history. Although not all participants took advantage of the opportunity for explicit comparisons to the extent hoped for and urged by the organizers, the materials for comparison are nevertheless available.

Before moving on to the comparative aspects, however, it is necessary to emphasize a fact already alluded to in different contexts: The primary function of banks on the international scene was the finance of international trade. In purely quantitative terms it was by far the most important function. Although the other international functions of banks, such as the underwriting and issue of government and corporate securities on international markets, may have provided more drama and more cause for public notice, they derived from and ultimately depended upon the primary function of financing international trade.

I

In the most general terms, *countries* may be compared with respect to their status as lenders (creditors) or borrowers (debtors), or in a few cases as both. Beyond that, they may be compared with respect to the consequences of foreign investment (whether inflow or outflow) for their domestic economies, and in particular their levels and rates of economic development. Moreover, national *banking systems* may be compared in terms of their origins and development (including the role of international influences therein), their roles in industrial finance, and (in at least some cases) their roles in international politics. (These headings do not exhaust the potential for comparison, but they are most relevant in terms of the parameters of this volume.) First the most general comparisons will be drawn. Subsequently, individual countries and banking systems will be compared with one another.

As is well known, at the beginning of the period Great Britain and France (and probably the Netherlands and Belgium) were already (or soon to be) "mature" creditor nations, in the sense that returns on previous foreign investments equaled or exceeded the net outflow of new foreign investments. Germany and the United States were the most obvious examples of nations whose positive trade balances gave them the resources to repatriate existing debts and become net foreign investors; Germany became a net creditor by the 1880s if not before, whereas the United States did not achieve that status until after the outbreak of World War I. All other nations (with the possible exception of Switzerland, whose situation was ambiguous) were for all or most of the period net debtors to one degree or another.

The debtor nations can be further classified with respect to the consequences of their foreign borrowings. They all obtained railways and other infrastructures; some saw the sources of their raw materials developed; and a few obtained manufacturing plants as a direct result of foreign investment. The efficacy of the investments varied enormously, however. Several debtor nations, notably the United States, Japan, the British dominions, and the Scandinavian countries, made good use of the funds, and in 1914 they were on their way to becoming creditor nations themselves. Others, including Russia, the Ottoman Empire, China, Brazil, and other Latin American countries, were sometimes obliged to borrow merely to pay interest and amortization on previous indebtedness.

Albert Fishlow distinguishes between "developmental borrowers," who used the borrowed funds for purposes of development, and "revenue borrowers," who merely consumed the proceeds of foreign loans.[2] Although the distinction is a useful one in principle, it is difficult to apply in specific cases. For example, Russia and even the Ottoman Empire, placed by Fishlow in the revenue borrower category, obtained railways, and Russia a substantial amount of heavy industry. Brazil and other Latin American countries considered by Fishlow as developmental borrowers, on the other hand, although they obtained some productive assets, in other instances exhibited the behavior of revenue borrowers.

Owing to their unique political and diplomatic circumstances, the cases of the Ottoman Empire and China can be set aside for further consideration in a different context. The purely economic consequences of foreign investment can best be observed in those smaller nations whose political histories were characterized by continuity. Within our sample those nations are represented by Sweden, Denmark, and Brazil.

At the beginning of our period Sweden and Denmark were on the periphery of Europe, economically as well as geographically. Both were predominantly agrarian and relatively poor. In the course of the next forty years or so, however, both developed rapidly. They exhibited high rates of economic growth, participated fully in the international economy along lines of comparative advantage, and spawned sophisticated industries. Denmark's highly productive agriculture dominated its list of exports, but it also produced a variety of manufactured consumer and capital goods for both domestic consumption and export. Sweden is perhaps the most outstanding example of "upstream industrialization," that is, of a country that once exported raw materials but then began to process them and export them in the form of semimanufactured and finished products. The timber industry is a case in point. In the beginning timber was exported as logs, to be sawed into boards in the importing country (Britain); in the 1850s Swedish entrepreneurs built sawmills to convert the timber into lumber in Sweden. In the 1860s and 1870s processes for making paper from wood pulp, at first by mechanical and subsequently by chemical means (the latter a Swedish invention), were introduced;

output of wood pulp grew rapidly for the remainder of the century. Well over half was exported, mainly to Great Britain and Germany, but the Swedes consumed an increasing amount themselves and exported the higher value-added paper.

The iron industry followed a similar pattern. Although Sweden's charcoal-smelted iron could not compete in price with coke-smelted iron or Bessemer steel, its higher quality made it especially valuable for such products as ball bearings, and after the advent of hydroelectricity Sweden, with its vast hydraulic resources, became one of the pioneers of electro-smelting. Sweden and Denmark also became important producers of electrical machinery. By 1914 they not only had sophisticated industries but also high levels of per capita income.

It would be fatuous to credit the banking systems exclusively for this performance. Many other factors contributed, especially the high levels of literacy and human capital, and sensible economic policies. But the banking systems also contributed. They did so in part by cooperation with the banks of the capital-exporting nations, and by directing imported capital into industries with high rates of return, such as hydroelectricity. Much imported capital also went into agricultural mortgages, directed by the mortgage banks and agricultural cooperatives, thus freeing domestic capital for other uses.

The comparison with Brazil, and with other nations of Latin America, is illuminating. Although those nations also specialized along lines of comparative advantage, with exports of foodstuffs and other primary products, productivity remained low and no upstream industrialization took place. (The import-substitution industrialization of the later twentieth century was something quite different.) Just as the banking systems of Denmark and Sweden do not deserve all the credit for their countries' development, that of Brazil should not be blamed for its failure to develop. Again, many factors were involved—notably the *low* levels of literacy and human capital, and the absence (on the whole) of sensible economic policies. But there was some connection between the two sets of factors. The higher literacy levels of the Scandinavian countries encouraged the "banking habit" among their populations, and this enabled the banks to perform their functions better, whereas the lower levels in Latin America discouraged the use of banks and deprived them of resources. Moreover, the dual nature of the banking systems of Latin America hampered their effectiveness. Foreign banks and bankers were concerned almost exclusively with international commerce and with loans to governments and large-scale enterprises, such as railways, whereas domestic banks lacked international connections and had limited opportunities as well as resources. And, as Professor Levy points out, the domestic banks suffered in times of uncertainty and crisis, when customers switched their deposits to the more highly regarded foreign banks.

Of the other nations in our sample, Australia and Canada most resembled Denmark and Sweden with respect to their utilization of foreign investment. Both experienced some balance-of-payments difficulties, and Australia actually had a negative growth rate of income for some years in the 1890s; but in both nations the investments proved productive on the whole and generated a flow of funds to cover both interest and amortization.

Japan also had a successful experience with imported capital, but that experience does not fit neatly into the categories of either developmental or revenue finance. Although some foreign capital entered Japan in the 1870s and before, the new Meiji government, fearing a loss of sovereignty, sought to limit and exclude it. The government itself borrowed abroad in the early 1870s for railway construction and to purchase the samurai feudal rights, but thereafter did not resort to foreign borrowing until 1896. It also discouraged private foreign borrowing. As a result, Japan's early industrialization was financed almost entirely with domestic capital (aided by the banks), and, as Professor Ishii reports, "the role of imported capital in promoting Japanese industrialization was comparatively limited."[3] After 1896 and especially from 1904 the government borrowed large sums from abroad, mainly for military purposes. In this way the government obtained its armaments, but the economy also obtained the foreign exchange to stave off a balance-of-payments crisis.

The Japanese case invites comparison with the Italian in that they were both relatively poor and relatively densely populated countries. As nations, they were also new actors on the international scene, with aspirations to great power status. Although Professor Hertner's contribution to this volume is limited to the role of foreign capital in the Italian banking system, enough is known about the role of foreign capital in the Italian economy as a whole to permit some limited generalizations.[4] Whereas Japan entered the modern era with no foreign indebtedness and no experience of foreign borrowing, the new Italian government of the 1860s inherited an enormous load of deadweight foreign debt and a long experience with foreign borrowing, mostly unhappy. Both were obliged to borrow anew, both for purposes of economic development and to support their political aspirations. The Japanese successfully limited their borrowing until the large-scale loans of the early twentieth century, but the Italians borrowed heavily on both public and private account from the very beginning of their nationhood. Both countries also experienced substantial periods of inconvertible paper currency as a result of political events, but neither actually defaulted on their international obligations. Both countries succeeded, with difficulty, in adhering to the gold standard by the end of the nineteenth century. On balance it would appear that both benefitted from foreign capital, although Japan probably obtained greater benefits from its more limited borrowing than did Italy with its more profligate policies.

By far the largest part of foreign investment went for railway construction. Overall, from 1870 to 1914, at least 60 percent and possibly more of the funds invested abroad had this destination. This included both private and public securities. In the United States privately issued securities of railway companies, primarily bonds and debentures, accounted for well over half of all foreign borrowing. In other countries government borrowing for railway construction, either directly or indirectly (via government-guaranteed securities, as in Russia and several other cou..tries), accounted for similar proportions. The interplay between public and private borrowing for purposes of railway construction is highlighted in the history of the Austro-Hungarian Empire where, as in other countries, more than half of all borrowed funds went into railways.

The Monarchy's first modern railway (apart from a short horse-drawn line from Budweiss to Linz dating from the 1820s) was the Kaiser Ferdinands-Nordbahn, conceded in 1836 to a company headed by Salomon Rothschild and financed by family connections in London, Paris, and Frankfurt. Shortly afterward, however, in 1842 the state undertook to construct all trunk lines, a policy that remained in effect until financial difficulties in the following decade obliged it to sell the state-owned railways and return to the policy of private ownership—but with state guarantees of interest and amortization. By 1854 the state had built less than 1,500 kilometers of railway and the construction program had come to a near standstill for want of resources. Under those circumstances the government sold a portion of the state-owned network to the French Crédit Mobilier and granted it concessions for new construction. The Crédit Mobilier promptly organized the Austrian State Railway Company (Österreichische Staats-Eisenbahn-Gesellschaft; Société Autrichienne des Chemins de fer de l'Etat) and issued its shares through the Paris Bourse. The original network consisted of 1,322 kilometers, of which 950 were in operation in three different sections. By 1870 the network exceeded 2,000 kilometers, with extensions to Silesia, Serbia, and Rumania, and was extended still further in subsequent years.

The Austrian government still owned several lines in various stages of completion, notably those in the Italian provinces of Lombardy and Venetia and the *Südbahn*, the main line from Vienna to Trieste and Venice. As part of his counterattack against the Pereires and the Crédit Mobilier, which included the formation of the Creditanstalt in 1855,[5] James de Rothschild succeeded in garnering those and concessions for still others, which he organized in 1858 as the South Austrian, Lombard-Venetian, and Central Italian Railway (the company also owned the main line from Milan down the Po Valley in the direction of Florence). Its network in 1858 amounted to more than 3,000 kilometers, of which 1,400 were in operation and 1,100 kilometers under construction. The company not only monopolized traffic in the southern half of the empire but also controlled the only two direct routes between Italy and Germany before the completion of the Gotthard Tunnel in 1882, the Semmering Pass on the *Südbahn*, opened in 1858, and the Brenner Pass in the Tyrol (1867). As a result of the wars of 1859 and 1866 the Lombard and Venetian lines, as well as those of Central Italy, fell to Italian sovereignty, but that did not interfere with the organization of the company. From 1860 the annual meetings of stockholders took place in Paris under the presidency of the chairman of the Committee of Paris, always a Rothschild, rather than in Vienna under the president of the company, required by law to be an Austrian citizen. The Rothschilds also controlled the Austrian *Westbahn*, from Vienna to Salzburg, as well as several lines in Hungary.

The Vienna-based companies, largely owned and controlled from abroad, did not build fast enough in Hungary to satisfy the nationalistic Magyars. After the Ausgleich (compromise) of 1867 they entered on a spree of railway construction of their own, financed mainly with foreign capital but with state-guaranteed interest. The result was overbuilding, bankruptcy, and eventual nationalization, epitomized by the fate of the Hungarian Eastern Railway.[6] The funds for nationalization came from the government, of course, which borrowed for the purpose, mostly in Vienna and abroad. In 1891 the Hungarian government nationalized the lines of the Austrian State Railway within its jurisdiction, after which it owned 85 percent of the railways on its territory, as compared with less than 50 percent in the Cisleithan provinces. Before World War I the government in Vienna also nationalized most of the remaining private railways on its territory, but, as Kövér reports, more than two-thirds of the bonds were still held abroad.[7]

At the level of individual nations the respective experiences of the United States and Russia invite comparison. Both were large nations in terms of area, population, and resources, the latter largely undeveloped in both at the beginning of the period. They were also the largest recipients of foreign investment during the period although, as already pointed out, the United States became a significant lender before the period was over. The United States was also one of the world's wealthiest nations, as measured by per capita income, whereas Russia lagged far behind the European average. The United States also already possessed a developed banking system. Although it owed something to Scottish and English examples and expertise in the first half of the century, by 1870 it had developed distinctive characteristics and behaviors that owed little to foreign influence, at least in the corporate sector. Among these characteristics was a pronounced domestic orientation, reenforced by both legislation and tradition. Only the relatively small number of unincorporated private bankers, mainly in New York City and other East Coast ports, played a significant role in international finance. That role, however, was all out of proportion to the number of firms. Those firms, with their international connections and contacts, were chiefly responsible for channeling the large volume of foreign investments into American securities, at first government securities, but, from the 1880s, predominantly railway bonds. Foreign direct investment in American industry and agriculture was also important but, as Professor Wilkins points out, those investments largely bypassed the domestic banking system. Although the American economy would undoubtedly have developed in the absence of foreign investment, that investment significantly hastened the process.

The Russian banking system, unlike the American, was still very much in its formative stages in 1870. Its development thereafter was rapid, especially from the 1880s, and owed much to both foreign examples and foreign capital. The Russian government, as is well known, likewise played a prominent role in the development of the economy. With respect to the banking system its role was manifested in the State Bank, wholly government-owned, which was in effect and became in fact an agent of the State Treasury. Throughout its existence the State Bank's primary concern was government finance, but it also granted commercial credit and increasingly acted as a banker's bank, especially during the crisis years between 1899 and 1903 and in the rapid upswing of Russian industry (supported by the banks) of 1909 to 1913.

The joint-stock banks at first dealt mainly in commercial discounts and, after the depression of 1873, in "safe" government and government-guaranteed securities. They cut their promotional teeth, as it were, with the promotion of railways (whose securities also carried a government guarantee), and that led them to cooperation with other European banks. The banks of Western Europe, for their part, entered Russia in increasing numbers in the 1870s, 1880s, and especially the 1890s. In some cases, notably the German banks in the 1880s, they did so as promoters and partners of Russian banks. In others they provided finance for Western entrepreneurs in Russian industry, especially the mining and metallurgical concerns of the southern Ukraine. By the early years of the twentieth century, and especially in the great industrial boom of 1909 to 1913, the foreign banks relied on their Russian partners (of which they were also generally part owners) for supervision and control of their industrial investments. In this way Russian banks became conduits not only for Western capital but also for Western entrepreneurial and managerial skill and expertise.

II

Although all banking systems have certain common features, determined by the functions they perform, systems also differ by nationality, since financial structure is determined primarily by legislation, which is influenced by historical evolution unique to each nation. The financial systems of the world in the period from 1870 to 1914 exhibited a broad array of patterns with respect to both the legal status of banking and the economic role they played within their respective economies. Details on these and other matters have already been presented in the chapters of Parts I and II. The purpose of this section is to compare the performance of the banking systems of the most important (or largest) nations in terms of their contributions to the economic development of both their own countries and the rest of the world, as a result of their international activities.

Of the major European industrial powers of the nineteenth century, the banking system of Germany is generally regarded as having been the most successful in contributing to economic growth; the British system as essentially neutral or permissive; and the French as the least dynamic and growth-inducing.[8] Is this assessment correct? How does it square with the findings presented in this volume?

With respect to the British experience, nothing presented here, either in Cottrell's chapter or elsewhere, contradicts the notion that the British system was essentially neutral, neither growth-inducing nor growth-retarding, as far as domestic industry was concerned, although it is clear that Britain's large foreign investments, guided in part by London's merchant bankers, had a positive impact in the regions to which they were directed. Whether or not this overseas benefit was at the expense of Britain's domestic economy cannot be definitively answered on the basis of the evidence herein; but it does not strongly support the arguments of those who contend that the London market at the end of the nineteenth century and beginning of the twentieth century was the best of all possible financial worlds.[9]

As for Germany, the information contained in Professor Tilly's chapter and other chapters, notably Professor Broder's on the electrical industry, as well as other recent publications by Professor Tilly,[10] reenforces the conventional wisdom regarding the effectiveness of Germany's "great banks" as promoters of industrialization. This is not to say that the German banks were all-powerful, or that they did not neglect some sectors of the economy, especially small business. But their policy of intimate, long-standing relations with industrial enterprises, exemplified by the numerous and interlocking memberships of bankers on the supervisory boards of industrial concerns, enabled the bankers to foresee the financial needs of industry and to participate in industrial decision making in a manner not envisioned by Schumpeter.[11] By and large, the banks followed the same policy with their foreign as with their domestic clients. (The relatively rapid withdrawal of the German banks from the Banca Commerciale Italiana and the Credito Italiano appears to contradict this generalization; but, as Professor Hertner makes clear, the Italian banks themselves adhered to the German model.)[12] The German example and influence was especially strong in the development of the Russian banking sector, even though the French banks commanded a larger share of the actual capital.

There is a long tradition of academic scholarship in France, of which Professor Bonin is the heir and executor, that denigrates the role of French banks, accusing them of timidity if not cowardice, of "Malthusianism," and so on. It is said that the banks engaged in "purely financial" transactions (e.g., loans to governments) unrelated to productive activities, that they systematically and on principle avoided industrial undertakings, and that they favored the export of capital to the detriment of the domestic economy. Various explanations of this bias of French historians of banking and finance may be offered—for example, their ignorance of economic theory, or their ideological proclivities—but that is not the concern here. What is relevant is to determine whether or not their characterization of the French banking system is correct and accurate. Unfortunately, the evidence presented in this volume is insufficient for that purpose. Professor Bonin's chapter raises more questions than it answers. While that is useful and even necessary as a first step, it would be desirable to have a more systematic survey of the subject. Instead, all that can be done here is to provide some counterexamples of the supposed debilities of the French banking system, particularly in the international context.

Although it is widely believed that the French banks, unlike the German, made no industrial investments and had no ties to industry, that notion is contradicted by numerous examples in the chapters above. The Banque de Paris et des Pays-Bas and other *banques d'affaires* made numerous industrial investments, of course, but even the large deposit banks also participated in industry. The French Société Générale, for example, was the first foreign bank to invest directly in Russian industry; it created the Société Industrielle Franco-Russe in 1872, which it reorganized the following year as the Société Minière et Industrielle.[13] The Société Générale also participated in the Krivoi Rog Company, one of the largest metallurgical concerns in the Donbas, and in several other companies as well. In time other French banks joined the Société Générale in financing Russian industry. For example, in 1877 the Crédit Lyonnais, generally regarded (thanks to Bouvier's work) as the leader of French banks opposed to industrial investments, issued the shares of the Société Anonyme des Forges et Aciéries de Huta-Bankova.[14] As Professors Anan'ich and Bovykin report, "Foreign banks at first tended to finance Russian industry independently of Russian banks, but from the mid-1890s began to cooperate with the major St. Petersburg banks. . . ."[15] That cooperation was faciliated by the fact that French banks also invested in Russian banks, using them, in fact, to manage their industrial investments as well as to cultivate contacts with the Russian government.

Russian industry came to be the prime field for French banks' industrial engagements, but it was by no means the only one. Earlier in the century French banks made industrial investments throughout Europe—in Belgium, Germany, Switzerland, and Austria-Hungary as well as the less developed countries of the Mediterranean and southeastern Europe.[16] After 1870 they continued to invest in industrial enterprises in Austria-Hungary, the Balkans, the Ottoman Empire, and overseas countries as well, as the chapters above make clear. It is, nevertheless, somewhat surprising to discover that supposed bellwether of anti-industrial investment banks, the Crédit Lyonnais, investing in the American aluminum industry in the early twentieth century![17] Clearly, the history of French banks, and of their industrial investments in particular, urgently requires revision.

Although this section has concentrated on the banking systems of the major European industrial powers, it should not be forgotten that Belgium was the pioneer not only of corporate investment banking but also one of the leaders in foreign investment. In many instances the French and German joint-stock banks merely applied financial techniques innovated by the Belgian Société Générale.

It remains to assess the effect of foreign investment on the economies of investing countries. As already indicated, our evidence is insufficient to judge whether or not

Britain's huge investments abroad came at the expense of the domestic economy, but probably it did not. There is no evidence of an unsatisfied demand for capital by British industry. Moreover, by developing overseas sources of supply of raw materials for that industry, and by creating markets for British manufactures (e.g., railway and mining equipment), foreign investment was probably a positive inducement for British industrial growth. The fact remains that Britain's relative economic superiority declined after 1870. To the extent that such relative decline was not inherent in the relative growth of other economies, the answer will have to be sought elsewhere.

French capital exports have long been subject to the charge, both contemporaneously and more recently in the writings of French historians alluded to above, that they deprived French industry of needed investment. But that indictment has already been conclusively refuted. The most decisive evidence is that periods of unusually large capital exports coincided with periods of prosperity and rapid domestic capital formation, whereas periods of weak foreign investment coincided with domestic depression or stagnation.[18]

The same argument has been made, then and more recently, with respect to German foreign investment. But, as Professor Tilly clearly shows, Germany's domestic need for capital always—or almost always—had first claim on Germany's own supplies of capital, at least as far as the banking system was concerned. The German banks even borrowed abroad at short term to support the demands of their domestic clients. On balance, Germany's investments abroad—like those of Britain, Belgium, and the United States, and usually even of France—served to stimulate the demand for products of domestic industry.

III

Finally, we must consider the political ramifications of international banking and foreign investment. It is well known that the period dealt with in this book witnessed the revival of Western imperialism. It is frequently alleged—even by some of the authors of this book—that the investments (or the interests of the investors) were the "cause" of the imperialist revival, and, insofar as the banks were the agents of investment, they too are implicated as "tools of imperialism." What is the evidence of this volume with respect to these allegations?

On the face of it, the facts dispute the allegations. Great Britain had both the largest foreign investments and the largest overseas empire, but over half of Britain's investments were in independent countries—the United States was the largest single recipient (as it was also for German and Dutch investment)—and in self-governing territories. France had the second largest empire, but less than 10 percent of French investments before 1914 went to the French colonies. The French invested mainly in other European countries; Russia alone, itself an imperialist nation, took more than a quarter of French foreign investments. German investments in German colonies were negligible, and even tiny Belgium and the Netherlands invested more in Europe than in their colonies. Some of the imperialist nations were actually net debtors; besides Russia, these included Italy, Spain, Portugal, Japan, and the United States.

If there were a systematic relationship between investment and imperialism one would expect to find evidence of it in the history of Great Britain. Cottrell, however, finds no such evidence. He takes explicit account of Gallagher and Robinson's revisionist "imperialism of free trade" argument and finds it wanting. "There was an informal empire in the mid-Victorian period but it had little to do with trade and finance."[19] Britain had an interest in protecting the "life line" to India, but that antedated by far the rise of financial investments there or elsewhere. That interest, unrelated to those of the investors, explains British diplomatic support for the decrepit regimes of the Ottoman and Persian empires as well as the Liberal Gladstone's intervention in Egypt, intended to be temporary. In the last decades before the Great War Britain did take a more activist role, in China and elsewhere, but the change in policy was not dictated by the interests of investors.

> The coming together of finance and British diplomacy in a few areas during the decades before World War I was not the relationship that Gallagher and Robinson have attempted to establish for the whole of the nineteenth century. Instead of the government using state power to open up the world for British commerce and finance, diplomats attempted to use British financial organs in a limited number of cases to augment British presence and secure [unrelated] goals of foreign policy.[20]

The governments of France and Germany occasionally intervened in the process of investment—but not always in the manner desired by investors. For example, Bismarck's famous *Lombardverbot* of 1887 was opposed by German bankers, including Bismarck's own personal banker and financial advisor, Gerson Bleichröder.[21] During the Moroccan crises of the early twentieth century both France and Germany sought Russia's diplomatic support; the French won that struggle because of Russia's dependence on the Paris Bourse. Russia itself, in somewhat different circumstances as a debtor nation, sought to use banks and investments as tools of policy in Persia and China, with indifferent results. These episodes reveal that although politicians and diplomats did not hesitate to use financial weapons as useful and—to them—costless instruments of foreign policy, the aims of those policies were determined by the governments independently of the wishes of the bankers and investors.

But what of those marginal areas, neither wholly dependent, like colonies, nor wholly independent, like the United States and Russia? Were investments in them either a cause or a result of imperialism?

As for the self-governing dominions of the British Empire, Professor Drummond is emphatic that the policies of Canada and Australia were set, not in London, but in their respective capitals. British annexation of southeastern New Guinea in 1884, after the Dutch had claimed the western half and the Germans the northeast, was a direct result of the agitation of the Queensland government of Australia, not of investors in Great Britain. Although we have not included South Africa in our sample of countries, we might remark in passing that the expansion of Britain's Cape Colony and its unfortunate consequence, the Boer War, took place as a result of South African initiative—chiefly that of one man, Cecil Rhodes—against the wishes and explicit instructions of the government in London.

Professor Levy finds that in Brazil—which in this instance, at least, may be taken as typical of Latin America as a whole—"it is clear that 'finance capital' in Hilferding's sense was not present. . . . The foreign banks had no interest whatever in dominating the Brazilian infant industries. They were, above all, tuned to international trade."[22]

The situation in China was characterized by the contradiction between foreign expectations relative to development and the insistence on large indemnity payments, which threatened its credit-worthiness. Nevertheless, traditional Chinese reluctance to borrow overseas, their desire to retain control of their infrastructure, especially railroads, combined with the determination of foreign banks and governments that China should not become a second "Ottoman" thus placed a limit on the frenetic ambitions of would-be concessionaires, imperialistic governments, and indeed of the more incautious Chinese. And the exchange banks not only facilitated the movement of development capital and financed resulting trade but themselves became involved in direct loans for fixed capital investment, despite frequent self-reminders that they ought to retain a more traditional (and conservative) role. Until the eve of World War I, China's international finances were, as Professor King describes, kept in some order, encouraged by the restraint in combination of major foreign banks as supported by their governments. But the pressures were great and the defenses crumbling. The War Lord period with its disastrous economic consequences was not far distant.

The situation in the Middle East was, if anything, even more complicated. Great power rivalry there long antedated the advent of European banks and investment. The banks and investors certainly sought the protection of and favors from their governments, just as the governments did not hesitate to use the banks and the claims of investors as pawns in their political and diplomatic rivalry. Committed as he is to an economic, or pecuniary, interpretation of imperialism, Professor Thobie nevertheless cannot find any simple chain of cause and effect. Can anyone?

In summary, there is no evidence in this volume, in the opinion of one of its editors, of a systematic relationship between foreign investment and imperialism. Professor Bovykin presents a somewhat different view in his own conclusion, based on different premises and a different reading of the evidence. That is his prerogative. It is for the reader to decide.

Notes

Introduction

1. By multinational business firms I mean enterprises that carried on productive activities beyond mere trade across political boundaries in two or more countries. See Mira Wilkins, *The Emergence of Multinational Enterprise: American Business Abroad from the Colonial Era to 1914* (Cambridge, MA, 1970), p. ix; and Peter Hertner and Geoffrey Jones, eds., *Multinationals: Theory and History* (Aldershot, UK, 1986), p. 1.
2. Robert-Henri Bautier, "Les foires de Champagne: recherches sur une evolution historique," *Bulletin de la Société Jean Bodin*, V, *La Foire* (1953), 97–145; trans. as "The Fairs of Champagne," in Rondo Cameron, ed., *Essays in French Economic History* (Homewood, IL, 1970), pp. 42–63.
3. A large literature is summarized in Michael Prestwich, "Italian Merchants in Late Thirteenth and Early Fourteenth Century England," in Center for Medieval and Renaissance Studies, University of California, Los Angeles, *The Dawn of Modern Banking* (New Haven and London, 1979), pp. 77–104.
4. Raymond de Roover, *The Rise and Decline of the Medici Bank, 1397–1494* (Cambridge, MA, 1963).
5. Barisa Krekić, "Italian Creditors in Dubrovnik (Ragusa) and the Balkan Trade, Thirteenth through Fifteenth Centuries," in *The Dawn of Modern Banking* (note 3), pp. 241–54.
6. Jean-François Bergier, "From the Fifteenth Century in Italy to the Sixteenth Century in Germany: A New Banking Concept?" in ibid, pp. 105–29.
7. Again, a large literature abounds; the Fuggers even merit a special series of publications, *Studien zur Fuggergeschichte*. Among the best sources, although dated, is Richard Ehrenberg, *Das Zeitalter der Fugger*, 3rd ed., 2 vols. (Jena, 1922); abbreviated trans. by H. M. Lucas, *Capital and Finance in the Age of the Renaissance: A Study of the Fuggers and Their Connections* (1928; reprinted New York, 1963). A somewhat more recent entry is Léon Schick, *Jacob Fugger: Un grand homme d'affaires au début du XVIe siècle* (Paris, 1957).
8. See the contributions by Oszkár Paulinyi, Sima Cirković, Ekkehard Westermann, Herman Van der Wee, and Hermann Kellenbenz in Hermann Kellenbenz, ed., *Precious Metals in the Age of Expansion: Papers of the XIVth International Congress of the Historical Sciences* (Stuttgart, 1981).
9. Herman Van der Wee, *The Growth of the Antwerp Market and the European Economy (fourteenth–sixteenth centuries)*, 3 vols., (The Hague, 1963), II, pp. 113–43.
10. Violet Barbour, *Capitalism in Amsterdam in the Seventeenth Century* (Baltimore, 1950), Chapter VI.
11. George Edmundson, "Louis de Geer," *English Historical Review*, VI (1891), 685–712.

12. James C. Riley, *International Government Finance and the Amsterdam Capital Market, 1740–1815* (Cambridge, 1980).
13. Marten G. Buist, *At Spes Non Fracta: Hope & Co. 1770–1815* (The Hague, 1974), p. 3.
14. Herbert Lüthy, *La Bangue Protestante en France de la Révocation de l'Edit de Nantes à la Révolution*, 2 vols. (Paris, 1959–61).
15. Stanley Chapman, *The Rise of Merchant Banking* (London, 1984).
16. Ibid., p. 39.
17. There is an enormous literature on the Rothschilds. Among better and more recent books are Bertrand Gille, *Histoire de la maison Rothschild*, 2 vols. (Geneva, 1965–67), and Jean Bouvier, *Les Rothschild* (Paris, 1967). Among the older works, E. C. Corti's two volumes, *The Rise of the House of Rothschild* and *The Reign of the House of Rothschild* (London, 1928), are still worth reading.
18. E. J. Perkins, *Financing Anglo-American Trade: The House of Brown, 1800–1880* (Cambridge, MA, 1975); see also Chapman, *Merchant Banking*, p. 41.
19. Vincent P. Carosso, *The Morgans: Private International Bankers, 1854–1913* (Cambridge, MA, 1987).
20. Chapman, *Merchant Banking*, p. 41.
21. Rondo Cameron, *France and the Economic Development of Europe, 1800–1914* (Princeton, NJ, 1961), pp. 107–9.
22. David S. Landes, "Vieille Banque et Banque Nouvelle: la Révolution financiére du dix-neuviéme siécle," *Revue d'histoire moderne et contemporaine*, III (juillet-septembre 1956).
23. Cameron, *France and Europe*, p. 113.
24. Ibid., pp. 119–25.
25. Ibid., pp. 129–31.
26. Ibid., pp. 148–50. Actually, the first one was the A. Schaaffhausen'scher Bankverein, created in the crisis year 1848 on the ruins of the bankrupt private bank, Abraham Schaaffhausen & Co. In the panic of the Revolution the Prussian administration departed temporarily from its firm rule against joint-stock banks, to which it soon returned, which is why the promoters of the Darmstädter could not locate their bank in Cologne, as they desired.
27. *Economist*, July 12, 1856.
28. Bertrande Gille, "La Fondation du Crédit Mobilier et les idées financières des frères Pereire", *Bullétin du Centre de Recherches sur l'Histoire des Entreprises*, III (1954), 16–18.
29. Cameron, *France and Europe*, p. 150.
30. Crédit Mobilier, annual report, April 30, 1855, quoted in Cameron, *France and Europe*, p. 151.
31. *Die Berliner Handels-Gesellschaft in einem Jahrhundert Deutscher Wirtschaft, 1856–1956* (Berlin, 1956), p. 16.
32. Jakob Riesser, *The German Great Banks and Their Concentration in connection with the Economic Development of Germany* (Publications of the National Monetary Commission, Vol. XIV, Washington, DC, 1911), Appendix II. In addition to those listed, several note-issuing banks were also created in 1855–56.
33. Jean Bouvier, *Le Crédit Lyonnais de 1863 á 1882*, 2 vols. (Paris, 1961).
34. See below, Chapter 1.
35. Karl Erich Born, *Geld und Banken im 19. und 20. Jahrhundert* (Stuttgart, 1977).
36. See Rondo Cameron, *A Concise Economic History of the World from Paleolithic Times to the Present* (New York and Oxford, 1989), Chapter 11.
37. This "balance sheet" of foreign investment was suggested by Mira Wilkins at the 1985 Bellagio Conference, who also supplied the initial figures. I have modified her format and

figures slightly. The figures refer to *gross* investments; some countries, notably the United States, were both borrowers and lenders, and every lending country, including the United Kingdom, employed some foreign capital. The figures have been rounded for convenience. In most instances the underlying data are too fragmentary and fragile for more precise statements, and in any case rough orders of magnitude are sufficient for the analysis.

38. Cameron, *France and Europe*, p. 487, Table 5.
39. See below, Chapter 6.
40. Ibid.
41. Ibid., Chapter 2.
42. Ibid., Chapter 21.
43. The House of Morgan and other leading banks had to engage in similar salvage operations on occasion; ibid., Chapter 2.
44. Ibid., Chapter 22.
45. Ibid., Chapter 20.

Chapter 1

1. This is a revised version of the paper presented to the Bellagio Conference, August 1985, and I am grateful to the other participants, especially Mira Wilkins and Richard Sylla, for their comments on the original and subsequent drafts. I have also benefitted from the Business History section of the Economic History Conference, Cheltenham, 1986, and the seminar arranged by J. J. van Helten at the Business History Unit, London School of Economics. The material contained in section I was given at the European University Institute, Florence, April 1986. The lively discussion and particularly the comments of Professor S. Pollard and Dr. M. Wagner assisted its further development. I would also like to acknowledge here a British Academy travel grant and the hospitality of the European University Institute.
2. For the relative decline of British industry see R. C. O. Matthews, C. H. Feinstein, and J. C. Olding-Smee, *British Economic Growth, 1856–1973* (Oxford, 1982 [the place of publication of all works cited is London, unless stated otherwise]), pp. 5, 22, 31. In terms of the absolute level of GDP per man-year, however, while Britain was overtaken by the United States in the 1880s, France and Germany did not exceed British levels until 1960 (ibid., p. 33).
3. Simon Kuznets, "Quantitative Aspects of the Economic Growth of Nations: VI. Long Term Trends in Capital Formation Proportions," *Economic Development and Cultural Change* (1961), 5, 38; B. J. Eichengreen, "The Proximate Determinants of Domestic Investment in Victorian Britain," *Journal of Economic History*, 42 (1982), 87; Sidney Pollard, "Capital Exports, 1870–1914: Harmful or Beneficial?," *Economic History Review*, 2nd ser., 38 (1985), 489.
4. Its exports of goods and services increased 2.6 percent per annum between 1873 and 1913, while its imports of goods and services rose 2.7 percent per annum in the same years. Its share in world exports of manufactures in the years from 1899 to 1913 was roughly one-third—far ahead of any other nation. Matthews, et al., *British Economic Growth*, pp. 428, 435.
5. P. N. Davies, "British Shipping and World Trade," in Tsunehiki Yui and Keiichiro Nakagawa, eds., *Business History of Shipping* (Tokyo, 1985), pp. 56–57.
6. Herbert Feis, *Europe the World's Banker, 1870–1914* (New York, 1965; a reprint of the edition of 1930), pp. 23, 27; see also Sir George Paish, "The Export of Capital and the Cost of Living," supplement to *The Statist*, 14, ii (1914), v–vi.

7. See P. L. Cottrell, *British Overseas Investment in the Nineteenth Century* (1975).
8. A. H. Imlah, *Economic Elements in the Pax Britannica* (Cambridge, MA, 1958), pp. 70–5. Here Imlah was following a path already laboriously trod by others: C. K. Hobson, *The Export of Capital* (1914, 1963 with a preface by Sir Roy Harrod); and A. K. Cairncross, *Home and Foreign Investment, 1870–1913* (Cambridge, 1953).
9. Matthew Edelstein, *Overseas Investment in the Age of High Imperialism* (1982), p. 18; C. H. Feinstein, *National Income, Expenditure and Output of the United Kingdom, 1855–1970* (Cambridge, 1972), pp. 37–38.
10. I am puzzled that Edelstein regards the Simon estimate as being "valued in nominal terms" (p. 18), when Simon's table has a column clearly headed "Money Calls," which is juxtaposed to a column headed "Creations," the latter being the nominal amount and the former the amount subscribed. See Matthew Simon, "The Pattern of New British Portfolio Foreign Investment, 1865–1914," in J. H. Adler with P. W. Kuznets, eds., *Capital Movements and Economic Development* (1967), Table 2; also "The Enterprise and Industrial Composition of New British Portfolio Foreign Investment, 1855–1914," *Journal of Development Studies*, III (1966–67); H. H. Segal and M. Simon, "British Foreign Capital Issues, 1865–1894," *Journal of Economic History*, 21 (1961).
11. L. E. Davis and R. A. Huttenback, *Mammon and the Pursuit of Empire* (Cambridge, 1986); also idem, "The Political Economy of British Imperialism: Measures of Benefits and Support," *Journal of Economic History*, 42 (March 1982), 119–30; "The Export of British Finance, 1865–1914," in A. N. Porter and R. F. Holland, eds., *Money, Finance and Empire, 1790–1960* (1985). The original Simon data are being reworked by Irving Stone.
12. Pollard, "Capital Exports," pp. 492–93.
13. D. C. M. Platt, "British Portfolio Investment before 1870: Some Doubts," *Economic History Review*, 2nd ser. 33 (1980); D. C. M. Platt, *Foreign Finance in Continental Europe and the USA, 1815–1870* (1984) and D. C. M. Platt, "Some Drastic Revisions in the Stock and Direction of British Investment Overseas, 31 December 1913," in R. V. Turell and J. J. Van Helten, eds., *The City and the Empire*, Collected Seminar Papers No. 35, Institute of Commonwealth Studies, University of London (1985). Subsequent to the writing of the first draft of this essay Platt's major monograph has been published, *Britain's Investment Overseas on the Eve of the First World War* (1986).
14. P. Svedberg, "The Portfolio-Direct Composition of Private Foreign Investment in 1914 Revisited," *Economic Journal*, 88 (1978).
15. Irving Stone, "British Long-term Investment in Latin America, 1865–1913," *Business History Review*, 13 (1968); "British Direct and Portfolio Investment in Latin American before 1914," *Journal of Economic History*, 37 (1977).
16. J. H. Dunning, "Changes in the Level and Structure of International Production," in M. Casson, ed., *The Growth of International Business* (1983).
17. Mira Wilkins, "Defining a Firm: History and Theory," in Peter Hertner and Geoffrey Jones, eds., *Multinationals: Theory and History* (Aldershot, UK, 1986); see also Mira Wilkins, "The Free-Standing Firm," *Economic History Review*, 2nd ser. 41 (May 1988), 259–82.
18. There are even earlier examples from the 1820s; see N. K. Hill, "The History of the Imperial Continental Gas Association, 1824–1900," unpublished Ph.D. thesis (University of London, 1950) and Anonymous, *Imperial Continental Gas Association, 1824–1974* (1974).
19. S. J. Nicholas, "British Multinational Investment before 1939," *Journal of European Economic History*, 11 (1982).
20. J. Stopford, "The Origins of British-based Multinational Manufacturing Enterprises," *Business History Review*, 48 (1974); see also L. G. Franko, *The European Multinationals*

(Stamford, CT, 1976), and Mira Wilkins, "Multinational Enterprises," in Herman Daems and Herman van der Wee, eds., *The Rise of Managerial Capitalism* (Louvain, 1974).

21. Geoffrey Jones, "British Multinationals: Origins, Management and Performance," paper presented to the Business History Section of the Economic History Society Conference, Cheltenham, 1986.

22. A point well made in Mira Wilkins, "Modern European Economic History and the Multi-nationals," *Journal of European Economic History*, 6 (1977), and "The History of Euro-pean Multinationals: A New Look," ibid., 15 (1986).

23. See David S. Landes, *Bankers and Pashas* (1958), especially Chapter I; N. S. Buck, *The Development and Organization of Anglo-American Commerce* (1925, New Haven, CT, reprinted 1969); W. Hunt, *Heirs of Great Adventure. The History of Balfour, Williamson and Company* (1951); M. Greenberg, *British Trade and the Opening of China 1800–42* (Cambridge, 1951).

24. B. Williams, *The Making of Manchester Jewry, 1740–1875* (Manchester, 1976); [S. D. Chapman], *N. M. Rothschild, 1777–1836* (London, privately printed, 1977); P. L. Cot-trell, "The Businessman and Financier," Sonia and V. D. Lipman, eds., *The Century of Moses Montefiore* (1985); A. J. Murray, *Home from the Hill* (1971), a history of F. Huth and Company; and Paul Emden, *Money Powers of Europe in the 19th and 20th Centuries* (1938). For a British international network see J. A. Gibbs, *The History of Antony and Dorothea Gibbs* (1922).

25. E. J. Perkins, *Financing Anglo-American Trade. The House of Brown, 1800–1880* (Cambridge, MA, 1975); H. D. Woodman, *King Cotton and His Retainers. Financing and Marketing the Cotton Crop of the South, 1800–1925* (Lexington, KY, 1968); R. H. Hidy, *The House of Baring in American Trade and Finance* (Cambridge, MA, 1949).

26. S. D. Chapman, "The International Houses; the Continental Contribution to British Com-merce in the Industrial Revolution Period," *Journal of European Economic History* (1977); P. L. Cottrell, "Commercial Enterprise," in Roy Church, ed., *The Dynamics of Victorian Business* (1980).

27. See A. J. Baster, *The International Banks* (1935); David Joslin, *A Century of Banking in Latin America* (1963); Geoffrey Jones, *Banking and Empire in Iran: The History of The British Bank of the Middle East* (Cambridge, 1986); and P. L. Cottrell, "London Financiers and Austria 1863–1875; the Anglo-Austrian Bank," *Business History*, 11 (1969).

28. R. P. T. Davenport-Hines and J. J. van Helten, "Concessions, Chartered Companies and Monopolies: Some Aspects of British Business Imperialism, 1880–1930," paper presented to the Business History Section of the Economic History Society Conference, Cheltenham, 1986.

29. A description of Sir Harry Parkes by E. V. G. Kiernan, "Diplomats in Exile," in R. M. Halton and M. S. Anderson, eds., *Studies in Diplomatic History in Memory of D. B. Horn* (1970), p. 303.

30. S. Nishimura, *The Decline of Inland Bills of Exchange in the London Money Market, 1855–1913* (Cambridge, 1971), Table 1, pp. 80–81.

31. J. Sykes, *The Amalgamation Movement in English Banking, 1825–1924* (1926), pp. 48–60; C. A. E. Goodhart, *The Business of Banking, 1891–1914* (1972), pp. 51–59; Nishimura, *Inland Bills*, p. 85.

32. Goodhart, *Business of Banking*, pp. 125, 130–33, 143–46.

33. R. S. Sayers, *Gilletts in the London Money Market, 1867–1967* (Oxford, 1968), pp. 46–47.

34. *The Bankers' Magazine* (1906), pt. II, p. 20. More generally see W. T. C. King, *History of the London Discount Market* (1936; reprinted 1972).

35. Stanley Chapman, *The Rise of Merchant Banking* (1984), pp. 105–6.

36. King, *London Discount Market*, p. 280.

37. Chapman, *Merchant Banking*, p. 121.
38. See Peter H. Lindert, *Key Currencies and Gold, 1900–1913* (Princeton, NJ, 1969).
39. A. R. Hall, *The London Capital Market and Australia, 1870–1914* (Canberra, 1963), p. 72.
40. On some aspects of the activities of the Crown Agents, see R. M. Kesner, "Builders of Empire: the Role of the Crown Agents in Imperial Development, 1880–1914," *Journal of Imperial and Commonwealth History*, 5 (1973); and A. W. Abbott, *A Short History of the Crown Agents and Their Office* (1952).
41. See Baster, *International Banks;* Joslin, *Century of Banking,* and Cottrell, "London Financiers and Austria."
42. Richard T. Stillson, "The Financing of Malayan Rubber, 1905–1923," *Economic History Review*, 2nd ser., 24 (November 1971), 589–98.
43. S. D. Chapman, "British-Based Investment Groups before 1914," *Economic History Review*, 2nd ser., 38 (1985).
44. See W. A. Thomas, *The Provincial Stock Exchanges* (1973).
45. W. L. Ken, *The Malayan Tin Industry to 1914* (Tucson, AZ, 1965).
46. D. S. Macmillan, *Scotland and Australia, 1788–1850; Emigration, Commerce and Investment* (Oxford, 1967); idem, "Scottish Enterprise in Australia, 1789–1879," in P. L. Payne, ed., *Studies in Scottish Business History* (1976).
47. W. T. Jackson, *The Enterprising Scot; Investors in the American West after 1873* (Edinburgh, 1968).
48. J. D. Bailey, "Australian Borrowing in Scotland in the Nineteenth Century," *Economic History Review*, 2nd ser., 12 (December 1959), 268–79.
49. B. Lenman and K. Donaldson, "Partners' Incomes, Investment and Diversification in the Scottish Linen Area, 1850–1921," *Business History*, 13 (1971).
50. R. S. Sayers, *Lloyds Bank in the History of English Banking* (1957), pp. 183–85.
51. Goodhart, *Business of Banking*, pp. 120, 124.
52. "The New Banking," *The Bankers' Magazine*, I (1896), 197–98.
53. Goodhart, *Business of Banking*, pp. 134–36.
54. *Bankers' Magazine* (1876), pp. 517–18.
55. For full documentation see P. L. Cottrell, *Investment Banking in England, 1856–1881: A Case Study of the International Financial Society* (1985) II, p. 505.
56. See below, Chapter 18, for a discussion of this process in the Ottoman Empire and Egypt.
57. Cottrell, *Investment Banking*, pp. 508–11.
58. Ibid., pp. 624–26.
59. Chapman, *Merchant Banking*, p. 160.
60. Gyorgi Ranki, "The Hugarian General Credit Bank in the 1920s," in Alice Teichova and P. L. Cottrell, eds., *International Business and Central Europe, 1918–1939* (Leicester, 1983).
61. Davis and Huttenback, *Mammon . . . ,* Chapter 7, "The Shareholders in Imperial Enterprises."
62. W. D. Rubinstein, "The Victorian Middle Classes: Wealth, Occupation and Geography," *Economic History Review*, 2nd ser., 30 (1977); and "Modern Britain" in W. D. Rubenstein, ed., *Wealth and the Wealthy in the Modern World* (1980).
63. Y. Cassis, "Bankers in English Society in the Late Nineteenth Century," *Economic History Review*, 2nd ser., 38 (1985); see also J. Harris and P. Thane, "British and European bankers 1880–1914: an 'Aristocratic Bourgeoisie'?" in P. Thane, G. Crossick, and R. Floud, eds., *The Power of the Past* (1985); M. Lisle-Williams, "Beyond the Market: The Survival of Family Capitalism in the English Merchant Banks," *British Journal of Sociology*, 35 (1984), and idem, "Merchant Banking Dynasties in the English Class Structure," *British Journal of Sociology*, 35 (1984). For a note of dissent see S. D. Chapman, "Aristocracy and Meritocracy in Merchant Banking," *British Journal of Sociology*, 37 (1986).

64. John Gallagher and Ronald Robinson, "The Imperialism of Free Trade," *Economic History Review*, 2nd ser., 6 (1953); idem, *Africa and the Victorians* (1967). See also R. J. Moore, "Imperialism and 'Free Trade' Policy in India, 1853–54," *Economic History Review*, 2nd ser., 17 (1964); Bernard Semmel, *The Rise of Free Trade Imperialism: Classical Political Economy, the Empire of Free Trade and Imperialism, 1750–1950* (Cambridge, 1970); A. G. Shaw, ed., *Great Britain and the Colonies, 1815–1865* (1970).

65. O. McDonagh, "The Anti-Imperialism of Free Trade," *Economic History Review*, 2nd ser., 14 (1962), and D. C. M. Platt, "The Imperialism of Free Trade: Some Reservations," *Economic History Review*, 2nd ser., 21 (1968); idem, *Finance, Trade and Politics in British Foreign Policy, 1815–1914* (Oxford, 1968); and "Economic Factors in British Policy during the 'New Imperialism,'" *Past and Present*, 34 (1968). See also D. K. Fieldhouse, "Imperialism: An Historiographical Revision," *Economic History Review*, 2nd ser. 14 (1961); idem, *Economics and Empire, 1830–1914* (1973), and W. M. Mathew, "The Imperialism of Free Trade: Peru, 1820–70," *Economic History Review*, 2nd ser., 21 (1968).

66. D. C. M. Platt, "Further Objections to an 'Imperialism of Free Trade,' 1830–60," *Economic History Review* 26 (1973); see also Cottrell, "Commercial Enterprise."

67. David McLean "Finance and 'Informal Empire' before the First World War," *Economic History Review*, 2nd ser., 29 (1967); see also below, Chapters 17 and 18.

68. See David McLean, "British Finance and Foreign Policy in Turkey: The Smyrna–Aden Railway Settlement, 1913–14," *Historical Journal*, 19 (1976). For the interests of the other powers, see below, Chapter 18.

69. See Chapter 17. Also David McLean, "Commerce, Finance and British Diplomatic Support in China, 1885–8," *Economic History Review*, 2nd ser., 26 (1973).

70. E. W. Edwards, "The Origins of British Financial Cooperation with France in China, 1903–06," *English Historical Review*, 86 (1971).

71. K. C. Chan, "British Policy in the Reorganisation Loan to China, 1912–13," *Modern Asian Studies*, 5 (1971).

72. See K. L. Wong, "Anglo-Chinese Trade and Finance, 1854–1914," unpublished doctoral dissertation (University of Leicester, 1976). For a fresh critique see P. J. Cain and A. G. Hopkins, "Gentlemanly Capitalism and British Expansion Overseas, I. The Old Colonial System, 1688–1850," *Economic History Review*, 2nd ser., 39 (November 1986), 501–25, and "II. New Imperialism, 1850–1945," ibid., 40 (February 1987), 1–26.

Chapter 2

1. The percentages presented are from the often-cited study by Folke Hilgert, *Industrialization and Foreign Trade* (Geneva, 1945), p. 13.

2. See Sidney Ratner, James H. Soltow, and Richard Sylla, *The Evolution of the American Economy* (New York, 1979), p. 384.

3. See Lance E. Davis, Richard A. Easterlin, William N. Parker et al., *American Economic Growth: An Economist's History of the United States* (New York, 1972), Table 14.4, p. 568.

4. See above, p. 13.

5. Jonathan R. T. Hughes, *American Economic History* (Glenview, IL, 1983), p. 413.

6. Cleona Lewis, *America's Stake in International Investments* (Washington, DC, 1938), p. 558.

7. Ibid., p. 605.

8. The Visible Hand reference is, of course, to Alfred D. Chandler, *The Visible Hand: The Managerial Revolution in American Business* (Cambridge, MA, 1977).

9. Karl Erich Born, *International Banking in the 19th and 20th Centuries* (New York, 1983),

p. 95; originally published as *Geld und Banken in 19. und 20. Jahrhundert* (Stuttgart, 1977).

10. See Richard Sylla, *The American Capital Market, 1846–1914* (New York, 1975), Chapter 2.

11. Clyde William Phelps, *The Foreign Expansion of American Banks: American Branch Banking Abroad* (New York, 1927; reprinted 1976), pp. 92–94.

12. For the New York call loan rates, see Sidney Homer, *A History of Interest Rates*, 2nd ed. (New Brunswick, NJ, 1977), Table 44, pp. 319–20 and Table 51, pp. 372–73; for the London market rate of discount, see B. R. Mitchell with Phyllis Deane, *Abstract of British Historical Statistics* (Cambridge, 1971), p. 460.

13. For the U.S. bond yields, see Homer, *History of Interest Rates*, Table 42, p. 309, and Table 46, p. 344; for the U.K. consol yields, see Mitchell with Deane, *Abstract of British Historical Statistics*, p. 455. Comparison of interest rates between two nations' capital markets is not easy for the period 1870 to 1914. Friedman and Schwartz find that U.S. rates were above U.K. rates throughout the period. But they use annual data that mask within-year variations. In addition, they compare U.S. commercial paper rates with U.K. bill rates at the short end of the market, and U.S. corporate and railroad bond rates with U.K. consol (government) bond rates. That is acceptable for studying *trends* in U.S.–U.K. interest differentials, which is what Friedman and Schwartz do. But it is not acceptable— because the financial instruments are not equivalent—for drawing inferences about the *level* of interest differentials at a particular time. (The comparison made here between U.S. and U.K. government bond interest yields is also subject to this criticism because the U.S. bonds were subject to some special influences in these years: They were demanded by national banks as collateral for note issues and their outstanding stock was shrinking as the U.S. government used budget surpluses to redeem its debt.) Both Friedman and Schwartz and, in another study, Michael Edelstein document the narrowing of U.S.–U.K. interest differentials to relative insignificance over the course of the 1870–1914 period. See Milton Friedman and Anna J. Schwartz, *Monetary Trends in the United States and the United Kingdom: Their Relation to Income, Prices and Interest Rates, 1867–1975* (Chicago and London, 1982), Chapters 4 and 10; and Michael Edelstein, *Overseas Investment in the Age of High Imperialism: The United Kingdom, 1850–1914* (New York, 1983), Chapter 10 and pp. 295–96.

14. Lewis, *America's Stake in International Investments*, Chapter 16, pp. 335–38; see also below, Chapter 11.

15. Ibid., pp. 338–41.

16. The best modern treatment of the U.S. correspondent banking network in the 1870–1914 period is in John A. James, *Money and Capital Markets in Postbellum America* (Princeton, NJ, 1978), Chapter 4. America's struggle with the branch banking issue is ably set forth by Eugene Nelson White, *The Regulation and Reform of the American Banking System, 1900–1929* (Princeton, NJ 1983).

17. James, *Money and Capital Markets*, pp. 146–48; Sylla, *American Capital Market*, p. 126.

18. On the estimated number and capital of America's private banks between 1870 and 1910, see Sylla, *American Capital Market*, pp. 266–78.

19. Fritz Redlich, *The Molding of American Banking: Men and Ideas*, 2 vols. (New York, 1947, 1951), II, pp. 60–84, provides a general account of private banking developments in the United States. See also the following more specialized accounts: Henrietta M. Larson, *Jay Cooke: Private Banker* (Cambridge, MA, 1936); Edwin J. Perkins, *Financing Anglo-American Trade: The House of Brown, 1800–1880* (Cambridge, MA, 1975); Vincent P. Carosso, *The Morgans: Private International Bankers, 1854–1913*, (Cambridge, MA, 1987); and Dolores Greenberg, *Financiers and Railroads, 1869–1889: A Study of Morton, Bliss & Co.* (Newark, DE 1980). Consult also Marshall W. Stevens, "History of Lee,

Higginson and Company" (typescript [1927], Baker Library, Harvard Graduate School of Business Administration, Boston); Linton Wells, "The House of Seligman," 3 vols. (New York [1931], typescript, New-York Historical Society, New York City); and Wilkins, below, Chapter 11.

20. Perkins, *Financing Anglo-American Trade*, pp. 40, 64, and John C. Brown, *A Hundred Years of Merchant Banking: A History of Brown Brothers and Company, Brown, Shipley & Company and the Allied Firms* (New York, 1909), Chapters v–viii.

21. [J. P. Morgan & Co.], "Co-Partnerships Notices . . . 1852–1929" (2 vols), Morgan Family Papers, The Pierpont Morgan Library, New York City. Hereafter cited as MFP/PML. Permission to use and cite from the Morgan Papers was generously granted by the late Henry S. Morgan of Morgan Stanley & Co. On the organization of other American private banking offices in Europe, see: Dolores Greenberg, "Yankee Financiers and the Establishment of Trans-Atlantic Partnerships: A Reexamination," *Business History*, XVI (January 1974), 17–35; Charles P. Kindleberger, "Origins of United States Direct Investment in France," *Business History Review*, XLVIII (Autumn 1974), 383–88; Vincent P. Carosso, "A Financial Elite: New York's German-Jewish Investment Bankers," *American Jewish Historical Quarterly*, LXVI (September 1976), 67–83; and Wilkins, below, Chapter 11.

22. U.S. Senate, Committee on Finance, 72nd Cong., 1st Sess., *Sale of Foreign Bonds or Securities in the United States: Hearings . . . ,* 4 parts (Washington, DC, 1931–32, II, pp. 608–09. See also Paul H. Emden, *Money Powers of Europe in the Nineteenth and Twentieth Centuries* (London, 1938), pp. 274–77; *New York Evening Post*, October 5, 1926, and *The New York Times*, November 1, 1941.

23. Irving Katz, *August Belmont: A Political Biography* (New York, 1968), pp. 5–7, and Vincent Carosso, *More Than a Century of Investment Banking: The Kidder, Peabody & Co. Story* (New York, 1979), 17, 33–34.

24. Copy of updated typescript, "Baring Brothers & Co., Kidder, Peabody & Co., and Baring, Magoun & Co.," Kidder, Peabody & Co. Papers, Baker Library, Harvard Graduate School of Business Administration, Boston. Hereafter cited as KPP/Baker. See also Carosso, *More Than a Century of Investment Banking*, pp. 33–34, 188 n. 49.

25. [J. P. Morgan & Co], "Firms in New York, Philadelphia, London and Paris," typescript dated September 23, 1929, MFP/PML.

26. Ibid.

27. Carosso, *The Morgans*.

28. Thomas W. Lamont, "J. P. Morgan & Co. and Their Relations to the Public," typescript dated June 1934, File 110-2, Thomas W. Lamont Papers, Baker Library, Harvard Graduate School of Business Administration, Boston.

29. Perkins, *Financing Anglo-American Trade*, p. 209.

30. Ibid., p. 1.

31. J. S. Morgan & Co. to Drexel, Morgan & Co. and M. K. Jesup & Co., August 1, 1871, and Dabney, Morgan & Co. to J. S. Morgan & Co., December 31, 1882, J. S. Morgan Papers, Morgan, Grenfell & Co., London. Hereafter cited as JSMP/MG&Co. Permission to use and cite from the J. S. Morgan & Co. and Morgan, Grenfell & Co. papers was granted by the late Henry S. Morgan and Bryan J. Pennington of Morgan Grenfell & Co., Ltd. See also Ann M. Scanlon, "The Building of the New York Central: A Study in the Development of the International Iron Trade," in Joseph R. Frese and Jacob Judd, eds., *An Emerging Independent American Economy* (Tarrytown, NY, 1980), pp. 99–117.

32. J. S. Morgan & Co. to C. H. McCormick, August 25, 1877 (cables September 17 and 21), September 22 (cables September 25, 28, October 4), October 18, November 14 (cables November 26, December 12), November 26, December 7, 19, 28, 1877, January 11, February 11, March 22, 1878, 1A/Box 69 and 1A/Box 72 Cyrus H. McCormick Papers, State Historical Society of Wisconsin, Madison; see Chapter 22.

33. Redlich, *Molding of American Banking*, II, pp. 365–69, provides a good summary of the international banking groups that participated in the Treasury's refunding operations.

34. The details of the loan's negotiations are covered in U.S. Senate, Committee on Finance, 54th Cong. 2nd Sess., *Investigation of the Sale of Bonds During the Years 1894, 1895, and 1896* (Washington, DC, 1896). The syndicate's allocations are listed in J. P. Morgan & Co., "Syndicates I," MFP/PML.

35. Undated memorandum, "United States of Mexico 5% External Consolidated Gold Loan of 1899," and undated memorandum "Mexican Conversion Syndicate," JSMP/MG&Co.

36. *The Daily Mail* (London), June 8, 1899.

37. *The Commercial & Financial Chronicle*, LXX (September 22, 1900), 579; *The New York Times*, April 1, 1905, and [Kuhn, Loeb & Co.], *Investment Banking Through Four Generations* (New York, 1955), pp. 17–18. On the Japanese loan, see also Cyrus Adler, *Jacob H. Schiff: His Life and Letters*, 2 vols. (Garden City, NY, 1929), I, pp. 212–40.

38. Vincent P. Carosso, *Investment Banking in America: A History* (Cambridge, MA, 1970), pp. 81–82.

39. *The Commercial & Financial Chronicle*, LXX (May 12, 1900), 925, and Walter S. S. Case, "Canada—An Opportunity for J. P. Morgan & Co.," undated typescript memorandum (September 1913?) in Morgan, Grenfell & Co. Papers, London. Hereafter cited as MGP/MG&Co.

40. There is a large secondary literature on the Taft-Knox policies. For a useful introduction to the subject, see Clarence B. Davis, "Financing Imperialism: British and American Bankers as Vectors of Imperial Expansion in China, 1908–1920," *Business History Review*, LVI (September 1982), 236–64; see also below, Chapter 17.

41. J. P. Morgan & Co., "Syndicates, VI," MFP/PML, and "Mexican External 4% Loan of 1910," undated memorandum in MGP/MG&Co.

42. Philander C. Knox to J. P. Morgan & Co., July 21, 1909, U.S. Department of State RG 59 (20606), National Archives, Washington, DC.

43. J. P. Morgan & Co., "Syndicates VI," MFP/PML.

44. Larson, *Jay Cooke*, pp. 429–31.

45. J. S. Morgan to E. P. Fabbri, January 14, 1870, JSMP/MG&Co.

46. J. P. Morgan to J. S. Morgan, September 10, 1875, MFP/PML. See also ibid., March 10, 1880, and Dorothy R. Adler (Muriel E. Hidy, ed.), *British Investment in American Railways, 1834–1898* (Charlottesville, VA, 1970), p. 79.

47. [J. S. Morgan & Co.], "Loans Issued by J. S. Morgan & Co. 1865/1885 & Approximate Results," undated (December 1885?) typescript, JSMP/MG&Co.

48. Carosso, *More Than a Century of Investment Banking*, pp. 20–24, and Arthur M. Johnson and Barry E. Supple, *Boston Capitalists and Western Railroads: A Study in the Nineteenth Century Investment Process* (Cambridge, MA, 1967), pp. 318–29.

49. Dietrich G. Buss, *Henry G. Villard: A Study of Transatlantic Investments and Interests, 1870–1895* (New York, 1978), pp. 218–20, and Chandler, *Visible Hand*, pp. 427–28. For a dissenting view, see Forrest McDonald, *Insull* (Chicago, 1962), pp. 50–52.

50. Chandler, *Visible Hand*, p. 428; see also below, Chapter 4.

51. U.S. House of Representatives, 62nd Cong., 3rd Sess., *Report of the Committee Appointed . . . to Investigate the Concentration of the Control of Money and Credit* (Washington, DC, 1913), p. 159.

52. J. S. Morgan & Co. to Samuel B. Hale & Co., April 13, 1891, JSMP/MG&Co.

53. Argentina Great Western Railway Co. to J. S. Morgan & Co., May 12, 1897, ibid.

54. J. S. Morgan & Co., "Loans & Options," ibid.

55. Undated memorandum (June 1909?), "Alaska Syndicate," in J. P. Morgan & Co., "Syndicates, V," MFP/PML.

56. The rise of trust companies as competitors of commercial banks in the U.S. domestic

market (but not internationally) is discussed by Larry Neal, "Trust Companies and Financial Innovation, 1897–1914," *Business History Review*, 45 (Spring 1971), pp. 35–51.

57. Phelps, *Foreign Expansion of American Banks*, pp. 133–35.
58. Ibid., pp. 136–42.
59. Ibid., pp. 147–49, 154; on the IBC in China, see below, Chapter 17.
60. Phelps, *Foreign Expansion of American Banks*, p. 142.
61. Harold Van B. Cleveland and Thomas F. Huertas, *Citibank, 1812–1970* (Cambridge, MA, 1985), Chapter 3.
62. Lewis, *America's Stake in International Investments*, p. 338.
63. Cleveland and Huertas, *Citibank*, Chapter 3.
64. Ibid., Chapter 4.
65. Ibid.
66. Phelps, *Foreign Expansion of American Banks*, p. 211.
67. Cleveland and Huertas, *Citibank*, Chapter 5.
68. See Mira Wilkins, *The Emergence of Multinational Enterprise: American Business Abroad from the Colonial Era to 1914* (Cambridge, MA, 1970), pp. 73–75, for a general discussion of this point. For specific examples of the U.S. government–U.S. business relationship in foreign investment, see ibid., pp. 60–71, 131–34, 139, 153–57.

Chapter 3

1. Jean Bouvier, *Le Crédit Lyonnais de 1863 á 1882: les années de formation d'une banque de dépôts* (Paris, 1961); Jean Dagneau, *De la maison de banque au réseau bancaire: Le Crédit Lyonnais des années 1870–1914* (Thése sur microfiche, Paris, 1975). See also Jean Bouvier, *Un siècle de banque française* (Paris, 1973); Bouvier, "L'extension des réseaux de circulation de la monnaie et de l'épargne," in Fernand Braudel and Ernest Labrousse, eds., *Histoire économique et sociale de la France*, Tome 4-1, (Paris, 1979); Alain Plessis, "La Banque de France et les relations monétaires internationales," *Relations internationales*, 29 (Spring 1982), 3–23; Bouvier, "La monnaie et les banques," in Pierre Léon, ed., *Histoire économique et sociale du monde*, tome 4, *La domination du capitalisme, 1840–1914* (Paris, 1978); and Bertrand Gille, *La banque et le crédit en France de 1815 á 1848* (Paris, 1959).

2. Jean Bouvier, "Recherches sur l'histoire des mécanismes bancaires en France dans le dernier tiers du XIXé siécle: Sources et problémes," in idem, *Histoire économique et histoire sociale* (Geneva, 1968). See also Hubert Bonin, "Banques," in Jeannine Brémond, ed., *Dictionnaire d'histoire économique de 1800 à nos jours* (Paris, 1987).

3. Rondo Cameron et al., *Banking in the Early Stages of Industrialization: A Study in Comparative Economic History* (London and New York, 1967), Chapter 4; R. J. Barker, "The Perier Bank During the Restoration, 1815–1830," *Journal of European Economic History*, 2 (Winter 1973), 641–56; Maurice Levy-Leboyer, *Les banques européennes et l'industrialisation internationale* (Paris, 1964).

4. Anthony Rowley, "Deux crises économiques modernes: 1846 et 1848?," *1848: Révolutions et mutations au XIXè siècle, Bulletin de la Société d'histoire de la révolution de 1848 et des révolutions du XIXé siècle*, (1986), 81–90.

5. David S. Landes, "Vielle Banque et Banque Nouvelle: la révolution financière du XIXé siècle," *Revue d'histoire moderne et contemporaine*, 3 (juillet-septembre 1956) 204–22; but see Alain Plessis, "La révolution du crédit en France (1852–1857)?" *1848: Révolution et mutations au XIXè siècle. Bulletin de la Société d'histoire de la révolution de 1848 et des révolutions du XIXè siècle* (1987), 31–40.

6. See above, Introduction.

7. Edmond Lebée, "Le groupe des banques affiliées au C.I.C. Ses origines et son dévoloppement," *Histoire des entreprises,* 7 (mai 1961), 5–40; G. Beaujouan and E. Lebée, "La fondation du C.I.C.," *Histoire des entreprises,* 6 (novembre 1960), 5–40.

8. Bertrand Gille, "La formation de la Société Générale" and "Les premières années de la Société Générale," in idem, *La banque en France au XIXè siècle* (Geneva, 1970).

9. Jean Autin, *Les frères Pereire: Le bonheur d'entreprendre* (Paris, 1984).

10. Jean Bouvier, *Les Rothschild* (Paris, 1960; new ed., 1983); Alain Plessis, *Régents et Gouverneurs de la Banque de France sous le Second Empire* (Geneva, 1985); Bertrand Gille, *Histoire de la Maison Rothschild* (Geneva, 1967).

11. Maurice Lévy-Leboyer, "Le crédit et la monnaire," in Braudel and Labrousse, eds., *Histoire économique et sociale de la France,* Tome 3-1.

12. Jean Bouvier, *Le krach de l'Union Générale, 1878–1885* (Paris, 1960); also idem, *Le Crédit Lyonnais;* idem, "Les crises économiques: Problématique des crises économiques du XIXè siècle et analyses historiques: le cas de la France," in P. Nora and Jacques le Goff, eds., *Faire de l'histoire,* vol. II, *Nouvelles approches* (Paris, 1974).

13. Michel Lescure, "Banques régionales et croissance économique au XIXè siècle: L'exemple de la Société Marseillaise de Crédit," in *Bangue et investissements en Méditerranée á l'époque contemporaine,* Actes du colloque de février 1982 (Marseille, Chambre de commerce et d'industrie de Marseille, 1985).

14. See below, Chapter 18.

15. Raymond Poidevin, *Les relations commerciales et financières entre la France et l'Allemagne de 1898 à 1914* (Paris, 1969); see also idem, "La puissance financiére de l'Allemagne, 1890–1914," *Relations internationales,* 29 (Spring 1982), 65–87; idem, *Finances et relations internationales, 1887–1914* (Paris, 1970); Bouvier, "Les interventions des banques françaises dans quelques grandes affaires de l'Unité italienne, 1863–1970," and idem, "La 'grande crise' des compagnies ferroviaires suisses: Les groupes bancaires et la lutte pour le trafic trans-alpin, 1875–1882," in *Histoire économique et histoire sociale.*

16. Rondo Cameron, *France and the Economic Development of Europe, 1800–1914* (Princeton, NJ, 1961) pp. 130, 201; see also below, Chapter 14.

17. See below, Chapter 15.

18. Quoted by Poidevin, *France et Allemagne;* see also Frederic Mauro, "Les investissements français au Brésil," in idem, ed., *La préindustrialisation du Brésil* (Paris, 1984).

19. Poidevin, *France et Allemagne,* p. 83.

20. Ibid., p. 401.

21. Réné Girault, "Le milieu bancaire française face aux relations internationales avant 1914," *Relations internationales,* 1 (mai 1974), 27–37; Jacques Attali, *Sir Siegmund Warburg, 1902–1982: Un homme d'influence* (Paris, 1985); Bernard Michel, *Banques et banquiers en Autriche au début du 20è siècle* (Paris, 1976); see also below, Chapter 11.

22. Gille, *Histoire de la Maison Rothschild;* Bouvier, *Les Rothschild.*

23. Poidevin, *France et Allemagne,* p. 401. See also idem, "Fabricants d'armes et relations internationales au début du 20è siècle," *Relations internationales,* 1 (mai 1974), 39–56.

24. Jean Bouvier, "Les traits majeurs de l'impérialisme français avant 1914," *Le mouvement social,* (jan–mars 1974).

25. Réné Girault, *Emprunts russes et investissements français en Russie, 1887–1914* (Paris, 1973), p. 344.

26. Rondo Cameron, "L'exportation des capitaux français (1850–1880), *Revue d'histoire économique et sociale,* 33 (1955), 347–53, and idem, *La France et le développement économique de l'Europe, 1800–1914* (Paris, 1971), Chapter 17.

27. Maurice Lévy-Leboyer, "La capacité financière de la France au début du 20é siècle," and "La balance des paiements et l'exportation des capitaux français," in idem, ed., *La position internationale de la France: aspects économiques et financiers, 19é–20é siècle* (Paris, 1977).

28. Calculated from figures in Girualt, "Emprunts russes, p. 84; see also Jean Bouvier, "L'installation du Crédit Lyonnais en Russie et la préhistoire des emprunts russes," *Revue d'histoire économique et sociale,* (1961).

29. Lévy-Leboyer, "La capacité financière."

30. Jacques Thobie, *Intérêts et impérialisme français dans l'Empire ottoman, 1895–1914* (Paris, 1977), pp. 301–2; see also idem, "Economie, mouvements de capitaux, imperialisme: le cas français jusqu'á la première Guerre mondiale," *Relations internationales,* 29 (Spring 1982), 25–52.

31. Girault, *Emprunts russes,* p. 399.

32. See below, Chapter 18.

33. Girault, *Emprunts russes,* p. 214; see also idem, "Place et rôle des échanges extérieurs", in Braudel and Labrousse, eds., *Histoire économique et sociale de la France,* Tome 4-1, pp. 199–230.

34. Poidevin, *France et Allemagne*; see also idem, "Les intérêts financiers francais et allemands en Serbie," *Revue historique* (juillet-septembre 1964).

35. Thobie, *Imperialisme français,* p. 719; see also idem, "Finance et politique: Le refus en France de l'emprunt ottoman en 1910," *Revue historique,* (1968), and "L'emprunt ottoman 4% 1901–1905: Le triptyque finance-industrie-diplomatie," *Relations internationales,* 1 (Mai 1974), 71–85.

36. Albert Broder, "Les investissements français en Espagne au XIXè siècle," in Lévy-Leboyer, ed., *La position internationale de la France;* also Broder, "Les investissements étrangers en Espagne: méthodologie et quantification," *Revue d'histoire économique et sociale de la France,* (1976), 29–62.

37. Albert Broder, "La multinationalisation de l'industrie électrique français, 1880–1931: Causes et pratiques d'une dépendance," *Annales,* (E.S.C.), (1984) and Broder, "L'expansion internationale de l'industrie allemande dans le dernier tiers du XIXè siècle: le cas de l'industrie électrique," *Relations internationales,* 29 (Spring 1982), 65–87.

38. Bouvier, "Les traits majeurs."

39. Hubert Bonin, *Les banques françaises dans la crise* (Paris, 1985).

40. Paul Bairoch, *Commerce extérieur et développement économique de l'Europe au XIXè siècle* (Paris, 1976), and idem, "La place de la France sur les marchés internationaux au XIXè siècle," in Lévy-Leboyer, ed., *La position internationale de la France.*

41. Quoted by Poidevin, *France et Allemagne,* p. 558.

42. See below, Chapter 19.

43. See below, Chapter 20.

44. Jean Bouvier, "Systémes bancaires et entreprises industrielles dans la croissance européenne au XIXè siècle," *Annales* (E.S.C.) (janvier-férrier 1972) 117. See also Broder, "Le commerce extérieur: l'échec de la conquête d'une position internationale," in Braudel and Labrousse, eds., *Histoire économique et sociale de la France,* Tome 3-1, 305–342.

45. Girault, *Emprunts russes,* p. 85; but see below, Chapter 6, for a different view.

46. Bouvier, "La 'grande crise' des compagnies ferroviaires suisses."

47. Poidevin, *France et Allemagne,* p. 44.

48. See the analysis of Girault, *Emprunts russes,* p. 296.

49. Ibid.

50. Ibid., pp. 450, 538.

51. Ibid., p. 69.

52. See below, Chapter 18. See also Thobie, "Conjoncture et stratégie: Le groupe financier de l'Ottomane en 1914," in *Economie et sociétés dans l'Empire Ottoman (fin du XVIIIé–début du XXè siècles),* Colloque international de Strasbourg (Paris, 1983), pp. 471–83.

53. See Hubert Bonin, *La Banque Nationale de Crédit (1913–1932)* (Lyon, 1983), and idem, "Les banques françaises de la seconde industrialisation," *Revue historique,* 543 (juillet-septembre 1982), 205–24.

54. Thobie, *Imperialisme français*, pp. 722–23.
55. See below, Chapter 19.
56. Gille, "Les premières années de la Sociètè Génerale" and "La formation de la Société Génerale"; also Girault, *Emprunts russes*, p. 60.
57. See below, Chapter 12.
58. Girault, *Emprunts russes*, p. 538.
59. On the expansion of French civil engineering firms, see Dominique Barjot, "An opportunity seized early: French entrepreneurs in the export market for major public works (1857–1919)," in Wolfram Fischer, R. Marvin McInnis, and Jürgen Schneider, eds., *The Emergence of a World Economy (1900–1914)* (Wiesbaden, 1986).
60. Girault, "Finances internationales et relations internationales: A propos des usines Poutiloff," *Revue d'histoire moderne et contemporaine*, (juillet-septembre 1966), 217–36. See also Girault, "Portrait de l'homme d'affaires francais en 1914," *Revue d'histoire moderne et contemporaine* (1969).
61. Quoted by Bouvier, "Encore sur l'impérialisme: des rapports entre banque et industrie dans l'expansion française au dehors, 1880–1914," *Revue française d'histoire d'outre-mer*, 248–249 (1980), 217–26.
62. Bouvier, "Rapports entre systémes bancaires," p. 117.
63. See Hubert Bonin, "Les banques face au cas Citroën: Essai d'appréciation de la puissance bancaire," *Revue d'histoire moderne et contemporaine*, 32 (janvier-mars 1985), 75–98; also idem, "Banques," in J. Brémond, ed., *Dictionnaire d'histoire économique de 1800 a nos jours* (Paris, 1987).
64. Bouvier, "Encore sur l'impérialisme," pp. 224–25.
65. Bouvier, "Les traits majeurs." See also Thobie, *La France impériale, 1880–1914* (Paris, 1983), and Jean Bouvier, Rene Girault, and Jacques Thobie, *L'impérialsme à la française, 1914–1960* (Paris, 1986).

Chapter 4

1. Rudolph Eberstadt's book, *Der deutsche Kapitalmarkt* (Leipzig, 1901), pp. 3–13, discusses the contemporary debate, concluding that the demands of foreign investment were paltry in comparison with those of urban real estate. Jacob Riesser's *Die deutschen Grossbanken und ihre Konzentration*, 3rd ed. (Jena, 1910), contains several elaborate justifications for foreign investment. A modern criticism of German foreign investment on the basis of the "capital shortage" theory is in P.-C. Witt's book: *Die Finanzpolitik des Deutschen Reiches von 1903 bis 1913* (Lübeck and Hamburg, 1970), especially pp. 143–52.
2. Walther G. Hoffmann et al., *Die Wachstum der deutschen Wirtschaft seit der Mitte des 19. Jahrhunderts* (Berlin, Heidelberg, New York, 1965), pp. 261–63, 506–10. Hoffmann's estimate may be too low. Mira Wilkins places Germany's gross foreign investments as of 1913 ahead of those of the United States. See Mira Wilkins, *The History of Foreign Investment in the U.S. to 1914* (Cambridge, MA, 1989).
3. Hoffmann, *Wachstum*, pp. 149–52.
4. According to the monetary theory of the balance of payments, gold flows responded to shifts within the domestic monetary system. For an application of this theory to German economic history in our period, see Andrea Sommariva and Giuseppe Tullio, *German Macroeconomic History, 1880–1979* (London, 1987), especially Chapter 2.
5. Richard Tilly, "Zeitreihen zum Geldumlauf in Deutschland, 1870–1913," *Jahrbücher für Nationalökonomie und Statistik*, 187 (1973), 331–63, especially 337.
6. Knut Borchardt, "Währung und Wirtschaft," in Deutsche Bundesbank, ed., *Währung und Wirtschaft in Deutschland 1876–1875* (Frankfurt/Main, 1976), p. 46.

7. See B. H. Brockhage, "Zur Entwicklung des preussisch-deutschen Kapitalexports (1.Teil)," in Gustav Schmoller and Max Sering, eds., *Staats- und Sozialwissenschaftliche Forschungen*, Vol. 148 (Leipzig, 1910); also Helmut Böhme, *Frankfurt und Hamburg* (Frankfurt, 1968), and Udo E. G. Heyn, *Private Banking and Industrialization: The Case of Frankfurt am Main, 1825–1875* (New York, 1981).

8. Richard Tilly, *Financial Institutions and Industrialization in the Rhineland, 1815–1870* (Madison, WI, 1966), Chapter 7.

9. In addition to the sources mentioned in the previous two notes, see Charles P. Kindleberger, *A Financial History of Western Europe*, (London, 1984), pp. 228–30.

10. For a case study see Rondo Cameron, *France and the Economic Development of Europe, 1800–1914*, (Princeton, NJ, 1961), Chapter XII; see also Pierre Benaerts, *Les Origines de la grande industrie allemande* (Paris, 1933).

11. For a crude estimate see Richard Tilly, "Los von England: Probleme des Nationalismus in der deutschen Wirtschaftsgeschichte," *Zeitschrift für die gesamte Staatswissenschaft*, 124 (1968), especially pp. 191–94.

12. See Ernst Engel, *Die erwerbstätigen juristischen Personen, insbes. die Aktiengesellschaften im preussischen Staate* (Berlin, 1876), and Robert van den Borght, *Statistische Studien über die Bewährung der Aktiengesellschaften* (Jena, 1883).

13. See Table 4–1; also Tilly, "Zeitreihen," pp. 340–41.

14. For one statement by an interested contemporary, see Hermann Wallich, "Aus meinem Leben," in Henry C. Wallich, ed., *Zwei Generationen im deutschen Bankwesen, 1823–1914* (Frankfurt/Main, 1978), p. 186. For the history of the Deutsche Bank see Franz Seidenzahl, *Hundert Jahre Deutsche Bank, 1870–1970* (Frankfurt/Main, 1970); also Karl Helfferich, *Georg von Siemens. Ein Lebensbild aus Deutschlands grosser Zeit*, 3 vols. (Berlin, 1921) I, especially Chapter 3.

15. Wallich, "Aus meinem Leben," pp. 122–24; also Helfferich, *Georg von Siemens*, I, especially pp. 317–20. Here it is shown how conflict between top management and representatives of the shareholders, sharpened by an organizational structure that gave those representatives far-reaching powers over the former (through the *Verwaltungsrat*, rather like a board of directors), was gradually overcome in the 1870s.

16. See M. S. Alberty, *Der übergang zum Staatsbahnensystem in Preussen* (Jena, 1911); also the London *Economist* in the 1880s; and Herbert Feis, *Europe, the World's Banker* (New York, 1930, 1965), especially Chapter 3.

17. See below, Chapter 6.

18. The Berlin financial journal, *Der Deutsche Ökonomist*, published numerous articles in the early 1890s on these details. As late as 1896 they were still attacking Greece, for which country they went so far as to recommend the sending of gunboats! See *Deutsche Ökonomist*, 1896, p. 578. The Argentinian debt posed a problem for German bankers sufficiently serious to induce Adolph Hansemann, head of the Diskonto-Gesellschaft of Berlin, to pay the London Rothschilds a visit and demand instant action. See the account of this episode in Walther Däbritz, *David Hansemann und Adolph von Hansemann* (Krefeld, 1954), pp. 104–5, and Hermann Münch, *Adolph von Hansemann* (Munich, 1932), especially pp. 206–10.

19. Regressing Foreign Issues (Log FI) on Total Issues (Log TI), Time (T), the Lombard Loan rate of interest (L), and a dummy variable for price level swings (D) for the 1883–1913 period yielded the following results (t-statistics in parentheses):

$$\text{Log FI} = 0.385 + 1.083 \text{ Log TI} - 0.293 \text{ L}$$
$$(0.201) \quad (3.589) \qquad (-2.533)$$
$$-0.042\,\text{T} -0.117 \text{ D}$$
$$(-2.375) \quad (0.393)$$
$$R^2 = 0.316 \qquad D-W = 1.734$$

Strictly speaking, these results do not rule out possibly significant changes in foreign opportunities.

20. In addition to the estimate made by Hoffman et al. (cited in n. 2), see the discussion by Karl-Erich Born, *Geld und Banken im 19, und. 20. Jahrhundert* (Stuttgart, 1977), pp. 262–64, where he supports the older estimate of Feis cited in n. 16.

21. Observations on ownership of existing securities for these years and for 1918 suggest an even more substantial diminution of portfolio investments in the United States. On this and other questions concerning German investment in America, see T. R. Kabisch, *Deutsches Kapital in den U.S.A.* (Stuttgart, 1982), pp. 26–27 and especially pp. 113–28. According to Mira Wilkins, however (see n. 2), German direct investments grew significantly between 1900 and 1913.

22. M. Edelstein, "Realized Rates of Return on U.K. Home and Overseas Portfolio Investment in the Age of High Imperialism," *Explorations in Economic History,* 13 (1976), 283–329; also idem, *Overseas Investment in the Age of High Imperialism: The United Kingdom, 1850–1914* (London, 1982).

23. See, e.g., Riesser, *Die deutschen Grossbanken,* pp. 297, 301; for Russian investments, see below, Chapter 12, and Table 4–5.

24. The return on Prussian consols is calculated from data in Spiethoff, *Wechsellagen,* II (cited under Table 4–2); that on domestic industrial shares (of 9.35 percent per annum) from Richard Tilly, "German Banking, 1850–1914: Development Assistance for the Strong," *Journal of European Economic History,* 15 (1986), 113–52. The figure of 6.7 percent cited is an average of the *yearly* weighted averages; the average of the period returns for each security is 5.81 percent. Selection of securities is believed to correspond roughly to the geographical and functional distribution of German foreign portfolio investment and is based on the author's assessment of the reports on these securities in the *Deutsche Ökonomist,* 1883–1913, and *Salings Börsenjahrbuch,* 1890–91, 1900–01, and 1910–11. Though it is not mentioned explicitly in the text, German foreign portfolio investment largely financed social overhead capital; and even a good share of the foreign government securities sold in Germany represented this kind of capital formation. That deserves consideration in any comparison of foreign and domestic returns.

25. See Barry Supple, "A Business Elite: German-Jewish Financiers in Nineteenth-Century New York," *Business History Review,* XXXI (1957), 143–77; also Vincent Carosso, *Investment Banking in America: A History* (Cambridge, MA, 1970) and F. H. Brunner, *Juden als Bankiers* (Tel Aviv, 1962). See also above, Chapter 2, and below, Chapter 11.

26. Eduard Rosenbaum and H. J. Sherman, *M. M. Warburg & Co., 1798–1938: Merchant Bankers of Hamburg* (London, 1979), p. 94; Walter Otto, *Anleiheübernahme-, Gründungs- und Beteiligungsgeschäfte der deutschen Grossbanken in Übersee* (doctoral dissertation, University of Würzburg, Berlin, 1910), gives examples of German involvement in American railroads going back to the 1850s.

27. Kabisch, *Deutsches Kapital,* p. 184; Arthur von Gwinner, *Lebenserinnerungen* (Frankfurt/Main, 1975), p. 52.

28. Kabisch, *Deutsches Kapital,* p. 189; Carl Fürstenberg, *Die Lebensgeschichte eines deutschen Bankiers, 1870–1919* (Berlin, 1931), pp. 330, 531.

29. This account is based on the summaries in Born (cited in n. 20), pp. 259–60; Kabisch, *Deutsches Kapital,* pp. 185–87, 198–201; and Seidenzahl, *Deutsche Bank,* Chapter 5.

30. Since this account is based on German sources, it is likely that the role of the Germans is somewhat overstated. See also above, Chapter 2; and below, Chapter 11, Vincent P. Carosso, *The Morgans: Private International Bankers, 1854–1913* (Cambridge, MA, 1988), pp. 383–86; and Albro J. Martin, *James J. Hill and The Opening of the Northwest* (New York, 1976), pp. 440–59.

31. Seidenzahl, *Deutsche Bank,* p. 100. On Villard's role as middleman between the Deutsche Bank and the U.S. General Electric Company at this same time, see ibid., pp. 123–25; also

Helfferich, *Georg von Siemens,* I, pp. 272–74; and above, Chapter 2, and below, Chapter 11.

32. For instance, M. M. Warburg & Co. and Kuhn, Loeb & Co. cooperated long before marriages "tightened up" the relationship in 1895.

33. Däbritz, *Hansemann,* pp. 91, 124; Born, *Geld und Banken,* pp. 249–51; Seidenzahl, *Deutsche Bank,* pp. 38–39, and Otto, *Anleiheübernahme,* pp. 88, 95–96, 106–07. The Diskonto-Gesellschaft operated in Argentina through a Buenos Aires banking firm, Ernesto Tornquist & Co. (a *Kommanditgesellschaft*), 1889–1897.

34. According to Hermann Wallich, who should have known, the Deutsche Bank liquidated the Laplata Bank without loss. Wallich, "Aus meinem Leben," pp. 141–42.

35. Seidenzahl, *Deutsche Bank,* pp. 116–18; Wallich, "Aus meinem Leben," pp. 141–58.

36. Riesser, *Die deutschen Grossbanken,* pp. 327–18, 333–34; also Däbritz, *Hansemann,* pp. 124–25. See also below, Chapter 16, for references to some of these banks in Brazil.

37. See Otto, *Anleiheübernahme,* pp. 69–83.

38. And also as proof of the German founders' commitment to the country in question, a prominently displayed calling card, as it were.

39. Moreover, it seems that these banks were used as pawns in the larger business strategy of the home country bank. For an interesting example of how the Deutsche Bank could employ its authority over the Deutsche-Übersee-Bank see Hugh Neuburger, *German Banks and German Growth from Unification to World War I* (New York, 1977), p. 89; also Siegfried Pudel, *Die Organisation des deutschen Übersee-, Kolonial- und Auslandsbankwesens* (doctoral dissertation, University of Berlin, 1924), pp. 124–25. The same seems true of German banks in Asia. See below, Chapter 17.

40. This enterprise and its South American context are discussed by Gerhart Jacob-Wendler, *Deutsche Elektroindustrie in Latinamerika. Siemens und AEG (1890–1914)* (Stuttgart, 1982), especially Chapters 3 and 4; financial aspects are discussed by Seidenzahl, *Deutsche Bank,* pp. 125–31.

41. The syndicate did not undertake a public issue until 1905, though large blocks of shares undoubtedly were sold to customers privately. A significant share was reportedly sold in the Swiss market where the A.E.G.-allied bank, Bank für elektrische Unternehmungen, was domiciled. On these points see Jacob-Wendler, *Elektroindustrie,* p. 87, and Seidenzahl, *Deutsche Bank.*

42. According to Paul Wallich, Hermann Wallich's son, who toured South America during 1909–10 and reported on the D.U.B.'s operations there, the local representative was not very effective; Paul Wallich, "Bericht über eine Reise zu den Filialen des Banco Aleman Translatantico, 1909–10," unpublished manuscript, pp. 47, 66.

43. The syndicate changed composition from issue to issue, but the Duetsche Bank was always its organizer. Seidenzahl, *Deutsche Bank,* pp. 125–31.

44. Ibid., p. 130.

45. Jacob-Wendler, *Elektroindustrie,* pp. 72, 79. In its first two years of operation it paid no dividends; in its third year, 3 percent; over the entire 1900–1909 period it paid an average of 6.8 percent. *Salings Börsenjahrbuch,* 1910–11 (Berlin, 1911). It is also significant that a long-term contract with the city of Buenos Aires was not concluded until 1907, nine years after operations had begun. That is an indication of the riskiness of the D.U.E.G. operations. See Otto, *Anleiheübernahme,* pp. 100–104.

46. Wallich, "Aus meinem Leben," p. 147. By 1913 these deposits amounted to 146 million marks.

47. D.U.B., *50 Jahre Deutsche Überseeische Bank 1886–1936* (Berlin, 1936), pp. 32–33.

48. Wallich, "Aus meinem Leben," p. 157.

49. See Fritz Stern, *Gold and Iron: Bismarck, Bleichröder and the Building of the German Empire* (New York, 1977), p. 18.

50. Rosenbaum and Sherman, *Warburg & Co.,* p. 40.

51. Ibid., pp. 46–48 and 94–95.
52. Riesser, *Die deutschen Grossbanken,* pp. 311–12.
53. Ibid., pp. 313–14; Born, *Geld und Banken,* p. 257. See also below, Chapter 14.
54. The shift of the AEG from the Deutsche Bank to the Berliner Handelsgesellschaft in 1897 followed from the Deutsche Bank's close association with Siemens & Halske in that year (in which Siemens & Halske became a joint-stock company with the Deutsche Bank organizing the accompanying issue of shares).
55. Riesser, *Die deutschen Grossbanken,* pp. 48–59, 327–43; Alfred Krüger, *Das Kölner Bankiergewerbe vom Ende des 18. Jahrhunderts bis 1875* (Essen, 1925).
56. Riesser, *Die deutschen Grossbanken,* Appendix IV; Manfred Pohl, *Konzentration im deutschen Bankwesen, 1848–1980* (Frankfurt, 1982); *Salings Börsenjahrbuch,* 1870–1913. It is not possible to give a full picture here of its development in the period between 1870 and 1914. A rough idea of its extent, however, is easily obtainable from an examination of the lists of banking firms taken over or controlled by German banks after 1870 compiled by Pohl or Riesser, and from the lists of directorships in foreign banks held by German bankers in Riesser, Krüger, or in that contemporary business publication, *Salings Börsenjahrbuch.*
57. For example, Feis, *Europe,* and Born, *Geld und Banken,* especially Chapter 5; for a more recent sophisticated survey see Wolfgang J. Mommsen, "Europäischer Finanzimperialismus vor 1914," *Historische Zeitschrift,* 224 (1977), 17–81.
58. One qualifying statement may be in order. Bankers were not above pressuring the leaders of second-rate powers into undertaking investments that were not clearly in the latters' interests but that would be profitable for bankers as long as the governments could be made to pay—even if gunboats were necessary to ensure payment. See the insightful comments of Franz Urbig in Henz Müller-Jabusch, *Franz Urbig* (Berlin, 1954), pp. 38–43, where a Chinese railroad project organized by German banks in 1898 is discussed. See also below, Chapter 14. China was not Europe, of course, but there are European parallels (e.g., Turkey).
59. Feis, *Europe,* especially Chapters 3, 12, and 13, is still worth reading on this topic. More recent (and rather different in emphasis) is Fritz Fischer, *Griff nach der Weltmacht,* 3rd ed. (Dusseldorf, 1964). See especially pp. 19–20, where the prominence of German bankers in the *Mitteleuropäische Verein* in the period from 1900 to 1914 is emphasized; pp. 26–27, where the expansion of German industrial interests in southeast Europe is discussed; and pp. 51–58, where a contradiction between foreign policy ambitions and financial capacity of the German banks is argued with special reference to the "Balkan Question" and Austria-Hungary's aims. But neither this particular discussion nor any other with which I am familiar would seem to permit more than the rather lame conclusion that financial and political commitments were mutually reinforcing.
60. On the 1860s see Münch, *Adolph von Hansemann,* pp. 82–84. For the 1900 (and 1913) estimates of German holdings see John Komlos, *The Habsburg Monarchy as a Customs Union, Economic Development in Austria-Hungary in the Nineteenth Century* (Princeton, NJ, 1983), pp. 162–206, especially Tables. 4.28, 4.35, and 4.38. This estimate is well below an alternative one by Bernard Michel, *Banques and banquiers en Autriche au debut de 20e siècle* (Paris, 1976) of 5 billion crowns (cited by Komlos on p. 197), but it tends to enhance the importance of Austria-Hungary as a field for German foreign investment relative to other authors such as Feis. See also below, Chapter 14.
61. On these Komlos, *Customs Union,* pp. 182, 184, 196–200; Richard Rudolph, "Austria, 1800–1914," in Rondo Cameron, ed., *Banking and Economic Development* (New York, 1972), p. 47; also Ivan Berend and Gyorgy Ranki, *Economic Development in East-Central Europe in the Nineteenth and Twentieth Centuries* (New York, 1974), especially Chapter 5 (and pp. 93–111).

62. Komlos, *Customs Union*, especially pp. 186–206; also David Good, *The Economic Rise of the Habsburg Empire* (Berkeley, CA, 1984), pp. 156–61 and Chapter 7. See also Josef Wysocki, *Infrastruktur und wachsende Staatsausgaben. Das Fallbeispiel Österreich, 1868–1913* (Stuttgart, 1975), where Austrian fiscal policy is discussed.

63. Münch, *Adolph von Hansemann*, pp. 113, 148–54; Stern, *Gold and Iron*, especially Chapter 14.

64. Berend and Ranki, *East-Central Europe*, pp. 106–10; John Lampe and Marvin Jackson, *Balkan Economic History, 1550–1950* (Bloomington, IN, 1982), pp. 210, 227–28, 262–64. Also Maurice Pearton, *Oil and the Romanian State* (Oxford, 1971), Chapter 2. See also below, Chapters 14 and 19.

65. Lampe and Jackson, *Balkan Economic History*, pp. 227–28 and 232–33, appear to conclude that the German banks' failure to penetrate the Balkans more effectively was owing to politically conditioned riskiness of the business; and indirectly, I think, they are saying that French banks did more because here, as in Russia, they could offer cheaper capital. For more on this, see Chapter 3 in this text.

66. "Heavy industry" is defined for present purposes as mining, metals production, heavy engineering (including electrical engineering), and heavy chemicals. To some extent this represented portfolio investment since German-run firms issued securities on German stock exchanges; or at least the large ones like A.E.G. or Siemens did. On German banks in Russia generally, see Chapters 6 and 12.

67. A student at the University of Münster, Wilfried Reininghaus, took the trouble to comb through the issues of the contemporary Berlin financial journal *Der Deutsche Ökonomist*, 1883–1913, as well as sift through a substantial German and English language literature to develop the data on which the cited figure—and others that follow it—are based. Note the discrepancy between this figure and that of Table 4–3 in this text. Repatriation of Russian securities over the period could be one reason. The following account draws on Reininghaus's *Diplomarbeit:* "Der deutsche Kapitalexport nach Russland, 1870–1913" (Münster, 1973); it also utilizes the useful study by Joachim Mai, *Das Deutsche Kapital in Russland, 1850–1894* (Berlin, 1970); but see the new estimates of bond issues in Chapter 12 of this text.

68. Mai, *Kapital*, pp. 63–73.

69. Ibid., pp. 63–65; also below, Chapter 6.

70. See Olga Crisp, "Russian Financial Policy and the Gold Standard at the End of the Nineteenth Century," *Economic History Review*, VI (1953), where Russia's step toward the gold standard at this time is discussed. See also Gerhart von Schulze-Gaevernitz, *Volkswirtschaftliche Studien aus Russland* (Leipzig, 1899), pp. 555.

71. Ibid.; Fürstenberg, *Lebensgeschichte*, p. 108; Mai, *Kapital*, p. 115. See also below, Chapter 12.

72. They are discussed in the sources cited in the previous notes as well as by Reininghaus, "Der deutsche Kapitalexport."

73. On this episode, see Sigrid Kumpf-Korfes, *Bismarcks Draht nach Russland* (Berlin, 1968); also Stern, *Gold and Iron*, especially pp. 439–43.

74. A very clear statement of this aspect of the government loan business by Carl Fürstenberg of the Berliner Handelsgesellschaft in 1909 is reproduced by Neuburger, *German Banks*, pp. 52–57 (in connection with a Serbian loan).

75. Stern, *Gold and Iron*, pp. 445–46.

76. Ibid., pp. 446–47, Mai, *Kapital*, pp. 15–53.

77. Witt, *Finanzpolitik*, pp. 157ff.

78. Olga Crisp, "Russia," in Rondo Cameron et al., *Banking in the Early Stages of Industrilization* (Oxford, 1967), p. 224.

79. Ibid., p. 227; and Reininghaus, "Der deutsche Kapitalexport."

80. This is based on Reininghaus's work. It assumes that German investors took the share of each Russian issue the *Deutsch Ökonomist* attributed to them and held on to it until conversion (accounted for) or 1913, with the exception of the loans contracted before the "Lombardverbot" of 1887, which are assumed to have been sold out in 1887. The securities were estimated at market value.

81. Stern, *Gold and Iron*, p. 286, suggests that Bismarck's return on his investments so well administered by Bleichröder was 4 or 5 percent per year in interest plus a 4 percent capital gain *per year!* That might be a rough indication of what bankers with resources and good information might expect to earn—as a minimum. Stern also notes the profitability of the Russian loan business for Bleichröder (Ibid., p. 447) as did Mai (*Kapital*, pp. 152–53).

82. Reininghaus, "Der deutsche Kapitalexport, Table 22. This is based on evidence in John McKay, *Pioneers for Profit: Foreign Entrepreneurship and Russian Industrialization, 1885–1913* (Chicago and London, 1970), especially pp. 24–39. See also below, Chapter 12, and for evidence of direct investment, Chapter 21.

83. Part of this import surplus was no doubt paid for by services not calculated here, e.g., shipping, insurance, and short-term trade finance. This "balance" is only significant as an indication of Russia's ability to earn claims on Germany in the period, for that ability helped determine the riskiness of German portfolio investments there. Of course, in a world of risk-free multilateral payments settlement, such bilateral accounting would be superfluous; but the Russian business did not belong to that world in this period, except perhaps ephemerally.

84. Richard Rosendorff, "Die deutschen Banken im überseeischen Verkehr," *Schmollers Jahrbuch,* 21 (1904), 101, where a German consulate report for 1888 is cited.

85. Franz Urbig, the banker cited in n. 58, believed the figure to be around 5 million per year in the 1880s; Müller-Jabusch, *Franz Urbig,* p. 73. But Urbig did not believe in the theory that these were a drain on, or loss to, the German economy. See also Riesser, *Die deutschen Grossbanken,* pp. 58–59.

86. Richard Hauser, *Die deutschen überseebanken* (Jena, 1906), pp. 14–15, suggests that British banks deliberately "manipulated" the exchanges so as to channel the German overseas business through London. His entire account, however, indicates that British banks were cheaper than German ones for given credit risks in this period, and that this followed from the more developed financial markets in which they operated. See also Otto, *Anleiheübernahme,* pp. 84–85, where the "thinness" of the Hamburg market for overseas bills in the 1880s is emphasized.

87. Franz Gutmann, *Das Französische Geldwesen im Kriege (1870–1878)* (Strassburg, 1913), p. 196; Kindleberger, *A Financial History,* p. 242.

88. Ibid., pp. 240–51 for the entire episode; also Gutmann, *Französische Geldwesen.*

89. Rosenbaum and Sherman, *Warburg & Co.,* pp. 72–73.

90. Kindleberger, *A Financial History,* pp. 240–49; and Gutmann, *Französische Geldwesen,* p. 87.

91. According to Gutmann, ibid., p. 272, Rosenbaum and Sherman, *Warburg & Co.,* p. 73, and Kindleberger, *A Financial History,* p. 248, both Hamburg and London, two pivots in the transfer, experienced temporary liquidity pressures.

92. Wallich, "Aus meinem Leben," pp. 121–26; Seidenzahl, *Deutsche Bank,* p. 36.

93. Seidenzahl, *Deutsche Bank,* p. 37. See also Helfferich, *Georg von Siemens,* I, pp. 267–68.

94. Wallich, "Aus meinem Leben," p. 143; also in the same vein, Müller-Jabusch, *Franz Urbig,* pp. 46–47.

95. Ibid. See also Hauser, *Überseebanken,* pp. 23–31.

96. Of great interest in this connection are the observations made by Paul Wallich on his tour of the D.Ü.B.'s South American branches during 1909–10. They are collected in an unpublished manuscript (cited in n. 42). See also Hermann Wallich's remarks, "Aus meinem Leben," pp. 141–58 and those of Franz Urbig; also Hauser, *Überseebanken,* p. 32.

97. Riesser, *Die deutschen Grossbanken*, p. 334; *Salings Börsenjahrbuch 1910–11*.
98. These domestic enterprise estimates are discussed in Richard Tilly, "Banken und Industrialisierung in Deutschland: Quantitizierungsversuche," in Friedrich-Wilhelm Henning, ed., *Entwicklung und Aufgaben von Verisicherungen und Banken in der Industrielisierung* (Berlin, 1980).
99. This entire account is based on Manfred Pohl, "100 Jahre Deutsche Bank London Agency," *Beiträge zu Wirtschafts- und Währungsfragen und zur Bankgeschichte*, nr. 10 (1973). In 1879 the Deutsche Bank sold its share in the German Bank of London; also Helfferich, *Georg von Siemens*, I, pp. 243–45.
100. There were two exceptions: the Imperial Ottoman Bank and the Comptoir d'Escompte de Paris; Pohl, "London Agency," p. 26. For the link among British banks, the London money market, and German banks, see also above, Chapter 1.
101. Riesser, *Die deutschen Grossbanken*, p. 369; and Müller-Jabusch, *Franz Urbig*, pp. 56–57; Siegfried Pudel, *Die Organisation des deutschen Übersee-, Kolonial- und Auslandsbankwesens* (dissertation, University Berlin, 1924), p. 31.
102. Peter Lindert, *Key Currencies and Gold, 1900–1913* (Princeton, NJ, 1969), especially Table 1 and pp. 18–19; Rosendorff, "Die deutschen Banken," p. 102; Müller-Jabusch, *Franz Urbig*, pp. 76–78. See also above, Chapter 7, Table 7–5.
103. Rosendorff, "Die deutschen Banken," p. 102ff; Wallich, "Aus meinem Leben," p. 122.
104. Müller-Jabusch, *Franz Urbig*, pp. 73–78.
105. Borchardt, "Währung und Wirtschaft," p. 33; Arthur Bloomfield, *Short-Term Capital Movements Under Pre-1914 Gold Standard* (Princeton Studies in International Finance No. 11, Princeton, NJ, 1963), particularly pp. 77–78; see also above, Chapter 3.
106. Both Borchardt and Bloomfield cite 1 billion marks in short-term credits owed French banks by German banks at unspecified times in the years just before World War I.
107. Bloomfield, *Capital Movements*, p. 78. Experience of the Warburg bank in Hamburg (which had a large bill acceptance business) confirms this view: "Foreign banks bought large quantities of German trade bills on a commission basis, usually one-sixth to one-fifth of the prevailing official discount rate, and brisk trading developed through Rothschilds and other London friends in trade bills denominated in marks, considered such an excellent investment for foreign banks that they came to be called 'Zuckerbrot' ('Sugarbread')." Rosenbaum and Sherman, *Warburg & Co.*, p. 98.
108. Lindert, *Key Currencies*, pp. 53–54, 78. According to Arthur von Gwinner's recollections (*Lebenserinnerungen*, pp. 103–4), the position of German banks was strong enough to help out J. P. Morgan's attempts to stop the panic of 1907 with a shipment of about $50 million in gold!
109. Paul Wallich, "Lehr- und Wanderjahre eines Bankiers," in H. C. Wallich, ed., *Zwei Generationen*, pp. 404–16, provides interesting observations of the prewar short-term capital shortage in Germany (Berlin), the competitive wiring by Berlin bankers to other financial centers for short-term funds, which drove interest rates up, and also on the consultations among the banks leading to a number of cartel-like agreements to raise commission rates and also, under pressure from the Reichsbank, to raise their cash reserves (including giro deposits with the Reichsbank).
110. Bloomfield, *Capital Movements*, p. 93.

Chapter 5

1. Raymond W. Goldsmith, "The Dimensions of International Capital Movements in the 1875–1913 Period: A Background Sketch"; this paper, prepared for the Bellagio Conference, has been omitted from the published version.
2. B. S. Chelpner, *Le marché financier belge depuis cent ans* (Brussels, 1930), p. 86.

According to Ginette Kurgan-Van Henterrijk, the Belgian foreign interests would have amounted to about 860 million Belgian francs; *Leopold II et les groupes financiers belges en Chine: La politique royale et ses prolongements (1895–1914)* (Brussels, 1972), p. 47.

3. Based on Herman Van der Wee, "Investment Strategy of Belgian Industrial Enterprise between 1830 and 1890 and Its Influence on the Economic Development of Europe," in *Belgium and Europe: Proceedings of the International Francqui Colloquium,* Brussels and Ghent, Nov. 12–14, 1981; and Julienne Laureyssens, "Le crédit industriel et la Société Générale des Pays-Bas pendant le régime hollandais," *Belgisch Tijdschrift voor Nieuwste Geschidenis,* 3 (1972), 119–25. See also Rondo Cameron et al., *Banking in the Early Stages of Industrialization* (Oxford, 1967), Chapter 5.

4. The Congress of Vienna (1815) united the Southern and Northern Netherlands in the Kingdom of the United Netherlands under the reign of William I. The revolution of 1830 created the independent Belgian state.

5. As was proclaimed in the foundation act of the Société Générale, "le but de cette société sera de favoriser les intérêts de l'agriculture, des fabriques et du commerce . . ."; quoted by Laureyssens, "Le crédit industriel," p. 129.

6. Before the creation of the National Bank of Belgium as the central bank, nearly every bank could issue bank notes.

7. Herman Van der Wee, "La politique d'investissements de la Société Générale de Belgique, 1822–1913," *Histoire, Economie et Société,* 1 (1982), 608.

8. Ibid., p. 605.

9. Laureyssens, "Le crédit industriel," p. 129–34; Van der Wee, "Investment Strategy," pp. 78–79.

10. Robert Durviaux, *La banque mixte, origine et soutien de l'expansion économique* (Brussels, 1947), pp. 33–51. For the evolution of the industrial portfolio of the Société Générale in the period 1822 to 1830, see Marc De Troyer, *Financiële intermediatiepolitiek van de Société Générale, 1822–1850* (unpublished dissertation, K. U. Leuven, Department of Economics, 1974).

11. William had donated these crownlands to the Société Générale at its foundation in 1822. The revenue of this real estate was to be attributed to the king as part of the civil list; Julienne Laureyssens, "The Société Générale and the Origin of Industrial Investment Banking," *Belgisch Tijdschrift voor Nieuwste Geschiedenis,* 6 (1975), 93–115.

12. Ibid., p. 103–15; Van der Wee, "La politique d'investissments," p. 608.

13. Ginette Kurgan-Van Hentenrrijk, "Geld en Bankwezen, 1830–1873," *Nieuwe Algemene Geschiedenis der Nederlanden,* vol. 12 (Haarlem, 1977), p. 43 (hereafter cited as "1830–1873").

14. Van der Wee, "La politique d'investissements," p. 610.

15. Kurgan-Van Henterrijk, "1830–1873," p. 44.

16. Ibid., p. 44; Van der Wee, "Investment Strategy," p. 80; Chlepner, *Le marché financier belge,* pp. 24–25; Durviaux, *La banque mixte,* pp. 37–38.

17. According to Joel Mokyr, however, external finance was not important for Belgian industrialization; in his model, capital accumulation was caused by ploughing back; see *Industrialization in the Low Countries, 1795–1850* (New Haven and London, 1976), pp. 51–68.

18. Term used by Pierre Lebrun in *Essai sur la révolution industrielle en Belgique, 1770–1847* (Brussels, 1979).

19. Van der Wee, "Investment Strategy," pp. 80–81.

20. Chlepner, *La marché financier belge,* p. 47.

21. Ibid., p. 37.

22. Ibid., p. 32.

23. Ibid., p. 37; Kurgan-Van Henterrijk, "1830–1873," pp. 43–44.

24. Hendricus M. H. A. Van der Valk, *De betrekkingen tussen Banken en Industrie in België* (Haarlem, 1932), p. 34.
25. Kurgan-Van Hentenrijk, "1830–1873," p. 45.
26. Durviaux, *La banque mixte*, p. 36.
27. Chlepner, *Le marché financier belge*, p. 49.
28. Rondo Cameron, *La France et le développement économique de l'Europe, 1800–1914* (Paris, 1971), pp. 270–71; Maurice Levy-Leboyer, *Les banques européennes et l'industrialisation internationale dans la première moitié du XIXè siècle* (Paris, 1964), p. 600; Bertrand Gille, ed., *Lettres adressées à la maison Rothschild de Paris par son représentant à Bruxelles*, 2 vols. (Louvain and Paris, 1961–1963).
29. Chlepner, *Le marché financier belge*, p. 49; Lévy-Leboyer, *Les banques européennes*, p. 616. Specifically on the French industrial participations see Karel Veraghtert, "Les participations française aux S. A. belges (1830–1970)," *Revue du Nord*, 5 (1975), 43–52. For the English interests in the financial sector, see Julienne Laureyssens, "Het ontstaan van de Banque de Flandres: onverwacht eindresultaat van het project Banque Anglo-Belge," *Handelingen van de Maatschappij voor Geschiedensis en Oudheidkunde van Gent*, 21 (1967), 191–221.
30. Van der Wee, "La politique d'investissements," p. 612.
31. Marie-Anna Trooskens, *De Société Générale als Promotor van de Belgische Industriële Ontwikkeling* (unpublished dissertation, K. U. Leuven, History Department, 1974), pp. 66, 185.
32. Ibid., p. 155; Chlepner, *Le marché financier belge*, p. 53.
33. The declining share, 1851–1870, was due to the liquidation of the subsidiary companies (the financial trusts).
34. Trooskens, *De Société Générale*, p. 164; Kurgan-Van Hentenrijk, "1830–1873," p. 46.
35. Chlepner, *Le marché financier belge*, p. 66.
36. Trooskens, *De Société Générale*, p. 157; Kurgan-Van Hentenrijk, "1830–1873," p. 46.
37. Cameron, *France et . . . l'Europe*, p. 214.
38. Kurgan-Van Hentenrijk, "1830–1873," p. 47.
39. Trooskens, *De Société Générale*, pp. 157–58.
40. Chlepner, *Le marche financier belge*, p. 68.
41. Durviaux, *La banque mixte*, p. 65.
42. Ibid., pp. 66–68; Ginette Kurgan-van Hentenrijk, "Geld en Bankwezen, 1873–1885," *Nieuwe Algemene Geschiedenis der Nederlanden*, vol. 12 (Haarlem, 1973), p. 25.
43. Jacqueline Lebrun, "Panorama des banques hainuyères de la seconde moitié du dix-neuvième siècle," in Jean M. Cauchies and Jean M. Duvosquel, eds., *Recueil d'études d'histoire hainuyère offertes à M. A. Arnould* (Mars, 1983), pp. 744–45, 747, 756.
44. Durviaux, *La banque mixte*, p. 56.
45. Chlepner, *Le marché financier belge*, p. 61.
46. B. S. Chlepner, "L'Etranger dans l'histoire économique de la Belgique," *Revue de l'Institut de Sociologie*, 4 (1931), 725–28; Michel Dumoulin, "Het Belgische zakenleven in Italië, 1861–1914," *Spieghel Historiael*, 18 (1983), 530.
47. Chlepner, *Le marché financier belge*, p. 87.
48. Van der Valk, *Banken en Industrie en België*, p. 42.
49. Chlepner, "L'Etranger," p. 728.
50. Kurgan-Van Hentenrijk, *Léopold II et les groupes financiers belges en Chine*, pp. 82–182.
51. Van der Wee, "La politique d'investissements," p. 615; Aldegonde Deville, *De Société Générale als promotor van de Belgische Industriële Ontwikkeling van 1880 tot 1913* (unpublished dissertation, K. U. Leuven, History Department, 1975), pp. 108–9; Chlepner, *Le marché financier belge*, p. 78.
52. In fact, the Société Belge was not the first modern holding company of Belgium. Although

it had been created in 1865, the Société Belge, because of special circumstances, did not start investing heavily in railway companies before 1877. As a modern holding company the Société Belge was, strictly speaking, preceded by the Société Générale des Tramways, which was founded in 1874 by the Banque de Bruxelles and J. Errera explicitly for exploiting tramway concessions in foreign countries (Durviaux, *La banque mixte*, p. 85). However, one could argue that the Société Générale des Tramways was itself modeled on the example of the Société Belge.

53. Between 1880 and 1913 the Société Générale participated in the following foreign companies or specialized holdings for the construction of railways abroad: in Spain, Société des Chemins de Fer du Nord de l'Espagne, Société de Construction de Chemin de Fer en Espagne, Société du Chemin de Fer du Central Aragon; in Italy, Société du Chemin de Fer du Nord-Milan, Société du Chemin de Fer Appenin-Central, Société du Chemin de Fer Napolitain, Société des Chemins de Fer du Tessin; in France, Société des Chemins de Fer de l'Est de Lyon; in Austria, Société du Chemin de Fer Vienne à Aspaing, Société Austro-Belge de Chemin de Fer; in Russia, Compagnie du Chemin de fer du Nord-Donetz; in Mexico, Société Belge de Chemin de Fer au Mexique; in China, Société d'Etude de Chemin de Fer en Chine; in Brazil, Compagnie Auxiliare de Chemin de Fer au Brésil, Compagnie du Chemin de Fer au Brésil; in the Congo, Compagnie du Chemin de Fer du Bas-Congo au Katanga; in Argentina, Compagnie Générale de Chemin de Fer dans la Province de Buenos-Aires. This list is not complete, for it only concerns shares that were held for at least three years (Deville, *De Société Générale*, p. I–III). The historical development of the Belgian holding company is also discussed in Herman Daems, *The Holding Company. Essays on Financial Intermediation, Concentration and Capital Market Imperfections in the Belgian Economy* (doctoral dissertation, K. U. Leuven, Department of Economics, 1975). In his explanation of the phenomenon of the holding company, Daems refers to "national" causes: Daems states that the Belgian holding company arose and has remained viable because it has been able to coordinate and control the flow of new equity capital to Belgian industry, which had a relatively high demand for external funds because of its traditional concentration on the capital-intensive basic industries (p. 239). This explanation refers to our own explanation for the success of the mixed banks from which the holding company emanated, and is thus not in contradiction with our explanation.

54. There were a few tramway participations: the Compagnie Générale du Tramway de Buenos-Aires and the Odessa Tramway Company; John McKay, *Pioneers for Profit: Foreign Entrepreneurship and Russian Industrialization, 1884–1912* (Chicago and London, 1970), p. 86; Deville, *De Société Générale*, p. III.

55. See above, Chapter 3.

56. Ginette Kurgan-Van Hentenrijk, "Les activités bancaires de la Société Générale de Belgique de 1900 á 1935," *Histoire économique de la Belgique: Traitement des sources et état des questions. Actes du colloque de Bruxelles, 17–19 Nov. 1972* (Brussels, 1973), pp. 61–63.

57. Deville, *De Société Générale*, pp. VIII–X.

58. Jean-Claude Allain, "Les Belges au Maroc à la veille du Protectorat francaise (1906–1912)," *Revue d'histoire diplomatique*, (1973), pp. 330–33; Deville, *De Société Générale*, p. IX.

59. G. Kurgan-Van Hentenrijk, "Geld en Bankwezen, 1895–1914," *Nieuwe Algemene Geschiedenis der Nederlanden*, vol. 13 (Haarlem, 1978), p. 240 (hereafter cited as "1895–1914").

60. Deville, *De Société Générale*, p. 114.

61. Ibid., p. 132; René Girault, *Emprunts russes et investissements français en Russie, 1887–1914* (Paris, 1973), pp. 367–72. See also below, Chapter 12.

62. M. E. Falkus, *The Industrialization of Russia, 1700–1914* (London, 1972), p. 70; see also below, Chapter 12.
63. The *Moniteur des intérêts matériels'* data refer only to industrial securities.
64. Quoted in Durviaux, *La banque mixte*, p. 71. The estimated value of 1.3 million francs refers to securities of 50 metallurgical companies, 19 mining companies, 6 glass companies, 7 companies for the distribution of gas and electricity, 8 construction companies, and 8 miscellaneous companies.
65. McKay, *Pioneers for Profit*, p. 86.
66. Ibid., pp. 50–52.
67. In fact, the Dnieper Metallurgical Company was a fusion of two earlier companies. For a more detailed description of the development of the Cockerill interests in Russia, see McKay, *Pioneers for Profit*, pp. 297–318.
68. Ibid., p. 298.
69. Ibid., p. 84. The Belgian interests in Russia during the last decade of the nineteenth century are also described in, among others, Chlepner, *Le marché financier belge*, pp. 81–83; Falkus, *Industrialization of Russia*, pp. 69–71; Girault, *Emprunts russes*, pp. 367–73, 481–84; Fernand Baudhuin, *Le Capital de la Belgique et le rendement de son industrie avant la guerre* (Leuven, 1924), pp. 165–67.
70. See below, Chapter 12.
71. Girault, *Emprunts russes*, pp. 62, 481–84.
72. Deville, *De Société Générale*, pp. 125–40. Especially for the interests in the Chinese Charbonnages de Kaiping, see Kurgan-Van Hentenrijk, *Léopold II et les groupes financiers belges en Chine*, pp. 687–716.
73. Deville, *De Société Générale*, p. XI.
74. B. S. Chlepner, "Esquisse de l'évolution bancaire en Belgique," *Revue de la Banque*, 17 (1953), 401; Durviaux, *La banque mixte*, p. 78–81; Kurgan-Van Hentenrijk, "1895–1914," p. 237.
75. Until 1873 the government had to approve the founding of a joint-stock company; because of their sometimes risky undertakings, financial joint-stock companies were often refused; Chlepner, *Le marché financier belge*, pp. 47–49.
76. Van der Wee, "La politique d'investissements," pp. 46–47.
77. Durviaux, *La banque mixte*, p. 83. Apart from banks, private industrialists were also engaged in international industrial affairs.
78. Dumoulin, "Het Belgische zakenleven," p. 530; Chlepner, *Le marché financier belge*, p. 99.
79. Chlepner, *Le marché financier belge*, p. 99.
80. Ibid., p. 100; Kurgan-Van Hentenrijk, *Léopold II et les groupes financiers belges en Chine*, pp. 208–17, 687–716.
81. Van der Wee, "La politique d'investissements," pp. 48–49.
82. Dumoulin, "Het Belgische zakenleven," p. 530.
83. Ibid., pp. 530–31.
84. Chlepner, *Le marché financier belge*, pp. 78, 108; Van der Valk, *Banken en Industrie in België*, pp. 48–52; Durviaux, *La banque mixte*, pp. 84–86.
85. Chlepner, *Le marché fancier belge*, p. 112.
86. Ibid., p. 85; Kurgan-Van Hentenrijk, "1895–1914," p. 240; Hugo Veulemans, *Gemeende banken en holdings in België tijdens de 19de en begin 20ste eeuw* (unpublished dissertation, K. U. Leuven, Department of Economics, 1974), p. 20.
87. Kurgan-Van Hentenrijk, "1895–1914," p. 239.
88. For example, the Société Internationale d'Entreprises et d'Exploitation Electrique, which was active in Belgium, Russia, and Algeria; Chlepner, *Le marché financier belge*, p. 110–12.

89. Not all investment trusts were creations of the banks; some were founded by industrial companies, but in this case they usually got assistance from the banks.

90. Jacques Thobie, "Intérêts belges et intérêts français dans l'empire Ottoman (1880–1914)," *Les relations franco-belges de 1830 à 1914. Actes du colloque du 15–16 novembre 1974* (Metz, 1975), p. 14; McKay, *Pioneers for Profit*, p. 278.

91. Theodore Heyse, "L'Allemagne et les finances belges," *Revue belge des livres et documents relatifs à la guerre*, 9 (1933), 78–81.

92. Ibid.

93. Chlepner, "L'Etranger," p. 730.

94. Ibid.

95. Theodore Heyse, "L'Allemagne et les finances belges," *Revue belge*, 11 (1936), 381.

96. Chlepner, "L'Etranger," p. 37, cites the *Financial Times* of March 6, 1914, where the term *vasselage industriel* was used when referring to the German interests in Belgian industries.

97. Theodore Heyse, "L'Allemagne et les finances belges," *Revue belge*, 12 (1937), 170.

98. Ibid., p. 171.

99. Heyse, "L'Allemagne et les finances belges," *Revue belge*, (1933), pp. 78–80.

Chapter 6

Section II was written by B. V. Anan'ich and Sections I, III, and IV by V. I. Bovkyin. We wish to acknowledge the assistance of Professor Gregory C. Freeze of Brandeis University in improving our English exposition.

1. *Opyt ischisleniia narodonogo dokhoda 50 gubernii Evropeiskoi Rossii v 1900–1913 gg.* (An attempt to calculate the national income of 50 provinces of European Russia in 1900–1913), S. N. Prokopovich, ed. (Moscow, 1918).

2. *Perspektivy razvertyvaniia narodnogo khoziaistva SSSR na 1926/27–1930/31* (Prospects of the development of the national economy of the USSR for 1926/27–1930/31). S. G. Strumilin, ed. (Moscow, 1927).

3. M. E. Falkus, "Russia's National Income, 1913: A Revaluation," *Economica*, N. S., Vol. 35, (1968), No. 137.

4. Paul R. Gregory, *Russian National Income, 1885–1913* (Cambridge, London, New York, 1982), p. 132.

5. Sources of the data contained in Table 6–2: cols. 1, 2, 7, 8, P. A. Khromov, *Ekonomicheskoe razvitie Rossii v XIX–XX vekakh* (Russia's economic development in the nineteenth and twentieth centuries) (Moscow, 1950); col. 3, *Russkie aktsionernye kommercheskie banki po otchetam za 1914 g.* (Russian joint-stock commercial banks according to the reports for 1914) (St. Petersburg, 1915); col. 4, A. S. Nifontov, *Zernovoe proizvodstvo Rossii vo vtoroi polovine XIX veka* (Russia's grain production in the second half of the nineteenth century) (Moscow, 1974); P. A. Khromov, *Ekonomicheskoe razvitie Rossii . . .* ; col. 5, Table 3; col. 6, S. G. Strumilin, *Statistika i ekonomika* (Statistics and economics), (Moscow, 1979).

6. In compiling the table we used three statistical publications, the data of which are concordant: *Svod dannykh o fabrichno-zavodskoi promyshlennosti v Rossii za 1867–1888 gg.* (A summary of data on factory industry in Russia for 1867–1888) (St. Petersburg, 1890); *Obzor deiatel'nosti Ministerstva finansov v tsarstvovanie imperatora Aleksandra III (1881–1894)* (Survey of the activity of the Finance Ministry during the reign of Emperor Alexander III [1881–1894]) (St. Petersburg, 1902); *Dinamika rossiiskoi i sovetskoi promyshlennosti v sviazi s razvitiem narodnogo khoziaistva za sorok let (1887–1926)* (Dynamics of the Russian and Soviet industry in connection with the development of the national

economy over forty years [1887–1926], Vol. I, Parts 1–3 (Moscow-Leningrad, 1929/30). It should be borne in mind that in Russia registration of the output of mining and manufacturing branches subject to taxation was conducted separately, in terms of the physical volume of output. Its value indicators are available only from 1880 on. The absence of data for 1867 about some other branches is explained by the fact that at that time they had not yet come into their own as branches of factory production.

7. Yearly statistical publication: *Obzor vneshnei torgovli Rossii po evropeiskim i aziatskim granitsam* (Survey of Russia's foreign trade in European and Asian frontiers).

8. Indicators of the ratio between production and export and also between consumption and import in Russia will be found in V. E. Den, *Polozhenie Rossii v mirovom khoziaistve* (Russia's position in the world economy) (Petrograd, 1922); E. S. Gorfinkel, *SSR v sisteme mirovogo khoziaistva* (USSR in the system of the world economy) (Moscow, 1929).

9. Here we deal only with some features of the development of the banking system in Russia, which are important for understanding the problem under consideration. A general survey of its history will be found in Olga Crisp, "Russia, 1860–1914," in Rondo Cameron et al., *Banking in the Early Stages of Industrialization* (Oxford, 1967), pp. 183–238.

10. I. I. Levin, *Aktsionernie kommercheskie banki v Rossii* (Joint stock commercial banks in Russia) (Petrograd, 1917), pp. 139ff.

11. The early period in the history of joint-stock commercial banks in Russia is examined in detail in I. I. Levin's work cited previously. The following stages are described more circumstantially in I. F. Gindin's study, *Russkie kommercheskie banki* (Russian commercial banks) (Moscow, 1948).

12. I. F. Gindin, *Gosudarstvennyi bank i ekonomicheskaia politika tsarskogo pravitelstva (1861–1892)* (The State Bank and the economic policy of the tsarist government [1861–1892]) (Moscow, 1960).

13. Ibid., p. 119.

14. *Ezhegodnik russkikh kreditnykh uchrezhdenii* (Yearbook of Russian credit institutions), issues 1–4, (St, Petersburg, 1880–1886.

15. I. F. Gindin, *Russkie kommercheskie banki*, p. 90.

16. Levin, *Aktsionernie kommercheskie banki v Rossii*.

17. A vivid example of such assimilation is furnished by the activity of the director of the St. Petersburg International Bank, A. I. Rothstein, a German by origin.

18. A. M. Solov'eva, *Zheleznodorozhnyi transport Rossii vo vtoroi polovine XIX v.* (Russia's railway transport in the second half of the nineteenth century) (Moscow, 1975), p. 67. See also Rondo Cameron, *France and the Economic Development of Europe, 1800–1914* (Princeton, NJ, 1961), pp. 275–82, and S. J. Rieber, "The Formation of La Grand Société des Chemins de fer Russes," *Jahrbücher für Geschichte Osteuropos*, 21, No. 3 (1973).

19. P. P. Migulin, *Russkii gosudarstvennyi kredit (1769–1899)* (Russian state credit [1769–1899]) (Kharkov, 1899), Vol. I, pp. 348–61.

20. Ibid., p. 355.

21. Solov'eva, *Zheleznodorozhnyi transport Rossii*, p. 108.

22. Central State Historical Archives (henceforth TsGIA SSSR), f. (fund) 258; op. (inventory) 3; d. (file) 2289; l. (folio) 147.

23. P. P. Migulin, *Russkii gosudarstvennyi kredit*, (Kharkov, 1900), Vol. II, p. 283.

24. TsGIA SSSR, f. 563; op. 2; d. 286; ll. 1–10. Migulin also mentions E. Hoskier as a syndicate participant. See Migulin, *Ruskii gosudarstvennyi credit*, p. 285.

25. Solov'eva, *Zheleznodorozhnyi transport Rossii*, p. 186.

26. TsGIA SSSR, f. 626; op. I; d. 709; ll. 16–19 (the syndicate agreement of banks signed in Paris on December 30, 1893, and approved by the Russian Finance Minister on January 8, 1894).

27. Solov'eva, *Zheleznodorozhnyi transport Rossii*, p. 188.

28. TsGIA SSSR, f. 583; op. 4; d. 276; ll. 192–93.
29. J. Mai, *Das deutsche Kapital in Russland, 1850–1894* (Berlin, 1970), p. 74.
30. Ibid., p. 76.
31. TsGIA SSSR, f. 626; op. I; d. 110; l. 88.
32. The operation testified to the intense activity and collaboration of the banking houses of St. Petersburg and southern Russia. The bank was founded with the participation of the following St. Petersburg commercial houses: Vineken and Co.; I. E. Günzburg; S. K. Gweier and Co.; Eliseev Brothers; Clemenz and Co.; I. E. Kondoianaki; E. M. Meyer and Co.; F. P. Rodokonaki; K. Feleizen; Egor Brant; E. G. Brant and Co. (commercial houses in St. Petersburg and Archangel); Scaramanga and Co. (commercial houses in St. Petersburg and Taganrog); and commercial houses in Odessa: Ephrussi and Co.; Raffalovich Brothers; T. P. Rodokonaki. TsGIA SSSR, f. 1152; op. 8; d. 1873; ll. 29–32.
33. TsGIA SSSR, f. 583; op. 4; d. 286; ll. 56–58.
34. TsGIA SSSR, f. 626; op. I; d. 183; ll. 29–32.
35. Migulin, *Russkii gosudarstvennyi kredit*, Vol., I, p. 287.
36. Ibid., p. 275.
37. Well-known Russian railway contractors Mekk and Derviz were credited with opening the German market for Russian railway securities (TsGIA SSSR, f. 268; op. 3; d. 1115; l. 39; report by an engineer, A. A. Bublikov, "On the Forms of State Support for Railway Enterprises" submitted in March 1907).
38. TsGIA SSSR, f. 268; op. I; d. 476; l. 50.
39. *S.-Peterburgskii Chastnyi bank za 50-letie ego sushchestvovaniia 1864–1914 gg.* (St. Petersburg Private Bank during the fifty years of its existence). See also Gindin, *Russkie kommercheskie banki*, pp. 51–52.
40. I. N. Shemiakin, "O nekotorykh ekonomicheskikh predposylkakh Velikoi Oktiabr'skoi sotsialisticheskoi revoliutsii" (Some economic prerequisites of the Great October Socialist Revolution), in *Sotsialisticheskie preobrazovaniia v SSSR i ikh ekonomicheskie predposylki* (Socialist transformations in the USSR and their economic prerequisites) (Moscow, 1959), pp. 19–21. See also V. I. Bovykin, *Zarozhdenie finansovogo kapitala v Rossii* (The rise of finance capital in Russia) (Moscow, 1967), p. 212.
41. Levin, *Aktsionernie kommercheskie banki v Rossii*, p. 247.
42. TsGIA SSSR, f. 583; op. 5; d. 107; f. 560; d. 21; l. 680 (contracts).
43. H. Lemke, "Die Zusammenarbeit der Peterburger internationalen Handelsbank mit Mendelssohn and Co. bei Emission russischer Eisenbahnleiden in Deutschland Ende des 19 Jh."; idem., "Verbindungen der Peterburger internationalen Handelsbank zu deutschen Banken Ende des 19 Jh." Both essays appeared in *Jahrbuch für Geschichte der sozialistischen Länder Europas*, Vols. 27–28 (Berlin, 1983–84).
44. Ibid.
45. A. M. Solov'eva, "K voprosu o roli finansovogo kapitala v zheleznodorozhnom stroitel'stve Rossii nakanune pervoi mirovoi voiny" (Concerning the role of finance capital in railway construction in Russia on the eve of the First World War), *Istoricheskie zapiski*, Vol. 55, (Moscow, 1956), pp. 180–81.
46. Ibid., p. 199; TsGIA SSSR, f. 597; op. 2; d. 170; ll. 69–72; f. 616; op. I; d. 464; ll. 1–4 (contracts).
47. TsGIA SSSR, f. 595; op. 2; d. 164; l. 22.
48. B. V. Anan'ich, *Rossiia i mezhdunarodnyi kapital, 1897–1914* (Russia and international capital) (Leningrad, 1970, p. 123.
49. TsGIA SSSR, f. 595; op. 2; d. 37; l. 17 (rough syndicate register).
50. I. F. Gindin, *Banki i promyshlennost' v Rossii* (Banks and industry in Russia) (Moscow-Leningrad, 1927), pp. 48–58; Bovykin, *Zarozhdenie finansovogo kapitala v Rossii*, pp. 208–69.

51. V. I. Bovykin, *Formirovanie finansovogo kapitala v Rossii* (Formation of finance capital in Russia) (Moscow, 1984), pp. 119–21.

52. Bovykin, *Zarozhdenie finansovogo kapitala*, pp. 216–17, 220–22, 225–26, 228–230, 252–53, 255–59.

53. Iu. B. Solove'v, "Petersburgskii Mezhdunarodnyi bank i frantsuzskii finansovyi kapital v gody pervogo promyshlennogo pod'ema v Rossii (obrazovanie i deiatel'nost' 'General'nogo obshchestva dlia razvitiia promyshlennosti v Rossii')" (The St. Petersburg International Bank and French finance capital during the years of the first industrial upsurge in Russia [Formation and activity of the Société Générale pour l'industrie en Russie]), *Monopolii i inostrannyi kapital v Rossii* (Monopolies and foreign capital in Russia) (Moscow-Leningrad, 1962); Bovykin, *Zarozhdenie finansovogo kapitala v Rossii*, pp. 240–50; R. Girault, *Emprunts russes et investissements français en Russie, 1887–1914*, (Paris, 1973), pp. 301–4.

54. V. S. Diakin, *Germanskie kapitaly v Rossii. Elektroindustriia i elektricheskii transport* (German capital in Russia. Electrical engineering and electrical transport) (Leningrad, 1971), pp. 66–73.

55. See works by Iu. B. Solove'v, V. I. Bovykin, and V. S. Diakin cited above.

56. Bovykin, *Zarozhdenie finansovogo kapitala*, p. 289.

57. H. Lemke, "Verbindungen der Peterburger Internationalen Handelsbank zu deutschen Banken Ende des 19 Jh, *Jahrbuch für Geschichte der sozialistischen Länder Europas*, Bd. 28 (Berlin, 1984); H. Lemke, *Finanztransaktionen und Aussenpolitik. Deutsche Banken und Russland im Jahrzehnt vor dem ersten Weltkreig* (Berlin, 1985).

58. B. A. Romanov, *Rossiia v Manchzhurii (1892–1906)* (Russia in Manchuria [1892–1906] (Leningrad, 1928); R. Girault, *Emprunts russes . . .* , pp. 305–8; R. Quested, *The Russo-Chinese Bank* (Birmingham, UK, 1977).

59. Girault, *Emprunts russes*, pp. 358–63, 468; Bovykin, *Formirovanie finansovogo kapitala* pp. 191–92.

60. Girault, *Emprunts russes*, pp. 500–502, 506–8.

61. Ibid., pp. 504–5.

62. Characteristically, in 1911, when French and Russian banking groups apportioned among themselves the concessions for railway construction in Russia, the St. Petersburg Private Bank was in the Crédit Mobilier Français group, with A. A. Davydov acting as representative for the latter. *Materialy po istorii SSSR* (Materials on the history of the USSR), Vol. VI (Moscow, 1959), pp. 575–602.

63. S. Ronin, *Inostrannyi kapital i russkie banki* (Foreign capital and Russian banks) (Moscow, 1926), pp. 78–79.

64. Ibid., pp. 74–75; Girault, *Emprunts russes*, p. 511.

65. John P. McKay, *Pioneers for Profit: Foreign Entrepreneurship and Russian Industrialization, 1885–1913* (Chicago, London, 1970), p. 375; Girault, *Emprunts russes*, pp. 501–11.

66. Girault, *Emprunts russes*, p. 511.

67. Archives Société Générale, D. F. 5969 (A. I. Putilov's letters for August 1911).

68. Ibid.

69. See V. I. Bovykin, "Banki i voennaia promyshlennost' Rossii nakanune pervoi mirovoi voiny" (Banks and war industry of Russia on the eve of the First World War), *Istoricheskie zapiski*, 64 (1959).

70. Literature on the Russo-Chinese Bank was indicated above, n. 58. For the Persian Discount and Loan Bank, see B. V. Anan'ich, *Rossiiskoe samoderzhavie i vyvoz kapitalov, 1895–1914 gg.* (Russian autocracy and the export of capital, 1895–1914) (Leningrad, 1975).

71. In a number of articles published in the periodical press E. M. Epstein expressed the view subsequently reiterated in his *Les banques de commerce russe* [Paris, 1925] that the foreign

branches of Russian banks provided large-scale credit for export and import. In I. I. Levin's view, however, the primary objective of these branches was to "draw closer to the world money market." He argued that the branches in London, Paris, and Brussels "develop their operations for assisting export and so on only as a sideline, for they yield far smaller profits than large financial operations" (I. I. Levin, *Banki i eksport* [Banks and export] [St. Petersburg, 1913], p. 13). Diverging opinions were also later expressed.

72. This was convincingly demonstrated by I. F. Gindin, *Russkie kommercheskie banki*, pp. 277–79.

73. Archives Nationales (France), Série AQ 65, A 746 (Rapports du Conseil d'Administration).

74. Archives PARIBAS. Archives anciennes, Russie, 190/14.

75. TsGIA SSSR, f.638; op. 1; d. 10; ll. 253–54 (The protocols of Board of the Siberian Trading Bank).

76. *Monopolisticheskii kapital v neftianoi promyshlennosti Rossii* (Monopoly capital in the oil industry of Russia) (Moscow-Leningrad, 1961), pp. 730–32. See also below, Chapter 19.

77. E. E. Kruze, "Tabachnyi i nitochnyi tresty" ("The Tobacco and Thread-Making Trusts"), *Iz istorii imperializma v Rossii* (From the history of imperialism in Russia) (Moscow-Leningrad, 1959); A. A. Arakelov, "Monopolizatsiia tabachnoi promyshlennosti v Rossii" (Monopolization of the tobacco industry in Russia), *Voprosy istorii,* 9 (1981).

Chapter 7

1. Foreign trade was very important to the country with an export ratio of nearly 20 percent of GNP. The foreign trade per capita was one of the highest in Europe.

2. Most of the dairies and slaughterhouses were relatively small and consequently needed little capital for their construction. It has been estimated that they only took up about 5 percent of total agricultural investment. When mortgages were needed for them, they were normally supplied by the savings banks.

3. There were also a few active merchant bankers, mainly in Copenhagen. Their international transactions were limited to transfers of payments connected with foreign trade and interest payments, and their importance was much more modest than in earlier periods.

4. Shareholders in both these banks were also Banque de Commerce de l'Azov-Don in St. Petersburg and Banque de Paris et des Pays-Bas in Paris, and also in the French one, C. J. Hambro & Son of London.

Chapter 8

1. Olle Krantz, *Utrikeshandel, ekonomisk tillväxt och strukturförändring efter 1950* (Stockholm, 1987, pp. 9–11. Earlier comparisons with other countries show Sweden far below the average for Europe in 1870, reaching only around 70 percent, and well above the average, around 30 percent, by the time of World War I. See Paul Bairoch, "Europe's Gross National Product, 1800–1975," *Journal of European Economic History,* 5 (Fall 1976), 273–340. The new estimates would raise the level of Swedish GNP in 1870 to one approaching the European average.

2. Lennart Jörberg, *Growth and Fluctuations of Swedish Industry, 1869–1912* (Stockholm, 1961), pp. 44–49.

3. Ibid., p. 386ff., Erik Lindahl et al., *National Income of Sweden, 1861–1930,* Part II (Stockholm, 1937), p. 326ff.

4. Jörberg, *Growth and Fluctuations,* p. 27; Krantz, *Utrikeshandel,* p. 32ff.

5. Jörberg, *Growth and Fluctuations;* Ö. Johansson, *The Gross Domestic Product of Sweden and Its Composition, 1861–1955* (Uppsala, 1967), p. 130ff.

6. Hans Modig, *Järnvägarnas efterfragan och den svenska industrin, 1861–1914* (Stockholm, 1971).

7. E. F. Söderlund, *Skandinaviska Banken i det svenska bankväsendets historia, 1864–1914* (Stockholm, 1964), p. 102.

8. Ibid.

9. Ibid., p. 70ff.

10. Ibid., p. 78; BiSOS, *Riksbankens och Enskilda Bankers stallning, 1874.*

11. E.g., Söderlund, *Skandinaviska Banken;* S. Brisman, *Sveriges affärsbanker,* I (Stockholm, 1924); Olle Gasslander, *Bank och industriellt genombrott, Stockholms Enskilda Bank kring sekelskiftet 1900* (Stockholm, 1956). The fullest account is in G. B. Nilsson, *Banker i brytningstid, A. O. Wallenberg i svensk bankpolitik 1850–1856* (Stockholm, 1981); idem, *André Oscar Wallenberg, I. Odyséernas ar 1816–1856* (Arlöv, 1984).

12. The greater elasticity is a point particularly stressed by Erik Dahmén in his "Innovationer i kreditväsendet under den svenska industrialiseringen," *Money, Growth and Methodology and Other Essays in Honour of Johan Akerman* (Lund, 1961), pp. 441–52.

13. *Sveriges Bankmatrikel* (Stockholm, 1886).

14. T. Gardlund, *Svenska industrifinansiering under genombrottsskedet 1830–1913* (Stockholm, 1947), passim. In the firms investigated by Gardlund, the importance of the private credit market decreased from 58 percent of external financing in 1850 to 43 percent in 1870 (p. 77ff.).

15. This is apparent from Söderlund, *Skandinaviska Banken,* passim.

16. Gardlund, *Svenska industrifinansiering,* p. 80.

17. Gasslander, *Bank och industriellt genombrott,* p. 76ff; Söderlund, *Skandinaviska Banken,* p. 45ff.

18. Cf. Lars Sandberg, "Banking and Economic Growth in Sweden before World War I," *Journal of Economic History,* 38 (September 1978), 650–80.

19. Estimates of domestic investments from Johansson, *Gross Domestic Product,* p. 130ff.; for the banks' foreign accounts, see BiSOS, *Riksbanken och Enskilda Banker,* 1893.

20. Figures on share loans in BiSOS, *Uppgifter om bankerna.* The Bank Inspector in his reports shows such suspicions.

21. *Sveriges Nationalförmögenhet ombring ar 1908* (Stockholm, 1912), pp. 714–45. This is also used for figures on Swedish debt in 1908 below.

22. *Översikt över obligationsmarknaden i Sverige 1924 utgiven av Göteborgs Bank* (Stockholm, 1925), p. 7.

23. Rondo Cameron, *France and the Economic Development of Europe, 1800–1914* (Princeton, NJ, 1961), p. 129.

24. K.-G. Hildebrand, *I omvandlingens tjänst: Svenska Handelsbanken, 1871–1955* (Stockholm, 1971), passim.

25. Gasslander, *Bank och industriellt genombrott,* II, p. 321ff., and own research in Stockholms Enskilda Bank archive.

Chapter 9

1. Public Record Office, Kew, Colonial Office Papers, CO 201/614, pp. 87–101, 111–24, and CO 309/139, pp. 150–56: dispatches and minutes, 8 May through 13 June 1893. The Agent-General of New South Wales, unlike the Colonial Office and the acting governors, was not averse to the use of the telegraph.

2. E. P. Neufeld, *The Financial System of Canada* (Toronto, 1972), Table 6:1.
3. *Canada Gazette, Supplement,* December 1913.
4. This sentence draws to some extent on the unpublished researches of Dr. Neil Quigley, of Victoria University, Wellington, New Zealand.
5. On these and other such banks see Ron Rudin, *Banking en français: the French Banks of Quebec, 1835–1925* (Toronto, 1985).
6. *Canada Gazette,* Vol. 4 (1870/1), p. 8; *Canada Year Book* (1936), p. 915.
7. Neufeld, *Financial System,* p. 168.
8. Idem.
9. For such firms see Donald Paterson, *British Direct Investment in Canada* (Toronto, 1976), particularly Chapter 2.
10. Ontario Registrar of Loan Corporations, *Reports: Loan Company Statements . . .* (in Legislature of Ontario, *Sessional Papers*). The figures in this paragraph do not include all loan companies, in that firms which did no business in Ontario were not obliged to file returns with the Provincial Registrar. They do, however, cover the vast bulk of loan company business in the Dominion.
11. See Ian M. Drummond, "Capital Markets in Canada and Australia, 1895–1914" (unpublished doctoral dissertation, Yale University, 1959), and "Canadian Life insurance Companies and the Capital Market, 1890–1914," *Canadian Journal of Economics and Political Science,* 28 (1962), 204–24, and Neufeld, *Financial System,* Chapter 8.
12. On the monetary chaos in Canada during the early days of commercial banking see A. B. McCullough, *Money and Exchange in Canada to 1900* (Toronto and Charlottetown, 1984), Introduction and Chapter 2.
13. I owe this observation to Dr. Neil Quigley.
14. M. C. Urquhart and K. A. H. Buckley, eds., *Historical Statistics of Canada,* 1st ed. (Toronto, 1965), Series F 195; Drummond, "Capital Markets," pp. 105, 117.
15. Ibid., p. 149.
16. Canadian Northern Railway System, *Second Annual Report, 1915/16* (consolidating the reports and debts of affiliated and subsidiary companies). See also T. D Regehr, *The Canadian Northern Railway* (Toronto, 1976), p. 479.
17. Penelope Hartland, "The Canadian Balance of Payments since 1868," *Trends in the American Economy in the Nineteenth Century (Studies in Income and Wealth, Vol. 24)* (Princeton, NJ, 1960).
18. Mathew Simon, "New British Investments in Canada, 1865–1914," *Canadian Journal of Economics,* 3 (1970), Tables III, VI: Neufeld, *Financial System,* Table 7:4. The mortgage company figures cover firms registered in Ontario.
19. Urquhart and Buckley, *Historical Statistics,* Series F 204; Paterson, *British Direct Investment,* Table 2.4.
20. Urquhart and Buckley, *Historical Statistics,* Series F 164, 172, 201, 204.
21. Kris Inwood, "The Decline and Rise of Charcoal Iron in Canada, 1870–1914," (unpublished doctoral dissertation, University of Toronto, 1984), Chapter 4.
22. The origin of SIH appears to be M. H. Watkins, "A Staple Theory of Economic Growth," *Canadian Journal of Economics and Political Science,* 29 (1963), 141–58, reprinted in W. T. Easterbrook and M. H. Watkins, *Approaches to Canadian Economic History,* (Toronto, 1967), pp. 49–73. The idea has been much elaborated and converted into a semi-Marxist argument by R. T. Naylor, especially in his *History of Canadian Business* (Toronto, 1975). It has become common currency among Canada's social scientists, especially among those who worry about the present-day extent of foreign direct investment, and among those who know little of Canadian economic history.
23. Because of changes in coverage the 1900 and 1910 figures are slightly understated in comparison to the figures for 1870, 1880, and 1890. In addition, there are problems about

valuation and reporting and accounting practices. Nevertheless, the numbers are suffi-ciently robust for our present purposes.

24. Peter George, "Ontario's Mining Industry, 1870–1940," in Ian M. Drummond, ed., *Progress without Planning* (Toronto, 1987), Chapter 4.
25. "The Ontario Oil and Gas Industry," ibid., Chapter 5.
26. Drummond, "Capital Markets," p. 123.
27. Urquhart and Buckley, *Historical Statistics,* Series S 71, S 72; 2nd ed. (Ottawa, 1982), Series J 163, J 164.
28. Regehr, *Canadian Northern;* A. W. Currie, *The Grand Trunk Railway of Canada* (Toronto, 1957); G. R. Stevens, *Canadian National Railways* (Toronto, 1960–62); Merril Denison, *Canada's First Bank* (Toronto, 1966/67).
29. J. Castel Hopkins, *Canadian Annual Review, 1908* (Toronto, 1909), p. 623.
30. Drummond, "Capital Markets," p. 54–56.
31. On the bankers' eagerness to transcend the several local banking codes, see Robin Gollan, *The Commonwealth Bank of Australia: Origins and Early History* (Canberra, 1968).
32. See ibid., pp. 46, 53–55, 59–65. See also S. J. Butlin, *Australia and New Zealand Bank, The Bank of Australasia, and the Union Bank of Australia Limited, 1828–1951* (London, 1961), pp. 341–51.
33. Reserve Bank of Australia, *Australian Banking and Monetary Statistics 1817–1945, Occasional Paper 4A* (Sydney, 1971), pp. 131–32. The figures relate to the assets in Australia of the country's check-payment banks, most of which had, before 1910, issued their own paper currency as well.
34. Ibid., pp. 103–6.
35. S. J. Butlin, "Australian Bank Branches, 1817–1914," *Australian Economic History Review,* XVII (2) (September 1977), 166–69. The figures cover only the trading banks; they include all agencies, and all Australian head offices, as well as branches narrowly defined.
36. Butlin, *Australia and New Zealand Bank,* p. 273; Geoffrey Blainey and Geoffrey Hutton, *Gold and Paper: A History of the National Bank of Australisia Limited* (South Melbourne, 1983), pp. 37–39.
37. The first and apparently the only full-length scholarly study of an Australian building society is Maurice French, *A Century of Homemaking: A History of the Toowoomba Permanent Building Society, 1875–1975* (Toowoomba, 1979).
38. See, for instance, the account of the largest such firm in Wynford Vaughan-Thomas, *Dalgety* (London, 1984).
39. J. Baxter, *Banking in Australia* (London, 1983), p. 79.
40. Ibid., p. 72. The data on companies include the four New Zealand firms, demonstrating even more forcibly the preponderance of the private pastoral finance firms.
41. See J. D. Bailey, *A Hundred Years of Pastoral Banking* (Oxford, 1966), pp. 55, 134–46.
42. The public flotation raised £500,000 in perpetual debenture stock, and sold 70 percent of the authorized shares by public subscription not only in London but also in Sydney and Melbourne. The result was to release the firm from dependence on the banks, and on the retention of earnings, for the financing of its expansion. See Vaughan-Thomas, *Dalgety,* p. 57.
43. Alan Barnard, *The Australian Wool Market, 1840–1900* (Melbourne, 1958), p. 224.
44. Butlin, *Australia and New Zealand Bank,* pp. 236–41.
45. *Statistical Register of the Colony of Victoria* (Melbourne, annual). See also Blainey and Hutton, *Gold and Paper,* p. 79, and Butlin, *Australia and New Zealand Bank,* p. 236.
46. Cited by R. J. Holder, *Bank of New South Wales* (Sydney, 1970), p. 44.
47. Henry Gyles Turner, *A History of the Colony of Victoria* (London, New York, and Bombay, 1904), Chapter 10.
48. T. A. Coghlan, *Labour and Industry in Australia,* (London, 1918), pp. 1669–71.

49. Ibid., p. 1774.
50. Coghlan, *Labour and Industry,* Part VI, Chapter 9.
51. Butlin, *Australia and New Zealand Bank,* pp. 279–97, 306–7.
52. Ibid., p. 302.
53. N. G. Butlin, *Australian Domestic Product, Investment, and Foreign Borrowing, 1861–1938/9* (Cambridge, 1962).
54. A. R. Hall, *The London Capital Market and Australia, 1870–1914* (Canberra, 1963), p. 103.
55. Ibid., p. 104.
56. Ibid., Appendix III, Tables I, II.
57. Blainey and Hutton, *Gold and Paper,* p. 39.
58. Holder, *Bank of New South Wales,* p. 543.
59. Ibid., pp. 531, 547.
60. Ibid., p. 547. All the data exclude unproductive loans.
61. Reserve Bank of Australia, *Occasional Paper 4A,* Table 8A, p. 555.
62. Drummond, "Capital Markets," p. 123.
63. On the change in the behavior of the Australian trading banks after the crisis, see C. B. Schedvin, "A Century of Money in Australia," *Economic Record* 49 (1973), 588–605, especially pp. 595–96: "it is likely that this long monetary depression slowed the pace of structural change and retarded general economic recovery."

Chapter 10

All of the books and articles by Japanese scholars are written in the Japanese language.

1. Takafusa Nakamura, *The Economic Growth of Prewar Japan* (Tokyo, 1971).
2. Kazushi Ohkawa et al., *National Income* (Tokyo, 1974).
3. Takafusa Nakamura, *The Economy of Japan* (Tokyo, 1979).
4. Hugh T. Patrick, "Japan, 1868–1914," in Rondo Cameron et al., *Banking in the Early Stages of Industrialization* (Oxford, 1967), p. 242.
5. Ibid., pp. 244–74.
6. The Sumitomo Bank, the Thirteenth National Bank (later the Konoike Bank), the Kajima Bank, and the Thirty-second National Bank (later the Naniwa Bank).
7. Kanji Ishii, "The relations with foreign trade of Yokohama," Society for the study of the history of Chogin, ed., *A Merchant in the Transition Period* (Tokyo, 1984).
8. Historical materials of Chogin kept in the archives of an Ohmi merchant.
9. Naomi Nakamura, *A study on the Public Finance by Okuma* (Tokyo, 1968), pp. 182–201.
10. Kanji Ishii, "Reorganization of British Colonial Banks in Japan and China from the 1870s to the 1880s," *The Journal of Economics,* 45, No. 1, No. 3, (1979).
11. F. H. H. King, ed., *Eastern Banking* (London, 1983), p. 43; and see below, Chapter 17.
12. Kanji Ishii and Hisashi Sekiguchi, eds., *The World Market and the Opening of the Ports at the end of the Tokugawa Era* (Tokyo, 1982), pp. 280–81.
13. Japanese Ministry of Finance, *History of the Public Finance in Meiji Period,* Vol. 13.
14. Shinya Sugiyama, "Glover and Co.," *Journal of Modern Japanese Studies,* No. 3 (1981), No. 4 (1982).
15. Tokihiko Tanaka, *The Political Situation of the Meiji Restoration and the Construction of Railway* (Tokyo, 1963).
16. Kanji Ishii, *Modern Japan and British Merchants* (Tokyo, 1984), Chapter 2.
17. Kanji Ishii, "The Crises of the Mitsui-gumi When They Established the Mitsui Bank," *Journal of Mitsui Research Institute for Social and Economic History,* No. 17 (1983).

18. Kanji Ishii, "The Structure of Credit System," Kaichiro Oishi, ed., *A Study on Japanese Industrial Revolution,* Vol. 1 (Tokyo, 1975).

19. The Bank of Tokyo, ed., *A Complete History of the Yokohama Specie Bank,* Vol. 2 (Tokyo, 1981), pp. 91, 213.

20. See n. 10.

21. Kozo Furusawa, "Enactment of the Ordinance of the Yokohama Specie Bank and the Policy of Foreign Exchange," in Ryuichi Shibuya, ed., *The History of the Special Legislation of the Finance in Meiji Era* (Tokyo, 1977), pp. 96–99.

22. See n. 10; also below, Chapter 17.

23. Kanji Ishii, *The Economic History of Japan* (Tokyo, 1976).

24. Makoto Takahashi, *A Study on the History of the Public Finance in Meiji Period* (Tokyo, 1964).

25. Yoshio Asai, "The Import of Capital after the Sino-Japanese War," *The Socio-Economic History,* 50, No. 6, (1985).

26. Yoshio Asai, "A Study on the Incorporation of the Industrial Bank of Japan," *The Journal of Agrarian History,* No. 68 (1975).

27. Kiyoshi Noichi, "The Political and Economic Policies after the Sino- and Russo-Japanese War and the Foreign Public Finance 1896–1913," *The Journal of Agrarian History,* No. 92 (1981).

28. Hitoshi Kojima, *The Gold Standard of Japan, 1897–1917* (Tokyo, 1981), Chapter 2.

29. Tomoyuki Taira, "The Yokohama Specie Bank under the International Gold Standard before the First World War," *The Journal of Financial Economics,* Nos. 208, 209 (1984).

30. Tsukasa Uetsuka, ed., *Autobiography of Korekiyo Takahashi* (Tokyo, 1936).

31. Akihiko Ishizaki, "Capital Imports to Japan," in Giichi Miyazaki, ed., *Foreign Capital* (Tokyo, 1965).

32. Yoshio Asai, "From Dependent Imperialism to Independent Imperialism, 1895–1931," *Journal of Historical Studies,* No. 511 (1982).

33. Patrick, "Japan, 1868–1914"; Kozo Yamamura, "Japan, 1868–1930: A Revised View," in Rondo Cameron, ed., *Banking and Economic Development* (Oxford, 1972).

34. Naosuke Takamura, *History of Japanese Capitalism* (Tokyo, 1980), p. 83.

35. The Osaka Spinning Co. and the Mie Spinning Co. merged as the Toyo Spinning Co. in 1914, and the Amagasaki Spinning Co. and the Settsu Spinning Co. merged as the Dai Nippon Spinning Co. in 1918.

36. Kazuo Yamaguchi, ed., *History of Industrial Finance in Japan (cotton-spinning industry)* (Tokyo, 1970); Naosuke Takamura, *History of the Cotton Spinning Industry of Japan* (Tokyo, 1971).

37. Kanji Ishii, "The Industrial Finance of the Bank of Japan," *The Socio-Economic History,* 38, No. 2 (1972).

38. Kanji Ishii, "Industrial Capital (2), Silk Industry," in Kaichiro Oishi, ed., *A Study on Japanese Industrial Revolution,* Vol. 1 (Tokyo, 1975).

39. Kanjii Ishii, "Management of the Filature of the Hayashi Family," in Kazuo Yamaguchi, ed., *The History of Industrial Finance in Japan (silk-reeling industry)* (Tokyo, 1966), pp. 242–45.

40. Kanjii Ishii, *Analysis of the History of the Silk Reeling Industry and the Sericulture of Japan* (Tokyo, 1972), Chapter 2.

41. Ishii, "Management of the Filature of the Hayashi Family," p. 272.

42. Yasuzo Horie, *Review and Prospect of Capital Imports* (Tokyo, 1950), pp. 52–53.

43. The Bank of Japan, ed., *The Centennial History of the Bank of Japan,* Vol. 2 (Tokyo, 1983).

44. Kanji Ishii, "Investment to the Ohmi Railway Company," Society for the study of the history of Chogin, ed., *A Merchant in the Transition Period* (Tokyo, 1984).

45. *Osaka Ginko Tsushin-Roku,* March 1901.
46. Masanori Sato, "Lending policy of Korekiyo Takahashi, the Vice-President of the Bank of Japan, before and after 1901," *The Socio-Economic History,* 50, No. 5 (1985).
47. Ryumonsha, ed., *The Biographical Materials of Eiichi Shibusawa,* Vol. 16 (Tokyo, 1957), pp. 9–10.
48. Masaaki Takashima, *A Study of the History of Colonial Finance in Korea* (Tokyo, 1978).
49. Katsuhiko Murakami, "The Korea Affiliate of the Dai-ich Bank and Colonial Finance," *The Journal of Agrarian History,* No. 61 (1973).
50. Kanji Ishii, "An Aspect of Japanese Imperialism in its Formative Period," *Journal of Historical Studies,* No. 383 (1972).
51. Shigenori Moriyama, "Japan and the Belgian Syndicate in Korea—The Failure of their Economic Cooperation," *Journal of Modern Japanese Studies,* No. 2 (1980).
52. Katsuhiko Murakami, "The Colonies of Japan," in Kaichiro Oishi, ed., *Japanese Industrial Revolution,* Vol. 2 (Tokyo, 1975).
53. Murakami, "The Korea Affiliate."
54. Shoichi Namigata, "Enactment of the Law of the Bank of Taiwan and the Reform of the Standard Currency System," in Ryuichi Shibuya, ed., *The History of the Special Legislation of the Finance in Meiji Era* (Tokyo, 1977).
55. Naosuke Takamura, *History of Japanese Capitalism* (Tokyo, 1980), p. 138.
56. Shoichiro Sato, "A Note on Loan for Iron Ore with Special Reference to the Finance of State Iron Works," *The Journal of Agrarian History,* No. 32 (1966).
57. Yurio Mukai, "Yokinbu of the Ministry of Finance," in Shibuya, ed., *History of the Special Legislation of the Finance in Meiji Era.*
58. Tenko Go, *History of the Formation of American Financial Capital* (Tokyo, 1971), pp. 311–13.
59. Fumio Kaneko, "Japanese Imperialism in Manchuria in the Post Russo-Japanese War and the Yokohama Specie Bank," *The Journal of Agrarian History,* No. 74 (1977).

Chapter 11

1. Mira Wilkins, *The History of Foreign Investment in the United States to 1914* (Cambridge, MA, 1989). My paper was written while this book was under preparation. Both used the same material. While the present paper is self-contained, it often cites the book where fuller details on foreign investment are to be found.
2. Ibid., pp. 147, 155, 159. Wilkins settled on a figure of about $7.1 billion that coincides with the earlier findings of Cleona Lewis, *America's Stake in Foreign Investments* (Washington, DC, Brookings Institution, 1938), p. 546. Lewis found America's long-term investments abroad to be $3.5 billion. Ibid., p. 605. If we subtract that figure from the $7.1 billion foreign investment in the United States, this would make the United States a *net* debtor nation to the extent of $3.6 billion, as of July 1, 1914.
3. Wilkins, *History of Foreign Investment,* p. 145. See also Rondo Cameron, "Introduction," in this volume, Table 1.
4. Wilkins, *History of Foreign Investment,* pp. 159, 155–74.
5. I use the term "foreign direct investment" in its modern usage—that is, to denote foreign investment that carries with it management and control, or at least the potential for management and control. Multinational enterprises make foreign direct investments.
6. America was a country of immigrants. Some carried capital from abroad; many made money in the United States. In defining the level of "foreign" investment in the United States, I look at the obligations to *nonresident* foreign investors. An immigrant who settled

in the United States became an American and the monies he (or she) brought in and then made in America created no obligations to anyone abroad. They are "American" investments—and thus are excluded from my study.

7. Report of the Special Commissioner of Revenue (David Wells), for the Year 1869, p. xxvii, reprinted in Mira Wilkins, ed., *Foreign Investments in the United States* (New York, 1977). Lewis, *America's Stake*, p. 546.

8. See Wilkins, *History of Foreign Investment*, pp. 91, 147, 150, 159–61. D. C. M. Platt, in *Foreign Finance in Continental Europe and the USA, 1814–1870* (London, 1984), and idem., *Britain's Investment Overseas on the Eve of the First World War* (New York, 1986), has challenged all our established numbers—arguing that the foreign investment figures are inflated. Platt is not the first to do so. Although I have doubts on the figures' accuracy, I am not convinced by Platt's arguments on foreign investment in the United States. I do *not* believe the totals of David Wells and Cleona Lewis are high; indeed, I uncovered investments that both had omitted.

9. I use the word "productive" in the broad sense of production of goods and services (including transportation services, i.e., railroads), as distinct from public finance investments, which could be "productive"—or, as in the case of Civil War finance, often were nonproductive (or only residually productive). Albert Fishlow, "Lessons from the Past: Capital Markets during the 19th Century and Interwar Period," *International Organization*, XXXIX (Summer 1985), 392–416, makes the distinction between "developmental finance" and "revenue finance." By his definitions, America's international borrowings between 1880 and 1914 were almost exclusively developmental.

10. Matthew Simon, *Cyclical Fluctuations and the International Capital Movements of the United States, 1865–1897* (New York, 1979), pp. 78–105.

11. Leland H. Jenks, *The Migration of British Capital to 1875* (New York, 1973), pp. 423–24 (on size of refunding issues). See list in Baring Archives London, AC 29, of "Foreign, Colonial, and Commercial Loans," in which the Barings participated, and Philip Ziegler, *The Sixth Great Power* (New York, 1988), p. 216; Hope & Co. to Thomas Baring, March 15, 1871, Baring Archives, Ottawa, Vol. lll, p. 06270 for Hope & Co.'s decision not "to accept the agency." Also on the 1871 and 1873 refunding issues, see Henrietta Larson, *Jay Cooke* (Cambridge, MA, 1936), pp. 318–21; Julius Grodinsky, *Jay Cooke* (Philadelphia, 1957), pp. 270, 278–94; and Linton Wells, "House of Seligman," unpublished typescript (1931), pp. 142–50, copy in New York Historical Society Library.

12. U.S. Treasury, *Specie Resumption and Refunding of National Debt*, H. Exec. Doc. 9, 46th Cong., 2nd sess. (1880); Wilkins, *History of Foreign Investment*, pp. 184–85.

13. Wilkins, *History of Foreign Investment*, pp. 185–86; Fritz Redlich, *The Molding of American Banking* (New York, 1968), Part 2, p. 370, and data in Rothschild Archives London. The Morgans in both New York and London were also involved in this operation; see Vincent P. Carosso, *The Morgans: Private International Bankers, 1854–1913* (Cambridge, MA, 1987).

14. *Stock Exchange Official Intelligence*, 1914.

15. *Commercial and Financial Chronicle*, XIX (November 14, 1874), 483, is useful on foreign holdings of state securities and the pattern of default. See also Wilkins, *History of Foreign Investment*, pp. 111–13.

16. In 1835 America had *no* federal government debt. In the 1830s most of the government securities of Americans sold abroad were those of the various states. On this, see Reginald C. McGrane, *Foreign Bondholders and American State Debts* (New York, 1935) and Wilkins, *History of Foreign Investment*, pp. 50–51, 54–59, 67–71.

17. On foreign purchases of New York City securities, see Paul D. Dickens, "The Transition Period in American International Financing: 1897 to 1914" (doctoral dissertation, George

Washington University, 1933), pp. 248, 250, 251, 252–55, 263, 264, 266, 269, and Wilkins, *History of Foreign Investment*, pp. 187–88.

18. John J. Madden, *British Investment in the United States, 1860–1880* (New York, 1985), pp. 78–79, has figures that suggest the change occurred in the early 1870s. Madden's dissertation covers continental European as well as British investment in the United States in these years. On the inflow into the railroad sector, see Jeffrey G. Williamson, *American Growth and the Balance of Payments, 1820–1913* (Chapel Hill, NC, 1964).

19. U.S. Bureau of the Census, *Historical Statistics of the United States* (Washington, DC, 1960), pp. 427, 429. For the importance of railroads in American development in these years see Alfred D. Chandler, *The Visible Hand* (Cambridge, MA, 1977).

20. See Wilkins, *History of Foreign Investment*, Chapter 6, and Dorothy Adler, *British Investment in American Railways, 1834–1898* (Charlottesville, VA, 1970); Dolores Greenberg, *Financiers and Railroads 1869–1889: A Study of Morton, Bliss & Co.* (Newark, DE, 1980); Vincent P. Carosso, *The Morgans* (Cambridge, MA, 1987); idem., *Investment Banking in America* (Cambridge, MA, 1970); Michael Edelstein, *Overseas Investment in the Age of High Imperialism: The United Kingdom, 1850–1914* (New York, 1982); Wells, "House of Seligman"; Thomas R. Kabisch, *Deutsches Kapital in den USA* (Stuttgart, 1982), pp. 183–97. This is but a sample of the huge literature.

21. Stanley D. Chapman, "The Evolution of Merchant Banking in Britain in the Nineteenth Century," in V. I. Bovykin, ed., *Transformation of Bank Structures in the Industrial Period* (Budapest, 1982), p. 25. Adler, *British Investment*, pp. 203–10, lists the public issues from 1865 to 1880.

22. See also Stanley D. Chapman, *The Rise of Merchant Banking* (London, 1984), p. 97, which covers the years 1865 to 1890, but Canadian as well as U.S. railroad issues. The period is still too limited. On J. S. Morgan & Co., see Carosso, *The Morgans*. The international banking networks handling American railway securities were extensive. Ruth Roosa, for example, found in Russian archives data on the participation of the St. Petersburg International Bank in an 1898 issue of $3\frac{1}{2}$ percent gold bonds of the Illinois Central. I am indebted to Dr. Roosa for sharing with me her notes on this transaction. See also her "Banking and Financial Relations between Russia and the United States," in this volume (Chapter 13). (The participation was a very small one—$35,000; nonetheless, her findings show the wide market for such bonds.)

23. Cyrus Adler, *Jacob H. Schiff*, Vol. I (Garden City, NY, 1928), pp. 78–79. See Hans Bauer, *Swiss Bank Corporation, 1872–1972* (Basel, 1972), p. 188, who writes of that bank's greatly increased loan-issuing activities between 1907 and 1914: American railways "were very much in favor."

24. See any edition of the *Stock Exchange Official Intelligence*, London, for the wide variety of bonds of American railroads.

25. Based on data in Baring Archives, Ottawa (BAO) and London (BAL). See, for instance, Memorandum of Agreement between H. D. Newcomb, President of the Louisville & Nashville Railroad Co., and Baring Brothers, July 14, 1871, Vol. 12, pp. 011965–65, BAO. See also Newcomb to Baring Bros., October 17, 1871 and November 4, 1871, Vol. 23, pp. 011998–2001, BAO.

26. See *Stock Exchange Official Intelligence, 1914*, p. 275.

27. Conversely, in England, stockbrokers, such as Foster & Braithwaite and Heseltine, Powell, acted on occasion as issue houses. These two stockbrokers were, for example, involved in marketing a Pennsylvania Railroad sterling bond issue in 1875; Adler, *British Investment*, p. 209. Professor Anan'ich asked me whether I could present a table comparable to the superb one that appears on railroads in the Anan'ich–Bovykin chapter (12) in this volume. Adler, *British Investment*, pp. 203–10, did prepare a table on publicly issued American

railway securities in London during the years 1865 to 1880 (her seven printed pages covered only ten years of our 1870 to 1914 period; only public issues; and only those in London). She also provides (pp. 211–13) a roster from the *Economist,* October 2, 1886, of 105 different U.S. railway securities *not* listed on the London Stock Exchange yet "known" in London in 1886. A table containing all issues of different securities of every American railroad offered or available abroad between 1870 and 1914 could easily run in excess of fifty pages and *then* would probably not be meaningful because, owing to the complexity of the process, allocations of American securities to individual bankers or individual foreign countries in no way reflected the actual sales of those securities to nationals of that country, much less the changing level of foreign investments through time.

28. E. Victor Morgan and W. A. Thomas, *The Stock Exchange: Its History and Functions* (London, 1962), pp. 280–81.
29. In 1875, sixty-three American railroad securities were quoted on the Amsterdam exchange. In 1914 the number was 194; K. D. Bosch, *Nederlandse Beleggingen in de Verenigde Staten* (Amsterdam, 1948), p. 139.
30. There were fewer American railroads on the Frankfurt, Berlin, and Paris exchanges than there were on the London and Amsterdam ones. As indicated in n. 27, a security could be "known" in a city and *not* listed on the exchange.
31. *Stock Exchange Official Intelligence, 1914,* p. 312.
32. Ibid., pp. 276, 300. The "agents" seem to have aided in security transfers.
33. Ellis T. Powell, *The Evolution of the Money Market (1885–1913)* (London, 1915), p. 389.
34. See Adler, *British Investment;* Stuart Daggett, *Railroad Reorganization* (Boston, 1908); and E. G. Campbell, *The Reorganization of the American Railroad System, 1893–1900* (New York, 1938).
35. Robert T. Swaine, *The Cravath Firm,* Vol. I (New York, 1946), pp. 499–501. On Dutch bankers and the Kansas City Southern railroad, see Augustus J. Veenendaal, Jr., "The Kansas City Southern Railway and the Dutch Connection," *Business History Review,* LXI (Summer 1987), 291–316. Dr. Veenendaal is at present doing research on Dutch investments in American railroads, and his work is uncovering all kinds of important banking connections.
36. See Wilkins, *History of Foreign Investment,* pp. 213–14, 221; see also above, Chapter 4.
37. Wilkins, *History of Foreign Investment,* pp. 208, 217–18.
38. See, for example, C. A. E. Goodhart, *The Business of Banking, 1891–1914* (London, 1972), pp. 508–13, on American railroads in the portfolio of the Union Bank of London and its successor, 1894 to 1914. Midland Bank archivist Edwin Green has provided me with data on the American railroads in the investment portfolio of London City and Midland. Likewise, J. M. L. Booker, Lloyds Bank archivist, found U.S. railroads in the 1913/14 portfolio of Lloyds Bank. So, too, Dr. Geoffrey Jones confirmed my assumption that the Imperial Bank of Persia would have American railroads in its 1913 portfolio; he found it owned securities of the Pennsylvania Co. (the Pennsylvania Railroad); the Rock Island, Arkansas & Louisiana Railway; the Baltimore & Ohio; the Illinois Central; the Minneapolis, Sault St. Marie and Atlantic Railway; and the Northern Pacific. I have evidence of such holdings by banks on the European Continent and Canada as well.
39. Harry H. Pierce has a good description in English of the Dutch bankers' administrative offices. See his discussion comments in David T. Gilchrist and W. David Lewis, *Economic Change in the Civil War Era* (Greenville, DE, 1965), p. 56. Pierce noted that German and Swiss banks had similar types of arrangements. Ibid., p. 57. See also Wilkins, *History of Foreign Investment,* pp. 210–11.
40. Wilkins, *History of Foreign Investment,* pp. 206–7, has details on all these bankers and their activities vis-à-vis American railroad finance.

41. See R. C. Michie, *The London and New York Stock Exchanges, 1850–1914* (London, 1987), pp. 46–47.

42. Thanks to the work of those mentioned in n. 20 and many others. Nonetheless, despite the vast literature on railroads, no single book has been written on foreign investment in American railroads, 1870 to 1914. Such a volume would be extremely useful.

43. Adler, *British Investment,* p. 205.

44. P. L. Cottrell, *Industrial Finance, 1830–1914* (London, 1980), pp. 113–39.

45. J. Henry Schroeder and Co., London, handled the issue.

46. American Smelting and Refining Company, for example, had Kleinwort Sons & Co. as its London agents; *Stock Exchange Official Intelligence, 1914,* p. 538.

47. Dickens, "The Transition Period," p. 258. On this, see S. Japhet, *Recollections from My Business Life* (London, 1931), p. 106.

48. See *Stock Exchange Official Intelligence, 1914.*

49. On the Amsterdam stock exchange, in particular, American industrials came to be important in the early twentieth century; Bosch, *Nederlandse Beleggingen,* p. 139.

50. Walter Däbritz, *Fünfzig Jahre Metallgesellschaft, 1881–1931* (Frankfurt, 1931) and Seymour S. Bernfeld, "A Short History of American Metal Climax," in American Metal Climax, Inc., *World Atlas* (n.p., n.d. [1962]).

51. For the Paris Rothschilds' involvement in metals, see John P. McKay, "The House of Rothschild (Paris) as a Multinational Industrial Enterprise, 1875–1914," in Alice Teichova, Maurice Lévy-Leboyer, and Helga Nussbaum, eds., *Multinational Enterprise in Historical Perspective* (Cambridge, 1986), pp. 74–86. My comments on both Rothschild houses' participation in American business are based on data in the London and Paris Rothschild archives. See Wilkins, *History of Foreign Investment,* pp. 241, 243, 246, 265–69, 279 for some of their investments in America.

52. A number of British merchant bankers had *their* origins in financing the raw cotton trade (Chapman, *Rise of Merchant Banking*), but in the period 1870 to 1914 no British merchant banker to my knowledge had any investments arising from trade in U.S. spinning, weaving, or any other aspect of U.S. cotton textiles. Baring Brothers did have an interest in the New England Yarn Company, but I do not believe this was a *trader-banker* relationship. The New England Yarn Company was an 1899 merger of nine American mills. It was promoted by Kidder, Peabody, which had brought in Baring Brothers. Some $5 million in first mortgage bonds and cumulative preferred shares were sold in London; Wilkins, *History of Foreign Investment,* pp. 360, 811 n. 64. Ziegler, *The Sixth Great Power,* p. 340, notes that in the 1920s the Barings had a $2.5 million interest in the successor to this firm (undoubtedly a carry-over from 1899). See also Vincent P. Carosso, *More Than a Century of Investment Banking. The Kidder, Peabody & Co. Story* (New York, 1979), p. 59. Other foreign investments existed in the American cotton textile industry, *not* associated with any trader-banker relationship. While the Dreyfus bank had some U.S. holdings, they do not appear to have been in flour mills. See Philippe Chalmin, *Negociants et chargeurs* (Paris, 1985) for excellent data on the commodity traders. Morton Rothstein, "Multinationals in the Grain Trade, 1850–1914," in *Business and Economic History,* 2nd ser., XII (1983), 85–93, does not suggest any such connections. Nonetheless, the British board of Pillsbury-Washburn Flour Mills Co., Ltd., British-owned (as of 1889), did come to include Richard H. Glyn of R. J. Wigram & Co., merchants; Glyn was also a director of the Bank of British North America; Sidney T. Klein of William Klein & Sons, "merchants and foreign bankers," London; and William B. Forwood of Leech, Harrison & Forwood, merchants Liverpool, and also important in the Bank of Liverpool. *Directory of Directors, 1892.*

53. The Rothschilds were involved in gold and silver. Leopold Hirsch & Co. took part in both South African and American gold mining; it was connected with Wernher, Beit & Co., another important "Rand" firm, which had some U.S. interests.

54. See my "Defining a Firm: History and Theory," in Peter Hertner and Geoffrey Jones, eds., *Multinationals: Theory and History* (Aldershot, UK, 1986), pp. 80–95, and my "The Free-Standing Company, 1870–1914: An Important Type of British Foreign Direct Investment," *Economic History Review*, 2nd ser. XLI (May 1988), 259–82.

55. See comments of Andrew Carnegie, quoted in Joseph Wall, *Andrew Carnegie* (New York, 1970), p. 292; Carnegie was selling U.S. railroad bonds in Britain and would not touch this other class of securities, fearing that he would alienate conservative merchant bankers.

56. Clark C. Spence, *British Investments and the American Mining Frontier, 1860–1901* (Ithaca, 1958), Chapter 8.

57. See Wilkins, *History of Foreign Investment*, pp. 320–23.

58. Ibid., pp. 313–14.

59. Ibid., pp. 324–31, and Thomas C. Cochran, *The Pabst Brewing Co.* (New York, 1948), pp. 405–6.

60. For example, when Pillsbury-Washburn was in difficulty, Gaspard Farrer, of Baring Brothers, tried to aid the British investors. See Gaspard Farrer (G.F.) to Thomas Skinner, September 8 and 10, 1908; G.F. to [Richard A.] Glyn, September 25, 1908; G.F. to Robert Meighen, September 29, 1908; G.F. to Lord Mount Stephen, October 8, 1908; G.F. to Meighen, November 3, 1908—all in Gaspard Farrer Letterbooks, Baring Archives London. The individuals he was aiding had *not* acquired the securities through Baring Brothers in the first instance.

61. There were French and Dutch "free-standing" companies that did business in America with securities denominated in francs and florins, but the truly typical (and most numerous) ones were the British firms.

62. I wonder how they fit into Fishlow's distinction between "developmental" and "revenue" finance? (See n. 9 above.)

63. Dr. R. Lundström has been extremely helpful to me on this Swedish investment.

64. See Wilkins, *History of Foreign Investment*, pp. 434–36; also above, Chapter 4, on the Deutsche Bank and electrical industry finance.

65. Clive Trebilcock, *Vickers Brothers* (London, 1977), p. 100.

66. Dr. Harm Schröter discovered in the Siemens Archives, Munich, copies of correspondence from Edward D. Adams, the Deutsche Bank representative in the United States, to the Deutsche Bank Secretariat, Berlin, dealing with Adams' role in handling Siemens & Halske matters in the United States. See Adams to Deutsche Bank, April 17, 1903, SAA 4/LK 77 (Wilhelm von Siemens) and Arthur von Gwinner to Wilhelm von Siemens, April 27, 1903, in ibid. This was *after* Siemens & Halske had retreated from its foreign direct investment in Siemens & Halske Electric Company of America. This was a different investment from the bank-led one in Edison General Electric Company. The problems concerned the Siemens name (rights over it) and patent questions. I am indebted to Dr. Schröter for copies of these letters.

67. C. J. Gignoux, *Histoire d'une entreprise française* (Paris, 1955), p. 116.

68. This was par value. *Bradstreet's*, October 24, 1914, p. 690.

69. Wilkins, *History of Foreign Investment*, p. 262.

70. Ibid., p. 289. It was a short-lived direct involvement on the part of the Paris Rothschilds, for in 1913 Royal Dutch-Shell obtained full control. Ibid., p. 291. The French Rothschilds had close relations with the Royal Dutch-Shell Group. Late in 1911 or early in 1912, the Paris Rothschilds had sold controlling interest in their Russian oil operations to Royal Dutch-Shell, in exchange for a sizable minority holding in the giant British-Dutch firm. Robert W. Tolf, *The Russian Rockefellers* (Stanford, CA, 1976), pp. 189–90; see also below, Chapter 19. In America, the brief participation of the Paris Rothschilds seems to have been complementary to that of Royal Dutch-Shell; it was far from decisive or vital—as witnessed by the brevity of the involvement.

71. Home construction and furniture manufacture were two of the very few sectors that did not receive foreign investment.

72. Wilkins, *History of Foreign Investment,* pp. 477, 749, 863–64.

73. See below, p. 243, on the 1906 A.T.&T. issue.

74. See Marquess of Reading, *Rufus Isaacs, First Marquess of Reading* (London, 1942), pp. 232–34.

75. Wilkins, *History of Foreign Investment,* pp. 528–35.

76. The overview is by no means comprehensive. There were many other foreign investments—from those in American retailing to those in American power plants. For a much fuller rendition, consult Wilkins, *History of Foreign Investment.*

77. Bauer, *Swiss Bank Corporation,* p. 137.

78. Especially good in showing the international character of banking in this period is the popular Paul H. Emden, *Money Powers of Europe in the Nineteenth and Twentieth Centuries* (1937; reprinted New York, 1983). Barry E. Supple, "A Business Elite: German-Jewish Financiers in Nineteenth Century New York," *Business History Review,* XXXI (Spring 1957), 143–78, after documenting some of the associations, concludes "a remarkable feature of the bankers' operations was their cosmopolitan outlook" (p. 176). This was the case not only of the German-Jewish financiers, but also of the Yankee ones.

79. The best source on the Barings before 1861 is Ralph W. Hidy, *The House of Baring in American Trade and Finance: English Merchant Bankers at Work, 1763–1861* (Cambridge, MA, 1949). Because Hidy paid attention to the Barings in pre–Civil War America, it has often been assumed that the Barings had little interest in the United States in the later period. This was *not* the case. The Barings retained important interests in American activities. Ziegler, *The Sixth Great Power,* and John Orbell, *Baring Brothers & Co., Ltd. A History to 1939* (London, 1985), have good data on the Barings' U.S. business before *and* after 1861.

80. I have deciphered all of this with the help of Hidy, *House of Baring,* p. 43, *Burke's Peerage,* and Dr. John Orbell, archivist, Baring Archives, London. My thanks go to the latter for his assistance. See also Ziegler, *The Sixth Great Power,* and Orbell, *Baring Brothers & Co.,* which were not available to me when I wrote this chapter. Gaspard Farrer retained "his partnership and pecuniary interest in Lefevres" after joining Baring Brothers. Gaspard Farrer to F. W. Warren, Birmingham, January 1, 1901, Gaspard Farrer Letterbooks, Baring Archives London.

81. See House Correspondence—North American, New York HC. 5.2.30 (1872–1886), Baring Archives London (BAL), and Hidy, *House of Baring,* p. 98.

82. House Correspondence 5.1.27, BAL. Carosso, *More Than a Century* and Arthur M. Johnson and Barry E. Supple, *Boston Capitalists and Western Railroads* (Cambridge, MA, 1967), p. 319.

83. Carosso, *More Than a Century,* pp. 17, 33; Johnson and Supple, *Boston Capitalists,* p. 319; *Burke's Peerage* and *Bankers' Magazine* (London), CXVI (July 1923), 28, on Thomas Baring.

84. Carosso, *More Than a Century,* pp. 33–34, 188; Heather Gilbert, *End of the Road* (Aberdeen, 1977), II, p. 256n; and Ziegler, *The Sixth Great Power,* pp. 299–302 (on the Hugo Baring era).

85. Swaine, *The Cravath Firm,* I, pp. 734–35.

86. See John A. Garver, *John William Sterling* (New Haven, CT, 1929), passim.

87. Albro Martin, *James J. Hill* (New York, 1976).

88. In this brief rendition, it is impossible to deal with all the various involvements. Barings' latest historian, Ziegler, *The Sixth Great Power,* p. 291, writes that "between 1890 and 1914 the house [Barings] handled twenty United States issues and had a finger in the pie of many more."

89. See quotation in Jenks, *Migration of British Capital*, p. 106.
90. Jean Bouvier, *Les Rothschild* (Paris, 1967), p. 296.
91. The correspondence in the Rothschild Archives London is splendid. I am indebted to Dr. Gerschom Knight and Ms. Yvonne Moss for assistance in using these archives.
92. Benjamin Davidson, formerly of the Rothschild agency in Mexico, opened the Rothschild office in San Francisco. Ira B. Cross, *Financing an Empire*, Vol. I (Chicago, 1927), p. 57, and Bertrand Gille, *Histoire de la Maison Rothschild*, Vol. II (Geneve, 1965), pp. 552–54, 582–83. Richard Davis, *The English Rothschilds* (Chapel Hill, NC, 1983), pp. 31, 131 (on the Davidsons).
93. The latest biography of August Belmont, Sr., is David Black, *The King of Fifth Avenue: The Fortunes of August Belmont* (New York, 1981).
94. Davidson & Co. closed its doors in 1878, and its business was taken over until 1880 by A. Gansl & J. Cullen. Gansl had come from the Rothschild agency in Naples. Cross, *Financing an Empire*, p. 51. Cross spells it *Gansel,* while data in the Rothschild archives use the spelling *Gansl.* In September 1880 the Bank of California agreed to act as correspondent for N. M. Rothschild & Sons, London. See Bank of California to N. M. Rothschild & Sons, September 7, 1880, in Rothschild Archives London (RAL) II/50/0.
95. The Rothschild Archives in Paris and London have sizable quantities of Belmont correspondence.
96. See correspondence in RAL XI/130A/1, especially Nathaniel Meyer Rothschild to Cousins, Paris, November 18 and 19, 1907, on Belmont's difficulties, and Wilkins, *History of Foreign Investment*, pp. 552–53.
97. Lee, Higginson & Co., Boston, to Lord Rothschild, November 6, 1901, RAL II/53/OB. See also 1913 American Accounts RAL II/3/27.
98. Edward D. Adams, *Niagara Power*, Vol. I (Niagara Falls, NY, 1927), p. 297.
99. Wilkins, *History of Foreign Investment*, p. 186; Adler, *Jacob Schiff*, p. 194.
100. Chapman, *Rise of Merchant Banking;* see also Herbert Feis, *Europe, The World's Banker, 1870–1914* (1930; reprinted New York, 1965), p. 87.
101. Data from Annual Reports of London & Midland Bank Ltd., 1893–1897, and London City and Midland Bank, 1898–1914, sent to me by Midland Bank archivist Edwin Green (letter of April 15, 1985); on Lloyds Bank, 1913–1914 data sent to me by the bank archivist, J. M. L. Booker (letter of June 3, 1985).
102. On Villard, see Dietrich F. Buss, *Henry Villard* (New York, 1978); see also Chapter 4; Fritz Seidenzahl, *100 Jahre Deutsche Bank, 1870–1970* (Frankfurt, 1970) is also useful. I have collected materials on Adams from a wide variety of sources.
103. August Belmont wrote to N. M. Rothschild & Sons, London, February 19, 1880, RAL T59/33, on the "immense transactions" in U.S. government bonds between the First National Bank, New York, and "the Raphaels in London and their agents v. Hoffman here [in New York]."
104. Gaspard Farrer to Lord Roberts, September 4, 1901, Gaspard Farrer Letterbook, September 4, 1901, Baring Archives London.
105. Emden, *Money Powers of Europe*, p. 399; see also Chapter 4.
106. Emden, *Money Powers of Europe*, p. 239.
107. Several, however, may have acted on behalf of banks that did serve that role.
108. See *Annual Reports of the Superintendent of Banks in the State of New York*, 1911–1914.
109. Ibid.
110. On the National Bank of Cuba, see Henry C. Wallich, *Monetary Problems of an Export Economy: The Cuban Experience, 1914–1947* (Cambridge, MA, 1950), pp. 52–53, 56. Vincent Carosso found, however, that there was substantial *European* capital involved in the ownership of this bank in the early twentieth century; Carosso, *The Morgans*, p. 851 n. 163.

111. Jean Bouvier, *Le Crédit Lyonnais de 1863 à 1882*, 2 vols. (Paris, 1961), Vol. I, p. 252; Vol. II, pp. 569–72.

112. *Commercial and Financial Chronicle*, XXXII (January 1, 1881), 24; *Bankers' Magazine* (New York), XXIII (February 1879), 648.

113. Eugene Kaufmann, *La Banque en France* (Paris, 1914), pp. 249–50.

114. Cross, *Financing an Empire*, Vol. III, p. 145; Vol. II, p. 641. Data from the Hongkong bank historian Frank H. H. King, June 24, 1984: J. R. Jones, "History of the Bank in California," ca. 1964, File J4, Archives Hongkong and Shanghai Banking Corporation. King has written to me that the Hongkong Bank in San Francisco was not a deposit-taking institution. King to Wilkins, June 24, 1984.

115. F. Cyril James, *The Growth of Chicago Banks*, Vol. II (New York, 1938), p. 836.

116. Ibid., p. 1211. James calls it a "branch." Kaufmann, *La Banque en France*, p. 237, says the Chicago "agency" was liquidated in 1899.

117. Adler, *British Investment*, p. 147.

118. J. Riesser, *The German Great Banks and Their Concentration* (1911; reprinted New York, 1977), pp. 435, 502, 680.

119. Ibid., pp. 447, 435.

120. See "History of Hallgarten & Co.," typescript, April 28, 1950 (copy from Moseley, Hallgarten, Estabrook & Weeden Holding Co.); Hans Fürstenberg, *Carl Fürstenberg* (Berlin, 1931), pp. 197, 330, 449, 525–31; and Hermann Wallich and Paul Wallich, *Zwei Generationen im deutschen Bankwesen, 1833–1914* (Frankfurt, 1978), p. 301.

121. Bauer, *Swiss Bank Corporation*, p. 161; Winterfeldt also served as that bank's "representative" in New York. Ibid., p. 169.

122. Emden, *Money Powers of Europe*, pp. 274–77.

123. Ibid., p. 397.

124. Stephen A. Caldwell, *A Banking History of Louisiana* (Baton Rouge, LA, 1935), pp. 109–10. The longevity of this interest seems exceptional.

125. On The London and San Francisco Bank's British and German connections, see A. S. J. Baster, *The International Banks* (1935; reprinted New York, 1977), p. 158; *Stock Exchange Yearbook, 1875;* and P. L. Cottrell, "Investment Banking in England, 1856–1882: A Case Study of the International Financial Society" (doctoral dissertation, University of Hull, 1969), pp. 269–71. On the bank's California history, see Cross, *Financing an Empire*, Vol. I, pp. 257–58, 411; Vol. II, pp. 884–85.

126. Ibid., Vol. I, pp. 220–21, 389, 423; Vol. II, p. 884; and Bauer, *Swiss Bank Corporation*, p. 368. The Hentsch family and Lombard, Odier & Co. were involved.

127. M. George Aubert, *La Finance américaine* (Paris, 1910), p. 163, and Gignoux, *Histoire d'une enterprise française*, p. 116.

128. Clyde W. Phelps, *Foreign Expansion of American Banks* (New York, 1917), p. 92.

129. Ibid.

130. W. P. G. Harding, "The Results of the European War on America's Financial Position," *The Annals of the American Academy of Political and Social Science*, LX (July 1915), 113.

131. Ibid.

132. Powell, *Evolution of the Money Market* (published in 1915), pp. 375–76, wrote of the key importance of "the great English accepting firms and banks," adding "There is no reason, on the face of things, why American private financial firms should not do a large acceptance business. (The American national banks are forbidden by law to give acceptances.) But the fact is that they do not attempt it because the endeavour would bring their credit, excellent as it is, into disadvantageous contrast with that of London houses. . . ." By 1915 national banks could give acceptances in international transactions. Likewise, some American private banks had done this for years. Nonetheless, despite the exaggeration, and failure to update his book, Powell's point is well taken.

133. Letter in FO 5/2043, Public Record Office, London.
134. *Annual Report of Superintendent of Banks, 1911,* dated January 3, 1912, p. 14.
135. Under this licensing law, one Connecticut bank received rights to set up an agency; the rest were out-of-country banks.
136. *Annual Report of Superintendent of Banks, 1914.*
137. Harding, "Results of the European War," p. 113.
138. In this chapter I am only going to discuss the laws during the period 1870 to 1914. Those in states where foreign banks were present are given in Wilkins, *History of Foreign Investment,* pp. 456–62. Herein I am presenting the same material.
139. James, *Growth of Chicago Banks,* Vol. I, p. 495, and State of Illinois Banking Department to Bureau of Foreign and Domestic Commerce, June 9, 1919, RG 151, 600 US 1919–1935, National Archives, Washington.
140. Chamber of Commerce of the United States, Finance Department, *Laws and Practices Affecting the Establishment of Foreign Branches of Banks* (Washington, DC, 1923), p. 15. This 1902 law was amended in 1906, but no changes were made in these provisions.
141. Ibid.
142. Baster, *International Banks,* p. 159, and Cross, *Financing an Empire,* Vol. III, p. 50.
143. For California's 1913 law see Chamber of Commerce, *Laws and Practices,* pp. 15–16.
144. U.S. Senate, National Monetary Commission, *Digest of State Bank Statutes,* Sen. Doc. 353, 61st Cong., 2nd sess. (1910), p. 693.
145. In the *international* sphere they served other functions as well. For example, in the early twentieth century the United States was both an exporter and importer of capital. The Yokohama Specie Bank in New York saw to it that interest on *Japanese* government loans was paid promptly.
146. Federal Trade Commission, *Report on Cooperation in American Export Trade,* Vol. I (Washington, DC, 1916), pp. 22, 40–44.
147. Ibid., p. 17.
148. Carosso, *Investment Banking in America.*
149. Chapman, *Rise of Merchant Banking,* p. 44.
150. Buss, *Henry Villard,* and Seidenzahl, *100 Jahre Deutsche Bank.*
151. Adler, *Jacob Schiff,* p. 195.
152. For the U.S. securities it was introducing in France, see Edmond Baldy, *Les Banques d'affaires en France depuis 1900* (Paris, 1922), p. 160.
153. On this involvement, see Nathaniel M. Rothschild to cousins, October 27, 1907, RAL XI/130A/1.
154. See Richard Eugene Sylla, *The American Capital Market, 1846–1914* (New York, 1975).
155. Of the fifteen original members of the San Francisco Clearing House Association (1876), six were known to have important foreign ownership. Cross, *Financing an Empire,* Vol. II, p. 884, gives the list.
156. It was said, in fact, that the London and San Francisco Bank, for example, was at a disadvantage because all decisions had to be approved in London. Ibid., Vol. 1, p. 258.
157. Measured by capital and surplus, it was in 1914 the largest commercial bank in Chicago. James, *Growth of Chicago Banks,* Vol. II, pp. 826, 834 (for comparisons).
158. John A. James, *Money and Capital Markets* (Princeton, NJ, 1978), pp. 172–73, looked at the ownership of national banks and never even hinted that any portion of out-of-state ownership was held out-of-country. Nathaniel T. Bacon, "American International Indebtedness," *Yale Review,* IX (November 1900), 266, described the amount, in 1899, as "infinitesimal."
159. See Wilkins, *History of Foreign Investment,* for the many such investments.
160. Barbara Stalling, *Banker to the Third World: U.S. Portfolio Investment in Latin America, 1900–1986* (Berkeley, CA, 1987), p. 102, makes the point that in the lending to Latin America in the 1980s, there was a shift from pre–World War II *bond lending* to present-day

bank lending; from the debt being held by individuals to its being held by the banks themselves. While in the years 1870 to 1914 there was foreign bank lending, it is true that, in the main, long-term American railroad debt was in the form of bonds.

Chapter 12

Sections II and IV were written by B. V. Anan'ich; Sections I and III by V. I. Bovykin. We wish to acknowledge the assistance of Professor Gregory Freeze of Brandeis University in improving our English exposition.

1. For a comparative analysis of available estimates of Russia's balance of payments, see V. I. Bovykin, "K voprosu o roli inostrannogo kapitala v Rossii" (Concerning the role of foreign capital in Russia), *Vestnik Moskovskogo Universiteta,* Ser. IX (1964), No. 1, 55–83. For more recent studies see Paul R. Gregory, "The Russian Balance of Payments, the Gold Standard, and Monetary Policy: A Historical Example of Foreign Capital Movements," *The Journal of Economic History,* 39 (June 1979), 379–99.

2. See I. F. Gindin, *Russkie kommercheskie banki* (Russian commercial banks) (Moscow, 1948), Chapter VI; V. I. Bovykin, "Probleme der industriellen Entwicklung Russlands," *Wirtschaft und Gesellschaft in vorrevolutionaren Russland* (Köln, 1975); Paul R. Gregory, *Russian National Income, 1885–1913* (Cambridge, 1982).

3. B. V. Anan'ich, *Rossiia i mezhdunarodnyi Kapital* (Russia and international capital) (Leningrad, 1970).

4. Publications of the Finance Ministry: *Russkii denezhnyi rynok, 1908–12* (n.p., n.d.); L. E. Shepelev's estimates are to be found in his article "Aktsionernoe unchreditel'stvo v Rossii" (Joint-stock promotion activity in Russia) in *Iz istorii imperializma v Rossii* (From the history of imperialism in Russia) (Moscow-Leningrad, 1959). For a detailed substantiation of calculations in Table 12–1 see V. I. Bovykin, *Formirovanie finansovogo kapitala v Rossii* (The formation of finance capital in Russia) (Moscow, 1984), pp. 157–68.

5. Gindin, *Russkie Kommercheskie banki,* p. 395–403.

6. For the results of the registration, see France, Archives Nationales, *sous-série* F30.1091. For the account of the results, see René Girault, *Emprunts russes et investissements français en Russie, 1887–1914* (Paris, 1973), pp. 72–73.

7. *Russkii denezhnyi rynok, 1908–12,* diagram 22; The Finance Ministry, 1903–13, diagram 14; see also *Russkie birzhevye tsennosti, 1914–15* (Petrograd, 1915), pp. 173–76.

8. I. I. Levin, *Germanskie kapitaly v Rossii* (German capital in Russia) (Petrograd, 1918), pp. 6–7.

9. Central State Historical Archives of the USSR (TsGIA SSSR) f. (fund) 268; op. (inventory) 1; d. (file) 235; l. (folio) ll.

10. P. P. Migulin, *Russkii gosudarstvennyi kredit* (Russian state credit) Vol. I, (Kharkov, 1899), pp. 391–94, 407.

11. TsGIA SSSR, f. 563; op, 2; d. 228; ll. 4–5 (Finance Minister's report to the Finance Committee).

12. Migulin, *Russkii gosudarstvennyi kredit,* Vol. I, pp. 407–8.

13. TsGIA SSSR, f. 563; op, 2; d. 243; l. 5 (Finance Minister's report to the Finance Committee).

14. Migulin, *Russki gosudarstvennyi kredit,* p. 459.

15. Ibid., p. 539–42. Along with Bleichröder, participants in the realization of the loan were Seehandlung (Berlin) and Lippmann, Rosenthal (Amsterdam).

16. TsGIA SSSR, f. 583; op. 11; d. 288; l. 43 (Finance Minister's report, February 3/15, 1878).

17. TsGIA SSSR, f. 583; op. 4; d. 287; ll. 202–3.
18. TsGIA SSSR, f. 583; op. 4; d. 267; ll. 121–29 (Witte's report on the attitude toward Hope and Co., February 18/March 2, 1894).
19. TsGIA SSSR, f. 583; op. 4; d. 288; ll. 178–79; see also above, Chapter 4.
20. *Die Diskonto-Gesellschaft 1851 bis 1901. Denkschrift zum 50 jährigen Jubiläum* (Berlin 1901), p. 54.
21. TsGIA SSSR, f. 268; op. 3; d. 1381; l. 14.
22. Levin, *Germanskie kapitaly v Rossii,* pp. 6–7.
23. Siegrid Kumpf, "K voprosu o prichinakh i sledstviiakh zapreshcheniia Bizmarkom priema v zalog russkikh tsennostei germanskimi bankami (noiabr' 1887)" (Concerning the causes and effects of Bismarck's banning German banks' loans based on Russian securities [November 1887]), *Vestnik Moskovskogo Universiteta,* Seriia, 1968, No. 3, p. 74.
24. S. Wegner-Korfes, "The Cooperation between Russian and German Bank Capital to Finance Russian Railway Construction from the Eighties of the Nineteenth Century up to the Outbreak of World War I," Eighth International Economic History Congress, Budapest, 1982, Sec. B 10, *Transformation of Bank Structures in the Industrial Period* (Budapest, 1982), pp. 16–17.
25. See Part 1, "The Role of International Factors in the Formation of the Banking System in Russia."
26. Siegrid Kumpf, "K voprosu o prichinakh," p. 73.
27. See "Doklad inzhenera A. A. Bublikova "O formakh gosudarsteennoi podderzhki zheleznodorozhnykh predpriiatii. Mart 1907 g." (Engineer A. A. Bublikov's Report "Forms of State Support for Railway Enterprises. March 1907") TsGIA SSSR, f. 268; op. 3; d. 1115; l. 39.
28. Migulin, *Russkii gosudarstvennyi kredit,* Vol. II, p. 35.
29. For information about this operation see A. L. Sidorov, "Konversii vneshnikh zaimov Rossii v 1888–90 gg" (Conversion of Russia's external loans in 1888–90), *Istoricheskii arkhiv,* No. 3, (1959), 99, 125. See also above, Chapter 4.
30. Ibid., p. 104.
31. Migulin, *Russkii gosudarstvennyi kredit,* vol. 2, pp. 88–89.
32. TsGIA SSSR, f. 583; op. 19; d. 58; l. 10; *Istoricheskii arkhiv,* No. 3, (1959), pp. 112–18.
33. Ibid., p. 119.
34. Anan'ich, *Rossiia . . . Kapital,* pp. 24–26.
35. Migulin, *Russkii gosudarstvennyi kredit,* vol. 3, pp. 474–75.
36. Anan'ich, *Rossia . . . Kapital,* p. 37.
37. See below, Ruth A. Roosa, "Banking and Financial Relations between Russia and the United States."
38. Anan'ich, *Rossia . . . Kapital,* p. 111.
39. Ibid., pp. 39–40.
40. Concerning the conversion of urgently redeemed internal loans and their replacement with the 4 percent rente, see Migulin, *Russkii gosudarstvennyi kredit,* Vol. 3, pp. 24–50; also *Spravochnaia knizhka dlia derzhatelei russkikh gosudarstvennykh i garantirovannykh pravitelstvom protsentnykh bumag* (A guide for the holders of Russian state and government-guaranteed interest-bonds) (St. Petersburg, 1913), pp. 70–74.
41. Anan'ich, *Rossia . . . Kapital,* pp. 50–52.
42. Ibid., pp. 86–88.
43. *Russkie finansy i evropeiskaia birzha v 1904–06 gg.* (Russian finances and the European stock exchange in 1904–06), B. A. Romanov, ed. (Moscow-Leningrad, 1926), pp. 375–76.
44. Ibid.
45. Ibid., pp. 378–82.

46. Anan'ich, *Rossia . . . Kapital*, p. 202.
47. Ibid., p. 267.
48. A. M. Solove'va, *Rol' finansovogo kapitala v zheleznodorozhnom stroitel'stve Rossii. Istoricheskie zapiski* (The role of financial capital in railway construction in Russia. Historical notes), Vol. 55 (Moscow, 1956), pp. 197–98; A. P. Pogrebinskii, *Gosudarstvennye finansy tsarskoi Rossii v epokhu imperializma* (Tsarist Russia's state finance in the age of imperialism) (Moscow, 1968), pp. 107–8; see also minutes of the meeting, TsGIA SSSR, f. 597; op. 2; d. 170; ll. 270–77.
49. Anan'ich, *Rossiia . . . Kapital*, p. 283–84.
50. Levin, *Germanskie kapitaly*, p. 12.
51. TsGIA SSSR, f. 616; op. 1; d. 62; l. 2 (minutes of the Azov-Don Bank council's meeting, April 28/May 11, 1912).
52. For weekly surveys of the world money market situation compiled by Mendelssohn and sent to the Finance Ministry, see TsGIA SSSR, f. 583; op. 1; d. 59.
53. Anan'ich, *Rossiia . . . Kapital*, p. 268.
54. TsGIA SSSR, f. 630; op. 2; d. 297, 969.
55. Levin, *Germanskie kapitaly*, p. 84.
56. A. Breiterman, *Obligatsionnye zaimy russkikh gorodov* (Bond loans of Russian cities) (St. Petersburg, 1913), p. 17.
57. TsGIA SSSR, f. 595; op. 2; d. 179; ll. 1–4, 12.
58. M. I. Bogolepov, *Russkie birzhevye tsennosti* (Russian exchange securities) (St. Petersburg, 1915), pp. 94, 113, 115, 174.
59. TsGIA SSSR, f. 565; op. 2; d. 498; ll. 15–21; f. 630, op. 2 d. 114 (Kontrakt [Contract]).
60. B. A. Romanov, *Rossiia v Manchzhurii, 1892–1906* (Russia in Manchuria) (Leningrad, 1928), pp. 90–91. Concerning the Russo-Chinese Bank see also Rosemary Quested, *The Russo-Chinese Bank* (Birmingham Slavonic Monographs, No. 2; Birmingham, UK, 1977).
61. TsGIA SSSR, f. 583; op. 1; d.453; ll. 36–37.
62. Ibid., ll. 37–40 (report from the Finance Ministry's agent in Paris to the Finance Minister, September 30/October 1, 1912.
63. TsGIA SSSR, f. 626; op. 1; d. 1181; l. 1 and others.
64. B. V. Anan'ich, "Iz istorii anglo-russkikh ontoshenii na rubezhe XX stoletiia" (From the history of Anglo-Russian relations at the turn of the century), *Problemy istorii mezhdunarodnykh ontoshenii* (Problems of the history of international relations) (Leningrad, 1972), pp. 198–99.
65. B. V. Anan'ich, *Rossiiskoe samoderzhavie i vyvoz kapitalov 1895–1914,* (The Russian autocracy and export of capital), (Leningrad, 1975), pp. 198–99.
66. Ibid.
67. From January 1878 until the summer of 1879 the Petersburg branch operated under the name of the banking firm Au. Cellerier.
68. Jean Bouvier, *Le Crédit Lyonnais de 1863 á 1882* (Paris, 1961); René Girault, *Emprunts russes.*
69. Jean Bouvier, "Uchrezhdenie otdeleniia Lionskogo kredita v tsarskoii Rossii i predystoriia "russkikh zaimov" (The formation of the Crédit Lyonnais branch in tsarist Russia and the story of Russian loans, *Frantsuzskii ezhegodnik* (French Yearbook for 1961), (Moscow, 1962), p. 155.
70. Girault, *Emprunts russes,* pp. 48, 496–97.
71. Bouvier, Formation of the Crédit Lyonnais branch, p. 155.
72. Scholars have long ago noticed this unique collection of materials on the history of Russian industry. See John P. McKay, *Pioneers for Profit: Foreign Entrepreneurship and Russian Industrialization, 1885–1913* (Chicago, London, 1970); also Girault, *Emprunts russes.*

73. Correspondence between the bank's management and its St. Petersburg branch for 1901, in particular, testifies to it. See the Archives of the Crédit Lyonnais, 3761, Correspondence, Saint-Petersbourg.

74. Not all of the foreigners who founded industrial, commercial, or other enterprises in Russia brought the required capital from abroad. Many acquired it in Russia using technical know-how and their connections with foreign firms. But it is impossible to draw a clear distinction between them.

75. L. E. Shepelev estimated that by 1861 over one hundred joint-stock companies operated in Russia; *Aktsionernye kompanii v Rossii* (Joint-stock companies in Russia) (Leningrad, 1973), pp. 63, 66.

76. *Statistika aktsionernogo dela v Rossii. Vyp. 1, Sostav direktorov pravlenii na 1897* (Statistics of joint-stock business in Russia: Part 1. Board directors for 1897) (St. Petersburg, 1897), pp. 122–3, 127.

77. Well-known companies are meant here. Possibly their number was greater. Only nine of those companies that started their operations in Russia between 1875 and 1881 continued to exist at the end of the nineteenth century. See *Statistika aktsionernogo dela v Rossii. Vyp. 1.*

78. *Société Générale, 1864–1964* (Paris, 1964), p. 68.

79. Out of twelve German companies that started operations in Russia between 1884 and 1890, ten represented firms that operated in Germany and aimed at establishing Russian branches of their German enterprises.

80. Shepelev, *Aktsionernye kompanii v Rossii*, pp. 94, 139.

81. For details see McKay, *Pioneers for Profit.*

82. Bertrand Gille, *La banque en France au XIX siécle* (Geneva, 1970), p. 263.

83. *Société Générale, 1864–1964* p. 68; Archives de la Société Générale, 5593.

84. One of these companies, the Moscow Steamship Company, still existed at the beginning of the twentieth century. See Statistics of Joint-stock business in Russia, Part I, p. 50.

85. McKay, *Pioneers for Profit,* p. 64; Archives du Crédit Lyonnais, Etudes financiéres, 30130.

86. A detailed picture of foreign entrepreneurship in Russia at this stage is given by McKay in his work mentioned above.

87. Judging from the list of the company shareholders for 1886, it had a family character until the end of the 1890s. Of 2,000 shares comprising its initial capital, 1,650 shares belonged to Carl Siemens; Leningrad State Historical Archives, f. 1243; op. 1; d. 2; l. 3.

88. See McKay, *Pioneers for Profit,* Chapter 11; see also Chapter 21 in this text where participation by the Crédit Lyonnais and the Banque Franco-Italienne is indicated.

89. Jean Bouvier, *Le krach de l'Union Générale, 1878–85,* (Paris, 1960), p. 57.

90. *Société Générale, 1864–1964,* p. 68; Bouvier, *Union Générale,* pp. 56–57; McKay, *Pioneers for Profit,* p. 41.

91. Bouvier, *Union Générale,* p. 125.

92. Ibid., Chapter VI. The collapse of the Banque de Lyon et de la Loire immediately entailed the ruin of both new companies. Subsequently, the Société Franco-Russe de l'Oural also ceased to exist, but its properties passed to the Bonnardel group, which in 1883 established the above-mentioned Société des forges et acierie de la Kama. See Jean Bouvier, "Une dynastie d'affaires lyonnaise au XIX siécle: Les Bonnardel," *Revue d'histoire moderne et contemporaine,* No. 2, (1955).

93. Archives, SG, DF, 5684, 5898, 6418, 6461, 6548.

94. *Société Générale, 1864–1964,* pp. 22, 68; Archives SG, DF, 5684, "Note sur la Société anonyme des Usines Franco-Russe," Juin 1916; Rondo Cameron, *La France et le développement économique de l"Europe, 1800–1914* (Paris, 1971), pp. 105–6.

95. For information about St. Paul de Sinçay see Cameron, *La France et le développment économique de l'Europe*, pp. 282–83, 301, 303.
96. McKay, *Pioneers for Profit*, p. 67; TsGIA SSSR, Leningrad, f. 23; op. 24; d. 4.
97. Girault, *Emprunts russes*, pp. 153, 257, 282.
98. Ibid., p. 296.
99. See A. A. Fursenko "Parizhskie Rotshil'dy i Russkaia neft'," (The Paris Rothschilds and Russian oil), *Voprosy istorii* (Problems of history) No. 8 (1962), also below, Chapter 19.
100. TsGIA, f. 20; op. 4; d. 3729.
101. This summary is based on the studies by McKay and Girault and also of works by Iu. B. Solov'ev: "Mezhdunarodnye finansovye otnosheniia i frantsuzskii denezhnyi rynok v kontse XIX v. (International financial relations and the French money-market at the end of the nineteenth century), in *Problemy istorii mezhdunarodnyh otnoshenii* (Problems of the history of international relations) (Leningrad, 1972); Russkie banki i frantsuzskii kapital v kontse XIX v." (Russian banks and French capital at the end of the nineteenth century), *Frantsuzskii ezhegodnik* (French Yearbook), 1974 (Moscow, 1976). See also Chapter 3.
102. Iu. B. Solov'ev, "Petersburgskii mezhdunarodnyi bank i frantsuzskii finansovyi kapital v gody pervogo promyshlennogo pod'cma v Rossii (obrazovanie i deiatel'nost' "General'nogo obshchestva dlia razvitiia promyshlennosti v Rossii") (St. Petersburg International Bank and French finance capital in the years of the first industrial upsurge in Russia/Formation and activity of the "Société Générale pour l'industrie en Russie"/, in *Monopolii i inostrannyi kapital v Rossii* (Monopolies and foreign capital in Russia) (Moscow-Leningrad, 1962); V. I. Bovykin, *Zarozhdenie finansovogo kapitala v Rossii* (The birth of finance capital in Russia) (Moscow, 1967), pp. 140–250); Girault, *Emprunts russes*, pp. 301–4.
103. V. I. Bovykin, *Formirovanie finansovogo kapitala v Rossii* (Formation of finance capital in Russia) (Moscow, 1984), pp. 186–87.
104. McKay, *Pioneers for Profit*, p. 58; also Girault, *Emprunts Russes*, pp. 300–301; Solov'ev, "Russkie banki i frantsuzskii kapital" (Russian banks and French capital), pp. 146–47.
105. V. S. Diakin, *Germanskie kapitaly v Rossii. Elektroindustriia i elektricheskii transport* (German capital in Russia. Electrical industry and electric transport) (Leningrad, 1971); J. Mai, *Deutscher Kapitalexport nach Russland, 1896 bis 1907: Russisch-Deutsche Beziechungen von der Kiever Rus' bis zur Oktoberrevolution* (Berlin, 1976).
106. A. A. Fursenko *Neftianye tresty i mirovaia politika, 1880-e gody–1918* (Oil trusts and world politics. 1880s–1918) (Moscow-Leningrad, 1965), pp. 107–8; see also Chapter 19 in this text.
107. TsGIA, f. 626 (St. Petersburg International Bank), op. l; d. 477; ll, 104–5.
108. Diakin, *Germanskie kapitaly*, pp. 66–81.
109. Bovykin, *Formirovanie finansovogo kapitala v Rossii*, pp. 188–91.
110. McKay, *Pioneers for Profit*, pp. 368–78.
111. Girault, *Emprunts russes*, pp. 493–540.
112. Ibid., in which Girault writes in detail about the activity of this bank.
113. McKay, *Pioneers for Profit*, pp. 368–78.
114. V. I. Bovykin, "Rossiiskaia neft'i Rotshil'dy" (Russian oil and the Rothschilds), *Voprosy istorii*, No. 4 (1978); see also Chapter 19 in this text.
115. Diakin, *Germanskie Kapitaly*, pp. 138–211.
116. *The Stock Exchange Official Intelligence* (hereafter *SEOI*), Vol. 21, p. 1211.
117. J. B. A. Sykes, *The Amalgamation Movement in English Banking, 1835–1924* (London, 1926), p. 65.
118. *SEOI*, Vol. 22, p. 1742.
119. Ibid., p. 1271.

120. Ibid., Vol. 24, p. 1722.

121. Ibid., Vol. 28, p. 1031.

122. Ibid., p. 1116.

123. *Russian Yearbook for 1912* (London), pp. 681–82.

124. M. Y. Lachaeva, "Angliiskii kapital v mezhdunarodnoi promyshlennosti Urala i Sibiri v nachale XX v" (English capital in the international industry of the Urals and Siberia at the beginning of the twentieth century), *Istoricheskie zapiski*, 108, (1982).

125. *SEOI*, Vol. 31, p. 1047.

126. See works cited by Solov'ev, Diakin, and Fursenko.

127. Bovykin, *Zarozhdenie finansovogo kapitala*, p. 288.

128. Girault, *Emprunts russes*, pp. 358–61.

129. TsGIA, f. 637 (Northern Bank); op. 1; d. 90.

130. S. Ronin, *Inostrannyi kapital i russkie banki* (Foreign capital and Russian banks) (Moscow, 1926).

131. V. I. Bovykin, "Banki i voennaia promyshlennost' Rossii nakanune pervoi mirovoi voiny" (Banks and military industry of Russia on the eve of the First World War), *Istoricheskie zapiski*, 64, (1969).

Chapter 13

I wish to thank Donald Ross, Chairman of the New York Life Insurance Company, and George Trapp, also of New York Life, and their staff for their most generous assistance in making the archives of the company available to me. John M. Meyer, Jr., the former chairman of the Morgan Guaranty Trust Company, as well as C. A. Ryskamp and David Wright of the Pierpont Morgan Library were also most generous in giving me the opportunity to make use of archival material. I am also indebted to the Rare Book and Manuscript Library of Columbia University for making the Vanderlip Collection available to me. Rachel Stauber of the Citibank has been most helpful.

In addition, I wish to express my most sincere gratitude and thanks to those Soviet historians who assisted me in obtaining access to the Central State Archives of the City of Moscow and the Central State Historical Archives in Leningrad, namely V. I. Bovykin of the University of Moscow and the Institute of History of the USSR in the Academy of Sciences in Moscow; A. A. Fursenko and B. V. Anan'ich, both of the Leningrad Institute of History in the Academy of Sciences—all contributors to this volume. I owe a debt of thanks especially to B. V. Anan'ich for his invaluable assistance in helping me to explore the wealth of material available in the historical archives in Leningrad. I. A. D'iakonova of the Institute of History of the USSR in Moscow was also extremely helpful. Finally, I wish to express my appreciation to the staffs of the State Archives and also to those of the Lenin Library in Moscow and the Saltykov-Shchedrin Library in Leningrad.

My warm thanks are extended to Alexander Elkin, CMG of London, for reading the manuscript and for his most insightful criticism. My husband, Robert V. Roosa, has been exceedingly helpful in a variety of ways, too many to enumerate here. Betsy Campbell has displayed most admirable patience and efficiency in typing this chapter through several versions.

Finally, the International Research and Exchanges Board (IREX) is owed a sincere debt of gratitude for helping to make possible my stay in the USSR for research purposes.

The Library of Congress system of transliteration has been followed throughout this chapter. It should also be noted that dates referring to Russia before 1914 and derived from both Russian (and sometimes from foreign sources in Russia) and from Soviet sources follow the Julian calendar, which was twelve days behind the Western calendar in the nineteenth century and thirteen days behind in the twentieth century.

1. V. I. Bovykin, *Formirovanie finansovogo kapitala v Rossii: Konets XIX v.–1908* g. (The formation of financial capital in Russia: The end of the XIXth century–1908) (Moscow, 1984), pp. 157–61. See also: *Massovye istochniki po sotsial'no–ekonomisheskoi istorii Rossii perioda kapitalizma.* Ot. redaktor I.D. Koval'chenko (Moscow, 1979), pp. 150–55.
2. Douglass C. North, "International Capital Movements in Historical Perspective," in Raymond F. Mikesell, ed., *U.S. Private and Government Investment Abroad* (Eugene, OR, 1962), p. 24, and idem. "International Capital Movements to 1913," in John H. Adler with the assistance of Paul W. Kuznets, ed., *Capital Movements and Economic Development* (London, 1970), Chapters 2 and 11.
3. North, "International Capital Movements in Historical Perspective," p. 24, Chapter 17.
4. Arcadius Kahan, "Capital Formation during the Period of Early Industrialization in Russia, 1890–1913," *The Cambridge Economic History of Europe*, Vol. VII, Part 2, (Cambridge, London, New York, Melbourne, 1978), p. 519.
5. Leo Pasvolsky and Harold Moulton, *Russian Debts and Russian Reconstruction* (New York, 1924), p. 181. Also, p. 16.
6. John P. McKay, *Pioneers for Profit: Foreign Entrepreneurship and Russian Industrialization, 1885–1913* (Chicago and London, 1970), p. 34. For a general survey, the reader is referred to Peter I. Lyashchenko, *History of the National Economy of Russia to the 1917 Revolution*, trans. L. M. Herman (New York, 1949), pp. 712–717. Various efforts have been made, both by Soviet and American historians, to estimate Russia's dependence on foreign capital before the war, but the United States is included in few of these estimates. Banking investments, also, are usually omitted. According to Pasvolsky and Moulton, Russia's total foreign debt in 1914 amounted to 4,229 million rubles or 48 percent of its total state debt—figures that included state-guaranteed bonds of private railroads and other property as well as borrowing abroad by municipal and other local governments and private industrial enterprise. This debt was held largely in France (80 percent) and in Great Britain (14 percent). American investors held only 6 percent of the industrial securities and an unknown quantity of state and government-guaranteed railroad and other bonds. (Pasvolsky and Moulton, *Russian Debts*, pp. 17–22, 177–181. These figures are subject to some variations, apparently owing to the procedural methods used.) A more recent study by Arcadius Kahan indicates that Russia's foreign debt added up to 6,507 million rubles in January 1914 as against 3,818 million in January 1893. (Kahan, "Capital Formation," p. 273. The total debt during those years, according to Kahan's calculations, increased from 6,090 million to 12,745 million rubles in January 1914.) In contrast, early Soviet historians offer much lower estimates of Russia's total foreign indebtedness. V. S. Ziv, for example, estimated Russia's total capital imports as of 1914 at 1,532 million rubles, of which 250 million constituted banking capital. (Lyashchenko, *History of the National Economy*, p. 714. The exchange rate throughout the years 1899 to 1914 was $1:1.9434 rubles.) Still another Soviet historian estimated total Russian imports of foreign capital in 1914 at 2,807 million rubles, of which 117.7 million or 5.2 percent was American. (L. Ia. Eventov, *Inostrannye kapitaly v russkoi promyshlennosti* [Foreign capital in Russian industry] (Moscow-Leningrad, 1931), pp. 20, 29. Also Lyashchenko, *History of the National Economy*, p. 716.) V. I. Bovykin, on the other hand, whose conclusions, unfortunately for our purpose, relate only to 1908 as the latest date with which he is concerned, estimates the total amount of foreign capital at 6,479 million rubles. (Bovykin, *Formirovanie finansovogo kapitala*, pp. 157–69.) However, in Chapter 12 of the present text (written jointly by Bovykin and B. V. Anan'ich) Table 12–1 gives the equivalent figures for 1913. The total amount of foreign capital is 7,585 million rubles, of which 5,275 million (as against 5,170 million in 1908) is represented by government bonds and government-guaranteed railroad obligations; 186 million (as against 96 million) is represented by foreign investment in the Peasants' and Nobles' Land Banks; and 1,960 million (as against 1,187) were

invested in joint-stock enterprises. I cite these figures with Professor Bovykin's kind authorization, for which I am most grateful.

7. William Howard Taft Papers, Series 6, case file 250, n.d., Manuscript Division, U.S. Library of Congress, Washington, DC. The Hanseatic Company, which had worldwide connections, had established a branch in the United States. The President was much interested in the advancement of U.S. economic interests abroad, and this report was no doubt submitted in response to his request. I am indebted to A. Fursenko for this information.

8. Ibid.

9. Leonard J. Lesery, *Foreign Investments in Russian Industries and Commerce*, U.S. Department of Commerce, Miscellaneous Series, No. 124. (Washington, DC, 1923), p. 27. This reference to a lack of investment in Russian railroads shows an ignorance that cannot but cast doubt on the validity of its overall statements, while the ambivalence of its concluding sentence must raise questions in the mind of any reader.

10. Mira Wilkins, *The Emergence of Multilateral Enterprise: American Business Abroad from the Colonial Era to 1914* (Cambridge, MA, 1970), pp. 17–18, 29. In the late 1870s, when Russia was engaged in war with the Turks, its armies were equipped with American small arms.

11. Ibid., p. 45; also Vincent P. Carosso, *Investment Banking in America: A History* (Cambridge, MA, 1970), p. 30.

12. The Vanderlip Collection, D3, the Rare Book and Manuscript Library, Columbia University; and Frank A. Vanderlip, "The American 'Commercial Invasion' of Europe," pp. 62–68 and 509, ibid. Also Fred V. Carstensen, *American Enterprise in Foreign Markets: Studies of Singer and International Harvester in Imperial Russia* (Chapel Hill, NC, and London, 1984), pp. 27–103. See Chapter 22 in this volume.

13. Their total funds quadrupled between 1875 and 1900, rising from $403 million to $1.7 billion. Their investments were principally in railroad bonds, amounting by 1904 to one-third of their total assets—a fact that was significant, inasmuch as their investments in Russia followed much the same pattern. See Carosso, *Investment Banking*, pp. 47–48.

14. Mira Wilkins and Frank Ernest Hill, *American Business Abroad: Ford on Six Continents* (Detroit, 1964), p. 8.

15. Wilkins, *Emergence of Multinational Enterprise*, p. 8.

16. Carosso, *Investment Banking*, pp. 79–81.

17. Eventov, *Inostrannye kapitaly*, p. 29. Witte was appointed Minister of Finance in August 1892, an office that he held until 1903. Prior to this appointment he served as Minister of Communications. For an account of the Russian banking structure, and especially for the predominant role of the State Bank, see George Garvy, "Banking under the Tsars and Soviets," *Journal of Economic History*, XXXII, No. 4 (December 1972), and I. F. Gindin, *Gosudarstvennyi Bank i Ekonomicheskaia Politika Tsarskogo Pravitel'stva (1861–1892 gody)* (The State Bank and the economic policy of the tsarist government [1861–1892]) (Moscow, 1960). Also, I. F. Gindin, *Russkie Kommercheskie Banki* (Russian commercial banks) (Moscow, 1948) and Olga Crisp, *Studies in the Russian Economy before 1914* (New York, 1976). The commercial banking system was relatively well-developed by the turn of the century when its ties with expanding industry, its growing network of branches throughout the Russian Empire, and its new connections with European and American bankers were becoming a part of Russian economic life. It was an essential link in the chain through which foreign investments were channeled from the State Bank to the railroads, industry, and other branches of the economy. The St. Petersburg banks were more active than were the Moscow banks in international affairs.

18. For an account of the long history of this reform, going back to the early 1860s, the reader

is referred to B. V. Anan'ich, *Rossiia i mezhdunarodnyi kapital, 1897–1914* (Russia and international capital, 1897–1914), (Leningrad, 1870), pp. 9–19.

19. R. Goldsmith, "The Economic Growth of Tsarist Russia, 1860–1913," *Economic Development and Cultural Change*, IX (1961), 465.

20. Eventov, *Inostrannye kapitaly*, p. 11.

21. Archives of N.Y. Life, Folio 2578. Also The New York Life Insurance Company, *Facts on New York Life's Foreign Business: Expansion and Liquidation*. The first places in which New York Life was active were England, France, and British Columbia.

22. "Statement of the chairman by the N.Y. Life Insurance Company against the Russian Socialist Federation of the Soviet Republic and/or the Union of Soviet Socialist Republics," addressed to the Hon. Henry L. Stimson, U.S. Secretary of State, by Walker Buchner, vice president of N.Y. Life, March 5, 1933, Archives of N.Y. Life. See also "Draft Reply to the Honorable E. T. Cantrell," folio 2578.

23. The conflicting interests of the two ministries have been confirmed by L. E. Shepelev of the Leningrad Institute of History in personal conversation.

24. H. G. Homans, General Manager for Europe, to William H. Beers, President, Paris, February 26, 1887; Archives of N.Y. Life, *Pravila File*, Drawer No. 20, Folder I: 1880–October 1887.

25. P. Moeller to H. G. Homans., St. Petersburg, February 1887, Archives of N.Y. Life, *Pravila File*, Drawer No. 20, Folder I: 1880–1887. Also "Memorandum for His Excellency Baron Rosen, Envoy Extraordinary," October 10, 1910, Archives of N.Y. Life, Box 410–108, pp. 1–2. The *Pravila*, an extremely detailed little booklet containing the text of the rules approved by the Ministry of Internal Affairs, was to be attached to each policy issued by N.Y. Life. It was modified and supplemented on three occasions: April 4, 1896; April 16, 1897; and May 24, 1897. None of the changes introduced redounded to the benefit of N.Y. Life, however.

26. "Statement of the Chairman by the N.Y. Life Insurance Company," Archives of N.Y. Life. Also "Draft to the Honorable E. T. Cantrell," folio 2578.

27. TsGIA, f. 626; op. 1; d. 1100; ll. 1–8. The loan was received by the Ministry of Internal Affairs and turned over to the State Chancellery, with the provision that 50,000 rubles must be deposited in the State Bank.

28. H. A. Homan to William H. Beers, Paris, December 15, 1886; Archives of N.Y. Life, Drawer 20, Folder I: 1880–October 1887.

29. Ibid., Homand (*sic*) to Beers; Paris, February 21, 1887.

30. "Memorandum on Russian Business," Archives of N.Y. Life, Box 410–106.

31. The Mutual Life Insurance Company "New York," *General Report from January 1st to December 31st, 1888* (translated from Russian), Archives of N.Y. Life. These figures have been converted from rubles at an exchange rate of 1.964 rubles to $1.

32. *Annual Statement of the New York Life Insurance Company of the City of New York,* December 31, 1898, Archives of N.Y. Life.

33. New York Life Insurance Company, *Finansovyi Otchet za 1913 god* (Financial report for 1913), TsGIA, f. 602; op. 1; d.7; ll. 44–49. The required deposits in the State Bank were as follows: Deposit Guarantee, $253,212; Reserve Capital, $740,949; and Reserve Fund, $19,782,507. Somewhat different figures are given in the N.Y. Life's *Annual Statement . . . for the year ending December 31, 1913*, Archives of N.Y. Life, Box 410–106. According to the latter, the Deposit Guarantee amounted to $286,822; Reserve Capital, $534,672; and Reserve Fund, $22,591,560, totaling $23,413,054. According to data available as of July 10, 1914 (Russian Old Style) and thus reflecting the position on the immediate eve of the war, the company's required deposits in the State Bank totaled $24,180,081, divided into Deposit Guarantees of $286,822, Reserve Capital of $534,717, and Reserve Funds of $23,358,542 (*Certificate*, Archives of N.Y. Life, Box 410–106). All of these figures were presented in rubles and have been converted to dollars at the going

rate of exchange, i.e., $1 = 1.9434$ rubles. See also "Memorandum on Russian Business," Archives of N.Y. Life, Box 410–106; and "General Journal", June 1913–October 1914, Box 461-B. According to these sources, by the beginning of 1914 the company had only 34,822 policies in force with a total value of $81,526,070. Its reserve deposits in the State Bank totaled $23,413,054. V. V. Lebedev gives still another account in his *Russko-Amerikanskie ekonomicheskie otnosheniia, 1900–1917gg* (Russo-American economic relations, 1900–1917) (Moscow, 1964), p. 142, where he states that in 1910 the assets of N.Y. Life in Russia amounted to 39,133,000 rubles ($20,134,000) and its profits amounted to 988,000 rubles ($405,474). Deposits in the State Bank in the form of guaranteed reserve capital and the reserve fund amounted to about 15 million rubles ($7,718,421). By 1913 N.Y. Life's assets, according to Lebedev, had grown to about 48,266,000 rubles ($24,835,854), of which 37,107,000 rubles ($19,093,856) were held, in 1912, in the State Bank. By contrast, he lists Equitable's assets on the eve of the war as amounting to only 194,600 rubles ($100,134) (p. 144).

34. *Annual Statement of the New York Life Insurance Company in the State of New York,* Deposits by the New York Life Insurance Company, Archives of N.Y. Life, (Foreign Business File), December 31, 1894.

35. *Annual Statement of the New York Life Insurance Company of the City of New York, December 31, 1904,* Archives of N.Y. Life.

36. "Deposits as of December 31, 1913," Archives of N.Y. Life. All of these amounts are at par value. Slightly different figures are given in "The Certificate, as of January 1, 1914," Box 410–106, Archives of N.Y. Life, and in TsGIA, f. 602; op. 1; d. 7; l. 48. The "Certificate," for example, lists the total value in "1/15 Imperial Roubles" as $23,413,055. The most notable difference is the $3,853,900, which it attributes to the Nobles' Land Bank. This statement also does not include government bonds or policy loans. All the railroad bonds were issued at a rate of 4 percent interest and had unusually long maturities, although all were also issued with early call features permitting amortization through serial drawings. Few carried final maturities of less than fifty years, and the government bonds of 1894 were scheduled to run until 1970! All were subject to rather large movements in price as relatively small changes occurred in the market rates of interest, a circumstance that accounted for the relatively large number of purchases at times of market lows, most notably in 1905 and 1908. Some railroad bonds were linked with German marks or French francs, which gave them an added attraction for N.Y. Life.

37. Second Vice President V. P. Ingersoll to Vice President George W. Perkins, Paris, March 16, 1905, N.Y. Life Archives, Box 2—410-107.

38. Correspondence between N.Y. Life and Volga-Kama Bank, 1907–1919, TsGia, f. 595; op. 5; d. 30; ll. 2–411. Also Director General for Europe, N.Y. Life, to the Volga-Kama Bank, January 26, 1910, TsGia, f. 595; op. 5; d. 31; ll. 8, 213, 301, 315. The total sums involved in such transactions were apparently so substantial as to be of both commercial and official concern. Thus in late 1909 and again in 1910, the American Express Co. wrote to the head of the Russian State Savings Funds (Gosudarstvennye Sberegatel'nye Kassy) proposing the creation of a system of sending postal remittances directly to the addressee, rather than having to go through the German postal service, as was the current practice. No reply was evidently received. (TsGIA, f. 581; op. 1; d.1630; ll. 1–2.) Late in 1910 Wells Fargo and Co. proposed, again unsuccessfully, that a system of travelers' checks be instituted. (TsGIA, f. 620; op. 1; d. 6; l. 67.) The fact that a large share of these remittances went through the postal services rather than through private banks was clearly revealed in a proposal of the State Savings Funds that Russian consulates in the United States establish facilities for handling such transfers of money.

39. See TsGIA, f. 588; op. 2; d. 1106; ll. 1–5 for the text of this agreement. These amounts were calculated at an exchange rate of 2 rubles to the dollar.

40. Ibid., l. 609, correspondence between the Ministry of Internal Affairs and the St. Pe-

tersburg office of the State Bank, and between The International Bank and the St. Petersburg office of the State Bank.

41. TsGIA. f, 626; op. 1; d. 768; ll. 2–3. Letter dated February 18, 1897.

42. John A. Garraty, *Right-Hand Man: The Life of George W. Perkins* (New York, 1960), pp. 64–65. See also *The Ledger*, Vol. IX, No. 4, p. 22 (Drexel Institute of Technology); and the Archives of N.Y. Life: G. W. Perkins, 4/12/93–7/2/06. See also Wilkins, *Emergence of Multinational Enterprise*, pp. 105–7.

43. Perkins to the International Commercial Bank, October 7, 1899; and Rothstein to Minister of Finance, October 7/19, 1899, TsGIA, f. 626; op. 1; d. 767; ll. 1–5. The quotations have been translated from their original French.

44. Ibid., ll. 6–13, correspondence among Witte, Perkins, and Rothstein.

45. Text of the contract between N.Y. Life and the International Bank, as approved by Witte, ibid., ll. 15–17 and TsGIA, f. 626; op. 1; d. 768; ll. 5–7. Also Archives of N.Y. Life, Finance Committee, Record, January 1898–April 1, 1901, p. 176.

46. B. A. Romanov and B. V. Anan'ich, "Popytki S. Iu. Vitte otkryt' amerikanskii denezhnyi rynok dlia russkikh zaimov (1898–1902 gg)" (The attempts of S. Iu. Witte to open the American money market for Russian loans [1892–1902]), *Istoricheskii Arkhiv* (Historical Archive], No. 1, (1959), 124.

47. A. A. Fursenko, "Iz istorii Russko-Amerikanskikh otnoshenii na rubezhe XIX-XX vv" (The history of Russo-American relations at the turn of the XIX-XX centuries), in *Iz Istorii Imperializma v Rossii* (The History of Imperialism in Russia), ed. M. P. Viadkin et al. (Moscow-Leningrad, 1959), p. 242.

48. Wilkins, *Emergence of Multinational Enterprise*, pp. 105–6.

49. *Annual Statement of the New York Life Insurance Company of the City of New York for the year ending December 31, 1894*, Archives of N.Y. Life.

50. *Annual Statement of the New York Life Insurance Company of the City of New York for the year ending December 31, 1913*, Archives of N.Y. Life.

51. A two-page flier, published March 19, 1887, entitled "The Supreme authorization of October 10, 1885 for the operation in Russia of the New York Life Insurance Society." TsGIA, f. 609; op. 1; d. 8; ll. 108. The ambivalence of this objective, at least in its operations in the United States, has been explored in detail by Carosso, *Investment Banking*, pp. 113–26.

52. Printed flier, entitled: "What did the 'New York' Society do in 1911?" TsGIA, f. 595; op. 5; d. 31; l. 213.

53. "A New Tax for the 'New York' Society," 1894. TsGIA, f. 623; op. 1; (no d.); ll. 1–7. See also; ll. 126ff., referring to other materials advertising the insurance offered by N.Y. Life.

54. TsGIA, f. 623; op. 1; d. 1; ll. 4–5. It is not strange that there is no mention of the Equitable Insurance Company here, as it did not become a Russian company until 1918. See N. S. B. Gras and Henrietta M. Larson, *Casebook in American Business History,* (New York, 1939), p. 542.

55. N.Y. Life's St. Petersburg office to the Board of Directors of the Volga-Kama Bank, May 29, 1913. TsGIA, f. 609; op. 1; d. 6, ll. 1–3.

56. A statement signed by James I. McIntosh, General Counsel of New York Life Insurance Company in New York, and dated November 2, 1910, while primarily concerned with the new tax laws that had recently been introduced, stated bluntly that the terms of the 1887 *Pravila* imposing restrictions on profits were still resented. *Memorandum Relating to Taxation of the New York Life Insurance Company by the Imperial Russian Government*. Archives of N.Y. Life, pp. 7–8, 21.

57. Ibid., pp. 1–22. According to figures presented in this document, the annual amount of taxation had increased from 1902, when it totaled 27,120 rubles to 40,865 rubles in 1910. In August 1910 the Russian Treasury had served notice on N.Y. Life that it owed in back

taxes, fines, and interest a total of 676,838 rubles. Of this sum, the lowest figure was for 1902, 14,336 rubles; in 1906 the annual accumulation was 18,260 rubles.

58. Archives of N.Y. Life, Box 410–106.

59. *Memorandum for His Excellency Baron Rosen, Envoy Extraordinary, etc., etc.*, Archives of N.Y. Life, Box 410–108, pp. 1–6.

60. *Trade Laws on "Profits."* Archives of N.Y. Life, Box 410–106.

61. A. A. Fursenko, "Proekt amerikanskogo banka v Moskve," (A projected American bank in Moscow) *Istoriia SSSR*, 3, (1986) 142–45.

62. Correspondence between N.Y. Life and the Volga-Kama Bank, 1907–1913. TsGIA, f. 595; d. 5; op. 30; ll. 2–411 and op. 31; ll. 8–315.

63. *Russian Bondholder's Manual. Loans issued or Guaranteed by the Imperial Government*, 1913, pp. 21–24, 26–27, 67, 87, 89, Archives of N.Y. Life. According to this source, Kidder, Peabody participated in the sale of Russian 4 percent bonds in 1889, 1890, 1893, 1894, and 1898. It also purchased part of the gold bond issues in 1891 and 1894.

64. *Russian Bondholder's Manual*, Archives of N.Y. Life.

65. TsGIA, f. 626; op. 1; d. 1002; ll. 3–4. In contrast with his relative indifference to Russia was Morgan's interest in China. In 1896 he headed a syndicate of banks that was arranging a loan of 200 million taels for China. TsGIA, f. 626; op. 1; d. 1183; no. 1.

66. TsGIA, f. 626; op. 1; d. 1186; ll. 1–7. Warburg's efforts on behalf of Illinois Central began with a letter to Rothstein on June 11, 1897, and continued throughout the following two years. In a letter dated June 2, 1899 he reported that Kuhn, Loeb & Co. had brought the operations of the syndicate to an end (l. 5).

67. Deutsche Vereinsbank to the International Bank, August 30, 1897. TsGIA, f. 626; op. 1; d. 229 (no. 1).

68. National City Bank to Volga-Kama Bank (n.d.). TsGIA, f. 595; op. 5; d. 19; l. 264. The date was probably late 1910. Also, l. 261. There is evidence, however, that National City Bank continued to deal with the Volga-Kama, at least in part, through the Deutsche Bank's London agency. (City Bank to Volga-Kama, March 4, 1914. TsGIA, f. 595; op. 5; d. 20; l. 125.)

69. Harold van B. Cleveland and Thomas F. Huertas, *Citibank, 1812–1970* (Cambridge, MA, and London, 1985), pp. 16–71.

70. Correspondence between National City Bank and the Volga-Kama Bank for 1907 and 1909–1911. Ibid., ll. 1–293. Also: f. 595; op. 5; d. 18 (1907–1909); f. 595; op. 5; d. 20 (1913–1914); and d. 21 (1914).

71. The Vanderlip Collection, B-1-1. The Rare Books and Manuscripts Library, Columbia University.

72. For all of this information I am indebted to Rachel Strauber of Citibank.

73. The Vanderlip Collection, B-1-4. The Rare Books and Manuscripts Library.

74. Ibid., B-1-3.

75. Ibid., B-1-5. Its investments, however, did include two in China and Manchuria and many more in Latin America. This information is contained in a letter from Vanderlip to Samuel Untermyer, of the U.S. Congress (Committee on Banking and Currency of the House of the Representatives), who was conducting an investigation of American banking. See also: Otchet buzhgalterii pri 2oi otdelenii osobennoi kantseliarii po kreditnam chasti ob oiaotazhe po prikhodu 1 raskhodu summi gosudarstvennogo kaznacheistva nakhodiasdh-chikeia v bankirov zagranitsei—za 1911 (Report of the chief of the second division of the special chancellery on credits concerning arbitrage on income and outflow of sums of the state treasury among bankers abroad—for 1911), TsGIA, f. 568; op. 14; d. 5033; l. 68.

76. Fursenko, "Iz istorii Russko-Amerikanskikh otnoshenii," p. 247. Cf. also Lebedev, *Russko-Amerikanskie ekonomicheskie otnosheniia*, pp. 33–34.

77. Smith to Rothstein, December 14, 1896. TsGIA, f. 626; op,. 1; d. 532; l. 11.

78. Fursenko, "Iz istorii Russko-Amerikanskikh otnoshenii," p. 247.
79. Rothstein to Hollister, president of the Russian-American Manufacturing Co., and Hollister to Rothstein. TsGIA, f. 626; op. 1; d. 532; ll. 39, 41. Soon after this fiasco, Smith accepted an offer by the International Bank to become managing director of the Nikopol-Mariupol firm, and he moved to Russia for this purpose. By January 1898, however, this had also become a most disillusioning experience. A year later, he was apparently once again on reasonably friendly terms with the directors of the Fourth Street Bank and was attempting to revive his old friendship with Rothstein. Ibid., ll. 51–118.
80. Romanov and Anan'ich, "Popytki," pp. 123, 126–28. See also Vincent P. Carosso, *The Morgans: Private International Bankers, 1854–1913* (Cambridge, MA, and London, 1987), pp. 399–403.
81. Fursenko, "Iz istorii Russko-Amerikanskikh otnoshenii," pp. 235–36.
82. Rutkovskii, who was the agent of the Ministry of Finances at the Washington embassy, actually was the first to arrive and to begin negotiations, but he was soon joined by Vyshnegradskii, a high official of the Ministry.
83. Lebedev, *Russko-Amerikanskie ekonomicheskie otnosheniia,* pp. 34–35.
84. TsGIA, f. 626; op. 1; d. 1132: l. 1.
85. Ibid., l. 2.
86. Ibid. According to this account, the Russians had originally said they would accept only 97.
87. Fursenko, "Iz istorii Russko-Amerikanskikh otnoshenii," p. 246.
88. TsGIA, f. 626; op. 1; d. 1132; l. 3.
89. Ibid., l. 5.
90. Lebedev, *Russko-Amerikanskie ekonomicheskie otnosheniia,"* p. 37. E. A. Hitchcock was about to leave his post in St. Petersburg, having already been appointed Secretary of the Interior.
91. Ibid. The copy of the letter was unsigned, but in view of the subsequent correspondence it seems almost certain to have come from Peirce.
92. TsGIA, f. 626; op. 1; d. 1132; ll. 11–12.
93. Ibid., l. 24.
94. Ibid., l. 16. The letter was written in German.
95. Ibid., l. 27.
96. Ibid., ll. 30–31.
97. Fursenko's view seems to be confirmed by an undated telegram sent by Morgan, finally agreeing to the meeting in Brussels and adding: "I much desire it look prospect future business will gladly meet brussels." Ibid., l. 38.
98. TsGIA, f. 626; op. 1; d. 1136; l. 8. Also: f. 560; op. 22; d. 200; l. 3. The Morgan offer was reported to Witte by Rothstein on June 16, 1900.
99. Correspondence between Rothstein and Witte, June 18/19, 1900. Ibid., ll. 9–16. Also, f. 560; op. 22; d. 200; ll. 10–18.
100. Correspondence between Rothstein and Witte and between Witte and Morgan. TsGIA, f. 626; op. 1; d. 1136; ll. 17–30. The reference to pounds sterling was to Morgan's insistence that at a later date Grenfell should be allowed to share in the operation.
101. Ibid., l. 54.
102. Lebedev, *Russko-Amerikanskie ekonomicheskie otnosheniia,* p. 58.
103. TsGIA, f. 626; op. 1; d. 1136; ll. 61–63.
104. Ibid., l. 64. Morgan to Rothstein, August 7, 1900.
105. Ibid., ll. 65–76. Rothstein to Morgan.
106. Anan'ich, *Rossiia i mezhdunarodnyi kapital,* p. 48. Anan'ich provides an excellent account of these negotiations (pp. 26–48).
107. Romanov and Anan'ich "Popytki," pp. 125, 133.

108. TsGIA, f. 626; op. 1; d. 8; l. 3. Porter was planning to publish a book to be entitled *Economic Russia* (to be published by G. P. Putnum's Sons) in which he paid the highest compliments to Witte, who "has placed Russia on the highest fiscal plane and attracted the world to the possibilities which she offers for foreign capital" (p. 5).

109. Ibid., l. 11.

110. TsGIA, f. 626; op. 1; d. 8; l. 3. Correspondence between A. Korobhoff, a member of the St. Petersburg International Commercial Bank, who was in close touch with Rothstein, and James Stillman, president of National City Bank, as well as a letter, written evidently by Rothstein himself, to Adolf Werth in Vienna on April 24, 1900. TsGIA, f. 626; op. 1; d. 253; ll. 2–10.

111. Fursenko, "Iz istorii Russko-Amerikanskikh otnoshenii," p. 248ff.

112. TsGIA, f. 626; op. 1; d. 253; l. 11.

113. Ibid., l. 13.

114. Ibid., l. 26.

115. Ibid., l. 45.

116. Ibid., ll. 66–67.

117. The Board of Directors of National City Bank included, as of September 1900, Robert Bacon of J. P. Morgan & Co.; Edward H. Harriman, chairman of Union Pacific Railroad; John A. McCall, president of New York Life; William Rockefeller, president of Standard Oil Co.; and Jacob H. Schiff of Kuhn, Loeb. George W. Perkins also became a director in 1900, and several years later a partner in J. P. Morgan as well. Thus, there can be no doubt as to National City Bank's influence in the New York financial world. Stillman, as well as several other directors of National City Bank, were also directors of N.Y. Life. Ibid., ll. 52–53. Also see Garraty, *Right-Hand Man,* pp. 81–88.

118. Archives of N.Y. Life, Finance Committee, *Record,* January 1898–April 1, 1901, p. 176.

119. Vanderlip Collection, Diary, D-4, pp. 100–102, 150. The Rare Books and Manuscripts Library, Columbia University.

120. Ibid., p. 146.

121. Ibid., p. 111.

122. Ibid., pp. 149–54.

123. "The American 'Commercial Invasion' of Europe," ibid., D-3, n.p.; and *Diary,* D-4, pp. 147, 150.

124. Ibid., Group B, Series 1, Box 1. Nevertheless, City Bank did, in November 1904, join in a syndicate, which included Britain, Germany, and various firms in New York, especially Kuhn, Loeb, which issued a very successful loan to Japan. Kuhn, Loeb, according to Vanderlip, expressed its "very sincere pleasure at our activity."

125. J. P. Morgan, Jr. Papers, Box 31. Pierpont Morgan Library, Morgan Archives.

126. B. V. Anan'ich, "Finansovyi kriziz tsarizma v 1905–1906 gg." (The financial crisis of tsarism during 1905–1906), *Vnutrenniaia Politika Tsarizma (seredina XIX–nachalo XX v)* (The internal policy of tsarism [the mid-nineteenth to the beginning of the twentieth centuries]) (Leningrad, 1967), pp. 283–97; and Anan'ich, *Rossiia i mezhdunarodnyi kapital.,* pp. 128–44. During the period of crisis Russia had also received a loan from German bankers, but there was no hope for a second. The state of Russian relations with England precluded any assistance from that quarter.

127. Vanderlip Collection, B-1-1. The Rare Books and Manuscripts Library, Columbia University. The substance of these talks was not made entirely clear in a letter from Vanderlip to Witte dated August 3, 1905.

128. Lebedev, *Russko-Amerikanskie ekonomicheskie otnosheniia,* pp. 87–88.

129. J. P. Morgan, Jr. (London) to J. P. Morgan, Sr. (New York), October 4, 1905. *J. P. Morgan, Jr. Papers,* Box 31 (cables). Morgan Archives. An account of the events that followed is available in Carosso, *The Morgans,* pp. 516–22.

130. Ibid. J. P. Morgan, Sr. to J. P. Morgan, Jr., October 5, 1905.
131. Ibid. J. P. Morgan, Jr. to J. P. Morgan, Sr., October 17, 1905. Under the preliminary terms of the syndicate that was to be formed, France and Holland would each contribute 950 million francs and England 250 million francs. Germany was expected to provide 500 million.
132. Ibid. Perkins and J. P. Morgan, Jr. to J. P. Morgan, Sr., October 17, 1905.
133. Lebedev, *Russko-Amerikanskie ekonomicheskie otnosheniia,* p. 87–88.
134. J. P. Morgan, Sr. to George Perkins and J. P. Morgan, Jr., October 17, 1905. J. P. Morgan, Jr. Papers, Box 31. Morgan Archives.
135. Carosso, *Investment Banking,* p. 81.
136. Perkins and J. P. Morgan, Jr. to J. P. Morgan, Sr., October 21, 1905. Also: cables between J. P. Morgan, Sr. and Perkins and J. P. Morgan, Jr., October 22, 1905. Morgan Archives, J. P. Morgan, Jr. Box 31. The British and German foreign ministers had insisted, according to Perkins and J. P. Morgan, Jr., that American participation "would have the best possible effect on the situation for the peace of the whole world and we see great possibilities for help from the U.S.A." J. P. Morgan, Sr.'s reply to Witte's plea for American participation was as follows:

> We have received your cable of today. It is not a question of taking 100,000,000 francs but in the present situation here, which certainly is not improving but rather growing more acute for reasons previously stated, an issue just now would have a very injurious effect in future upon what we so much desire, and that is, to open American market to Russian loans. This is independent of unwillingness on our own part to face an unsuccessful issue. We therefore think it best to adhere to our decision. Express to Witte and Minister of Finance deep regrets that circumstances absolutely beyond our control make any other decision impossible.

137. Ibid. Perkins and J. P. Morgan, Jr. to J. P. Morgan, Sr., October 23, 1905.
138. Ibid. Perkins and J. P. Morgan, Jr. to J. P. Morgan, Sr., October 31 and November 1, 1905. A brief account of these events is described by John Douglas Forbes, *J. P. Morgan, Jr., 1867–1943* (Charlottesville, VA, 1981), pp. 56–58. A detailed account, based on Soviet archival sources, is provided by Romonov and Anan'ich, "Popytki."
139. See the accounts in Anan'ich, *Rossiia i mezhdunarodnyi kapital,* pp. 145–52; and Anan'ich, "Finansovyi kriziz tsarizma," pp. 299–302. Also B. A. Romanov, *Ocherki Diplomaticheskoi Istorii Russko-Iaponskoi Voiny: 1895–1907* (Outlines of the diplomatic history of the Russo-Japanese War: 1895–1907), 2nd ed. (Moscow-Leningrad, 1955), pp. 601–2.
140. J. P. Morgan, Jr., Papers, Box 31, Morgan Archives. The cable went on to say that an unnamed friend of J. P. Morgan, Jr. would soon be in London to deliberate on this matter.
141. Ibid.
142. Ibid. See also: Anan'ich, "Popytki," No. 2 (1959).
143. Lebedev, *Russko-Amerikanskie ekonomicheskie otnosheniia,* p. 115.
144. Vanderlip Collection, B-1-5. The Rare Books and Manuscripts Library, Columbia University.
145. TsGIA, f. 568; op. 14; d. 5033; l. 68; and f. 588; op. 5; d. 133; ll. 95–101. Also, *The Russian Bondholder's Manual, Loans issued or guaranteed by the Imperial Government* (1913) pp. 21–67, 78–89. Archives of N.Y. Life.
146. Kokovtsov served as Minister of Finance continually from 1904 until 1914, except for one brief interval between October 1905 and April 1906. He also served as Chairman of the Council of Ministers from 1911 until his removal from office in February 1914.
147. Ruth AmEnde Roosa, "Russian Industrialists Look to the Future: Thoughts on Economic Development, 1906–1917," in *Essays in Russian and Soviet History,* John Shelton Curtiss, ed. (New York, 1963), pp. 198–218.

148. Vanderlip Collection, B-1-4. The Rare Books and Manuscripts Library, Columbia University. In a letter to Stillman on April 15, 1911, Vanderlip wrote:

> One of the reasons why President Taft believes he cannot be reelected is a factor that I have heard very little about. He thinks there is a strong demand from Hebrews for the abrogation of our treaties with Russia. He is determined not to yield to this demand and he feels that, in the end, he will have the whole Hebrew sentiment against him.

It is noteworthy that, in another letter to Stillman, Vanderlip wrote that "all of Wall Street," including himself, was "intensely anti-Roosevelt." Ibid., B-1-3.

Chapter 14

At the 1985 conference in Bellagio Jan Hájek of the Czechoslovak Academy of Science presented a paper on "International Factors in the Forming of Cisleithanian Banking." It has been published in Czech in *Hospdárské Dejiny* (Economic history), Vol. 14, pp. 91–110, and in English in ibid., Vol. 15, pp. 433–55.

1. László Katus, *Economic Growth in Hungary during the Age of Dualism (1867–1913): A Quantitative Analysis,* Studia Historica Accademiae Scientiarum Hungaricae No. 62. (Budapest, 1970), pp. 113.
2. William Ashworth, "Typologies and Evidence: Has Nineteenth Century Europe a Guide to Economic Growth?" *Economic History Review,* 30 (1977), 140–58.
3. John Komlos, *The Habsburg Monarchy as a Customs Union: Economic Development in Austria-Hungary in the Nineteenth Century* (Princeton, NJ, 1983), 280–321.
4. Scott M. Eddie, "The Terms and Patterns of Hungarian Foreign Trade, 1882–1913," *Journal of Economic History,* 37 (1977), 329–58.
5. W. Arthur Lewis, *Growth and Fluctuations* (London, 1978), p. 164.
6. Paul Bairoch, "European Foreign Trade in the XIX Century: The Development of the Value and Volume of Exports (Preliminary Results)," *Journal of European Economic History,* 2 (1973), 5–37.
7. B. R. Mitchell, "Statistical Appendix, 1700–1914," in Carlo M. Cipolla, ed., *The Fontana Economic History of Europe, 4/2, The Emergence of Industrial Societies* (London and Glasgow, 1973), pp. 738–820.
8. Comte de Mülinen, *Les finances de l'Autriche* (Paris and Vienna, 1875), p. 130; Gÿorgy Kövér "The London Stock Exchange and the Credit of Austria-Hungary (1867–1871)," *Acta Historica* (1987).
9. Franz Bartsch, *Statistische Daten über die Zahlungsbilanz Österreich-Ungarns vor Ausbruch des Krieges,* Mitteilungen des K. K. Finanzministeriums, XXII (Vienna, 1917), 198; Frigyes Fellner, *A nemzetkozi fizetési merleg es alakasa Magyarorszagon* (The international balance of payments and its development in Hungary) (Budapest, 1908), pp. 80–81.
10. Scott Eddie, "Limits on the Fiscal Independence of Sovereign States in Customs Union: 'Tax Union' Aspects of the Austro-Hungarian Monarchy, 1868–1911," *Hungarian Studies Review* (1982), 7–29.
11. Hungarian National Archive [HNA], Budapest.
12. Gyorgy Kövér, "Az Osztrak Magyar Monarchia bankrendszerenek fejlodesne" (The development of the banking system in the Austro-Hungarian monarchy), *Kozgazdasagi Szemli,* 33 (1986), Table 1.
13. Eduard März and Karl Socher, "Wahrung und Banken in Cisleithanien in Die Habsburg

monarchie 1848–1918," in Alois Brusatti, ed., *Die wirtschaftliche Entwicklung* (Vienna, 1973), pp. 323–69.

14. Gyula Varga, *A magyar hitelugy es hitelintezetek tortenette* (The history of Hungarian credit-system and banking institutions) (Budapest, 1896), p. 84.

15. Bernard Michel, *Banques et banquiers en Autriche au debut de 20ᵉ siècle* (Paris, 1976), pp. 106–9.

16. Fritz Schulte, *Die Bodenkreditinstitute der Österreichisch-Ungarischen Monarchie, 1841 bis 1910* (Munich-Leipzig, 1912); and Michel, *Banques et banquiers en Autriche*, pp. 27–28.

17. Michel, *Banques et banquiers en Autriche*, p. 40.

18. David Landes, "The Old Bank and the New: The Financial Revolution of the Nineteenth Century," in Francois Crouzet et al., eds., *Essays in European Economic History, 1789–1914* (London, 1969), pp. 112–127.

19. Eduard März, *Österreischische Industrie und Bankpolitik in der Zeit Franz Josephs I* (Vienna, 1968), p. 111.

20. Hungarian National Archive [HNA], Budapest, 51 56-831; Michel, *Banques et banquiers en Autriche*, pp. 227–228; Gyorgy Ránki, "The Hungarian General Credit Bank in the 1920s," in Alice Teichova and P. L. Cottrell, eds., *International Business and Central Europe, 1918–1939* (Leicester, 1983), pp. 355–74.

21. P. L. Cottrell, "London Financiers and Austria, 1863–1875: The Anglo-Austrian Bank," *Business History,* 11 (1969), 106–20.

22. Richard L. Rudolph, *Banking and Industrialization in Austria-Hungary: The Role of Banks in the Industrialization of the Czech Crownlands, 1873–1914* (Cambridge, 1976), p. 72.

23. März and Socher, "Wahrung und Banken in Cisleithanien," p. 358.

24. Ibid., p. 349.

25. Michel, *Banques et banquiers en Autriche*, p. 37.

26. März, *Österreichische Industrie*, p. 296; Rudolph, *Banking and Industrialization in Austria-Hungary*, p. 145; Geza Zsoldos, *A bankkoncentracio* (The concentration of banks) (Budapest, 1914), p. 61.

27. Franz Baltzarek, *Die Geschichte der Wiener Börse* (Vienna, 1973), p. 9; S. D. Chapman, "The International Houses: The Continental Contribution to British Commerce, 1800–1860," *Journal of European Economic History,* 6 (1977), 5–49.

28. David S. Landes, *Bankers and Pashas: International Finance and Economic Imperialism in Egypt* (New York, 1969), p. 16.

29. Bertrand Gille, *Histoire de la Maison Rothschild, Vol. II: 1848–1870* (Geneva, 1967), p. 571.

30. Gyorgy Kövér, "A brit tokepiac es Magyarorszag: az Anglo-magyar bank 1868–1879" (The British capital market and Hungary: The Anglo-Hungarian Bank, 1868–1879), *Szazadok,* 118 (1984), 492, 509.

31. Rudolph, *Banking and Industrialization in Austria-Hungary,* p. 76.

32. Rondo Cameron, *France and the Economic Development of Europe, 1800–1914* (Princeton, NJ, 1961), p. 152; see also above, Introduction.

33. März, "*Österreichische Industrie*, pp. 37–38.

34. Cameron, *France and the Economic Development of Europe*, pp. 149–51; Paul H. Emden, *Money Powers of Europe* (London, 1938), p. 88; and Introduction in this volume.

35. Gille, *Histoire de la Maison Rothschild*, p. 237; März, *Österreichische Industrie*, pp. 55–56.

36. Gille, *Histoire de la Maison Rothschild*, p. 239.

37. Fritz G. Steiner, *Die Entwicklung des Mobilbankwesens in Osterreich* (Vienna, 1913), p. 72; Marz, *Osterreischische Industrie*, p. 39.

38. Gille, *Histoire de la Miason Rothschild*, p. 240.

39. N. M. Rothschild and Sons Ltd. Archives, London [RAL], Extracts T 10.100, Alphonse to his cousins in London and Paris, July 10, 1872.

40. Bartsch, *Statistische Daten uber die Zahlungsbilanz*, p. 143.

41. Steiner, *Die Entwicklung des Mobilbankwesens*, p. 162; Cameron, *France and the Economic Development of Europe*, p. 130; Bertrand Gille, *La Banque en France* au XIXᵉ siècle (Geneva & Paris, 1970), p. 171.

42. Michel Lescure, *Les banques, l'Etat et le marché immobilier en France a l'Epoque contemporaine, 1820–1940* (Paris, 1982), pp. 88–96.

43. Cameron, *France and the Economic Development of Europe*, p. 130.

44. Fritz Schulte, *Die Bodenkreditinstitute der Osterreichische-Ungarischen Monarchie, 1841 bis 1910* (Munich-Leipzig, 1912), p. 97.

45. Michel, *Banques et banquiers en Autriche*, p. 140; Bartsch, *Statistische Daten uber die Zahlungsbilanz*, p. 143.

46. Cameron, *France and the Economic Development of Europe*, p. 130; Henri Claude, *Histoire, realité, et destin d'un monopole: La Banque de Paris et des Pays-Bas et son groupe, 1872–1968*, (Paris, 1969), pp. 16–17.

47. Carl Morawitz, *50 Jahre Geschichte einer Wiener Bank* (Vienna, 1914), p. 10.

48. A. S. J. Baster, *The International Banks* (London, 1935), p. 46.

49. Williams and Glyn's Bank Archive, London: G. C. Glyn to Madame de Bury, January 11, 1863, Letter Book.

50. Cottrell, "London Financiers and Austria," p. 112.

51. Ibid., p. 113.

52. Kövér, "A brit tokepiac es Magyarorszag," p. 493.

53. Bartsch, *Statistische Daten uber die Zahlungsbilanz*, p. 143.

54. Emden, *Money Powers of Europe*, pp. 397–98.

55. Steiner, *Die Entwicklung des Mobilbankwesens*, pp. 217–18; John R. Lampe, "Serbia," in Rondo Cameron, ed., *Banking and Economic Development* (New York, 1972), p. 136.

56. März, *Osterreichische Industrie*, p. 224.

57. Michel, *Banques et banquiers en Autriche*, p. 240; Bartsch, *Statistische Daten uber die Zahlungsbilanz*, p. 243.

58. März, *Österreichische Industrie*, pp. 222–23; Heinrich Benedikt, *Die wirtschaftliche Entwicklung in der Franz-Joseph-Zeit* (Vienna and Munich, 1958), pp. 112–14; Jean Bouvier, *Le Krach de l'Union Generale (1878–1885)* (Paris, 1960), pp. 58–71; Gyorgy Ranki, "Le capital francais en Hongrie avant 1914," in Maurice Levy-Leboyer, ed., *La position internationale de la France: Aspects économiques et financiers, XIXᵉ–XXᵉ siecle*, (Paris, 1977), pp. 235–37.

59. Vilmos Sandor, *Nagyipari fejlodes Magyarorszagon (1867–1900)* (The development of big industry in Hungary) (Budapest, 1954), p. 265.

60. Lampe, "Serbia," p. 137; Michel, *Banques et banquiers en Autriche*, p. 263.

61. Michel, *Banques et banquiers en Autriche*, p. 265.

62. Ibid., p. 264.

63. Bartsch, *Statistische Daten uber die Zahlungsbilanz*, p. 144.

64. Lorant Hegedus, *A Pesti Magyar Kereskedelmi Bank keletkezesenek es fennallasanak tortenete II.k., 1892–1917* (The history of the origin and existence of the Hungarian Commercial Bank of Pest), (Budapest, 1922) pp. 238–39.

65. Lampe, "Serbia," pp. 157–59.

66. Michel, *Banques et banquiers en Autriche*, p. 264; HNA Z 34 49-2032, 2086.

67. Rudolph, *Banking and Industrialization in Austria-Hungary*, p. 179.

68. Quotation from D. C. M. Platt, "British Portfolio Investment Overseas before 1870: Some Doubts," *Economic History Review*, 33 (1980), 3, citing the *Economist*, 17 July 1869.

69. Cameron, *France and the Economic Development of Europe*, p. 419.

70. Joseph Puregger, *Funfzig Jahre Staatsschuld, 1862–1912*, (Vienna, 1912), p. 567.

71. Fellner, *A menzetkozi fizetesi merleg es alakulasa Magyarorszagon*, Appendix.
72. Katus, "Magyarorszag Gazdasag: Fejlodese," p. 287.
73. Bartsch, *Statistische Daten uber die Zahlungsbilanz*, p. 34.
74. John Lampe and Marvin Jackson, *Balkan Economic History, 1550–1950: From Imperial Borderlands to Developing Nations* (Bloomington, IN, 1982), p. 208.
75. Geza Ujhely, *A vasutugy tortenete* (The history of railways) (Budapest, 1910), p. 494.
76. Gille, *La Banque en France*, p. 261.
77. Ludwig Schonberger, *Die Actionare der ungarischen Ostbahn und der ungarischen Staat: Ein Drama* (Vienna, 1875), p. 34.
78. László Katus, "Transport Revolution and Economic Growth in Hungary," in John Komlos, ed., *Economic Development in the Habsburg Monarchy in the Nineteenth Century. Essays.* (Boulder, CO, 1983), p. 192; and Josef Wysocki, *Intfrastruktur und wachsende Staatsausgaben: Das Fallbeispiel Osterreich, 1868–1913* (Stuttgart, 1975), p. 60.
79. Ivan T. Berend and György Ránki, *Economic Development in East-Central Europe in the 19th and 20th Centuries* (New York, 1974), p. 97; Bartsch, *Statistische Datcn uber die Zahlungsbilanz*, p. 136.
80. Rudolph, *Banking and Industrialization in Austria-Hungary*, pp. 174–75.
81. Lampe and Jackson, *Balkan Economic History*, p. 225; Michel, *Banques et banquiers en Autriche*, pp. 274–79, 299–305.
82. Rudolph, *Banking and Industrialization in Austria-Hungary*, pp. 152–55; Lampe and Jackson, *Balkan Economic History*, pp. 260–64.
83. Michel, *Banques et banquiers en Autriche*, p. 121.
84. *Die Diskonto-Gesellschaft, 1851 bis 1901: Denkschrift zum 50 Jahrigen Jubilaum* (Berlin, 1901), p. 47.
85. David S. Landes, "The Bleichröder Bank: An Interim Report," *Leo Baeck Institute Yearbook*, V (1960), 211.
86. HNA K 269 359–343.
87. *Economist*, January 25, 1873, p. 101.
88. HNA K 255 1085-3563/1874.
89. Georges Diouritch, *L'expansion des banques allemandes á l'étranger* (Paris-Berlin, 1909), pp. 391–92; Claude, *Histoire, réalité, et destin d'un Monopole*, p. 16; *The Times*, January 19, 1877.
90. Michel, *Banques et banquiers en Autriche*, p. 244.
91. Ibid., pp. 124–26.
92. Egon Scheffer, *Das Bankwesen in Osterreich* (Vienna, 1924), pp. 279–83; Jurij Krizek, *Die wirtschaftliche Grundzuge des osterreichisch-ungarischen Imperialismus in der Vorkriegszeit (1900–1914)* (Prague, 1963), p. 47.
93. Michel, *Banques et banquiers en Autriche*, pp. 130–31.
94. Diouritch, *L'expansion des banques allemandes*, p. 440.
95. Raymond Poidevin, *Les rélations économiques et financiéres entre la France et l'Allemagne de 1898 a 1914* (Paris, 1969), p. 339; Simeon Damjanov, *Frenszkoto Ikonomicseszko Pronikvane v Bolgarija (1878–1914)* (The French economic penetration into Bulgaria) (Sofia, 1971), pp. 111–12; Svetlana Todorova, *Diplomaticheska istoria na vnushnite zaemi na Bulgaria, 1878–1912* (Sofia, 1971), pp. 110–40.
96. *Nagy Magyar Compass*, XLIII (1916) 1846; Eduard März, "Besonderheiten in der Entwicklung des osterreichischen Bankwesens," *Schmollers Jahrbuch fur Gesetzgebung, Verwaltung und Volkswirtschaft*, 77 (1957), 198.
97. David F. Good, "National Bias in the Austrian Capital Market before World War I," *Explorations in Economic History*, 14 (1977), 118–19.
98. Arthur I. Bloomfield, *Monetary Policy under the International Gold Standard, 1880–1914* (New York, 1959), p. 55; S. Pressburger, ed., *Oesterreichische Notenbank, 1816–1966* (Vienna, 1966), p. 264.

99. Leland B. Yeager, "Fluctuating Exchange Rates in the Nineteenth Century: The Experiences of Austria and Russia," in Robert A. Mundell and Alexander K. Swoboda, eds., *Monetary Problems of the International Economy* (Chicago, 1969), pp. 75–76.

100. Kövér, "A brit tokepiac es Magyarorszag," p. 506.

101. Manfred Pohl, "100 Jahre Deutsche Bank London Agency," *Beitrage zu Wirtschafts und Wahrungsfragen und zur Bankgeschichte,* No. 10 (1973), 256.

102. Stanley Chapman, *The Rise of Merchant Banking* (London, 1984), p. 121.

103. Bartsch, *Statistische Daten uber die Zahlungsbilanz,* p. 45.

104. HNA Z 40 130-2205.

105. Michel, *Banques et banquiers en Autriche,* pp. 302–4; Rudolph, *Banking and Industrialization in Austria-Hungary,* pp. 153–55.

106. HNA Z 34 48-108-1266.

107. HNA K 255 1085-1874-74; 1086-1874-74 and RAL XI/111/10.

108. HNA Z 51 16-226 and *Tabellen zur Wahrungs-Statistik,* Zweite Ausgabe, Zweiter Teil (Vienna, 1900–1904), pp. 468–81.

109. Franz Baltzarek, "Finanzplatz Wien—die innerstaatliche und internationale Stellung in historischer Perspektiv," *Quartalshefte der Girozentrale,* 15 (1980), 59; *Nagy Magyar Compass,* 1873–1916.

110. Bartsch, *Statistische Daten uber die Zahlungsbilanz,* pp. 87–88.

111. *Tabellen zur Wahrungs-Statistik,* pp. 504–6.

112. Karl Erich Born, *International Banking in the 19th and 20th Centuries* (London, 1983), pp. 45, 140; Fritz Seidenzahl, "Bank fur Orientalische Eisenbahnen (Eine Finanzholding und ihre Portfeuille)," *Beitrage zu Wirtschafts und Wahrungsfragen und zur Bankgeschichte,* No. 1 (1965), 15.

113. Robert Leifmann, *Beteiligungs- und Finanzierungs-gesellschaften,* 2nd ed. (Jena, 1913), pp. 482–83; Sandor, *Nagyipari fejlodes Magyarorszagon,* pp. 486–87.

114. Mira Wilkins, *The Emergence of Multinational Enterprise: American Business Abroad from the Colonial Era to 1914* (Cambridge, MA, 1970), p. 84; Aleksandr Fursenko, *Nieftjanue vojnu* (Oil wars), (Leningrad, 1985), pp. 101, 109; see also below, Chapter 19.

115. *Geschafts-Bericht der Direktion der Deutschen Bank AG, 1873–1910,* p. 7.

116. Jacob Riesser, *Die deutschen Grossbanken und ihre Konzentration* (Jena, 1912), p. 340; Diouritch, *L'expansion des banques allemandes,* pp. 406–7; Georg Siemens, *Geschichte des Hauses Siemens* (Munich, 1949), pp. 220–21; Michel, *Banques et banquiers en Autriche,* pp. 183–86; Harm Schroter, "Siemens and Central and South-East Europe between the Two World Wars," in Alice Teichova and P. L. Cottrell, eds., *International Business and Central Europe, 1918–1939* (Leicester, 1983), pp. 173–77.

117. Liefmann, *Beteiligungs- und Finanzierungs-gesellschaften,* p. 459.

118. *Tabellen zur Wahrungs-Statistik,* p. 744; HNA Z 62-2-22.

119. Leifmann, *Beteiligungs- und Finanzierungs-gesellschaften* 458; Sandor, *Nagyipari fejlodes Magyarorszagon,* p. 467.

120. Jacques Thobie, "Interêts belges et interêts français dans l'Empire Ottomane, 1900–1914," in *Les relations franco-belges de 1830 à 1934* (Metz, 1975), pp. 213–43.

121. März, *Osterreichische Industrie,* p. 343.

122. Eduard März "Besonderheiten in der Entwicklung des osterreichischen Bankwesens," *Schmollers Jahrbuch fur Gesetzgebung, Verwaltung und Volkswirtschaft,* 77 (1957), 70–71.

Chapter 15

1. J. S. Cohen, "Italy, 1861–1914," in Rondo Cameron, ed., *Banking and Economic Development: Some Lessons of History* (New York, London, Toronto, 1972), pp. 58–90.

2. Antonio Confalonieri, *Banca e industria in Italia 1894–1906*, 3 vols. (Milano, 1974–76).

3. Peter Hertner, "Banken und Kapitalbildung in der Giolitti-Ära," *Quellen und Forschungen aus italienischen Archiven und Bibliotheken*, 58 (1978), 466–565; "Das Vorbild deutscher Universalbanken bei der Gründung und Entwicklung italienischer Geschäftsbanken neuen Typs, 1894–1914," in F. W. Henning, ed., *Entwicklung und Aufgaben von Versicherungen und Banken in der Industrialisierung* (Berlin, 1980), pp. 195–282.

4. See Rondo Cameron, "French Finance and Italian Unity: The Cavourian Decade," *American Historical Review*, 62 (1957), 552–69; idem, *France and the Economic Development of Europe, 1800–1914* (Princeton, NJ, 1961), Chapter 16; and Rosario Romeo, *Cavour e il suo tempo (1842–1854)*, Vol. 2 (Bari, 1977), p. 645.

5. P. Norsa, "Finanziamenti stranieri nel periodo del Risorgimento e dell'Unitá d'Italia, 1832–1863," typescript (Milano, 1959), p. 45.

6. Bertrand Gille, *Les investissements français en Italie (1815–1914)* (Turin, 1968), p. 132ff.; M. da Pozzo and G. Felloni, *La borsa valori di Genova nel secolo XIX*, (Torino, 1964) (Archivio Economica dell'Unificazione Italiana, serie II, Vol. X), p. 343ff.

7. Gille, *Investissements francais*, pp. 140.

8. Ibid., p. 229.

9. Ibid., p. 334; Cameron, *France and the Economic Development of Europe*, p. 180ff.; Confalonieri, *Banca e industria*, Vol. 1, p. 275.

10. Da Pozzo and Felloni, *La borsa valori*, p. 321.

11. A. J. S. Baster, *The International Banks* (London, 1935), p. 47.

12. P. L. Cottrell, "Anglo-French Financial Cooperation, 1850–1880," *The Journal of European Economic History*, 3 (1974), 65.

13. Baster, *International Banks*, p. 48; P. L. Cottrell, "Investment Banking in England, 1856–1882: A Case Study of the International Financial Society" (doctoral thesis, University of Hull, 1974), p. 288; "London Financiers and Austria, 1863–1875: The Anglo-Austrian Bank," *Business History*, 11 (1969), 106–19; see also Chapter 1 in this volume.

14. Peter Hertner, "Deutsches Kapital im italienischen Bankensektor und die deutsch-italienischen Finanzbeziehungen in der zweiten Hälfte des 19. Jahrhundert," *Bankhistorisches Archiv*, 2 (1977), 1–29; Gino Luzzatto, *L'economia italiana dal 1861 al 1894*, (Turin, 1968), p. 76.

15. See Confalonieri, *Banca e industria*, Vol. 1, p. 276.

16. Peter Hertner, *Il capitale tedesco in Italia dall' Unità alla Prima Guerra Mondiale*, (Bologna, 1984), p. 70.

17. Alexander Gerschenkron, *Economic Backwardness in Historical Perspective* (Cambridge, MA, 1962), p. 13.

18. Alexander Gerschenkron, "The Industrial Development of Italy: A Debate with Rosario Romeo," in *Continuity in History and Other Essays* (Cambridge, MA, 1968), pp. 98–124, particularly p. 108; idem, "Notes on the Rate of Industrial Growth in Italy, 1881–1913," *Economic Backwardness*, p. 88.

19. Hertner, *Il capitale tedesco*, p. 74; idem, *Die Deutsche Bank in Italien und ihre Beziehungen zum italienischen Kapitalmarkt bis zum Ausbruch des Ersten Weltkrieges* (Frankfurt/Main, 1985).

20. Hertner, *Il capitale tedesco*, p. 26.

21. Ibid., p. 74.

22. Ibid., p. 93.

23. Ibid., p. 177.

24. Ibid., p. 101.

25. Ibid., p. 104.

26. Confalonieri, *Banca e industria*, Vol. 3, pp. 73, 77, n. 2.

27. Hertner, "Das Vorbild deutscher Universalbanken."

28. Hertner, *Il capitale tedesco*, p. 132.
29. Ibid., p. 196.
30. Ibid., p. 133.
31. See Chap. 20 in this volume.
32. Hertner, *Il capitale tedesco*, pp. 124, 191ff.
33. J. S. Cohen, "Financing Industrialization in Italy, 1894–1914: The Partial Transformation of a Late-comer," *Journal of Economic History*, 27 (1967), 369.

Chapter 16

1. The first Banco do Brasil's role in monetary policy is summarized from Maria Bárbara Levy and Ana Maria Andrade, "A gestão monetária na formacão do Estado Nacional," *Revista Brasileira de Mercado de Capitais*, 6 (May/August 1980), 138–52, which includes quantitative data.
2. The analysis of the private banking system in this period is summarized from Maria Bárbara Levy and Ana Maria Andrade, "Fundamentos do sistema bancário no Brasil," *Estudos Econômicos*, 15 (1985), 17–48, which includes quantitative data.
3. Maria Bárbara Levy, *História do Direito Societário no Brasil* (Rio de Janeiro, 1983), p. 14.
4. David Joslin, *A Century of Banking in Latin America* (London, 1963), pp. 65–66, 80, 84.
5. Ibid., p. 168.
6. Steven Topik, "Capital estrangeiro no sistema bancário brasileiro, 1889–1930," *Revista Brasileira de Mercado de Capitais*, 5 (September/December 1979), p. 132.
7. Richard Graham, *Gran-Bretanha e o início da modernizacâo do Brasil, 1850–1914* (Sâo Paulo, 1973), p. 28.
8. Rui Granziera, *A guerra do Paraguai e o capitalismo no Brasil* (São Paulo, 1973), p. 157.
9. *Annuário Estatístico*, 1939/1940.
10. Raymond Goldsmith, *Desenvolvimento financeiro sob um século de inflacáo (1850–1984)* (Rio de Janeiro, 1986).
11. Ibid.
12. See Chapter 4 in this volume.
13. Maria Bárbara Levy, *História da Bolsa de Valores do Rio de Janeiro* (Rio de Janeiro, 1977), p. 298.
14. Maria Bárbara Levy et al., *Sul America: 90 anos de seguros* (mimeo, 1985), p. 11.
15. Levy, *Bolsa de Valores*, p. 252.
16. Ministério da Fazenda, *Serviço de Estatística Enconômica e Financeira*, various years.
17. Ana Celia Castro, *As empresas estrangeiras no Brasil (1860–1913)* (Rio de Janeiro, 1979), p. 39.
18. Irving Stone, "British Direct and Portfolio Investment in Latin America before 1914," *Journal of Economic History*, 37 (September 1977), 690–722.
19. Marcelo Paiva Abreu, *A Dívida pública externa do Brasil, 1824–1931* (Pontificia Universidade Católica do Rio de Janeiro, 1985, mimeo).
20. *Annuário Estatística*, 1939/1940.
21. Goldsmith, *Desenvolvimento financeiro*.
22. Claudio Contador and Claudio Haddad, "Real Income, Money and Prices: The Brazilian Experience, 1891–1970," (University of Chicago, 1972, mimeo).
23. Goldsmith, *Desenvolvimento financeiro*, p. 25.
24. Ibid., p. 26.
25. Albert Fishlow, "Origins and Consequences of Import Substitution in Brazil," in Luis Eugenio Di Marco, ed., *International Economic Development: Essays in Honor of Raul Prebisch* (New York, 1972).

26. Maria Bárbara Levy, "O Encilhamento," in Paulo Neuhaus, ed., *Economica Brasileira: uma visão historica* (Rio de Janeiro, 1980).

27. Carlos Pelaez and Wilson Suzigan, *História Monetária do Brasil* (Rio de Janeiro, 1976), p. 38.

28. Maria Bárbara Levy, "Banco do Brasil," entry in *Enciclopédia de História Contemporânea do Brasil*, I. Beloch, ed. (Rio de Janeiro, 1984).

29. Wilson Suzigan and Anibal Villela, *A politica do Governo e crescimento da economia brasileira (1889/1945)* (Rio de Janeiro, 1975), p. 87.

30. Levy, *Bolsa de Valores*, p. 297.

31. *Gazeta de Commercio e Finanças*, September 2, 1905, p. 1.

32. Brasil. Congresso. Câmera dos Deputados, *Annais*, Vol. 2, p. 107.

33. "Banking," *The Brazilian Review*, November 26, 1901.

34. Joslin, *Banking in Latin America*, p. 127, and Edward Hurley, *Banking and Credit in Argentia, Brazil, Chile and Peru* (Washington, DC, 1914), p. 4.

35. The London and Brazilian Bank functioned in the cities of Rio de Janeiro, Belém, Recife, São Paulo, Santos, Campinas, Porto Alegre, Rio Grande, and Pelotas. In 1901 it established an agency in Manaus, in the state of Amazonas.

36. After 1891 the English Bank of Rio de Janeiro continued its activities under the name of the British Bank of South America, Ltd., and it established itself in Salvador (1895) and Manaus (1901).

37. The Brasilianische Bank für Deutschland received authorization in 1897 to operate in Porto Alegre. In 1900 it became affiliated with the Banque d'Anvers.

38. The London and River Plate Bank began operations in 1891. Its founding partners were all bankers and businessmen established in London. In 1901 the bank paid a dividend of 20 percent.

39. The Banque Française du Brésil started its activities in 1897 with an office in Rio de Janeiro and agencies in Santos and São Paulo. It was formed by the Comptoir Nationale d'Escompte and the Société Générale de France.

40. The Banque Belge de Prêts Fonciers began operations in 1900 in Rio de Janeiro. The preferred stock was held by the Banque d'Anvers and the commercial enterprise Vande Put Heirman and Frédéric Jacobs. Among the ordinary shareholders were the Cie Anversoise d'Entreprises Coloniales and the Brasilianische Bank für Deutschland.

41. See Table A16–1 for further details.

42. The London and Brazilian Bank expanded south (Paranágua and Curitiba) in the state of Paraná, as well as to the north (São Luis do Maranhão) and northeast (Fortaleza in Ceará). The British Bank of South America augmented its capital, and the Brasilianische Bank für Deutschland expanded through agencies in the south and northeast.

43. Maria Bárbara Levy, *Estrutura e Funcionamento dos Bancos Comerciais, Traços históricos* (Rio de Janeiro, 1977, mimeo), p. 264.

44. Levy, *Sul América: 90 anos de seguros*, p. 158.

45. Levy, *Bolsa de Valores*, p. 387.

46. Abreu, *A divida publica externa do Brasil*.

47. Castro, *As empresas estrangeiras*, pp. 64–66.

48. Ibid., pp. 78–84.

49. Ibid., pp. 116–22.

50. Ibid., p. 98.

51. Flavio Saes and Tamas Szmreczanyi, "O capital estrangeiro no Brasil, 1880–1930," *Estudos Economicos*, 15 (May–August 1985), No. 2.

52. Stone, "British Direct and Portfolio Investment," p. 706.

Chapter 17

1. "Six-Power Groups" is a clumsy terminology. Some contemporary sources prefer "consortium," but officially this term was not used until 1920 with the formation of the "New" China Consortium. The several national groups were associated by agreements, but their involvement in any specific projects was separately negotiated. Thus the Five-Power Groups Agreement bound five groups in the Reorganization Loan of 1913 at the same time as the Four-Power Groups Agreement bound another combination of these groups in the Hukuang Railways Loan of 1911. Although such terms as "Sextuple" are more convenient, the longer form was used more consistently. See Table 17–1.

2. Chinese names and terms are romanized as follows: (1) commonly known geographical names and familiar persons are spelled as was usual at the time, i.e., a variation of Wade-Giles or a form adopted consciously by the person involved, and (2) modified Wade-Giles. For those requiring *pinyin*, see Appendix 17B.

3. Carl Meyer (1851–1922) was born in Hamburg and was associated for many years with N. M. Rothschild & Sons with special interest in South African mining. From this his independent interests spread to China, and Chinese mining and associated railways. He was chairman for a time of the Pekin (*sic*) Syndicate, which joined with the British and Chinese Corporation to found the Chinese Central Railways, Ltd. In this latter capacity he was invited to join the Hongkong Bank's London Consultative Committee.

4. As described by W. F. Spalding of the Hongkong Bank's London office, the duties of the compradore were to transact business for the bank with other Chinese; to look after all monetary affairs connected therewith, such as the receipt and payment of money and the collection of drafts and notes; to offer advice to the bank regarding the condition of local markets; to compile commercial information as to the standing of Chinese borrowers; and to recommend, control, and guarantee the Chinese staff of the bank.

5. Following the failure of Chinese-owned and Chinese-administered customs banks, the disappearance of Chinese customs officials, and other irregularities in consequence of the disturbances following the 1911 Revolution, the Chinese Foreign Ministry took steps to ensure that the revenues be deposited in those foreign banks interested in China's foreign debt servicing. These temporary arrangements continued, however, until the establishment of the National Government in Nanking in 1927.

Chapter 18

1. The following results, in percentage, were obtained at the moment of registration of the securities during conversion operations after the bankruptcy: France, 40; Great Britain, 29; Turkey, 7.93; Belgium, 7.20; Netherlands, 7.59; Germany, 4.70; Italy; 2.62; Austria-Hungary, 0.96. (*Source:* Archives de la Dette, P.V. 1301, Annee 1885/86.)

2. For more ample information on the B.I.O., see Jacques Thobie, *Intérêts et impérialisme français dans l'Empire ottoman*, especially p. 81.

3. Extraordinary General Meeting of August 12, 1874; Archives of the B.I.O. in Istanbul, proceedings of the General Meetings.

4. Generally issued at 6 percent and well below par, the effective yield of these loans oscillated between 8.5 and 11 percent at the time of issue; but their often steep fall at the Stock Exchange sometimes drove real interest above 20 percent. Such figures underlined the fragility of Ottoman "credit."

5. With the exception of the 1870 loan, which produced a premium and was devoted to

railway construction in the European part of Turkey (9 percent of the total), no part of these loans was invested in the Ottoman economy.

6. See David S. Landes, *Bankers and Pashas: International Finance and Economic Imperialism in Egypt* (London and Cambridge, MA, 1958).

7. Which had to close in 1873 the branch it had opened in Alexandria in 1869.

8. See above, Chapter 3.

9. Neither the French government nor the Crédit Foncier opposed the sale. Decazes did not want to displease Britain, the only relatively friendly country in a period of isolation; and since the Crédit Foncier was preparing to put forward the khedive's Suez shares as collateral for a financial operation, it opposed the Dervieu-Société Générale project to acquire these very shares. The Crédit Lyonnais and de Lesseps expressed their satisfaction with the added security resulting from the British purchase. Bouvier rightly states: "In Paris as in London, the governments and bankers initiated a decisive collaboration. At once, financial interests became the main element of high politics"; Jean Bouvier "Les intérêts financiers et la question d'Egypte, 1875–1876," *Revue Historique,* 1960, 75–104.

10. The British objected that the debt was too great and the "floating" too favored.

11. This commission was entrusted with the administration of the railways and the port of Alexandria, whose revenues were assigned to the Privileged.

12. Bouvier, "Intérêts financiers," p. 100.

13. For retail trade, the *medjidié* at 20 meant a Turkish pound worth 108 piasters; for the State Administration and the Treasury, the *medjidié* at 19 pence the pound at 102.6 piasters; the free exchange of the *medjidié* whose value oscillated around 108 piasters to the pound. Minting of silver coins was stopped in 1884. In certain provinces there still circulated gold Louis, which was worth 20 francs, and Austrian thalers, Persian krans, etc.

14. Whereas the par value of the pound sterling in relation to the Turkish pound was 110 gold piasters, the exchange rate was 120 piasters while the Turkish pound was worth 108, a premium of 9 percent.

15. Salgur Kancal, "Note on the Dualization of the Ottoman Monetary Space from 1880 to 1913," typescript, 13 p., 1981, p. 8.

16. A totally floating exchange system would have meant a great element of risk for foreign trade, unfavorable speculation of the balance of payments, the necessity for a sudden transfer of resources from the domestic to the external sector with the attendant acute social tensions; a totally fixed, classical, gold exchange standard would have led the indebted Ottoman Empire to lower its prices and reduce its revenues, which would have been fatal to the "sick man."

17. At the time of its reform in 1834.

18. See Samir Saul, "La France et l'Egypte a l'áube du XXè siècle, les difficultiés d'une jonction," *Le Miroir égyptien* (Marseille, 1984), pp. 109–24.

19. Nearly 2 million Egyptian pounds in 1913.

20. Emile Antonini, *Le crédit et la banque en Egypte* (Lausanne, 1927), p. 86.

21. In his *Banking and Empire in Iran, 1889–1952: The Imperial Bank of Persia* (Cambridge, U.K., 1986), that I closely follow here.

22. "A Banknote which can only be cashed where it is issued," observed the British consul at Mashad in 1919, "is not money at all and will never do the work of money"; ibid., p. 126. The notes were denominated in *tomans*, a unit of account, one toman being equal to ten krans.

23. About this evolution, see Thobie, *Intérêts et impérialisme*, pp. 457–59.

24. These banks were sometimes small, such as the French provincial banks, but large ones were involved, such as the Banque de l'Union Anversoise, the Banque d'Outre-Mer of Brussels, the Union Financiére of Geneva, the Société de Crédit Suisse of Zurich, the Wiener Bankverein, the Creditanstalt of Vienna, the Banca Commerciale Italiana, the

Credito Italiano, and the Banque Hypothécaire d'Espagne. The U.S. participant was the Equitable Trust Co. of New York.

25. "Ferdinand Perier . . . is a knight of the Légion d'Honneur and a member of the Automobile Club Circle. He belongs to the Société Hippique and to the Union Artistic Club. He is everywhere considered quite a gallant man. He is director of the Compagnie Hâvraise, of the Soleil (Grêle), of the Chantiers et Ateliers de Gironde, of the Gaz de Mulhouse, of the Union Maritime, of the Caisse Mutuelle, etc. His son married Miss Charlotte Billet, daughter of the former General Councillor of the Nord"; inquiry by the Department of Finance, May 22, 1913, Archives des Affaires Etrangéres Paris, Turquie, carton 47.

26. Sir Ernest Cassel to P. Cambon, December 15, 1908, Archives Nationales, Paris, F 30. 361.

27. The names of the main ones are given in n. 24.

28. Samir Saul, a Canadian historian, is completing a *doctorat d'Etat* on French interests in Egypt from 1882 to 1914, which should fill the gap.

29. At the request of France, a German and a Russian commissioner entered the Caisse de la Dette.

30. At the head of a group of bankers, Sir Ernest Cassel carried out a successful coup by commiting himself in 1898 to pay back the Daria debt by October 1905. The operation was made easy by the value that land gained from the construction of dams at Aswan and Asyut; the profit amounted to £6.8 million; J. Ducruet, *Les capitaux européens au Proche-Orient* (Paris, 1962), p.63.

31. In 1899 the bank still held £122,100 of the loan.

32. The margin of 9 points between firm purchase and subscription was more than twice the margin in similar Ottoman loans.

33. Quoted by Geoffrey Jones, *Banking and Empire,* p. 55.

34. Antonini, *Le crédit et la banque en Egypte,* p. 30; the Crédit Lyonnais opened a sub-branch in Jerusalem in 1892.

35. Thobie, *Intéréts et impérialisme,* p. 9.

36. There were local private bankers, or rather merchant bankers, mostly from the minority communities, some of whom were correspondents or representatives of European banks.

37. The Anglo-Palestine Bank, an establishment whose capital was of British origin, found its customers among the Zionist Jews of Palestine. Founded in 1899, it opened a branch in Jaffa in 1902 and in Jerusalem in 1904.

38. D. Grange, "La premiere expansion de capitaux italiens en Méditerranée," in *Banque et investissements en Méditerranée à l'epoque contemporaine* (Actes du colloque de Marseille, Fevrier, 1982), p. 43.

39. The capital of the Bank of Athens was of British and Greek origin; the B.U.P. entered in 1904 with two directors. In 1905 the Banque de Crédit Industriel d'Athènes opened a branch in the Ottoman capital, but it had to merge the following year with the Bank of Athens. The capital of the Banque d'Orient was of German (Nationalbank für Deutschland) and Greek origin in 1905; after 1906 it was under the influence of French capital (Comptoir d'Escompte).

40. On the role of the Banco di Roma in the occupation of Libya, see D. Grange, "La premiere expansion . . ." , pp. 42–47.

41. Ibid., p. 43. According to S. I. Minerbi, *L'Italie et la Palestine, 1914–1920* (Paris, 1970), p. 224, the Jerusalem branch in fact opened only in 1918.

42. The Ottoman diversion resulted in losses of at least £84,000, or 8.4 percent of the capital; Jones, *Banking and Empire,* p. 66.

43. The Banque de Métélin was formed in 1891 with a capital belonging to Levantine Greeks of Smyrna (6 million francs). It opened branches in Constantinople, Smyrna, Salonica, Athens, and Piraeus. Poorly managed, bogged down in the affairs of a navigation company

(the Egée) and mines (in Heraklea), it experienced difficulties in 1904, and was felled by the crisis of 1907; archives of the Crédit Lyonnais, Agences Etrangères, 1913.

44. The Crédit Agricole was a state institution whose capital was constituted by a tax on crops (*dime*). In 1913 it had 355 branches, and used 82 percent of its effective capital (120 million francs) in mortgage loans; Archives Nationales Paris, F. 30 361, J. M. Méasché (correspondent of the B.F.C.I.) to ambassador Bompard, May 17, 1913.

45. On this question, see Thobie, *Intérêts et imperialisme*, pp. 472–75.

46. The remarks below are based on Saul, "La France et l'Egypte."

47. It then became the Banque Internationale de Paris.

48. Paribas, the Société Générale, the Crédit Lyonnais, and the C.N.E.P. were able to float 100 million francs of bonds on the French market, while the advance promoted by the Bank of England failed.

49. Saul, "La France et l'Egypte," p. 10.

50. A. Forte, *Les Banques en Egypte* (Paris, 1938), p. 96. A part of the Bank of Egypt, the Banque Zervoudaki disappeared in 1911, to be followed in 1912 by the Banque Tilche.

51. Antonini, *Le crédit et la banque en Egypte*, p. 94.

52. On this question refer to Jacques Thobie, *L'impérialisme à la française, La France impériale* (Paris, 1982), Chapter 1.

53. P. Cambon, ambassador in Constantinople, to the Minister of Foreign Affairs, February 26, 1893.

54. See Chapter 3 in this volume.

55. The B.I.O. and the Régie Générale had directors in the Société for a while; moreover, Cail obtained an order of eight locomotives. See also Rondo Cameron, *France and the Economic Development of Europe, 1800–1914* (Princeton, NJ, 1961), pp. 324–25.

56. No bank was part of the syndicate formed by W. K. d'Arcy to search for oil in Persia, but he had the good fortune of finding oil quickly and thus meeting the Admiralty's requirements. See Chapter 19 in this volume.

57. This company is analyzed in some detail in Jacques Thobie, "Intérêts belges et intérêts français dans l'Empire Ottomane," *Les relations franco-belges de 1830 à 1934* (Metz, 1975), pp. 213–43.

58. Belgian banks almost never appeared in the front ranks for important affairs in the Ottoman Empire, but they were quite active as intermediaries in the sector of municipal service companies, and in the supply of transport material, especially tramways.

59. On the economic-financial and political meaning of this failure, and the famous controversy between Rouvier and Delcassé, see Thobie, *Intérêts et impérialisme*, pp. 592–608.

60. Jacques Thobie, "Conjoncture et strategie: le groupe financier de l'Ottomane en 1914," *Economie et Société dans l'Empire Ottoman* (Paris, 1983), pp. 470–83.

61. The withdrawal of the B.I.O. from the Baghdad railway was underway. The B.I.O. played an active role in the establishment of the Crédit Foncier Ottoman and the Consortium de Constantinople.

62. The National Bank of Turkey had a minority share in the Tigris and Euphrates Transports.

63. S. Saul, "La France et l'Egypte," p. 12.

64. Jones, *Banking and Empire*, p. 127.

65. Ibid., p. 124.

66. "Political considerations," S. F. Rogers, the bank's Deputy Chief Manager, wrote to Newell, Secretary of the Board, in November 1909, "do not pay our dividends." And the Chief Manager Wood wrote to Newell in November 1910: "You see how we dance to the piping from Downing Street and get more kicks than ha'pence for our trouble, and yet we must maintain in *all* quarters these good relations which are a *sine qua non* to our best interests"; quoted by Jones, *Banking and Empire*, pp. 127–28.

67. Ibid., p. 60. These interests were liquidated in 1901.

68. The loss for the bank was £88,000. Ibid., p. 62.
69. Ibid., p. 129.
70. These were the Anglo-Persian Oil Company, F. Strick and Co., the Persian Transport Co., Lynch and Co., Gray Paul, Ellerman Shipping Lines, the British India Steam Navigation Co., and S. Pearson and Co. (oil business in Mexico).
71. Réné Girault, *Emprunts russes et investissements français en Russie, 1887–1914* (Paris, 1973), p. 938.
72. The Persian Railways Syndicate continued in existence until 1939, but it never built any railways.

Chapter 19

The author would like to express his gratitude to Professor Gregory C. Freeze of Brandeis University for editorial assistance in preparing the English translation of the present essay.

Works frequently cited in this chapter have been identified by the following abbreviations:

MKNPR	*Monopolisticheskiy Kapital v Noftjanoy Dromishlennosty Rossii* (Monopoly capital in Russian oil industry). Collection of Documents and Commentaries, Leningrad, 1961.
TsGIA SSSR	Tcentralnyi Gosudarstvennye Archiv SSSR (USSR Central Historical Archives). Leningrad.
TsGIA Gruz. SSR	Tsentralnyi Gosudarstvennyi Archiv Gruzinskoy SSR (Georgian SSR Historical Archives). Tbilisi.
TsGAVMF	Tsentralnyi Gosudarstvennyi Archiv Voenno-Morskogo Flota (Central USSR Navy Archives). Leningrad.
LGIA	Leningradskii Gosudarstvennyi Istoricheskii Arkhiv (Leningrad State Historical Archives). Leningrad.
f.	fond (record group).
op.	opis' (inventory).
d.	delo (file).
l.	list (page).

1. Allan Nevins, *A Study in Power* (New York, 1953), Chapter 2–5.
2. A. L. Moore, *John D. Archbold and the Early Development of Standard Oil* (New York, n.d.), pp. 115–121.
3. Harold F. Williamson et al., *A History of the American Petroleum Industry* (Evanston, IL, 1959), Vol. I, p. 471.
4. Ibid., pp. 360–66.
5. Harvey O'Connor, *World Crisis in Oil* (London, 1963), p. 61.
6. Ralph and Muriel Hidy, *Pioneering in Big Business* (New York, 1955), pp. 271, 407.
7. Williamson et al., *Petroleum Industry,* Vol. I, pp. 466–70.
8. Hidy and Hidy, *Pioneering,* pp. 611–12.
9. Mira Wilkins, *The Emergence of Multinational Enterprise* (Cambridge, MA, 1970), pp. 84–85.
10. MKNPR, p. 662; Robert W. Tolf, *The Russian Rockefellers* (Stanford, CA, 1976), p. 79.
11. Irina A. Diakonova, *Nobelevskaia korporatsiia v Rossii* (Nobel Corporation in Russia) (Moscow, 1980), p. 66.
12. Ibid.; Tolf, *Russian Rockefellers,* pp. 79–80.
13. Joachim Mai, *Das Deutsche Kapital in Russland, 1850–1895* (Berlin, 1970), p. 177.

14. L. Nobel to St. Petersburg Office of the State Bank, 9/21 June 1884, TsGIA SSSR, f.588; op. 1; d. 121; l. 41a.
15. E. Nobel to V. A. Lasky, (St. Petersburg International Bank) 19 June/1 July 1889, TsGIA SSSR, f. 626; op. 1; d. 121; l. 41a.
16. Adolf von Hansemann (Diskonto-Gesellschaft) to Lasky, 9/21 June 1884, TsGIA SSSR, f. 626; op. 1; d. 107; l. 1.
17. Hansemann to Lasky, 20 April 2 May 1899; Ibid., d. 121; l. 418.
18. Hansemann to Lasky, 26 April/8 May, 2/14 July 1899; Ibid. ll. 45a, 87.
19. Valeria A. Nardova, *Nachalo monopolisatsii neftianoi promyshlennosti Rossii* (The beginning of oil business monopolization in Russia) (Leningrad, 1974).
20. MKNPR, p. 750 (statistical appendix).
21. Nardova, *Nachalo monopolisatsii,* pp. 9–11; Diakonova, *Nobelevskaia korporatsiia,* p. 59–60; Tolf, *Russian Rockefellers,* pp. 50–67.
22. MKNPR, p. 754 (statistical appendix); Diakonova, *Nobelevskaia korporatsiia,* pp. 62–63.
23. MKNPR, pp. 753–54 (statistical appendix).
24. Ibid.
25. Alexander A. Fursenko, *Mozhno li schitat' kompaniiu Nobelia russkim koncernom* (Can the Nobel Co. be considered a Russian concern?), in *Issledovaniia po sotsial'no-politicheskoi istorii Rossii* (Studies in Russian sociopolitical history) (Leningrad, 1971), p. 352–61.
26. Tolf, *Russian Rockefellers,* p. 82.
27. MKNPR, Journal of State Bank Council, July 29, 1905, pp. 340–41.
28. E. Nobel's receipts 10/22 August 1898, 3/15 May, 10/22 August 1899; TsGIA SSSR, f. 626; op. 1, 353; ll. 3, 5–6.
29. Volga-Kama Bank board proceedings, 9/22 April 1915; ibid., f. 595; op. 2; d. 102; ll. 46–48.
30. Tolf, *Russian Rockefellers,* pp. 89–91.
31. MKNPR, p. 665 (comment).
32. Russian Foreign Trade Bank to St. Petersburg International Commercial Bank, 3/15 July 1898; TsGIA SSSR, f. 626; op. 1; d. 366; ll. 1, 9.
33. MKNPR, S. Markoff (Chief of Caucasian and Caspian excise office) to V. Andreef (Ministry of Finance), January 12, 1889, pp. 118–21.
34. Obzor bakinskoi neftianoi promyshlennosti za 1901 god. (Report of Baku oil business in 1901) (Baku, 1902), Part 1, p. 431; Part 2, pp. 10, 213, 226, 230; Report of 1914, Part 1, pp. 8–9; Nardova, *Nachalo monopolisatsii,* p. 140; MKNPR, pp. 752–54; Lev Eventov, *Inostrannyi kapital v neftianoi promyshlennesti Rossii* (Foreign capital in Russian oil industry) (Moscow, Leningrad, 1925), pp. 39–41; Sergei and Ludwig Perschke, *Russkaia neftianaia promyshlennost, ee razvitie i sovremennoe polozhenie v statisticheskich dannych* (Russian oil industry, its development and present condition in statistics) (Tiflis, 1913), pp. 191–93.
35. Proceedings of "A. I. Mantashoff and Co. Stockholders Meeting," 29 June/10 July 1899, TsGIA SSSR, f. 23; op. 24; d. 620; ll. 70, 74.
36. List of "A. I. Mantashoff and Co." Stockholders 2/11 June July 1899; Volga-Kama Bank Baku branch to "A. I. Mantashoff and Co." 20 September/2 October 1899 (ibid., ll. 70, 117).
37. Perschke, *Russkaia neftianaia promyshlennost,* p. 29; Hidy and Hidy, *Pioneering,* pp. 132, 153.
38. Nevins, *Study in Power,* Vol. II, pp. 115–16.
39. J. D. Rockefeller to J. Archbold, 14 June 1889; Rockefeller Archive Center (Tarrytown, NY).

40. Final Report of the Industrial Commission, Vol. XIX, (Washington, DC, 1902), pp. 579–80.

41. Hidy and Hidy, *Pioneering*, pp. 144–54, 533–46; Wilkins, *Emergence of Multinational Enterprise*, pp. 83–84.

42. Chu-yuan Chen, "The United States Petroleum Trade with China, 1876–1949," and Mira Wilkins, "The Impacts of American Multinational Enterprise on American-Chinese Economic Relations, 1786–1914," in Ernest R. May and John K. Fairbank, eds., *America's China Trade in Historical Perspective* (Cambridge, MA 1986), pp. 211–13, 264–66.

43. A. A. Fursenko, "Pervyi neftianoi exportnyi syndikat v Rossii" (The first Russian oil export syndicate), in *Monopolii i inostrannyi kapital v. Rossii* (Monopolies and foreign capital in Russia) (Moscow, Leningrad, 1962), pp. 4–58.

44. A. Bompar (French Ambassador in Petersburg) to Boujois (French Ministry of Foreign Affairs), 29 March 1906. Paris, Archives des Affaires Etrangéres, Correspondance politique, Russie, N. S., T. 57, pp. 49–50. See also Chapter 6 in this volume.

45. Banque de Rothschild to Petersburg International Bank, 1896. TsGIA SSSR, f. 626; op. 1; d. 286; ll. 82–83.

46. Jules Aron to Adolf Rothstein 24 March 1896. Ibid., d. 352; ll. 6–7.

47. A. de Rothschild to Adolf Rothstein, 3 March and 30 November 1897; ibid., d. 224; ll. 14, 15, 70.

48. List of the Mazut Stockholders, 28 March/10 April 1898; International Bank Circular, 1/13 February 1898 and Responses from Petersburg Discount and Loan Bank, 4/16 February; Russian Foreign Trade Bank, 5/17 February; M. Warburg bank, 4/16 April 1898. Ibid., d. 363; ll. 2, 3, 5, 33.

49. Savely Pollack (of Mazut) to Rothstein, 15/28 July 1898; Mazut to International Bank, 8/21 August 1902; 21 February/3 March 1904; International Bank to Mazut, 20 January/2 February 1904; 9/22 September 1914. Ibid., f. 37; d. 372; ll. 5, 8, 9, 11, 18.

50. Pollack to Rothstein, 28 October/9 November 1899. Ibid., f. 626; op. 1; d. 363; l. 120.

51. Witte to E. Hubbard (Bank of England), 13/25 May 1898; *Istoricheskii arkhiv* (1960) No. 6, 85–86.

52. Boris V. Anan'ich; *Rossija i mezjdunarodnij capital* (Russia and international finances) (Leningrad, 1970), p. 32.

53. E. Cassel to E. Noetzlin (of the Banque de Paris et des Pays-Bas), 1/13 May 1899; copy in TsGIA SSSR, f. 626; op. 1; d. 247; l. 43.

54. Agreement between St. Petersburg International Bank and London Bibi-Eibat Petroleum Co., 12/25 October 1900; ibid., d. 371; l. 200.

55. Rothstein to A. Koch (of St. Petersburg International Bank for Panmure Gordon, Hill and Co.), 12–15 October 1900; ibid., l. 209.

56. B. Redwood report, 2/15 October 1900; ibid., ll. 145–50.

57. Proceedings of agreement, 30 June/12 July 1904; ibid., f. 1425; op. 1; d. 76; ll. 286–87.

58. A. A. Fursenko, *Neftianye tresti i mirovaia politika* (World oil trusts and world politics) (Moscow, Leningrad, 1965), p. 134.

59. M. Warburg to Rothstein, 12 September 1898; TsGIA SSSR, f. 626; op. 1; d. 136; ll. 170–71.

60. V. I. Timirjasev (Berlin agent of Russian Ministry of Finance) to V. I. Kovalevsky (Director of Trade Dept. of Ministry of Finance), 15/27 August 1898; ibid., f. 20; op. 7; d. 195; l. 252.

61. Rothstein to Aron, 8/20 June 1899; ibid., f. 626; op. 1; d. 270; l. 30.

62. Aron to H. Spitzer (of St. Petersburg International Bank), 18 September 1899; MKNPR, p. 238.

63. Pavel V. Volobuev, *Iz istorii monopolizatzii neftianoi promyshlennosti dorevoliutsionnoi*

Rossii (From the History of Monopolization of the Oil Industry in Prerevolutionary Russia), *Istoricheskie zapiski,* 52 (1955); Valeri I. Bovykin, *Formirovanie finansovogo capitala v Rossii* (The formation of financial capital in Russia) (Moscow, 1984), p. 205.

64. 1899 report; TsGIA Gruzinskoi SSR, f. 370; d. 822; l. 20.
65. Report on Baku Oil Industry in 1901 (Baku, 1902), Part 2, pp. 237–39.
66. Rothstein to Aron, 15/27 June 1899; TsGIA SSSR, f. 626; op. 1; d. 370; l. 32.
67. Frederick C. Gerretson; *History of the Royal Dutch,* Vol. 2 (Leiden, 1958), p. 351.
68. *The Mineral Resources of the United States, 1899,* (Washington, DC, 1900), p. 201.
69. Gerretson, *History of the Royal Dutch,* p. 351.
70. Ibid., Vol. 1, p. 282.
71. Hidy and Hidy, *Pioneering,* pp. 265–67; Gerretson, *History of the Royal Dutch,* Vol. 2, pp. 46, 68–69, 94–96.
72. Kendall Beaton, *Enterprise in Oil* (New York, 1957), pp. 44–45.
73. Gerretson, *History of the Royal Dutch,* Vol. 2, p. 238.
74. Report of the conversations between Mr. Rockefeller and Mr. Inglis, 14 November 1908, Rockefeller Archive Center.
75. *Moniteur du Petrole roumain,* 10/23 November 1908.
76. Yuri I. Vinzer, *Angliiskie kapitalovlozheniia za granitsei* (English investments abroad) (Moscow, 1960), p. 34.
77. Gerretson, *History of the Royal Dutch,* Vol. 4, p. 136.
78. Mazut to Ministry of Finance, 1916; TsGIA SSSR, f. 1450; op. 1; d. 27; l. 444.
79. V. I. Bovykin, "Rossiskaia neft' i Rotshildi" (Russian oil and Rothschilds), *Voprosy istorii* No. 4, (1978), 41; Eventov, *Inostrannyi kapital,* p. 92.
80. Beaton, *Enterprise in Oil,* pp. 76–80, 129, 167.
81. T[homas] A. B. Corley, *A History of the Burmah Oil Company, 1886–1924* (London, 1983), Chapter 4.
82. Ronald W. Ferrier, *The History of the British Petroleum Company* (London, 1982), pp. 32–42; see also Geoffrey Jones, *The State and Emergence of the British Oil Industry* (London, 1981), p. ix.
83. Ferrier, *History of British Petroleum,* pp. 70–72; Henry Longhurst, *Adventure in Oil* (London, 1959), p. 23.
84. Ferrier, *History of British Petroleum,* p. 88.
85. Ibid., p. 107.
86. Ibid., p. 110.
87. Ibid., pp. 194–201; Gerretson, *History of the Royal Dutch,* Vol. 4, p. 293.
88. Marian Kent, *Oil and Empire* (London, 1976), pp. 74–89.
89. Friedrich Haase, *Die Erdöl Interessen der Deutschen Bank und der Direction der Disconto-Gesellschaft in Rumänien* (Berlin, 1922), p. 42.
90. Ulrich Brack, *Deutsche Erdölpolitik von 1914* (Hamburg, 1977), pp. 169, 178.
91. MKNPR, p. 706 (comment).
92. U.S. Office of Naval Intelligence, RG 38, box 838, file 1623; National Archives, Washington, DC.
93. Brack, *Deutsche Erdólpolitik,* p. 506; Inge von Baumgart and Horst Benneckenstein, "Der Kampf des deutschen Finanzkapitals in den Jahren 1897 bis 1914 für ein Reichspetroleummonopol," *Jahrbuch für Wirtschaftsgeschichte,* Vol. 2 (Berlin, 1980), p. 102.
94. Diakonova, *Nobelevskaia korporatsia,* pp. 107–8; MKNPR, p. 750.
95. Bovykin, "Rossiiskaia neft'," pp. 30–31.
96. Baumgart and Benneckenstein, "Der Kampf des deutschen Finanzkapitals," p. 112; Brack, *Deutsche Erdölpolitik,* p. 351.
97. George S. Gibb and Evelyn H. Knowlton, *The Resurgent Years* (New York, 1956), pp. 208–19.

98. Ibid., pp. 219–20; Gh. Dobrovici, *Istoria dezvoltarii economice di financiare a Rominei* (Bucharest, 1935), p. 244, quoted in G. Ravas, *Iz istorii rumynskoii nefti* (From the history of Rumanian oil) (Moscow, 1958), pp. 58–59.

99. Nobel-Diskonto-Gesellschaft agreement, 18–31 December 1911; TsGIA SSSR, f. 630; op. 2; d. 297; ll. 7–8.

100. E. Solomonson (of Diskonto-Gesellschaft) to Nobel, 6 July 1912; 30 September 1913; LGIA, f. 1258; op. 2; d. 268; ll. 250–51; d. 273; l. 135.

101. MKNPR, K. Henninghausen (of Diskonto-Gesellschaft) to Nobel, 21 May 1912, p. 531; also p. 750 (statistical appendix).

102. V. N. Kokovtsov (Chairman, Council of Ministers) to Th. Bethmann-Hollweg (German Chancellor), September 16/29, 1912; Bethmann-Hollweg to Kokovtsov, November 25/December 8, 1912; MKNPR, pp. 538, 548–49.

103. Memo, 3 February 1912; TsCAVMF, f. 418; op. 1; d. 3920; l. 23.

104. *Stenographische Bericht über die Verhandlungen des Deutschen Reichstages*, 7 December 1912, Bd. 286, S. 2633–2638.

105. U.S. Office of Naval Intelligence; RG 38, box 838, file 1623; National Archives, Washington, DC.

106. Memo on foreign capital in the Russian oil industry belonging to the subjects whose countries participated in the war against Russia; TsGIA SSSR, f. 37; op. 77; d. 877; l. 1.

107. Book of sales of "Neft'" shares 1913–1917; ibid., f. 1459; op. 1; d. 28.

108. Tolf, *Russian Rockefellers*, p. 194.

109. Hidy and Hidy, *Pioneering*, p. 637.

110. Wilkins, *Emergence of Multinational Enterprise*, p. 84.

111. Gibb and Knowlton, *The Resurgent Years*.

112. MKNPR, p. 750 (statistical appendix); Diakonova, *Nobelevskaia korporatsiia*, pp. 125–26.

113. William Howard Taft Papers, Series 6, f. 205; Library of Congress, Washington, DC. See also Chapter 13 in this volume.

114. Diakonova, *Nobelevskaia korporatsiia*, pp. 114–15.

115. MKNPR, p. 727 (comment).

116. Syndicate agreement, 18–31 December 1911; TsGIA SSSR, f. 630; op. 2; d. 297; ll. 5–6.

117. Eventov, *Inostrannyi kapital*, p. 94.

118. List of Nobel Co. stockholders, 13–26 May 1914; TsGIA SSSR, f. 595; op. 2; d. 203; ll. 55–57.

119. Eventov, *Inostrannyi kapital*, p. 96.

120. List of "Noblessner" stockholders, 8/21 January 1913, 38 May/11 June 1915; TsGIA SSSR, f. 23; op. 12; d. 1588; ll. 53, 103–4.

121. MKNPR, pp. 730–31 (comment).

122. Eventov, *Inostrannyi kapital*, pp. 80–84.

123. Ernst Agahd, *Grossbanken und Weltmarkt* (Berlin, 1914), p. 186.

124. MKNPR, pp. 738–39 (comment).

125. Letter of an anonymous Russian stockholder of RGO ("X") to the French journal *L'Evolution économique*, October 1913; Ibid., pp. 610–12.

126. O. Rosenberg (of O. A. Rosenberg and Co. in Paris) to A. Putilof (Chairman, Russo-Asiatic Bank), and A. Vyshnogradsky (Chairman, St. Petersburg International Bank), 22 August/4 September 1913; TsGIA SSSR, f. 630; op. 2; d. 313; ll. 315, 319.

127. RGO press release, early 1914; Ibid., p. 624.

128. S. Penaccio (Vice-Director, Russo-Asiatic Bank) to A. Raffalovich (Paris agent of Russian Ministry of Finance), 27 February/12 March 1914; MKNPR, p. 629.

129. A. Raffalovich to M. E. Verstrat (Director, Russo-Asiatic Bank) 1/14 May 1914; TsGIA SSSR, f. 630; op. 2; d. 313; ll. 344–46.

130. International Bank to Midland Bank, 3/16 March 1914; ibid., f. 638; op. 1; d. 98; l. 13.
131. MKNPR, pp. 738–39 (comment).
132. Alfred D. Chandler, *The Visible Hand: The Managerial Revolution in American Business* (Cambridge, MA, 1977), p. 424.

Chapter 20

This chapter has been freely translated and heavily edited by Rondo Cameron.

1. See the chapters in Part I.
2. This appears clearly in Rondo Cameron et al., *Banking in the Early Stages of Industrialization* (New York and Oxford, 1967).
3. A large part of British railway investments in the United States, Latin America, and India, and of French and Belgian in Spain, were offset by shipments of rails and other equipment. Many government loans merely offset deficits in the balance of payments, especially in the first half of the century; see Albert Broder, *Le rôle des intérêts étrangers dans la croissance économique de l'Espagne, 1767–1924*, 7 vols. (Lille, 1982, microfilm), Vol. 1.
4. The well-known work of Jakob Riesser, *Die Deutsche Grossbanken*, 3rd ed. (Jena, 1912), is still indispensable for Germany. For France the best available is Jean Bouvier, *Le Crédit Lyonnais, 1863–1882*, 2 vols. (Paris, 1961). A recent interesting work on Britain is Youssef Cassis, *Les Banquiers de la City á l'Epoque Edouardienne* (Geneva, 1984).
5. Fritz Fasolt, *Die sieben Grösten deutschen elektrizitäts Gesellschaften* (Dresden, 1904), p. 38.
6. Riesser, *Grossbanken*, p. 666; Jürgen Kocka, *Unternehmungsverwaltung und Angestelltenschaft am beispiel Siemens* (Stuttgart, 1969).
7. Otto Jeidels, *Das Verhältnis der deutschen Grossbanken zur Industrie* (Leipzig, 1913), p. 231.
8. Riesser, *Grossbanken;* Felix Pinner, *Industrie und Banken* (Berlin, 1933).
9. Albert Broder, "L'Industrie electrotechnique en France, 1880–1913," *Revue du Nord* (1989), 1–5 and Table 12; Albert Beltran, "L'Energie electrique à Paris, 1878–1907," *L'Information Historique* (1986), 369–88.
10. Cassis, *Les Banquiers de la City*, pp. 124–25 and Table 2.5.
11. See Bouvier, *Crédit Lyonnais*, for the case of *fuchsine*.
12. See Chapter 1 in this volume.
13. The official announcements do not mention an issue, nor is there any trace in the documents that the CIC furnished us.
14. Formed May 23, 1881, with the English patents of Reynier and Wergemann. Durrieu at that time was president of the CIC.
15. Paul Leroy Beaulieu, in *L'Economiste français*, I (1882) 65, 97.
16. See Mira Wilkins, *The Emergence of Multinational Enterprise: American Business Abroad from the Colonial Era to 1914* (Cambridge, MA, 1970), p. 57.
17. Calculated from published figures of the era.
18. Alfred Neymarck, "Conseil aux rentiers," (1892) in his *Finances contemporaines*, I (Paris, 1902), 100–07.
19. W. G. Hoffmann et al., *Das Wachstum der deutschen Wirtschaft seit der Mitte des 19. Jahrhundert* (Berlin, Heidelberg, New York, 1965).
20. Riesser, *Grossbanken*.
21. Cf. the famous work of E. E. Williams, *Made in Germany*, and the numerous notations by Raffalovitch in his annual Paris publication, *le Marché financier;* also the remarkable book by G. Diouritch, *L'Expansion des banques allemandes à étranger* (Paris, 1909).

22. Franz Eulenburg, "Die Aufsichtsräte der deutschen Aktien Gesellschaften," *Jahrbuch für Nationaloekonomie und Statistik* 32 (1906), 98.

23. Albert Broder, "Investissements européens dasn l'electricité en Amerique du Sud avant 1914," First Congress on Energy and History in Brazil, Sao Paulo, September 1986.

24. Pinner, *Industrie und Banken*, p. 209.

25. Jeidels, *Verhältnis*, p. 267.

26. Albert Broder, "L'Expansion internationale de l'industrie allemande," *Relations internationales*, 43 (1985), 269–87.

27. On the connections between the Banca Commerciale and the A.E.G. see Claudio Pavese, "Le origini della società Edison e il suo sviluppo," in Bruno Bezza, ed., *Energia e Sviluppo* (Turin, 1986), p. 76–79.

28. Peter Hertner, "Il capitale tedesco nell' industria elettrica italiana fino alla primera guerra mondiale," in ibid., pp. 213–58.

29. Broder, *Le rôle des intérêts étrangers*, pp. 1660–1808.

30. Idem.

31. I. C. R. Byatt, *The British Electrical Industry, 1875–1914* (Oxford, 1979); Lesley Hannah, *Electricity before Nationalisation* (London, 1979).

32. R. P. T. Davenport-Hines, *Dudley Docker: The Life and Times of a Trade Warrior* (Cambridge, 1984), p. 155, quoting A. L. Levine, *Industrial Retardation in Britain, 1880–1914* (London, 1967), p. 31. I should like to thank Dr. Geoffrey Jones for bringing this quotation to my attention.

33. Broder, "L'Industrie electrotechnique en France."

34. Ibid.

35. Maurice Lévy-Leboyer, "Histoire de l'entreprise et histoire de l'electricité," in *L'Electricité dans l'histoire* (Paris, 1985); for a discussion see Broder, "L'Industrie electotechnique."

36. Broder, "L'electricité en Amerique du Sud."

37. Olle Gasslander, *History of Stockholms Enskilda Bank to 1914* (Stockholm, 1962), pp. 174–75, 223–27, 292–95, 383–402, 405–08, 422–30, et passim.

Chapter 21

1. Examples of steel companies integrating forward into heavy engineering and investing abroad were Vickers-Terni in Italy and Schneider-Putilov in Russia. Although both Terni and Putilov did produce steel, the cooperation with the foreign firms was clearly limited to engineering and armaments production. For the most recent research in these two multinational cooperations see Luciano Segreto, "The Investments of Vickers in Italy (1906–1939)," European University Institute, Florence, DOC.IUE 154/84 (Col. 23), 1984, and Claude Beaud, "Schneider en Russie (1896–1914)," European University Institute, Florence, DOC.IUE 153/84 (Col. 22), 1984.

2. On the development of production organization and technology see Ulrich Wengenroth, "Technologietransfer als multilateraler Austauschprozess: Die Entstehung der modernen Stahlwerkskonzeption im späten 19 Jahrhundert," *Technikgeschichte*, 50 (1983), 238–52, and Ulrich Wengenroth, *Unternehmensstrategien und technischer Fortschritt: Die deutsche und britische Stahlindustrie, 1865–1895* (Gottingen, 1986), Chapter 3.

3. Ulrich Wengenroth, "Raw Material Ventures: Multinational Activities in Acquiring and Processing of Iron Ore before World War I," European University Institute, Florence, DOC.IUE 158/84 (Col. 27), 1984.

4. The ores used for the acid Bessemer and Siemens-Martin processes, which dominated in Britain, had to be free from phosphorus whereas those for the basic Bessemer

or Thomas process used mainly on the Continent had to contain at least 1.8 percent phosphorus.

5. Personal communication by Albert Broder of the University of Lille, preparing a book on foreign investment in Spain, and Gerard Chastagneret of the University of Aix-en-Provence, preparing a book on Spanish mining in the nineteenth century. Their views are corroborated by the nonexistence of any references to banking activities in the hitherto most substantial work on foreign investment in Spanish ore by Michael Flinn, "British Overseas Investment in Iron Ore Mining, 1870–1914" (unpublished M.A. thesis, University of Manchester, 1952).

6. On the Orconera Iron Ore Company, see Wengenroth, "Raw Material Ventures," pp. 6–8. While there was no information traceable on the activities of the City, it can at least be established that the most prominent domestic partners in the major investment schemes in Spanish iron ore were among the founders of the banks of Bilbao, Urquijo and Barcelona. See Manuel Gonzalez Portilla, *La formacion de la sociedad capitalista en el pais vasco (1876–1913)*, 2 vols. (San Sebastian, 1981), Vol. 1, p. 117.

7. Martin Fritz, *Svensk Järnmalmsexport, 1883–1913* (Meddelanden fran Ekonomisk-historiska institutionen vid Göteborgs universitet, Vol. 12; Göteborg, 1967), pp. 99–100, and Friedhelm Plücker, "Der schwedische Eisenerzbergbau und seine Beziehungen zur westdeutschen Eisenindustrie 1880–1965" (unpublished doctoral thesis, Wirtschafts- und Sozialwissenschaftliche Fakultät, University of Cologne, 1968), pp. 44–48.

8. Plücker, "Der schwedische Eisenerzbergbau," p. 75.

9. In view of the Swedish government's policy the London Rothschild declared on the occasion that he would never again touch Swedish paper; Plücker, "Der schwedische Eisenerzbergbau," pp. 79–80.

10. Deutsche Bank AG, Historisches Archiv (hereafter: DB/HA), S 3610, Klönne to Thyssen, June 27, 1902.

11. DB/HA, S 3610, Klönne to Gwinner, January 14, 1903. On the French loan see Olle Gasslander, *History of Stockholms Enskilda Bank to 1914* (Stockholm, 1962), pp. 258–66.

12. DB/HA, S 3610, Deutsche Bank Berlin to Hamburger Filiale der Deutschen Bank, January 17, 1902.

13. The stipulations of this contract in DB/HA, S 3610, Notizen über Konsortialvertrag der Norddeutschen Bank mit deutschen Hüttenwerken, January 30, 1901.

14. See above, n. 12 and DB/HA, S 3610, Hamburger Filiale der Deutschen Bank to Direktion der Deutschen Bank, betr. Reorganisation der Gellivare und Luossavaara/Kiirunavaara-Erzgruben, July 12, 1902.

15. DB/HA, S 3610, Klönne to Thyssen, July 14, 1902, and Thyssen to Klönne, July 15, 1902.

16. DB/HA, S 3610, Klönne to Gwinner, January 14, 1903: Gasslander, *Stockholms Enskilda Bank*, p. 372.

17. DB/HA, S 3610, Thyssen to Klönne, December 17, 1902, and Klönne to Gwinner, January 14, 1903.

18. Martin Fritz, *Gustay Emil Broms och Norbottens järnmalm: En studie i finansierings-problematiken under exploateringstiden, 1891–1903*, (Meddelanden fran Ekonomisk-historiska institutionen vid Göteborgs universitet, Vol. 5; Göteborg, 1965), p. 42; Gasslander, *Stockholms Enskilda Bank*, p. 368.

19. DB/HA, S 3610, Vereinbarung der Firmen Fried. Krupp und Thyssen & Co. mit der Norddeutschen Bank und der Diskonto-Gesellschaft, Berlin, January 31/February 1, 1903.

20. Plücker, "Der schwedische Eisenerzbergbau," pp. 139–40; Fritz, *Svensk Järnmalmsexport*, p. 106.

21. The only major German bank archive to survive the war was that of the Deutsche Bank.

The direct investment in French iron ore, however, was handled by the Dresdner Bank from which we have very sparse documentation only.

22. DB/HA, Carl Klönne—Korrespondenzabschriften Klönne/Thyssen, Gwinner to Klönne, March 23, 1903, and Thyssen to Klönne, April 19, 1903. See also Chapter 3 in this volume.

23. Raymond Poidevin, *Les relations economiques et financiéres entre la France et l'Allemagne* (Paris, 1969), p. 206.

24. Valerii I. Bovykin, "Probleme der industriellen Entwicklung Russlands," in Karl Otmar Freiherr von Aretin and Werner Conze, eds., *Deutschland und Russland im Zeitalter des Kapitalismus, 1861–1914* (Wiesbaden, 1977), p. 105; Archiv der August-Thyssen-Hütte, Bestand Rheinstahl (hereafter: ATH/RS), 123 00 1 13, Errichtung eines Stahlwerke in Russland 1877.

25. Irena Pietrzak-Pawlowska, "L'expansion de la région Lyon-St. Etienne sur le territoire polonais après 1870," *Studia Historiae Oeconomicae* 1 (1966), 102.

26. See above, n. 2, and Alfred D. Chandler, Jr., *The Visible Hand: The Managerial Revolution in American Business* (Cambridge, MA, 1977), Chapter 8, especially pp. 258–69.

27. The Upper Silesian industry traditionally worked for a regional market extending into the neighboring Polish provinces. The border became economically important only after the new Russian tariff of 1877. When thereafter the Upper Silesian ironmasters invested "abroad" they still did this inside a very small and well-known territory. The regional character of this kind of investment and the banking operations involved were altogether more conspicuous than its "international" dimension; Joachim Mai, *Das deutsche Kapital in Russland 1850–1894* (Berlin, 1970), pp. 178–88; Waclaw Dlugoborski, "Wirtschaftliche Region und politische Grenzen: Die Industrialisierung des oberschlesischen Kohlenbeckens," in Sidney Pollard, ed., *Region und Industrialisierung: Studien zur Rolle der Region in der Wirtschaftsgeschichte der letzten zwei Jahrunderte* (Göttingen, 1980), pp. 142–69. A similar case though for different reasons was the "enforced multinationalization" of the French company de Wendel in Lorraine. After the German Reich had annexed Lorraine in 1871 de Wendel was cut off from a substantial part of his market. In 1882 he founded a subsidary across the new border on French territory with the help of Schneider of Creuzot and his banker Demachy-Seillière. De Wendel was now clearly a binational company, but this was a very peculiar case and had certainly not been the intention of Francois de Wendel. On the close relationship between the two companies of de Wendel see Henry Grandt, *Monographie d'un établissement métallurgique sis à la fois en France et en Allemagne* (Chartres, 1909), pp. 123–27.

28. The Suermondt family was in fact of Aachen, a few miles from the Belgian border, but since it operated mostly in the Belgian market it seems adequate to call Barthoid Suermondt a "Belgian" banker. The Suermondt and Cockerill families were relatives by marriage. Ernst Nagelmackers was married to the sister of the new company's general manager. In a way it was largely a family affair. Carl-Friedrich Baumann, "Gustave Léon Pastor, Technische-Reorganisator des Rheinischen Stahlwerke," *Niederrheinkammer* I (May 1987), 306.

29. The founders of the Société anonyme des Aciéries Rhénanes à Meiderich were Barthold, Henry, and William Suermondt of Aachen; Leon Donnat; the banker Albert de Marc, and the Comte de Rochechouart of Paris; Adolphe de Vaux and Georges Pasteur, both of Liége; the Russian prince Augustin Galitzin; and the German Max Haniel. Anton Hasslacher, *Der Werdegang der Rheinischen Stahlwerke* (Essen, 1936), pp. 5, 50.

30. From time to time the Rheinische Stahlwerke produced rails under the Angleur trademark, which were sold by Angleur on the Belgian market. The general managers of the two companies were both brothers of the Pastor family; ATH/RS 200 00 A5, Korrespondenz

zwischen Georg Pastor (Rheinische Stahlwerke) und Gustave Pastor (Angleur), 1875. When Georg left the German company in 1878 to look after the new Russian investment his brother, Gustave, followed him as general manager of the German steel works. The duo had been shifted eastward; Hasslacher, *Der Werdegang*, p. 7.

31. ATH/RS 126 00 2, Bericht des Vorstandes in der Generalversammlung am 29.11.1877.
32. Eventually the company had to be reorganized, with bonds and direct loans being converted into priority shares. ATH/RS 126 00 5, Bericht des Aufsichtsrats für die Generalversammlung am 31.10.1878.
33. ATH/RS 123 00 1 13, Errichtung eines Stahlwerke in Russland.
34. The cost per ton of steel rails was estimated to be 195.87 marks in the Dombrova against 177.96 in Praga. Ibid.
35. Zbigniew Pustula, *Poczatki kapitalu monopolistycznego w przemysle hutniczo-metalowym Królestwa Polskiego (1882–1900)* (Warsaw, 1968), p. 102.
36. Ibid., p. 224.
37. Ibid., p. 150. After moving from Belgium to Germany Georges Pasteur became Georg Pastor.
38. ATH/RS 126 00 5, Bericht des Aufsichtsrats für die Generalversammlung am 31.10.1878.
39. ATH/RS 126 00 5-10 and 126 01 11-17. Berichte des Aufsichtsrats an die Generalversammlung 1879–1889. According to Pustula, *Poczatki,* aneks 11, p. 254, who quotes Polish sources, the Rheinische Stahlwerke had only 100,000 rubles. The company's own documentation, however, is probably more reliable. The difference is not substantial anyway.
40. Pustula, *Poczatki,* pp. 218–20 and aneks 11, p. 254. Unfortunately we do not know anything about the quality of the shares as the right to first and second dividends and the right to vote. That there was not necessarily a close relationship between the number of shares and the influence on the company or the distribution of profits is well demonstrated in the better-documented case of the Huta-Bankova treated below.
41. Pustula, *Poczatki,* pp. 219–20.
42. ATH/RS 123 00 5 71–75, minutes of board meeting, July 21, 1886, September 28, 1886, and January 19, 1887.
43. John P. McKay, *Pioneers for Profit: Foreign Entrepreneurship and Russian Industrialization 1885–1913* (Chicago, 1970), p. 300.
44. *The Moscow Gazette,* quoted by McKay, *Pioneers for Profit,* p. 301.
45. ATH/RS 123 00 5 71, minutes of board meeting, July 21, 1886.
46. McKay, *Pioneers for Profit,* p. 303.
47. ATS 126 01 18, Bericht des Vorstandes zu der ordentlichen Generalversammlung vom 12, Oktober 1889.
48. Pustula, *Poczatki,* p. 205.
49. McKay, *Pioneers for Profit,* p. 305.
50. Ibid., p. 306.
51. Aldegonde Deville, "De Société Générale als promotor van de belgische industriele ontwikkeling van 1880 tot 1913" (unpublished lic. lett.-thesis, Fakulteit van de Wijsbegeerte en de Letteren, Katholieke Universiteit te Leuven, 1975), p. 132; J. B. Silly, "Capitaux français et sidérurgie russe," *Revue d'histoire de la sidérurgie,* 6 (1965), 40; McKay, *Pioneers for Profit,* p. 305.
52. The Praga steel works were not opened until 1880 but the decision to go there dated from 1877. See n. 33.
53. Pietrzak-Pawlowska, "L'expansion," pp. 103, 109. It is not quite clear whether the first name of this member of the ubiquitous Pasteur clan was Edouard or Eugène; McKay, *Pioneers for Profit,* pp. 351–54, opts for Edouard while Pustula, *Poczatki,* pp. 231, 259, calls him Eugène.
54. Pietrzak-Pawlowska, "L'expansion," pp. 109–10.

55. McKay, *Pioneers for Profit*, p. 342; Pietrzak-Pawlowska, "L'expansion," p. 107, gives the same account of the cooperation between the two Verdiés but says that they were brothers.
56. Bernard Griault, "La sidérurgie française de 1860 à 1880," *Revue d'histoire de la sidérurgie*, 6 (1965), 247–52.
57. Pietrzak-Pawlowska, "L'expansion," p. 107.
58. McKay, *Pioneers for Profit*, pp. 343–44.
59. Pietrzak-Pawlowska, "L'expansion," pp. 114–16.
60. Ibid.
61. McKay, *Pioneers for Profit*, p. 345. In 1877 the Crédit Lyonnais had refused to issue bonds on behalf of the Huta-Bankova; Pietrzak-Pawlowska, "L'expansion," pp. 119–20.
62. Jean Bouvier, "Une dynastie d'affaires lyonnaise au XIXè siècle: les Bonnardel," *Revue d'histoire moderne et contemporaine*, 2 (1955), 194–96; Pietrzak-Pawlowska, "L'expansion," p. 118.
63. McKay, *Pioneers for Profit*, pp. 351–54.
64. Silly, "Capitaux francais," p. 36.
65. Beaud, "Schneider en Russie," pp. 2–5.
66. Valerii I. Bovykin, *Formirovanie finansovogo kapitala v Rossii konets XIXv.–1908* (Moscow, 1984), p. 180, also describes the role of the French industrial enterprises largely as one of technical assistance given to banks. On the Upper Silesian companies see Mai, *Das deutsche Kapital*, pp. 181–85.
67. René Girault, *Emprunts russes et investissements français en Russie 1887–1914. Recherches sur l'investissement international* (Paris, 1973), p. 296; Griault, "La sidérurgie," p. 253; Silly, "Capitaux français," p. 30.
68. Girault, *Emprunts russes*, p. 231; Silly, "Capitaux francais," pp. 41–46; Bovykin, *Formirovanie*, p. 186. New problems arise, however, when a steel company becomes itself the center of a financial group and performs banking operations, like the Cockerill group in Belgium, for instance.
69. Heinrich Koch, *75 Jahre Mannesmann: Geschichte einer Erfindung und eines Unternehmens, 1890–1965* (Düsseldorf, 1965), p. 33.
70. Ibid., p. 42.
71. Ibid., p. 45.
72. Fritz Seidenzahl, *100 Jahre Deutsche Bank, 1870–1970* (Frankfurt am Main, 1970), p. 187.
73. Koch, *75 Jahre*, p. 46.
74. Hartmut Pogge von Strandmann, *Unternehmenspolitik und Unternehmensführung: Der Dialog zwischen Aufsichtsrat und Vorstand bei Mannesmann, 1900 bis 1919* (Düsseldorf, 1978), p. 18.
75. Koch, *75 Jahre*, pp. 63–66.
76. Quoted by Pogge von Strandmann, *Unternehmenspolitik*, p. 21.
77. Koch, *75 Jahre*, p. 76.
78. Ibid., p. 71.
79. DB/HA, Carl Klönne—Korrespondenzabschriften Klönne/Thyssen, undated minutes of late 1903.
80. Pogge von Strandmann, *Unternehmenspolitik*, pp. 50, 53.
81. Ibid., p. 70.
82. Alice Teichova, "The Mannesmann Concern in East Central Europe in the Inter-war Period," in Alice Teichova and Phillip Cottrell, eds., *International Business and Central Europe, 1918–1939* (Leicester, 1983), p. 105.
83. Peter Hertner, "Deutsches Kapital in Italien: Die 'Societá Tubi Mannesmann' in Dalmine bei Bergamo, 1906–1916," Part I, *Zeitschrift für Unternehmensgeschichte*, 22 (1977), 190–91.

84. Hertner "Deutsches Kapital," Part II, *Zeitschrift für Unternehmensgeschichte,* 23 (1978), 62–63.
85. Ibid.
86. Koch, *75 Jahre,* pp. 96–100.
87. There were exceptions to this rule, of course, like the promotion of a steel rail company by the Bochumer Verein in Savona, Italy. The Bochumer Verein, however, was also an outsider in domestic business strategies; Wengenroth, *Unternehmensstrategien,* Chapter 5.

Chapter 22

Works frequently cited have been identified by the following abbreviations:

MC   McCormick Collection at the State Historical Society of Wisconsin. There are numerous subcollections, such as 2X or 10C, often box numbers, and, irregularly, file names.

IH   International Harvester Corporation archives housed at that company's Chicago world headquarters. Files by number.

1. *London Times,* May 1, 1851.
2. McCormick had the foresight to send the "rough, homespun Yankee" D. C. McKenzie—an expert mechanic and seasoned raker—to England to adjust and operate the reaper.
3. Clippings file on the Great Exhibition, MC:2C:Bx 133. When Obed Hussey gave his machine proper attention, it defeated McCormick's in several later trials. See *London Times,* October 7, 1851.
4. Burgess & Key developed a screw device that delivered the grain in swath, but the egotistical McCormick resisted putting it on his reaper—he apparently preferred pride of authorship to sales; William T. Hutchinson, *Cyrus Hall McCormick,* Vol. II (New York, 1935), pp. 402, 411–12 [hereafter WH: II:]
5. WH: II:79–80, 413–14.
6. WH: II:411–15; Fred V. Carstensen, *American Enterprise in Foreign Markets* (Chapel Hill, NC, 1984), Chapter 7, passim.
7. WH: II:79–80.
8. WH: II:418–19.
9. *Mark Lane Express,* August 11, 1862; *London Times,* August 15, 1862.
10. *Bell's Weekly Messenger,* August 18 and September 8, 1862; WH: II:422.
11. WH: II:423–28. Market share calculation from Harvester Buildings (industry census for 1860–61, with aggregate data for 1864). MC:4X:BX 4:F: Production, Reports, Misc. Data.
12. WH: II:437–40.
13. WH:II:455–56; MC:3X:Sales Ledgers; IH: Competitors Advertising (bound volumes).
14. C. A. Spring to C. H. McCormick, July 5, 1871, MC:2A:Bx 35.
15. Reminiscences of Cyrus H. McCormick, by Wm. R. Selleck; MC:1A:BX 122.
16. In 1869 McCormick had a net wealth of $5.5 million; in 1875 of $6.8 million; WH:II:749 n. 42. (There are annual financial statements for both the company and Cyrus's personal finances, but they are scattered; e.g., 1876: MC:1A:Bx 63:F: C. H. & L. J. McCormick; 1877: MC:2A:Bx 68F: C. H. & L. J. McCormick; 1879: MCX:2A:Bx 53: F:McC. Harv. Mach. Co.—1880.) Just his Chicago real estate was worth more than twice the cost of the factory. In 1879 he owed Connecticut Life Insurance Co. $540,000 on mortgages taken out in 1872/73. The insurance company valued the lots at $1.28 million. In 1876 McCormick valued his real estate at $2.6 million. Annual Statement, 1879: Schedule B, Connecticut Life Insurance Co.; IH:760.

valued his real estate at $2.6 million. Annual Statement, 1879: Schedule B, Connecticut Life Insurance Co.; IH:760.

17. Carryover inventory was a serious problem from 1871 through 1877, except for 1872 when, because of the fire, the company simply had very few machines to sell.

18. Carstensen, *American Enterprise*, p. 113. Hutchinson largely ignored Butler's role in the reconstruction of the McCormick company.

19. WH:II:606–7. The company did borrow from Cyrus McCormick himself. The statement for August 1, 1876, shows the company owing Cyrus $1.38 million—probably a long-term loan—while identifying no outstanding loans to banks; MC:1A:Bx 63:F:C.H. & L. J. McCormick.

20. Proposed agreement, C. H. McCormick and R. F. Mason, 11-16-76; MC:2A:Bx 56:F:1876; F. C. Newell to C. H. McCormick, 7-15-77; MC:2A:Bx 56:F:1877. MHMCo. to Morrow, Bassett & Co., 11-14-78; MC:1X:V:185:427, 437; WH: II:662, 675.

21. WH: II:669–72.

22. Harvester reminiscences of William H. Town; MC:AD:Bx 8: Gorham Pool.

23. But they did not provide any credit to the farmers, so that their costs were limited to that of carrying the inventory that dealers held. This did not seem to be a cost large enough to put significant financial pressure on the manufacturers.

24. *Farm Implement News*, VIII:9 (September 1887), 11; X:11 (November 1889), 30.

25. The only salaried foreign representative during these years was in Russia, a consequence more of Cyrus Sr.'s ego than business acumen. In 1879 Cyrus contracted with Alexis Victor Perrin, a "stirring young man" of immense self-confidence, who came to Chicago after Waite, Burnell, Huggins & Co. had failed to live up to a contract for Perrin to show a McCormick self-binder in Russia. Initially, Perrin got a commission contract, but by 1881 an experienced American had replaced Perrin and the business was on the same cash-only basis as other foreign sales. The 1879 agreement initiated McCormick's presence in Russia, but the company provided few resources and the Russian agency remained largely undeveloped until 1895; See Carstensen, *American Enterprise*, Chapter 8, passim.

26. C. H. McCormick to P. Lankester & Co., 7-14-81, MC:IX: V:455; Carstensen, *American Enterprise*, p. 113.

27. C. H. McCormick to MHMCo, 8-13-87, MC:3B:BX 7; E. K. Butler to E. Ackerman, 8-18-87, MC:IX:V, 459.

28. *Farm Implement News*, VIII:9 (September 1887), 11.

29. C. H. McCormick to MHMCo, 8-23-87, MC:2X:Bx 286; E. K. Butler to W. H. Grossman & Bros., 5-5-87, MC: special collections.

30. *Farm Implement News*, IX:1 (January 1888), 21; C. H. McCormick to MHMCo, 9-12-88; 9-19-88; to P. Lankester, 10-13-88; MC:2X:BX 286.

31. *Farm Implement News*, X:11 (November 1889), 29–30. Statement, 1889, in file of C. H. McCormick correspondence detailing his 1889 European trip; MC:10C.

32. E. K. Butler to C. H. McCormick, 10-5-91, MC:8C:BX 11: F: 3.

33. In fairness to Freudenreich, McCormick's trade had been built on the success of the twine binder, which brought the self-raker and mower in its wake. But in Russia labor had remained so cheap that there was no sustained demand for binders; Russian farmers stayed with a primitive hand-rake reaper similar to McCormick's original design.

34. Carstensen, *American Enterprise*, pp. 125–31.

35. Ibid.

36. Based on financial records in McCormick papers, primarily series 3X. Deering sales data in privately held collection; photocopies now in the International Harvester archives.

37. Carstensen, *American Enterprise*, p. 115.

38. Ibid., pp. 115–16.

39. Based on financial records in MC:3X and MC:M/I.

40. Guthrie, Cravath, and Henderson to IHC, April 25, 1903, IH F:208.
41. Roberts Walker's Report, IH F:208.
42. Carstensen, *American Enterprise,* p. 139.
43. Fred V. Carstensen, "'. . . a dishonest man is at least prudent': George W. Perkins and the International Harvester Steel Properties," *Business and Economic History,* 9 (1980), 87–102, provides details on the earliest conflict, from September 1902 through mid-1903. Additional detail in U.S. Bureau of Corporations, *International Harvester Company* (Washington, DC, 1913).
44. Carstensen, *American Enterprise,* Chapter 10.
45. C. H. Haney to A. E. Mayer, 1-03-07, IH: 1228.
46. Testimony of C. H. Haney, in Guy E. Snider, *Selling in Foreign Markets* (Dept. of Commerce, Miscellaneous Series No. 81, Washington, DC, 1919).
47. W. V. Couchman to IH European branches, 6-15-09, IH: F:919.
48. Minutes, Board of Directors, IH: F: 16228; C. H. McCormick, Jr., to G. W. Perkins, 10/2/1902, MC:2C:Bx 31: F: IHC:Consolidation:Comptroller.
49. C. H. McCormick, Jr., to H. F. McCormick, 7/10/1911, MC:2C:Bx 35: F: IHC-J. See also chapter on London banking practice.
50. F. T. Gates to J. D. Rockefeller, n.d., reproduced in full in F. T. Gates to C. H. & H. F. McCormick, 11/14/1910, MC:2C:Bx 34:F: IHC:Finances; C. H. McCormick to F. T. Gates, 11/19/1902, MC:M/I:Bx 21:F: 1; Agreement between John D. Rockefeller and International Harvester Company, February 16, 1911, National Archives, Washington, DC: International Harvester Investigation, 4921/25.
51. J. E. Blunt to H. F. McCormick, June 10, 1911, IH:17058.
52. Ibid.
53. C. H. McCormick, Jr., to G. W. Perkins, December 21, 1911; to Mrs. S. McCormick, January 2, 1912, MC:2C:Bx 34: IHC: Finances.

Conclusion

1. I should make clear that by "the organizers" and "our" I refer primarily to Professor Bovykin and me (R. C.). Professor Wilkins is emphatic that she shared no such illusion, and she attributes our preconception—or misconception—to the fact that historians of banking and historians of multinational corporations are disjunctive sets that do not read each other's books and articles! If this text remedies that defect it will have performed a service.
2. Albert Fishlow, "Lessons from the Past: Capital Markets during the 19th Century and the Interwar Period," *International Organization,* 39 (Summer 1985), 383–439.
3. See Chap. 10 in this volume.
4. E.g., Rondo Cameron, *France and the Economic Development of Europe, 1800–1914* (Princeton, NJ, 1961), Chapter XIV.
5. See Introduction to this volume.
6. See Chapter 14 above.
7. Ibid.
8. See Rondo Cameron et al., *Banking in the Early Stages of Industrailization* (Oxford, 1971), Chapter 9, summarized in Rondo Cameron, *A Concise Economic History of the World* (Oxford, 1989), Chapter 12, sec. 2. It should be noted that in this comparison the banking systems of Sweden and Japan (and Scotland before 1845) received even higher marks than did Germany; but they were not major industrial powers before 1914.
9. For contrasting viewpoints on this question see, on the one hand, Donald N. McCloskey,

Enterprise and Trade in Victorian Britain (London, 1981), and on the other, M. W. Kirby, *The Decline of British Economic Power since 1870* (London, 1981), and W. P. Kennedy, *Industrial Structure, Capital Markets and the Origins of British Economic Decline* (New York, 1987).

10. Richard H. Tilly, "German Banking, 1850–1914: Development Assistance for the Strong," *Journal of European Economic History*, 15 (1986), 113–52; idem, "Banking Institutions in Historical and Comparative Perspective: Germany, Great Britain and the United States in the Nineteenth and Early Twentieth Century," *Journal of Institutional and Theoretical Economics*, 145 (1989), 189–209.

11. Joseph A. Schumpeter, *Business Cycles: A Theoretical and Statistical Analysis of the Capitalist Process*, 2 vols. (New York and London, 1939), Vol. I, 118, 251; idem., *The Theory of Economic Development* (Cambridge, MA, 1933), Chapter 3; see also Rondo Cameron, "The Banker as Entrepreneur," *Explorations in Entrepreneurial History*, 2nd ser., I (1963), 50–55.

12. See Chapter 15 in this volume.

13. Chapter 12.

14. Chapter 21. Significantly, this episode is not mentioned by Bonin in his chapter [3] on French banks.

15. See Chapter 12.

16. Cameron, *France and the Economic Development of Europe*, passim.

17. See Chapter 11.

18. Cameron, *France and the Economic Development of Europe*, pp. 504–5.

19. See Chapter 1.

20. Ibid.

21. Chapter 4.

22. Chapter 16.

Index